Basic Federal Income Taxation

ASPEN PUBLISHERS

Basic Federal Income Taxation

Sixth Edition

William D. Andrews
Eli Goldston Professor of Law Emeritus
Harvard University

Peter J. Wiedenbeck
Joseph H. Zumbalen Professor of the Law of Property
Washington University in St. Louis

Wolters Kluwer
Law & Business

AUSTIN   BOSTON   CHICAGO   NEW YORK   THE NETHERLANDS

>Aspen Publishers
Attn: Permissions Department
76 Ninth Avenue, 7th Floor
New York, NY 10011-5201

To contact Customer Care, e-mail customer.care@aspenpublishers.com, call 1-800-234-1660, fax 1-800-901-9075, or mail correspondence to:

>Aspen Publishers
Attn: Order Department
PO Box 990
Frederick, MD 21705

Printed in the United States of America.

1 2 3 4 5 6 7 8 9 0

ISBN 978-0-7355-7768-8

Library of Congress Cataloging-in-Publication Data

Andrews, William D., 1931–
    Basic federal income taxation/William D. Andrews, Peter J. Wiedenbeck. — 6th ed.
        p.   cm.
    ISBN-13: 978-0-7355-7768-8
    ISBN-10: 0-7355-7768-4
    1. Income tax — Law and legislation — United States — Cases.
I. Wiedenbeck, Peter J., 1953– II. Title.
KF6369.A953 2009
343.7305'2 — dc22

2009000914

This book contains paper from well-managed forests to SFI standards.

About Wolters Kluwer Law & Business

Wolters Kluwer Law & Business is a leading provider of research information and workflow solutions in key specialty areas. The strengths of the individual brands of Aspen Publishers, CCH, Kluwer Law International, and Loislaw are aligned within Wolters Kluwer Law & Business to provide comprehensive, in-depth solutions and expert-authored content for the legal, professional, and education markets.

CCH was founded in 1913 and has served more than four generations of business professionals and their clients. The CCH products in the Wolters Kluwer Law & Business group are highly regarded electronic and print resources for legal, securities, antitrust and trade regulation, government contracting, banking, pension, payroll, employment and labor, and healthcare reimbursement and compliance professionals.

Aspen Publishers is a leading information provider for attorneys, business professionals, and law students. Written by preeminent authorities, Aspen products offer analytical and practical information in a range of specialty practice areas from securities law and intellectual property to mergers and acquisitions and pension/benefits. Aspen's trusted legal education resources provide professors and students with high-quality, up-to-date, and effective resources for successful instruction and study in all areas of the law.

Kluwer Law International supplies the global business community with comprehensive English-language international legal information. Legal practitioners, corporate counsel, and business executives around the world rely on the Kluwer Law International journals, loose-leafs, books, and electronic products for authoritative information in many areas of international legal practice.

Loislaw is a premier provider of digitized legal content to small law firm practitioners of various specializations. Loislaw provides attorneys with the ability to quickly and efficiently find the necessary legal information they need, when and where they need it, by facilitating access to primary law as well as state-specific law, records, forms, and treatises.

Wolters Kluwer Law & Business, a unit of Wolters Kluwer, is headquartered in New York and Riverwoods, Illinois. Wolters Kluwer is a leading multinational publisher and information services company.

To
S.H.A.

Summary of Contents

Contents

Preface

Many tax professors and not a few practitioners have long considered William D. Andrews's *Basic Federal Income Taxation* to be the most insightful, policy-oriented, and coherent treatment of the field. The prospect of losing such a remarkable tool upon retirement was not a happy one, but fortunately Professor Andrews decided to update the book with the assistance of a coauthor. Under such circumstances the role of a coauthor is to be a faithful steward, not an innovator; the cardinal rule of revision is, do no harm. With Professor Andrews's input and oversight, I trust that this sixth edition of *Basic Federal Income Taxation* achieves that goal, updating a classic while preserving its distinctive attributes.

The style of the book has been retained, with its focus on cases and tax policy. Its basic organization is the same, but users of the prior edition will notice two significant changes in ordering. First, the materials on alimony, child support, divorce property settlements, and the kiddie tax, which appeared in scattered locations throughout the fifth edition, have been collected in a new chapter, titled "Taxation and the Family," where they are presented in conjunction with the cases on interspousal income attribution and the treatment of the marriage penalty and bonus. (Although placed as Chapter 17, the material on taxation and the family could be taken up at any time after Chapter 4 on gifts.) Second, Chapter 6, titled "Return of Capital and Timing Issues," provides a conceptual overview of return of capital alternatives (basis recovery techniques) and gathers together the many important issues relating to accounting methods (constructive receipt, original issue discount, prepayments, security deposits, inventories, etc.). This consolidated approach to tax timing includes a number of advanced topics from earlier editions, and so instructors may want to be selective. (We suspect that many instructors will cover Chapter 6A-C only, then skip to Chapter 7 on loans.)

The passage of ten years since publication of the fifth edition has of course occasioned many changes to reflect new developments, both legislative and judicial. Among the most notable developments are the 2001 and 2003 tax and capital gains rate reductions (Chapters 1, 8, 19, and pervasively throughout); taxing qualified dividends at capital gain rates (Chapter 5);

the D.C. Circuit's *Murphy* decision concerning the taxation of damages for nonphysical injuries (Chapter 3B); and the increasingly threatening specter of the alternative minimum tax (Chapter 16D). More attention is given to the tax treatment of health care (including health savings accounts, Chapter 3C), and the proliferation of tax benefits for education (Chapter 12H). The 2005 proposals by the President's Advisory Panel on Federal Tax Reform for changes in the tax treatment of home ownership have been included (Chapter 10C). Overall, the last decade has seen the continued unraveling of the grand compromise of the Tax Reform Act of 1986 (lower rates for a broader base), as both the Clinton and Bush Administrations have sought to advance contested policy priorities piecemeal through tax incentives. Viewed at large, Congress seems engaged in a halting semi-conscious (intermittently candid?) conversion of the federal revenue system from a realization-based income tax to a covert personal consumption tax.

Some observations from the preface to the fifth edition remain apt:

> We are teaching students for a career at the bar, not just a season, and one of the challenges is to sort out and focus on things that are likely to be of lasting importance. I try to think what students will most need to know and understand ten years from now. From this perspective the main objective is to teach students about persistent underlying problems, to which current legislation may be only an ephemeral response. But ephemeral or not, it is the authoritative text through which the persistent problems are currently revealed.
>
> Cases, text, and problems — this book has all of these. What appears to distinguish it now is more cases and less text than some other books. For students just coming to the subject, selected cases often represent by far the most efficient way to arouse interest and define the problems with which the statute and administrative authorities must deal. Even cases that turn closely on superseded provisions offer a good base for evaluating subsequent legislative provisions, actual and potential. In a sense, cases provide a proxy for the actual experience seasoned professionals will bring to bear in studying the statute. There may be other proxies, but good law students respond to judicial opinions in a lively, interactive way that is hard to duplicate with any other materials.

A note about conventions: Where footnotes from excerpted material (cases, committee reports, etc.) are reproduced, the original numbering is retained. Authors' footnotes are numbered consecutively within each chapter, except that authors' footnotes added to excepted material are indicated with an asterisk (*) and the notes appear in square brackets with an indication of source (— EDS.). All section references in this book, unless otherwise indicated, are to the Internal Revenue Code of 1986, which is Title 26 of the United States Code. References to Treasury regulations, which are in Title 26 of the Code of Federal Regulations, are given as "Reg. §".

We are grateful to Jessica I. Rothschild for outstanding research and editorial assistance.

Peter J. Wiedenbeck
St. Louis, Missouri

I am very thankful for Peter Wiedenbeck's indefatigable energy, consummate skill, and patient good spirits in producing this new edition, and delighted with the result.

William D. Andrews
Cambridge, Massachusetts
February 2009

Chapter 1 — *Introduction*

A. *IN GENERAL*

The federal income tax is imposed annually on the taxable income of every individual who is either a citizen or resident of the United States. §1.[1] (In certain circumstances and subject to special limitations, U.S. federal income tax is also imposed on nonresident aliens. §2(d).) The current statutory rates are 10, 15, 25, 28, 33, and 35 percent. Look at §1(a) and (i) to see how these apply in steps to successive layers of income. The *marginal* rate applicable to an additional dollar of taxable income received by an individual taxpayer will be either 10, 15, 25, 28, 33, or 35 percent, depending on the taxpayer's total taxable income for the year, but the taxpayer's *average* rate is lower because the amount of income that is less than the starting point of the taxpayer's top bracket continues to be taxed at the lower rates applicable to the prior brackets.

Taxable income (the tax base) is computed by subtracting personal exemptions ($3,650 per individual taxpayer and dependent in 2009) and a standard deduction ($11,400 for a married couple; $5,700 for an unmarried individual in 2009), which have the effect of specifying a basic amount not subject to tax at all—a zero percent rate bracket as it were. §§63(b), (c), 151. In 2009 that amount for an unmarried individual without dependents is generally $9,350 ($3,650 exemption plus $5,700 standard deduction); for a married couple with two children it is $26,000 ($14,600 for four personal exemptions plus $11,400 standard deduction).[2]

---

1. All section references in this book, unless otherwise indicated, are to the Internal Revenue Code of 1986, which is Title 26 of the United States Code.

2. The amount of the personal exemption is reduced for high-income taxpayers. In 2009 the reduction for unmarried taxpayers begins at $166,800 of adjusted gross income, and for married couples the cut back starts at $250,200. §151(d)(3). Every taxpayer is allowed to claim either the standard deduction or

The foregoing dollar amounts are all for the year 2009 and they, together with the applicable dollar amounts in the rate schedules in §1, are derived by applying annual inflation adjustments to the figures in the statute. §§1(f), 63(c)(4), 151(d)(4). Note that the statutory figures are dated differently, and that annual inflation adjustments have to be made in different amounts to reflect different lengths of subsequent time. For most individual taxpayers this is an invisible complexity because the applicable adjustments are all incorporated in the tax return forms and instructions each year.[3]

In 1997, Congress enacted a Child Tax Credit that is now set at $1,000 per qualifying child. §24. The definition of qualifying child is similar to that for personal exemptions but with an age limit of 16 years. This credit is given in addition to the deduction for personal exemptions. A credit is subtracted from the tax otherwise due — $1,000 of credit saves $1,000 of tax. At a 10 percent rate of tax, it takes $10,000 of income to produce $1,000 of tax, so in general the credit will increase the amount of income one can receive without tax by $10,000 for the first qualifying child. Taking account of this credit, the amount of income that a couple with two qualifying children can receive free of tax in 2009 is $44,900 ($14,600 for four personal exemptions plus $11,400 standard deduction, while two child credits eliminate tax on the first $18,900 of taxable income).

The combined effect of the foregoing provisions in 2009 is illustrated in Table 1-1.[4]

Some curious features of Table 1-1 have been highlighted with shading. The careful observer will notice that three of the marginal rates shown in the table do not correspond with any rate specified in §1(i) (these three entries appear against a dark gray background). In two of those instances the reported marginal rate exceeds the marginal rate applicable to the next highest income level. These cases seem to contradict the statutory rate schedule, according to which marginal tax rates increase monotonically with income. What's going on? The answer lies in provisions that reduce the benefit of personal exemption deductions and child tax credits for high-income taxpayers. As Table 1-1 illustrates, in the ranges where they apply these income-based phase-outs impose disguised rate increases.

---

the amount of his or her itemized deductions, whichever is more advantageous. Compare §63(a) with §63(b). Most high-income taxpayers have itemized deductions in excess of the standard deduction and so the standard deduction becomes less relevant at upper income levels. Itemizers by and large tend to be homeowners because some of the largest itemized deductions are for home mortgage interest and property taxes.

3. Inflation adjustment figures are announced shortly before the beginning of the calendar year to which they relate. Those for 2009 are in Revenue Procedure 2008-66, 2008-45 I.R.B. 1107. The annual Revenue Procedures announcing these inflation adjustments are generally reproduced either at the beginning or in an appendix to students' selected sections editions of the income tax statute and regulations.

4. There is another credit called the earned income credit that would further reduce (or eliminate) income taxes for some low-income taxpayers in Table 1-1. But the purpose of that credit is in part to offset Social Security taxes imposed by the Federal Insurance Contributions Act (FICA), which are withheld from employees' wages. This table and discussion do not take account of either the Social Security taxes or the earned income credit.

TABLE 1-1
Illustrative Rates of Tax — 2009

	Unmarried Individual			Married Couple with Two Children		
Income ($)	Tax ($)	Average Rate (%)	Marginal Rate (%)	Tax ($)	Average Rate (%)	Marginal Rate (%)
10,000	65	0.7	10	0	0.0	0
20,000	1,180	5.9	15	0	0.0	0
30,000	2,680	8.9	15	0	0.0	0
40,000	4,180	10.5	15	0	0.0	0
50,000	6,350	12.7	25	765	1.5	15
60,000	8,850	14.8	25	2,265	3.8	15
80,000	13,850	17.3	25	5,265	6.6	15
100,000	19,102	19.1	28	8,875	8.9	25
120,000	24,702	20.6	28	14,375	12.0	30
200,000	48,169	24.1	33.3	36,984	18.5	28
300,000	81,459	27.2	33	68,883	23.0	34.3
400,000	114,837	28.7	35	102,966	25.7	35
1,000,000	324,837	32.5	35	312,966	31.3	35

Source: Rate schedules, standard deduction, personal exemption amount, and phase-out ranges for personal exemptions from Rev. Proc. 2008-66, 2008-45 I.R.B. 1107.

Assumes that "Income" is composed entirely of includible ordinary income (not capital gains or dividends), that there are no nonitemized deductions (i.e., "Income" here is adjusted gross income), and that the taxpayers take the standard deduction rather than itemizing their deductions.

The 30 percent marginal rate reported for the married couple with two children and $120,000 of income is the combination of the 25 percent rate prescribed by §1 and the phase-out of the child tax credits, which are reduced at the rate of $50 for each $1,000 of income in excess of $110,000 (in the case of a married couple filing jointly). §24(b)(1), (2). A credit reduction is merely a tax increase described differently, and the take-back at the rate of $50 per each $1,000 of additional income yields an average tax rate increase of 5 percent.[5] Due to the phase-out this couple (two children and $120,000 income) receives child tax credits of only $1,500, not $2,000. Observe that each $1,000 credit is eliminated over an income range of $20,000 so that a couple with two qualifying children receives no credit if their income exceeds $149,000. The phase-out of the child tax credit was designed to focus tax relief on low- and middle-income taxpayers. Observe that tax liability and average tax rates increase dramatically for the married couple with income above the

5. This describes a kind of average marginal rate effect. Because the credit goes down in $50 steps, at certain income levels one additional dollar of income will produce a $50 increment in tax — a marginal rate of 5,000 percent! But then the credit will be unaffected by the next $999 of income, so the average effective marginal rate is only 5 percent.

What reason(s) can you imagine for imposing the phase-out in $50 steps instead of proportionately?

phase-out range ($200,000 or more in Table 1-1; see the entries that appear against a light gray background).

Personal exemption deductions are also reduced at high incomes, but the reduction starts at higher incomes than the phase-out threshold of the child tax credit and extends over a much broader income range ($122,500). §151(d)(3). Because of this broader income range and because reducing a deduction increases tax indirectly by increasing the tax base, the impact on marginal rates of the personal exemption reduction is much less dramatic that the 5 percent rate hike caused by the child tax credit phase-out. The single individual with income of $200,000 loses only $341 of her exemption, while the married couple with two children and $300,000 income has each of four exemptions lowered by $487. The impact on each of these taxpayers is to cause the otherwise-applicable 33 percent marginal rate to increase by 0.321 percent times the number of exemptions. Reduction of the personal exemption deduction, which dates from 1990, seems to have had no justification other than the political imperative to increase revenue somewhat without explicitly raising the top nominal tax rates. Until 2006 personal exemptions could be entirely eliminated for high-income taxpayers, but the cutback is limited for tax years from 2006 through 2009 (yes, the phase-out is being phased out!), and is scheduled to expire in 2010. §151(d)(3)(E), (F).

In 1990 another disguised rate increase was introduced in §68 which disallows specified personal deductions in an amount up to 3 percent of the excess of income over $100,000 (inflation adjusted to $166,800 for 2009). Most high-income taxpayers have deductions substantially in excess of that 3 percent figure, and for them this provision imposes a 3 percent increase in marginal rates of tax on income (but not on deductions). (That is, $1.00 more income causes $0.03 more of deduction to be disallowed, with the result that taxable income goes up by $1.03.) The 1990 Act was therefore generally described as imposing a real marginal rate of 31.93 percent (1.03×31 percent) on ordinary income of the highest income taxpayers. The cut back of itemized deductions is also limited for tax years between 2006 and 2009 and is scheduled to expire in 2010. §68(f), (g). In 2009 it raises the top nominal rate of 35 percent to an effective marginal rate of 35.35 percent. Unlike the child credit phase-out and personal exemption reduction, this provision works as a disguised marginal rate increase for many taxpayers even at the very highest income levels. Section 68 has not been taken into account in Table 1-1 because it is there assumed that deductions were not itemized.

Even taking such disguised rate increases into account, the top rate has been considerably lower since 1986 than at any time in the past half century. From 1981 through 1986 the top rate was 50 percent; prior to 1969 it was 70 percent. From 1969 to 1980 it was 70 percent on investment income and 50 percent on compensation for services. During wartime, top rates have risen up to 90 percent.

Corporate income is subject to income tax at a top rate of 35 percent. Before 1986, the basic corporate rate was 46 percent. For corporate income below $10,000,000 the rate is 34 percent. For income below $75,000 the rates are 15 percent and 25 percent. Note the bubbles prescribed in the flush language following the nominal rates in §11(b)(1). What are their purpose and effect? (Two answers!)

Undistributed income of trusts and estates is taxed at the same marginal rates as individual income but with very narrow brackets for the lower rates. §1(e).

Revenues from the federal individual income tax are estimated to be $1,259 billion for fiscal year 2009, with another $339 billion coming from the corporate income tax. Individual income taxes have been somewhat less than half of total federal government receipts (not including borrowing) since the end of World War II. Corporate income taxes now account for about 12 percent, but they used to contribute much more.[6] Taking federal, state, and local governments together, in 2004 individual income taxes account for about 26 percent of total tax revenue, and corporate income taxes account for another 6 percent.[7]

Figure 1-1[8]
Total Tax Receipts as a Percentage of GDP, 1929-2003

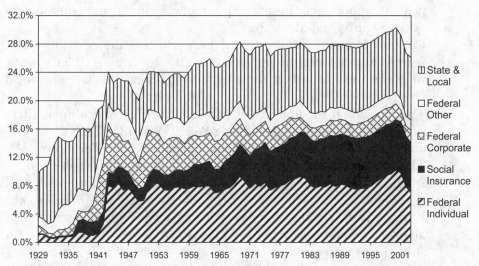

Note: "Federal Other" includes federal estate taxes, gift taxes, and custom duties plus employer contributions for federal unemployment tax, railroad unemployment insurance, and federal worker's compensation. Excludes federal nontaxes. Projected 2002 levels for Social Insurance, State & Local, and for some subcategories under "Federal Other" based on 2001 levels as a contant ratio to GDP.

6. Office of Management and Budget, Historical Tables: Budget of the United States Government—Fiscal Year 2009, Tables 2.1 & 2.2 (2008). Corporate income taxes exceeded personal taxes until 1944. By the 1960s the personal income tax raised about twice as much as the corporate tax; in the 1970s it was raised to about three times as much; in the 1980s it was more than four times as much; and by the early 2000s it was about five times as much. The corporate income tax has come back a little since then.
7. U.S. Census Bureau, Dept. of Commerce, Statistical Abstract of the United States: 2008, Tables 421, 461 (2007).
8. Figure 1-1 was prepared by and is reproduced with the courtesy of the Tax Policy Center, a joint venture of the Urban Institute and the Brookings Institution. See *http://www.taxpolicycenter.org/index.cfm.*

In relation to the whole economy, the federal individual income tax has for several years been very close to 10 percent of total personal income—a tithe in the aggregate, although not for each individual taxpayer.[9] As a share of the overall economy federal individual income tax receipts have been remarkably stable — running about 8 to 9 percent of gross domestic product (GDP) — since World War II, despite repeated bouts of major reform and readjustments of the rate schedules. As Figure 1-1 shows, over the long term the share of GDP absorbed by the federal government has also been surprisingly constant, about 18 percent, year in and year out since the 1940s. Figure 1-1 reveals several other noteworthy facts.

- While overall federal revenues and individual income tax receipts have been quite stable for decades, there has been a dramatic shift in contributions from other sources of revenue. In particular, the corporate income tax, which took about 5 percent of GDP in the early 1950s and thereafter ran around 4 percent through the 1960s, has since fallen to about 1.5 percent of GDP. Receipts from excise taxes and the federal wealth transfer taxes also fell over this period. Offsetting those declines has been a substantial increase in payroll taxes to support social insurance programs, including most importantly Social Security and Medicare.
- Contrary to popular assumptions, there is little evidence of the much-feared expansion of the public sector (the Leviathan). What growth in government that has occurred is actually at the state and local levels.
- The individual income tax, which has been in effect since 1913, underwent a major change during World War II (in 1942, to be precise) when it first became the principal source of federal revenues. This war-time transformation from a "class tax" that targeted only a small group of the highest-income Americans (less than 10 percent of the population) to a "mass tax" that reached the middle class brought with it many changes (e.g., wage withholding, taxation of alimony, medical expense deduction) that will be explored in subsequent chapters.

Federal estate and gift taxes produce little more than 1 percent of total revenues but they are quite important for the small group of people on whom they fall.[10] They are closely related to the individual income tax in their impact on the planning of property arrangements in well-to-do families

---

9. U.S. Census Bureau, Dept. of Commerce, Statistical Abstract of the United States: 2008, Tables 651, 656 (2007).

10. Id., Table 466.

and in their contribution of an element of progressivity to the tax system as a whole.

As Figure 1-1 dramatically illustrates, the prominence of the federal income tax as a revenue source is a product of World War II, as is the size and the economic importance of the federal government. During the Civil War there was an income tax that accounted for a significant portion of federal government revenue, but it was repealed in 1872. In 1894 a tax of 2 percent was imposed on incomes in excess of $4,000, but it was held unconstitutional the next year. Pollock v. Farmers' Loan & Trust Co., 157 U.S. 429, aff'd on rehearing, 158 U.S. 601 (1895). The major sources of federal revenues throughout the nineteenth century were customs duties and excises.

A corporate income tax was imposed in 1909. In 1913 the Sixteenth Amendment to the Constitution was adopted, overruling *Pollock*, and Congress then levied an income tax on both corporate and individual incomes. The individual income tax was at first another low-rate, low-yield tax on relatively high incomes, but it was soon called into service as a major revenue source during World War I, with a top rate as high as 77 percent in 1918. The income tax has remained a major revenue source ever since and has been predominant since World War II.

In addition to being the principal source of federal revenues, the income tax is also a popular tax in the sense that it is imposed on most of the people. For example, in 1981 nearly four-fifths of the population was covered by taxable income tax returns.[11] This extensive coverage of the income tax is even more recent than its emergence as a major revenue source. Prior to World War II, only about 5 percent of the population was covered by taxable returns, except from 1918 to 1920 when the figure was about 10 percent.[12]

Apart from its coverage and prominence as a revenue source, the income tax is immensely important because of its impact on the whole range of commercial, financial, economic, and property relationships in our society. The tax applies to income from whatever source derived; there is hardly any property or economic transaction that does not have its income tax aspects and implications to be considered. The high rates of tax that were prescribed for upper-income brackets prior to 1986 had much more of an impact on transactions than on the amount of revenue raised. In this respect they were like the gift and estate taxes.

11. U.S. Bureau of the Census, Dept. of Commerce, Statistical Abstract of the United States: 1984, 6, 327 (1983). Persons "covered by taxable income tax returns" are individuals filing taxable returns (that is, returns showing income tax *after* credits) and persons claimed as dependents on those returns.

12. Goode, The Individual Income Tax 302 (Table A-3) (rev. ed. 1976); Seltzer, The Place of Personal Exemptions in the Present-Day Income Tax, in House Comm. on Ways and Means, 86th Cong., Tax Revision Compendium 493 (1959).

There are several purposes to be served, or at least observed, in constructing, interpreting, and administering a tax law.

(a) *Financing government expenditures* is the principal purpose of any general tax, including the federal income tax. For a long time it was thought that taxes had to be set nearly equal to government expenditures on an immediate current basis. Today we know that governments, like private persons, can sometimes spend before receiving revenues by borrowing to cover the difference. Indeed, the national government can perhaps do that more readily than private persons or local governments can because the national government controls the supply of currency in which the debts are required to be paid and there is no risk of death, disability, or bankruptcy to limit what lenders will advance.

But deficit financing is not costless. At a minimum, continued deficit financing means an increase in national debt and in interest payments due; consequently, future taxes will have to be higher just to meet those interest charges than if government expenditures had been kept lower or taxes higher in the deficit years.[13] In that way tax and government expenditure levels are tied to one another over the long haul even if there is some flexibility in relative timing.

(b) *Promoting economic stability and growth* is a second, more recently recognized, objective. In a period of recession or excessive unemployment, a government deficit may operate to restore equilibrium between general levels of supply and demand. On the other hand, an increase in taxes relative to government expenditures is one tool with which to fight inflation. To some extent the income tax functions as a built-in stabilizer because collections will increase or decrease automatically as economic activity, which is reflected in incomes, goes up or down. But the government has sometimes gone further by deliberately reducing taxes in the face of an existing deficit for the purpose of stimulating the economy.

During the 1980s we had continuing large deficits even though there was no recession from 1983 through 1989. These deficits did not result in the excessive inflation some had predicted. In part at least this was because

---

13. Debt and interest obligations have risen in recent years as follows. Note that while deficits were reduced and at the turn of the century temporarily eliminated, tax cuts and spending increases since 2001 have brought them back. Debt and interest charges remain high.

	1970	1980	1985	1990	1995	2000	2005	2010*
Debt (percent of GDP)	37.6	33.3	43.9	55.9	67.2	58.0	64.6	69.5
Deficit (percent of GDP)	−0.3	−2.7	−5.1	−3.9	−2.2	2.4	−2.6	−1.0
Interest paid								
Percent of GDP	1.6	2.0	3.2	3.5	3.6	2.9	2.2	2.6
Billions of dollars	15.9	54.9	133.6	200.3	265.4	282.7	275.8	411.4
Percent of income taxes collected	12.9	17.8	33.7	35.7	35.5	23.3	22.9	23.4

Source: Office of Management and Budget, Historical Tables: Budget of the United States Government — Fiscal Year 2009, Tables 1.2, 2.3, 3.1, 7.1 (2008).
  * Data for 2010 are estimates.

foreigners showed a willingness to finance our spending by buying our bonds (and stocks, real estate, and art treasures).

(c) *Equity* means fairness in distribution of the burdens of government expenditures or of economic stabilization, as the case may be, and it must be an objective of any acceptable taxing system. *Horizontal equity* is imposing similar burdens on people in like circumstances; *vertical equity* is creating an appropriate differential in burdens for people in unlike circumstances. These formulations raise questions, of course, rather than settle them: What are the like circumstances? And what are appropriate differentials in burdens for people in different circumstances?

(d) *Redistributing income or wealth* is another matter. Or is it? (1) Is redistributing wealth a legitimate object of taxation? (2) Can redistribution of wealth be distinguished from distribution of the burdens of government expenditure or fiscal control? Or, put the other way, can tax burdens be distributed without wealth being redistributed? (3) Can a graduated income tax be defended and rationalized without admitting redistribution of wealth to be an objective? (4) What information would one need to have and what judgments would one need to make to decide whether present taxes do effect any substantial redistribution of wealth?

(e) *Neutrality* means avoiding or minimizing distortions of normal economic incentives, and it is another crucial objective. Virtually any tax will distort market incentives to some extent, but some taxes are worse than others in this respect, and we should prefer the latter on that account. In part, distortion varies because different aspects of economic behavior vary in their sensitivity to costs and prices. This criterion provides some reason for avoiding taxes on particularly sensitive items, and for concentrating taxes on particularly insensitive ones.

Some would argue, for example, that investment is particularly sensitive to after-tax rates of return and that capital gains cannot be subjected to high graduated tax rates without impairing the normal flow of capital into new enterprises. Therefore, the argument concludes, capital gains should be given special protection against ordinary income tax rates. Others are skeptical of that argument at several points, but it is important to keep in mind the extent to which various aspects of the tax system may alter the economic choices that would be made in its absence.

(f) *Creating special incentives* not generated by the market alone, like redistributing income, is more problematic. (1) Is it legitimate and desirable to use the general tax system to create special incentives for particularly desirable forms of conduct? (2) Can any satisfactory line be drawn between the business of creating special incentives and that of protecting normal incentives? (3) Are there special advantages and disadvantages to using the tax system rather than government expenditures to provide special incentives?

What about special *disincentives*, like an emissions tax based on the amount of pollutants emitted by a business firm? These have mostly been proposed as separate taxes, not parts of the general income tax. Yet because they take the form of taxes rather than regulations, they may come within the jurisdiction of tax-writing committees in Congress and be thought of as part of the tax system and thereby subjected to criteria appropriate for the design of general taxes. Does this make sense?

(g) *Administrability*, finally, is the sine qua non for sound tax legislation. None of the other objectives can be achieved unless the tax imposed is capable of reasonably fair and efficient administration. This is no more of an absolute than any of the other characteristics, but difficulty of administration must constantly be taken into account with respect to any proposal that may be made. Under this general heading, everyone suffers from excessive *complexity* and *simplification* is a commonly stated aim of tax legislation.

A practicing lawyer must have a working knowledge of the federal income tax for several strictly professional reasons. Occasionally, clients may be in trouble for income tax violations. More often, clients will want to know how to comply with the income tax law. With luck, some clients will have the foresight to seek advice not only on compliance with the income tax law but also on arranging their affairs in advance to make such compliance less burdensome; the lawyer will thus be called on to play a creative planning role and will need a broad sense of the limitations and the possibilities that are implicit in the tax law. Finally, the lawyer will have clients who seek advice generally without realizing that they have income tax problems. This will require sensitivity to a range of income tax implications — both the pitfalls and the opportunities for creative planning — to serve the clients' interests well.

Beyond these primary professional concerns, there are many other reasons for studying the income tax. First, the lawyer as a citizen should be concerned with the quality of the income tax law because of its pervasive influence. The tax law requires more from more people in the way of conscious compliance than any other statute. Furthermore, it represents the most general, single, positive attempt to face the question of how the burdens (and benefits) of our society should be distributed among its members. The quality of the income tax law and its administration is a fair index of our social and political morality and should be of concern for that reason.

Another reason to study the income tax in law school is to develop some skill and experience in dealing with statutory materials. The income tax law is essentially and originally statutory because it all arises out of the legislative act of imposing taxes. In this respect it is quite different from subjects in which rules of decision have been codified after initial development in the courts and scholarly treatises. Moreover, the tax statute is repeatedly revisited by Congress.

The tax statute is the work of many people working at different times and with different purposes and it speaks with many voices that are sometimes not easy to reconcile. As a treatise or model statute it might not get high marks, but it all speaks with the authority of congressional enactment (*not* revelation) and we are therefore obliged to study the comical as well as the profound.

A lawyer has to learn to work with legislative materials as creatively and critically as with judicial opinions. Indeed, many lawyers in practice will spend more time working with legislative materials than with judicial opinions. Particularly in newly developing subjects, legislation is likely to dominate because it leads the way and is general in its application; judicial opinions come later and are narrower in focus. One must learn to read with a sense for the inherent ambiguity in general formulations, with a sense for the variety of potential meanings in particular formulations, and with a sense of the imaginative creativity that enters into the business of construction and interpretation. A lawyer must also learn not only how context gives meaning to terms but also about the ambiguities of context itself and the extent to which skillful advocacy may give context its meaning. The possibility of identifying and working with underlying purposes and principles should also be considered. A student of the law is accustomed to distilling a common theme or underlying idea from a collection of cases; when a statute is written in very particular terms, the question arises whether it is possible to read those particular provisions, like cases, as exhibiting or reflecting a deeper meaning that is not expressed directly. Finally, one simply needs practice at reading and making sense of highly complicated statutory provisions.

Beyond working with given statutory materials, a thoughtful student should also be concerned with legislation from a drafter's viewpoint. Are there good and bad techniques in legislation? Is the fearful complexity of many of the present provisions of the tax law necessary or desirable? Are there limits to what can be done by legislation, and how? Are there categories of problems that will not yield to statutory resolution, and, if so, is it possible to generalize about them? Can one develop any skill or general knowledge to foresee the kinds of administrative or interpretive problems that a particular legislative enactment will produce? Should legislation be highly articulated and particularized, or should it be general in its terms? Or does that vary with subject matter, and if so, how? What is the relationship between differences in legislative style and differences in allocation of authority among agencies of government, and what considerations should influence judgments about that allocation?

These questions concern us because a large part of any lawyer's function is to order affairs by verbal generalization. Few, perhaps, will be directly concerned with tax legislation, although the tax bar collectively has a considerable share of responsibility for the quality of tax legislation. But skill with words and a sense of what is feasible in the way of verbal formulation is an indispensable part of the stock in trade of any lawyer involved in drafting contracts, wills, corporate papers, collective bargaining agreements, consent decrees, and so on.

Another reason to study the tax law is for what it can show about problems of administration. What are the relationships between substantive provisions and the necessities of administration? What limits are imposed by administrative requirements? Again, these very practical questions — and a sense for what is feasible within a given institutional framework — affect lawyers in many of the contexts in which they work, even if they are never directly involved in tax administration.

Finally, the income tax law provides a superb vantage point from which to study many related subjects. Tax cases represent the application of the tax statute to the whole panorama of economic and property relations and transactions that characterize our society, and the basic income tax course cannot help but serve as a survey of those relations. Furthermore, the tax question typically offers an unusually illuminating perspective on those transactions. As between the parties, there are often persuasive reasons to let their choice of labels and characterizations control their rights and obligations. But the tax collector is not a party, so tax administrators and tax lawyers and courts in tax cases need to be ever vigilant, skeptical of parties' labels, and prepared to search for deeper characterizations. The courts and administrators have not always been up to the task (nor, indeed, has Congress) but a careful, critical discussion of income tax issues always raises challenging problems of objective evaluation of transactions.

The study of income taxation of corporate transactions is a good way to learn about corporate transactions themselves. Tax lawyers have found themselves among the leaders of the business law bar partly because tax considerations play such a prominent part in that practice. But another reason is that a good tax lawyer's habit of mind equips her to cut through the layers of documentation that typically surround complex corporate transactions—even if, too often, the tax result ultimately does turn on that documentation.

B. PROCEDURE AND ADMINISTRATION

1. The Internal Revenue Service

Administration and enforcement of the federal income tax are committed by statute to the Secretary of the Treasury. §7801(a). The statute further provides for a Commissioner of Internal Revenue who shall have such duties and powers as may be prescribed by the Secretary. §7803(a). In practice the Commissioner is the chief full-time tax administrator.

The Commissioner has long had authority to employ and supervise such number of persons as he deems proper for the administration and enforcement of the internal revenue laws.[14] These persons constitute the Internal Revenue Service (IRS). In the early years it was called the Bureau of Internal Revenue.

In the summer of 1998 Congress enacted the IRS Restructuring and Reform Act. This legislation followed extended hearings that featured

---

14. §7804.

testimony by taxpayers (and a few former IRS personnel) concerning alleged abuses of taxpayer rights by IRS personnel. Some incidents of abuse undoubtedly did occur, and for these the Commissioner has apologized. On the other hand, many professionals dealing regularly with the IRS would estimate that incidents of serious abuse have been remarkably rare. (At least one disaffected ex-employee alleged that IRS instructions were to behave less aggressively in the case of taxpayers who had professional representation.)

Some of the congressional critics of the IRS are also champions of radical tax change and reduction. Some have announced goals of eliminating the income tax and of "eliminating the Internal Revenue Service as we know it." One peculiar locution is to refer to the Internal Revenue Code (IRC) as the "IRS Code." The fact is, of course, that only Congress can make or change the IRC, and most informed observers would judge that complications and inconsistencies and other defects in the Code are a substantial part of the reason for taxpayer frustrations and any deficiencies there are in IRS performance.

The statutory revisions resulting from all these charges are less dramatic. The Commissioner has been given a five-year term.[15] An oversight board has been established to "oversee the Internal Revenue Service in its administration, management, conduct, direction, and supervision of the execution and application of the internal revenue laws."[16] Membership on the board is to include the Secretary or Deputy Secretary of the Treasury, the Commissioner, one "full–time Federal employee or a representative of employees," and six individuals who are not otherwise Federal officers or employees. All except the ex-officio members are to be "appointed by the President, by and with the advice and consent of the Senate," for five-year terms. See generally §7802.

The Office of the Taxpayer Advocate and the National Taxpayer Advocate who supervises that office have had their authority and responsibilities spelled out at greater length.[17]

For many years IRS field personnel and taxpayers have been divided into regions and districts, with each district being under the charge of a District Director. §7621. The 1998 statute directs the Commissioner to develop and implement a plan to reorganize the IRS that will:

(1) supersede any organization or reorganization of the Internal Revenue Service based on any statute or reorganization plan applicable on the effective date of this section;

(2) eliminate or substantially modify the existing organization of the Internal Revenue Service, which is based on a national, regional, and district structure;

15. §7301(a)(1)(A).
16. §7802(a), (c)(1)(A).
17. §7803(c).

(3) establish organizational units serving particular groups of taxpayers with similar needs; and

(4) ensure an independent appeals function within the Internal Revenue Service. . . . [Internal Revenue Service Restructuring and Reform Act of 1998, Pub. L. No. 105-206, §1001, 112 Stat. 685, 689.]

Prior to enactment of the statute the Commissioner had identified four different groups of taxpayers with similar needs: individual taxpayers, small businesses, large businesses, and the tax-exempt sector, and the statute is apparently intended to encourage him to proceed along these or similar lines.

Another theme in the criticism of the IRS has been its failure to move more rapidly in adopting and adapting modern computer technology. The restructuring legislation identifies upgrading information technology and promotion of electronic filing as primary goals.

Another change was to shift the burden of proof in tax litigation from the taxpayer to the Commissioner. But the shift only occurs if the taxpayer presents credible evidence in support of her position, keeps adequate records, and cooperates reasonably in the IRS examination. §7491.

2. Annual Returns

Administration of the federal income tax revolves around the filing of returns by taxpayers. §6011. Every individual subject to tax is required to file a return for each taxable year. §6012. In general, returns are due three and one-half months after the end of the taxable year, although it is not hard to secure extensions of time. §§6072, 6081. The return contains a report of the taxpayer's income and deductions together with a computation of the tax due, and payment is required to accompany the return. §6151. In most individual cases, the taxpayer's own computation of tax on the return is the last as well as the first computation; the IRS simply cannot audit a major share of returns. There are now more than 130 million individual income tax returns filed annually, and the percentage of those examined by the IRS (including examinations by correspondence) is only about 1 percent.[18] The system is sometimes therefore called a self-assessment system, although technically assessment refers to a procedure instituted by the government to collect deficiencies in tax, not to the initial determination of liability or payment of tax by the taxpayers. §§6201-6204.

18. U.S. Census Bureau, Dept. of Commerce, Statistical Abstract of the United States: 2008, Table 467 (2007).

3.   Investigation, Assessment, and Collection of Deficiencies

It would hardly work, however, to leave all returns unexamined, so the IRS has extensive authority to investigate and examine taxpayers and their books of account and other sources of information to determine if taxes have been properly paid. §§7601-7612. If a return has not been filed, the Secretary has authority to make one on behalf of a taxpayer. §6020(b). If examination reveals that taxes have not been paid in full, then procedures may be invoked to assess a deficiency. §§6201-6204. After a deficiency is assessed, the government is given various more-or-less summary procedures for collecting the assessed amount. §6303 (notice and demand); §6321 (lien for assessed taxes); §6331 (levy and distraint); §6335 (sale of seized property).

The government can assess and collect deficiencies without resorting to the courts, but aggrieved taxpayers may go to court to contest the government's determinations. There are two principal ways to do so: (1) by suit for a refund after paying the tax or (2) by petition to the Tax Court for redetermination of a deficiency prior to assessment.

4.   Refund Procedure

Refund procedure begins with a claim for refund filed by the taxpayer with the IRS. The Secretary has authority to refund overpayments or to credit them against other amounts due. §6402. Sometimes a claimed overpayment results from payment of a deficiency asserted by the IRS, and sometimes it results from the taxpayer's original or subsequent payment of an excessive amount, either by mistake or because the taxpayer decides to pay on a disputed or doubtful item. A claim for refund is appropriate in any of these cases.

If a claim for refund is rejected or unanswered for six months then the taxpayer may bring suit in court. §§7422, 6532(a).

Originally there was no remedy against the sovereign government itself, but an aggrieved taxpayer was allowed to bring suit against the Collector for taxes wrongfully collected. Although this was formally a suit against the Collector personally for his wrongful conduct in collecting taxes that were not due, statutes have long provided that the government would pay judgments rendered against its tax collectors and defend them against such litigation, so such actions have long been recognized in substance as suits against the government. Now suits are conducted directly against the government in name as well as substance. These may be brought in the United States Court of Federal Claims, 28 U.S.C. §1491(a)(1) (2006), or in a federal district court for the district in which the taxpayer resides or has his primary place of business. 28 U.S.C. §§1340, 1346(a) (jurisdiction), 1402 (venue). In a federal district court the taxpayer may choose to have the case tried before a jury.

5. The Tax Court

In 1924 Congress provided for the establishment of a Board of Tax Appeals to give taxpayers an opportunity for an impartial determination of their tax liabilities prior to payment. The Board of Tax Appeals, later renamed the Tax Court, is now an Article I court and an independent agency in the legislative branch of the government. §7441. Even though it is not an Article III Court, the Tax Court commands wide respect for the impartiality and competence of its decisions. It is currently authorized to have 19 judges appointed for terms of 15 years. §7443(a), (e). Several of its members have served more than a single term.

The jurisdiction of the Tax Court is confined to tax cases and consists primarily of hearing taxpayers' petitions for redetermination of deficiencies preliminarily determined by the IRS. §§6213-6214. The Tax Court also has jurisdiction to review certain other administrative determinations besides deficiencies. See, for example, §§7428 (qualified status of charitable organizations), 7476 (qualification of retirement plans), 7478 (tax-exempt status of state or municipal bonds). The Tax Court is the only court with general power to review determinations of tax liability prior to payment of the tax. Indeed, §7421(a) provides that "no suit for the purpose of restraining the assessment or collection of any tax shall be maintained in any court by any person, whether or not such person is the person against whom such tax was assessed." Tax Court redeterminations of deficiencies are among the things excepted from this prohibition.

There are strict procedural requirements for bringing matters before the Tax Court. §§6212-6213. After opportunities for several rounds of consideration of a matter in the IRS, if agreement has not been reached, a preliminary determination of deficiency is sent to the taxpayer. §6212(a). The preliminary determination letter is commonly referred to as a "90-day letter" since the taxpayer has just 90 days from the mailing of that letter to file a petition with the Tax Court for review of the preliminary determination. §6213(a). That 90-day requirement is strictly construed; it is said to be a matter of jurisdiction.

Except in cases of jeopardy (when there appears to be reason to fear that the taxpayer will otherwise abscond without paying; see §6861), the government is prohibited from assessing a deficiency (and thus invoking the summary collection procedures available after assessment) until it has sent a 90-day letter and either the 90 days have expired without any petition to the Tax Court or a decision has been rendered by the Tax Court and has become final. §6213(a).

6. Appellate Review

Tax Court decisions may be appealed by either the taxpayer or the government (or both) to the federal court of appeals for the circuit in which the taxpayer resides. §7482. For a corporation it is the circuit that includes the principal place of business or the principal office or the office from which the return was filed. §7482(b)(1)(B). Thus, decisions of a single court of specialized competence and national jurisdiction are subject to review by a dozen appellate courts of general subject matter but limited geographical jurisdiction. Decisional conflicts among courts of appeals can only be settled by the Supreme Court, which grants certiorari in a limited number of tax cases mostly to resolve such conflicts.

In general, an appeal from a Tax Court decision is likely to go to the same court of appeals as if the taxpayer had paid the tax and sued for a refund in the appropriate federal district court. The United States Court of Federal Claims, however, is another matter; its decisions are subject to review by the Court of Appeals for the Federal Circuit wherever the taxpayer may reside. 28 U.S.C. §1295(a)(3). If a taxpayer has an issue, therefore, on which the court of appeals for his circuit has taken a position adverse to his claim, he may find it worthwhile to bring the action in the Court of Federal Claims just to avoid direct application of that precedent. The Tax Court has taken the position that it will decide cases in accord with precedents of the court to which an appeal would lie even if it has decided to reject those decisions in subsequent cases arising in other circuits. Jack E. Golsen, 54 T.C. 742, affd. 445 F.2d 985 (10th Cir.), cert. denied, 404 U.S. 940 (1971). But no such doctrine prevents the Court of Federal Claims and the Federal Circuit from rendering superior justice in comparable circumstances, and once they do, other taxpayers may well choose to follow the same route.

7.   Statutes of Limitations

The most generally applicable limitation periods in the determination of income tax liability are three years. If a return is filed on time and tax is paid therewith, then the taxpayer must file a claim for refund with the IRS within three years of the due date of the return for the government or any court to have authority to award or pay a refund. §6511(a)-(c). If a claim is timely filed, then the taxpayer must wait six months or until the IRS denies the claim before bringing suit; no suit may be brought more than two years after the claim is denied. §6532. If all or part of the tax was paid more than a year after the return was filed, then a claim for refund of the amount so paid is timely if filed within two years of such payment.

So far as the government is concerned, the statute provides that deficiencies must be assessed within three years after the return is filed, §6501, but the statute is tolled when a 90-day letter is sent, so in effect it is the sending of that letter that must be accomplished within the three-year period. §6503(a).

There are several exceptions to the three-year limit on assessment of deficiencies. Most importantly, there is no statute of limitations against assessment if no return is filed or if the deficiency is attributable to the tax-payer's fraud or willful attempt to evade tax. §6501(c). Of course the existence of fraud may be a more problematic matter of proof than the underlying tax liability itself. Because of this provision, the government may assess a deficiency at any time; it is just that if the assessment procedure is begun too late the government will have to prove fraud or willful attempt to evade to make the assessment stick.

The other major exception relates simply to substantial omissions: If there is an omission from gross income of more than 25 percent, then the government has six years instead of three to determine a deficiency. §6501(e).

8.   Interest, Penalties, and Costs

In general, interest accrues in favor of the government on underpayments of tax, §§6601, 6602, and in favor of the taxpayer on overpayments, §6611, at rates redetermined quarterly to stay close to the commercial prime rate. Interest is compounded daily. §6622.

Penalties come in a variety of strengths and sizes. The IRS may simply assess additions to tax: the oldest and most general additions are: (1) 20 percent of the amount of any underpayment due to negligence or disregard of rules or regulations; and (2) 75 percent of the amount of any underpayment due to fraud. §§6662(b)(1), 6663. There are many other penalties as well, and some of them are very specific. See generally §§6651-6725. The penalty provisions have been the subject of extensive legislative activity in recent years.

The Tax Court and other courts are authorized to assess damages against any taxpayer if it appears that proceedings have been instituted by the taxpayer primarily for delay or that the taxpayer's position is frivolous or groundless. §6673. On the other hand, there is currently in effect a statutory provision under which any court can award reasonable litigation costs to a taxpayer who has substantially prevailed in litigation in which the position of the United States is established to have been unreasonable. §7430. For more serious offenses there are criminal penalties imposed in criminal proceedings, with all the attendant procedural protections. §§7201-7232. Administration of the criminal provisions is under the supervision of the Assistant Attorney General in charge of the Tax Division of the Department of Justice.

9.   Withholding and Estimated Taxes

While returns and final payments are not due until after year-end, most income taxes are actually collected during the taxable year for which they are incurred. First, employers are required to withhold income taxes from employees' wages and salaries and pay them directly to the government. §3402(a). Employees then, of course, are entitled to a credit for the amounts withheld when they come to compute the taxes due with their returns. §31(a). Wage withholding accounts for almost four-fifths of total individual income tax liability.[19]

Second, taxpayers whose tax liabilities are not substantially covered by withholding are required to make quarterly estimated tax payments during the taxable year. §§6654, 6315. Sometimes withholding and estimated tax payments exceed a taxpayer's tax liability, in which case the taxpayer may secure either a refund of the excess or a credit against tax obligations for the succeeding taxable year. §6402. Indeed more than 75 percent of returns filed are to claim a refund.[20]

C. CONSTITUTIONAL BACKGROUND

Article I, Section 2, Clause 3:

Representatives and direct Taxes shall be apportioned among the several States which may be included within this Union, according to their respective Numbers, which shall be determined by adding to the whole Number of free Persons, including those bound to Service for a Term of Years, and excluding Indians not taxed, three-fifths of all other Persons.

Article I, Section 8, Clause 1:

The Congress shall have Power to lay and collect Taxes, Duties, Imposts and Excises, to pay the Debts and provide for the common Defence and general Welfare of the United States; but all Duties, Imports and Excises shall be uniform throughout the United States.

Article I, Section 9, Clause 4:

No capitation, or other direct, Tax shall be laid, unless in Proportion to the Census or Enumeration herein before directed to be taken.

Sixteenth Amendment:

The Congress shall have power to lay and collect taxes on incomes, from whatever source derived, without apportionment among the several States, and without regard to any census or enumeration.

---

19. IRS, Individual Income Tax Returns 2005, Table 3.3 (2007). Data also available at: *http://www.irs.gov/pub/irs-soi/05in02ar.xls*
  20. Id.

There has never been any substantial doubt about the power of Congress to impose an income tax under Article I, §8. However, the Supreme Court did hold a tax on income from property to be a direct tax on the property itself requiring apportionment under Article I, §§2 and 9. Pollack v. Farmer's Loan and Trust Co., 157 U.S. 429, aff'd on rehearing, 158 U.S. 601 (1895). An income tax on earned income alone would have been politically unfeasible, and an income tax apportioned among the states according to population would have been wholly impractical. The effect of *Pollock* was therefore to prevent enactment of any federal individual income tax until approval of the Sixteenth Amendment in February 1913.

The Revenue Act of 1913, which was enacted after the effective date of the Sixteenth Amendment, was upheld against a variety of constitutional claims in Brushaber v. Union Pacific R.R., 240 U.S. 1 (1916). Among the arguments rejected were (1) that the tax was repugnant to the Due Process clause of the Fifth Amendment by reason of the exemption of income below $3,000 (or $4,000 for married persons) and the graduated surtax on income above $20,000; (2) that "discrimination and want of due process [result] from the fact that the owners of houses in which they live are not compelled to estimate the rental value in making up their incomes, while those who are living in rented houses and pay rent are not allowed, in making up their taxable income, to deduct rent which they have paid," 240 U.S. at 23-24; and (3) that the statute was invalid under both the Fifth Amendment and Sixteenth Amendment because it retroactively taxed all income received between March 1, 1913, and October 3 of that year (the date of its passage).

Pollack also held a federal income tax on interest from state and municipal bonds invalid because such a tax infringed on the states' sovereign power to borrow money. Earlier the Court had held that a federal income tax could not be imposed on the salaries of state judicial officers. Collector v. Day, 78 U.S. (11 Wall.) 113 (1870). The exemption of state salaries from federal income tax was put to rest in Helvering v. Gerhardt, 304 U.S. 405 (1938). The exemption of state and municipal bond interest is still in the statute, §103, although the Supreme Court has now made clear that it too is not required by the constitution. South Carolina v. Baker, Chapter 8A below.

D.   SOURCES OF FEDERAL INCOME TAX LAW

The Internal Revenue Code is, of course, the primary authority. The present statute is the Internal Revenue Code of 1986, which is Title 26 of the United States Code. Prior to 1986, there were the Internal Revenue Codes of 1954 and 1939, and before that there were individual revenue acts, which were usually passed every other year. Much of the language was repeated from one act to the next so that the difference between adopting new acts and amending a code was not as radical as it might appear. Indeed the section numbering had a persistent general pattern through successive acts and the 1939 Code.

The 1954 Code contained new material, some of which codified existing interpretations. Although it introduced a wholly new numbering scheme, it did not introduce any radical substantive changes to most provisions. In 1986 there were important substantive changes but again most of the statute remained unchanged. It was not even reenacted as a new code; its name was just altered by substituting "1986" for "1954" in the title. Other years of extensive and important revision were 1942, 1969, and 2001, but the tax reductions and amendments made in the latter year were enacted subject to a 10-year sunset provision and so are scheduled to vanish for years beginning after December 31, 2010. Economic Growth and Tax Relief Reconciliation Act of 2001, Pub. L. No. 107-16, §901, 115 Stat. 38, 150.

In general, the present statute should be thought of as originating in 1913, with subsequent changes representing growth without loss of identity. (Some might go further, asserting that the vigorous growth came mostly in the statute's youth, that it reached full height by World War II, and that too many of the subsequent changes, particularly those since 1969, represent gain in weight, healing of wounds, hardening of arteries, and loss of some vital functions. Try to keep your eyes open to the genealogy of particular provisions as you study them, and consider whether this is a fair suggestion.)

Treasury regulations are the most formal and authoritative administrative interpretation of the tax statute. After the statute itself, a practicing lawyer or revenue agent is likely to turn to them. (The revenue agent may indeed begin with the regulations, leaving the statute for lawyers to argue about.) The regulations are all promulgated under the general statutory authority conferred in §7805(a); some are also specifically authorized in the substantive provisions to which they relate. The regulations are intended to resolve doubtful questions of interpretation of the statute and to provide instruction and explanation to the IRS. Students will find the regulations very helpful simply in understanding and working through complex statutory provisions.

Revenue rulings and procedures are less formal and comprehensive than Treasury regulations. Revenue rulings contain interpretations of substantive provisions usually in relation to particular factual situations that are described. Statements describing IRS practice are called *revenue procedures*. These had a wide variety of other names in the early years. They are published periodically in the Internal Revenue Bulletin, available in PDF format on the IRS Web site, at *http://www.irs.gov/businesses/lists/0,,id=98230,00.html*, and compiled semiannually in the Cumulative Bulletin.

Private letter rulings. Most rulings and technical advice memoranda are not *officially* published by the government; these are often called "private letter rulings." They are now required to be released to public view, however, under the Freedom of Information laws, and several private publishers have undertaken to make them generally available.

Judicial opinions. Opinions by the Supreme Court, courts of appeals, district courts, and the United States Court of Federal Claims are published in the usual places. Some Tax Court opinions are officially reported in Reports of the United States Tax Court. §7462. Others, usually called memorandum opinions, are unofficially reported by the loose-leaf services.

Legislative history. Committee reports and hearings, floor debates, and bills may all help in understanding the tax laws as they are enacted. Committee reports are the most important. For convenience, these are republished in the Cumulative Bulletin. In addition, the Cumulative Bulletins for 1939 and immediately succeeding years contain the committee reports for all the Revenue Acts from 1913 down to that date. Prior to 1939 these were not readily available.

In recent years, the staff of the Joint Committee on Taxation has often prepared and published general explanations of major tax statutes after enactment. Often incorporating explanatory materials from the committee reports that have been selected and modified to refer to the statute as finally passed, the general explanation has regularly borne a blue cover and so is sometimes referred to as the "blue book." This term has also become a colloquial verb that refers to the activity of congressional committee staffs in clarifying the intention and effect of last-minute statutory changes by the composition and publication of blue book explanations.

Secondary sources. Literature on the income tax is extensive. There is a brief general bibliography at the end of this chapter, and selective, more particular references appear at the end of each of the other chapters in this book.

E.   A GLOSSARY OF BASIC TERMS AND ISSUES

It is difficult to understand any part of the income tax law without knowing something of the whole structure. The next few pages contain a very condensed outline of the whole subject that is intended to provide an introduction to major issues and common terms. It may be helpful to return to this discussion from time to time after studying particular issues in greater detail.

Taxes are generally computed by applying a rate or rate schedule to some *base:* value of property in the case of a real estate tax, retail sales in the case of a sales tax, and so forth. The *tax base* on which the income tax is computed is *taxable income,* which is defined as *gross income* minus allowable *deductions.*[21] The statute specifies a number of particular items to be

---

21. §§1, 11, 63.

included[22] or excluded[23] in computing gross income, but many issues remain to be resolved under the general statutory language that "gross income means all income from whatever source derived."[24]

Deductions[25] are specifically allowed for some items[26] and specifically disallowed for a number of others.[27] There is no general all-inclusive provision authorizing deductions, but there are some general ideas that run through a number of them. Several provisions authorize deductions of expenses and losses incurred in a trade or business[28] or in the production of income.[29] These function to make taxable income akin to net income or profit.[30]

Personal expenses[31] and capital expenditures[32] are generally disallowed, but personal deductions are specifically allowed for a number of items.[33]

It is often convenient to think of income and deduction items separately, but it is only a convenience. Sometimes if an item is included in gross income, it will provide the basis for an offsetting deduction.[34] Exclusion from gross income and allowance of a deduction therefore may represent alternative ways of excluding a particular real item from the tax base, and *both* inclusion in gross income and disallowance of any offsetting deduction are required to establish ultimate inclusion in taxable income. Questions of inclusion and deduction frequently involve the same (or very closely related) underlying issues seen from slightly differing points of view. In any event, it is important to remember that the computation of gross income and the allowance of deductions are interrelated steps in the computation of taxable income, and that gross income itself has only limited independent significance.[35]

22. E.g., §§61, 71-90, 301(c)(1), 652, 662, 671, 702, 1366.
23. E.g., §§101-134.
24. §61(a). Gross income is generally the subject of Part I of this book.
25. Deductions are generally the subject of Part II.
26. E.g., §§162-199, 212-223, 243-248, 651, 661.
27. E.g., §§262-280H.
28. E.g., §§162, 165(c)(1), 167(a)(1).
29. E.g., §§212, 165(c)(2), 167(a)(2).
30. Indeed, the statutory term was "net income" instead of "taxable income" prior to 1954. I.R.C. §21(a) (1939).
31. §262.
32. §263.
33. For example, §§164 and 166 allow deductions for taxes and bad debt losses that may or may not be business connected or profit motivated, while §§170, 213, and 215 allow deductions for charitable contributions, medical expenses, and alimony, which usually would not arise out of a business or profit-oriented transaction. Section 163 originally contained a general deduction for interest paid. It now disallows personal interest, except for interest on qualified home mortgage and educational loans. §163(h), 221.
34. If an employer pays an employee's business travel expenses, for example, the payment might be included in the employee's gross income but also be deductible by the employee as a business expense under §162(a)(2).
35. E.g., §§6012(a)(1) (persons required to file returns), 6501(e)(1)(A) (extension of statute of limitations for omission amounting to 25 percent of gross income). Adjusted gross income, defined in §62, has certain other consequences. See, e.g., §§170(b)(1)(G), 213(a).

If an item is included in gross income without any offsetting deduction it will usually cause an increase in the tax. It is sometimes convenient to speak of that increase in tax as a tax on the item itself, but that is merely a shorthand form of expression. It is important to remember that the rate of tax (and indeed whether any tax is payable at all) depends on the aggregate of all income and deduction items for the taxpayer for the taxable year in question.

Allowance of a deduction or exclusion of an item from gross income will usually reduce the income tax below what it otherwise would be, and it is possible to speak of this tax reduction as an implicit subsidy for the deductible or excludible expenditure or receipt. Such implicit subsidies are now called *tax expenditures* and are required to be estimated and tabulated as part of the government's annual budgeting procedure. Whether characterization of a particular provision as a tax expenditure is appropriate apparently depends on its purpose.[36]

In certain cases, the statute allows a *credit* rather than a deduction for an expenditure.[37] A credit is subtracted from the tax otherwise payable and does not enter into the computation of taxable income. It operates to give every taxpayer a tax reduction equal to the dollar amount of the allowable credit, whereas a deduction only reduces taxes by the amount of the allowable deduction multiplied by the taxpayer's marginal tax rate. In general, therefore, deductions are relatively more valuable to high-bracket taxpayers, and credits are relatively more valuable to low-bracket taxpayers.

A personal exemption is allowed for each individual taxpayer (one for each spouse in the case of a joint return) and for each dependent child or other qualified dependent. Each exemption is allowed as a deduction in computing taxable income. The amount deductible for each exemption was set at $2,000 in 1989, and is adjusted for changes in the cost of living thereafter.[38]

There is also a standard deduction that functions to exempt a further limited amount from tax: $5,000 for a married couple and $3,000 for an unmarried individual in 1988. These amounts are subject to upward inflation adjustments after 1988,[39] and are somewhat different for heads of households, married individuals filing separate returns, and taxpayers who are over 64 years old or who are blind.

Capital gains. The principal rules that govern the income taxation of capital appreciation can be summarized as follows:

Unrealized appreciation in the value of property is not taxed.[40] However, income may be *realized* from an item of appreciated property by sale, by

---

36. See Chapters 3D.2, 8B, 10, and 11 below.
37. §§21-54.
38. §151. With inflation adjustments the exemption amount is $3,650 for 2009.
39. §63(c). Inflation adjustments have already increased these amounts to $11,400 for a married couple and $5,700 for an unmarried individual for 2009.
40. Chapter 5A.

exchange for other property, or in a variety of other ways. Just what is required to constitute a realization of gain has been a controversial issue in some cases.[41]

Even if gain is realized, the statute has special provisions under which it is sometimes not *recognized*.[42] Under these provisions, taxation of gain is postponed or, in some cases, effectively eliminated. Nonrecognition provisions usually apply to exchanges in which it is deemed appropriate to treat the property received as taking the place of the property given up.

Recognized gain may be classified as *long-term capital gain* if it arises from the sale or exchange of a *capital asset* held for more than a year. During most of the history of the income tax, long-term capital gain was taxed at half the rate on ordinary income (sometimes less). Immediately prior to 1986, the differential took the form of a deduction of 60 percent of net capital gain. Therefore, a net capital gain of $1,000 would produce a net increment to taxable income of $400: $1,000 income minus $600 of capital gain deduction. For a taxpayer in the top marginal rate bracket of 50 percent, this produced an increment to tax of $200, or 20 percent of the capital gain itself. It was therefore said that the top rate of tax on long-term capital gain was 20 percent while that for ordinary income was 50 percent. The deduction mechanism automatically gave proportionate rate reductions to taxpayers in lower brackets too.

The Tax Reform Act of 1986 reduced the top rate from 50 to 28 percent on ordinary income; it also eliminated the capital gain deduction, with the result that the effective rate on capital gains was raised from 20 to 28 percent. Elimination of the capital gain differential was perhaps the most significant structural change in the 1986 Act; doing this in exchange for such a dramatic decrease in the top rate was its central political compromise. The 1986 law contained a provision that if the rate on ordinary income were ever raised above 28 percent, that increase would not apply to capital gains.

Almost from the beginning there were calls from different quarters to raise the marginal rate on high-income taxpayers above 28 percent and to reduce the ceiling rate on capital gains to something less than 28 percent. The former call drew support from the burgeoning government deficits of the time. Enthusiasts for capital gain tax reductions claimed that such reductions would also help reduce deficits by inducing investors to realize more gains.

Reinstatement of higher rates came first: a marginal rate of 31 percent was enacted in 1990, and in 1993 marginal rates of 36, 39, and 39.6 were added. Section 1(h) operated to preserve a top rate of 28 percent on capital gains despite these changes, and so a differential for upper-bracket taxpayers reemerged.

41. Chapter 5C.
42. E.g., §§1031, 1033, 351, 354, 361.

In 1997 Congress moved the basic ceiling on capital gain rates back down to 20 percent, where it was prior to 1986. But this was not done by restoring the capital gain deduction; instead §1(h) was amended to prescribe a ceiling rate of 20 percent, along with a small assortment of other rates for particular categories of capital gain. Legislation enacted in 2001 called for a gradual reduction of tax rates above 15 percent and instituted a new 10 percent bracket.[43] When that general rate reduction was accelerated in 2003 Congress also reduced the basic capital gain rate to 15 percent. For taxpayers whose capital gain would have been taxed at 15 percent if it were ordinary income, §1(h)(B) provides a special lower capital gain rate of 5 percent, or zero for tax years beginning after 2007.

Gain on the sale or other disposition of any property is the *amount realized* on the disposition, less the taxpayer's *adjusted basis.*[44] *Basis* is usually cost,[45] but there are a number of important exceptions.[46]

Capital losses are subtracted from capital gains before applying any of the special capital gain rate provisions. If capital losses exceed capital gains, deductibility of the excess losses is generally limited to $3,000 a year.[47] If there are net gains in some capital gain categories and net losses in others, then complications may arise about what is to be set off against what and in what order. These complications are dealt with as between short- and long-term capital gains and losses by the definitions in §1222, which is an old pre-1986 provision. How to untangle this web for the new categories introduced in 1997 is dealt with in §1(h).

Annual accounting. Income taxes are returned, settled, audited, and litigated on an annual basis.[48] The *taxable year* for most taxpayers is the calendar year, but a business whose books are kept on some other fiscal year may have its taxable income computed on a fiscal year basis.[49]

Annual accounting requires accounting rules to determine in what year income and deduction items should be reported in computing taxable income. Most individual taxpayers use the *cash receipts and disbursements method* of accounting, which means that items are reflected when actually or constructively received, or when paid.[50] But books of account for a business are often kept on an *accrual* basis, with income and expenses recorded when earned or incurred, even if payment has not been made. In such a case, the accrual method may be acceptable and indeed required for computing taxable income as well.[51] Frequently, however, particular items

---

43. §1(i).
44. §1001.
45. §1012.
46. E.g., §§1013-1023, 358, 362, 1031(d).
47. §§1211, 1212.
48. Chapters 3B and 7B.
49. §441.
50. §446(c)(1).
51. §446(a), (c)(2).

are permitted or required to be treated differently for tax purposes than under normal financial accounting practice.

The annual accounting requirement sometimes produces harsh results, either by causing deduction items to fall in no-income or low-rate years or by causing income items to be bunched together in a single year. Special relief provisions apply to a number of such situations.[52] On the other hand, accounting methods and disparities among them have been subject to tax-payer exploitation, and there are now a number of provisions intended to curb abuses.[53]

Corporate earnings are in general subject to corporate income tax when received or accrued by the corporation, whether or not distributed.[54] Payments of interest, rent, and salaries, if reasonable, are deductible in computing corporate taxable income,[55] but dividends to shareholders are not.

An individual is not generally taxed on his or her share of undistributed corporate earnings,[56] even in the case of a one-person corporation. Individual taxable income does include corporate dividends,[57] however, as well as interest, rent, and salaries received. Historically, dividends have been taxed as ordinary income, like interest, rent, and salaries, but in 2003 Congress made most corporate dividends taxable at the lower rates (15 percent or zero) applicable to capital gains.[58]

As a result of these rules, corporate revenues may enter into the tax base in three different ways. (1) Corporate revenues distributed as dividends effectively enter into the tax base twice, once as corporate income and again as individual income to the shareholders. (2) On the other hand, corporate revenues distributed as salaries, rent, or interest enter into the tax base only as individual income to the employee, lessor, or lender to whom distributed. (3) Finally, corporate revenues that are not distributed enter into the corporate tax base but not, immediately at least, into individual income. Freedom from individual income tax will be only temporary if distribution occurs later. Furthermore, accumulated corporate earnings may be reflected, in whole or in part, in appreciation in the value of shares. If that appreciation is realized, such as on a sale of shares, the accumulated earnings may in a sense enter into the individual income tax base, usually to be taxed at capital gain rates, at that time.

The questions of what constitutes a taxable distribution of corporate earnings and what adjustments will trigger recognition of gain or loss by a corporation and by its stockholders and security holders are among

---

52. E.g., §§111, 172, 1341.
53. See, e.g., §§267, 448, 461(h), 467, 1272.
54. §11.
55. §§162, 163.
56. Chapter 5A.
57. §301.
58. §1(h)(1)(B), (C), (h)(3), (h)(11).

the oldest, hardest, and most important questions in the income tax. They have been the subject of extensive and highly articulated legislation and judicial exegesis.[59]

Penalty taxes are imposed on the use of a corporation to accumulate earnings for the purpose of avoiding individual income taxes[60] and on the use of a corporation whose stock is wholly or partly held by a small number of shareholders (closely held) to accumulate passive or personal service income, whatever the purpose or motive.[61]

The rules that govern corporate earnings should be compared with those that govern partnerships and trusts and estates. A partnership is not taxed as such, but partnership income is taxed to the partners individually when received by the partnership, whether distributed or not.[62] Income of trusts and estates is taxed to the beneficiaries if currently distributed or distributable, and only otherwise to the trust or estate as such.[63] Partnerships and trusts are both said to be *pass-through entities* because the aim is to tax their income only once at rates appropriate for their individual partners or beneficiaries.

Rates. The tax is a function of the tax base and the applicable rate schedule specified in the statute. The rate schedules in the individual income tax have always been graduated. The percentages in any such schedule specify *marginal* rates — the rate at which additional amounts of income will be taxed. An individual's *average* or *effective* rate of tax would always be less than the marginal rate because income below an individual's top bracket would be taxed at lower rates.

For example, if the rate on the first $40,000 were 15 percent and the rate on the rest were 25 percent, then the tax on $50,000 of taxable income would be 15 percent of $40,000 plus 25 percent of $10,000, or $8,500. That represents an average rate of 17 percent ($8,500/$50,000). As income increases the average rate rises because a higher and higher portion of income is taxed at the higher rate. However, the average will never quite reach the highest marginal rate as long as some income is still taxed at the lower rates.

It is sometimes useful to distinguish *graduation* from *progression*. A tax is graduated if it has a schedule of graduated marginal rates. It is progressive, on the other hand, if the total tax imposed represents a greater percentage of income for higher-income taxpayers than for lower-income taxpayers. A tax may be graduated without being progressive if it contains deductions and exclusions that operate disproportionately to favor high-income taxpayers, since these may offset the higher *nominal rates* (rates specified in the statutory rate schedule). On the other hand, exemptions and certain

---

59. I.R.C. Subchapter C, beginning at §301.
60. §531.
61. §541.
62. §§701-702.
63. §§641, 651-652, 661-662.

other deductions give the tax a degree of progressivity even without graduated rates since they represent a higher portion of income for low-income than for high-income taxpayers.

Progressivity of a tax may be measured in relation to income, wealth, or aggregate personal consumption, and a judgment about progressivity depends on how the chosen base for comparison is defined. "Income" for the purpose of judging progressivity would often be defined differently (usually more broadly) than taxable income. For example, total income might be defined to include interest on state and municipal securities[64] and the full amount of realized capital gains, and not to allow deductions for accelerated depreciation[65] or charitable contributions.[66] As so computed, income for many high-bracket taxpayers would be much more than taxable income under the statute, and the effective rate of tax in relation to income so defined would be much lower than the nominal statutory rates. Whether our income tax has actually ever been significantly progressive at all, and if so how much, in relation to a more comprehensive income base is not clear.

The question of progressivity is often discussed in relation to the aggregate burden of all taxes rather than any single tax such as the income tax alone. In that perspective, the purpose of progressivity in the income tax may be partly to offset regressivity in other taxes, especially sales taxes and other general excises.

Rates, in some sense, raise political, economic, and social rather than legal issues. They are specified in the statute and changed by legislation, not litigation. But there is much more real difference between a 14 percent tax and a 50 percent tax, for instance, than there is between a 14 percent tax and none at all. It is unrealistic, therefore, not to keep rates and the differences in rates constantly in mind.

The existence of a graduated rate schedule has had a profound effect on the whole structure of the tax and on the impact of other more clearly legal issues. In particular, rate graduation has made important both the definition of the taxpaying unit—individual or family—and in whose income particular items are included. It has spawned a school of devices and plans for making income in high-income families taxable to those family members subject to the lowest marginal rates, and a network of legal provisions, judicial and congressional, for attributing income items to taxpayers other than the actual recipient.[67] Rate graduation has also often made it important whether an item is included in taxable income for one year rather than another. Furthermore, many have asserted that the whole special treatment of capital gains was largely a matter of relief from highly graduated rates on certain kinds of income.

64. Cf. §103.
65. Cf. §§167(b), 168(b).
66. Cf. §170.
67. See Chapters 17 and 18 below.

Bibliography

Treatises and Texts: Boris I. Bittker & Lawrence Lokken, Federal Taxation of Income, Estates, and Gifts (3d ed. 1999) and Jacob Mertens, The Law of Federal Income Taxation (loose-leaf), are the two most comprehensive and frequently cited treatises. Marvin A. Chirelstein, Federal Income Taxation (10th ed. 2005), probably the most popular and useful student aid, is a kind of insider's exposé of what law school tax teachers typically try to teach.

History: There is no general up-to-date history of the income tax. For an account of the early years, see R. Paul, Taxation in the United States (1954). For early judicial and theoretical developments see R. Magill, Taxable Income (rev. ed. 1945), and J. Sneed, The Configurations of Gross Income (1967). For an interesting special view see J. Witte, The Politics and Development of the Federal Income Tax (1985).

Tax Policy: It is not yet too late to begin with U.S. Department of the Treasury, Tax Reform for Fairness, Simplicity, and Economic Growth (Nov. 1984). This document resulted from President Reagan's call, early in 1984, for a study of general income tax reform, to be delivered immediately after the elections. Generally regarded as a high-level piece of staff work, relatively free from political restraints, it is colloquially known as *Treasury I.*

The President's Tax Proposals to the Congress for Fairness, Growth, and Simplicity (May 1985) is a sequel to *Treasury I,* also produced in the Treasury Department, taking reactions to the earlier document into account. It is sometimes called *Treasury II,* even though it appeared over the President's signature. It was the principal source from which Congress put together the Tax Reform Act of 1986.

There are a host of other books about what the tax law ought to be. See particularly D. Bradford, Untangling the Income Tax (1986). Also, Inflation and the Income Tax (H. Aaron ed. 1976); W. Blum & H. Kalven, The Uneasy Case for Progressive Taxation (1953) (originally published in 19 U. Chi. L. Rev. 417 (1952)); L. Eisenstein, The Ideologies of Taxation (1961); M. Feldstein, Capital Taxation (1983); R. Goode, The Individual Income Tax (rev. ed. 1976); M. Graetz, The Decline (and Fall?) of the Income Tax (1997); M. Graetz, 100 Million Unnecessary Returns (2008); N. Kaldor, An Expenditure Tax (1955); R. Musgrave & P. Musgrave, Public Finance in Theory and Practice (5th ed. 1989); J. Pechman, Federal Tax Policy (5th ed. 1988); H. Simons, The Definition of Income As a Problem of Fiscal Policy (1938); H. Simons, Federal Tax Reform (1950); J. Slemrod & J. Bakija, Taxing Ourselves (4th ed. 2008); S. Surrey, Pathways to Tax Reform: The Concept of Tax Expenditures (1973); E. Steuerle, Contemporary U.S. Tax Policy (2004); W. Vickrey, Agenda for Progressive Taxation (1947).

There are also useful collections of shorter pieces, including: W. Andrews, D. Bradford, R. Goode, M. Graetz, E. Howrey, S. Hymans, & J. Minarik, What Should Be Taxed: Income or Expenditure (J. Pechman ed. 1980); B. Bittker, C. Galvin, R. Musgrave, & J. Pechman, A Comprehensive Tax Base? (1968) (originally published in large part in 80 and 81 Harv. L. Rev. (1967-1968)); Comprehensive Income Taxation (J. Pechman ed. 1977); Does Atlas Shrug? The Economic Consequences of Taxing the Rich (J. Slemrod ed. 2000); Tax Justice (J. Thorndike & D. Ventry Jr. eds. 2002).

Possibilities for sweeping revision of the income tax are described in D. Bradford & U.S. Department of the Treasury Tax Policy Staff, Blueprints for Basic Tax Reform (2d ed. 1984); Options for Tax Reform: Papers (J. Pechman ed., Brookings Institution 1984). Most recent proposals for major reform are based on one of two models: a comprehensive income tax that would combine elimination of many deductions and tax preferences with lower rates, and a tax focused on consumption as measured by cash flow. The latter would differ from an income tax by excluding savings and investment but taxing withdrawal of savings for personal consumption. See D. Bradford, Taxation, Wealth, and Saving (2000); D. Bradford, The X Tax in the World Economy (2004). Another approach to consumption taxation that has attracted considerable political interest among Republicans is described in Robert E. Hall & Alvin Rabushka, The Flat Tax (2d ed. 1995).

Periodicals: Tax Notes, a weekly magazine published by Tax Analysts, provides a full report of news, analysis, and opinion concerning taxes. It focuses particularly on political and legislative developments, but it also reports judicial and administrative decisions and contains some interesting essays on matters of tax policy. There is also a Daily Tax Reporter, published by the Bureau of National Affairs. Articles and notes about the tax law appear in almost all the law reviews. Journals devoted exclusively to federal tax law include Journal of Taxation, Taxes, The Tax Lawyer (the journal of the Tax Section of the American Bar Association), Tax Law Review, Florida Tax Review, Virginia Tax Review, while the Journal of Corporate Taxation, Journal of Individual Taxation, Journal of Passthrough Entities, and Journal of Real Estate Taxation are more specialized. National Tax Journal is oriented more toward economic than legal analysis of tax problems. Selected law review articles are cited at the end of each chapter in this book.

Loose-leaf Services: There are several loose-leaf compendia of federal tax law that are kept up to date with weekly supplements. The most frequently cited are Commerce Clearing House, Standard Federal Tax Reporter; Research Institute of America, The United States Tax Reporter (formerly Prentice Hall); and J. Rabkin & M. Johnson, Federal Income, Gift and Estate Taxation (Matthew Bender). Serious students will want to learn to use one or more of these services with ease.

Part I — *Income*

Chapter 2 — *Income in Kind*

A. *NONCASH RECEIPTS IN GENERAL*

Most income is received in the form of cash (including checks) — salaries, wages, dividends, interest, sales proceeds, and so forth. But the value of money is what it will buy, so the direct provision in kind of items that would otherwise be purchased may be a substitute for money income. More fundamentally, perhaps, money may be viewed as a symbol for the real goods and services it will buy; real income, then, is real goods and services consumed or accumulated rights to such goods and services whether they are purchased with money income or received in kind.

For all that, there are practical difficulties and perhaps some theoretical problems in taxing nonmoney income. In practice, a variety of quite substantial items are omitted from the income tax base. This chapter is about those difficulties, problems, and omissions.

OLD COLONY TRUST CO. v. COMMISSIONER
279 U.S. 716 (1929)

Mr. Chief Justice TAFT delivered the opinion of the Court. . . . William M. Wood was president of the American Woolen Company during the years 1918, 1919, and 1920. In 1918 he received as salary and commissions from the company $978,725, which he included in his federal income tax return for 1918. In 1919 he received as salary and commissions from the company $548,132.27, which he included in his return for 1919.

August 3, 1916, the American Woolen Company had adopted the following resolution, which was in effect in 1919 and 1920:

Voted: That this company pay any and all income taxes, State and Federal, that may hereafter become due and payable upon the salaries of all the officers of the company, including the president, William M. Wood; the comptroller, Parry C. Wiggin; the auditor, George R. Lawton; and the following members of the staff, to wit: Frank H. Carpenter, Edwin L. Heath, Samuel R. Haines, and William M. Lasbury, to the end that said persons and officers shall receive their salaries or other compensation in full without deduction on account of income taxes, State or Federal, which taxes are to be paid out of the treasury of this corporation.

This resolution was amended on March 25, 1918, as follows:

Voted: That, in referring to the vote passed by this board on August 3, 1916, in reference to income taxes, State and Federal, payable upon the salaries or compensation of the officers and certain employees of this company, the method of computing said taxes shall be as follows, viz:

"The difference between what the total amount of his tax would be, including his income from all sources, and the amount of his tax computed upon his income excluding such compensation or salaries paid by this company."

Pursuant to these resolutions, the American Woolen Company paid to the collector of internal revenue Mr. Wood's federal income and surtaxes due to salary and commissions paid him by the company, as follows:

Taxes for 1918 paid in 1919	$681,169.88
Taxes for 1919 paid in 1920	351,179.27

The decision of the Board of Tax Appeals here sought to be reviewed was that the income taxes of $681,169.88 and $351,179.27 paid by the American Woolen Company for Mr. Wood were additional income to him for the years 1919 and 1920.

The question certified by the Circuit Court of Appeals for answer by this Court is:

"Did the payment by the employer of the income taxes assessable against the employee constitute additional taxable income to such employee?" . . .

Coming now to the merits of this case, we think the question presented is whether a taxpayer, having induced a third person to pay his income tax or having acquiesced in such payment as made in discharge of an obligation to him, may avoid the making of a return thereof and the payment of a corresponding tax. We think he may not do so. The payment of the tax by the employer was in consideration of the services rendered by the employee and was a gain derived by the employee from his labor. The form of the payment is expressly declared to make no difference. Section 213, Revenue Act of 1918, ch. 18, 40 Stat. 1065. It is therefore immaterial that the taxes were directly paid over to the Government. The discharge by a third person of an obligation to him is equivalent to receipt by the person taxed. The certificate shows that the taxes were imposed upon the employee, that the taxes were actually paid by the employer and that the employee entered upon his duties in the years in question under the express agreement that his income taxes would be paid by his employer. This is evidenced by the terms of the resolution passed August 3, 1916, more than one year prior to the year in which the taxes were imposed. The taxes were paid upon a valuable consideration, namely, the services rendered by the employee and as part of the compensation therefor. We think therefore that the payment constituted income to the employee. . . .

Nor can it be argued that the payment of the tax was a gift. The payment for services, even though entirely voluntary, was nevertheless compensation within the statute. . . .

It is next argued against the payment of this tax that if these payments by the employer constitute income to the employee, the employer will be called upon to pay the tax imposed upon this additional income, and that the payment of the additional tax will create further income which will in turn be subject to tax, with the result that there would be a tax upon a tax. This it is urged is the result of the Government's theory, when carried to its logical conclusion, and results in an absurdity which Congress could not have contemplated.

In the first place, no attempt has been made by the Treasury to collect further taxes, upon the theory that the payment of the additional taxes creates further income, and the question of a tax upon a tax was not before the Circuit Court of Appeals and has not been certified to this Court. We can settle questions of that sort when an attempt to impose a tax upon a tax is undertaken, but not now. United States v. Sullivan, 274 U.S. 259, 264; Yazoo & Mississippi Valley R.R. v. Jackson Vinegar Co., 226 U.S. 217, 219. It is not, therefore, necessary to answer the argument based upon an algebraic formula to reach the amount of taxes due. The question in this case is, "Did the payment by the employer of the income taxes assessable against the employee constitute additional taxable income to such employee?" The answer must be "Yes."

[Separate opinion of Mr. Justice McReynolds omitted.]

Questions

1. Section 22(a) of the Internal Revenue Code of 1939 read as follows:

"Gross income" includes gains, profits, and income derived from salaries, wages, or compensation for personal service (including personal service as an officer or employee of a State, or any political subdivision thereof, or any agency or instrumentality of any one or more of the foregoing), of whatever kind and in whatever form paid, or from professions, vocations, trade, businesses, commerce, or sales, or dealings in property, whether real or personal, growing out of the ownership or use of or interest in such property; also from interest, rent, dividends, securities, or the transaction of any business carried on for gain or profit, or gains or profits and income derived from any source whatever. . . . [Internal Revenue Code of 1939, §22(a).]

Why does §61(a) of the present code omit the phrase "in whatever form paid"? The Senate Finance Committee said that while "the section 22(a) phrase 'in whatever form paid' has been eliminated statutory gross income will continue to include income realized in any form." S. Rep. No. 83-1622, at 168 (1954). The Treasury responded with a regulation that provides in part: "Gross income includes income realized in any form, whether in money, property, or services." Reg. 1.61-1(a) (1957).

2. What about the tax on the tax on the tax? Was the government right to be satisfied with one round? Is it true that the total tax attributable to a particular year's salary would never be fully paid if each payment of the tax were subject to a further tax payable in the next year? See §6313. Even without §6313, would the total tax be unlimited? Why not?

Zeno's paradox asserts that a moving animal shot from behind will never be hit because when the arrow gets to where the animal originally was, the animal will be at a new place; and when the arrow gets to the new place, the animal will be at a newer place, and so on. Is that the same problem as pyramiding the tax on the tax?

Can the pyramiding of tax be dismissed as insubstantial? Consider, for example, a taxpayer subject to tax at a marginal rate of 66.67 percent. (This is higher than the top individual rate under present law, but somewhat below the ratio between tax and income exhibited in the *Old Colony* case itself.) Suppose his employer pays him $100 and pays the government $66.67 of tax. Now if *Old Colony* is applied once, that would represent an additional $44.44 of tax. How much more would be involved if *Old Colony* were applied to require the tax on the tax on the tax ad infinitum? What is the right amount?

3. Since 1942 employers generally have been required by law to withhold employee income taxes and to pay them over to the government. Employees are entitled to a credit for the taxes so paid on their behalf but the income on which tax is based is the full amount of their salary, including what was withheld and what was paid them in cash. See §§31, 3402(a).

Is this essentially the same as what was done by directors' resolution instead of statute in *Old Colony*? One important difference is that the imposition of withholding ordinarily causes a decrease in what is paid in cash to the employee, while in *Old Colony* the intention was to keep the employee's net after-tax income undiminished. The intended effect of the arrangement in *Old Colony* was to shift the burden of the tax from employee to employer, while withholding is assumed and intended to leave the burden on the employee. Does *Old Colony* manifest any policy against the shifting of income tax burdens from employee to employer? Would any such policy be appropriate?

4. Why was the 1916 directors' resolution amended in 1918? As lawyer for the company, would you have recommended the amendment that was adopted?

5. What is the relevance of §§164 and 275? The 1913 income tax allowed a deduction for the federal income tax itself,[1] but it was dropped in 1917. Senator Hollis said, "It is a pure matter of expediency. If you so arrange the income tax this year that you allow those who pay it to take back a third of it next year, you have simply got to put on a bigger tax. . . ."[2]

The resolution in *Old Colony* called for the company to pay "any and all income taxes, State and Federal, that may hereafter become due. . . ." Would payment of *state* income taxes of an employee pursuant to this resolution be *federal* taxable income to the employee? What does *Old Colony* indicate about this?

6. Is *Old Colony* confined to taxes? What if an employer made direct payments to an employee's mortgagee for home mortgage payments or to her landlord for rent?

ARTHUR BENAGLIA
36 B.T.A. 838 (1937), acq. 1940-1 C.B. 1

The Commissioner determined a deficiency in the petitioners' joint income tax for 1933 of $856.68, and for 1934 of $1,001.61, and they contest the inclusion in gross income each year of the alleged fair market value of rooms and meals furnished by the husband's employer.

FINDINGS OF FACT . . .

The petitioner has, since 1926 and including the tax years in question, been employed as the manager in full charge of the several hotels in Honolulu owned and operated by Hawaiian Hotels, Ltd., a corporation of Hawaii, consisting of the Royal Hawaiian, the Moana and bungalows, and the Waialae Golf Club. These are large resort hotels, operating on the American plan. Petitioner was constantly on duty, and, for the proper performance of his duties and entirely for the convenience of his employer, he and his wife occupied a suite of rooms in the Royal Hawaiian Hotel and received their meals at and from the hotel.

---

1. Act of October 3, 1913, ch. 16, §2(B), 38 Stat. 167 (repealed 1917).
2. 55 Cong. Rec. 6324 (1917); see C. Kahn, Personal Deductions in the Federal Income Tax 67 (1970).

Petitioner's salary has varied in different years, being in one year $25,000. In 1933 it was $9,625, and in 1934 it was $11,041.67. These amounts were fixed without reference to his meals and lodging, and neither petitioner nor his employer ever regarded the meals and lodging as part of his compensation or accounted for them.

OPINION

STERNHAGEN, Judge: The Commissioner has added $7,845 each year to the petitioner's gross income as "compensation received from Hawaiian Hotels, Ltd.," holding that this is "the fair market value of rooms and meals furnished by the employer." In the deficiency notice he cites article 52[53], Regulations 77, and holds inapplicable Jones v. United States, 60 Ct. Cls. 552; I.T. 2232; G.C.M. 14710; G.C.M. 14836. The deficiency notice seems to hold that the rooms and meals were not in fact supplied "merely as a convenience to the hotels" of the employer.

From the evidence, there remains no room for doubt that the petitioner's residence at the hotel was not by way of compensation for his services, not for his personal convenience, comfort or pleasure, but solely because he could not otherwise perform the services required of him. The evidence of both the employer and employee shows in detail what petitioner's duties were and why his residence in the hotel was necessary. His duty was continuous and required his presence at a moment's call. He had a lifelong experience in hotel management and operation in the United States, Canada, and elsewhere, and testified that the functions of the manager could not have been performed by one living outside the hotel, especially a resort hotel such as this. The demands and requirements of guests are numerous, various, and unpredictable, and affect the meals, the rooms, the entertainment, and everything else about the hotel. The manager must be alert to all these things day and night. He would not consider undertaking the job and the owners of the hotel would not consider employing a manager unless he lived there. This was implicit throughout his employment, and when his compensation was changed from time to time no mention was ever made of it. Both took it for granted. The corporation's books carried no accounting for the petitioner's meals, rooms, or service.

Under such circumstances, the value of meals and lodging is not income to the employee, even though it may relieve him of an expense which he would otherwise bear. In Jones v. United States, supra, the subject was fully considered in determining that neither the value of quarters nor the amount received as commutation of quarters by an Army officer is included within his taxable income. There is also a full discussion in the English case of Tennant v. Smith, H.L. (1892) App. Cas. 150, III British Tax Cases 158. A bank employee was required to live in quarters located in the bank building, and it was held that the value of such lodging was not taxable income.

The advantage to him was merely an incident of the performance of his duty, but its character for tax purposes was controlled by the dominant fact that the occupation of the premises was imposed upon him for the convenience of the employer. The Bureau of Internal Revenue has almost consistently applied the same doctrine in its published rulings.

The three cases cited by the respondent, Ralph Kitchen, 11 B.T.A. 855; Charles A. Frueauff, 30 B.T.A. 449; and Fontaine Fox, 30 B.T.A. 451, are distinguishable entirely upon the ground that what the taxpayer received was not shown to be primarily for the need or convenience of the employer. Of course, as in the Kitchen case, it can not be said as a categorical proposition of law that, where an employee is fed and lodged by his employer, no part of the value of such perquisite is income. If the Commissioner finds that it was received as compensation and holds it to be taxable income, the taxpayer contesting this before the Board must prove by evidence that it is not income. In the Kitchen case the Board held that the evidence did not establish that the food and lodging were given for the convenience of the employer. In the present case the evidence clearly establishes that fact, and it has been so found.

The determination of the Commissioner on the point in issue is reversed.

Reviewed by the Board.

Judgment will be entered under Rule 50.

MURDOCK, Judge, concurs only in the result.

ARNOLD, Judge dissenting: I disagree with the conclusions of fact that the suite of rooms and meals furnished petitioner and his wife at the Royal Hawaiian Hotel were entirely for the convenience of the employer and that the cash salary was fixed without reference thereto and was never regarded as part of his compensation.

Petitioner was employed by a hotel corporation operating two resort hotels in Honolulu — the Royal Hawaiian, containing 357 guest bed rooms, and the Moana, containing 261 guest bed rooms, and the bungalows and cottages in connection with the Moana containing 127 guest bed rooms, and the Waialae Golf Club. His employment was as general manager of both hotels and the golf club.

His original employment was in 1925, and in accepting the employment he wrote a letter to the party representing the employer, with whom he conducted the negotiations for employment, under date of September 10, 1925, in which he says: "Confirming our meeting here today, it is understood that I will assume the position of general manager of both the Royal Waikiki Beach Hotel (now under construction) and the Moana Hotel in Honolulu, at a yearly salary of $10,000.00, payable monthly, together with living quarters, meals, etc., for myself and wife. In addition I am to receive $20.00 per day while traveling, this however, not to include any railroad or steamship fares, and I [am] to submit vouchers monthly covering all such expenses."

While the cash salary was adjusted from time to time by agreement of the parties, depending on the amount of business done, it appears that the question of living quarters, meals, etc., was not given further consideration and was not thereafter changed. Petitioner and his wife have always occupied living quarters in the Royal Hawaiian Hotel and received their meals from the time he first accepted the employment down through the years before us. His wife performed no services for the hotel company.

This letter, in my opinion, constitutes the basic contract of employment and clearly shows that the living quarters, meals, etc., furnished petitioner and his wife were understood and intended to be compensation in addition to the cash salary paid him. Being compensation to petitioner in addition to the cash salary paid him, it follows that the reasonable value thereof to petitioner is taxable income. Cf. Ralph Kitchen, 11 B.T.A. 855; Charles A. Frueauff, 30 B.T.A. 449.

Conceding that petitioner was required to live at the hotel and that his living there was solely for the convenience of the employer, it does not follow that he was not benefited thereby to the extent of what such accommodations were reasonably worth to him. His employment was a matter of private contract. He was careful to specify in his letter accepting the employment that he was to be furnished with living quarters, meals, etc., for himself and wife, together with the cash salary, as compensation for his employment. Living quarters and meals are necessities which he would otherwise have had to procure at his own expense. His contract of employment relieved him to that extent. He has been enriched to the extent of what they are reasonably worth.

The majority opinion is based on the finding that petitioner's residence at the hotel was solely for the convenience of the employer and, therefore, not income. While it is no doubt convenient to have the manager reside in the hotel, I do not think the question here is one of convenience or of benefit to the employer. What the tax law is concerned with is whether or not petitioner was financially benefited by having living quarters furnished to himself and wife. He may have preferred to live elsewhere, but we are dealing with the financial aspect of petitioner's relation to his employer, not his preference. He says it would cost him $3,600 per year to live elsewhere.

It would seem that if his occupancy of quarters at the Royal Hawaiian was necessary and solely for the benefit of the employer, occupancy of premises at the Moana would be just as essential so far as the management of the Moana was concerned. He did not have living quarters or meals for himself and wife at the Moana and he was general manager of both and both were in operation during the years before us. Furthermore, it appears that petitioner was absent from Honolulu from March 24 to June 8 and from August 19 to November 2 in 1933, and from April 8 to May 24 and from September 3 to November 1 in 1934—about 5 months in 1933 and 3½ months in 1934. Whether he was away on official business or not we do not know. During his absence both hotels continued in operation. The $20 per day travel allowance in his letter of acceptance indicates his duties were not confined to managing the hotels in Honolulu, and the entire letter indicates he was to receive maintenance, whether in Honolulu or elsewhere, in addition to his cash salary.

At most the arrangement as to living quarters and meals was of mutual benefit, and to the extent it benefited petitioner it was compensation in addition to his cash salary, and taxable to him as income.

The Court of Claims in the case of Jones v. United States, relied on in the majority opinion, was dealing with a governmental organization regulated by military law where the compensation was fixed by law and not subject to private contract. The English case of Tennant v. Smith involved the employment of a watchman or custodian for a bank whose presence at the bank was at all times a matter of necessity demanded by the employer as a condition of the employment.

The facts in both these cases are so at variance with the facts in this case that they are not controlling in my opinion.

SMITH, TURNER, and HARRON agree with this dissent.

Questions

1. Is this case essentially any different from *Old Colony*?
2. What does it mean to say that housing was provided for the convenience of the employer? Why is that condition relevant to the *employee's* income tax treatment?
3. If Benaglia had been taxed, how should the amount of his tax be determined?

REGINALD TURNER
T.C. Mem. 1954-38

MEMORANDUM FINDINGS OF FACT AND OPINION

The Commissioner determined a deficiency of $388.96 in the income tax of the petitioners for 1948. The only question for decision is the amount which should be included in income because of the winning by Reginald of steamship tickets by answering a question on a radio program.

FINDINGS OF FACT

The petitioners are husband and wife who filed a joint return for 1948 with the collector of internal revenue for the District of North Carolina. They reported salary of $4,535.16 for 1948.

Reginald, whose name had been selected by chance from a telephone book, was called on the telephone on April 18, 1948 and was asked to name a song that was being played on a radio program. He gave the correct name of the song and then was given the opportunity to identify a second song and thus to compete for a grand prize. He correctly identified the second song and in consideration of his efforts was awarded a number of prizes, including two round trip first-class steamship tickets for a cruise between New York City and Buenos Aires. The prize was to be one ticket if the winner was unmarried, but if he was married, his wife was to receive a ticket also. The tickets were not transferable and were good only within one year on a sailing date approved by the agent of the steamship company.

The petitioners reported income on their return of $520, representing income from the award of the two tickets. The Commissioner, in determining the deficiency, increased the income from this source to $2,220, the retail price of such tickets.

Marie was born in Brazil. The petitioners had two sons. Reginald negotiated with the agent of the steamship company, as a result of which he surrendered his rights to the two first-class tickets, and upon payment of $12.50 received four round trip tourist steamship tickets between New York City and Rio de Janeiro. The petitioners and their two sons used those tickets in making a trip from New York City to Rio de Janeiro and return during 1948.

The award of the tickets to Reginald represented income to him in the amount of $1,400.

OPINION

MURDOCK, Judge: Persons desiring to buy round trip first-class tickets between New York and Buenos Aires in April 1948, similar to those to which the petitioners were entitled, would have had to pay $2,220 for them. The petitioners, however, were not such persons. The winning of the tickets did not provide them with something which they needed in the ordinary course of their lives and for which they would have made an expenditure in any event, but merely gave them an opportunity to enjoy a luxury otherwise beyond their means. Their value to the petitioners was not equal to their retail cost. They were not transferable and not salable and there were other restrictions on their use. But even had the petitioner been permitted to sell them, his experience with other more salable articles indicates that he would have had to accept substantially less than the cost of similar tickets purchased from the steamship company and would have had selling expenses. Probably the petitioners could have refused the tickets and avoided the tax problem. Nevertheless, in order to obtain such benefits as they could from winning the tickets, they actually took a cruise accompanied by their two sons, thus obtaining free board, some savings in living expenses, and the pleasure of the trip. It seems proper that a substantial amount should be included in their income for 1948 on account of the winning of the tickets. The problem of arriving at a proper fair figure for this purpose is difficult. The evidence to assist is meager, perhaps unavoidably so. The Court, under such circumstances, must arrive at some figure and has done so. Cf. Cohan v. Commissioner [Chapter 12D below].

Decision will be entered under Rule 50.

Notes and Questions

1. Does this case provide a viable solution for the valuation problem in *Benaglia*? *Turner* has been frequently cited in theoretical and policy discussions of the fringe benefit problem, but not in judicial opinions. Why?

2. Suppose Benaglia could show that living in a hotel was for him no boon but a burden. Would that justify, either in theory or in practice, excluding or assigning a low value to the lodging provided him?

3. Suppose it could be shown that Benaglia had a passion for hotels and that living in a hotel was worth much more to him than the price of a room. (Suppose, for example, that he had turned down other higher-paying jobs in order to live in the hotel.) Would it then be justifiable to tax Benaglia on more than the established room rent?

Economists use the term "consumer surplus" for the excess of satisfactions derived from a product over its market price. Are there convincing reasons for categorically excluding consumer surplus from taxable income?

4. Is difficulty of valuation a reason for omitting a noncash benefit from income entirely? Conversely, is ease of valuation a reason for taxation?

5. Does the fact that an item is supplied *for the convenience of* an employer, or other payor, bear significantly on the question of valuation? Does it bear on any other relevant question?

In this connection, consider a person who loves to travel and becomes an airline pilot to indulge that love: Is she taxable on the value of her travel? Why not? Is *Benaglia* significantly different from this case?

Or consider this conundrum:

We are asked to measure the relative incomes of an ordinary officer serving with his troops and a *Flugeladjutant* to the sovereign. Both receive the same nominal pay; but the latter receives quarters in the palace, food at the royal table, servants, and horses for sport. He accompanies the prince to theater and opera, and, in general, lives royally at no expense to himself and is able to save generously from his salary. But suppose, as one possible complication, that the *Flugeladjutant* detests opera and hunting. [H. Simons, Personal Income Taxation 53 (1938).]

6. Turner's prize was not from his employer, as were the items in *Old Colony Trust Co.* and *Benalgia*. Does that change the analysis in any way?

Should he have argued that the prize was not income to him at all since it just came without effort or investment?[3]

HAVERLY v. UNITED STATES
513 F.2d 224 (7th Cir.), cert. denied, 423 U.S. 912 (1975)

Before Hastings, Senior Circuit Judge, Swygert and Cummings, Circuit Judges.

HASTINGS, Senior Circuit Judge:

During the years 1967 and 1968 Charles N. Haverly was the principal of the Alice L. Barnard Elementary School in Chicago, Illinois. In each of these years publishers sent to the taxpayer unsolicited sample copies of textbooks which had a total fair market value at the time of receipt of $400. The samples were given to taxpayer for his personal retention or for whatever disposition he wished to make. The samples were provided, in the hope of receiving favorable consideration, to give taxpayer an opportunity to examine the books and determine whether they were suitable for the instructional unit for which he was responsible. The publishers did not intend that the books serve as compensation.

In 1968 taxpayer donated the books to the Alice L. Barnard Elementary School Library. The parties agreed that the donation entitled the taxpayer to a charitable deduction under 26 U.S.C. §170, in the amount of $400, the value of the books at the time of the contribution.[2] . . .

Taxpayer's report of his 1968 income did not include the value of the textbooks received, but it did include a charitable deduction for the value of the books donated to the school library. The Internal Revenue Service assessed a deficiency against the taxpayer representing income taxes on the value of the textbooks received. Taxpayer paid the amount of the deficiency, filed a claim for refund and subsequently instituted this action to recover that amount.[3] . . .

The Supreme Court has frequently reiterated that it was the intention of Congress "to use the full measure of its taxing power" and "to tax all gains except those specifically exempted." James v. United States, 366 U.S. 213, 218-219 (1961). The Supreme Court has also held that the language of Section 61(a) encompasses all "accessions to wealth, clearly realized, and

---

3. See, e.g., Webster's Tenth Collegiate Dictionary 588 (1997), wherein income is defined as "a gain or recurrent benefit usually measured in money that derives from capital or labor."

Since 1954 inclusion of prizes has been specifically dealt with in §74. See Chapter 4C.1 below.

2. Since the tax year at issue in this litigation is 1968, the amount of charitable deduction which could be taken was unaffected by 26 U.S.C. §170(e)(1) which was added by the Tax Reform Act of 1969, Pub. L. No. 91-172, 83 Stat. 487.

3. Taxpayer originally sought a refund of $288.76 and sought to recover that amount in this action. This amount reflected taxpayer's contentions that the books were not income and that he was entitled to a charitable deduction for $430 worth of books which had been given directly to the school by the publishers. In proceedings in the district court, taxpayer conceded that he was not entitled to a deduction for the books which the publishers had sent to the school.

over which the taxpayers have complete dominion." Id. at 219; Commissioner v. Glenshaw Glass Co., 348 U.S. 426, 431 (1955).

There are no reported cases which have applied these definitions of income to the questions of the receipt of unsolicited samples. . . .

The receipt of textbooks is unquestionably an "accession to wealth." Taxpayer recognized the value of the books when he donated them and took a $400 deduction therefor. Possession of the books increased the taxpayer's wealth. Taxpayer's receipt and possession of the books indicate that the income was "clearly realized." Taxpayer admitted that the books were given to him for his personal retention or whatever disposition he saw fit to make of them. Although the receipt of unsolicited samples may sometimes raise the question of whether the taxpayer manifested an intent to accept the property or exercised "complete dominion" over it, there is no question that this element is satisfied by the unequivocal act of taking a charitable deduction for donation of the property.

The district court recognized that the act of claiming a charitable deduction does manifest an intent to accept the property as one's own. It nevertheless declined to label receipt of the property as income because it considered such an act indistinguishable from other acts unrelated to the tax laws which also evidence an intent to accept property as one's own, such as a school principal donating his sample texts to the library *without* claiming a deduction. We need not resolve the question of the tax consequences of this and other hypothetical cases discussed by the district court and suggested by the taxpayer. To decide the case before us we need only hold, as we do, that when a tax deduction is taken for the donation of unsolicited samples the value of the samples received must be included in the taxpayer's gross income.

This conclusion is consistent with Revenue Ruling 70-498, 1970-2 Cum. Bull. 6, in which the Internal Revenue Service held that a newspaper's book reviewer must include in his gross income the value of unsolicited books received from publishers which are donated to a charitable organization and for which a charitable deduction is taken. This ruling was issued to supersede an earlier ruling, Rev. Rul. 70-330, 1970-1 Cum. Bull. 14, that mere retention of unsolicited books was sufficient to cause them to be gross income.

The Internal Revenue Service has apparently made an administrative decision to be concerned with the taxation of unsolicited samples only when failure to tax those samples would provide taxpayers with double tax benefits. It is not for the courts to quarrel with an agency's rational allocation of its administrative resources.

In light of the foregoing, the judgment appealed from is reversed and the case is remanded to the district court with directions to enter judgment for the United States. Reversed.

Notes and Questions

1. Do you suppose that Mr. Haverly could have sold the textbooks for $400? How much could you get for a dozen elementary school social studies textbooks, all by different authors, if none of them has been adopted by the local school district? (Remember, this was the era before eBay®.) Was $400 really the books' "fair market value"? What was the extent of Haverly's accession to wealth?

2. In view of the decision in *Haverly*, how should a law professor treat sample casebooks sent to him by publishers? What if he adopts such a book for use in his class? What if he does not adopt it, but puts it on his shelf and uses it as a reference source for additional information and views on the subject he teaches? What if he gives such a book to his daughter who is attending law school and taking a course for which the book has been adopted?

3. Observe that *Haverly*, like *Turner*, concerns a valuable receipt that was not earned as compensation for services, either as an employee (as in *Old Colony Trust Co.* and *Benaglia*) or an independent contractor. Are windfalls (fortuitous gains) income? See Commissioner v. Glenshaw Glass Co., Chapter 3A below. Special rules now govern the amount and timing of income in the case of in-kind compensation for services, such as stock-based compensation of corporate executives. See §83, examined Chapter 6F.3 below.

B. STATUTORY EXCLUSIONS

Sometimes Congress undertakes to prescribe specific answers to some of the questions considered in this chapter. Here are two prominent examples. In examining the following materials try to begin to think about when a statutory solution (?) is likely to be an improvement over administrative and judicial responses to tax problems. In what respects are statutory solutions likely to be better or worse?

1. Meals and Lodging: §119

In 1954 Congress enacted §119 codifying (and modifying) the rule in *Benaglia.* Read §119 and the regulations thereunder and figure out how they affect the following situations.

Problems

1. Anderson was a motel manager who lived in the motel until his family outgrew their quarters. The motel had a high occupancy rate, and so instead of giving him more space in the motel, the owner purchased a house in a tract two short blocks from the motel and required him to live there.[4]

2. Dole was hired as assistant superintendent of Packard Mills, and he was told he would be on call 24 hours a day and that he would have to live in a company-owned house approximately one mile from the mill so that he would be readily available for emergencies and conferences. Other supervisory personnel were also required to live in company houses at the same location. The company houses were nearer to the mill than any other available housing, and Packard's supervisory personnel were frequently called on outside regular hours.[5]

3. A Veteran's Administration doctor lives in a home on hospital grounds about a mile from the hospital itself where he works. A so-called housing allowance is deducted from his regular salary grade and would be deducted as long as government housing were available, whether or not he occupied it.[6]

4. Taxpayers, husband and wife, accept jobs as domestic cook and gardener for a wealthy couple who provide them a room in their house and meals in their kitchen.

5. Must a university president report as gross income the rental value of an official residence located adjacent to campus that is furnished free of charge by the institution?

6. Consult §107, which was enacted in 1921, and answer the following problems.

(a) A minister is furnished with a home next door to the parish church. Is the rental value included in the minister's income? What result if the parish pays the minister $12,000 annually as a housing allowance, which the minister uses to rent a house in a neighborhood located several miles from the church?

(b) Assume now that the parishioners pay the minister an annual rental allowance of $24,000, which the minister uses to rent a small farm. The parish serves a rural community and the minister uses the farmhouse as her residence. Is any amount includible in the minister's gross income? What statutory term is at issue here? See Reg. §1.107-1(c).

(c) What if the minister is a nationally syndicated "televangelist" whose church provides him the use of a 50-room mansion situated on a 100-acre estate in Florida? Why wasn't §107 repealed in 1954 when Congress added §119?

4. Charles N. Anderson, 42 T.C. 410 (1964), rev'd, 371 F.2d 59 (6th Cir. 1966), cert. denied, 387 U.S. 906 (1967).
5. Gordon S. Dole, 43 T.C. 697 (1965), aff'd, 351 F.2d 308 (1st Cir. 1965).
6. Boykin v. Commissioner, 260 F.2d 249 (8th Cir. 1958).

(d) While continuing his job as an electrician, Hector establishes the Universal Laugh Church and becomes its first ordained minister. Thereafter, Hector contributes half of his $50,000 salary to the Church and claims a charitable contribution deduction therefor. The Universal Laugh Church, in turn, pays its minister a $25,000 parsonage allowance, which Hector uses to pay off the mortgage and for home repair, furniture, and the like. What is the purpose of this arrangement? Do you see the role of §107? As a revenue agent auditing Hector's return, would you raise any objections? Cf. Reg. §1.107-1(a).

7. Make a critical evaluation of §119. Note that it was newly adopted as part of the Internal Revenue Code of 1954. Congressional intent in 1954 was to put pesky problems like *Benaglia* to rest by adopting specific statutory provisions to settle what appeared to be debatable under more general provisions. Is this a well-conceived objective? Is it well executed?

8. State police in New Jersey used to return to their barracks for meals. Is this excludible under §119? In order to avoid a hiatus in police coverage on the highway during the noon meal hour, a change was made requiring police *not* to return to the barracks but authorizing them instead to eat in public restaurants and to turn in their meal receipts for reimbursement. Is this excludible?[7]

COMMISSIONER v. KOWALSKI
434 U.S. 77 (1977)

Mr. Justice BRENNAN delivered the opinion of the Court.

This case presents the question whether cash payments to state police troopers, designated as meal allowances, are included in gross income under §61(a) of the Internal Revenue Code of 1954, 26 U.S.C. §61(a), and if so, are otherwise excludable under §119 of the Code.

I

The pertinent facts are not in dispute. Respondent is a state police trooper employed by the Division of State Police of the Department of Law and Public Safety of the State of New Jersey. During 1970, the tax year in question, he received a base salary of $8,739.38, and an additional $1,697.54 designated as an allowance for meals.

The State instituted the cash meal allowance for its state police officers in July 1949. Prior to that time, all troopers were provided with mid-shift[5]

---

7. See Saunders v. Commissioner, 215 F.2d 768 (1954); but cf. Commissioner v. Kowalski [next case].

5. While on active duty, New Jersey troopers are generally required to live in barracks. Meals furnished in kind at the barracks before or after a patrol shift are not involved in this case. Nor is the meal

meals in kind at various meal stations located throughout the State. A trooper unable to eat at an official meal station could, however, eat at a restaurant and obtain reimbursement. The meal-station system proved unsatisfactory to the State because it required troopers to leave their assigned areas of patrol unguarded for extended periods of time. As a result, the State closed its meal stations and instituted a cash-allowance system. Under this system, troopers remain on call in their assigned patrol areas during their mid-shift break. Otherwise, troopers are not restricted in any way with respect to where they may eat in the patrol area and, indeed, may eat at home if it is located within that area. Troopers may also bring their mid-shift meal to the job and eat it in or near their patrol cars.

The meal allowance is paid biweekly in advance and is included, although separately stated, with the trooper's salary. The meal allowance money is also separately accounted for in the State's accounting system. Funds are never commingled between the salary and meal-allowance accounts. Because of these characteristics of the meal-allowance system, the Tax Court concluded that the "meal allowance was not intended to represent additional compensation." 65 T.C. 44, 47.

Notwithstanding this conclusion, it is not disputed that the meal allowance has many features inconsistent with its characterization as a simple reimbursement for meals that would otherwise have been taken at a meal station. For example, troopers are not required to spend their meal allowances on their mid-shift meals, nor are they required to account for the manner in which the money is spent. With one limited exception not relevant here,[6] no reduction in the meal allowance is made for periods when a trooper is not on patrol because, for example, he is assigned to a headquarters building or is away from active duty on vacation, leave, or sick leave. In addition, the cash allowance for meals is described on a state police recruitment brochure as an item of salary to be received in addition to an officer's base salary and the amount of the meal allowance is a subject of negotiations between the State and the police-troopers' union. Finally, the amount of an officer's cash meal allowance varies with his rank,[7] and is included in his gross pay for purposes of calculating pension benefits.

On his 1970 income-tax return, respondent reported $9,066 in wages. That amount included his salary plus $326.45 which represented cash meal allowances reported by the State on respondent's Wage and Tax Statement (Form W-2).[8] The remaining amount of meal allowance, $1,371.09, was

---

allowance intended to pay for meals eaten before or after a shift in those instances in which the trooper is not living in the barracks. However, because of the duration of some patrols, a trooper may be required to eat more than one meal per shift while on the road.

6. The amount of the allowance is adjusted only when an officer is on military leave.

7. Troopers, such as respondent and other noncommissioned officers received $1,740 per year; lieutenants and captains received $1,776, majors $1,848, and the Superintendent $2,136.

8. On October 1, 1970, the Division of State Police began to withhold income tax from amounts paid as cash meal allowances. No claim has been made that the change in the Division's withholding policy has any relevance for this case.

not reported. On audit, the Commissioner determined that this amount should have been included in respondent's 1970 income and assessed a deficiency. . . .

II

A

The starting point in the determination of the scope of "gross income" is the cardinal principle that Congress in creating the income tax intended "to use the full measure of its taxing power." Helvering v. Clifford [infra Chapter 18A at pp. 1024, 1025] (1940). . . .

In applying this principle to the construction of §22(a) of the Internal Revenue Code of 1939[12] this Court stated that "Congress applied no limitations as to the source of taxable receipts, nor restrictive labels as to their nature[, but intended] to tax all gains except those specifically exempted." Commissioner v. Glenshaw Glass Co. [infra Chapter 3A at pp. 90, 91-92] (1955), citing Commissioner v. Jacobson, 336 U.S. 28, 49 (1949), and Helvering v. Stockholms Enskilda Bank, 293 U.S. 84, 87-91 (1934). Although Congress simplified the definition of gross income in §61 of the 1954 Code, it did not intend thereby to narrow the scope of that concept. See Commissioner v. Glenshaw Glass Co., supra, at [93] and n.11; H.R. Rep. No. 1337, 83d Cong., 2d Sess., A18 (1954); S. Rep. No. 1622, 83d Cong., 2d Sess., 168 (1954).[13] In the absence of a specific exemption, therefore, respondent's meal-allowance payments are income within the meaning of §61 since, like the payments involved in Glenshaw Glass Co., the payments are "undeniabl[y] accessions to wealth, clearly realized, and over which the [respondent has] complete dominion." Commissioner v. Glenshaw Glass Co., supra, at [92]. See also Commissioner v. LoBue, 351 U.S. 243, 247 (1956); Van Rosen v. Commissioner, 17 T.C. 834, 838 (1951).

Respondent contends, however, that §119 can be construed to be a specific exemption covering the meal-allowance payments to New Jersey troopers. Alternatively, respondent argues that notwithstanding §119 a specific exemption may be found in a line of lower-court cases and administrative rulings which recognize that benefits conferred by an employer on

12. 53 Stat. 9. as amended, 53 Stat. 574. This section provided: "(a) General Definition — 'Gross income' includes gains, profits, and income derived from salaries, wages, or compensation for personal service or gains or profits and *income derived from any source whatever*. . . ." (Emphasis added.)

13. The House and Senate Reports state: "[Section 61] corresponds to section 22(a) of the 1939 Code. While the language in existing section 22(a) has been simplified, the all-inclusive nature of statutory gross income has not been affected thereby. Section 61(a) is as broad in scope as section 22(a)."

an employee "for the convenience of the employer" — at least when such benefits are not "compensatory" — are not income within the meaning of the Internal Revenue Code. . . .

B

Section 119 provides that an employee may exclude from income "the value of any meals furnished to him by his employer, but only if the meals are furnished on the business premises of the employer. . . ." By its terms, §119 covers *meals* furnished by the employer and not *cash* reimbursements for meals. This is not a mere oversight. As we shall explain at greater length below, the form of §119 which Congress enacted originated in the Senate and the Report accompanying the Senate bill is very clear: "Section 119 applies only to meals or lodging furnished in kind." S. Rep. No. 1622, 83d Cong., 2d Sess., 190 (1954). See also Treas. Regs. §1.119-1(c)(2). Accordingly, respondent's meal allowance payments are not subject to exclusion under §119.

C

The convenience of the employer doctrine is not a tidy one. The phrase "convenience of the employer" first appeared in O.D. 265, 1 Cum. Bull. 71 (1919), in a ruling exempting from the income tax board and lodging furnished seamen aboard ship. The following year, T.D. 2992, 2 Cum. Bull. 76 (1920), was issued and added a convenience of the employer section to Article 33 of Regulations 45, the income tax regulations then in effect. As modified, Art. 33 stated: "Art. 33. *Compensation paid other than in cash. . . .* When living quarters such as camps are furnished to employees for the convenience of the employer, the ratable value need not be added to the cash compensation of the employee, but where a person receives as compensation for services rendered a salary and in addition thereto living quarters, the value to such person of the quarters furnished constitutes income subject to tax. . . ." While T.D. 2992 extended the convenience of the employer test as a general rule solely to items received in kind, O.D. 514, 2 Cum. Bull. 90 (1920), extended the convenience of the employer doctrine to cash payments for "supper money."[15]

The rationale of both T.D. 2992 and O.D. 514 appears to have been that benefits conferred by an employer on an employee in the designated circumstances were not compensation for services and hence not income. Subsequent rulings equivocate on whether the noncompensatory character of a

---

15. "'Supper money' paid by an employer to an employee, who voluntarily performs extra labor for his employer after regular business hours, *such payment not being considered additional compensation and not being charged to the salary account*, is considered as being paid for the convenience of the employer. . . ." (Emphasis added.)

benefit could be inferred merely from its characterization by the employer or whether there must be additional evidence that employees are granted a benefit solely because the employer's business could not function properly unless an employee was furnished that benefit on the employer's premises. O.D. 514, for example, focuses only on the employer's characterization. Two rulings issued in 1921, however, dealing respectively with cannery workers[17] and hospital employees,[18] emphasize the necessity of the benefits to the functioning of the employer's business, and this emphasis was made the authoritative interpretation of the convenience of the employer provisions of the regulations in Mim. 5023, 1940-1 Cum. Bull. 14.

Adding complexity, however, is Mim. 6472, 1950-1 Cum. Bull. 15, issued in 1950. This Mimeograph states in relevant part: "The 'convenience of the employer' rule is simply an administrative test to be applied only in cases in which the compensatory character of benefits is not otherwise determinable. It follows that the rule should not be applied in any case in which it is evident from the other circumstance involved that the receipt of quarters or meals by the employee represents compensation for services rendered." 1950-1 Cum. Bull., at 15.

Mim. 6472 expressly modified all previous rulings which had suggested that meals and lodging could be excluded from income upon a simple finding that the furnishing of such benefits was necessary to allow an employee to perform his duties properly.[20] However, the ruling apparently did not affect O.D. 514, which, as noted above, creates an exclusion from income based solely on an employer's characterization of a payment as noncompensatory.

Coexisting with the regulations and administrative determinations of the Treasury, but independent of them, is a body of case law also applying the "convenience of the employer" test to exclude from an employee's statutory income benefits conferred by his employer.

An early case is Jones v. United States, 60 Ct. Cl. 552 (1925). There the Court of Claims ruled that neither the value of quarters provided an Army officer for nine months of a tax year nor payments in commutation of quarters paid the officer for the remainder of the year were includable in income. The decision appears to rest both on a conclusion that public quarters by

---

17. "Where, from the location and nature of the work, it is necessary that employees engaged in fishing and canning be furnished with lodging and sustenance by the employer, the value of such lodging and sustenance may be considered as being furnished for the convenience of the employer and need not, therefore, be included in computing net income. . . ." O.D. 814, 4 Cum. Bull. 84, 84-85 (1921).

18. "Where the employees of a hospital are subject to immediate service on demand at any time during the twenty-four hours of the day and on that account are required to accept quarters and meals at the hospital, the value of such quarters and meals may be considered as being furnished for the convenience of the hospital and does not represent additional compensation to the employees. On the other hand, where the employees could, if they so desired, obtain meals and lodging elsewhere than in the hospital and yet perform the duties required of them by such hospital, the ratable value of the board and lodging furnished is considered additional compensation." O.D. 915, 4 Cum. Bull 85, 85-86 (9121).

20. See 1950-1 Cum. Bull., at 16.

tradition and law were not "compensation received as such" within the meaning of §213 of the revenue act of 1921, 42 Stat. 237, and also on the proposition that "public quarters for the housing of officer is as much a military necessity as the procurement of implements of warfare or the training of troops." 60 Ct. Cl., at 569; see id. at 565-568. The Court of Claims, in addition, rejected the argument that money paid in commutation of quarters was income on the ground that it was not "gain derived from labor" within the meaning of Eisner v. Macomber [Chapter 5A below] (1920), but apparently was at most a reimbursement to the officer for furnishing himself with a necessity of his job in those instances in which the Government found it convenient to leave the task of procuring quarters to an individual officer. 60 Ct. Cl., at 574-578.

Subsequent judicial development of the convenience of the employer doctrine centered primarily in the Tax Court. In two reviewed cases decided more than a decade apart, Benaglia v. Commissioner, 36 B.T.A. 838 (1937), and Van Rosen v. Commissioner, 17 T.C. 834 (1951), that court settled on the business necessity rationale for excluding food and lodging from an employee's income. *Van Rosen's* unanimous decision is of particular interest in interpreting the legislative history of the 1954 recodification of the Internal Revenue Code since it predates that recodification by only three years. There, the Tax Court expressly rejected any reading of *Jones*, supra, that would make tax consequences turn on the intent of the employer, even though the employer in *Van Rosen* as in *Jones* was the United States and, also as in *Jones* the subsistence payments involved in the litigation were provided by military regulation. In addition, *Van Rosen* refused to follow *Jones* holding with respect to cash allowances. . . . *

Two years later, the Tax Court in an unreviewed decision in Doran v. Commissioner, 21 T.C.374 (1953), returned in part to the employer's characterization rationale rejected by *Van Rosen*. In *Doran*, the taxpayer was furnished lodging in kind by a state school. State law required the value of the lodging to be included in the employee's compensation. Although the court concluded that the lodging was furnished to allow the taxpayer to be on 24-hour call, a reason normally sufficient to justify a convenience of the employer exclusion, it required the value of the lodging to be included in income on the basis of the characterization of the lodgings as compensation under state law. The approach taken in *Doran* is the same as that in Mim. 6472, supra. However, the Court of Appeals for the Second Circuit, in Diamond v. Sturr, 221 F.2d 264 (1955), on facts indistinguishable from *Doran*, reviewed the law prior to 1954 and held that the business necessity view of the convenience of the employer test, "having persisted through the interpretations of the Treasury and the Tax Court throughout years of

---

* Van Rosen was a civilian employee of the Army Transportation Corps who received a cash allowance "in lieu of subsistence and quarters." The allowance was held taxable. — EDS.

re-enactment of the Internal Revenue Code," was the *sole* test to be applied. 221 F.2d, at 268.

D

Even if we assume that respondent's meal-allowance payments could have been excluded from income under the 1939 Code pursuant to the doctrine we have just sketched, we must nonetheless inquire whether such an implied exclusion survives the 1954 recodification of the Internal Revenue Code. Cf. Helvering v. Winmill, 305 U.S. 79, 83 (1938). Two provisions of the 1954 Code are relevant to this inquiry: §119 and §120,[25] now repealed,[26] which allowed police officers to exclude from income subsistence allowances of up to $5 per day.

In enacting §119, the Congress was determined to "end the confusion as to the tax status of meals and lodging furnished an employee by his employer." H.R. Rep. No. 1337, 83d Cong., 2d Sess., 18 (1954); S. Rep. No. 1622, 83d Cong., 2d Sess., 19 (1954). However, the House and Senate initially differed on the significance that should be given the convenience of the employer doctrine for the purposes of §119. As explained in its Report, the House proposed to exclude meals from gross income "if they [were] furnished at the place of employment and the employee [was] required to accept them at the place of employment as a condition of his employment." H.R. Rep. No. 1337, supra, at 18; see H.R. 8300, 83d Cong., 2d Sess., §119 (1954). Since no reference whatsoever was made to the concept, the House view apparently was that a statute "designed to end the confusion as to the tax status of meals and lodging furnished an employee by his employer" required complete disregard of the convenience of the employer doctrine.

The Senate, however, was of the view that the doctrine had at least a limited role to play. After noting the existence of the doctrine and the Tax Court's reliance on state law to refuse to apply it in Doran v. Commissioner, supra, the Senate Report states:

> Your committee believes that the House provision is ambiguous in providing that meals or lodging furnished on the employer's premises, which the employee is required to accept as a condition of his employment, are excludable from income whether or not furnished as compensation. Your committee has provided that the basic test of

---

25. Sec. 120. Statutory Subsistence Allowance Received By Police.

(a) General Rule. — Gross income does not include any amount received as a statutory subsistence allowance by an individual who is employed as a police official. . . .

(b) Limitations. —

(1) Amounts to which subsection (a) applies shall not exceed $5 per day.

(2) If any individual receives a subsistence allowance to which subsection (a) applies, no deduction shall be allowed under any other provision of this chapter for expenses in respect of which he has received such allowance, except to the extent that such expenses exceed the amount excludable under subsection (a) and the excess is otherwise allowable as a deduction under this chapter.

Pub. L. No. 83-591, §120. 68A Stat. 39.

26. See Technical Amendments Act of 1958, §3, 72 Stat. 1607.

exclusion is to be whether the meals or lodging are furnished primarily for the convenience of the employer (and thus excludable) or whether they were primarily for the convenience of the employee (and therefore taxable). However, in deciding whether they were furnished for the convenience of the employer, the fact that a State statute or an employment contract fixing the terms of the employment indicate the meals or lodging are intended as compensation is not to be determinative. This means that employees of State institutions who are required to live and eat on the premises will not be taxed on the value of the meals and lodging even though the State statute indicates the meals and lodging are part of the employee's compensation. [S. Rep. No. 1622, supra, at 19.]

In a technical appendix, the Senate Report further elaborated that: "Section 119 applies only to meals or lodging furnished in kind. Therefore, any cash allowances for meals or lodging received by an employee will continue to be includable in gross income to the extent that such allowances constitute compensation." Id., at 190-191.

After conference, the House acquiesced in the Senate's version of §119. Because of this, respondent urges that §119 as passed did not discard the convenience of the employer doctrine, but indeed endorsed the doctrine shorn of the confusion created by Mim. 6472 and cases like *Doran*. Respondent further argues that, by negative implication, the technical appendix to the Senate Report creates a class of noncompensatory cash meal payments that are to be excluded from income. We disagree.

The Senate unquestionably intended to overrule *Doran* and rulings like Mim. 6472. Equally clearly the Senate refused completely to abandon the convenience of the employer doctrine as the House wished to do. On the other hand, the Senate did not propose to leave undisturbed the convenience of the employer doctrine as it had evolved prior to the promulgation of Mim. 6472. The language of §119[27] quite plainly rejects the reasoning behind rulings like O.D. 514, see n.15, supra, which rest on the employer's characterization of the nature of a payment.[28] This conclusion is buttressed by the Senate's choice of a term of art, "convenience of the employer," in describing one of the conditions for exclusion under §119. In choosing, the Senate obviously intended to adopt the meaning of that term as it had developed over time, except, of course, to the extent §119 overrules decisions like *Doran*. As we have noted above, Van Rosen v. Commissioner, 17 T.C. 834 (1951), provided the controlling court definition at the time of the 1954 recodification and it expressly rejected the *Jones*' theory of "convenience of the employer" — and by implication the theory of O.D. 514 — and adopted as the exclusive rationale the business necessity theory. See 17 T.C., at 838-840. The business necessity theory was also the controlling

---

27. "[T]he provisions of an employment contract shall not be determinative of whether meals are intended as compensation."

28. We do not decide today whether, notwithstanding §119, the "supper money" exclusion may be justified on other grounds. See, e.g., Treasury Department Proposed Fringe Benefit Regulations, 40 Fed. Reg. 41118, 41121 (1975) (example 8). Nor do we decide whether sporadic meal reimbursements may be excluded from income. Cf. United States v. Correll [Chapter 12C below].

administrative interpretation of "convenience of the employer" prior to Mim. 6472. See ante, at 8-9, and n.19. Finally, although the Senate Report did not expressly define "convenience of the employer" it did describe those situations in which it wished to reverse the courts and create an exclusion as those where "an employee must accept meals or lodging in order properly to perform his duties." S. Rep. No. 1622, supra, at 190.

As the last step in its restructuring of prior law, the Senate adopted an additional restriction created by the House and not theretofore a part of the law, which required that meals subject to exclusion had to be taken on the business premises of the employer. Thus §119 comprehensively modified the prior law, both expanding and contracting the exclusion for meals and lodging previously provides, and it must therefore be construed as its drafts-men obviously intended it to be — as a replacement for the prior law, designed to "end [its] confusion."

Because §119 replaces prior law, respondent's further argument — that the technical appendix in the Senate Report recognized the existence under §61 of an exclusion for a class of noncompensatory cash payments — is without merit. If cash meal reimbursements could be excluded on the mere showing that such payments served the convenience of the employer, as respondent suggests, then cash would be more widely excluded from income than meals in kind, an extraordinary result given the presumptively compensatory nature of cash payments and the obvious intent of §119 to narrow the circumstance in which meals could be excluded. Moreover, there is no reason to suppose that Congress would have wanted to recognize a class of excludable cash meal payments. The two precedents for the exclusion of cash — O.D. 514 and Jones v. United States — both rest on the proposition that the convenience of the employer can be inferred from the character-ization given the cash payments by the employer, and the heart of this prop-osition is undercut by both the language of §119 and the Senate Report. *Jones* also rests on Eisner v. Macomber, 252 U.S. 189 (1920), but Congress had no reason to read *Eisner's* definition of income into §61 and, indeed, any assumption that Congress did is squarely at odds with United States v. Glenshaw Glass Co., 348 U.S. 426 (1955).[29] See id., at 430-431. Finally, as petitioner suggests, it is much more reasonable to assume that the cryptic statement in the technical appendix — "cash allowance will continue to be includable in gross income to the extend that such allowances constitute compensation" — was meant to indicate only that meal payments otherwise

---

29. Moreover, it must be recognized that §213 of the Revenue Act of 1921, 42 Stat. 237, which was involved in Jones v. United States, made a distinction by its terms between "gross income" which included "salaries, wages, or compensation for personal service" and the "compensation received as such" by an officer of the United State. See 60 Ct. Cl., at 563. The Court of Claims assumed that Congress by so distinguishing intended to tax United States officers more narrowly than other taxpayers by levying the income tax only on amounts expressly characterized by Congress as compensation. See ibid. For this reason, *Jones* is of limited value in construing §61 which contains no language even remotely similar to §213.

deductible under §162(a)(2) of the Internal Revenue Code, as amended, 26 U.S.C.A. §162(a)(2) (Supp. 1977), were not affected by §119.

Moreover, even if we were to assume with respondent that cash meal payments made for the convenience of the employer could qualify for an exclusion notwithstanding the express limitations upon the doctrine embodied in §119, there would still be no reason to allow the meal allowance here to be excluded. Under the pre-1954 convenience of the employer doctrine respondent's allowance is indistinguishable from that in Van Rosen v. Commissioner, 17 T.C. 834 (1951), and hence it is income. Indeed, the form of the meal allowance involved here has drastically changed from that passed on in Saunders v. Commissioner, 215 F.2d 768 (1954), relied on by the Third Circuit below, see ante, and in its present form the allowance is not excludable even under *Saunders'* analysis. In any case, to avoid the completely unwarranted result of creating a larger exclusion for cash than kind, the meal allowance here would have to be demonstrated to be necessary to allow respondent "properly to perform his duties." There is not even a suggestion on this record of any such necessity.

Finally, respondent argues that it is unfair that members of the military may exclude their subsistence allowances from income while respondent cannot. While this may be so, arguments of equity have little force in construing the boundaries of exclusions and deductions from income many of which, to be administrable, must be arbitrary. In any case, Congress has already considered respondent's equity argument and has rejected it in the repeal of §120 of the Internal Revenue Code of 1954. That provision as enacted allowed state troopers like respondent to exclude from income up to $5 of subsistence allowance per day. Section 120 was repealed after only four years, however, because it was "inequitable since there are many other individual taxpayers whose duties also require them to incur subsistence expenditures regardless of the tax effect. Thus, it appears that certain police officials by reason of this exclusion are placed in a more favorable position taxwise than other individual income taxpayers who incur the same types of expense. . . ." H.R. Rep. No. 775, 85th Cong., 1st Sess., 7 (1957).

Reversed.

Mr. Justice BLACKMUN, with whom The Chief Justice joins, dissenting.

More than a decade ago the United States Court of Appeals for the Eighth Circuit, in United States v. Morelan, 356 F.2d 199 (1966), held that the $3 per day subsistence allowance paid Minnesota state highway patrolmen was excludable from gross income under §119 of the Internal Revenue Code of 1954, 26 U.S.C. §119. . . . I sat as a Circuit Judge on that case. I was happy to join Chief Judge Vogel's opinion because I then felt, and still do, that it was correct. . . .

I have no particular quarrel with the conclusion that the payments received by the New Jersey troopers constituted income to them under §61. I can accept that, but my stance in *Morelan* leads me to disagree with the Court's conclusion that the payments are not excludable under §119.

The Court draws an in-cash or in-kind distinction. This has no appeal or persuasion for me because that statute does not speak specifically in such terms. It does no more than refer to "meals furnished on the business premises of the employer," and from those words the Court draws the in-kind consequence. I am not so sure. In any event, for me, as was the case in *Morelan*, the business premises of the State of New Jersey, the trooper's employer, are wherever the trooper is on duty in that State. The employer's premises are statewide.

The Court in its opinion makes only passing comment, with a general reference to fairness, on the ironical difference in tax treatment it now accords to the paramilitary New Jersey state trooper structure and the federal military. The distinction must be embarrassing to the Government in its position here, for the Internal Revenue Code draws no such distinction. . . .

I fear that state troopers the country over, not handsomely paid to begin with, will never understand today's decision. And I doubt that their reading of the Court's opinion — if, indeed, laymen can be expected to understand its technical wording — will convince them that the situation is as clear as the Court purports to find it.

SIBLA v. COMMISSIONER
611 F.2d 1260 (9th Cir. 1980)

Before Kennedy and Tang, Circuit Judges, and Curtis,* District Judge.
CURTIS, District Judge: . . .

FACTS

During the relevant period the taxpayers were employed as firemen by the Los Angeles Fire Department and were assigned to Fire Station No. 89 in North Hollywood, California. They normally worked 24-hour shifts and were not permitted to leave the fire station on personal business while on duty.

In the late 1950's a desegregation plan was implemented by the Fire Department. Previously segregated posts were consolidated in order to eliminate segregation within a post. The Board of Fire Commissioners adopted rules requiring all firemen at each fire station to participate in a nonexclusionary organized mess at the station house, unless officially excused. The only recognized grounds for nonparticipation was a physical ailment verified by the city's own examining physician.

---

* Honorable Jesse W. Curtis, United States District Judge, Central District of California, sitting by designation.

The Fire Department provided kitchen facilities, but the firemen them-selves generally organized the activities themselves — they provided dishes and pots, purchased and prepared the food, assessed members for the cost of the meals and collected the assessments. Meal expenses averaged about $3.00 per man for each 24-hour shift which the taxpayers were required to pay even though they were at times away from the station on fire depart-ment business during the mess period.

In 1973, the appellant Sibla deducted his total payments for the year. The appellant Cooper deducted the amounts he had paid into the organized mess expense in the years 1972 and 1973. Both appellants claim the deduc-tion as an ordinary and necessary business expense under section 162(a). In both cases the Commissioner disallowed the deduction as a non-deductible personal expense. The Commissioner was overruled, but by a divided court. The majority consisting of seven judges allowed the deduction under section 162(a). A concurring opinion written by Judge Simpson, although allowing the deduction, chose to do so under the provisions of section 119 . . . and would have disallowed it under section 162(a). The concurring opinion was signed by five other judges, two judges dissented.

ISSUE ON APPEAL

The issue on appeal therefore is "whether the tax court erred in holding that taxpayer's share of the expenses of the organized mess at the firehouse was deductible under section 162(a) or section 119 of the Internal Revenue Code of 1954." We hold that such expenses are both deductible under section 162(a) and excludable under section 119.

BUSINESS EXPENSE DEDUCTION UNDER SECTION 162

Section 162(a) provides a deduction for all the "ordinary and necessary expenses paid or incurred in carrying on any trade or business. . . ."

Section 262 provides: "Except as otherwise expressly provided in this chapter, no deduction shall be allowed for personal, living, or family expenses."

The Commissioner argues that an expense is "personal" rather than "business" if it is personal in character and could be incurred whether or not the taxpayer engaged in business activity. An expense for meals or groceries is generally considered a non-deductible personal expense. Here the tax-payer would have incurred a similar expense whether or not he ate at work. Consequently, the Commissioner contends the fact that the taxpayer incurred the expense while at work does not change the personal character of the expenditure.

In allowing the deduction, Judge Fay speaking for the majority observed initially that:

> [M]any expenditures possess both personal and business attributes. In these situations placement of that often thin line which distinguishes a "personal expense" from a "business expense" depends primarily upon the facts and circumstances of each particular case. Cf. Robert J. Kowalski, 65 T.C. 44, 63 (1975) (Drennen, J., concurring and dissenting), revd. 544 F.2d 686 (3d Cir. 1976). For example, Rev. Rul. 75-316, 1975-2 C.B. 54, provides in part as follows:
>
>> "The fact that a particular expense may under certain circumstances be a nonde-ductible personal expense does not preclude the deduction of such an expense as an ordinary and necessary business expense under other circumstances."

As the tax court has indicated, that which may be a personal expense under some circumstances can, when circumscribed by company regulations, directives, and conditions, lose its character as a personal expense and take on the color of a business expense. Recognizing the "unusual nature of petitioner's employment, the involuntary nature of the expense incurred, petitioner's limited ability to physically participate in the mess, and his employer's lack of intent to compensate or otherwise benefit petitioner for enacting the requirement, . . ." the court said, "upon consideration of the entire record, we find that the amounts in issue constitute business expenses rather than personal expenses."

In reaching such a determination, we consider that the tax court has exercised that degree of special expertise which Congress has intended to provide in that tribunal, and that this court should not overrule that body, unless some unmistakable question of law mandates such a decision. . . .

Those judges who dissented from this view express the fear that, "If a deduction is allowed under section 162(a) for this personal expenditure, we may be launched down a slippery slope, and it may be difficult to find a rational basis for drawing a line in other cases involving personal expenditures." Although we recognize the court's concern, we do not consider the task so difficult as to justify abdicating what we believe is the court's duty to try to find the congressional intent in these complex statutes. The tax laws are shot through with instances in which courts are called upon to make delicate factual assessments and interpretive decisions in areas where rational distinctions are difficult to establish. And we think the task of doing so here is no greater than that often encountered by courts working in this field of the law. . . .

MEAL EXCLUSION UNDER SECTION 119

The concurring judges would allow such payment to be excluded from gross income under section 119. This section allows an employee to exclude the value of meals or lodging furnished him by his employer for the convenience of the employer. In summarizing the regulations section 1.119-1(a)(3), Income Tax Regulations, the court pointed out that employees are not taxable on amounts charged for meals if four conditions exist: (1) The meals are furnished by the employer, (2) there is a charge for the meals which must be paid irrespective of how much he eats, (3) the meals are furnished for the convenience of the employer, and (4) the charge equals the value of the meals. From that the court reasons that while "[t]he employer did not purchase and supervise the preparation of the meals in this case and did not withhold the charge from the compensation paid the petitioner, the employer furnished the facility for preparing the meals and required the employees to participate in the meals as a condition for their employment." The concurring court further pointed out:

> There can be no question but that, if the meals were furnished in kind, they would qualify for the exclusion. During his tour of duty, the petitioner is not allowed to leave the fire station for personal purposes — not allowed to leave to eat elsewhere; he must remain available at all times to respond to emergency calls. Such circumstances satisfy the requirements concerning meals furnished for the convenience of the employer. Sec. 1.119-1(a)(2)(ii)(a), Income Tax Regs.

The court concludes, "In substance, there is no difference between this situation and the typical situation in which the employer directs the preparation of the meals."

We agree, especially in the light of other similarities appearing in the record.

Admittedly, the record is sketchy, but it appears that meals are actually provided by the cook, in the sense that he selects the menus, supervises the purchase of the groceries, and cooks and serves the meals. The cook is appointed by the Fire Chief or the highest ranking officer at the station, presumably by some direction or authority from the employer. The money is collected by one "delegated by the chief." There is no evidence that the cook receives extra pay for his work, but it appears almost certain that he would be relieved of other duties in exchange for his culinary activities, from which it may well be argued that he is compensated by the employer. And the plan, whereby the meals are furnished, has been established by the management.

Relying upon these facts, a strong argument could have been made that the meals were in fact "furnished in kind" by the employer. The tax court found otherwise and we are of course bound by the ruling, nor are we critical of the tax court for so finding, for the evidence is ample to support it. We simply refer to these facts to show the faint line of difference between the two concepts. We think it too slender a reed upon which to hang tax liability.

The Commissioner places heavy reliance upon Commissioner v. Kowalski, 434 U.S. 77 (1977), in which the Supreme Court held that "cash meal allowances" were not excludable under section 119. . . .

Kowalski is of course distinguishable upon the facts. The state troopers could eat any place they wanted, and they had complete dominion over their cash allowances and could spend it as they pleased. In the case before us the fire fighters were required to eat their meals on the employer's premises, and were required to pay for them whether they ate them or not.

The language in the *Kowalski* opinion however presents a more difficult problem. In interpreting section 119, the Court would allow deductions for meals "furnished by the employer in kind" but would disallow the deductions for "cash advances for food." It seems clear throughout the opinion and in the cases the Court discusses that the concept of "cash allowances" assumes an allowance over which the taxpayer has complete dominion. That is, he may eat as little or as much as he wants, or not at all if he wishes, and he may spend any unused portion any way he desires. We do not believe that the Court intended to rule that an allowance otherwise excludable should be denied excludability simply because it was paid in cash. We think the true holding of *Kowalski* can best be demonstrated by the following example. Let us assume that the taxpayers were given scrip for the purpose of paying for their meals. If the scrip were redeemable at any eating establishment in the vicinity or could be exchanged for cash at a bank or elsewhere, there is little doubt in the *Kowalski* factual setting but that the Court would have reached the same result. However, if the scrip were issued in the precise amount of the meal assessment; was redeemable only at the mess; and had to be surrendered whether the fireman ate or not, such an allowance in our view whether paid in scrip or cash would be deductible and we do not read *Kowalski* to the contrary.

In the light of all the circumstances in this case, the meals in question in a very real sense were "furnished in kind by the employer" upon the "business property" by means of a device conceived and established by the employer for its convenience. This being so, the taxpayers should be permitted to exclude from their gross income under the provision of section 119 the value of these meals notwithstanding the fact that cash has been used as a simple method of implementing the plan.

We hold therefore that taxpayers may elect either to deduct the mess fees under section 162(a) or to exclude them from income under section 119.

We therefore affirm.

KENNEDY, Circuit Judge, dissenting:

I respectfully disagree with the majority's holding. In my view the taxpayers' expenses for meals in common with co-employees are neither business expenses deductible under I.R.C. §162 nor meals furnished by the employer excludable under I.R.C. §119. . . .

A result contrary to the one reached by the Tax Court does not depend upon an overly literal reading of the statute. Although deductibility under section 162, rather than exclusion of income under section 119, presents the more substantial argument for the taxpayers here, under either provision the underlying principle is the idea that forced consumption should in some cases be treated as a transaction that is not dependent on significant elements of personal choice. That is, if the convenience of the employer dictates a certain type of consumption that is likely to be different from that which a taxpayer would normally prefer, this restriction of the taxpayer's preferences is an occasion for an "accession to wealth" over which the taxpayer does not "have complete dominion." Cf. Commissioner v. Glenshaw Glass Co., 348 U.S. 426, 431 (1955) (defining gross income in terms of quoted phrases). It appears from the record that such a restriction on the taxpayers' consumption preferences was not present in this case: the only aspect of the common dining arrangement that suited the employer was its location. The firemen were apparently free to suit their own tastes in the groceries purchased and the food prepared. This freedom points up the critical omission in the majority's hypothetical, which is the failure to specify the amount of the individual taxpayer's participation in either the choice of food or the decision of how much to spend on the meals.

The necessity in cases like these to focus on such minutiae to determine the degree of taxpayer control suggests the hairsplitting artificiality of isolating an otherwise clear type of personal expense which all taxpayers must incur in the ordinary course of living and labeling that expense "business" and therefore nontaxable for a particular, and to that extent special, class of taxpayers. Legislative exceptions such as section 119 should not be broadened beyond their explicit terms by judicial interpretation. . . .

Questions

1. What is the purpose of section 119(b)(3)? Compare the tax treatment of the following two employees.

A is paid $30,000 in *stated* wages, but $1,000 is withheld as payment for meals furnished by the employer on business premises for the convenience of the employer. Section 119(b)(3).

B is paid $29,000 in stated wages, and is furnished *free* meals worth $1,000 by the employer on business premises for the convenience of the employer. Section 119(a)(1).

Note that although added in 1978, the effective date Congress prescribed for section 119(b)(2) and (3) is retroactive to 1954, the date of enactment of section 119 in its original form. Why?

2. Consider this situation.

Department employees work 24-hour duty shifts that begin at 8:00 a.m. and end at 8:00 a.m. the following day. During the duty shifts employees perform tasks such as firefighting, inspecting buildings for fire hazards, and participating in training and testing programs. Department employees are on duty at all times during the 24-hour shifts and are only allowed to leave the fire station on business or if they are ill.

As required by a collective bargaining agreement, petitioner's employer provided certain cooking and eating facilities at #14 Fire Station such as a stove, two refrigerators, and a table and chairs. During 1976 there were 12 persons working each shift and, generally, meals were prepared as a common mess with one person designated as the cook and two others as helpers on a rotation system. The person designated as the cook for a particular day bought the groceries and prepared the meals. The cook divided the total grocery bill by the number of employees participating in the meals that day and collected a ratable portion from each. Thus, the amount contributed by each employee varied from day to day. In addition, employees were assessed 35 cents per day for a "house fund" which was used to defray the cost of coffee, pots, appliances, and other cooking utensils.

A similar system was in effect in the other 15 fire stations in the city with the exception of a few stations that employed only three persons per shift. However, participation in the common mess was not mandatory and some employees did not participate, such as individuals with diet restrictions. Although not as practical under the circumstances, employees also had the option of bringing food already prepared or bringing groceries and preparing their own meals at work. [Thomas J. Duggan, 77 T.C. 911, 912-913 (1981).]

Would you agree with petitioner's characterization of the differences between this and *Sibla* as "minor variations" or "distinctions without a difference"?

3. Suppose the senior partner of a law firm of litigators required partners and associates to meet daily for lunch at a restaurant near the courthouse so that they could arrange work assignments and discuss settlements. Does *Sibla* indicate that the cost of meals could be deducted or excluded from taxable income under these circumstances? John D. Moss, Jr. [Chapter 12D below.]

4. Suppose a state were to contract with a number of restaurants to supply meals to police officers on their request, the restaurant then billing the state directly for such meals. Would the meals supplied then be income to the officers in question?

5. Are the restaurants at which police officers take meals on the business premises of the employer? In Wilson v. United States, 412 F.2d 694 (1st Cir. 1969), the court said,

The statute upon which taxpayer [a state policeman] relies, 1954 I.R.C. §119, excludes ". . . the value of any meals furnished to him by his employer for the convenience of the employer, but only if the meals are furnished on the business premises of the employer." Taxpayer would have this read, ". . . the cost of any meals repaid by his employer if for the convenience of the employer the meals are eaten near the taxpayer's place of work." Each of these transpositions, individually, enlarges the scope of the exclusion, and cumulatively they enlarge it entirely beyond its intended meaning. Rather, we agree with the Commissioner that the statute means, and therefore is limited to, meals served in kind on the employer's business premises. We find this interpretation supported by the language, the intendment, and the relevant legislative history.

Other courts have thought, like the dissenters in *Kowalski*, that the business premises of a state police officer's employer included every place within the territory of the state.

6. Where does *Kowalski* leave the exclusion of supper money? If a law firm reimburses associates for a good dinner whenever they work at night, how should this matter be treated for income tax purposes?

2.   Certain Other Fringe Benefits: §132

In 1984, Congress enacted §132, titled, "Certain Fringe Benefits." Read through §132 (and §117(d)) and then through the explanation in the following excerpts from the House Committee Report. Are the grounds for exclusion set forth in this legislation sound in principle? Are they expedient politically or administratively? Are they a satisfactory rationalization for preserving present practice?

FRINGE BENEFITS PROVISIONS
[NEW §§132 AND 117(d)]

Supplemental Report of the House Comm. on Ways and Means on the Tax Reform Act of 1984, H.R. Rep. No. 432, 98th Cong., 2d Sess. 1590-1610 (1984)

A. PRESENT LAW

GENERAL RULES

The Internal Revenue Code defines gross income for purposes of the Federal income tax as including "all income from whatever source derived," and specifies that it includes "compensation for services" (sec. 61). Treasury regulations provide that gross income includes compensation for services paid other than in money (Reg. sec. 1.61-1 (a)). Further, the U.S. Supreme Court has stated that Code section 61 "is broad enough to include in taxable income any economic or financial benefit conferred on the employee as compensation, whatever the form or mode by which it is effected."[1] . . .

Certain employee benefits, such as health plan benefits, are excluded by statute from gross income and wages. Nontaxable benefits offered under a plan which offers a choice between taxable and nontaxable benefits (a "cafeteria plan") may be excluded from gross income if certain conditions are met (sec. 125).*

MORATORIUM ON ISSUANCE OF REGULATIONS

In 1975, the Treasury Department issued a discussion draft of proposed regulations which contained a number of rules for determining whether various nonstatutory fringe benefits constitute taxable compensation.[2]

---

1. Commissioner v. Smith, 324 U.S. 177, 181 (1945). Similarly, the Court has stated: "Congress applied no limitations as to the source of taxable receipts, nor restrictive labels as to their nature. And the Court has given a liberal construction to this broad phraseology in recognition of the intention of Congress to tax all gains except those specifically exempted." Commissioner v. Glenshaw Glass Co. [Chapter 3A below, at pp. 90, 91-92.]

 * See Chapter 3C.1 below. — EDS.

2. 40 Fed. Reg. 4118 (Sept. 5, 1975). The discussion draft was later withdrawn (41 Fed. Reg. 5634, Dec. 28, 1976). On January 15, 1981, the Treasury Department forwarded to the Committee on Ways and Means a revised discussion draft of proposed regulations on the tax treatment of fringe benefits. This

Public Law 95-427, enacted in 1978, prohibited the Treasury Department from issuing, prior to 1980, final regulations under section 61 of the Internal Revenue Code relating to the income tax treatment of fringe benefits. That statute further prohibited Treasury from proposing regulations relating to the treatment of fringe benefits under Section 61 which would be effective prior to 1980. . . .

The Economic Recovery Tax Act of 1981 (Public Law 97-34) extended the moratorium on issuance of fringe benefit regulations through December 31, 1983. . . .

B. REASONS FOR CHANGE

In providing statutory rules for exclusion of certain fringe benefits for income and payroll tax purposes, the committee has attempted to strike a balance between two competing objectives.

First, the committee is aware that in many industries, employees may receive, either free or at a discount, goods and services which the employer sells to the general public. In many cases, these practices are long established, and have been treated by employers, employees, and the IRS as not giving rise to taxable income. Although employees may receive an economic benefit from the availability of these free or discounted goods or services, employers often have valid business reasons, other than simply providing compensation, for encouraging employees to avail themselves of the products which they sell to the public. For example, a retail clothing business will want its salespersons to wear, when they deal with customers, the clothing which it seeks to sell to the public. In addition, the fact that the selection of goods and services usually available from a particular employer usually is restricted makes it appropriate to provide a limited exclusion, when such discounts are generally made available to employees, for the income employees realize from obtaining free or reduced-cost goods or services. The committee believes, therefore, that many present practices under which employers may provide to a broad group of employees, either free or at a discount, the products and services which the employer sells or provides to the public do not serve merely to replace cash compensation. These reasons support the committee's decision to codify the ability of employees to continue these practices without imposition of income or payroll taxes.

The second objective of the committee's bill is to set forth clear boundaries for the provision of tax-free benefits. Because of the moratorium on the issuance of fringe benefit regulations, the Treasury Department has been precluded from clarifying the tax treatment of many of the forms of noncash

---

discussion draft was not reviewed by the Secretary of Treasury and was not published in the Federal Register. The discussion draft was reprinted in various publications, including Bureau of National Affairs, Daily Executive Report (Jan. 16, 1981), at p. J-14.

compensation commonly in use. As a result, the administrators of the tax law have not had clear guidelines in this area, and hence taxpayers in identical situations have been treated differently. The inequities, confusion, and administrative difficulties for business, employees, and the IRS resulting from this situation have increased substantially in recent years. The committee believes that it is unacceptable to allow these conditions—which have existed since 1978—to continue any longer.

In addition, the committee is concerned that without any well-defined limits on the ability of employers to compensate their employees tax-free by using a medium other than cash, new practices will emerge that could shrink the income tax base significantly, and further shift a disproportionate tax burden to those individuals whose compensation is in the form of cash. A shrinkage of the base of the social security payroll tax could also pose a threat to the viability of the social security system above and beyond the adverse projections which the Congress recently addressed in the Social Security Amendments of 1983. Finally, an unrestrained expansion of non-cash compensation would increase inequities among employees in different types of businesses, and among employers as well.

The nondiscrimination rule is an important common thread among the types of fringe benefits which are excluded under the bill from income and employment taxes. Under the bill, most fringe benefits may be made available tax-free to officers, owners, or highly compensated employees only if the benefits are also provided on substantially equal terms to other employees. The committee believes that it would be fundamentally unfair to provide tax-free treatment for economic benefits that are furnished only to highly paid executives. Further, where benefits are limited to the highly paid, it is more likely that the benefit is being provided so that those who control the business can receive compensation in a nontaxable form; in that situation, the reasons stated above for allowing tax-free treatment would not be applicable. Also, if highly paid executives could receive free from taxation economic benefits that are denied to lower-paid employees, while the latter are compensated only in fully taxable cash, the committee is concerned that this situation would exacerbate problems of noncompliance among taxpayers. In this regard, some commentators argue that the current situation—in which the lack of clear rules for the tax treatment of nonstatutory fringe benefits encourages the nonreporting of many types of compensatory benefits—has led to nonreporting of types of cash income which are clearly taxable under present-law rules, such as interest and dividends.

In summary, the committee believes that providing rules which essentially codify many present practices under which employers provide their own products and services tax-free to a broad group of employees, and by ending the uncertainties arising from a moratorium on the Treasury Department's ability to clarify the tax treatment of these benefits, the bill substantially improves the equity and administration of the tax system.

C. EXPLANATION OF PROVISIONS

1. OVERVIEW

Under the bill, certain fringe benefits provided by an employer are excluded from the recipient employee's gross income for Federal income tax purposes and from the wage base (and, if applicable, the benefit base) for purposes of income tax withholding, FICA [Federal Insurance Contributions Act, the tax side of Social Security], FUTA [Federal Unemployment Tax Act], and RRTA [Railroad Retirement Tax Act].

The excluded fringe benefits are those benefits that qualify under one of the following five categories as defined in the bill: (1) a no-additional-cost service, (2) a qualified employee discount, (3) a working condition fringe, (4) a de minimis fringe, and (5) a qualified tuition reduction. Special rules apply with respect to certain parking or eating facilities provided to employees, on-premises athletic facilities, and demonstration use of an employer-provided car by auto salespersons. Some of the exclusions under the bill apply to benefits provided to the spouse and dependent children of a current employee, to former employees who separated from service because of retirement or disability (and their spouses and dependent children), and to the widow(er) of a deceased employee (and the dependent children of deceased employees).

In the case of a no-additional-cost service, a qualified employee discount, employee . . . eating facilities, or a qualified tuition reduction, the exclusion applies with respect to benefits provided to officers, owners, or highly compensated employees only if the benefit is made available to employees on a basis which does not discriminate in favor of officers, owners, or highly compensated employees.

Any fringe benefit that does not qualify for exclusion under the bill (for example, free or discounted goods or services which are limited to corporate officers) and that is not excluded under another statutory fringe benefit provision of the Code is taxable to the recipient under Code sections 61 and 83, and is includible in wages for employment tax purposes, at the excess of its fair market value over any amount paid by the employee for the benefit. . . .

Notes and Questions

1. Derek is Vice President for Design and Product Planning of Ford Motor Company. Each month Derek is provided with a new Ford automobile for both business and personal use. Each month a different model vehicle selected by the company is provided. Derek is required to submit a detailed record of his own and his family's evaluation of each model based on a minimum of 1,000 miles driven.

(a) Is the personal use of the cars income to Derek? What arguments would you make based on *Benaglia?*

(b) On audit, the revenue agent adds $3,000 to Derek's gross income, representing the value of the personal use of the Ford cars. The IRS agent asserts that only the exclusions from gross income set forth in the Code and regulations are allowable. What result under §132 and the House report thereon? See §61(a)(1).

(c) And if some amount is includible in Derek's gross income, what should be the measure: the rental rate for similar brand-new cars or the cost of operating Derek's personal vehicle, a six-year-old Taurus?

2. Ella is an associate with a large law firm in New York. In order to encourage its associates to put in the time necessary to produce high-quality legal work, the firm follows a policy of reimbursing its associates for the cost of a restaurant meal (not exceeding $50) and taxi fare home on any day on which the associate works past 8 p.m. Following the routine of the majority of associates, Ella arrives at the law office about 9:30 a.m. and works until 8 p.m. four or five nights a week. What are the tax consequences, if any, of Ella's receipt of supper money and cab fare reimbursement? §132(e)(1). Compare §132(e)(2) and (f). What justifies these provisions?

3. Deuce Hardware allows employees to purchase its merchandise at a discount equal to 5 percent multiplied by the number of years the employee has worked for Deuce, but not exceeding 60 percent. Deuce is a local establishment with only five employees: a president who has worked for the company for 10 years, and four low-paid retail clerks, whose length of service varies from one to four years. The gross profit percentage on all of Deuce's merchandise is approximately 15 percent.

(a) How much of the discount is tax free to the president? To the retail clerks? Why? §132(a), (c), (j)(1), (j)(6), 414(q). Precisely what statutory term is at issue here?

(b) What results if Deuce changes its policy and makes a flat 20 percent discount available on all purchases by employees with four or more years of service?

(c) What is the policy behind the nondiscrimination requirement?

4. Hugo, who works as a sales representative of a software development company, travels frequently on business. These trips, which are paid for by Hugo's employer, generate a lot of airline frequent-flyer miles issued in the traveler's name. Are there tax consequences if the employer has a policy that:

(a) Allows Hugo to use frequent-flyer credits to obtain first-class upgrades on business trips?

(b) Allows Hugo to apply the credits to obtain free or discounted personal travel (e.g., vacation trips) for himself or members of his immediate family? If Hugo's daughter uses the credits, who has income, how much, and when? For the time being, the IRS has declined to insist on inclusion. Announcement 2002-18, 2002-1 C.B. 621. If that forbearance ended, what rules would apply? See §83(a).

C. IMPUTED INCOME

Another form of income in kind does not even involve a receipt: It is the imputed income that results from the investment of capital or performance of services for one's own personal or family use. No effort has ever been made to tax imputed income generally, and its omission represents such a settled interpretation that any substantial inclusion of such income now would require legislation.

1. Owner-Occupied Housing

Suppose a taxpayer invests funds in a house, which she then rents to someone else for use as a personal residence. The rent she receives is clearly taxable income (after deduction of expenses and depreciation). And the tenant who lives in the house would have no deduction for rental payments since they are a personal expense unconnected with any income-producing activity on his part.

Now suppose the tenant leaves and the taxpayer begins to live in the house herself. Is her real income any less? Or has she simply begun to receive her return on her investment in kind in the form of housing services (which she used to sell) instead of cash rental income?

In real terms, assuming the owner is happy with the house, there is no decrease in either production or consumption of housing services or in any other aspect of personal welfare.

An estimate of the rental of owner-occupied housing is included in computing the gross national product and net personal income in the national income accounts.[8] Imputed rental value has been included in taxable income in some other countries but never in the United States. There is even some indication that imputed rental income might once have been held to be outside the constitutional meaning of income in the sixteenth amendment. Helvering v. Independent Life Insurance Co., 292 U.S. 371 (1934).

Omission of imputed rent of homeowners from taxable income affects many more people and involves much larger aggregate amounts than does the statutory exclusion of lodging provided by an employer. Does that omission provide a persuasive unstated reason for the statutory exclusion in §119?

A homeowner does incur costs, of which some are nondeductible, and to that extent pays for housing out of after-tax income. The omission of imputed rental income is only a matter of excluding the net return on

---

8. In 2005 owner-occupied housing accounted for $832 billion of total nonfarm housing output of $1,123 billion. U.S. Census Bureau, Dept. of Commerce, Statistical Abstract of the United States: 2008, 436 (Table 655) (2007).

the investment, not the whole gross value of housing services received. But our tax law further favors homeowners by allowing deductions for two of the most significant expenses of homeownership: mortgage interest and real estate taxes. The treatment of homeowners is taken up in more detail in Chapter 10C.

2.   Other Consumer Durables

Imputed income arises from investment in a whole range of other consumer durables, including automobiles, appliances, yachts, jewelry, paintings, and so forth. Does the impracticality of taxing all these things comprehensively offer a convincing reason for continuing the exclusion of homeowners' imputed rental income?

3.   Household Services

Another sort of imputed income arises from the performance of services within the household, including care of the home, preparation of meals, and care and education of children. Economists regard the performance of such services as a substantial component in total income and production. On the other hand, until recently there was some inclination to believe that imputed income from such services was relatively evenly distributed within income classes, and, if anything, more prevalent among the less well-to-do because the affluent were more apt to hire help to perform such functions. In any event, it is commonly considered that difficulties of valuation would interpose an insuperable obstacle to any direct inclusion of such items in taxable income.

But is the problem just a practical one of valuation or does it go deeper? If one were to set out to include imputed income from services, what should be included? What about the value of a shampoo that a taxpayer could have hired a hairdresser or barber to do? What about the value of vegetables grown in a home garden? Are flowers any different? Or what about the pleasure and entertainment one produces for oneself (and others) by playing the piano, or playing tennis, or teaching someone else to play? Who had income, and how much, when Leopold Mozart taught Wolfgang to play the piano?

4.   Leisure

As some of these questions may suggest, leisure itself can be thought of as a component of imputed income. Surely, it is an economic good, a component of total personal utility or welfare, and one that a person may effectively buy at a market price by withholding services from the employment market.

B and *C* each had an annual salary of $40,000 and each inherited securities yielding $40,000. *C* continued working, and increased her expenditures for entertainment, travel, and whatnot, and even saved a little. *B* continued her previous level of expenditure but quit work so she would have more time to entertain herself. Are *B* and *C* now at different levels of economic welfare or are they effectively just spending their resources differently? Their taxable incomes under existing law will be quite different.

Imputed income from leisure and from services are closely related because a taxpayer may substitute either for the other without changing hours of employment. The exclusion of one may therefore tend to offset exclusion of the other in the measurement of relative incomes, but there still are important differences among households in what is available either for leisure or for household services because of differences in employment patterns. Careful economists who specify family welfare or utility functions regularly include a negative term for the sacrifice of time and energy involved in any employment. But then what about people who are delighted with their work?

It would undoubtedly be impractical to try to reflect either the value of leisure or the cost of its sacrifice in taxable income, but differences among households could be taken into account indirectly by reducing the rate of tax on personal earnings as compared with property income or by differentiating among households in which different numbers of persons go to work.

Would it be fairer to tax people on what they could earn instead of what they do? Consider the following: (a) schemes requiring everyone to work for a certain numbers of days on the highway; (b) universal military service; (c) selective service.

5. Borderlines

If two homemakers each do their own laundry and cooking, no taxable income results. Suppose one cooks for both in exchange for the other doing the laundry; then each has performed compensated services for the other, and is taxable on the value of what is received in kind. This has not been clear to everyone, and so-called barter clubs have sometimes been promoted on the basis that they will enable participants to trade professional services free of tax. The Commissioner has consistently ruled that benefits derived from such a club are taxable. (The only tricky question is when, if services performed and services received are in different years.) See Rev. Rul. 83-163, 1983-2 C.B. 26; Rev. Rul. 80-52, 1980-1 C.B. 100; Rev. Rul. 79-24, 1979-1 C.B. 60.

What if people just help one another out from time to time without keeping accounts? What if they work at common enterprises together, like bringing food to a cookout and sharing it? What if people organize a cooperative nursery school to which each parent contributes services at assigned times?

What about exchanges within the family? Suppose it is formally agreed that one spouse will keep house for both in exchange for which the other will go to work and pay the household bills: does the homemaker have taxable income? Why not?

Notes and Questions

1. Assume that A and B each have $300,000 in savings and that each is in the 30 percent tax bracket. A invests her $300,000 in a house that she uses as a residence for herself and her family. Because the house is well built and located in a desirable neighborhood, A expects to be able to sell the house for $300,000 at the end of 20 years (the period during which her family is likely to need a house of this size). B invests her $300,000 savings in corporate bonds that pay interest at the rate of 10 percent, with principal repayment in 20 years. B uses the $30,000 annual interest to rent a house.

(a) What is the difference, if any, between the tax treatment of A and B? Is this result justified? Why or why not? What real-life consequences would you expect to flow from this state of affairs?

(b) How could the tax treatment of A and B be equalized? Two different methods could be used to achieve tax equity. What are the advantages and disadvantages of the two approaches?

(c) Both the Union and the Confederacy resorted to income taxes to help finance the Civil War. The federal government's first experiment with personal income taxation expired at the end of 1872, but in its final years the law expressly provided that income shall not include "the rental value of the homestead used or occupied by any person, or by his family." On the other hand, "the amount paid for the rent of the house or premises occupied as a residence for himself or his family" was deductible. Act of July 14, 1870, §§7, 9, ch. 255, 16 Stat. 256.

2. Now assume that C and D are each in the 50 percent tax bracket and that each is married, works at the same job, and has two preschool-aged children. C's spouse works at home caring for the children, doing house-work, shopping, and so on. D's spouse also works at home, but has just been offered a job that would pay a $40,000 salary. However, D has calculated that it would cost $24,000 annually for childcare and domestic services to replace their lost household services. Purely as a matter of after-tax incomes, should D's spouse accept the employment? If not, how much would the job have to

pay in order to induce *D*'s spouse into the marketplace? Do you see any problem with this result? Should it be addressed, and if so, how? Consult §21, which was enacted in 1976 in place of a limited itemized deduction for child and dependent care expenses. Why was the prior deduction converted into a tax credit?

3. *E* agrees with his neighbor that he will mow both of their equal-sized lawns every second week. *E*'s neighbor will cut the grass on the alternate weeks. Last summer, *E* paid $1,200 to have his lawn mowed every week. What are the tax consequences, if any, of *E*'s arrangement? See Reg. §§1.61-1(a), -2(d)(1).

4. What about exchanges within the virtual economy? Devotees of massive multiplayer online games such as EverQuest and World of Warcraft meet in virtual worlds where they can interact through "avatars" (an *avatar* is a player's chosen character or visual representation in the game), explore their universe, and participate in the quest or journey that is the central storyline of the game. In the process, a player may discover or capture virtual objects (loot) that enhance the avatar's power, allowing it to advance in the game. Players may also trade goods or services, and many of the games have their own currency to facilitate sales within the game. "Most game makers . . . try to thwart what gamers call real money trade, or RMT. The most valuable items are now bound to the avatars that find them and cannot be traded. That means most internet sales now consist of the sale of whole accounts containing any avatars that have acquired valuable items." Dustin Stamper, Taxing Ones and Zeros: Can the IRS Ignore Virtual Economies?, 114 Tax Notes 149 (2007).

(a) What are a gamer's tax consequences, if any, assuming that she deals only in the game's currency and accumulates only virtual assets? What if she sells her avatar on eBay®?

(b) Other virtual worlds, such as The Sims Online and Second Life, are unscripted environments in which participants interact, undertake activities, and pursue a (virtual) life plan of their own design. Second Life, for example has "a thriving real estate market and a currency that is directly exchangeable for U.S. dollars through [its maker,] Linden Lab itself." Id. Does one's "second life" entail real-world income tax obligations?

D.   *ALTERNATIVE FORMULATIONS*

It is sometimes said that in principle, gross income for tax purposes includes all gain in whatever form received, in cash or in kind, but that administrative considerations justify omission of some items received in kind. Along this line, it is sometimes asserted that §61 embraces all forms of gain, leaving it to the Commissioner to determine what is to be left out as a matter of simple practicality.

Another formulation starts from the observation that comprehensive inclusion in taxable income of all the good things in life is out of the question. It would certainly be impractical, and it is not even clear that it would be desirable as a matter of principle. Money income in an exchange economy is a convenient and reasonable index, however, of economic power and well being, and therefore of taxpaying ability, even if it does not embrace or reflect everything. The problem with income in kind is one of distortion, stemming from the fact that income in kind may be a substitute for money income or that differences in money income may be offset by countervailing differences in income in kind. In this view, taxable income should be thought of as money income plus such items of income in kind as it is necessary and practical to include in order to avert excessive distortion by substitution of the latter for the former.

Are these two formulations substantially different, or do they just say the same thing in different ways? Which is preferable?

It may help to think in terms of economic organization. Economic activity includes production and consumption of goods and services. To a considerable extent production is a business function while consumption is a household function. Households provide services to business firms through employment and investment; for that they receive remuneration with which they then can purchase their share of total output for consumption.

Money income in this description is a measure of a household's total economic activity or capacity as reflected in the market value of the services it exports and the goods and services it is accordingly able to import. That is what makes it a good general measure of taxpaying capacity. However, it also makes clear what the income tax does not automatically embrace: production within the home and consumption on the job. Inevitably, a substantial amount of productive activity occurs within households for consumption in kind therein, and taxable income will not reflect the value of such activity or the consumption it supports. Similarly, some individuals will derive considerable satisfactions and gratifications from various aspects of their employment or other business activities, and differences in welfare attributable to such gratifications ordinarily will not be reflected in taxable income.

To a considerable extent this account just identifies built-in limitations or shortcomings in a personal income tax: It would be impossible to tax all intra-household production and on-the-job gratifications, particularly if one thinks of relatively intangible goods and satisfactions. But there remains a constant question of whether inclusion in taxable income of particular items of job gratification or household production would make the line between taxable and nontaxable fairer or less distorting, or both, without unreasonable administrative cost.

E. DEDUCTIONS

Consider lawyers in practice by themselves whose clients all pay their fees in cash. Everything they receive from clients will be included in their gross income, and they will apparently not be able to share in the game of tax-free fringe benefits as such. Suppose, for example, one such lawyer had decided to attend the 2006 annual meeting of the American Bar Association, which was held in Honolulu. The lawyer's fees would still be fully included in gross income even if used partly to pay for this trip.

But look at §162. Would it authorize deduction of the cost of the trip in computing taxable income? If so, the end result is the same as if the taxpayer had had the trip provided by someone else as a tax-free fringe benefit. So exclusion of fringe benefits and deduction of business expenses represent two facets of the same underlying problem. The deduction question is taken up at greater length in Part II, particularly in Chapter 12.

F. MICROECONOMIC EFFECTS

Omission of noncash items in the computation of taxable income is unfair because it imposes a smaller burden on some taxpayers than on others in similar overall circumstances. It may also be inefficient, inducing a mis-allocation of real resources.

Suppose, for example, that it costs an employer $5.00 to provide a meal for which employees would be willing to pay only $4.00. (If there is any benefit to the employer except by way of employee gratification then suppose the cost exceeds that benefit by $5.00 — in other words, that $5.00 is the net cost to the employer.) Would the employer provide the meal under these conditions, or would that represent a pointless waste of resources?

But what if an income tax is imposed? Suppose first that the cost or value of the meal is included in taxable income. In that case, as in the absence of tax, the employer can deliver more to employees at the same cost to itself by paying cash than by providing the meal. But if the meal in kind is excluded from gross income and the employee's tax rate exceeds 20 percent then the employer can deliver more by providing the meal because the tax saving exceeds the waste loss. The waste is a burden on taxpayers without any corresponding revenue benefit to the government; it is called *excess burden* (or *deadweight loss*). For example, at a 28 percent rate:

	Taxable Salary	Exempt Meal
Employer Pays	−5.00 cash	−5.00 cost
IRS Collects	1.40 tax	0
Employee Enjoys	<u>3.60</u> net	<u>4.00</u> value
Net Total	0	**−1.00 Deadweight Loss**

Some such distortion of allocation of resources seems to be an inevitable consequence of an income tax. At a minimum the tax decreases the price of leisure as compared with money income from personal services, which may induce some people to prefer leisure even when the social value of their services exceeds the private value of their leisure.

A professional person, for example, may face a choice of whether to work an additional ten hours a month at $50 an hour: Society apparently values these professional services at $500, but if the professional is in a 40 percent marginal tax bracket, work will only increase his disposable income by $300. If one further supposes that the ten hours a month in question are worth $350 to the person himself when devoted to his own private affairs, he will not work professionally, and there will be a deadweight loss of $150.

But while an income tax clearly distorts relative prices in favor of leisure (defined broadly to include all nonincome-producing activities) over remunerative uses of time, it is not clear that the net effect of the tax is to diminish remunerative work effort. A person may have a very strong desire to maintain consumption expenditures at a certain level, enjoying leisure only after that level has been reached. An income tax might well make such a person work harder than in the absence of the tax to make up for what the tax takes away. This effect is called the *income effect* of the tax (in contrast to its *price effect* or *substitution effect*) because it simply reflects the necessity for the taxpayer to cut consumption of something if his or her disposable income (income left after taxes) is reduced. Leisure is one of the goods that may be given up, in which case the taxpayer's work will have increased as a result of the tax.

When price and income effects conflict, as in the case of work and leisure, it is theoretically indeterminate and often empirically very difficult to determine which will prevail.

G.   TAXING EMPLOYERS IN LIEU OF EMPLOYEES

1.   Withholding

If a noncash item constitutes wages subject to withholding within the meaning of §3401(a), then the government can proceed against an employer on the basis of the employer's duty to withhold and pay over to the government without proceeding directly against individual employees. This may provide the only practical way for the government to deal with common fringe benefits. Should the question of what constitutes wages subject to withholding be any different from what constitutes income to the employee? When §132 was enacted, §3401(a) was amended by inserting "(including benefits)" into the definition of wages subject to withholding.

Suppose the government were to succeed in establishing that an item was wages subject to withholding and accordingly collected an appropriate tax from the employer. This result might not be achieved until several years after the tax year in question. Would it then be necessary or desirable to allocate the amount of the item among individual employees and recalculate their taxes, giving credit for the increased withholding? How much distortion would result from neglecting to make such an allocation?

2. Other Possibilities

Would it be desirable to try to deal with some problems that involve fringe benefits by taxing the employer in lieu of the employee? One possibility is just to deny an employer any deduction for fringe benefits not reported as income to employees. Along this line, §132 omits any nondiscrimination requirement in connection with employee athletic facilities on the ground that §274 will deny any employer deduction if access to the facilities discriminates in favor of highly paid employees. How close a substitute is denial of an employer deduction for inclusion in employee income?

Another possibility would be just to impose an excise at a specified rate on the value of any fringe benefit not reported as income to employees. Such an excise would impose a tax burden independent of the employer's tax bracket or status; it would reach benefits, for example, provided to employees of tax-exempt employers or net loss corporations; it could be assessed on value (while a denial of deduction only effectively taxes the cost of benefits provided); and it would avoid the necessity of allocating value among employees in the case of benefits whose utilization may vary and be difficult to track.

What would be an appropriate rate for an excise designed to take the place of an income tax on top-bracket employees? (Do not neglect the implications of *Old Colony* in answering this question!)

H. OTHER ITEMS

This chapter is only introductory; we will encounter many more issues about income in kind. The general question of capital appreciation — saved income in kind — is considered in Chapter 5. Other statutory exclusions for fringe benefits include those for health and medical benefits, taken up in Chapter 3, and qualified retirement savings arrangements, which are briefly introduced in Chapter 6C.1, below.

References

A. Noncash Receipts in General: Henry C. Simons, Personal Income Taxation 110-124 (1938).

B. Statutory Exclusions: Dodge, Joseph M., How to Tax Frequent Flyer Miles, 48 Tax Notes 1301 (1990); Hickman, The Outlook for Fringe Benefits, 29 S. Cal. Tax Inst. 459 (1977); Kies, Analysis of the New Rules Governing the Taxation of Fringe Benefits, 24 Tax Notes 981 (1984); Wasserman, Principles in Taxation of Nonstatutory Fringe Benefits, 32 Tax Law. 137 (1979); Note, Federal Income Taxation of Employee Fringe Benefits, 89 Harv. L. Rev. 1141 (1976).

C. Imputed Income: Keller, The Taxation of Barter Transactions, 67 Minn. L. Rev. 441 (1982); Leandra Lederman, "Stranger Than Fiction": Taxing Virtual Worlds, 82 N.Y.U. L. Rev., 1620 (2007).

Chapter 3 — *Compensation for Losses*

Suppose a taxpayer sells shares of stock to pay living expenses during an extended absence from gainful employment. Are the sale proceeds taxable as income? Should they be?

Insofar as the sale proceeds represent recovery of a prior investment they are not income, regardless of whether they are reinvested or used for consumption. A central defining characteristic of income is gain or enrichment, and sale proceeds are therefore not taxed except to the extent that they exceed prior investment.

This is affirmed quite specifically in the Code itself. Read §§1001 (a), 1001(b), 1011, and 1012. Try to get an initial idea of the terms *amount realized, adjusted basis, fair market value,* and *cost.* If a piece of property is sold for no more than its fair market value, is there no gain?

Similarly, compensation for a loss or injury may seem not to involve gain, at least if the compensation and loss are considered together, and in some circumstances such compensation is therefore not taxable.

The ideas of return of capital and compensation for losses are interrelated in theory and practice as we shall see here and in Chapter 6.

A.   DAMAGE PAYMENTS (IN GENERAL)

EDWARD H. CLARK
40 B.T.A. 333(1939), acq. 1957-1 C.B.4

OPINION

LEECH: This is a proceeding to redetermine a deficiency in income tax for the calendar year 1934 in the amount of $10,618.87. The question presented is whether petitioner derived income by the payment to him of an amount of $19,941.10, by his tax counsel, to compensate him for a loss suffered on account of erroneous advice given him by the latter. The facts were stipulated and are so found. The stipulation, so far as material, follows: . . .

"3. The petitioner during the calendar year 1932, and for a considerable period prior thereto, was married and living with his wife. He was required by the Revenue Act of 1932 to file a Federal Income Tax Return of his income for the year 1932. For such year petitioner and his wife could have filed a joint return or separate returns.

"4. Prior to the time that the 1932 Federal Income Tax return or returns of petitioner and/or his wife were due to be filed, petitioner retained experienced tax counsel to prepare the necessary return or returns for him and/or his wife. Such tax counsel prepared a joint return for petitioner and his wife and advised petitioner to file it instead of two separate returns. In due course it was filed with the Collector of Internal Revenue for the first District of California. . . .

"5. Thereafter on or about the third day of February, 1934, a duly appointed revenue agent of the United States audited the aforesaid 1932 return and recommended an additional assessment against petitioner in the sum of $34,590.27, which was subsequently reduced to $32,820.14. This last mentioned sum was thereafter assessed against and was paid by petitioner to the Collector of Internal Revenue for the First District of California.

"6. The deficiency of $32,820.14 arose from an error on the part of tax counsel who prepared petitioner's 1932 return. The error was that he improperly deducted from income the total amount of losses sustained on the sale of capital assets held for a period of more than two years instead of applying the statutory limitation required by Section 101(b) of the Revenue Act of 1932.

"7. The error referred to in paragraph six above was called to the attention of the tax counsel who prepared the joint return of petitioner and his wife for the year 1932. Recomputations were then made which disclosed that if petitioner and his wife had filed separate returns for the year 1932 their combined tax liability would have been $19,941.10 less than that which was finally assessed against and paid by petitioner.

"8. Thereafter, tax counsel admitted that if he had not erred in computing the tax liability shown on the joint return filed by the petitioner, he would have advised petitioner to file separate returns for himself and his wife, and accordingly tax counsel tendered to petitioner the sum of $19,941.10, which was the difference between what petitioner and his wife would have paid on their 1932 returns if separate returns had been filed and the amount which petitioner was actually required to pay on the joint return as filed. Petitioner accepted the $19,941.10.

"9. In his final determination of petitioner's 1934 tax liability, the respondent included the aforesaid $19,941.10 in income.

"10. Petitioner's books of account are kept on the cash receipts and disbursements basis and his tax returns are made on such basis under the community property laws of the State of California. . . ."

The theory on which the respondent included the above sum of $19,941.10 in petitioner's gross income for 1934, is that this amount constituted taxes paid for petitioner by a third party and that, consequently, petitioner was in receipt of income to that extent. The cases of Old Colony Trust Co. v. Commissioner [Chapter 2A above]; United States v. Boston & Maine Railroad, 279 U.S. 732, are cited as authority for his position. Petitioner, on the contrary, contends that this payment constituted compensation for damages or loss caused by the error of tax counsel, and that he therefore realized no income from its receipt in 1934.

We agree with petitioner. The cases cited by the respondent are not applicable here. Petitioner's taxes were not paid for him by any person — as rental, compensation for services rendered, or otherwise. He paid his own taxes.

When the joint return was filed, petitioner became obligated to and did pay the taxes computed on that basis. John D. Biggers, 39 B.T.A. 480. In paying that obligation, he sustained a loss which was caused by the negligence of his tax counsel. The $19,941.10 was paid to petitioner, not qua taxes (cf. T. G. Nicholson, 38 B.T.A. 190), but as compensation to petitioner for his loss. The measure of that loss, and the compensation therefor, was the sum of money which petitioner became legally obligated to and did pay because of that negligence. The fact that such obligation was for taxes is of no moment here.

It has been held that payments in settlement of an action for breach of promise to marry are not income. Lyde McDonald, 9 B.T.A. 1340. Compromise payments in settlement of an action for damages against a bank on account of conduct impairing the taxpayer's good will by injuring its reputation are also not taxable. Farmers' & Merchants' Bank of Catlettsburg, Ky. v. Commissioner, 59 Fed.(2d) 912. The same result follows in the case of payments in settlement for injuries caused by libel and slander. C.A. Hawkins, 6 B.T.A. 1023. Damages for personal injury are likewise not income. Theodate Pope Riddle, 27 B.T.A. 1339.

The theory of those cases is that recoupment on account of such losses is not income since it is not "derived from capital, from labor or from both combined." See Merchants Loan & Trust Co. v. Smietanka, 255 U.S. 509; United States v. Safety Car Heating & Lighting Co., 297 U.S. 88. And the fact that the payment of the compensation for such loss was voluntary, as here, does not change its exempt status. Rice, Barton & Fales Inc. v. Commissioner, 41 Fed.(2d) 339. It was, in fact, compensation for a loss which impaired petitioner's capital.

Moreover, so long as petitioner neither could nor did take a deduction in a prior year of this loss in such a way as to offset income for the prior year, the amount received by him in the taxable year, by way of recompense, is not then includable in his gross income. Central Loan & Investment Co., 39 B.T.A. 981.

Decision will be entered for the petitioner.

Note and Question

The *Clark* problem recurs with interesting variations. Here are excerpts from a recent private letter ruling, IRS Priv. Ltr. Rul. 98-33-007 (May 13, 1998).

> After winning $x in the State lottery in Year [1], you consulted attorneys for tax preparation advice. You were not advised to maximize your deductible expenses for federal income tax purposes by paying State income tax in Year [1] on your winnings. This resulted in your paying $y more federal income tax than you otherwise would have been required to pay. You have computed your economic detriment to be somewhat less, $z, and you are negotiating with your attorneys' malpractice insurer for an indemnification payment that will reimburse you for this amount. . . .
>
> . . . In *Clark* and Rev. Rul. 57-47, the preparers' errors in filing returns or failing to claim refunds caused the taxpayers to pay more than their minimum proper federal income tax liabilities based on the underlying transaction for the years in question. However, your payment of additional federal income tax was not due to an error made . . . on the return itself but on an omission to provide advice that would have reduced your federal income tax liability. Thus, unlike the situations in *Clark* and Rev. Rul. 57-47 you are not paying more than your minimum proper federal income tax liability based on the taxation for the tax year to which the tax reimbursement relates. Therefore, under section 1.61-14(a) the indemnity payment that you receive for the additional federal income tax you pay represents a gain that is includible in your gross income. . . .

How would you advise the recipient of this ruling?

RAYTHEON PRODUCTION CORP. v. COMMISSIONER
144 F.2d 110 (1st Cir.), cert. denied, 323 U.S. 779 (1944)

Before Magruder, Mahoney, and Woodbury, Circuit Judges.

Mahoney, Circuit Judge. This case presents the question whether an amount received by the taxpayer in compromise settlement of a suit for damages under the Federal Anti-Trust Laws, 15 U.S.C.A. §1 et seq., is a non-taxable return of capital or income. If the recovery is non-taxable, there is a second question as to whether the Tax Court erred in holding that there was insufficient evidence to enable it to determine what part of the lump sum payment received by the taxpayer was properly allocable to compromise of the suit and what part was allocable to payment for certain patent license rights which were conveyed as part of the settlement.

Petitioner, Raytheon Production Corporation, came into existence as result of a series of what both parties as well as the Tax Court have treated as tax free reorganizations. Since we think such is the proper treatment, we shall simplify the facts by referring to any one of the original and successor companies as Raytheon. The original Raytheon Company was a pioneer manufacturer of a rectifying tube which made possible the operation of a radio receiving set on alternating current instead of on batteries. In 1926 its profits were about $450,000; in 1927 about $150,000; and in 1928, $10,000. The Radio Corporation of America had many patents covering radio circuits and claimed control over almost all of the practical circuits. Cross-licensing agreements had been made among several companies including R.C.A., General Electric Company, Westinghouse, and American Telephone & Telegraph Company. R.C.A. had developed a competitive tube which produced the same type of rectification as the Raytheon tube. Early in 1927, R.C.A. began to license manufacturers of radio sets and in the license agreement it incorporated "Clause 9", which provided that the licensee was required to buy its tubes from R.C.A. In 1928 practically all manufacturers were operating under R.C.A. licenses. As a consequence of this restriction, Raytheon was left with only replacement sales, which soon disappeared. When Raytheon found it impossible to market its tubes in the early part of 1929, it obtained a license from R.C.A. to manufacture tubes under the letters patent on a royalty basis. The license agreement contained a release of all claims of Raytheon against R.C.A. by reason of the illegal acts of the latter under Clause 9 but by a side agreement such claims could be asserted if R.C.A. should pay similar claims to others. The petitioner was informed of instances in which R.C.A. had settled claims against it based on Clause 9. On that ground it considered itself released from the agreement not to enforce its claim against R.C.A. and consequently, on December 14, 1931, the petitioner caused its predecessor, Raytheon, to bring suit against R.C.A. in the District Court of Massachusetts alleging that the plaintiff had by 1926 created and then possessed a large and valuable good will in interstate commerce in rectifying tubes for radios and had a large and profitable established business therein so that the net profit for the year 1926 was $454,935; that the business had an established prospect of large increases and that the business and good will thereof was of a value of exceeding $3,000,000; that by the beginning of 1927 the plaintiff was doing approximately 80 percent of the business of rectifying tubes of the entire United States; that the defendant conspired to destroy the business of the plaintiff and others by a monopoly of such business and did suppress and destroy the existing companies; that the manufacturers of radio sets and others ceased to purchase tubes from the plaintiffs; that by the end of 1927 the conspiracy had completely destroyed the profitable business and that by the early part of 1928 the tube business of the plaintiff and its property and good will had been totally destroyed at a time when it had a present value in excess of $3,000,000, and thereby the plaintiff was injured in its business and property in a sum in excess of $3,000,000. The action against R.C.A. was referred to an auditor who found that Clause 9 was not the cause of damage to the plaintiff but that the decline in plaintiff's business was due to advancement in the radio art and competition. The auditor, however, also found that if it should be decided that Clause 9 had turned the development of the radio art away from plaintiff's type of tube, then the damages would be $1,000,000.

In the spring of 1938, after the auditor's report and just prior to the time for the commencement of the trial before a jury, the Raytheon affiliated companies began negotiations for the settlement of the litigation with R.C.A. In the meantime a suit brought by R.C.A. against the petitioner for the non-payment of royalties resulted in a judgment of $410,000 in favor of R.C.A. R.C.A. and the petitioner finally agreed on the payment by R.C.A. of $410,000 in settlement of the antitrust action. R.C.A. required the inclusion in the settlement of patent license rights and sublicensing rights to some thirty patents but declined to allocate the amount paid as between the patent license rights and the amount for the settlement of the suit. The agreement of settlement contained a general release of any and all possible claims between the parties.

The officers of the Raytheon companies testified that $60,000 of the $410,000 received from R.C.A. was the maximum worth of the patents, basing their appraisal on the cost of development of the patents and the fact that few of them were then being used and that no royalties were being derived from them. In its income tax return the petitioner returned $60,000 of the $410,000 as income from patent licenses and treated the remaining $350,000 as a realization from a chose in action and not as taxable income. The Commissioner determined that $350,000 constituted income on the following ground contained in the statement attached to his notice of deficiency:

> It is the opinion of this office that the amount of $350,000 constitutes income under §22(a) of the Revenue Act of 1936. There exists no clear evidence of what the amount was paid for so that an accurate apportionment can be made as to a specific consideration for patent rights transferred to Radio Corporation of America and a consideration for damages. The amount of $350,000 has therefore been included in your taxable income. . . .

Damages recovered in an antitrust action are not necessarily nontaxable as a return of capital. As in other types of tort damage suits, recoveries which represent a reimbursement for lost profits are income. . . . The reasoning is that since the profits would be taxable income, the proceeds of litigation which are their substitute are taxable in like manner.

Damages for violation of the anti-trust acts are treated as ordinary income where they represent compensation for loss of profits. . . .

The test is not whether the action was one in tort or contract but rather the question to be asked is "In lieu of what were the damages awarded?" Farmers' & Merchants' Bank v. Commissioner, 6 Cir., 1932, 59 F.2d 912. . . . Where the suit is not to recover lost profits but is for injury to good will, the recovery represents a return of capital and, with certain limitations to be set forth below, is not taxable. Farmers' & Merchants' Bank v. Commissioner, supra. . . . "Care must certainly be taken in such cases to avoid taxing recoveries for injuries to good will or loss of capital." 1 Paul and Mertens Law of Federal Income Taxation §6.48.

Upon examination of Raytheon's declaration in its anti-trust suit we find nothing to indicate that the suit was for the recovery of lost profits. The allegations were that the illegal conduct of R.C.A. "completely destroyed the profitable interstate and foreign commerce of the plaintiff and thereby, by the early part of 1928, the said tube business of the plaintiff and the property good will of the plaintiff therein had been totally destroyed at a time when it then had a present value in excess of three million dollars and thereby the plaintiff was then injured in its business and property in a sum in excess of three million dollars." This was not the sort of antitrust suit where the plaintiff's business still exists and where the injury was merely for loss of profits. The allegations and evidence as to the amount of profits were necessary in order to establish the value of the good will and business since that is derived by a capitalization of profits. A somewhat similar idea was expressed in Farmers' & Merchants' Bank v. Commissioner, supra, 59 F.2d at page 913. "Profits were one of the chief indications of the worth of the business; but the usual earnings before the injury, as compared with those afterward, were only an evidential factor in determining actual loss and not an independent basis for recovery." Since the suit was to recover damages for the destruction of the business and good will, the recovery represents a return of capital. Nor does the fact that the suit ended in a compromise settlement change the nature of the recovery; "the determining factor is the nature of the basic claim from which the compromised amount was realized." . . .

But, to say that the recovery represents a return of capital in that it takes the place of the business good will is not to conclude that it may not contain a taxable benefit. Although the injured party may not be deriving a profit as a result of the damage suit itself, the conversion thereby of his property into cash is realization of any gain made over the cost or other basis of the good will prior to the illegal interference. Thus A buys Blackacre for $5,000. It appreciates in value to $50,000. B tortiously destroys it by fire. A sues and recovers $50,000 tort damages from B. Although no gain was derived by A from the suit, his prior gain due to the appreciation in value of Blackacre is realized when it is turned into cash by the money damages.

Compensation for the loss of Raytheon's good will in excess of its cost is gross income. . . .

Since we assume with the parties that the petitioner secured the original Raytheon's assets through a series of tax free reorganizations, petitioner's basis for the good will is the same as that of the original Raytheon. As the Tax Court pointed out, the record is devoid of evidence as to the amount of that basis and "in the absence of evidence of the basis of the business and good will of Raytheon, the amount of any nontaxable capital recovery cannot be ascertained." 1 T.C. 952. . . .

Where the cost basis that may be assigned to property has been wholly speculative, the gain has been held to be entirely conjectural and not taxable. In Strother v. Commissioner, 4 Cir., 1932, 55 F.2d 626, affirmed on other grounds, 1932, 287 U.S. 308, a trespasser had taken coal and then destroyed the entries so that the amount of coal taken could not be determined. Since there was no way of knowing whether the recovery was greater than the basis for the coal taken, the gain was purely conjectural and not taxed. Magill explains the result as follows: "as the amount of coal removed could not be determined until a final disposition of the property, the computation of gain or loss on the damages must await that disposition." Taxable Income, pp. 339-340. The same explanation may be applied to Farmers' & Merchants' Bank v. Commissioner, supra, which relied on the Strother case in finding no gain. The recovery in that case had been to compensate for the injury to good will and business reputation of the plaintiff bank inflicted by defendant reserve banks' wrongful conduct in collecting checks drawn on the plaintiff bank by employing "agents who would appear daily at the bank with checks and demand payment thereof in cash in such a manner as to attract unfavorable public comment." Since the plaintiff bank's business was not destroyed but only injured and since it continued in business, it would have been difficult to require the taxpayer to prove what part of the basis of its good will should be attributed to the recovery. In the case at bar, on the contrary, the entire business and good will were destroyed so that to require the taxpayer to prove the cost of the good will is no more impractical than if the business had been sold.

Inasmuch as we conclude that the portion of the $410,000 attributable to the suit is taxable income, the second question as to allocation between this and the ordinary income from patent licenses is not present.

The decision of the Tax Court is affirmed.

COMMISSIONER v. GLENSHAW GLASS CO.
348 U.S. 426 (1955)

Mr. Chief Justice WARREN delivered the opinion of the Court. . . . Commissioner v. Glenshaw Glass Co. — The Glenshaw Glass Company, a Pennsylvania corporation, manufactures glass bottles and containers. It was engaged in protracted litigation with the Hartford-Empire Company, which manufactures machinery of a character used by Glenshaw. Among the claims advanced by Glenshaw were demands for exemplary damages for fraud and treble damages for injury to its business by reason of Hartford's violation of the federal antitrust laws. In December, 1947, the parties concluded a settlement of all pending litigation, by which Hartford paid Glenshaw approximately $800,000. Through a method of allocation which was approved by the Tax Court, 18 T.C. 860, 870-872, and which is no longer in issue, it was ultimately determined that, of the total settlement, $324,529.94 represented payment of punitive damages for fraud and antitrust violations. Glenshaw did not report this portion of the settlement as income for the tax year involved. The Commissioner determined a deficiency claiming as taxable the entire sum less only deductible legal fees. As previously noted, the Tax Court and the Court of Appeals upheld the taxpayer.

Commissioner v. William Goldman Theaters, Inc. — William Goldman Theatres, Inc., a Delaware corporation operating motion picture houses in Pennsylvania, sued Loew's Inc., alleging a violation of the federal antitrust laws and seeking treble damages. After a holding that a violation had occurred, William Goldman Theatres, Inc. v. Loew's, Inc., 150 F.2d 738, the case was remanded to the trial court for a determination of damages. It was found that Goldman had suffered a loss of profits equal to $125,000 and was entitled to treble damages in the sum of $375,000. William Goldman Theatres, Inc. v. Loew's, Inc., 69 F. Supp. 103, aff'd, 164 F.2d 1021, cert. denied, 334 U.S. 811. Goldman reported only $125,000 of the recovery as gross income and claimed that the $250,000 balance constituted punitive damages and as such was not taxable. The Tax Court agreed, 19 T.C. 637, and the Court of Appeals, hearing this with the Glenshaw case, affirmed. 211 F.2d 928.

It is conceded by the respondents that there is no constitutional barrier to the imposition of a tax on punitive damages. Our question is one of statutory construction: are these payments comprehended by §22(a)?

The sweeping scope of the controverted statute is readily apparent:

SEC. 22. GROSS INCOME

(a) General Definition — "Gross income" includes gains, profits, and income derived from salaries, wages, or compensation for personal service . . . of whatever kind and in whatever form paid, or from professions, vocations, trades, businesses, commerce, or sales, or dealings in property, whether real or personal, growing out of the ownership or use of or interest in such property; also from interest, rent, dividends, securities, or the transaction of any business carried on for gain or profit, *or gains or profits and income derived from any source whatever.* . . . (Emphasis added.)

This Court has frequently stated that this language was used by Congress to exert in this field "the full measure of its taxing power." Helvering v. Clifford [Chapter 18A at pp. 1024, 1025]; Helvering v. Midland Mutual Life Ins. Co., 300 U.S. 216, 223; Douglas v. Willcuts [Chapter 18A below]; Irwin v. Gavit [Chapter 4A below]. Respondents contend that punitive damages, characterized as "windfalls" flowing from the culpable conduct of third parties, are not within the scope of the section. But Congress applied no limitations as to the source of taxable receipts, nor restrictive labels as to their nature. And the Court has given a liberal construction to this broad phraseology in recognition of the intention of Congress to tax all gains except those specifically exempted. Commissioner v. Jacobson, 336 U.S. 28, 49; Helvering v. Stockholms Enskilda Bank, 293 U.S. 84, 87-91. Thus, the fortuitous gain accruing to a lessor by reason of the forfeiture of a lessee's improvements on the rented property was taxed in Helvering v. Bruun [Chapter 5C.1 below]. Cf. Robertson v. United States, 343 U.S. 711; Rutkin v. United States, 343 U.S. 130; United States v. Kirby Lumber Co. [Chapter 7A below]. Such decisions demonstrate that we cannot but ascribe content to the catchall provision of §22(a), "gains or profits and income derived from any source whatever." The importance of that phrase has been too frequently recognized since its first appearance in the Revenue Act of 1913 to say that it adds nothing to the meaning of "gross income."

Nor can we accept respondents' contention that a narrower reading of §22(a) is required by the Court's characterization of income in Eisner v. Macomber [infra Chapter 5A at pp. 207, 212] as "the gain derived from capital, from labor, or from both combined."[6] The Court was there endeavoring to determine whether the distribution of a corporate stock dividend constituted a realized gain to the shareholder, or changed "only the form, not the essence," of his capital investment. Id., at [214]. It was held that the taxpayer had "received nothing out of the company's assets for his separate use and benefit." Id., at [214]. The distribution, therefore, was held not a taxable event. In that context — distinguishing gain from capital — the definition served a useful purpose. But it was not meant to provide a touchstone to all future gross income questions. Helvering v. Bruun [Chapter 5C.1 below]; United States v. Kirby Lumber Co. [Chapter 7A below].

Here we have instances of undeniable accessions to wealth, clearly realized, and over which the taxpayers have complete dominion. The mere fact that the payments were extracted from the wrongdoers as punishment for unlawful conduct cannot detract from their character as taxable income to the recipients. Respondents concede, as they must, that the recoveries are taxable to the extent that they compensate for damages actually incurred. It would be an anomaly that could not be justified in the absence of clear congressional intent to say that a recovery for actual damages is taxable but not the additional amount extracted as punishment for the same conduct which caused the injury. And we find no such evidence of intent to exempt these payments.

It is urged that re-enactment of §22(a) without change since the Board of Tax Appeals held punitive damages nontaxable in Highland Farms Corp.,

---

6. The phrase was derived from Stratton's Independence, Ltd. v. Howbert, 231 U.S. 399, 415, and Doyle v. Mitchell Bros. Co., 247 U.S. 179, 185, two cases construing the Revenue Act of 1909, 36 Stat. 11, 112. Both taxpayers were "wasting asset" corporations, one being engaged in mining, the other in lumbering operations. The definition was applied by the court to demonstrate a distinction between a return on capital and "a mere conversion of capital assets." Doyle v. Mitchell Bros. Co., supra, at 184. The question raised by the instant case is clearly distinguishable.

42 B.T.A. 1314, indicates congressional satisfaction with that holding. Re-enactment—particularly without the slightest affirmative indication that Congress ever had the Highland Farms decision before it—is an unreliable indicium at best. Helvering v. Wilshire Oil Co., 308 U.S. 90, 100-101; Koshland v. Helvering, 298 U.S. 441, 447. Moreover, the Commissioner promptly published his nonacquiescence in this portion of the Highland Farms holding[7] and has, before and since, consistently maintained the position that these receipts are taxable. It therefore cannot be said with certitude that Congress intended to carve an exception out of §22(a)'s pervasive coverage. Nor does the 1954 Code's legislative history, with its reiteration of the proposition that statutory gross income is "all inclusive," give support to respondents' position. The definition of gross income has been simplified, but no effect upon its present broad scope was intended.[11] Certainly punitive damages cannot reasonably be classified as gifts, cf. Commissioner v. Jacobson, 336 U.S. 28, 47-52, nor do they come under any other exemption provision in the Code. We would do violence to the plain meaning of the statute and restrict a clear legislative attempt to bring the taxing power to bear upon all receipts constitutionally taxable were we to say that the payments in question here are not gross income. See Helvering v. Midland Mutual Life Ins. Co., supra, at 223.

Reversed.

Mr. Justice DOUGLAS dissents.

Mr. Justice Harlan took no part in the consideration or decision of this case.

Notes and Questions

1. Why wasn't *Old Colony Trust Co.* (Chapter 2A above) controlling authority in *Clark*? Both cases, after all, involved third-party payment of the taxpayer's federal income tax liability. Compare Clark with a similarly situated taxpayer who makes the same mistake but who prepared his own return. When the dust settles, do they end up in the same economic position? Should they be taxed the same? Should a deduction be allowed for unreimbursed overpayments of tax? Is there a better solution to the horizontal equity problem?

---

7. 1941-1 Cum. Bull. 16.

11. In discussing §61(a) of the 1954 Code, the House Report states:

"This section corresponds to section 22(a) of the 1939 Code. While the language in existing section 22(a) has been simplified, the all-inclusive nature of statutory gross income has not been affected thereby. Section 61(a) is as broad in scope as section 22(a).

"Section 61(a) provides that gross income includes 'all income from whatever source derived.' This definition is based upon the 16th Amendment and the word 'income' is used in its constitutional sense." H.R. Rep. No. 1337, [83d Cong., 2d Sess.] at 18.

A virtually identical statement appears in S. Rep. No. 1622, [83d Cong., 2d Sess.] at 168.

2. Does *Clark* stand for the proposition that damages are not income? What, if anything, do *Raytheon* and *Glenshaw Glass* leave of *Clark?* What of the notion that income is only gain "derived from capital, from labor or from both combined"?

3. *Income from sales and other dispositions.* Under *Raytheon,* compensatory payments for an involuntary conversion are to be taxed like sale proceeds on a voluntary sale. The basic statutory provisions for determining gain or loss on a sale or other disposition are §§1001(a), 1001(b), 1011, and 1012. Suppose a taxpayer owns stock with an adjusted basis of 20 and a fair market value of 90. She sells the stock for 88 and claims a deduction for a loss of 2 on the sale (90 minus 88). Do the relevant statutory provisions allow for that loss, or do they have the effect of imposing a tax on the transaction even though it does not enrich the taxpayer at all? Why?

What is *cost* as used in §1012? Suppose a taxpayer purchased land for $5,000 and built a house thereon, spending $10,000 for materials and $5,000 for labor and contributing $15,000 worth of his own time and effort. How much gain or loss would be realized if he subsequently sold for $50,000? Why?

4. Why did the taxpayer fail to show any basis for the goodwill in *Raytheon?* What is a taxpayer's basis for goodwill built up in the course of conducting a business? Section 1012 specifies that basis for determining gain or loss is ordinarily cost, but how would one compute cost for goodwill generated in the course of conduct of a business? Many of the expenses that may in fact go into generating goodwill are currently deductible; should they give rise to a cost basis for goodwill?

5. Consider carefully the court's example in *Raytheon* of the burning of Blackacre. Is taxation in such a case too harsh? Look at §1033. What is its rationale? Should Raytheon be given some relief like that provided in §1033? How?

6. Apply the *Raytheon* replacement rule ("in lieu of what were the damages received") to determine whether in each of the following situations the compensation is gross income under section 61.

(a) Damages for breach of an employment contract. Assume for example that a college football coach is fired with three years left on his contract.

(b) Damages for wrongful destruction of property. Suppose that a building burns down as a result of a tenant's negligence and the landlord recovers $300,000. What is the proper tax treatment of the recovery? (Assume that landlord's adjusted basis in building at time of fire was $200,000.)

(c) Malpractice damages in *Clark.* What was being replaced?

(d) Compensation for breach of a promise to marry. (*Hint:* Describe the likely basis for recovery, or types of compensable injury.)

(e) Suppose a taxpayer accepts payment for a release of any right he might have to prevent the making of a motion picture about his family.

Could he exclude that payment from income as damages for invasion of privacy?[1]

7. A special problem arises when property is damaged but not destroyed. Consider the following cases.

(a) *A* bought land and building many years ago for $40,000. Later the building burned, but not completely, and *A* collected insurance proceeds of $40,000. Suppose it were shown that the land and building were worth $100,000 before the fire and $60,000 thereafter. Are the insurance proceeds taxable, in full or in part? Try to think of alternative possible solutions to this problem and grounds for choosing among them. Cf. Reg. §1.165-7(b)(2). Why do these regulations treat a personal residence differently from business or investment property?

(b) *B* purchased an estate of land for use as a fishing preserve. Thereafter commercial interests developed upstream, polluting the water and impairing the fishing. *B* sued and subsequently settled, releasing all claims in exchange for a payment equal to her cost for the land, which she kept. Is the recovery taxable? Inaja Land Co. v. Commissioner, 9 T.C. 727 (1947). See Fairfield Plaza v. Commissioner and Rev. Rul. 70-510, Chapter 6A below.

8. *Record-setting baseballs.* In September 1998 Mark McGuire of the St. Louis Cardinals tied, then broke Roger Maris's long-standing single-season record of 61 home runs. It was estimated that the 62nd home-run ball was worth at least $1 million, and McGuire's record-setting 70th was sold a few months after the season for more than $3 million. Under Major League Baseball rules, a ball hit out of the field of play becomes the property of the fan who catches it. In the thick of the 1998 McGuire-Sosa home run derby, the IRS issued a press release that stated in part:

> In response to press speculation resulting from events in Major League Baseball, the Internal Revenue Service today provided a brief explanation of the basic income and gift tax principles that would apply to a baseball fan who catches a home run ball and immediately returns it.
>
> In general, the fan in these circumstances would not have taxable income. This conclusion is based on an analogy to principles of tax law that apply when someone immediately declines a prize or returns unsolicited merchandise. There would likewise be no gift tax in these circumstances. The tax results may be different if the fan decided to sell the ball. [IR-98-56 (Sept. 8, 1998), *http://www.irs.gov/pub/irs-news/ir-98-56.pdf.*]

Do you agree? What if the fan does not immediately return the ball, but instead retains it as a keepsake?

9. Note Justice Douglas's lone dissent, without opinion, in *Glenshaw Glass.* Why? See Wolfman, Silver, and Silver, Dissent Without Opinion, the Behavior of Justice William O. Douglas in Federal Tax Cases (1975) (originally published in 122 U. Pa. L. Rev. 235 (1973)).

1. Meyer v. United States, 173 F. Supp. 920 (E.D. Tenn. 1959); Runyon, Jr. v. United States, 52-2 USTC 619 (S.D. FLA 1959), affd. 281 F.2d 590 (5th Cir. 1960).

B. PERSONAL INJURIES

1. In General

Consider a taxpayer injured in an automobile accident who recovers $800,000 from the other driver, identified as follows.

$150,000	medical expenses
30,000	loss of earnings while hospitalized
120,000	permanent loss of earning power (present discounted value of estimated loss of $10,000 per year during remaining working years resulting from loss of a finger)
200,000	pain and suffering
300,000	punitive damages
$800,000	

Under the principles examined so far, which elements of this recovery, if any, would be taxable? Why?

If the recovery in this case had been an undifferentiated settlement for $500,000, how should it be taxed? What if the taxpayer received general jury verdict for $1,000,000?

Now look at §104(a)(2). How does this alter the results? How are the alterations best explained?

Notes and Questions

1. As a technical matter, what is the relationship between *Raytheon* and §104(a)(2)?

2. In fixing the amount of damages in a personal injury action, particularly for loss of earnings, what account should be taken of the fact that the damages are themselves not taxable? Would it make sense to award only what the plaintiff would have had left after taxes if he had continued to work? See Norfolk & Western Ry. Co. v. Liepelt, 444 U.S. 490, rehg. denied, 445 U.S. 972 (1980).

3. *Structured settlements.* Does it matter whether a tort judgment is paid in a lump sum or in periodic payments, perhaps over the lifetime of the tort victim? In the case of loss of earnings, it may seem particularly appropriate to "structure" a settlement to replace the earnings over the period in which they would have been received. Section 104(a)(2) was amended in 1983 by adding the parenthetical expression "(whether by suit or agreement and whether as lump sums or as periodic payments)." This apparently codifies the position previously taken by the IRS under the older statute. Is this development sound? See Frolick, The Convergence of I.R.C. §104(a)(2), Norfolk & Western Railway Co. v. Liepelt and Structured Tort Settlements: Tax Policy

"Derailed," 51 Fordham L. Rev. 565 (1983). Compare §§101(c) and 101(d). With respect to the payor of a structured settlement see Chapter 6D.4 below.

4. *P* was injured as a result of a tort chargeable to *D*, a municipality. The parties have agreed to settle on the basis of a predicted loss of earnings for *P* of $6,000 per year for 20 years of remaining employment. *D* has estimated that it can invest at 8 percent per annum and has computed that at that interest rate it would need to set aside $59,777.15 today to finance 240 monthly payments of $500 each. *D* is willing either to make that investment itself and then make monthly payments of $500 to *P*, or to pay *P* $60,000 forthwith as a lump sum settlement. Advise *P* about how to choose.

2. Nonphysical Injuries and Nonphysical Sickness

In 1996 §104(a)(2) was amended to apply only to *physical* injuries or *physical* sickness. Some description of the judicial developments that led to this amendment is in order.

Damages for Libel, Slander, Alienation of Affections, and Loss of Child Custody. Solicitor's Memorandum 957, 1 C.B. 65 (1919) reads in its entirety "Money recovered as damages in libel proceedings is subject to income tax." Solicitor's Memorandum 1384, 2 C.B. 71 (1920) deals at a little greater length with "a sum received by a taxpayer as damages on account of the alienation of the affections of his wife." It cites the predecessor of §104(a)(2) as controlling authority, and indicates that if the language "personal injury" were taken by itself it might well be held to apply to alienation of a wife's affections, but "it appears more probable from the language . . . taken as a whole, referring as it does, to accident and health insurance and workmen's compensation Acts, that the term 'personal injuries', as used therein means physical injuries only. . . ."

Solicitor's Opinion 32, 1-1 C.B. 92 (1922) deals with "(1) Damages for alienation of affections; (2) damages for slander or libel of personal character; and (3) money received by a parent in consideration of the surrender of his right to the custody of his minor child."

It asserts that Solicitor's Memorandum 1384 . . . correctly held that the exemption contained in section [104(a)(2)] does not include damages for alienation of affections, but the question is really more fundamental, namely, whether such damages are within the legal definition of income. Similarly, Solicitor's Memorandum 957 may have been correct in holding that damages received by a lawyer for libel of his professional reputation constitute income. Business libel may be distinguished from ordinary defamation of character and is not here under consideration. The ruling in Solicitor's Memorandum 957, however, was not limited but apparently applied to libel generally.

The opinion then goes on to cite Supreme Court opinions for the conclusion that "without gain of some sort no income within the meaning of the sixteenth amendment can be said to be realized," and concludes that "there is no gain, and therefore no income, derived from the receipt of damages for alienation of affections or defamation of personal character." Accord C.A. Hawkins, 6 B.T.A. 1023 (1927).

Subsequent citations to these authorities for the conclusion that defamation was within §104 are inaccurate. Nevertheless, many subsequent authorities came to treat defamation as within §104(a)(2) to the extent it represented injury to personal as compared with professional or business reputation. In Paul F. Roemer, Jr., 79 T.C. 398 (1982), rev'd, 716 F.2d 693 (9th Cir. 1983), an insurance broker recovered damages for a false and defamatory report by a credit agency, as a result of which he lost business, including an opportunity to enter into a new business venture. The Tax Court held the recovery taxable since the injury complained of was primarily to Roemer's business rather than his personal reputation. Some dissenters in the Tax Court thought it was unrealistic to draw any such distinction in view of the fact that Roemer's social friends and business clients were largely the same people.

The court of appeals decided, on the basis of an extensive review of California law, that defamation was an attack on character and good name and therefore a personal injury, and that harm to personal and professional reputations were just different consequences, compensation for both of which were within §104. That conclusion was enthusiastically adopted by the Tax Court itself in James E. Threlkeld, 87 T.C. 1294 (1986). Business losses due to defamation were likened to the loss of earnings of a young surgeon who loses a finger in an accident, compensation for which had long been regarded as exempt under §104(a)(2).

Employment discrimination. A number of statutes prohibit employment discrimination on various bases. The commonest form of damages for violation of these statutes is back pay, in which an employer is effectively compelled to pay what he should have paid just as if he had complied with the law. In a case of wage discrimination, this will be the difference between what was paid and what should have been paid; in cases of discriminatory firing, it may be the whole amount of wages that would have been paid but for the firing. How should such damage awards be taxed? Citing *Threlkeld*, a number of successful discrimination plaintiffs excluded such damages from gross income, and they met with considerable tax success in the courts of appeals.

Commissioner v. Burke, 504 U.S. 229 (1992), involved employees who secured back pay in settlement of a claim of sex-based wage discrimination under Title VII of the Civil Rights Act of 1964. The employer withheld taxes from the payments, and taxpayers sued for a refund. The court of appeals held that the discrimination constituted a personal, tort-like injury, and that compensation was therefore exempt. The Supreme Court concluded, with dissents, that since relief under this statute was confined to back pay and injunctions, the statute did not redress a tort-like personal injury within the meaning of §104(a)(2). The IRS responded dutifully by ruling, under the reasoning in *Burke*, that (1) damages for sex discrimination under Title VII, as amended in 1991 to grant additional remedies; (2) damages for racial discrimination under Title VII; and (3) damages under the Americans with Disabilities Act would all be exempt under §104(a)(2). Rev. Rul. 93-88, 199-2 C.B. 61.

Commissioner v. Schleier, 515 U.S. 323 (1995) involved pilots of Eastern Airlines whose service was routinely terminated at age 60. Taxpayers received back pay in settlement of a suit for discriminatory firing under the Age Discrimination in Employment Act (ADEA) of 1967, and the lower courts held these excludible under §104. The Supreme Court reversed, partly on the ground that remedies available under ADEA still lacked the critical elements of a tort-type right, but primarily because a back pay award was not "on account of" any personal injury that might have occurred even if there was one. "The amount of back wages recovered is completely independent of the existence or extent of any personal injury." 515 U.S. at 330.

Questions

1. One can readily sympathize with the judgment that somehow when an employee simply secures from his *employer* what the employer should have paid him for his work, he should be taxed the same as if he had been treated lawfully in the first place. But the courts did not have an easy time reaching that result. Where, if anywhere, do you think they went wrong?

2. Given the decision in *Schleier*, do you think the congressional limitation of §104(a)(2) to *physical* injury or *physical* sickness was a desirable change?

3. How do we distinguish between physical and nonphysical injuries? Consider a mother who, while strolling down the sidewalk with her five-year-old child, sees the child run over and killed by a drunk driver. The mother requires extensive medical and psychological treatment for depression and loses her job as a result of sleeplessness and inability to concentrate. If the mother recovers damages for her medical expenses, pain and suffering, and lost wages from the tortfeasor (or his insurer), how will they be taxed? Read the final two sentences of §104(a). Does your answer change if the mother's symptoms include gastric ulcers? And what if the vehicle that killed her child had also struck the mother's arm, bruising it and dislocating her shoulder?

4. Is there room left to argue for exclusion of some damages for defamation under the definition of gross income apart from §104? How should any such argument be answered and ruled on?

REVENUE RULING 74-77
1974-1 C.B. 33

An individual taxpayer received certain amounts in settlement of his suit for damages on account of alienation of affections and in consideration for the surrender of the custody of his minor child. These items relate to personal or family rights, not property rights, and may be treated together. None of the amounts received constituted exemplary or punitive damages.

Held, amounts received by the taxpayer as damages for alienation of affections or for the surrender of the custody of his child, whether under agreement of the parties or pursuant to judgment of the court, are not income.

Sol. Op. 132, I-1 C.B. 92 (1922), is hereby superseded since the position stated therein is set forth under the current statute and regulations in this Revenue Ruling.

MURPHY v. INTERNAL REVENUE SERVICE
493 F.3d 170 (D.C. Cir. 2007), cert. denied,
128 S.Ct. 2050 (2008)

ON REHEARING

GINSBURG, Chief Judge:

Marrita Murphy brought this suit to recover income taxes she paid on the compensatory damages for emotional distress and loss of reputation she was awarded in an administrative action she brought against her former employer. Murphy contends that under §104(a)(2) of the Internal Revenue Code (IRC), 26 U.S.C. §104(a)(2), her award should have been excluded from her gross income because it was compensation received "on account of personal physical injuries or physical sickness." She also maintains that, in any event, her award is not part of her gross income as defined by §61 of the IRC, 26 U.S.C. §61. Finally, she argues that taxing her award subjects her to an unapportioned direct tax in violation of Article I, Section 9 of the Constitution of the United States.

We reject Murphy's argument in all aspects. We hold, first, that Murphy's compensation was not "received . . . on account of personal physical injuries" excludable from gross income under §104(a)(2). Second, we conclude gross income as defined by §61 includes compensatory damages for non-physical injuries. Third, we hold that a tax upon such damages is within the Congress's power to tax.

I. BACKGROUND

In 1994 Marrita Leveille (now Murphy) filed a complaint with the Department of Labor alleging that her former employer, the New York Air National Guard (NYANG), in violation of various whistle-blower statutes, had "blacklisted" her and provided unfavorable references to potential employers after she had complained to state authorities of environmental hazards on a NYANG airbase. The Secretary of Labor determined the NYANG had unlawfully discriminated and retaliated against Murphy, ordered that any adverse references to the taxpayer in the files of the Office of Personnel Management be withdrawn, and remanded her case to an Administrative Law Judge "for findings on compensatory damages."

On remand Murphy submitted evidence that she had suffered both mental and physical injuries as a result of the NYANG's blacklisting her. A psychologist testified that Murphy had sustained both "somatic" and "emotional" injuries, basing his conclusion in part upon medical and dental records showing Murphy had "bruxism," or teeth grinding often associated with stress, which may cause permanent tooth damage. Noting that Murphy also suffered from other "physical manifestations of stress" including "anxiety attacks, shortness of breath, and dizziness," and that Murphy testified she "could not concentrate, stopped talking to friends, and no longer enjoyed 'anything in life,' " the ALJ recommended compensatory damages totaling $70,000, of which $45,000 was for "past and future emotional distress," and $25,000 was for "injury to [Murphy's] vocational reputation" from having been blacklisted. None of the award was for lost wages or diminished earning capacity.

In 1999 the Department of Labor Administrative Review Board affirmed the ALJ's findings and recommendations. See Leveille v. N.Y. Air Nat'l Guard, 1999 WL 966951, at *2-*4 (Oct. 25, 1999). On her tax return for 2000, Murphy included the $70,000 award in her "gross income" pursuant to §61 of the IRC. See 26 U.S.C. §61(a) ("[G]ross income means all income from whatever source derived"). As a result, she paid $20,665 in taxes on the award.

Murphy later filed an amended return in which she sought a refund of the $20,665 based upon §104(a)(2) of the IRC, which provides that "gross income does not include ... damages ... received ... on account of personal physical injuries or physical sickness." In support of her amended return, Murphy submitted copies of her dental and medical records. Upon deciding Murphy had failed to demonstrate the compensatory damages were attributable to "physical injury" or "physical sickness," the Internal Revenue Service denied her request for a refund. Murphy thereafter sued the IRS and the United States in the district court.

In her complaint Murphy sought a refund of the $20,665, plus applicable interest, pursuant to the Sixteenth Amendment to the Constitution of the United States, along with declaratory and injunctive relief against the IRS pursuant to the Administrative Procedure Act and the Due Process Clause of the Fifth Amendment. She argued her compensatory award was in fact for "physical personal injuries" and therefore excluded from gross income under §104(a)(2). In the alternative Murphy asserted taxing her award was unconstitutional because the award was not "income" within the meaning of the Sixteenth Amendment. The Government moved to dismiss Murphy's suit as to the IRS, contending the Service was not a proper defendant, and for summary judgment on all claims.

The district court denied the Government's motion to dismiss, holding that Murphy had the right to bring an "action[ ] for declaratory judgments or . . . [a] mandatory injunction" against an "agency by its official title," pursuant to §703 of the APA [Administrative Procedure Act], 5 U.S.C. §703. Murphy v. IRS, 362 F.Supp.2d 206, 211-12, 218 (2005). The court then rejected all of Murphy's claims on the merits and granted summary judgment for the Government and the IRS. Id.

Murphy appealed the judgment of the district court with respect to her claims under §104(a)(2) and the Sixteenth Amendment. In Murphy v. IRS, 460 F.3d 79 (2006), we concluded Murphy's award was not exempt from taxation pursuant to §104(a)(2), id. at 84, but also was not "income" within the meaning of the Sixteenth Amendment, id. at 92, and therefore reversed the decision of the district court. The Government petitioned for rehearing en banc, arguing for the first time that, even if Murphy's award is not income, there is no constitutional impediment to taxing it because a tax on the award is not a direct tax and is imposed uniformly. In view of the importance of the issue thus belatedly raised, the panel sua sponte vacated its judgment and reheard the case. See Consumers Union of U.S., Inc. v. Fed. Power Comm'n, 510 F.2d 656, 662 (D.C.Cir. 1975) ("[R]egarding the contents of briefs on appeal, we may also consider points not raised in the briefs or in oral argument. Our willingness to do so rests on a balancing of considerations of judicial orderliness and efficiency against the need for the greatest possible accuracy in judicial decisionmaking. The latter factor is of particular weight when the decision affects the broad public interest.") (footnotes omitted); see also Eli Lilly & Co. v. Home Ins. Co., 794 F.2d 710, 717 (D.C.Cir. 1986) ("The rule in this circuit is that litigants must raise their claims on their initial appeal and not in subsequent hearings following a remand. This is a specific application of the general waiver rule, which bends only in 'exceptional circumstances, where injustice might otherwise result.' ") (quoting Dist. of Columbia v. Air Florida, Inc., 750 F.2d 1077, 1085 (D.C.Cir. 1984)) (citation omitted). In the present opinion, we affirm the judgment of the district court based upon the newly argued ground that Murphy's award, even if it is not income within the meaning of the Sixteenth Amendment, is within the reach of the congressional power to tax under Article I, Section 8 of the Constitution.

II. ANALYSIS

We review the district court's grant of summary judgment de novo, Flynn v. R.C. Tile, 353 F.3d 953, 957 (D.C.Cir. 2004), bearing in mind that summary judgment is appropriate only "if there is no genuine issue as to any material fact and if the moving party is entitled to judgment as a matter of law," Anderson v. Liberty Lobby, Inc., 477 U.S. 242, 250, 106 S.Ct. 2505, 91 L.Ed.2d 202 (1986). Before addressing Murphy's claims on their merits, however, we must determine whether the district court erred in holding the IRS was a proper defendant.

A. THE IRS AS A DEFENDANT

The Government contends the courts lack jurisdiction over Murphy's claims against the IRS because the Congress has not waived that agency's immunity from declaratory and injunctive actions pursuant to 28 U.S.C. §2201(a) (courts may grant declaratory relief "except with respect to Federal taxes") and 26 U.S.C. §7421(a) ("no suit for the purpose of restraining the assessment or collection of any tax shall be maintained in any court by any person"); and insofar as the Congress in 28 U.S.C. §1346(a)(1) has waived immunity from civil actions seeking tax refunds, that provision on its face applies to "civil action[s] against the United States," not against the IRS. In reply Murphy argues only that the Government forfeited the issue of sovereign immunity because it did not cross-appeal the district court's denial of its motion to dismiss. See FED. R.APP. P. 4(a)(3). Notwithstanding the Government's failure to cross-appeal, however, the court must address a question concerning its jurisdiction. See Occidental Petroleum Corp. v. SEC, 873 F.2d 325, 328 (D.C.Cir. 1989) ("As a preliminary matter . . . we must address the question of our jurisdiction to hear this appeal").

Murphy and the district court are correct that §703 of the APA does create a right of action for equitable relief against a federal agency but, as the Government correctly points out, the Congress has preserved the immunity of the United States from declaratory and injunctive relief with respect to all tax controversies except those pertaining to the classification of organizations under §501(c) of the IRC. See 28 U.S.C. §2201(a); 26 U.S.C. §7421(a). As an agency of the Government, of course, the IRS shares that immunity. See Settles v. U.S. Parole Comm'n, 429 F.3d 1098, 1106 (D.C.Cir.2005) (agency "retains the immunity it is due as an arm of the federal sovereign"). Insofar as the Congress in 28 U.S.C. §1346(a)(1) has waived sovereign immunity with respect to suits for tax refunds, that provision specifically contemplates only actions against the "United States." Therefore, we hold the IRS, unlike the United States, may not be sued eo nomine in this case.

B. SECTION 104(a)(2) OF THE IRC

Section 104(a) ("Compensation for injuries or sickness") provides that "gross income [under §61 of the IRC] does not include the amount of any damages (other than punitive damages) received . . . on account of personal physical injuries or physical sickness." 26 U.S.C. §104(a)(2). Since 1996 it has further provided that, for purposes of this exclusion, "emotional distress shall not be treated as a physical injury or physical sickness." Id. §104(a). The version of §104(a)(2) in effect prior to 1996 had excluded from gross income monies received in compensation for "personal injuries or sickness," which included both physical and nonphysical injuries such as emotional distress. Id. §104(a)(2) (1995); see United States v. Burke, 504 U.S. 229, 235 n.6 (1992) ("[section] 104(a)(2) in fact encompasses a broad range of physical and nonphysical injuries to personal interests"). In Commissioner v. Schleier, 515 U.S. 323 (1995), the Supreme Court held that before a taxpayer may exclude compensatory damages from gross income pursuant to §104(a)(2), he must first demonstrate that "the underlying cause of action giving rise to the recovery [was] 'based upon tort or tort type rights.'" Id. at 337. The taxpayer has the same burden under the statute as amended. See, e.g., Chamberlain v. United States, 401 F.3d 335, 341 (5th Cir. 2005).

Murphy contends §104(a)(2), even as amended, excludes her particular award from gross income. First, she asserts her award was "based upon . . . tort type rights" in the whistle-blower statutes the NYANG violated — a position the Government does not challenge. Second, she claims she was compensated for "physical" injuries, which claim the Government does dispute.

Murphy points both to her psychologist's testimony that she had experienced "somatic" and "body" injuries "as a result of NYANG's blacklisting [her]," and to the American Heritage Dictionary, which defines "somatic" as "relating to, or affecting the body, especially as distinguished from a body part, the mind, or the environment." Murphy further argues the dental records she submitted to the IRS proved she has suffered permanent damage to her teeth. Citing Walters v. Mintec/International, 758 F.2d 73, 78 (3d Cir.1985), and Payne v. Gen. Motors Corp., 731 F.Supp. 1465, 1474-75 (D.Kan.1990), Murphy contends that "substantial physical problems caused by emotional distress are considered physical injuries or physical sickness."

Murphy further contends that neither §104 of the IRC nor the regulation issued thereunder "limits the physical disability exclusion to a physical stimulus." In fact, as Murphy points out, the applicable regulation, which provides that §104(a)(2) "excludes from gross income the amount of any damages received (whether by suit or agreement) on account of personal injuries or sickness," 26 C.F.R. §1.104-1(c), does not distinguish between physical injuries stemming from physical stimuli and those arising from emotional trauma; rather, it tracks the pre-1996 text of §104(a)(2), which the IRS agrees excluded from gross income compensation both for physical and for nonphysical injuries.

For its part, the Government argues Murphy's focus upon the word "physical" in §104(a)(2) is misplaced; more important is the phrase "on account of." In O'Gilvie v. United States, 519 U.S. 79 (1996), the Supreme Court read that phrase to require a "strong[ ] causal connection," thereby making §104(a)(2) "applicable only to those personal injury lawsuit damages that were awarded by reason of, or because of, the personal injuries." Id. at 83. The Court specifically rejected a "but-for" formulation in favor of a "stronger causal connection." Id. at 82-83. The Government therefore concludes Murphy must demonstrate she was awarded damages "because of" her physical injuries, which the Government claims she has failed to do.

Indeed, as the Government points out, the ALJ expressly recommended, and the Board expressly awarded, compensatory damages "because of" Murphy's nonphysical injuries. The Board analyzed the ALJ's recommendation under the headings "Compensatory damage for emotional distress or mental anguish" and "Compensatory damage award for injury to professional reputation," and noted such damages compensate "not only for direct pecuniary loss, but also for such harms as impairment of reputation, personal humiliation, and mental anguish and suffering." *Leveille,* 1999 WL 966951 at *2. In describing the ALJ's proposed award as "reasonable," the Board stated Murphy was to receive "$45,000 for mental pain and anguish" and "$25,000 for injury to professional reputation." Although Murphy may have suffered from bruxism or other physical symptoms of stress, the Board focused upon Murphy's testimony that she experienced "severe anxiety attacks, inability to concentrate, a feeling that she no longer enjoyed 'anything in life,' and marital conflict" and upon her psychologist's testimony about the "substantial effect the negative references had on [Murphy]." Id. at *3. The Board made no reference to her bruxism, and acknowledged that "[a]ny attempt to set a monetary value on intangible damages such as mental pain and anguish involves a subjective judgment," id. at *4, before concluding the ALJ's recommendation was reasonable. The Government therefore argues "there was no direct causal link between the damages award at issue and [Murphy's] bruxism."

Murphy responds that it is undisputed she suffered both "somatic" and "emotional" injuries, and the ALJ and Board expressly cited to the portion of her psychologist's testimony establishing that fact. She contends the Board therefore relied upon her physical injuries in determining her damages, making those injuries a direct cause of her award in spite of the Board's labeling the award as one for emotional distress.

Although the pre-1996 version of §104(a)(2) was at issue in *O'Gilvie,* the Court's analysis of the phrase "on account of," which phrase was unchanged by the 1996 Amendments, remains controlling here. Murphy no doubt suffered from certain physical manifestations of emotional distress, but the record clearly indicates the Board awarded her compensation only "for mental pain and anguish" and "for injury to professional reputation." Id. at *5. Although the Board cited her psychologist, who had mentioned her physical aliments, in support of Murphy's "description of her mental anguish," we cannot say the Board, notwithstanding its clear statements to the contrary, actually awarded damages because of Murphy's bruxism and other physical manifestations of stress. Id. at *3. At best — and this is doubtful — at best the Board and the ALJ may have considered her physical injuries indicative of the severity of the emotional distress for which the damages were awarded, but her physical injuries themselves were not the reason for the award. The Board thus having left no room for doubt about the grounds for her award, we conclude Murphy's damages were not "awarded by reason of, or because of, . . . [physical] personal injuries," *O'Gilvie*, 519 U.S. at 83. Therefore, §104(a)(2) does not permit Murphy to exclude her award from gross income.[1]

C. SECTION 61 OF THE IRC

Murphy and the Government agree that for Murphy's award to be taxable, it must be part of her "gross income" as defined by §61(a) of the IRC, which states in relevant part: "gross income means all income from whatever source derived." The Supreme Court has interpreted the section broadly to extend to "all economic gains not otherwise exempted." Comm'r v. Banks, 543 U.S. 426, 433 (2005); see also, e.g., James v. United States, 366 U.S. 213, 219 (1961) (Section 61 encompasses "all accessions to wealth") (internal quotation mark omitted); Com'r v. Glenshaw Glass Co., 348 U.S. 426, 430 ("the Court has given a liberal construction to ["gross income"] in recognition of the intention of Congress to tax all gains except those specifically exempted"). "Gross income" in §61(a) is at least as broad as the meaning of "incomes" in the Sixteenth Amendment.[2] See *Glenshaw Glass*, 348 U.S. at 429, 432 n.11 (quoting H.R. Rep. No. 83-1337, at A18 (1954), reprinted in 1954 U.S.C.C.A.N. 4017, 4155); Helvering v. Bruun, 309 U.S. 461, 468 (1940).

Murphy argues her award is not a gain or an accession to wealth and therefore not part of gross income. Noting the Supreme Court has long recognized "the principle that a restoration of capital [i]s not income; hence it [falls] outside the definition of 'income' upon which the law impose[s] a tax," *O'Gilvie*, 519 U.S. at 84; see, e.g., Doyle v. Mitchell Bros. Co., 247 U.S. 179, 187-88 (1918); S. Pac. Co. v. Lowe, 247 U.S. 330, 335 (1918), Murphy contends a damage award for personal injuries — including nonphysical injuries — should be viewed as a return of a particular form of capital — "human capital," as it were. See Gary S. Becker, Human Capital (1st ed. 1964); Gary S. Becker, The Economic Way of Looking at Life, Nobel Lecture (Dec. 9, 1992), in Nobel Lectures In Economic Sciences 1991-1995, at 43-45 (Torsten Persson ed., 1997). In her view, the Supreme Court in *Glenshaw Glass* acknowledged the relevance of the human capital concept

---

1. Insofar as compensation for nonphysical personal injuries appears to be excludable from gross income under 26 C.F.R. §1.104-1, the regulation conflicts with the plain text of §104(a)(2); in these circumstances the statute clearly controls. See Brown v. Gardner, 513 U.S. 115, 122 (1994) (finding "no antidote to [a regulation's] clear inconsistency with a statute").

2. The Sixteenth Amendment provides: "The Congress shall have power to lay and collect taxes on incomes, from whatever source derived, without apportionment among the several States, and without regard to any census or enumeration."

for tax purposes. There, in holding that punitive damages for personal injury were "gross income" under the predecessor to §61, the Court stated:

> The long history of . . . holding personal injury recoveries nontaxable on the theory that they roughly correspond to a return of capital cannot support exemption of punitive damages following injury to property. . . . Damages for personal injury are by definition compensatory only. Punitive damages, on the other hand, cannot be considered a restoration of capital for taxation purposes.

348 U.S. at 432 n.8. By implication, Murphy argues, damages for personal injury are a "restoration of capital."

As further support, Murphy cites various administrative rulings issued shortly after passage of the Sixteenth Amendment that concluded recoveries from personal injuries were not income, such as this 1918 Opinion of the Attorney General:

> Without affirming that the human body is in a technical sense the "capital" invested in an accident policy, in a broad, natural sense the proceeds of the policy do but substitute, so far as they go, capital which is the source of future periodical income. They merely take the place of capital in human ability which was destroyed by the accident. They are therefore "capital" as distinguished from "income" receipts.

31 Op. Att'y Gen. 304, 308; see T.D. 2747, 20 Treas. Dec. Int. Rev. 457 (1918); Sol. Op. 132, I-1 C.B. 92, 93-94 (1922) ("[M]oney received . . . on account of . . . defamation of personal character . . . does not constitute income within the meaning of the sixteenth amendment and the statutes enacted thereunder"). She also cites a House Report on the bill that became the Revenue Act of 1918. H.R. Rep. No. 65-767, at 9-10 (1918) ("Under the present law it is doubtful whether amounts received . . . as compensation for personal injury . . . are required to be included in gross income"); see also Dotson v. United States, 87 F.3d 682, 685 (5th Cir. 1996) (concluding on basis of House Report that the "Congress first enacted the personal injury compensation exclusion . . . when such payments were considered the return of human capital, and thus not constitutionally taxable 'income' under the 16th amendment").

Finally, Murphy argues her interpretation of §61 is reflected in the common law of tort and the provisions in various environmental statutes and Title VII of the Civil Rights Act of 1964, all of which provide for "make whole" relief. See, e.g., 42 U.S.C. §1981a; 15 U.S.C. §2622. If a recovery of damages designed to "make whole" the plaintiff is taxable, she reasons, then one who receives the award has not been made whole after tax. Section 61 should not be read to create a conflict between the tax code and the "make whole" purpose of the various statutes.

The Government disputes Murphy's interpretation on all fronts. First, noting "the definition [of gross income in the IRC] extends broadly to all economic gains," *Banks*, 543 U.S. at 433, the Government asserts Murphy "undeniably had economic gain because she was better off financially after receiving the damages award than she was prior to receiving it." Second, the Government argues that the case law Murphy cites does not support the proposition that the Congress lacks the power to tax as income recoveries for personal injuries. In its view, to the extent the Supreme Court has addressed at all the taxability of compensatory damages, see, e.g., *O'Gilvie*, 519 U.S. at 86; *Glenshaw Glass*, 348 U.S. at 432 n. 8, it was merely articulating the Congress's rationale at the time for not taxing such damages, not the Court's own view whether such damages could constitutionally be taxed.

Third, the Government challenges the relevance of the administrative rulings Murphy cites from around the time the sixteenth amendment was ratified; Treasury decisions dating from even closer to the time of ratification treated damages received on account of personal injury as income. See T.D. 2135, 17 Treas. Dec. Int. Rev. 39, 42 (1915); T.D. 2690, Reg. No. 33 (Rev.), art. 4, 20 Treas. Dec. Int. Rev. 126, 130 (1918). Furthermore, administrative rulings from the time suggest that, even if recoveries for physical personal injuries were not considered part of income, recoveries for nonphysical personal injuries were. See Sol. Mem. 957, 1 C.B. 65 (1919) (damages for libel subject to income tax); Sol. Mem. 1384, 2 C.B. 71 (1920) (recovery of damages from alienation of wife's affections not regarded as return of capital, hence taxable). Although the Treasury changed its position in 1922, see Sol. Op. 132, I-1 C.B. at 93-94, it did so only after the Supreme Court's decision in Eisner v. Macomber, 252 U.S. 189 (1920), which the Court later viewed as having established a definition of income that "served a useful purpose [but] was not meant to provide a touchstone to all future gross income questions." *Glenshaw Glass*, 348 U.S. at 430-431. As for Murphy's contention that reading §61 to include her damages would be in tension with the common law and various statutes providing for "make whole" relief, the Government denies there is any tension and suggests Murphy is trying to turn a disagreement over tax policy into a constitutional issue.

Finally, the Government argues that even if the concept of human capital is built into §61, Murphy's award is nonetheless taxable because Murphy has no tax basis in her human capital. Under the IRC, a taxpayer's gain upon the disposition of property is the difference between the "amount realized" from the disposition and his basis in the property, 26 U.S.C. §1001, defined as "the cost of such property," id. §1012, adjusted "for expenditures, receipts, losses, or other items, properly chargeable to [a] capital account," id. §1016(a)(1). The Government asserts, "The Code does not allow individuals to claim a basis in their human capital"; accordingly, Murphy's gain is the full value of the award. See Roemer v. Comm'r, 716 F.2d 693, 696 n.2 (9th Cir.1983) ("Since there is no tax basis in a person's health and other personal interests, money received as compensation for an injury to those interests might be considered a realized accession to wealth") (dictum).

Although Murphy and the Government focus primarily upon whether Murphy's award falls within the definition of income first used in *Glenshaw*

Glass,[3] coming within that definition is not the only way in which §61(a) could be held to encompass her award. Principles of statutory interpretation could show §61(a) includes Murphy's award in her gross income regardless whether it was an "accession to wealth," as *Glenshaw Glass* requires. For example, if §61(a) were amended specifically to include in gross income "$100,000 in addition to all other gross income," then that additional sum would be a part of gross income under §61 even though no actual gain was associated with it. In other words, although the "Congress cannot make a thing income which is not so in fact," Burk-Waggoner Oil Ass'n v. Hopkins, 269 U.S. 110, 114 (1925), it can *label* a thing income and tax it, so long as it acts within its constitutional authority, which includes not only the Sixteenth Amendment but also Article I, Sections 8 and 9. See Penn Mut. Indem. Co. v. Comm'r, 277 F.2d 16, 20 (3d Cir. 1960) ("Congress has the power to impose taxes generally, and if the particular imposition does not run afoul of any constitutional restrictions then the tax is lawful, call it what you will") (footnote omitted). Accordingly, rather than ask whether Murphy's award was an accession to her wealth, we go to the heart of the matter, which is whether her award is properly included within the definition of gross income in §61(a), to wit, "all income from whatever source derived."

Looking at §61(a) by itself, one sees no indication that it covers Murphy's award unless the award is "income" as defined by *Glenshaw Glass* and later cases. Damages received for emotional distress are not listed among the examples of income in §61 and, as Murphy points out, an ambiguity in the meaning of a revenue-raising statute should be resolved in favor of the taxpayer. See, e.g., Hassett v. Welch, 303 U.S. 303, 314 (1938); Gould v. Gould, 245 U.S. 151, 153 (1917); see also United Dominion Indus., Inc. v. United States, 532 U.S. 822, 839 (2001) (Thomas, J., concurring); id. at 839 n.1 (Stevens, J., dissenting); 3A Norman J. Singer, Sutherland Statutes & Statutory Construction §66:1 (6th ed. 2003). A statute is to be read as a whole, however, see, e.g., Alaska Dep't of Envtl. Conservation v. EPA, 540 U.S. 461, 489 n.13 (2004), and reading §61 in combination with §104(a)(2) of the Internal Revenue Code presents a very different picture — a picture so clear that we have no occasion to apply the canon favoring the interpretation of ambiguous revenue-raising statutes in favor of the taxpayer.

As noted above, in 1996 the Congress amended §104(a) to narrow the exclusion to amounts received on account of "personal physical injuries or physical sickness" from "personal injuries or sickness," and explicitly to provide that "emotional distress shall not be treated as a physical injury or physical sickness," thus making clear that an award received on account

---

3. Murphy also suggests further insight into whether her award is income can be gleaned from application of the "in lieu of" test. See Raytheon Prod. Corp. v. Comm'r, 144 F.2d 110, 113 (1st Cir. 1944). As she acknowledges, however, we would still be required to determine whether her award was compensatory or an accession to wealth, which is the same analysis *Glenshaw Glass* and its progeny demand. As discussed below, it is unnecessary to determine if there was an accession to wealth in this case; §61 encompasses Murphy's award regardless.

of emotional distress is not excluded from gross income under §104(a)(2). Small Business Job Protection Act of 1996, Pub. L. 104-188, §1605, 110 Stat. 1755, 1838. As this amendment, which narrows the exclusion, would have no effect whatsoever if such damages were not included within the ambit of §61, and as we must presume that "[w]hen Congress acts to amend a statute, . . . it intends its amendment to have real and substantial effect," Stone v. INS, 514 U.S. 386, 397 (1995), the 1996 amendment of §104(a) strongly suggests §61 should be read to include an award for damages from nonphysical harms.[4] Although it is unclear whether §61 covered such an award before 1996, we need not address that question here; even if the provision did not do so prior to 1996, the presumption indicates the Congress implicitly amended §61 to cover such an award when it amended §104(a).

We realize, of course, that amendments by implication, like repeals by implication, are disfavored. United States v. Welden, 377 U.S. 95, 103 n.12 (1964); Cheney R.R. Co. v. R.R. Ret. Bd., 50 F.3d 1071, 1078 (D.C.Cir. 1995). The Supreme Court has also noted, however, that the "classic judicial task of reconciling many laws enacted over time, and getting them to 'make sense' in combination, necessarily assumes that the implications of a statute may be altered by the implications of a later statute." United States v. Fausto, 484 U.S. 439, 453 (1988); see also FDA v. Brown & Williamson Tobacco Corp., 529 U.S. 120, 133 (2000) ("[T]he meaning of one statute may be affected by other Acts, particularly where Congress has spoken subsequently and more specifically to the topic at hand"); Almendarez-Torres v. United States, 523 U.S. 224, 237 (1998) (suggesting later enacted laws "depend[ing] for their effectiveness upon clarification, or a change in the meaning of an earlier statute" provide a "forward looking legislative mandate, guidance, or direct suggestion about how courts should interpret the earlier provisions"); cf. Franklin v. Gwinnett County Pub. Sch., 503 U.S. 60, 72-73 (1992) (amendment of Title IX abrogating States' Eleventh Amendment immunity validated Court's prior holding that Title IX created implied right of action); id. at 78 (Scalia, J., concurring in judgment) (amendment to Title IX was an "implicit acknowledgment that damages are available").

This "classic judicial task" is before us now. For the 1996 amendment of §104(a) to "make sense," gross income in §61(a) must, and we therefore hold it does, include an award for nonphysical damages such as Murphy received, regardless whether the award is an accession to wealth. *Cf.* Vermont Agency of Natural Res. v. United States ex rel. Stevens, 529 U.S. 765, 786 & n. 17 (2000) (determining meaning of "person" in False Claims Act, which was originally enacted in 1863, based in part upon definition of "person" in

_____

4. As evidence the presumption is well-founded in this case, we note the House Report accompanying the 1996 amendment to §104 explicitly presumes recoveries for nonphysical injuries would be included in gross income: Part of the section explaining the effect of the amendment is entitled "Include in income damage recoveries for nonphysical injuries." H.R. Rep. No. 104-586, at 143-144 (1996), reprinted in 1996-3 C.B. 331, 481-482.

Program Fraud Civil Remedies Act of 1986, which was "designed to operate in tandem with the [earlier Act]").

D. The Congress's Power to Tax

The taxing power of the Congress is established by Article I, Section 8 of the Constitution: "The Congress shall have power to lay and collect taxes, duties, imposts and excises." There are two limitations on this power. First, as the same section goes on to provide, "all duties, imposts and excises shall be uniform throughout the United States." Second, as provided in Section 9 of that same Article, "No capitation, or other direct, tax shall be laid, unless in proportion to the census or enumeration herein before directed to be taken." See also U.S. Const. art. I, §2, cl. 3 ("direct taxes shall be apportioned among the several states which may be included within this union, according to their respective numbers").[5] We now consider whether the tax laid upon Murphy's award violates either of these two constraints.

1. a direct tax?

Over the years, courts have considered numerous claims that one or another nonapportioned tax is a direct tax and therefore unconstitutional. Although these cases have not definitively marked the boundary between taxes that must be apportioned and taxes that need not be, see Bromley v. McCaughn, 280 U.S. 124, 136 (1929); Spreckels Sugar Ref. Co. v. McClain, 192 U.S. 397, 413 (1904) (dividing line between "taxes that are direct and those which are to be regarded simply as excises" is "often very difficult to be expressed in words"), some characteristics of each may be discerned.

Only three taxes are definitely known to be direct: (1) a capitation, U.S. Const. art. I, §9, (2) a tax upon real property, and (3) a tax upon personal property. See Fernandez v. Wiener, 326 U.S. 340, 352 (1945) ("Congress may tax real estate or chattels if the tax is apportioned"); Pollock v. Farmers' Loan & Trust Co., 158 U.S. 601, 637 (1895) (*Pollock II*).[6] Such direct taxes are laid upon one's "general ownership of property," *Bromley*, 280 U.S. at 136; see also Flint v. Stone Tracy Co., 220 U.S. 107, 149 (1911), as contrasted with excise taxes laid "upon a particular use or enjoyment of property or the shifting from one to another of any power or privilege incidental to the ownership or enjoyment of property." *Fernandez*, 326 U.S. at 352; see also Thomas v. United States, 192 U.S. 363, 370 (1904) (excises cover "duties imposed on importation, consumption, manufacture and sale of certain

5. Though it is unclear whether an income tax is a direct tax, the Sixteenth Amendment definitively establishes that a tax upon income is not required to be apportioned. See Stanton v. Baltic Mining Co., 240 U.S. 103, 112-113 (1916).

6. *Pollock II* also held that a tax upon the income of real or personal property is a direct tax. 158 U.S. at 637. Whether that portion of *Pollock* remains good law is unclear. See Graves v. New York ex rel. O'Keefe, 306 U.S. 466, 480 (1939).

commodities, privileges, particular business transactions, vocations, occupations and the like"). More specifically, excise taxes include, in addition to taxes upon consumable items, see Patton v. Brady, 184 U.S. 608, 617-618 (1902), taxes upon the sale of grain on an exchange, Nicol v. Ames, 173 U.S. 509, 519 (1899), the sale of corporate stock, *Thomas,* 192 U.S. at 371, doing business in corporate form, *Flint,* 220 U.S. at 151, gross receipts from the "business of refining sugar," *Spreckels,* 192 U.S. at 411, the transfer of property at death, Knowlton v. Moore, 178 U.S. 41, 81-82 (1900), gifts, *Bromley,* 280 U.S. at 138, and income from employment, see Pollock v. Farmers' Loan & Trust Co., 157 U.S. 429, 579 (1895) (*Pollock I*) (citing Springer v. United States, 102 U.S. 586 (1881)).

Murphy and the amici supporting her argue the dividing line between direct and indirect taxes is based upon the ultimate incidence of the tax; if the tax cannot be shifted to someone else, as a capitation cannot, then it is a direct tax; but if the burden can be passed along through a higher price, as a sales tax upon a consumable good can be, then the tax is indirect. This, she argues, was the distinction drawn when the Constitution was ratified. See Albert Gallatin, A Sketch of the Finances of the United States (1796), reprinted in 3 The Writings Of Albert Gallatin 74-75 (Henry Adams ed., Philadelphia, J.P. Lippincott & Co. 1879) ("The most generally received opinion . . . is, that by direct taxes . . . those are meant which are raised on the capital or revenue of the people; by indirect, such as are raised on their expense"); The Federalist No. 36, at 225 (Alexander Hamilton) (Jacob E. Cooke ed., 1961) ("internal taxes[ ] may be subdivided into those of the *direct* and those of the *indirect* kind . . . by which must be understood duties and excises on articles of consumption"). But see Gallatin, supra, at 74 ("[Direct tax] is used, by different writers, and even by the same writers, in different parts of their writings, in a variety of senses, according to that view of the subject they were taking"); Edwin R.A. Seligman, The Income Tax 540 (photo. reprint 1970) (2d ed. 1914) ("there are almost as many classifications of direct and indirect taxes are there are authors"). Moreover, the amici argue, this understanding of the distinction explains the different restrictions imposed respectively upon the power of the Congress to tax directly (apportionment) and via excise (uniformity). Duties, imposts, and excise taxes, which were expected to constitute the bulk of the new federal government's revenue, see Erik M. Jensen, The Apportionment of "Direct Taxes": Are Consumption Taxes Constitutional?, 97 Colum. L. Rev. 2334, 2382 (1997), have a built-in safeguard against oppressively high rates: Higher taxes result in higher prices and therefore fewer sales and ultimately lower tax revenues. See The Federalist No. 21, supra, at 134-135 (Alexander Hamilton). Taxes that cannot be shifted, in contrast, lack this self-regulating feature, and were therefore constrained by the more stringent requirement of apportionment. See id. at 135 ("In a branch of taxation where no limits to the discretion of the government are to be found in the nature of things, the establishment of a fixed rule . . . may be attended with fewer inconveniences than to leave that discretion altogether at large"); see also Jensen, supra, at 2382-2384.

Finally, the amici contend their understanding of a direct tax was confirmed in *Pollock II*, where the Supreme Court noted that "the words 'duties, imposts, and excises' are put in antithesis to direct taxes," 158 U.S. at 622, for which it cited The Federalist No. 36 (Hamilton). *Pollock II,* 158 U.S. at 624-625. As it is clear that Murphy cannot shift her tax burden to anyone else, per Murphy and the amici, it must be a direct tax.

The Government, unsurprisingly, backs a different approach; by its lights, only "taxes that are capable of apportionment in the first instance, specifically, capitation taxes and taxes on land," are direct taxes. The Government maintains that this is how the term was generally understood at the time. See Calvin H. Johnson, Fixing the Constitutional Absurdity of the Apportionment of Direct Tax, 21 Const. Comm. 295, 314 (2004). Moreover, it suggests, this understanding is more in line with the underlying purpose of the tax and the apportionment clauses, which were drafted in the intense light of experience under the Articles of Confederation.

The Articles did not grant the Continental Congress the power to raise revenue directly; it could only requisition funds from the States. See Articles Of Confederation art. VIII (1781); Bruce Ackerman, Taxation and the Constitution, 99 Colum. L. Rev. 1, 6-7 (1999). This led to problems when the States, as they often did, refused to remit funds. See Calvin H. Johnson, The Constitutional Meaning of "Apportionment of Direct Taxes," 80 Tax Notes 591, 593-594 (1998). The Constitution redressed this problem by giving the new national government plenary taxing power. See Ackerman, supra, at 7. In the Government's view, it therefore makes no sense to treat "direct taxes" as encompassing taxes for which apportionment is effectively impossible, because "the Framers could not have intended to give Congress plenary taxing power, on the one hand, and then so limit that power by requiring apportionment for a broad category of taxes, on the other." This view is, according to the Government, buttressed by evidence that the purpose of the apportionment clauses was not in fact to constrain the power to tax, but rather to placate opponents of the compromise over representation of the slave states in the House, as embodied in the Three-fifths Clause.[7] See Ackerman, supra, at 10-11. See generally Seligman, supra, at 548-555. As the Government interprets the historical record, the apportionment limitation was "more symbolic than anything else: it appeased the anti-slavery sentiment of the North and offered a practical advantage to the South as long as the scope

---

7. Many Northern delegates were opposed to the three-fifths compromise on the ground that if slaves were property, then they should not count for the purpose of representation. Apportionment effectively meant that if the slaveholding states were to receive representation in the House for their slaves, then because apportioned taxes must be allocated across states based upon their representation, the slaveholding states would pay more in taxes to the national government than they would have if slaves were not counted at all in determining representation. See Ackerman, supra, at 9. Apportionment was then limited to direct taxes lest it drive the Congress back to reliance upon requisitions from the States. See id. at 9-10.

of direct taxes was limited." See Ackerman, supra, at 10. But see Erik M. Jensen, Taxation and the Constitution: How to Read the Direct Tax Clauses, 15 J.L. & Pol. 687, 704 (1999) ("One of the reasons [the direct tax restriction] worked as a compromise was that it had teeth — it made direct taxes difficult to impose — and it had teeth however slaves were counted").

The Government's view of the clauses is further supported by the near contemporaneous decision of the Supreme Court in Hylton v. United States, 3 U.S. (3 Dall.) 171 (1796), holding that a national tax upon carriages was not a direct tax, and thus not subject to apportionment. Justices Chase and Iredell opined that a "direct tax" was one that, unlike the carriage tax, as a practical matter could be apportioned among the States, id. at 174 (Chase, J.); id. at 181 (Iredell, J.), while Justice Paterson, noting the connection between apportionment and slavery, condemned apportionment as "radically wrong" and "not to be extended by construction," id. at 177-178.[8] As for Murphy's reliance upon *Pollock II*, the Government contends that although it has never been overruled, "every aspect of its reasoning has been eroded," see, e.g., Stanton v. Baltic Mining Co., 240 U.S. 103, 112-113 (1916), and notes that in *Pollock II* itself the Court acknowledged that "taxation on business, privileges, or employments has assumed the guise of an excise tax," 158 U.S. at 635. *Pollock II*, in the Government's view, is therefore too weak a reed to support Murphy's broad definition of "direct tax" and certainly does not make "a tax on the conversion of human capital into money . . . problematic."

Murphy replies that the Government's historical analysis does not respond to the contemporaneous sources she and the amici identified showing that taxes imposed upon individuals are direct taxes. As for *Hylton*, Murphy argues nothing in that decision precludes her position; the Justices viewed the carriage tax there at issue as a tax upon an expense, see 3 U.S. (3 Dall.) at 175 (Chase, J.); see also id. at 180-181 (Paterson, J.), which she agrees is not a direct tax. See *Pollock II*, 158 U.S. at 626-627. To the extent *Hylton* is inconsistent with her position, however, Murphy contends her references to the Federalist are more authoritative evidence of the Framers' understanding of the term.

Murphy makes no attempt to reconcile her definition with the long line of cases identifying various taxes as excise taxes, although several of them seem to refute her position directly. In particular, we do not see how a known excise, such as the estate tax, see, e.g., New York Trust Co. v. Eisner, 256 U.S. 345, 349 (1921); *Knowlton*, 178 U.S. at 81-83, or a tax upon income from employment, see *Pollock II*, 158 U.S. at 635; *Pollock I*, 157 U.S. at 579; cf. Steward Mach. Co. v. Davis, 301 U.S. 548, 580-581 (1937) (tax upon employers based upon wages paid to employees is an excise), can be shifted to another person, absent which they seem to be in irreconcilable conflict

---

8. The other Justice to hear the case, Wilson, J., had previously determined while sitting on the Circuit Court of Virginia, that the tax was not direct and so he did not write a full opinion. Id. at 183-184.

with her position that a tax that cannot be shifted to someone else is a direct tax. Though it could be argued that the incidence of an estate tax is inevitably shifted to the beneficiaries, we see at work none of the restraint upon excessive taxation that Murphy claims such shifting is supposed to provide; the tax is triggered by an event, death, that cannot be shifted or avoided. In any event, *Knowlton* addressed the argument that *Pollock I* and *II* made ability to shift the hallmark of a direct tax, and rejected it. 178 U.S. at 81-82. Regardless what the original understanding may have been, therefore, we are bound to follow the Supreme Court, which has strongly intimated that Murphy's position is not the law.

That said, neither need we adopt the Government's position that direct taxes are only those capable of satisfying the constraint of apportionment. In the abstract, such a constraint is no constraint at all; virtually any tax may be apportioned by establishing different rates in different states. See *Pollock II*, 158 U.S. at 632-633. If the Government's position is instead that by "capable of apportionment" it means "capable of apportionment in a manner that does not unfairly tax some individuals more than others," then it is difficult to see how a land tax, which is widely understood to be a direct tax, could be apportioned by population without similarly imposing significantly non-uniform rates. See *Hylton*, 3 U.S. (3 Dall.) at 178-179 (Paterson, J.); Johnson, Constitutional Absurdity, supra, at 328. But see, e.g., *Hylton*, 3 U.S. (3 Dall.) at 183 (Iredell, J.) (contending land tax is capable of apportionment).

We find it more appropriate to analyze this case based upon the precedents and therefore to ask whether the tax laid upon Murphy's award is more akin, on the one hand, to a capitation or a tax upon one's ownership of property, or, on the other hand, more like a tax upon a use of property, a privilege, an activity, or a transaction, see *Thomas*, 192 U.S. at 370. Even if we assume one's human capital should be treated as personal property, it does not appear that this tax is upon ownership; rather, as the Government points out, Murphy is taxed only after she receives a compensatory award, which makes the tax seem to be laid upon a transaction. See Tyler v. United States, 281 U.S. 497, 502 (1930) ("A tax laid upon the happening of an event, as distinguished from its tangible fruits, is an indirect tax which Congress, in respect of some events . . . undoubtedly may impose"); Simmons v. United States, 308 F.2d 160, 166 (4th Cir. 1962) (tax upon receipt of money is not a direct tax); cf. *Penn Mut.*, 277 F.2d at 20. Murphy's situation seems akin to an involuntary conversion of assets; she was forced to surrender some part of her mental health and reputation in return for monetary damages. Cf. 26 U.S.C. §1033 (property involuntarily converted into money is taxed to extent of gain recognized).

At oral argument Murphy resisted this formulation on the ground that the receipt of an award in lieu of lost mental health or reputation is not a transaction. This view is tenable, however, only if one decouples Murphy's injury (emotional distress and lost reputation) from her monetary award, but that is not beneficial to Murphy's cause, for then Murphy has nothing to offset the obvious accession to her wealth, which is taxable as income. Murphy also suggested at oral argument that there was no transaction because she did not profit. Whether she profited is irrelevant, however, to whether a tax upon an award of damages is a direct tax requiring apportionment; profit is relevant only to whether, if it is a direct tax, it nevertheless need not be apportioned because the object of the tax is income within the meaning of the Sixteenth Amendment. Cf. *Spreckels,* 192 U.S. at 412-413 (tax upon gross receipts associated with business of refining sugar not a direct tax); *Penn Mut.,* 277 F.2d at 20 (tax upon gross receipts deemed valid indirect tax despite taxpayer's net loss).

So we return to the question: Is a tax upon this particular kind of transaction equivalent to a tax upon a person or his property? Cf. *Bromley,* 280 U.S. at 138 (assuming without deciding that a tax "levied upon all the uses to which property may be put, or upon the exercise of a single power indispensable to the enjoyment of all others over it, would be in effect a tax upon property"). Murphy did not receive her damages pursuant to a business activity, cf. *Flint,* 220 U.S. at 151; *Spreckels,* 192 U.S. at 411, and we therefore do not view this tax as an excise under that theory. See Stratton's Independence, Ltd. v. Howbert, 231 U.S. 399, 414-415 (1913) ("The sale outright of a mining property might be fairly described as a mere conversion of the capital from land into money"). On the other hand, as noted above, the Supreme Court several times has held a tax not related to business activity is nonetheless an excise. And the tax at issue here is similar to those.

Bromley, in which a gift tax was deemed an excise, is particularly instructive: The Court noted it was "a tax laid only upon the exercise of a single one of those powers incident to ownership," 280 U.S. at 136, which distinguished it from "a tax which falls upon the owner merely because he is owner, regardless of the use or disposition made of his property," id. at 137. A gift is the functional equivalent of a below-market sale; it therefore stands to reason that if, as *Bromley* holds, a gift tax, or a tax upon a below-market sale, is a tax laid not upon ownership but upon the exercise of a power "incident to ownership," then a tax upon the sale of property at fair market value is similarly laid upon an incidental power and not upon ownership, and hence is an excise. Therefore, even if we were to accept Murphy's argument that the human capital concept is reflected in the Sixteenth Amendment, a tax upon the involuntary conversion of that capital would still be an excise and not subject to the requirement of apportionment. But see *Nicol,* 173 U.S. at 521 (indicating pre-*Bromley* that tax upon "every sale made in any place . . . is really and practically upon property").

In any event, even if a tax upon the sale of property is a direct tax upon the property itself, we do not believe Murphy's situation involves a tax "upon the sale itself, considered separate and apart from the place and the circumstances of the sale." Id. at 520. Instead, as in *Nicol,* this tax is more akin to "a duty upon the facilities made use of and actually employed in the transaction." Id. at 519. To be sure, the facility used in *Nicol* was a commodities exchange whereas the facility used by Murphy was the legal system, but that hardly seems a significant distinction. The tax may be laid upon the proceeds received when one vindicates a statutory right, but the right is nonetheless a "creature of law," which *Knowlton* identifies as a "privilege" taxable by excise. 178 U.S. at 55 (right to take property by inheritance is granted by law and therefore taxable as upon a privilege);[9] cf. *Steward*, 301 U.S. at 580-581 ("[N]atural rights, so called, are as much subject to taxation as rights of less importance. An excise is not limited to vocations or activities that may be prohibited altogether. . . . It extends to vocations or activities pursued as of common right.") (footnote omitted).

2. UNIFORMITY

The Congress may not implement an excise tax that is not "uniform throughout the United States." U.S. Const. art. I, §8, cl. 1. A "tax is uniform when it operates with the same force and effect in every place where the subject of it is found." United States v. Ptasynski, 462 U.S. 74, 82 (1983) (internal quotation marks omitted); see also *Knowlton,* 178 U.S. at 84-86. The tax laid upon an award of damages for a nonphysical personal injury operates with "the same force and effect" throughout the United States and therefore satisfies the requirement of uniformity.

III. CONCLUSION

For the foregoing reasons, we conclude (1) Murphy's compensatory award was not received on account of personal physical injuries, and therefore is not exempt from taxation pursuant to §104(a)(2) of the IRC; (2) the award is part of her "gross income," as defined by §61 of the IRC; and (3) the tax upon the award is an excise and not a direct tax subject to the apportionment requirement of Article I, Section 9 of the Constitution. The tax is uniform throughout the United States and therefore passes constitutional muster. The judgment of the district court is accordingly

Affirmed.

Note

In the founding era the term *direct tax* lacked a generally understood meaning, and as a result the scope of apportionment has never been clear. Indeed, Madison's notes on debates in the Constitutional Convention report that Rufus King "asked what was the precise meaning of *direct* taxation?" to

---

9. For the same reason, we infer from *Knowlton* that a tax laid upon an amount received in settlement of a suit for a personal nonphysical injury would also be an excise. See 178 U.S. at 55.

which "No one answ[ere]d." 2 Records of the Federal Convention of 1787, at 350 (Max Farrand ed. 1966). What is clear is that apportionment is antithetical to fairness in the distribution of the tax burden. In Pollock v. Farmers' Loan & Trust Co., 158 U.S. 601 (1895), the Supreme Court held the 1894 income tax unconstitutional because its tax on income from real and personal property (rents and dividends) amounted to an unapportioned direct tax on the property itself. Under existing precedents, Congress had the power to immediately reenact a uniform nationwide income tax simply by exempting income from property, yet it declined to do so, instead waiting almost 20 years until ratification of the Sixteenth Amendment allowed it to impose an unapportioned tax on income from both labor and capital. This reluctance shows that the Sixteenth Amendment was not required to enable Congress to raise revenue by income taxation, but to empower it to raise revenue *fairly*. Unfortunately, however, the Sixteenth Amendment, by its terms, does not repeal the direct tax clause, it merely exempts income taxes from population apportionment. Consequently, if Congress were to adopt an alternative tax base, such as a value-added tax or a progressive consumption tax, there would surely be a constitutional challenge to the new system with debate centering on the meaning of direct tax.

3. Punitive Damages

The treatment of punitive damages under §104(a)(2) has been one of continual controversy, and somewhat intertwined with the treatment of nonphysical injuries. Indeed, in *Roemer* (discussed at p. 98 above) there were punitive damages that the Tax Court held taxable citing *Glenshaw Glass*. The court of appeals asserted that §104(a)(2) took them out of *Glenshaw*. In 1989, §104(a)(2) was amended by providing that it would not apply to punitive damages for nonphysical injuries. That amendment was read by some of the Justices as implying or confirming that compensatory damages for nonphysical injuries and punitive damages for physical injuries were within the protection of §104(a)(2). Nevertheless the Supreme Court ruled (6-3) in O'Gilvie v. United States, 519 U.S. 79 (1996), that punitive damages in a tort action for death, brought by the surviving husband and the decedent's estate, were not received "on account of" personal injuries within the meaning of §104(a)(2) and were therefore taxable. This decision came at the end of the year in which the Congress had come to the same conclusion, for the future, by legislation. Note what §104(c) has to say about punitive damages in some wrongful death actions.

Question

The exclusion of "any damages" received on account of physical injuries or physical sickness obviates serious administrative problems that would arise in applying the *Raytheon* test to a general jury verdict or an unallocated settlement. To what extent does the exception for punitive damages reintroduce these problems?

C. INSURANCE

Damages are not the only means of relief from the burden of losses imposed by personal or business injuries. For some types of loss, insurance compensation is commonly available. (Indeed, insurance typically provides the funds to finance a personal injury settlement or damage award.) How should insurance proceeds be taxed? Does the *Raytheon* replacement rule hold sway? Does the type of insurance — property, casualty, medical, disability, or life insurance — matter? Does the tax status of policy proceeds depend on the treatment of insurance premiums, and is the payment of premiums deductible? Should the purchase of insurance be viewed as an investment, with the policyholder deriving a gain or loss according to whether she receives proceeds that are greater or less than the amount paid for coverage?

Here we briefly explore the tax treatment of medical, disability, and life insurance, and we compare the deduction for extraordinary medical expenses (the self-insurance alternative).

1. Medical Insurance

There are three common ways to finance the cost of health care. Many taxpayers participate in employer-provided group health insurance plans, others purchase individual health insurance policies, and some simply pay for their health care expenses out of their salary, savings, or other resources as they are incurred (i.e., self-insurance). How does the tax treatment of these alternative funding methods compare?

Funding Method	Tax Treatment of Insurance for "Medical Care"	
	Premiums	*Proceeds*
Employer-Provided Coverage	Excluded, §106	Excluded, §105(b)
Individually Purchased Insurance	Limited Deduction, §213(d)(1)(D)	Excluded, §104(a)(3)
Self-Insurance	N/A	Limited Deduction, §213(a)

Does this pattern make sense? Observe that all amounts actually expended for medical care are tax free, if one ignores the limits of section 213.

- Proceeds of employer-provided insurance excluded by §105(b);
- proceeds of individual insurance policy excluded by §104(a)(3);
- individual payment of medical expenses (self insurance) deductible by §213; and
- proceeds of PI tort claim excluded by §104(a)(2).

The section 213 medical expense deduction is subject to two important limits, however, that are designed to distinguish ordinary from extraordinary medical expenses. First, a deduction is allowed only to the extent that the aggregate of all medical expenses within the year exceed 7.5 percent of adjusted gross income (AGI). Second, the medical expense deduction is itemized, §§63(d), 62, so that there is no tax savings unless the aggregate of all itemized deductions exceeds the standard deduction ($5,000 for a joint return, indexed for inflation to $11,400 in 2009).

Notes and Questions

1. *Incentive effects.* Consider both ends of the insurance transaction: premiums *and* proceeds. Observe that employer-paid premiums are excludible in full, but individually paid premiums are "excludible" only via a limited deduction. Clearly, coverage under an employer-provided group health insurance program is the most advantageous alternative because both ends of the transaction are entirely tax free! Consequently, employment-based health benefits are the most prevalent form of health care coverage in the United States. In 2007, 62.2 percent of the nonelderly (i.e., younger than 65 years) population had employment-based health benefits, while the rate of individually purchased health coverage consistently hovers around 7 percent. About 18 percent of the nonelderly population is uninsured, or "self insured." (The rest of the population receives some form of public coverage, such as Medicaid or the State Children's Health Insurance Program.) Paul Fronstin, Sources of Health Insurance and Characteristics of the Uninsured: Analysis of the March 2008 Current Population Survey, EBRI Issue Brief No. 321 (Sep. 2008). Recently, "exclusion of employer contributions for medical insurance premiums and medical care" has been identified as the single largest tax expenditure in the budget of the United States, estimated to cost $168 billion in lost tax revenue for Fiscal Year 2009 (and $1,052 billion over the five years 2009-2013). See Table [8-2] in Chapter 8B below.

2. *Second best.* Of the remaining alternatives (individually provided health insurance and self-insurance), the tax code actually favors self-insurance. Do you see why? Over the long haul and on average, policyholders

will pay about as much in premiums as the amount of their covered medical expenses (ignoring the insurer's administrative costs and profit), but this is not true on an annual basis. Consider a taxpayer who pays premiums of $6,000 per year for five years but has no covered expenses until year five, in which she incurs $30,000 in medical bills. If she buys insurance, the non-deductible 7.5 percent AGI floor under the section 213 deduction affects this taxpayer every year as she pays her premiums, but if she self-insures she is caught by it only once, in year five when she pays the medical bills out of her own pocket.

3. *Health benefit costs.* In 2007 health care benefits contributed 7.1 percent of total compensation cost for workers in private industry (10.0 percent of average wages). Employee Benefit Research Institute, EBRI Databook on Employee Benefits, Table 3.2c (April 2008), *http:// www.ebri.org/pdf/publications/books/databook/DB.Chapter%2002.pdf.* The Kaiser Family Foundation reports that the average annual total health care premium contribution for covered workers in 2007 was $4,479 for worker-only coverage and $12,106 for family coverage. Workers contributed $3,281 toward the total family coverage premium, while employers paid $8,824. Kaiser Family Foundation & Health Research and Educational Trust, Employer Health Benefits: 2007 Annual Survey, Exhibit B at 2 (2008), *http://www.kff.org/insurance/7672/ upload/76723.pdf.* Perhaps most alarming is the rapid growth rate of health insurance costs relative to income and consumer prices generally. According to a study commissioned by the Robert Wood Johnson Foundation, the national average cost of family health insurance coverage increased from $8,281 in 2001 to $10,728 in 2005, a 30 percent increase over a four-year period, during which the median income of those with family health insurance coverage increased only 3 percent. State Health Access Data Assistance Center, Squeezed: How Costs for Insuring Families are Outpacing Income (April 2008), *http://www.rwjf.org/coverage/product.jsp?id=28711.*

4. *Contributory plans: premium cost sharing and §125.* Wholly employer-financed health care (noncontributory coverage) has become rare as costs have risen. On average, workers must contribute more than 25 percent of the cost of employment-based family health care coverage, or about 15 percent for worker-only coverage. The employee's share of the cost of coverage will qualify as "medical care" under §213(d)(1)(D), but the presence of insurance makes it unlikely that the employee will have other substantial unreimbursed medical care expenses for the year, with the result that her contribution toward the premiums will generate little or no medical expense deduction (i.e., will not surpass 7.5 percent of AGI). If the employer has a written plan that allows employees to elect to pay their share of premiums by salary reduction, however, the arrangement may qualify as a cafeteria plan under §125, and payments made pursuant to such an election are treated as pre-tax employer contributions rather than after-tax employee contributions (i.e., §106 rather than §213 will apply). How does §125 relate to *Old Colony Trust Co.* (Chapter 2A above)?

5. *Out-of-pocket expenses: flexible spending arrangements.* Regardless of who pays the premiums, most health care plans do not offer complete protection; instead they include coinsurance features to encourage cost consciousness. Covered individuals may bear part of the cost of their care because the plan imposes "deductibles" (e.g., first $200 per person of annual expenses not insured), requires fixed copayments for certain services or goods (e.g., patient pays $20 per physician office visit, $75 per emergency room visit, or $15 per prescription), or pays only a specified percentage of certain costs (e.g., 80 percent of inpatient hospital charges). Such out-of-pocket costs constitute medical care expenses but are unlikely to exceed the non-deductible floor of §213, even if combined with a share of the premiums. Here again, with proper planning, the cafeteria plan rules of §125 can come to the rescue, magically transforming nondeductible employee expenses into excludible employer-provided health benefits.

The regulations under §125 authorize an employer-created program known as a flexible spending arrangement (FSA), which can be used to pay or reimburse otherwise uninsured out-of-pocket employee medical care expenses. The FSA is typically funded by participating employees, who elect to forego a portion of their pay for the upcoming year, directing it instead to their FSA accounts, although the employer may make non-elective contributions as well. (The salary reduction election, which is a choice between cash and a qualified benefit (health care), satisfies the definition of a cafeteria plan.) A health FSA (often called a medical care spending account) generally may reimburse only substantiated out-of-pocket medical expenses (as defined by §213) incurred during a 12-month coverage period, although the plan may allow unused amounts to be paid for medical expenses incurred during a grace period of not more than two months and fifteen days following the close of the plan year. Adequate substantiation generally requires a receipt or other written statement from an independent third-party showing the expense that was incurred (i.e., nature, date, and amount of medical care provided), together with a written statement from the participant that the expense is not covered by any other health insurance. If special substantiation rules are followed, participants may be issued debit cards to pay for medical services and eligible drug store and pharmacy purchases directly, instead of requesting reimbursement by submitting receipts to the plan administrator after the fact. The amount of coverage selected for the year (generally, the amount of salary reduction) must be available to reimburse eligible expenses without regard to the time they are incurred during the year, and so an employee who elects $600 in coverage and has major uninsured dental work in January must be reimbursed up to the annual account limit ($600) even though she is funding her account by salary reduction only at the rate of $50 per month. Any unused amount remaining in the account at the end of the coverage period (12-month plan year, plus grace period, if applicable) must be forfeited under a use-it-or-lose-it rule; the residue cannot be carried over to the following period or refunded to the account holder. The election to contribute to the FSA generally must be made in advance of the coverage year and is irrevocable, but mid-year changes in response to certain family and employment status changes are permitted. Prop. Reg. §§1.125-5 (general FSA requirements), -1(e) (grace period), -6 (substantiation, including debit card rules), -2 (election rules). Although used to pay out-of-pocket health care costs, FSA contributions are characterized for tax purposes as employer-provided health care coverage (excludible under §106), while payments from the account are viewed as proceeds of employer-provided medical care insurance (excludible under §105(b)).

In 2007, 51 percent of individuals who worked in private industry for an establishment having at least 100 employees were offered medical spending accounts, but only 17 percent of those working for firms with less than 100 employees had access to such accounts. Bureau of Labor Statistics, U.S. Department of Labor, National Compensation Survey: Employee Benefits in Private Industry in the United States, March 2007, at 34, available at *http://stats.bls.gov/ncs/ebs/sp/ebsm0006.pdf.*

6. *Cap on coverage exclusion.* Despite coinsurance features in health care plans, many analysts are convinced that widespread group insurance has actually increased health care cost inflation by stimulating excessive demand due to the phenomenon know as *moral hazard.* Moral hazard refers to the tendency of insurance to induce excessive risk taking as a result of the insured's insulation from the full cost of his actions. An individual with health care coverage has little incentive to forego additional procedures or to take precautions that would reduce the need for medical care (for example, smoking cessation, controlling diet and exercise, or limiting participation in risky activities such as certain sports). The Treasury's 1984 tax reform study included a proposal to limit the exclusion of employee medical coverage to $70 per month for individual medical coverage and $175 per month for family coverage.[2] The thinking was that limiting the preferential tax treatment of health care coverage would create pressure to keep employer contributions under the cap, because workers would prefer additional wages to nonessential health benefits if the cost of the latter were, like wages, fully taxable. This pressure would induce cost-saving changes that would reorient health benefit programs to focus on the core function of insurance, protection from extraordinary and unpredictable medical care needs. Plans might be amended by dropping some coverage (e.g., vision or dental care), by increasing employee out-of-pocket expenses (raising insurance deductibles and copayments), or by encouraging preventive care. While not enacted in

---

2. U.S. Department of the Treasury, Tax Reform for Fairness, Simplicity, and Economic Growth 23-27 (1984). This document was the work of a team of economists and lawyers in the Treasury Department charged with indicating just how our income tax ought ideally to be reformed. It was produced in an atmosphere that appears to have been quite effectively isolated from immediate political pressures, and it has been generally applauded by tax policy professionals. It served to a very considerable extent as a starting point for the complex political negotiations that culminated in the Tax Reform Act of 1986.

1986, similar proposals have been advanced by succeeding Administrations, both Republican and Democratic. A recent version of the proposal would have placed an annual cap on the §106 exclusion set at $5,000 for individual coverage and $11,500 for family coverage in 2006. Paul Fronstin, The Tax Treatment of Health Insurance and Employment-Based Health Benefits, EBRI Issue Brief No. 294 (June 2006). Although mandatory across-the-board limits on §106 have not passed, Congress and the Bush Administration have each authorized new optional cost-containment strategies of their own: health savings accounts and health reimbursement arrangements.

7. *Health savings accounts, §223.* An individual who has only high deductible health plan coverage (major medical insurance covering only extraordinary costs) is permitted to save for routine medical care expenses through a tax-preferred health savings account (HSA). A high deductible health plan is defined under §223(c)(2)(A) as a plan with an annual deductible that is not less than $1,150 for self-only coverage or $2,300 for family coverage (in 2009), which provides that the maximum annual out-of-pocket expenses (deductibles, copayments, and other amounts, but not premiums) may not exceed $5,800 for self-only coverage or $11,600 for family coverage. In 2009 an individual with self-only coverage under a high deductible heath plan may deduct up to $3,000 in contributions to an HSA, while an individual with family coverage under a high deductible health plan can make up to $5,950 in deductible HSA contributions regardless of whether the taxpayer itemizes deductions. §§223(b)(2), 62(a)(19); Rev. Proc. 2008-29, 2008-22 I.R.B. 1039. (Observe that the deduction for HSA contributions is not subject to §213's limits on the deduction of health insurance premiums.) Investment earnings of an HSA are not taxed, and distributions used to pay for uninsured medical care for the account beneficiary or his spouse or dependents are not included in gross income. §223(e)(1), (f)(1). In other words, both HSA contributions and proceeds may be entirely tax free. Cost consciousness (consumer discipline) is achieved in two ways: first, amounts saved on health care now continue to be available to fund more urgent needs in the future, and second, amounts not ultimately needed for health care can be used for other purposes. Distributions not used to pay for medical care are included in gross income, and an additional (penalty) tax of 10 percent is imposed to discourage use of an HSA as a tax-deferral vehicle, but the penalty tax is waived once the account beneficiary is eligible for Medicare (i.e., reaches the age of 65), becomes disabled, or dies. An employer may contribute to an eligible employee's HSA (instead of the account beneficiary contributing his own resources), and such employer funding is treated as excludible employer-provided health care coverage per §106(d).

8. *Health reimbursement arrangements.* In 2002 the IRS announced that a certain type of medical expense reimbursement program, which it labeled a "health reimbursement arrangement" (HRA), would be treated as employer-provided accident or health plan benefits excludible under

§§106 and 105(b). Rev. Rul. 2002-41, 1002-28 I.R.B. 75; Notice 2002-45, 2002-28 I.R.B. 93. An HRA reimburses the employee for medical care expenses (as defined in §213(d)) incurred by the employee or her spouse or dependents up to a maximum dollar amount per coverage period, and provides that any unused allowance at the end of the period is carried forward to increase the maximum reimbursement amount in subsequent periods. This carryforward may even continue past the worker's retirement or other termination of employment, and the resulting savings feature creates the incentive to economize (induces participants to act as price-sensitive health care consumers, that is). Unlike a flexible spending arrangement, an HRA is not subject to the use-it-or-lose-it principle (contrast §125(d)(2) and Prop. Reg. §1.125-5(c)), and unlike a health savings account, HRA balances may not be used for any purpose other than medical care (contrast §223(f)). An HRA must be funded solely by the employer (elective salary reduction would trigger the cafeteria plan rules and their prohibition on deferred compensation), but it may be combined with other employer-provided health benefit programs, such as major medical insurance or other limited or catastrophic coverage.

9. *Information and adverse selection.* Both health savings accounts and health reimbursement arrangements tend to instill an incentive to shop wisely. (Query whether consumers have access to adequate information about the quality of medical services, or the ability to evaluate price-quality trade-offs?) These devices may be attractive to small employers who cannot afford to provide their workers with a comprehensive health benefit package. Some companies that have traditional broad-based health coverage in place have begun to allow their workers to choose a high deductible health plan combined with coverage under either HSA or HRA as an alternative to continued coverage under the traditional plan. Optional institution of such "consumer-driven health plans" (as the combination of high deductible coverage with an HSA or HRA program is sometimes called) raises concerns about adverse selection: Relatively healthy workers can be expected to select the consumer-driven plan, leaving a group of employees covered under the traditional plan that is likely to make greater than average demands on the health care system. Insuring the pool of higher-risk employees raises the cost of traditional coverage, inducing more workers to select the consumer-driven alternative, which might lead to the eventual unraveling of the traditional health insurance coverage.

10. *Proposed standard deduction for health insurance.* In 2007 the Bush Administration proposed a radical change in the tax treatment of health care. Its plan would repeal the existing exclusion for employment-based health benefits, §§105 and 106, the itemized deduction for extraordinary medical expenses, §213, as well as §162(*l*), which allows self-employed individuals to deduct their health insurance premiums. Those allowances would be replaced with a new "standard deduction for health insurance" in the amount of $15,000 for family coverage or $7,500 for single coverage. The

standard deduction would be allowed only to individuals that have certain qualifying health insurance coverage (determined on a monthly basis, with one-twelfth of the specified annual deduction granted per month), whether that coverage is individually purchased or employer-provided (the value of employer coverage would be included in gross income due to the repeal of §106). The amount deductible, however, would not be tied to the actual cost of insurance — the deduction would be set at the specified dollar amount ($15,000/$7,500) regardless of whether the taxpayer (or her employer) actually spent more or less than that amount on health insurance.

> The new SDHI [Standard Deduction for Health Insurance] would address the rising cost of health insurance by removing the tax bias for more expensive insurance, while also providing a potent incentive for the uninsured to purchase insurance. The proposal would break the link between the value of the tax subsidy and the amount of insurance a worker purchases. The proposal also would level the playing field between less expensive and more expensive health insurance, and between wages and employer-provided health insurance.
>
> Individuals and families would have a strong incentive to purchase insurance under the proposal. However, the insurance they choose to purchase would be based on their needs and circumstances rather than the tax bias in favor of health insurance and against wages. The tax bias for overly generous insurance would be eliminated. This change would translate into greater price sensitivity for health care consumers. Many of those with employer-based insurance would take advantage of the level playing field between wages and health insurance by receiving higher wages in exchange for less expensive health insurance.

U.S. Department of the Treasury, General Explanation of the Administration's Fiscal Year 2008 Revenue Proposals 18-24 (Feb. 2007), available at *http://www.ustreas.gov/offices/tax-policy/library/bluebk07.pdf.* Evaluate this recommendation from the standpoint of both tax policy and national health care policy. Do you agree with Senator Edward M. Kennedy's observation, made in 1976, that "We already have a national health insurance program and its being run by the Internal Revenue Service"? Edward M. Kennedy, Second Thoughts — The IRS Health Insurance Program, Human Behavior (Sept. 1976).

2. Deducting Extraordinary Medical Expenses (Self-Insurance)

In the case of extraordinary medical expenses, the statute takes a step beyond excluding compensation: If there is no compensation, by insurance or otherwise, the statute allows a deduction. This has the same effect, essentially, as allowing an exclusion of an amount of income equal to the deduction, without regard to its source; the taxpayer is treated as using part of her income to offset the loss and accordingly is relieved of tax, whether or not any income was paid for that purpose.

The statutory provision for deducting medical expenses is §213. Enacted in 1942 (a year when many refinements of the income tax were made in connection with the introduction of wartime rates), it has raised its share of both interpretive and policy questions.

OCHS v. COMMISSIONER
195 F. 2d 692 (2d Cir.), cert. denied, 344 U.S. 827 (1952)

Before Augustus N. Hand, Chase and Frank, Circuit Judges.

AUGUSTUS N. HAND, Circuit Judge. The question raised by this appeal is whether the taxpayer Samuel Ochs was entitled under [§213] to deduct the sum of $1,456.50 paid by him for maintaining his two minor children in day school and boarding school as medical expenses incurred for the benefit of his wife. The pertinent sections of the Internal Revenue Code and the Regulations are [§§213, 262; Reg. §1.213-1(e)(1)].

The Tax Court made the following findings:

"During the taxable year petitioner was the husband of Helen H. Ochs. They had two children, Josephine age six and Jeanne age four.

"On December 10, 1943, a thyroidectomy was performed on petitioner's wife. A histological examination disclosed a papillary carcinoma of the thyroid with multiple lymph node metastes, according to the surgeon's report. During the taxable year the petitioner maintained his two children in day school during the first half of the year and in boarding school during the latter half of the year at a cost of $1,456.50. Petitioner deducted the sum from his income for the year 1946 as a medical expense under [§213].

"During the taxable year, as a result of the operation on December 10, 1943, petitioner's wife was unable to speak above a whisper. Efforts of petitioner's wife to speak were painful, required much of her strength, and left her in a highly nervous state. Petitioner was advised by the operating surgeon that his wife suffered from cancer of the throat, a condition which was fatal in many cases. He advised extensive X-ray treatment after the operation. Petitioner became alarmed when, by 1946, his wife's voice had failed to improve, and believed that the irritation and nervousness caused by attempting to care for the children at a time when she could scarcely speak above a whisper might cause a recurrence of the cancer. Petitioner and his wife consulted a reputable physician and were advised by him that if the children were not separated from petitioner's wife she would not improve and her nervousness and irritation might cause a recurrence of the cancer. Petitioner continued to maintain his children in boarding school after the taxable year here involved until up to the end of five years following the operation of December 10, 1943, petitioner having been advised that if there was no recurrence of the cancer during that time his wife could be considered as having recovered from the cancer.

"During the taxable year petitioner's income was between $5,000 and $6,000. Petitioner's two children have not attended private school but have lived at home and attended public school since a period beginning five years after the operation of December 10, 1943. Petitioner's purpose in sending the children to boarding school during the year 1946 was to alleviate his wife's pain and suffering in caring for the children by reason of her inability to speak above a whisper and to prevent a recurrence of the cancer which was responsible for the condition of her voice. He also thought it would be good for the children to be away from their mother as much as possible while she was unable to speak to them above a whisper.

"Petitioner's wife was employed part of her time in 1946 as a typist and stenographer. On account of the impairment which existed in her voice she found it difficult to hold a position and was only able to do part-time work. At the time of the hearing of this proceeding in 1951, she had recovered the use of her voice and seems to have entirely recovered from her throat cancer."

The Tax Court said in its opinion that it had no reason to doubt the good faith and truthfulness of the taxpayer and that his devotion and consideration for his wife were altogether admirable, but it nevertheless held that the expense of sending the children to school was not deductible as a medical expense under the provisions of [§213].

In our opinion the expenses incurred by the taxpayer were non-deductible family expenses within the meaning of [§262] of the Code rather than medical expenses. Concededly the line between the two is a difficult one to draw, but this only reflects the fact that expenditures made on behalf of some members of a family unit frequently benefit others in the family as well. The wife in this case had in the past contributed the services of caring for the children — for which the husband was required to pay because, owing to her illness, she could no longer care for them. If, for example, the husband had employed a governess for the children, or a cook, the wages he would have paid would not be deductible. Or, if the wife had died, and the children were sent to a boarding school, there would certainly be no basis for contending that such expenses were deductible. The examples given serve to illustrate that the expenses here were made necessary by the loss of the wife's services, and that the only reason for allowing them as a deduction is that the wife also received a benefit. We think it unlikely that Congress intended to transform family expenses into medical expenses for this reason. The decision of the Tax Court is further supported by its conclusion that the expenditures were to some extent at least incurred while the wife was acting as a typist in order to earn money for the family. We do not think that the decisions discussed in the opinion of the Tax Court and the briefs of the parties have any real bearing upon the issues involved in this appeal.

The decision is affirmed.

FRANK, Circuit Judge (dissenting). Human considerations in revenue laws are undeniably exceptional. But there is no good reason why, when, for once, Congress, although seeking revenue, shows it has a heart, the courts should try to make it beat feebly. Here is a man earning between $5,000 and $6,000 a year. His wife was operated on for cancer three years earlier and has still not regained the use of her voice. The doctor says that she will not get any better—may indeed have a recurrence of the cancer, this time surely fatal—unless she is separated from her two children, aged six and four. The children are young, healthy, active and irrepressible; their mother cannot speak above a whisper without pain. She becomes ever more nervous and irritable when they are around; her voice does not improve when it should. The father (instead of sending her to a sanitarium) sends the children away to school and seeks to deduct the cost therefor as a "medical expense."

The Commissioner, the Tax Court, and now my colleagues, are certain Congress did not intend relief for a man in this grave plight. The truth is, of course, no one knows what Congress would have said if it had been faced with these facts. The few paltry sentences of Congressional history for [§213] do not lend strong support—indeed any support at all—to a strict construction theory:

> This allowance is granted in consideration of the heavy tax burden that must be borne by industry during the existing emergency and of the desirability of maintaining the present high level of public health and morale. . . . The term "medical care" is broadly defined to include amounts paid for the diagnoses, care, mitigation, treatment, or prevention of disease, or for the purpose of affecting any structure or function of the body. It is not intended, however, that a deduction should be allowed for any expense that is not incurred primarily for the prevention or alleviation of a physical or mental defect or illness.[1]

I think that Congress would have said that this man's expense fell within the category of "mitigation, treatment, or prevention of disease," and that it was for the "purpose of affecting [a] structure or function of the body." The Commissioner argued, successfully in the Tax Court, that, because the money spent was only indirectly for the sake of the wife's health and directly for the children's maintenance, it could not qualify as a "medical expense." Much is made of the fact that the children themselves were healthy and normal—and little of the fact that it was their very health and normality which were draining away the mother's strength. The Commissioner seemingly admits that the deduction might be a medical expense if the wife were sent away from her children to a sanitarium for rest and quiet, but asserts that it never can be if, for the very same purpose, the children are sent away from the mother—even if a boarding-school for the children is cheaper than a sanitarium for the wife. I cannot believe that Congress intended such a meaningless distinction, that it meant to rule out all kinds of therapeutic treatment applied indirectly rather than directly—even though indirect treatment be "primarily for the . . . alleviation of a physical or mental defect

1. Sen. Rep. 1631, 77th Cong., 2d Sess. (1942) 95-96.

or illness."[2] The cure ought to be the doctor's business, not the Commissioner's.

The only sensible criterion of a "medical expense"—and I think this criterion satisfies Congressional caution without destroying what little humanity remains in the Internal Revenue Code—should be that the taxpayer, in incurring the expense, was guided by a physician's bona fide advice that such a treatment was necessary to the patient's recovery from, or prevention of, a specific ailment.

Indeed, a test for [§213] applicability, much akin to the one I have in mind, was adopted by the Tax Court in Havey v. Commissioner, 12 T.C. 409, 412:

> In determining allowability, many factors must be considered. Consideration should be accorded the motive or purpose of the taxpayer, but such factor is not alone determinative. To accord it conclusive weight would make nugatory the prohibition against allowing personal, living, or family expenses. Thus also it is important to inquire as to the origin of the expense. Was it incurred at the direction or suggestion of a physician; did the treatment bear directly on the physical condition in question; did the treatment bear such a direct or proximate therapeutic relation to the bodily condition as to justify a reasonable belief the same would be efficacious; was the treatment in proximate time so near to the onset or recurrence of the disease or condition as to make one the true occasion of the other, thus eliminating expense incurred for general, as contrasted with some specific physical improvement.

This taxpayer can, I think, meet every requirement of the *Havey* test. (1) *Motive:* Ochs could have no motive but his wife's health in sending the children away. They had never attended before—nor have they attended since—private schools. A man earning less than $6,000 with three dependents would not normally send his children to boarding school. The four-year-old would most likely have stayed home; the six-year-old, if she went to school at all, would have gone to a free public school. Day school and boarding school were indispensable only because they filled up the children's play and leisure hours—when they would have harassed their mother. The Commissioner doesn't argue that Ochs chose a more expensive school than he had to; nor even that the wife might have been more economically sent away from home. He does suggest, however, that, since the change benefitted the children as well as the mother, it cannot be considered a medical expense

2. The Commissioner has, in the past, shown more liberal tendencies in sanctioning somewhat unorthodox kinds of treatment as contemplated by the statute: He has allowed the deduction of fees paid to chiropractors and Christian Science practitioners. I.T. 3598, 1943 CB 157. Bureau letter, February 2, 1943. 433 CCH, Fed. Tax. Rep. §6175. He should not, in this context, lag behind the progress of the medical art. Especially in this case should the Commissioner realize the growing emphasis placed by medical practitioners upon peace of mind as a major factor in the recovery of patients from what were formerly thought to be entirely organic diseases. If the wife here had been recovering from a nervous breakdown, it could not be sensibly argued that the cure did not fit the disease. Are we ready now to discount the uncontroverted evidence of the doctor in this case that peace of mind and body (it takes not only mental but physical gymnastics to keep up with two children aged four and six) was essential to recovery from, and prevention of, a throat cancer?

because [it was] not incurred solely for the mother's recovery. Congress required only that medical expenses be "primarily" for the patient's recovery. The evidence here, moreover, establishes (and the Tax Court so found) that the effect on the wife's health was the sole consideration inducing her husband's action even if it was not the sole result. (2) *Doctor's advice:* Ochs' action was precipitated by the strong warning of a physician. The doctor predicted that the wife might not recover if the children stayed at home. (3) *Relation between illness and treatment:* The physician advised sending the children away because their presence required vocal exertion on the mother's part — strain and pain in the vulnerable throat region. The advice was aimed to aid the mother's specific throat condition and not just her general well-being or disposition. The physician's warning was certainly ominous enough to instill in the taxpayer a "reasonable belief that the 'treatment' would be efficacious." (4) *Proximity in time of treatment to illness:* The children were sent away as soon as possible after the doctor's advice. They were kept in schools until the five-year danger period of cancer recurrence was over. Then they were brought home, and have never been to private schools since. It is true that the children were kept at home for three years after the cancer operation. But the doctor who counseled their separation was not consulted until 1946, when Mrs. Ochs' lack of improvement became very noticeable.[3]

In the final analysis, the Commissioner, the Tax Court and my colleagues all seem to reject Mr. Ochs' plea because of the nightmarish spectacle of opening the floodgates to cases involving expense for cooks, governesses,

---

3. See how these tests have been applied in other [§213] cases: Usually when such deductions are disallowed, the taxpayers have failed to prove that the expenses were incurred primarily to alleviate a specific illness of the body or mind, i.e., they have not met the motive-test or the relation-test laid down in *Havey.*

The majority of [§213] cases seems to have dealt, strangely enough, with Florida or Arizona winter vacations. One taxpayer closed up his business after a coronary occlusion and, in effect, retired to Florida. He wanted to deduct his year's rent and payment to a cleaning woman; Brody v. Commissioner, 8 T.C.M. 288. A second taxpayer and his wife took an extended holiday in the sunshine as an aftermath of ulcers and pneumonia; Keller v. Commissioner, 8 T.M.C. 685. Dobkin v. Commissioner, 15 T.C. 886, concerned a heart patient who took annual Florida vacations. Havey v. Commissioner, 12 T.C. 409, involved another heart patient who returned to old vacation haunts in New Jersey and Arizona as late as two years after the attack. All these five taxpayers were halted by the same stumbling block: None of them could show a direct relation between (1) the heart condition or the ulcers and (2) the Florida sunshine. The inference was unavoidable that the patient enjoyed a relief from the cold winds of winter for his general well-being; in some cases, he might very well have made the trip anyway according to his long-established vacation practices. The Commissioner and the Tax Court, on the other hand, have sanctioned deductions of funds paid for southern exposures in cases where the patients went South for relief from asthma, hay fever, or respiratory infections, i.e., where a direct relation was proved between the southern climate and treatment of the disease. Stringham v. Commissioner, 12 T.C. 580, affirmed 6 Cir., 183 F.2d 579.

One [§213] case of disallowance of an alleged medical expense involved the installation of an oil furnace in war-time 1944. The taxpayer had always wanted one, and with the help of his physician's certification that it was bad for his sinuses to stoke a coal furnace, he finally got authorization from the authorities for an oil furnace. "Capital expenditures of permanent benefit to a property, such as is the present item," said the Tax Court, are not deductible as current expenses. "Not every expenditure," it warned, "prescribed by a physician is to be catalogued under this term." Seymour v. Commissioner, 14 T.C. 1111.

baby-sitters, nourishing food, clothing, frigidaires, electric dishwashers — in short, allowances as medical expenses for everything "helpful to a convalescent housewife or to one who is nervous or weak from past illness." I, for one, trust the Commissioner to make short shrift of most such claims.[4] The tests should be: Would the taxpayer, considering his income and his living standard, normally spend money in this way regardless of illness? Has he enjoyed such luxuries or services in the past? Did a competent physician prescribe this specific expense as an indispensable part of the treatment? Has the taxpayer followed the physician's advice in the most economical way possible? Are the so-called medical expenses over and above what the patient would have to pay anyway for his living expenses, i.e., room, board, etc? Is the treatment closely geared to a particular condition and not just to the patient's general good health or well-being?

My colleagues are particularly worried about family expenses, traditionally non-deductible, passing as medical expenses. They would classify the children's schooling here as a family expense, because, they say, it resulted from the loss of the wife's services. I think they are mistaken. The Tax Court specifically found that the children were sent away so they would not bother the wife, and not because there was no one to take care of them. Ochs' expenditures fit into the Congressional test for medical deductions because he was compelled to go to the expense of putting the children away primarily for the benefit of his sick wife. Expenses incurred solely because of the loss of the patient's services and not as a part of his cure are a different thing altogether. Wendell v. Commissioner, 12 T.C. 161, for instance, disallowed a deduction for the salary of a nurse engaged in caring for a healthy infant whose mother had died in childbirth. The case turned on the simple fact that, where there is no patient, there can be no deduction.

Thus, even here, expense attributed solely to the education, at least of the older child, should not be included as a medical expense. See Stringham v. Commissioner, supra. Nor should care of the children during that part of the day when the mother would be away, during the period while she was working part-time. Smith v. Commissioner, 40 B.T.A. 1038, aff'd, 2 Cir., 113 F.2d 114. The same goes for any period when the older child would be away at public school during the day. In so far as the costs of this private schooling are thus allocable, I would limit the deductible expense to the care of the children at the times when they would otherwise be around the mother. If my views prevailed, this might require a remand to the Tax Court for such allocation.

Line-drawing may be difficult here as everywhere, but that is what courts are for. See Lavery v. Purssell, 399 Ch.D. 508, 517: ". . . courts of justice ought not be puzzled by such old scholastic questions as to where a horse's tail

---

4. He has so handled the Florida vacationers and the oil-furnace purchaser. See note 3 supra.

begins and where it ceases. You are obliged to say, this is a horse's tail at some time."

Notes

1. A special problem relates to travel for medical care. Section 213(d)(1)(B) allows a deduction for amounts paid for "transportation primarily for and essential to medical care"; use of the word *transportation* instead of *travel* is to prevent deduction of meals and lodging, except in a hospital or similar institution or as provided in §213(d)(2).

Mr. Kelly went from Milwaukee to New York on business, and while there he contracted acute appendicitis and underwent an appendectomy. Because the hospital was full, he was discharged and told to stay for a week at a hotel next door. His wife came in from Milwaukee to care for him in the hotel. While there, he was seen by his surgeon four times.

Can Mr. Kelly deduct the cost of his meals and lodging in the hotel? What about his wife's meals and lodging and transportation? Kelly v. Commissioner, 440 F.2d 307 (7th Cir. 1971).

2. Another special problem relates to capital expenditures for medical purposes. Suppose a taxpayer builds a pool in his or her home on doctor's orders to deal with a particular illness. The IRS position is to allow whatever deduction is to be allowed in the year of expenditure, not by way of amortization, but to allow only the excess of the expenditure over the increase in value of the property that results from the expenditure. For example, a taxpayer was allowed an $82,000 deduction for a swimming pool that cost $194,660, despite the Commissioner's claim that the taxpayer's medical needs could have been met with a $70,000 pool that would have increased property value by $31,000, limiting the deduction to $39,000. Collins H. Ferris T.C. Memo 1977-186, rev'd and rem'd, 582 F.2d 1112 (7th Cir. 1978) (to determine minimum reasonable cost of a functionally adequate pool and housing structure).

3. *Long-term care.* What about the cost of nursing home care or fees for an assisted-living facility paid by an elderly and disabled individual who cannot perform routine personal maintenance tasks for himself? Is this a medical expense, or is it core consumption — "personal, living, or family expenses" disallowed by §262? Is it necessary (or feasible) to segregate the portion of the cost attributable to the provision of food and shelter from personal assistance and medical services? Compare §213(d)(6). Now read §§213(d)(1), (10), 7702B. What are the effects of these provisions? What are the policy implications? Observe that under §7702B(a) employer-provided coverage under a qualified long-term care insurance contract triggers the exclusions of §§105 and 106.

One effect of the medical expense deduction is, for some taxpayers, to reduce the marginal cost of medical care. For a taxpayer in the 35 percent tax bracket, provided he is an itemizer and already has enough medical expenses to overcome the floor, the after-tax cost of additional medical care is only 65 percent of its pretax price.

That consideration might lead one to think of the medical expense deduction as essentially a subsidy for medical expenses rather than a proper part of the income tax system. Professor Stanley Surrey and others have developed and promoted this idea skillfully and energetically, with the result that *tax expenditure* is now a common term for provisions of this sort, and they are required to be listed in the annual Budget of the United States in order to provide a basis for getting a more comprehensive view of total government resources devoted to healthcare, for example.

Tax expenditures are taken up more generally in Chapter 8B below. That chapter contains a list of tax expenditures from the FY 2009 Budget (Table [8-2]), in which you can find the magnitude of the tax revenues estimated to be lost by reason of the medical expense deduction as well as various other provisions.

Surrey suggested that one ought to judge a tax expenditure by considering what an equivalent direct expenditure would look like. So the medical expense deduction might be thought of as a form of national health insurance. As such, it is surely cock-eyed:

1. It is run by the IRS instead of the Department of Health and Human Services, the cabinet department which runs the Centers for Medicare & Medicaid Services.
2. More significantly, no one qualifies for it unless he has enough income to owe taxes; the poor are systematically excluded.
3. Even among taxpayers, it is only itemizers who qualify; to a considerable extent that means only homeowners, since home mortgage interest and real estate tax deductions are what generally make a person an itemizer. So the IRS health insurance program is basically only for homeowners, not renters.
4. Next there is quite a high deductible. Reimbursement for medical expenses is only available to the extent they exceed 7.5 percent of taxable income. (This feature in fact keeps the medical expense deduction from being regressive; in practice, the amount claimed on high-income returns is very limited.)
5. There is also coinsurance, with an upside-down sliding scale: for high-income taxpayers (if they exceed the deductible) the coinsurance — what is not reimbursed through a tax deduction — is 65 percent. For poorer persons, as indicated by their income tax brackets, the coinsurance is higher: 67, 72, 75, 85, or for some even 90 percent.

So the deduction is clearly inadequate and indeed perverse as a health insurance program. But is that the only way to look at it? Or do complicated matters have to be looked at from different perspectives for different purposes? For the purpose of evaluating national health policy, the Surrey perspective looks dead right indeed. But if our purpose is income tax policy, perhaps we should take the absence or inadequacy of comprehensive health insurance as a given and observe that some people do bear the burden of extraordinary medical expenses. Moreover, we have an income tax because such a tax is supposed to tax people according to their ability to pay, and therefore it should be considered whether income minus extraordinary medical expenses gives a better index of ability to pay than would income without that deduction. Tax expenditure zealots have sometimes seemed to think this is somehow an impermissible perspective even for purposes of implementing an income tax. Are they right?

3. Disability Insurance

The proceeds of employer-provided accident or health insurance coverage are excluded from gross income under §105(b) only if the amount is paid "for the medical care (as defined in section 213(d)) of the taxpayer, his spouse, and his dependents." In contrast, the proceeds of individually purchased accident or health insurance are excluded from gross income under §104(a)(3) without regard to whether the amount is paid for medical care. This distinction has important consequences for the tax treatment of payments made to replace wages or salary lost as a result of the inability to work due to personal injury or sickness (so-called sick pay coverage or disability insurance). Such income-replacement payments are "amounts received through accident or health insurance for personal injuries or sickness" but they are not paid for medical care. Consequently, they are excludible if received under an individually purchased policy, but if they are attributable to employer-provided coverage they fall within the express inclusion rule of §105(a).

This disparity in the taxation of income-continuation benefits tracks a difference in treatment of the cost of coverage. Premiums paid by an individual for disability income protection are not deductible even if the coverage is contained in an individually purchased accident or health insurance policy that is primarily aimed at funding medical care expenses. §213(d)(1)(D), (d)(6). The cost of employer-provided disability insurance, on the other hand, is paid with pre-tax dollars: Amounts expended are deductible by the employer and excludible by covered workers. Observe that §106(a) exempts "employer-provided coverage under an accident or health plan" without insisting that the coverage be for medical care. Hence, one end or the other of the disability insurance transaction is taxed.

Funding Method	Accident or Health Insurance Not for "Medical Care" (e.g., Sick Pay)	
	Premiums	*Proceeds*
Employer-Provided Coverage	Excluded, §106	Included, §105(a) [but see §22]
Individually Purchased Insurance	No Deduction, §213(d)(1)(D)	Excluded, §104(a)(3)

Notes and Questions

1. Revenue-wise, the Treasury is apparently indifferent as between these approaches, but does that hold true for an individual worker? Workers in most occupations never become disabled. Which would you prefer, employer or individual disability insurance coverage?

2. If an individual buys his own disability insurance coverage (perhaps because his employer does not provide this benefit), how much of his income should he insure?

3. *Contributory plans.* Corporation *D* provides every employee with insurance that pays two-thirds of his or her wages or salary for any period of absence from work due to disability. *D* requires that employees pay half of the premiums, however, which the company collects by wage withholding. Employee *E*, whose salary is $90,000, is injured and receives benefits this year of $60,000. How should *E* report this transaction? Reg. §1.105-1(c).

4. *Permanent disability credit.* Until repealed in 1983, §105(d) granted an exclusion for sick pay or disability income up to a maximum of $100 per week. The excludible amount was reduced dollar-for-dollar as the taxpayer's adjusted gross income, including disability income, exceeded $15,000. The dollar limit was apparently thought to take care of the problem of wealthy executives "recuperating" in Arizona. But is there any adequate reason for treating pay despite not working more favorably than pay for work performed? A remnant of the prior sick pay exclusion persists in the 15 percent credit of §22, which also contains an income phase out.

4. Life Insurance

Look at §101(a)(1) and consider whether this provision makes sense in relation to a *term life insurance* policy. A term policy is one that insures only against death during a specified limited period, like one year or five years. If the insured survives to the end of the period, no benefit is paid. Essentially, the insurance company ascertains from a mortality table what portion of its policyholders in a particular age category will die during the term, and then it collects enough premiums from all of them to pay the promised benefits for those who die. With respect to term life insurance one might assert that §101(a)(1) is a logical extension of the rule in §104(a)(3), death being simply the ultimate personal injury.

The premium cost of term insurance increases with age of the insured since a higher proportion of the people in older age categories will die during the policy term. Often a term insurance policy gives the insured the right to renew the policy at the end of the term, but renewal will be at the higher premium rate prescribed for the insured's older age during the renewal term and is ordinarily not permitted at all after about age 65. To avoid this increase in premiums and ultimate termination of coverage, much life insurance is written on something other than a term basis.

Whole-life insurance, for example, provides a fixed benefit payable on death of the insured, whenever it may occur, with premiums payable for life at a fixed rate that does not increase with age. The amount of the premium will vary, of course, with the age of the insured when the policy is taken out, but once that occurs the premium will be fixed for life. To provide such whole-life coverage, the insurance company charges more initially than it would have charged for a term policy of the same amount. Premiums collected from a given age category, therefore, in the early years of coverage, will substantially exceed benefits paid on account of deaths in that category. The excess is held by the insurance company as a fund with which to pay increasing death benefits without increasing premiums as the insureds grow older. The funds required to be accumulated on account of outstanding policies are called *reserves*, and the reserve value of a particular policy is the amount of reserves allocable to that policy.

Since the insurance company collects more in premiums earlier in order to pay out more in benefits later, it finds itself with substantial accumulations of money to invest. The investment earnings of the insurance company then become an important source of funds in addition to premium receipts for paying benefits. The insurance company makes some estimate of earnings on reserve funds in computing what it has to charge in premiums for any particular level of insurance coverage, and so in effect the benefit of earnings on reserve funds is largely passed through to policyholders.[3]

The accumulation of a reserve under a whole-life policy is analogous to what a policyholder could do for himself by purchasing renewable term insurance and putting the difference between the term premium and a whole-life premium into a savings account. The insurance could then be reduced each year by the amount of increase in the savings account balance so that the sum available from the savings account plus the term policy would be held constant. The increase in the savings account balance would result

---

3. Some insurance companies have stockholders who will get at least some of the benefit of earnings in excess of the rate of return employed in computing premiums. Many insurance companies, however, are mutual companies, without stockholders, in which the policyholders are thought of as the owners; in these companies all investment earnings, minus expenses, will ultimately redound to the benefit of policyholders.

partly from continuing contributions by the insured but also, increasingly, from the accumulation of interest earned on the account. If the amount to save were correctly chosen, the savings account would eventually contain the whole amount originally provided by insurance, and the insurance policy itself could be allowed to lapse.

A person proceeding in this manner would be taxed, of course, on the interest on the savings account, currently as that interest was earned and credited to the account. But no analogous tax is imposed on the holder of a whole-life insurance policy because the insurance company earns income from investing its reserves, and §101 operates to exempt the whole proceeds from tax when paid by reason of the death of the insured. The result is that very substantial amounts of ordinary investment income escape income tax altogether by being accumulated in life insurance reserves paid out on death.

Consider carefully whether this treatment is sound both theoretically and in practical terms. Should the interest component in life insurance proceeds be taxed? How and when? To whom?

The problem does not end with whole-life insurance because some life insurance products have an even higher ratio of investment return to pure insurance. It is quite common to write policies to be paid up by retirement so that an insured will be relieved of the cash drain of premium payments when salary payments are no longer being received. Moreover, some policies are written to be paid up forthwith on the payment of a single premium. Such policies depend proportionately more on investment income and less on premium receipts to fund payment of benefits. Still, the assumption has been that the whole proceeds would go untaxed under §101.

More recently, insurance companies have introduced flexible premium life insurance contracts, which have sometimes been sold on the basis that they offer an opportunity to wrap investment earnings in the tax-exempt mantle of a life insurance contract. Congress reacted in 1982 by enacting what is now §7702, titled "Life insurance contract defined." Despite the label, this section contains substantive provisions concerning the treatment of policies that do not meet the statutory requirements for exclusion as life insurance. In explanation of the 1982 change it was stated that:

> Congress believed that flexible premium life insurance contracts should have the same tax treatment as traditional level-premium whole life insurance contracts if they are substantially comparable to traditional contracts. However, Congress was concerned by the fact that some flexible premium contracts can be overly investment oriented by allowing large cash value build-ups without requiring a continued reasonable amount of pure insurance protection. In the case of such contracts, the traditional use of life insurance as financial protection against early death could be overshadowed by the use of the contract as the vehicle for tax-favored investment.
>
> Because the uncertain tax treatment of flexible premium life insurance contracts has caused significant confusion among consumers and life insurance companies, Congress believed that it should resolve the tax treatment of these contracts, at least temporarily, by legislation. [Staff of the Joint Committee on Taxation, General

Explanation of the Revenue Provisions of the Tax Equity and Fiscal Responsibility Act of 1982, 367 (1982).]

Is it useful to try to distinguish between "the traditional use of life insurance as financial protection against early death" and "use of the contract as a vehicle for tax-favored investment"? Or would it be simpler and preferable to sort out the investment return on every life insurance contract and make it fully taxable?

Employee life insurance. If an employer pays premiums on an individual life insurance policy that belongs to an employee, those premium payments will be taxed to the employee. If an employer pays death benefits directly to employees, those benefit payments are taxable to the recipients. There used to be an exclusion for the latter, in §101(b), limited to $5,000 per employee.

If life insurance is provided for employees through a group life policy and eligibility and coverage meet the nondiscrimination requirements of §79(d) then benefits will be exempt under §101 and payment of premiums or provision of insurance coverage will be excluded under §79 but only for coverage up to $50,000. The value of coverage above that figure is taxable.

Accelerated death benefits and viatical settlements. The exclusion of life insurance proceeds is restricted to amounts "paid by reason of the death of the insured." §101(a)(1). What about a policy that allows payment of proceeds to the insured during life if the insured is shown to be terminally ill? Policy provisions that allow such accelerated payment of death benefits have become fairly common in recent years, apparently in response to demand created by the AIDS crisis. The insured may desperately need policy proceeds to finance end-of-life hospital or hospice care, but pre-death distribution negates the tax exemption. In 1992 the Treasury proposed regulations that would have extended the exclusion to cover proceeds paid prior to death under circumstances in which death was reasonably expected to occur within one year. Congress confirmed this liberalization with the enactment of §101(g) in 1996. What if a terminally ill individual owns a life insurance policy that does not contain an accelerated payment rider, and, finding herself in exigent circumstances, she is forced to sell her policy to an investor? See §101(g)(2), on viatical settlements.

Problems

1. *A* purchased a $100,000 life endowment insurance policy. At age 65, after *A* had paid total premiums of $80,000, the policy matured and the insurance company began to make payments to *A* under the policy. *A* will be paid $10,000 a year for as long as she lives; if she dies before age 75, any excess of $100,000 over what has previously been paid to her will be paid to her estate or designated beneficiary. How are periodic payments under this policy taxed? How much, if any, of the lump-sum payment will be taxed if *A* dies before age 75? See Rev. Rul. 55-313, 1955-1 C.B. 219.

2. *B* owned a life insurance policy on his own life. In order to remove it from his estate for federal estate tax purposes, *B* transferred the policy to his daughter in exchange for securities worth $45,000. Shortly thereafter, *B* died and the policy was paid off at the face amount of $100,000. Is any part of the proceeds taxable as income?

3. *C* had $100,000 to invest. She purchased a $100,000 paid-up life insurance policy for $60,000. With the remaining $40,000 she purchased a life annuity, which will pay $5,000 a year. *C* then transferred the life insurance policy as a gift to her daughter, retaining the annuity contract. How will payments under the annuity contract and the life insurance policy be taxed? Would it matter if *C*'s health were such that an insurance company would not issue the life insurance policy unless *C* also purchased the annuity contract? Kess v. United States, 72-1 USTC (6th Cir. 1971); Rev. Rul. 65-67, 1965-1 C.B. 56. But compare Fidelity-Philadelphia Trust Co. v. Smith, 356 U.S. 274 (1958).

4. National Bank lent *D* $100,000 and required *D* to purchase credit life insurance in that amount, payable to the bank. *D* defaulted, and Bank deducted $100,000 as a bad debt loss. Subsequently *D* died, and Bank collected $100,000 from the insurer. Is that recovery taxable to Bank? McCamant v. Commissioner, 32 T.C. 824 (1959).

D. PREVIOUSLY DEDUCTED LOSSES

1. Annual Accounting

BURNET v. SANFORD & BROOKS CO.
282 U.S. 359 (1931)

Mr. Justice STONE delivered the opinion of the Court. . . . From 1913 to 1915, inclusive, respondent, a Delaware corporation engaged in business for profit, was acting for the Atlantic Dredging Company in carrying out a contract for dredging the Delaware River, entered into by that company with the United States. In making its income tax returns for the years 1913 to 1916, respondent added to gross income for each year the payments made under the contract that year, and deducted its expenses paid that year in performing the contract. The total expenses exceeded the payments received by $176,271.88. The tax returns for 1913, 1915 and 1916 showed net losses. That for 1914 showed net income.

In 1915 work under the contract was abandoned, and in 1916 suit was brought in the Court of Claims to recover for a breach of warranty of the character of the material to be dredged. Judgment for the claimant, 53 Ct. Cls. 490, was affirmed by this Court in 1920. United States v. Atlantic Dredging Co., 253 U.S. 1. It held that the recovery was upon the contract and was "compensatory of the cost of the work, of which the government got the benefit." From the total recovery, petitioner received in that year the sum of $192,577.59, which included the $176,271.88 by which its expenses under the contract had exceeded receipts from it, and accrued interest amounting to $16,305.71. Respondent having failed to include these amounts as gross income in its tax returns for 1920, the Commissioner made the deficiency assessment here involved, based on the addition of both items to gross income for that year.

The Court of Appeals ruled that only the item of interest was properly included, holding, erroneously as the government contends, that the item of $176,271.88 was a return of losses suffered by respondent in earlier years and hence was wrongly assessed as income. Notwithstanding this conclusion, its judgment of reversal and the consequent elimination of this item from gross income for 1920 were made contingent upon the filing by respondent of amended returns for the years 1913 to 1916, from which were to be omitted the deductions of the related items of expenses paid in those years. Respondent insists that as the Sixteenth Amendment and the Revenue Act of 1918, which was in force in 1920, plainly contemplate a tax only on net income or profits, any application of the statute which operates to impose a tax with respect to the present transaction, from which respondent received no profit, cannot be upheld.

If respondent's contention that only gain or profit may be taxed under the Sixteenth Amendment be accepted without qualification, see Eisner v. Macomber, 252 U.S. 189, Doyle v. Mitchell Brothers Co., 247 U.S. 179, the question remains whether the gain or profit which is the subject of the tax may be ascertained, as here, on the basis of fixed accounting periods, or whether, as is pressed upon us, it can only be net profit ascertained on the basis of particular transactions of the taxpayer when they are brought to a conclusion.

All the revenue acts which have been enacted since the adoption of the Sixteenth Amendment have uniformly assessed the tax on the basis of annual returns showing the net result of all the taxpayer's transactions during a fixed accounting period, either the calendar year, or, at the option of the taxpayer, the particular fiscal year which he may adopt. Under §§230, 232 and 234(a) of the Revenue Act of 1918, 40 Stat. 1057, respondent was subject to tax upon its annual net income, arrived at by deducting from gross income for each taxable year all the ordinary and necessary expenses paid during that year in carrying on any trade or business, interest and taxes paid, and losses sustained, during the year. By §§233(a) and 213(a) gross income "includes . . . income derived from . . . business . . . or the transaction of any business carried on for gain or profit, or gains or profits and income derived from any source whatever." The amount of all such items is required to be included in the gross income for the taxable year in which received by the taxpayer, unless they may be properly accounted for on the accrual basis under §212(b). See

United States v. Anderson, 269 U.S. 422; Aluminum Castings Co. v. Routzahn [282 U.S. 92 (1930)].

That the recovery made by respondent in 1920 was gross income for that
year within the meaning of these sections cannot, we think, be doubted. The
money received was derived from a contract entered into in the course of
respondent's business operations for profit. While it equalled, and in a loose
sense was a return of, expenditures made in performing the contract, still,
as the Board of Tax Appeals found, the expenditures were made in defraying
the expenses incurred in the prosecution of the work under the contract, for
the purpose of earning profits. They were not capital investments, the cost of
which, if converted, must first be restored from the proceeds before there is a
capital gain taxable as income. See Doyle v. Mitchell Brothers Co., supra,
p. 185.

That such receipts from the conduct of a business enterprise are to be
included in the taxpayer's return as a part of gross income, regardless of
whether the particular transaction results in net profit, sufficiently appears
from the quoted words of §213(a) and from the character of the deductions
allowed. Only by including these items of gross income in the 1920 return
would it have been possible to ascertain respondent's net income for the
period covered by the return, which is what the statute taxes. The excess of
gross income over deductions did not any the less constitute net income for
the taxable period because respondent, in an earlier period, suffered net
losses in the conduct of its business which were in some measure attributable
to expenditures made to produce the net income of the later period.

Bowers v. Kerbaugh-Empire Co., 271 U.S. 170, on which respondent
relies, does not support its position. In that case the taxpayer, which had
lost, in business, borrowed money, which was to be repaid in German marks,
and which was later repaid in depreciated currency, had neither made a
profit on the transaction, nor received any money or property which
could have been made subject to the tax.

But respondent insists that if the sum which it recovered is the income
defined by the statute, still it is not income, taxation of which without apportionment is permitted by the Sixteenth Amendment, since the particular
transaction from which it was derived did not result in any net gain or profit.
But we do not think the amendment is to be so narrowly construed. A taxpayer may be in receipt of net income in one year and not in another. The
net result of the two years, if combined in a single taxable period, might still
be a loss; but it has never been supposed that that fact would relieve him from
a tax on the first, or that it affords any reason for postponing the assessment
of the tax until the end of a lifetime, or for some other indefinite period, to
ascertain more precisely whether the final outcome of the period, or of a
given transaction, will be a gain or a loss.

The Sixteenth Amendment was adopted to enable the government to
raise revenue by taxation. It is the essence of any system of taxation that it
should produce revenue ascertainable, and payable to the government, at

regular intervals. Only by such a system is it practicable to produce a regular flow of income and apply methods of accounting, assessment, and collection capable of practical operation. It is not suggested that there has ever been any general scheme for taxing income on any other basis. The computation of income annually as the net result of all transactions within the year was a familiar practice, and taxes upon income so arrived at were not unknown, before the Sixteenth Amendment. See Bowers v. Kerbaugh-Empire Co., supra, p. 174; Pacific Insurance Co. v. Soule, 7 Wall. 433; Pollock v. Farmers' Loan & Trust Co., 158 U.S. 601, 630. It is not to be supposed that the amendment did not contemplate that Congress might make income so ascertained the basis of a scheme of taxation such as had been in actual operation within the United States before its adoption. While, conceivably, a different system might be devised by which the tax could be assessed, wholly or in part, on the basis of the finally ascertained results of particular transactions, Congress is not required by the amendment to adopt such a system in preference to the more familiar method, even if it were practicable. It would not necessarily obviate the kind of inequalities of which respondent complains. If losses from particular transactions were to be set off against gains in others, there would still be the practical necessity of computing the tax on the basis of annual or other fixed taxable periods, which might result in the taxpayer being required to pay a tax on income in one period exceeded by net losses in another.

Under the statutes and regulations in force in 1920, two methods were provided by which, to a limited extent, the expenses of a transaction incurred in one year might be offset by the amounts actually received from it in another. One was by returns on the accrual basis under §212(b), which provides that a taxpayer keeping accounts upon any basis other than that of actual receipts and disbursements, unless such basis does not clearly reflect its income, may, subject to regulations of the Commissioner, make its return upon the basis upon which its books are kept. See United States v. Anderson, and Aluminum Castings Co. v. Routzahn, supra. The other was under Treasury Regulations (Art. 121 of Reg. 33 of Jan. 2, 1918, under the Revenue Acts of 1916 and 1917; Art 36 of Reg. 45, Apr. 19, 1919, under the Revenue Act of 1918) providing that in reporting the income derived from certain long term contracts, the taxpayer might either report all of the receipts and all of the expenditures made on account of a particular contract in the year in which the work was completed, or report in each year the percentage of the estimated profit corresponding to the percentage of the total estimated expenditures which was made in that year.

The Court of Appeals said that the case of the respondent here fell within the spirit of these regulations. But the court did not hold, nor does respondent assert, that it ever filed returns in compliance either with these regulations, or §212(b), or otherwise attempted to avail itself of their provisions; nor on this record do any facts appear tending to support the burden, resting on the taxpayer, of establishing that the Commissioner erred in failing to apply them. See Niles Bement Pond Co. v. United States, 281 U.S. 357, 361.

The assessment was properly made under the statutes. Relief from their alleged burdensome operation which may not be secured under these provisions, can be afforded only be legislation, not by the courts.

Reversed.

Notes

1. *The taxable year.* Look at §§441-443. Would it be a fair generalization to say that the calendar year is the basic taxable year but that others are permitted where considerations of taxpayer convenience justify the variation? Note that a taxpayer can initially establish a fiscal year without consent but that a change requires approval. Could an individual whose only business consists of the performance of services as an employee adopt a fiscal year? How? Would it be a good idea? See §31(a).

The vast majority of individuals use a calendar year for computing taxable income while a substantial number of corporations and partnerships employ fiscal years. Careful consideration should be given to the choice of a fiscal year whenever a corporation is organized.

Why are income taxes computed on an *annual* basis? Would a quarterly basis be acceptable? A monthly basis? Why?

2. It is usually said that *Sanford & Brooks* involved a conflict between equitable considerations on the taxpayer's side and administrative considerations on the government's side. Try to define those considerations on both sides as exactly as you can.

3. *Net operating losses.* Section 172 now allows a net operating loss to be carried over and deducted in other taxable years — two years back, and twenty years forward for most taxpayers. Does this provision deal adequately with the taxpayer's problem in *Sanford & Brooks*? If so, at what administrative cost?

4. *Accounting methods.* Look at §446. Most individuals compute taxable income from employment and from investments on the cash receipts and disbursements method. This means that income items are included in income for the year in which they are received. See §451. In a few situations, an item may be included on the basis of constructive receipt prior to actual receipt. See Reg. §1.451-2 and Chapter 6A.1 below. Deductible expenses are allowed in the year actually paid.

Taxpayers involved in more complex business activities, however, are apt to keep their books by some more sophisticated method. In particular, accrual methods allow income to be recorded when earned and expenses when incurred, even if receipt or payment is delayed. In general, taxpayers are permitted to use the same method for computing taxable income as they use in keeping their books. Taxpayers who make money from selling goods are indeed usually required to use an accrual method, at least with respect to sales and cost of goods sold. See Reg. §§1.446-1(a)(4)(i) and 1.446-1(c)(2)(i). A taxpayer starting a business of providing services can generally choose whether to use the cash receipts and disbursements method or an accrual method, but a later change in method will require the Commissioner's consent. See §446(e). What happens if a taxpayer changes the method by which he computes income in keeping his books and then simply declines to seek permission to change for tax purposes?

There are many special methods or techniques of accounting for particular kinds of business transactions, some but not all of which have been found acceptable for income tax purposes. Note, for example, the Court's reference to regulations that authorize special methods of reporting income from long-term contracts. Accounting rules for long-term contracts are now set forth in §460 and regulations thereunder.

It is sometimes suggested that accrual accounting is the only true way to measure income and that cash receipts and disbursements accounting is only allowed because it represents a much simpler method of bookkeeping for unsophisticated taxpayers. On the other hand, it can be argued that payment of taxes should follow receipt of income and that actual receipts and disbursements are therefore the natural basis for computing taxable income. In this view, accrual methods represent a concession to practicality. How much truth is there in either of these views of the relation between cash and accrual accounting? See Chapter 6C and 6D below.

5. Think about *Sanford & Brooks* from the perspective of cost instead of income. Essentially, the question is what allowance to make for the tax-payer's expenses in 1913-1916, and the holding is that a deduction in those years is sufficient.

What alternative forms of allowance, if any, would also be sufficient? Is some form of allowance necessary, or could the government tax receipts without any allowance for costs and expense?

2. Tax-Benefit Limitations

DOBSON v. COMMISSIONER
320 U.S. 489 (1943)

Mr. Justice JACKSON delivered the opinion of the Court. These four cases were consolidated in the Court of Appeals. The facts of one will define the issue present in all.

The taxpayer, Collins, in 1929 purchased 300 shares of stock of the National City Bank of New York which carried certain beneficial interests in stock of the National City Company. The latter company was the seller and the transaction occurred in Minnesota. In 1930 Collins sold 100 shares, sustaining a deductible loss of $41,600.80, which was claimed on his return for that year and allowed. In 1931 he sold another 100 shares, sustaining a deductible loss of $28,163.78, which was claimed in his return and allowed. The remaining 100 shares he retained. He regarded the purchases and sales as closed and completed transactions.

In 1936 Collins learned that the stock had not been registered in compliance with the Minnesota Blue Sky Laws and learned of facts indicating that he been induced to purchase by fraudulent representations. He filed suit against the seller alleging fraud and failure to register. He asked rescission of the entire transaction and offered to return the proceeds of the stock, or an equivalent number of shares plus such interest and dividends as he had received. In 1939 the suit was settled, on a basis which gave him a net recovery of $45,150.63, of which $23,296.45 was allocable to the stock sold in 1930 and $6,454.18 allocable to that sold in 1931. In his return for 1939 he did not report as income any party of the recovery. Throughout that year adjustment of his 1930 and 1931 tax liability was barred by the statute of limitation.

The Commissioner adjusted Collins' 1939 gross income by adding as ordinary gain the recovery attributable to the shares sold, but not that portion of it attributable to the shares unsold. The recovery upon the shares sold was not, however, sufficient to make good the taxpayer's original investment in them. And if the amounts recovered had been added to the proceeds received in 1930 and 1931 they would not have altered Collins' income tax liability for those years, for even if the entire deductions claimed on account of these losses had been disallowed, the returns would still have shown net losses.

Collins sought a redetermination by the Board of Tax Appeals, now the Tax Court. He contended that the recovery of 1939 was in the nature of a return of capital from which he realized no gain and no income either actually or constructively, and that he had received no tax benefit from the loss deductions. In the alternative he argued that if the recover could be called income at all it was taxable as capital gain. The Commissioner insisted that the entire recovery was taxable as ordinary gain and that it was immaterial whether the taxpayer had obtained any tax benefits from the loss deduction reported in prior years. The Tax Court sustained the taxpayer's contention that he realized no taxable gain from the recovery.[1]

The Court of Appeals concluded that the "tax benefit theory" applied by the Tax Court "seems to be injection into the law of an equitable principle, found neither in the statutes nor in the regulations." Because the Tax Court's reasoning was not embodied in any statutory precept, the court held that the Tax Court was not authorized to resort to it in determining whether the recovery should be treated as income or return of capital. It held as matter of law that the recoveries were neither return of capital nor

---

1. Estate of Collins v. Commissioner, 46 B.T.A. 765.

capital gain, but were ordinary income in the year received.[2] Questions important to tax administration were involved, conflict was said to exist, and we granted certiorari. . . .[3]

The court below thought that the Tax Court's decision "evaded or ignored" the statute of limitation, the provision of the Regulations that "expenses, liability, or deficit of one year cannot be used to reduce the income of a subsequent year," and the principle that recognition of a capital loss presupposes some event of "realization" which closes the transaction for good. We do not agree. The Tax Court has not attempted to revise liability for earlier years closed by the statute of limitation, nor used any expenses, liability, or deficit of a prior year to reduce the income of a subsequent year. It went to prior years only to determine the nature of the recovery, whether return of capital or income. Nor has the Tax Court reopened any closed transaction; it was compelled to determine the very question whether such a recognition of loss had in fact taken place in the prior year as would necessitate calling the recovery in the taxable year income rather than return of capital.

The 1928 Act provides that "The Board in redetermining a deficiency in respect of any taxable year shall consider such facts with relation to the taxes for other taxable years as may be necessary correctly to redetermine the amount of such deficiency. . . ." The Tax Court's inquiry as to past years was authorized if "necessary correctly to redetermine" the deficiency. The Tax Court thought in this case that it was necessary; the Court of Appeals apparently thought it was not. This precipitates a question not raised by either counsel as to whether the court is empowered to revise the Tax Court's decision as "not in accordance with law" because of such a difference of opinion.

With the 1926 Revenue Act, Congress promulgated, and at all times since has maintained, a limitation on the power of courts to review Board of Tax Appeals (now the Tax Court) determinations. "Such courts shall have power to affirm or, if the decision of the Board is not in accordance with law, to modify or to reverse the decision of the Board. . . ." However, even a causal survey of decisions in tax cases, now over 5,000 in number, will demonstrate that courts, including this Court, have not paid the scrupulous deference to the tax laws' admonitions of finality which they have to similar provisions in statutes relating to other tribunals. After thirty years of income tax history the volume of tax litigation necessary merely for statutory interpretation would seem due to subside. That it shows no sign of diminution suggests that many decisions have no value as precedents because they determine only fact questions peculiar to particular cases. Of course frequent amendment of the statute causes continuing uncertainty and litigation, but all too often amendments are themselves made necessary by court decision. Increase of potential tax litigation due to more taxpayers and higher rates lends new

2. 133 F.2d 732.
3. 319 U.S. 739.

importance to observance of statutory limitations on review of tax decisions. No other breach of the law touches human activities at so many points. It can never be made simple, but we can try to avoid making it needlessly complex.

It is more difficult to maintain sharp separation of court and administrative functions in tax than in other fields. One reason is that tax cases reach circuit courts of appeals from different sources and do not always call for observance of any administrative sphere of decision. Questions which the Tax Court considers at the instance of one taxpayer may be considered by many district courts at the instance of others. . . .

Another reason why courts have deferred less to the Tax Court than to other administrative tribunals is the manner in which Tax Court finality was introduced into the law.

The courts have rather strictly observed limitations on their reviewing powers where the limitation came into existence simultaneously with their duty to review administrative action in new field of regulation. But this was not the history of the tax law. Our modern income tax experience began with the Revenue Act of 1913. The World War soon brought high rates. The law was an innovation, its constitutional aspects were still being debated, interpretation was just beginning, and administrators were inexperienced. The Act provided no administrative review of the Commissioner's determinations. It did not alter the procedure followed under the Civil War income tax by which an aggrieved taxpayer could pay under protest and then sue the Collector to test the correctness of the tax. The courts by force of this situation entertained all manner of tax question, and precedents rapidly established a pattern of judicial thought and action whereby the assessments of income tax were reviewed without much restraint or limitation. Only after that practice became established did administrative review make its appearance in tax matters.

Administrative machinery to give consideration to the taxpayer's contentions existed in the Bureau of Internal Revenue from about 1918 but it was subordinate to the Commissioner.[13] In 1923, the situation was brought to the attention of Congress by the Secretary of the Treasury, who proposed creation of a Board of Tax Appeals, within the Treasury Department, whose decision was to conclude Government and taxpayer on the question of assessment and leave the taxpayer to pay the tax and then test its validity by suit against the Collector. Congress responded by creating the Board of Tax Appeals as "an independent agency in the executive branch of the Government." The Board was to give hearings and notice thereof and "make a report in writing of its findings of fact and decision in each case." But Congress dealt cautiously with finality for the Board's conclusions, going only so far as to provide that in later proceedings the findings should be "prima facie evidence of the facts therein stated." So the Board's decision first came

13. For an account thereof, see opinion of Mr. Justice Brandeis in Williamsport Wire Rope Co. v. United States, 277 U.S. 551, 562, n. 7.

before the courts under a statute which left them free to go into both fact and law questions. Two years later Congress reviewed and commended the work of the new Board, increased salaries and lengthened the tenure of its members, provided for a direct appeal from the Board's decisions to the circuit court of appeals or the Court of Appeals of the District of Columbia, and enacted the present provision limiting review to questions of law.

But this restriction upon judicial review of the Board's decisions came only after thirteen years of income tax experience had established a contrary habit. . . .

The court is independent, and its neutrality is not clouded by prosecuting duties. Its procedures assure fair hearings. Its deliberations are evidenced by careful opinions. All guides to judgment available to judges are habitually consulted and respected. It has established a tradition of freedom from bias and pressures. It deals with a subject that is highly specialized and so complex as to be the despair of judges. It is relatively better staffed for its task than is the judiciary. Its members not infrequently bring to their task long legislative or administrative experience in their subject. The volume of tax matters flowing through the Tax Court keeps its members abreast of changing statutes, regulations, and Bureau practices, informed as to the background of controversies and aware of the impact of their decisions on both Treasury and taxpayer. Individual cases are disposed of wholly on record publicly made, in adversary proceedings, and the court has no responsibility for previous handling. Tested by every theoretical and practical reason for administrative finality, no administrative decisions are entitled to higher credit in the courts. Consideration of uniform and expeditious tax administrations require that they be given all credit to which they are entitled under the law.

Tax Court decisions are characterized by substantial uniformity. Appeals fan out into courts of appeal of ten circuits and the District of Columbia. This diversification of appellate authority inevitably produces conflict of decision, even if review is limited to questions of law. But conflicts are multiplied by treating as questions of law what really are disputes over proper accounting. The mere number of such questions and the mass of decision, they call forth become a menace to the certainty and good administration of the law.

To achieve uniformity by resolving such conflicts in the Supreme Court is at best slow, expensive, and unsatisfactory. Students of federal taxation agree that the tax system suffers from delay in getting the final word in judicial review, from retroactivity of the decision when it is obtained, and from the lack of a roundly tax-informed viewpoint of judges.[26]

---

26. Paul, Selected Studies in Federal Taxation (1938) 204, n.18, comments on the number and variety of the sources contributing to tax law.

Perhaps the chief difficulty in consistent and uniform compliance with the congressional limitation upon court review lies in the want of a certain standard for distinguishing "questions of law" from "questions of fact." This is the test Congress has directed, but its difficulties in practice are well known and have been the subject of frequent comment. Its difficulty is reflected in our labeling some questions as "mixed questions of law and fact" and in a great number of opinions distinguishing "ultimate facts" from evidentiary facts. . . .

Congress has invested the Tax Court with primary authority for redetermining deficiencies, which constitutes the greater part of tax litigation. This requires it to consider both law and facts. Whatever latitude exists in resolving questions such as those of proper accounting, treating a series of transactions as one for tax purposes, or treating apparently separate ones as single in their tax consequences, exists in the Tax Court and not in the regular courts; when the court cannot separate the elements of a decision so as to identify a clear-cut mistake of law, the decision of the Tax Court must stand. . . .

The Government says that "the principal question in this case turns on the application of the settled principle that the single year is the unit of taxation." But the Tax Court was aware of this principle and in no way denied it. Whether an apparently integrated transaction shall be broken up into several separate steps and whether what apparently are several steps shall by synthesized into one whole transaction is frequently a necessary determination in deciding tax consequences. Where no statute or regulation controls, the Tax Court's selection of the course to follow is no more reviewable than any other question of fact. Of course we are not here considering the scope of review where constitutional questions are involved. The Tax Court analyzed the basis of the litigation which produced the recovery in this case and the obvious fact that "regarding the series of transactions as a whole it is apparent that no gain was actually realized." It found that the taxpayer had realized no tax benefits from reporting the transaction in separate years. It said the question under these circumstances was whether the amount the taxpayer recovered in 1939 "constitutes taxable income, even though he realized no economic gain." It concluded that the item should be treated as a return of capital rather than as taxable income. There is no statute law to the contrary, and the administrative rulings in effect at the time tended to support the conclusion. It is true that the Board in a well considered opinion reviewed a number of court holdings, but it did so for the purpose of showing that they did not fetter its freedom to reach the decision it thought sound. With this we agree.

Viewing the problem from a different aspect, the Government urges in this Court that although the recovery is capital return, it is taxable in its entirety because taxpayer's basis for the property in question is zero. The argument relies upon [§1016(a)(1)] of the Internal Revenue Code, which provides for adjusting the basis of property for "expenditures, receipts, losses, or other items, properly chargeable to capital account." This provision, it is said, requires that the right to a deduction for a capital loss be treated as a return of capital. Consequently, by deducting in 1930 and 1931 the entire difference between the cost of his stock and the proceeds of the sales, taxpayer reduced his basis to zero. But the statute contains no such fixed rule as the Government would have us read into it. It does not specify the circumstances or manner in which adjustments of the basis are to be made, but merely provides that "Proper adjustment . . . shall in all cases be made" for the items named if "properly chargeable to capital account." What, in the circumstances of this case, was a proper adjustment of the basis was thus purely an accounting problem and therefore a question of fact for the Tax Court to determine. Evidently the Tax Court thought that the previous deductions were not altogether "properly chargeable to capital account" and that to treat them as an entire recoupment of the value of taxpayer's stock would not have been a "proper adjustment." We think there was substantial evidence to support such a conclusion.

The Government relies upon Burnet v. Sanford & Brooks Co., 282 U.S. 359, for the proposition that losses of one year may not offset receipts of another year. But the case suggested its own distinction: "While [the money received] equaled, and in a loose sense was a return of, expenditures made in performing the contract, still as the Board of Tax Appeals found, the expenditures were made in defraying the expenses. . . . They were not capital investments, the cost of which, if converted, must first be restored from the proceeds before there is a capital gain taxable as income." 282 U.S. at 363-364. It is also worth noting that the Court affirmed the Board's decision, which had been upset by the circuit court of appeals, and answered, in part, the contention of the circuit court that certain regulations were applicable by saying, "nor on this record do any facts appear tending to support the burden, resting on the taxpayer, of establishing that the Commissioner erred in failing to apply them." 282 U.S. at 366-367.

It is argued on behalf of the Commissioner that the Court should over-rule the Board by applying to this question rules of law laid down in decisions on the analogous problem raised by recovery of bad debts charged off without tax benefit in prior years. The court below accepted the argument. However, instead of affording a reason for overruling the Tax Court, the history of the bad debt recovery question illustrates the mischief of over-ruling the Tax Court in matters of tax accounting. Courts were persuaded to rule as matter of law that bad debt recoveries constitute taxable income, regardless of tax benefit from the charge-off.[31] The Tax Court had first made a similar holding,[32] but had come to hold to the contrary.[33] Substitution of

31. Commissioner v. United States & International Securities Corp., 130 F.2d 894; Helvering v. State-Planters Bank & Trust Co., 130 F.2d 44.
32. Lake View Trust & Savings Bank v. Commissioner, 27 B.T.A. 290.
33. Central Loan & Investment Co. v. Commissioner, 39 B.T.A. 981; Citizens State Bank v. Commissioner, 46 B.T.A. 964.

the courts' rule for that of the Tax Court led to such hardships and inequities that the Treasury appealed to Congress to extend relief.[34] It did so.[35] The Government now argues that by extending legislative relief in bad debt cases Congress recognized that in the absence of specific exemption recoveries are taxable as income. We do not find that significance in the amendment. A specific statutory exception was necessary in bad debt cases only because the courts reversed the Tax Court and established as matter of law a "theoretically proper" rule which distorted the taxpayer's income. Congress would hardly expect the courts to repeat the same error in another class of cases, as we would do were we to affirm in this case.[36]

The Government also suggested that "If the tax benefit rule were judicially adopted the question would then arise of how it should be determined," and the difficulties of determining tax benefits, it says, create "an objection in itself to an attempt to adopt such a rule by judicial action." We are not adopting any rule of tax benefits. We only hold that no statute or regulation having the force of one and no principle of law compels the Tax Court to find taxable income in a transaction where as matter of fact it found no economic gain and no use of the transaction to gain tax benefit. The error of the court below consisted of treating as a rule of law what we think is only a question of proper tax accounting.

There is some difference in the facts of these cases. In two of them the Tax Court sustained deficiencies because it found that the deductions in prior years had offset gross income for those years and therefore concluded that the recoveries must to that extent be treated as taxable gain.[37] The taxpayers object that this conclusion disregards certain exemptions and credits which would have been available to offset the increased gross income in the prior years, so that the deductions resulted in no tax savings.

In determining whether the recoveries were taxable gain, however, the Tax Court was free to decide for itself what significance it would attach to the previous reduction of taxable income as contrasted with reduction of tax. The statute gives no inkling as to the correctness or incorrectness of the Tax Court's view, and we can find no compelling reason to substitute our judgment. . . .

No. 47 affirmed.

---

34. Mr. Randolph Paul, Tax Adviser to the Secretary of the Treasury, in a statement to the House Committee on Ways and Means said: "The Secretary has pointed out that wartime rates make it imperative to eliminate as far as possible existing inequities which distort the tax burden of certain taxpayers. I should like to discuss the inequities which the Secretary mentioned, as well as a few additional hardships. . . ."

35. Revenue Act of 1942 §116, 56 Stat. 798, 812.

36. The question of whether a recovery is properly accounted for as income in the year received or should be related to a previous reported deduction without tax benefit is one with a long history and much conflict. It arises not only in case of recoveries of previously charged-off bad debts and recoveries of the type we have here. It is also present in case of refund of taxes or cancellation of expenses or interest previously reported as accrued, adjustments of depreciation and depletion or amortization, and other similar situations.

37. Dobson v. Commissioner, 46 B.T.A. 770.

Nos. 44, 45, 46 reversed.

Notes

1. *Appellate review.* Consider carefully Justice Jackson's attempt here to curtail the scope of appellate review of Tax Court decisions. This aspect of *Dobson* was very unpopular with the tax bar and was soon repudiated by the statutory provision now in §7482, which provides for appellate review of Tax Court decisions "in the same manner and to the same extent as decisions of the district courts in civil actions tried without a jury."

Does the opinion in *Dobson* hold matters of accounting to be questions of fact rather than law? Or do questions of accounting constitute a third category? Could it be said that questions of accounting are factual in a sense similar to the way that questions of medical inference are factual: that is, that the court wants to rely on expert judgment from professionals other than lawyers? If not strictly factual, are matters of accounting nonlegal in this sense: that they are beyond the special competence of ordinary lawyers and judges?

On the other hand, the issue in *Dobson* is legal in the sense that it must be resolved by adopting a rule to be applied in all like cases. Therefore, even if the judgment to be made is one to which the accountant's training and experience are more relevant than the lawyer's, it is a judgment that must be incorporated into the law of the subject. In that sense the law incorporates a great many nonlegal judgments, does it not? And the judges derive their authority and responsibility to decide not so much from any special competence as from the necessity that the matter be settled authoritatively after taking the best counsel available.

Would this aspect of the *Dobson* decision have had more viability if it was expressed in terms of deference to the Tax Court rather than jurisdiction or scope of review? Compare Justice Jackson's dissent in *Arrowsmith*, Chapter 20A below.

2. *Statutory provisions.* The legislation referred to by the Court in which Congress enacted a tax benefit limitation for recovery of bad debts, prior taxes, and delinquency amounts is now in §111. This continued until 1984 to refer only to bad debts, taxes, and delinquency amounts, although regulations under it were written more broadly so as to embrace *Dobson* as well.

Would §111 now cover *Sanford & Brooks* and *Dobson?* Should it? How about §186, which was added in 1969? Is there any significant reason for separating §§111 and 186?

3. *The tax-benefit rule — equitable considerations.* Define precisely the hardship to which the tax-benefit rule is responsive. Is the response too narrow? Is the definition of the hardship too narrow?

In Perry v. United States, 160 F. Supp. 270 (1958), the taxpayer had, over a period of years, made and deducted contributions to a town for the construction of a library. The town decided not to construct the library and returned the taxpayer's contributions. The Court of Claims held that the return of the contributions was taxable income but that the tax should be limited to the amount of the aggregate tax reduction attributable to the earlier deductions. No other court interpreted the tax-benefit rule this way, and in Alice Phelan Sullivan Corp. v. United States, 381 F.2d 399 (1967), the Court of Claims specifically overruled this aspect of its own ruling in *Perry.* If there is to be a tax-benefit rule, is there any reason not to have the *Perry* version of it? Cf. §1341; Chapter 7B below.

What about people who simply have bad debt losses in a net loss year and never recover them? Are they any less deserving of relief than those who subsequently recover? Is the tax-benefit rule inequitable in that it gives relief to only a small fraction of the people who suffer the hardship of net losses? Does it in effect just substitute another arbitrary accounting rule for the strict annual rule? Is the tax-benefit rule better or worse than no relief in any such cases?

In a sense, the tax-benefit rule and the net operating loss deduction deal with the same hardship: the occurrence of deduction items in a net loss year. But relief is granted on quite different conditions. Give examples showing how the tax-benefit rule may grant relief while the net operating loss deduction would not, and vice versa. Which represents a better way to grant relief? Are both necessary? Should a broader form of relief be adopted that would encompass both? What happens under present law if the conditions are met for relief under both the tax-benefit rule and §172? See §111(c).

4. *The tax-benefit rule — administrative considerations.* Consider the extent to which the tax-benefit rule interferes with orderly tax administration. Read §111 and the regulations thereunder and the last paragraph in *Dobson.* Does the tax-benefit rule make it impossible in effect to close a loss year?

5. *Tax detriment.* In 1937 a taxpayer received oil royalties of $5,000 on account of a certain Texas property. He reported the $5,000 as income for 1937. The taxpayer had a net loss of $17,000 from other items, so he paid no tax for that year.

Subsequently, taxpayer's title to the Texas property was challenged, and litigation followed that finally resulted in a judgment adverse to the taxpayer. In 1941, the taxpayer surrendered the property and also paid the plaintiff $5,000 representing the 1937 royalties, plus interest. Should a deduction for this payment be disallowed on the grounds that the taxpayer suffered no tax burden or detriment on account of the prior receipt? Maurice P. O'Meara, 8 T.C. 622 (1947).

3. The Inclusionary Side of the Tax-Benefit Rule

In the preceding materials there is a straightforward cash recovery that would be taxed but for the tax-benefit rule; the tax-benefit rule is an *exclusionary* rule that applies to *prevent* taxation of the recovery if there was *no tax benefit* from the prior deduction.

But suppose there is no recovery in any simple sense. Suppose, for example, a taxpayer purchases business supplies and deducts the cost, but then in a subsequent year gives the materials away to a personal friend. Is the government then entitled to impose a tax to make up for the deduction that now appears unjustified?

This question has come to litigation in the context of certain corporate transactions. For example, Hillsboro National Bank paid a state property tax imposed on its shareholders and claimed a federal income tax deduction for it under §164(e). The state tax was subsequently held invalid and refunded directly *to the shareholders*. The IRS asserted that the bank had taxable income in the year of the repayment to its shareholders.

In another example, Bliss Dairy deducted the cost of dairy feed on purchase; it subsequently made a liquidating distribution of all its assets, including the feed. The IRS charged Bliss with taxable income in the amount of the prior deduction, notwithstanding the provision in §336, as it then read, that no gain or loss shall be recognized to a corporation on a liquidating distribution of property.

The *Bliss Dairy* and *Hillsboro National Bank* cases both went all the way to the Supreme Court, where they were consolidated. In both cases the government assessed a tax on the basis of a tax-benefit rule, which it asserted required current taxation of the previously deducted item even though it was not recovered in cash by the taxpayer corporation itself. The taxpayers argued that such a recovery was a prerequisite to application of the rule, and the government argued that it was enough if later events were inconsistent with the earlier deduction. The Supreme Court concluded that the purpose of the rule was to "achieve rough transactional parity in tax," and that such parity requires that "a careful examination shows that the later event is indeed fundamentally inconsistent with the premise on which the deduction was initially based. That is, if that event had occurred within the same taxable year, it would have foreclosed the deduction." And it concluded that this showing was made with respect to Bliss Dairy but not Hillsboro Bank because the focus in §164(e) is on payment by the corporation and not retention of funds by the state. Hillsboro National Bank v. Commissioner, 457 U.S. 1103 (1983).

Compare the problems discussed here with that in *Haverly*, Chapter 2A above. Should the holding in that case be described in terms of tax benefit?

Now compare the introductory clauses of §§104(a), 105(b), and 213(a). In plain English, what do these statutory provisions say?

References

A. Damage Payments: Founts, Payments Received in Settlement of Litigation and Claims, 25 N.Y.U. Inst. on Fed. Taxn. 555 (1967); Huff, Tax Aspects of Litigated Awards and Settlements Involving Real Estate, 40 N.Y.U. Inst. on Fed. Taxn. 25 (1982); Note, The Tax Consequences of a Punitive Damages Award, 31 Hastings L.J. 909 (1980).

B. Personal Injuries: Stephen B. Cohen & Laura Sager, Discrimination Against Damages for Unlawful Discrimination: The Supreme Court, Congress, and the Income Tax, 35 Harv. J. Legis. 447 (1998); Joseph M. Dodge, *Murphy* and the Sixteenth Amendment in Relation to the Taxation of Non-Excludable Personal Injury Awards, 8 Fla. Tax Rev. 369-427 (2007); Jaeger, Taxation of Punitive Damage Awards After the Revenue Reconciliation Act of 1989, 68 Tax Notes 368 (1990).

C. Insurance: Bradley W. Joondeph, Tax Policy and Health Care Reform: Rethinking the Tax Treatment of Employer-Sponsored Health Insurance, 1995 B.Y.U. L. Rev. 1229; IRS, Health Savings Accounts and Other Tax-Favored Health Plans (Pub. 969) (2007); Feld, Abortion to Aging: Problems of Definition in the Medical Expense Deduction, 58 B.U.L. Rev. 165 (1978); Newman, The Medical Expense Deduction: A Preliminary Postmortem, 53 S. Cal. L. Rev. 787 (1980); Chieche & Adney, An Analysis of the Effects of the Life Insurance and Annuity Provisions of TEFRA, 57 J. Tax'n 338 (1982); Goode, Policyholders' Interest Income from Life Insurance Under the Income Tax, 16 Vand. L. Rev. 33 (1962); Irenas, Life Insurance Interest Income Under the Federal Income Tax, 21 Tax L. Rev. 297 (1966); Pike, Reflections on the Meaning of Life: An Analysis of Section 7702 and the Taxation of Cash Value Life Insurance, 43 Tax L. Rev. 491 (1988); Richey, Life Insurance: The Investment of Your Life (How to Pick What Is Best for the Client), 41 N.Y.U. Inst. on Fed. Taxn. 33 (1983).

D. Previously Deducted Losses: Bittker & Kanner, The Tax Benefit Rule, 26 U.C.L.A. L. Rev. 265 (1978); Rice, Law, Fact, and Taxes: Review of Tax Court Decisions Under Section 1141 of the Internal Revenue Code, 51 Colum. L. Rev. 439 (1951); Wilkinson, The Net Operating Loss Deduction and Related Income Tax Devices, 45 Tex. L. Rev. 809 (1967).

Chapter 4 — *Gifts and Kindred Items*

Read §102(a). What is the policy behind it? Does the policy behind it give any clues as to how it should be interpreted?

A. *INCOME INTERESTS*

IRWIN v. GAVIT
268 U.S. 161 (1925)

Mr. Justice HOLMES delivered the opinion of the Court. . . . The question is whether the sums received by the plaintiff under the will of Anthony N. Brady in 1913, 1914 and 1915 were income and taxed. The will, admitted to probate August 12, 1913, left the residue of the estate in trust to be divided into six equal parts, the income of one part to be applied so far as deemed proper by the trustees to the education and support of the testator's granddaughter, Marcia Ann Gavit, the balance to be divided into two equal parts and one of them to be paid to the testator's son-in-law, the plaintiff, in equal quarter-yearly payments during his life. But on the granddaughter's reaching the age of twenty-one or dying the fund went over, so that, the granddaughter then being six years old, it is said, the plaintiff's interest could not exceed fifteen years. The Courts below held that the payments received were property acquired by bequest, were not income and were not subject to tax.

The statute in Section II, A, subdivision 1, provides that there shall be levied a tax "upon the entire net income arising or accruing from all sources in the preceding calendar year to every citizen of the United States." If these payments properly may be called income by the common understanding of that word and the statute has failed to hit them it has missed so much of the general purpose that it expresses at the start. Congress intended to use its power to the full extent. Eisner v. Macomber, 252 U.S. 189, 203. By B. the net income is to include "gains or profits and income derived from any source whatever, including the income from but not the value of property acquired by gift, bequest, devise or descend." By D. trustees are to make "return of the net income of the person for whom they act, subject to this tax," and by E. trustees and others having the control or payment of fixed or determinable gains, & c., of another person who are required to render return on behalf of another are "authorized to withhold enough to pay the normal tax." The language quoted leaves no doubt in our minds that if a fund were given to trustees for A for life with remainder over, the income received by the trustees and paid over to A would be income of A under the statute. It seems to us hardly less clear that even if there were a specific provision that A should have no interest in the corpus, the payments would be income none the less within the meaning of the statute and the Constitution, and by popular speech. In the first case it is true that the bequest might be said to be of the corpus for life, in the second it might be said to be of the income. But we think that the provision of the act that exempts bequests assumes the gift of a corpus and contrasts it with the income arising from it, but was not intended to exempt income properly so-called simply because of a severance between it and the principal fund. No such conclusion can be drawn from Eisner v. Macomber, 252 U.S. 189, 206, 207. The money was income in the hands of the trustees and we know of nothing in the law that prevented its being paid and received as income by the donee.

The Courts below went on the ground that the gift to the plaintiff was a bequest and carried no interest in the corpus of the fund. We do not regard those considerations as conclusive, as we have said, but if it were material a gift of the income of a fund ordinarily is treated by equity as creating an interest in the fund. Apart from technicalities, we can perceive no distinction relevant to the question before us between a gift of the fund for life and gift of the income from it. The fund is appropriated to the production of the same result whichever form the gift takes. Neither are we troubled by the question where to draw the line. That is the question in pretty much everything worth arguing in the law. . . . Day and night, youth and age are only types. But the distinction between the cases put of a gift from the corpus of the estate payable in instalments and the present seems to us not hard to draw, assuming that the gift supposed would not be income. This is a gift from the income of a very large fund, as income. It seems to us immaterial that the same amounts might receive a different color from their source. We are of opinion that quarterly payments, which it was hoped would last for fifteen years, from the income of an estate intended for the plaintiff's child, must be regarded as income within the meaning of the Constitution and the law. It is said that the tax laws should be construed favorably for the taxpayers. But that is not a reason for creating a doubt or for exaggerating one when it is no greater than we can bring ourselves to feel in this case.

Judgment reversed.

Mr. Justice SUTHERLAND, dissenting. By the plain terms of the Revenue Act of 1913, the value of property acquired by gift, bequest, devise, or descent is not to be included in net income. Only the income derived from such property is subject to the tax. The question, as it seems to me, is really a very simple one. Money, of course, is property. The money here sought to be taxed as income was paid to respondent under the express provisions of a will. It was a gift by will — a bequest. United States v. Merriam, 263 U.S. 179, 184. It, therefore, fell within the precise letter of the statute; and, under well settled principles, judicial inquiry may go no further. The taxpayer is entitled to the rigor of the law. There is no latitude in a taxing statute — you must adhere to the very words. United States v. Merriam, supra, pp. 187-188.

The property which respondent acquired being a bequest, there is no occasion to ask whether, before being handed over to him, it had been carved from the original corpus of, or from subsequent additions to, the estate. The corpus of the estate was not the legacy which respondent received, but merely the source which gave rise to it. The money here sought to be taxed was not the fruits of a legacy; it was the legacy itself. Matter of Stanfield, 135 N.Y. 292, 294.

With the utmost respect for the judgments of my brethren to the contrary, the opinion just rendered, I think without warrant, searches the field of argument and inference for a meaning which should be found only in the strict letter of the statute.

Mr. Justice BUTLER concurs in this dissent.

Notes

1. *Life tenants. Gavit* exhibits the tax treatment that applies in the very common situation of income-producing property put in trust for *A* for life, with remainder to *B*. In such a situation the income is distributed and taxed to *A*; the corpus distribution to *B*, on *A*'s death, would be exempt from income tax under §102. Is this a sound way to treat that situation? Why? What alternatives should be considered?

2. *Gavit.* How is the situation in *Gavit* different? Did the taxpayer in *Gavit* argue to distinguish his case from that of an ordinary life tenant, or did he argue that an ordinary life tenant would not be taxable on income distributed to him? How would you characterize the taxpayer's argument? This kind of argument is not uncommon, especially in the early cases. Justice Holmes' answer to the taxpayer's argument is twofold. Again it is not atypical. Articulate and evaluate each branch of his reasoning: Which is the stronger?

Is it consistent with the statutory structure to reason, as in *Gavit*, that an item is not a gift because it *is* income? The holding in *Gavit* is now codified in §102(b)(2).

3. *Whitehouse.* Suppose *T* holds property in trust under instructions to pay *B* $5,000 a year out of income if sufficient and otherwise out of corpus. In a particular year *T* receives $6,000 in income and distributes $5,000 to *B.* How will *B* be taxed? In Burnet v. Whitehouse, 283 U.S. 148 (1931), such a distribution was held not taxable. The penultimate sentence in §102(b) overrules *Whitehouse.*

4. *Subchapter J.* Beginning at §641, subchapter J now prescribes a highly articulated scheme for determining taxable income of trusts and beneficiaries and, in some circumstances, grantors. The basic pattern is that income is currently taxed to beneficiaries to whom distributable or distributed and otherwise to the trust itself. This basic objective is achieved by making the trust taxable, §641, but allowing it a deduction for whatever is currently distributable or distributed and so taxable to beneficiaries. §§651, 661. Complications arise in determining what is distributed or distributable, determining who is taxable if distributions exceed trust income, and reconciling differences in the definition of income for trust accounting and income tax purposes. For slightly more detailed material on subchapter J, see Chapter 18B below.

Look at §663(a)(1) and consider its relation to the decisions in *Gavit* and *Whitehouse.*

5. Would it be a more accurate treatment of life tenants to let them have the value of their life interests tax-free by way of amortization? For example, if when *L* is 50 years old a fund is left to *L* for life with remainder to *R*, then one would ascertain the actuarial value of the life interest and allow this amount to be deducted ratably over *L*'s life expectancy. *L* would thus be treated essentially as if he had received cash tax-free as an inheritance and had then used the cash to purchase a life annuity. Section 273 clearly disallows any such treatment. Why?

COMMISSIONER v. EARLY
445 F.2d 166 (5th Cir. 1971)

Before Coleman, Ainsworth and Godbold, Circuit Judges.

GODBOLD, Circuit Judge: . . . Taxpayers Allen and Jeanette Early are husband and wife, reside in Dallas, Texas, and filed joint returns for the tax years in question. Both were friends of Sam and Rose Van Wert. For several years prior to 1954, taxpayer acted as Sam Van Wert's accountant. Following Van Wert's death in that year, taxpayer performed the same services for Mrs. Van Wert until her death. At her husband's death Mrs. Van Wert was left with real and intangible personal property of substantial value, including 70,000 shares of stock in El Paso Natural Gas Company. By and large, the certificates and instruments evidencing her ownership of these assets, together with her books and records, were in taxpayer's possession.

In November, 1957 Mrs. Van Wert executed stock powers, covering certificates representing the 70,000 shares of El Paso stock in taxpayer's possession, in favor of taxpayer (50,000 shares) and Mrs. Early (20,000 shares). Mrs. Van Wert's 1957 federal gift tax return, prepared and filed by taxpayer, did not reflect these transactions.

Mrs. Van Wert died August 12, 1958. She left a will and codicil in which she appointed taxpayer and another as co-executors, made various specific and monetary bequests, expressly pretermitted all relatives in "blood or law," and directed that the residue of her estate be placed in trust with the income to be paid to her physician and his wife for their joint lives, the remainder to specified charitable donees. The will and codicil did not specifically mention the 70,000 shares of El Paso stock. Taxpayers claimed ownership of the shares, asserting that in executing the stock powers Mrs. Van Wert had intended to make them a gift[2] of the stock.

Mrs. Van Wert's will and codicil were contested by 44 intestate heirs on the grounds of undue influence and lack of testamentary capacity, and several parties to the controversy objected to taxpayers' retention of the El Paso stock. A settlement was reached in November, 1959 which in part provided that in return for the surrender of the El Paso stock to the estate, and destruction of the stock powers, taxpayers would be accorded a joint life interest in 32 percent of the income from the trust reduced by $4,000 during each of the first four years. Taxpayers incurred legal fees of $20,000 in connection with this settlement.

The El Paso stock transferred to the estate had a fair market value at the date of transfer of $2,288,125, and it was included in the estate for federal estate tax purposes as a transfer by gift with the retention of a life interest. The value of the El Paso stock comprised about 53 percent of the corpus delivered to the testamentary trust. The commuted value of taxpayers' joint life estate in the trust income was $716,919.91, based upon an expected joint life of 31.16 years, calculated through the use of the Commissioner's tables. . . .

During the years 1961-1965 taxpayers reported as income the payments they received from the Van Wert testamentary trust. They also took periodic deductions for amortization of the cost basis of the life estate. These annual deductions for amortization were calculated by combining the commuted value of the life estate at the time taxpayers acquired it with the $20,000 legal fee incurred in connection with the settlement, Pennroad Corp., 21 T.C. 1087 (1954); Jones Estate v. C.I.R. 127 F.2d 231 (5th Cir. 1942), and dividing this by the expected duration of taxpayers' joint life, 31.16 years. However, since the Van Wert trust received part of its income in the form of interest in tax-exempt obligations, taxpayers allocated part of the annual amortization to taxable income and part to income from tax-exempt sources, and did not

---

2. A bank guaranteed Mrs. Van Wert's signature on the stock powers to be genuine.

claim deductions for that part of the amortization allocated to tax-exempt income.

The Commissioner disallowed the deductions for amortization on the ground that taxpayers' life interest was "acquired by gift, bequest, or inheritance" and that the deductions were therefore prohibited by §273 of the Code. . . .

Central to a resolution of the disputed applicability of §273 is whether the rationale of Lyeth v. Hoey, 305 U.S. 188 (1938), compels the conclusion that for income tax purposes taxpayers acquired their life interest by "gift, bequest, or inheritance." *Lyeth* held that an heir who contested his grandmother's will, and who, as a result of a compromise of that contest, received property from the grandmother's estate which he would not have received had the will gone uncontested, acquired that property "by bequest, devise, or inheritance," and was therefore not liable for federal income taxes. See I.R.C. §102. The Court observed that

> Petitioner was concededly an heir of his grandmother under the Massachusetts statute. It was by virtue of that heirship that he opposed probate of her alleged will which constituted an obstacle to the enforcement of his right. . . .
>
> There is no question that petitioner obtained that portion, upon the value of which he is sought to be taxed, because of his standing as an heir and of his claim in that capacity. . . .
>
> Whether he would receive any property [as an heir] depended upon the validity of his ancestor's will and the extent to which it would dispose of his ancestor's estate. When, by compromise and the decree enforcing it, that disposition was limited, what he got from the estate came to him because he was heir. . . . 305 U.S. at 195-197.

The Commissioner contends that taxpayers here acquired their life interest under circumstances analogous to those in *Lyeth*, that since the nature of their claim to the stock was as donees their life interest should also be treated as having been acquired by gift, and that §273 therefore prohibits amortization.

However, the Tax Court held, and taxpayers contend, that *Lyeth* is inapplicable because taxpayers "sold or exchanged" the stock, to which they had bona fide claims of title through an alleged prior gift, for their life interest. To characterize the transaction with a different label, it is their contention that they "purchased" their joint life interest, and that §273 does not apply to "purchased" life estates. See Gist v. United States, 296 F. Supp. 526 (S.D. Cal. 1968), aff'd. 423 F.2d 1118 (9th Cir. 1970); Bell v. Harrison, 212 F.2d 253 (7th Cir. 1954).

A taxpayer may legitimately amortize the cost basis of a purchased life interest. But we think that for income tax purposes these taxpayers must be treated as having acquired their life estates by gift and not by sale or exchange, or purchase. It is undisputed that whatever claim they may have had to the El Paso stock was acquired by a purported gift. It was this claim to ownership through an assertedly donative transaction which, among other things, was put in issue by the controversy over the Van Wert estate. The thrust of taxpayers' position in this controversy was that they were donees. We cannot conclude otherwise than that, when the dispute was compromised, whatever taxpayers took they took for income tax purposes as donees. . . .

There are circumstances under which the donee of another may through an exchange of rights or property with the donor also acquire a life interest which may be said to be purchased, and which is therefore amortizable notwithstanding §273. See Gist v. United States, supra; see also, Bell v. Harrison, supra; William N. Fry, Jr., 31 T.C. 522 (1958), aff'd. 293 F.2d 869 (6th Cir. 1960). And we think that this may be so where that which the donee exchanges consists of rights or property previously acquired from the donor. Cf. Sherman Ewing, 40 B.T.A. 912 (1939); C.I.R. v. Matheson, 82 F.2d 380 (5th Cir. 1936). It is also true that unlike Lyeth, who had an inchoate claim as an heir against his grandmother's estate, taxpayers here had claims of full ownership to stock which was in their possession, and that, therefore, the settlement involved some exchange of property rights, and in some degree resembled a "sale or exchange" of stock for life estate.

But all compromises, and therefore all transactions within the potential ambit of Lyeth v. Hoey, are in some measure exchanges. We believe it is not sufficient to render *Lyeth* inapplicable that taxpayers' status as purported donees took the form of claims to ownership of the stock, which resulted in the settlement resembling a sale of the stock and purchase of the life estate. Whether one relinquishes the right to litigate a suit contesting a will to judgment, as in *Lyeth*, or the claimed right to the possession, use and benefit of stock, as here, we have concluded that so long as the settlement is in substantial measure to resolve an underlying and disputed claim based upon a purported gift, bequest, inheritance or the like, what is received in settlement must be characterized, for tax purposes, by the nature of the underlying and disputed claim resolved.[6] Thus, in circumstances such as those presented by this record, where the rationale of *Lyeth* is implicated but where, in addition, the transaction resembles a sale or exchange of property, we think that *Lyeth* governs unless it may be said that the circumstances surrounding the transaction fairly exclude the possibility that the exchange is in reality a compromise of an underlying and controverted claim such as one of gift, bequest or inheritance.

---

6. We are not prepared to accept the somewhat broader proposition suggested in the Commissioner's brief, that the nature of the transaction by which taxpayers acquired their interest in the stock governs the tax treatment of the life interest. It is the nature of the underlying and disputed claim resolved by the settlement which is crucial, and the nature of the transaction by which taxpayers asserted ownership of the stock is only relevant here because it was the validity of that precise transaction which was in dispute and was resolved by the compromise.

That this broader proposition may have been advanced inadvertently by the Commissioner is indicated by his apparent acceptance of *Ewing*, supra, and *Matheson*, supra, as correct, but distinguishable from the case under consideration because the taxpayers in each of those decisions had a clear and pre-existing right to that which they exchanged.

Indeed, in the decisions relied upon by the Tax Court majority, and by taxpayers here, there existed no dispute which the exchange may be said to have compromised. Each taxpayer's right to that which he gave up in the exchange was unquestioned. In Gist v. United States, supra, a widow in a community property jurisdiction was put to an election by her husband's will. If she took against the will she retained fee simple title to her share in the community and received nothing from her husband. If she elected to take under the will she received a life interest in the income from her husband's share of the community but acceded to her husband's disposition of the remainder interest in her share. In short, she exchanged the remainder interest in her share of the community for a life interest in her husband's share. It was held that the widow acquired the life interest in the income from her husband's share by purchase and that §273 did not prohibit amortization of the commuted value of that interest.[7] However *Gist*, by reference to such decisions as C.I.R. v. Siegel, 250 F.2d 339, 345-347 (9th Cir. 1957), relied upon the undisputed and vested character of the wife's community interest, which was exchanged for the life interest. 296 F. Supp. at 528. Similarly, Sherman Ewing, supra, and C.I.R. v. Matheson, supra, which hold that the discharge of a monetary legacy by the transfer of securities constitutes a sale or exchange of the securities, involve legatees whose right to take was not in dispute.

Taxpayers here had no such clearcut right. The Tax Court held that they had a bona fide claim of title to the stock, but refrained from holding that they were undisputed owners by virtue of the purported gift. Their claim of ownership was very much in dispute. . . .

Taxpayers urge that White v. Thomas, 116 F.2d 147 (5th Cir. 1940), cert. denied, 313 U.S. 581 (1941), is to the contrary. The taxpayer there claimed ownership of a decedent's ranch through a prior inter vivos gift. In compromise of this claim the estate paid the taxpayer a sum of money. Taxpayer contended that the money received was not includable in gross income for federal tax purposes since it was received in compromise of a claim which he asserted as a donee, and under *Lyeth* should be treated as having been acquired by gift. We held that "[w]hen what is received by a compromise is a part of the very thing claimed, the assertion is correct," but that since taxpayer had not received a part of that claimed, i.e., the ranch, *Lyeth* was inapplicable.

We think that White v. Thomas is inapplicable. When taxpayers surrendered the El Paso stock to the Van Wert estate the estate in turn transferred it to the testamentary trust from which taxpayers were to receive their income interest. As we have pointed out, the value of the stock comprised some 53 percent of the trust corpus. When taxpayers received income from the

---

7. She was not permitted to amortize that portion of the life interest in the community property which was attributable to her share of the community, for she was entitled to that in any event and in no sense acquired it by either "purchase" or "compromise." 296 F. Supp. 529.

trust they were in part receiving income from the stock they had relinquished. . . .

Since, under the rationale of Lyeth v. Hoey, taxpayers must be treated for income tax purposes as having acquired their joint life estate by gift, §273 of the Code prohibits any deductions for amortization of the cost basis of the life estate. The decision of the Tax Court is therefore

Reversed.

Question

What implications does the resolution of the issue in this case have in computing the taxable income of the estate?

B. APPRECIATED PROPERTY

Suppose property is purchased by *T* for $1,000, goes up in value to $3,000, and is then transferred to *R* either by inter vivos gift or by bequest or inheritance on *T*'s death. Is there taxable income to either *T* or *R* on account of the transfer? If *R* sells the property for $3,500, does he then have any taxable gain, and if so, how much?

Under existing law, neither *T* nor *R* is thought to have taxable gain on the transfer; *R* because he is covered by §102, and *T* because she does not realize anything on the transfer. See §1001(b). It has been repeatedly urged that *T* should be made taxable on the $2,000 appreciation when she disposes of the property, if not before, but that argument is one of policy concerned with amending the statute, not interpreting it as it stands.

On *R*'s subsequent sale of the property the matter is considerably more complex.

1. Inter Vivos Gifts: §1015

TAFT v. BOWERS
278 U.S. 470 (1929)

Mr. Justice McReynolds delivered the opinion of the Court. . . . Abstractly stated, this is the problem —

In 1916 *A* purchased 100 shares of stock for $1,000 which he held until 1923 when their fair market value had become $2,000. He then gave them to *B* who sold them during the year 1923 for $5,000. The United States claims that, under the Revenue Act of 1921, *B* must pay income tax upon $4,000, as realized profits. *B* maintains that only $3,000 — the appreciation during her ownership — can be regarded as income; that the increase during the donor's ownership is not income assessable against her within intendment of the Sixteenth Amendment. . . .

We think the manifest purpose of Congress expressed in [§1015] was to require the petitioner to pay the exacted tax.

The only question subject to serious controversy is whether Congress had power to authorize the exaction.

It is said that the gift became a capital asset of the donee to the extent of its value when received and, therefore, when disposed of by her no part of that value could be treated as taxable income in her hands.

The Sixteenth Amendment provides

"The Congress shall have power to lay and collect taxes on incomes from whatever source derived, without apportionment among the several States, and without regard to any census or enumeration."

Income is the thing which may be taxed — income from any source. The Amendment does not attempt to define income or designate how taxes may be laid thereon, or how they may be enforced.

Under former decisions here the settled doctrine is that the Sixteenth Amendment confers no power upon Congress to define and tax as income without apportionment something which theretofore could not have been properly regarded as income.

Also, this Court has declared — "Income may be defined as the gain derived from capital, from labor, or from both combined, provided it be understood to include profit gained through a sale or conversion of capital assets." Eisner v. Macomber [Chapter 5A below]. The "gain derived from capital," within the definition, is "not a gain accruing to capital, nor a growth or increment of value in the investment, but a gain, a profit, something of exchangeable value proceeding from the property, severed from the capital however invested, and coming in, that is, received or drawn by the claimant for his separate use, benefit and disposal." United States v. Phellis, 257 U.S. 156.

If, instead of giving the stock to petitioner, the donor had sold it at market value, the excess over the capital he invested (cost) would have been income therefrom and subject to taxation under the Sixteenth Amendment. He would have been obliged to share the realized gain with the United States. He held the stock — the investment — subject to the right of the sovereign to take part of any increase in its value when separated through sale or conversion and reduced to his possession. Could he, contrary to the express will of Congress, by mere gift enable another to hold his stock free from such right, deprive the sovereign of the possibility of taxing the appreciation when actually severed, and convert the entire property into a capital asset of the donee, who invested nothing, as though the latter had purchased at the market price? And after a still further enhancement of the property, could the donee make a second gift with like effect, etc.? We think not.

In truth the stock represented only a single investment of capital — that made by the donor. And when through sale or conversion the increase was separated therefrom, it became income from that investment in the hands of the recipient subject to taxation according to the very words of the Sixteenth Amendment. By requiring the recipient of the entire increase to pay a part into the public treasury, Congress deprived her of no right and subjected her to no hardship. She accepted the gift with knowledge of the statute and, as to the property received, voluntarily assumed the position of her donor. When she sold the stock she actually got the original sum invested, plus the entire appreciation; and out of the latter only was she called on to pay the tax demanded.

The provision of the statute under consideration seems entirely appropriate for enforcing a general scheme of lawful taxation. To accept the view urged in behalf of petitioner undoubtedly would defeat, to some extent, the purpose of Congress to take part of all gain derived from capital investments. To prevent that result and insure enforcement of its proper policy, Congress had power to require that for purposes of taxation the donee should accept the position of the donor in respect of the thing received. And in so doing, it acted neither unreasonably nor arbitrarily.

The power of Congress to require a succeeding owner, in respect of taxation, to assume the place of his predecessor is pointed out by United States v. Phellis, 257 U.S. 156 —

> Where, as in this case, the dividend constitutes a distribution of profits accumulated during an extended period and bears a large proportion to the par value of the stock, if an investor happened to buy stock shortly before the dividend, paying a price enhanced by an estimate of the capital plus the surplus of the company, and after distribution of the surplus, with corresponding reduction in the intrinsic and market value of the shares, he were called upon to pay a tax upon the dividend received, it might look in his case like a tax upon his capital. But it is only apparently so. In buying at a price that reflected the accumulated profits, he of course acquired as a part of the valuable rights purchased the prospect of a dividend from the accumulations — bought "dividend on" as the phrase goes — and necessarily took subject to the burden of the income tax proper to be assessed against him by reason of the dividend if and when made. He simply stepped into the shoes, in this as in other respects, of the stockholder whose shares he acquired, and presumably the prospect of a dividend influenced the price paid, and was discounted by the prospect of an income tax to be paid thereon. In short, the question whether a dividend made out of company profits constitutes income of the stockholder is not affected by antecedent transfers of the stock from hand to hand.

There is nothing in the Constitution which lends support to the theory that gain actually resulting from the increased value of capital can be treated as taxable income in the hands of the recipient only so far as the increase occurred while he owned the property. And Irwin v. Gavit [Chapter 4A above] is to the contrary.

The judgments below are
Affirmed.
The Chief Justice took no part in the consideration or decision of these cases.

Questions

1. The Court's opinion in Taft v. Bowers suggests that §1015 is acceptable because it is necessary to prevent tax avoidance that would result from the realization requirement announced in Eisner v. Macomber, Chapter 5A below. Could Congress instead tax appreciation to the donor at the time the gift is made? As to the donor, the transaction (property ownership) is completed on making the gift, but has the donor obtained the value of the appreciation for his own use and enjoyment, separate from the risks of the investment? See Helvering v. Bruun, Chapter 5C below; Helvering v. Horst, Chapter 18A below.

2. Taft v. Bowers involved an attempt to obtain exemption from tax. Section 1015 implicates questions of the proper taxpayer, tax rates, and tax timing. Explain.

3. Is there a common theme in Irwin v. Gavit and Taft v. Bowers?

4. By the combined operation of the §102(a) exclusion and the absence of a deduction for gifts given, money gifts to individuals are taxed to the donor only. What about gifts in kind?

Problems

Look in §1015 and work out these problems:

1. *A* purchased shares of stock for $10,000. In 1996, when they were worth $16,000 he gave them to *B*, who sold the shares in 2008 for $15,000. How much gain (or loss) did *B* realize?

2. *C* purchased shares for $1,000. In 2005, when the shares were worth $600, she gave them to *D*. How much gain or loss will *D* realize if he subsequently sells for $500? For $900? For $1,400?

2. Property Acquired from Decedents: §§1014, 1022, & 691

Under our concept of realization and §102(a), the tax treatment of both the decedent and the recipient of a death-time donative transfer (whether bequest, devise, or inheritance) is the same as the treatment of an inter vivos gift: Neither party is taxed at the time of the transfer. The subsequent tax treatment of the recipient is very different, however. Compare §1014(a)(1) and (b)(1) with §1015(a). How do we treat the recipient upon the subsequent sale of inherited appreciated property? What if the property declined in value during the decedent's lifetime? Wealthy individuals commonly hold a diversified portfolio composed of stocks, bonds, real estate, and other investment assets, and at any given time some items in the portfolio will have appreciated while others will have declined in value. From a tax standpoint, should a wealthy elderly taxpayer adjust such a portfolio? Explain. Most property that is owned by taxpayers at death is in fact appreciated, and in consequence section 1014 is often referred to as a stepped-up basis.

Section 1014 means that some income is not taxed—it converts the deferral inherent in the realization requirement into outright tax forgiveness, thereby greatly increasing the tax preference for the wealthy. Partly for this reason, the IRS strictly applies statutory nonrecognition rules because nonrecognition is not just a matter of timing and who has temporary use of the tax dollars. See Reg. §1.1002-1(b) ("exceptions from the general rule requiring the recognition of all gains and losses . . . are strictly construed and do not extend beyond the words or the underlying assumptions and purposes of the exception"). Rather, any appreciation that is not taxed upon the disposition of property may escape tax entirely because, even if the gain is initially preserved by assigning an exchanged basis to some other asset, section 1014 may intervene to wipe out that appreciation on the owner's death.

According to congressional estimates, the failure to tax capital gains at death is expected to cause a revenue loss of about $60 billion in Fiscal Year 2010. This is the fifth largest tax expenditure on the list prepared by the Joint Committee on Taxation and is eclipsed only by (1) the reduced rates of tax afforded dividends and long-term capital gains, (2) the tax exemption granted employer-provided health care, (3) the deferral accorded qualified retirement savings, and (4) the mortgage interest deduction. Staff of the Joint Committee on Taxation, 110th Cong., Estimates of Federal Tax Expenditures for Fiscal Years 2007-2011, at 28, 24-36 (2007). Each of those larger tax expenditures finds some justification in either tax policy norms (reduced rates for long-term capital gains mitigate the lock-in caused by the realization requirement) or social policy goals extrinsic to the tax system (encouraging widespread health insurance, retirement savings, or home ownership). In an era when federal budget deficits of several hundred billion dollars annually are forecast for the long-term, what policies support the stepped-up basis rule? Is there a good reason to encourage people to hold on to their appreciated property until death?

To take a different tack on this problem, consider the likely consequences of repealing §1014. Appreciation in property owned at death could be taxed either by giving the recipient a carryover basis (as per §1015), or by treating the appreciation as realized at death so that the gains are included on the decedent's final income tax return. As for inter vivos gifts, the carryover basis approach may be criticized for taxing the appreciation at the wrong time, to the wrong person, and at the wrong rate. Perhaps more serious from an economic perspective would be the tendency of a carryover basis regime to indefinitely prolong the capital lock-in effect of the realization doctrine — at least §1014 wipes the slate clean at death and thereby prevents inter-generational capital lock in. Taxing appreciation to the property owner at death (sometimes called constructive realization, or realization at death), in contrast, sets a definite endpoint for the duration of tax deferral accorded unrealized gains. Realization at death would not only prevent the inter-generational capital lock in that is inherent in the carryover basis alternative, it would eliminate the capital lock in that is currently *caused* by §1014: elderly taxpayers are often deterred from selling appreciated assets, even when they need the money for their own support, so that their children can get the benefit of tax forgiveness at death. Unfortunately, there is a catch. Collecting tax on the appreciation from the decedent's estate would frequently require asset sales to raise money to pay the tax, and such forced liquidations outrage taxpayers. We shall see that this liquidity concern, with its focus on convenience in the timing of tax liability, is a common justification of nonrecognition rules, such as §1031 on like-kind exchanges. See Chapter 5D. (It has also long been a rallying point for opposition to the federal estate tax.) This line of reasoning suggests that §1014 may have survived because it offers a taxpayer-friendly second-best solution to the economic and compliance problems that would be posed by either a carryover basis or a constructive realization regime.

Pause for a moment to consider whether this is a false dilemma. Realization at death would surely force asset sales if the tax so computed is immediately payable in full by the decedent's estate. Must the tax obligation be collected in such an inflexible manner? Would a long-term installment payment obligation adequately respond to liquidity concerns? What explains the staying power of §1014?

In 2001 Congress amended the federal estate tax, increasing the estate tax exclusion (i.e., the exempt amount of wealth transfers) in stages from $675,000 in 2001 to $3.5 million in 2009, and phasing down the maximum rate from 55 percent in 2001 to 45 percent for decedents who died in 2007, 2008, or 2009. The 2001 legislation also prospectively repealed the estate tax as of January 1, 2010. For budget reasons, however, these and other tax reductions that were enacted in 2001 were made effective for only 10 years so that, absent further legislation extending or making permanent the 2001 tax reductions, the law in effect in 2001 will come back into force in 2011. In that event, the estate tax would reappear with renewed vigor (the exclusion level would drop back to $675,000 and the top rate would jump up to 55 percent) after a one-year "repeal" (hiatus, really). Congress tied the elimination of the estate tax to the prospective repeal of the stepped-up basis rule. See §1014(f). In place of §1014, a "modified carryover basis" rule is scheduled to apply to property acquired from decedents who die after December 31, 2009. Read and evaluate §1022. Observe that while 2.4 million individuals (citizens or residents) died in the United States during calendar year 2004, the IRS reports that only 11,399 estate tax returns were filed reporting property owned at death with a value in excess of $3.5 million. What do you make of this state of affairs?

There is an important exception to the fair market value basis if the property in question is *income in respect of a decedent*. That phrase is not defined in the statute. It includes any naked right to receive income, such as a doctor's uncollected fees, an employee's uncollected wages, pension rights that survive a retiree's death, interest due on a bond or any other debt, dividends declared on stock, or rent due from a tenant. Most income in respect of a decedent is ordinary income, but if a capital asset is sold during life and payment is not received until after death, then the appreciation is taxable as capital gain income in respect of a decedent. Section 691(a) states that all these items will be taxed when collected or disposed of, and both §1014(c) and §1022(f) confirm that this means such items do not qualify for a basis step up. Examine and consider the correlative deductions allowed by §691(b) and (c); what is their rationale?

Problems

Look in §§1014 and 691 and work out the following problems.

1. *TP*, a high-income retiree, owns blocks of stock in three large publicly traded corporations, General Electric (GE), General Foods (GF), and General Motors (GM). His holdings in each company have a current market value of $100,000, but they were purchased at different times for different amounts. Specifically, the GE stock was bought for $60,000, the GF for $100,000, and the GM shares were acquired at a price of $150,000. *TP* plans to sell one block of stock because he needs $100,000 to fund his retirement travel and recreation. His holdings in the other corporations will be used to make (1) a gift to his children this year, and (2) a bequest (i.e., gift under a will) to his grandchildren. From a tax standpoint, what disposition should *TP* make of each block of stock?

2. *A* purchased shares of stock for $10,000. In 1997, when they were worth $16,000, he gave them to *B* subject to a reserved life income interest. *A* later transferred the life estate to *B* in 1999, when the stock was worth $17,000. *A* died in 2001 and the property, which was then worth $19,000, was includible in his gross estate pursuant to §§2035(a) and 2036(a). *B* sold the shares in 2008 for $24,000. How much gain or loss did *B* realize?

3. *C* purchased shares for $1,000. In 2009, when the shares were worth $600, *C* died, leaving the shares to *D*. How much gain or loss will *D* realize if he subsequently sells for $500? For $900? For $1,400?

4. *E*, a doctor, died suddenly in the prime of life. Among the assets in her estate were $10,000 worth of accounts receivable for services performed for patients. These were valued in her estate at $9,800, and the executor

subsequently sold them all to a collection agency for $9,500. How much gain or loss is realized on the sale?

Notes on the Federal Transfer Taxes

1. *Estate tax.* The federal estate tax, §§2001 *et seq.*, is principally a tax on net wealth owned at death. Section 2001 imposes the tax at graduated rates on the taxable estate, §§2031-2046 enumerate the property interests included in the gross estate, and §§2053-2058 prescribe the deductions allowable in arriving at the taxable estate. Section 2010 allows a credit that effectively exempts from the tax the estates of all but the wealthiest individuals: In recent years less than 1 percent of decedents have left estates that actually incurred tax liability.

The estate tax applies to the value of all property owned at death, regardless of its adjusted basis for income tax purposes. §2031(a). Does the existence of the estate tax provide an adequate justification for §1014? To bar easy avoidance, the taxable estate is defined to include the value of property given away during life but in which the decedent retained specified sorts of interests. §§2036-2040, 2042, 2044.

2. *Gift tax.* The federal gift tax, §§2501 *et seq.*, further protects the estate tax by imposing some burden with respect to property given away during life with no strings attached. Indeed, the gift and estate taxes are now generally integrated with one another by using of the same rate schedule and taking a decedent's lifetime taxable gifts into account in computing the amount of his estate tax. §§2502(a), 2001(b). They also share the same unified credit, which for individuals dying in 2009 exempts $3.5 million of cumulative donative transfers during life and at death.

The gift tax has also been thought to have a protective function with respect to the income tax by imposing some immediate tax cost when a wealthy taxpayer transfers large amounts of income-producing property to relatives in lower income tax brackets. For this reason the 2001 legislation, which is scheduled to eliminate the estate and generation skipping transfer taxes for decedents who die in 2010, left the federal gift tax in place but with its top rate reduced to 35 percent. Should the gift tax survive solely as an adjunct to the income tax? Would expansion of the scope of the "kiddie tax," §1(g), be a better solution?

3. *Generation-skipping transfer (GST) tax.* The GST tax, §§2601 *et seq.*, further backstops the estate and gift taxes by assuring that transfers accomplished through the use of trusts or future interests do not allow large fortunes to pass through multiple generations at the cost of only a single round of transfer taxation. If a settlor, *S*, places property in trust with income to her child for life, principal to her grandchildren, the transfer will be subject to either estate or gift taxation (typically depending on whether *S* may amend or revoke the trust during life), but the distribution of principal to the

grandchildren would not trigger taxation in the child's estate. (The child was not the transferor of the property and so the child's income interest is not a retained life estate or power that would trigger inclusion in the child's gross estate, §2036.) In contrast, if *S* had given fee ownership to her child, who later passed the property on to the next generation, two rounds of transfer tax would have been due. The GST tax prevents such dynastic wealth transfer tax minimization. §§2601, 2611(a), 2612(a), 2613, 2651.

C.   *GRATUITOUS TRANSFERS OUTSIDE THE FAMILY*

The gift provisions of the income tax undoubtedly have their primary application in the context of intra-family property transfers, but they are not limited to such transfers. They clearly apply to extra-familial transfers made in a noncommercial context, such as gifts among social friends. But they are not limited to family or social contexts, so various other payments have been sought to be brought within the gift exclusion.

In 1954 two subjects were carved out for separate statutory treatment: prizes and awards, and scholarships and fellowships. The separate statutory exclusions for these have been subsequently narrowed quite substantially. Important matters, particularly involving transfers to employees and their families, were left to be governed by §102. That exclusion, too, has been narrowed by subsequent legislation.

Let us look first at the matters separately dealt with in 1954 before returning to §102.

1.   Prizes and Awards

PAULINE C. WASHBURN
5 T.C. 1333 (1945)

Van Fossan, Judge: . . .

The petitioner was sitting at home during the evening of March 12, 1941, when the telephone rang. A guest in the house answered the phone and stated that the call was for the petitioner. Petitioner went to the telephone and a man's voice said, "Congratulations, Mrs. Washburn." Petitioner inquired, "What for?" The voice said, "Haven't you been listening to your radio?" When petitioner replied that she had not, the voice said, "Well, you have won the Pot O' Gold." Petitioner did not know what he meant, but thought it was someone perpetrating a joke. She inquired, "What is this and what is it all about?" The voice repeated, "You have won the Pot O' Gold." Petitioner asked what she should do. The voice answered, "Nothing. Within a half hour you will receive the money." Petitioner asked how much money, and she was told $900.

Petitioner remained at home and within a half hour a telegraph messenger brought her a telegram which read as follows:

> Herewith draft for nine hundred dollars outright cash gift with our compliments presented by Tums Pot O' Gold program. Congratulations from Tommy Tucker and ourselves.
>
>   LEWIS HOWE COMPANY, MAKERS OF TUMS.

The boy also handed the petitioner a draft for $900. Petitioner deposited the money in the bank the following day.

A day or two later, while petitioner was absent from her home, a man called her home by telephone and asked if petitioner would care to appear on the "Tums" program. When this message was relayed to petitioner, the man was advised by telephone in the negative and that petitioner would not be interested. Petitioner never appeared on the program and has never had any other connection with the "Pot O' Gold" program or with the company that manufactures "Tums." She has never bought or used the product nor has she given a testimonial with regard to it. Petitioner never authorized anyone to announce that she had received the money.

The petitioner's name was chosen by the following method: The selection is made by the use of a spinning wheel bearing numbers. The company has in its possession telephone directories listing all telephones of the Bell System. These telephone books and listings are all numbered. The wheel first selects the telephone book to be used, next the page in the book, and then the line on the page on which the number of the telephone is given. The telephone number is called and, if answered by anyone, the party whose name appears as owner of the telephone receives the gift. If the person is not at home it makes no difference as long as the telephone is answered. The party called has no knowledge that he is going to be called.

Under the above set of facts, we conclude without difficulty that the $900 received by the petitioner was an outright gift, without any of the earmarks of income. The sum was not a gain from capital, for petitioner employed no capital; nor from labor, for petitioner contributed no labor; nor from both combined. It came to petitioner without expectation or effort. It was not the result of a wager. The receipt of the payment involved no subsequent obligation on petitioner's part and petitioner in no wise undertook to justify the payment by appearing on the program or authorizing the use of her name in advertising the fact of receipt. She gave no endorsement of the product.

The telegram accompanying the draft in payment denominated the payment an "outright cash gift." We think this correctly characterized the payment and accordingly hold that it did not constitute income to the petitioner.

Note

In 1954 the Congress reacted to this case, among others, by enacting §74(a) and the exception in §74(b), but the condition now appearing as (b)(3) was not added until 1986. How would *Glenshaw Glass* (Chapter 3A above) have affected *Washburn* if §74 had not been enacted?

PAUL V. HORNUNG
47 T.C. 428 (1967)

HOYT, Judge. . . .

. . . Each year *Sport Magazine* (hereinafter sometimes referred to as Sport or the magazine) awards a new Corvette automobile to the player selected by its editors (primarily by its editor in chief) as the outstanding player in the National Football League championship game. . . .

On December 31, 1961, petitioner played in the National Football League championship game between the Green Bay Packers and the New York Giants. The game was played in Green Bay, Wis. Petitioner scored a total of 19 points during this game and thereby established a new league record. At the end of this game petitioner was selected by the editors of Sport as the most valuable player and the winner of the Corvette, and press releases were issued announcing the award. . . .

The dominant motive and purpose of McFadden-Bartell in awarding the Corvette to petitioner was to promote and benefit their business of publishing Sport Magazine. . . .

. . . Petitioner's offensive strategy . . . is two-pronged. He contends (1) that the car was received as a gift and therefore properly excluded from gross income under section 102(a), and (2) that the car was received as a nontaxable prize or award under section 74.

It is our opinion that certainly the donor's motive here precludes a determination that Sport made a gift of the Corvette to petitioner in 1962. It is clear that there was no detached and disinterested generosity. It also seems clear that the enactment of section 74 has had the desirable effect of eliminating the theory of gift exclusions from the field of prizes and awards. The Supreme Court has stated in Commissioner v. Duberstein, 363 U.S. 278, 290 (1960), with regard to gift exclusions that:

> If there is fear of undue uncertainty or overmuch litigation, Congress may make more precise its treatment of the matter by singling out certain factors and making them determinative of the matter, as it has done in one field of the "gift" exclusion's former application, that of prizes and awards. [Footnote omitted.]

Petitioner undeniably received an award for his outstanding performance in the National Football League championship game. Under the provisions of section 74, gross income includes amounts received as prizes and awards unless section 117 (relating to scholarships and fellowship grants), or the exception set forth in subsection (b) is applicable. Therefore, petitioner is precluded from effectively arguing that the award constituted a gift, and he can only hope to score on his argument that the award qualifies as an exception under section 74(b). In making this argument, petitioner shifts into a shotgun formation, contending that his accomplishments in the championship football game constitute educational, artistic, scientific, and civic achievements within the meaning of section 74(b). We believe that petitioner should be caught behind the line of scrimmage on this particular offensive maneuver.

. . . Petitioner relies primarily upon the opinions and beliefs of the editor in chief of Sport to establish the applicability of section 74(b).

In the opinion of this witness, the game of football is educational because it is taught in accredited colleges as part of certain physical education courses. Moreover, being a star football player is said to be an artistic achievement since such status "calls for a degree of artistry." Finally, since the skills of a football player are based upon techniques which encompass certain "scientific" principles, it is contended that petitioner's ability to excel in the execution of these techniques is a scientific achievement worthy of recognition by means of the award presented by Sport. Petitioner also argues that the award was made in recognition of civic achievement due to the alleged interest of the President of the United States in petitioner's application for leave from the Army to allow participation in the championship game.

We believe that the words "educational," "artistic," "scientific," and "civic" as used in section 74(b) should be given their ordinary, everyday meaning in the context of defining certain types of personal achievement. Legislative history supports our belief. For example, the Senate report states that the provisions of section 74(b) are intended to exempt from taxation such awards as the Nobel Prize. See S. Rept. No. 1622, to accompany H.R. 8300 (Pub. L. 591), 83d Cong., 2d Sess., p. 178 (1954).

The legislative history of section 74 has been judicially interpreted as indicating that "only awards for genuinely meritorious achievements were to be freed from taxation." Simmons v. United States, 308 F.2d 160, 163 (C.A. 4, 1962). It was further stated in *Simmons* that all of the types of achievements singled out in section 74(b) resemble each other in general character since "they all represent activities enhancing in one way or another the public good." This interpretation is consistent with our view that the field of activity here in question, professional football, is not an activity which is "educational," "artistic," "scientific," or "civic" in the traditional, ordinarily understood, and intended sense of these words.

We feel confident that Congress had no intention of allowing professional football to constitute a type of activity for which proficiency could be recognized with an exempt award under section 74(b). . . .

MAURICE M. WILLS
48 T.C. 308 (1967), aff'd, 411 F.2d 537 (9th Cir. 1969)

FAY, Judge. . . . In 1962, petitioner broke the major league baseball record for the most stolen bases in one season, a record that had been set some 47 years earlier by Ty Cobb. In the same year, petitioner had a 299 batting average and tied with three other ball players for the most triples hit in the National League. Petitioner led the Dodgers in most games played, most times at bat, and most runs scored. . . .

In January 1963, petitioner received the S. Rae Hickok belt awarded annually to the outstanding professional athlete of the prior year.[1] . . .

Petitioner opines that the fair market value of the Hickok belt is not includable in his taxable income. In support of this position, he argues that the award of the Hickok belt was made "primarily in recognition of religious, charitable, scientific, educational, artistic, literary, or civic achievement." . . .

Petitioner vainly attempts to distinguish the facts in *Hornung* from those surrounding the award of the Hickok belt in the instant case by contending that "stealing bases over a complete major league schedule is quite different from playing one football game." The mere fact that the Hickok belt was awarded for petitioner's athletic skill and prowess exhibited over an entire season does not seem to make the award any the less "athletic" in nature than had the Hickok belt been awarded for petitioner's performance in a single game. Moreover, "stealing bases" is no less exclusively an "athletic" skill than being a good halfback. . . .

Petitioner argues that the Hickok belt is nontaxable on the ground that the belt is a "trophy;" that section 74 is silent on the question of a trophy; and that the belt has no fair market value because recipients intend to treat it as a "trophy." Respondent counters this argument by noting that petitioner was not subject to any restrictions as to possible disposition of the belt after receipt and that it had an actual value of over $6,000.

Petitioner's position is equitable. The receipt of an award like the Hickok belt is not equivalent to the receipt of a car or any other like item which the recipient would ordinarily find useful in his daily affairs and which he might purchase on his own. The fact that a recipient of an award having utilitarian value would commonly purchase a similar item tends to mitigate the harshness of imposing a tax upon its receipt. Clearly, the Hickok belt, being large and cumbersome, made out of gold and studded with gems, is of no utilitarian value. Its purpose is honorary and decorative. Although the Hickok belt is a valuable item, it is hardly one which the recipient would be

---

1. The S. Rae Hickok belt was jewel-studded, contained 27 one and one-half carat diamonds, simulated stones, and had a 3½-pound gold belt buckle. It is stipulated that the value of the belt at the time of receipt was $6,038.19. One of the gems in the belt was subsequently removed by and used in a ring for petitioner's wife.

likely to purchase in the absence of award. Thus, if taxable, the taxpayer-recipient would be required to pay for the privilege of retaining a trophy.

Despite our solicitude for petitioner's position, we do not believe that the fair market value of the Hickok belt is excludable from gross income. . . .

Decision will be entered under Rule 50.

Questions

1. Is an Olympic gold medal taxable income to the medal winner? How much? How about Super Bowl rings for professional football players?

2. In the span of one week, the ABC television show *Extreme Makeover: Home Edition* will completely renovate and refurbish the home of a selected family. Sometimes the existing structure is torn down and replaced with a much larger new home built on the site. Families selected to receive this home "makeover" are typically needy and deserving. Assume that the construction and new furnishings have a value of $600,000. If the homeowner was selected without action on her part, what are the tax consequences? Does it matter whether the homeowner was chosen to receive the makeover based on her selfless good works in the community or because of crushing medical expenses of a severely disabled child? Apparently, the network's lawyers have taken the position that the value of the home improvements is tax-free on the authority of §280A(g). Evaluate that argument.

3. Is there any persuasive reason that a Nobel prize should be exempt from income tax? The limitation in §74(b)(3) was not added until 1986. At least some Nobel laureates transferred their prizes to exempt institutions anyway; how would they have been treated under the income tax? Is the limitation a good idea?

4. Is enactment of §74(c) consistent with the general trend of legislation in this area? Is it sound policy?

2.   Scholarships and Fellowship Grants

Prior to 1954 the taxability of scholarships and fellowship grants was judged, uneasily, under §102. In 1954 §117 was enacted to deal more specifically with this particular problem. Prior to 1986 the exclusion was available in a limited amount for grants to persons who were not degree candidates and it was not limited to qualified tuition and related expenses. As a consequence, the exclusion could cover grants for living and travel expenses, sometimes in rather generous amounts. The exclusion was a matter of continuing controversy as applied to payments to students who performed teaching, laboratory, or hospital duties. The term "scholarship or fellowship grant" was interpreted not to embrace payments made primarily to secure the taxpayer's services, but the payor's motives for payment were sometimes obscure and often debatable (or at least debated; most decisions seemed to go in favor of the government).

In principle (i.e., ignoring §117 for the moment), should it matter whether a scholarship is awarded on the basis of need or merit (academic or athletic achievement)? Should it matter whether the scholarship is provided by the educational institution at which the student is enrolled? Is such a "scholarship" really just differential pricing in disguise? (Compare airline ticket pricing.) Should it matter whether the "scholarship" is provided by an educational institution that employs the student's parent?

Turning now to §117, is the limitation to tuition and related expenses sound? Why did Congress enact §117(d) instead of simply leaving these arrangements to be handled under §132?

Would it make sense to repeal the exclusion altogether and to substitute a deduction for tuition and related expenses? Or at least to repeal §117(c)? Or to allow a deduction, but one limited to the earned income of the student herself? Cf. §63(c)(5).

There is an array of other provisions that grant tax relief for educational expenditures. These are discussed briefly in Chapter 12H below.

3.   Commercial and Compensatory Gifts

COMMISSIONER v. DUBERSTEIN
363 U.S. 278 (1960)

Mr. Justice BRENNAN delivered the opinion of the Court. . . . No. 376, Commissioner v. Duberstein. The taxpayer, Duberstein, was president of the Duberstein Iron & Metal Company, a corporation with headquarters in Dayton, Ohio. For some years the taxpayer's company had done business with Mohawk Metal Corporation, whose headquarters were in New York City. The president of Mohawk was one Berman. The taxpayer and Berman had generally used the telephone to transact their companies' business with each other, which consisted of buying and selling metals. The taxpayer testified, without elaboration, that he knew Berman "personally" and had known him for about seven years. From time to time in their telephone conversations, Berman would ask Duberstein whether the latter knew of potential customers for some of Mohawk's products in which Duberstein's company itself was not interested. Duberstein provided the names of potential customers for these items.

One day in 1951 Berman telephoned Duberstein and said that the information Duberstein had given him had proved so helpful that he wanted to give the latter a present. Duberstein stated that Berman owed him nothing. Berman said that he had a Cadillac as a gift for Duberstein, and that the latter should send to New York for it; Berman insisted that Duberstein accept the car, and the latter finally did so, protesting however that he had not intended to be compensated for the information. At the time Duberstein already had a Cadillac and an Oldsmobile, and felt that he did not need another car. Duberstein testified that he did not think Berman would have sent him the Cadillac if he had not furnished him with information about the customers. It appeared that Mohawk later deducted the value of the Cadillac as a business expense on its corporate income tax return.

Duberstein did not include the value of the Cadillac in gross income for 1951, deeming it a gift. The Commissioner asserted a deficiency for the car's value against him, and in proceedings to review the deficiency the Tax Court affirmed the Commissioner's determination. It said that "The record is significantly barren of evidence revealing any intention on the part of the payor to make a gift. . . . The only justifiable inference is that the automobile was intended by the payor to be remuneration for services rendered to it by Duberstein." The Court of Appeals for the Sixth Circuit reversed. 265 F.2d 28.

No. 546, Stanton v. United States. The taxpayer, Stanton, had been for approximately 10 years in the employ of Trinity Church in New York City. He was comptroller of the Church corporation, and president of a corporation, Trinity Operating Company, the church set up as a fully owned subsidiary to manage its real estate holdings, which were more extensive than simply the church property. His salary by the end of his employment there in 1942 amounted to $22,500 a year. Effective November 30, 1942, he resigned from both positions to go into business for himself. The Operating Company's directors, who seem to have included the rector and vestrymen of the church, passed the following resolution upon his resignation:

> Be it resolved that in appreciation of the services rendered by Mr. Stanton . . . a gratuity is hereby awarded to him of Twenty Thousand Dollars, payable to him in equal instalments of Two Thousand Dollars at the end of each and every month commencing with the month of December, 1942; provided that, with the discontinuance of his services, the Corporation of Trinity Church is released from all rights and claims to pension and retirement benefits not already accrued up to November 30, 1942.

The Operating Company's action was later explained by one of its directors as based on the fact that, "Mr. Stanton was liked by all of the Vestry personally. He had a pleasing personality. He had come in when Trinity's affairs were in a difficult situation. He did a splendid piece of work, we felt. Besides that . . . he was liked by all the members of the Vestry personally." And by another: "[W]e were all unanimous in wishing to make Mr. Stanton a gift. Mr. Stanton had loyally and faithfully served Trinity in a very difficult time. We thought of him in the highest regard. We understood that he was going in business for himself. We felt that he was entitled to that evidence of good will."

On the other hand, there was a suggestion of some ill-feeling between Stanton and the directors, arising out of the recent termination of the services of one Watkins, the Operating Company's treasurer, whose departure was evidently attended by some acrimony. At a special board meeting on October 28, 1942, Stanton had intervened on Watkins' side and asked reconsideration of the matter. The minutes reflect that "resentment was expressed as to the 'presumptuous' suggestion that the action of the Board, taken after long deliberation, should be changed." The Board adhered to its determination that Watkins be separated from employment, giving him an opportunity to resign rather than be discharged. At another special meeting two days later it was revealed that Watkins had not resigned; the previous resolution terminating his services was then viewed as effective; and the Board voted the payment of six months' salary to Watkins in a resolution similar to that quoted in regard to Stanton, but which did not use the term "gratuity." At the meeting, Stanton announced that in order to avoid any such embarrassment or question at any time as to his willingness to resign if the Board desired, he was tendering his resignation. It was tabled, though not without dissent. The next week, on November 5, at another special meeting, Stanton again tendered his resignation which this time was accepted.

The "gratuity" was duly paid. So was a smaller one to Stanton's (and the Operating Company's) secretary, under a similar resolution, upon her resignation at the same time. The two corporations shared the expense of the payments. There was undisputed testimony that there were in fact no enforceable rights or claims to pension and retirement benefits which had not accrued at the time of the taxpayer's resignation, and that the last proviso of the resolution was inserted simply out of an abundance of caution. The taxpayer received in cash a refund of his contributions to the retirement plans, and there is no suggestion that he was entitled to more. He was required to perform no further services for Trinity after his resignation.

The Commissioner asserted a deficiency against the taxpayer after the latter had failed to include the payments in question in gross income. After payment of the deficiency and administrative rejection of a refund claim, the taxpayer sued the United States for a refund in the District Court for the Eastern District of New York. 137 F. Supp. 803. The trial judge, sitting without a jury, made the simple finding that the payments were a "gift," and judgment was entered for the taxpayer. The Court of Appeals for the Second Circuit reversed. 268 F.2d 727. . . .

The exclusion of property acquired by gift from gross income under the federal income tax laws was made in the first income tax statute passed under the authority of the Sixteenth Amendment, and has been a feature of the income tax statutes ever since. The meaning of the term "gift" as applied to particular transfers has always been a matter of contention. Specific and illuminating legislative history on the point does not appear to exist. Analogies and inferences drawn from other revenue provisions, such as the estate and gift taxes, are dubious. . . . The meaning of the statutory term has been shaped largely by the decisional law. With this, we turn to the contentions made by the Government in these cases.

First. The Government suggests that we promulgate a new "test" in this area to serve as a standard to be applied by the lower courts and by the Tax Court in dealing with the numerous cases that arise.[6] We reject this invitation. We are of opinion that the governing principles are necessarily general and have already been spelled out in the opinions of this Court, and that the problem is one which, under the present statutory framework, does not lend itself to any more definitive statement that would produce a talisman for the solution of concrete cases. The cases at bar are fair examples of the settings in which the problem usually arises. They present situations in which payments have been made in a context with business overtones — an employer making a payment to a retiring employee; a businessman giving something of value to another businessman who has been of advantage to him in his business. In this context, we review the law as established by the prior cases here.

The course of decision here makes it plain that the statute does not use the term "gift" in the common-law sense, but in a more colloquial sense. This Court has indicated that a voluntarily executed transfer of his property by one to another, without any consideration or compensation therefor, though a common-law gift, is not necessarily a "gift" within the meaning of the statute. For the Court has shown that the mere absence of a legal or moral obligation to make such a payment does not establish that it is a gift. Old Colony Trust Co. v. Commissioner, 279 U.S. 716, 730. And, importantly, if the payment proceeds primarily from "the constraining force of any moral or legal duty," or from "the incentive of anticipated benefit" of an economic nature, Bogardus v. Commissioner, 302 U.S. 34, 41, it is not a gift. And, conversely, "[w]here the payment is in return for services rendered, it is irrelevant that the donor derives no economic benefit from it." Robertson v. United States, 343 U.S. 711, 714.[7] A gift in the statutory sense, on the other hand, proceeds from a "detached and disinterested generosity," Commissioner v. LoBue, 351 U.S. 243, 246; "out of affection, respect, admiration, charity or like impulses." Robertson v. United States, supra, at 714. And in this regard, the most critical consideration, as the Court was agreed in the leading case here, is the transferor's "intention." Bogardus v. Commissioner, 302 U.S. 34, 43. "What controls is the intention with which payment, however voluntary, has been made." Id., at 45 (dissenting opinion).[8]

6. The Government's proposed test is stated: "Gifts should be defined as transfers of property made for personal as distinguished from business reasons."

7. The cases including "tips" in gross income are classic examples of this. See, e.g., Roberts v. Commissioner, 9 Cir., 176 F.2d 221.

8. The parts of the *Bogardus* opinion which we touch on here are the ones we take to be basic to its holding, and the ones that we read as stating those governing principles which it establishes. As to them we see little distinction between the views of the Court and those taken in dissent in *Bogardus*. The fear expressed by the dissent at 302 U.S. at 44, that the prevailing opinion "seems" to hold "that every payment which in any aspect is a gift is . . . relieved of any tax" strikes us now as going beyond what the opinion of the Court held in fact. In any event, the Court's opinion in *Bogardus* does not seem to have been so interpreted afterwards. The principal difference, as we see it, between the Court's opinion and the dissent lies in the weight to be given the findings of the trier of fact.

The Government says that this "intention" of the transferor cannot mean what the cases on the common-law concept of gift call "donative intent." With that we are in agreement, for our decisions fully support this. Moreover, the *Bogardus* case itself makes it plain that the donor's characterization of his action is not determinative — that there must be an objective inquiry as to whether what is called a gift amounts to it in reality. 302 U.S. at page 40. It scarcely needs adding that the parties' expectations or hopes as to the tax treatment of their conduct in themselves have nothing to do with the matter.

It is suggested that the *Bogardus* criterion would be more apt if rephrased in terms of "motive" rather than "intention." We must confess to some skepticism as to whether such a verbal mutation would be of any practical consequence. We take it that the proper criterion, established by decision here, is one that inquires what the basic reason for his conduct was in fact — the dominant reason that explains his action in making the transfer. Further than that we do not think it profitable to go.

Second. The Government's proposed "test," while apparently simple and precise in its formulation, depends frankly on a set of "principles" or "presumptions" derived from the decided cases, and concededly subject to various exceptions; and it involves various corollaries, which add to its detail. Were we to promulgate this test as a matter of law, and accept with it its various presuppositions and stated consequences, we would be passing far beyond the requirements of the cases before us, and would be painting on a large canvas with indeed a broad brush. The Government derives its test from such propositions as the following: That payments by an employer to an employee, even though voluntary, ought, by and large, to be taxable; that the concept of a gift is inconsistent with payment's being a deductible business expense; that a gift involves "personal" elements; that a business corporation cannot properly make a gift of its assets. The Government admits that there are exceptions and qualifications to these propositions. We think, to the extent they are correct, that these propositions are not principles of law but rather maxims of experience that the tribunals which have tried the facts of cases in this area have enunciated in explaining their factual determinations. Some of them simply represent truisms: it doubtless is, statistically speaking, the exceptional payment by an employer to an employee that amounts to a gift. Others are overstatements of possible evidentiary inferences relevant to a factual determination on the totality of circumstances in the case: it is doubtless relevant to the overall inference that the transferor treats a payment as a business deduction, or that the transferor is a corporate entity. But these inferences cannot be stated in absolute terms. Neither factor is a shibboleth. The taxing statute does not make nondeductibility by the transferor a condition on the "gift" exclusion; nor does it draw any distinction, in terms, between transfers by corporations and individuals, as to the availability of the "gift" exclusion to the transferee. The conclusion whether a transfer amounts to a "gift" is one that must be reached on consideration of all the factors.

Specifically, the trier of fact must be careful not to allow trial of the issue whether the receipt of a specific payment is a gift to turn into a trial of the tax liability, or of the propriety, as a matter of fiduciary or corporate law, attaching to the conduct of someone else. The major corollary to the Government's suggested "test" is that, as an ordinary matter, a payment by a corporation cannot be a gift, and, more specifically, there can be no such thing as a "gift" made by a corporation which would allow it to take a deduction for an ordinary and necessary business expense. As we have said, we find no basis for such a conclusion in the statute; and if it were applied as a determinative rule of "law," it would force the tribunals trying tax cases involving the donee's liability into elaborate inquiries into the local law of corporations or into the peripheral deductibility of payments as business expenses. The former issue might make the tax tribunals the most frequent investigators of an important and difficult issue of the laws of the several States, and the latter inquiry would summon one difficult and delicate problem of federal tax law as an aid to the solution of another.[9] Or perhaps there would be required a trial of the vexed issue whether there was a "constructive" distribution of corporate property, for income tax purposes, to the corporate agents who had sponsored the transfer.[10] These considerations, also, reinforce us in our conclusion that while the principles urged by the Government may, in nonabsolute form as crystallizations of experience, prove persuasive to the trier of facts in a particular case, neither they, nor any more detailed statement than has been made, can be laid down as a matter of law.

Third. Decision of the issue presented in these cases must be based ultimately on the application of the fact-finding tribunal's experience with the mainsprings of human conduct to the totality of the facts of each case. The nontechnical nature of the statutory standard, the close relationship of it to the data of practical human experience, and the multiplicity of relevant factual elements, with their various combinations, creating the necessity of ascribing the proper force to each, confirm us in our conclusion that primary weight in this area must be given to the conclusions of the trier of fact. . . .

This conclusion may not satisfy an academic desire for tidiness, symmetry and precision in this area, any more than a system based on the determinations of various fact-finders ordinarily does. But we see it as implicit in the present statutory treatment of the exclusion for gifts, and in the variety of forums in which federal income tax cases can be tried. If there is fear of undue uncertainty or overmuch litigation, Congress may make more precise its treatment of the matter by singling out certain factors and making them

---

9. Justice Cardozo once described in memorable language the inquiry into whether an expense was an "ordinary and necessary" one of a business: "One struggles in vain for any verbal formula that will supply a ready touchstone. The standard set up by the statute is not a rule of law; it is rather a way of life. Life in all its fullness must supply the answer to the riddle." Welch v. Helvering, 290 U.S. 111, 115. The same comment well fits the issue in the cases at bar.

10. Cf., e.g., Nelson v. Commissioner, 203 F.2d 1.

determinative of the matter, as it has done in one field of the "gift" exclusion's former application, that of prizes and awards.[12] Doubtless diversity of result will tend to be lessened somewhat since federal income tax decisions, even those in tribunals of first instance turning on issues of fact, tend to be reported, and since there may be a natural tendency of professional triers of fact to follow one another's determinations, even as to factual matters. But the question here remains basically one of fact, for determination on a case-by-case basis.

One consequence of this is that appellate review of determinations in this field must be quite restricted. Where a jury has tried the matter upon correct instructions, the only inquiry is whether it cannot be said that reasonable men could reach differing conclusions on the issue. . . . Where the trial has been by a judge without a jury, the judge's findings must stand unless "clearly erroneous." Fed. Rules Civ. Proc. 52(a). "A finding is 'clearly erroneous' when although there is evidence to support it, the reviewing court on the entire evidence is left with the definite and firm conviction that a mistake has been committed." . . . The rule itself applies also to factual inferences from undisputed basic facts . . . as will on many occasions be presented in this area. . . . And Congress has in the most explicit terms attached the identical weight to the findings of the Tax Court. I.R.C. §7482(a). . . .

Fourth. A majority of the Court is in accord with the principles just outlined. And, applying them to the *Duberstein* case, we are in agreement, on the evidence we have set forth, that it cannot be said that the conclusion of the Tax Court was "clearly erroneous." It seems to us plain that as trier of the facts it was warranted in concluding that despite the characterization of the transfer of the Cadillac by the parties and the absence of any obligation, even of a moral nature, to make it, it was at bottom a recompense for Duberstein's past services, or an inducement for him to be of further service in the future. We cannot say with the Court of Appeals that such a conclusion was "mere suspicion" on the Tax Court's part. To us it appears based in the sort of informed experience with human affairs that fact-finding tribunals should bring to this task.

As to *Stanton*, we are in disagreement. To four of us, it is critical here that the District Court as trier of fact made only the simple and unelaborated finding that the transfer in question was a "gift." To be sure, conciseness is to be strived for and prolixity avoided, in findings; but, to the four of us, there comes a point where findings become so sparse and conclusory as to give no revelation of what the District Court's concept of the determining facts and legal standard may be. Such conclusory, general findings do not constitute compliance with Rule 52's direction to "find the facts specially and state

12. I.R.C. §74, which is a provision new with the 1954 Code. Previously there had been holdings that such receipts as the "Pot O' Gold" radio giveaway, Washburn v. Commissioner, 5 T.C. 1333, and the Ross Essay Prize, McDermott v. Commissioner, 80 U.S. App. D.C. 176, 150 F.2d 585, were "gifts." Congress intended to obviate such rulings. S. Rep. No. 1622, 83d Cong., 2d Sess., p. 178. We imply no approval of those holdings under the general standard of the "gift" exclusion. Cf. Robertson v. United States, supra.

separately . . . conclusions of law thereon." While the standard of law in this area is not a complex one, we four think the unelaborated finding of ultimate fact here cannot stand as a fulfillment of these requirements. It affords the reviewing court not the semblance of an indication of the legal standard with which the trier of fact has approached his task. For all that appears, the District Court may have viewed the form of the resolution or the simple absence of legal consideration as conclusive. While the judgment of the Court of Appeals cannot stand, the four of us think there must be further proceedings in the District Court looking toward new and adequate findings of fact. In this, we are joined by Mr. Justice Whittaker, who agrees that the findings were inadequate, although he does not concur generally in this opinion. . . .

Accordingly, in No. 376, the judgment of this Court is that the judgment of the Court of Appeals is reversed, and in No. 546, that the judgment of the Court of Appeals is vacated, and the case is remanded to the District Court for further proceedings not inconsistent with this opinion.

It is so ordered.

Mr. Justice HARLAN concurs in the result in No. 376. In No. 546, he would affirm the judgment of the Court of Appeals for the reasons stated by Mr. Justice Frankfurter.

Mr. Justice WHITTAKER, agreeing with *Bogardus* that whether a particular transfer is or is not a "gift" may involve "a mixed question of law and fact," 302 U.S., at 39, concurs only in the result of this opinion.

Mr. Justice DOUGLAS dissents, since he is of the view that in each of these two cases there was a gift under the test which the Court fashioned nearly a quarter of a century ago in Bogardus v. Commissioner, 302 U.S. 34.

Mr. Justice BLACK, concurring and dissenting. I agree with the Court that it was not clearly erroneous for the Tax Court to find as it did in No. 376 that the automobile transfer to Duberstein was not a gift and so I agree with the Court's opinion and judgment reversing the judgment of the Court of Appeals in that case.

I dissent in No. 546, Stanton v. United States. The District Court found that the $20,000 transferred to Mr. Stanton by his former employer at the end of ten years' service was a gift and therefore exempt from taxation under [§102(a)]. I think the finding was not clearly erroneous and that the Court of Appeals was therefore wrong in reversing the District Court's judgment. While conflicting inferences might have been drawn, there was evidence to show that Mr. Stanton's long services had been satisfactory, that he was well liked personally and had given splendid service, that the employer was under no obligation at all to pay any added compensation, but made the $20,000 payment because prompted by a genuine desire to make him a "gift," to award him a "gratuity." Cf. Commissioner v. LoBue, 351 U.S. 243, 246-247. The District Court's finding was that the added payment "constituted a gift to the taxpayer, and therefore need not have been reported by him as income. . . ." The trial court might have used more words, or discussed the facts set out above in more detail, but I doubt if this would have made its crucial, adequately supported finding any clearer. For this reason I would reinstate the District Court's judgment for petitioner.

Mr. Justice FRANKFURTER, concurring in the judgment in No. 376 and dissenting in No. 546. As the Court's opinion indicates, we brought these two cases here partly because of a claimed difference in the approaches between two Courts of Appeals but primarily on the Government's urging that, in the interest of the better administration of the income tax laws, clarification was desirable for determining when a transfer of property constitutes a "gift" and is not to be included in income for purposes of ascertaining the "gross income" under the Internal Revenue Code. As soon as this problem emerged after the imposition of the first income tax authorized by the Sixteenth Amendment, it became evident that its inherent difficulties and subtleties would not easily yield to the formulation of a general rule or test sufficiently definite to confine within narrow limits the area of judgment in applying it. While at its core the tax conception of a gift no doubt reflected the non-legal, non-technical notion of a benefaction unentangled with any aspect of worldly requital, the divers blends of personal and pecuniary relationships in our industrial society inevitably presented niceties for adjudication which could not be put to rest by any kind of general formulation.

Despite acute arguments at the bar and a most thorough reexamination of the problem on a full canvass of our prior decisions and an attempted fresh analysis of the nature of the problem, the Court has rejected the invitation of the Government to fashion anything like a litmus paper test for determining what is excludable as a "gift" from gross income. Nor has the Court attempted a clarification of the particular aspects of the problem presented by these two cases, namely, payment by an employer to an employee upon the termination of the employment relation and nonobligatory payment for services rendered in the course of a business relationship. While I agree that experience has shown the futility of attempting to define, by language so circumscribing as to make it easily applicable, what constitutes a gift for every situation where the problem may arise, I do think that greater explicitness is possible in isolating and emphasizing factors which militate against a gift in particular situations.

Thus, regarding the two frequently recurring situations involved in these cases — things of value given to employees by their employers upon the termination of employment and payments entangled in a business relation and occasioned by the performance of some service — the strong implication is that the payment is of a business nature. The problem in these two cases is entirely different from the problem in a case where a payment is made from one member of a family to another, where the implications are directly otherwise. No single general formulation appropriately deals with both types of cases, although both involve the question whether the payment was a "gift." While we should normally suppose that a payment from father to son was a gift, unless the contrary is shown, in the two situations now before us the business implications are so forceful that I would apply a presumptive rule placing the burden upon the beneficiary to prove the payment wholly unrelated to his services to the enterprise. The Court, however, has declined so to analyze the problem and has concluded "that the governing principles are necessarily general and have already been spelled out in the opinions of this Court, and that the problem is one which, under the present statutory framework, does not lend itself to any more definitive statement that would produce a talisman for the solution of concrete cases."

The Court has made only one authoritative addition to the previous course of our decisions. Recognizing Bogardus v. Commissioner, 302 U.S. 34, as "the leading case here" and finding essential accord between the Court's opinion and the dissent in that case, the Court has drawn from the dissent in *Bogardus* for infusion into what will now be a controlling qualification, recognition that it is "for the triers of the facts to seek among competing aims or motives the ones that dominated conduct." 302 U.S. 34, 45 (dissenting opinion). All this being so in view of the Court, it seems to me desirable not to try to improve what has "already been spelled out" in the opinions of this Court but to leave to the lower courts the application of old phrases rather than to float new ones and thereby inevitably produce a new volume of exegesis on the new phrases.

Especially do I believe this when fact-finding tribunals are directed by the Court to rely upon their "experience with the mainsprings of human conduct" and on their "informed experience with human affairs" in appraising the totality of the facts of each case. Varying conceptions regarding the "mainsprings of human conduct" are derived from a variety of experiences or assumptions about the nature of man, and "experience with human affairs" is not only diverse but also often drastically conflicting. What the Court now does sets fact-finding bodies to sail on an illimitable ocean of individual beliefs and experiences. This can hardly fail to invite, if indeed not encourage, too individualized diversities in the administration of the income tax law. I am afraid that by these new phrasings the practicalities of tax administration, which should be as uniform as is possible in so vast a country as ours, will be embarrassed. By applying what has already been spelled out in the opinions of this Court, I agree with the Court in reversing the judgment in Commissioner v. Duberstein.

But I would affirm the decision of the Court of Appeals for the Second Circuit in Stanton v. United States. I would do so on the basis of the opinion of Judge Hand and more particularly because the very terms of the resolution by which the $20,000 was awarded to Stanton indicated that it was not a "gratuity" in the sense of sheer benevolence but in the nature of a generous lagniappe, something extra thrown in for services received though not legally nor morally required to be given. This careful resolution, doubtless drawn by a lawyer and adopted by some hardheaded businessmen, contained a proviso that Stanton should abandon all rights to "pension and retirement benefits." The fact that Stanton had no such claims does not lessen the significance of the clause as something "to make assurance double sure." 268 F.2d 728. The business nature of the payment is confirmed by the words of the resolution, explaining the "gratuity" as "in appreciation of the services rendered by Mr. Stanton as Manager of the Estate and Comptroller of the Corporation of Trinity Church throughout nearly ten years, and as President of Trinity Operating Company, Inc." The force of this document, in light of all the factors to which Judge Hand adverted in his opinion, was not in the least diminished by testimony at the trial. Thus the taxpayer has totally failed to sustain the burden I would place upon him to establish that the payment to him was wholly attributable to generosity unrelated to his performance of his secular business functions as an officer of the corporation of the Trinity Church of New York and the Trinity Operating Co. Since the record totally fails to establish taxpayer's claim, I see no need of specific findings by the trial judge.

STANTON v. UNITED STATES
186 F. Supp. 393 (E.D.N.Y. 1960), aff'd per curiam,
287 F.2d 876 (2d Cir. 1961)

BYERS, District Judge. . . . Mr. Stanton so discharged the duties committed to him, that on November 19, 1942 the resolution heretofore quoted was unanimously adopted by the directors of the Operating Company. His salary for the year 1942 was $22,500 and there is no suggestion that it was less than commensurate with his task. The witness Hasler testified (Record, p. 37): "We were all unanimous in wishing to make Mr. Stanton a gift. Mr. Stanton had loyally and faithfully served Trinity in a difficult time. We thought of him in the highest regard.

"We understood he was going in business for himself.

"We felt that he was entitled to that evidence of good will."

The foregoing, coupled with the statements made by Mr. Sheppard in his deposition on this subject, enter into this "fact-finding tribunal's experience with the mainsprings of human conduct to the totality of facts . . ." (186 F. Supp. 396) in this wise:

The Vestrymen of Trinity Church as trustees of its very considerable properties, were deeply concerned that their fiduciary duties should be rendered so as to meet the most exact requirements of a sensitive conscience that each is assumed to have possessed.

The individual to whom the supervisory task was committed performed so genuine a stewardship that they could not suffer the closing of his association with them to be marked by the mere adoption of formal resolutions.

Something more was owing to their own sense of the fitness of things, as this record is understood.

Such a situation seems to have been conceived of in *Bogardus* in the then Circuit Court of Appeals, 2 Cir., 88 F.2d 646, at page 648:

> We will assume that the gift would be nothing more, if for instance the donor believed that what he had paid in the past was the full measure of anything that the employee was then "entitled to"; that in fairness he did not "owe" a cent; and that anything he might give was not only beyond what the law would exact, but what the employee could in justice demand. Even so the past services would be the cause of the gift in the sense that except for them the donor would never have been moved to spontaneous generosity, but the gift would not pay for the services.

Such is the frame of mind that actuated the mental processes of the Vestry of Trinity Church, as this court perceives them, when the original finding was made, but which was insufficiently disclosed therein.

The reference in the opinion written for reversal (268 F.2d 727, 729) to "the success of his (Stanton's) real estate ventures" is unsatisfactory unless it is borne in mind that there is no suggestion in the testimony that Stanton conducted any real estate "ventures" in the sense of seeking a profit for the benefit of anyone whomsoever, save those to and among whom lay the ultimate spiritual ministry of the Church.

Thus it is clear to this court that the members of the Vestry of Trinity Church took the action under scrutiny because they were grateful to a man whom they had found to be a friend to them and also to the cause in which their talents were enlisted; who had enabled them the more adequately to perform the exacting duties of their office than had been possible before his advent as comptroller and active administrator of the parish realty holdings.

Thus the corporate action was not only the gratification of a kindly impulse present in the minds of the Vestry, but also the exercise of the considered judgment of fiduciaries concerning a proper and circumspect administration of corporate property entrusted to their care.

The action itself therefore did not differ in principle from a gift to a rector, a choir-master or a parish visitor who might be withdrawing from active participation in a common task.

The foregoing is written in answer to the Government's argument submitted with its proposed findings, that the members of the Vestry were either making a gift that was purely personal to them, and therefore converting Church property to their own use, or they were voting severance pay to Mr. Stanton. That argument is deemed to be fallacious for reasons that it has been the effort to demonstrate; and for the added reason that the manner in which the Vestry here functioned is scarcely to be determined by the test of whether we are dealing with a non-taxable gift, or a taxable severance pay. . . .

In my opinion the presence of good will, esteem and kindliness in the minds of the Vestry of Trinity Church is demonstrated by the evidence; and also the reason that called into existence that purpose, namely, something over and above a mere whim or transitory emotion, but was rather a deep sense of appreciation for the way in which Mr. Stanton had enabled the members of the Vestry to rise to the requirement of their high office.

It does not aid in the solution of the question here presented, to rely upon what has been written in cases that involve the taxable consequences flowing from the disposition of funds of a corporation conducted purely for the financial profit of stockholders.

It is in light of the foregoing opinion that the findings submitted by the plaintiff have been signed with one amendment, and those submitted for the defendant have not.

Questions

What more do we learn on remand in *Stanton*? Is the district judge saying, in effect, "Would the Pope lie to me?"

UNITED STATES v. KAISER
363 U.S. 299 (1960)

[In this companion case the Court upheld a jury verdict finding union strike assistance in the form of room rent and food vouchers to be a gift. Assistance was not confined to union members; indeed, Kaiser himself was not a member when the strike began.]

Mr. Justice BRENNAN. . . . In the absence of specific objection at trial, or of demonstration of any compelling reason for dispensing with such objection, we do not here notice any defect in the charge, in the light of the controlling legal principles as we have reviewed them in *Duberstein*.

We think, also, that the proofs were adequate to support the conclusion of the jury. Our opinion in *Duberstein* stresses the basically factual nature of the inquiry as to this issue. The factual inferences to be drawn from the basic facts were here for the jury. They had the power to conclude, on the record, taking into account such factors as the form and amount of the assistance and the conditions of personal need, of lack of other sources of income, compensation, or public assistance, and of dependency status, which surrounded the program under which it was rendered, that while the assistance was furnished only to strikers, it was not a recompense for striking. They could have concluded that the very general language of the Union's constitution, when considered with the nature of the Union as an entity and with the factors to which we have just referred, did not indicate that basically the assistance proceeded from any constraint of moral or legal obligation, of a nature that would preclude it from being a gift. And on all these circumstances, the jury could have concluded that assistance, rendered as it was to a class of persons in the community in economic need, proceeded primarily from generosity or charity, rather than from the incentive of anticipated economic benefit. We can hardly say that, as a matter of law, the fact that these transfers were made to one having a sympathetic interest with the giver prevents them from being a gift. This is present in many cases of the most unquestionable charity.

We need not stop to speculate as to what conclusion we would have drawn had we sat in the jury box rather than those who did. The question is one of the allocation of power to decide the question; and once we say that such conclusions could with reason be reached on the evidence, and that the District Court's instructions are not overthrown, our reviewing authority is exhausted, and we must recognize that the jury was empowered to render the verdict which it did.

Affirmed.

Mr. Justice FRANKFURTER, whom Mr. Justice CLARK joins, concurring in the result. [There is first a long refutation of the taxpayer's argument that strike assistance was beyond the concept of income in §61(a). The opinion concludes, however, as follows.]

... As a matter of ordinary reading of language I could not conclude that all strike benefits are, as a matter of law, "gifts." I should suppose that a strike benefit does not fit the notion of "gift." A union surely has strong self-interest in paying such benefits to strikers. The implications arising out of the relationship between a union which calls a strike and its strikers are such that, without some special circumstances, it would be unrealistic for a court to conclude that payments made by the union for which only strikers qualify, even though based upon need, derive solely from the promptings of benevolence.

In this case, however, under instructions to the jury that

> [t]he term "gift" as here used denotes the receipt of financial advantage gratuitously, without obligation to make the payment, either legal or moral, and without the payment being made as remuneration for something that the Union wished done or omitted by the plaintiff. To be a gift, the payments must have been made with the intent that there be nothing of value received, or that they were not made to repay what was plaintiff's due but were bestowed only because of personal regard or pity or from general motives or philanthropy or charity. If the plaintiff received this assistance simply and solely because he and his family were in actual need and not because of any obligations, as above referred to, or any expectation of anything in return, then such payments were gifts,

the jury found in a special verdict that the strike benefit payments to taxpayer were a "gift." These instructions certainly were not unfavorable to the Government. . . .

On the evidence in this case, may the jury's verdict stand? There was evidence justifying the view that in the particular circumstances existing in Sheboygan at the time these benefits were paid, the union had assumed the functions normally exercised by private charitable organizations and governmental relief programs, in view of the excessive difficulty in getting adequate relief from them, so that these benefits were dispensed pursuant to such a charitable relief program in what, because of the strike, was a distressed area. The mere fact that the payments were made by the union to men participating in the strike called by the union does not as a matter of tax law conclude the case against a "gift." When the circumstances negating the business nature of the payment were strong enough, the Commissioner has ruled that even payments by an employer to his employees were gifts. See ruling Number 13 in the Appendix, and see also Rev. Rul. 59-58, 1959-1 Cum. Bull. 17, holding that the value of turkeys, hams, etc., given by an employer to employees at Christmas or some other holiday need not be reported as income. Although it is for me a very close question I find sufficient evidence in the record to support the theory that in making these payments the union was exercising a wholly charitable function. On this view, restricted to the particular set of circumstances under which the special verdict was rendered, I would therefore hold the payment in this case to be a gift and would affirm the judgment below.

I am well aware that this disposition of the case does not preclude different juries reaching different conclusions on the same facts. Some individualization of result is inevitable so long as it is left to courts to determine what is or is not a "gift." The diversities that may thus result are all the more inevitable in view of the scope left to the fact-finders—whether courts or jury—by our decision today in Commissioner v. Duberstein and Stanton v. United States, ante. . . .

[Mr. Justice DOUGLAS wrote a separate concurring opinion, and Mr. Justice WHITTAKER wrote a dissenting opinion, joined by Justices HARLAN and STEWART.]

Question

What should the IRS have done with other strikers following the decision in *Kaiser*?

REVENUE RULING 61-136
1961-2 C.B. 20

. . . In the *Kaiser* case a labor union furnished strike benefits, by way of room rent and food vouchers, to a needy worker participating in a strike although he was not a member of the union during the early period of the strike. The Supreme Court held that, on consideration of all of the circumstances presented, the jury in the lower court acted within its province in concluding that the strike benefits were gifts within the meaning of section 102(a) of the Internal Revenue Code of 1954 and, hence, were not includible in the worker's gross income. Emphasizing that the question in such cases is essentially a factual one to be resolved by the trier of facts, the Supreme Court noted that the lower court had taken into account such factors as the form and the amount of the benefits, the conditions of personal need, the lack of other sources of income, and the availability of public assistance.

In view of the foregoing, it is held that in cases presenting facts substantially like those in the *Kaiser* case, strike benefit payments will be regarded as gifts and, therefore, exempt from Federal income tax. Other cases will be scrutinized to determine whether the payments constitute gross income for Federal income tax purposes. However, the fact that benefits are paid only to union members will not, in and of itself, be considered determinative of whether such benefits will be regarded as gifts or as gross income. . . .

Notes and Questions

1. What are "facts substantially like those in the *Kaiser* case"? The government continued to litigate strike benefits and has won a number of cases; e.g., Richard A. Osborne, T.C. Memo 1995-71.

2. *Employee gifts.* In 1986 the Congress added §102(c), which provides that §101(a) "shall not exclude from gross income any amount transferred by or for an employer to, or for the benefit of, an employee." This section was enacted in connection with §74(c), presumably to ensure that §102 would not be used to circumvent the limitations in that provision, but it does not appear to be confined to such cases. Would it now cover *Duberstein? Kaiser? Stanton?* Does "employee" include *former* employees?

3. *Deductibility by the donor.* What precisely is the relationship between excludability under §102 and deductibility by the donor? If the gift exclusion was intended to prevent double taxation of income earned by one and spent by another, then does it not follow that excludability and deductibility should not extend to the same payment?

In the case of a corporate payment the matter is more complex because a distribution of profits is normally taxable to shareholders *and* is not deductible by the corporation. Therefore, if a corporation purchased an automobile for its sole shareholder's daughter, for example, that might well be a nontaxable gift to the daughter; however, it should probably be nondeductible by the corporation *and* taxable to the shareholder-parent, just as if the car had been distributed to the parent as a dividend and given by the parent to the daughter.

Part of the government's argument in *Duberstein* seems to reflect this reasoning. The government's test, as elaborated, included the propositions that payments deductible by the payor and payments by corporations could not be gifts. Does the Court's rejection of the government's test mean that deductibility by the payor is irrelevant? Or is it only insufficient by itself to establish taxability to the recipient? Does deductibility by the payor, in other words, remain an important, relevant factor if not a dispositive test? Or at least should the same factors be taken into account on both sides so that a substantial payment will not be likely to be held simultaneously deductible by the payor and excludible by the recipient?

Of course, the relationship between deductibility and excludability, even if admitted, would not solve problems of excludability because the issue of deductibility is often not clear. Sometimes the issue of deductibility is unimportant, as in *Stanton* and *Kaiser*, because the payor is exempt from tax. On the other hand, there seems to be considerable force to the notion that the value of the Cadillac in *Duberstein* represents a distribution of business profits that ought to be taxable to someone.

If Berman had reported the value of the Cadillac as income to himself (either as a dividend or salary from Mohawk) and had claimed no offsetting deduction, would it follow that Duberstein should be able to exclude it as a gift?

Should there be a procedure by which the government could bring both Duberstein and Berman into court, taking the position that the value of the Cadillac is taxable to one of them, and leaving it to them to fight it out?

Look at §274(b), which was added in 1962. This rule was intended to reduce litigation and to prevent the government from getting whipsawed in cases like *Duberstein*, in which the transferor claims a business expense deduction and the transferee claims the gift exclusion. Does §274(b) really prevent the parties from taking inconsistent positions? Observe that §274(b) defines "gift" as an item that is "excludable from gross income of the recipient under section 102" not according to whether the item is actually "excluded." What is likely to happen if the parties try to have it both ways (i.e., both deduct and exclude the transfer)?

4. *Form of receipt.* Is it important that Duberstein received a Cadillac while Stanton and Kaiser received cash? What if Duberstein and his wife had been taken on a week's cruise aboard a yacht? Would Scrooge's gift of a turkey to Bob Cratchit have been taxable income under our present law?

In Revenue Ruling 59-58, 1959-1 C.B. 17, the IRS held that "the value of a turkey, ham, or other item of merchandise purchased by an employer and distributed generally to each of the employees engaged in his business at Christmas, or a comparable holiday . . . need not be treated as taxable income by the employee who receives it." The ruling is not conditioned on any particular finding as to the employer's intention, purpose, state of mind, or state of grace.

What is the import of §§102(c) and 132 in relation to these matters? See IRS Tech. Adv. Mem. 2004-37-030 (Apr. 30, 2004), involving a tax-exempt organization's distribution to its employees of $35 gift coupons redeemable at local grocery stores in lieu of the employer's prior practice of annually distributing a ham, turkey, or gift basket to employees as a holiday gift.

5. *Oprah's largess.* In September 2004 television talk show host and celebrity Oprah Winfrey marked the premiere of her show's nineteenth

season by giving every member of the studio audience — all 276 of them — a new Pontiac G6 sedan with a manufacturer's suggested retail price of about $28,000. Oprah instructed her staff to find deserving recipients and the audience included 57 people in desperate need of transportation. Ann Oldenburg, $7M Car Giveaway Stuns TV Audience; Oprah Calls It "Greatest Day," USA Today, Sept. 14, 2004, at A1. An advertising firm that works for General Motors initiated the idea of the Oprah car giveaway, GM paid for the vehicles, and the event happened at the start of the week when GM gathered journalists in Michigan to test drive the newly redesigned model. How should a recipient of one of new cars report the transaction? Does it matter whether the recipient was one of the needy audience members?

6. At an April 2005 party celebrating the fifth anniversary of O, The Oprah Magazine (which is published by Hearst Corporation), Oprah Winfrey gave 100 magazine employees checks of $5,000 each. The Big Five-0's Oprah's magazine marks a milestone, New York Daily News, Apr. 20, 2005, at 41. Ms. Winfrey reportedly paid the money out of her personal account in the expectation that the payments would be treated as gifts rather than compensation. Do you agree? Cf. §118. Would the result differ if Ms. Winfrey were the majority shareholder of the magazine publisher?

7. *Statutory purpose.* Why should gifts and bequests be excluded from the recipient's taxable income in any event? Is it fair to tax one who works but not one who receives funds or property free of toil? Do the problems raised by commercial and compensatory gifts (and by prizes, awards, and scholarships) suggest that the gift exclusion is fundamentally overbroad? Should §102 be restricted to transfers within the household? Between members of the same family?

Is support of a husband, wife, or child taxable income to the dependent? Why not? What is the relationship between this question and the question whether a spouse's performance of domestic services gives rise to imputed income?

8. *Intention and motive.* "What controls is the intention with which payment, however voluntary, has been made." *Duberstein* at p. 182. Is this an illuminating formula?

Is the Court right to reject a distinction between intention and motive? Intention traditionally has to do with the intended immediate consequences of an action, whatever its purpose or motivation. The intention in each of these cases is clearly to transfer the money or property in question, but intention in that sense does not serve to identify a gift for income tax purposes, and the Court seems to recognize that. What does intention mean in the Court's formulation?

What is the meaning of "the basic reason for his conduct . . . in fact — the dominant reason that explains his action"? *Duberstein* at p. 183. Does that formulation come near to making the test motive after all? And aren't we really dealing with mixed motives in all these cases? Why do we impose a binary test instead of treating such transfers as part gift, part compensation for services?

Whatever the term, is the proper inquiry directed to the state of mind of the transferor or to an objective appraisal of circumstances surrounding the transfer? Is there a difference? Does "the dominant reason" mean the reason or circumstance that was dominant in the mind of the transferor, or that is dominant in the mind of the person deciding the case in explaining the action of the transferor?

9. *Rules versus guidelines.* How should a lawyer now advise a client with a case like *Duberstein*? *Kaiser*? *Stanton*? "[T]o take pot luck in the courts"? Commissioner v. Bagley, 374 F.2d 204, 207 (1st Cir. 1967). Need the issue in these cases be left in such a state of disorder? How could the Court and the government best have promoted greater order?

The important part of the government's new test proposed in *Duberstein* was apparently a highly articulated set of rigid, definitive statements about what are and are not gifts. If accepted, these would have operated to translate the inquiry about an alleged gift into one of a number of simpler ones — was the payment made by a corporation, for example — from which the conclusion that it was not a gift would follow as a matter of deductive logic. Was this attempt to restate the law well conceived? Would it be well conceived if offered for Congressional enactment rather than judicial adoption? Would it be accurate to say that the government in these cases asked the Court to deal with the problem of gifts too abstractly?

Even if the subject does not lend itself to definitive restatement, Justice Frankfurter is surely right in saying that "greater explicitness is possible in isolating and emphasizing factors which militate against a gift in particular situations." Cannot some of the government's proposed tests be usefully restated as identifying relevant, if not dispositive, factors to be taken into account?

10. *Discretion to decide.* Although the gift exclusion is important, *Duberstein* has as much to do with the distribution of authority to decide on tax matters generally. It is frequently cited in upholding trial court verdicts and judgments on a variety of tax issues. Is this aspect of the *Duberstein* decision sound? Is there any reason why an appellate court should not itself weight and reach a judgment on the competing factors in the cases before it? If the problem of defining gifts will not yield to abstract restatement, might it not nevertheless yield to concrete judgment in particular cases? And wouldn't concrete judgments in the cases at hand serve as landmarks from which to reason analogically, if not deductively, in subsequent cases? Is there anything about concrete judgment and analogical reasoning that is inappropriate for appellate courts? Is it that such courts are too far removed from "experience with the mainsprings of human conduct" to deal with "the totality of the facts" of concrete cases? But what else is law about?

(a) The Court says its "conclusion that primary weight in this area must be given to the conclusions of the trier of fact" is "implicit . . . in the variety of forums in which federal income tax cases can be tried." The point is highlighted by the procedural aspects of the cases before the Court: *Duberstein* was a Tax Court decision, *Stanton* was tried before a district judge, and *Kaiser* turned on a jury verdict.

But how does this variety of forums imply that primary weight is to be given to the conclusions of the trier of fact? Would it make more sense to give primary weight to the findings of the trier of fact if all tax cases were tried in the Tax Court? Should it be granted exclusive original jurisdiction over all tax cases? Given the present distribution of original jurisdiction, would it make sense to defer to Tax Court judgments more than those of other triers of fact? Cf. Dobson v. Commissioner, Chapter 3D.2 above.

(b) The burden of proof in tax litigation has traditionally been put on the taxpayer. The court of appeals originally decided against the taxpayer in *Stanton* on the ground that he had failed to sustain his burden of proof.[1]

Putting the burden of proof on the taxpayer has often been described in terms of a presumption that the Commissioner's determination of tax liability is correct. *Duberstein* could be described as creating a presumption of correctness for trial court determinations of gift characterization.

What is to be said for (and against) giving primary weight to determinations by the Commissioner rather than the trial court? The Commissioner has the opportunity and duty to make an initial determination in every tax controversy whether or not it is subsequently litigated, so consistency in treatment of all taxpayers might be best served by giving primary weight to his determinations. On the other hand, the Commissioner does not hold hearings with confrontation and cross-examination of witnesses. Is the absence of a formal hearing important? Or does that vary with the nature of the issue?

Recent critics of the IRS picked on the taxpayer burden of proof as an instrument of taxpayer oppression, tacitly suggesting that honest taxpayers were being treated more harshly in this regard than common criminals. But taxes are not criminal penalties. Taxpayers have control of most of the relevant evidence and a duty to produce it, and the burden of proof in civil tax litigation is a relatively benign way of enforcing that obligation.

The traditional assignment of burden of proof has been revised by enactment of §7491 in 1998. This provision puts the burden of proof on the Commissioner if the taxpayer meets specified conditions. One of these is the presentation of credible evidence in support of the taxpayer's position,

---

1. The court of appeals said:

The Supreme Court has several times said that a taxpayer has the burden of proving that the Commissioner's determination is wrong. Welch v. Helvering, 290 U.S. 111, 115; Helvering v. Taylor, 293 U.S. 507, 515; his decision is prima facie correct; Wickwire v. Reinecke, 275 U.S. 101, 105. Certainly the taxpayers in the case at bar did not prove that to any substantial degree the "honorarium" was more than an expression of gratitude for exceptional services rendered.

We are indeed acutely aware that such a test goes far to leave the issue always in the hands of the taxing authorities, but it is, as we have tried to show, inherently incapable of exact definition, and we can think of no better standard.

Stanton v. United States, 268 F.2d 727, 729 (2d Cir. 1959).

so in effect the burden of producing some evidence remains on the taxpayer. Others are compliance with substantiation and record-keeping requirements in the Code and regulations and "cooperat[ion] with reasonable requests by the Secretary for witnesses, information, documents, meetings, and interviews . . ." §7491(a)(2)(B). The Finance Committee report asserts that "A necessary element of cooperating with the Secretary is that the taxpayer must exhaust his or her administrative remedies (including any appeal rights provided by the IRS)." S. Rep. No. 105-704. Some practitioners have worried that complying with these conditions may prove more onerous than the burden of proof itself.

The new provision does not apply to a partnership, corporation, or trust whose net worth exceeds $7 million.

(c) Does proper allocation of primary authority to decide depend on the nature of the issue involved? Or vice versa? Or both?

Some cases depend, inevitably, on witness credibility. In these cases there are good reasons to give primary weight to the findings of the trier of fact after a hearing at which witnesses are presented subject to cross-examination. Does this reason apply to any of the present cases?

Sometimes issues are defined abstractly, as the government sought to do in *Duberstein*. The acceptance or rejection of abstract formulations is apparently subject to unfettered review, and therefore ultimately for the appellate courts. But cf. Dobson v. Commissioner, Chapter 3D.2 above.

Many tax controversies, however, turn on issues like those in the present cases, which are not particularly (or necessarily) dependent on witness credibility but will not yield to abstract formulation. These are questions of classification in which the problem is to weigh and evaluate conflicting factors, about which generalization is difficult because significance depends on particular factual contexts. These issues might be called discretionary issues in the rather literal sense that there is no escape from the need for an exercise of discretion in each particular case that arises. (Is there ever?)

Duberstein says in effect that for this type of issue primary weight is to be given to the findings of the trier of fact. Discretion is thus effectively assigned to the triers of fact, whoever they may be, rather than the appellate courts or the Commissioner. Is there anything about this kind of issue that makes such an assignment necessary or desirable?

In some areas scope of review may be restricted for the purpose of implementing policy by conferring discretion on a particular trier of fact, and thus incorporating that trier's perspective and value scale into the substance of the law. That is probably true for administrative agencies like the National Labor Relations Board that are given exclusive or primary jurisdiction to make certain findings. It is likewise the case, quite intentionally if not avowedly, with juries in criminal and negligence cases. But is it a good idea for the differing perspectives and outlooks of juries, district judges, Tax Court judges, and the Court of Claims to be incorporated into the stuff of the tax law in a similar manner (to be chosen among by taxpayers in the course of deciding where to sue)? Insofar as there is policy to be made through findings of fact, that points much more in the direction of upholding the Commissioner's determinations, than the determinations of such varied triers of fact.

11. How will the allocation of discretion between trier of fact and appellate court prescribed by *Duberstein* ultimately reflect back on the administration of the law prior to litigation? On the practice of tax professionals advising taxpayers? On the conduct of taxpayers in paying their taxes? Aren't these the central institutional issues in the case?

12. Reconsider the government's attempt in *Duberstein* to persuade the Court to adopt a set of objective, categorical rules defining "gift" for income tax purposes (discussed in note 3 above). In light of §§274(b) and 102(c), has that position been vindicated in the long run?

ESTATE OF SYDNEY CARTER v. COMMISSIONER
453 F.2d 61 (2d Cir. 1971)

Before Friendly, Chief Judge, Feinberg, Circuit Judge, and Davis, Associate Judge.*

FRIENDLY, Chief Judge: . . . Sydney J. Carter had been employed by the New York City financial house of Salomon Bros. & Hutzler ("Salomon Bros.") for 38 years when he died on March 1, 1960. At that time he was working under a yearly employment contract entitling him to an annual salary of $15,000 and, if he was still in the firm's employ on September 30, 1960, the end of its fiscal year, to an additional amount equal to .55 percent of the firm's net profits. During his employment he had required hospitalization more than 20 times and had undergone seven major operations. On many of these occasions partners of Salomon Bros. called Mrs. Carter[1] to offer financial assistance; the Carters declined, preferring to manage on their own. Most of the Salomon Bros. partners attended Mr. Carter's funeral, two having flown in from Chicago despite a blizzard. Some of the partners later suggested that the Carters' son come to work for the firm, which he did for a while.

In 1960 Salomon Bros. was managed by an administrative committee, consisting of a number of the general partners. At a meeting of this committee held shortly after Mr. Carter's death, it was decided to pay Mrs. Carter what her husband would have earned under his contract if he had lived until the end of the firm's fiscal year. These payments amounted to $60,130.84, of which $8,653.80 (paid in 15 biweekly checks of $576.92) constituted what would have been Mr. Carter's salary and $51,477.04 was what would have been his .55 percent share in the firm's profits.

---

* Of the United States Court of Claims, sitting by designation.

1. Mrs. Carter was personally acquainted with many of the partners, in part because she had served as secretary to the manager of the firm's Cleveland office from November, 1929 to December, 1932, when she married Mr. Carter.

While no minutes were kept of the administrative committee meeting at which the payments to Mrs. Carter were authorized, two members of the committee testified before the Tax Court. They agreed that at the time of Mr. Carter's death, Salomon Bros. had no established plan or policy with respect to payments to the survivors of valued employees; indeed, Mr. Carter was the first "contract employee" to have died. Both attested to the affection and esteem in which Mr. Carter was held. One, Mr. William J. Salomon, now the managing partner, who was called by the Commissioner, testified that he felt sympathy for the widow, that this did not enter into the particular decision since "we would be sympathetic to any widow," but that, on the other hand, he doubted whether the payment would have been made if Mr. Carter had not been survived by a wife and son. He said further that, as was fairly obvious, Mr. Carter's past services were a factor in arriving at the decision. . . .

The joint returned for 1960 filed by Mrs. Carter as executrix and for herself did not report as income the payments of $60,130.84. . . . The Commissioner assessed a deficiency . . . : Mrs. Carter petitioned the Tax Court to reconsider this; that court sustained the Commissioner; and this appeal followed. We reverse.

The Commissioner expectably relies on Commissioner v. Duberstein, which included Stanton v. United States, and United States v. Kaiser. We believe he reads somewhat more into those decisions than they held. Apart from the fact that none of the three cases involved payments to a survivor of a deceased employee, we do not understand the Court's opinion to mean that every trier of the facts was to be free for all future time to disregard guidelines that other trial and appellate courts had developed concerning the weight to be given to recurring "relevant factual elements, with their various combinations; . . . ." In refusing to adopt the Government's proposal that *any* business reason for a payment would prevent it from being considered a gift . . . and requiring inquiry in each case into "the dominant reason that explains his [the payor's] action in making the transfer," the Court scarcely intended to sanction disregard of the teaching of one of its greatest members: "It will not do to decide the same question one way between one set of litigants and the opposite way between another." Cardozo, The Nature of the Judicial Process 33 (1921). See also H.L.A. Hart, The Concept of Law 155-162 (1961).

When the Supreme Court decided *Duberstein, Stanton* and *Kaiser*, the Tax Court had already gone a considerable way toward structuring its position with respect to the taxable status of payments to the survivor of a deceased employee. In the often cited case of Estate of Hellstrom v. Commissioner, 24 T.C. 916 (1955), it held that payments to the widow of the president of a corporation of the amount the president would have received in salary if he had lived out the year constituted a gift. The court specifically gave no weight to the facts that the corporation took a deduction or that the gift was a function of the deceased's salary. It found the controlling facts to be that (1) the gift was made to the widow, rather than to the estate; (2) there was no obligation on the part of the corporation to make any further payments to the deceased; (3) the widow had never worked for the corporation; (4) the corporation received no economic benefit; and (5) the deceased had been fully compensated for his services. Applying a test of principal motive and thus anticipating *Duberstein*, the court found this to be a desire of the corporation to do an act of kindness for the widow. . . . In Estate of Luntz v. Commissioner, 29 T.C. 647 (1958), the Tax Court held that payments to the widow of a sum equivalent to two years salary of her husband, a former president, were a gift, despite the fact that at the same time the corporation also provided for the wives of two living officers at the time of their death. In finding that the payments were a gift, the Tax Court repeated the five factors noted in *Hellstrom*.

Despite the fact that *Duberstein* had approved the substantive test applied in *Hellstrom* and *Luntz*, the Tax Court took an abrupt swerve in Estate of Pierpont v. Commissioner, 35 T.C. 65 (1960), decision of which had been postponed pending the Supreme Court's decision in *Duberstein* and which was reviewed by the full court. The majority, seeing in the Supreme Court's summarization of older cases an indication, not perceptible to us, that the Court was adopting a more restrictive notion of what constitutes a gift, found payments to a survivor to be income, despite the presence of the five factors held in *Hellstrom* and *Luntz* to point to a gift, because of the authorizing resolution's having used the phrases "in recognition of the services rendered," a factor obviously present in every such case — whether mentioned or not — and having described the payment as "a continuation" of decedent's salary, as the payments held to be gifts in *Hellstrom, Foote* and *Luntz* had also been, and of the absence of "solid evidence" that the payments "were motivated in any part by the widow's needs or by a sense of generosity or the like." 35 T.C. at 68.

The Tax Court's decision in *Pierpont* was reversed and remanded by the Fourth Circuit, Poyner v. Commissioner, 301 F.2d 287 (4 Cir. 1962). Chief Judge Sobeloff, writing for a strong court, said, id. at 291-292 (footnote omitted):

> In every prior Tax Court case, essentially identical facts were held sufficient to support the conclusion that the dominant motive was sympathy for the taxpayer's widowed position. The only evidence on which the Tax Court specifically relies for its contrary finding is the wording of the authorizing corporate resolutions. While the language of the resolutions certainly merits consideration, never before has such language been deemed sufficient by itself, and in the face of the other above specified factors, to support a finding that the payments were compensation for services rendered. As the facts stipulated in this case do not differ from those deemed conclusive in past cases, a contrary finding seems to us without warrant.

. . . Since *Pierpont* the Tax Court seems to have found almost uniformly that payments to survivors constituted income. . . . While in most instances there were special factors making the conclusion plainly correct, in others . . . the decision seems in clear conflict with *Hellstrom* and

Luntz: the effect of *Pierpont*, doubtless inevitable in light of the review of reports of a single judge by the Chief Judge of the Tax Court with a view to maintaining consistency, I.R.C. §7460(b), has been to establish what amounts in that court to a rule that, in the absence of unusual circumstances demonstrating compassion, all payments to survivors of deceased employees are considered to be compensation.

As previously noted, the Tax Court's finding of income has been upset in two cases since *Poyner*. . . .

The course of decision in the district courts has been quite different from that in the Tax Court.[7] Payments to a survivor, not specifically characterized as compensation, have been rather consistently held to be gifts except when the corporation was dominated by the decedent's immediate family or there was a plan, formal or informal, for making such payments. . . . Our own case of Fanning v. Conley, 357 F.2d 37 (2 Cir. 1966), affirmed a finding of a gift where a corporation had paid the widow an amount equal to a half year's salary "as a salary continuation," the payments were charged to "miscellaneous expense" and a tax deduction was claimed under the heading "Other Deductions" — despite evidence that this was not the first payment to a survivor. Where courts of appeals have affirmed district courts' findings of income or reversed their findings of gift, the facts have been far more favorable to the Government than here. . . . Quite obviously, the Tax Court and the district courts have been traveling different paths.

If Mrs. Carter had paid the tax here at issue and sued for a refund, the odds that a district court would have found the payments constituted a gift would thus have been overwhelming. If it had done so, Fanning v. Conley, supra, 357 F.2d 37, is proof positive that we would have affirmed. Not content with reliance on the "unless clearly erroneous" rule, F.R. Civ. P. 52(a), we went to pains to point out for the guidance of the district courts that the very factors here principally relied upon by the Commissioner to negate the inference of gift — the references to salary continuation, the deduction of the payment as a business expense, although not as compensation, and the failure to investigate the widow's financial circumstances — "should not be the controlling or determinative factor," 357 F.2d at 41. Indeed, on the last item Mrs. Carter stands rather better than did Mrs. Fanning, in light of Salomon Bros.' knowledge of the heavy costs entailed by her husband's many hospitalizations. We cannot believe the Supreme Court intended that, at least in an area where, in contrast to the entire field of controversy with respect to gifts versus compensation, similar fact patterns tend to recur so often, the result should depend on whether a widow could afford to pay the tax and sue for a refund rather than avail herself of the salutary remedy Congress intended to afford in establishing the Tax Court and permitting determination before payment. The "mainsprings of human conduct," 363 U.S. at 289 do not differ so radically according to who tries the facts.

---

7. We omit discussion of cases tried to a jury since the reports generally do not give sufficient facts.

Beyond all this, we join in Chief Judge Soboloff's belief, expressed in Poyner v. C.I.R. supra, 301 F.2d at 291-292, that when the Supreme Court wrote as it did in *Duberstein*, it could reasonably have expected the Tax Court to continue to observe the sensible guidelines last enunciated in Luntz v. C.I.R., 29 T.C. 647, 650 (1958), supplemented by such others as experience should prove to be relevant, as aids to determining "the dominant reason that explains his [the payor's] action in making the transfer," 363 U.S. at 286. Each of the factors mentioned in *Luntz* as pointing to a gift is present here unless the one reading "the wife performed no services for the corporation" were to be read to include services that had ended 28 years before her husband's death, a construction that is patently unreasonable. . . .

. . . Applying the criterion of United States v. United States Gypsum Co., 333 U.S. 364, 395 . . . (1948), approved for use in this context by the Court in *Duberstein*, . . . we are "left with the definite and firm conviction that a mistake has been committed."

The judgment is reversed, with instructions to enter judgment annulling the determination of a deficiency.

DAVIS, Judge (dissenting): Chief Judge FRIENDLY's comprehensive opinion demonstrates at least these two things: first, that since Commissioner v. Duberstein . . . , there has been a perhaps unfortunate variety of judicial answers to the question whether payments to survivors were compensation or gifts, and, second, that in this case the trier of facts could have come to the other conclusion as many other judges probably would. Nevertheless, I depart from the court because the standards set by the Supreme Court, in delineating the roles of trier and reviewing tribunal, seem to me to call for affirmance of the Tax Court's result here, regardless of what we or some others would do as fact-finders. . . .

. . . As for the implied suggestion that the Tax Court should, in a case like this, bow to the assumed trend in the district courts, I see two obstacles: first, that nothing in the federal model of tax-determination sets one group of triers above another; and, second, that *Duberstein* contemplated lack of "symmetry" between "the variety of forums in which federal income tax cases can be tried."

Notes and Questions

1. In Bank of Palm Beach & Trust Co. v. United States, 201 Ct. Cl. 325, 476 F.2d 1343 (1973), Salomon Bros. was allowed a deduction for these payments to Mrs. Carter. The Court of Claims said the prior holding with respect to Mrs. Carter did not preclude deduction because "symmetry of treatment with respect to the recipient and the payor is not required." Nevertheless its holding is based on findings that "the dominant motivation prompting the payments was a business motivation" whose aspects "include the award of additional compensation as well as a general policy directed

toward the increased morale of similarly situated employees"; and there are indications in the opinion that gift and business treatment are conceived as dichotomous.

Judge Davis, who dissented in Mrs. Carter's case (sitting on the Second Circuit by designation), concurred in the result "on the ground that the payments to Mrs. Carter were (at the least) business-motivated gifts. . . . Because of that conclusion, I need not and do not reach the separate question, discussed in the court's opinion, whether these sums were not gifts at all but additional compensation for Mr. Carter's work."

Would §274(b) now prevent the decision in *Bank of Palm Beach & Trust Co.*?

2. Did Judge Friendly read *Duberstein* correctly about allocation of authority between trial and appellate courts? For an earlier Friendly opinion on this aspect of *Duberstein*, compare Bessenyey v. Commissioner, Chapter 12E (determining whether an activity was carried on for profit so that net losses could be deducted against other income).

3. Note the emphasis on the fact that Salomon Bros. had no plan to pay bonuses to widows and had never before made any such payment. How many such payments could be made before a plan would be inferred? Despite the large number of litigated cases on this question, it does not appear to be an exclusion that can be systematically exploited.

4. In Estate of William Enyart, T.C. Mem. 1965-266, a widow's bonus of $10,000 was voted by the directors of the corporation for which her husband had worked at a meeting held immediately after his funeral. Should the bonus be held to be a gift on the ground that the "Board meeting was held in an atmosphere of complete sadness, gloom, and grief"? Should the result be different than if the directors had wept at the funeral but put off voting a bonus until the next regular business meeting?

5. Look at §102(c); how should it affect the decision in a case like *Carter's Estate*?

4. Social Insurance and Welfare Payments

How should unemployment benefits be taxed? Social Security benefits? Government and philanthropic welfare payments? If such payments are made on a basis of need, then recipients often would not have enough income to be taxed in any event; but if that condition is not met, should such receipts be excluded from gross income?

The IRS originally ruled that many such items are to be excluded, citing no authority and elaborating no reasons to support its conclusion. E.g., IT 3194, 1938-1 C.B. 114 (lump-sum social security benefits); IT 3447, 1941-1 C.B. 191 (monthly Social Security benefits); IT 3229, 1938-2 C.B. 136 (social security death benefits); IT 3230, 1938-2 C.B. 136 (government unemployment benefits to private employees); Rev. Rul. 55-652, 1953-2 C.B. 21

(unemployment benefits to federal employees). These rulings, among others, are described and discussed at some length in Justice Frankfurter's concurring opinion in United States v. Kaiser, 363 U.S. 299, 312-314 (1960).

In 1978, Congress enacted §85, imposing some tax on unemployment benefits; in 1986 the section was amended to make them fully taxable.

With respect to Social Security benefits, look at §86, which was adopted in 1983. How should Social Security benefits be taxed? And how should Social Security taxes (contributions) be treated? The principal Social Security contribution is a tax on wages paid half by the employee and half by the employer. The whole tax is paid to the government by the employer, but the employee half is deducted from wage payments so that it is imposed quite explicitly on the employee. Employees currently get no deduction for the Social Security tax withheld from their wages, but are not taxed on the employer's Social Security contribution paid on account of their employment. Does that treatment of contributions justify the statutory treatment of benefits in §86?

References

A. Income Interests: Joseph M. Dodge, A Deemed Realization Approach Is Superior to Carryover Basis (and Avoids Most of the Problems of the Estate and Gift Tax), 54 Tax. L. Rev. 421 (2001).

B. Appreciated Property: Lewis, Taxing Unrealized Gains: The Nettle and the Flower, 34 Rec. A.B. City N.Y. 355 (1979); Lewis, Exploring Section 1015 and Related Topics, 43 Tax Law. 241 (1990).

C. Gratuitous Transfers Outside the Family: Blum, Motive, Intent and Purpose in Federal Income Taxation, 34 U. Chi. L. Rev. 485 (1967); Griswold, Foreword: Of Time and Attitudes — Professor Hart and Judge Arnold, 74 Harv. L. Rev. 81, 88-91 (1960); Klein, An Enigma in the Federal Income Tax: The Meaning of the Word "Gift," 48 Minn. L. Rev. 215 (1963).

Chapter 5 — *Capital Appreciation*

A. *UNREALIZED GAINS*

EISNER v. MACOMBER
252 U.S. 189 (1920)

Mr. Justice PITNEY delivered the opinion of the court. This case presents the question whether, by virtue of the Sixteenth Amendment, Congress has the power to tax, as income of the stockholder and without apportionment, a stock dividend made lawfully and in good faith against profits accumulated by the corporation since March 1, 1913.

It arises under the Revenue Act of September 8, 1916, ch. 463, 39 Stat. 756, et seq., which, in our opinion (notwithstanding a contention of the Government that will be noticed), plainly evinces the purpose of Congress to tax stock dividends as income.[1]

The facts, in outline, are as follows:

On January 1, 1916, the Standard Oil Company of California, a corporation of that State, out of an authorized capital stock of $100,000,000, had shares of stock outstanding, par value $100 each, amounting in round figures to $50,000,000. In addition, it had surplus and undivided profits invested in plant, property, and business and required for the purposes of the corporation, amounting to about $45,000,000, of which about

---

1. TITLE I. — INCOME TAX.

PART I. — ON INDIVIDUALS

Sec. 2(a) That, subject only to such exemptions and deductions as are hereinafter allowed, the net income of a taxable person shall include gains, profits, and income derived . . . , also from interest, rent, dividends, securities, or the transaction of any business carried on for gain or profit, or gains or profits and income derived from any source whatever: *Provided*, That the term "dividends" as used in this title shall be held to mean any distribution made or ordered to be made by a corporation, . . . out of its earnings or profits accrued since March first, nineteen hundred and thirteen, and payable to its shareholders, whether in cash or in stock of the corporation, . . . which stock dividend shall be considered income, to the amount of its cash value.

$20,000,000 had been earned prior to March 1, 1913, the balance thereafter. In January, 1916, in order to readjust the capitalization, the board of directors decided to issue additional shares sufficient to constitute a stock dividend of 50 percent of the outstanding stock, and to transfer from surplus account to capital stock account an amount equivalent to such issue. Appropriate resolutions were adopted, an amount equivalent to the par value of the proposed new stock was transferred accordingly, and the new stock duly issued against it and divided among the stockholders.

Defendant in error, being the owner of 2,200 shares of the old stock, received certificates for 1,100 additional shares, of which 18.07 percent, or 198.77 shares, par value $19,877, were treated as representing surplus earned between March 1, 1913, and January 1, 1916. She was called upon to pay, and did pay under protest, a tax imposed under the Revenue Act of 1916, based upon a supposed income of $19,877 because of the new shares; and an appeal to the Commissioner of Internal Revenue having been disallowed, she brought action against the Collector to recover the tax. In her complaint she alleged the above facts, and contended that in imposing such a tax the Revenue Act of 1916 violated Art. I, §2, cl. 3, and Art I, §9, cl. 4, of the Constitution of the United States, requiring direct taxes to be apportioned according to population, and that the stock dividend was not income within the meaning of the Sixteenth Amendment. A general demurrer to the complaint was overruled upon the authority of Towne v. Eisner; and, defendant having failed to plead further, final judgment went against him. To review it, the present writ of error is prosecuted.

The case was argued at the last term, and reargued at the present term, both orally and by additional briefs.

We are constrained to hold that the judgment of the District Court must be affirmed: First, because the question at issue is controlled by Towne v. Eisner, supra; secondly, because a reexamination of the question, with the additional light thrown upon it by elaborate arguments, has confirmed the view that the underlying ground of that decision is sound, that it disposes of the question here presented, and that other fundamental considerations lead to the same result.

In Towne v. Eisner, the question was whether a stock dividend made in 1914 against surplus earned prior to January 1, 1913, was taxable against the stockholder under the Act of October 3, 1913, ch. 16, 38 Stat. 114, 166, which provided (§B, p. 167) that net income should include "dividends," and also "gains or profits and income derived from any source whatever." Suit having been brought by a stockholder to recover the tax assessed against him by reason of the dividend, the District Court sustained a demurrer to the complaint. 242 Fed. Rep. 702. The court treated the construction of the act as inseparable from the interpretation of the Sixteenth Amendment; and, having referred to Pollock v. Farmers' Loan & Trust Co., 158 U.S. 601, and quoted the Amendment, proceeded very properly to say (p. 704): "It is manifest that the stock dividend in question cannot be reached by the

Income Tax Act, and could not, even though Congress expressly declared it to be taxable as income, unless it is in fact income." It declined, however, to accede to the contention that in Gibbons v. Mahon, 136 U.S. 549, "stock dividends" had received a definition sufficiently clear to be controlling, treated the language of this court in that case as obiter dictum in respect of the matter then before it (p. 706), and examined the question as res nova, with the result stated. When the case came here, after overruling a motion to dismiss made by the Government upon the ground that the only question involved was the construction of the statute and not its constitutionality, we dealt upon the merits with the question of construction only, but disposed of it upon consideration of the essential nature of a stock dividend, disregarding the fact that the one in question was based upon surplus earnings that accrued before the Sixteenth Amendment took effect. Not only so, but we rejected the reasoning of the District Court, saying (245 U.S. 426):

> Notwithstanding the thoughtful discussion that the case received below we cannot doubt that the dividend was capital as well for the purposes of Income Tax Law as for distribution between tenant for life and remainderman. What was said by this court upon the latter question is equally true for the former. "A stock dividend really takes nothing from the property of the corporation, and adds nothing to the interests of the shareholders. Its property is not diminished, and their interests are not increased. . . . The proportional interest of each shareholder remains the same. The only change is in the evidence which represents that interest, the new shares and the original shares together representing the same proportional interest that the original shares represented before the issue of the new ones." Gibbons v. Mahon, 136 U.S. 549, 559, 560. In short, the corporation is no poorer and the stockholder is no richer than they were before. Logan County v. United States, 169 U.S. 255, 261. If the plaintiff gained any small advantage by the change, it certainly was not an advantage of $417,450, the sum upon which he was taxed. . . . What has happened is that the plaintiff's old certificates have been split up in effect and have diminished in value to the extent of the value of the new.

This language aptly answered not only the reasoning of the District Court but the argument of the Solicitor General in this court, which discussed the essential nature of a stock dividend. And if, for the reasons thus expressed, such a dividend is not to be regarded as "income" or "dividends" within the meaning of the Act of 1913, we are unable to see how it can be brought within the meaning of "incomes" in the Sixteenth Amendment; it being very clear that Congress intended in that act to exert its power to the extent permitted by the Amendment. In Towne v. Eisner it was not contended that any construction of the statute could make it narrower than the constitutional grant; rather the contrary.

The fact that the dividend was charged against profits earned before the Act of 1913 took effect, even before the Amendment was adopted, was neither relied upon nor alluded to in our consideration of the merits in that case. Not only so, but had we considered that a stock dividend constituted income in any true sense, it would have been held taxable under the

Act of 1913 notwithstanding it was based upon profits earned before the Amendment. We ruled at the same term, in Lynch v. Hornby, that a cash dividend extraordinary in amount, and in Peabody v. Eisner, 247 U.S. 347, that a dividend paid in stock of another company, were taxable as income although based upon earnings that accrued before adoption of the Amendment. In the former case, concerning "corporate profits that accumulated before the Act took effect," we declared (pp. 343-344): "Just as we deem the legislative intent manifest to tax the stockholder with respect to such accumulations only if and when, and to the extent that, his interest in them comes to fruition as income, that is, in dividends declared, so we can perceive no constitutional obstacle that stands in the way of carrying out this intent when dividends are declared out of a preexisting surplus. . . . Congress was at liberty under the Amendment to tax as income, without apportionment, everything that became income, in the ordinary sense of the word, after the adoption of the Amendment, including dividends received in the ordinary course by a stockholder from a corporation, even though they were extraordinary in amount and might appear upon analysis to be a mere realization in possession of an inchoate and contingent interest that the stockholder had in a surplus of corporate assets previously existing." In Peabody v. Eisner (pp. 349-350), we observed that the decision of the District Court in Towne v. Eisner had been reversed "only upon the ground that it related to a stock dividend which in fact took nothing from the property of the corporation and added nothing to the interest of the shareholder, but merely changed the evidence which represented that interest"; and we distinguished the *Peabody* Case from the *Towne* Case upon the ground that "the dividend of Baltimore & Ohio shares was not a stock dividend but a distribution in specie of a portion of the assets of the Union Pacific."

Therefore, Towne v. Eisner cannot be regarded as turning upon the point that the surplus accrued to the company before the act took effect and before adoption of the Amendment. And what we have quoted from the opinion in that case cannot be regarded as obiter dictum, it having furnished the entire basis for the conclusion reached. We adhere to the view then expressed, and might rest the present case there; not because that case in terms decided the constitutional question, for it did not; but because the conclusion there reached as to the essential nature of a stock dividend necessarily prevents its being regarded as income in any true sense.

Nevertheless, in view of the importance of the matter, and the fact that Congress in the Revenue Act of 1916 declared (39 Stat. 757) that a "stock dividend shall be considered income, to the amount of its cash value," we will deal at length with the constitutional question, incidentally testing the soundness of our previous conclusion.

The Sixteenth Amendment must be construed in connection with the taxing clauses of the original Constitution and the effect attributed to them before the Amendment was adopted. In Pollock v. Farmers' Loan & Trust Co., 158 U.S. 601, under the Act of August 27, 1894, ch. 349, §§27, 28 Stat.

509, 553, it was held that taxes upon rents and profits of real estate and upon returns from investments of personal property were in effect direct taxes upon the property from which such income arose, imposed by reason of ownership; and that Congress could not impose such taxes without apportioning them among the States according to population, as required by Art. I, §2, cl. 3, and §9, cl. 4, of the original Constitution.

Afterwards, and evidently in recognition of the limitation upon the taxing power of Congress thus determined, the Sixteenth Amendment was adopted, in words lucidly expressing the object to be accomplished: "The Congress shall have power to lay and collect taxes on incomes, from whatever source derived, without apportionment among the several States, and without regard to any census or enumeration." As repeatedly held, this did not extend the taxing power to new subjects, but merely removed the necessity which otherwise might exist for an apportionment among the States of taxes laid on income. Brushaber v. Union Pacific R.R. Co., 240 U.S. 1, 17-19; Stanton v. Baltic Mining Co., 240 U.S. 103, 112 et seq.; Peck & Co. v. Lowe, 247 U.S. 165, 172-173.

A proper regard for its genesis, as well as its very clear language, requires also that this Amendment shall not be extended by loose construction, so as to repeal or modify, except as applied to income, those provisions of the Constitution that require an apportionment according to population for direct taxes upon property, real and personal. This limitation still has an appropriate and important function, and is not to be overridden by Congress or disregarded by the courts.

In order, therefore, that the clause cited from Article I of the Constitution may have proper force and effect, save only as modified by the Amendment, and that the latter also may have proper effect, it becomes essential to distinguish between what is and what is not "income," as the term is there used; and to apply the distinction, as cases arise, according to truth and substance, without regard to form. Congress cannot by any definition it may adopt conclude the matter, since it cannot by legislation alter the Constitution, from which alone it derives its power to legislate, and within whose limitations alone that power can be lawfully exercised.

The fundamental relation of "capital" to "income" has been much discussed by economists, the former being likened to the tree or the land, the latter to the fruit or the crop; the former depicted as a reservoir supplied from springs, the latter as the outlet stream, to be measured by its flow during a period of time. For the present purpose we require only a clear definition of the term "income," as used in common speech, in order to determine its meaning in the Amendment; and, having formed also a correct judgment as to the nature of a stock dividend, we shall find it easy to decide the matter at issue.

After examining dictionaries in common use (Bouv. L.D.; Standard Dict.; Webster's Internat. Dict.; Century Dict.), we find little to add to the succinct definition adopted in two cases arising under the Corporation Tax

Act of 1909 (Stratton's Independence v. Howbert, 231 U.S. 399, 415; Doyle v. Mitchell Bros. Co., 247 U.S. 179, 185) — "Income may be defined as the gain derived from capital, from labor, or from both combined," provided it be understood to include profit gained through a sale or conversion of capital assets, to which it was applied in the *Doyle* Case (pp. 183, 185).

Brief as it is, it indicates the characteristic and distinguishing attribute of income essential for a correct solution of the present controversy. The Government, although basing its argument upon the definition as quoted, placed chief emphasis upon the word "gain," which was extended to include a variety of meanings; while the significance of the next three words was either overlooked or misconceived. "*Derived — from — capital*"; — "the *gain — derived — from — capital*," etc. Here we have the essential matter: *not* a gain *accruing to* capital, not a *growth* or *increment* of value *in* the investment; but a gain, a profit, something of exchangeable value *proceeding from* the property, *severed from* the capital however invested or employed, and *coming in*, being "*derived*," that is *received* or *drawn by* the recipient (the taxpayer) for his *separate* use, benefit and disposal; *that* is income derived from property. Nothing else answers the description.

The same fundamental conception is clearly set forth in the Sixteenth Amendment — "incomes, *from* whatever *source derived*" — the essential thought being expressed with a conciseness and lucidity entirely in harmony with the form and style of the Constitution.

Can a stock dividend, considering its essential character, be brought within the definition? To answer this, regard must be had to the nature of a corporation and the stockholder's relation to it. We refer, of course, to a corporation such as the one in the case at bar, organized for profit, and having a capital stock divided into shares to which a nominal or par value is attributed.

Certainly the interest of the stockholder is a capital interest and his certificates of stock are but the evidence of it. They state the number of shares to which he is entitled and indicate their par value and how the stock may be transferred. They show that he or his assignors, immediate or remote, have contributed capital to the enterprise, that he is entitled to a corresponding interest proportionate to the whole, entitled to have the property and business of the company devoted during the corporate existence to attainment of the common objects, entitled to vote at stockholders' meetings, to receive dividends out of the corporation's profits if and when declared, and, in the event of liquidation, to receive a proportionate share of the net assets, if any, remaining after paying creditors. Short of liquidation, or until dividend declared, he has no right to withdraw any part of either capital or profits from the common enterprise; on the contrary, his interest pertains not to any part, divisible or indivisible, but to the entire assets, business, and affairs of the company. Nor is it the interest of an owner in the assets themselves, since the corporation has full title, legal and equitable, to the whole. The stockholder has the right to have the assets employed in the enterprise, with the incidental rights mentioned; but, as stockholder, he has no right to withdraw, only the right to persist, subject to the risks of the enterprise, and looking only to dividends for his return. If he desires to dissociate himself from the company he can do so only by disposing of his stock.

For bookkeeping purposes, the company acknowledges a liability in form to the stockholders equivalent to the aggregate par value of their stock, evidenced by a "capital stock account." If profits have been made and not divided they create additional bookkeeping liabilities under the head of "profit and loss," "undivided profits," "surplus account," or the like. None of these, however, gives to the stockholders as a body, much less to any one of them, either a claim against the going concern for any particular sum of money, or a right to any particular portion of the assets or any share in them unless or until the directors conclude that dividends shall be made and a part of the company's assets segregated from the common fund for the purpose. The dividend normally is payable in money, under exceptional circumstances in some other divisible property; and when so paid, then only (excluding, of course, a possible advantageous sale of his stock or winding-up of the company) does the stockholder realize a profit or gain which becomes his separate property, and thus derive income from the capital that he or his predecessor has invested.

In the present case, the corporation had surplus and undivided profits invested in plant, property, and business, and required for the purposes of the corporation, amounting to about $45,000,000, in addition to outstanding capital stock of $50,000,000. In this the case is not extraordinary. The profits of a corporation, as they appear upon the balance sheet at the end of the year, need not be in the form of money on hand in excess of what is required to meet current liabilities and finance current operations of the company. Often, especially in a growing business, only a part, sometimes a small part, of the year's profits is in property capable of division; the remainder having been absorbed in the acquisition of increased plant, equipment, stock in trade, or accounts receivable, or in decrease of outstanding liabilities. When only a part is available for dividends, the balance of the year's profits is carried to the credit of undivided profits, or surplus, or some other account having like significance. If thereafter the company finds itself in funds beyond current needs it may declare dividends out of such surplus or undivided profits; otherwise it may go on for years conducting a successful business, but requiring more and more working capital because of the extension of its operations, and therefore unable to declare dividends approximating the amount of its profits. Thus the surplus may increase until it equals or even exceeds the par value of the outstanding capital stock. This may be adjusted upon the books in the mode adopted in the case at bar — by declaring a "stock dividend." This, however, is no more than a book adjustment, in essence not a dividend but rather the opposite; no part of the assets of the company is separated from the common fund, nothing distributed except paper certificates that evidence an antecedent increase in the value of the stockholder's capital interest resulting from an accumulation of profits by the company, but profits so far absorbed in the business as to render it impracticable to separate them for withdrawal and distribution. In order to make the adjustment, a charge is made against surplus account with corresponding credit to capital stock account, equal to the proposed "dividend"; the new stock is issued against this and the certificates delivered to the existing stockholders in proportion to their previous holdings. This, however, is merely bookkeeping that does not affect the aggregate assets of the corporation or its outstanding liabilities; it affects only the form, not the essence, of the "liability" acknowledged by the corporation to its own shareholders, and this through a readjustment of accounts on one side of the balance sheet only, increasing "capital stock" at the expense of "surplus"; it does not alter the preexisting proportionate interest of any stockholder or increase the intrinsic value of his holding or of the aggregate holdings of the other stockholders as they stood before. The new certificates simply increase the number of the shares, with consequent dilution of the value of each share.

A "stock dividend" shows that the company's accumulated profits have been capitalized, instead of distributed to the stockholders or retained as surplus available for distribution in money or in kind should opportunity offer. Far from being a realization of profits of the stockholder, it tends rather to postpone such realization, in that the fund represented by the new stock has been transferred from surplus to capital, and no longer is available for actual distribution.

The essential and controlling fact is that the stockholder has received nothing out of the company's assets for his separate use and benefit; on the contrary, every dollar of his original investment, together with whatever accretions and accumulations have resulted from employment of his money and that of the other stockholders in the business of the company, still remains the property of the company, and subject to business risks which may result in wiping out the entire investment. Having regard to the very truth of the matter, to substance and not to form, he has received nothing that answers the definition of income within the meaning of the Sixteenth Amendment.

Being concerned only with the true character and effect of such a dividend when lawfully made, we lay aside the question whether in a particular case a stock dividend may be authorized by the local law governing the corporation, or whether the capitalization of profits may be the result of correct judgment and proper business policy on the part of its management, and a due regard for the interests of the stockholders. And we are considering the taxability of bona fide stock dividends only.

We are clear that not only does a stock dividend really take nothing from the property of the corporation and add nothing to that of the shareholder, but that the antecedent accumulation of profits evidenced thereby, while indicating that the shareholder is the richer because of an increase of his capital, at the same time shows he has not realized or received any income in the transaction.

It is said that a stockholder may sell the new shares acquired in the stock dividend; and so he may, if he can find a buyer. It is equally true that if he does sell, and in doing so realizes a profit, such profit, like any other, is income, and so far as it may have arisen since the Sixteenth Amendment is taxable by Congress without apportionment. The same would be true were he to sell some of his original shares at a profit. But if a shareholder sells dividend stock he necessarily disposes of a part of his capital interest, just as if he should sell a part of his old stock, either before or after the dividend. What he retains no longer entitles him to the same proportion of future dividends as before the sale. His part in the control of the company likewise is diminished. Thus, if one holding $60,000 out of a total $100,000 of the capital stock of a corporation should receive in common with other stockholders a 50 percent stock dividend, and should sell his part, he thereby would be reduced from a majority to a minority stockholder, having six-fifteenths instead of six-tenths of the total stock outstanding. A corresponding and proportionate decrease in capital interest and in voting power would befall a minority holder should he sell dividend stock; it being in the nature of things impossible for one to dispose of any part of such an issue without a proportionate disturbance of the distribution of the entire capital stock, and a like diminution of the seller's comparative voting power — that "right preservative of rights" in the control of a corporation. Yet, without selling, the shareholder, unless possessed of other resources, has not the wherewithal to pay an income tax upon the dividend stock. Nothing could more clearly show that to tax a stock dividend is to tax a capital increase, and not income, than this demonstration that in the nature of things it requires conversion of capital in order to pay the tax.

Throughout the argument of the Government, in a variety of forms, runs the fundamental error already mentioned — a failure to appraise correctly the force of the term "income" as used in the Sixteenth Amendment, or at least to give practical effect to it. Thus, the Government contends that the tax "is levied on income derived from corporate earnings," when in truth the stockholder has "derived nothing except paper certificates which, so far as they have any effect, deny him present participation in such earnings. It contends that the tax may be laid when earnings "are received by the stockholder," whereas he has received none; that the profits are "distributed by means of a stock dividend," although a stock dividend distributes no profits; that under the Act of 1916 "the tax is on the stockholder's share in corporate earnings," when in truth a stockholder has no such share, and receives none in a stock dividend; that "the profits are segregated from his former capital, and he has a separate certificate representing his invested profits or gains," whereas there has been no segregation of profits, nor has he any separate certificate representing a personal gain, since the certificates, new and old, are alike in what they represent — a capital interest in the entire concerns of the corporation.

We have no doubt of the power or duty of a court to look through the form of the corporation and determine the question of the stockholder's right, in order to ascertain whether he has received income taxable by Congress without apportionment. But looking through the form, we cannot disregard the essential truth disclosed; ignore the substantial difference between corporation and stockholder; treat the entire organization as unreal; look upon stockholders as partners, when they are not such; treat them as having in equity a right to a partition of the corporate assets, when they have none; and indulge the fiction that they received and realized a share of the profits of the company which in truth they have neither received nor realized. We must treat the corporation as a substantial entity separate from the stockholder, not only because such is the practical fact but because it is only by recognizing such separateness that any dividend — even one paid in money or property — can be regarded as income of the stockholder. Did we regard corporation and stockholders as altogether identical, there would be no income except as the corporation acquired it; and while this would be taxable against the corporation as income under appropriate provisions of law, the individual stockholders could not be separately and additionally taxed with respect to their several shares even when divided, since if there were entire identity between them and the company they could not be regarded as receiving anything from it, any more than if one's money were to be removed from one pocket to another.

Conceding that the mere issue of a stock dividend makes the recipient no richer than before, the Government nevertheless contends that the new certificates measure the extent to which the gains accumulated by the corporation have made him the richer. There are two insuperable difficulties with this: In the first place, it would depend upon how long he had held the stock whether the stock dividend indicated the extent to which he had been enriched by the operations of the company; unless he had held it throughout such operations the measure would not hold true. Secondly, and more important for present purposes, enrichment through increase in value of capital investment is not income in any proper meaning of the term.

The complaint contains averments respecting the market prices of stock such as plaintiff held, based upon sales before and after the stock dividend, tending to show that the receipt of the additional shares did not substantially change the market value of her entire holdings. This tends to show that in this instance market quotations reflected intrinsic values — a thing they do not always do. But we regard the market prices of the securities as an unsafe criterion in an inquiry such as the present, when the question must be, not what will the thing sell for, but what is it in truth and in essence.

It is said there is no difference in principle between a simple dividend and a case where stockholders use money received as cash dividends to purchase additional stock contemporaneously issued by the corporation. But an actual cash dividend, with a real option to the stockholder either to keep the money for his own or to reinvest it in new shares, would be as far removed as possible from a true stock dividend, such as the one we have under consideration, where nothing of value is taken from the company's assets and transferred to the individual ownership of the several stockholders and thereby subjected to their disposal.

The Government's reliance upon the supposed analogy between a dividend of the corporation's own shares and one made by distributing shares owned by it in the stock of another company, calls for no comment beyond the statement that the latter distributes assets of the company among the shareholders while the former does not; and for no citation of authority except Peabody v. Eisner, 247 U.S. 347, 349-350.

Two recent decisions, proceeding from courts of high jurisdiction, are cited in support of the position of the Government.

Swan Brewery Co., Ltd. v. Rex [1914] A.C. 231, arose under the Dividend Duties Act of Western Australia, which provided that "dividend" should include "every dividend, profit, advantage, or gain intended to be paid or credited to or distributed among any members or directors of any company," except, etc. There was a stock dividend, the new shares being allotted among the shareholders pro rata; and the question was whether this was a distribution of a dividend within the meaning of the act. The Judicial Committee of the Privy Council sustained the dividend duty upon the ground that, although "in ordinary language the new shares would not be called a dividend, nor would the allotment of them be a distribution of a dividend," yet, within the meaning of the act, such new shares were an "advantage" to the recipients. There being no constitutional restriction upon the action of the lawmaking body, the case presented merely a question of statutory construction, and manifestly the decision is not a precedent for the guidance of this court when acting under a duty to test an act of Congress by the limitations of a written Constitution having superior force.

In Tax Commissioner v. Putnam (1917), 227 Massachusetts, 522, it was held that the 44th Amendment to the constitution of Massachusetts, which conferred upon the legislature full power to tax incomes, "must be interpreted as including every item which by any reasonable understanding can fairly be regarded as income" (pp. 526, 531); and that under it a stock dividend was taxable as income, the court saying (p. 535): "In essence the thing which has been done is to distribute a symbol representing an accumulation of profits, which instead of being paid out in cash is invested in the business, thus augmenting its durable assets. In this aspect of the case the substance of the transaction is no different from what it would be if a cash dividend had been declared with the privilege of subscription to an equivalent amount of new shares." We cannot accept this reasoning. Evidently, in order to give a sufficiently broad sweep to the new taxing provision, it was deemed necessary to take the symbol for the substance, accumulation for distribution, capital accretion for its opposite; while a case where money is paid into the hand of the stockholder with an option to buy new shares with it, followed by acceptance of the option, was regarded as identical in substance with a case where the stockholder receives no money and has no option. The Massachusetts court was not under an obligation, like the one which binds us, of applying a constitutional amendment in the light of other constitutional provisions that stand in the way of extending it by construction.

Upon the second argument, the Government, recognizing the force of the decision in Towne v. Eisner, supra, and virtually abandoning the contention that a stock dividend increases the interest of the stockholder or otherwise enriches him, insisted as an alternative that by the true construction of the Act of 1916 the tax is imposed not upon the stock dividend but rather upon the stockholder's share of the undivided profits previously accumulated by the corporation; the tax being levied as a matter of convenience at the time such profits become manifest through the stock dividend. If so construed, would the act be constitutional?

That Congress has power to tax shareholders upon their property interests in the stock of corporations is beyond question; and that such interests might be valued in view of the condition of the company, including its accumulated and undivided profits, is equally clear. But that this would be taxation of property because of ownership, and hence would require apportionment under the provisions of the Constitution, is settled beyond peradventure by previous decisions of this court.

The Government relies upon Collector v. Hubbard (1870), 12 Wall. 1, 17, which arose under §117 of the Act of June 30, 1864, ch. 173, 13 Stat. 223, 282, providing that "the gains and profits of all companies, whether incorporated or partnership, other than the companies specified in this section, shall be included in estimating the annual gains, profits, or income of any person entitled to the same, whether divided or otherwise." The court held an individual taxable upon his proportion of the earnings of a corporation although not declared as dividends and although invested in assets not in their nature divisible. Conceding that the stockholder for certain purposes had no title prior to dividend declared, the court nevertheless said (p. 18):

> Grant all that, still it is true that the owner of a share of stock in a corporation holds the share with all its incidents, and that among those incidents is the right to receive all future dividends, that is, his proportional share of all profits not then divided. Profits are incident to the share to which the owner at once becomes entitled provided he remains a member of the corporation until a dividend is made. Regarded as an incident to the shares, undivided profits are property of the shareholder, and as such are the proper subject of sale, gift, or devise. Undivided profits invested in real estate, machinery, or raw material for the purpose of being manufactured are investments in which the stockholders are interested, and when such profits are actually appropriated to the payment of the debts of the corporation they serve to increase the market value of the shares, whether held by the original subscribers or by assignees.

In so far as this seems to uphold the right of Congress to tax without apportionment a stockholder's interest in accumulated earnings prior to dividend
declared, it must be regarded as overruled by Pollock v. Farmers' Loan &
Trust Co., 158 U.S. 601, 627, 628, 637. Conceding Collector v. Hubbard was
inconsistent with the doctrine of that case, because it sustained a direct tax
upon property not apportioned among the States, the Government nevertheless insists the Sixteenth Amendment removed this obstacle, so that now
the Hubbard Case is authority for the power of Congress to levy a tax on the
stockholder's share in the accumulated profits of the corporation even
before division by the declaration of a dividend of any kind. Manifestly
this argument must be rejected, since the Amendment applies to income
only, and what is called the stockholder's share in the accumulated profits of
the company is capital, not income. As we have pointed out, a stockholder
has no individual share in accumulated profits, nor in any particular part of
the assets of the corporation, prior to dividend declared.

Thus, from every point of view, we are brought irresistibly to the conclusion that neither under the Sixteenth Amendment nor otherwise has
Congress power to tax without apportionment a true stock dividend made
lawfully and in good faith, or the accumulated profits behind it, as income of
the stockholder. The Revenue Act of 1916, in so far as it imposes a tax upon
the stockholder because of such dividend, contravenes the provisions of
Article I, §2, cl. 3, and Article I, §9, cl. 4, of the Constitution, and to this
extent is invalid notwithstanding the Sixteenth Amendment.

Judgment affirmed.

Mr. Justice HOLMES, dissenting. I think that Towne v. Eisner was right in
its reasoning and result and that on sound principles the stock dividend was
not income. But it was clearly intimated in that case that the construction of
the statute then before the Court might be different from that of the Constitution. 245 U.S. 425. I think that the word "incomes" in the Sixteenth
Amendment should be read in "a sense most obvious to the common
understanding at the time of its adoption." Bishop v. State, 149 Indiana,
223, 230; State v. Butler, 70 Florida, 102, 133. For it was for public adoption
that it was proposed. McCulloch v. Maryland, 4 Wheat. 316, 407. The known
purpose of this Amendment was to get rid of nice questions as to what might
be direct taxes, and I cannot doubt that most people not lawyers would
suppose when they voted for it that they put a question like the present to
rest. I am of opinion that the Amendment justifies the tax. See Tax Commissioner v. Putnam, 227 Massachusetts, 522, 532, 533.

Mr. Justice DAY concurs in this opinion.

Mr. Justice BRANDEIS, dissenting, delivered the following opinion, in
which Mr. Justice Clarke concurred. Financiers, with the aid of lawyers,
devised long ago two different methods by which a corporation can, without
increasing its indebtedness, keep for corporate purposes accumulated profits, and yet, in effect, distribute these profits among its stockholders. One
method is a simple one. The capital stock is increased; the new stock is paid

up with the accumulated profits; and the new shares of paid-up stock are then distributed among the stockholders pro rata as a dividend. If the stockholder prefers ready money to increasing his holding of the stock in the company, he sells the new stock received as a dividend. The other method is slightly more complicated. Arrangements are made for an increase of stock to be offered to stockholders pro rata at par and, at the same time, for the payment of a cash dividend equal to the amount which the stockholders will be required to pay to the company, if he avails himself of the right to subscribe for his pro rata of the new stock. If the stockholder takes the new stock, as is expected, he may endorse the dividend check received to the corporation and thus pay for the new stock. In order to ensure that all the new stock so offered will be taken, the price at which it is offered is fixed far below what it is believed will be its market value. If the stockholder prefers ready money to an increase of his holdings of stock, he may sell his right to take new stock pro rata, which is evidence by an assignable instrument. In that event the purchaser of the rights repays to the corporation, as the subscription price of the new stock, an amount equal to that which it had paid as a cash dividend to the stockholder.

Both of these methods of retaining accumulated profits while in effect distributing them as a dividend had been in common use in the United States for many years prior to the adoption of the Sixteenth Amendment. They were recognized equivalents. Whether a particular corporation employed one or the other method was determined sometimes by requirements of the law under which the corporation was organized; sometimes it was determined by preferences of the individual officials of the corporation; and sometimes by stock market conditions. Whichever method was employed the resultant distribution of the new stock was commonly referred to as a stock dividend. How these two methods have been employed may be illustrated by the action in this respect (as reported in Moody's Manual, 1918 Industrial, and the Commercial and Financial Chronicle), of some of the Standard Oil companies, since the disintegration pursuant to the decision of this court in 1911. Standard Oil Co. v. United States, 221 U.S. 1.

(a) Standard Oil Co. (of Indiana), an Indiana corporation. It had on December 31, 1911, $1,000,000 capital stock (all common), and a large surplus. On May 5, 1912, it increased its capital stock to $30,000,000, and paid a simple stock dividend of 2900 percent in stock.[1]

(b) Standard Oil Co. (of Nebraska), a Nebraska corporation. It had on December 31, 1911, $600,000 capital stock (all common), and a substantial surplus. On April 15, 1912, it paid a simple stock dividend of $33^1/_3$ percent, increasing the outstanding capital to $800,000. During the calendar year 1912 it paid cash dividends aggregating 20 percent; but it earned considerably more, and had at the close of the year again a substantial surplus.

1. Moody's, p. 1544; Commercial and Financial Chronicle, Vol. 94, p. 831; Vol. 98, pp. 1005, 1076.

On June 20, 1913, it declared a further stock dividend of 25 percent, thus increasing the capital to $1,000,000.[2]

(c) The Standard Oil Co. (of Kentucky), a Kentucky corporation. It had on December 31, 1913, $1,000,000 capital stock (all common), and $3,701,710 surplus. Of this surplus $902,457 had been earned during the calendar year 1913, the net profits of that year having been $1,002,457 and the dividends paid only $100,000 (10 percent). On December 22, 1913, a cash dividend of $200 per share was declared payable on February 14, 1914, to stockholders of record January 31, 1914; and these stockholders were offered the right to subscribe for an equal amount of new stock at par and to apply the cash dividend in payment therefore. The outstanding stock was thus increased to $3,000,000. During the calendar years 1914, 1915 and 1916, quarterly dividends were paid on this stock at an annual rate of between 15 percent and 20 percent, but the company's surplus increased by $2,347,614, so that on December 31, 1916, it had a large surplus over its $3,000,000 capital stock. On December 15, 1916, the company issued a circular to the stockholders, saying:

> The company's business for this year has shown a very good increase in volume and a proportionate increase in profits, and it is estimated that by Jan. 1, 1917, the company will have a surplus of over $4,000,000. The board feels justified in stating that if the proposition to increase the capital stock is acted on favorably, it will be proper in the near future to declare a cash dividend of 100%; and to allow the stockholders the privilege pro rata according to their holdings, to purchase the new stock at par, the plan being to allow the stockholders, if they desire, to use their cash dividend to pay for the new stock.

The increase of stock was voted. The company then paid a cash dividend of 100 percent, payable May 1, 1917, again offering to such stockholders the right to subscribe for an equal amount of new stock at par and to apply the cash dividend in payment therefore.

Moody's Manual, describing the transaction with exactness, says first that the stock was increased from $3,000,000 to $6,000,000, "a cash dividend of 100%, payable May 1, 1917, being exchanged for one share of new stock, the equivalent of a 100% stock dividend." But later in the report giving, as customary in the Manual, the dividend record of the company, the Manual says: "A stock dividend of 200% was paid Feb. 14, 1914, and one of 100% on May 1, 1917." And in reporting specifically the income account of the company for a series of years ending December 31, covering net profits, dividends paid and surplus for the year, it gives, as the aggregate of dividends for the year 1917, $660,000; (which was the aggregate paid on the quarterly cash dividend — 5 percent January and April; 6 percent July and October); and adds in a note: "In addition a stock dividend of 100% was paid during

---

2. Moody's, p. 1548; Commercial and Financial Chronicle, Vol. 94, p. 771; Vol. 96, p. 1428; Vol. 97, p. 1434; Vol. 98, p. 1541.

the year."[3] The Wall Street Journal of May 2, 1917, p. 2, quotes the 1917 "High" price for Standard Oil of Kentucky as "375 Ex. Stock Dividend."

It thus appears that among financiers and investors the distribution of the stock by whichever method effected is called a stock dividend; that the two methods by which accumulated profits are legally retained for corporate purposes and at the same time distributed as dividends are recognized by them to be equivalents; and that the financial results to the corporation and to the stockholders of the two methods are substantially the same — unless a difference results from the application of the federal income tax law.

Mrs. Macomber, a citizen and resident of New York, was, in the year 1916, a stockholder in the Standard Oil Company (of California) a corporation organized under the laws of California and having its principal place of business in that State. During that year she received from the company a stock dividend representing profits earned since March 1, 1913. The dividend was paid by direct issue of the stock to her according to the simple method described above, pursued also by the Indiana and Nebraska companies. In 1917 she was taxed under the federal law on the stock dividend so received at its par value of $100 a share, as income received during the year 1916. Such a stock dividend is income as distinguished from capital both under the law of New York and under the law of California; because in both States every dividend representing profits is deemed to be income whether paid in cash or in stock. It had been so held in New York, where the question arose as between life-tenant and remainderman, Lowry v. Farmers' Loan & Trust Co., 172 N.Y. 137; Matter of Osborne, 209 N.Y. 450; and also, where the question arose in matters of taxation. People v. Glynn, 130 App. Div. 332; 198 N.Y. 605. It has been so held in California, where the question appears to have arisen only in controversies between life-tenant and remainderman. Estate of Duffill, 58 Cal. Dec. 97; 180 California, 748.

It is conceded that if the stock dividend paid to Mrs. Macomber had been made by the more complicated method pursued by the Standard Oil Company of Kentucky, that is, issuing rights to take new stock pro rata and paying to each stockholder simultaneously a dividend in cash sufficient in amount to enable him to pay for this pro rata of new stock to be purchased — the dividend so paid to him would have been taxable as income, whether he retained the cash or whether he returned it to the corporation in payment for his pro rata of new stock. But it is contended that, because the simple method was adopted of having the new stock issued direct to the stockholders as paid-up stock, the new stock is not to be deemed income, whether she retained it or converted it into cash by sale. If such a different result can flow merely from the difference in the method pursued, it must be because Congress is without power to tax as income of the stockholder either the

[3]. Moody's, p. 1547; Commercial and Financial Chronicle, Vol. 97, pp. 1589, 1827, 1903; Vol. 98, pp. 76, 457; Vol. 103, p. 2348. Poor's Manual of Industrials (1918), p. 2240, in giving the "Comparative Income Account" of the company describes the 1914 dividend as "Stock Dividend paid (200%) — $2,000,000"; and describes the 1917 dividend as "$3,000,000 special cash dividend."

stock received under the latter method or the proceeds of its sale; for Congress has, by the provisions in the Revenue Act of 1916, expressly declared its purpose to make stock dividends, by whichever method paid, taxable as income.

The Sixteenth Amendment proclaimed February 25, 1913, declares:

"The Congress shall have power to lay and collect taxes on incomes, from whatever source derived, without apportionment among the several States, and without regard to any census or enumeration."

The Revenue Act of September 8, 1916, ch. 463, 39 Stat. 756, 757, provided:

> That the term "dividends" as used in this title shall be held to mean any distribution made or ordered to be made by a corporation, . . . out of its earnings or profits accrued since March first, nineteen hundred and thirteen, and payable to its shareholders, whether in cash or in stock of the corporation . . . which stock dividend shall be considered income, to the amount of its cash value.

Hitherto powers conferred upon Congress by the Constitution have been liberally construed, and have been held to extend to every means appropriate to attain the end sought. In determining the scope of the power the substance of the transaction, not its form, has been regarded. Martin v. Hunter, 1 Wheat. 304, 326; McCulloch v. Maryland, 4 Wheat. 316, 407, 415; Brown v. Maryland, 12 Wheat. 419, 446; Craig v. Missouri, 4 Pet. 410, 433; Jarrolt v. Moberly, 103 U.S. 580, 585, 587; Legal Tender Case, 110 U.S. 421, 444; Burrow-Giles Lithographic Co. v. Sarony, 111 U.S. 53, 58; United States v. Realty Co., 163 U.S. 427, 440, 441, 442; South Carolina v. United States, 199 U.S. 437, 448-449. Is there anything in the phraseology of the Sixteenth Amendment or in the nature of corporate dividends which should lead to a departure from these rules of construction and compel this court to hold, that Congress is powerless to prevent a result so extraordinary as that here contended for by the stockholder?

First: The term "income" when applied to the investment of the stockholder in a corporation, had, before the adoption of the Sixteenth Amendment, been commonly understood to mean the returns from time to time received by the stockholder from gains or earnings of the corporation. A dividend received by a stockholder from a corporation may be either in distribution of capital assets or in distribution of profits. Whether it is the one or the other is in no way affected by the medium in which it is paid, nor by the method or means through which the particular thing distributed as a dividend was procured. If the dividend is declared payable in cash, the money with which to pay it is ordinarily taken from surplus cash in the treasury. But (if there are profits legally available for distribution and the law under which the company was incorporated so permits) the company may raise the money by discounting negotiable paper; or by selling bonds, scrip or stock of another corporation then in the treasury; or by selling its own bonds, scrip or stock then in the treasury; or by selling its own bonds, scrip or stock issued expressly for that purpose. How the money shall be raised is wholly a matter of financial management. The manner in which it is raised in no way affects the question whether the dividend received by the stockholder is income or capital; nor can it conceivably affect the question whether it is taxable as income.

Likewise whether a dividend declared payable from profits shall be paid in cash or in some other medium is also wholly a matter of financial management. If some other medium is decided upon, it is also wholly a question of financial management whether the distribution shall be, for instance, in bonds, scrip or stock of another corporation or in issues of its own. And if the dividend is paid in its own issues, why should there be a difference in result dependent upon whether the distribution was made from such securities then in the treasury or from others to be created and issued by the company expressly for the purpose? So far as the distribution may be made from its own issues of bonds, or preferred stock created expressly for the purpose, it clearly would make no difference in the decision of the question whether the dividend was a distribution of profits, that the securities had to be created expressly for the purpose of distribution. If a dividend paid in securities of that nature represents a distribution of profits Congress may, of course, tax it as income of the stockholder. Is the result different where the security distributed is common stock?

Suppose that a corporation having power to buy and sell its own stock, purchases, in the interval between its regular dividend dates, with monies derived from current profits, some of its own common stock as a temporary investment, intending at the time of purchase to sell it before the next dividend date and to use the proceeds in paying dividends, but later, deeming it inadvisable either to sell this stock or to raise by borrowing the money necessary to pay the regular dividend in cash, declares a dividend payable in this stock: Can anyone doubt that in such a case the dividend in common stock would be income of the stockholder and constitutionally taxable as such? See Green v. Bissell, 79 Connecticut, 547; Leland v. Hayden, 102 Massachusetts, 542. And would it not likewise be income of the stockholder subject to taxation if the purpose of the company in buying the stock so distributed had been from the beginning to take it off the market and distribute it among the stockholders as a dividend, and the company actually did so? And proceeding a short step further: Suppose that a corporation decided to capitalize some of its accumulated profits by creating additional common stock and selling the same to raise working capital, but after the stock has been issued and certificates therefor are delivered to the bankers for sale, general financial conditions make it undesirable to market the stock and the company concludes that it is wiser to husband, for working capital, the cash which it had intended to use in paying stockholders a dividend, and, instead, to pay the dividend in the common stock which it had planned to sell: Would not the stock so distributed be a distribution of profits — and, hence, when received, be income of the stockholder and taxable as such? If this be conceded, why should it not be equally income of the stockholder, and taxable as such, if the common stock created by capitalizing profits, had been originally created for the express purpose of being distributed as a dividend to the stockholder who afterwards received it?

Second: It has been said that a dividend payable in bonds or preferred stock created for the purpose of distributing profits may be income and taxable as such, but that the case is different where the distribution is in common stock created for that purpose. Various reasons are assigned for making this distinction. One is that the proportion of the stockholder's ownership to the aggregate number of the shares of the company is not changed by the distribution. But that is equally true where the dividend is paid in its bonds or in its preferred stock. Furthermore, neither maintenance nor change in the proportionate ownership of a stockholder in a corporation has any bearing upon the question here involved. Another reason assigned is that the value of the old stock held is reduced approximately by the value of the new stock received, so that the stockholder after receipt of the stock dividend has no more than he had before it was paid. That is equally true whether the dividend be paid in cash or in other property, for instance, bonds, scrip or preferred stock of the company. The payment from profits of a large cash dividend, and even a small one, customarily lowers the then market value of stock because the undivided property represented by each share has been correspondingly reduced. The argument which appears to be most strongly urged for the stockholders is, that when a stock dividend is made, no portion of the assets of the company is thereby segregated for the stockholder. But does the issue of new bonds or of preferred stock created for use as a dividend result in any segregation of assets for the stockholder? In each case he receives a piece of paper which entitles him to certain rights in the undivided property. Clearly segregation of assets in a physical sense is not an essential of income. The year's gains of a partner are taxable as income, although there, likewise, no segregation of his share in the gains from that of his partners is had.

The objection that there has been no segregation is presented also in another form. It is argued that until there is a segregation, the stockholder cannot know whether he has really received gains; since the gains may be invested in plant or merchandise or other property and perhaps be later lost. But is not this equally true of the share of a partner in the year's profits of the firm or, indeed, of the profits of the individual who is engaged in business alone? And is it not true, also, when dividends are paid in cash? The gains of a business, whether conducted by an individual, by a firm or by a corporation, are ordinarily reinvested in large part. Many a cash dividend honestly declared as a distribution of profits proves later to have been paid out of capital, because errors in forecast prevent correct ascertainment of values. Until a business adventure has been completely liquidated, it can never be determined with certainty whether there have been profits unless the returns have at least exceeded the capital originally invested. Businessmen, dealing with the problem practically, fix necessarily periods and rules for determining whether there have been net profits—that is income or gains. They protect themselves from being seriously misled by adopting a system of depreciation charges and reserves. Then, they act upon their own determination, whether profits have been made. Congress in legislating has wisely adopted their practices as its own rules of action.

Third: The Government urges that it would have been within the power of Congress to have taxed as income of the stockholder his pro rata share of undistributed profits earned, even if no stock dividend representing it had been paid. Strong reasons may be assigned for such a view. See Collector v. Hubbard, 12 Wall. 1. The undivided share of a partner in the year's undistributed profits of his firm is taxable as income of the partner, although the share in the gain is not evidenced by any action taken by the firm. Why not the stockholder's interest in the gains of the company? The law finds no difficulty in disregarding the corporate fiction whenever that is deemed necessary to attain a just result. Linn & Lane Timber Co. v. United States, 236 U.S. 574; see Morawetz on Corporations, 2d ed., §§227-231; Cook on Corporations, 7th ed., §§663, 664. The stockholder's interest in the property of the corporation differs, not fundamentally but in form only, from the interest of a partner in the property of the firm. There is much authority for the proposition that, under our law, a partnership or joint stock company is just as distinct and palpable an entity in the idea of the law, as distinguished from the individuals composing it, as is a corporation.[4] No reason appears, why Congress, in legislating under a grant of power so comprehensive as that authorizing the levy of an income tax, should be limited by the particular view of the relation of the stockholder to the corporation and its property which may, in the absence of legislation, have been taken by this court. But we have no occasion to decide the question whether Congress might have taxed to the stockholder his undivided share of the corporation's earnings. For Congress has in this act limited the income tax to that share of the stockholder in the earnings which is, in effect, distributed by means of the stock dividend paid. In other words, to render the stockholder taxable there must be both earnings made *and* a dividend paid. Neither earnings without dividend—nor a dividend without earnings—subjects the stockholder to taxation under the Revenue Act of 1916.

Fourth: The equivalency of all dividends representing profits, whether paid in cash or in stock, is so complete that serious question of the taxability of stock dividends would probably never had been made, if Congress had undertaken to tax only those dividends which represented profits earned during the year in which the dividend was paid or in the year preceding.

4. See Some Judicial Myths, by Francis M. Burdick, 22 Harvard Law Review, 393, 394-396; The Firm as a Legal Person, by William Hamilton Cowles, 57 Cent. L.J., 343, 348; The Separate Estates of Non-Bankrupt Partners, by J.D. Brannan, 20 Harvard Law Review, 589-592; compare Harvard Law Review, Vol. 7, p. 426; Vol. 14, p. 222; Vol. 17, p. 194.

But this court, construing liberally not only the constitutional grant of power but also the Revenue Act of 1913, held that Congress might tax, and had taxed, to the stockholder dividends received during the year, although earned by the company long before; and even prior to the adoption of the Sixteenth Amendment. Lynch v. Hornby.[5] That rule, if indiscriminatingly applied to all stock dividends representing profits earned, might, in view of corporate practice, have worked considerable hardship, and have raised serious questions. Many corporations, without legally capitalizing any part of their profits, had assigned definitely some part or all of the annual balances remaining after paying the usual cash dividends, to the uses to which permanent capital is ordinarily applied. Some of the corporations doing this, transferred such balances on their books to "Surplus" account, — distinguishing between such permanent "Surplus" and the "Undivided Profits" account. Other corporations, without this formality, had assumed that the annual accumulating balances carried as undistributed profits were to be treated as capital permanently invested in the business. And still others, without definite assumption of any kind, had so used undivided profits for capital purposes. To have made the revenue law apply retroactively so as to reach such accumulated profits, if and whenever it should be deemed desirable to capitalize them legally by the issue of additional stock distributed as a dividend to stockholders, would have worked great injustice. Congress endeavored in the Revenue Act of 1916 to guard against any serious hardship which might otherwise have arisen from making taxable stock dividends representing accumulated profits. It did not limit the taxability to stock dividends representing profits earned within the tax years or in the year preceding; but it did limit taxability to such dividends representing profits earned since March 1, 1913. Thereby stockholders were given notice that their share also in undistributed profits accumulating thereafter was at some time to be taxed as income. And Congress sought by §3 to discourage the postponements of distribution for the illegitimate purpose of evading liability to surtaxes.

Fifth: The decision of this court, that earnings made before the adoption of the Sixteenth Amendment but paid out in cash dividend after its adoption were taxable as income of the stockholder, involved a very liberal construction of the Amendment. To hold now that earnings both made and paid out after the adoption of the Sixteenth Amendment cannot be taxed as income of the stockholder, if paid in the form of a stock dividend, involves an exceedingly narrow construction of it. As said by Mr. Chief Justice Marshall in Brown v. Maryland, 12 Wheat. 419, 446: "To construe the power so as to impair its efficacy, would tend to defeat an object, in the attainment of which the American public took and justly took, that strong interest which arose from a full conviction of its necessity."

---

5. The hardship supposed to have resulted from such a decision has been removed in the Revenue Act of 1916, as amended, by providing in §31(b) that such cash dividends shall thereafter be exempt from taxation, if before they are made, all earnings made since February 28, 1913, shall have been distributed. Act of October 3, 1917, ch. 63, §1211, 40 Stat. 338; Act of February 24, 1919, ch. 18, §201(b), 40 Stat. 1059.

No decision heretofore rendered by this court requires us to hold that Congress, in providing for the taxation of stock dividends, exceeded the power conferred upon it by the Sixteenth Amendment. The two cases mainly relied upon to show that this was beyond the power of Congress are Towne v. Eisner, which involved a question not of constitutional power but of statutory construction, and Gibbons v. Mahon, 136 U.S. 549, which involved a question arising between life-tenant and remainderman. So far as concerns Towne v. Eisner, we have only to bear in mind what was there said [245 U.S. 418, 425] (p. 425): "But it is not necessarily true that income means the same thing in the Constitution and the [an] act.[6]" Gibbons v. Mahon is even less an authority for a narrow construction of the power to tax incomes conferred by the Sixteenth Amendment. In that case the court was required to determine how, in the administration of an estate in the District of Columbia, a stock dividend, representing profits, received after the decedent's death, should be disposed of as between life-tenant and remainderman. The question was in essence: What shall the intention of the testator be presumed to have been? On this question there was great diversity of opinion and practice in the courts of English-speaking countries. Three well-defined rules were then competing for acceptance; two of these involve an arbitrary rule of distribution, the third equitable apportionment. See Cook on Corporations, 7th ed., §§552-558.

1. The so-called English rule, declared in 1799, by Brander v. Brander, 4 Ves. Jr. 800, that a dividend representing profits, whether in cash, stock or other property, belongs to the life-tenant if it was a regular or ordinary dividend, and belongs to the remainderman if it was an extraordinary dividend.

2. The so-called Massachusetts rule, declared in 1868 by Minot v. Paine, 99 Massachusetts, 101, that a dividend representing profits, whether regular, ordinary or extraordinary, if in cash belongs to the life-tenant, and if in stock belongs to the remainderman.

3. The so-called Pennsylvania rule declared in 1857 by Earp's Appeal, 28 Pa. St. 368, that where a stock dividend is paid, the court shall inquire into the circumstances under which the fund had been earned and accumulated out of which the dividend, whether a regular, an ordinary or an extraordinary one, was paid. If it finds that the stock dividend was paid out of profits earned since the decedent's death, the stock dividend belongs to the life-tenant; if the court finds that the stock dividend was paid from capital or from profits earned before the decedent's death, the stock dividend belongs to the remainderman.

[6]. Compare Rugg, C.J., in Tax Commissioner v. Putnam, 227 Massachusetts, 522, 533: "However strong such an argument might be when urged as to the interpretation of a statute, it is not of prevailing force as to the broad considerations involved in the interpretation of an amendment to the Constitution adopted under the conditions preceding and attendant upon the ratification of the Forty-fourth Amendment."

This court adopted in Gibbons v. Mahon as the rule of administration for the District of Columbia the so-called Massachusetts rule, the opinion being delivered in 1890 by Mr. Justice Gray. Since then the same question has come up for decision in many of the States. The so-called Massachusetts rule, although approved by this court, has found favor in only a few States. The so-called Pennsylvania rule, on the other hand, has been adopted since by so many of the States (including New York and California), that it has come to be known as the "American Rule." Whether, in view of these facts and the practical results of the operation of the two rules as shown by the experience of the thirty years which have elapsed since the decision in Gibbons v. Mahon, it might be desirable for this court to reconsider the question there decided, as some other courts have done (see 29 Harvard Law Review, 551), we have no occasion to consider in this case. For, as this court there pointed out (p. 560), the question involved was one "between the owners of successive interests in particular shares," and not, as in Bailey v. Railroad Co., 22 Wall. 604, a question "between the corporation and the government, and [which] depended upon the terms of a statute carefully framed to prevent corporations from evading payment of the tax upon their earnings."

We have, however, not merely argument, we have examples which should convince us that "there is no inherent, necessary and immutable reason why stock dividends should always be treated as capital." Tax Commissioner v. Putnam, 227 Massachusetts, 522, 533. The Supreme Judicial Court of Massachusetts has steadfastly adhered, despite ever-renewed protest, to the rule that every stock dividend is, as between life-tenant and remainderman, capital and not income. But in construing the Massachusetts Income Tax Amendment, which is substantially identical with the Federal Amendment, that court held that the legislature was thereby empowered to levy an income tax upon stock dividends representing profits. The courts of England have, with some relaxation, adhered to their rule that every extraordinary dividend is, as between life-tenant and remainderman, to be deemed capital. But in 1913 the Judicial Committee of the Privy Council held that a stock dividend representing accumulated profits was taxable like an ordinary cash dividend, Swan Brewery Co., Ltd., v. Rex. [1914] A.C. 231. In dismissing the appeal these words of the Chief Justice of the Supreme Court of Western Australia were quoted (p. 236), which show that the facts involved were identical with those in the case at bar: "Had the company distributed the 101,450 among the shareholders and had the shareholders repaid such sums to the company as the price of the 81,160 new shares, the duty on the 101,450$L would clearly have been payable. Is not this virtually the effect of what was actually done? I think it is."

Sixth: If stock dividends representing profits are held exempt from taxation under the Sixteenth Amendment, the owners of the most successful businesses in America will, as the facts in this case illustrate, be able to escape taxation on a large part of what is actually their income. So far as their profits are represented by stock received as dividends they will pay these taxes not upon their income but only upon the income of their income. That such a result was intended by the people of the United States when adopting the Sixteenth Amendment is inconceivable. Our sole duty is to ascertain their intent as therein expressed.[7] In terse, comprehensive language befitting the Constitution, they empowered Congress "to lay and collect taxes on incomes, from whatever source derived." They intended to include thereby everything which by reasonable understanding can fairly be regarded as income. That stock dividends representing profits are so regarded, not only by plain people but by investors and financiers, and by most of the courts of the country, is shown, beyond peradventure, by their acts and by their utterances. It seems to me clear, therefore, that Congress possesses the power which it exercised to make dividends representing profits, taxable as income, whether the medium in which the dividend is paid be cash or stock and that it may define, as it has done, what dividends representing profits shall be deemed income. It surely is not clear that the enactment exceeds the power granted by the Sixteenth Amendment. And, as this court has so often said, the high prerogative of declaring an act of Congress invalid, should never be exercised except in a clear case.[8] "It is but a decent respect due to the wisdom, the integrity and the patriotism of the legislative body, by which any law is passed, to presume in favor of its validity, until its violation of the Constitution is proved beyond all reasonable doubt." Ogden v. Saunders, 12 Wheat. 213, 270.

Mr. Justice CLARKE concurs in this opinion.

Notes and Questions

1. If Macomber had received a cash dividend and used it to purchase additional shares, she would have been taxed on the dividend. Why should receipt of the additional shares in kind produce a different result? How can this case be reconciled with *Old Colony*, Chapter 2A above?

[7]. Compare Rugg, C.J., Tax Commissioner v. Putnam, 227 Mass. 522, 524:

"It is a grant from the sovereign people and not the exercise of a delegated power. It is a statement of general principles and not a specification of details. Amendments to such a charter of government ought to be construed in the same spirit and according to the same rules as the original. It is to be interpreted as the Constitution of a State and not as a statute or an ordinary piece of legislation. Its words must be given a construction adapted to carry into effect its purpose."

8. "It is our duty, when required in the regular course of judicial proceedings, to declare an act of Congress void if not within the legislative power of the United States; but this declaration should never be made except in a clear case. Every possible presumption is in favor of the validity of a statute, and this continues until the contrary is shown beyond a rational doubt. One branch of the government cannot encroach on the domain of another without danger. The safety of our institutions depends in no small degree on a strict observance of this salutary rule." Sinking-Fund Cases, 99 U.S. 700, 718 (1878). See also Legal Tender Cases, 12 Wall. 457, 531 (1870); Trade-Mark Cases, 100 U.S. 82, 96 (1879). See American Doctrine of Constitutional Law, by James B. Thayer, 7 Harvard Law Review, 129, 142.

"With the exception of the extraordinary decree rendered in the Dred Scott Case, . . . all of the acts or the portions of the acts of Congress invalidated by the courts before 1868 related to the organization of courts. Denying the power of Congress to make notes legal tender seems to be the first departure from this rule." Haines, American Doctrine of Judicial Supremacy, p. 288. The first legal tender decision was overruled in part two years later (1870), Legal Tender Cases, 12 Wall. 457; and again in 1882, Legal Tender Case, 110 U.S. 421.

Apparently the competing (and prevailing) analogy is this: If Macomber had received nothing but merely continued to hold on to her old shares, enhanced in value by corporate accumulation of earnings, she would not be taxed, at least yet. A stock dividend of the kind involved here does not effect any change in Macomber's rights sufficient to justify imposition of a tax.

How should the choice be made between these analogies? Who should make it? Or is it a matter of choice? What do the opinions in *Macomber* say about these questions?

2. Justice Pitney's opinion treats the matter as if it were one of logical deduction. First, what is needed is "only a clear definition of the term 'income,' as used in common speech, in order to determine its meaning in the [Sixteenth] Amendment"; second, "a correct judgment as to the nature of a stock dividend"; and then "we shall find it easy to decide the matter at issue." Page 211 above.

He finds the clear definition by examining common (nonlegal) dictionaries:

> Income may be defined as the gain derived from capital, from labor, or from both combined," provided it be understood to include profit gained through a sale or conversion of capital assets. . . . [Ibid.]

For purposes of this case, the aspect of the definition to be emphasized is the requirement of realization; income must be *derived from* capital; mere appreciation in value will not do. This is in effect the major premise of the argument.

Most of the opinion is then devoted to the minor premise, which is the proposition that neither a stock dividend nor the realization of earnings by the corporation answers to the requirement that income be "*derived— from— capital*" before it can be taxed.

One should focus primarily on the major premise that mere appreciation in value of property (including corporate shares) is not taxable to the owner as income, although its effect is essentially the same as that of realized income spent for the acquisition of investment assets. Is that difference in treatment justified? How? What difficulties will it raise?

3. Unrealized appreciation is in some respects analogous to imputed income, which, as we have seen, is not taxed. First, it involves no exchange of one thing for another, like the exchange of services for relief from tax liability in *Old Colony*. Exchange, or receipt, seems to be an essential ingredient of taxable income as the concept has so far developed. Consider whether this is essentially a substantive or a formal requirement.

Second, as with imputed income, a kind of reductio ad absurdum would occur if one set out to tax all unrealized appreciation. Consider the following examples:

(a) *A* is the sole shareholder of *X* Company, whose stock went up in value by $5,000 because of retained earnings in that amount.

(b) *B* is a one percent shareholder in *Y* Corporation, a listed, publicly held corporation. His stock went up in value by 30 percent due partly to accumulated earnings, partly to a general rise in stock prices, and partly to good earnings prospects.

(c) *C* is a majority shareholder in *Z* Company, a privately held corporation whose stock went up in value because oil was discovered on company land.

(d) *D* is sole proprietor of a small electronics business. Her total investment in it is $200,000, but earnings are $100,000 a year and have risen rapidly. An underwriter has offered to sell a 33⅓ percent stock interest to the public at a price of $500,000 (so that *D*'s remaining shares at that price would be worth $1,000,000) if *D* will incorporate the business.

(e) *E* has just graduated from law school. This enhances her future earning power by several times the amount of tuition paid.

(f) *F* has just been accepted as a freshman at Princeton. Statistics indicate that Princetonians earn more than the rest of us on average.

4. *Exemption or deferral.* Is the failure to tax unrealized appreciation ultimately a matter of exemption from tax or only deferral? What about the failure to tax Macomber?

Suppose, for example, that Macomber had originally purchased 100 shares of stock for $10,000 ($100 a share) and then had received a stock dividend of 50 shares. Suppose that she subsequently sold all 150 shares for $16,500 ($110 per share). Pursuant to the logic of the *Macomber* opinion, what would be her gain on that sale? What would it be if she had received a $5,000 cash dividend instead of stock and used the cash to purchase an additional 50 shares? Or if the stock dividend had been held to be a taxable stock dividend? (See §307.) Is it the case that her gain on sale would then be $5,000 less, so that the total gain taxed over the course of her investment would be the same either way? It is sometimes said that the issue in *Macomber* is only "sooner or later," not "now or never," as in cases like *Old Colony.*

But while deferral is worth less than exemption, it is not unimportant. Indeed it has now become a major preoccupation of tax policy and practice, identified by the phrase *Time Value of Money.* We will return to it presently in Section B of this chapter.

5. *Other stock dividends and stock redemptions.* The Court in *Macomber* established a persistent rule for the nontaxation of dividends of common stock on common stock, but the taxation of related forms of transactions has been a matter of continuing controversy throughout the history of the income tax.

First, what if a corporation buys back the stock it issues as a stock dividend? The combined effect of the stock dividend and the repurchase would be quite the same as a cash dividend, but the shareholder's tax on a sale of shares would be considerably less than that on a dividend. The statute has therefore long provided that under certain circumstances the redemption of stock by a corporation shall be taxed as a dividend. The current provision is §302.

Even stock dividends, however, while they do not involve any distribution of corporate assets out of corporate solution, may effect changes in the interests of shareholders if there are different classes of stock. That takes them outside the scope of the *Macomber* decision. The statutory treatment of such stock dividends has varied through the years; currently (since 1969) it is rather stringent. See §305.

What would you expect to be the principal effect of an ordinary income tax on stock dividends?

6. *The corporate income tax.* What is the relation between the individual income tax on corporate dividends and the corporate income tax on corporate earnings?

Early integration. In the beginning the individual income tax was made up of two parts: a flat-rate normal tax, and a surtax applicable only to income above $20,000 (intended to introduce an element of graduation). Corporate dividends were exempt from normal tax and the corporate income tax was assessed at the same rate as the individual normal tax. This represented a somewhat integrated scheme, therefore, in which the equivalent of a normal tax was collected at the corporate level when earnings were realized by the corporation and the surtax was collected upon distribution. The ultimate burden on distributed corporate earnings was thus roughly the same as on earnings realized by an individual proprietor without the interposition of a corporation. (Why *roughly?*)

The exemption of corporate dividends from normal tax ended in 1936. Long before that the integration in the original statute had been eroded by rate changes in which the corporate rate became substantially higher than the individual normal rate.

The present corporate income tax. For many years the corporate income tax was absolute in the sense that individual income taxes from corporate investments were computed without any allowance for the fact that corporate earnings had already been taxed at the corporate level. Corporate dividends paid to individuals were taxed at the full progressive rates of §1 like other items of ordinary income (wages, interest, rents), despite the fact that dividends come from after-tax corporate profits (generally, corporations are not allowed to deduct dividend payments). If profits are reinvested at the corporate level instead of being distributed to shareholders as dividends, the retained earnings increase the value of the corporation's stock and so will be taxed as gain on the sale or disposition of the shares. Stock sale gain is generally classified as capital gain, which during most periods of U.S. tax history has been taxed at lower rates than ordinary income. The resulting "double tax" on corporate profits (at the corporate level when earned and again at the shareholder level either when distributed as dividends or as gain upon the sale of shares) created several serious distortions. It can influence the choice between conducting business as a corporation and employing an unincorporated form of business organization, such as a partnership or sole proprietorship.[1] Within the corporate sector, it affects the choice between debt and equity financing because corporate interest payments are deductible while dividend payments are not. Moreover, the rate differential between ordinary income and capital gain favored retention or corporate profits over dividend distributions.

In 2003 Congress enacted a provision that taxes most dividends at the favorable rates applicable to net capital gain. Consequently, dividends may be taxed to shareholders at 15 percent even though their tax rate on ordinary income would be 25 percent or higher. If the taxpayer would otherwise be taxed at a rate below 25 percent (if the dividends would fall in the 10- or 15-percent bracket, that is), the tax rate is zero. §1(h)(1)(B) and (C), (h)(3), (h)(11). To what extent does this cure the distortions described above? The reduced tax rate on dividends is scheduled to expire for tax years beginning in 2011, at which time dividends would again be taxed at the progressive rates applicable to wages, interest, rent, and other sources of ordinary income. Tax Increase Prevention and Reconciliation Act of 2005, Pub. L. No. 109-222, §102, 120 Stat. 345, 346 (2006).

Proposals for future integration. There has been recent widespread discussion inside the government and out of various forms of partial integration. The most widely supported scheme is one in which dividend recipients would be given a credit for all or part of the corporate tax paid on the earnings out of which dividends are paid. Similar systems are now in effect in several European countries and Japan, and eventual adoption of such a system here is not unlikely.

Deductible payments to shareholders. Some of the earnings of an unincorporated business such as a partnership or individual proprietorship, for example, might well be paid out to the owners as salaries if the business were incorporated. Compare the income tax treatment of corporate revenues (a) distributed as salaries (or other deductible expenses), (b) distributed as dividends, or (c) accumulated in the corporation. Are the differences justified? What problems will they create?

Penalty taxes on undistributed corporate earnings. Payment of the corporate income tax does not confer a license to accumulate earnings and avoid payment of individual taxes. Look at §§531, 532, 541, 542(a), 543(a) to get a general sense of what they are about.

Other entities. Compare the tax treatment of corporate earnings with the treatment of partnership earnings and trust income. The general rule for partnership income is in §§701 and 702. The general rule for trust income is that income currently distributable or distributed is taxed to the beneficiaries and that the trust as such is taxed only on undistributed income. See Chapter 18B.

---

1. The influence did not necessarily weigh against incorporation. Over long periods the top rate of the corporate income tax, §11, was set below the top tax rate for individuals, §1, and under those circumstances a corporation that retained its earnings could often be used to reduce the tax burden on business income despite the double tax. The use of corporations as a tax-reduction vehicle is a story best left to a course on business or corporate taxation, however.

7. *Constitutional aspects.* Does the holding in *Macomber* make sense as a constitutional limitation? Should the constitutional question be stated as whether a stock dividend *is* income or whether it can reasonably be classed and treated by the legislature as income? Doesn't the power to tax income necessarily include the power, within limits, to define it? Could the Congress impose a tax simply on "all income within the meaning of the sixteenth amendment"?

In any event, if a tax on stock dividends is not an income tax, what is it? Why is it not then an excise? If it is not an income tax, on what theory is it a direct tax?

Macomber is apparently the only Supreme Court decision holding an item exempt from income tax solely because it was outside the concept of income in the Sixteenth Amendment. While *Macomber* has not been directly overruled, its present validity as a constitutional decision is very dubious. See Helvering v. Bruun, Chapter 5C.1 below; Helvering v. Griffiths, 318 U.S. 371 (1943), Cottage Savings Ass'n v. Commissioner, Chapter 5C.2 below. Also look at §951(a)(1). Is it unconstitutional? See President's 1961 Tax Recommendations: Hearings Before the H. Comm. on Ways and Means, 87th Cong. 313 (1961).

8. *Comprehensive income definitions. Macomber* used to be frequently cited for its dictionary definition of income as gain derived from capital, from labor, or from both combined. The definition obviously has implications far beyond the issue in the present case, particularly as it limits income to gain or receipts from labor or investment. The Court has not attempted a comprehensive definition since and is usually thought both to have repudiated the *Macomber* definition and given up the attempt at comprehensive definition in subsequent cases. See United States v. Kirby Lumber Co., Chapter 7A below, and Commissioner v. Glenshaw Glass Co., Chapter 3A above.

The other most frequently cited attempt at a comprehensive definition is that of the economist Henry Simons:

> Personal income may be defined as the algebraic sum of (1) the market value of rights exercised in consumption and (2) the change in the value of the store of property rights between the beginning and end of the period in question. [Henry C. Simons, Personal Income Taxation 50 (1938).]

Is this more helpful than the definition in *Macomber*? Carefully state the differences between the Simons definition and the *Macomber* definition and the arguments on each side of each difference.

B.   TIME VALUE OF MONEY

The fact that nontaxation of unrealized capital appreciation is essentially one of deferral rather than exemption has led some to argue that it is not very important.[2] But there are at least two serious objections to this conclusion.

First, deferral may turn into exemption, whole or partial, if the taxpayer never sells, realizes no gain on sale, or if the gain on the sale for some reason goes untaxed or is taxed at a lower rate. If a taxpayer holds appreciated property until her death, the appreciation in value will escape income tax altogether pursuant to §1014. If she gives it away during life the appreciation may subsequently be taxed but only if and when the donee sells and at the donee's rates, which may be lower than the donor's. If the donee is a tax-exempt charity, the gain will escape tax altogether. Even if the taxpayer sells the property herself, she may sell after the property has fallen in value, in a year in which she has a net loss, or in a year in which her tax rate is lower. In any event, her gain on sale may be taxed at the lower rate applicable to long-term capital gains. For these reasons, deferral may be desirable because of its potential exemption or rate-reduction effect.

Second, even if all gain were ultimately taxed and without any reduction in rate, deferral for a substantial period of time is tantamount to a reduction in tax for the simple reason that the present value (or burden) of a dollar payable at some future date is less than that of a dollar due currently. Deferral of income tax thus has value in itself wholly apart from any resulting exemption or rate reduction. This is now commonly called the *time value of money*.

Whether for evaluating tax policy, for assessing the effect of judicial decisions, or for counseling clients, a sound appreciation of the time value of money is an absolute prerequisite to the understanding of much of current tax policy and practice.

In an effort to begin to appreciate the value of deferral, consider it from the following viewpoints.

1. Interest

Essentially the value of deferral is a matter of interest. A taxpayer who can defer $1,000 of tax for one year and invest the retained funds at 6 percent interest will earn or save $60.

Interest varies with time and rate, of course, and the value of deferral depends on how soon the tax will have to be paid and how the taxpayer employs the funds. If the $1,000 of tax were deferred for ten years instead of one, the interest earned (or saved) would be $600. And if the taxpayer were a successful and aggressive business person, he might hope to earn a return of 20 percent on funds invested in his own business. At 20 percent for ten years, the simple interest return on deferral would amount to 200 percent, or $2,000 for $1,000 of tax. At 20 percent interest compounded annually, $1,000 would earn $5,192.

Of course, the interest earned on deferred taxes may itself be subject to income tax. The degree of impact depends on the rate of tax and also, to

2. E.g., Henry C. Simons, Personal Income Taxation 168, 169 (1938).

some extent, on whether the taxpayer can defer the tax on that as well as on the original income item.

2.   Present Discounted Value

Another way to measure the value of deferral is by comparing the present discounted values (or burdens) of immediate and future payment.

Discount is just another way of describing interest so it too is a function of time and rate of return. If taxes can be put off for only one year and funds invested at 6 percent, then the present value of the future payment is about 94.3 percent of immediate payment (94.3 = 100/1.06) and the value of deferral is only about 5.7 percent.

If a $100 tax can be put off for ten years, however, and funds invested at 20 percent per annum, compounded semiannually, the present discounted value of that future payment is only $14.86. In other words, $14.86 set aside today and invested at 20 percent, compounded semiannually, for 10 years, would produce $100 with which to pay the deferred tax at that time. (A 10 percent increase in each of 20 periods, compounded, yields total growth factor of $(1.10)^{20}$, or 6.73; $14.86 = $100/$(1.10)^{20}$.) Based on these figures, 85.14 percent of the tax burden is eliminated by "mere" deferral.

In general, if x is the percentage growth per period and y is the number of compounding periods, then at the end of y periods an initial amount will have grown by a factor of $(1 + (x/100))^y$. The reciprocal of this growth factor gives the discount factor. If one does not have a calculator handy, there is a marvelously convenient rule of thumb called the *Rule of 72* that says money invested at x percent per annum compound interest will double in $72/x$ years. At 6 percent interest it takes 12 years for a compounding deposit to double; at 12 percent, 6 years; at 8 percent, 9 years; and so forth. This rule is reasonably accurate for any period in excess of about three years or even for shorter periods if interest is compounded more often than annually.[3]

In discount terms this means that the present discounted burden of a tax payment will be cut in half if payment can be deferred for a period equal to $72/x$ years and funds invested at a return (after tax) of x percent per year. For a business person who hopes to make 20 percent per annum, deferral for three and a half years is tantamount to reduction by 50 percent.

3.   After-Tax Returns

Another way to measure the value of deferral is to compare after-tax returns if the tax is paid currently or later. For example:

A1, who is in a 33 percent marginal income tax bracket, invests $10,000 in a savings bank at 9 percent interest. Each year she withdraws one-third of

---

3. The actual times are 11.90, 6.12, and 9.01 years, respectively, for annual compounding, and 11.72, 5.94, and 8.84 years, respectively, for semiannual compounding — all within 2.5 percent of the Rule of 72 estimates.

the interest to pay her tax. The fund thus grows at 6 percent per annum and will double in about 12 years.

In 24 years *A1*'s deposit would double twice and her net after-tax profit will be $30,000.

A2 invests $10,000 in a deferred annuity bond that earns and accumulates at the rate of 9 percent. Interest earned on the bond is not taxed until paid. At 9 percent, *A2*'s investment will roughly double in 8 years and will multiply eight-fold in 24 years. If *A2* then receives a distribution of his investment ($80,000) and is taxed at 33 percent on his profit ($70,000), he will have $56,900 left and a net after-tax profit of $46,900.

A2's net after-tax return is thus 156 percent of *A1*'s.

B1 owns GM, which she bought at $40 and which is now selling for $100. She decides to hold her GM until it goes to $200, then sell. How much will be left after selling at $200 if *B1* has to pay a tax on her profit at the rate of 20 percent?

B2 owns GM, which he bought at $40 and which is now selling for $100. He decides to sell his GM now, use part of the proceeds to pay the tax at a 20 percent rate on his profit, and invest the rest of the proceeds in GE. If he holds the GE until it doubles, sells, and again pays tax at 20 percent on his profit, how much will he have left?

Is the difference between the outcome for *B1* and *B2* serious? Would it be serious at higher rates? What can and should be done about it?

It has become common to analyze projections of investment returns in terms of after-tax rate of return, particularly in the case of real estate and other items that may produce accelerated tax deductions. The Appendix contains an illustration of such analysis for a simple real estate investment.

4.   Effective Tax Rates

Analysis of after-tax returns can be carried further by computing the effective rate of tax, which is the difference between the after-tax rate of return on an investment and the rate of return if there were no income tax, expressed as a percentage of the latter. *A1*, for example, has an effective rate of tax of 33 percent since her after-tax rate of return (6 percent) is two-thirds of the tax-free rate of return (9 percent). This effective rate just equals her nominal tax rate.

A2 on the other hand has an effective rate of tax of only 16.52 percent. His after-tax return is 469 percent in 24 years, which represents an annual rate of 7.513 percent. The effect of the tax therefore is to reduce the rate of return from 9 percent to 7.513 percent, or by 16.52 percent (1.487/9). Deferral thus has the effect of reducing the tax burden from a nominal rate of 33 percent to an effective rate of 16.52 percent.

The illustration in the Appendix contains some further examples of effective rate computations in the context of a real estate investment.

5.   Tax Deferral as a Source of Capital

Another way to look at tax deferral is as a source of equity capital. Accumulated earnings are commonly viewed as such a source, effectively contributed by the investors to whom they would otherwise be distributed. Deferral of taxes, in this view, similarly represents a source of capital that has been contributed by the government, to which they would be paid if taxation were not deferred.

It may help to think of the government as an uninvited partner in every taxable transaction. The government makes no initial capital contribution. (Its contribution is services in the form of military defense, air pollution control, and the like.) But if the other participants allow their profits to accumulate, and if their profits go untaxed until withdrawn, then the effect of deferral is to make the government bear its share of this mode of financing.

For example, consider a person who invests $40,000 in TX common. Over a period of years the value of his investment goes up to $100,000. At the end of that period he looks at this as an investment of $100,000 because this is the amount on which he should rationally expect a current return, and this is the amount he could take out and invest elsewhere.

But if he looks more closely, he might analyze the $100,000 into components. His original investment is $40,000; the other $60,000 is in effect unwithdrawn profit. Furthermore, the $60,000 is not all his. If his tax on this sort of profit would be at a 20 percent rate then in effect only $48,000 is his and $12,000 is the government's. Under present law the government's share will remain invested until there is a taxable sale or exchange of the shares.

This could all be represented by the balance sheet shown in Table 5-1.

TABLE 5-1

Asset		*Proprietorship*	
TX stock	$100,000	Original investment	$ 40,000
		Appreciation — taxpayer's share	48,000
		Appreciation — government's share	12,000
			$100,000

Of course, the allocation of appreciation between the taxpayer's share and the government's share is provisional and subject to change if the effective rate of tax changes. Under current law the government will forfeit its share and the whole appreciation will go to the taxpayer's successors if he holds the stock until death.[4]

---

4. This form of accounting is not generally applied in financial accounting practice partly because appreciated assets are usually shown conservatively at cost rather than current value. But something akin to this is used in accounting for deferred income tax obligations in circumstances where generally accepted accounting principles (financial accounting) require recognition of income or gain earlier than the tax law. See Financial Accounting Standards Board, Statement of Financial Accounting Standards No. 109, Accounting for Income Taxes (1992).

Viewing tax deferral as a source of capital provides another way to analyze the value of deferral. Assume that TX stock goes up 40 percent so that the investment shown above becomes $140,000, as shown in Table 5-2.

TABLE 5-2

Asset		*Proprietorship*	
TX stock	$140,000	Original investment	$ 40,000
		Appreciation — taxpayer's share	80,000
		Appreciation — government's share	20,000
			$100,000

Comparing the two balance sheets reveals a total increase of $40,000, allocated $8,000 (20 percent) to the government and $32,000 (80 percent) to the taxpayer.

But if the $40,000 is further analyzed as a 40 percent return on each component of proprietorship as shown in the first balance sheet, $4,800 of the $8,000 credited to the government is seen simply as its return on its $12,000 share of invested capital. The other $3,200 is 20 percent of the 40 percent return on the $40,000 original investment. Under this form of analysis the return on the taxpayer's share of appreciation is credited 100 percent to the taxpayer and is thus in effect untaxed — the effective rate of tax on this portion of the taxpayer's investment return is reduced to zero. Table 5-3 summarizes this result.

TABLE 5-3

	Total	Allocated to government	Allocated to taxpayer
40 percent return on $40,000 original investment	$16,000	$3,200	$12,800
40 percent return on $48,000 taxpayer share of prior unrealized appreciation	19,200	—	19,200
40 percent return on $12,000 government share of prior unrealized appreciation	4,800	4,800	—
Total return	$40,000	$8,000	$32,000

After sale, payment of tax, and reinvestment of proceeds net of tax, the government will of course continue to claim 20 percent of further appreciation even though its share of the investment has been withdrawn. Thus, the effect of realizing gain and terminating tax deferral is to terminate this effective tax exemption.

6.   Fruits and Trees

For a more rural example, consider an orange grower who sets out 100 trees. If her rate of tax is 15 percent then the government will take the oranges from 15 trees, leaving her with the oranges from the other 85. If the government were to treat the growing of the trees as income, however, it would take 15 trees and then would also take 15 percent of the fruit from the remaining trees. The taxpayer would then be left with the fruit from only 72 trees instead of 85. Full accretion taxation would thus increase the effective rate of tax on her final output from 15 to 28 percent.

This result is sometimes asserted to be double taxation, and the example is given as an argument against taxing capital gains at all. Is that argument sound? Even if not, is the result objectionable?

Is the farmer's investment in fruit trees essentially different from any other investment in income-producing property?

7.   The Equivalence of Tax Deferral and Yield Exemption

The value of pure tax deferral can be quantified, in the abstract, as follows.

The effect of deferring tax on an item of accumulation is the same as exempting from tax the yield from investment of that item, throughout the period of deferral.

To illustrate, consider a $1,000 payment owed to a taxpayer, which she might receive and be taxed on this year, or on which she might defer recognition of gain for a year. In either case the taxpayer plans to invest the item at 12 percent interest. If tax is deferred then the amount invested will be $1,000, which will produce interest of $120, and the taxpayer will receive a total of $1,120 at the end of the year. The whole amount will be taxable at that time, and so if the applicable tax rate were 33 percent, for example, there would be a tax of $370 leaving $750 after tax.

If, on the other hand, the taxpayer had been taxed on the $1,000 initially, she would have had a tax of $330 and only $670 to invest. Twelve percent interest on $670 would be $80, and so if the interest were tax free the taxpayer would again come out with $750 of disposable income. *Exemption of the interest and deferral of tax on the principal produce exactly the same effect.*

If the interest were not tax exempt and the $1,000 were taxed before investment then the taxpayer would have a second tax to pay of $26.40 (33 percent of $80) and would be left with only $723.60 instead of $750. Her after-tax return would indeed be cut from 12 to 8 percent, which some would say is exactly the right effect for a 33 percent income tax.

The difference between $750 and $723.60 is not very dramatic, but this example involves only a single year's deferral at a very modest interest rate. In actual practice, this effect has often been exploited to produce quite spectacular reductions in tax burdens.

The equivalence between deferral and yield exemption is not unconditional: it depends, primarily, on constancy of rates. If tax rates on an accumulated item go down during the period of deferral then the savings from deferral will be more than yield exemption. Mere postponement without reduction in tax rate produces a savings equivalent to yield exemption; the tax rate reduction is an additional saving.

The equivalence also depends on equality of rates on the item itself and on its yield. If the item is taxable at 15 percent as a capital gain and the yield from investing it is taxable at 35 percent as ordinary income then deferral of the capital gain tax is equivalent to eliminating only a 15 percent tax on yield. A 35 percent tax is equivalent to a 15 percent tax and a 23.5 percent tax imposed in succession (in either order),[5] and so deferral of the 15 percent capital gains tax would be equivalent to reducing the tax on yield from 35 to 23.5 percent.

C. REALIZATION

Macomber established the need for realization of gain as a precondition to taxation, and it seems to take a restrictive view of what constitutes realization. But subsequent cases have indicated that realization may be found in events that are much less indicative of profit than a stock dividend. Sometimes Congress has felt impelled to offer relief. Here are a couple of notable examples from outside the corporate sphere.

1. Leasehold Improvements

HELVERING v. BRUUN
309 U.S. 461 (1940)

Mr. Justice ROBERTS delivered the opinion of the Court. The controversy had its origin in the petitioner's assertion that the respondent realized

---

5. A 15 percent tax leaves (1 − .15) = .85; a 23.5 percent tax leaves (1 − .235) = .765; the two taxes in succession will leave .85 times .765 which is .650, which equals (1 − .35).

taxable gain from the forfeiture of a leasehold, the tenant having erected a new building upon the premises. The court below held that no income had been realized.[1] Inconsistency of the decisions on the subject led us to grant certiorari.

The Board of Tax Appeals made no independent findings. The cause was submitted upon a stipulation of facts. From this it appears that on July 1, 1915, the respondent, as owner, leased a lot of land and the building thereon for a term of ninety-nine years.

The lease provided that the lessee might, at any time, upon giving bond to secure rentals accruing in the two ensuing years, remove or tear down any building on the land, provided that no building should be removed or torn down after the lease became forfeited, or during the last three and one-half years of the term. The lessee was to surrender the land, upon termination of the lease, with all buildings and improvements thereon.

In 1929 the tenant demolished and removed the existing building and constructed a new one which had a useful life of not more than fifty years. July 1, 1933, the lease was cancelled for default in payment of rent and taxes and the respondent regained possession of the land and building.

The parties stipulated "that as at said date, July 1, 1933, the building which had been erected upon said premises by the lessee had a fair market value of $64,245.68 and that the unamortized cost of the old building, which was removed from the premises in 1929 to make way for the new building, was $12,811.43, thus leaving a net fair market value as at July 1, 1933, of $51,434.25, for the aforesaid new building erected upon the premises by the lessee."

On the basis of these facts, the petitioner determined that in 1933 the respondent realized a net gain of $51,434.25. The Board overruled his determination and the Circuit Court of Appeals affirmed the Board's decision. The course of administrative practice and judicial decision in respect of the question presented has not been uniform. In 1917 the Treasury ruled that the adjusted value of improvements installed upon leased premises is income to the lessor upon the termination of the lease. The ruling was incorporated in two succeeding editions of the Treasury Regulations. In 1919 the Circuit Court of Appeals for the Ninth Circuit held in Miller v. Gearin, 258 F. 225, that the regulation was invalid as the gain, if taxable at all, must be taxed as of the year when the improvements were completed.

The regulations were accordingly amended to impose a tax upon the gain in the year of completion of the improvements, measured by their anticipated value at the termination of the lease and discounted for the duration of the lease. Subsequently the regulations permitted the lessor to

---

1. Helvering v. Bruun, 105 F.2d 442.

spread the depreciated value of the improvements over the remaining life of the lease, reporting an aliquot part of each year, with provision that, upon premature termination, a tax should be imposed upon the excess of the then value of the improvements over the amount theretofore returned.

In 1935 the Circuit Court of Appeals for the Second Circuit decided in Hewitt Realty Co. v. Commissioner, 76 F.2d 880, that a landlord received no taxable income in a year, during the term of the lease, in which his tenant erected a building on the leased land. The court, while recognizing that the lessor need not receive money to be taxable, based its decision that no taxable gain was realized in that case on the fact that the improvement was not portable or detachable from the land, and if removed would be worthless except as bricks, iron, and mortar. It said (p. 884): "The question as we view it is whether the value received is embodied in something separately disposable, or whether it is so merged in the land as to become financially a part of it, something which, though it increase its value, has no value of its own when torn away."

This decision invalidated the regulations then in force.

In 1938 this court decided M. E. Blatt Co. v. United States, 305 U.S. 267. There, in connection with the execution of a lease, landlord and tenant mutually agreed that each should make certain improvements to the demised premises and that those made by the tenant should become and remain the property of the landlord. The Commissioner valued the improvements as of the date they were made, allowed depreciation thereon to the termination of the leasehold, divided the depreciated value by the number of years the lease had to run, and found the landlord taxable for each year's aliquot portion thereof. His action was sustained by the Court of Claims. The judgment was reversed on the ground that the added value could not be considered rental accruing over the period of the lease; that the facts found by the Court of Claims did not support the conclusion of the Commissioner as to the value to be attributed to the improvements after a use throughout the term of the lease; and that, in the circumstances disclosed, any enhancement in the value of the realty in the tax year was not income realized by the lessor within the Revenue Act.

The circumstances of the instant case differentiate it from the *Blatt* and *Hewitt* cases; but the petitioner's contention that gain was realized when the respondent, through the forfeiture of the lease, obtained untrammeled title, possession and control of the premises, with the added increment of value added by the new building, runs counter to the decision in the *Miller* case and to the reasoning in the *Hewitt* case.

The respondent insists that the realty, — a capital asset at the date of the execution of the lease, — remained such throughout the term and after its expiration; that improvements affixed to the soil became part of the realty indistinguishably blended in the capital asset; that such improvements cannot be separately valued or treated as received in exchange for the improvements which were on the land at the date of the execution of the lease; that they are, therefore, in the same category as improvements added by the respondent to his land, or accruals of value due to extraneous and adventitious circumstances. Such added value, it is argued, can be considered capital gain only upon the owner's disposition of the asset. The position is that the economic gain consequent upon the enhanced value of the recaptured asset is not gain derived from capital or realized within the meaning of the Sixteenth Amendment and may not, therefore, be taxed without apportionment.

We hold that the petitioner was right in assessing the gain as realized in 1933.

We might rest our decision upon the narrow issue presented by the terms of the stipulation. It does not appear what kind of a building was erected by the tenant or whether the building was readily removable form the land. It is not stated whether the difference in value between the building removed and that erected in its place accurately reflects an increase in the value of land and building considered as a single estate in land. On the facts stipulated, without more, we should not be warranted in holding that the presumption of the correctness of the Commissioner's determination has been overborne.

The respondent insist, however, that the stipulation was intended to assert that the sum of $51,434.25 was the measure of the resulting enhancement in value of the real estate at the date of cancellation of the lease. The petitioner seems not to contest this view. Even upon this assumption we think that gain in the amount named was realized by the respondent in the year of repossession.

The respondent can not successfully contend that the definition of gross income in §22(a) or the Revenue Act of 1932 is not broad enough to embrace the gain in question. That definition follows closely the Sixteenth Amendment. Essentially the respondent's position is that the Amendment does not permit the taxation of such gain without apportionment amongst the states. He relies upon what was said in Hewitt Reality Co. v. Commissioner, supra, and upon expressions found in the decisions of this court dealing with the taxability of stock dividends to the effect that gain derived from capital must be something of exchangeable value proceeding from property, severed from the capital, however invested or employed, and received by the recipient for his separate use, benefit, and disposal.[8] He emphasizes the necessity that the gain be separate from the capital and separately disposable. These expressions, however, were used to clarify the distinction between an ordinary dividend and a stock dividend. They were

8. See Eisner v. Macomber [Chapter 5A above]: United States v. Phellis, 257 U.S. 156.

meant to show that in the case of a stock dividend, the stockholder's interest in the corporate assets after receipt of the dividend was the same as and inseverable from that which he owned before the dividend was declared. We think they are not controlling here.

While it is true that economic gain is not always taxable as income, it is settled that the realization of gain need not be in cash derived from the sale of an asset. Gain may occur as a result of exchange of property, payment of the taxpayer's indebtedness, relief from a liability, or other profit realized from the completion of a transaction. The fact that the gain is a portion of the value of property received by the taxpayer in the transaction does not negative its realization.

Here, as a result of a business transaction, the respondent received back his land with a new building on it, which added an ascertainable amount to its value. It is not necessary to recognition of taxable gain that he should be able to sever the improvement begetting the gain from his original capital. If that were necessary, no income could arise from the exchange of property; whereas such gain has always been recognized as realized taxable gain.

Judgment reversed.

The Chief Justice concurs in the result in view of the terms of the stipulation of facts.

Mr. Justice McReynolds took no part in the decision of this case.

Notes

1. *Statutory response.* Look at §§109 and 1019. They were enacted rather promptly after *Bruun*. Why?

2. Is the issue in *Bruun* and §109 one of exemption or deferral? Explain.

3. If one buys stock of a corporation shortly before payment of a large dividend he may well have taxable income without gain when the dividend is paid. Does *Bruun* involve some similar likelihood of rental income without gain? Is that a reason for §109?

4. What is "rent" in the parenthetical in §109? Suppose clients are about to build on some unimproved land for rental to a designated tenant; then they learn of §109 and decide to let the tenant build, reducing the rent by an amount representing the cost of construction. How will they then be taxed? What do they have to look out for? Cf. I.T. 4009, 1950-1 C.B. 13.

Note the description in *Bruun* of the holding in *Blatt,* "that the added value could not be considered rental accruing over the period of the lease. . . ." Might "rent" in the statute be sensibly interpreted as incorporating whatever meaning the term had in that decision?

5. How would the *Bruun* case have come out under the government's prior schemes for taxing lessee improvements?

2. Mortgage Participation Exchanges

COTTAGE SAVINGS ASSN. v. COMMISSIONER
499 U.S. 554 (1991)

Justice MARSHALL delivered the opinion of the court. . . .

I

Petitioner Cottage Savings Association (Cottage Savings) is a savings and loan association (S & L) formerly regulated by the Federal Home Loan Bank Board (FHLBB).[1] Like many S & L's, Cottage Savings held numerous long-term, low-interest mortgages that declined in value when interest rates surged in the late 1970's. These institutions would have benefited from selling their devalued mortgages in order to realize tax-deductible losses. However, they were deterred from doing so by FHLBB accounting regulations, which required them to record the losses on their books. Reporting these losses consistent with the then-effective FHLBB accounting regulations would have placed many S & L's at risk of closure by the FHLBB.

The FHLBB responded to this situation by relaxing its requirements for the reporting of losses. In a regulatory directive known as "Memorandum R-49," dated June 27, 1980, the FHLBB determined that S & L's need not report losses associated with mortgages that are exchanged for "substantially identical" mortgages held by other lenders.[2] The FHLBB's acknowledge purpose for Memorandum R-49 was to facilitate transactions that would generate tax losses but that would not substantially affect the economic position of the transacting S & L's.

This case involves a typical Memorandum R-49 transaction. On December 31, 1980, Cottage Savings sold "90% participation interests" in

---

1. Congress abolished the FHLBB in 1989. See §401 of the Financial Institutions Reform, Recovery, and Enforcement Act of 1989, Pub. L. 101-73, 103 Stat. 354.

2. Memorandum R-49 listed 10 criteria for classifying mortgaging as substantially identical.

"The loans involved must:
  "1. involve single-family residential mortgages,
  "2. be of similar type (e.g., conventionals for conventionals),
  "3. have the same stated terms to maturity (e.g., 30 years),
  "4. have identical stated interest rates,
  "5. have similar seasoning (i.e., remaining terms to maturity),
  "6. have aggregate principle amounts within the lesser of $2^{1}/_{2}\%$ or $100,000 (plus or minus) on both sides of the transaction, with any additional consideration being paid in cash,
  "7. be sold without recourse,
  "8. have similar fair market values,
  "9. have similar loan-to-value ratios at the time of the reciprocal sale, and
  "10. have all security properties for both sides of the transaction in the same state." Record, Exh. 72-BT.

252 mortgages to four S & L's. It simultaneously purchased "90% participation interests" in 305 mortgages held by these S & L's.[3] All of the loans involved in the transaction were secured by single-family homes, most in the Cincinnati area. The fair market value of the package of participation interests exchanged by each side was approximately $4.5 million. The face value of the participation interests Cottage Savings relinquished in the transaction was approximately $6.9 million. See 90 T.C. 372, 378-382 (1988).

On its 1980 federal income tax return, Cottage Savings claimed a deduction for $2,447,091, which represented the adjusted difference between the face value of the participation interests that it treated and the fair market value of the participation interests that it received. As permitted by Memorandum R-49, Cottage Savings did not report these losses to the FHLBB. After the Commissioner of Internal Revenue disallowed Cottage Savings' claimed deduction, Cottage Savings sought a redetermination in the Tax Court. The Tax Court held that the deduction was permissible. See 90 T.C. 372 (1988).

On appeal by the Commissioner, the Court of Appeals reversed. 890 F.2d 848 (CA6 1989). The Court of Appeals agreed with the Tax Court's determination that Cottage Savings had realized its losses through the transaction. See id., at 852. However, the court held that the Cottage Savings was not entitled to a deduction because its losses were not "actually" sustained during the 1980 tax year for purposes of 26 U.S.C. §165(a). See 890 F.2d, at 855.

Because of the importance of this issue to the S & L industry and the conflict among the Circuits over whether Memorandum R-49 exchanges produce deductible tax losses,[4] we granted certiorari. 498 U.S. 808 (1990). We now reverse.

II

Rather than assessing tax liability on the basis of annual fluctuations in the value of a taxpayer's property, the Internal Revenue Code defers the tax consequences of a gain or loss in property value until the taxpayer "realizes" the gain or loss. The realization requirement is implicit in §1001(a) of the Code, 26 U.S.C. §1001(a), which defines "the gain [or loss] from the sale or other disposition of property" as the difference between "the amount realized" from the sale or disposition of the property and its "adjusted basis." As this Court has recognized, the concept of realization is "founded on

3. By exchanging merely participation interests rather than the loans themselves, each party retained its relationship with the individual obligors. Consequently, each S & L continued to service the loans on which it had transferred the participation interests and made monthly payments to the participation-interest holders. See 90 T.C. 372, 381 (1988).

4. The two other Courts of Appeals that have considered the tax treatment of Memorandum R-49 transactions have found that these transactions do give rise to deductible losses. See Federal Nat. Mortgage Assn. v. Commissioner, 283 U.S. App. D. C. 53, 56-58, 896 F.2d 580, 583-584 (1990); San Antonio Savings Assn. v. Commissioner 887 F.2d 577 (CA5 1989).

administrative convenience." Helvering v. Horst, 311 U.S. 112, 116 (1940). Under an appreciation-based system of taxation, taxpayers and the Commissioner would have to undertake the "cumbersome, abrasive, and unpredictable administrative task" of valuing assets on an annual basis to determine whether the assets had appreciated or depreciated in value. See 1 B. Bittker & L. Lokken, Federal Taxation of Income, Estate and Gifts para. 5.2, p. 5-16 (2d ed. 1989). In contrast, "[a] change in the form or extent of an investment is easily detected by a taxpayer or an administrative officer." R. Magill, Taxable Income 79 (rev. ed. 1945).

Section 1001(a)'s language provides a straightforward test for realization: to realize a gain or loss in the value of property, the taxpayer must engage in a "sale or other disposition of [the] property." The parties agree that the exchange of participation interests in this case cannot be characterized as a "sale" under §1001(a); the issue before us is whether the transaction constitutes a "disposition of property." The Commissioner argues that an exchange of property can be treated as a "disposition" under §1001(a) only if the properties exchanged are materially different. The Commissioner further submits that, because the underlying mortgages were essentially economic substitutes, the participation interests exchanged by Cottage Savings were not materially different from those received from the other S & L's. Cottage Savings, on the other hand, maintains that any exchange of property is a "disposition of property" under §1001(a), regardless of whether the property exchanged is materially different. Alternatively, Cottage Savings contends that the participation interests exchanged were materially different because the underlying loans were secured by different properties. . . .

A

Neither the language nor the history of the Code indicates whether and to what extend property exchanged must differ to count as a "disposition of property" under §1001(a). Nonetheless, we readily agree with the Commissioner that an exchange of property gives rise to a realization event under §1001(a) only if the properties exchanged are "materially different." The Commissioner himself has by regulation construed §1001(a) to embody a material difference requirement;

> "Except as otherwise provided . . . the gain or loss realized form the conversion of property into cash, or from the exchange of property for other property *differing materially either in kind or in extent*, is treated as income or as loss sustained." Treas. Reg. §1.1001-1, 26 CFR §1.1001-1 (1990) (emphasis added).

Because Congress had delegated to the Commissioner the power to promulgate "all needful rules and regulations for the enforcement of [the Internal Revenue Code]," 26 U.S.C. §7805(a), we must defer to his regulatory interpretations of the Code so long as they are reasonable, see National Muffler Dealers Assn., Inc. v. United States, 440 U.S. 472, 476-477 (1979).

We conclude that Treasury Regulation §1.1001-1 is a reasonable interpretation of §1001(a). Congress first employed the language that now comprises §1001(a) of the Code in §202(a) of the Revenue Act of 1924, ch. 234, 43 Stat. 253; that language has remained essentially uncharged through various reenactments.[5] And since 1934, the Commissioner has construed the statutory term "disposition of property" to include a "material difference" requirement.[6] As we have recognized, " 'Treasury regulations and interpretations long continued without substantial change, applying to unamended or substantially reenacted statutes, are deemed to have received congressional approval and have the effect of law.' " United States v. Correll, 389 U.S. 299, 305-306 (1967), quoting Helvering v. Winmill, 305 U.S. 79, 83 (1938).

Treasury Regulation §1.1001-1 is also consistent with our landmark precedents on realization. In a series of early decisions involving the tax effects of property exchanges, this Court made clear that a taxpayer realizes taxable income only if the properties exchanged are "materially" or "essentially" different. See United States v. Phellis, 257 U.S. 156, 173 (1921); Weiss v. Stearn, 265 U.S. 242, 253-254 (1924); Marr v. United States, 268 U.S. 536, 540-542 (1925); see also Eisner v. Macomber, 252 U.S. 189, 207-212 (1920) (recognizing realization requirement). Because these decisions were part of the "contemporary legal context" in which Congress enacted §202(a) of the 1924 Act, see Cannon v. University of Chicago, 441 U.S. 677, 698-699 (1979), and because Congress has left undisturbed through subsequent reenactments of the Code the principles of realization established in these case, we may presume that Congress intended to codify these principles in §1001(a), see Pierce v. Underwood, 487 U.S. 552, 567 (1988); Lorillard v. Pons, 434 U.S. 575, 580-581 (1978). The Commissioner's construction of the statutory language to incorporate these principles certainly was reasonable.

---

5. Section 202(a) of the 1924 Act provided:

"Except as hereinafter provided in this section, the gain from the sale or other disposition of property shall be the excess of the amount realized therefrom over the basis provided in subdivision (a) or (b) of section 204, and the loss shall be the excess of such basis over the amount realized."

The essence of this provision was reenacted in §111(a) or Revenue Act of 1934, ch. 277, 48 Stat. 703; and then in §111(a) of the Internal Revenue Code of 1939, ch. 1, 53 Stat. 36; and finally in §1001(a) of the Internal Revenue Code of 1954, Pub. L. 591, 68A Stat. 295.

6. What is now Treas. Reg. §1.1001-1 originated as Treas. Reg. 86, Art. 111-1, which was promulgated pursuant to the Revenue Act of 1934. That regulation provided:

"Except as otherwise provided, the Act regards as income or as loss sustained, the gain or loss realized from the conversion of property into cash, *or from the exchange of property for other property differing materially either in kind or in extent*" (emphasis added).

B

Precisely that constitutes a "material difference" for purposes of §1001(a) of the Code is a more complicated question. The Commissioner argues that properties are "materially different" only if they differ in economic substance. To determine whether the participation interests exchanged in this case were "materially different" in this sense, the Commissioner argues, we should look to the attitudes of the parties, the evaluation of the interests by the secondary mortgage market, and the views of the FHLBB. We conclude that §1001(a) embodies a much less demanding and less complex test.

Unlike the question whether §1001(a) contains a material difference requirement, the question of what constitutes a material difference is not one on which we can defer to the Commissioner, for the Commissioner has not issued an authoritative, prelitigation interpretation of what property exchanges satisfy this requirement. Thus, to give meaning to the material difference test, we must look to the case law from which the test derives and which we believe Congress intended to codify in enacting and reenacting the language that now comprises §1001(a). See Lorillard v. Pons, supra, at 580-581.

We start with the classic treatment of realization in Eisner v. Macomber, supra. In *Macomber*, a taxpayer who owned 2,200 shares of stock in a company received another 1,100 shares from the company as part of a prorata stock dividend meant to reflect the company's growth in value. As issue was whether the stock dividend constituted taxable income. We held that it did not, because no gain was realized. See id., at 207-212. We reasoned that the stock, see id., at 211-212, and that a taxpayer realizes increased worth of property only by receiving "something of exchangeable value proceeding from the property," see id., at 207.

In three subsequent decisions — United States v. Phellis; Weiss v. Stearn, supra; and Marr v. United States, supra — we refined *Macomber*'s conception of realization in the context of property exchanges. In each case, the taxpayer owned stock that had appreciated in value since its acquisition. And in each case, the corporation in which the taxpayer held stock had reorganized into a new corporation, with the new corporation assuming the business of the old corporation. While the corporations in *Phellis* and *Marr* both changed from New Jersey to Delaware corporations, the original and successor corporations in *Weiss* both were incorporated in Ohio. In each case, following the reorganization, the stockholders of the old corporation received shares in the new corporation equal to their proportional interest in the old corporation.

The question in these cases was whether the taxpayers realized the accumulated gain in their shares in the old corporation when they received in return for those shares stock representing an equivalent proportional interest in the new corporations. In *Phellis* and *Marr*, we held that the transaction were realization, events. We reasoned that because a company incorporated in one State has "different rights and powers" from one incorporated in a different State, the taxpayers in *Phellis* and *Marr* acquired through the transaction property that was "materially different" from what they previously had. United States v. Phellis; 257 U.S., at 169-173; see Marr v. United States, supra, at 540-542 (using phrase "essentially different"). In contrast, we held that no realization occurred in *Weiss*. By exchanging stock in the predecessor corporation for stock in the newly recognized corporation, the taxpayer did not receive "a thing really different from what he theretofore had." Weiss v. Stearn, supra, at 254. As we explained in *Marr*, our determination that the reorganized company in *Weiss* was not "really different" from its predecessor turned on the fact that both companies were incorporated in the same State. See Marr v. United States, supra, at 540-542 (outlining distinction between these cases).

Obviously, the distinction in *Phellis* and *Marr* that made the stock in the successor corporations materially different from the stock in the predecessors was minimal. Taken together, *Phellis*, *Marr*, and *Weiss* stand for the principle that properties are "different" in the sense that is "material" to the Internal Revenue Code so long as their respective possessors enjoy legal entitlements that are different in kind or extent. Thus, separate groups of stock are not materially different if they confer "the same proportional interest of the same character in the same corporation." Marr v. United States, 268 U.S., at 540. However, they are materially different if they are issued by different corporations, id., at 541; United States v. Phellis, supra, at 173, or if they confer "different rights and powers" in the same corporation, Marr v. United States, supra, at 541. No more demanding a standard than this is necessary in order to satisfy the administrative purposes underlying the realization requirement in §1001(a). See Helvering v. Horst, 311 U.S., at 116. For, as long as the property entitlements are not identical, their exchange will allow both the Commissioner and the transacting taxpayer easily to fix the appreciated or depreciated values of the property relative to their tax bases.

In contrast, we find no support for the Commissioner's "economic substitute" conception of material difference. According to the Commissioner, differences between properties are material for purposes of the Code only when it can be said that the parties, the relevant market (in this case the secondary mortgage market), and the relevant regulatory body (in this case the FHLBB) would consider them material. Nothing in *Phellis*, *Weiss*, and *Marr* suggests that exchanges of properties must satisfy such a subjective test to trigger realization of a gain or loss.

Moreover, the complexity of the Commissioner's approach ill serves the goal of administrative convenience that underlies the realization requirement.

In order to apply the Commissioner's test in a principled fashion, the Commissioner and the taxpayer must identify the relevant market, establish whether there is a regulatory agency whose views should be taken into account, and then assess how the relevant market participants and the agency would view the transaction. The Commissioner's failure to explain how these inquiries should be conducted further calls into question the workability of his test.

Finally, the Commissioner's test is incompatible with the structure of the Code. Section 1001(c) of Title 26 provides that a gain or loss realized under §1001(a) "shall be recognized" unless one of the Code's nonrecognition provisions applies. One such nonrecognition provision withholds recognition of a gain or loss realized from an exchange of properties that would appear to be economic substitutes under the Commissioner's material difference test. This provision, commonly known as the "like kind" exception, withholds recognition of a gain or loss realized "on the exchange of property held for productive use in a trade or business or for investment . . . for property of like kind which is to be held either for productive use in a trade or business or for investment." 26 U.S.C. §1031(a)(1). If Congress had expected that exchanges of similar properties would not count as realization events under §1001(a), it would have had no reason to bar recognition of a gain or loss realized from these transactions.

C

Under our interpretation of §1001(a), an exchange of property gives rise to a realization event so long as the exchanged properties are "materially different" — that is, so long as they embody legally distinct entitlements. Cottage Savings' transactions at issue here easily satisfy this test. Because the participation interests exchanged by Cottage Savings and the other S & L's derived from loans that were made to different obligors and secured by different homes, the exchanged interests did embody legally distinct entitlements. Consequently, we conclude that Cottage Savings realized its losses at the point of the exchange.

The Commissioner contends that it is anomalous to treat mortgages deemed to be "substantially identical" by the FHLBB as "materially different." The anomaly, however, is merely semantic; mortgages can be substantially identical for Memorandum R-49 purposes and still exhibit "differences" that are "material" for purposes of the Internal Revenue Code. Because Cottage Savings received entitlements different from those it gave up, the exchange put both Cottage Savings and the Commissioner in a position to determine the change in the value of Cottage Savings' mortgages relative to their tax bases. Thus, there is no reason not to treat the exchange of these interests as a realization event, regardless of the status of the mortgages under the criteria of Memorandum R-49.

III

Although the Court of Appeals found that Cottage Savings' losses were realized, it disallowed them on the ground that they were not sustained under §165(a) of the Code, 26 U.S.C. §165(a). . . .

The Commissioner offers a minimal defense of the Court of Appeals' conclusion . . . state[ed] . . . in one sentence in a footnote in his brief without offering further explanation. . . .

IV

For the reasons set forth above, the judgment of the Court of Appeals is reversed, and the case is remanded for further proceedings consistent with this opinion.

So ordered.

Justice BLACKMUN, with whom Justice WHITE joins, concurring in part and dissenting in part . . .

That the mortgage participation partial interests exchanged in these cases were "different" is not in dispute. The materiality prong is the focus. A material difference is one that has the capacity to influence a decision. See, e.g., Kungys v. United States, 485 U.S. 759, 770-771 (1988); Basic Inc. v. Levinson, 485 U.S. 224, 240 (1988); TSC Industries, Inc. v. Northway, Inc., 426 U.S. 438, 449 (1976).

The application of this standard leads, it seems to me, to only one answer — that the mortgage participation partial interests released were not materially different from the mortgage participation partial interests received. Memorandum R-49, as the Court notes, Opinion in No. 89-1965, ante, at 2, n. 2, lists 10 factors that, when satisfied, as they were here, serve to classify the interests as "substantially identical." These factors assure practical identity; surely, they then also assure that any difference cannot be of consequence. Indeed, nonmateriality is the full purpose of the Memorandum's criteria. The "proof of the pudding" is in the fact of its complete accounting acceptability to the FHLBB. Indeed, as has been noted, it is difficult to reconcile substantial identity for financial accounting purposes with a material difference for tax accounting purposes. See First Federal Savings & Loan Assn. v. United States, 694 F. Supp. 230, 245 (WD Tex. 1988), aff'd., 887 F. 2d 593 (CA5 1989), cert. pending No. 89-1927. Common sense so dictates.

This should suffice and be the end of the analysis. Other facts, however, solidify the conclusion: The retention by the transferor of 10% interests, enabling it to keep on servicing its loans; the transferor's continuing to collect the payments due from the borrowers so that, so far as the latter were concerned, it was business as usual, exactly as it had been; the obvious lack of concern or dependence of the transferor with the "differences" upon which the Court relies (as transferees, the taxpayers made no credit checks and no appraisals of collateral, see 890 F.2d 848, 849 (CA6 1989)); 90 T. C. 372, 382 (1988); 682 F. Supp. 1389, 1392 (ND Tex. 1988); the selection of the loans by computer programmed to match mortgages in accordance with the Memorandum R-49 criteria; the absence of even the names of the borrowers in the closing schedules attached to the agreements; Centennial's receipt of loan files only six years after its exchange, 682 F. Supp., at 1392, n.5; the restriction of the interests exchanged to the same State; the identity of the respective face and fair market values; and the application by the parties of common discount factors to each side of the transaction — all reveal that any differences that might exist made no difference whatsoever and were not material. This demonstrates the real nature of the transactions, including nonmateriality of the claimed differences.

We should be dealing here with realities and not with superficial distinctions. As has been said many times, and as noted above, in income tax law we are to be concerned with substance and not with mere form. When we stray from that principle, the new precedent is likely to be a precarious beacon for the future.

I respectfully dissent on this issue.

Questions

1. Does *Cottage Savings* stand for the proposition that only a very small modification in an investment is needed to constitute a realization event, or that a change in the identify of the obligor[s] is a relatively substantial change for tax law purposes even if its economic impact is very limited? Or does it stand for both?

2. What if a single loan contract is modified by mutual consent of a borrower and lender? When, if ever, will such a modification constitute a realization of gain or loss for the parties to the contract? This problem came to be referred to as the *Cottage Savings* problem, and it is dealt with now by a new regulation, §1.1001-3, titled, "Modification of Debt Instruments," under which "a significant modification of a debt instrument, within the meaning of this section, results in an exchange of the original debt instrument for a modified instrument that differs materially either in kind or in extent." The regulation defines modification broadly and then specifies what modifications are significant, again rather broadly. A change in interest rate, for example, is a significant modification if the change can reasonably be expected to affect the annual yield on the instrument by more than 5 percent of the yield before modification (or, if greater, one-fourth of one percent (25 basis points)). On the other hand a change that was provided for in the original instrument, as in the case of a variable rate mortgage, is not a modification at all. If the instrument makes a change in terms available at the option of either party alone such a change is not a modification, but a change that requires the consent of both parties is.

3. Constructive Sales

Suppose an investor has purchased WBX stock from time to time in 100 share lots at prices varying between $20 and $45 per share. And then, holding 800 shares, she calls her broker and tells him to sell 200 shares, which he does, at the current market price of $48. How is one to determine which shares were sold in order to know which cost to apply as the basis in computing her gain? See Reg. §1012-1(c) and (e). The basic premise seems to be that the seller can choose which lots to sell as if they were separate things; the problems are how the choice is to be expressed and what to do if no choice is expressed.

Does the basic premise make sense? Is there any economic (i.e., nontax) difference between selling lots that cost $20 and selling lots that cost $45? Should immediate tax results vary substantially between forms of transaction that are economically indistinguishable? If not, what should the rule be for determining the applicable basis in this case? In recent years the administration has proposed legislation that would eliminate this taxpayer choice.

A short sale is a sale of shares one does not own. The broker lends the customer shares to sell. Typically the broker keeps the sale proceeds as security for the customer's obligation to return the borrowed shares. So the result of the short sale is that the customer has cash being held by the broker and an obligation to return borrowed shares. The burden of that obligation will go up and down with the market value of the shares. Since it is a burden, the short seller's net wealth will go up when the market for these shares goes down and will go down when it goes up. The short seller is said to have a short position, or simply to be short, in the shares sold. (Correlatively, an owner of shares is said to be long or to have a long position in the stock.) A short position can be closed out by purchasing shares and delivering them to the broker in place of the shares that were originally borrowed. (Obviously the loan of shares was one permitting return of any identical shares in the borrowed amount.) Alternatively, the short sale can usually be closed out by a simple cash settlement with the broker, paying him the amount by which the value of the underlying shares exceeds the deposit retained by the broker or receiving from him the amount of any excess of that deposit over the current price. The net effect is the same except perhaps for transaction costs, and the net overall effect is that the short seller will profit by the amount the stock went down while he was short or will lose by the amount the stock went up.

How is *taxable* gain or loss to be determined on a short sale? Normally the tax law recognizes gain or loss on the sale of property, and traditionally the short sale has been regarded as the sale. But at the time of a short sale one does not know the identity or cost basis or acquisition date of the shares sold, so the tax law waits until the short position is closed.

Now what happens if a taxpayer makes a short sale of shares identical to shares she already owns? Such a sale is called a short sale *against the box*. (One use of a short sale might be to accommodate an owner whose share certificates are locked up in a box where she cannot get at them to deliver as required in a normal sale.) A short sale against the box can be closed by delivering the appropriate number of shares already owned, by payment or receipt of cash, or by acquiring and delivering new shares in satisfaction of the short-sale obligation.

How is a short sale against the box to be treated for income tax purposes? Economically it could be argued that the short sale is equivalent to a sale of an equivalent number of the shares already owned, and that a subsequent closing of the short position with cash is equivalent to a repurchase of those shares. But how is it treated for income tax purposes?

Prior to 1997, no gain or loss was recognized on the short sale itself, presumably because it was then unknown and indeterminable whether the taxpayer would satisfy her obligation under the short sale by delivering shares already owned. Accordingly, a short sale against the box has long been recognized as a device for locking in a gain on stock immediately while postponing recognition of gain (or loss) to a subsequent year. Transaction costs used to be such that most people would think of this only as a device for short-term deferral. But recent innovations in securities practice have brought such costs down, at least for substantial transactions, and so there have been a few widely publicized instances of prominent shareholders disposing of substantial investments apparently for the long haul by means of short sales against the box.

Congress responded in 1997 (and 1998) by enacting §1259, titled, "Constructive Sales Treatment for Appreciated Financial Positions."

Notes and Questions

1. Read through §1259 and try to describe the new treatment of a short sale against the box. What is the point of the exceptions in paragraphs (c)(2) and (3)? Note the statutory definitions of a forward contract and a notional principal contract. Are they different from a short sale in any way that ought to warrant some difference in treatment?

2. Note the fifth subparagraph in the specification of a constructive sale, (c)(1)(E), and try to think of how more than one transaction or position might have substantially the same effect as one of the previously described transactions.

First consider a single transaction called a *put*. A put is an option to sell a specified quantity of a specified underlying property at a specified price (the *strike price*) until a specified expiration date. Suppose one has a substantially appreciated long position in a certain stock and then purchases a put entitling the purchaser for a year to sell that stock at a strike price that is about equal to the current market value when the put is acquired. This has the effect of locking in the holder's gain on the shares for the duration of the put, without giving up the opportunity for further gain. Should purchase of a put be treated as a constructive sale? Is it? The legislative history of §1259 indicates that it should not be so treated because continued enjoyment of the opportunity to gain is a substantial element of continued ownership.

One might dispose of the opportunity to gain by writing a *call.* A call is an option to buy a specified quantity of a specified underlying property at a specified strike price for a specified period. "Writing a call" means granting such an option to buy, agreeing to deliver the shares in exchange for payment of the strike price if the call is exercised. One who buys a call pays the price of the call to the one who writes it, to be kept by the writer whether or not the call is exercised.

Consider a stock selling for $100. The owner might write a call at $110 and buy a put at $95. This will mean that if the stock goes over $110 he will lose it but will receive $110 from the holder of the call; if the stock goes below $95, he will exercise his put and sell the stock for $95; if the stock stays between $95 and $110 both options will expire unexercised and he will enjoy or suffer whatever gain or loss that occurs between those limits. This combination of options is called a *collar.* If the strike prices are chosen correctly one can find a put whose cost just equals what one gets for writing the call; then the combination is called a *costless collar.*

If the holder of a block of substantially appreciated securities enters into a collar, should that constitute a constructive sale of the securities? The legislative history describes collars and indicates that the Treasury is expected to study them and to develop objective criteria for answering those questions. Factors to be taken into account are how tight the collar is and how long it is to endure. The implication is clear that if the collar is tight enough and lasts long enough it should be treated as a constructive sale. How tight and how long are for the Treasury to determine in the course of writing regulations.

What should the answers be?

3. What other problems will the implementation of this provision involve?

D.   NONRECOGNITION EXCHANGES

1. Like-Kind Exchanges

ALDERSON v. COMMISSIONER

317 F.2d 790 (9th Cir. 1963)

Before Barnes and Merrill, Circuit Judges, and Crary, District Judge.

CRARY, District Judge. . . . The question presented is whether the transactions whereby taxpayers transferred one parcel of realty and acquired another constituted a sale, the gain from which is recognizable under

Section [1001(c)] of the Internal Revenue Code of 1954, or a nontaxable exchange within the meaning of Section 1031 of said Code.

On May 21, 1957, following negotiations between petitioners and Alloy Die Casting Company, hereinafter referred to as Alloy, representatives of petitioners and Alloy executed escrow instructions to the Orange County Title Company, hereinafter referred to as Orange, constituting a purchase and sale agreement whereby petitioners agreed to sell their Buena Park property, consisting of 31.148 acres of agricultural property, to Alloy for $5,500.00 per acre, a total price of $172,871.40. Pursuant to the terms of said agreement, Alloy deposited $17,205.00 in the Orange escrow toward purchase of the Buena Park property.

Some time after the execution of the May 21st escrow petitioners located 115.32 acres of farming land in Monterey County, California, hereinafter referred to as the Salinas property, which they desired to obtain in exchange for their Buena Park property.

On August 19, 1957, petitioners and Alloy executed an amendment to their May 21, 1957, escrow providing that "the Salinas property be acquired by Alloy and exchanged for the Buena Park property in lieu of the original contemplated cash transaction." (R. 21). The amendment further provides that if the exchange was not effected by September 11, 1957, the original escrow re the purchase for cash would be carried out. On the same day (August 19th) petitioners' daughter, Jean Marie Howard, acting for petitioners, executed escrow instructions to the Salinas Title Guarantee Company, hereinafter referred to as Salinas Title, in the form of "Buyer's Instructions." The parties have agreed that the acts of petitioners' daughter, Jean Marie Howard, with respect to the transactions here involved, are to be considered as acts of the petitioners, and any acts of said daughter are hereinafter referred to as acts of petitioners. The escrow instructions last mentioned provided for payment of $190,000.00 for the Salinas property, that title was to be taken in the name of Salinas Title, that $19,000.00 had been deposited with Orange and that the remaining $171,000.00 would also be deposited with Orange. The instructions also stated that Salinas Title was authorized to deed the Salinas property to Alloy, provided Salinas Title could "immediately record a deed from Alloy . . . to James Alderson and Clarissa F. Alderson, his wife, issuing final title evidence in the last mentioned grantees." (R. 21-22, R. Br. 5).

On August 20, 1957, petitioners authorized Orange to pay $19,000.00 into the Salinas escrow, which was done, and directed Orange to pay $171,000.00 into the Salinas escrow when these funds became available. (R. 22).

On August 22, 1957, Alloy, by letter to petitioners, summarized the agreements of the parties *re the manner of accomplishing the transfer of the properties between them.* (R. Br. 6). The letter further stated that Alloy's representative would deposit $172,871.40 (the cash amount for the Buena Park property as per May 21st escrow) with Salinas Title on assurance that the agreements would be effected. The letter was countersigned by petitioners.

By deed dated August 20, 1957, title to the Salinas property was transferred to Salinas Title. By deed dated August 21, 1957, Salinas Title conveyed the Salinas property to Alloy. By deed dated August 26, 1957, petitioners conveyed the Buena Park property to Alloy and deed dated August 29, 1957, conveyed the Salinas property from Alloy to petitioners. All four of these deeds were recorded September 4, 1957. (R. Br. 6).

On September 3, 1957, Alloy, acting through its attorney, Elliott H. Pentz, deposited $172,871.40, *belonging to Alloy,* in the Salinas escrow, *on Alloy's behalf,* with instruction that said sum should be used to complete the purchase of the Salinas property. (R. 17, 24, 72-73). The said $172,871.40, plus the $19,000.00 previously deposited with Salinas Title by Orange, made up something more than the $190,000.00 purchase price for the Salinas property, and the excess was returned to the petitioners. Alloy's original deposit of $17,205.00 in the Orange escrow was returned to it sometime after August 28, 1957. (R. 23).

The petitioners paid approximately $10,000.00 into the Orange escrow for real estate commissions and escrow charges and paid for documentary stamps on the transfer of the Buena Park property to Alloy, and $471.80 into the Salinas escrow for fees and escrow charges together with cost of documentary stamps on the transfer of the Salinas property from Salinas Title to Alloy.

Alloy paid $106.38 to Orange for escrow charges and paid nothing to Salinas Title for escrow charges or stamps.

The Commissioner determined that the transfer of the Buena Park property to Alloy constituted a sale upon which petitioners realized a long term capital gain (R. 9) and the Tax Court sustained the decision of the Commissioner (R. 27) holding "... that the transactions in which petitioners disposed of the Buena Park property and acquired the Salinas property did not constitute an exchange within the meaning of Section 1031(a)."

In considering the question involved, there are certain findings of the Tax Court which this court believes to be particularly pertinent. Said findings are as follows:

> From the outset, petitioners desired to exchange their Buena Park property for other property of a like kind. They intended to sell the property for cash only if they were unable to locate a suitable piece of property to take in exchange. (R. 20) (Emphasis ours.)
>
> The deposit by Alloy of $172,871.40 in the Salinas escrow was made by Elliott Pentz, an attorney, pursuant to the commitment of his client, Alloy. The funds were received from Alloy by Pentz; *were the property of Alloy;* and *were deposited by him in Alloy's behalf.*
>
> Alloy acquired title to the Salinas property solely to enable it to perform its agreement to exchange that property for the Buena Park property. (R. 24) (Emphasis ours.)
>
> The Buena Park property and the Salinas property were of like kind. (R. 24).

By the finding of the Tax Court, supra, it was determined that there was from the outset no intention on the part of the petitioners to sell the Buena Park property for cash if it could be exchanged for other property of like kind. There is no question that the desired property of like kind was located (Salinas property) and that, as determined by the findings, petitioners had no intention other than to exchange the Buena Park property for the Salinas property. It also follows from the findings that petitioners had no intention to purchase the Salinas property and that title to the Salinas property was to come to the petitioners by exchange thereof for the Buena Park property. The intention of the parties and what actually occurred re the obtaining of the Salinas property for the exchange is further established by the finding that the $172,871.40 deposited by Alloy's attorney, Pentz in the Salinas escrow was the "*property of Alloy*" and deposited by Pentz "*in Alloy's behalf.*" Further, "Alloy acquired title to the Salinas property solely to enable it to perform its agreement to exchange the property for the Buena Park property."

Respondent concedes that an exchange is not vitiated because cash is received in addition to property held for productive use or investment, but asserts that the $19,000.00 deposited by petitioners with Orange escrow was transmitted by Orange to Salinas escrow, whereas Alloy's initial deposit of $17,205.00 into the Orange escrow was returned by Orange to Alloy, and that if petitioners were not the purchasers of the Salinas property that Orange would have returned the $19,000.00 to petitioners and deposited the $17,205.00 with Salinas escrow in payment of the difference between the value of the Buena Park property and the purchase price of the Salinas property.

It is the position of respondent that from the facts and circumstances outlined above it must be concluded the Buena Park property was sold by petitioners to Alloy and the Salinas property was purchased by petitioners, not Alloy. However, it does not appear from the terms of the amended Orange escrow (August 19, 1957) that there was ever any obligation on the part of Alloy to pay cash for the Buena Park property or for the petitioners to receive cash for said property as provided in the May 21, 1957, escrow, by reason of the fact that *prior* to September 11, 1957, Alloy did deposit with Orange a deed to the Salinas property conveying same to petitioners. Neither liability of Alloy to petitioners for payment of cash for the Buena Park property nor liability of petitioners to sell the said property to Alloy for money ever matured because under no conditions was there to be a sale of the Buena Park property for cash until September 11, 1957, and *then only* if the Salinas property *was not* acquired by Alloy and exchanged for the Buena Park property as of that date (R. 21). Deed of Alloy to petitioners conveying the Salinas property and deed of petitioners to Alloy conveying the Buena Park property were exchanged and recorded September 4, 1957. Consequently, an agreement on the part of petitioners to sell to Alloy the Buena Park property for money did not come into being.

Petitioners, on finding the Salinas property, took steps to make it available to Alloy for the exchange by signing buyer's instructions in the escrow of August 19, 1957, opened at Salinas Title, but the fact is, as found by the Tax Court, that petitioners at that time intended to accomplish an exchange of properties and that the Salinas property was "acquired by Alloy" for the sole purpose of such exchange.

True, the intermediate acts of the parties could have hewn closer to and have more precisely depicted the ultimate desired result, but what actually occurred on September 3 or 4, 1957, was an exchange of deeds between petitioners and Alloy which effected an exchange of the Buena Park property for the Salinas property. It is also noted by the court that the buyer's instructions in the Salinas escrow did not conform to the seller's instructions although the transfer from the original owner of the Salinas property to Salinas Title was, as to the provision at variance, pursuant to the terms of the buyer's instructions. If Alloy had signed the said "Buyer's Instructions" this litigation would have been avoided, but even in the circumstances here involved the court concludes that the intended exchange was accomplished.

Respondent argues the Tax Court found only that petitioners from the outset "desired" to exchange their Buena Park property and not that from the outset they "intended" to do so. This would appear in the circumstances to be a distinction without a difference since it does not seem logical that one would intentionally take steps to accomplish a result not desired, and that, therefore, all acts of the petitioners may be considered as having been performed with the intent to accomplish their desired result, to wit, "exchange their Buena Park property for other property of a like kind." ...

Referring again to the Salinas escrow and the instructions to Orange, it is to be noted that the terms of the buyer's instructions in the Salinas escrow and the instructions to Orange were not carried out in important details not heretofore mentioned. Although the petitioners authorized Orange to pay $19,000.00 into the Salinas escrow and to pay $171,000.00, when available, into the Salinas escrow, and although the Salinas escrow provided for the depositing of $171,000.00 into the Orange escrow (R. Br. 5), *this was not done.* The $171,000.00 nor any part thereof was ever paid into the Orange escrow, but on the contrary $172,871.40, *property of Alloy,* was by its attorney, Pentz, deposited in the Salinas escrow *in Alloy's behalf.*

The court concludes the holding of the Tax Court, "that in essence petitioners acquired the Salinas property in a separate transaction; that payment of the $172,871.40, made by Alloy, was a payment made for petitioners" (R. 32), is not supported by the Tax Court's Findings of Fact, Stipulation of Facts or by the evidence in the case when considered in all of its aspects.

The court further concludes that there was no sale by petitioners of the Buena Park property to Alloy, but that the pertinent transactions resulted in an exchange of the Buena Park property for property of like kind to be held either for productive use in trade or for investment, and that by reason thereof there was no gain or loss from said exchange which should be recognized for income tax purposes. For the reasons set forth above, the Decision of the Tax Court of the United States, entered herein May 8, 1962, "That there is a deficiency in the income tax for the taxable year 1957 in the amount of $39,530.58" (R. 33), is reversed.

Questions

1. *The exchange requirement.* Does the whole controversy in *Alderson* seem excessively technical? If a person can exchange appreciated property for other property of a like kind without tax, why should there be any difficulty over refinements of title and mechanics? Is anything of real importance except that the taxpayer ends up with his investment transferred from one piece of property to another, not liquidated?

2. *Boot.* When cash or other nonqualifying property enters into a like-kind exchange, be sure to understand exactly how it is treated.

(a) *A* owns Blackacre with a basis of $10,000. It is worth considerably more. He transfers Blackacre in exchange for Greenacre plus $7,000 cash. How will this exchange be taxed? What will be *A*'s basis for Greenacre?

(b) *B* owns Whiteacre with a basis of $24,000. She disposes of Whiteacre together with $17,000 cash in exchange for Purpleacre. How will that exchange be taxed? What will be *B*'s basis for Purpleacre?

(c) One of the purposes of §1031 is said to be to avoid the necessity for fixing any exact value on property received in a like-kind exchange. Is that objective achieved? Within what limits or under what circumstances?

3. *Related party exchanges.* *E* owns a farm whose market value has recently increased sharply because of the possibility of residential development. *E*'s sister *F* recently inherited a farm of equal market value, but greater agricultural utility. *F* does not want a farm and plans to sell. *E* wants to exchange farms with *F*. He asserts that under §1031(a) neither he nor *F* would recognize gain on the exchange, and that under §1031(d) *F* would retain her stepped-up fair market value basis, enabling her to sell *E*'s farm without taxable gain.

(a) Is *E*'s analysis correct? Look at §1031(f) and (g). Are they justified?

(b) What if *F* were *E*'s wife, not his sister?

4. *Deferred exchanges.* Suppose Alderson had failed to locate a suitable replacement property before he had to deliver the parcel that he was exchanging. Would it still be possible to avoid gain recognition if his intention was to invest the sale proceeds in like-kind replacement property? How?

In Starker v. United States, 602 F.2d 1341 (9th Cir. 1979), a taxpayer transferred real estate in exchange for a promise by the transferee to acquire and deliver replacement properties subsequently designated by the taxpayer, and the court held this to be within §1031. The matter is now regulated by §1031(a)(3), enacted in 1984, which requires that replacement property be identified within 45 days and received within 180 days of the taxpayer's disposition of property on which nonrecognition is sought. Are there strong reasons for this limitation?

5. *Electivity.* Section 1031 is not explicitly elective but some of its conditions are sufficiently formal that taxpayers, with adequate advance advice, can often arrange to bring themselves within or without their coverage. *Alderson* is illustrative; clearly the taxpayer there could have arranged the

transaction to avoid §1031. Is there any reason not to give the taxpayer an express election in these situations?

6. *"Realization" and "recognition."* Notice the two-level analysis implicit in the statute. Gain on a like-kind exchange is *realized* in an amount equal to the excess of the value of property received over the basis of the property transferred. §1001(a) and (b). Section 1031 only provides that the gain shall not be *recognized*.

What is the status of realized but unrecognized gain? If gain is unrecognized, does it make any difference whether it is realized? Why does the statute introduce the idea of recognition? Why not simply provide that no gain is realized on a like-kind exchange? Is it because *Macomber* made realization into a constitutional concept to be defined by the courts rather than the Congress?

7. Smith bought parcel *A* for $45,000. He then sought a way to liquidate his half-interest in parcel *B* without tax. On his attorney's advice he sold 8/9 of parcel *A* to the other co-owner of parcel *B* for $40,000, and then exchanged his half interest in parcel *B* for the 8/9 of parcel *A* just conveyed. Smith's basis for his half interest in parcel *B* was $10,000. What taxable gain, if any, will result from this series of transactions? Smith v. Commissioner, 537 F.2d 972 (8th Cir. 1976). Cf. Crenshaw v. United States, 450 F.2d 472 (5th Cir. 1971), cert. denied, 408 U.S. 923 (1972).

8. Look at §1031(e). Can you figure out what it was designed to deal with?

REVENUE RULING 79-143
1979-1 C.B. 264

... An individual taxpayer who is not a dealer in foreign or domestic coins purchased United States $20 gold coins as an investment. After the coins had appreciated in value, the taxpayer exchanged them for South African Krugerrand gold coins of equal total fair market value. A gain was realized by the taxpayer as a result of the exchange. The taxpayer will hold the South African Krugerrand gold coins as an investment.

The United States $20 gold coins exchanged by the taxpayer are numismatic-type coins. The value of numismatic-type coins is determined by their age, number minted, history, art and aesthetics, condition, and metal content. The South African Krugerrand gold coins received by the taxpayer are bullion-type coins. The value of bullion-type coins is determined solely on the basis of their metal content. ...

Section 1.1031(a)-1(b) of the Income Tax Regulations provides that as used in section 1031(a) of the Code, the words "like kind" have reference to the nature or character of the property and not to its grade or quality. One kind or class of class of property may not, under that section, be exchanged for property of a different kind or class.

Section 1031(e) of the Code provides that the exchange of livestock of one sex for livestock of the other sex is not an exchange of property of like kind for purposes of the nonrecognition provision of section 1031(a), because, as the committee report cited below points out, the different sexes of livestock represent investments of different types, in one case an investment of breeding purposes, in the other an investment in livestock raised for slaughter. Section 1031(e) was enacted to clarify what was considered to be the correct interpretation of section 1031(a). See S. Rep. No. 91-552, 91st Cong., 1st Sess. (1969), 1969-3 C.B. 423, 488-489.

Similarly, in this case although the coins appear to be similar because they both contain gold, they actually represent totally different types of underlying investment, and therefore are not of the same nature or character. The bullion-type coins, unlike the numismatic-type coins, represent an investment in gold on world markets rather than in the coins themselves. Therefore, the bullion-type coins and the numismatic-type coins are not property of like kind. . . .

Note

In the case of tangible personal property that is subject to depreciation, a regulation promulgated in 1991 provides concrete guidance in the form of categorical bright-line rules that define like-kind property. Two items of depreciable tangible personal property are of like kind if they are "either within the same General Asset Class or within the same Product Class." Reg. 1.1031-2(b)(1). The asset and product classes involve quite broad groupings, such that, for example, all office furniture, fixtures, and equipment fall within one asset class, while another comprehends all computers and peripherals. (Compare the rule for realty swaps.) If the items don't share a common asset or product class, it is still open to the taxpayer to argue that the exchange is nevertheless like kind; the categorical approach merely provides a safe harbor, it does not venture to say what properties are not like kind. Id. -2(a) ("no inference is to be drawn from the fact that the properties are not of a like class"). No more specific guidance or safe harbor is specified, however, if the personal property exchanged is either intangible or nondepreciable. Id. -2(c).

JORDAN MARSH CO. v. COMMISSIONER
269 F.2d 453 (2d Cir. 1959)

Before Hincks, Lumbard and Moore, Circuit Judges.

Hincks, Circuit Judge. . . . The transactions giving rise to the dispute were conveyances by the petitioner in 1944 of the fee of two parcels of property in the city of Boston where the petitioner, then as now, operated a department store. In return for its conveyances the petitioner received $2,300,000 in cash which, concededly, represented the fair market value of the properties. The conveyances were unconditional, without provision of any option to repurchase. At the same time, the petitioner received back from the vendees leases of the same properties for terms of 30 years and 3 days, with options to renew for another 30 years if the petitioner-lessee should erect new buildings thereon. The vendees were in no way connected with the petitioner. The rentals to be paid under the leases concededly were full and normal rentals so that the leasehold interested which devolved upon the petitioner were of no capital value.

In its return for 1944, the petitioner, claiming the transaction was a sale . . . sought to deduct from income the difference between the adjusted basis of the property and the cash received. The Commissioner disallowed the deduction, taking the position that the transaction represented an exchanged of property for other property of like kind. Under [§1031] such exchanges are not occasions for the recognition of gain or loss; and even the receipt of cash or other property in the exchange of the properties of like kind is not enough to permit the taxpayer to recognize loss. [§1031(c)]. Thus the Commissioner viewed the transaction, in substance, as an exchange of a fee interest for a long term lease, justifying his position by [Reg. §1031(a)-1(c)], which provides that a leasehold of more than 30 years is the equivalent of a fee interest . . . .

The controversy centers around the purposes of Congress in enacting [§1031] dealing with non-taxable exchanges. The section represents an exception to the general rule . . . that upon the sale or exchange of property the entire amount of gain or loss is to be recognized by the taxpayer. . . . Congress was primarily concerned with the inequity, in the case of an exchange, of forcing a taxpayer to recognize a paper gain which was still tied up in a continuing investment of the same sort. If such gains were not to be recognized, however, upon the ground that they were theoretical, neither should equally theoretical losses. And as to both gains and losses the taxpayer should not have it within his power to avoid the operation of the section by stipulating for the addition of cash, or boot, to the property received in exchange. These considerations, rather than concern for the difficulty of the administrative task of making the valuations necessary to compute gains and losses,[5] were at the root of the Congressional purpose in enacting [§1031] . . . .

---

5. In Century Electric Co. v. Commissioner, supra, 192 F.2d at page 159, the court thought that in the enactment of §112 Congress "was concerned with the administrative problem involved in the computation of gain or loss in transactions of the character with which the section deals." But so far as appears from the opinion the attention of the court had not been called to the legislative history of the section set forth earlier in this opinion.

That such indeed was the legislative objective is supported by Portland Oil Co. v. Commissioner, 1 Cir., 109 F.2d 479. There Judge Magruder, in speaking of a cognate provision . . . said at page 488:

> It is the purpose of Section [351] to save the taxpayer form an immediate recognition of a gain, or to intermit the claim of loss, in certain transactions where gain or loss may have accrued in a constitutional sense, but where in a popular and economic sense there has been a mere change in the form of ownership and the taxpayer has not really "cashed in" on the theoretical gain, or closed out a losing venture.

In conformity with this reading of the statute, we think the petitioner here, by its unconditional conveyances to a stranger, had done more than make a change in the *form of ownership*: it was a change as to the *quantum* of ownership whereby, in the words just quoted, it had "closed out a losing venture." By the transaction its capital invested in the real estate involved had been completely liquidated for cash to an amount fully equal to the value of the fee. This, we hold, was a sale — not an exchange within the purview of [§1031].

The Tax Court apparently thought it of controlling importance that the transaction in question involved no change in the petitioner's possession of the premises: it felt that the decision in Century Electric Co. v. Commissioner [192 F.2d 155 (8th Cir. 1951), cert. denied, 342 U.S. 954 (1951)] controlled the situation here. We think, however, that that case was distinguishable on the facts. For notwithstanding the lengthy findings made with meticulous care by the Tax Court in that case, 15 T.C. 581, there was no finding that the cash received by the taxpayer was the full equivalent of the value of the fee which the taxpayer had conveyed to the vendee-lessor, and no finding that the lease back called for a rent which was fully equal to the rental value of the premises. Indeed, in its opinion the Court of Appeals pointed to evidence that the fee which the taxpayer had "exchanged" may have had a value substantially in excess of the cash received. And in the *Century Electric* case, the findings showed, at page 585, that the taxpayer-lessee, unlike the taxpayer here, was not required to pay "general state, city and school taxes" because its lessor was an educational institution which under its charter was exempt from such taxes. Thus the leasehold interest in *Century Electric* on this account may well have had a premium value. In the absence of findings as to the values of the properties allegedly "exchanged," necessarily there could be no finding of a loss. And without proof of a loss, of course, the taxpayer could not prevail. Indeed, in the Tax Court six of the judges expressly based their concurrences on that limited ground. 15 T.C. 596.

In the *Century Electric* opinion it was said, 192 F.2d at page 159:

> Subsections [1031(a) and (c)] indicate the controlling policy and purpose of the section, that is, the nonrecognition of gain or loss in transactions where neither is readily measured in terms of money, where in theory the taxpayer may have realized gain or loss but where in fact his economic situation is the same after as it was before the transaction. See Fairfield S.S. Corp. v. Commissioner, 2 Cir., 157 F.2d 321, 323; Trenton Cotton Oil Co. v. Commissioner, 6 Cir., 147 F.2d 33, 36.

But the *Fairfield* case referred to was one in which the only change in taxpayer's ownership was through the interposition of a corporate title accomplished by transfer to a corporation wholly owned by the taxpayer. And in the *Trenton Cotton Oil* case, the court expressly relied on Portland Oil Co. v. Commissioner, supra, as stating correctly the purpose of [§351], but quoted only the first of the two requisites stated in *Portland*. As we have already observed, in that case Judge Magruder said that it was the purpose of [§351] "to intermit the claim of a loss" not only where the economic situation of the taxpayer is unchanged but also "*where . . . the taxpayer has not . . . closed out a losing venture.*" Here plainly the petitioner by the transfer finally closed out a losing venture. And it cannot justly be said that the economic situation of the petitioner was unchanged by a transaction which substituted $2,300,000 in cash for its investment in real estate and left it under a liability to make annual payments of rent for upwards of thirty years. Many bona fide business purposes may be served by such a transaction. Cary, Corporate Financing through the Sale and Lease-Back of Property: Business, Tax, and Policy Considerations, 62 Harv. L. Rev. 1.

In ordinary usage, an "exchange" means the giving of one piece of property in return for another—not, as the Commissioner urges here, the return of a lesser interest in a property received from another. It seems unlikely that Congress intended that an "exchange" should have the strained meaning for which the Commissioner contends. For the legislative history states expressly an intent to correct the indefiniteness of prior versions of the Act by excepting from the general rule "specifically and in definite terms those cases of exchanges in which it is not desired to tax the gain or allow the loss."

But even if under certain circumstances the return of a part of the property conveyed may constitute an exchange . . . we think that in this case, in which cash was received for the full value of the property conveyed, the transaction must be classified as a sale. Standard Envelope Manufacturing Co. v. C.I.R., 15 T.C. 41; May Department Stores Co. v. C.I.R., 16 T.C. 547.

Reversed.

Questions

1. Does this case suggest that §1031 has any effective role to play in preventing deductions for losses that have not been *economically* realized (whatever that might mean)?

2. Why do you suppose the lease was for just over 30 years instead of just under? Can you imagine reasons why a taxpayer might wish to come under §1031 on a transaction of this kind? Are there tax motivations that might underlie a sale and leaseback such as this even if §1031 could not be avoided?

3. Why didn't §1031 operate to prevent recognition of the losses in *Cottage Savings*?

2. Nonrecognition on Dispositions for Cash

(a) *Involuntary conversions.* Suppose a taxpayer has a warehouse used in its business that is taken from it by eminent domain. The governmental unit that is taking the warehouse is unlikely to be able or willing to produce other property to convey to the taxpayer in a like-kind exchange. Does that mean the taxpayer will be unable to postpone its gain even if it replaces the taken property?

Look at §1033. The property that will qualify for reinvestment is property "similar or related in service or use." How does that compare with like-kind property in §1031?

What happens if more or less than all the proceeds of the original disposition are reinvested in qualifying property? Look particularly at (a)(1), (a)(2)(A), (b)(1), and (b)(2). Is the treatment prescribed exactly equivalent to the treatment of boot under §1031?

Consider for example a property with an adjusted basis of $100x$ taken by eminent domain for a price of $260x$. Suppose suitable replacement properties are located, one at a cost of $200x$, the other for $300x$. Describe the tax consequences for either replacement. Are these consequences different in any significant respect than if the replacement had been effected by a like-kind exchange prior to condemnation?

If the replacement is for $300x$, the taxpayer can elect to recognize none of the condemnation gain because the condemnation proceeds ($260x$) do not exceed the replacement price ($300x$). Basis for the replacement property then will be cost ($300x$), reduced by the amount of gain not recognized on the condemnation ($160x$), which equals $140x$.

An equivalent like-kind exchange would be one in which the taxpayer would have to pay $40x$ along with his property to get the replacement property. On such an exchange, no gain would be recognized since the taxpayer receives nothing but like-kind property, and basis would be the basis of the like-kind property transferred ($100x$) plus the amount of cash, for a total of $140x$ (same result).

Work out the consequences of the $200x$ replacement for yourself. If the result for cash replacement differs from a like-kind exchange, keep working.

Would you favor a proposal to make these mechanics for cash replacement more broadly available for voluntary as well as involuntary conversions? What problems would such an extension raise?

(b) *Principal residences.* Until May 7, 1997, these mechanics were generally available upon any sale of a principal residence. The statutory provision was §1034, and the only eligible replacement property was a new principal residence acquired by purchase (including construction) within two years before or after sale of the old residence. The provision could be used any number of times during a lifetime, but not more than once in any two-year period (with a possible exception if the second sale was sufficiently connected with commencement of work at a new principal place of work). There was no dollar limit on the amount of gain that could be postponed pursuant to this provision.

As under §1033, if sale proceeds from the old residence (with some adjustment for expenses of sale) exceeded cost of the new residence, then gain would be recognized to the extent of that excess. And basis, similarly, was prescribed as cost of the new residence reduced by the amount of gain unrecognized on the old.

For example, *C*'s principal residence had a cost basis of $120,000. She sold it for $220,000, realizing a gain of $100,000. Within two years she bought a new principal residence for $250,000. Since her investment in the new home (250) exceeds the sale price received for the old (220), she recognized no gain, and her basis in the new home was $150,000 (250 cost of the new minus 100 unrecognized gain on the old). The result can be confirmed by noting that her unrealized gain — the excess of value over basis — is $100,000 before and after the two transactions, which is what ought to happen when no gain (or loss) has been recognized. Or one might just observe that *C*'s basis for her residence was $120,000 before the transaction and $150,000 afterward, which is perfectly consistent with the fact that she increased her investment by putting $30,000 more into the new home than she got from selling the old.

If *C*'s new residence had cost only $200,000, she would have recognized gain to the extent of $20,000 (220 sales proceeds minus 200 reinvestment) on sale of the old residence and her basis for the new would have been $120,000 (200 cost minus 80 gain not recognized). In this case the spread between basis and value will have been reduced from $100,000 before to $80,000 after, which is wholly consistent with gain recognition of $20,000. Basis is unchanged at $120,000 before and after; this is consistent with the fact that gain recognition just equals net disinvestments (excess of sale proceeds of the old over cost basis of the new residence).

One shortcoming of this provision was that it left a tax, sometimes quite substantial, on people selling and then buying a less expensive replacement home. Older people might do that because their children have left home and they want something smaller; because on retirement they move to a region where real estate prices are lower; or just because dwindling funds make a reduction in investment necessary.

Do these represent convincing reasons for broader relief?

Congress apparently thought so, and therefore provided a limited exemption for taxpayers selling their homes after reaching age 55.[6] This exemption could be taken only once in a lifetime, and was limited to $125,000 (or $250,000 for a married couple filing a joint return).

In 1997, in connection with the restoration of a 20 percent top rate on capital gains, §121 was expanded and §1034 was repealed. The expansion of §121 consisted of doubling the dollar limits on the amount excludable,

---

6. §121 (prior to its amendment in 1997).

eliminating the age-55 restriction, and ameliorating the once-in-a-lifetime restriction by making it once every two years. As a result, a taxpayer can apparently exclude an unlimited amount of gain on principal residences at the rate of $250,000 ($500,000 on a joint return) every two years without any overall dollar limitation. Even a sale within two years of a prior sale will qualify for a proportionately smaller exclusion if it is occasioned by a change in the taxpayer's principal place of work. As this brief description indicates, the new version of §121 is in several respects a kind of combination of the old versions of §§121 and 1034.

The main reason given for this change was that calculating capital gain from the sale of a principal residence is among the most complex tasks faced by a typical taxpayer, and that excluding gains below a relatively high threshold would eliminate this complexity for all but a few taxpayers. Furthermore, the old provision may have encouraged some taxpayers to purchase a more expensive house than they otherwise would in order to avoid tax liability, and it may have discouraged some older taxpayers from selling their homes.

Questions

1. Read §121 and figure out just how much a wealthy taxpayer would have to move around to take full advantage of this new provision.

2. In what respects, if any, is the new provision an improvement over the older law? In what respects is it worse?

3. Numerous questions have arisen under the old law about what is a taxpayer's principal residence. Presumably some of the old learning will survive under the new provision, but some is superseded. One recurring issue under §1034 arose when a taxpayer moved out of his old residence and then leased it for a short period pending sale: Did it remain his principal residence when a sale was finally accomplished? And what was to be done about changes in value and basis during the period of time between when the taxpayer moved out of the old residence and when it was sold? What if a taxpayer had substantial renovations to make on a new residence and moved into much cheaper substitute housing pending their completion? Might that substitute housing be identified as the replacement principal residence? How are these questions affected by the 1997 revision?

4. Who are the winners and losers, if any, from the 1997 change? Do any of the losers have an appealing claim for relief? What relief, if any, would make sense? Would you expect that there would be more winners than losers?

(c) *Wash sales of stock or securities.* If loss is realized on the sale or other disposition of shares of stock or securities and the taxpayer acquires substantially identical stock or securities within the 61-day period starting 30 days before and ending 30 days after the sale or disposition, then §1091(a) denies a loss deduction. The substantially identical stock or securities acquired within that period are assigned a basis that preserves the loss for possible future recognition so that the deduction is merely deferred, not disallowed. §1091(d). The wash sale rule is examined further in Chapter 14B. What does it indicate about the difference between a technical realization event and a substantial change in the underlying risks of the investment? And why doesn't the wash sale rule apply to gains?

3. Corporate Reorganizations and Transfers to Controlled Corporations

The management of a New Jersey corporation concludes that it would be desirable to reincorporate in Delaware. To that end, a Delaware corporation is organized; the New Jersey shareholders transfer their shares to the Delaware corporation in exchange for its stock; finally, the New Jersey corporation is liquidated so that its assets pass, subject to its liabilities, to the Delaware corporation.

Is taxable gain realized on the exchange of New Jersey shares for Delaware shares?

In a series of early cases it was argued that transactions of this kind produced only formal changes in evidences of ownership and therefore came under the umbrella of *Macomber*. For the most part the Supreme Court rejected that argument, apparently confining *Macomber* to changes in form of ownership of a single continuing corporate entity. Marr v. United States, 268 U.S. 536 (1925), involved substantially the case stated, the company being General Motors, and the Court held the shareholders taxable on their whole gain. Note that this series of cases is discussed in Part IIB of *Cottage Savings Ass'n*, Chapter 5C.2 above, and is relied on for the proposition that properties are materially different whenever "their respective possessors enjoy legal entitlements that are different in kind or extent."

Section 1031 will not cover an exchange of this sort since stocks, bonds, and other securities are expressly excluded from its coverage. Why? An exchange of the kind described would today be covered by §354 if the transaction met the statutory definition of a reorganization in §368(a)(1).

The reorganization provisions date from 1918; they are extremely complex; and they have been the object of a long history of esoteric judicial interpretation full of surprises and mysteries, even for those who have made their living from them for years. The provisions cover much more than the mere formal reincorporation of a single enterprise — a merger of two corporations or a division of a single corporation into two or more separately owned enterprises may qualify as a reorganization. In general, however, stock or securities received on a nonrecognition basis under the reorganization provisions must represent a continuing investment in the old enterprise, or part of it, or an enterprise into which the old enterprise has been merged.

Section 351 is closely related to the reorganization provisions but often operates independently. It can and should be read at this point. The related basis provisions are in §§358 and 362(a).

Problem

An individual owns a building worth $100,000 with an adjusted basis of $40,000. He transfers it to a newly organized corporation in exchange for all the corporate stock. How much gain, if any, is realized on this exchange? How much is recognized? How much will be recognized and by whom if the corporation subsequently sells the building for $110,000? How much will be recognized and by whom if the individual subsequently sells the stock for $95,000?

There are many wrinkles in the text and interpretation of §351; this problem only illustrates its operation in the simplest situation.

E.   DEFERRED AND CONTINGENT PAYMENT SALES

BERNICE PATTON TESTAMENTARY TRUST v. UNITED STATES

*2001-1 U.S. Tax Cas. (CCH) ¶50,332 (Fed. Cl. 2001),
aff'd, without opinion, 2002-1 U.S. Tax Cas.
(CCH) ¶50,277 (Fed. Cir. 2002)*

FUTEY, Judge.

This tax refund case is before the court on the parties' cross-motions for summary judgment. Plaintiff asserts a promissory note it received in 1990 for the sale of stock did not have an ascertainable value, and therefore, the Internal Revenue Service (IRS) should not have considered it taxable income for the 1990 tax year. Plaintiff invokes the open transaction method for reporting taxable income. Defendant contends the fair market value of the note was reasonably ascertainable at the time of sale, so the open transaction doctrine does not apply. Defendant asserts the Commissioner of the IRS (Commissioner) was correct in determining the proper method for reporting this transaction was as an installment sale.

FACTUAL BACKGROUND

Plaintiff is Bernice Patton Testamentary Trust with Moody Patton as trustee. Plaintiff was established in the last will and testament of Bernice Patton, who died January 5, 1981. Plaintiff formerly owned 25% of the common stock of Western Packing Company (Western) and Braunfel Meats, Inc. (Braunfel). Moody Patton, acting individually, also owned 25% and Dick Patton owned 50%. Western and Braunfel were located in Sealy, Texas and were in the business of slaughtering cattle and processing beef for sale. Compared to other businesses in this industry, Western and Braunfel were relatively small, slaughtering approximately 400 head of cattle per day while larger packers slaughtered 10,000 to 12,000 head per day. Dick Patton ran the processing end of the business while sales were handled by both Dick and Moody Patton via telephone.

In 1990, a group of investors located in Chicago formed W-B Acquisition Corporation (W-B) for the purpose of acquiring Western and Braunfel stock. The Pattons were experiencing financial troubles and were interested in selling the two businesses.[4] An outside party did an independent appraisal to determine the value of the companies.[5] The Pattons and the investors from W-B executed documents in 1990 transferring the Pattons' stock to W-B in exchange for cash and a seller's note. Plaintiff's portion was $317,140 in cash and a note (Note) with the face amount of $507,424. Dick and Moody Patton continued to run Western and Braunfel on behalf of W-B after this transaction.

Plaintiff's basis in the common stock of Western and Braunfel was $299,322. Plaintiff reported the sale on its 1990 income tax return as an open transaction with the Note having no ascertainable value. The $317,140 plaintiff received from the buyer was reduced by plaintiff's basis, leaving an excess amount of $17,818, which plaintiff reported as long term capital gain.

W-B was to pay the Note in full by September 1, 1995. Plaintiff would receive payments before that date if certain conditions materialized with respect to the net income of the business. Specifically, plaintiff was entitled to receive 40% of the remaining cash flow each year after a $150,000 management fee was allotted to the buyer. Also, plaintiff's rights were subordinated to Greyhound Financial Corporation and Creekwood Capital Corporation (Senior Lenders). In 1991, plaintiff and W-B modified the buyer's obligation by increasing the amount owed to plaintiff to $661,712.[7] Plaintiff received no payment on the Note between 1990 and 1994 because the operations of the companies were insufficient to require annual payments.

In 1993, W-B's successor, Carlton Foods, Inc., assumed the buyer's obligation to the Pattons. Plaintiff and Carlton Foods modified the Note, effective January 15, 1993, reducing the required payment to $107,916

---

4. At this time, small meat packing companies like Western and Braunfel were becoming obsolete as they could not compete with larger companies, and strict environmental standards were making it difficult to generate a profit. Also, in 1986 an ammonia explosion at one of the plants resulted in extensive litigation that drained the Pattons' financial resources.

5. Plaintiff has been unable to locate a copy of this outside appraisal but contends it is irrelevant. . . . Defendant maintains that since an appraisal was done it was possible to ascertain the fair market value of the companies at the time of sale . . . .

7. The stock purchase agreement allowed for increasing or decreasing the Note to reflect operational changes . . . .

principal, $23,067 in interest and $2,914 in default interest. Carlton Foods paid plaintiff $14,116 in 1995, $104,704 in 1996, and $85,350 in 1997, upon which the buyer's obligations were released.

Upon audit of plaintiff's 1990 return, the IRS determined the buyer's obligation had an ascertainable value equal to the face amount of the Note given to plaintiff. The IRS also concluded plaintiff was entitled to use the installment sale method to report the resulting long term capital gain of $202,344. Plaintiff paid the resulting deficiency of $56,656, filed a timely claim for refund, which was denied, and then filed a complaint in this court on January 29, 1996, seeking a refund of the $56,656 as well as $12,126.53 in interest. Plaintiff filed a motion for summary judgment on July 5, 2000, asserting the Note had no ascertainable value in 1990 based on the open transaction doctrine. On October 26, 2000, defendant submitted its cross-motion for summary judgment claiming: (1) the IRS properly determined that plaintiff should report the Note using the installment sale method, and (2) the tax assessed in 1990 was proper. The court heard oral argument on Thursday, March 8, 2001.

DISCUSSION . . .

Plaintiff maintains the Note should not be included when computing its 1990 income tax because it was uncertain when the Note would be paid in full. Plaintiff relies on the open transaction method of tax valuation when making its assertion. Defendant contends the open transaction method is limited to rare circumstances that do not exist in this case. Defendant also asserts plaintiff has failed to prove, either through evidence or expert testimony, that the Note had no ascertainable value in 1990. The proper method for reporting income from the Note, according to defendant, is to consider the transaction an installment sale.

The United States Supreme Court established the open transaction method in Burnet v. Logan, 283 U.S. 404 (1936). The doctrine applies in deferred payment cases with so much uncertainty that it is impossible to determine whether any profit will be realized, because income is contingent upon unknown factors. Id. at 413. Under these circumstances, the taxpayer first applies any payments received to his or her basis. Once they have recovered their basis, they report any additional payments as income. The taxpayer is not taxed on this income until there is certainty as to the amount of payments, if any, that should be taxed. Id. at 413-414.[8]

---

8. For example, a person sells property in a deferred payment sale for $1,000 in which the person's basis is $300. Under the open transaction method, the first $300 the person receives over time will be applied to the basis and is not reported as taxable income. Any remaining payments are then considered taxable income.

Since *Burnet v. Logan*, however, statutes, regulations and the courts have severely limited the use of the open transaction method. The doctrine now applies only in "rare and extraordinary cases," and is generally rejected "in favor of the best estimate of fair market value which the circumstances allow." Rosenberg v. United States, 3 Cl. Ct. 432, 438 (1983) (citing Campbell v. United States, 228 Ct. Cl. 661, 670-671, 661 F.2d 209 (1981); Estate of Bird v. United States, 534 F.2d 1214, 1218 (6th Cir. 1976); McCormac v. United States, 191 Ct. Cl. 483, 424 F.2d 607 (1970); Denver & Rio Grande W. R.R. v. United States, 162 Ct. Cl. 1, 318 F.2d 922 (1963); Grill v. United States, 157 Ct. Cl. 804, 303 F.2d 922 (1962); Garvey, Inc. v. United States, 1 Cl. Ct. 108, 123 (1983)).

In lieu of the open transaction doctrine, courts and the IRS favor reporting these transactions, in which the fair market value can be reasonably ascertained, as installment sales. Section 453(b)(1) of the Internal Revenue Code defines "installment sale" as "a disposition of property where at least 1 payment is to be received after the close of the taxable year in which the disposition occurs." I.R.C. §453(b)(1) (2000). The taxable income from an installment sale for a particular year is the "proportion of the payments received . . . which the gross profit . . . bears to the total contract price." I.R.C. §453(c). Thus, a taxpayer is only taxed for payments he or she received in a particular tax year. The taxable gain from these payments is determined by subtracting a proportion of the taxpayer's basis from the income received.[9] The purpose of installment sale reporting is "to relieve taxpayers . . . from having to pay an income tax in the year of sale based on the full amount of anticipated profits when in fact they had received in cash only a small portion of the sales price." Comm'r v. S. Texas Lumber Co., 333 U.S. 496 (1948).

Plaintiff relies heavily on *Burnet v. Logan*, maintaining the open transaction doctrine has retained viability and applies to this case. Plaintiff asserts the Note had no ascertainable value in 1990 because its payment was conditional on the future cash flow of Western and Braunfel, which were becoming economically obsolete. Plaintiff contends it was very uncertain whether it would ever receive payments because it was only entitled to 40% of the remaining cash flow after the buyer: (1) received a $150,000 management fee, and (2) paid principal and interest to the Senior Lenders. Indeed, plaintiff received no payments until five years after the closing.

This court has never found the open transaction doctrine to apply in a tax refund suit as it applies only in rare and extraordinary circumstances. This case is not one of those exceptional instances. A comparison to other

---

9. Defendant offered an example in its brief to clarify installment sale reporting. Suppose a taxpayer sells for $1,000 property in which his basis is $300. His total gain is $700, and tax will eventually be due on that income. If he receives the $1,000 purchase price in five equal installments of $200 per year for five years, he will report $140 ($200 times 300/1,000 [sic: 700/1,000—Eds.]) each year as income from the transaction ($60 of his basis is subtracted from the income each year). The entire $700 gain is dispersed over the five years the taxpayer receives payments . . . .

cases makes this clear. In *McCormac*, the Court of Claims rejected the application of the open transaction doctrine in a case similar to the one before this court. The taxpayers in *McCormac* had transferred the stock of a cemetery corporation to a non-profit corporation, in exchange for an agreement to receive 40% of the transferee's gross sales for the life of the cemetery. 191 Ct. Cl. at 490-491. The amount of gross sales was uncertain, and the life of the cemetery was an indefinite period. Id. The court agreed with the position of the IRS, set forth in Rev. Rul. 58-402, 1958-2 C.B. 15, that "contracts and claims to receive indefinite amounts, such as those received in exchange for stock in liquidation of a corporation, must be valued for Federal income tax purposes except in rare and extraordinary cases." Id. at 499. The court held: (1) the transfer constituted a closed transaction and (2) the entire proceeds the taxpayer received in the year the agreement was executed had an ascertainable fair market value. Id. at 497.

The present case involves the same type of transaction as *McCormac*— the transfer of stock in exchange for a promise to repay in amounts dependent on the corporation's financial success. In fact, the present case contains even less uncertainty than *McCormac* because the Note was due in full by September 1, 1995. Plaintiff was well aware of the amount of the Note and the deadline for repayment. As held in *McCormac*, the entire proceeds plaintiff received in 1990 had an ascertainable fair market value. The face value of the Note represented this value.

In addition, another case directly on point is *Campbell*. Like the present case, it involved a testamentary trust selling stock for a small, family-owned business in return for cash, several notes, and stock in the purchasing corporation. 228 Ct. Cl. at 665. The Court of Claims rejected plaintiff's assertion that it was impossible to know whether plaintiff would ever receive payment because the future of the business was uncertain. Id. at 671. The sale was in fact not an "inherently speculative undertaking" that involved "a totally new and untested business whose only backing lay in the hope of things to come." Id. The business had been in operation for years, so it was somewhat predictable what its current value and potential was. Id. The court denied open transaction treatment because it "is not warranted every time . . . operations are deemed speculative." Id. at 670-671. The sale contained sufficient information "from which willing buyers and willing sellers could construct soundly based equations of value." Id. at 671.

Although the future success of Western and Braunfel was in doubt at the time of sale, this alone is not enough to require open transaction treatment. Plaintiff's business was not new and untested as it had been in operation for quite some time. Like the transaction in *Campbell*, the sale was not an inherently speculative undertaking. There was enough information in place at the time of sale for plaintiff and W-B to determine the value of the company, as evident in the outside appraisal done for W-B. Plaintiff and W-B agreed on a sale price, and the Note reflects a portion of this price. The fair market value of the Note in 1990, therefore, was its face value.

At oral argument, plaintiff asked the court to consider what actually happened to the value of the Note after the 1990 transaction, as proof that its value was unascertainable. In particular, plaintiff emphasized the modifications made to the Note's value and the actual dates payments were received. This argument is unpersuasive. At issue in this case is plaintiff's 1990 tax liability. Therefore, the court will only look at the particular tax year in question and not consider events happening subsequent to that period. Modifications made to the Note's value in later years would presumably be taken into account in plaintiff's income tax liability for those particular years. Plaintiff has not contested its income tax liability for years other than 1990, so it is unnecessary for the court to consider these later periods.

The court determines, therefore, that plaintiff cannot invoke the open transaction doctrine in this case. The proper way for plaintiff to report the income from this transaction was as an installment sale. Indeed, this is what the Commissioner concluded when determining plaintiff owed a $56,656 deficiency. Plaintiff has failed to offer enough proof to rebut the presumption that the decision of the Commissioner was correct. Plaintiff solicited no expert testimony on valuation and offers no evidence, besides a naked assertion of the facts, to support its claim that the value of the Note was unascertainable in 1990. When considered in light of the large body of case law discouraging the use of the open transaction doctrine, this assertion is insufficient for plaintiff to rebut the presumption of correctness. See Celotex Corp. v. Catrett, 477 U.S. 317 (1986) ("the plain language of Rule 56(c) mandates the entry of summary judgment, after adequate time for discovery and upon motion, against a party who fails to make a showing sufficient to establish the existence of an element essential to that party's case, and on which the party will bear the burden of proof at trial.").

CONCLUSION

For the above-stated reasons, defendant's motion for summary judgment is hereby allowed. Plaintiff's motion for summary judgment is denied. Accordingly, the Clerk is directed to dismiss plaintiff's complaint. No costs.

It is so ordered.

Notes and Questions

1. *Contingent payment sales.* An independent appraiser was able to put a value on the businesses in *Bernice Patton Testamentary Trust*. Why then was the amount of the note left subject to adjustment?

Sales with contingent terms are quite common when the parties cannot agree on price. Often, the seller of a business is far more optimistic about its future prospects than the buyer, and she will demand a higher price than the buyer is willing to pay. The buyer might pay the higher price if he were certain that the seller's expectations would materialize, but this will not be known until after the business is transferred. Making a part of the purchase price contingent on future profits bridges the gap—if the profits the seller anticipates materialize, the seller receives additional consideration; if the profits fail to materialize, the buyer's cost does not increase.

Jeffrey L. Kwall, Out with the Open-Transaction Doctrine: A New Theory for Taxing Contingent Payment Sales, 81 N.C. L. Rev. 977, 979 (2003) (footnotes omitted). Business people often refer to such contingent payment arrangements as "earn outs." Observe that while the Pattons continued to run the businesses for the new owners after the sale, their right to a share of its cash flow was subordinated to the new owners and their outside lenders. Why?

  2. *Open transaction doctrine.* Burnet v. Logan, 283 U.S. 404 (1931), concerned the sale of stock of a corporation that owned an interest in an iron mine in return for an immediate cash payment plus subsequent annual production-based payments (cents per ton of ore). The IRS computed the value of the production payments by estimating the mine's ore reserves and the rate at which they would be extracted, and used that value to determine the amount of realized gain or loss for the year of the stock sale, 1916. See §1001(b). The taxpayer, who used the cash receipts and disbursements method of accounting, reported no gain in 1916, nor did she include as income any of the annual production payments received from 1917 to 1920, on the grounds that until the total payments actually received by virtue of the sale equaled her basis in the stock, she had no gain.

> As annual payments on account of extracted ore come in they can be readily apportioned first as return of capital and later as profit. The liability for income tax ultimately can be fairly determined without resort to mere estimates, assumptions and speculation. When the profit, if any, is actually realized, the taxpayer will be required to respond. The consideration for the sale was $2,200,000.00 in cash and the promise of future money payments wholly contingent upon facts and circumstances not possible to foretell with anything like fair certainty. The promise was in no proper sense equivalent to cash. It had no ascertainable fair market value. The transaction was not a closed one. Respondent might never recoup her capital investment from payments only conditionally promised. Prior to 1921 all receipts from the sale of her shares amounted to less than their value on March 1, 1913. She properly demanded the return of her capital investment before assessment of any taxable profit based on conjecture.

283 U.S. at 412-413. By allowing tax-free return of capital first, the open transaction doctrine granted some sellers maximum tax deferral. The test for open transaction reporting, whether the contingent payments have an "ascertainable fair market value," was not further defined, and for many years thereafter the tax authorities were at pains to reign in this exception to immediate reckoning of gain or loss.

3. *Installment sales.* Even if the amount of future payments is fixed, immediate inclusion of the full realized gain can present a hardship where the seller receives insufficient cash in the year of sale to pay the tax. Such liquidity problems are often avoided by §453, which provides that the gain on an installment sale of property is to be reported year by year according to the proportion of the total payments received each year. §453(a)-(c). While categorized as a method of accounting, installment reporting functions as a nonrecognition rule. See §453(c) ("income recognized"). The installment method is not available for dispositions of publicly traded securities, inventories of personal property, or dealer dispositions of personal or real property other than farming property, residential time shares, and residential lots, §453(b)(2), (k), (l), and any depreciation recapture triggered by the sale must be immediately recognized, §453(i).

The current version of §453, enacted by the Installment Sales Revision Act of 1980, applies the installment method to contingent payment sales. See §453(f)(8)(B), (k)(2). The regulations provide timing rules for contingent payment sales where there is (1) a stated maximum selling price, (2) a fixed maximum payment period, and (3) neither a stated maximum selling price nor a fixed maximum period. Reg. §15a.453-1(c). Where there is a stated maximum selling price, the normal installment reporting method (pro-rata return of capital) is applied by using the stated maximum price calculate to the gain and total payments to be received. Where there is no stated maximum selling price but payments are to be received over a maximum period, basis is recovered in equal amounts each year within that period. If the sale agreement specifies neither a maximum selling price nor a maximum payment period, then basis is recovered in equal increments over a 15-year period, commencing with the year of sale. The regulation warns, however, that a contract that provides neither a maximum price nor a maximum period presents the question "whether a sale realistically has occurred or whether, in economic effect, payments received under the agreement are in the nature of rent or royalty income. Arrangements of this sort will be closely scrutinized." Reg. §15a.453-1(c)(4). What, if anything, remains of the open transaction doctrine?

4. *Election out.* The installment method applies generally to both individual and business taxpayers, regardless of whether they otherwise employ cash or accrual-basis accounting. Installment reporting, however, is subject to an election out, §453(d), so pro-rata cost recovery is the default rule. A seller might elect out to avoid an anticipated increase in the capital gain tax rate or because the taxpayer has losses for the year of sale that would shelter the gain. But can one elect out in the case of a contingent payment sale to obtain the benefits of open transaction reporting? That is, can election out be employed to defer rather than accelerate gain inclusion? The regulations warn, "Only in rare and extraordinary cases will the fair market value of the contingent payments be treated as not reasonably ascertainable." In that elusive (nonexistent?) case, however, open transaction reporting apparently survives. Reg. §1.1001-1(g)(2)(ii), -1(g)(3).

5. *Interest on deferred payments.* If a deferred payment sale does not call for adequate stated interest then in most cases interest will be imputed and a portion of the contract price recharacterized for tax purposes as interest rather than sale proceeds. Such interest imputation may affect the character of the income (ordinary income versus capital gain) and might also alter the timing of income inclusion. See Chapter 6C.2 below, concerning original issue discount. In applying the installment sale rules, "[n]either interest, whether stated or unstated, nor original issue discount is considered to be part of the selling price" used to compute gain and apportion it among taxable years. Reg. §15a.453-1(b)(2)(ii).

Problems

1. *A* sells property to *B* in year 1 for $25,000 plus interest. The principal is payable $5,000 at the time of sale and $10,000 in each of years 2 and 3. *A*'s adjusted basis in the property is $15,000. What is *A*'s gain from the sale in each of years 1, 2, and 3 under the installment method of §453?

2. *C* sells property to *D* in year 1 for $25,000 cash plus assumption of a $30,000 mortgage. The cash is to be paid $5,000 in year 1 and $10,000 in each of years 2 and 3, with interest payable annually on the unpaid balance. *C*'s basis is $45,000. When will *C*'s gain be taxed under §453?

3. *E* sold the stock of his closely held corporation to *F* for a promise to pay $2,000,000 ratably over ten years ($200,000 per year), with interest each year on the unpaid balance. In addition, *F* is to pay 1 percent of profits from the acquired business, for ten years, but not more than a total (under this provision) of $3,000,000. Profits have recently run around $3,000,000 per year, and *E's* basis is $1,200,000. How will *E* and *F* be taxed?

4. What if the facts were as in Problem 3 but with all the dollar figures multiplied by ten? Consult §453A.

5. Assume that the facts are as in Problem 1, but that *B* is *A*'s brother. What if at the start of year 2 *B* sells the property to an unrelated party, *G*, for an immediate cash payment of $27,000? §453(e), (f)(1). Does it matter whether the sale to *G* was contemplated or arranged at the time of *A*'s sale to *B*?

F.   CAPITAL GAINS

From 1921 through 1986, long-term capital gains, even if realized and recognized, were taxed at bargain rates, generally half or less than half of the rate applicable to ordinary income. In 1986 the top rate on ordinary income was 50 percent; the top rate on net capital gain was 20 percent. That differential was implemented by allowing a deduction for 60 percent of net capital gain.

The 1986 Act repealed this differential, adopting a top rate of 28 percent for all income, ordinary and capital gain alike. Repeal of the capital gain preference was perhaps the single most significant structural change in the 1986 Act.

Capital gains accrue disproportionately to very high income taxpayers. For taxpayers with incomes over $200,000, a substantial portion of their total income, in the aggregate, was capital gain. For such taxpayers, in the aggregate, therefore, one may think of the radical reduction in the top ordinary income rate from 50 percent to 28 percent as having been substantially offset by a rate increase on capital gain income from 20 percent to 28 percent. That trade was perhaps the central political deal in getting the 1986 Act adopted.

But it has come undone. First, in response to growing deficits the top rate on ordinary income was raised to 31 percent in 1990. In 1993 ordinary income brackets of 36 and 39.6 were added. The top rate for capital gains remained at 28 percent, and so a rate differential of 11.6 percentage points was reinstated.[7]

In 1997 the basic capital gain rate itself was reduced from 28 percent to 20 percent. This is the same top rate as before 1986 and is just a hair above half of 39.6, which was then the top rate on ordinary income. By 2003 the top rate on ordinary income had been reduced to 35 percent, §1(i)(2), while the basic capital gain rate had come down to 15 percent, §1(h)(1)(C), less than half the top bracket rate, or a differential of 20 percentage points.

Even while there was not a substantial rate differential, capital gains were still highly preferred for a few taxpayers due to the continuation of the capital loss limitation in §1211. Losses from the sale or exchange of capital assets held for business or investment are deductible, but only to the extent of capital gains plus $3,000 per year. For a taxpayer with excess capital losses, therefore, capital gains are effectively tax free because every extra dollar of capital gain permits the deduction of an additional dollar of capital loss.

One of the functions of the capital loss limitation is to assure that the preferential rate on capital gains applies only to net capital gain. Without it, taxpayers could separate capital gains and losses into alternate years, applying the bargain rate to gross capital gains and deducting capital losses against ordinary income. But the capital loss limitation was not relaxed in 1986 or thereafter. Apparently it has a broader function than just protecting the capital gain rate. At least part of that broader function is to limit deductions for taxpayers who sell their losing investments while simply holding onto

---

7. Indeed, the statute as enacted in 1986 specified that if the rates in the rate schedules were ever increased to more than 28 percent the rate on capital gains would be limited to 28 percent. It is hard to see how that provision was anything more than a nonbinding statement of intention, but its force was not put to the test.

their winners. The matter of limitations on loss deductions generally is taken up in Chapter 14.

Questions of timing are often mitigated or aggravated by special treatment of capital gains because timing may affect capital gain characterization. The questions of realization and recognition raised in this chapter are often suffused with capital gain significance: Lessee improvements treated as rent, for example, would be taxable as ordinary income while gain on subsequent sale of the real estate would probably be capital gain. In such cases, capital gain treatment would likely add to the value of deferral. In general, in thinking about particular questions of the timing of income or deductions, one needs to be alert to the possible characterization effects of the timing decision. (*Characterization* is a nonstatutory word of art referring to the sorting out of capital gain or loss items from ordinary income items.)

In order to have a capital gain, a taxpayer must first have owned something that qualifies as a *capital asset*. Gain from a sale of inventory, for example, is not capital gain because inventory is not a capital asset. §1221(1). But ownership of a capital asset is not enough; capital gain treatment applies only to gain from a *sale or exchange*. For example, interest is ordinary income even though it represents gain from investments in bonds, which do qualify as capital assets.

A host of statutory provisions outside §§1201-1223 (and not a few judicial and administrative interpretations of the basic provisions) prescribe that various specific transactions shall or shall not be treated as involving sales or exchanges or as involving capital assets, but the root idea is one of liquidation, complete or partial, of some sort of an investment.

Are there any persuasive justifications for taxing capital gains at a lower rate than ordinary income? We will return to this topic in greater detail in Chapters 19 to 21, but it is not too soon to start thinking about this question. Consider particularly the following possibilities:

1. Capital gains should be taxed at lower rates to alleviate the burden on a taxpayer whose property has increased in value over many years from having the profits on sale taxed at graduated tax rates designed for a single year's income.

2. Capital gains should be taxed at lower rates because otherwise the tax will create an excessive deterrent to realization of gains. An investor who is deterred from selling by the prospect of a tax that can be avoided more-or-less indefinitely by holding onto her present investment is said to be *locked in.* Lower tax rates on capital gains are defended as mitigating such capital lock-in. Some economists have argued that a reduction in capital gain rates would actually increase tax collections by virtue of the increase in realizations it would encourage. (Others have argued that any such increase in taxes collected would be only temporary.)

3. Capital gains should be taxed at lower rates than ordinary income since often they represent only paper gains due to inflation, not real income.

4. Capital gains sometimes represent only paper profits in another sense when they reflect changes in capitalization rates. Consider, for example, a bondholder whose bonds go up in value because of a drop in market interest rates. Is such an investor any better off than if interest rates had remained unchanged? Even if he sells at a gain, he will only be able to reinvest at the new lower interest rate. Insofar as he measures his well-being in terms of the level of income he can maintain indefinitely, therefore, the rise in capital value does not represent a substantial change.

5. Lower rates for capital gains are desirable because they encourage private investment — particularly speculative investment — which is good for the economy.

G.   *INFLATION*

The inflation argument deserves elaboration. Inflation affects income taxes in two quite different ways.

1.   Bracket Creep

The first way inflation affects income tax is through the phenomenon of "bracket creep." Throughout most of the history of our income tax, rates, as a function of real income, were raised automatically over time by the operation of inflation because the real-dollar value of each rate bracket was reduced.

Consider, for example, an unmarried taxpayer with a salary of $22,000. Applying the rate schedule in §1(c), without inflation adjustments, would produce a tax of $2,350. (Fifteen percent of $17,000, the amount by which $22,000 exceeds $5,000 of personal exemption and standard deduction.)

Now suppose salary goes up 20 percent, to $24,400, in a period when the cost of living also goes up by just 20 percent. In the absence of inflation adjustments, that would produce taxable income of $19,400 and a tax of $3,111.50. Part of the increase in tax bill just reflects inflation, but part of it is real, resulting from the fact that a smaller portion of real income now falls within the exemption and standard deduction, and the fact that part of the income has now advanced to the 28 percent bracket. If $3,111.50 is itself restated in terms of earlier year dollars (divide by 120 percent), the amount is $2,592.92, an advance of 242.92, or 10.3 percent over the earlier figure.

Now the statute contains provisions to eliminate bracket creep by indexing the relevant dollar figures in the Code. See §1(f) (rate brackets),

§63(c)(4) (standard deduction), and §151(d)(3) (personal exemptions). Many other dollar figures that impose limitations, for example, are similarly subject to indexing.

Is this indexation of figures in the Code itself a good idea? Does it accomplish anything that could not have been done by the Congress amending the Code from time to time? Has it contributed to the persistent government deficit problem? Is it likely ever to be repealed? One suggestion for achieving deficit reduction in 1990 was to postpone inflation adjustments for a year; would that be a good way to move?

2. Income Mismeasurement

Quite apart from bracket creep, inflation causes a mismeasurement of income from capital by including unreal gains. Thus if Genevra buys stock for $100 and sells it for $150 she will have a taxable gain of $50, even if price levels have gone up 20 percent (or 40 to 60) during the time she has held the stock. Her real gain in that case would be only $30 (or $10 or –$10), but she will be taxed on her full nominal gain of $50. If her tax rate is 20 percent, the tax will be $10 and her after-tax gain will be nominally $40, but really only $20 (or $0 or –$20), and so her effective rate of tax in real terms will be 33.3 percent (or 100 percent, or –100 percent!). This last figure does not denote a negative tax but rather a positive tax on a negative real gain.

What is the correct cure for this problem? Should capital gain rates be reduced generally to deal with it? Would indexation of basis be too complicated to administer and audit? Are there other objections to that fix? The House of Representatives once passed a general basis indexing provision, but none has yet found its way into the law. Indexing basis is regularly discussed as an alternative (or a supplement!) to capital gain rate reductions.

Gains on sale are not the only item of income subject to mismeasurement by reason of inflation. Consider an ordinary savings account paying 6 percent interest, while inflation proceeds at an annual rate of 4 percent. How much real income does such an account produce? How will it be taxed? What is the real effective rate of income tax if the nominal rate is 15 percent? 25 percent?

What would be required to measure income accurately in this regard? Would that be practical?

Consider deductions. Interest expense will tend to be overstated as a result of inflation while depreciation expense will get understated. What sorts of adjustments would be required to get rid of these mismeasurements?

What would be involved in a comprehensive elimination of inflation effects from the income tax base? Would anything less than comprehensive elimination be desirable?

H.   TAXING CONSUMPTION INSTEAD OF TOTAL ACCRETION

Reconsider the famous definition of personal income formulated by the economist Henry Simons:

> Personal income may be defined as the algebraic sum of (1) the market value of rights exercised in consumption and (2) the change in the value of the store of property rights between the beginning and end of the period in question. [Henry C. Simons, Personal Income Taxation 50 (1938)]

The principal purpose of the Simons definition is to eliminate conditions as to source of funds from the income definition, not to introduce distinctions as to use. Cash receipts are to be taxed whether spent or saved and from whatever source derived. But of course the tax does not attach to all receipts, as we have seen particularly in Chapters 3 and 4. And it has to include some things or benefits received in kind, without any cash receipt. Chapter 2 is largely about the taxability of consumption benefits received in kind, and this chapter is about accumulation benefits. So the Simons definition can be taken initially as rhetoric about a comprehensive income tax, but when one looks at it harder, it becomes an assertion that in judging individual hard cases of inclusion in or exclusion (or deduction) from the income tax base, the underlying issue is whether the item in question represents either consumption or accumulation.

Can the issues that arise under an income tax be usefully restated as issues of defining consumption and accumulation? Which issues in this and prior chapters are consumption issues? Which are accumulation issues? Are there general differences between the two? Is it true that problems of tax deferral are generally problems of defining the accumulation component of taxable income and vice versa?

Approaching the matter from this direction at least raises the question of whether these two components should be aggregated and treated as one. Would it be a better idea to focus the personal income tax on total personal consumption instead of accretion? The personal income tax could be transformed into a graduated personal consumption expenditure tax by allowing an immediate deduction for all business and investment expenditures, including accumulation of substantial bank balances. The corollary of immediate deduction would be a zero basis for all such investments so that on sale or other disposition the whole proceeds would be taxable. In addition, substantial loan proceeds would be taxable and repayments deductible. The tax would be based simply on net aggregate cash flow from all business and investment activities, plus such noncash consumption items as are decided to be included. The net effect would be an extension to all savings of the treatment now given to unrealized capital appreciation and qualified retirement savings.

The present income tax is sometimes now described as a mongrel hybrid of accretion income taxation and a consumption tax. Full-blown accretion taxation would involve problems of valuation and liquidity that have led to the present compromises. Cash-flow taxation would generally avoid those problems and arguably achieve a more comprehensive taxation of the consumption component of accretion. Would that represent a desirable way to go?

In present political discourse some have advocated replacing the income tax with other sorts of consumption taxes. The most familiar, perhaps, is a retail sales tax, which many of our states already impose. This tax is paid to the government by retail sellers, but they collect it from their customers. The tax does not normally involve private persons in tax reporting or collection activities. It also cannot be conveniently graduated in relation to customer wealth or well being as reflected by aggregate income or consumption levels.

Other national governments rely on a value added tax (VAT) for a substantial part of their tax revenues. A VAT is similar to a retail sales tax, but is collected in stages from producers and others in the chain of distribution of goods, so that enforcement does not depend entirely on catching the retail seller. Each seller subject to the tax typically takes credit, immediately, for the tax paid by those from whom it buys inventories, supplies, or capital equipment. As a result the burden of the tax falls only on final sales even though each seller is charged for all his sales without distinction between final and intermediate sales.

When most people think of taxing consumption they probably think of a VAT or retail sales tax. One advantage of such taxes is that they are collected from business firms and do not require individual or household returns. But a corresponding disadvantage is that such taxes cannot be graduated by reference to total individual or household consumption because sellers have no way of knowing whether the purchasers to whom they sell are big spenders overall or not. (Some of those currently advocating replacement of the income tax undoubtedly regard this as an advantage.)

One particularly ingenious proposal is that of Hall and Rabushka for a graduated Flat Tax.[8] This is essentially like a VAT with an additional wrinkle: business firms would deduct wages and salaries but recipients would be taxed on these items at the general VAT rate. In effect, workers are added to the chain of VAT payers at the earliest stage.

This wrinkle has two notable advantages. First, it facilitates the provision of a rather generous exemption on a one-per-worker basis, which has the effect of making the average tax rate a significantly rising function of worker income at lower income levels. Second, it increases the chance that workers generally will accept a continuation of present price levels under the new tax regime. Without this wrinkle it is widely assumed that workers would resist any cut in pre-tax pay to reflect elimination of the income tax and that consumer prices would have to go up to pay for the new VAT; while this

8. Robert E. Hall & Alvin Rabushka, The Flat Tax (2d ed. 1995).

would itself be only a one-time jolt of inflation, it could have undesirable destabilizing effects.

One question raised by the Flat Tax proposal is whether the public would ever buy a personal tax on wages and salaries but not on interest, dividends, rent, capital gains, and other returns to investment. In theory, with no deduction for payors, such items are effectively taxed at the business firm level, at the (top) single Flat Tax rate. What do you think of that theory? If you believe it, what do you think the prospects are for getting a substantial number of people to understand and believe it?

A second question is whether a majority wants to abandon graduation of rates and the effort to make the well-to-do pay tax at rates significantly higher than any widely applicable general rate. Many of those currently advocating a retail sales tax, VAT, or Flat Tax to replace the present income tax (and estate and gift taxes) are doubtless pleased by this feature of the proposed taxes. If an effective majority insists on preserving upward graduation, then a VAT or Flat Tax could be combined with a graduated, personal cash-flow tax for higher income taxpayers. One proposal along these lines is titled "The USA Tax System," in which "USA" stands for Unlimited Savings Account.[9] In addition to combining a VAT-type business tax with a graduated consumption-type personal tax, this proposal attempts to preserve certain popular features of the present income tax (like the mortgage interest deduction).

References

A. Unrealized Gains: Powell, Stock Dividends, Direct Taxes, and the Sixteenth Amendment, 20 Colum. L. Rev. 536 (1920); Seligman, Implications and Effects of the Stock Dividend Decision, 21 Colum. L. Rev. 313 (1921); Shakow, Taxation Without Realization: A Proposal for Accrual, U. Pa. L. Rev. 1111 (1986); Slawson, Taxing as Ordinary Income the Appreciation of Publicly Held Stock, 76 Yale L. J. 623 (1967).

B. Time Value of Money: Cannellos & Kleinbard, The Miracle of Compound Interest, 38 Tax. L. Rev. 565 (1983); Halperin, Interest in Disguise: Taxing the "Time Value of Money," 95 Yale L. J. 506 (1986); Lokken, The Time Value of Money Rules, 42 Tax L. Rev. 1 (1986).

C. Realization: Asimow, Section 1041 Needs No Cure, 69 Taxes 37 (1991); Burford, Tax Treatment of Tenant-Added Leasehold Improvements, 16 S. Cal Tax Inst. 183 (1964); Warren, Financial Contract Innovation and Income Tax Policy, 107 Harv. L. Rev. 460-492 (1993); James M. Peaslee,

---

9. See the report prepared for Alliance USA by Ernest S. Christian and George J. Schutzer, Unlimited Savings Allowance (USA) Tax System, 66 Tax Notes 1481 (1995).

Modifications of Nondebt Financial Instruments as Deemed Exchanges, 95 Tax Notes 737 (2002).

D. Nonrecognition Exchanges: Duhl, Like-Kind Exchanges Under Section 1031: Multiparty Exchanges, Nonsimultaneous Exchanges, and Exchanges of Partnership Interests, 58 Taxes 949 (1980); Gannet, Tax Advantages and Risks in Real Property Exchanges: Voluntary and Involuntary, 25 N.Y.U. Inst. on Fed. Taxn. 1 (1967); Goldstein & Lewis, Tax Treatment of Like-Kind Exchanges of Property Used in a Trade or Business or for Investment, 5 Rev. Taxn. Individuals 195 (1981); Guerin, A Proposed Test for Evaluating Multiparty Like-Kind Exchanges, 35 Tax L. Rev. 545 (1980); Mandell, Tax Aspects of Sales and Leasebacks as Practical Devices for Transfer and Operation of Real Property, 18 N.Y.U. Inst. on Fed. Taxn. 17 (1960); Fellows & Yuhas, Like-Kind Exchanges and Related Parties Under New Section 1031(f), 68 Tax Notes 352 (1990).

E. Deferred and Contingent Payment Sales: Note, Fairness and Tax Avoidance in the Taxation of Installment Sales, 100 Harv. L. Rev. 403 (1986); David C. Garlock et al., Federal Income Taxation of Debt Instruments (5th ed. 2005).

F. Capital Gains: Blum, A Handy Summary of the Capital Gains Argument, 35 Taxes 247 (1957); Clark, The Paradox of Capital Gains: Taxable Income That Ought Not to Be Currently Taxed, 2 House Comm. on Ways and Means, Tax Revision Compendium 1243 (1959); Gravelle & Lindsey, Capital Gains, 38 Tax Notes 397 (1988); Noël B. Cunninghan & Deborah H. Schenck, The Case for a Capital Gains Preference, 48 Tax L. Rev. 319 (1993).

G. Inflation: New York State Bar Assoc., Report on Inflation Adjustment to the Basis of Capital Assets, 48 Tax Notes 759 (1990).

H. Taxing Consumption Instead of Total Accretion: David Bradford & U.S. Department of the Treasury, Blueprints for Basic Tax Reform (2d ed. 1984); W. Andrews, D. Bradford, R. Goode, M. Graetz, E. Howrey, S. Hymans, & J. Minarik, What Should Be Taxed: Income or Expenditure? (J. Pechman ed., 1980); N. Kaldor, An Expenditure Tax (1955); Andrews, A Consumption Type or Cash Flow Personal Income Tax, 87 Harv. L. Rev. 1113 (1974); Warren, Fairness and a Consumption-Type or Cash Flow Personal Income Tax, 88 Harv. L. Rev. 931 (1975); Andrews, Fairness and the Personal Income Tax: A Reply to Professor Warren, 88 Harv. L. Rev. 947 (1975); Warren, Would A Consumption Tax Be Fairer Than an Income Tax?, 89 Yale L.J. 1081 (1980); Shachar, From Income to Consumption Tax: Criteria for Rules of Transition, 97 Harv. L. Rev. 1581 (1984); Kotlikoff, The Case for the Value-Added Tax, 39 Tax Notes 239 (1988). Warren, How Much Capital Income Taxed under an Income Tax Is Exempt under a Cash Flow Tax?,

52 Tax L. Rev. 1 (1996); Warren, The Proposal for an "Unlimited Savings Allowance," 68 Tax Notes 1103 (August 28, 1995); Warren, Three Versions of Tax Reform, 39 Wm. & Mary L. Rev. 157 (1997); David F. Bradford, The X Tax in the World Economy (2004); Edward J. McCaffery, A New Understanding of Tax, 103 Mich. L. Rev. 807 (2005).

Chapter 6 — *Return of Capital and Timing Issues*

A. RETURN OF CAPITAL

1. Timing Alternatives

Assume that *B* enters into an agreement with an insurance company under which the company promises to pay him $1,000 on each of the first five anniversaries of the date of contracting. This arrangement is known as a term-certain annuity because it calls for annual (i.e., annuity) payments over a fixed period of years (a term certain). (In contrast, under the more common life annuity contract, explored below in Chapter 6B, the duration of the annuity is tied to the life-span of one or more individuals.) The insurance company charges *B* a single premium price of $3,790. This price guarantees *B* a 10 percent compound annual rate of return. How should the payments *B* receives under the contract be taxed?

One thing that we can say for sure is that over the life of the contract, *B* will receive $1,210 more than his premium ($5,000 − $3,790 = $1,210). Over the five-year period, this $1,210 is the extent of *B*'s enrichment; the remaining amount received, $3,790, simply returns *B*'s invested capital and so should not be taxed. While these aggregate results seem indisputable, the federal income tax is an annual levy, and it is not so clear how the payment received in a particular year should be allocated between income and return of capital.

There are a number of reasonable alternatives. At one extreme, the taxpayer might argue that he has not experienced a gain until such time as he has gotten back the full amount invested in the contract while thereafter all amounts received are income. This view supports a return-of-capital (ROC) first approach to tax timing. As applied to the five $1,000 annual payments received by *B*, the following amounts would be excludible.

Method	Year 1	2	3	4	5	Total
ROC first	$1,000	$1,000	$1,000	$790	$0	$3,790

Accordingly, *B* would owe no tax on the annuity payments received in the first three years, but $210 of the year four payment would be included in income, as would the full $1,000 received in year five.

On these facts the government might argue that *B* is assured a $1,210 gain the moment the contract is signed, and under a receipts-based annual income tax, that increase in wealth is most accurately reflected by attributing the first dollars received as income. Taxing the income component first is equivalent to providing tax-free return of capital last, and *B*'s annual exclusion would look like this.

Method	Year 1	2	3	4	5	Total
ROC last	$0	$790	$1,000	$1,000	$1,000	$3,790

Intermediate approaches are possible, of course. The most obvious compromise would be to treat an appropriate fixed proportion of each payment as excludible (return of capital) and the remainder income, with the proportion determined by the ratio of the amount invested to the total payments to be received. In *B*'s case, the proportion is $3,790/$5,000, or 75.8 percent, and this pro-rata return of capital approach yields these annual exclusions.

Method	Year 1	2	3	4	5	Total
Pro-rata ROC	$758	$758	$758	$758	$758	$3,790

These three timing rules (ROC first, last, and pro rata) represent the extremes and the midpoint, but they do not exhaust the set of defensible candidates. Notice that the annuity purchaser (*B*, in our example) is in effect lending money to the contract issuer in return for the insurance company's promise to pay back the amount borrowed together with 10 percent interest in five equal annual installments. Each annual payment, therefore, might be thought to consist of interest on the outstanding amount of the loan plus a partial repayment of principal. In the first year, B has $3,790 on loan at 10 percent, so $379 of the first-year payment is interest income and the balance ($621) is principal repayment. Consequently, in the second year the loan balance is only $3,169 (= $3,790 − $621), and B earns only $316.90 interest, making $683.10 of the year two annuity payment principal. That principal repayment in turn reduces the outstanding balance of the loan in year three to $2485.90, and so on. Conceptualizing the annuity contract as a loan to the insurance company repaid via level amortization yields an annual exclusion that increases year by year. As under the typical home mortgage, the payment made in the first year (when the loan balance is highest) largely consists of interest, but over time the small annual reductions in principal cause each succeeding payment to be composed of less interest and more principal. Hence, this mortgage amortization approach produces a schedule of exclusions that taxes more of the income in the early years and gives the taxpayer back-loaded return of capital.

	Year					
Method	1	2	3	4	5	Total
Back-loaded ROC	$621	$683	$751	$826	$909	$3,790

Finally, note that B's five-year term-certain annuity contract could be viewed as the combination or bundling of five $1,000 endowment contracts. Instead of buying the right to this series of payments from one company, B might have bought five separate contracts from five different companies, each giving him the right to a single payment (endowment) of $1,000 on specified future dates. B might buy a contract that pays out in one year from Insurer One, an endowment that matures in two years from Insurer Two, etc. Assume that each insurance company is willing to pay B 10 percent interest compounded annually for the use of his money. Then Insurer One would charge a premium of $909 for the commitment to pay $1,000 one year hence ($909 × 1.10 = $1,000); Insurer Two has use of the premium for two years before making the $1,000 payment and so would charge a premium of only $826 ($826 × $(1.10)^2$ = $1,000); Insurer Three would charge only $751 today in exchange for a payment of $1,000 three years hence ($751 × $(1.10)^3$ = $1,000); and so on. Thus, disaggregating the annuity contract into independent endowment contracts produces a set of premiums that is exactly the reverse of the mortgage amortization schedule. Viewed from this perspective, B's exclusion should give him front-loaded return of capital.

	Year					
Method	1	2	3	4	5	Total
Front-loaded ROC	$909	$826	$751	$683	$621	$3,790

To summarize, in the simple term-certain annuity transaction there are at least five plausible candidates for allocating each annuity payment between the interest (income) component and (excludible) return of capital, as shown in Table 6-1.

TABLE 6-1

Method	Year					Total
	1	2	3	4	5	
ROC first	$1,000	$1,000	$1,000	$790	$0	$3,790
Front-loaded ROC	$909	$826	$751	$683	$621	$3,790
Pro-rata ROC	$758	$758	$758	$758	$758	$3,790
Back-loaded ROC	$621	$683	$751	$826	$909	$3,790
ROC last	$0	$790	$1,000	$1,000	$1,000	$3,790

These methods all have in common the taxation of $1,210 in total gain over the life of the contract, but the allocation of any particular payment between income and return of capital is somewhat arbitrary. (Because money is fungible tracing is not possible — the dollar bills that *B* receives from the insurance company do not come with labels attached that would allow him to tell whether this is the money he used to buy the contract originally.)

Questions

1. What is at stake in the choice between these alternatives? In general, which method would taxpayers prefer? Which would the Treasury prefer?

2. If we are dealing with a life annuity rather than a term-certain annuity, the ROC last method becomes impractical. Do you see why?

FAIRFIELD PLAZA, INC. v. COMMISSIONER
39 T.C. 706 (1963)

BRUCE, *Judge:* Respondent determined deficiencies in income taxes of the petitioner for the years 1957 and 1958 in the amounts of $413.74 and $17,669.70, respectively.

We are called upon to determine (1) the proper allocation of the basis of a single tract of real estate to two portions of that tract, one of which was sold in 1957, the other in 1958, and (2) whether any part of an amount of $50,000 placed in escrow for improvements to the retained center portion, or the $40,146.32 actually expended for such improvements, is allocable to the basis of the parcel sold in 1957 or to the basis of that parcel and the parcel sold in 1958. . . .

OPINION

In 1955 petitioner purchased a 10-acre tract of real estate, located between 16th and 17th Streets in Huntington, W. Va., with the intention of developing the property into a shopping center. After grading had been completed, negotiations were begun with Big Bear Stores Co. pursuant to which petitioner was to build and lease to Big Bear a store on approximately 30 percent of the property, which portion has frontage on 17th Street.

Petitioner had difficulty in obtaining financing for the building, and in 1957 sold this easterly portion of the tract to Big Bear for $100,000, $50,000 of which was placed in escrow pending petitioner's completion of paving and lighting on the remainder of the tract.

In 1958 the western 30 percent of the tract, which has frontage on 16th Street, was sold to Paisley and associates for $150,000.

The parties agree that the $50,000 placed in escrow in the Big Bear sale should be taken into income in 1958.

The purchase price to petitioner in 1955 of the whole tract, including the basic cost of the land, commissions, interest, taxes, and legal fees and insurance, was $110,941.12. In addition, petitioner spent a net of $29,584.64 for engineering, grading, and other miscellaneous items which are to be capitalized. The first issue involves the allocation of the above amounts in the computation of the bases of the two parcels sold to Big Bear and Paisley, respectively.

It is the position of respondent that the allocation must be made as of the 1955 purchase date and that since the petitioner then intended to use the land for a shopping center the only proper method of allocation is on the basis of square footage. Respondent reasons that reciprocal easements for access and the very nature of a shopping center support his assertion that no portion of the property has a value greater than that of any other.

We agree with respondent that the allocation of basis is to be made as of 1955. Wellesley A. Ayling, 32 T.C. 704. It is the proper method of allocation which remains in issue.

Section 1.61-6, Income Tax Regs., provides that "When a part of a larger property is sold, the cost or other basis of the entire property shall be equitably apportioned among the several parts, ..." Such "equitable" apportionment demands that relative values be reflected. Accordingly, if one parcel is of greater value than another, apportionment solely on the basis of square footage appears inappropriate. Biscayne Bay Islands Co., 23 B.T.A. 731; Cleveland-Sandusky Brewing Corp., 30 T.C. 539; and see 3-A Mertens, Law of Federal Income Taxation, sec. 21.12, p. 43. It is, of course, true that

petitioner bears the burden of demonstrating the applicability of an allocation of basis other than that reflected in respondent's determinations.

We are satisfied from the evidence presented that despite the fact the
property was to be used as a shopping center, thus having an integrated
value, each lot or portion thereof reflecting upon each other portion, the
land fronting on 16th Street, which was sold to the Paisley group, had a
greater value than that reflected by a simple allocation of cost on the basis
of square footage. Sixteenth Street is one of Huntington's main thorough-
fares. Any business fronting thereon is inevitably in the public eye. Two
expert witnesses testified that the Paisley property had a value equal to
the remainder of the tract. Despite petitioner's intentions in 1955, we are
satisfied that this property had a fair market value in excess of the approximately 30.9 percent of original cost assigned thereto by respondent. On the
basis of all of the evidence, we have concluded that 40 percent of cost is
allocable to the Paisley parcel. While we have not rested our conclusion
thereon, it is significant that the sales price of the Paisley portion in 1958
was 50 percent greater than the price realized on the sale of the Big Bear
parcel which fronts on the less-traveled 17th Street. Nothing in the evidence
warrants a conclusion that the value of the 16th Street property increased so
markedly from 1955 to 1958 that such a percentage difference is explained
thereby. Yet, respondent valued the Big Bear and Paisley parcels almost
equally.

The opinion of the experts did not differ greatly with respect to the
relative value of the Big Bear parcel. Taking into account its frontage on 17th
Street as well as its accessibility by reason of easements across the remainder
of the tract, we have determined that the Big Bear parcel had a basis of
30 percent of the cost of the entire tract.

Respondent has argued that since the witnesses called by petitioner did
not specifically testify with respect to allocation as of 1955, their testimony
should be wholly disregarded. Petitioner contends, however, that there was
little or no change in the relative values of the parcels between 1955 and
1959. Such a posture of the facts is consistent with respondent's own
position, for his valuation as of 1955 reflects relative values which very closely
parallel the relative values disclosed by the county assessor's records as of
1959, upon which respondent places some emphasis. Thus, we are satisfied
that the relative values of the properties remained fairly constant over the
period in question and that the testimony of the expert witnesses called by
petitioner is not to be disregarded.

What we have said thus far resolves the allocation issue only in connection with those costs incurred as part of the purchase price or clearly measurable thereby. Such costs total $110,941.12. There remains $29,584.64,
consisting of grading and leveling expenses, engineering costs, and other
related amounts incurred after purchase of the property. Petitioner has
introduced no evidence to demonstrate that these costs may be apportioned
or allocated to the Big Bear and Paisley tracts in any proportions other than

those originally determined by respondent. Moreover, since these costs appear to have been incurred principally to fill and grade the excavation in the center parcel [i.e., the portion of the tract retained by petitioner], allocation of some 41 percent thereof to that portion of the tract does not seem excessive. Accordingly, respondent's determinations with respect to allocation of these costs, to wit, 27.567 percent to the Big Bear parcel and 30.942 percent to the Paisley parcel, are sustained. . . .

The remaining question involves the $50,000 placed in escrow in 1957 upon sale of the Big Bear parcel. The parties now agree that the amount in question is $40,146.32, the actual cost to petitioner for paving and lighting the center tract. While it has been held that improvements made to specific parcels or contracted for with respect to specific parcels may be added to the basis thereof, Milton A. Mackay, 11 B.T.A. 569; Cambria Development Co., 34 B.T.A. 1155, and that costs of improvements to a subdivision as a whole may be allocated among the parcels thereof, *Biscayne Bay Islands Co.*, supra, improvements to property retained by the petitioner which may be sold at a later date may not be added to basis of another parcel in the tract. Colony, Inc., 26 T.C. 30, aff'd., 244 F. 2d 75 (C.A. 6, 1957), reversed on other grounds 357 U.S. 28. Cf. *Biscayne Bay Islands Co.*, supra. Cf. also Estate of M. A. Collins, 31 T.C. 238. Accordingly, since it is uncontested that the $40,146.32 was spent entirely on improvements placed on the center or retained parcel of the tract, no portion of that amount may be allocated to the basis of the Big Bear tract alone or to the Big Bear and Paisley parcels.

The matter of a net operating loss carryover from 1957 to 1958 depends upon the disposition of the above issues.

Decision will be entered under Rule 50.

REVENUE RULING 70-510
1970-2 C.B. 159

The purpose of this Revenue Ruling is to update and restate, under the current statute and regulations, the position set forth in G.C.M. 23162, C.B. 1942-1, 106.

The question presented is whether the amounts received by the taxpayer under the circumstances described below constitute a reduction in the basis of property within the meaning of section 1016 of the Internal Revenue Code of 1954.

The taxpayer, a domestic corporation, received a payment from the Federal Government in connection with the Government's flood control project. The payment made was consideration for a "flowage deed" whereby the Government was granted the perpetual right, under certain conditions, to flood designated portions of the taxpayer's property. The taxpayer retained title to the land and had full use thereof except when flooded.

The payment received by the taxpayer was less than its basis in the land and improvements to which the agreement applied.

The taxpayer's plant is constructed on a portion of the land covered by the "flowage deed." As protection for the properties, there is a four foot seawall and the plant is constructed on pillars three feet off the ground. The taxpayer's use of the properties has not thus far been changed or affected in any way whatsoever as a result of the flowage easement granted by the taxpayer.

According to the district engineer for the Department of the Army, the elevation of the land is such that an overflow of the river should occur once a year for the low areas and about once every 160 years for high areas. It is anticipated that there would be some flooding of the property by ordinary high waters every year, but with no damage to the plant and that only in the event of an unusual flood every 10 or 15 years would there be damage to the plant.

The amount paid by the Government for the flowage easement in the instant case represented 20 percent of the fee value, which was determined from a fee appraisal of the land and improvements, and was the maximum amount considered reasonable by the Government. The acquisition of easements in the area where the taxpayer's property is located is discretionary and condemnation to acquire title would not be resorted to should a property owner refuse to execute an agreement, in which event claims for damages would have to be entertained in case of overflow. In other words, the consideration for the "flowage deed" was measured, at least in so far as was possible, by negotiation and without resort to the right of eminent domain or litigation, by the estimated diminution in value of the affected properties (for any and all purposes for which they were or might be utilized) caused by the burden of the flowage easement.

Section 1001(a) of the Code of 1954 provides, in part, that the gain from the sale or other disposition of property shall be the excess of the amount realized therefrom over the adjusted bases provided in section 1011 of the Code.

Section 1011(a) of the Code provides, in pertinent part, the adjusted bases for determining gain or loss from the sale or other disposition of property, whenever acquired, shall be the basis, adjusted as provided in section 1016 of the Code.

Section 1016(a) of the Code provides, in pertinent part, that proper adjustments in respect of the property shall be made for receipts properly chargeable to capital account.

Under the "flowage deed" executed by the taxpayer in consideration of the payment of a specific sum of money, it granted, sold, and conveyed to the United States a perpetual easement to flood the designated properties at such infrequent intervals as not to deprive the taxpayer of any substantial beneficial use of the properties. The taxpayer did not, in form or effect, sell and dispose of the land and improvements concerned, nor merely receive payment in advance for anticipated future damages to its trade or business.

Accordingly, the amount received should be applied by the taxpayer against the cost or other basis of the properties to which the easement appertains in determining gain or loss from subsequent sale or other disposition of the properties. If the amount received had exceeded the taxpayer's basis for determining gain or loss on the properties affected by the easement, the excess would have constituted recognized gain for the taxable year in which the payment was received or accrued.

G.C.M. 23162 is hereby superseded, since the position stated therein is restated under the current law in this Revenue Ruling.

Notes and Questions

1. Why wasn't part of the overall cost of the land assigned to the flowage easement in Revenue Ruling 70-510, while the overall land cost was allocated between the parcels in *Fairfield Plaza?* See Inaja Land Co. v. Commissioner, 9 T.C. 727, 735-736 (1947). Are these decisions related to the open transaction doctrine and Burnet v. Logan (Chapter 5E above)? What is the result if the fee owner of Blackacre, which was purchased for $400,000, conveys a life estate to the purchaser for $500,000 at a time when the land had doubled in value?

2. Blocks of the same class of stock of a corporation may be acquired on different dates for varying prices. Assume that O purchased 100 shares of XYZ Corporation in 2003 for $20 per share, and another 200 shares in 2008 for $32 per share. In early 2009, O sells 100 shares of XYZ for $30 per share. What is O's gain (loss)? Read Reg. §1.1012-1(c). Do these rules make sense? What if XYZ is a mutual fund? Id. -1(e).

2. Capital Expenditures, Depreciation, and Loss Deductions

The term-certain annuity nicely illustrates the range of reasonable return of capital methods (see Table 6-1 above), but the tax timing problem is not confined to annuities. Indeed, the need to allocate a stream of receipts between income and return of capital is a pervasive problem under an income tax. At different times and in various contexts, Congress has prescribed one or another of the five reasonable timing methods described above. Prior to 1934, annuities were taxed using the ROC-first method. Similarly, in situations in which the total amount to be received (and hence the extent of gain or loss) from the sale of property was uncertain courts sometimes allowed taxation to be postponed until full recovery of invested capital.[1] See Chapter 5E above.

At the other extreme, ROC last is the general rule for taxing investments in nondepreciable property such as unimproved land or corporate stock. The owner's periodic receipts from these assets are taxed in full as rent or dividends, §61(a)(5), (7); return of capital is postponed until the very end of the investment transaction when gain or loss is computed on disposition of the property, §1001. Ditto for government or corporate bonds.

Property that declines in value through use or the passage of time (so-called wasting assets) presents a challenge for an exclusion-based cost recovery system. At the end of the taxpayer's ownership the property may have little or no remaining value, in which case there will be little or no proceeds from the sale or disposition of the property, and an exclusion tied to receipts on disposition would be inadequate. Immunizing final receipts from tax is possible where the property produces a fixed payment stream (as with the ROC-last approach applied to a term-certain annuity) but not where the amount or duration of the receipts is uncertain.

Consider, for example, a self-employed taxicab driver, *D*, who operates a vehicle that he purchased for $30,000. The taxicab wears out through use in the production of income (fares). It will never be re-sold for $30,000; after several years of service and with 200,000 miles on the odometer, it may have only scrap value. In contrast to the term-certain annuity, we cannot exclude the "last" $30,000 in fares because we do not know how long the vehicle will be used or what fares it will produce. Thus it might seem that uncertainty in the amount or duration of receipts forces us to allow the owner to exclude the first $30,000 in fares (ROC first). Instead of excluding receipts, however, we could simply allow the owner to deduct the cost of the vehicle, thereby freeing $30,000 of gross income from tax without regard to whether the deduction offsets income from fares or other sources. (Recall that deductions and exclusions are functionally equivalent.) The deduction mechanism obviates concerns over unpredictable or contingent receipts. (Not only can deductions ordinarily offset unrelated income, if total income for the year is insufficient, excess deductions may be available as a net operating loss carryover to another year, §172.) The deduction mechanism also reinstates the timing question because the full cost of the property could be allowed as a deduction on purchase (ROC first), or postponed until the property is disposed of (ROC last), or allocated in some manner over the anticipated period of use of the property. If the owner expects to use

---

1. This treatment, which came to be known as "open transaction" reporting, is now largely foreclosed. Reg. §15a.453-1(d)(2)(iii) provides in part:

> Only in those rare and extraordinary cases involving sales for a contingent payment obligation in which the fair market value of the obligations (determinable under the preceding sentence) cannot reasonably be ascertained will the taxpayer be entitled to assert that the transaction is "open." Any such transaction will be carefully scrutinized to determine whether a sale in fact has taken place.

the taxicab in business for five years, pro-rata return of capital could be approximated by allowing a deduction of 20 percent ($6,000) annually, which is known as straight-line depreciation, but front- or back-loaded depreciation schedules are also possible.

Tax-free return of capital is necessary to correctly measure the *increase* in resources available for consumption or saving (net income). Timing questions arise where a given investment or expenditure produces returns over multiple years. Because we tax income *annually* (Burnet v. Sanford & Brooks Co., Chapter 3D.1 above, §441) according to a set of progressive rates, taxable income should be defined so as to provide an accurate measure of year-by-year enrichment. This simple principle explains both the nondeductibility of capital expenditures and the variation in methods of cost recovery available for depreciable and nondepreciable property.

Speaking generally, a capital expenditure is any outlay that will yield benefits for a period extending substantially beyond the close of the current taxable year. It may be the acquisition price of long-lived income-producing property, the cost of a personal residence or other consumer durable, or the cost of long-lasting additions or improvements to property. (In the language of §263, capital expenditures include "Any amount paid out for new buildings or for permanent improvements or betterments made to increase the value of any property or estate.") While the costs of producing income are ordinarily deductible, §§162(a), 212, costs that will yield income over multiple years are not — deductions for capital expenditures are barred by §§263 and 263A. Capital expenditures are made nondeductible for reasons of tax timing even though they are legitimate costs of producing income. The bar to deduction of capital expenditures says, in effect, that return-of-capital first is not a permissible method for recovery of multi-year costs. Instead, capital expenditures generate a cost basis (§1012) or an upward adjustment to the basis of the property improved (§1016(a)(1)), and this "capitalization" (that is, inclusion in adjusted basis) preserves the outlay for possible future cost recovery. Such future cost recovery is ordinarily accomplished either through depreciation deductions or via the computation of gain or loss on the sale or disposition of the property (or both).

For property that is subject to "exhaustion, wear and tear [or] obsolescence" — property that declines in value over time or through use such as machinery and buildings — §167(a) authorizes a depreciation deduction provided that the property is used to produce income. The decline in value of such property is a real economic cost of producing income from the property, and depreciation deductions allocate that cost over the years in which the property is producing income. By roughly matching gross income with the costs of producing it (the decline in value of wasting assets), depreciation yields a better approximation of annual enrichment than would a regime that calls for ROC first or ROC last.

Returning to our taxicab operator (*D*), he deducts his gasoline, tolls, traffic fines, and other current costs when paid, §162. The $30,000 cost of his vehicle is a capital expenditure, and so is not immediately deductible, §263. The deterioration and decline in value of the car through use is a real cost of earning his fares, and so an annual depreciation deduction is allowed to (roughly) reflect this cost, §§167, 168. Observe that if *D* leased a taxicab instead of operating his own vehicle, the annual rental cost would be deductible, §163(a)(3). This comparison indicates that depreciation allowances, by spreading the cost of wasting assets over the period of business use, promote parity in tax timing (economic neutrality) between owners and renters. See Commissioner v. Idaho Power Co., Chapter 13C below. Nor could a taxicab driver who leased his vehicle obtain more favorable results (ROC first) by prepaying all rent due under a three-year lease: the prepayment would be a capital expenditure (it creates a long-lived intangible asset), the capitalized cost of which would be recoverable via depreciation over the lease term. Commissioner v. Boylston Market Association, 131 F.2d 966 (1st Cir. 1942).

Spreading the cost of a wasting asset over its period of service gives a better picture of annual enrichment than lumping the cost at the beginning or end of the period (ROC first or ROC last), but there are many possible methods of cost spreading (compare front-loaded, pro-rata, and back-loaded ROC). Accurate measurement of annual enrichment would call for the deduction of the actual decline in market value of the asset during the taxable year, necessitating yearly appraisals, which clearly would be unworkable. Instead, Congress permits deduction of a "reasonable allowance" for depreciation, §167(a). That allowance is determined by application of categorical rules rather than being tethered to actual yearly diminution in value. What considerations or criteria should have shaped those rules?

The depreciation deduction (authorized by §167(a), but modified and elaborated at length elsewhere in §167 and §168), while not a measure of the actual decline in value of the property during the taxable year (true economic depreciation), could be constructed to approximate that quantity. At one time, taxpayers computed depreciation by predicting how long they would actually use the property to produce income (useful life) and estimating what the property would be worth when retired from service (salvage value); the difference between initial cost and salvage value, divided by the useful life of the property, gave the annual depreciation deduction. Assuming that the property produced the same amount of income during each year of its useful life, this "straight-line depreciation" accomplished pro-rata ROC. In 1962 Congress authorized accelerated depreciation, allowing taxpayers to deduct a larger portion of the anticipated total cost in the early part of the property's useful life, which corresponded to front-loaded ROC. In 1986 Congress enacted §168, which decoupled depreciation allowances from anticipated useful life and salvage value (taxpayer-specific facts that were rife with controversy), allowing taxpayers to deduct the full cost of property over specified recovery periods that are substantially shorter than the actual experience of property longevity in business. This dramatic further acceleration of depreciation was enacted as an investment incentive: by deducting the costs of a machine over five years when the machine will actually be producing widgets for ten years, income from depreciable property is granted tax deferral. Of course, maximum tax deferral would be accomplished by the immediate deduction of the full cost of the property, known as "expensing" (in contrast to "capitalizing" under §263), which is equivalent to ROC first. Within limits, Congress has even gone to this extreme. Read §263(a)(1)(G) and skim §179. Is there any downside to a more general adoption of expensing?

Notice that depreciation is allowable only for property used in a trade or business or held for the production of income, §167(a), not for consumer durables such as owner-occupied housing or a personal automobile, even though the cost of consumer durables is a capital expenditure that generates basis (or an increase in adjusted basis). The depreciation deduction is so limited because the decline in value through use of one's house, car, appliances, or clothing is a cost of *consumption*, not a cost of earning income, and consumption is the core of the tax base.[2]

For property that does not wear out over time, cost recovery is accomplished principally via the definition of gain in §1001(a). By exempting from tax a portion of the sales proceeds ("amount realized") equal to the seller's remaining tax-paid investment (adjusted basis) in the property, the owner is assigned ROC-last cost recovery. If nondepreciable income-producing property such as land or corporate stock is sold for less than cost, then the entire proceeds will be tax free (i.e., no gain), and the seller is allowed a loss deduction for the diminution in value of the property. The loss deduction reduces the seller's taxable income to reflect the decrease in wealth (disenrichment) attributable to the investment, which was a cost of owning the property, and which (due to the realization doctrine) also receives ROC-last treatment.

Where depreciable property is sold, cost recovery is accomplished by the combination of depreciation allowances and the treatment of gain or loss on disposition. The two systems are coordinated by §1016(a)(2): Each year that the property is used to produce income a depreciation deduction provides partial cost recovery and the permissible deduction ("allowable" depreciation) also triggers a corresponding reduction in the owner's adjusted basis in the property. Consequently, at any given time, adjusted basis reflects the owner's unrecovered after-tax investment in the property, so that the remaining investment can be recovered upon sale or disposition. Assume that a piece of office equipment (classified as 5-year property for purposes of computing depreciation under §168) was purchased for $10,000 and placed

---

2. Even if section 167 were not limited to income-producing property, depreciation deductions for consumer durables would presumably be disallowed either as a "personal, living, or family expense," §262(a), or as a cost of producing tax-free imputed income, §265(a).

in service in year one, and that it is sold for $3,000 some time during year three. The owner would be entitled to depreciation deductions of $2,000 in year one, $3,200 in year two, and $960 in year three, which would reduce the equipment's adjusted basis to $3,840 at the time of sale. The $3,000 sale proceeds are received tax free under §1001, and the loss of $840 is deductible in year three under §165(c). If the equipment had instead been worth $5,000 the sale would yield a gain of $1,160 (= $5,000 − $3,840), indicating that the actual decline in value through use in the production of income (economic depreciation) was less than the depreciation allowed, and the excessive prior depreciation is, in effect, recaptured (retrospectively offset) by the gain on sale.

Consumer durables, as noted earlier, are not depreciable even though they suffer "exhaustion, wear and tear, [or] obsolescence," because the diminution in value is a cost of consumption, not of producing income. But what happens when long-lived consumption property is sold? The capitalization requirement (§263) applies to consumer durables as well as business and investment property, so the cost of consumer durables generates basis (§1012). Because depreciation deductions are not allowed, basis is not adjusted downward (§1016(a)(2)) even though the property is losing value year by year. Accordingly, upon the sale or disposition of the property, the adjusted basis used for determining gain or loss (§1001(a)) will typically be the original (historical) cost of the property, with the result that sale of the well-worn item will generally produce a loss. Sale proceeds will be received tax free but the "loss" — which reflects diminution in value attributable to consumption (prior nondeductible depreciation) — is nondeductible by operation of the limits of §165(c). This is, of course, the correct result because wear and tear attributable to consumption use should never be deductible (§262). Hence, the limits of §167(a) and §165(c) operate in tandem to assure that any deduction traceable to diminution in value of consumer durables is permanently disallowed, not simply deferred until disposition.

This simple approach to consumer durables (i.e., barring both depreciation and loss deductions) works well for items that uniformly decline in value over time, such as personal automobiles, household furnishings and appliances, and clothing. Arguably, however, it does not accurately measure income in the case of owner-occupied housing. Housing is, of course, subject to physical exhaustion, which depresses its value, but it also frequently benefits from increased market demand due to population growth and land scarcity. Historically, home prices in many metropolitan areas of the United States have experienced long-term appreciation. Such gains are currently excluded (§121), but even if they were subject to tax, the homeowner's income would be understated. Overall gain or loss, as computed under §1001, is a composite of diminution in value due to consumption use (nondeductible depreciation) and market appreciation. Because basis is not adjusted downward to reflect the value-depressing effects of physical deterioration and obsolescence, sale of a personal residence at zero gain (as defined by §1001) effectively allows the homeowner to offset prior depreciation (the cost of prior consumption) against market appreciation.

B. ANNUITY CONTRACTS

1. Life Annuities

A simple life annuity contract is one under which an issuer, usually a life insurance company, promises to make periodic payments for the life of an annuitant. Such a contract may be purchased by payment of a single premium immediately before annuity payments commence. More often, perhaps, the annuity is purchased by paying one or more premiums considerably in advance of the annuity starting date. If an annuity is to provide retirement income, it may make very good sense to pay for it by periodic payments throughout active employment. The insurance company then will pay for the use of the investor's money by charging smaller total dollar amounts as premiums for any given level of benefit payment the longer in advance the premiums are paid.

Variations on a simple life annuity include joint and survivor annuities, under which payments will continue as long as either of two annuitants survives (sometimes in a reduced amount after one dies), and refund annuities, under which the insurer guarantees to pay some minimum total amount even if the annuitant(s) die before receiving it.

The basic problem in taxing life annuitants lies in making appropriate provision for tax-free return of investment. Annuity payments are income to the recipient, but only to the extent they represent some gain over what was paid for the contract. Whether there is ultimately any gain to a particular annuitant, however, and how much, may not be known until he or she dies. The problem has been how to treat each payment when made, in view of this uncertainty.

1. *Return of capital treatment.* Until 1934 all payments received under an annuity were exempt from tax until the annuitant had received back the aggregate premiums paid for the contract. This ROC-first approach to taxation led to "an increasing amount of capital going into the purchase of annuities, with the result that income taxes are postponed indefinitely." H.R. Rep. No. 73-704, at 21 (1934). What, if anything, was wrong with this simple treatment?

2. *The 3 percent rule.* In 1934, Congress abandoned the ROC-first method of annuity taxation and instead adopted the 3 percent rule under which annuity payments were treated as taxable income to the extent of 3 percent of an annuitant's investment in the contract. Any excess over 3 percent was treated as excludible (return of capital).

The constitutionality of this provision was challenged in Egtvedt v. United States, 112 Ct. Cl. 80 (1948). In 1937 Egtvedt was 45 years old with a life expectancy of 28 years when he paid $100,000 for a single-premium life annuity that paid $4,884 per year. Under the 3 percent rule he would get back only $1,884 per year tax free, and it would take him 53 years to recover his whole investment at that rate. According to the American Annuitants' Male Select Table of Mortality, the probability of his living so long was less than one-half of 1 percent. The statute was nevertheless upheld, partly on the basis of a congressional finding that 3 percent was generally the average rate of return in annuity contracts.

Even if the 3 percent rule was constitutional, does Egtvedt's case give some indication of what was wrong with it? Was the rule generally as harsh as in Egtvedt's case? Or are there other cases in which its application would be more reasonable or even excessively lenient? Suppose Egtvedt had paid for his annuity contracts several years in advance of the annuity starting date at a total cost of $50,000 instead of $100,000. How then would the 3 percent rule have applied? As a policy matter, is there any good reason to tax Egtvedt on a higher portion of his annuity payments than one who bought his annuity earlier for less? Is there a persuasive reason for taxing him on a lower portion of his payments?

3. *The exclusion-ratio rule.* Look at §72(a), (b)(1), and (c), which were adopted in 1954, and work out the following problems. You will need to look at the appropriate table in Reg. §1.72-9.

(a) *A* purchases a simple life annuity to pay $5,000 per year for life, commencing with the year of purchase (an immediate annuity). The cost is $70,000 and *A* is 65 years old. How much of each payment is subject to tax under §72? What if *A* dies at age 82?

(b) *B* purchases the same contract ($5,000 simple life annuity commencing at age 65) when he is 45 years old and pays for it in installments (annual premiums) of $2,400 per year until the annuity starting date (a deferred annuity). How much of each annuity payment is subject to tax?

(c) How would *A* and *B* have been taxed under the 3 percent rule?

4. *Mortality gains and losses.* It is simplest to think of §72 as providing a statutory formula for allocating annuity payments between income (interest) and return of capital. It is more accurate to analyze the return on a life annuity contract into three components: (1) interest income, (2) return of capital, and (3) mortality gain or loss (i.e., the profit under such a contract if the annuitant lives long and the loss if death comes early). If the return is so analyzed, how does §72 treat mortality gains and losses?

From 1954 to 1986 the exclusion ratio was applied to all annuity payments received, however few or many. Therefore, annuitants who outlived their life expectancy got back more than their investment tax free, and those who died early got less. This was not generally thought to be a problem, since the effect was that the government just took on a mortality risk exactly proportional to that borne by the insurance company. For annuitants it had the considerable advantage of making their after-tax income constant for as long as they live, which is consistent with the purpose of purchasing a life annuity.

In 1989, Congress added §72(b)(2), (3), and (4). These will tend to cause an increase in income taxes, resulting in a drop in after-tax income whenever an annuitant outlives her life expectancy. In exchange, they create a deduction for estates of annuitants who die early. Is anybody's interest served by this trade-off?

This 1986 change is something of a mystery; there is no account for it in the committee reports and its reasons are entirely obscure. Was it an improvement?

5. *Employee annuities.* What happens if all or part of the consideration for an annuity is paid by a taxpayer's employer? See §72(d) and (f). The principal reason employer premium payments might not be includible in the gross income of the employee would be that they were made pursuant to a qualified retirement plan meeting the requirements referred to in §403(a)(1) or by an employer described in §403(b)(1).

6. *Joint and survivor annuities.* Life annuities are most commonly purchased to provide secure retirement income because they offer insurance against outliving one's savings. A married couple will commonly want annuity payments to provide lifetime support for both spouses, and so they will buy a joint and survivor annuity under which payments continue for as long as either spouse is alive. Sometimes payments to the survivor continue at the same level as when both are alive or they may be reduced to a fraction (often to 75 or 50 percent) of the annuity paid during their joint lives. The anticipated duration of payments under a joint and survivor annuity depends on the ages of both annuitants, and the expected return is calculated as explained in Reg. §1.72-5(b), using Table VI of Reg. §1.72-9. Assume that *C* pays a premium of $200,000 for an annuity that will pay $1,000 monthly for as long as either *C* or his wife, *D*, are alive. At the annuity starting date *C* is 65 years old and *D* is 63 years old. What is their exclusion ratio? What would be the exclusion ratio if the premium were $180,000 but the level of the survivor annuity was dropped from $1,000 (during their joint lives) to $500 per month?

7. *Refund annuities.* Many people find simple life annuities unattractive because of loss aversion — they are deterred by the possibility that they might die shortly after the annuity starting date and so will receive little or no payout under the contract. To ameliorate this concern, many annuity contracts contain a refund feature, which (for an increase in premiums) guarantees that the contract will yield some minimum number of payments or minimum total payout (typically tied to the amount paid for the contract). If the annuitant(s) die before the guarantee is met, the remainder is paid to the annuitant's estate or beneficiaries. Such a refund annuity may be viewed as the composite of a simple life annuity and declining life insurance. So viewed, the portion of the premiums paid for the life insurance should not be taken into account in computing the annuity exclusion ratio. The statute

mandates such an adjustment, §72(c)(2), and Reg. §1.72-7 specifies the computational gymnastics.

8. *Depreciation.* Suppose a taxpayer were to purchase the interest of a life beneficiary in a trust. The purchase price of the income interest would be a nondeductible capital expenditure, §263, and would generate a cost basis, §1012. The purchaser would then include the trust income in her gross income but would deduct her purchase price as depreciation ratably over the life expectancy of the life beneficiary, §167. Cf. Commissioner v. Early, Chapter 4A. How does this treatment differ, if at all, from the treatment of an annuity contract under §72?

2. Deferred Annuities

The foregoing discussion concerns taxation of annuity payments. Until 1982 other payments under an annuity contract were treated as reductions in investment if received prior to the annuity starting date and were fully taxable if received thereafter. Some insurance companies then promoted an investment like the following.

A taxpayer pays $100,000 for a deferred annuity with payments to begin on his 95th birthday. The cash surrender value is $99,000 right off the bat, and it goes up $7,000 per annum. At the end of each year after purchasing the contract, the annuitant will take $7,000 out, thus returning the cash surrender value to $99,000. Advertised result: 142/7 years of tax-free 7 percent cash return. (Everything will be taxable after that.)

Consider the statutory changes described in the following excerpt. Do they deal adequately with the problem identified? What would you recommend?

DEFERRED ANNUITIES [§72]

Staff of Joint Comm. on Taxation, 97th Cong., 2d Sess.,
Explanation of the Revenue Provisions of the Tax Equity and Fiscal
Responsibility Act of 1982, 360-362 (Comm. Print 1982)

PRIOR LAW

The taxation of interest or other current earnings on a policyholder's investment in an annuity contract generally is deferred until annuity payments are received or amounts characterized as income are withdrawn (secs. 72(a) and (e)). A portion of each amount paid to a policyholder as an annuity generally is taxed as ordinary income under an "exclusion ratio" (sec 72(b)) computed to reflect the projected nontaxable return of investment in the contract and the taxable growth on the investment. Policy dividends paid after annuity payments begin are not subject to the "exclusion ratio" but are taxable in full to the policy holder as ordinary income.

Under prior law, amounts paid out under a contract before the annuity payments began, such as payments upon partial surrender of a contract, were first treated as a return of the policyholder's capital and were taxable (as ordinary income) only after all of the policyholder's investments in the contract had been recovered.

REASONS FOR CHANGE

Traditionally, annuity contracts have been safe, conservative, but low-yielding investments purchased by individuals who wish both to provide for income during their retirement and to insure against the possibility of out-living their assets. Deferred annuities typically guaranteed and limited both the rate of interest at which the principal would grow during the accumulation period and the rate at which that amount could be converted to annuity payments at the end of that period. Although taxes were deferred during the accumulation period, the relatively low yields and high commissions made deferred annuities less attractive for short-term investment by comparison with other investment alternatives.

In recent years, however, the life insurance industry has developed new products that provide an investment yield for the policyholder that is competitive with other commercial investments that do not enjoy the same tax treatment. By emphasizing the benefits of tax deferral during the accumulation period, the tax-favored treatment of partial surrenders, and options for lump-sum settlements, deferred annuities have been actively marketed as "tax shelters." Although the current tax rules were enacted when deferred annuities were used to provide long-term income security, variations on traditional products have been developed that are comparable to short-term money market investments.

Congress believed that the use of deferred annuity contracts to meet long-term investment and retirement goals, such as income security, was still a worthy ideal. However, Congress believed that their use for short-term investment and income tax deferral should be discouraged.

EXPLANATION OF PROVISION

CASH WITHDRAWALS

... The first change made by the Act is that partial surrenders or cash withdrawals prior to the annuity starting date are income to the extent that the cash value of the contract (determined immediately before the amount is received and without regard to any surrender charge) exceeds the investment in the contract. To the extent that such cash value does not exceed the investment in the contract, such withdrawals are a return of capital to the policyholder and reduce the taxpayer's investment in the contract.

Policyholder dividends received prior to the annuity starting date are cash withdrawals subject to the new rules. Such policyholder dividends are not included in the taxpayer's income to the extent they are retained by the insurer as premiums or other consideration paid for the contract. However, the retained policyholder dividends do not increase the taxpayer's investment in the contract since such amounts received under the contract are excludable from gross income. Likewise, for purposes of this new rule, loans against a contract or pledging an annuity contract are treated the same as a cash withdrawal. Thus, a loan or pledge for a specific amount will be treated as a cash withdrawal of that amount when the loan or pledge is made. If the taxpayer pledges the entire contract, he will be treated as having received a cash withdrawal at the time of the initial pledge; moreover, whenever the contract is credited with additional income, which becomes subject to the pledge, then such additional income will be treated as additional cash withdrawals and taxed accordingly. . . .

Questions

1. Does this change prevent the marketing of "variations on traditional products . . . that are comparable to short-term money market investments" as "tax shelters" "emphasizing the benefits of tax deferral during the accumulation period"? Speaking broadly, is it fair to say that Congress closed down a deferral tax shelter by replacing ROC-first cost recovery with ROC-last?

2. What about policyholder dividends received prior to the annuity starting date in the case of "deferred annuity contracts [purchased in fact] to meet long-term investment and retirement goals"? It used to be thought that such dividends were essentially reductions in premium payments; why is that not an adequate reason for excluding them from income?

3. Can a better job be done in confining deferral to good or true annuity contract investments? Would it help to distinguish between single-premium and multiple-premium contracts? How and why? How about simply allowing dividends (or other withdrawals) to be netted against premiums paid in the same taxable year before being subject to tax?

4. The deferred annuity episode suggests a larger question: Is taxation necessarily postponed until payment is received? Even after the 1982 reform the interest earned on a deferred annuity is includible only when some amount is withdrawn or paid under the contract. §72(e)(1). In contrast, if money is deposited in a savings account, whether at a bank, savings and loan association, or credit union, the interest is taxable each year as it is earned even if it is not withdrawn. Why is the taxation of interest deferred throughout the accumulation period under an annuity, life insurance, or endowment contract, but not in the case of a savings account? How does this disparity affect savings behavior? Demand for financial products?

C. *CASH METHOD ACCOUNTING AND ITS LIMITS*

Most individuals derive their income predominately from the performance of services and compute their taxable income using the cash receipts and disbursements method. §446(c)(1). In the case of a business with books of account, taxable income is to be computed by the method used in keeping those books. §446(a). This effectively gives many taxpayers engaged in service businesses a kind of restrained choice between cash and accrual accounting in computing taxable income. Taxpayers who derive income from the production, purchase, or sale of goods, however, are required to keep inventories and to compute their income from merchandise dealings under the accrual method. §417; Reg. §§1.471-1, 1.446-1(c)(2)(i).

Under the cash receipts and disbursements method (often referred to simply as the "cash method" or "cash basis accounting") income is includible in the year in which the item is received by the taxpayer, and deductions are ordinarily claimed for the year in which the amount is paid. Reg. §1.446-1(c)(1)(i). The straightforward admonition of the cash method: Follow the money. Yet each prong of that simple rule is subject to an important limitation. Income is reported when received, but receipt may be actual or constructive. Id.; §1.451-1(a). Deductions are to be claimed for the year when the amount is paid, but if "an expenditure results in the creation of an asset having a useful life which extends substantially beyond the close of the taxable year, such an expenditure may not be deductible, or may be deductible only in part, for the taxable year in which made" because of the capitalization rules. Reg. §1.461-1(a)(1). These limitations are necessary to prevent the cash method from giving taxpayers unilateral control over tax timing. Without the constructive receipt and capitalization rules, cash-basis taxpayers could choose to pay tax in a later year by simply deferring collections or accelerating payment of deductible items.

Capitalization issues will be taken up in Chapter 13C. Here we turn to constructive receipt, followed by consideration of situations in which Congress has mandated inclusion in advance of either actual or constructive receipt.

1. Constructive Receipt

REVENUE RULING 60-31
1960-1 C.B. 174

Advice has been requested regarding the taxable year of inclusion in gross income of a taxpayer, using the cash receipts and disbursements method of accounting, of compensation for services received under the circumstances described below.

(1) On January 1, 1958, the taxpayer and corporation X executed an employment contract under which the taxpayer is to be employed by the corporation in an executive capacity for a period of five years. Under the contract, the taxpayer is entitled to a stated annual salary and to additional compensation of $10x$ dollars for each year. The additional compensation will be credited to a bookkeeping reserve account and will be deferred, accumulated, and paid in annual installments equal to one-fifth of the amount in the reserve as of the close of the year immediately preceding the year of first payment. The payments are to begin only upon (a) termination of the taxpayer's employment by the corporation; (b) the taxpayer's becoming a part-time employee of the corporation; or (c) the taxpayer's becoming partially or totally incapacitated. Under the terms of the agreement, corporation X is under a merely contractual obligation to make the payments when due, and the parties did not intend that the amounts in the reserve be held by the corporation in trust for the taxpayer.

The contract further provides that if the taxpayer should fail or refuse to perform his duties, the corporation will be relieved of any obligation to make further credits to the reserve (but not of the obligation to distribute amounts previously contributed); but, if the taxpayer should become incapacitated from performing his duties, then credits to the reserve will continue for one year from the date of the incapacity, but not beyond the expiration of the five-year term of the contract. There is no specific provision in the contract for forfeiture by the taxpayer of his right to distribution from the reserve; and, in the event he should die prior to his receipt in full of the balance in the account, the remaining balance is distributable to his personal representative at the rate of one-fifth per year for five years, beginning three months after his death.

(2) The taxpayer is an officer and director of corporation A, which has a plan for making future payments of additional compensation for current services to certain officers and key employees designated by its board of directors. This plan provides that a percentage of the annual net earnings (before Federal income taxes) in excess of $\$4,000x$ dollars is to be designated for division among the participants in proportion to their respective salaries. This amount is not currently paid to the participants; but, the corporation has set up on its books a separate account for each participant and each year it credits thereto the dollar amount of his participation for the year, reduced by a proportionate part of the corporation's income taxes attributable to the additional compensation. Each account is also credited with the net amount, if any, realized from investing any portion of the amount in the account.

Distributions are to be made from these accounts annually beginning when the employee (1) reaches age 60, (2) is no longer employed by the company, including cessation of employment due to death, or (3) becomes totally disabled to perform his duties, whichever occurs first. The annual distribution will equal a stated percentage of the balance in the employee's account at the close of the year immediately preceding the year of first payment, and distributions will continue until the account is exhausted. However, the corporation's liability to make these distributions is contingent upon the employee's (1) refraining from engaging in any business competitive to that of the corporation, (2) making himself available to the corporation for consultation and advice after retirement or termination of his services, unless disabled, and (3) retaining unencumbered any interest or benefit under the plan. In the event of his death, either before or after the beginning of payments, amounts in an employee's account are distributable in installments computed in the same way to his designated beneficiaries or heirs-at-law. Under the terms of the compensation plan, corporation A is under a merely contractual obligation to make the payments when due, and the parties did not intend that the amounts in each account be held by the corporation in trust for the participants.

(3) On October, 1, 1957, the taxpayer, an author, and corporation Y, a publisher, executed an agreement under which the taxpayer granted to the publisher the exclusive right to print, publish and sell a book he had written. This agreement provides that the publisher will (1) pay the author specified royalties based on the actual cash received from the sale of the published work, (2) render semiannual statements of the sales, and (3) at the time of rendering each statement make settlement for the amount due. On the same day, another agreement was signed by the same parties, mutually agreeing that, in consideration of, and notwithstanding any contrary provisions contained in the first contract, the publisher shall not pay the taxpayer more than $100x$ dollars in any one calendar year. Under this supplemental contract, sums in excess of $100x$ dollars accruing in any one calendar year are to be carried over by the publisher into succeeding accounting periods; and the publisher shall not be required either to pay interest to the taxpayer on any such excess sums or to segregate any such sums in any manner.

(4) In June 1957, the taxpayer, a football player, entered into a two-year standard player's contract with a football club in which he agreed to play football and engage in activities related to football during the two-year term only for the club. In addition to a specified salary for the two-year term, it was mutually agreed that as an inducement for signing the contract the taxpayer would be paid a bonus of $150x$ dollars. The taxpayer could have demanded and received payment of this bonus at the time of signing the contract, but at his suggestion there was added to the standard contract form a paragraph providing substantially as follows:

> The player shall receive the sum of $150x$ dollars upon signing of this contract, contingent upon the payment of this $150x$ dollars to an escrow agent designated by him. The escrow agreement shall be subject to approval by the legal representatives of the player, the Club, and the escrow agent.

Pursuant to this added provision, an escrow agreement was executed on June 25, 1957, in which the club agreed to pay $150x$ dollars on that date to the *Y* bank, as escrow agent; and the escrow agent agreed to pay this amount, plus interest, to the taxpayer in installments over a period of five years. The escrow agreement also provides that the account established by the escrow agent is to bear the taxpayer's name; that payment from such account may be made only in accordance with the terms of the agreement; that the agreement is binding upon the parties thereto and their successors or assigns; and that in the event of the taxpayer's death during the escrow period the balance due will become part of his estate. . . .

Section 1.451-1 (a) of the Income Tax Regulations provides in part as follows:

"Gains, profits, and income are to be included in gross income for the taxable year in which they are actually or constructively received by the taxpayer unless includible for a different year in accordance with the taxpayer's method of accounting. . . . " And, with respect to the cash receipts and disbursements method of accounting, section 1.446-1(c)(1)(i) provides in part — "Generally, under the cash receipts and disbursements method in the computation of taxable income, all items which constitute gross income (whether in the form of cash, property, or services) are to be included for the taxable year in which actually or constructively received. . . . "

As previously stated, the individual concerned in each of the situations described above, employs the cash receipts and disbursements method of accounting. Under the method, as indicated by the above-quoted provisions of the regulations, he is required to include the compensation concerned in gross income only for the taxable year in which it is actually or constructively received. Consequently, the question for resolution is whether in each of the situations described the income in question was constructively received in a taxable year prior to the taxable year of actual receipt.

A mere promise to pay, not represented by notes or secured in any way, is not regarded as a receipt of income within the intendment of the cash receipts and disbursements method. See United States v. Christine Oil & Gas Co., 269 Fed. 458; William J. Jackson v. Smietanka, 272 Fed. 970 (1921); and E. F. Cremin v. Commissioner, 5 B.T.A. 1164, acquiescence, C.B. VI-1, 2 (1927). Also C. Florian Zittel v. Commissioner, 12 B.T.A. 675, in which, holding a salary to be taxable when received, the Board said: "Taxpayers on a receipts and disbursements basis are required to report only income actually received no matter how binding any contracts they have to receive more."

This should not be construed to mean that under the cash receipts and disbursements method income may be taxed only when realized in cash. For, under that method a taxpayer is required to include in income that which is received in cash or cash equivalent. W.P. Henritze v. Commissioner, 41 B.T.A. 505. And, as stated in the above-quoted provisions of the regulations, the "receipt" contemplated by the cash method may be actual or constructive.

With respect to the constructive receipt of income, section 1.451-2(a) of the Income Tax Regulations (which accords with prior regulations extending back to, and including, Article 53 of Regulation 45 under the Revenue Act of 1918) provides, in part, as follows:

> Income although not actually reduced to a taxpayer's possession is constructively received by him in the taxable year during which it is credited to his account or set apart for him so that he may draw upon it at any time. However, income is not constructively received if the taxpayer's control of its receipt is subject to substantial limitations or restrictions. Thus, if a corporation credits its employees with bonus stock, but the stock is not available to such employees until some future date, the mere crediting on the books of the corporation does not constitute receipt.

Thus, under the doctrine of constructive receipt, a taxpayer may not deliberately turn his back upon income and thereby select the year for which he will report it. The Hamilton National Bank of Chattanooga, as Administrator of the Estate of S. Strang Nicklin, Deceased, v. Commissioner, 29 B.T.A. 63. Nor may a taxpayer, by a private agreement, postpone receipt of income from one taxable year to another. James E. Lewis v. Commissioner, 30 B.T.A. 318.

However, the statute cannot be administered by speculating whether the payor would have been willing to agree to an earlier payment. See, for example, J.D. Amend, et ux., v. Commissioner, 13 T.C. 178, acquiescence, C.B. 1950-1, 1; and C.E. Gullett, et al., v. Commissioner, 31 B.T.A. 1067, in which the court, citing a number of authorities for its holdings, stated:

> It is clear that the doctrine of constructive receipt is to be sparingly used; that amounts due from a corporation but unpaid, are not to be included in the income of an individual reporting his income on a cash receipts basis unless it appears that the money was available to him, that the corporation was able and ready to pay him, that his right to receive was not restricted, and that his failure to receive resulted from exercise of his own choice.

Consequently, it seems clear that in each case involving a deferral of compensation a determination of whether the doctrine of constructive receipt is applicable must be made upon the basis of the specific factual situation involved.

Applying the foregoing criteria to the situations described above, the following conclusions have been reached:

(1) The additional compensation to be received by the taxpayer under the employment contract concerned will be includible in his gross income only in the taxable years in which the taxpayer actually receives installment payments in cash or other property previously credited to his account. To hold otherwise would be contrary to the provisions of the regulations and the court decisions mentioned above.

(2) For the reasons in (1) above, it is held that the taxpayer here involved also will be required to include the deferred compensation concerned in his gross income only in the taxable years in which the taxpayer actually receives installment payments in cash or other property credited to his account.

In arriving at this conclusion and the conclusion reached in case "(1)," consideration has been given to section 1.402(b)-1 of the Income Tax Regulations and to Revenue Ruling 57-37, C.B. 1957-1, 18, as modified by Revenue Ruling 57-528, C.B. 1957-2, 263. Section 1.402(b)-1(a)(1) provides in part, with an exception not here relevant, that any contribution made by an employer on behalf of an employee to a trust during a taxable year of the employer which ends within or with a taxable year of the trust for which the trust is not exempt under section 501(a) of the Code, shall be included in income of the employee for his taxable year during which the contribution is made if his interest in the contribution is nonforfeitable at the time the contribution is made. Revenue Ruling 57-37, as modified by Revenue Ruling 57-528, held, inter alia, that certain contributions conveying fully vested and nonforfeitable interests made by an employer into separate independently controlled trusts for the purpose of furnishing unemployment and other benefits to its eligible employees constituted additional compensation to the employees includible, under section 402(b) of the Code and section 1.402(b)-1(a)(1) of the regulations, in their income for the taxable year in which such contributions were made. These Revenue Rulings are distinguishable from cases "(1)" and "(2)" in that, under all the facts and circumstances of these cases, no trusts for the benefit of the taxpayers were created and no contributions are to be made thereto. Consequently, section 402(b) of the Code and section 1.402(b)-1(a)(1) of the regulations are inapplicable.

(3) Here the principal agreement provided that the royalties were payable substantially as earned, and this agreement was supplemented by a further concurrent agreement which made the royalties payable over a period of years. This supplemental agreement, however, was made before the royalties were earned; in fact, it was made on the same day as the principal agreement and the two agreements were a part of the same transaction. Thus, for all practical purposes, the arrangement from the beginning is similar to that in (1) above. Therefore, it is also held that the author concerned will be required to include the royalties in his gross income only in the taxable years in which they are actually received in cash or other property.

(4) In arriving at a determination as to the includibility of the $150x$ dollars concerned in the gross income of the football player, under the circumstances described, in addition to the authorities cited above, consideration also has been given to Revenue Ruling 55-727, C.B. 1955-2, 25, and to the decision in E. T. Sproull v. Commissioner, 16 T.C. 244.

In Revenue Ruling 55-727, the taxpayer, a professional baseball player, entered into a contract in 1953 in which he agreed to render services for a baseball club and to refrain from playing baseball for any other club during the term of the contract. In addition to specified compensation, the contract provided for a bonus to the player or his estate, payable one-half in January 1954 and one-half in January 1955, whether or not he was able to render services. The primary question was whether the bonus was capital gain or ordinary income; and, in holding that the bonus payments constituted ordinary income, it was stated that they were taxable for the year in which received by the player. However, under the facts set forth in Revenue Ruling 55-727 there was no arrangement, as here, for placing the amount of the bonus in escrow. Consequently, the instant situation is distinguishable from that considered in Revenue Ruling 55-727.

In E. T. Sproull v. Commissioner, 16 T.C. 244, affirmed, 194 Fed. (2d) 541, the petitioner's employer in 1945 transferred in trust for the petitioner the amount of $10,500. The trustee was directed to pay out of principal to the petitioner the sum of $5,250 in 1946 and the balance, including income, in 1947. In the event of the petitioner's prior death, the amounts were to be paid to his administrator, executor, or heirs. The petitioner contended that the Commissioner erred in including the sum of $10,500 in his taxable income for 1945. In this connection, the court stated:

> . . . it is undoubtedly true that the amount which the Commissioner has included in petitioner's income for 1945 was used in that year for his benefit . . . in setting up the trust of which petitioner, or, in the event of his death then his estate, was the sole beneficiary. . . .
>
> The question then becomes . . . was "any economic or financial benefit conferred on the employee as compensation" in the taxable year. If so, it was taxable to him in that year. This question we must answer in the affirmative. The employer's part of the transaction terminated in 1945. It was then that the amount of the compensation was fixed at $10,500 and irrevocably paid out for petitioner's sole benefit. . . .

Applying the principles stated in the *Sproull* decision to the facts here, it is concluded that 150x-dollar bonus is includible in the gross income of the football player concerned in 1957, the year in which the club unconditionally paid such amount to the escrow agent. . . .

As previously stated, in each case involving a deferral of compensation, a determination of whether the doctrine of constructive receipt is applicable must be made upon the basis of the specific factual situation involved. . . .

With respect to deductions for payments made by an employer under a deferred compensation plan, see section 404(a)(5) of the 1954 Code and section 1.404(a)-12 of the Income Tax Regulations.

In the application of those sections to unfunded plans, no deduction is allowable for any compensation paid or accrued by an employer on account of any employee under such a plan except in the year when paid and then only to the extent allowable under section 404(a). Thus, under an unfunded plan, if compensation is paid by an employer directly to a former employee, such amounts are deductible under section 404(a)(5) when *actually* paid *in cash or other property to the employee,* provided that such amounts meet the requirements of section 162 or section 212.

Advance rulings will not be issued in specific cases involving deferred compensation arrangements.

Notes and Questions

1. *Constructive receipt and tax policy.* Assume that in Situation 1 it could be shown that corporation *X,* the employer, originally proposed to pay the additional compensation to the executive as a cash year-end bonus, but the executive insisted that the contract call for deferral. Given those additional facts, would the executive be taxable on the additional compensation each year as it was earned? Wouldn't such facts show that the employer was "ready, willing, and able to pay" and that the executive had "deliberately turn[ed] his upon income" in order to "select the year for which he will report it"? In such circumstances, is there any need to "speculat[e] whether the payor would have been willing to agree to an earlier payment"? If not, might there nevertheless be administrative reasons to permit deferral?

2. *Time of commitment to defer.* Is it important that the deferral provision in Situation 1 was negotiated as part of the original five-year employment contract?

(a) Assume that the contract originally called for payment of the additional compensation as a cash bonus payable on the last business day of the calendar year, but at the end of the second year of employment, corporation *X* and the executive agree to modify the contract so that payment of the additional compensation earned in years three, four, and five will be deferred. When would amounts so deferred be taxable?

(b) What if the contract modification was instead entered into in November of the third year of the executive's employment, and the new deferred payment provision applied to the additional compensation earned in that year?

(c) Assume again that the contract initially provided for a cash bonus payable on the last business day of the calendar year, but in practice corporation *X* typically delivers the check in early January. If in January of year four, before the additional compensation earned in year three is paid, the parties modify their contract to require deferred payment of the additional compensation for years three, four, and five. When would the amounts so deferred be taxable?

The IRS did not object to delayed reporting where the deferral arrangement was entered into before the beginning of the taxable year in which the employee would earn the compensation to be deferred. Where the agreement called for deferred payment of amounts that had been earned but were not yet payable, the IRS asserted that the agreement was ineffective to defer taxation, but the courts were not receptive to the constructive receipt argument. E.g., Oates v. Commissioner, 18 T.C. 570 (1952), aff'd 207 F.2d 711 (7th Cir. 1953), acq., 1960-1 C.B. 5; Martin v. Commissioner, 96 T.C. 814 (1991); Childs v. Commissioner, 103 T.C. 634, 654-55 (1994) (deferred payment of contingent attorneys' fees under structured settlement of personal injury claims); but see Palmer v. Commissioner, T.C. Memo 2000-228, 80 T.C.M. (CCH) 101 (2000) (despite contract amendment that gave consultant right to specify whether invoice for services would be paid within 30 days of submission or at some later date specified in the invoice, deferred fees were constructively received 30 days after invoicing).

3. *Substantial restrictions or limitations.* Reg. §1.451-2(a) provides in part:

> Income although not actually reduced to a taxpayer's possession is constructively received by him in the taxable year during which it is credited to his account, set apart for him, or otherwise made available so that he may draw upon it at any time, or so that he could have drawn upon it during the taxable year if notice of intention to withdraw had been given. However, income is not constructively received if the taxpayer's control of its receipt is subject to substantial limitations or restrictions.

Assume that an employee or independent contractor has performed services that are to be paid for in a subsequent year. In addition, the contract provides that the worker can have immediate access to all or any portion of the deferred compensation upon request, but at the cost of forfeiting 10 percent of the amount distributed early. When are the deferred amounts taxable? What if the penalty for early withdrawal (the "haircut") were only 5 percent? Two percent? What if an employer contributes 7 percent of each employee's monthly salary to a deferred profit-sharing plan and allows employees to withdraw without penalty any part of their current balance, but any worker who makes such a withdrawal receives no employer contributions to his account for the succeeding six months? What if the suspension or hold-out period were only three months?

4. *Economic benefit doctrine.* Did the football player in Situation 4 have a legal right to receive any part of the bonus in the year of signing? If not, why is current inclusion required?

Observe that the recitations of facts for Situations 1 and 2 of Revenue Ruling 60-31 stipulate that the employer "is under a merely contractual obligation to make the payments when due, and the parties did not intend the amounts [credited on the company's books] be held by the corporation in trust for [the employees]." Why?

The economic benefit doctrine says, in effect, that some promises to pay money in the future amount in substance to current payment in kind. The elements of the economic benefit doctrine are (1) that a fund has been irrevocably set aside for the taxpayer (in trust, escrow, or the like) and (2) that the fund is beyond the reach of the payor's creditors. Pulsifer v. Commissioner, 64 T.C. 245 (1975) (child's share of Irish Sweepstakes prize taxable in year won, although Irish law required it to be put on deposit with the Bank of Ireland to be paid out with interest upon attaining age 21).

5. *Restricted property.* Since the enactment of the restricted property rules in 1969, most economic benefit questions have been subsumed within the operation of §83.

> For purposes of section 83 and the regulations thereunder, the term "property" includes real and personal property other than either money or an unfunded and unsecured promise to pay money or property in the future. The term also includes a beneficial interest in assets (including money) which are transferred or set aside from the claims of creditors of the transferor, for example, in a trust or escrow account.

Reg. §1.83-3(e). See below Chapter 6F.3. Where a promise of deferred compensation, instead of being a "merely contractual obligation to make the payments when due," is backed by a transfer of assets in trust for the benefit of the employee, §83 supplies the tax timing rules. See §402(b)(1). If the employee's right to such funded deferred compensation becomes "transferable or not subject to a substantial risk of forfeiture" before the amount is distributed from the trust, then §83(a) will require taxation in advance of receipt.

6. *Rabbi trusts.* What if the employer takes steps to finance deferred compensation as it is earned without protecting the funding vehicle from the company's creditors? The employer might, for example, buy an annuity contract or life insurance policy to provide a ready source of funds with which to pay its deferred compensation obligations, but retain ownership of the contract. Under such circumstances the promise of future payments might be considered "funded" in a colloquial or pragmatic sense, but the assets are not immune from the claims of the employer's creditors so that in the event of insolvency the employee entitled to deferred compensation would have only a general creditor's claim. Where assets dedicated to financing deferred compensation remain subject to the claims of general creditors of the promisor (are unsecured, that is), the cases hold that the promise to pay is "unfunded" for tax purposes so that there is no transfer of "property" that would trigger §83. Childs v. Commissioner, 103 T.C. 634 (1994). Consequently, cash method accounting (constructive receipt) governs the time for taxation of the deferred compensation, notwithstanding the set aside of (unprotected) assets.

If the promise of deferred compensation is backed by assets placed in trust and the service provider (employee or independent contractor) entitled to future payments is the trust beneficiary, then the advance funding is a transfer of property subject to the timing rules of §83. If assets are put in trust under an instrument that obligates the trustee, in the event of the employer's insolvency, to suspend distributions of deferred compensation and hold the trust fund for the benefit of all general creditors of the employer, does §83 or the cash method supply the timing rule? Such arrangements, commonly known as "rabbi trusts," became popular components of executive deferred compensation programs once the IRS concluded that the employee was not taxable until distribution (or in other words, that a properly structured rabbi trust would not trigger §83). See Rev. Proc. 92-64, 1992-2 C.B. 422 (model rabbi trust); Rev. Proc. 92-65, 1992-2 C.B. 428. By definition, rabbi trusts afford no protection against employer insolvency; their attraction lies in the protection they offer executives in the event of a change of ownership or control of the employer corporation. Incumbent management is often replaced on a change of control, but the rabbi trust can prevent the new owners from reneging on promised deferred compensation that has already been earned, which obviates the need for discharged former managers to resort to costly litigation.

7. *Cash equivalence doctrine.* Is receipt of the employer's promissory note taxable in-kind compensation to a cash basis employee? Is the note payment or a means of putting off payment? Does it matter whether the note is a negotiable instrument? In Cowden v. Commissioner, 289 F.2d 20 (5th Cir. 1961), the court explained that receipt of a note is the equivalent of cash in some circumstances.

> A promissory note, negotiable in form, is not necessarily the equivalent of cash. Such an instrument may have been issued by a maker of doubtful solvency or for other reasons such paper might be denied a ready acceptance in the market place. We think the converse of this principle ought to be applicable. We are convinced that if a promise to pay of a solvent obligor is unconditional and assignable, not subject to set-offs and is of a kind that is frequently transferred to lenders or investors at a discount not substantially greater than the generally prevailing premium for the use of money, such promise is the equivalent of cash and taxable in like manner as cash would have been taxable had it been received by the taxpayer rather than the obligation. The principle that negotiability is not the test of taxability in an equivalent of cash case such as is before us * * * points up the doctrine that substance and not form should control in the application of the income tax laws.

289 F.2d at 24. See Williams v. Commissioner, 28 T.C. 1000 (1957), acq., 1958-1 C.B. 6 (no income on receipt of a note where the maker was without funds and taxpayer's repeated attempts to sell the note were unsuccessful). Wholesale application of the cash equivalence doctrine would largely obliterate the distinction between cash and accrual accounting. (Can you explain why?) It functions as a deterrent — an anti-abuse sledge hammer that can be invoked in egregious cases. The IRS will not issue favorable rulings on constructive receipt questions or rabbi trusts unless the arrangement expressly provides that the employee's rights to deferred compensation are inalienable. Rev. Proc. 92-64, §13(b), 1992-2 C.B. 422 (model rabbi trust); Rev. Proc. 92-65, §3(e), 1992-2 C.B. 428.

8. *ERISA and tax timing.* The Employee Retirement Income Security Act of 1974 (ERISA), 29 U.S.C. §1001 et. seq., requires that an employee's interest in certain deferred compensation arrangements be protected in various ways, including insulation from the employer's creditors and limiting the duration of forfeiture conditions. ERISA §§403(c)(1), 203(a), 29 U.S.C.

§§1103(c)(1), 1053(a). Observe that security from creditors makes for "property" subject to §83, while limiting the duration of forfeiture conditions extinguishes any substantial risk of loss, which may make deferred compensation taxable years in advance of actual distribution. As such, federal labor law (ERISA) can sometimes force deferred compensation into a mold that triggers taxation under the restricted property rules, trumping constructive receipt. Sometimes, but not always. In three notable situations ERISA does not accelerate inclusion.

First, ERISA's advance funding and anti-forfeiture rules apply to "pension" plans, defined as arrangements that either provide retirement income or defer compensation to the termination of employment (or longer). ERISA §3(2)(A), 29 U.S.C. §1002(2)(a). Consequently, short-term deferred compensation programs that are structured so that the employee is likely to receive in-service distributions are not pension plans within ERISA's ambit.

Second (and more importantly), a pension plan that is "unfunded and maintained by an employer primarily for the purpose of providing deferred compensation for a select group of management or highly compensated employees" is excused from ERISA's funding and security rules that would trigger inclusion under §83. ERISA §§201(2), 401(a)(1), 29 U.S.C. §§1051(2), 1101(a)(1). This so-called top hat plan exception allows constructive receipt principles to govern tax timing of certain executive deferred compensation programs. The Labor Department has interpreted "unfunded" consistently with the IRS's rabbi trust rulings, as meaning not protected from the payor's general creditors (unsecured), even though the statutes have quite different histories and purposes.

Third, pension plans that satisfy the Internal Revenue Code's intricate definition of a qualified pension, profit-sharing, stock bonus, or annuity plan, §§401(a), 404(a)(2), are subject to special tax provisions that override §83 and defer inclusion until actual distribution. §§83(e)(2), 402(a), 403(a)(1). Such qualified retirement plans (often simply referred to as "qualified plans") are fully subject to ERISA's worker-protection rules. Additional tax law conditions apply as well, most importantly the nondiscrimination rules, which require that plan membership not favor highly compensated employees and that contributions or benefits provided under the plan, when expressed as a share of total compensation, not discriminate in favor of the highly compensated segment of the workforce. §§401(a)(3), (4), (5), 410(b).

9. *Qualified retirement plans.* Favorable tax treatment is accorded retirement savings accumulated through a qualified plan. There are three major components of the preferential tax treatment of qualified deferred compensation. First, the employer receives a current deduction (subject to certain limits) for amounts actually contributed to the plan. §404(a)(1)-(3). Second, the trust that holds the plan assets is generally exempt from taxation on its investment income. §501(a). Third, any amount contributed on behalf

of an individual employee is not included in gross income until actually distributed by the plan; upon distribution, trust earnings are taxable to the recipient as well. §§83(e)(2), 402(a). In some circumstances distributions may be eligible for further tax deferral if they are directly transferred to or promptly reinvested in another qualified plan or an individual retirement account (so-called rollovers, §§402(c), 401(a)(31)). Observe that these rules grant the employer a deduction upon contribution even though the employee does not simultaneously report income — the tax deferral provided by that offset is the source of the qualified plan tax preference. Because the deferral may extend over decades, its value is immense. Recall that deferral is, assuming constant tax rates, equivalent to exempting the investment's yield from tax. In 2005 the value of assets held in qualified trusts was $5,082 billion;[3] assuming an average 10 percent return and 25 percent tax rate, the tax subsidy for qualified plan savings is worth about $130 billion *annually*.

10. *Employee elections.* In applying the constructive receipt doctrine in Revenue Ruling 60-31, the IRS declined to look behind the parties' agreement because "the statute cannot be administered by speculating whether the payor would have been willing to agree to an earlier payment." What if no such speculation is necessary because the payor did in fact agree to earlier payment? For instance, an employer might allow certain executives either to receive their full salary or bonus currently, or instead to elect to defer payment of a designated portion. Assume that an election to defer an amount earned and otherwise payable in a particular year must be made before the start of the year, that any compensation deferred will be paid with interest upon separation from service, and that the employer is under a merely contractual obligation to make the payments when due. There is no moment in time when an executive who elects deferral has a current right to payment (the election must be made before the compensation is earned or payable), so inclusion would not be required under a strict interpretation of constructive receipt. Yet there is also no question that the employer was ready, willing, and able to pay for the work currently. Hence the employee's election could be characterized as "deliberately turn[ing] his back upon income" because "his failure to receive resulted from the exercise of his own choice." In 1978 the Treasury proposed a regulation that provided that a taxpayer who elects to defer payment of compensation under a plan or arrangement that gives the taxpayer the unilateral option to defer must include the amount as income for the taxable year in which, but for the election, it would otherwise have been payable. Prop. Reg. §1.61-16(a), 43 Fed. Reg. 4638 (1978).

The attempted expansion of constructive receipt stirred up a hornet's nest. The Revenue Act of 1978 repudiated the innovation. The 1978 legislation went further by authorizing cafeteria plans, which allow employees to

---

3. Employee Benefit Research Institute, EBRI Databook on Employee Benefits, Table 11.3(c) (Feb. 2007), at *http://www.ebri.org/pdf/publications/books/databook/DB.Chapter%2011.pdf*

choose between receiving cash and certain excludible benefits without being deemed (by virtue of that election) to have constructively received cash. §125; Prop. Reg. §1.125-2(a) (election timing). In addition, the Revenue Act of 1978 sanctioned cash-or-deferred arrangements — commonly known as 401(k) plans — that permit employees to elect to defer part of their current compensation by having the employer contribute it instead to a qualified retirement plan. If certain conditions are satisfied, the amount contributed to the retirement plan is deemed an (excludible) employer contribution rather than receipt of includible compensation (constructive receipt) that is used to make an after-tax employee contribution. §§401(k), 402(e)(3).

11. *Reigning in nonqualified deferred compensation — §409A.* In 2004 Congress revisited constructive receipt and its relation to §83 and concluded that aggressive tax planners had gone too far. The result, §409A, imposes new limits on nonqualified deferred compensation plans. The limits are of two sorts. First, the participant's control over distribution timing is cabined: (1) the election to defer must generally be made before the start of the taxable year in which the services are performed, (2) the plan must provide that deferred amounts cannot be distributed earlier than six specified times (separation from service, disability, death, a time specified when the compensation is deferred, change of ownership or control of the corporate payor, or an unforeseeable emergency), and (3) subsequent elections to further delay payment must generally be made at least 12 months before the payment is due and in some cases (distributions tied to separation from service, change of control, or a date fixed by the plan) must call for at least five years of additional deferral. §409A(a)(2)-(4). Second, certain rabbi trusts that offer de facto creditor protection, including offshore trusts and trusts that restrict assets to payment of benefits if the employer's financial health deteriorates, are treated as funded. Failure to comply with these requirements triggers taxation of the deferred compensation as soon as it is not subject to a substantial risk of forfeiture, regardless of whether any assets are set aside to finance future payment. This will often require deferred amounts to be included in gross income far in advance of actual payment. §409A(a)(1)(A), (b)(1). Moreover, if the plan fails to comply with the timing controls, interest is charged from the time the compensation was earned and a 20 percent penalty tax is imposed. §409A(a)(1)(B). The interest and penalty exaction biases the tax system against deferred compensation, violating economic neutrality. See Chapter 6E below.

2. Inclusion in Advance of Receipt: Debt Instruments

If a taxpayer simply puts her money in a savings account and lets the interest pile up from year to year, indefinitely, tax is not deferred until she makes a withdrawal. Annual interest credits are constructively received because they are credited to the account and made available so that the taxpayer could draw on them at any time, or could do so if notice of intention to withdraw were given. Reg. §1.451-2(a).

Would constructive receipt apply if instead the taxpayer put her money in a three-year bank certificate of deposit (CD) that calls for payment of accumulated interest at maturity and imposes a penalty for early withdrawal? Is tax timing just a matter of proper planning? Should the owner of the CD be treated as constructively receiving the (lesser) amount of interest, which the bank would have paid each year on a savings account? (As to that amount, there's no need to speculate whether the payor would have been willing to agree to an earlier payment.)

Suppose the taxpayer bought zero-coupon bonds. These are bonds on which the stated interest (coupon) is zero. With no stated interest, such bonds sell at a substantial discount from face. The longer their term, the bigger the original discount. It is well recognized that in economic terms the discount — or more precisely the excess of stated redemption price over issue price — is interest, payable on maturity of the bond. The discount will normally diminish with time as maturity draws nearer, and the value of the bond will rise accordingly. Is the bondholder taxed on this appreciation in value prior to maturity under the constructive receipt doctrine? Should she be taxed each year on the increase in value of the bond? Does Congress have the power to impose tax in advance of receipt? Is the annual increment in the bond's value any different from appreciation of real estate or corporate stock, which is tax deferred under the realization doctrine of Eisner v. Macomber?

Now look at §§1272 and 1273. These require that interest be accrued on most discount bond transactions, even by taxpayers using the cash receipts and disbursements method. In the case of a bond issued for cash, the discount can be measured in cash terms, converted into an equivalent rate of interest, and then income is imputed at that rate, all on a compound basis.

It took some time to arrive at this solution. Prior to 1969 the only concern was one of characterization. The statute did not require recognition of income prior to receipt of payment at maturity, but it did insist that the gain then recognized, to the extent of original issue discount, be recognized as interest income, not capital gain. Section 1271(c)(2)(A) preserves this rule for bonds issued prior to the effective date of §1272. In 1969 the statute was amended to require inclusion of original issue discount in the income of a holder allocated over the period of his holding. From 1969 to 1982 the requirement was that original issue discount be allocated ratably over the period from acquisition to maturity. See §1272(b). Since 1982 the rule has required allocation of interest on the basis of a compound interest computation prescribed in §1272(a)(3).

In general, the compound interest computation produces a slower recognition of income than a ratable allocation, since it reflects the fact that income should be less in the early years because the bondholder has less invested. For example, consider a $1,000 bond issued for $250 payable in 18 years. Ratable allocation of $750 over 18 years is $41.67 a year (which is 16.67 percent simple interest on $250). But at compound interest, money will quadruple in 18 years at about 8 percent. More precisely, at 7.85 percent compounded semiannually the interest accruable under §1272(a) in the first year would be only $20.01, less than half the $41.67 required under ratable allocation.[4]

The change from ratable allocation to compound interest computation operated as a sensible relief measure for bondholders, but its chief purpose was apparently to prevent borrowers from taking inflated interest deductions in the early years of a bond issue.

Why is interest thus treated so radically differently from dividends and equity earnings? A partial answer may be that creditors are *entitled* to receive interest and principal while shareholders are only entitled to such dividends as corporate directors may in their discretion declare. Even preferred shareholders are not entitled to dividends until declared; their preference only takes the form of a prohibition against payment of dividends on common shares unless dividends due on the preferred have been paid.

A more specifically tax-oriented factor may be that interest is deductible by the payor. Many corporate borrowers compute taxable income on an accrual basis, and so interest will be deductible by them as it accrues, despite the fact that payment is deferred. It may seem unacceptable to let people create transactions in which lenders can defer taxes on interest income while borrowers are allowed an immediate deduction for the corresponding expense. There is no equivalent deduction for anyone on the payment of a corporate dividend, nor on the appreciation of property values that makes it possible. Similarly, there is no obligor's deduction in the case of simple appreciation in the value of ownership interests in real estate or other property.

Notes

1. *Interest deduction timing.* By forcing inclusion of original issue discount in advance of receipt, §1272 requires cash-method lenders to report interest using the accrual method. If the borrower uses the cash method, will the interest be taxed before it becomes deductible? See §163(e). The cash method override works both ways.

2. *Scope of OID rules.* Section 1272 requires the holder of "any debt instrument" to pay tax on post-paid interest as it accrues. Debt instrument is defined by §1275(a)(1) to mean "any bond, debenture, note, or certificate or other evidence of indebtedness." This definition comprehends the

---

4. Section 1272 requires semiannual compounding, §1272(a)(5), and the bond issued for $250 quadruples in value over 18 years (36 periods). If $x^{36} = 4$, then $x = 4^{-36}$, so $x = 1.03926$. A six-month interest rate of 3.926 percent corresponds to an annual interest rate of 7.85 percent.

three-year bank certificate of deposit (CD), which calls for payment of accumulated interest at maturity (mentioned earlier), and the depositor must include accrued interest each year over the life of the CD. What about the deferred annuity contract, Chapter 6B.2 above? Isn't an annuity contract in substance a loan transaction? Do the OID rules demand taxation of the year-by-year increase in contract value during the accumulation period, even if no amounts are withdrawn? §1275(a)(1)(b).

Besides preserving the tax-preferred status of annuities, Congress also moved to protect the market for its own debt obligations. Traditional (paper) U.S. savings bonds (series EE) are sold to the public at a price equal to half of their denominated face value, with all interest paid at redemption (the bonds may be redeemed for their face value at maturity). §1272(a)(2)(B). What explains the other exceptions to current inclusion?

3. *Market discount.* Assume that a bond pays interest at a rate equal to the market rate at the time of issue and so sells at par (with no discount). But then suppose market interest rates go up, and so the value of the bond in question goes down. This is called market discount, as distinguished from original issue discount. How should the purchaser of a bond with market discount be treated? People buying and selling such bonds will regularly describe them in terms of "yield to maturity," a figure that makes no distinction between market discount and original issue discount.

Until comparatively recently, the tax statute had no provisions for market discount. Indeed the excess of redemption price over a lower market purchase price was capital gain. See §1271. But now we have §§1276 and 1278, which take a cautious shot at market discount after all. List and evaluate the conditions and qualifications on the taxation of market discount as interest income.

4. *Deferred payment sales.* Do the original issue discount rules apply to a deferred payment sale of property (seller financing)? The OID computation in §§1272 and 1273 depends on knowing the issue price of an obligation. That is relatively easy to determine if the obligation was issued for cash. What if an obligation is issued for property? The problem then is much more difficult since it requires putting a cash value on the property. If either the property or the debt instrument with which it is acquired is publicly traded, the OID rules apply as usual. §1273(b)(3). In other cases, §1274 is used to determine the value of the property. All payments due under the contract (whether denominated interest or principal) are discounted to present value using prevailing interest rates and the result, called the "imputed principal amount," is treated as the property's value if it is less than the stated principal amount of the debt. (If the imputed principal amount is greater than the stated principal amount of the debt, then the contract provides adequate stated interest and the stated principal amount is treated as the property's value.) The property value so determined is treated as the issue price of the debt instrument for purposes of applying the OID rules. §§1274(a), 1273(a)(1). The OID rules then mandate annual inclusion

of accrued interest regardless of whether the seller receives any payments under the contract during the year.

Some deferred payment sales are excepted from §1274, including certain sales of farms for less than $1 million, sales of principal residences, sales involving total payments of $250,000 or less, and sales of patents. §1274(c)(3). In such cases, the technique of discounting payments to present value is still used to identify the interest component (determine the property's imputed value), but the interest so identified is taxed only as payments are received; inclusion of accrued interest is not required. §483(a), (b), (d)(1). In addition, if section 1274 applies but the stated principal amount of the debt instrument is $2 million or less, interest accrual is not required if the seller is not a dealer in the property and does not use the accrual method and if the buyer and seller jointly elect cash method treatment of the debt instrument. §1274A(c).

5. *Post-paid rent.* Property sales are not the only instance in which deferred payments might postpone taxation of income that has been fully earned. Suppose that the owner of Blackacre, a cash-basis taxpayer, signs a three-year lease of the property under which the tenant's only rental obligation is to pay a lump sum of $1.2 million on termination of the lease. Look at §467, enacted in 1984, which prescribes another legislative override of cash-method accounting.

D. ACCRUAL METHOD ACCOUNTING AND ITS LIMITS

Most individual taxpayers compute taxable income by the cash receipts and disbursements method. §446(c)(1). But in the case of a business with books of account, taxable income is to be computed by the method used in keeping those books. §446(a). This effectively gives many taxpayers a kind of restrained choice between cash and accrual accounting for taxable income.

A taxpayer's accounting method can be rejected if it "does not clearly reflect income." §446(b). Under this standard, taxpayers whose incomes arise from selling goods have long been required to keep inventories and to account for inventory sales and costs by an accrual accounting method, while businesses selling services rather than goods were allowed to utilize cash receipts and disbursements accounting. Farmers, however, have long been excepted from many of the requirements of normal accrual accounting, even though they do sell goods. See Reg. §1.162-12.

More recent statutory provisions have required accrual accounting, however, for certain farming operations and for some service businesses in which the sale of goods is not a material factor. §§447, 448. In 1986 it was even proposed to require accrual accounting for large law firms; the proposal was strenuously resisted, and what emerged is in §448. Should large professional firms be required to account on an accrual basis?

Beyond the choice of overall method, there are numerous variations and particular rules about accounting for specific items. Interest, in particular, is now required to be accounted for on a strict economic accrual basis in many transactions regardless of a taxpayer's general method of accounting for other items.

This section is only a thin sample of accrual accounting problems. It deals with prepaid income, security deposits, inventories, and accrual of future expenses. A closely related topic already covered is compulsory accrual accounting for bond interest (Chapter 6C.2 above). All these topics raise the recurring issue of the relationship between tax and financial accounting practices.

1. Prepaid Income

AMERICAN AUTOMOBILE ASS'N v. UNITED STATES
367 U.S. 687 (1961)

Mr. Justice Clark delivered the opinion of the Court. . . . The Association is a national automobile club organized as a nonstock membership corporation with its principal office in Washington, D.C. It provides a variety of services to the members of affiliated local automobile clubs and those of ten clubs which taxpayer itself directly operates as divisions, but such services are rendered solely upon a member's demand. Its income is derived primarily from dues paid one year in advance by members of the clubs. Memberships may commence or be renewed in any month of the year. For many years, the association has employed an accrual method of accounting and the calendar year as its taxable year. It is admitted that for its purposes the method used is in accord with generally accepted commercial accounting principles. The membership dues, as received, were deposited in the Association's bank accounts without restriction as to their use for any of its corporate purposes. However, for the Association's own accounting purposes, the dues were treated in its books as income received ratably[3] over the 12-month membership period. The portions thereof ratably attributable to membership months occurring beyond the year of receipt, i.e., in a second calendar year, were reflected in the Association's books at the close of the first year as unearned or deferred income. Certain operating expenses were

---

3. In 1952 and 1953 dues collected in any month were accounted as income to the extent of one-twenty-fourth for that month (on the assumption that the mean date of receipt was the middle of the month), one-twelfth for each of the next eleven months, and again one-twenty-fourth in the anniversary month. In 1954, however, guided by its own statistical average experience, the Association changed its system so as to more simply reach almost the same result by charging to year of receipt, without regard to month of receipt, one-half of the entire dues payment and deferring the balance to the following year.

chargeable as prepaid membership cost and deducted ratably over the same periods of time as those over which dues were recognized as income.

The Court of Claims bottomed its opinion on Automobile Club of Michigan v. Commissioner, 353 U.S. 180 (1957), finding that "the method of treatment of prepaid automobile club membership dues employed [by the Association here was,] ... for Federal income tax purposes, "purely artificial." 181 F. Supp. 255, 258. It accepted that case as "a rejection by the Supreme Court of the accounting method advanced by plaintiff in the case at bar." Ibid. The Association does not deny that its accounting system is substantially identical to that used by the petitioner in Michigan. It maintains, however, that Michigan does not control this case because of a difference in proof, i.e., that in this case the record contains expert accounting testimony indicating that the system used was in accord with generally accepted accounting principles; that its proof of cost of member service was detailed; and that the correlation between that cost and the period of time over which the dues were credited as income was shown and justified by proof of experience. The holding of Michigan, however, that the system of accounting was "purely artificial" was based upon the finding that "substantially all services are performed only upon a member's demand and the taxpayer's performance was not related to fixed dates after the tax year." 353. U.S. 180, 189, n.20. That is also true here.[4] As the Association's own accounting expert testified:

> You are dealing with a group or pool. Any pooling or risk situation, particular members may in a particular year require very little of a specific service that is rendered to certain other members. I wouldn't know what the experience on that would be, but I would think it would be rather irregular between individual members. . . . I am buying the availability of services, the protection. . . . Frankly, the irregularity of the actual furnishing of the maps and helping you out when you run out of gasoline and so on, I frankly don't think that has a blessed thing to do with the over all accounting.

It may be true that to the accountant the actual incidence of cost in serving an individual member in exchange for his individual dues is inconsequential, or, from the viewpoint of commercial accounting, unessential to determination and disclosure of the overall financial condition of the Association. That "irregularity," however, is highly relevant to the clarity of an accounting system which defers receipt, as earned income, of dues to a taxable period in which no, some, or all the services paid for by those dues may or may not be rendered. The Code exacts its revenue from the individual member's dues which, no one disputes, constitute income. When their receipt as earned income is recognized ratably over two calendar years, without regard to correspondingly fixed individual expense or performance justification,

4. Beacon Publishing Co. v. Commissioner, 218 F.2d 697, and Schuessler v. Commissioner, 230 F.2d 722, may be distinguished from the present case on the same grounds which made them distinguishable in Automobile Club of Michigan v. Commissioner, 353 U.S. 180, 189, n.20.

but consistently with overall experience, their accounting doubtless presents a rather accurate image of the total financial structure, but fails to respect the criteria of annual tax accounting and may be rejected by the Commissioner.

The Association further contends that the findings of the court below support its position. We think not. The Court of Claims' only finding as to the accounting system itself is as follows:

> 22. The method of accounting employed by plaintiff during the years in issue has been used regularly by plaintiff since 1931 and is in accord with generally accepted commercial accounting principles and practices and was, prior to the adverse determination by the Commissioner of the Internal Revenue, customarily and generally employed in the motor club field.

This is only to say that in performing the function of business accounting the method employed by the Association "is in accord with generally accepted commercial accounting principles and practices." It is not to hold that for income tax purposes it so clearly reflects income as to be binding on the Treasury. Likewise, other findings merely reflecting statistical computations of average monthly cost per member on a group or pool basis are without determinate significance to our decision that the federal revenue cannot, without legislative consent and over objection of the Commissioner, be made to depend upon average experience in rendering performance and turning a profit. Indeed, such tabulations themselves demonstrate the inadequacy from an income tax standpoint of the pro rata method of allocating each year's membership dues in equal monthly installments not in fact related to the expenses incurred. Not only did individually incurred expenses actually vary from month to month, but even the average expense varied — recognition of income nonetheless remaining ratably constant. . . .

Whether or not the Court's judgment in Michigan controls our disposition of this case, there are other considerations requiring our affirmance. They concern the action of the Congress with respect to its own positive and express statutory authorization of employment of such sound commercial accounting practices in reporting taxable income. In 1954 the Congress found dissatisfaction in the fact that "as a result of court decisions and rulings, there have developed many divergencies between the computation of income for tax purposes and income for business purposes as computed under generally accepted accounting principles. The areas of difference are confined almost entirely to questions of when certain types of revenue and expenses should be taken into account in arriving at net income." House Ways and Means Committee Report, H.R. Rep. No. 1337, 83d Cong., 2d Sess. 48. As a result, it introduced into the Internal Revenue Code of 1954 §452 and §462, which specifically permitted essentially the same practice as was employed by the Association here. Only one year later, however, in June 1955, the Congress repealed these sections retroactively. It appears that in this action Congress first overruled the long administrative practice of the Commissioner and holdings of the courts in disallowing such deferral of income for tax purposes and then within a year reversed its own action. This repeal, we believe, confirms our view that the method used by the Association could be rejected by the Commissioner. While the claim is made that Congress did not "intend to disturb prior law as it affected permissible accrual accounting provisions for tax purposes," H.R. Rep. No. 293, 84th Cong., 1st Sess. 4-5, the cold fact is that it repealed the only law incontestably permitting the practice upon which the Association depends. To say that, as to taxpayers using such systems, Congress was merely declaring existing law when it adopted §452 in 1954, and that it was merely restoring unaffected the same prior law when it repealed the new section in 1955 for good reason, is a contradiction in itself, "varnishing nonsense with the charm of sound." . . . We are further confirmed in this view by consideration of the even more recent action of the Congress in 1958, subsequent to the decision in Michigan, supra. In that year §455 was added to the Internal Revenue Code of 1954. It permits publishers to defer receipt of income of prepaid subscriptions of newspapers, magazines and periodicals. An effort was made in the Senate to add a provision in §455 which would extend its coverage to prepaid automobile club membership dues. However, in conference the House Conferees refused to accept this amendment. Senator Byrd explained the rejection of the amendment to the Senate (104 Cong. Rec., Part 14, p. 17744): "It was the position of the House conferees that this matter of prepaid dues and fees received by nonprofit service organizations was a part of the entire subject dealing with the treatment of prepaid income and that such subject should be left for study of this entire problem. . . . " It appears, therefore, that, pending its own further study, Congress has given publishers but denied automobile clubs the very relief that the Association seeks in this Court.

To recapitulate, it appears that Congress has long been aware of the problem this case presents. In 1954 it enacted §452 and §462, but quickly repealed them. Since that time Congress has authorized the desired accounting only in the instance of prepaid subscription income, which, as was pointed out in Michigan, is ratably earned by performance on "publication dates after the tax year." 353 U.S. 180, 189, note 20. It has refused to enlarge §455 to include prepaid membership dues. At the very least, this background indicates congressional recognition of the complications inherent in the problem and its seriousness to the general revenue. We must leave to the Congress the fashioning of a rule which, in any event, must have wide ramifications. The Committees of the Congress have standing committees expertly grounded in tax problems, with jurisdiction covering the whole field of taxation and facilities for studying considerations of policy as between the various taxpayers and the necessities of the general revenues. The validity of the long-established policy of the Court in deferring, where possible, to congressional procedures in the tax field is clearly indicated in this case.[12] Finding only that, in light of existing provisions not specifically authorizing it, the exercise of the Commissioner's discretion in rejecting the Association's accounting system was not unsound, we need not anticipate what will be the product of further "study of this entire problem."

Affirmed.

Mr. Justice STEWART, whom Mr. Justice DOUGLAS, Mr. Justice HARLAN and Mr. Justice WHITTAKER join, dissenting. . . .

I

The Commissioner's basic argument against the deferred reporting of prepayments has traditionally been that such a method conflicts with a series of decisions of this Court which establish the so-called "claim of right doctrine." In this case the Government abandoned that argument, with good reason. As four Circuits have correctly held, the claim of right doctrine furnishes no support for the Government's position. . . . A claim of right without "restriction on use" may be the crucial factor in determining that particular funds are includable in gross income. . . . But it hardly follows that all such funds must necessarily be reported by an accrual basis taxpayer as income in the year of receipt, whether or not then earned.

The Government shifted its argument in this case to the contention that the "annual accounting requirement" demands that "[n]either income nor deduction items may be accelerated or postponed from one taxable year to another in order to reflect the long-term economic result of a particular transaction or group of transactions." The Government finds a basis for this argument in such cases as Security Mills Co. v. Commissioner, 321 U.S. 281; Brown v. Helvering, 291 U.S. 193; Burnet v. Sanford & Brooks Co., 282 U.S. 359; Guaranty Trust Co. v. Commissioner, 303 U.S. 493; and Heiner v. Mellon, 304 U.S. 271.

The Court today does not base its decision on this theory, presumably because the Court believes, as I do, that the theory is not valid. Putting to one side the point that many of the cases relied on involved cash basis taxpayers, these decisions no more pertain to deferred reporting of totally unearned receipts than do the claim of right decisions. These cases, like the claim of right cases, start from the premise that the income in question has been fully earned. The underlying premise of the annual accounting requirement is that *otherwise reportable income* derived from a transaction cannot be excluded

---

12. In 1955 it was estimated that transitional loss of revenue under §452 and §462, repealed that year, would total in excess of a billion dollars. H.R. Rep. No. 293, 84th Cong., 1st Sess. 3. That this impact on the revenue continues to be an important factor in congressional consideration of the problem is indicated by the observation of the House Committee on Ways and Means that a "transitional rule" is necessary "to minimize the initial revenue impact" of the measure currently pending. H.R. Rep. No. 381, 87th Cong., 1st Sess. 4. That the system used by petitioner here is, perhaps, presently not uncommon may be indicated by the fact that during this Term alone several cases involving similar systems have reached this Court.

from gross income in order to let the taxpayer wait to see in a later year how the over-all transaction turns out. That is not the issue in this case. The question here is whether any reportable income has been derived from a transaction when payments are received in advance of performance.

Although wisely rejecting the claim of right and annual accounting arguments, the Court decides this case upon grounds which seem to me equally invalid. I can find nothing in Automobile Club of Michigan which controls disposition of this case. And the legislative history upon which the Court alternatively relies seems to me upon examination to be singularly unconvincing.

In Michigan there was no offer of proof to show the rate at which the taxpayer fulfilled its obligations under its membership contracts. . . .

As to the enactment and repeal of §452 and §462, upon which the Court places so much reliance, there are, at the outset, obvious difficulties in relying on what happened in 1954 and 1955 to ascertain the meaning of §41 of the 1939 Code. . . . But these problems aside, I think that the enactment and subsequent repeal of §452 and §462 give no indication of Congressional approval of the position taken by the Commissioner in this case. If anything, the legislative action leads to the contrary impression. . . .

Although §452 and §462 were short-lived, the shape of the decisional law with respect to §41 of the 1939 Code changed considerably during the interval between the passage and repeal of the new sections. In Beacon Publishing Co. v. Commissioner, 218 F.2d 697, the Tenth Circuit rejected the Commissioner's reliance on the claim of right rationale and found that the deferment of advances in accord with accrual principles did "clearly reflect . . . income" under §41. At about the same time a Ninth Circuit decision permitted income received from the sale of goods to be offset by a deduction for the future expense of shipping the goods. Pacific Grape Products Co. v. Commissioner, 219 F.2d 862.

When Congress repealed §452 and §462, the record shows that it was fully aware of these decisions. Congress recognized that the rationale of these cases would produce a complete reversal of the previous administrative position with respect to the reporting of unearned receipts under §41 and its counterpart under the 1954 Code, §446. Congressional intent with respect to this possibility was entirely clear — the trend of judicial decisions should be allowed to run its course *without any inference of disapproval being drawn from the repeal of §452 and §462*. This intent was evidenced in the assurances which the House Ways and Means Committee demanded and received from the Secretary of the Treasury, who had sought the repeal of the two sections. . . .

To my mind, this legislative history shows that Congress made every effort to dissuade the courts from doing exactly what the Court is doing in this case — drawing from the repeal of §452 an inference of Congressional disapproval of deferred reporting of advances. But even if the legislative history on this point were hazy, the same conclusion would have to be reached upon examination of Congressional purpose in repealing §452 and §462. Cf. United States v. Benedict, 338 U.S. 692, 696. For the fact of the matter is, contrary to the impression left by the Court's opinion, that the reasons for rejecting §452 and §462 were entirely consistent with accepting the deferred reporting of receipts in a case like this. Sections 452 and 462 were repealed *solely* because of a prospective loss of revenue during the first year in which taxpayers would take advantage of the new sections. Insofar as the reporting of advances was concerned, that loss of revenue would have occurred solely as a consequence of taxpayers changing their method of reporting, without the necessity of securing the Commissioner's consent, to that authorized under §452 and §462. The taxpayer who shifted his basis for reporting advances would have been allowed what was commonly termed a "double deduction" during the transitional year. . . .

The Congressional purpose in repealing §452 and §462 — maintenance of the revenues — does not, however, require disapproval of sound accounting principles in cases of taxpayers who, like the petitioner, have customarily and regularly used a sound accrual accounting method in reporting advance payments. No transition is involved, and no "double deduction" is possible. Moreover, taxpayers formerly reporting advances as income in the year of receipt can now shift to a true accrual system of reporting only with the approval of the Commissioner. See Treas. Reg. 111, §29.41-2 (1943); Treas. Reg. 118, §39.41-2(c) (1953); Int. Rev. Code of 1954, §446(e). Before giving his approval the Commissioner can be expected to insist upon adjustments in the taxpayer's transition year to forestall any revenue loss which would otherwise result from the change in accounting method. . . .

II

I think the Government's position in this case is at odds with the statutes, regulations, and court decisions, which, since 1916, have recognized that realistic accrual accounting does "clearly reflect income." If I am correct, the law did not give the Commissioner any "discretion . . . not to accept the taxpayer's accounting system."

The basic concept of including advances in gross income only as they are earned is but an aspect of accrual accounting principles which have consistently received judicial approval. . . . Indeed, "accrual" of income has been commonly defined in terms of "earnings" from the sale of goods or the performance of services. See, e.g., Spring City Co. v. Commissioner, 292 U.S. 182, 184-185; Stanley and Kilcullen, *The Federal Income* Tax (3d ed., 1955), 190. In rejecting petitioner's method of allocating prepaid advances, the Court, I think, disregards these basic principles.

The net effect of compelling the petitioner to include all dues in gross income in the year received is to force the petitioner to utilize a hybrid accounting method — a cash basis for dues and an accrual basis for all other items. . . .

The Court suggests that the application of sound accrual principles cannot be accepted here because deferment is based on an estimated rate of earnings, and because this estimate, in turn, is based on average, not individual, costs. It is true, of course, that the petitioner cannot know what service an individual member will require or when he will demand it. Accordingly, in determining the portion of its outstanding contractual obligations which have been discharged during a particular period (and hence the portion of receipts earned during that period), the petitioner can only compare the total expenditures for that period against estimated average expenditures for the same number of members over a full contract term. But this use of estimates and averages is in no way inconsistent with long-accepted accounting practices in reflecting and reporting income. . . .

Similarly, it is not relevant that the petitioner "defers receipt . . . of dues to a taxable period in which no, some, or all the services paid for by those dues may or may not be rendered." The fact of the matter is that what the petitioner has an obligation to provide, i.e., the constant readiness of services if needed, will with certainty be provided during the period to which deferment has been made. Averages are frequently utilized in tax reporting. In computing the value of work in progress, in distributing overhead to product cost, and in various other areas, the use of averages has long been accepted. See, e.g., Rookwood Pottery Co. v. Commissioner, 45 F.2d 43; Eatonville Lumber Co. v. Commissioner, 10 B.T.A. 232. The use of an "average cost" is particularly appropriate here where the dues are earned by making services continuously available. The cost of doing so must necessarily be based on composite figures.

For these reasons I think that the petitioner's original returns clearly reflected its income, that the Commissioner was therfore without authority under the law to override the petitioner's accounting method, and that the judgment should be reversed.

Notes and Questions

1. In Schlude v. Commissioner, 372 U.S. 128 (1963), the Court considered an Arthur Murray dance studio operator who deferred payments received for lessons not yet given. The deferral was based on an analysis of individual customers' contracts, not a statistical summary. Again the Court held that the income must be reported in the year received; again the Court's opinion seemed to say both that there was no adequate authority for deferral of income in any event and that there were particular defects in the taxpayer's method of determining how much to defer; and again four justices dissented with an opinion by Justice Stewart.

Among the particular defects in Schlude's accounting to which the Court referred were: (1) the failure to reduce deferrals by the amount of lessons that the taxpayer could estimate, on a statistical basis, would never be claimed; and (2) the failure to capitalize or defer sales commissions and royalties paid to Arthur Murray, both of which were paid and deducted in the year in which lessons were sold. What arguments and reflections do each of these aspects of the taxpayer's accounting suggest?

Consider particularly the Arthur Murray royalty provision. Suppose in renegotiating its franchise contract Schlude were to demand that royalties be based on fees earned and that prepaid fees be deferred. Would this demand be acceptable to Arthur Murray? Do the considerations that would militate against Arthur Murray's accepting this demand have any bearing on the tax problem? Is the tax collector's relation to Schlude's enterprise analogous to Arthur Murray's relation in any relevant respects?

2. In all three cases — *Automobile Club of Michigan, AAA,* and *Schlude* — the Court's opinion is partly devoted to criticism of the proof or of the particular accounting method before it. Accountants and taxpayers thought the failures in proof in *Michigan* had been cured in *AAA*, and that the defect of depending on estimates and averages in *AAA* had been cured in *Schlude.* Even in *Schlude* the Court's finding fault with particular aspects of the accounting suggests that some system of deferral might pass muster. This aspect of the Court's decisions has helped to stimulate continuing litigation.

What do you think of the Court's performance on this level? Are its criticisms of accounting techniques in these cases sound? In which of these cases is deferral most justified? Most questionable? Would it be fair to say that the chief significance of the Court's accounting analysis is to show why the tax law should be written and interpreted, if possible, in a way that eliminates such issues?

3. Perhaps the criticisms of accounting techniques are only meant to indicate the existence of plausible grounds for the Commissioner's action in rejecting the taxpayers' accounting. The tenuous quality of the reasoning is then like that in opinions upholding jury verdicts, where the Court purports not to be giving its own analysis but only to be indicating how the jury may have reasoned. But the Commissioner seems to have exercised whatever discretion he has pretty much across the board, not on the narrower grounds suggested by the Court's analysis.

In any event one gets the feeling that the Court majority would like to be rid of the problem by deferring to either the Commissioner or the Congress. These issues are somehow not what the Supreme Court was created to resolve. Congress did in fact overrule the Court's decision in *AAA* by enacting §456. The Court in *Schlude* took comfort from this action as "continuing, at least so far, the congressional policy of treating this problem by precise provisions of narrow applicability" and thus condoning and approving the "long-established policy of the Court in deferring, where possible, to congressional procedures in the tax field." 372 U.S. at 135.

4. *AAA* and *Schlude* seem to raise an underlying issue about the relation between tax accounting and financial income accounting that could be dealt with in much more fundamental terms than the Court employed. What is

that relationship? Are taxable income and income as computed in financial reports variants of the same concept, or are they related only by name and analogy? Should all the rules and practices of financial accounting be made presumptively applicable to the computation of taxable income, or are the purposes of computing taxable and financial income too different to permit such a presumption?

Accountants have generally thought that the computation of taxable income should follow financial accounting practice in matters of interperiod allocation, except where clear considerations of tax policy demand a departure. Whatever the Court says, sound financial accounting practice would not only authorize but require deferral of income in both *AAA* and *Schlude*. The distortion of income described by Justice Stewart would be wholly unacceptable for financial reporting purposes.

But is this distortion unacceptable for income tax purposes? After all, the primary question in tax controversies is when the tax is to be paid. With respect to that question, what reason is there to defer recognition of income after receipt? Why is it a distortion at all, for tax purposes, to show a high income in the early years of a business when receipts exceed expenses, and a low income, or net loss, in the later years if and when expenses are more and receipts are less?

It is tempting to try to justify the results in *AAA* and *Schlude* by drawing a general, tentative distinction between interpersonal accounting, which affects allocation of income between persons, and interperiod accounting, which affects only matters of timing. With respect to the former, something approaching scientific precision has to be sought, even if it does entail difficult questions of judgment. With respect to the latter, such precision is unnecessary, and considerations of simplicity and convenience should dictate accounting procedures.

An example of interpersonal accounting is the allocation of trust receipts and expenditures between income and corpus, when there is one beneficiary entitled to income and another entitled to the remainder. On the other hand, the decision to take a dividend into trust income one year or the next is generally only an interperiod problem.

Of course, the computation of income for corporate financial reporting purposes is on its face a matter of interperiod accounting, since all income is that of the corporation. But the effects of financial reporting are largely interpersonal because of the uses people make of financial statements. The financial accountant must make the rather sophisticated adjustments involved in *AAA* and *Schlude* because people may make interpersonal allocations on the basis of financial statements through the purchase and sale of shares and other interests. The deferral of income in *Schlude* warns that there are outstanding obligations to perform services for which payment has already been received and that the owner has in a sense already borrowed against the future earnings of the business. Investors need to take that information into account in deciding whether to provide capital (debt or equity) to the business, negotiating terms and setting the price, and monitoring their investment.

Today interperiod allocations of corporate income are likely to have a multiplied interpersonal effect because of the tendency to trade on earnings multiples. Consider a business with $200,000 of earnings for several years. Suppose that in 2007, without any general expansion of capacity, the business collects an additional $20,000 for services to be performed in subsequent years. If the business would sell for five times its earnings, then a failure to defer that item could bring about a $100,000 increase in the price at which the business would sell.

Indeed, the situation is worse than that because failure to defer would produce both higher earnings and an upward trend. If an unwary purchaser would have paid five times the steady earnings of $200,000, he might pay six times the rising earnings of $220,000, thus producing an increase in price from $1,000,000 to $1,320,000. The need for deferral is patent.

But none of these effects generally attaches to questions of tax accounting. The effect of failure to defer is an increase in current tax collections, with a generally corresponding decrease in future collections.

There are other instances of interperiod accounting without likely interpersonal effects, and it is common to use something much nearer a cash or modified cash method in those situations. For instance, general partnership interests are not commonly bought and sold, and the use of cash accounting is much more common in partnerships than in public corporations. There may, indeed, be something very like a one-shot accrual, taking account of receivables and payables and evaluating work in process when one of the partners is to be bought out, but for ordinary periodic accounting purposes a simple cash accounting method may be perfectly acceptable.

Because interperiod allocations of taxable income do not have primary interpersonal effects, tax administration should not concern itself with such relatively sophisticated year-end adjustments as those in *AAA* and *Schlude*.

5. In appraising the general question of the relation between financial accounting and tax accounting, consider the effects of accelerated depreciation and of various nonrecognition provisions that authorize deferral for tax purposes of income that would be recognized for financial accounting purposes. Such provisions have accounted for most of the discrepancy between tax and financial accounting. The claim that tax accounting should conform to financial accounting is made more often in relation to cases like *AAA* and *Schlude*, where the effect of the financial accounting rule would be to defer payment of taxes, than in relation to depreciation and nonrecognition. Is there any more reason for tax accounting to follow financial accounting in one situation than in the other?

Consider also the general problem of distinguishing between current expenses (deductible) and capital expenditures (not immediately deductible). To what extent should answers to this problem, for tax purposes, be controlled by financial accounting practice? See Chapter 13C.

6. Ebasco performed engineering services for clients. It had a

long-consistent method of accounting under which receipts are accrued and reported as income only at the time the engineering and similar services which generate such receipts are rendered. In many cases, Ebasco's right to bill or receive payment arose prior to the annual accounting period in which the related services were to be performed. In other cases, the right to bill or receive payment arose subsequent to the annual accounting period in which the services were performed.

When under the terms of a contract Ebasco billed a client prior to the accounting period in which the related services were rendered, Ebasco debited the amount billed to accounts receivable and credited it to a balance sheet liability account called "Unearned Income." Subsequently, when the services were rendered, the income earned was debited to the "Unearned Income" account and credited to the income account "Service Revenues." The amounts recorded in the "Service Revenues" account were reported as income for both book and tax purposes. All of the amounts which were included in the "Unearned Income" account at the end of a taxable year were earned through the performance of services in the next succeeding year and were accrued and reported as income in such next succeeding taxable year for both book and tax purposes.

When services were performed in an annual accounting period and Ebasco was not entitled to bill a client for such services until a subsequent annual accounting period under the terms of a contract, Ebasco debited the amount attributable to such services to the balance sheet account "Unbilled Charges" and credited a like amount to "Service Revenues." The amount recorded in the "Service Revenues" account was reported as income for both book and tax purposes. Ebasco's cost of rendering the services which produced the amounts recorded in the "Unbilled Charges" account were deducted from gross income for that year for both book and tax purposes.

Thus, it can readily be seen that, under Ebasco's system, all amounts reported as income were determined with reference to the related services performed within the annual accounting period. The record clearly establishes that such system is a generally accepted accounting method for a business such as Ebasco's. Does it clearly reflect income as required by section 446 of the Code? [Boise Cascade Corp. v. United States, 530 F.2d 1367, 1372-1373 (Ct. Cl.), cert. denied, 429 U.S. 867 (1976)].

REVENUE PROCEDURE 2004-34
2004-1 C.B. 991

SECTION 1. PURPOSE

This revenue procedure allows taxpayers a limited deferral beyond the taxable year of receipt for certain advance payments. Qualifying taxpayers generally may defer to the next succeeding taxable year the inclusion in gross income for federal income tax purposes of advance payments (as defined in section 4 of this revenue procedure) to the extent the advance payments are not recognized in revenues (or, in certain cases, are not earned) in the taxable year of receipt. Except as provided in section 5.02(2) of this revenue procedure for certain short taxable years, this revenue procedure does not permit deferral to a taxable year later than the next succeeding taxable year. This revenue procedure neither restricts a taxpayer's ability to use the methods provided in §1.451-5 of the Income Tax Regulations regarding advance payments for goods nor limits the period of deferral available under §1.451-5.

This revenue procedure also provides the exclusive administrative procedures under which a taxpayer within the scope of this revenue procedure may obtain consent to change to a method of accounting provided in section 5 of this revenue procedure.

SECTION 2. BACKGROUND AND CHANGES

.01 In general, §451 of the Internal Revenue Code provides that the amount of any item of gross income is included in gross income for the taxable year in which received by the taxpayer, unless, under the method of accounting used in computing taxable income, the amount is to be properly accounted for as of a different period. Section 1.451-1(a) provides that, under an accrual method of accounting, income is includible in gross income when all the events have occurred that fix the right to receive the income and the amount can be determined with reasonable accuracy. All the events that fix the right to receive income generally occur when (1) the payment is earned through performance, (2) payment is due to the taxpayer, or (3) payment is received by the taxpayer, whichever happens earliest. *See* Rev. Rul. 84-31, 1984-1 C.B. 127.

.02 Section 1.451-5 generally allows accrual method taxpayers to defer the inclusion in gross income for federal income tax purposes of advance payments for goods until the taxable year in which they are properly accruable under the taxpayer's method of accounting for federal income tax purposes if that method results in the advance payments being included in gross income no later than when the advance payments are recognized in revenues under the taxpayer's method of accounting for financial reporting purposes.

.03 Rev. Proc. 71-21, 1971-2 C.B. 549, was published to implement an administrative decision of the Commissioner in the exercise of his discretion under §446 to allow accrual method taxpayers in certain specified and limited circumstances to defer the inclusion in gross income for federal income tax purposes of payments received (or amounts due and payable) in one taxable year for services to be performed by the end of the next succeeding taxable year. Rev. Proc. 71-21 was designed to reconcile the federal income tax and financial accounting treatment of payments received for services to be performed by the end of the next succeeding taxable year without permitting extended deferral of the inclusion of those payments in gross income for federal income tax purposes.

.04 Considerable controversy exists about the scope of Rev. Proc; 71-21. In particular, advance payments for non-services (and often, for combinations of services and non-services) do not qualify for deferral under Rev. Proc. 71-21, and taxpayers and the Internal Revenue Service frequently disagree about whether advance payments are, in fact, for "services." In addition to the issue of defining "services" for purposes of Rev. Proc. 71-21, questions also arise about whether advance payments received under a series of agreements, or under a renewable agreement, are within the scope of Rev. Proc. 71-21. In the interest of reducing the controversy surrounding these issues, the Service has determined that it is appropriate to expand the scope of Rev. Proc. 71-21 to include advance payments for certain non-services and combinations of services and non-services. Additionally, the Service has determined that it is appropriate to expand the scope of Rev. Proc. 71-21 to include advance payments received in connection with an agreement or series of agreements with a term or terms extending beyond the end of the next succeeding taxable year. The Service has determined, however, that for taxpayers deferring recognition of income under this revenue procedure it is appropriate to retain the limited one-year deferral of Rev. Proc. 71-21 (except as provided in section 5.02(2) of this revenue procedure for certain short taxable years).

SECTION 3. SCOPE

This revenue procedure applies to taxpayers using or changing to an overall accrual method of accounting that receive advance payments as defined in section 4 of this revenue procedure.

SECTION 4. DEFINITIONS.

The following definitions apply solely for purposes of this revenue procedure —

.01 *Advance Payment.* Except as provided in section 4.02 of this revenue procedure, a payment received by a taxpayer is an "advance payment" if —

(1) including the payment in gross income for the taxable year of receipt is a permissible method of accounting for federal income tax purposes (without regard to this revenue procedure);

(2) the payment is recognized by the taxpayer (in whole or in part) in revenues in its applicable financial statement (as defined in section 4.06 of this revenue procedure) for a subsequent taxable year (or, for taxpayers without an applicable financial statement as defined in section 4.06 of this revenue procedure, the payment is earned by the taxpayer (in whole or in part) in a subsequent taxable year); and

(3) the payment is for —

    (a) services;

    (b) the sale of goods (other than for the sale of goods for which the taxpayer uses a method of deferral provided in §1.451-5(b)(1)(ii));

(c)   the use (including by license or lease) of intellectual property as defined in section 4.03 of this revenue procedure;

(d)   the occupancy or use of property if the occupancy or use is ancillary to the provision of services (for example, advance payments for the use of rooms or other quarters in a hotel, booth space at a trade show, campsite space at a mobile home park, and recreational or banquet facilities, or other uses of property, so long as the use is ancillary to the provision of services to the property user);

(e)   the sale, lease, or license of computer software;

(f)   guaranty or warranty contracts ancillary to an item or items described in subparagraph (a), (b), (c), (d), or (e) of this section 4.01(3);

(g)   subscriptions (other than subscriptions for which an election under §455 is in effect), whether or not provided in a tangible or intangible format;

(h)   memberships in an organization (other than memberships for which an election under §456 is in effect); or

(i)   any combination of items described in subparagraphs (a) through (h) of this section 4.01(3).

.02 *Exclusions From Advance Payment.* The term "advance payment" does not include—

(1)   rent (except for amounts paid with respect to an item or items described in subparagraph (c), (d), or (e) of section 4.01(3));

(2)   insurance premiums, to the extent the recognition of those premiums is governed by Subchapter L;

(3)   payments with respect to financial instruments (for example, debt instruments, deposits, letters of credit, notional principal contracts, options, forward contracts, futures contracts, foreign currency contracts, credit card agreements, financial derivatives, etc.), including purported prepayments of interest;

(4)   payments with respect to service warranty contracts for which the taxpayer uses the accounting method provided in Rev. Proc. 97-38, 1997-2 C.B. 479;

(5)   payments with respect to warranty and guaranty contracts under which a third party is the primary obligor;

(6)   payments subject to §871(a), 881, 1441, or 1442; and

(7)   payments in property to which §83 applies.

.03 *Intellectual Property.* The term "intellectual property" includes copyrights, patents, trademarks, service marks, trade names, and similar intangible property rights (such as franchise rights and arena naming rights).

.04 *Received.* Income is "received" by the taxpayer if it is actually or constructively received, or if it is due and payable to the taxpayer.

.05 *Next Succeeding Taxable Year.* The term "next succeeding taxable year" means the taxable year immediately following the taxable year in which the advance payment is received by the taxpayer.

.06 *Applicable Financial Statement.* The taxpayer's applicable financial statement is the taxpayer's financial statement listed in paragraphs (1) through (3) of this section 4.06 that has the highest priority (including within paragraph (2)). A taxpayer that does not have a financial statement described in paragraphs (1) through (3) of this section 4.06 does not have an applicable financial statement for purposes of this revenue procedure. The financial statements are, in descending priority—

(1) a financial statement required to be filed with the Securities and Exchange Commission ("SEC") (the 10-K or the Annual Statement to Shareholders);

(2) a certified audited financial statement that is accompanied by the report of an independent CPA (or in the case of a foreign corporation, by the report of a similarly qualified independent professional), that is used for—
    (a) credit purposes,
    (b) reporting to shareholders, or
    (c) any other substantial non-tax purpose;

(3) a financial statement (other than a tax return) required to be provided to the federal or a state government or any federal or state agencies (other than the SEC or the Internal Revenue Service).

SECTION 5. PERMISSIBLE METHODS OF ACCOUNTING FOR ADVANCE PAYMENTS

.01 *Full Inclusion Method.* A taxpayer within the scope of this revenue procedure that includes the full amount of advance payments in gross income for federal income tax purposes in the taxable year of receipt is using a proper method of accounting under §1.451-1, regardless of whether the taxpayer recognizes the full amount of advance payments in revenues for that taxable year for financial reporting purposes and regardless of whether the taxpayer earns the full amount of advance payments in that taxable year.

.02 *Deferral Method.*

(1) In general.

(a) A taxpayer within the scope of this revenue procedure that chooses to use the Deferral Method described in this section 5.02 is using a proper method of accounting under §1.451-1. Under the Deferral Method, for federal income tax purposes the taxpayer must—

(i) include the advance payment in gross income for the taxable year of receipt (and, if applicable, in gross income for a short taxable year described in section 5.02(2) of this revenue procedure) to the extent provided in section 5.02(3) of this revenue procedure, and

(ii) except as provided in section 5.02(2) of this revenue procedure, include the remaining amount of the advance payment in gross income for the next succeeding taxable year.

(b) Except as provided in section 5.02(3)(b) of this revenue procedure, a taxpayer using the Deferral Method must be able to determine—

(i) the extent to which advance payments are recognized in revenues in its applicable financial statement (as defined in section 4.06 of this revenue procedure) in the taxable year of receipt (and a short taxable year described in section 5.02(2) of this revenue procedure, if applicable), or

(ii) if the taxpayer does not have an applicable financial statement (as defined in section 4.06 of this revenue procedure), the extent to which advance payments are earned (as described in section 5.02(3)(b) of this revenue procedure), in the taxable year of receipt (and a short taxable year described in section 5.02(2) of this revenue procedure, if applicable).

(2) *Short taxable years.* If the next succeeding taxable year is a taxable year (other than a taxable year in which the taxpayer dies or ceases to exist in a transaction other than a transaction to which §381(a) applies) of 92 days or less, a taxpayer using the Deferral Method must include the portion of the advance payment not included in the taxable year of receipt in gross income for the short taxable year to the extent provided in section 5.02(3) of this revenue procedure. Any amount of the advance payment not included in the taxable year of receipt and the short taxable year must be reported in gross income for the taxable year immediately following the short taxable year.

(3) *Inclusion of advance payments in gross income.*

(a) Except as provided in paragraph (b) of this section 5.02(3), a taxpayer using the Deferral Method must—

(i) include the advance payment in gross income for the taxable year of receipt (and, if applicable, in gross income for a short taxable year described in section 5.02(2) of this revenue procedure) to the extent recognized in revenues in its applicable financial statement (as defined in section 4.06 of this revenue procedure) for that taxable year, and

(ii)   include the remaining amount of the advance payment in gross income in accordance with section 5.02(1)(a)(ii) of this revenue procedure.

(b) If the taxpayer does not have an applicable financial statement (as defined in section 4.06 of this revenue procedure), or if the taxpayer is unable to determine, as required by section 5.02(1)(b)(i) of this revenue procedure, the extent to which advance payments are recognized in revenues in its applicable financial statements for the taxable year of receipt (and a short taxable year described in section 5.02(2) of this revenue procedure, if applicable), a taxpayer using the Deferral Method must include the advance payment in gross income for the taxable year of receipt (and, if applicable, in gross income for a short taxable year described in section 5.02(2)) to the extent earned in that taxable year and include the remaining amount of the advance payment in gross income in accordance with section 5.02(1)(a)(ii) of this revenue procedure. The determination of whether an amount is earned in a taxable year must be made without regard to whether the taxpayer may be required to refund the advance payment upon the occurrence of a condition subsequent. If the taxpayer is unable to determine the extent to which a payment (such as a payment for contingent goods or services) is earned in the taxable year of receipt (and, if applicable, in a short taxable year described in section 5.02(2)), the taxpayer may determine that amount—

(i)   on a statistical basis if adequate data are available to the taxpayer;

(ii)   on a straight line ratable basis over the term of the agreement if the taxpayer receives advance payments under a fixed term agreement and if it is not unreasonable to anticipate at the end of the taxable year of receipt that the advance payment will be earned ratably over the term of the agreement; or

(iii) by the use of any other basis that in the opinion of the Commissioner results in a clear reflection of income.

(4) *Allocable payments.*

(a) *General rule.* A taxpayer that receives a payment that is partially attributable to an item or items described in section 4.01(3) of this revenue procedure may use the Deferral Method for the portion of the payment allocable to such item or items and, with respect to the remaining portion of the payment, may use any proper method of accounting (including the Deferral Method if the remaining portion of the advance payment is for an item or items described in section 4.01(3) of this revenue procedure with a different deferral period (based on the taxpayer's applicable financial statement or the earning of the payment, as applicable)), provided that the taxpayer's method for determining the portion of the payment allocable to such item or items is based on objective criteria.

(b) *Advance payments under section 4.01(3)(i)*. An advance payment under section 4.01(3)(i) that is wholly attributable to two or more items described in subparagraphs (a) through (h) of section 4.01(3) of this revenue procedure that have the same deferral period (based on the taxpayer's applicable financial statement or the earning of the payment, as applicable) is not an allocable payment under section 5.02(4)(a) of this revenue procedure.

(c) *Allocation deemed to be based on objective criteria*. A taxpayer's allocation method with respect to an allocable payment described in section 5.02(4)(a) of this revenue procedure will be deemed to be based on objective criteria if the allocation method is based on payments the taxpayer regularly receives for an item or items it regularly sells or provides separately.

(5) *Acceleration of advance payments*. Notwithstanding section 5.02(1) of this revenue procedure, a taxpayer using the Deferral Method must include in gross income for the taxable year of receipt (or, if applicable, for a short taxable year described in section 5.02(2) of this revenue procedure) all advance payments not previously included in gross income—

(a)   if, in that taxable year, the taxpayer either dies or ceases to exist in a transaction other than a transaction to which §381(a) applies, or

(b)   if, and to the extent that, in that taxable year, the taxpayer's obligation with respect to the advance payments is satisfied or otherwise ends other than in—

(i)   a transaction to which §381(a) applies, or

(ii)   a §351(a) transfer in which (a) substantially all assets of the trade or business (including advance payments) are transferred, (b) the transferee adopts or uses the Deferral Method in the year of transfer, and (c) the transferee and the transferor are members of an affiliated group of corporations that file a consolidated return, pursuant to §§1504-1564.

.03 *Examples*. In each example below, the taxpayer uses an accrual method of accounting for federal income tax purposes and files its returns on a calendar year basis. Except as stated otherwise, the taxpayer in each example has an applicable financial statement as defined in section 4.06 of this revenue procedure.

> *Example 1*. On November 1, 2004, *A*, in the business of giving dancing lessons, receives an advance payment for a 1-year contract commencing on that date and providing for up to 48 individual, 1-hour lessons. *A* provides eight lessons in 2004 and another 35 lessons in 2005. In its applicable financial statement, *A* recognizes 1/6 of the payment in revenues for 2004, and 5/6 of the payment in revenues for 2005. *A* uses the Deferral Method. For federal income tax purposes, *A* must include 1/6 of the payment in gross income for 2004, and the remaining 5/6 of the payment in gross income for 2005.

Example 2. Assume the same facts as in *Example 1*, except that the advance payment is received for a 2-year contract under which up to 96 lessons are provided. *A* provides eight lessons in 2004, 48 lessons in 2005, and 40 lessons in 2006. In its applicable financial statement, *A* recognizes 1/12 of the payment in revenues for 2004, 6/12 of the payment in revenues for 2005, and 5/12 of the payment in gross revenues for 2006. For federal income tax purposes, *A* must include 1/12 of the payment in gross income for 2004, and the remaining 11/12 of the payment in gross income for 2005.

Example 3. On June 1, 2004, *B*, a landscape architecture firm, receives an advance payment for goods and services that, under the terms of the agreement, must be provided by December 2005. On December 31, 2004, *B* estimates that 3/4 of the work under the agreement has been completed. In its applicable financial statement, *B* recognizes 3/4 of the payment in revenues for 2004 and 1/4 of the payment in revenues for 2005. *B* uses the Deferral Method. For federal income tax purposes, *B* must include 3/4 of the payment in gross income for 2004, and the remaining 1/4 of the payment in gross income for 2005, regardless of whether *B* completes the job in 2005.

Example 4. On July 1, 2004, *C*, in the business of selling and repairing television sets, receives an advance payment for a 2-year contract under which *C* agrees to repair or replace, or authorizes a representative to repair or replace, certain parts in the customer's television set if those parts fail to function properly. In its applicable financial statement, *C* recognizes 1/4 of the payment in revenues for 2004, 1/2 of the payment in revenues for 2005, and 1/4 of the payment in revenues for 2006. *C* uses the Deferral Method. For federal income tax purposes, *C* must include 1/4 of the payment in gross income for 2004 and the remaining 3/4 of the payment in gross income for 2005.

Example 5. On December 2, 2004, *D*, in the business of selling and repairing television sets, sells for $200 a television set with a 90-day warranty on parts and labor (for which *D*, rather than the manufacturer, is the obligor). *D* regularly sells television sets without the warranty for $188. In its applicable financial statement, *D* allocates $188 of the sales price to the television set and $12 to the 90-day warranty, recognizes 1/3 of the amount allocable to the warranty ($4) in revenues for 2004, and recognizes the remaining 2/3 of the amount allocable to the warranty ($8) in revenues for 2005. *D* uses the Deferral Method. For federal income tax purposes, *D* must include the $4 allocable to the warranty in gross income for 2004 and the remaining $8 allocable to the warranty in gross income for 2005.

Example 6. *E*, in the business of photographic processing, receives advance payments for mailers and certificates that oblige *E* to process photographic film, prints, or other photographic materials returned in the mailer or with the certificate. *E* tracks each of the mailers and certificates with unique identifying numbers. On July 20, 2004, *E* receives payments for 2 mailers. One of the mailers is submitted and processed on September 1, 2004, and the other is submitted and processed on February 1, 2006. In its applicable financial statement, *E* recognizes the payment for the September 1, 2004, processing in revenues for 2004 and the payment for the February 1, 2006, processing in revenues for 2006. *E* uses the Deferral Method. For federal income tax purposes, *E* must include the payment for the September 1, 2004, processing in gross income for 2004 and the payment for the February 1, 2006, processing in gross income for 2005.

Example 7. *F*, a hair styling salon, receives advance payments for gift cards that may later be redeemed at the salon for hair styling services or hair care products at the face value of the gift card. The gift cards look like standard credit cards, and each gift card has a magnetic strip that, in connection with *F*'s computer system, identifies the available balance. The gift cards may not be redeemed for cash, and have no expiration date. In its applicable financial statement, F recognizes advance payments for gift cards in revenues when redeemed. F is not able to determine the extent to which advance payments are recognized in revenues in its applicable financial statement for the taxable year of receipt and therefore does not meet the requirement of section 5.02(1)(b)(i) of this revenue procedure. Further, F does not determine under a basis described in section 5.02(3)(b) of this revenue procedure the extent to which payments are earned for the taxable year of receipt. Therefore, F may not use the Deferral Method for these advance payments.

Example 8. Assume the same facts as in *Example 7*, except that the gift cards have an expiration date 12 months from the date of sale, F does not accept expired gift cards, and F recognizes unredeemed gift cards in revenues in its applicable financial statement for the taxable year in which the cards expire. Because F tracks the sale date and the expiration date of the gift cards for purposes of its applicable financial statement, F is able to determine the extent to which advance payments are recognized in revenues for the taxable year of receipt. Therefore, F meets the requirement of section 5.02(1)(b)(i) of this revenue procedure and may use the Deferral Method for these advance payments.

Example 9. G, a video arcade operator, receives payments in 2004 for game tokens that are used by customers to play the video games offered by G. The tokens cannot be redeemed for cash. The tokens are imprinted with the name of the video arcade, but they are not individually marked for identification. For purposes of its applicable financial statement, G completed a study that determined that for payments received for tokens in the current year, x percent of tokens are expected to be used in the current year, y percent of tokens are expected to be used in the next year, and z percent of tokens are expected to never be used. Based on the study, in its applicable financial statement G recognizes in revenues for 2004 x percent (tokens expected to be used in 2004) and z percent (tokens expected never to be used) of the payments received in 2004 for tokens; G recognizes in revenues for 2005 the remaining y percent of the payments received in 2004 for tokens. G uses the Deferral Method. Using the study, G determines the extent to which advance payments are recognized in revenues in its applicable financial statement for the taxable year of receipt and therefore meets the requirement of section 5.02(1)(b)(i) of this revenue procedure. Under section 5.02(3)(a) of this revenue procedure, G must include advance payments in gross income in accordance with its applicable financial statement in the taxable year of receipt, provided that any portion of the payment not included in income in the taxable year of receipt is included in gross income for the next succeeding taxable year. Thus, for federal income tax purposes, G must include x percent and z percent of the advance payments in gross income for 2004, and y percent of the advance payments in gross income for 2005. . . .

Example 13. In 2004, J, in the business of operating tours, receives payments from customers for a 10-day cruise that will take place in April 2005. Under the agreement, J charters a cruise ship, hires a crew and a tour guide, and arranges for entertainment and shore trips for the customers. In its applicable financial statement, J recognizes the payments in revenues for 2005. J uses the Deferral Method. For federal income tax purposes, J must include the payments in gross income for 2005.

Example 14. On November 1, 2004, K, a travel agent, receives payment from a customer for an airline flight that will take place in April 2005. K purchases and delivers the airline ticket to the customer on November 14, 2004. K retains a portion of the customer's payment (the excess of the customer's payment over the cost of the airline ticket) as its commission. Because K is not required to provide any services after the ticket is delivered to the customer, K earns its commission when the airline ticket is delivered. The customer may cancel the flight and receive a refund from K only to the extent the airline itself provides refunds. *K* does not have an applicable financial statement (as defined in section 4.06 of this revenue procedure), but, in its unaudited financial statements, *K* recognizes its commission in revenues for 2005. The commission is not an advance payment as defined in section 4.01 of this revenue procedure because the payment is not earned by *K*, in whole or in part, in a subsequent taxable year. Thus, *K* may not use the Deferral Method for this payment. . . .

SECTION 8. CHANGE IN METHOD OF ACCOUNTING

.01 *In General.* A change in a taxpayer's treatment of advance payments to either of the methods described in section 5 of this revenue procedure is a change in method of accounting to which the provisions of §§446 and 481, and the regulations thereunder, apply. A taxpayer may adopt any permissible method of accounting for advance payments for the first taxable year in which the taxpayer receives advance payments. A taxpayer that seeks to change its method of accounting for advance payments must use Form 3115, *Application for Change in Accounting Method,* and complete all applicable parts thereof. *See* §1.446-1(e).

.02 *Automatic Change.* Except with respect to a change in method to which section 8.03 or 8.04(2) of this revenue procedure applies, a taxpayer within the scope of this revenue procedure that wants to change to one of the methods of accounting provided in section 5 of this revenue procedure must follow the automatic change in method of accounting provisions in Rev. Proc. 2002-9 (or its successor) with the following modifications—. . . .

Notes and Questions

1. See also Reg. §1.451-5, which deals with advance payments for goods as compared with services. Should goods and services be dealt with differently? Are they? Why is one covered by regulation while the other is dealt with by Revenue Procedure?

2. How would this Revenue Procedure affect Ebasco in Question 6 on p. 340 above? The Court of Claims opinion noted that "Ebasco's counsel are astonished that defendant could in this case interpret *American Automobile* and *Schlude* as preventing any income deferral when, as recently as 1971, the Commissioner, in Rev. Proc. 71-21 [the predecessor to Rev. Proc. 2004-34, reproduced above] has held that taxpayer may defer the inclusion in income of payments received in one taxable year for services to be performed in the next succeeding year." Boise Cascade Corp., 530 F.2d at 1373. Why, in view of these revenue procedures, did the government litigate the Ebasco matter, even to the point of filing a petition for certiorari? See IRS Action on Dec. 1986-014, 1986 AOD Lexis 13 (Feb. 19, 1986).

2.   Security Deposits

E is the lessor of a small store building on a five-year lease. She collects a security deposit from the tenant equal to one year's rent. The lease provides that in the absence of prior defaults the deposit is to be returned to the lessee at the end of the lease term. There are no restrictions on *E*'s use of the money. Is she taxable on receipt of it?

Would the case be any different if the lease simply provided for payment of two years' rent in the first year, one year's rent in the second, third, and fourth, and nothing in the fifth?

What if *E* and the tenant had talked in advance about two years' rent in the first year but then the lease was written in terms of a security deposit?[5]

COMMISSIONER v. INDIANAPOLIS POWER & LIGHT CO.

493 U.S. 203 (1990)

Justice BLACKMUN delivered the opinion of the Court. . . .

I

IPL is a regulated Indiana corporation that generates and sells electricity in Indianapolis and its environs. It keeps its books on the accrual and calendar year basis. During the years 1974 through 1977, approximately 5 percent of IPL's residential and commercial customers were required to make deposits "to insure prompt payment," as the customers' receipts stated, of future utility bills. These customers were selected because their credit was suspect. Prior to March 10, 1976, the deposit requirement was imposed on a case-by-case basis. IPL relied on a credit test but employed no fixed formula. The amount of the required deposit ordinarily was twice the customer's estimated monthly bill. IPL paid 3 percent interest on a deposit held for six months or more. A customer could obtain a refund of the deposit prior to termination of service by requesting a review and demonstrating acceptable credit. The refund usually was made in cash or by check, but the customer could choose to have the amount applied against future bills.

In March 1976, IPL amended its rules governing the deposit program. See Title 170, Ind. Admin. Code §4-1-15 (1988). Under the amended rules, the residential customers from whom deposits were required were selected

5. Compare John Mantell, 17 T.C. 1143 (1952) (acq.) (Arundell, J.) with Jack August, 17 T.C. 1165 (1952) (Arundell, J.). But cf. §467(f). Also see and cf. Commissioner v. Indianapolis Power & Light Co., the next case.

on the basis of a fixed formula. The interest rate was raised to 6 percent but was payable only on deposits held for 12 months or more. A deposit was refunded when the customer made timely payments for either nine consecutive months, or for 10 out of 12 consecutive months so long as the two delinquent months were not themselves consecutive. A customer could obtain a refund prior to that time by satisfying the credit test. As under the previous rules, the refund would be made in cash or by check, or, at the customer's option, applied against future bills. Any deposit unclaimed after seven years was to escheat to the State. See Ind. Code §32-9-1-6(a) (1988).[1]

IPL did not treat these deposits as income at the time of receipt. Rather, as required by state administrative regulations, the deposits were carried on its books as current liabilities. Under its accounting system, IPL recognized income when it mailed a monthly bill. If the deposit was used to offset a customer's bill, the utility made the necessary accounting adjustments. Customer deposits were not physically segregated in any way from the company's general funds. They were commingled with other receipts and at all times were subject to IPL's unfettered use and control. It is undisputed that IPL's treatment of the deposits was consistent with accepted accounting practice and applicable state regulations.

Upon audit of respondent's returns for the calendar years 1974 through 1977, the Commissioner asserted deficiencies. . . .

In a reviewed decision, with one judge not participating, a unanimous Tax Court ruled in favor of IPL. 88 T.C. 964 (1987). . . .

The United States Court of Appeals for the Seventh Circuit affirmed the Tax Court's decision. 857 F.2d 1162 (1988). The court stated that "the proper approach to determining the appropriate tax treatment of a customer deposit is to look at the primary purpose of the deposit based on all the facts and circumstances. . . ." Id., at 1167. The court appeared to place primary reliance, however, on IPL's obligation to pay interest on the deposits. . . .

II

We begin with the common ground. IPL acknowledges that these customer deposits are taxable as income upon receipt if they constitute advance payments for electricity to be supplied.[3] The Commissioner, on his part,

---

1. During the years 1974 through 1977, the total amount that escheated to the State was less than $9,325. Stipulation of Facts ¶25.

3. This Court has held that an accrual-basis taxpayer is required to treat advance payments as income in the year of receipt. See Schlude v. Commissioner, 372 U.S. 128 (1963); American Automobile Assn. v. United States, 367 U.S. 687 (1961); Automobile Club of Michigan v. Commissioner, 353 U.S. 180 (1957). These cases concerned payments—nonrefundable fees for services—that indisputably constituted income; the issue was when that income was taxable. Here, in contrast, the issue is whether these deposits, as such, are income at all.

concedes that customer deposits that secure the performance of non-income-producing covenants—such as a utility customer's obligation to ensure that meters will not be damaged—are not taxable income. And it is settled that receipt of a loan is not income to the borrower. See Commissioner v. Tufts, 461 U.S. 300, 307 (1983) ("Because of [the repayment] obligation, the loan proceeds do not qualify as income to the taxpayer"); James v. United States, 366 U.S. 213, 219 (1961) (accepted definition of gross income "excludes loans"); Commissioner v. Wilcox, 327 U.S. 404, 408 (1946). IPL, stressing its obligation to refund the deposits with interest, asserts that the payments are similar to loans. The Commissioner, however, contends that a deposit which serves to secure the payment of future income is properly analogized to an advance payment for goods or services. See Rev. Rul. 72-519, 1972-2 Cum. Bull. 32, 33 ("[W]hen the purpose of the deposit is to guarantee the customer's payment of amounts owed to the creditor, such a deposit is treated as an advance payment, but when the purpose of the deposit is to secure a property interest of the taxpayer the deposit is regarded as a true security deposit").

In economic terms, to be sure, the distinction between a loan and an advance payment is one of degree rather than of kind. A commercial loan, like an advance payment, confers an economic benefit on the recipient: a business presumably does not borrow money unless it believes that the income it can earn from its use of the borrowed funds will be greater than its interest obligation. See Illinois Power Co. v. Commissioner of Internal Revenue, 792 F.2d 683, 690 (CA7 1986). Even though receipt of the money is subject to a duty to repay, the borrower must regard itself as better off after the loan than it was before. The economic benefit of a loan, however, consists entirely of the opportunity to earn income on the use of the money prior to the time the loan must be repaid. And in that context our system is content to tax these earnings as they are realized. The recipient of an advance payment, in contrast, gains both immediate use of the money (with the chance to realize earnings thereon) and the opportunity to make a profit by providing goods or services at a cost lower than the amount of the payment.

The question, therefore, cannot be resolved simply by noting that respondent derives some economic benefit from receipt of these deposits.[4] Rather, the issue turns upon the nature of the rights and obligations that IPL assumed when the deposits were made. In determining what sort of economic benefits qualify as income, this Court has invoked various formulations. It has referred, for example, to "undeniable accessions to wealth, clearly realized, and over which the taxpayers have complete dominion."

---

4. See Illinois Power Co., 792 F.2d, at 690. See also Burke & Friel, Recent Developments in the Income Taxation of Individuals, Tax-Free Security: Reflections on Indianapolis Power & Light, 12 Rev. of Taxation of Individuals 157, 174 (1988) (arguing that economic-benefit approach is superior in theory, but acknowledging that "an economic-benefit test has not been adopted, and it is unlikely that such an approach will be pursued by the Service or the courts").

Commission v. Glenshaw Glass Co., 348 U.S. 426, 431 (1955). It also has stated: "When a taxpayer acquires earnings, lawfully or unlawfully, without the consensual recognition, express or implied, of an obligation to repay and without restriction as to their disposition, 'he has received income. . . . ' " James v. United States, 366 U.S., at 219, quoting North American Oil Consolidated v. Burnet, 286 U.S. 417, 424 (1932). IPL hardly enjoyed "complete dominion" over the customer deposits entrusted to it. Rather, these deposits were acquired subject to an express "obligation to repay," either at the time service was terminated or at the time a customer established good credit. So long as the customer fulfills his legal obligation to make timely payments, his deposit ultimately is to be refunded, and both the timing and method of that refund are largely within the control of the customer.

The Commissioner stresses the fact that these deposits were not placed in escrow or segregated from IPL's other funds, and that IPL therefore enjoyed unrestricted use of the money. That circumstance, however, cannot be dispositive. After all, the same might be said of a commercial loan; yet the Commissioner does not suggest that a loan is taxable upon receipt simply because the borrower is free to use the funds in whatever fashion he chooses until the time of repayment. In determining whether a taxpayer enjoys "complete dominion" over a given sum, the crucial point is not whether his use of the funds is unconstrained during some interim period. The key is whether the taxpayer has some guarantee that he will be allowed to keep the money. IPL's receipt of these deposits was accompanied by no such guarantee.

Nor is it especially significant that these deposits could be expected to generate income greater than the modest interest IPL was required to pay. Again, the same could be said of a commercial loan, since, as has been noted, a business is unlikely to borrow unless it believes that it can realize benefits that exceed the cost of servicing the debt. A bank could hardly operate profitably if its earnings on deposits did not surpass its interest obligations; but the deposits themselves are not treated as income.[5] Any income that the utility may earn through use of the deposit money of course is taxable, but the prospect that income will be generated provides no ground for taxing the principal.

The Commissioner's advance payment analogy seems to us to rest upon a misconception of the value of an advance payment to its recipient. An advance payment, like the deposits at issue here, concededly protects the seller against the risk that it would be unable to collect money owed it after it has furnished goods or services. But an advance payment does much more: it protects against the risk that the purchaser will back out of the deal before the seller performs. From the moment an advance payment is made, the

---

5. Cf. Rev. Rul. 71-189, 1971-1 Cum. Bull. 32 (inactive deposits are not income until bank asserts dominion over the accounts). See also Fidelity-Philadelphia Trust Co. v. Commissioner, 23 T.C. 527 (1954).

seller is assured that, so long as it fulfills its contractual obligation, the money is its to keep. Here, in contrast, a customer submitting a deposit made no commitment to purchase a specified quantity of electricity, or indeed to purchase any electricity at all. IPL's right to keep the money depends upon the customer's purchase of electricity, and upon his later decision to have the deposit applied to future bills, not merely upon the utility's adherence to its contractual duties. Under these circumstances, IPL's dominion over the fund is far less complete than is ordinarily the case in an advance-payment situation.

The Commissioner emphasizes that these deposits frequently will be used to pay for electricity, either because the customer defaults on his obligation or because the customer, having established credit, chooses to apply the deposit to future bills rather than to accept a refund. When this occurs, the Commissioner argues, the transaction, from a cash-flow standpoint, is equivalent to an advance payment. In his view this economic equivalence mandates identical tax treatment.[7]

Whether these payments constitute income when received, however, depends upon the parties' rights and obligations at the time the payments are made. The problem with petitioner's argument perhaps can best be understood if we imagine a loan between parties involved in an ongoing commercial relationship. At the time the loan falls due, the lender may decide to apply the money owed to him to the purchase of goods or services rather than to accept repayment in cash. But this decision does not mean that the loan, when made, was an advance payment after all. The lender in effect has taken repayment of his money (as was his contractual right) and has chosen to use the proceeds for the purchase of goods or services from the borrower. Although, for the sake of convenience, the parties may combine the two steps, that decision does not blind us to the fact that in substance two transactions are involved. It is this element of choice that distinguishes an advance payment from a loan. Whether these customer deposits are the economic equivalents of advance payments, and therefore taxable upon receipt, must be determined by examining the relationship between the parties at the time of the deposit. The individual who makes an advance payment retains no right to insist upon the return of the funds; so long as the recipient fulfills the terms of the bargain, the money is its to keep. The customer who submits a deposit to the utility, like the lender in the previous hypothetical, retains the right to insist upon repayment in cash; he may choose to apply the money to the purchase of electricity, but he assumes no obligation to do so, and the utility therefore acquires no unfettered "dominion" over the money at the time of receipt.

7. The Commissioner is unwilling, however, to pursue this line of reasoning to the limit of its logic. He concedes that these deposits would not be taxable if they were placed in escrow, Tr. of Oral Arg. 4; but from a cash flow standpoint it does not make much difference whether the money is placed in escrow or commingled with the utility's other funds. In either case, the utility receives the money and allocates it to subsequent purchases of electricity if the customer defaults or chooses to apply his refund to a future bill.

When the Commissioner examines privately structured transactions, the true understanding of the parties, of course, may not be apparent. It may be that a transfer of funds, though nominally a loan, may conceal an unstated agreement that the money is to be applied to the purchase of goods or services. We need not, and do not, attempt to devise a test for addressing those situations where the nature of the parties' bargain is legitimately in dispute. This particular respondent, however, conducts its business in a heavily regulated environment; its rights and obligations vis-a-vis its customers are largely determined by law and regulation rather than by private negotiation. That the utility's customers, when they qualify for refunds of deposits, frequently choose to apply those refunds to future bills rather than taking repayment in cash does not mean that any customer has made an unspoken commitment to do so.

Our decision is also consistent with the Tax Court's longstanding treatment of lease deposits—perhaps the closest analogy to the present situation. The Tax Court traditionally has distinguished between a sum designated as a prepayment of rent—which is taxable upon receipt— and a sum deposited to secure the tenant's performance of a lease agreement. See, e.g., J. & E. Enterprises, Inc. v. Commissioner, 26 T.C.M. 944 (1967).[9] In fact, the customer deposits at issue here are less plausibly regarded as income than lease deposits would be. The typical lease deposit secures the tenant's fulfillment of a contractual obligation to pay a specified rent throughout the term of the lease. The utility customer, however, makes no commitment to purchase any services at all at the time he tenders the deposit.

We recognize that IPL derives an economic benefit from these deposits. But a taxpayer does not realize taxable income from every event that improves his economic condition. A customer who makes his deposit reflects no commitment to purchase services, and IPL's right to retain the money is

---

9. In J. &. E. Enterprises the Tax Court stated:

> If a sum is received by a lessor at the beginning of a lease, is subject to his unfettered control, and is to be applied as rent for a subsequent period during the term of the lease, such sum is income in the year of receipt even though in certain circumstances a refund thereof may be required. . . . If, on the other hand, a sum is deposited to secure the lessee's performance under a lease, and is to be returned at the expiration thereof, it is not taxable income even though the fund is deposited with the lessor instead of in escrow and the lessor has temporary use of the money. . . . In this situation the acknowledged liability of the lessor to account for the deposited sum on the lessee's performance of the lease covenants prevents the sum from being taxable in the year of receipt.

26 T.C.M. at 945-946.

In Rev. Rul. 72-519, 1972-2 Cum. Bull. 32, the Commissioner relied in part on *J. & E. Enterprises* as authority for the proposition that deposits intended to secure income-producing covenants are advance payments taxable as income upon receipt, while deposits intended to secure nonincome-producing covenants are not. Id., at 33. In our view, neither *J. & E. Enterprises* nor the other cases cited in the Revenue Ruling support that distinction. See Hirsch Improvement Co. v. Commissioner, 143 F.2d 912 (2d Cir. 1944), cert. denied, 323 U.S. 750 (1944); Mantell v. Commissioner, 17 T.C. 1143 (1952); Gilken Corp. v. Commissioner, 10 T.C. 445 (1948), aff'd. 176 F.2d 141 (6th Cir. 1949). These cases all distinguish between advance payments and security deposits, not between deposits that do and do not secure income-producing covenants.

contingent upon events outside its control. We hold that such dominion as IPL has over these customer deposits is unsufficient for the deposits to qualify as taxable income at the time they are made.

The judgment of the Court of Appeals is affirmed.

It is so ordered.

3. Inventories

Suppose a manufacturer spends $100,000 producing widgets. He collects only $90,000 for the sale of widgets. But he has on hand at the end of the year an inventory of widgets whose cost of manufacture was $30,000. In that case, assuming he had no inventory at the beginning of the year, he earned $20,000 because his cost of goods sold was only $70,000 for sales of $90,000. The $30,000 closing inventory, which is subtracted in determining cost of goods sold for the current period, will be added as opening inventory for the next period, so the effect is simply to defer the cost of goods on hand from period to period, as follows.

	Year 1		Year 2	
Sales		$90,000		$140,000
Cost of goods sold				
Cost of manufacturing	$100,000		$105,000	
Plus opening inventory	0		30,000	
Total	100,000		135,000	
Minus closing inventory	30,000		25,000	
Cost of goods sold	70,000	70,000	110,000	110,000
Gross profit		$20,000		$ 30,000

The most prevalent technique for determining or verifying goods on hand is to count them — take inventory at the period's end. Then there is the question of assigning an appropriate value. In general, inventory is valued at cost since the main objective is to defer costs for matching against sales in a subsequent period. In a sales business, cost means purchase price. In a manufacturing business it is cost of manufacturing, but that can be a matter of some complexity to determine since it involves potentially difficult questions of cost allocation. What part of office expenses and overhead, for example, should be treated as part of manufacturing cost?

Price level changes present special problems. When price levels decline it is common practice to value inventories at the lower of cost or market. If market value is lower than cost, the effect is to charge the inventory loss in computing gross profit from sales for the period during which the loss in value occurs. Some people consider this illogical, but it is a conservative and widely accepted practice.

When prices increase, a problem arises of whether to charge against income the older or the newer costs. FIFO means the problem is resolved on the assumption that goods move First-In-First-Out; LIFO means Last-In-First-Out; average cost means that costs are averaged for purposes of computing both closing inventory and cost of goods sold.

Consider a merchant with an opening inventory of 1,000 pairs of shoes that cost $5 each. During the period she sells 1,000 pairs at $10 and purchases 1,000 pairs at $7. What is her gross income from sale of shoes for the period? What is her closing inventory? What does §472 indicate? What are the strongest arguments for and against §472? Notice the conformity condition of §472(c). In recent years there have been a number of announcements that attempt to accommodate this requirement with the full-disclosure requirements of the federal securities laws.

Retail method. In some cases, like that of a large department store, it would be impractical to identify goods on hand with particular purchase transactions on either a LIFO or FIFO basis. When inventory is counted the only readily available valuation figure is the retail sale price. The retail method is a way of reasoning back from retail sale price to inventory cost by computing and subtracting an average mark-on percentage. See Reg. §1.471-8. A combination of the retail method and LIFO was approved in Hutzler Brothers Co., 8 T.C. 14 (1947), which contains a remarkably good discussion of an extraordinarily complicated problem.

In general, any taxpayer who holds goods for sale is required to count inventories and defer their cost from period to period. §471; Reg. §§1.471-1, 1.446-1(a)(4)(i). Moreover, since inventories are determined or verified by counting goods on hand, such a taxpayer must account for credit sales and costs of goods sold or manufactured on an accrual basis. Reg. §1.446-1(c)(2)(i). This is one general case in which cash receipts and disbursements accounting is not permitted.

A major exception has been made, however, for farmers using the cash method. They are permitted to deduct costs of raising crops and livestock in the year paid even if the crops or livestock remain on hand at the end of the year. See Reg. §§1.61-4, 1.162-12. These provisions are of ancient origin and their purpose is apparently just to relieve farmers of the need for sophisticated accounting techniques in determining their taxes.

How should these provisions be applied in the case of a syndicated investment in cattle or citrus groves or rosebushes? Is an investor in such a syndicate, or the syndicate itself, a farmer within the meaning of the regulations? In general it has been so treated, and in years gone by that treatment provided part of the basis for extensive tax shelter investments in farming activities, together with some quite particularized statutory responses thereto. §§1252, 464, 447.

Look particularly at §464(a) and think about it. Feed may be purchased in Year 1 and consumed by animals in Year 2 and the animals sold in Year 3 (often several years later). Section 464(a) requires capitalization of the purchase price in Year 1 but then apparently permits deduction in Year 2. Does that make sense? How much sense? Why? Compare the treatment of prepaid interest in §461(g).

Section 263A, added in 1986, is intended to prescribe more uniform rules for determining what expenditures must be capitalized as cost of inventory and other property. Take a look at §263A. How much does it settle, and how much does it just set a general direction for the Treasury to pursue?

THOR POWER TOOL CO. v. COMMISSIONER
439 U.S. 522 (1979)

Mr. Justice BLACKMUN delivered the opinion of the Court. . . .

A

Taxpayer is a Delaware corporation with principal place of business in Illinois. It manufactures hand-held power tools, parts and accessories, and rubber products. At its various plants and service branches, Thor maintains inventories of raw materials, work-in-process, finished parts and accessories, and completed tools. At all times relevant, Thor has used, both for financial accounting and for income tax purposes, the "lower of cost or market" method of valuing inventories. App. 23-24. See Treas. Reg. §1.471-2(c), 26 CFR §1.471-2(c) (1978).

Thor's tools typically contain from 50 to 200 parts, each of which taxpayer stocks to meet demand for replacements. Because of the difficulty, at the time of manufacture, of predicting the future demand for various parts, taxpayer produced liberal quantities of each part to avoid subsequent production runs. Additional runs entail costly retooling and result in delays in filling orders. App. 54-55.

In 1960, Thor instituted a procedure for writing down the inventory value of replacement parts and accessories for tool models it no longer produced. It created an inventory contra account and credited that account with 10 percent of each part's cost for each year since production of the parent model had ceased. 64 T.C., at 156-157; App. 24. The effect of the procedure was to amortize the cost of these parts over a 10-year period. For the first nine months of 1964, this produced a write-down of $22,090. 64 T.C., at 157; App. 24.

In late 1964, new management took control and promptly concluded that Thor's inventory in general was overvalued. After "a physical inventory taken at all locations" of the tool and rubber divisions, id., at 52, management wrote off approximately $2.75 million of obsolete parts, damaged or defective tools, demonstration or sales samples, and similar items. Id., at 52-53. The Commissioner allowed this writeoff because Thor scrapped most of the articles shortly after their removal from the 1964 closing inventory. Management also wrote down $245,000 of parts stocked for three unsuccessful products. Id., at 56. The Commissioner allowed this write-down, too, since Thor sold these items at reduced prices shortly after the close of 1964. Id., at 62.

This left some 44,000 assorted items, the status of which is the inventory issue here. Management concluded that many of these articles, mostly spare parts, were "excess" inventory, that is, that they were held in excess of any reasonably forseeable future demand. It was decided that this inventory should be written down to its "net realizable value," which, in most cases, was scrap value. 64 T.C., at 160-161; Brief for Petitioner 9; Tr. of Oral Arg. 11.

Two methods were used to ascertain the quantity of excess inventory. Where accurate data were available, Thor forecast future demand for each item on the basis of actual 1964 usage, that is, actual sales for tools and service parts, and actual usage for raw materials, work-in-process, and production parts. Management assumed that future demand for each item would be the same as it was in 1964. Thor then applied the following aging schedule: the quantity of each item corresponding to less than one year's estimated demand was kept at cost; the quantity of each item in excess of two years' estimated demand was written off entirely; and the quantity of each item corresponding to from one to two years' estimated demand was written down by 50 percent or 75 percent. App. 26. Thor presented no statistical evidence to rationalize these percentages or this time frame. In the Tax Court, Thor's president justified the formula by citing general business experience, and opined that it was "somewhat in between" possible alternative solutions. This first method yielded a total write-down of $744,030. 64 T.C., at 160.

At two plants where 1964 data were inadequate to permit forecasts of future demand, Thor used its second method for valuing inventories. At these plants, the company employed flat percentage write-downs of 5 percent, 10 percent, and 50 percent for various types of inventory. Thor presented no sales or other data to support these percentages. Its president observed that "this is not a precise way of doing it," but said that the company "felt some adjustment of this nature was in order, and these figures represented our best estimate of what was required to reduce the inventory to net realizable value." App. 67. This second method yielded a total write-down of $160,832. 64 T.C. at 160.

Although Thor wrote down all its "excess" inventory at once, it did not immediately scrap the articles or sell them at reduced prices, as it had done with the $3 million of obsolete and damaged inventory, the write-down of which the Commissioner permitted. Rather, Thor retained the "excess" items physically in inventory and continued to sell them at original prices. Id., at 160-161. The company found that, owing to the peculiar nature of the articles involved,[7] price reductions were of no avail in moving this "excess" inventory. As time went on, however, Thor gradually disposed of some of these items as scrap; the record is unclear as to when these dispositions took place.

Thor's total write-down of "excess" inventory in 1964 therefore was:

Ten-year amortization of parts for discontinued tools	$ 22,090
First method (aging formula based on 1964 usage)	744,030
Second method (flat percentage write-downs)	160,832
Total	$926,952

Thor credited this sum to its inventory contra account, thereby decreasing closing inventory, increasing cost of goods sold, and decreasing taxable income for the year by that amount.[9] The company contended that, by writing down excess inventory to scrap value, and by thus carrying all inventory at "net realizable value," it had reduced its inventory to "market" in accord with its "lower of cost or market" method of accounting. On audit, the Commissioner disallowed the write-down in its entirety, asserting that it did not serve clearly to reflect Thor's 1964 income for tax purposes.

The Tax Court, in upholding the Commissioner's determination, found as a fact that Thor's write-down of excess inventory did conform to "generally accepted accounting principles"; indeed, the court was "thoroughly convinced . . . that such was the case." Id., at 165. The court found that if Thor had failed to write down its inventory on some reasonable basis, its accountants would have been unable to give its financial statements the desired certification. Id., at 161-162. The court held, however, that conformance with "generally accepted accounting principles" is not enough; §446(b), and §471 as well, of the 1954 Code, 26 U.S.C. §446(b) and 471, prescribe, as an independent requirement, that inventory accounting methods must "clearly reflect income." The Tax Court rejected Thor's argument that its write-down of "excess" inventory was authorized by Treasury Regulations, 64 T.C., at 167-171, and held that the Commissioner had not abused

7. The Tax Court found that the finished tools were too specialized to attract bargain hunters; that no one would buy spare parts, regardless of price, unless they were needed to fix broken tools; that work-in-process had no value except as scrap; and that other manufacturers would not buy raw materials in the secondary market. 64 T.C., at 160-162.

9. For a manufacturing concern like Thor, Gross Profit basically equals Sales minus Cost of Goods Sold. Cost of Goods Sold equals Opening Inventory, plus Cost of Inventory Acquired, minus Closing Inventory. A reduction of Closing Inventory, therefore, increases Cost of Goods Sold and decreases Gross Profit accordingly.

his discretion in determining that the write-down failed to reflect 1964 income clearly.

B

Inventory accounting is governed by §§446 and 471 of the Code, 26 U.S.C. §§446 and 471. Section 446(a) states the general rule for methods of accounting: "Taxable income shall be computed under the method of accounting on the basis of which the taxpayer regularly computes his income in keeping his books." Section 446(b) provides, however, that if the method used by the taxpayer "does not clearly reflect income, the computation of taxable income shall be made under such method as, in the opinion of the [Commissioner], does clearly reflect income." Regulations promulgated under §446, and in effect for the taxable year 1964, state that "no method of accounting is acceptable unless, in the opinion of the Commissioner, it clearly reflects income." Treas. Reg. §1.446-1(a)(2), 26 CFR §1.446-1(a)(2) (1964).

Section 471 prescribes the general rule for inventories. It states:

> Whenever in the opinion of the [Commissioner] the use of inventories is necessary in order clearly to determine the income of any taxpayer, inventory shall be taken by such taxpayer on such basis as the [Commissioner] may prescribe as conforming as nearly as may be to the best accounting practice in the trade or business and as most clearly reflecting the income.

As the Regulations point out, §471 obviously establishes two distinct tests to which an inventory must conform. First, it must conform "as nearly as may be" to the "best accounting practice," a phrase that is synonymous with "generally accepted accounting principles." Second, it "must clearly reflect the income." Treas. Reg. §1.471-2(a)(2), 26 CFR §1.471-2(a)(2) (1964).

It is obvious that on their face, §§446 and 471, with their accompanying Regulations, vest the Commissioner with wide discretion in determining whether a particular method of inventory accounting should be disallowed as not clearly reflective of income. This Court's cases confirm the breadth of this discretion. In construing §446 and its predecessors, the Court has held that "[t]he Commissioner has broad powers in determining whether accounting methods used by a taxpayer clearly reflect income." Commissioner v. Hansen, 360 U.S. 446, 467 (1959). Since the Commissioner has "[m]uch latitude for discretion," his interpretation of the statute's clear-reflection standard "should not be interfered with unless clearly unlawful." Lucas v. American Code Co., 280 U.S. 445, 449 (1930). To the same effect are United States v. Catto, 384 U.S. 102, 114 (1966); Schlude v. Commissioner, 372 U.S. 128, 133-134 (1963); American Automobile Assn. v. United States, [Chapter 6D.1 above] (1961); Automobile Club of Michigan v.

Commissioner, 353 U.S. 180, 189-190 (1957); Brown v. Helvering, 291 U.S. 193, 203 (1934). In construing §203 of the Revenue Act of 1918, 40 Stat. 1060, a predecessor of §471, the Court held that the taxpayer bears a "heavy burden of [proof]," and that the Commissioner's disallowance of an inventory accounting method is not to be set aside unless shown to be "plainly arbitrary." Lucas v. Structural Steel Co., 281 U.S. 264, 271 (1930).

As has been noted, the Tax Court found as a fact in this case that Thor's write-down of "excess" inventory conformed to "generally accepted accounting principles" and was "within the term, 'best accounting practice,' as that term is used in section 471 of the Code and the regulations promulgated under that section." 64 T.C., at 161, 165. Since the Commissioner has not challenged this finding, there is no dispute that Thor satisfied the first part of §471's two-pronged test. The only question, then, is whether the Commissioner abused his discretion in determining that the write-down did not satisfy the test's second prong in that it failed to reflect Thor's 1964 income clearly. Although the Commissioner's discretion is not unbridled and may not be arbitrary, we sustain his exercise of discretion here, for in this case the write-down was plainly inconsistent with the governing Regulations which the taxpayer, on its part, has not challenged.

It has been noted above that Thor at all pertinent times used the "lower of cost or market" method of inventory accounting. The rules governing this method are set out in Treas. Reg. §1.471-4, 26 CFR §1.471-4 (1964). The Regulation defines "market" to mean, ordinarily, "the current bid price prevailing at the date of the inventory for the particular merchandise in the volume in which usually purchased by the taxpayer." §1.471-4(a). The courts have uniformly interpreted "bid price" to mean replacement cost, that is, the price the taxpayer would have to pay on the open market to purchase or reproduce the inventory items. Where no open market exists, the Regulations require the taxpayer to ascertain "bid price" by using "such evidence of a fair market price at the date or dates nearest the inventory as may be available, such as specific purchases or sales by the taxpayer or others in reasonable volume and made in good faith, or compensation paid for cancellation of contracts for purchase commitments." §1.471-4(b).

The Regulations specify two situations in which a taxpayer is permitted to value inventory below "market" as so defined. The first is where the taxpayer in the normal course of business has actually offered merchandise for sale at prices lower than replacement cost. Inventories of such merchandise may be valued at those prices less direct cost of disposition, "and the correctness of such prices will be determined by reference to the actual sales of the taxpayer for a reasonable period before and after the date of the inventory." Ibid. The Regulations warn that prices "which vary materially from the actual prices so ascertained will not be accepted as reflecting the market." Ibid.

The second situation in which a taxpayer may value inventory below replacement cost is where the merchandise itself is defective. If goods are "unsalable at normal prices or unusable in the normal way because of damage, imperfections, shop wear, changes of style, odd or broken lots, or other similar causes," the taxpayer is permitted to value the goods "at bona fide selling prices less direct cost of disposition." §1.471-2(c). The Regulations define "bona fide selling price" to mean an "actual offering of goods during a period not later than 30 days after inventory date." Ibid. The taxpayer bears the burden of proving that "such exceptional goods as are valued upon such selling basis come within the classifications indicated," and is required to "maintain such records of the disposition of the goods as will enable a verification of the inventory to be made." Ibid.

From this language, the regulatory scheme is clear. The taxpayer must value inventory for tax purposes at cost unless the "market" is lower. "Market" is defined as "replacement cost," and the taxpayer is permitted to depart from replacement cost only in specified situations. When it makes any such departure, the taxpayer must substantiate its lower inventory valuation by providing evidence of actual offerings, actual sales, or actual contract cancellations. In the absence of objective evidence of this kind, a taxpayer's assertions as to the "market value" of its inventory are not cognizable in computing its income tax.

It is clear to us that Thor's procedure for writing down the value of its "excess" inventory were inconsistent with this regulatory scheme. Although Thor conceded that "an active market prevailed" on the inventory date, see 64 T.C., at 169, it "made no effort to determine the purchase or reproduction cost" of its "excess" inventory. Id., at 162. Thor thus failed to ascertain "market" in accord with the general rule of the Regulations. In seeking to depart from replacement cost, Thor failed to bring itself within either of the authorized exceptions. Thor is not able to take advantage of §1.471-4(b) since, as the Tax Court found, the company failed to sell its excess inventory or offer it for sale at prices below replacement cost. 64 T.C., at 160-161. Indeed, Thor concedes that it continued to sell its "excess" inventory at original prices. Thor also is not able to take advantage of §1.471-2(c) since, as the Tax Court and the Court of Appeals both held, it failed to bear the burden of proving that its excess inventory came within the specified classifications. 64 T.C., at 171; 563 F.2d, at 867. Actually, Thor's "excess" inventory was normal and unexceptional, and was indistinguishable from and intermingled with the inventory that was not written down.

More importantly, Thor failed to provide any objective evidence whatever that the "excess" inventory had the "market value" management ascribed to it. The Regulations demand hard evidence of actual sales and further demand that records of actual dispositions be kept. The Tax Court found, however, that Thor made no sales and kept no records. 64 T.C., at 171. Thor's management simply wrote down its closing inventory on the basis of a well-educated guess that some of it would never be sold. The formulae governing this write-down were derived from management's collective "business experience"; the percentages contained in those formulae seemingly were chosen for no reason other than that they were multiples of five and embodied some kind of anagogical symmetry. The Regulations do not permit this kind of evidence. If a taxpayer could write down its inventories on the basis of management's subjective estimates of the goods' ultimate salability, the taxpayer would be able, as the Tax Court observed, id., at 170, "to determine how much tax it wanted to pay for a given year."

For these reasons, we agree with the Tax Court and with the Seventh Circuit that the Commissioner acted within his discretion in deciding that Thor's write-down of "excess" inventory failed to reflect income clearly. In the light of the well-known potential for tax avoidance that is inherent in inventory accounting, the Commissioner in his discretion may insist on a high evidentiary standard before allowing write-downs of inventory to "market." Because Thor provided no objective evidence of the reduced market value of its "excess" inventory, its write-down was plainly inconsistent with the Regulations, and the Commissioner properly disallowed it.

C

The taxpayer's major argument against this conclusion is based on the Tax Court's clear finding that the write-down conformed to "generally accepted accounting principles." Thor points to language in Treas. Reg. §1.446-1(a)(2), 26 CFR §1.446-1(a)(2) (1964), to the effect that "[a] method of accounting which reflects the consistent application of generally accepted accounting principles ... *will ordinarily be regarded* as clearly reflecting income" (emphasis added). Section 1.471-2(b), 26 CFR §1.471-2(b) (1964), of the Regulations likewise stated that an inventory taken in conformity with best accounting practice "can, *as a general rule,* be regarded as clearly reflecting ... income" (emphasis added). These provisions, Thor contends, created a *presumption* that an inventory practice conformable to "generally accepted accounting principles" is valid for income tax purposes. Once a taxpayer has established this conformity, the argument runs, the burden shifts to the Commissioner affirmatively to demonstrate that the taxpayer's method does *not* reflect income clearly. Unless the Commissioner can show that a generally accepted method "demonstrably distorts income," Brief for Chamber of Commerce of the United States as Amicus Curiae 3, or that the taxpayer's adoption of such method was "motivated by tax avoidance," Brief for Petitioner 25, the presumption in the taxpayer's favor will carry the day. The Commissioner, Thor concludes, failed to rebut that presumption here.

If the Code and Regulations did embody the presumption petitioner postulates, it would be of little use to the taxpayer in this case. As we have noted, Thor's write-down of "excess" inventory was inconsistent with the Regulations; any general presumption obviously must yield in the face of such particular inconsistency. We believe, however, that no such presumption is present. Its existence is unsupportable in light of the statute, the Court's past decisions, and the differing objectives of tax and financial accounting.

First, as has been stated above, the Code and Regulations establish two distinct tests to which an inventory must conform. The Code and Regulations, moreover, leave little doubt as to which test is paramount. While §471 of the Code requires only that an accounting practice conform "as nearly as may be" to best accounting practice, §1.446-1(a)(2) of the Regulations states categorically that "*no* method of accounting is acceptable unless, in the opinion of the Commissioner, it clearly reflects income" (emphasis added). Most importantly, the Code and Regulations give the Commissioner broad discretion to set aside the taxpayer's method if, "in [his] opinion," it does not reflect income clearly. This language is completely at odds with the notion of a "presumption" in the taxpayer's favor. The Regulations embody no presumption; they say merely that, in most cases, generally accepted accounting practices will pass muster for tax purposes. And in most cases they will. But if the Commissioner, in the exercise of his discretion, determines that they do not, he may prescribe a different practice without having to rebut any presumption running against the Treasury.

Second, the presumption petitioner postulates finds no support in this Court's prior decisions. It was early noted that the general rule specifying use of the taxpayer's method of accounting "is expressly limited to cases where the Commissioner believes that the accounts clearly reflect the net income." Lucas v. American Code Co., 280 U.S., at 449. More recently, it was held in American Automobile Assn. v. United States that a taxpayer must recognize prepaid income when received, even though this would mismatch expenses and revenues in contravention of "generally accepted commercial accounting principles." 367 U.S., at 690. "[T]o say that in performing the function of business accounting the method employed by the Association 'is in accord with generally accepted commercial accounting principles and practices,'" the Court concluded, "is not to hold that for income tax purposes it so clearly reflects income as to be binding on the Treasury." Id., at 693. "[W]e are mindful that the characterization of a transaction for financial accounting purposes, on the one hand, and for tax purposes, on the other, need not necessarily be the same." Frank Lyon Co. v. United States, 435 U.S. 561, 577 (1978). See Commissioner v. Idaho Power Co., 418 U.S. 1, 15 (1974). Indeed, the Court's cases demonstrate that divergence between tax and financial accounting is especially common when a taxpayer seeks a current deduction for estimated future expenses or losses. E.g., Commissioner v. Hansen, 360 U.S. 446 (1959) (reserve to cover contingent liability in event of nonperformance of guaranty); Brown v. Helvering, 291 U.S. 193 (1934) (reserve to cover expected liability for unearned commissions on anticipated insurance policy cancellations); Lucas v. American Code Co., supra (reserve to cover expected liability on contested lawsuit). The rationale of these cases amply encompasses Thor's aim. By its president's concession, the company's write-down of "excess" inventory was founded on the belief that many of the articles inevitably would become useless due to breakage, technological change, fluctuations in market demand, and the like. Thor, in other words, sought a current "deduction" for an estimated future loss. Under the decided cases, a taxpayer so circumstanced finds no shelter beneath an accountancy presumption.

Third, the presumption petitioner postulates is insupportable in light of the vastly different objectives that financial and tax accounting have. The primary goal of financial accounting is to provide useful information to management, shareholders, creditors, and others properly interested; the major responsibility of the accountant is to protect these parties from being misled. The primary goal of the income tax system, in contrast, is the equitable collection of revenue; the major responsibility of the Internal Revenue Service is to protect the public fisc. Consistently with its goals and responsibilities, financial accounting has as its foundation the principle of conservatism, with its corollary that "possible errors in measurement [should] be in the direction of understatement rather than overstatement of net income and net assets."[18] In view of the Treasury's markedly different goals and responsibilities, understatement of income is not destined to be its guiding light. Given this diversity, even contrariety of objectives, any presumptive equivalency between tax and financial accounting would be unacceptable.

This difference in objectives is mirrored in numerous differences of treatment. Where the tax law requires that a deduction be deferred until "all the events" have occurred that will make it fixed and certain, United States v. Anderson, 269 U.S. 422, 441 (1926), accounting principles typically require that a liability be accrued as soon as it can reasonably be estimated. Conversely, where the tax law requires that income be recognized currently under "claim of right, "ability to pay," and "control" rationales, accounting principles may defer accrual until a later year so that revenues and expenses may be better matched. Financial accounting, in short, is hospitable to estimates, probabilities, and reasonable certainties; the tax law, with its mandate to preserve the revenue, can give no quarter to uncertainty. This is as it should be. Reasonable estimates may be useful, even essential in giving shareholders and creditors an accurate picture of a firm's overall financial health; but the accountant's conservatism cannot bind the Commissioner in his efforts to collect taxes. "Only a few reserves voluntarily established as a matter of conservative accounting," Mr. Justice Brandeis wrote for the Court, "are authorized by the Revenue Acts." Brown v. Helvering, 291 U.S., at 201-202.

Finally, a presumptive equivalency between tax and financial accounting would create insurmountable difficulties of tax administration.

---

18. AICPA Accounting Principles Board, Statement No. 4, Basic Concepts and Accounting Principles Underlying Financial Statements of Business Enterprises §171 (1970), reprinted in 2 APB Accounting Principles 9089 (1973). See Sterling, Conservatism: The Fundamental Principle of Valuation in Traditional Accounting, 3 Abacus 109-113 (1967).

Accountants long have recognized that "generally accepted accounting principles" are far from being a canonical set of rules that will ensure identical accounting treatment of identical transactions. "Generally accepted accounting principles," rather, tolerate a range of "reasonable" treatments, leaving the choice among alternatives to management. Such, indeed, is precisely the case here. Variances of this sort may be tolerable in financial reporting, but they are questionable in a tax system designed to ensure as far as possible that similarly situated taxpayers pay the same tax. If management's election among "acceptable" options were dispositive for tax purposes, a firm, indeed, could decide unilaterally — within limits dictated only by its accountants — the tax it wished to pay. Such unilateral decisions would not just make the Code inequitable; they would make it unenforceable.

D

Thor complains that a decision adverse to it poses a dilemma. According to the taxpayer, it would be virtually impossible for it to offer objective evidence of its "excess" inventory's lower value, since the goods cannot be sold at reduced prices; even if they could be sold, says Thor, their reduced-price sale would just "pull the rug out" from under the identical "non-excess" inventory Thor is trying to sell simultaneously. The only way Thor could establish the inventory's value by a "closed transaction" would be to scrap the articles at once. Yet immediate scrapping would be undesirable, for demand for the parts ultimately might prove greater than anticipated. The taxpayer thus sees itself presented with "an unattractive Hobson's choice: either the unsalable inventory must be carried for years at its cost instead of net realizable value, thereby overstating taxable income by such overvaluation until it is scrapped, or the excess inventory must be scrapped prematurely to the detriment of the manufacturer and its customers." Brief for Petitioner 25.

If this is indeed the dilemma that confronts Thor, it is in reality the same choice that every taxpayer who has a paper loss must face. It can realize its loss now and garner its tax benefit, or it can defer realization, and its deduction, hoping for better luck later. Thor, quite simply, has suffered no present loss. It deliberately manufactured its "excess" spare parts because it judged that the marginal cost of unsalable inventory would be lower than the cost of retooling machinery should demand surpass expectations. This was a rational business judgment and, not unpredictably, Thor now has inventory it believes it cannot sell. Thor, of course, is not so confident of its prediction as to be willing to scrap the "excess" parts now; it wants to keep them on hand, just in case. This, too, is a rational judgment, but there is no reason why the Treasury should subsidize Thor's hedging of its bets. There is also no reason why Thor should be entitled, for tax purposes, to have its cake and to eat it too. . . .

[Discussion of bad debt deduction omitted.]

The judgment of the Court of Appeals is affirmed.

Questions

Would the taxpayer's argument be more persuasive if focused more on cost instead of loss? The Court said that parts were cheap to produce in quantity. Suppose it were shown that most of the cost was tooling up to produce a particular part and that the marginal cost of producing a large quantity of a particular part was very small. If this were the case, could the taxpayer assign his tooling-up costs to the first few items used and carry the rest at the low marginal cost that led to their production? Would this be an acceptable mode of inventory cost accounting for most goods produced for sale? If not, is there something different about replacement parts?

Does the last part of the Court's opinion represent a necessary or sufficient response to the taxpayer's dilemma (as there described)?

4. Accruing Future Expenses

UNITED STATES v. GENERAL DYNAMICS CORP.
481 U.S. 239 (1987)

Marshall, J., delivered the opinion of the Court, in which Rehnquist, C. J., and Brennan, White, Powell, and Scalia, J. J., joined. O'Connor, J., filed a dissenting opinion, in which Blackmun and Stevens, J. J., joined.

Justice MARSHALL delivered the opinion of the Court. The issue in this case is whether an accrual-basis taxpayer providing medical benefits to its employees may deduct at the close of the taxable year an estimate of its obligation to pay for medical care obtained by employees of their qualified dependents during the final quarter of the year, claims for which have not been reported to the employer.

I

... General Dynamics uses the accrual method of accounting for federal tax purposes; its fiscal year is the same as the calendar year. From 1962 until October 1, 1972, General Dynamics purchased group medical insurance for its employees and their qualified dependents from two private insurance carriers. Beginning in October 1972, General Dynamics became a self-insurer with regard to its medical care plans. Instead of continuing to purchase insurance from outside carriers, it undertook to pay medical claims out of its own funds, while continuing to employ private carriers to administer the medical care plans.

To receive reimbursement of expenses for covered medical services, respondent's employees submit claims forms to employee benefits personnel, who verify that the treated persons were eligible under the applicable plan as of the time of treatment. Eligible claims are then forwarded to the plan's administrators. Claims processors review the claims and approve for payment those expenses that are covered under the plan.

Because the processing of claims takes time, and because employees do not always file their claims immediately, there is a delay between the provision of medical services and payment by General Dynamics. To account for this time lag, General Dynamics established reserve accounts to reflect its liability for medical care received, but still not paid for, as of December 31, 1972. It estimated the amount of those reserves with the assistance of its former insurance carriers. . . .

II

As we noted in United States v. Hughes Properties, Inc., 476 U.S. 593, 600 (1986), whether a business expense has been "incurred" so as to entitle an accrual-basis taxpayer to deduct it under §162(a) of the Internal Revenue Code, 26 U.S.C. §162(a), is governed by the "all events" test that originated in United States v. Anderson, 269 U.S. 422, 441 (1926). In Anderson, the Court held that a taxpayer was obligated to deduct from its 1916 income a tax on profits from munitions sales that took place in 1916. Although the tax would not be assessed and therefore would not formally be due until 1917, all the events which fixed the amount of the tax and determined the taxpayer's liability to pay it had occurred in 1916. The test is now embodied in Treas. Reg. §1.461-1(a)(2), 26 CFR §1.461-1(a)(2) (1986), which provides that "[u]nder an accrual method of accounting, an expense is deductible for the taxable year in which all the events have occurred which determine the fact of the liability and the amount thereof can be determined with reasonable accuracy."[3]

_____

3. The regulation in force in 1972 was identical to the present version. See 26 CFR §1.461-1(a)(2) (1972).

The "all events" test has been incorporated into the Internal Revenue Code by the Deficit Reduction Act of 1984, Pub. L. 98-369, 98 Stat. 598, 607, 26 U.S.C. §461(h)(4) (1982 ed., Supp. III). Section 461(h) imposed limits on the application of the test, providing that "in determining whether an amount has been incurred with respect to any item during any taxable year, the all events test shall not be treated as met any earlier than when economic performance with respect to such item occurs." §461(h)(1). The pertinent portions of the 1984 amendments were retained in the Tax Reform Act of 1986.

Section 461(h) does not apply in this case. It became effective as of July 18, 1984, the date of the enactment of the Deficit Reduction Act. See §91(g)(1)(A), 26 U.S.C. §461 note (1982 ed., Supp. III). While that statute permits a taxpayer to elect the application of §461(h) to amounts incurred on or before July 18, 1984, see §91(g)(2), there is no indication that the taxpayer here has done so. We do not address how this case would be decided under §461(h), but note that the legislative history of the Act indicates that, "[i]n the case of . . . employee benefit liabilities, which require a payment by the taxpayer to another person, economic performance occurs as the payments to such person are made." H.R. Rep. No. 98-432, pt. 2, p. 1255 (1984); see also H. Conf. Rep. No. 98-861, p. 872 (1984).

It is fundamental to the "all events" test that, although expenses may be deductible before they have become due and payable, liability must first be firmly established. This is consistent with our prior holdings that a taxpayer may not deduct a liability that is contingent, see Lucas v. American Code Co., 280 U.S. 445, 452 (1930), or contested, see Security Flour Mills Co. v. Commissioner of Internal Revenue, 321 U.S. 281, 284 (1944). Nor may a taxpayer deduct an estimate of an anticipated expense, no matter how statistically certain, if it is based on events that have not occurred by the close of the taxable year. Brown v. Helvering, 291 U.S. 193, 201 (1934); cf. American Automobile Assn. v. United States, 367 U.S. 687, 693 (1961).

We think that this case, like *Brown*, involves a mere estimate of liability based on events that had not occurred before the close of the taxable year, and therefore the proposed deduction does not pass the "all events" test. We disagree with the legal conclusion of the courts below that the last event necessary to fix the taxpayer's liability was the receipt of medical care by covered individuals.[4] A person covered by a plan could only obtain payment for medical services by filling out and submitting a health-expense-benefits claim form. App. 23. Employees were informed that submission of satisfactory proof of the charges claimed would be necessary to obtain payment under the plans. Id., at 58. General Dynamics was thus liable to pay for covered medical services only if properly documented claims forms were filed.[5] Some covered individuals, through oversight, procrastination, confusion over the coverage provided, or fear of disclosure to the employer of the extent or nature of the services received, might not file claims for reimbursement to which they are plainly entitled. Such filing is not a mere technicality. It is crucial to the establishment of liability on the part of the taxpayer. Nor does the failure to file a claim represent the type of "extremely remote and speculative possibility" that we held in Hughes, supra, at 601, did not render an otherwise fixed liability contingent. Cf. Lucas v. North Texas Lumber Co., 281 U.S. 11, 13 (1930) (where executory contract of sale was created in 1916 but papers necessary to effect transfer were not prepared until 1917, unconditional liability for the purchase price was not created in 1916, and the gain from the sale was therefore not realized until 1917). Mere receipt of services for which, in some instances,

---

4. We do not challenge the Claims Court's factual conclusion that the processing of the claims was "routine," "clerical," and "ministerial in nature," 6 Cl. Ct. 250, 254 (1984). The Claims Court did not, however, make any factual findings with respect to the filing of claims. We conclude that, as a matter of law, the filing of a claim was necessary to create liability.

5. General Dynamics could not avoid its obligation to pay for services after they were received by, for example, discharging the employee. If an employee were terminated after receiving covered services but before filing a claim, the taxpayer would still be obliged to reimburse that employee, App. 22 — but only in the event that the employee filed a claim form. The filing of the claim is thus a true condition precedent to liability on the part of the taxpayer.

claims will not be submitted does not, in our judgment, constitute the last link in the chain of events creating liability for purposes of the "all events" test.

The parties stipulated in this case that as of December 31, 1972, the taxpayer had not received all claims for medical treatment services rendered in 1972, and that some claims had been filed for services rendered in 1972 that had not been processed. App. 26. The record does not reflect which portion of the claims against General Dynamics for medical care had been filed but not yet processed and which portion had not even been filed at the close of the 1972 tax year. The taxpayer has the burden of proving its entitlement to a deduction. Helvering v. Taylor, 293 U.S. 507, 514 (1935). Here, respondent made no showing that, as of December 31, 1972, it knew of specific claims which had been filed but which it had not yet processed. Because the taxpayer failed to demonstrate that any of the deducted reserve represented claims for which its liability was firmly established as of the close of 1972, all the events necessary to establish liability were not shown to have occurred, and therefore no deduction was permissible.

This is not to say that the taxpayer was unable to forecast how many claims would be filed for medical care received during this period, and estimate the liability that would arise from those claims. Based on actuarial data, General Dynamics may have been able to make a reasonable estimate of how many claims would be filed for the last quarter of 1972. But that alone does not justify a deduction. In Brown, supra, the taxpayer, a general agent for insurance companies, sought to take a deduction for a reserve representing estimated liability for premiums to be returned on the percentage of insurance policies it anticipated would be cancelled in future years. The agent may well have been capable of estimating with a reasonable degree of accuracy the ratio of cancellation refunds to premiums already paid and establishing its reserve accordingly. Despite the "strong probability that many of the policies written during that taxable year" would be cancelled, 291 U.S., at 201, the Court held that "no liability accrues during the taxable year on account of cancellations which it is expected may occur in future years, since the events necessary to create the liability do not occur during the taxable year." Id., at 200. A reserve based on the proposition that a particular set of events is likely to occur in the future may be an appropriate conservative accounting measure, but does not warrant a tax deduction. See American Automobile Assn. v. United States, supra, at 692; Lucas v. American Code Co., 280 U.S., at 452.

That these estimated claims were not intended to fall within the "all events" test is further demonstrated by the fact that the Internal Revenue Code specifically permits insurance companies to deduct additions to reserves for such "incurred but not reported" (IBNR) claims. See 26 U.S.C. §832(b)(5) (providing that an insurance company may treat as losses incurred "all unpaid losses outstanding at the end of the taxable year"); §832(c)(4) (permitting deduction of losses incurred as defined in

§832(b)(5)).[6] If the "all events" test permitted the deduction of an estimated reserve representing claims that were actuarially likely but not yet
reported, Congress would not have needed to maintain an explicit provision
that insurance companies could deduct such reserves.[7]

General Dynamics did not show that its liability as to any medical care
claims was firmly established as of the close of the 1972 tax year, and
is therefore entitled to no deduction. The judgment of the Court of Appeals is
   Reversed.

Justice O'CONNOR, with whom Justice BLACKMUN and Justice STEVENS join,
dissenting.

Section 446(a) of the Internal Revenue code of 1954 provides that taxable income "shall be computed under the method of accounting on the
basis of which the taxpayer regularly computes his income in keeping his
books." The code specifically recognizes the use of "an accrual method," 26
U.S.C. §446(c)(2), under which a taxpayer is permitted to deduct an
expense in the year in which it is "incurred," regardless of when it is actually
paid. §162(a). Under the "all events" test, long applied by this Court and the
Internal Revenue Service, an expense may be accrued and deducted when all
the events that determine the fact of liability have occurred, and the amount
of the liability can be determined with reasonable accuracy. Treas. Reg.
§1.461-1, 26 CFR §1.461-1(a)(2) (1986). Because the Court today applies a
rigid version of the "all events" test that retreats from our most recent application of that test, and unnecessarily drives a greater wedge between tax and
financial accounting methods, I respectfully dissent.

This case calls for the Court to revisit the issue addressed only last Term
in United States v. Hughes Properties, Inc., 476 U.S. 593 (1986). At issue in
Hughes Properties was whether a casino operator utilizing the accrual
method of accounting could deduct amounts guaranteed for payment
on "progressive" slot machines but not yet won by a playing patron.
A progressive slot machine has a jackpot whose size increases as money is
gambled on the machine. Under Nevada law, a casino operator is prohibited
from reducing the amount of the progressive jackpot. We concluded, therefore, that all the events had occurred that determine the fact of the casino
operator's liability despite the fact that the jackpot might not be won for as
long as four years. We rejected the argument made by the United States that
the casino operator's obligation to pay the jackpot arose only upon a winning
patron's pull of the handle, even though it was conceivable that the jackpot
might never be won:

"There is always a possibility, of course, that a casino may go out of
business, or surrender or lose its license, or go into bankruptcy, with the

---

6. During the time that private insurance carriers provided insurance coverage for General Dynamics
employees, the insurers maintained reserves for IBNR claims and deducted those reserves in the tax year
in which the services were received. 6 Cl. Ct., at 252.

7. Respondent has never sought to be treated as an insurance company entitled to take IBNR
deductions under the provisions of Subchapter L.

result that the amounts shown on the jackpot indicators would never be won by playing patrons. But this potential nonpayment of an incurred liability exists for every business that uses an accrual method, and it does not prevent accrual. See. e.g., Wien Consolidated Airlines, Inc. v. Commissioner, 528 F.2d 735 (CA9 1976). 'The existence of an absolute liability is necessary; absolute certainty that it will be discharged by payment is not.' Helvering v. Russian Finance & Constr. Corp., 77 F.2d 324, 327 (CA2 1935)." United States v. Hughes Properties, Inc., supra, at 605-606.

In my view, the circumstances of this case differ little from those in Hughes Properties. The taxpayer here is seeking to deduct the amounts reserved to pay for medical services that are determined to have been provided to employees in the taxable year, whether or not the employees' claims for benefits have been received. The taxpayer's various medical benefits plans provided schedules for the medical and hospital benefits, and created a contractual obligation by the taxpayer to pay for the covered services upon presentation of a claim. The courts below found that the obligation to pay became fixed once the covered medical services were received by the employee. See App. 25. Once the medical services were rendered to an employee while the relevant benefit plan was in effect, General Dynamics could not avoid liability by terminating the plan prior to the filing of a claim. Id., at 133-134. Neither could General Dynamics extinguish its liability by firing an employee before the employee filed a claim for benefits. Id., at 87.

It is true, of course, that it was theoretically possible that some employees might not file claim forms. In my view, however, this speculative possibility of nonpayment differs not at all from the speculation in Hughes Properties that a jackpot might never be paid by a casino. As we observed in Hughes Properties, the potential of nonpayment of a liability always exists, and it alone does not prevent accrual. The beneficiary of a liability always has the option of waiving payment, but a taxpayer is still unquestionably entitled to deduct the liability. An injured employee entitled absolutely to reimbursement for medical services under a worker's compensation statute, for example, may fail to utilize the medical services. The employer, however, has been held to be entitled to deduct the expected medical expenses because the worker's compensation law creates liability. See Wien Consolidated Airlines, Inc. v. Commissioner, 528 F.2d 735 (CA9 1976) (holding that accrual basis taxpayer may deduct expected worker's compensation payments in year of injury even though injured workers may not utilize medical benefits). Similarly, any business liability could ultimately be discharged in bankruptcy, or a check might never be cashed by its recipient. There can be no doubt, however, that these remote possibilities alone cannot defeat an accrual basis taxpayer's right to deduct the liability when incurred.

The Claims Court found that the processing of the employees' claims was "routine" and "ministerial in nature," 6 Cl. Ct. 250, 254 (1984), and the majority does not question that finding. Ante, at 244, n. 4. Instead, the majority holds that "as a matter of law, the filing of a claim was necessary to create liability." Ibid. Even if, in a technical sense, the Court is correct that the filing of a claim is a necessary pre-condition to liability as a matter of law, the failure to file a claim is at most a "merely formal contingenc[y], or [one] highly improbable under the known facts," that this Court has viewed as insufficient to preclude accrual and deductibility. 2 J. Mertens, Law of Federal Income Taxation §12.62, p. 241 (M. Weinstein, R. Donovan, P. Gaveras, H. Piech, & R. Neeld rev. 1985). Indeed, in the very case that first announced the "all events" test, United States v. Anderson, 269 U.S. 422 (1926), this Court concluded that a taxpayer should deduct a federal munitions tax before the year in which the tax was even assessed — in effect before the Government had made a claim for the tax. The Court recognized that "[i]n a technical legal sense it may be argued that a tax does not accrue until it has been assessed and becomes due," but concluded that otherwise all the events that determined the liability for the munitions tax had occurred. Id., at 441. Similarly, in Continental Tie & Lumber Co. v. United States, 286 U.S. 290 (1932), the Court held that an accrual basis taxpayer should immediately include as income a federal payment to railroads created by statute, but neither claimed by the taxpayer nor awarded by the Federal Government until years later. The court explained that although no railroad had any vested right to payments under the statute until a claim was made by the railroad and awarded by the Interstate Commerce Commission, "[t]he right to the award was fixed by the passage of the Transportation Act. What remained was mere administrative procedure to ascertain the amount to be paid." Id., at 295. Clearly, the right to reimbursement for medical benefits under any of the medical benefits plans at issue in this case arises once medical services are rendered; the filing and processing of a claim is purely routine and ministerial, and in the nature of a formal contingency, as correctly perceived by the courts below.

The holding of the Court today unnecessarily burdens taxpayers by further expanding the difference between tax and business accounting methods without a compelling reason to do so. Obviously, tax accounting principles must often differ from those of business accounting. The goal of business accounting "is to provide useful and pertinent information to management, shareholders, and creditors," while "the responsibility of the Internal Revenue Service is to protect the public fisc." United States v. Hughes Properties, Inc., 476 U.S., at 603. Therefore, while prudent businesses will accrue expenses that are merely reasonably foreseeable, for tax purposes the liability must be fixed. But Congress has expressly permitted taxpayers to use the accrual method of accounting, and from its inception in United States v. Anderson, supra, the "all events" test has been a practical adjustment of the competing interests in permitting accrual accounting and protecting the public fisc. Unfortunately, the Court today ignores the pragmatic roots of the "all events" test and instead applies it in an essentially mechanistic and wholly unrealistic manner. Because the liability in this case was fixed with no less certainty than the range of expenses both routinely accrued by accrual method taxpayers and approved as deductible for tax purposes by this Court and other courts in a variety of circumstances, I respectfully dissent.

PREMATURE ACCRUALS [§461(h)]

Staff of Joint Comm. on Taxation, 98th Cong., General Explanation of the Revenue Provisions of the Deficit Reduction Act of 1984, 258-263 (Comm. Print 1984)

GENERAL

Prior law provided that, under the accrual method of accounting, an expense was deductible for the taxable year in which all the events had occurred which determined the fact of the liability and the amount thereof could be determined with reasonable accuracy (the so-called "all events test") (Treas. Reg. sec. 1.461-1(a) (2)). If the "all events" test was satisfied, an accrual basis taxpayer generally could deduct the full face amount of the liability (ignoring any discounting of the amount to reflect the time value of money).

FACT OF LIABILITY

In a number of early cases, the courts held that expenditures are deductible only when the activities that the taxpayer is obligated to perform are in fact performed, not when the "fact" of the obligation to perform is determined. For example, in Spencer, White & Prentis, Inc. v. Commissioner, 144 F.2d 45 (2d Cir. 1944), a contractor, who was engaged in the construction of a subway system and who was required under contract to restore certain property damaged or otherwise affected by the construction, was denied deductions for the accrued estimated costs of restoration. The court held that the liability for work done after the end of the taxable year had not been incurred because the work had not been performed. The court also held that deductions were only allowable when the taxpayer's liability to pay became definite and certain.

More recently, the courts generally have reached a different conclusion: a taxpayer may deduct the amount of a liability if all the events that fix the liability have occurred and the amount can be determined with reasonable accuracy, even though the activities the taxpayer is obligated to perform are not actually performed until a later year. For example, the Fourth Circuit held that surface mining reclamation costs that could be estimated with reasonable accuracy were properly accrued when the land was stripped although the land was not reclaimed until a subsequent year. Harold v. Commissioner, 192 F.2d 1002 (4th Cir. 1951).

The position of the Fourth Circuit with respect to strip mining reclamation costs has been extended by other courts to certain other situations. For example, the Ninth Circuit held that the fact of the liability under workers' compensation laws[2] is determined in uncontested cases in the year in which injury occurs, even though medical services may be rendered at a future time. Crescent Wharf & Warehouse Co. v. Commissioner, 518 F.2d 772 (9th Cir. 1975).

A deduction for a contingent liability generally is not allowed under present or prior law, because all of the events necessary to fix the liability have not yet occurred. However, in one recent case, the Third Circuit held that a taxpayer was allowed to deduct amounts paid to a trust to fund benefits under a negotiated supplemental unemployment benefit plan, including amounts accrued in a "contingent liability account" (at a fixed rate for each hour worked by eligible employees until a target funding amount is reached). Lukens Steel Co. v. Commissioner, 442 F.2d 1131 (3d Cir. 1971). The fact that the liability was to a group, rather than a specific individual, and that the time of future payment was indefinite, did not bar, in the Court's view, a deduction under the all events test.

The courts generally have held that the length of time between accrual and performance does not affect whether an amount is properly accruable. However, in Mooney Aircraft, Inc. v. United States, 420 F.2d 400 (5th Cir. 1969), the court held that a taxpayer, who gave to purchasers of its airplanes a bond redeemable when the plane was permanently retired from service, was not allowed a deduction because the possible interval between accrual and payment was "too long"; the court concluded that the likelihood of payment decreases as the time between accrual and payment increases.

The Internal Revenue Service takes the position that, for an amount to be deductible, there must be a current liability to pay that amount, and there must not be a contingency as to payment (other than the ability of the obligor to pay). Rev. Rul. 72-34, 1972-1 C.B. 132.

AMOUNT OF LIABILITY

In order for an amount to be deductible under the all events test, the amount of a liability must be determinable with reasonable accuracy. The courts have held that this rule is satisfied if the amount of the liability, although not definitely ascertained, can be estimated with reasonable accuracy. Generally, estimates based on industry-wide experience or the experience of the taxpayer have been accepted by the courts as reasonable. In a recent case, the Ninth Circuit permitted the question of the reasonable accuracy of the amount reserved for anticipated liabilities to be determined

---

2. Under workers' compensation laws, employers generally are required to pay injured employees' medical expenses and disability benefits. In many cases, the employer's payments of the benefits extends over several years.

by estimating the amount of the liability on an aggregate rather than on an individual claim basis, as had generally been required in earlier cases. Kaiser Steel Corp. v. United States, 411 F.2d 235 (9th Cir. 1983).

The Internal Revenue Service generally takes a more restrictive position. Under their view, the exact amount of a liability must be determinable by a computation based on presently known or knowable factors. . . .

REASONS FOR CHANGE

Congress believed that the rules relating to the time for accrual of a deduction by a taxpayer using the accrual method of accounting should be changed to take into account the time value of money and the time the deduction is economically incurred. Recent court decisions in some cases permitted accrual method taxpayers to deduct currently expenses that were not yet economically incurred (i.e., that were attributable to activities to be performed or amounts to be paid in the future). Allowing a taxpayer to take deductions currently for an amount to be paid in the future overstates the true cost of the expense to the extent that the time value of money is not taken into account; the deduction is overstated by the amount by which the face value exceeds the present value of the expense. The longer the period of time involved, the greater is the overstatement. Congress was concerned about the potential revenue loss from such overstated deductions. In many everyday business transactions, taxpayers incur liabilities to pay expenses in the future. Congress believed that because of the large number of transactions in which deductions may be overstated and because of the high interest rates in recent years, the magnitude of the revenue loss could be significant.

Finally, the failure of prior law to take into account the time value of money had become the cornerstone for a variety of tax shelters. For example, a tax shelter partnership could obligate itself to pay someone to perform research and development in the future and claim a current deduction for the undiscounted amount of the future payments.

Congress recognized that, in the case of noncapital items, a taxpayer, theoretically, should be allowed a deduction for either the full amount of a liability when the liability is satisfied or a discounted amount at an earlier time. However, Congress also recognized that determining the discounted values for all kinds of future expenses would be extraordinarily complex and would be extremely difficult to administer. For instance, a system that allowed current deductions for discounted future expenses would have to include a complex set of rules for recalculating overstated and understated deductions when the future liabilities are reestimated or are actually satisfied at a time, or in an amount, different from that originally projected. Furthermore, in the case of future expenditures, an appropriate discounting system may be equally complex. Therefore, in order to prevent deductions for future expenses in excess of their true cost, while avoiding the complexity of a system of discounted valuation, Congress believed that expenses should be accrued only when economic performance occurs.

Congress recognized that in many ordinary business transactions, economic performance may not occur until the year following the year in which the deduction may be taken under the all events test. Therefore, to avoid disrupting normal business and accounting practices and imposing undue burdens on taxpayers, Congress believed that an exception to the economic performance requirement should be provided for certain recurring items.

EXPLANATION OF PROVISION

In General

The Act provides that, in determining whether an amount has been incurred with respect to any item during the taxable year by a taxpayer using the accrual method of accounting, all the events which establish liability for such amount generally are not to be treated as having occurred any earlier than the time economic performance occurs. The all events test is met if all events have occurred which determine the fact of liability and the amount of such liability can be determined with reasonable accuracy. If economic performance has occurred and the other requirements of the all events test are met, the amount is treated as incurred for all purposes of the Code. If amounts incurred are chargeable to a capital account or, under any other provision of the Code, are deductible in a taxable year later than the year when economic performance occurs then such other provisions apply in determining the amount deductible each year.

The Act provides special rules relating to nuclear power plant decommissioning costs and to costs associated with reclamation and closing of mine and solid waste disposal sites [see Codes §§468, 88, 468A].

Economic Performance

The Act provides a series of principles for determining when economic performance occurs. The principles provided by the Act describe the two most common categories of liabilities: first, cases where the liability arises as a result of another person providing goods and services to the taxpayer and, second, cases where the liability requires the taxpayer to provide goods and services to another person or undertake some activity as a result of its income-producing activities.

With respect to the first category of liabilities, if the liability arises out of the use of property, economic performance occurs as the taxpayer uses the property. If the liability requires a payment for the providing of property, economic performance occurs when the property is provided. However,

Congress intended that the Treasury Department issue regulations providing that the time at which property is provided should include the time of delivery, shipment, or other time so long as the taxpayer accounts for such items consistently from year to year. If the liability of the taxpayer requires a payment to another person for the providing of services to the taxpayer by another person, economic performance generally occurs when such other person provides the services.

With respect to the second category of liabilities, if the liability of the taxpayer requires the taxpayer to provide property or perform services, economic performance occurs as the taxpayer provides the property or performs the services. For this purpose, property does not include money; that is, economic performance generally does not occur as payments are made except as specifically provided in the Code or regulations. For example, if a contractor is engaged by a highway construction company to repair damaged properties, economic performance occurs as the contractor performs the work. Likewise, when the highway construction company itself repairs the damage, economic performance occurs as repairs are made.

Under a special rule for workers' compensation and tort liabilities requiring payments to another person, economic performance occurs as payments are made to that person. In the case of any other liability of the taxpayer, economic performance will occur at the time determined under regulations to be prescribed by the Treasury.

EXCEPTION FROM ECONOMIC PERFORMANCE REQUIREMENT FOR CERTAIN RECURRING ITEMS

IN GENERAL

The Act provides an exception under which certain expenses may be treated as incurred in the taxable year in which the all events test is otherwise met even though economic performance has not yet occurred. This exception applies if four conditions are met: (1) the all events test, without regard to economic performance, is satisfied with respect to the item during the taxable year; (2) economic performance occurs within a reasonable period (but in no event more than 8½ months) after the close of the taxable year; (3) the item is recurring in nature and the taxpayer consistently from year to year treats items of that type as incurred in the taxable year in which the all events test is met; and (4) either (a) the item is not material, or (b) the accrual of the item in the year in which the all events test is met results in a better matching of the item with the income to which it relates than would result from accruing the item in the year in which economic performance occurs.

This exception does not apply to workers' compensation or tort liabilities. . . .

Notes and Questions

1. Think hard about three concepts in these materials: the all-events test, time value of money, and economic performance. What is their relationship, if any?

2. What is the relationship, if any, between the traditional issues of certainty and the more recently focused problem of time value of money? Can serious time value problems arise even when liability to make a future payment is clear?

3. *Structured settlements.* Consider, for example, a taxpayer who admits liability for a serious personal injury to another, the liability having been incurred in the taxpayer's business. Assume then that the taxpayer is considering settling that liability by agreeing to pay $100,000 a year for 40 years. If that settlement is made, how much will be deductible and when?

Consider the effect if the whole $4,000,000 is deductible forthwith. If the taxpayer is a corporation in a 35 percent tax bracket with plenty of income to absorb the deduction, then the deduction will produce an immediate income tax saving of $1,400,000 (35 percent times $4,000,000). Now suppose that amount were invested to return 8 percent after taxes. How long would the taxpayer be able to finance payment of the liability solely out of the after-tax return from investment of the tax savings?

Would the taxpayer in this case be worse or better off if it negotiated its liability down to $3,000,000 over 30 years?

Does it make sense to have an income tax system under which a taxpayer is financially better off the longer it agrees to pay?

What about the recipient in this case? Is he better or worse off than if he received a lump sum equal to the present discounted value of the installment payments? See the parenthetical expression in §104(a)(2) and Chapter 3B.1 above.

4. Look carefully at §461(h)(2) defining time of economic performance. Does any coherent concept emerge? Is it easier to make sense of the separate strands than to unite them in a single idea?

5. Consider, in particular, §461(h)(2)(C)(ii), concerning tort and workers' compensation liabilities. Does the time of payment of such liabilities have anything to do with the economics of the taxpayer's business or profitability? Passing that question, is it a good idea for some other reason to postpone deduction until payment to the victim?

If the problem is time value of money, why not simply limit deductions to the present discounted value (burden?) of the liability? This would have the effect of treating the taxpayer just as if money had been borrowed, at interest, to pay off the liability forthwith. If the rate of discount was the pretax interest rate, the taxpayer should get further deductions for the interest component of his ultimate payments as they accrue. In the end, the taxpayer's total deductions would equal total payments, but would be timed in a much more realistic way than immediate deduction of the whole. The statute adopted is of course much harsher since it does not permit any deduction until payment.

The General Explanation of the new statute says discounting was rejected because it is too complex. Is that persuasive?

Another possibility is that postponing deduction until actual payment does indeed overtax the employer, but that this only serves to offset the undertaxation of the recipient that results from total exemption of periodic payments without separating out and taxing the interest component in them. Is this any more persuasive?

6. In 1980 Ford Motor Company entered into 24 structured settlements of tort suits on account of accidents involving its cars and trucks.[6] These committed Ford to pay $24.5 million over various periods, mostly more than 40 years.[7] To provide it with funds to cover the periodic payments, Ford purchased single premium annuity contracts at a cost of $4.4 million. The annuity contracts were structured so that the yearly annuity payments would equal the yearly amount owed to the claimants under the structured settlement agreements. None of the settlement agreements released Ford from liability following the purchase of the annuity contract, and, in the event of a default on an annuity, petitioner would be required to pay the remaining balance owed to the tort claimants. The parties stipulated that the present value of the deferred payments that petitioner agreed to make to the claimants did not exceed the cost of the annuity contracts. For financial accounting purposes, Ford reported the 1980 structured settlements by expensing the cost of the annuities in the year of the settlement.

Ford claimed a deduction in 1980 of the full $24.5 million due under the settlements.[8] It also reported the annuity income on its 1980 federal income tax return under §72.

The Commissioner determined that Ford's method of accounting for its structured settlements did not clearly reflect income under §446(b). The method of accounting that the Commissioner imposed was to allow Ford a deduction for the amount that it paid for the annuities with no further deductions for the future payments that Ford will make to the claimants. To offset her disallowance of future deductions, the Commissioner allowed Ford to exclude its income derived from the annuity contracts.

(a) Ford argued that because its accrual of deductions satisfied the all-events test, the Commissioner had no authority to invoke §446(b). The court ruled that the authorization of accrual methods in §446(c) is, by the terms of the statute, subordinate to the clear reflection requirements of §446(b).

---

6. Ford Motor Co. v. Commissioner, 71 F.3d 209 (6th Cir. 1995).

7. Many of the settlements were for payments during someone's life, with or without a minimum term of years. The $24.5 million figure was computed on the assumption that claimants would live just their life expectancies.

8. On its return as filed Ford deducted only $10.6 million, since the rest was contingent on payees' longevity. After being challenged, it filed an amended return claiming the whole $24.5 million.

(b) To demonstrate the distortion inherent in the taxpayer's account-ing, the Tax Court constructed an example showing how Ford would come out financially better off than if no accident had occurred. Ford objected to the example for using a pre-tax rate of return where it should have used an after-tax rate; its recomputation showed the taxpayer to be slightly worse off than if the accident had not occurred. The Commissioner in her brief offered a revised example in which there was a net gain from an accident using an after-tax rate of return, and the taxpayer found fault with that. The court of appeals concluded that conversion of the pre-tax tort loss into an after-tax profit was not determinative and that, "even viewing petitioner's numerical example as correct, the gross distortion of income that it demon-strates between the economic and tax results persuades us that the tax court's decision was not improper. Given the length of the payment periods, allowing a deduction for the full amount of liability in 1980 could lead to the result that the tax benefit from the deduction would fund the full amounts due in future years and leave petitioner with a profit. Such a result extends the accrual method of accounting beyond its inherent limitations."

(c) Ford objected to the Commissioner's remedy because (1) it imposes on Ford a present-value method of accounting that should only be imposed in the presence of a directive by Congress to do so; (2) it impermissibly allows Ford only to deduct the $4.2 million it paid for the annuities without ever allowing a deduction for the additional $20.1 million it will pay to the clai-mants in the future; and (3) it is arbitrary because it is not a method that Ford could have adopted on its own.

The Commissioner replied that her method of accounting was a modi-fied cash-basis method that allows Ford "a dollar for dollar deduction, albeit in the form of an offset against its annuity income, for the full face amount of its future payments of approximately $24 million." She pointed out that because she allowed Ford to deduct the full cost of the annuity contracts in 1980 Ford had no basis in the contracts and would be fully taxable on the annuity income of $24.5 million as it is received. However, the payments Ford is required to make to the tort claimants, which correspond exactly with the amount of its annuity income, give rise to deductions that offset the income and create a wash. The Commissioner argued that because she has relieved taxpayer of the obligation to report the annuity income as it is received she should not allow Ford any deductions for the required payments.

The court concluded that "[t]he Commissioner's discretion to impose an alternate method of accounting under §446(b) is not limited to methods that Ford could have adopted on its own. While we recognize that to require Ford to account for its tort obligations on the cash method might have been a more logical alternative, we cannot find that the Commissioner's exercise of her discretion was arbitrary because it resulted in an accounting treatment more favorable to Ford than a straight cash method would be. The only difference between the Commissioner's method of accounting and the cash basis method is that petitioner receives an immediate deduction for the cost of its annuities rather than recovering that cost over the terms of the annuities under §72, and this difference inures to Ford's benefit. We therefore conclude that the tax court's decision regarding the accounting method the Commissioner imposed was proper." 71 F.3d at 217.

Given this decision, what is now the net effect of §461(h)(2)(C)(ii)? Should it be repealed?

7. Nuclear decommissioning costs and mining reclamation expenditures in particular have provoked much controversy and comment. In both cases it seems clear that these items, although payable only in the future, are part of the cost of earning present income and should be taken into account somehow in measuring net income from present operations. They may of course present difficulties in estimation. Moreover, even if they could be estimated with precision, there would be an enormous time value of money problem if their full amount were currently deductible. (Indeed, whenever the time between accrual and payment is long enough for money to triple — 19 years at 6 percent, for example — immediate accrual in full by a 34 percent taxpayer would produce tax savings sufficient to finance the whole cost when due!) The specific provisions enacted in 1984 for nuclear decommissioning expenses are found at §§88 and 468A, and those for mining reclamation are at §468. These provisions are not easy to rationalize or to understand.

8. Another 1984 accounting change deals with distorted rental payments. §467. See Chapter 6C.2 above.

E.   INCONSISTENT METHODS AND MATCHING

1.   Related Party Transactions

One aspect of time value of money concerns is that a payor may be claiming a deduction while a payee is deferring income under a different method of accounting. Does it matter in this connection if the parties are related? How?

TREATMENT OF CERTAIN RELATED PARTY TRANSACTIONS [§267]

Staff of Joint Comm. on Taxation, 98th Cong., General Explanation of the Revenue Provisions of the Deficit Reduction Act of 1984, 541-543 (Comm. Print 1984)

PRIOR LAW

Under prior law, an accrual-basis taxpayer was denied a deduction for certain accrued expenses or interest owed to related persons who used the cash method of accounting (sec. 267(a)(2)). The disallowed interest and business expenses were those which were not paid to the related person within the taxable year in which the expenses accrued or within 2½ months thereafter. This provision prevented an accrual-basis taxpayer from claiming a deduction for an accrued expense which the related cash-basis payee was not required to take into income until some subsequent time, if at all.

Because an accrued expense is deductible by a taxpayer under the accrual method of accounting only in the taxable year in which it accrues, a deduction disallowed under section 267(a) was permanently lost. It could not be deducted at some subsequent time when payment was made. . . .

REASONS FOR CHANGE

Congress believed that persons who are related should be required to use the same accounting method with respect to transactions between themselves in order to prevent the allowance of a deduction without the corresponding inclusion in income. The failure to use the same accounting method with respect to one transaction involves unwarranted tax benefits, especially where payments are delayed for a long period of time, and in fact may never be paid.

Congress also believed that the prior rules denying a deduction entirely lead to an unduly harsh result where payment was in fact made more than 2½ months after the close of the taxable year, while allowing too much of a tax advantage (i.e., effectively a one year's deferral) for payments made within 2½ months after the close of a taxable year.

Finally, Congress believed that certain related parties, such as a partnership and its partners, and controlled corporations should be made subject to the related party rules in order to prevent tax avoidance on transactions between those parties.

EXPLANATION OF PROVISION

In General

Under the Act, a taxpayer is generally placed on the cash method of accounting with respect to the deduction of amounts owed to a related cash-basis taxpayer (sec. 267(a)(2)).[17] Thus, a taxpayer is allowed to deduct amounts owed to a related cash-basis taxpayer when payment is received

---

17. This provision will not apply, for example, to original issue discount allowable as a deduction under section 163(e) and required to be included in income of the related party creditor under the accrual method by reason of section 1272.

by the related party payee (whether or not paid within 2½ months after the close of the taxable year) or, if later, when otherwise deductible. In other words, the deduction by the payor is allowed no earlier than when the corresponding income is recognized by the payee. This provision applies to all deductible expenses (whether or not deductible under section 162, 163 or 212) the timing of which depends upon the taxpayer's method of accounting or upon the making of an election to expense an item. It does not apply, for example, to expenses such as the deductions for cost recovery or depreciation of an asset (other than an asset which is related to the performance (or nonperformance) of services by the payee).

TREATMENT OF PARTNERSHIPS AND S CORPORATIONS

The prior-law rules relating to accruals by subchapter S corporations to cash basis shareholders are extended to accruals by partnerships to cash basis partners, as well as to accruals by partners to cash basis partnerships and shareholders to cash basis subchapter S corporations (sec. 267(e))....

2.   Inconsistency Between Years

a. Erroneous Treatment in Closed Year

In 1935 Bennet suffered a loss on the worthlessness of 50 shares of stock. The trouble was that the shares were income to him when he received them and he had "innocently" failed to report them as such. "The Commissioner argued, and the Tax Court held, that the privilege of making such a deduction was a correlative of the payment of a tax upon the income when originally received; and that, since the husband had failed to pay any tax upon the shares at any time, he could not deduct the loss in the year when they became worthless."[9] The Court of Appeals rejected this argument, indicating that it would produce an equitable result only if the inclusion in income for the earlier year would have produced the same tax as the present deduction would save, in which case it would just be an indirect way around the statute of limitations with respect to the earlier year. Cases allowing a similar argument in refund suits were distinguished since the claim of a refund involves a claim of overall indebtedness of the government to the taxpayer; cases in other circuits allowing such an argument in deficiency litigation were rejected.

Congress has since enacted §§1311-1314, which proceed indeed by making an exception to the statute of limitations in specified cases of inconsistent treatment in another year. In Bennet's case, the claim of a loss involves a

---

9. Bennet v. Helvering, 137 F.2d 537 (2d Cir. 1943).

claim of basis for the stock that is inconsistent with the omission of the stock from income in the year it was received. Bennet has taken the position with respect to basis by claiming the loss. There is a final determination that the loss is allowable. The inconsistency seems to be described as a circumstance of adjustment in §1312(7)(A), (B)(i), and (C)(i). So if these provisions had been in effect, the government would have had a year from the final judgment as to 1935 in which to assert a deficiency with respect to the year the stock was acquired. §1314.

Does this relief depend on there having been litigation with respect to the year 1935 in order to have a determination for that year? No, but it appears to require something more than just an acceptance of a return as filed. Look at §1313(a). So the IRS would apparently have to assert a deficiency for 1935, as it did; and then the taxpayer would effectively have a choice whether or not to resist. If he does and the government accedes in a manner that constitutes a determination, then the taxpayer may lose more by reason of an adjustment to the closed year than he saves by deducting his full loss in the open year.

It is essential for a practitioner advising taxpayers to know these provisions are there and to have a general idea of what they provide. It is almost equally essential not to count on one's memory or intuition for details because they are complex and sometimes counterintuitive.

Problems

1. In 2002 *A*'s employer awarded him a bonus of $20,000, payable in five annual installments. *A* reported the whole bonus as income in 2002. In the course of auditing *A*'s 2006 return, an agent asserted that the installments are taxable when paid and proposed to recommend a deficiency determination for 2004, 2005, and 2006 for failure to include the $4,000 installment in each of those years. If *A* agrees to pay the proposed deficiencies, will he be able to secure a refund for 2002?

2. *B* is an officer of a closely held corporation who received salary payments of $60,000 from her corporation in 2004. She reported only $40,000. When the government asserted a deficiency, *B* took the position that the other $20,000 had been constructively received in 2003, although it had not in fact been reported for that year. The Tax Court upheld that position. If the statute of limitations had run for 2003, could the government nevertheless insist that 2003 be adjusted to include the $20,000?

3. *C* received a stock bonus in 2002, which he did not report as income. In 2008 he sold the stock for $20,000. If it now appears that the stock should have been reported as income in 2002 at a value of $8,000, what would you advise *C* to do? (Assume *C* is in the top marginal tax bracket for both years.)

4. *D* bought a bond in 2001 at a 10 percent premium. *D* deducted the whole amount of the premium in 2001. See §171. Then in 2002 *D* sold the

bond again at about a 10 percent premium and reported a capital gain. The government asserted a deficiency for 2001 on the theory that the deduction was improper. Simultaneously it issued an over-assessment for 2002 and refunded an amount equal to the tax that resulted from reporting the capital gain. Finally, in 2007 the Tax Court upheld the deduction for 2001. Can the government now recover the refund it erroneously made for 2002? See James Brennen, 20 T.C. 495 (1953).

5. *E* created an accumulation trust for her children. She then transferred some business assets to the trust, subject to a leaseback. Thereafter, *E* deducted the rental payments and the trustee reported them as income. The government asserted a deficiency against *E*, disallowing the deductions and simultaneously issued an over-assessment and refunded all taxes paid by the trust. Several years later *E*'s deduction was upheld by the Tax Court. Can the government now collect from the trust?

6. *F* reported taxable income of $60,000 for 2001, with a closing inventory of $40,000. The government claimed that closing inventory was undervalued, and income thereby understated, by $15,000. In 2007 the Tax Court decision in favor of the government on this issue became final. Can *F* now adjust 2002 by restating opening inventory at $55,000 instead of $40,000? See Gooch Milling & Elevator Co. v. United States, 111 Ct. Cl. 576, 78 F. Supp. 94 (1948).

7. An employee stole goods from *G* during the years 1958-1961. Since the stolen goods were missing when inventory was taken, closing inventory was down, cost of goods sold was up, and gross income was down by the amount of the theft. In 1965 the theft was discovered. Is *G* entitled to a deduction for 1965 under §165(e)? If *G* claims and is allowed a deduction for 1965, can *G*'s income be corrected for 1958-1961, assuming those years are otherwise closed? See B.C. Cook & Sons, Inc., 65 T.C. 422 (1975), aff'd per curiam, 584 F.2d 53 (5th Cir. 1978).

8. Can you state the rationale of §1311(b)(2)? Why is §1311(b)(1) not applicable in cases described in §1312(3)(B) and (4)?

9. *H* had $60,000 credited to him during 2008 under a deferred compensation plan. It is not clear, on all the facts, whether that amount was constructively received, and thus income to *H* for 2008, or will be taxable only when paid to him after retirement some 20 years hence.

(a) If *H* thinks this item is taxable to him now, and wants to report it that way, do §§1311-1314 protect him adequately against the risk of being taxed twice if the government ultimately asserts that the money is income to *H* later when paid to him?

(b) If *H* on the other hand were to omit this item from his 2008 return, would §§1311-1314 protect the government against double exclusion of the item both when earned and later when received?

(c)(1) Is *H* under any duty to report the item in 2008 if he is in genuine doubt about the year in which it should be included? (2) Will he be under any duty to report it when received?

b. Changes in Accounting Method

One particular way inconsistencies might arise is from a change in accounting method. Suppose some item has been accounted for on a cash receipts and disbursements method, but from now on is to be accounted for on an accrual method. Items that accrue before the change but are not collected or paid until after threaten to fall between the cracks. Does permanent exclusion (or disallowance in the case of deductions) reflect an inconsistency in treatment for which relief is or ought to be available?

Does it matter for this purpose whether the change in accounting method was instituted by the taxpayer or the Commissioner? Is a correction of accounting method different from a change in accounting method? If items of income that accrue while a taxpayer is on the cash method and are collected after he has gone on an accrual method are nevertheless required to be taken into income somehow, how should that be? Are there appropriate and effective measures, other than permanent exclusion, to provide relief against the hardship that might result from having to pay taxes on three years' income in a two-year period?

How are these questions affected by §481 and the regulations thereunder?

F. COMPENSATING EMPLOYEES

1. Deferred Compensation

ALBERTSON'S, INC. v. COMMISSIONER
42 F.3d 537 (9th Cir. 1994) (on rehearing) cert. denied, 516 U.S. 807 (1995)

REINHARDT, Circuit Judge: On December 30, 1993, we filed an opinion concerning various disputes between Albertson's and the Internal Revenue Service. . . . We granted the government's petition for rehearing as to Part II.B of the opinion, which concerned the appropriate tax treatment of deferred compensation agreements. Today we vacate Part II.B of the original opinion and affirm the Tax Court's decision.

I. BACKGROUND

Deferred compensation agreements ("DCAs") are agreements in which certain employees and independent contractors ("DCA participants") agree to wait a specified period of time ("deferral period") before receiving the annual bonuses, salaries, or director's fees that they would otherwise receive on a current basis. During the deferral period, the employer uses the basic amounts of deferred compensation ("basic amounts"), which accumulate on an annual basis, as a source of working capital. At the end of the deferral period, the employer pays the participating individuals the basic amounts and an additional amount for the time value of the deferred payments that have accumulated on the basic amounts ("additional amount"). The time-value-of-money sums are also computed on a yearly basis. The total of these basic amounts and the amounts attributable to compensation for the delay in payment of those amounts constitutes the whole of the deferred compensation ("deferred compensation"). The time-value-of-money component may be measured by interest rate indices, equity fund indices, or cost of living increases, or it may simply be included within a lump-sum payment.

Prior to 1982, Albertson's entered into DCAs with eight of its top executives and one outside director. The parties agreed that their deferred compensation would include the annual basic amounts plus additional amounts calculated annually in accordance with an established formula. Albertson's, Inc. v. Commissioner, 12 F.3d 1529, 1534 (9th Cir. 1993).[1] The DCA participants would be eligible to receive the deferred compensation (the total sum) upon their retirement or termination of employment with Albertson's. The DCA participants also had the option of further deferring payment for up to fifteen years thereafter. During that extra period, the additional amounts would continue to accrue on an annual basis. Id. at 1535.

In 1982, Albertson's requested permission from the IRS to deduct the additional amounts (but not the basic amounts) during the year in which they accrued instead of waiting until the end of the deferral period. Id. In 1983, the IRS granted Albertson's request. Accordingly, Albertson's claimed deductions of $667,142 for the additional amounts that had already accrued, even though it had not yet paid the DCA participants any sums under the deferred compensation agreements. Id. In 1987, the IRS changed its policy, however, and sought a deficiency for the additional amounts, contending that all amounts provided for in the deferred compensation agreements were deductible only when received by Albertson's employees. Albertson's filed a petition with the Tax Court, claiming that the additional amounts constituted "interest" and thus could be deducted as they accrued. Id.

---

1. The terms of the eight executives' agreements were as follows:

3.1 The *Company* agrees to defer payment of certain compensation earned by *Employee* during each fiscal year, such deferred compensation to be paid to *Employee* after *Employee's* employment is terminated. The compensation to be deferred shall be as set forth . . . below: . . .
3.2 The *Company* agrees to pay to *Employee* a further sum of money equal to the amount of interest accrued which shall be calculated by applying the rate of interest to the total accumulated amount of deferred compensation including accrued interest compounded monthly. The rate to be used will be the weighted average of the *Company's* long term borrowing rate for that current fiscal year. . . .

The outside director's additional amount was calculated at a rate equivalent to the rates for new certificates of deposit over $1,000,000 as published in the Wall Street Journal.

In a sharply divided opinion,[2] the Tax Court rejected Albertson's position. Albertson's, Inc. v. Commissioner, 95 T.C. 415 (1990). The court found that the additional amounts represented compensation, not interest, and were therefore not deductible until the end of the deferral period under I.R.C. §404(a)(5) & (d).

We reversed the decision of the Tax Court. Albertson's, Inc. v. Commissioner, 38 F.3d 1046 (9th Cir. 1993). We held that the additional amounts constituted interest within the definition of I.R.C. §163(a) and that interest payments were not governed by the timing restrictions of section 404. The government petitioned for rehearing due to the significant fiscal impact of the panel's opinion which it estimates will cause a $7 billion loss in tax revenues.

II. REHEARING

We agreed to rehear this issue after lengthy consideration and reflection. In our original opinion, we stated that the plain language of the statute strongly supported Albertson's interpretation and, accordingly, we adopted it. Nevertheless, we expressed sympathy for the Commissioner's argument that Congress intended the timing restrictions of I.R.C. §404 to apply to all payments made under a deferred compensation plan and recognized that our plain language interpretation seemed to undercut Congress' purpose.

We have now changed our minds about the result we reached in our original opinion and conclude that our initial decision was incorrect. The question is not an easy one, however. We have struggled with it unsuccessfully at least once, and it may, indeed, ultimately turn out that the United States Supreme Court will tell us that it is this opinion which is in error. This is simply one of those cases — and there are more of them than judges generally like to admit — in which the answer is far from clear and in which there are conflicting rules and principles that we are forced to try to apply simultaneously. Such accommodation sometimes proves to be impossible. In some cases, as here, convincing arguments can be made for both possible results, and the court's decision will depend on which of the two competing legal principles it chooses to give greater weight to in the particular circumstance. Law, even statutory construction, is not a science. It is merely an effort by human beings, albeit judges, to do their best with imperfect tools to arrive at a correct result.

---

2. The nine-member majority held that the additional amount was not currently deductible because it was not interest. The four-member concurrence argued that the additional amount was interest, but that section 404's timing restrictions applied to both compensation and interest. The five-member dissent argued that the additional amount was interest and that section 404's timing restrictions applied only to compensation. One judge did not participate, and one judge voted in favor of the majority and the concurrence. Thus, twelve judges agreed that the additional amounts were not deductible interest under section 404.

There is a question whether, having once decided a case, we should change our decision when we are not entirely certain that the result we reached is wrong. . . . [O]ur conclusion is that, while we should not ordinarily abandon the decisions we have just reached following full deliberation, we must be willing to take that unusual step — at least in cases of some significance — when ultimately we are fairly persuaded that our decision is in error. This is such a case.

In its petition for rehearing, the government, far more forcefully and clearly than it did originally, has articulated the purpose of the timing restrictions outlined in I.R.C. §404: to encourage employers to invest in qualified compensation plans by requiring inclusions and deductions of income and expense to be "matched" for nonqualified plans. See infra pp. 395-396. The matching principle, widely recognized to be the key to I.R.C. §404, provides significant tax incentives for employers to invest in qualified deferred compensation plans, which are nondiscriminatory and ensure that employees receive the compensation promised to them. See 2 Boris I. Bittker & Lawrence Lokken, Federal Taxation of Income, Estates & Gifts Par. 60.1 (2d ed., 1990) (noting that the "matching principle" is "the most consistent feature of the rules for nonqualified plans"). As the Commissioner forcefully argues, our original interpretation of I.R.C. §404 undercut the essential purpose of that provision by violating the matching principle and creating a taxation scheme that favors the type of plan that Congress intended to discourage. See infra pp. 394-398. For this reason, we granted the Commissioner's petition for rehearing. We now withdraw the portion of our earlier opinion that dealt with deferred compensation agreements, published at 12 F.3d at 1534-1539, and affirm the Tax Court's decision, although not for the reasons upon which the Tax Court majority relied.

III. ANALYSIS

Albertson's again urges this court (1) to characterize the additional amounts as interest as defined by I.R.C. §163(a),[4] and (2) to find that such "interest" payments are deductible under I.R.C. §404.[5] However, we have now concluded that, notwithstanding the statutory language on which

---

4. The relevant language of I.R.C. §163 is as follows:

(a) *General Rule*—There shall be allowed as deduction all interest paid or accrued within the taxable year on indebtedness.

5. The relevant provisions, at the time Albertson's filed its 1983 tax return, were:

Sec. 404. Deductions for . . . compensation under a deferred-payment plan.

(a) *General Rule*— . . . If compensation is paid or accrued on account of any employee under a plan deferring the receipt of such compensation such . . . compensation shall not be deductible under section 162 (relating to trade or business expenses) or section 212 (relating to expenses for the production of income); but if they satisfy the conditions of either such sections, they shall be deductible subject, however, to the following limitations as to the amounts deductible in any year. . . .

Albertson's relies, to hold the additional amounts to be deductible would contravene the clear purpose of the taxation scheme Congress created to govern deferred compensation plans. . . .

A.   A COMPARISON OF QUALIFIED AND NONQUALIFIED PLANS

An examination of the differences between qualified and nonqualified plans is essential to an understanding of the purpose of the congressional scheme governing deferred compensation agreements. Congress has imposed few restrictions upon nonqualified deferred compensation plans. An employer may limit participation in a nonqualified plan to highly paid executives, and it need not guarantee equal benefits for all participants. In addition, the employer is not required to set aside any funds or provide any guarantees (beyond the initial contractual promise) that its employees will receive the compensation. Thus, promised benefits for unfunded, non-qualified plans are subject to the claims of the employer's general creditors.

Under a qualified plan, in contrast, an employer may not discriminate in favor of officers, shareholders, or highly compensated employees. I.R.C. §401(a)(4) & (a)(5). In addition, a qualified plan must satisfy minimum participation and coverage standards concerning eligibility and actual rates of participation. I.R.C §§401(a)(2) & (a)(26), 410. The amounts which an employer may contribute to qualified plans and the benefits which qualified plans may provide are also restricted. I.R.C. §§401(a)(17), 415.

A qualified plan also provides significant guarantees that employees will receive the compensation promised to them. It generally must be funded through a trust. I.R.C. §401(a). Neither the corpus nor the income of the trust may be diverted for any purpose; they can only be used for the exclusive benefit of the participants. I.R.C. §401(a)(2). Under certain qualified plans, the employer's contributions must meet strict funding requirements, and minimum standards govern the vesting of participants' benefits. I.R.C. §§401(a)(1) & (a)(7), 411, 412; see also 29 U.S.C. §1082.

It is clear that few employers would adopt a qualified deferred compensation plan, with all of its burdensome requirements, if the taxation scheme favored nonqualified plans or treated nonqualified and qualified plans similarly. Although qualified plans provide significant benefits to employees, they allow employers little flexibility in structuring a plan, require them to provide extensive coverage, prevent them from discriminating in favor of highly

---

(5) If the plan is not one included in paragraph (1), (2), or (3) [relating to pension trusts, annuities, and stock bonus and profit-sharing trusts], in the taxable year in which an amount attributable to the contribution is includible in the gross income of employees participating in the plan. . . .

   (d) *Deductibility of payments of deferred compensation, etc., to independent contractors.*—If a plan would be described [as above] . . . [the] compensation—

      (1) shall not be deductible by the payor thereof under section 162 or 212, but

      (2) shall . . . be deductible under this subsection for the taxable year in which an amount attributable to the . . . compensation is includible in the gross income of the persons participating in the plan.

compensated employees, and involve a significant initial outlay of funds. Thus, the extensive regulations Congress has imposed upon qualified plans would serve little purpose unless employers had an incentive to adopt such plans. As we discuss in the next part, section 404 provides the incentive necessary to encourage employers to adopt qualified plans by providing significantly more favorable tax treatment of qualified plans than of nonqualified ones.

The most significant difference between the two types of plans, for purposes of tax deductibility, is that under a qualified plan the employer must turn over annually to a third party the basic amounts that are deferred and may not use those amounts for the employer's own benefit. Thus, the employer, in effect, is required to make the deferred payments at the time the employee is earning the compensation. It is only the employee's right to receive the funds that is delayed. In contrast, an employer with a nonqualified plan is not required to turn any funds over to anyone until the end of the deferred compensation period. Such an employer may use those funds for its own purposes for a period of many years. In a nonqualified plan, it is not only the employee's right to receive the funds that is deferred; the employer's obligation to part with the funds is deferred as well. If one could simply retain the funds and receive tax benefits similar to those one would receive if those amounts were paid out, there would clearly be little incentive to establish a qualified plan.

B. THE PURPOSE OF SECTION 404

Congress enacted section 23(p), the forerunner to section 404, in 1942. Prior to 1942, corporations were allowed to deduct DCA-related expenses as they accrued each year, even though employees did not recognize any income until a subsequent taxable year. In 1942, Congress eliminated this favorable treatment for deductions relating to "nonqualified" deferred compensation agreements, such as the DCAs at issue in this case.[6] In so doing, Congress forced employers who chose to retain their funds for their own use to wait until the end of the deferral period, when these amounts were includible in plan participants' taxable income, before they could take deductions for deferred compensation payments. However, employers who maintained a "qualified" plan that met the rigorous requirements of the Internal Revenue Code (and now ERISA), including turning over the sums involved to a

---

6. The relevant provision is as follows:

§23—Deductions from gross income
    (p) Contributions of an employer to an employees' trust or annuity plan and compensation under a deferred-payment plan.
    (1) General Rule.
    If . . . compensation is paid or accrued on account of any employee under a plan deferring the receipt of such compensation, such . . . compensation shall not be deductible under subsection (a) [business expenses] but shall be deductible, if deductible under subsection (1) without regard to this subsection, under this subsection.

I.R.C. §23 (1942).

trust fund (or purchasing an annuity), were allowed to continue to take the annual deductions even though their employees would not receive the deferred compensation until a later year. See, e.g., I.R.C. §§404(a) & (d); 29 U.S.C. §1082 (1988).

1. THE MATCHING PRINCIPLE

Congress provided a single explanation for the timing restrictions of section 404: to ensure matching of income inclusion and deduction between employee and employer under nonqualified plans. As both the House and Senate Reports note, "if an employer on the accrual basis defers paying any compensation to the employee until a later year or years . . . he will not be allowed a deduction until the year in which the compensation is paid." H.R. Rep. No. 2333, 77th Cong., 2d Sess. (1942), 1942-2 Cum. Bull. 372, 452; S. Rep. No. 1631, 77th Cong., 2d Sess. (1942), 1942-2 Cum. Bull. 504, 609.

Commentators have widely agreed that this "matching principle" is the key to section 404. As Boris Bittker and Lawrence Lokken have observed, "the most consistent feature for the rules for nonqualified plans is that the employer is ordinarily allowed no deduction for contribution, payments or benefits until they are taxed to the employee." 2 Boris I. Bittker & Lawrence Lokken, Federal Taxation of Income, Estates & Gifts Par. 60.1 (2d ed., 1990). Similarly, Daniel Halperin has noted that, in the case of deferred payment of compensation under nonqualified plans, Congress has imposed "a matching requirement, which denies an employer's deduction until the deferred amount is included in the employee's income." Daniel I. Halperin, Interest in Disguise: Taxing the "Time Value of Money," 95 Yale L.J. 506, 520 (1986) (discussing section 404). David Davenport also cites section 404 as the primary proof that "current law follows a matching principle and defers the employer's deduction until the year of payment." David S. Davenport, Education & Human Capital: Pursuing an Ideal Income Tax and a Sensible Tax Policy, 42 Case W. Res. L. Rev. 793, 865 (1992); see also Merten's Law of Federal Income Taxation, Comm. §404 (1990 & 1994 Supp.); Joseph L. Cummings, Jr., The Silent Policies of Conservation and Cloning of Tax Basis and Their Corporate Application, 48 Tax L. Rev. 113, 162 n.245 (1992) (noting that the matching principle governs section 404); Noel B. Cunningham, A Theoretical Analysis of the Tax Treatment of Future Costs, 40 Tax L. Rev. 577, 610 (1985) (same) Mark P. Gergen, Reforming Subchapter K: Compensating Service Partnerships, 48 Tax L. Rev. 69, 97 n.91 (1992) (same).

2. THE SIGNIFICANCE OF THE MATCHING PRINCIPLE

The significance of section 404's matching principle becomes evident when one compares the treatment of qualified and nonqualified plans under that section. Because section 404 requires employer deductions for contributions to nonqualified plans to be "matched," an employer cannot take tax deductions for payments to its employees until the DCA participants include those payments in their taxable income — that is, until the employees actually receive the compensation promised to them.

Qualified plans, in contrast, are not governed by the matching principle and consequently generate concurrent tax benefits to employers. Although employees are not taxed upon the benefits they receive from the plan until they actually receive them, an employer's contributions to a qualified plan are deductible when paid to the trust. I.R.C. §§402(a)(1) & 404(a). Thus, the employer may take an immediate, unmatched deduction for any contribution it makes to a qualified plan.[7]

By exempting contributions to qualified plans from the matching principle, Congress compensates employers for meeting the burdensome requirements associated with qualified plans by granting them favorable tax treatment. The current taxation scheme thus creates financial incentives for employers to contribute to qualified plans while providing no comparable benefits for employers who adopt plans that are unfunded or that discriminate in favor of highly compensated employees.

C.   The Effects of Albertson's Proposal

Albertson's maintains that section 404 only requires that the basic amounts of compensation be matched; it argues that all additional amounts paid to compensate an employee for the time value of money represent "interest" payments for which an employer may take an immediate deduction. In light of the clear purpose underlying section 404 — to encourage employers to create qualified plans for their employees — we decline to ascribe such an intention to Congress.

First, Albertson's proposal appears to undermine the effectiveness of the timing restrictions by reducing the significance of the incentive structure created by section 404. In order to adopt Albertson's proposal and allow employers to take current deductions for additional "interest" payments, we would be required to conclude that Congress created a system in which employers could deduct a substantial portion of the nonqualified deferred compensation package long before its employees had received any of those funds. For example, when the additional amounts are calculated for a compensation package deferred over a fifteen-year period using an interest rate similar to that used by Albertson's, an employer can classify more than seventy percent of the deferred compensation package as "interest payments."[8] If the additional amounts were calculated at an eight percent

---

7. In addition, the earnings of a trust established by a qualified plan are not taxable to the trust. I.R.C. §§401(a) & 501(a).

8. According to the record, it appears that Albertson's employees were compensated at a 14.8% interest rate, compounded monthly.

interest rate, compounded annually, almost fifty percent of the compensation package could be characterized as "interest" under Albertson's approach. Even under a deferred compensation package with an interest rate one-third as high as Albertson's, one-third of the amount paid to the employee at the end of a fifteen-year period would consist of "interest." Moreover, we note that, under Albertson's deferred compensation agreement, participants have the option of deferring payment of the total sum available to them upon retirement for an additional period of up to fifteen years. All payments during that additional period would also constitute "interest," and the deductible portion of the final compensation package would thus increase exponentially.

Albertson's has been unable to explain why Congress, in designing a taxation scheme to encourage the creation of qualified plans, would require an employer that maintains a nonqualified plan to defer taking a deduction on the basic amounts of a promised compensation package but nevertheless allow that employer to take current deductions on amounts that constitute a substantial portion of the compensation package, merely because that portion is classified as "interest." Given that the interest payments will often constitute the bulk of the total compensation package that an employee under a nonqualified plan ultimately receives, it would make little sense to impose a matching requirement upon "basic" payments but not upon "interest" payments. Albertson's interpretation of section 404 would seriously undermine the incentive structure designed by Congress to encourage employers to establish qualified plans.

An additional reason to reject Albertson's statutory interpretation of section 404 is that, in certain cases, Albertson's approach might actually create an incentive for employers to establish nonqualified plans. Whereas an employer who maintains a qualified plan may only take a current deduction for the basic amounts of promised compensation, an amount it actually has paid out, under Albertson's approach an employer that maintains a nonqualified plan could take current deductions for "interest" payments that substantially exceed the basic amounts even though it has paid out none of these funds. Moreover, the employer could take advantage of these tax benefits without being constrained by the burdensome requirements associated with qualified plans. For this reason, characterizing the additional amounts as deductible interest, as Albertson's suggest, would encourage employers to maintain nonqualified plans and thus directly contradict the statutory purpose underlying I.R.C. §404.[9] Thus, Albertson's proposal runs

9. We also note the government's argument concerning the possible consequences of a finding in favor of Albertson's. According to the Commissioner, under a long-standing administrative practice, employees are currently not taxed upon the benefits they receive from deferred compensation plans until they actually receive them, precisely because employers have not taken deductions for those amounts. Because section 404 only exempts payments under qualified plans from the matching principle, were we to uphold Albertson's approach, the Commissioner suggests that we would be required to conclude that employer deductions for interest accruing under nonqualified plans must be "matched" by the inclusion of those amounts in employees' current taxable income. As is clear from the foregoing

counter to the congressional scheme. It undermines Congress' attempts to encourage employers to adopt qualified plans and, in some cases, directly contradicts the purpose of section 404 by creating an incentive to create nonqualified plans.

D.   ALBERTSON'S RESPONSE

Albertson's has not been able to refute the argument that its interpretation of section 404 undercuts the provision's central purpose. Equally important, it offers us no reason why Congress would have wanted to treat the "interest" part of the deferred compensation package differently from the basic amounts for tax purposes.

Instead, Albertson's rests its argument upon its contention that, because the plain language of §404 only refers to "compensation" rather than "interest," the employers have a statutory right to deduct the additional amounts as interest under §163. In this connection, Albertson's points out that section 404 prohibits deduction under sections 162 and 212 but not under section 163, and it is the latter section that governs the deduction of interest. Albertson's argument as to the plain language of the statute is a strong one. We certainly agree that the additional payments resemble "interest" and that, under a literal reading of the statutory language, the deduction of interest is not affected by section 404. However, holding such payments to be deductible "interest" under section 404 would lead to an anomalous result: a taxation scheme designed to make nonqualified plans less attractive would in many cases provide incentives for adopting such plans, and a provision intended to apply the matching principle to non-qualified deferred compensation agreements would exempt substantial portions of DCA payments from its application.

In the end we are forced, therefore, to reject Albertson's approach. We may not adopt a plain language interpretation of a statutory provision that directly undercuts the clear purpose of the statute. In Brooks v. Donovan, 699 F.2d 1010 (9th Cir. 1983), we refused to adopt a plain language interpretation of a statute governing pension funds. We reasoned that the "court must look beyond the express language of a statute where a literal interpretation 'would thwart the purpose of the overall statutory scheme or lead to an absurd or futile result.'" Brooks, 699 F.2d at 1011 (quoting International Tel. & Tel. Corp. v. General Tel. & Elec. Corp., 518 F.2d 913, 917-918 (9th Cir. 1975)). In reaching our conclusion, we followed the Supreme Court's approach in United States v. American Trucking Ass'ns., 310 U.S. 534 (1940). There the Court noted that "when [a given] meaning has led to absurd results . . . this Court has looked beyond the words to the purpose of

---

discussion, such an unrealized addition to the employees' income for tax purposes would indeed be substantial and, as far as the employees are concerned, harshly inequitable. We express no opinion about the merits of the government's argument.

the act. Frequently, however, even when the plain meaning did not produce absurd results but *merely an unreasonable one 'plainly at variance with the policy of the legislation as a whole,'* this Court has followed that purpose, rather than the literal words." American Trucking Ass'ns., 310 U.S. at 543 (emphasis added; citations omitted).

The Supreme Court's decision in Bob Jones University v. United States, 461 U.S. 574 (1983), provides especially useful guidance in this regard. In Bob Jones University, the Supreme Court addressed the question of whether I.R.C. §501(c)(3) — which provides that "corporations . . . organized and operated exclusively for religious, charitable . . . or educational purposes" are entitled to tax exemption — included educational institutions with racially discriminatory policies. Even though Congress had explicitly out-lined eight categories of exempt organizations in section 501(c)(3) without making any mention of additional requirements beyond those outlined in the statute, the Supreme Court interpreted the statute to include an addi-tional requirement: the organization in question must serve a valid charita-ble purpose. Bob Jones University, 461 U.S. at 592 n.19. Thus, the Court was willing to read additional language into the text of the statute because an alternative interpretation would undermine the fundamental purpose of the legislation. As the Court itself noted, "it is a well-established canon of stat-utory construction that a court should go beyond the literal language of a statute if reliance on that language would defeat the plain purpose of the statute." Id. at 586.

In rejecting Albertson's appeal, we take heed of the Supreme Court's instructions concerning the proper interpretation of the Internal Revenue Code when the plain language of the provision leads to an unreasonable result and directly contradicts its underlying purpose: the provision "must be analyzed and construed within the framework of the Internal Revenue Code and *against the background of the congressional purposes.*" Id. (emphasis added). For the reasons we have expressed, we conclude that, despite the literal wording of the statute, Congress could not have intended to exclude interest payments, a substantial part of the deferred compensation package, from the rule prohibiting deductions until such time as the employee receives the benefits. Indeed, the matching principle would not be much of a principle if so substantial a part of the deferred compensation package were excluded from its operation.

IV. CONCLUSION

In sum, we decline to adopt Albertson's interpretation of I.R.C. §404. Whether or not the additional amounts constitute interest, allowing Albertson's to deduct them prior to their receipt by their employees would contravene the clear purpose of the taxation scheme governing deferred compensation agreements. Accordingly, we vacate the portion of our original opinion dealing with deferred compensation agreements and affirm the Tax Court's holding that Albertson's may not currently deduct the additional amounts.

Affirmed.

Notes and Questions

1. In advising taxpayers, how would you describe the difference in tax burden between a qualified retirement plan and what the *Albertson's* court refers to as a DCA? Does it capture the tax difference to say that the investment return on funds devoted to a qualified plan are effectively exempt from income tax while there is no similar exemption in the case of a DCA? Is the *Albertson's* decision essential to the preservation of that difference?

2. Do you agree with the court's suggestion that adoption of the taxpayer's position might make a DCA more attractive, in terms of tax burden, than a qualified retirement plan?

3. In advising taxpayers about composing a DCA, what would you say (as a tax lawyer) about choice of an interest rate? Cf. *Albertson's*, n.8 and accompanying text.

4. In view of *Albertson's*, would you characterize §404 as a tax penalty designed to push taxpayers into qualified retirement plans?

2. Stock Options and Restricted Property

COMMISSIONER v. LoBUE
351 U.S. 243 (1956)

Mr. Justice BLACK delivered the opinion of the Court. This case involves the federal income tax liability of respondent LoBue for the years 1946 and 1947. From 1941 to 1947 LoBue was manager of the New York Sales Division of the Michigan Chemical Corporation, a producer and distributor of chemical supplies. In 1944 the company adopted a stock option plan making 10,000 shares of its common stock available for distribution to key employees at $5 per share over a 3-year period. LoBue and a number of other employees were notified that they had been tentatively chosen to be recipients of nontransferable stock options contingent upon their continued employment. LoBue's notice told him: "You may be assigned a greater or less amount of stock based entirely upon your individual results and that of the entire organization." About 6 months later he was notified that he had been definitely awarded an option to buy 150 shares of stock in recognition of his "contribution and efforts in making the operation of the Company successful." As to future allotments he was told "It is up to you to justify your participation in the plan during the next two years."

LoBue's work was so satisfactory that the company in the course of 3 years delivered to him 3 stock options covering 340 shares. He exercised all these $5 per share options in 1946 and in 1947, paying the company only $1,700 for stock having a market value when delivered of $9,930. Thus, at the end of these transactions, LoBue's employer was worth $8,230 less to its stockholders and LoBue was worth $8,230 more than before. The company deducted this sum as an expense in its 1946 and 1947 tax returns but LoBue did not report any part of it as income. Viewing the gain to LoBue as compensation for personal services the Commissioner levied a deficiency assessment against him, relying on §22(a) of the Internal Revenue Code of 1939, 53 Stat. 9, as amended, 53 Stat. 574, which defines gross income as including "gains, profits, and income derived from . . . compensation for personal service . . . of whatever kind and in whatever form paid. . . . "

LoBue petitioned the Tax Court to redetermine the deficiency, urging that "The said options were not intended by the Corporation or the petitioner to constitute additional compensation but were granted to permit the petitioner to acquire a proprietary interest in the Corporation and to provide him with the interest in the successful operation of the Corporation deriving from an ownership interest." The Tax Court held that LoBue had a taxable gain if the options were intended as compensation but not if the options were designed to provide him with "a proprietary interest in the business." Finding after hearings that the options were granted to give LoBue "a proprietary interest in the corporation, and not as compensation for services" the Tax Court held for LoBue. 22 T.C. 440, 443. Relying on this finding the Court of Appeals affirmed, saying: "This was a factual issue which it was the peculiar responsibility of the Tax Court to resolve. From our examination of the evidence we cannot say that its finding was clearly erroneous." 223 F.2d 367, 371. Disputes over the taxability of stock option transactions such as this are longstanding. We granted certiorari to consider whether the Tax Court and the Court of Appeals had given §22(a) too narrow an interpretation. 350 U.S. 893.

We have repeatedly held that in defining "gross income" as broadly as it did in §22(a) Congress intended to "tax all gains except those specifically exempted." See, e.g., Commissioner v. Glenshaw Glass Co., 348 U.S. 426, 429-430. The only exemption Congress provided from this very comprehensive definition of taxable income that could possibly have application here is the gift exemption of §22(b)(3). But there was not the slightest indication of the kind of detached and disinterested generosity which might evidence a "gift" in the statutory sense. These transfers of stock bore none of the earmarks of a gift. They were made by a company engaged in operating a business for profit, and the Tax Court found that the stock option plan was designed to achieve more profitable operations by providing the employees "with an incentive to promote the growth of the company by permitting them to participate in its success," 22 T.C., at 445. Under these circumstances the Tax Court and the Court of Appeals properly refrained from treating this transfer as a gift. The company was not giving something away for nothing.

Since the employer's transfer of stock to its employee LoBue for much less than the stock's value was not a gift, it seems impossible to say that it was not compensation. The Tax Court held there was no taxable income, however, on the ground that one purpose of the employer was to confer a "proprietary interest." But there is not a word in §22(a) which indicates that its broad coverage should be narrowed because of an employer's intention to enlist more efficient service from his employees by making them part proprietors of his business. In our view there is no statutory basis for the test established by the courts below. When assets are transferred by an employer to an employee to secure better services they are plainly compensation. It makes no difference that the compensation is paid in stock rather than in money. Section 22(a) taxes income derived from compensation "in whatever form paid." And in another stock option case we said that §22(a) "is broad enough to include in taxable income any economic or financial benefit conferred on the employee as compensation, whatever the form or mode by which it is effected." Commissioner v. Smith, 324 U.S. 177, 181. LoBue received a very substantial economic and financial benefit from his employer prompted by the employer's desire to get better work from him. This is "compensation for personal service" within the meaning of §22(a).

LoBue nonetheless argues that we should treat this transaction as a mere purchase of a proprietary interest on which no taxable gain was "realized" in the year of purchase. It is true that our taxing system has ordinarily found an arm's length purchase of property even at a bargain price as giving rise to no taxable gain in the year of purchase. See Palmer v. Commissioner, 302 U.S. 63, 69. But that is not to say that when a transfer which is in reality compensation is given the form of a purchase the Government cannot tax the gain under §22(a). The transaction here was unlike a mere purchase. It was not an arm's length transaction between strangers. Instead it was an arrangement by which an employer transferred valuable property to his employees in recognition of their services. We hold that LoBue realized taxable gain when he purchased the stock.

A question remains as to the time when the gain on the shares should be measured. LoBue gave his employer promissory notes for the option price of the first 300 shares but the shares were not delivered until the notes were paid in cash. The market value of the shares was lower when the notes were given than when the cash was paid. The Commissioner measured the taxable gain by the market value of the shares when the cash was paid. LoBue contends that this was wrong, and that the gain should be measured either when the options were granted or when the notes were given.

It is of course possible for the recipient of a stock option to realize an immediate taxable gain. See Commissioner v. Smith, 324 U.S. 177, 181-182. The option might have a readily ascertainable market value and the recipient might be free to sell his option. But this is not such a case. These three options were not transferable and LoBue's right to buy stock under them was contingent upon his remaining an employee of the company until they were exercised. Moreover, the uniform Treasury practice since 1923 has been to measure the compensation to employees given stock options subject to contingencies of this sort by the difference between the option price and the market value of the shares at the time the option is exercised. We relied in part upon this practice in Commissioner v. Smith, 324 U.S. 177, 324 U.S. 695. And in its 1950 Act affording limited tax benefits for "restricted stock option plans" Congress adopted the same kind of standard for measurement of gains. §130A, Internal Revenue Code of 1939, as amended, 64 Stat. 942. And see §421, Internal Revenue Code of 1954, 68A Stat. 142. Under these circumstances there is no reason for departing from the Treasury practice. The taxable gain to LoBue should be measured as of the time the options were exercised and not the time they were granted.

It is possible that a bona fide delivery of a binding promissory note could mark the completion of the stock purchase and that gain should be measured as of that date. Since neither the Tax Court not the Court of Appeals passed on this question the judgment is reversed and the case is remanded to the Court of Appeals with instructions to remand the case to the Tax Court for further proceedings.

Reversed and remanded.

Mr. Justice FRANKFURTER and Mr. Justice CLARK, concurring. We join in the judgment of the Court and in its opinion on the main issue. However, the time when LoBue acquired the interest on which he is taxed was not in issue either before the Tax Court or the Court of Appeals. In the circumstances of this case, there certainly is no reason for departing from the general rule whereby this Court abstains from passing on such an issue in a tax case when raised here for the first time. See Helvering v. Minnesota Tea Co., 296 U.S. 378, 380; Helvering v. Tex-Penn Co., 300 U.S. 481, 498.

Mr. Justice HARLAN, whom Mr. Justice BURTON joins, concurring in part and dissenting in part. In my view, the taxable event was the grant of each option, not its exercise. When the respondent received an unconditional option to buy stock at less than the market price, he received an asset of substantial and immediately realizable value, at least equal to the then-existing spread between the option price and the market price. It was at that time that the corporation conferred a benefit upon him. At the exercise of the option, the corporation "gave" the respondent nothing; it simply satisfied a previously-created legal obligation. That transaction by which the respondent merely converted his asset from an option into stock, should be of no consequence for tax purposes. The option should be taxable as income when given, and any subsequent gain through appreciation of the stock, whether realized by sale of the option, if transferable, or by sale of the stock acquired by its exercise, is attributable to the sale of a capital asset and, if the other requirements are satisfied, should be taxed as a capital gain.

Any other result makes the division of the total gains between ordinary income (compensation) and capital gain (sale of an asset) dependent solely upon the fortuitous circumstance of when the employee exercises his option.[2]

The last two options granted to respondents were unconditional and immediately exercisable, and thus present no further problems. The first option, however, was granted under somewhat different circumstances. Respondent was notified in January 1945 that 150 shares had been "allotted" to him, but he was given no right to purchase them until June 30, 1945, and his right to do so then was expressly made contingent upon his still being employed at that date. His right to purchase the first allotment of stock was thus not vested until he satisfied the stated condition, and it was not until then that he could be said to have received income, the measure of which should be the value of the option on that date.

Accordingly, while I concur in the reversal of the judgment below and in the remand to the Tax Court, I would hold the granting of the options to be the taxable events and would measure the income by the value of the options when granted.

Note

Prior to 1969, the taxation of most compensatory stock options was governed by regulations.[9] Primarily, these regulations provided that an employee would be taxed on exercise of an option on the excess of fair market value over option price, as in *LoBue*. The employer would get a deduction at the same time and in the same amount, but there were two important exceptions or variations.

First, if an option had a readily ascertainable market value, then the employee would be taxable and the employer would be allowed a deduction on grant of the option. That would close the matter out as a compensatory item, and there would be no further tax or deduction on exercise of the option, but it has never been easy to establish that an option had a readily ascertainable value.

The second exception was that if stock received on exercise of the option was subject to substantial restrictions on disposition, then taxable gain would be deferred until the restrictions lapsed or the stock was disposed of. At that point, the amount taxable as compensation income and

2. Suppose two employees are given unconditional options to buy stock at $5, the current market value. The first exercises the option immediately and sells the stock a year later at $15. The second holds the option for a year, exercises it, and sells the stock immediately at $15. Admittedly the $10 gain would be taxed to the first as capital gain; under the Court's view, it would be taxed to the second as ordinary income because it is "compensation" for services. I fail to see how the gain can be any more "compensation" to one than it is to the other.

9. More favorable tax treatment is granted to options that satisfy certain special requirements. These so-called statutory or qualified stock options, the most important current incarnation of which is the Incentive Stock Option defined in §422, are discussed in the notes following *Alves*, the next case.

deductible by the employer was still limited to the spread at the time of exercise or when restrictions lapsed, whichever was lower. In the case of appreciating property, this meant that the restrictions would enable an employee to defer his or her tax without any offsetting increase in the amount subject to tax; restrictions were often cooperatively imposed just to achieve this effect. This ploy was terminated in 1969, by adoption of §83.

ALVES v. COMMISSIONER
734 F.2d 478 (9th Cir. 1984)

Before Kennedy, Schroeder, and Boochever, Circuit Judges.

SCHROEDER, Circuit Judge. . . . Section 83 requires that an employee who has purchased restricted stock in connection with his "performance of services" must include as ordinary income the stock's appreciation in value between the time of purchase and the time the restrictions lapse, unless at the time he purchased the stock he elected to include as income the difference between the purchase price and the fair market value at that time. The issue here is whether section 83 applies to an employee's purchase of restricted stock when, according to the stipulation of the parties, the amount paid for the stock equaled its full fair market value, without regard to any restrictions. The Tax Court, with two dissenting opinions, held that section 83 applies to all restricted stock that is transferred "in connection with the performance of services," regardless of the amount paid for it. 79 T.C. at 878. We affirm.

FACTS

General Digital Corporation (the company) was formed in April, 1970, to manufacture and market micro-electronic circuits. At its first meeting, the company's board of directors resolved to issue 90,000 shares of its common stock to its company president, and 66,000 shares to the company underwriter. The board also voted to sell an additional 264,000 shares of common stock to seven named individuals, including Alves. All seven became company employees.

Alves joined the company as vice-president for finance and administration. As part of an employment and stock purchase agreement dated May 22, 1970, the company agreed to sell Alves 40,000 shares of common stock at ten cents per share "in order to raise capital for the Company's initial operations while at the same time providing the Employee with an additional interest in the Company. . . . " 79 T.C. at 867. The six other named individuals signed similar agreements on the same day. The agreement divided Alves's shares into three categories: one-third were subject to repurchase by the company at ten cents per share if Alves left within four years; one-third were subject to repurchase if he left the company within five years; and one-third were unrestricted. In addition, the company retained an option to repurchase up to one-half of the shares for their fair market value at any time between July 1, 1973 and July 1, 1975.

In transactions not at issue here, Alves sold some of his shares to friends and relatives. In 1973 he sold 4,667 four-year shares to Technology Ventures, Inc. (TVI), the assignee of General Digital's repurchase option, for $18 per share, and in 1974 he sold TVI 2,240 five-year shares for $4 per share.[2]

On July 1, 1974, when the restrictions on the four-year shares lapsed, Alves still owned 4,667 four-year shares that had a fair market value at that time of $6 per share. On March 24, 1975, the restrictions on the 7,093 remaining five-year shares lapsed with the fair market value at $3.43 per share.

Although Alves reported the $8,736 of gain on the sale of the 2,240 five-year shares to TVI as ordinary income on his 1974 tax return, he did not report the difference between the fair market value of the four and five-year shares when the restrictions ended, and the purchase price paid for the shares. The Commissioner treated the difference as ordinary income in 1974 and 1975, pursuant to section 83(a).[3]

In proceedings before the Tax Court, the parties stipulated that: (1) General Digital's common stock had a fair market value of 10 cents per share on the date Alves entered into the employment and stock purchase agreement; (2) the stock restrictions were imposed to "provide some assurance that key personnel would remain with the company for a number of years"; (3) Alves did not make an election under section 83(b) when the restricted stock was received; (4) the free shares were not includable in gross income under section 83; and (5) the four and five-year restricted shares were subject to a substantial risk of forfeiture until July 1, 1974, and March 24, 1975, respectively.

The Tax Court sustained the Commissioner's deficiency determination. It found as a matter of fact that the stock was transferred to Alves in connection with the performance of services for the company, and, as a matter of law, that section 83(a) applies even where the transferee paid full fair market value for the stock. 79 T.C. at 874, 878.

DISCUSSION

Resolution of the legal issue presented here requires an understanding of section 83's background and operation. Congress enacted section 83 in 1969 in response to the existing disparity between the tax treatment of

---

2. No claim is made here with regard to any section 83 income Alves may have received during the 1973 tax year.

3. In his Tax Court petition, Alves claimed error in reporting as ordinary income the $8,736 gain on the 2,240 five-years shares sold to TVI in 1974. Our disposition here necessarily resolves that issue.

restricted stock plans and other types of deferred compensation arrangements. S. Rep. No. 552, 91st Cong., 1st Sess. 120-21, reprinted in 1969 U.S. Code Cong. & Admin. News 2027, 2150-2151 (Senate Report). Prior to 1969, an individual purchasing restricted stock was taxed either when the restrictions lapsed or when the stock was sold in an arm's length transaction. Tax was imposed upon the difference between the purchase price and the fair market value at the time of transfer or when the restrictions lapsed, whichever was less. See Cohn v. Commissioner, 73 T.C. 443, 446 (1979). This had both tax deferral and tax avoidance advantages over, for example, employer contributions to an employee's pension or profit sharing trust, which were immediately taxable in the year of receipt. H.R. Rep. No. 413, 91st Cong., 1st Sess. 86-87, reprinted in 1969 U.S. Code Cong. & Admin. News 1645, 1733-1734 (House Report); Senate Report at 120-121, reprinted in 1969 U.S. Code Cong. & Admin. News 2027, 2150-2151.

Section 83 resolved this disparity by requiring the taxpayer either to elect to include the "excess" of the fair market value over the purchase price in the year the stock was transferred, or to be taxed upon the full amount of appreciation when the risk of forfeiture was removed. 26 U.S.C. §§83(a), 83(b). See generally Sobeloff, Payment of Compensation in the Form of Restricted Property: Problems of Employer and Employee — The Rules of New Code Section 83, 28 Inst. on Fed. Taxn. 1041, 1042-1043 (1970). By its terms, the statute applies when property is: (1) transferred in connection with the performance of services; (2) subject to a substantial risk of forfeiture; and (3) not disposed of in an arm's length transaction before the property becomes transferable or the risk of forfeiture is removed. In the present case, it is undisputed that the stock in question was subject to a substantial risk of forfeiture, that it was not disposed of before the restrictions lapsed, and that Alves made no section 83(b) election. Alves's contention is that because he paid full fair market value for the shares, they were issued as an investment, rather than in connection with the performance of services.

The Tax Court concluded that Alves obtained the stock "in connection with the performance of services" as company vice-president. To the extent that this conclusion is a finding of fact, it is not clearly erroneous. Commissioner v. Duberstein, 363 U.S. 278, 291 (1960); Rockwell v. Commissioner, 512 F.2d 882, 884 (9th Cir.), cert. denied, 423 U.S. 1015 (1975). Although payment of full fair market value may be one indication that stock was not transferred in connection with the performance of services, the record shows that until the company sold stock to TVI, it issued stock only to its officers, directors, and employees, with the exception of the shares sold to the underwriter. Alves purchased the stock when he signed his employment agreement and the stock restrictions were linked explicitly to his tenure with the company. In addition, the parties stipulated that the restricted stock's purpose was to ensure that key personnnel would remain with the company. Nothing in the record suggests that Alves could have purchased the stock had he not agreed to join the company.

Alves maintains that, as a matter of law, section 83(a) should not extend to purchases for full fair market value. He argues that "in connection with" means that the employee is receiving compensation for his performance of services. In the unusual situation where the employee pays the same amount for restricted and unrestricted stock, the restriction has no effect on value, and hence, Alves contends, there is no compensation.

The plain language of section 83(a) belies Alves's argument. The statute applies to all property transferred in connection with the performance of services. No reference is made to the term "compensation." Nor is there any statutory requirement that property have a fair market value in excess of the amount paid at the time of transfer. Indeed, if Congress intended section 83(a) to apply solely to restricted stock used to compensate employees, it could have used much narrower language. Instead, Congress made section 83(a) applicable to all restricted "property," not just stock; to property transferred to "any person," not just to employees, and to property transferred "in connection with ... services" not just compensation for employment. See Cohn v. Commissioner, 73 T.C. 443, 446-447 (1979); Armantrout v. Commissioner, 67 T.C. 966 (1977), affd. 570 F.2d 210 (7th Cir. 1978) (per curiam). As the Second Circuit has noted, Congress drafted section 83(a) as a "blanket rule" in an effort to create "a workable, practical system of taxing employees' restricted stock options." Sakol v. Commissioner, 574 F.2d 694, 699-700 (2d Cir.) cert. denied, 439 U.S. 859 (1978).

Section 83's legislative history also reveals that while Congress was concerned primarily with the favorable tax treatment afforded restricted stock plans, it also was concerned that such plans were a means of allowing key employees to become shareholders in businesses without adhering to requirements in other sections of the Code. The Senate Report stated:

> To the extent that a restricted stock plan can be considered a means of giving employees a stake in the business, the committee believes the present tax treatment of these plans is inconsistent with the specific rules provided by Congress in the case of qualified stock options, which were considered by Congress as the appropriate means by which an employee could be given a shareholder's interest in the business.

Senate Report at 120-21, reprinted in 1969 U.S. Code Cong. & Admin. News 2027, 2152. Accord House Report at 90, reprinted in 1969 U.S. Code Cong. & Admin. News 1645, 1735. The legislative history reveals that Congress perceived restricted stock as more than a problem of deferred compensation. It also demonstrates that Congress intended section 83 to apply to taxpayers like Alves who allege that they purchased restricted stock as an investment.

Alves suggests that the language of section 83(b) indicates that Congress meant for that section to apply only to bargain purchases and that section 83(a) should be interpreted in the same way. Section 83(b) allows taxpayers to elect to include as income in the year of transfer "the excess" of the full fair market value over the purchase price. Alves contends that a taxpayer who pays full fair market value would have "zero excess," and would fall outside the terms of section 83(b).

Section 83(b), however, is not a limitation upon section 83(a). Congress designed section 83(b) merely to add "flexibility," not to condition section 83(a) on the presence or absence of an "excess." Senate Report at 123, reprinted in 1969 U.S. Code Cong. & Admin. News 2027, 2154.

Moreover, nothing in section 83(b) precludes a taxpayer who has paid full market value for restricted stock from making an 83(b) election. Treasury Regulations promulgated in 1978 and made retroactive to 1969[4] specifically provide that section 83(b) is available in situations of zero excess:

> If property is transferred . . . in connection with the performance of services, the person performing such services may elect to include in gross income under section 83(b) the excess (if any) of the fair market value of the property at the time of transfer . . . over the amount (if any) paid for such property. . . . *The fact that the transferee has paid full value for the property transferred, realizing no bargain element in the transaction, does not preclude the use of the election as provided for in this section.*

26 C.F.R. §1.83.2(a) (1983) (emphasis supplied). These regulations are consistent with the broad language of section 83 and, as the Tax Court stated, simply make "more explicit a fact which is inherent in the statute itself." 79 T.C. at 877-878 n. 7. See Fulman v. United States, 434 U.S. 528, 533 (1978).

Alves last contends that since every taxpayer who pays full fair market value for restricted stock would, if well informed, choose the section 83(b) election to hedge against any appreciation, applying section 83(a) to the unfortunate taxpayer who made no election is simply a trap for the unwary. The tax laws often make an affirmative election necessary. Section 83(b) is but one example of a provision requiring taxpayers to act or suffer less attractive tax consequences. A taxpayer wishing to avoid treatment of appreciation as ordinary income must make an affirmative election under 83(b) in the year the stock was acquired.

Other courts have considered and rejected even stronger attacks on the broad application of section 83. See Pledger v. Commissioner, 641 F.2d 287 (5th Cir.), cert. denied, 454 U.S. 964 (1981); Sakol v. Commissioner, 574 F.2d 694 (2d Cir.), cert. denied, 439 U.S. 859 (1978); Cohn v. Commissioner, 73 T.C. 443 (1979); Cassetta v. Commissioner, 39 T.C.M. (CCH) 188 (1979). As the Second Circuit pointed out, Congress was "solving a practical problem," by making a "gross accommodation to the economic reality." Sakol v. Commissioner, 574 F.2d at 700, quoting Fraser v. Commissioner, 25 F.2d 653, 655 (2d Cir. 1928) (L. Hand, J.). In the present case, the statutory language, legislative history, applicable regulations and the consistent refusal of courts to create exceptions to the statute's coverage, all compel the conclusion that section 83(a) applies to the income Alves received when the

---

4. Treas. Reg. §1.83.8(b)(1) (1983). The Commissioner has statutory authority under 26 U.S.C. §7805(b) to prescribe the retroactivity of regulations.

restrictions on his stock lapsed in 1974 and 1975. The decision of the Tax Court is affirmed.

Notes and Questions

1. *Scope.* Section 83 needs and deserves careful study. It now supplies the rule for the taxation of in-kind compensation for services (whether performed by an employee or an independent contractor) if no special exclusion applies. As in *Alves*, §83 is most commonly applied to stock or other equity-based compensation. Its scope, however, is much broader. "Property" is defined to encompass all "real and personal property other than either money or an unfunded and unsecured promise to pay money or property in the future," and specifically includes "a beneficial interest in assets (including money) which are transferred or set aside from the claims of creditors of the transferor, for example, in a trust or escrow account." Reg. §1.83-3(e). Consequently, a mere promise to pay in the future (contract right) does not trigger §83 (this limitation preserves the distinction between the cash and accrual methods of accounting, which were explored earlier in this chapter), but if that promise is backed by assets that are protected from the promisor's creditors, then a transfer of property has occurred and §83(a) might require the promisee to report income long before any payment is received. Section 83, in other words, applies not only to current in-kind compensation but also to "funded" deferred compensation (other than deferred compensation provided under a qualified pension, profit-sharing, or stock bonus plan, which is subject to special treatment). See §§83(e)(2), 402(b)(1).

2. *Substantial vesting.* The regulations under §83 introduce the concept of *substantial vesting* to determine when income is to be recognized. Property is substantially vested when it is transferable or not subject to a substantial risk of forfeiture. Reg. §1.83-3(b). Now look at the statutory definition of transferability, §83(c)(2). Is it fair to say that everything comes down to risk of loss? Why is that so important? And how "substantial" must the risk of loss be to delay inclusion of the transferred property in gross income? Congress specified that future service requirements generally create a substantial risk of forfeiture, but what about other conditions, such as forfeiture in the event the employee discloses a trade secret? See Reg. §1.83-3(c)(2).

3. *Valuation.* Fundamentally, §83 responds to the valuation problems frequently presented by in-kind compensation. Observe that it adopts a three-part solution. First, conditions that present a substantial risk of forfeiture trigger deferred taxation rather than discounted valuation. Thus, Congress adopted a wait-and-see approach to such contingencies: in the event of forfeiture no inclusion is required, but once it becomes clear that the recipient will get to keep the property it is taxed at fair market value. Second, temporary restrictions that do not constitute a substantial risk of forfeiture are ignored — the property is taxed at its fair market value "determined

without regard to any restriction other than a restriction which by its terms will never lapse." §83(a)(1). Third, permanent restrictions (so-called non-lapse restrictions, defined in §1.83-3(h)) affect valuation, and a mandatory formula price is treated as the value of the property. §83(a)(1), (d)(1).

4. *Section 83(b) election.* What would induce a taxpayer to choose to pay tax earlier than required? Compare the final sentence of §83(b)(1) with Reg. §1.83-2(a) (if the election is made "any subsequent appreciation in the value of the property is not taxable as compensation"). Would a timely election under §83(b) have avoided the taxpayer's predicament in *Alves*? At what cost?

5. *Nonqualified stock options.* How does §83 relate to *LoBue*? Both the grant of a stock option and the receipt of stock upon exercise of the option entail a transfer of property "in connection with the performance of services." Does §83 apply twice? Now read §83(e)(3) and compare it with §83(e)(4). In conjunction, what is the message of these provisions? Recall that in *LoBue* the majority observed that, "It is of course possible for the recipient of a stock option to realize an immediate taxable gain. . . . The option might have a readily ascertainable market value and the recipient might be free to sell his option. But this is not such a case." Regulations provide that "Options have a value at the time they are granted, but that value is ordinarily not readily ascertainable unless the option is actively traded on an established market." Reg. §1.83-7(b)(1). If an option is not actively traded, the option grant is not a taxable event if (1) the option is not transferable, (2) the option is not exercisable immediately in full, (3) the option or the property to which it relates is subject to any restriction or condition which has a significant impact on value, or (4) the value of the option privilege cannot be determined under established financial methods. Id. -7(b)(2), (3). Under this narrow definition, §83 ordinarily applies to the exercise rather than the grant of a compensatory stock option.

6. *Qualified stock options.* Instead of taxing the grant of an option or the receipt of stock upon its exercise, why not simply wait and tax gain on the sale of the stock? Under this approach, the stock's adjusted basis on sale would simply be its cost (the option price) without any increase to reflect prior inclusion of compensation. The compensatory component of the transaction would ordinarily be taxed (but see §1014), but the inclusion might be long-delayed and would get the advantage of the reduced rates applicable to capital gains. Now read §83(e)(1). Section 421 provides the rules governing so-called qualified stock options, which currently consist of "incentive stock options" (ISOs) and "employee stock purchase plans" (ESPPs), defined in §§421 and 422. Observe that no built-in discount is permissible under an ISO, §422(b)(4), and the value of stock subject to ISOs is limited, §422(d). In contrast, a built-in discount of up to 15 percent is permitted under an ESPP, §423(b)(6), but all full-time employees with at least two years of service must be granted options under an ESPP. The favorable treatment accorded stock-based compensation received under an ISO or ESPP is conditioned on

holding the stock for one year (or, if longer, at least until two years from the grant of the option) and continued employment from the time the option is granted until three months before exercise. §§422(a), 423(a). And there is another catch: no compensation deduction is allowed to the corporate employer. §421(a)(2).

7. *Payor's deduction.* When and how much is the employer or service recipient allowed to deduct with respect to contingent in-kind compensation? §83(h). Why? Compare §404(a)(5) and *Albertson's*, Chapter 6F.1 above.

Problems

How would §83 apply to the following cases?

1. *X* transferred 100 shares of TBM stock to its president, *P*, for $10,000 under an agreement requiring *P* to return the stock at cost if he left *X*'s employ within five years. After five years, *P* would be free to retain or sell the stock without restriction. The TBM stock was worth $15,000 when transferred and $35,000 five years later when the restrictions lapsed. *P* sold the shares two years after that for $50,000.

2. On July 1, 2009, Corporation *Y* transferred 100 shares of *Y* stock to a management employee, *M*, for $21 per share under a stock purchase plan that required *M* to return the stock to *Y* (for the price that had been paid for it) if *M*'s employment with *Y* terminated for any reason within one year. In addition, *M* was prohibited from selling or transferring registered ownership of the shares for a period of five years from the date of purchase, which limitation was noted on the share certificates. *Y* common stock (without such restrictions) traded on the New York Stock Exchange for $58 per share on July 1, 2009, $65 per share on July 1, 2010 (at which time *M* was still employed by *Y*), and $88 per share on July 1, 2014.

3. Same facts as in Problem 2, except that in December 2009 *M* sells the stock for $35 per share to an unrelated buyer for delivery in July 2014. See §83(a) (final sentence); Reg. §1.83-1(b)(1).

References

C. Cash Method Accounting and Its Limits

1. Constructive Receipt: Metzer, Constructive Receipt, Economic Benefit and Assignment of Income: A Case Study in Deferred Compensation, 29 Tax L. Rev. 525 (1974); Watts, Some Problems of Constructive Receipt of Income, 27 Tax Law. 23 (1973).

2. Inclusion in Advance of Receipt: Debt Instruments: Lokken, The Time Value of Money Rules, 42 Tax L. Rev. 1 (1986).

D. Accrual Accounting and Its Limits

1. Prepaid Income: David Hasen, The Tax Treatment of Advance Receipts, 61 Tax L. Rev. 395 (2008); Malman, Treatment of Prepaid Income — Clear Reflection of Income or Muddied Waters?, 37 Tax L. Rev. 103 (1982); Presellin & Greenstein, Security Deposit Issue, 68 Tax Notes 426 (1990); Schapiro, Prepayments and Distortion of Income Under Cash Basis Tax Accounting, 30 Tax L. Rev. 117 (1975); Stanger, Vander Kam, & Polifka, Prepaid Income and Estimated Expenses: Financial Accounting Versus Tax Accounting Dichotomy, 33 Tax Law. 403 (1980); Stewart & Woods, Analysis of the Trend Toward Deferring Recognition of Prepaid Income, 59 Taxes 400 (1981); Weary, IRS Creation of Hybrid Methods: Prepayment and the Accrual Method, 35 N.Y.U. Inst. on Fed. Taxn. 59, 71 (1977); Note, New Tax Rules Permitting Limited Deferral of Unearned Income, 55 Marq. L. Rev. 525 (1972).

3. Inventories: Mikalow, Inventory Write-Downs and *Thor Power Tool,* 57 Taxes 384 (1979); Young & Metz, Son of *Thor,* Taxes 324 (1980).

4. Accruing Future Expenses: Aidinoff & Lopata, Section 461 and Accrual-Method Taxpayers: The Treatment of Liabilities Arising from Obligations to Be Performed in the Future, 33 Tax Law. 789 (1980); Committee on Taxation of the Association of the Bar of the City of New York, Transactions Involving Deferred Payment of Accrued Liabilities: Federal Income Tax and the Time Value of Money, 22 Tax Notes 699 (1983); Halperin & Klein, Tax Accounting for Future Obligations: Basic Principles Revised, 38 Tax Notes 831 (1988); Stanger, Vander Kam, & Polifka, Prepaid Income and Estimated Expenses: Financial Accounting Versus Tax Accounting Dichotomy, 33 Tax Law. 403 (1980); Sunley, Observations on the Appropriate Tax Treatment of Future Costs, 23 Tax Notes 719 (1984); Note, A Suggestion for Federal Tax Treatment of Accrued Nuclear Power Plant Decommissioning Expenses, 35 Tax Law. 779 (1982).

Chapter 7 — *Receipts Subject to Offsetting Liabilities*

A taxpayer borrowing funds, for whatever purpose, is not considered to have income; on the other hand, the taxpayer is not allowed any deduction for repayment of the loan. The rule is simple enough on its face and apparently convenient and satisfactory, but what are its rationale and scope and corollaries?

The simplest explanation is that borrowing proceeds are offset by the borrower's liability to repay so that no net gain results from borrowing. But then what if the liability is subsequently altered or terminated? And what qualifies as a liability for this purpose besides an unconditional, consensual obligation to repay? Are there other reasons for the treatment of borrowing that will help to answer these questions, or perhaps even justify exclusion or deferral if the obligation to repay is doubtful?

A. CANCELLATION OF INDEBTEDNESS

UNITED STATES v. KIRBY LUMBER CO.
284 U.S. 1 (1931)

Mr. Justice HOLMES delivered the opinion of the Court. In July, 1923, the plaintiff, the Kirby Lumber Company, issued its own bonds for $12,126,800 for which it received their par value. Later in the same year it purchased in the open market some of the same bonds at less than par, the difference of price being $137,521.30. The question is whether this difference is a taxable gain or income of the plaintiff for the year 1923. By the Revenue Act of (November 23,) 1921, ch. 136, §213(a) gross income includes "gains or profits and income derived from any source whatever," and by the Treasury Regulations authorized by §1303, that have been in force through repeated reenactments, "If the corporation purchases and retires any of such bonds at a price less than the issuing price or face value, the excess of the issuing price or face value over the purchase price is gain or income for the taxable year." Article 545(1)(c) of Regulations 62, under Revenue Act of 1921. See Article 544(1)(c) of Regulations 45, under Revenue Act of 1918; Article 545(1)(c) of Regulations 65, under Revenue Act of 1924; Article 545(1)(c) of Regulations 69, under Revenue Act of 1926; Article 68(1)(c) of Regulations 74, under Revenue Act of 1928. We see no reason why the Regulations should not be accepted as a correct statement of the law.

In Bowers v. Kerbaugh-Empire Co., 271 U.S. 170, the defendant in error owned the stock of another company that had borrowed money repayable in marks or their equivalent for an enterprise that failed. At the time of payment the marks had fallen in value, which so far as it went was a gain for the defendant in error, and it was contended by the plaintiff in error that the gain was taxable income. But the transaction as a whole was a loss, and the contention was denied. Here there was no shrinkage of assets and the taxpayer made a clear gain. As a result of its dealings it made available $137,521.30 assets previously offset by the obligation of bonds now extinct. We see nothing to be gained by the discussion of judicial definitions. The defendant in error has realized within the year an accession to income, if we take words in their plain popular meaning, as they should be taken here. Burnet v. Sanford & Brooks, Co. [Chapter 3D.1 above].

Judgment reversed.

Notes

1. Note what the Court says in this case about judicial definitions of income. *Kirby Lumber* is frequently cited as one of the first cases in which the Supreme Court abandoned the effort to articulate any general definition of income for income tax purposes.

2. A variety of exceptions have arisen to the rule in *Kirby Lumber*. Bankruptcy statutes used to provide an exemption from income tax for discharge of debts in bankruptcy. A judicially created exception covered discharges of indebtedness of insolvent taxpayers outside bankruptcy proceedings: *Kirby Lumber* was read as predicating taxability on the presence of assets to be freed from the burden of indebtedness. Under some circumstances, discharge of a debt might be treated as a nontaxable contribution to the capital of a corporate debtor, and more rarely the cancellation of a debt might escape tax as a gift from creditor to debtor. Under other circumstances, discharge of a purchase money obligation might be treated as a retroactive reduction in purchase price and accounted for as a reduction in the basis of the

purchased property rather than income. There was no general requirement to reduce basis or any other tax attributes in connection with the other exceptions to the *Kirby Lumber* rule.

3. From 1942 to 1986 the tax code contained an election by which even a solvent taxpayer could elect to exclude cancellation-of-indebtedness income, reflecting it instead by a downward adjustment in basis of assets. In 1980, as described in the following report, that provision was restricted by requiring the adjustment to be in basis of depreciable property or realty held for sale to customers, and disallowing the exclusion itself in the absence of such property; all with the intended effect that cancellation of indebtedness income could not be deferred indefinitely or transformed into capital gain. In 1986, the provision for deferral by solvent taxpayers was largely eliminated, but a narrow exception for certain farmers survived. §108(a)(1)(C), (g).

In 1993, elective deferral was restored for noncorporate taxpayers in the case of qualified real property business indebtedness. §108(a)(1)(D) and (c). Read these provisions and consider whether there is any good reason such indebtedness should be distinguished from any other for this purpose.

4. In 1980 most of the foregoing exceptions were codified, with modifications, in §108. The general effect of the modifications is described in the following excerpt.

BANKRUPTCY TAX ACT OF 1980
S. Rep. No. 96-1035, at 9-11 (1980)

OVERVIEW . . .

The rules of the bill concerning income tax treatment of debt discharge in bankruptcy are intended to accommodate bankruptcy policy and tax policy. To preserve the debtor's "fresh start" after bankruptcy, the bill provides that no income is recognized by reason of debt discharge in bankruptcy, so that a debtor coming out of bankruptcy (or an insolvent debtor outside bankruptcy) is not burdened with an immediate tax liability. The bill provides that the debt discharge amount thus excluded from income is applied to reduce the taxpayer's net operating losses and certain other tax attributes, unless the taxpayer elects to apply the debt discharge amount first to reduce basis in depreciable assets (or in realty held as inventory). . . .

DEBTORS GIVEN FLEXIBILITY

The committee believes that these attribute-reduction provisions of the bill give flexibility to the debtor to account for a debt discharge amount in a manner most favorable to the debtor's tax situation. For example, a bankrupt or insolvent debtor which wishes to retain net operating losses and other carryovers will be able to elect to reduce asset basis in depreciable property (or in realty held as inventory). On the other hand, a debtor having an expiring net operating loss which otherwise would be "wasted" will be able (by not making the election) to apply the debt discharge amount first against the net operating loss. [Similarly, a solvent debtor can continue to defer recognition of income by electing to reduce basis of depreciable assets (or in realty held as inventory), or (by not electing) can include all or part of the debt discharge amount in income (for example, in order to offset an expiring net operating loss).]*

At the same time, in developing the rules of the bill, the committee recognized that the basis-reduction mechanism of present law fails to effectuate the Congressional intent of deferring, but eventually collecting tax on, ordinary income realized from debt discharge.

Thus present law permits both solvent and insolvent taxpayers to apply the amount of their discharged debts to reduce the basis of nondepreciable assets which may never be sold, such as stock in a subsidiary corporation or the land on which the company operates its business, thereby avoiding completely, rather than deferring, the tax consequences of debt discharge. Also under present law, a related party (such as the parent corporation of a debtor) can acquire the taxpayer's debt at a discount and effectively eliminate it as a real liability to outside interests, but the debtor thereby avoids the tax treatment which would apply if the debtor had directly retired the debt by repurchasing it. In other cases, the debtor may be able to convert ordinary income from discharge of indebtedness into capital gain, as where the debtor reduces basis in a nondepreciable capital asset.

DEFERRAL OF ORDINARY INCOME ON DEBT DISCHARGE

Accordingly, the rules of the bill are intended to carry out the Congressional intent of deferring, but eventually collecting within a reasonable period, tax on ordinary income realized from debt discharge. Thus in the case of a bankrupt or insolvent debtor, the debt discharge amount is applied to reduce the taxpayer's net operating losses and certain other tax attributes, unless the taxpayer elects to apply the amount first to reduce basis in depreciable assets. . . . Similarly, the debtor can defer immediate tax consequences of debt discharge by reducing basis in real property held as inventory. A subsequent disposition of such reduced-basis realty will result in recognition of a larger amount of ordinary income, just as reduction in basis of depreciable assets results in lower depreciation deductions to offset ordinary income.

---

* The general provision allowing solvent debtors to defer recognition was repealed in 1986. — EDS.

To insure that the debt discharge amount eventually will result in ordinary income (and cannot be converted to capital gain), the bill provides that any gain on a subsequent disposition of the reduced-basis property will be subject to a "recapture" under rules similar to those now applicable with respect to depreciation recapture. Also, the bill contains rules relating to discharge of indebtedness as a capital contribution, acquisition of debt by a related party, discharge of partnership debt, and other income tax aspects of discharge of indebtedness. . . .

Notes and Questions

1. What are the federal income tax consequences if a taxpayer is discharged of an obligation that was never previously deducted and for which no value was received? Consider the following examples.

(a) *A* promises under seal to make a gift to her son. Her son subsequently releases her from the promise.

(b) *B* promises to make a $1,000 contribution to a church's building fund. Subsequently the church agrees to accept $500 in full satisfaction of the pledge.

(c) *C* Corporation issues bonds in payment of a dividend. It subsequently buys back the bonds for 90 cents on the dollar.[1]

(d) *D* receives a bill from his lawyer for $1,000. In the following year *D* complains about the bill and the lawyer agrees to accept $600 instead of $1,000.

(e) *H* had borrowed $100,000 from a bank. In order to improve *H*'s credit standing, the bank surrendered *H*'s note in exchange for a $100,000 note executed by *H*'s wife, *W*. Later the bank sold *W*'s note to *H*'s brother, *X*, for $50,000. *X* obtained the funds for the purchase from *H* and *W* and tore up the note immediately after buying it.[2]

2. What would be the federal income tax consequences of the following transactions? How do they differ from *Kirby Lumber*?

(a) *A*'s employer pays all federal income taxes imposed on *A* by reason of *A*'s salary.

(b) *B*, a railroad company, leases its lines and equipment to another railroad on a perpetual lease under which the lessee agrees to pay a 6 percent dividend on all *B*'s outstanding stock. United States v. Joliet and Chicago R.R., 315 U.S. 44 (1942). (1) Is *B* taxable? (2) If so, who pays the tax? (3) Suppose as part of the lease the lessee has agreed to pay all taxes imposed on *B*:

---

1. See Commissioner v. Rail Joint Co., 61 F.2d 751 (2d Cir. 1932). See also Fashion Park, Inc., 21 T.C. 600 (1954).

2. See §108(e)(4); cf. Bradford v. Commissioner, 233 F.2d 935 (6th Cir. 1956).

Is the payment of *B*'s income taxes by the lessee further income to *B*?
(4) How much?[3]

(c) *C* issues bonds for cash. Subsequently *C*'s stockholders purchase the
bonds and cancel them. Does *C* have income from the cancellation?

(d) *D*, an amateur painter, receives a bill for $800 from his lawyer.
Being short of cash, he persuades the lawyer instead to accept one of his
paintings.

3. *Statute of limitations.* What is the tax effect if the statute of limitations
runs in favor of a taxpayer on a note? On a judgment? On an unliquidated
tort claim?

4. *Temporary relief provisions.* Recently Congress has taken to the practice
of excluding cancellation-of-indebtedness income associated with certain
calamities. This concession was granted to certain persons residing in the
area devastated by Hurricane Katrina and to loan forgiveness resulting from
deaths traceable to the terrorist attacks of September 11, 2001. Katrina Emergency Tax Relief Act of 2005, Pub. L. No. 109-73, §401, 119 Stat. 2016, 2026-
27; Victims of Terrorism Tax Relief Act of 2001, Pub. L. No. 107-134, §105,
115 Stat. 2427, 2432 (2002). The sub-prime mortgage crisis, which began in
2007, impacted banks and credit markets and depressed home prices and
economic conditions in many areas across the country. In response, Congress added §108(a)(1)(E) and (h), which exclude the discharge of acquisition indebtedness on a principal residence if the discharge occurs between
2007 and 2009 (inclusive) and is related to a decline in the value of the
residence or the financial condition of the borrower. Why are (solvent)
borrowers more sympathetic or deserving of relief than savers who suffer
similar financial reverses?

5. *Student loan forgiveness.* Concerned that high student debt loads
were steering students away from low-paying public service employment
into high-paying private sector jobs, some law schools adopted programs
that reduce student loan repayment obligations if the student works for
certain government or charitable organization employers for a specified
period of time. Read and evaluate §108(f). Does this provision make
sense? How does it compare with granting scholarships limited to entering
students who are interested in public service careers? And what about the
student who follows a different path to change the world, striking out on her
own as an entrepreneur, but who ends up in bankruptcy? Cf. 11 U.S.C.
§523(a)(8) (2006) (student loan debt non-dischargeable).

6. *Character of debt cancellation income.* Should the taxpayer's gain in *Kirby
Lumber* be taxed as ordinary income or capital gain? It is commonly assumed
that *Kirby Lumber* gain is ordinary income, not capital gain, and that assumption is clearly and repeatedly incorporated into the provisions of §108 as

---

3. United States v. Boston & Maine R.R., 279 U.S. 732 (1929), and Securities Co. v. United States, 85 F.
Supp. 532 (S.D.N.Y. 1948).

amended in 1980. But is it sound? Think about grounds on which an opposite conclusion might have been reached.

DAVID ZARIN
92 T.C. 1084 (1989), rev'd, 916 F.2d 110 (3d Cir. 1990)

COHEN, Judge: ... David Zarin (petitioner) was a professional engineer involved in the development, construction, and management of multi-family housing and nursing home facilities. In 1978, two years after New Jersey passed the Casino Control Act, N.J. Stat. Ann. sec. 5:12-101 et seq. (West 1988), legalizing casino gambling in Atlantic City, petitioner began developing various housing projects in Atlantic City, New Jersey.

Petitioner occasionally stayed at Resorts International Hotel, Inc. (Resorts), in Atlantic City in connection with his construction activities. Prior to 1978, petitioner had gambled on credit both in Las Vegas, Nevada, and in the Bahamas. In June 1978, petitioner applied to Resorts for a $10,000 line of credit to be used for gambling. After a credit check, which included inquiries with petitioner's banks and "Credit Central," an organization that maintains records of individuals who gamble in casinos, the requested line of credit was granted, despite derogatory information received from Credit Central.

The game most often played by petitioner, craps, creates the potential of losses or gains from wagering on rolls of dice. When he played craps at Resorts, petitioner usually bet the table limit per roll of the dice. Resorts quickly became familiar with petitioner. At petitioner's request, Resorts would raise the limit at the table to the house maximum. When petitioner gambled at Resorts, crowds would be attracted to his table by the large amounts he would wager. Gamblers would wager more than they might otherwise because of the excitement caused by the crowds and the amounts that petitioner was wagering. Petitioner was referred to as a "valued gaming patron" by executives at Resorts.

By November 1979, petitioner's permanent line of credit had been increased to $200,000. Despite this increase, at no time after the initial credit check did Resorts perform any further analysis of petitioner's creditworthiness. Many casinos extend complimentary services and privileges ("comps") to retain the patronage of their best customers. Beginning in the late summer of 1978, petitioner was extended the complimentary use of a luxury three-room suite at Resorts. Resorts progressively increased the complimentary services to include free meals, entertainment, and 24-hour access to a limousine. By late 1979, Resorts was extending such comps to petitioner's guests as well. By this practice, Resorts sought to preserve not only petitioner's patronage but also the attractive power his gambling had on others.

Once the line of credit was established, petitioner was able to receive chips at the gambling table. Patrons of New Jersey casinos may not gamble with currency, but must use chips provided by the casino. Chips may not be used outside the casino where they were issued for any purpose.

Petitioner received chips in exchange for signing counter checks, commonly known as "markers." The markers were negotiable drafts payable to Resorts drawn on petitioner's bank. The markers made no reference to chips, but stated that cash had been received.

Petitioner had an understanding with Gary Grant, the credit manager at Resorts, whereby the markers would be held for the maximum period allowable under New Jersey law, which at that time was 90 days, whereupon petitioner would redeem them with a personal check. At all times pertinent hereto, petitioner intended to repay any credit amount properly extended to him by Resorts and to pay Resorts in full the amount of any personal check given by him to pay for chips or to reduce his gambling debt. Between June 1978 and December 1979, petitioner incurred gambling debts of approximately $2.5 million. Petitioner paid these debts in full. . . .

By January 1980, petitioner was gambling compulsively at Resorts. Petitioner was gambling 12-16 hours per day, 7 days per week in the casino, and he was betting up to $15,000 on each roll of the dice. Petitioner was not aware of the amount of his gambling debts.

On April 12, 1980, Resorts increased petitioner's permanent credit line to $215,000, without any additional credit investigation. During April 1980, petitioner delivered personal checks and markers in the total amount of $3,435,000 that were returned to Resorts as having been drawn against insufficient funds. On April 29, 1980, Resorts cut off petitioner's credit. Shortly thereafter, petitioner indicated to the Chief Executive Officer of Resorts that he intended to repay the obligations.

On November 18, 1980, Resorts filed a complaint in New Jersey state court seeking collection of $3,435,000 from petitioner based on the unpaid personal checks and markers. On March 4, 1981, petitioner filed an answer, denying the allegations and asserting a variety of affirmative defenses.

On September 28, 1981, petitioner settled the Resorts suit by agreeing to make a series of payments totaling $500,000. Petitioner paid the $500,000 settlement amount to Resorts in accordance with the terms of the agreement. The difference between petitioner's gambling obligations of $3,435,000 and the settlement payments of $500,000 is the amount that respondent alleges to be income from forgiveness of indebtedness. . . .

INCOME FROM THE DISCHARGE OF INDEBTEDNESS

In general, gross income includes all income from whatever source derived, including income from the discharge of indebtedness. Sec. 61(a)(12). Not all discharges of indebtedness, however, result in income. See sec. 1.61-12(a), Income Tax Regs., "The discharge of indebtedness, in whole or in part, *may* result in the realization of income." (Emphasis supplied.) The gain to the debtor from such discharge is the resultant freeing up of his assets that he would otherwise have been required to use to pay the debt. See United States v. Kirby Lumber Co., 284 U.S. 1 (1931).

Respondent contends that the difference between the $3,435,000 in personal checks and markers that were returned by the banks as drawn against insufficient funds and the $500,000 paid by petitioner in settlement of the Resorts suit constitutes income from the discharge of indebtedness. Petitioner argues that the settlement agreement between Resorts and himself did not give rise to such income because, among other reasons, the debt instruments were not enforceable under New Jersey law and, in any event, the settlement should be treated as a purchase price adjustment that does not give rise to income from the discharge of indebtedness. . . .

ENFORCEABILITY

In United States v. Hall, [307 F.2d 238 (10th Cir. 1962)], the taxpayer transferred appreciated property in satisfaction of a gambling debt of an undetermined amount incurred in Las Vegas, Nevada. The Commissioner sought to tax as gain the difference between the amount of the discharged debt and the basis of the appreciated property. Although licensed gambling was legal in Nevada, gambling debts were nevertheless unenforceable. The Court of Appeals concluded that, under the circumstances, the amount of the gambling debt had no significance for tax purposes. The Court reasoned that, "The cold fact is that taxpayer suffered a substantial loss from gambling, the amount of which was determined by the transfer." 307 F.2d at 241. The Court of Appeals relied on the so-called "diminution of loss theory" developed by the Supreme Court in Bowers v. Kerbaugh-Empire Co., 271 U.S. 170 (1926). In that case, the taxpayer borrowed money that was subsequently lost in a business transaction. The debt was satisfied for less than its face amount. The Supreme Court held that the taxpayer was not required to recognize income from discharge of a debt because the transaction as a whole lost money.

The Court of Appeals for the Tenth Circuit in *Hall* quoted at length from Bradford v. Commissioner, 233 F.2d 935 (6th Cir. 1956), which noted that the *Kerbaugh-Empire* case was decided before United States v. Kirby Lumber Co., 284 U.S. 1 (1931), and Burnet v. Sanford & Brooks Co., 282 U.S. 359 (1931), and had been "frequently criticized and not easily understood." Subsequent developments further suggest that *Kerbaugh-Empire* has lost its vitality. See Vukasovich, Inc. v. Commissioner, 790 F.2d 1409 (9th Cir. 1986), revg. a Memorandum Opinion of this Court, discussed at length, infra. . . .

Petitioner argues that he did not get anything of value when he received the chips other than the "opportunity to gamble," and that, by reason of his addiction to gambling, he was destined to lose everything that he temporarily received. Thus, he is in effect arguing, based on *Hall,* that the settlement merely reduced the amount of his loss and did not result in income. . . .

We conclude here that the taxpayer did receive value at the time he incurred the debt and that only his promise to repay the value received prevented taxation of the value received at the time of the credit transaction. When, in the subsequent year, a portion of the obligation to repay was forgiven, the general rule that income results from forgiveness of indebtedness, section 61(a)(12), should apply.

Legal enforceability of an obligation to repay is not generally determinative of whether the receipt of money or property is taxable. James v. United States, 366 U.S. 213, 219 (1961). Under the "all events test," only the fact of liability and the amount owed need be fixed as of the end of a taxable year in order to give rise to a deduction by an accrual basis taxpayer; legal liability is not required. Burlington Northern Railroad v. Commissioner, 82 T.C. 143, 151 (1984). Unenforceability of an underlying gambling debt is not a bar to the recognition of income by an accrual method gambling casino. Flamingo Resort, Inc. v. United States, 664 F.2d 1387 (9th Cir. 1982). Enforceability may affect the timing of recognition of income; other factors fix the amount to be recognized. Cf. United States v. Hughes Properties, 476 U.S. 593, 602-604 (1986). . . .

DEDUCTIBILITY OF GAMBLING LOSSES

In several different ways, petitioner argues that any income from discharge of his gambling debt was income from gambling against which he may offset his losses; thus, he argues, he had no net income from gambling.

Section 165(d) provides that "Losses from wagering transactions shall be allowed only to the extent of the gains from such transactions." Neither section 165(d) nor section 1.165-10, Income Tax Regs., defines what items are included as gains from wagering transactions. The regulation, however, provides that wagering losses "shall be allowed as a deduction but only to the extent of the gains *during the taxable years* from such transactions." (Emphasis supplied.) Petitioner incurred gambling losses in 1980, but his gain from the discharge of his gambling debts occurred in 1981. That gain is separate and apart from the losses he incurred from his actual wagering transactions. We have no evidence of his actual wagering gains and losses for either year. If we were to effectively allow petitioner to deduct the value of the lost chips from the value of the discharge debt, we would ignore annual accounting and undermine section 165(d) by in effect allowing gambling losses in excess of gambling winnings.

PURCHASE MONEY DEBT REDUCTION

Petitioner argues that the settlement with Resorts should be treated as a purchase price adjustment that does not give rise to income from the discharge of indebtedness. He cites the parties' stipulation, which included a statement that, "Patrons of New Jersey casinos may not gamble with currency. All gambling must be done with chips provided by the casino. Such chips are property which are not negotiable and may not be used to gamble or for any other purpose outside the casino where they were issued." Respondent argues that petitioner actually received "cash" in return for his debts. . . .

Section 108(e)(5) was enacted "to eliminate disagreements between the Internal Revenue Service and the debtor as to whether, in a particular case to which the provision applies, the debt reductions should be treated as discharge income or a true price adjustment." S. Rept. No. 96-1035 (1980), 1980-2 C.B. 620, 628. Section 108(e)(5) applies to transactions occurring after December 31, 1980. S. Rept. No. 96-1035, supra, 1980-2 C.B. at 622-623. The provisions of this section are not elective.

For a reduction in the amount of a debt to be treated as a purchase price adjustment under section 108(e)(5), the following conditions must be met: (1) The debt must be that of a purchaser of property to the seller which arose out of the purchase of such property; (2) the taxpayer must be solvent and not in bankruptcy when the debt reduction occurs; and (3) except for section 108(e)(5), the debt reduction would otherwise have resulted in discharge of indebtedness income. Sec. 108(e)(5); 1 B. Bittker & L. Lokken, Federal Taxation of Income, Estates and Gifts, pp. 6-40, 6-41 (2d ed. 1989).

In addition to the literal statutory requirements, the legislative history indicates that section 108(e)(5) was intended to apply only if the following requirements are also met: (a) The price reduction must result from an agreement between the purchaser and the seller and not, for example, from a discharge as a result of the bar of the statute of limitations on enforcement of the obligation; (b) there has been no transfer of the debt by the seller to a third party; and (c) there has been no transfer of the purchased property from the purchaser to a third party. S. Rept. No. 96-1035 (1980), 1980-2 C.B. 620, 628; 1 B. Bittker & L. Lokken, supra at 6-40, 6-41.

It seems to us that the value received by petitioner in exchange for the credit extended by Resorts does not constitute the type of property to which section 108(e)(5) was intended to or reasonably can be applied. Petitioner argued throughout his briefs that he purchased only "the opportunity to gamble" and that the chips had little or no value. We agree with his description of what he bargained for but not with his conclusion about the legal effect. . . .

The "opportunity to gamble" would not in the usual sense of the words be "property" transferred from a seller to a purchaser. The terminology used in section 108(e)(5) is readily understood with respect to tangible property and may apply to some types of intangibles. Abstract concepts of property are not useful, however, in deciding whether what petitioner received is within the contemplation of the section.

Obviously the chips in this case were a medium of exchange within the Resorts casino, and in that sense they were a substitute for cash, just as Federal Reserve Notes, checks, or other convenient means of representing credit balances constitute or substitute for cash. Recognition that foreign currency has, for some purposes, been held to be "property" that qualifies as a capital asset is not in point here. See National-Standard Co. v. Commissioner, 80 T.C. 551 (1983), aff'd, 749 F.2d 369 (6th Cir. 1984). Foreign currency fluctuates in United States dollar value, whereas the chips in question do not.

We conclude that petitioner's settlement with Resorts cannot be construed as a "purchase-money debt reduction" arising from the purchase of property within the meaning of section 108(e)(5)....

Decision will be entered under Rule 155.

Reviewed by the Court.

NIMS, PARKER, KORNER, SHIELDS, HAMBLEN, CLAPP, GERBER, WRIGHT, PARR, and COLVIN, J.J., agree with the majority opinion.

TANNENWALD, J., dissenting: ... I think it highly significant that in all the decided cases involving the cancellation of indebtedness, the taxpayer had, in a prior year when the indebtedness was created, received a nontaxable benefit clearly measurable in monetary terms which would remain untaxed if the subsequent cancellation of the indebtedness were held to be tax free. Such is simply not the case herein. The concept that petitioner received his money's worth from the enjoyment of using the chips (thus equating the pleasure of gambling with increase in wealth) produces the incongruous result that the more a gambler loses, the greater his pleasure and the larger the increase in his wealth.[1] Under the circumstances, I think the issue of enforceability becomes critical. In this connection, the repeated emphasis by the majority on the stipulation that Mr. Zarin intended to repay the full amount at the time the debt was created is beside the point. If the debt was unenforceable under New Jersey law, that intent is irrelevant.

It is clear that respondent has not shown that the checks Mr. Zarin gave Resorts were enforceable under New Jersey law....

I would hold for petitioner.

WELLS, J., agrees with this dissent.

JACOBS, J., dissenting: ... In my opinion, petitioner's obligation to Resorts was void ab initio, and therefore, I would first hold that petitioner realized income (herein referred to as chip income) in 1980 (a year at issue) to the extent of the value of the chips received.

---

1. I think it clear that, although theoretically the chips could have been redeemed for cash instead of being used for gambling, any attempt by Mr. Zarin to follow this path would have been known to Resorts' personnel and strongly resisted.

It is apparent that petitioner left the chips he obtained through the extension of credit by Resorts on Resorts' gambling tables. For had he won, his markers undoubtedly would have been paid, and this case would not be before us. Accordingly, I would next hold that the amount of petitioner's losses from wagering activities in 1980 equalled or exceeded the amount of chip income.

I recognize that section 165(d) limits losses from wagering transactions to the extent of gains from such transactions. In my opinion, for purposes of section 165(d), the chip income constitutes gain from a wagering transaction, because no such income would have been realized but for the wagering transactions in which petitioner's losses occurred. Thus, I would hold that petitioner is entitled to deduct in 1980 his gambling losses to the extent of the chip income. . . .

I do not wish to be oblivious to the net effect of the transactions before us. I therefore dissent.

RUWE J., dissenting: Although I agree with much of the majority's reasoning in this case, I dissent from that portion of the opinion which holds that section 108(e)(5) is inapplicable to the transaction at issue. . . .

Section 108(e)(5) and the background giving rise to its enactment support its application to the facts in this case. Prior to enactment of section 108(e)(5), case law distinguished between true discharge of indebtedness situations which required recognition of income and purchase price adjustments. A purchase price adjustment occurred when a purchaser of property agreed to incur a debt to the seller but the debt was subsequently reduced because the value of the property was less than the agreed upon consideration. A mere purchase price adjustment does not result in discharge of indebtedness income. See N. Sobel, Inc. v. Commissioner, 40 B.T.A. 1263 (1939); B. Bittker & L. Lokken, Federal Taxation of Income, Estates and Gifts, pp. 6-39, 6-40 (2d ed. 1989).

Section 108(e)(5) was enacted "to eliminate disagreements between the Internal Revenue Service and the debtor as to whether, in a particular case to which the provision applies, the debt reductions should be treated as discharge income or a true price adjustment." S. Rept. No. 96-1035 (1980), 1980-2 C.B. 620, 628. Section 108(e)(5) applies to transactions occurring after December 31, 1980. S. Rept. No. 1035, supra, 1980-2 C.B. at 622-623. Its provisions are not elective. It is obvious from the portions of petitioner's brief, quoted in the majority opinion at pages 23 and 24, that one of petitioner's arguments is that the value of what he received was less than the amount of debt incurred. Respondent argues, and the majority finds, that the chips petitioner received were worth the full value of the debt. Thus, this case presents the very controversy that the above-quoted legislative history says Congress tried to eliminate by enacting section 108(e)(5). . . .

Respondent's brief makes only two arguments as to why section 108(e)(5) is inapplicable to this case. Respondent first argues that section 108 does not apply to this case because section 1.108(a)-1, Income Tax Regs., restricts its application to corporations or individuals in connection with property used in a trade or business and that section 1.108(a)-2, Income

Tax Regs., requires that a taxpayer must file a consent form with his return to have his property adjusted. The problem with this argument is that there are no such requirements in section 108(e)(5) and the regulations relied upon by the respondent clearly do not apply.

Section 1.108(a)-1, Income Tax Regs., was promulgated in 1956, over 23 years before enactment of the provisions of section 108(e)(5). The section of the regulations that respondent relies upon specifically applies to the then existing provisions of section 108(a) dealing with a situation completely separate from that covered in section 108(e)(5). Likewise, section 1.108(a)-2, Income Tax Regs., last amended in 1967, specifically applies to the then existing provision of section 108(a) and not to section 108(e)(5) which was enacted 13 years later. Respondent's arguments are without merit.

Respondent's second argument consists of only the following two sentences in his reply brief. "Furthermore, the liability in this case is based on the receipt of cash. A purchase price adjustment occurs when the dispute involves contract liability for the purchase of an asset." I am unable to discern any basis or rationale for this argument. Respondent stipulated to, and his brief requests, a finding of fact that property in the form of chips was received in exchange for petitioner's markers.[7]

The majority decides an issue of first impression by disregarding the plain language of the statute without any justification in the statute or legislative history. The result produced is ironic for both the Court and petitioner. The Court must decide the difficult factual issues that section 108(e)(5) was intended to eliminate while petitioner incurs a huge tax liability, the magnitude of which is in direct proportion to his losses.[8]

I would dispose of this case by assuming that there was a discharge of indebtedness income. I would then apply section 108(e)(5) to treat the discharge as a purchase price adjustment. This would result in no taxable income. I respectfully dissent.

CHABOT, SWIFT, WILLIAMS, and WHALEN, J.J., agree with this dissent.

ZARIN v. COMMISSIONER
916 F.2d 110 (3d Cir. 1990)

Before Stapleton, Cowen and Weis, Circuit Judges.

COWEN, Circuit Judge: . . . Initially, we find that sections 108 and 61(a)(12) are inapplicable to the Zarin/Resorts transaction. Section 61

---

7. We have recently described a seller-financed transaction as an "amalgam of two distinct transactions. First, there is a transfer of the asset from the seller to the buyer. Then, there is a 'loan' from the seller to the purchaser of all or a portion of the purchase price." Finkelman v. Commissioner, T.C. Memo. 1989-72. If respondent's "cash" argument is based on the second part of this bifurcated description of a seller-financed transaction, the result would completely nullify section 108(e)(5) since no transactions would ever qualify for section 108(e)(5) relief.

8. While I do not agree with Judge TANNENWALD's technical analysis of the discharge of indebtedness issue, the irony he points out is inescapable.

does not define indebtedness. On the other hand, section 108(d)(1), which repeats and further elaborates on the rule in section 61 (a)(12), defines the term as any indebtedness "(A) for which the taxpayer is liable, or (B) subject to which the taxpayer holds property." I.R.C. §108(d)(1). In order to come within the sweep of the discharge of indebtedness rules, then, the taxpayer must satisfy one of the two prongs in the section 108(d)(1) test. Zarin satisfies neither.

Because the debt Zarin owed to Resorts was unenforceable as a matter of New Jersey state law,[7] it is clearly not a debt "for which the taxpayer is liable." I.R.C. §108(d)(1)(A). Liability implies a legally enforceable obligation to repay, and under New Jersey law, Zarin would have no such obligation.

Moreover, Zarin did not have a debt subject to which he held property as required by section 108(d)(1)(B). Zarin's indebtedness arose out of his acquisition of gambling chips. The Tax Court held that gambling chips were not property, but rather, "a medium of exchange within the Resorts casino" and a "substitute for cash." Alternatively, the Tax Court viewed the chips as nothing more than "the opportunity to gamble and incidental services . . ." Zarin, 92 T.C. at 1099. We agree with the gist of these characterizations, and hold that gambling chips are merely an accounting mechanism to evidence debt. . . .

Instead of analyzing the transaction at issue as cancelled debt, we believe the proper approach is to view it as disputed debt or contested liability. Under the contested liability doctrine, if a taxpayer, in good faith, disputed the amount of a debt, a subsequent settlement of the dispute would be treated as the amount of debt cognizable for tax purposes. The excess of the original debt over the amount determined to have been due is disregarded for both loss and debt and accounting purposes. . . .

STAPLETON, Circuit Judge, dissenting. I respectfully dissent because I agree with the Commissioner's appraisal of the economic realities of this matter.

Resorts sells for cash the exhilaration and the potential for profit inherent in games of chance. It does so by selling for cash chips that entitle the holder to gamble at its casino. Zarin, like thousands of others, wished to purchase what Resorts was offering in the marketplace. He chose to make this purchase on credit and executed notes evidencing his obligation to repay the funds that were advanced to him by Resorts. As in most purchase money transactions, Resorts skipped the step of giving Zarin cash that he would only return to it in order to pay for the opportunity to gamble. Resorts provided him instead with chips that entitled him to participate in Resorts' games of chance on the same basis as others who had paid cash for that

---

7. The Tax Court held that the Commissioner had not met its burden of proving that the debt owed Resorts was enforceable as a matter of state law. Zarin, 92 T.C. at 1090. There was ample evidence to support that finding. In New Jersey, the extension of credit by casinos "to enable [any] person to take part in gaming activity as a player" is limited. N.J. Stat. Ann. §5:12-101(b) (1988). Under N.J. Stat. Ann. §5:12-101(f), any credit violation is "invalid and unenforceable for the purposes of collection. . . ."

privilege.[1] Whether viewed as a one or two-step transaction, however, Zarin received either $3.4 million in cash or an entitlement for which others would have had to pay $3.4 million.

Despite the fact that Zarin received in 1980 cash or an entitlement worth $3.4 million, he correctly reported in that year no income from his dealings with Resorts. He did so solely because he recognized, as evidenced by his notes, an offsetting obligation to repay Resorts $3.4 million in cash. See, e.g., Vukasovich, Inc. v. Commissioner, 790 F.2d 1409 (9th Cir. 1986); United States v. Rochelle, 384 F.2d 748 (5th Cir. 1967), cert. denied, 390 U.S. 946 (1968); Bittker and Thompson, Income from the Discharged Indebtedness: The Progeny of United States v. Kirby Lumber Co., 66 Calif. L. Rev. 159 (1978). In 1981, with the delivery of Zarin's promise to pay Resorts $500,000 and the execution of a release by Resorts, Resorts surrendered its claim to repayment of the remaining $2.9 million of the money Zarin had borrowed. As of that time, Zarin's assets were freed of his potential liability for that amount and he recognized gross income in that amount. Commissioner v. Tufts, 461 U.S. 300 (1983); United States v. Kirby Lumber Company, 284 U.S. 1 (1931); Vukasovich, Inc. v. Commissioner, 790 F.2d 1409 (9th Cir. 1986). But see United States v. Hall, 307 F.2d 238 (10th Cir. 1962).[2]

The only alternatives I see to this conclusion are to hold either (1) that Zarin realized $3.4 million in income in 1980 at a time when both parties to the transaction thought there was an offsetting obligation to repay or (2) that the $3.4 million benefit sought and received by Zarin is not taxable at all. I find the latter alternative unacceptable as inconsistent with the fundamental principle of the Code that anything of commercial value received by a taxpayer is taxable unless expressly excluded from gross income.[3] Commissioner v. Glenshaw Glass Co., 348 U.S. 426 (1955); United States v. Kirby Lumber Co., supra. I find the former alternative unacceptable

---

1. I view as irrelevant the facts that Resorts advanced credit to Zarin solely to enable him to patronize its casino and that the chips could not be used elsewhere or for other purposes. When one buys a sofa from the furniture store on credit, the fact that the proprietor would not have advanced the credit for a different purpose does not entitle one to a tax-free gain in the event the debt to the store is extinguished for some reason.

2. This is not a case in which parties agree subsequent to a purchase money transaction that the property purchased has a value less than thought at the time of the transaction. In such cases, the purchase price adjustment rule is applied and the agreed-upon value is accepted as the value of the benefit received by the purchaser; see e.g., Commissioner v. Sherman, 135 F.2d 68 (6th Cir. 1943); Commissioner v. N. Sobel, Inc., 40 B.T.A. 1263 (1939). Nor is this a case in which the taxpayer is entitled to rescind an entire purchase money transaction, thereby to restore itself to the position it occupied before receiving anything of commercial value. In this case, the illegality was in the extension of credit by Resorts and whether one views the benefit received by Zarin as cash or the opportunity to gamble, he is no longer in a position to return that benefit.

3. As the court's opinion correctly points out, this record will not support an exclusion under §108(a), which relates to discharge of debt in an insolvency or bankruptcy context. Section 108(e)(5) of the Code, which excludes discharged indebtedness arising from a "purchase price adjustment" is not applicable here. Among other things, §108(e)(5) necessarily applies only to a situation in which the debtor still holds the property acquired in the purchase money transaction. Equally irrelevant is §108(d)'s definition of "indebtedness" relied upon heavily by the court. Section 108(d) expressly defines that term solely for the purposes of §108 and not for the purposes of §61(a)(12).

as impracticable. In 1980, neither party was maintaining that the debt was unenforceable and, because of the settlement, its unenforceability was not even established in the litigation over the debt in 1981. It was not until 1989 in this litigation over the tax consequences of the transaction that the unenforceability was first judicially declared. Rather than require such tax litigation to resolve the correct treatment of a debt transaction, I regard it as far preferable to have the tax consequences turn on the manner in which the debt is treated by the parties. For present purposes, it will suffice to say that where something that would otherwise be includable in gross income is received on credit in a purchase money transaction, there should be no recognition of income so long as the debtor continues to recognize an obligation to repay the debt. On the other hand, income, if not earlier recognized, should be recognized when the debtor no longer recognizes an obligation to repay and the creditor has released the debt or acknowledged its unenforceability.[4]

In this view, it makes no difference whether the extinguishment of the creditor's claim comes as a part of a compromise. Resorts settled for 14 cents on the dollar presumably because it viewed such a settlement as reflective of the odds that the debt would be held to be enforceable. While Zarin should be given credit for the fact that he had to pay 14 cents for a release, I see no reason why he should not realize gain in the same manner as he would have if Resorts had concluded on its own that the debt was legally unenforceable and had written it off as uncollectible.[5]

I would affirm the judgment of the Tax Court.

B.   CLAIM OF RIGHT

NORTH AMERICAN OIL CONSOLIDATED v. BURNET
286 U.S. 417 (1932)

Mr. Justice BRANDEIS delivered the opinion of the Court. The question for decision is whether the sum of $171,979.22 received by the North American Oil Consolidated in 1917, was taxable to it as income of that year.

The money was paid to the company under the following circumstances. Among many properties operated by it in 1916 was a section of oil land, the legal title to which stood in the name of the United States. Prior to that year, the Government, claiming also the beneficial ownership, had instituted a

---

4. Cf. Bear Manufacturing Co. v. United States, 430 F.2d 152 (7th Cir. 1970) (termination of a liability for tax purposes turns not on running of applicable statute of limitations, but on conduct of the parties), cert. denied, 400 U.S. 1021 (1971).

5. A different situation exists where there is a bona fide dispute over the amount of a debt and the dispute is compromised. Rather than require tax litigation to determine the amount of income received, the Commission treats the compromise figure as representing the amount of the obligation. I find this sensible and consistent with the pragmatic approach I would take.

suit to oust the company from possession; and on February 2, 1916, it secured the appointment of a receiver to operate the property, or supervise its operations, and to hold the net income thereof. The money paid to the company in 1917 represented the net profits which had been earned from that property in 1916 during the receivership. The money was paid to the receiver as earned. After entry by the District Court in 1917 of the final decree dismissing the bill, the money was paid, in that year, by the receiver to the company. United States v. North American Oil Consolidated, 242 Fed. 723. The Government took an appeal (without supersedeas) to the Circuit Court of Appeals. In 1920, that Court affirmed the decree. 264 Fed. 336. In 1922, a further appeal to this Court was dismissed by stipulation. 258 U.S. 633.

The income earned from the property in 1916 had been entered on the books of the company as its income. It had not been included in its original return of income for 1916; but it was included in an amended return for that year which was filed in 1918. Upon auditing the company's income and profits tax returns for 1917, the Commissioner of Internal Revenue determined a deficiency based on other items. The company appealed to the Board of Tax Appeals. There, in 1927 the Commissioner prayed that the deficiency already claimed should be increased so as to include a tax on the amount paid by the receiver to the company in 1917. The Board held that the profits were taxable to the receiver as income of 1916; and hence made no finding whether the company's accounts were kept on the cash receipts and disbursements basis or on the accrual basis. 12 B.T.A. 68. The Circuit Court of Appeals held that the profits were taxable to the company as income of 1917, regardless of whether the company's returns were made on the cash or on the accrual basis. 50 F.2d 752. This Court granted a writ of certiorari. 284 U.S. 614.

It is conceded that the net profits earned by the property during the receivership constituted income. The company contends that they should have been reported by the receiver for taxation in 1916; that if not returnable by him, they should have been returned by the company for 1916, because they constitute income of the company accrued in that year; and that if not taxable as income of the company for 1916, they were taxable to it as income for 1922, since the litigation was not finally terminated in its favor until 1922.

First. The income earned in 1916 and impounded by the receiver in that year was not taxable to him, because he was the receiver of only a part of the properties operated by the company. . . . The language of the Section contemplates a substitution of the receiver for the corporation; and there can be such substitution only when the receiver is in complete control of the properties and business of the corporation. Moreover, there is no provision for the consolidation of the return of a receiver of part of a corporation's property or business with the return of the corporation itself. It may not be assumed that Congress intended to require the filing of two separate returns for the same year, each covering only a part of the corporate income, without making provision for consolidation so that the tax could be based upon the income as a whole.

Second. The net profits were not taxable to the company as income of 1916. For the company was not required in 1916 to report as income an amount which it might never receive. See Burnet v. Logan, 283 U.S. 404, 413. Compare Lucas v. American Code Co., 280 U.S. 445, 452; Burnet v. Sanford & Brooks Co., 282 U.S. 359, 363. There was no constructive receipt of the profits by the company in that year, because at no time during the year was there a right in the company to demand that the receiver pay over the money. Throughout 1916 it was uncertain who would be declared entitled to the profits. It was not until 1917, when the District Court entered a final decree vacating the receivership and dismissing the bill, that the company became entitled to receive the money. Nor is it material, for the purposes of this case, whether the company's return was filed on the cash receipts and disbursements basis, or on the accrual basis. In neither event was it taxable in 1916 on account of income which it had not yet received and which it might never receive.

Third. The net profits earned by the property in 1916 were not income of the year 1922 — the year in which the litigation with the Government was finally terminated. They became income of the company in 1917, when it first became entitled to them and when it actually received them. If a taxpayer receives earnings under a claim of right and without restriction as to its disposition, he has received income which he is required to return, even though it may still be claimed that he is not entitled to retain the money, and even though he may still be adjudged liable to restore its equivalent. See Board v. Commissioner, 51 F.2d 73, 75, 76. Compare United States v. S.S. White Dental Mfg. Co., 274 U.S. 398, 403. If in 1922 the Government had prevailed, and the company had been obliged to refund the profits received in 1917, it would have been entitled to a deduction from the profits of 1922, not from those of any earlier year. Compare Lucas v. American Code Co., supra.

Affirmed.

UNITED STATES v. LEWIS
340 U.S. 590 (1951)

Mr. Justice BLACK delivered the opinion of the Court. Respondent Lewis brought this action in the Court of Claims seeking a refund of an alleged overpayment of his 1944 income tax. The facts found by the Court of Claims are: In his 1944 income tax return, respondent reported about $22,000 which he had received that year as an employee's bonus. As a result of subsequent litigation in a state court, however, it was decided that respondent's bonus had been improperly computed; under compulsion of the state court's judgment he returned approximately $11,000 to his employer.

Until payment of the judgment in 1946, respondent had at all times claimed and used the full $22,000 unconditionally as his own, in the good faith though "mistaken" belief that he was entitled to the whole bonus.

On the foregoing facts the Government's position is that respondent's 1944 tax should not be recomputed, but that respondent should have deducted the $11,000 as a loss in his 1946 tax return. See G.C.M. 16730, XV-1 Cum. Bull. 179 (1936). The Court of Claims, however, relying on its own case, Greenwald v. United States, 102 Ct. Cl. 272, 57 F. Supp. 569, held that the excess bonus received "under a mistake of fact" was not income in 1944 and ordered a refund based on a recalculation of that year's tax. 117 Ct. Cl. 336, 91 F. Supp. 1017. We granted certiorari, 340 U.S. 903, because this holding conflicted with many decisions of the courts of appeals. See, e.g., Haberkorn v. United States, 173 F.2d 587, and with principles announced in North American Oil v. Burnet, 286 U.S. 417.

In the *North American Oil* case we said:

> If a taxpayer receives earnings under a claim of right and without restriction as to its disposition, he has received income which he is required to return, even though it may still be claimed that he is not entitled to retain the money, and even though he may still be adjudged liable to restore its equivalent. 286 U.S. at 424.

Nothing in this language permits an exception merely because a taxpayer is "mistaken" as to the validity of his claim. . . .

Income taxes must be paid on income received (or accrued) during an annual accounting period. Cf. I.R.C., §§41, 42; and see Burnet v. Sanford & Brooks Co. [Chapter 3D.1 above]. The "claim of right" interpretation of the tax laws has long been used to give finality to that period, and is now deeply rooted in the federal tax system. See cases collected in 2 Mertens, Law of Federal Income Taxation, §12.103. We see no reason why the Court should depart from this well-settled interpretation merely because it results in an advantage or disadvantage to a taxpayer.*

Reversed.

Mr. Justice DOUGLAS, dissenting. The question in this case is not whether the bonus had to be included in 1944 income for purposes of the tax. Plainly it should have been because the taxpayer claimed it as of right. Some years later, however, it was judicially determined that he had no claim to the bonus. The question is whether he may then get back the tax which he paid on the money.

Many inequities are inherent in the income tax. We multiply them needlessly by nice distinctions which have no place in the practical administration of the law. If the refund were allowed, the integrity of the taxable year would not be violated. The tax would be paid when due; but the

---

* It has been suggested that it would be more "equitable" to reopen respondent's 1944 tax return. While the suggestion might work to the advantage of this taxpayer, it could not be adopted as a general solution because, in many cases, the three-year statute of limitations would preclude recovery.

Government would not be permitted to maintain the unconscionable position that it can keep the tax after it is shown that payment was made on money which was not income to the taxpayer.

Notes

1. In one sense *North American Oil* and *Lewis* represent another way of accounting for funds received subject to an obligation to repay: Ignore the liability, tax the receipt of funds, and then allow a deduction if and when repayment is made. This is indeed the treatment prescribed if the taxpayer does not admit the asserted obligation to repay — if the funds are received, that is, under a claim of right to retain them.

The holding in *North American Oil* is of immense importance as a matter of administrative practicality, since it enables taxpayers and revenue officials to settle tax liabilities without reference to subtle and difficult questions about when a claim has been settled or abandoned. In *North American Oil* itself, the Supreme Court decision marked a definite end to overt litigation, but other situations would be much more ambiguous. How would one treat funds received as income if a claim to repayment was only asserted later in the year or in a subsequent year, and then how would one determine whether such a claim was bona fide and was being prosecuted diligently, or when it had been abandoned (forgiven within the meaning of *Kirby Lumber*), and so forth? The decision in *North American Oil* avoids these problems by focusing solely on payment and repayment.

2. What is the impact of accounting methods for these decisions? Read §§446 and 448. Many taxpayers, including almost all individuals whose income is from employment and investment, compute taxable income on a simple cash receipts and disbursements basis, reporting income when received (actually or constructively), and deducting expenses when paid. *North American Oil* and *Lewis* exhibit a spirit quite consistent with cash receipts and disbursements accounting.

But the statute authorizes, and taxpayers engaged in the sale of goods generally use, an accrual method of accounting to compute income for tax as well as financial purposes. What does this case indicate about accrual accounting for tax purposes? Under an accrual method, income is taxable in the year in which the taxpayer's right to receive it becomes fixed and unconditional, even if payment is deferred. But income does not accrue if the taxpayer's claim to it is subject to substantial dispute. Thus North American Oil's income did not accrue in 1916, and presumably would not have accrued, in the absence of payment, until termination of the litigation in 1922. One might think that under an accrual method receipt of payment should not alter the result, but the Court held that it did. Would it be accurate to say that in the face of dispute or uncertainty, tax accounting reverts to a cash receipts and disbursements basis even for an accrual method tax-payer? Would that be a sound rule? Why?

3. Is the rule of *North American Oil* applicable to deductions? Con Ed paid real estate taxes of $100 in 1946, but only admitted it owed $85 and sued to get the other $15 back. In 1951 the liability was settled at $95, and Con Ed received a refund of $5. The IRS took the position that $100 was deductible in 1946 and the $5 refund was income in 1951. Con Ed sought to deduct only $85 in 1946 and to deduct $10 in 1951, instead of reporting $5 income, presumably because its marginal rate was higher in 1951 than in 1946. The Supreme Court upheld the taxpayer's position in United States v. Consolidated Edison Co. of New York, Inc., 366 U.S. 380 (1961). This holding was very soon overruled by enactment of §461(f). Why? Should §461(f) be regarded as restoring the general rule of *North American Oil* with respect to deductions?

4. Why does the taxpayer care about how these cases come out? Consider each case separately in speculating about this question.

5. Look at §1341. Would it relieve the taxpayer's problem in *Lewis*? Explain. Would it provide any relief in *North American Oil*? Would it provide relief in *North American Oil* if the taxpayer had ultimately lost its case in the Supreme Court and had to pay the government back?

ALCOA, INC. v. UNITED STATES
509 F.3d 173 (3d Cir. 2007)

ROTH, Circuit Judge:

The issue before us is whether a taxpayer's expenses for environmental clean-up of its industrial sites, mandated by changes in environmental law, qualify for the beneficial tax treatment afforded by section 1341 of the Internal Revenue Code, 26 U.S.C. §1341. Section 1341 applies when a taxpayer must restore a substantial amount of money, which the taxpayer had received in a prior tax year under a claim of right. Section 1341 allows the taxpayer to take a deduction in the current tax year for the amount of taxes the taxpayer would have saved if the amount restored had not been included in its reported gross income in the prior tax year.

We hold that Alcoa's environmental clean-up expenses, incurred in the 1993 tax year for pollution created in past years, do not qualify as restored moneys under Section 1341.

I. FACTUAL AND PROCEDURAL BACKGROUND

The facts of this case are simple and mostly undisputed. Alcoa is a well-known producer of aluminum and aluminum products. From 1940 to 1987, Alcoa's operations produced waste byproducts, which Alcoa disposed of during the ordinary course of business. Alcoa claims that it included disposal costs for these waste byproducts in its Cost of Goods Sold (COGS) calculations for the relevant years, thereby excluding them from its reported income during those years.[1]

After the enactment of new environmental laws, including the Comprehensive Environmental Response, Compensation, and Liability Act of 1980 (CERCLA), state and federal agencies found that a number of Alcoa's industrial sites were polluted and ordered Alcoa to conduct environmental clean-up at these sites. As a result, in 1993 Alcoa expended substantial funds on environmental remediation.

In its 1993 tax return, Alcoa claimed these costs as a tax deduction; the Internal Revenue Service (IRS) did not challenge that treatment. Subsequently, however, Alcoa filed with the IRS a claim for a refund of over twelve million dollars. Alcoa maintained that under section 1341, Alcoa was entitled to enjoy not the tax benefit yielded by the 1993 deduction, but rather the much larger benefit (due to the then generally higher corporate tax rates) of a reduction of its 1940-1987 tax liability. The IRS disallowed the refund and Alcoa filed this action in the District Court.

After discovery the parties filed cross-motions for summary judgment. The District Court noted that a practically identical case had recently been decided in the United States District Court for the Eastern District of Virginia against the Reynolds Metal Company. See Reynolds v. United States, 389 F.Supp.2d 692 (E.D.Va.2005). Finding itself in full agreement with the opinion of the Virginia court, the District Court adopted that opinion as its own and granted summary judgment in favor of the government.

This timely appeal followed. . . .

III. DISCUSSION

The issue in this case is whether Alcoa's 1993 expenditure for environmental remediation qualifies for the beneficial tax treatment allowed by section 1341. If it does not qualify, as the government argues, Alcoa can reduce its tax liability for the year 1993 only to the extent it deducts its remedial expenses from its 1993 income which will be taxed at the 1993 corporate tax rate of 35%. If Alcoa's 1993 environmental expenses do qualify under section 1341, however, Alcoa is entitled to a deduction in 1993 equal to what it would have saved in taxes in the years 1940-1987 by excluding the

---

1. Expenses included in COGS are excluded from gross income because "in a manufacturing, merchandising, or mining business, 'gross income' means the total sales, less the costs of goods sold." 26 C.F.R. §1.61-3(a).

The government disputes that Alcoa included its waste disposal costs in the COGS calculation; since we are reviewing a grant of summary judgment for the government, however, we must credit Alcoa's version.

remediation expenses from its reported income for those prior tax years.[2] This treatment would be beneficial to Alcoa because corporate tax rates were generally far higher in 1940-1987 than in 1993. For the reasons we set out below, we conclude that the environmental remediation expenses that Alcoa incurred in 1993 do not qualify for beneficial tax treatment under section 1341. Alcoa's proposed interpretation of the statute, while artful, is not convincing.

A. The Claim of Right Doctrine and Section 1341

The United States Tax Code operates on an annual accounting system, under which "each year's tax must be definitively calculable at the end of the tax year." United States v. Skelly Oil Co., 394 U.S. 678, 684 (1969). Under the so-called "claim of right" doctrine, "[i]f a taxpayer receives earnings under a claim of right and without restriction as to its disposition, he has received income which he is required to return, even though it may still be claimed that he is not entitled to retain the money, and even though he may still be adjudged liable to restore its equivalent." Id. at 680 (internal quotation omitted). Thus, a taxpayer must include in his tax return even those items of income which are subject to competing claims, so long as he has full control of those moneys at the end of the tax year.

For many years, if a taxpayer filed a tax return but later was forced to relinquish some of the reported income, the taxpayer "would be entitled to a deduction in the year of repayment; the taxes due for the year of receipt would not be affected." Skelly Oil, 394 U.S. at 680-81. This system had the potential to create inequities because a taxpayer might be forced to pay taxes on the item of income at a certain tax rate and take a deduction at a lower rate (because of an intervening change either in the taxpayer's tax bracket or in the tax rates themselves). Id. at 681. The case which focused attention on these inequities is United States v. Lewis, 340 U.S. 590 (1951). In 1944, the taxpayer in *Lewis* had received a bonus from his employer, on which he had properly paid income taxes in the year of receipt. Two years later, in 1946, a state court ordered Lewis to repay his employer part of that bonus because it had been improperly computed. "Until payment of the judgment in 1946, [Lewis] had at all times claimed and used the full [bonus amount] unconditionally as his own, in the good faith though 'mistaken' belief that he was

---

2. Alcoa calculates the additional tax savings arising from section 1341 treatment at over twelve million dollars. It appears that it does so by apportioning its 1993 expenses among the years 1940 to 1987. There is a significant question, however, about whether the clean-up expenses in 1993 are in any meaningful sense the "same" costs Alcoa would have incurred in 1940-1987 if the remediation had been done over those years. It would be very difficult to establish what portion of the pollution that was eventually removed should be apportioned to each of the 47 years in question; and even if that were possible, it would then be necessary to calculate what it would have cost to remove the relevant pollutants under the economic and technological circumstances of each of those years. This is a highly speculative enterprise. For purposes of this discussion, however, we assume that Alcoa would be able to identify the exact amount it would have been able to exclude from income in each of the 47 years under review.

entitled to the whole bonus." Id. at 591. The government argued that Lewis should deduct the amount he returned to his employer as a loss from his 1946 tax return; Lewis wished to recompute his tax for 1944. The Court sided with the government and held that under the well-established claim of right doctrine, the tax year in which the contested amount was received could not be reopened, whether this would "result[ ] in an advantage or disadvantage to a taxpayer." Id. at 592.

In order to correct the inequities made apparent by the *Lewis* decision, Congress enacted section 1341, which, "as an alternative to the deduction in the year of repayment which prior law allowed, . . . permits certain taxpayers to recompute their taxes for the year of receipt." Skelly Oil, 394 U.S. at 682. Section 1341 is designed to put the taxpayer in essentially the same position he would have been in had he never received the returned income in the first place. Dominion Res., Inc. v. United States, 219 F.3d 359, 363 (4th Cir.2000). . . . The "net effect" of the provision is "that the taxpayer can recompute his taxes for the year in which he originally received the money, excluding from his income that amount which he later repaid." Reynolds, 389 F.Supp.2d at 698. By allowing the taxpayer the choice between a simple deduction and a recalculation of the prior year's tax liability, section 1341 ensures that any change in tax rates or in the taxpayer's tax bracket is a tax neutral event with respect to the disputed item of income.

For a taxpayer to qualify for the beneficial tax treatment of section 1341, (1) the taxpayer must have appeared to have an unrestricted right to an item included in gross income for a prior taxable year (i.e., must have included the item in income under a claim of right); (2) it must be established after the close of that prior year that the taxpayer did not have an unrestricted right to the item; (3) the taxpayer must be entitled to deduct the amount of the item in the year in which the taxpayer restored the item; and (4) the amount of the deduction must exceed $3,000. Dominion Res., 219 F.3d at 363. The taxpayer bears the burden of proving his eligibility for section 1341 treatment. Kappel v. United States, 437 F.2d 1222, 1227 (3d Cir.1971).

In the District Court, the government conceded (as it does here) that Alcoa has met the third and fourth requirements of section 1341 because it was entitled to a deduction in 1993 that exceeded $3,000. The government contended, however, that Alcoa could not satisfy the first or second requirement for eligibility under the provision, i.e., (1) inclusion of an item in gross income under claim of right, and (2) later determination that the taxpayer did not have an unrestricted right to that item (restoration of that item). The government argued that Alcoa could not characterize as an "item . . . included in gross income" the funds it did not spend in 1940-1987 on additional waste disposal activities. The government's position was that "gross income" means "gross receipts"; "gross income" does not include money the taxpayer failed to spend. Alcoa disagreed, reasoning its "gross income" for the years in question was overstated because Alcoa's cost of goods sold was understated.

The government's response to this argument was that, even if the amounts not spent by Alcoa could qualify as an "item included in gross income," the claim of right doctrine applied only when the taxpayer was subject to an adverse claim at the time it included the item in gross income—whether or not the taxpayer was aware of the adverse claim at the time of the initial return. In the government's view, section 1341 does not apply where the taxpayer had an *actual* and not simply an *apparent* right to the item, but later lost its right to the item through an intervening change in factual circumstances. Under this theory, even if Alcoa's insufficient waste disposal expenses could qualify as an "item included in gross income," Alcoa had an *actual*—not an *apparent*—claim to the funds it saved by failing to conduct proper waste disposal. This is so because there was no rival claim to those funds. Alcoa replied that something can be *apparent* and also be *true;* in Alcoa's view, all a taxpayer must show to qualify under section 1341 is that the taxpayer lost the right to the item at some point before claiming the deduction.[5]

The District Court, pursuant to the *Reynolds* decision, grudgingly accepted Alcoa's argument that its insufficient environmental expenditures during the 1940-1987 period amounted to the inclusion of an item in gross income under an apparent claim of right. See *Reynolds,* 389 F.Supp.2d at 702 (noting that the taxpayer had "skillfully co-opted the definition of gross income for its own means"). As for the requirement of a determination in a later year that the taxpayer did not have a claim of right to that item, however, the District Court held that Alcoa could not satisfy it and therefore could not avail itself of the beneficial treatment of section 1341.[6]

B. THE "SAME CIRCUMSTANCES, TERMS AND CONDITIONS" TEST

We agree with the District Court that Alcoa's clean-up expenditures in 1993 do not qualify as the restoration of income to which Alcoa found it did not have a claim of right. How then can a taxpayer satisfy section 1341's requirement that it "was established after the close of [a] prior taxable

5. The question of whether an *actual* claim of right can qualify as an *apparent* one under the statute has caused some disagreement in the federal courts. Compare *Dominion Res.*, 219 F.3d 359 (holding that a taxpayer may qualify for section 1341 treatment even if, during the year of receipt, he did in fact have an actual right to the item of income) with *Cinergy Corp. v. United States*, 55 Fed.Cl. 489 (Fed.Cl.2003) (holding that section 1341 treatment presupposes that the taxpayer's right to was "apparent," not "actual," in the year of receipt).

6. Because of the conclusion we come to in this appeal, we do not need to reach the question of whether the funds Alcoa did not spend in 1940-1987 on waste disposal qualify as "items included in gross income." We note, however, that the argument presents significant difficulties. As a practical matter, the relationship between Alcoa's expenditure in 1993, on the one hand, and whatever unspent moneys may have been included in the COGS for the years under review, on the other, is tenuous and speculative at best. The exact amount Alcoa expended on clean-up in 1993 cannot be simply apportioned among the 47 years at issue without regard to the difference in the kind of activity (immediate waste disposal vs. delayed cleanup), cost of labor, cost and availability of technology, etc. Moreover, it seems unlikely that the statute was intended to cover unspent money. What Congress had in mind was the situation where a taxpayer received income that it later had to relinquish. Alcoa's artful argument that waste disposal expenses would have been part of COGS, and thus an item of income, exploits technicalities at the expense of common sense.

year (or years) that the taxpayer did not have an unrestricted right" to an item of income or a portion of such item? 26 U.S.C. §1341(a)(2). The District Court, adopting *Reynolds*, held that a taxpayer's later arising obligation to remedy environmental ills is not a determination that the taxpayer did not have an unrestricted right to an item of income or to a portion of such item, as required by the statute, because the taxpayer had not demonstrated restoration of an item of income to an entity from whom the income was received or to whom the item of income should have been paid. *Reynolds*, 389 F.Supp.2d at 702; see also *Kappel*, 437 F.2d at 1226 ("[t]he requirement that a legal obligation exist to restore funds before a deduction is allowable under the claim of right doctrine is derived from the language of §1341(a)(2) of the Code").

On appeal, Alcoa argues that, in order to take advantage of section 1341, it needs to show only that it discovered it could not keep the money it had not spent on more effective clean-up in 1940-1987 because after the enactment of CERCLA and other environmental laws it was forced to spend the money on remediation efforts. The government responds that this interpretation would extend the benefits of section 1341 far beyond its intended scope and that a taxpayer must show it has "restored" the amount at issue to another claimant with actual right to it. The government urges that a taxpayer is entitled to section 1341 treatment if the repayment arose from the "same circumstances, terms and conditions" as the original payment of the item to the taxpayer. See, e.g., *Kraft v. United States*, 991 F.2d 292, 295 (6th Cir.1993); *Dominion Res.*, 219 F.3d at 367; *Cinergy Corp. v. United States*, 55 Fed.Cl. 489, 507 (Fed.Cl.2003); *Blanton v. Comm'r*, 46 T.C. 527, 530 (T.C.1966). In other words, there must be a "substantive nexus between the right to the income at the time of receipt and the subsequent circumstances necessitating a refund." *Dominion Res., Inc. v. United States*, 48 F.Supp.2d 527, 540 (E.D.Va.1999), aff'd, *Dominion Res.*, 219 F.3d 359.

Alcoa's claim fails under this "same circumstances, terms, and conditions" test. Even if we were to credit Alcoa's theory about its new obligation to engage in clean-up in 1993 — namely, that it is equivalent to the discovery that it did not have a claim of right on the money it saved by not engaging in more extensive environmental efforts in 1940-1987 — it is clear that the new obligations did not arise from the same *circumstances, terms,* and *conditions* as the initial failure to spend additional funds on environmental clean-up. Rather, the obligations were created by *new* circumstances, terms, and conditions, namely, by an intervening change in environmental legislation. There is no substantive nexus that can be recognized for our purposes between the waste disposal expenses Alcoa did not incur in 1940 to 1987 and its clean-up expenses in 1993.

Taxpayers' claims have been rejected in analogous situations. For instance, in *Cinergy*, the Court of Federal Claims held that a utility company's "refund" to current customers of payments for deferred taxes made by former customers arose from "subsequent and unrelated events."

55 Fed.Cl. at 508. The "refund" did not arise from a recognition that the "amounts originally collected were excessive or otherwise unneeded"; rather, customers began protesting the utility's rates and, faced with an investigation into the rates' reasonableness, the utility proposed a reduction but paired it with a plan for "accelerated reversal of certain tax reserves" so as to reduce the effect of the impending rate reduction on its equity. Id. The court found that the obligation to reverse the tax reserves did not arise from the same circumstances, terms, and conditions as the original accumulation of the reserves, but from the later dispute with customers and wrote that "nothing in the case law suggests that the requisite nexus is satisfied simply because the receipt of income and its later return both derived from the same regulatory process." Id. Here, the obligation to clean up certain sites — though undoubtedly connected in some way to the earlier polluting activities — did not arise from some inherent fault in Alcoa's waste management choices. The moneys not spent did not fall under the pall of a latent competing claim. Instead, the need to expend money for remediation arose from the more stringent regulations that were *later* enacted.

We conclude then, as the government proposes, that because Alcoa's expenditure of funds in 1993 was not the restoration of particular moneys to the rightful owner and did not arise from the same circumstances, terms, and conditions as Alcoa's original acquisition of the income, Alcoa's 1993 cleanup expenditures do not qualify for the beneficial tax treatment provided under section 1341. See id.

This conclusion appears to be consistent with the language of the statute — although the language of section 1341 is ambiguous in that it does not explain "how a taxpayer or the IRS is supposed to establish that the taxpayer does not have an unrestricted right to income." Chernin v. United States, 149 F.3d 805, 815 (8th Cir.1998). To resolve this ambiguity in the language of the statute, we will turn to the congressional intent revealed in the history and purpose of the statutory scheme. See Adams Fruit Co. v. Barrett, 494 U.S. 638, 642 (1990). The historical background of the statute, recounted in some detail above, strongly suggests that Congress intended to allow taxpayers to reverse their tax liability for funds received and included in the relevant tax return although they were the object of a competing claim. As the Court of Federal Claims found, at the time the statute was enacted, claim of right cases "tend[ed] to coalesce around some dispute over the ownership of income or a mistake of fact, deriving, for example, from a quarrel over the ownership of income producing property, the misapplication of a contract provision, or the payment of funds under a contingency based upon business expectations that were thought to, but actually did not, materialize." *Cinergy*, 55 Fed.Cl. at 500 (citations omitted). The purpose of section 1341 was, quite simply, to ensure that, when the taxpayer found itself to be the losing party in the dispute and had to turn over specific funds to the rightful owner, the taxpayer should be able to recompute its income for the year of receipt so as to entirely reverse the tax liability due to the disputed item.

Legislative history confirms this interpretation. It documents the section's enactment in reaction to the perceived inequity of *Lewis*, supra, and makes repeated references to repayment, restoration, and restitution. See, e.g., H.R.Rep. No. 83-1337, at 86-87, reprinted in 1954 U.S.C.C.A.N. 4017, 4113 ("The committee's bill provides that if the amount *restored* exceeds $3,000, the taxpayer may recompute the tax for the prior year, excluding from income the amount repaid"; "excluding the amount *repaid* from the earlier year's income is likely to have little, if any, tax advantage over taking a deduction in the year of restitution") (emphasis added); S.Rep. No. 83-1622, at 188, reprinted in 1954 U.S.C.C.A.N. 4621, 4751 (same).

> Similarly, the accompanying regulations explain that [i]f, during the taxable year, the taxpayer is entitled under other provisions of chapter 1 of the Internal Revenue Code of 1954 to a deduction of more than $3,000 because of the *restoration to another* of an item which was included in the taxpayer's gross income for a prior taxable year (or years) under a claim of right, the tax imposed by chapter 1 of the Internal Revenue Code of 1954 for the taxable year shall be the tax provided in paragraph (b) of this section.

26 C.F.R. §1.1341-1(a)(1) (emphasis added).[7] Clearly in order to qualify under the section, the taxpayer must show not simply that it is no longer entitled to keep money it has included in an earlier return, but also that it has "restored" it.

Alcoa argues, however, that, even if section 1341 includes a restoration requirement, it does not mean that restoration must be to the taxpayer's customers or to a connected third party. Rather, all the regulations require is restoration "to another," and therefore any "other" to whom moneys are paid will do.

We reject this argument. The requirement that there be a nexus is inherent in the concept of "restoration" itself. It is true, as Alcoa points out, that "restoration to another" is not further defined in the statute or the regulations; the latter merely state, somewhat tautologically, that "restoration to another means a restoration resulting because it was established after the close of [the] prior taxable year (or years) that the taxpayer did not have an unrestricted right to such item (or portion thereof)." 26 C.F.R. §1.1341-1(a)(2). For clarification then we will turn to the dictionary. See Perrin v. United States, 444 U.S. 37, 42 (1979) (it is a fundamental canon of statutory construction that "unless otherwise defined, words will be interpreted as taking their ordinary, contemporary, common meaning").

Webster's Third International Dictionary defines "restore" as: "1: to give back (as something lost or taken away); make restitution of; return . . . .

7. We also note, of course, that the title of section 1341, "Computation of tax where taxpayer restores substantial amount held under claim of right," uses the verb "restore." We do not rely on this, however; although generally "the title of a statute or section can aid in resolving an ambiguity in the legislative text," INS v. Nat'l Ctr. for Immigrants' Rights, 502 U.S. 183, 189 (1991), the Internal Revenue Code's rules of construction provide that no "legal effect" should be given to descriptive matter in the Code. 26 U.S.C. §7806(b).

2: to put or bring back; 3: to bring back to or put back into a former or original state." *Webster's Third International Dictionary Unabridged* 1936 (1971). The American Heritage Dictionary lists "4. To make restitution of; give back; [e.g.,] *restore the stolen funds.*" The American Heritage Dictionary of the English Language 1538 (3d ed., 1992). Clearly, to restore something to another means to give it to the person who either once had it or should have had it all along — in this case, the person with the actual claim of right to the item of income.

Alcoa's argument that the legislative history shows that Congress intended to extend section 1341 benefits to completely unconnected third parties is unavailing. Alcoa grounds its contention on the statement found in both the Senate and House reports that section 1341 would apply to cases of transferee liability such as Arrowsmith v. Comm'r, 344 U.S. 6 (1952). In *Arrowsmith*, a corporation was liquidated, but subsequent to the liquidation a judgment was rendered against it. As a result, the shareholders who had received capital gain income from the liquidation of the corporation were required to disgorge part of that income to satisfy a claim by the corporation's creditor. Somewhat puzzlingly, Alcoa presents this as evidence that Congress intended payments *to anyone* to count. But the references to *Arrowsmith* in the legislative history intimate precisely the opposite. In *Arrowsmith,* the funds received by the shareholders at the time of their corporation's liquidation were partly the object of a competing claim; when that competing claim was perfected, the shareholders were obligated to turn over the funds. There is nothing remarkable about the recognition that section 1341 applies to such an instance — and nothing at all that could be construed as analogous to Alcoa's situation here.

Moreover, for substantially the same reasons given by the District Court in *Reynolds* (and adopted by the District Court here), we decline Alcoa's invitation to follow the Court of Federal Claims' decision in Pennzoil-Quaker State Co. v. United States, 62 Fed.Cl. 689 (Fed.Cl. 2004). See *Reynolds,* 389 F.Supp.2d at 700-702. In *Pennzoil*, the taxpayer, Quaker State, had purchased crude oil from independent oil producers for a period of time. In 1994, a number of these independent producers brought an antitrust action against Quaker State, alleging that Quaker State had engaged in price-fixing of its own products, thereby reducing the price at which the producers could sell their oil to Quaker State. Eventually Quaker State settled the lawsuit for $4.4 million and claimed that the corresponding deduction on the year of the settlement was entitled to Section 1341 treatment. The Court of Federal Claims agreed. *Pennzoil* is both unpersuasive and distinguishable. It is unpersuasive because the decision is based on a number of problematic assumptions, including that Quaker State's COGS during the years of the price-fixing would have been higher without its alleged misconduct and that there was an ascertainable relationship between the settlement amount and the amount by which Quaker State's COGS would have been higher. In addition, *Pennzoil* is distinguishable because even if the *Pennzoil* court's understanding of the facts was correct, there was an identifiable entity—the wholesale oil merchants—who would have received the money had Quaker State not saved it by illegally keeping the wholesale prices down. In Alcoa's case, there simply was never any entity that had a better right to the funds Alcoa deducted in 1993 than Alcoa itself.[8]

The other case Alcoa relies on, Barrett v. Comm'r, 96 T.C. 713 (1991), is no more persuasive. The taxpayers in that case had bought and sold stock options and realized a large short-term capital gain. The Securities & Exchange Commission charged Barrett with using inside information to buy the options and instituted proceedings to cancel his broker's license. Certain other brokers filed suit against Barrett and others, seeking $10 million. The lawsuits were eventually settled, with Barrett paying about $54,000 to the plaintiffs. The Tax Court allowed Barrett to benefit from section 1341 treatment for the settlement amount. In doing so it treated the settlement as directly related to the profit, talking about "the $54,400 of the proceeds from the sale of the options." Id. at 718. After the Tax Court's decision, the I.R.S. declared its non-acquiescence with the decision. 1992-2 C.B. 1. The IRS noted that "[t]he Tax Court in the instant case failed to consider whether there was a nexus between the obligation to repay and the original option profits received by Barrett. Specifically, neither the plaintiffs' complaint nor any other evidence was introduced by either party to establish the grounds for the civil suit, the allegations made in the complaint or the focus of the plaintiffs' discovery." I.R.S. AOD 1992-08, 1992 WL 794825 (March 13, 1992). *Barrett,* like *Pennzoil,* appears to be based on the rationale that the settlement gave back certain funds to persons or entities that had a better right to them, but in each case the analysis was too imprecise to be followed.

In sum, only the most torturous reading of section 1341 could equate Alcoa's expenditures to clean up its sites with restoring moneys to the rightful owner. Under Alcoa's theory, a taxpayer may qualify under section 1341 almost any time that it is faced with an expense that can be related in any way to the fact that the taxpayer did not pay that expense in a prior year. This approach turns the annual accounting system into an illusion.[9]

8. Evidently aware that this is a significant weakness in Alcoa's theory, *amicus* Entergy Corporation argues that the restoration requirement is satisfied because the aim of CERCLA was "to restore to the public the income attributable to the producers' environmental consumption." Like Alcoa's own proposed interpretation of the statute, the argument that the amount not spent by Alcoa in 1940-1987 was somehow restored to "the public" in 1993 is creative but not convincing.

9. Because we reach this result without relying on Revenue Ruling 2004-17, which the IRS issued while the *Reynolds* litigation was ongoing and which addresses the precise issue presented both in *Reynolds* and here, we do not decide what deference it should be accorded. Compare Long Island Care at Home v. Coke, 127 S.Ct. 2339, 2349, 168 L.Ed.2d 54 (2007) (holding that an "Advisory Memorandum" of the Department of Labor, issued only to Department personnel and written in response to the litigation, should be afforded deference because it reflected the Department's fair and considered views developed over many years and did not appear to be a "*post hoc* rationalization" of past agency action) with AMP Inc. and Consol. Subsidiaries v. United States, 185 F.3d 1333, 1338-1339 (Fed.Cir. 1999) ("[a] revenue ruling issued at a time when the I.R.S. is preparing to litigate is often self-serving and not generally entitled to deference by the courts") and Catskill Mtns. Chapter of Trout Unltd. v. City of New York, 273 F.3d 481, 491 (2d Cir. 2001) ("a position adopted in the course of litigation lacks the indicia of expertise, regularity, rigorous consideration, and public scrutiny that justify *Chevron* deference").

IV. CONCLUSION

For the reasons stated above, we will affirm the District Court's grant of the government's motion for summary judgment motion and its denial of Alcoa's.

Note

The definition of "restoration" of an amount earlier included in gross income under claim of right for purposes of §1341 relief is the cognate of the definition of "recovery" for purposes of the exclusionary side of the tax benefit rule, §111(a). See Chapter 3D.2 above. Explain the relationship. Are the doctrines applied symmetrically?

C. *EMBEZZLED FUNDS*

JAMES v. UNITED STATES
366 U.S. 213 (1961)

Mr. Chief Justice WARREN announced the judgment of the Court and an opinion in which Mr. Justice BRENNAN, and Mr. Justice STEWART concur. . . . The petitioner is a union official who, with another person, embezzled in excess of $738,000 during the years 1951 through 1954 from his employer union and from an insurance company with which the union was doing business. Petitioner failed to report these amounts in his gross income in those years and was convicted for willfully attempting to evade the federal income tax due for each of the years 1951 through 1954 in violation of §145(b) of the Internal Revenue Code of 1939 and §7201 of the Internal Revenue Code of 1954. He was sentenced to a total of three years' imprisonment. The Court of Appeals affirmed. 273 F.2d 5. Because of a conflict with this Court's decision in Commissioner v. Wilcox, 327 U.S. 404, a case whose relevant facts are concededly the same as those in the case now before us, we granted certiorari, 362 U.S. 974.

In *Wilcox*, the Court held that embezzled money does not constitute taxable income to the embezzler in the year of the embezzlement under §22(a) of the Internal Revenue Code of 1939. Six years later, this Court held, in Rutkin v. United States, 343 U.S. 130, that extorted money does constitute taxable income to the extortionist in the year that the money is received under §22(a) of the Internal Revenue Code of 1939. In *Rutkin*, the Court did not overrule *Wilcox*, but stated:

"We do not reach in this case the factual situation involved in Commissioner v. Wilcox, 327 U.S. 404. We limit that case to its facts.

There embezzled funds were held not to constitute taxable income to the embezzler under §22(a)." Id., at 138.

However, examination of the reasoning used in *Rutkin* leads us inescapably to the conclusion that *Wilcox* was thoroughly devitalized.

The basis for the *Wilcox* decision was

> that a taxable gain is conditioned upon (1) the presence of a claim of right to the alleged gain and (2) the absence of a definite, unconditional obligation to repay or return that which would otherwise constitute a gain. Without some bona fide legal or equitable claim, even though it be contingent or contested in nature, the taxpayer cannot be said to have received any gain or profit within the reach of section 22(a). [Commissioner v. Wilcox, supra, at p. 408.]

Since Wilcox embezzled the money, held it "without any semblance of a bona fide claim of right," ibid., and therefore "was at all times under an unqualified duty and obligation to repay the money to his employer," ibid., the Court found that the money embezzled was not includible within "gross income." But, Rutkin's legal claim was no greater than that of Wilcox. It was specifically found "that petitioner had no basis for his claim . . . and that he obtained it by extortion." Rutkin v. United States, supra, at p. 135. Both *Wilcox* and *Rutkin* obtained the money by means of a criminal act; neither had a bona fide claim of right to the funds. Nor was Rutkin's obligation to repay the extorted money to the victim any less than that of Wilcox. The victim of an extortion, like the victim of an embezzlement, has a right to restitution. Furthermore, it is inconsequential that an embezzler may lack title to the sums he appropriates while an extortionist may gain a voidable title. Questions of federal income taxation are not determined by such "attenuated subtleties." Lucas v. Earl, 281 U.S. 111, 114; Corliss v. Bowers, 281 U.S. 376, 378. Thus, the fact that Rutkin secured the money with the consent of his victim . . . is irrelevant. Likewise unimportant is the fact that the sufferer of an extortion is less likely to seek restitution than one whose funds are embezzled. What is important is that the right to recoupment exists in both situations.

Examination of the relevant cases in the courts of appeals lends credence to our conclusion that the *Wilcox* rationale was effectively vitiated by this Court's decision in *Rutkin*. Although this case appears to be the first to arise that is "on all fours" with *Wilcox*, the lower federal courts, in deference to the undisturbed *Wilcox* holding, have earnestly endeavored to find distinguishing facts in the cases before them which would enable them to include sundry unlawful gains within "gross income."[9]

---

9. For example, Kann v. Commissioner, 3 Cir., 210 F.2d 247, was differentiated on the following grounds: the taxpayer was never indicted or convicted of embezzlement; there was no adequate proof that the victim did not forgive the misappropriation; the taxpayer was financially able to both pay the income tax and make restitution; the taxpayer would have likely received most of the misappropriated money as dividends. . . .

It had been a well-established principle, long before either *Rutkin* or *Wilcox*, that unlawful, as well as lawful, gains are comprehended within the term "gross income." Section II B of the Income Tax Act of 1913 provided that "the net income of a taxable person shall include gains, profits, and income . . . from . . . the transaction of any *lawful* business carried on for gain or profit, or gains or profits and income derived from any source whatever. . . ." (Emphasis supplied.) 38 Stat. 167. When the statute was amended in 1916, the one word "lawful" was omitted. This revealed, we think, the obvious intent of that Congress to tax income derived from both legal and illegal sources, to remove the incongruity of having the gains of the honest laborer taxed and the gains of the dishonest im-mune. . . . Thereafter, the Court held that gains from illicit traffic in liquor are includible within "gross income." . . . And, the Court has pointed out, with approval, that there "has been a widespread and settled administrative and judicial recognition of the taxability of unlawful gains of many kinds." Rutkin v. United States, supra, at p. 137. These include protection payments made to racketeers, ransom payments paid to kidnappers, bribes, money derived from the sale of unlawful insurance policies, graft, black market gains, funds obtained from the operation of lotteries, income from race track bookmaking and illegal prize fight pictures. Ibid.

The starting point in all cases dealing with the question of the scope of what is included in "gross income" begins with the basic premise that the purpose of Congress was "to use the full measure of its taxing power." . . .

When a taxpayer acquires earnings, lawfully or unlawfully, without the consensual recognition, express or implied, of an obligation to repay and without restriction as to their disposition, "he has received income which he is required to return, even though it may still be claimed that he is not entitled to retain the money, and even though he may still be adjudged liable to restore its equivalent." North American Oil v. Burnet, [Chapter 7B above]. In such case, the taxpayer has "actual command over the property taxed — the actual benefit for which the tax is paid," Corliss v. Bowers, supra. This standard brings wrongful appropriations within the broad sweep of "gross income"; it excludes loans. When a law-abiding taxpayer mistakenly receives income in one year, which receipt is assailed and found to be invalid in a subsequent year, the taxpayer must nonetheless report the amount as "gross income" in the year received. . . . We do not believe that Congress intended to treat a lawbreaking taxpayer differently. Just as the honest taxpayer may deduct any amount repaid in the year in which the repayment is made, the Government points out that, "If, when, and to the extent that the victim recovers back the misappropriated funds, there is of course a reduction in the embezzler's income." Brief for the United States, p. 24.

Petitioner contends that the *Wilcox* rule has been in existence since 1946; that if Congress had intended to change the rule, it would have done so; that there was a general revision of the income tax laws in 1954 without mention of the rule; that a bill to change it was introduced in the Eighty-sixth Congress but was not acted upon; that, therefore, we may not change the rule now. But the fact that Congress has remained silent or has reenacted a statute which we have construed, or that congressional attempts to amend a rule announced by this Court had failed, does not necessarily debar us from re-examining and correcting the Court's own errors. . . . There may have been any number of reasons why Congress acted as it did. . . . One of the reasons could well be our subsequent decision in *Rutkin* which has been thought by many to have repudiated *Wilcox*. Particularly might this be true in light of the decisions of the Courts of Appeals which have been riding a narrow rail between the two cases and further distinguishing them to the disparagement of *Wilcox*. . . .

We believe that *Wilcox* was wrongly decided and we find nothing in congressional history since then to persuade us that Congress intended to legislate the rule. Thus, we believe that we should now correct the error and the confusion resulting from it, certainly if we do so in a manner that will not prejudice those who might have relied on it. . . . We should not continue to confound confusion, particularly when the result would be to perpetuate the injustice of relieving embezzlers of the duty of paying income taxes on the money they enrich themselves with through theft while honest people pay their taxes on every conceivable type of income.

But, we are dealing here with a felony conviction under statutes which apply to any person who "willfully" fails to account for his tax or who "willfully" attempts to evade his obligation. In Spies v. United States, 317 U.S. 492, 499, the Court said that §145(b) of the 1939 Code embodied "the gravest of offenses against the revenues," and stated that willfulness must therefore include an evil motive and want of justification in view of all the circumstances. Id., at 498. Willfulness "involves a specific intent which must be proved by independent evidence and which cannot be inferred from the mere understatement of income." Holland v. United States, 348 U.S. 121, 139.

We believe that the element of willfulness could not be proven in a criminal prosecution for failing to include embezzled funds in gross income in the year of misappropriation so long as the statute contained the gloss placed upon it by *Wilcox* at the time the alleged crime was committed. Therefore, we feel that petitioner's conviction may not stand and that the indictment against him must be dismissed.

Since Mr. Justice HARLAN, Mr. Justice FRANKFURTER, and Mr. Justice CLARK agree with us concerning *Wilcox*, that case is overruled. Mr. Justice BLACK, Mr. Justice DOUGLAS, and Mr. Justice WHITTAKER believe that petitioner's conviction must be reversed and the case dismissed for the reasons stated in their opinions.

Accordingly, the judgment of the Court of Appeals is reversed and the case is remanded to the District Court with directions to dismiss the indictment.

It is so ordered.

Mr. Justice BLACK, whom Mr. Justice DOUGLAS joins, concurring in part and dissenting in part. . . .

. . . The whole picture can best be obtained from the court's opinion in McKnight v. Commissioner,* written by Judge Sibley, one of the ablest circuit judges of his time. He recognized that the taxpayer could not rely upon the unlawfulness of his business to defeat taxation if the ordinary embezzler "got no title, void or voidable, to what he took. He was still in possession as he was before, but with a changed purpose. He still had no right nor color of right. He claimed none."[10] Judge Sibley's opinion went on to point out that the "first takings [of an embezzler] are, indeed, nearly always with the intention of repaying, a sort of unauthorized borrowing. It must be conceded that no gain is realized by borrowing, because of the offsetting obligation." Approaching the matter from a practical standpoint, Judge Sibley also explained that subjecting the embezzled funds to a tax would amount to allowing the United States "a preferential claim for part of the dishonest gain, to the direct loss and detriment of those to whom it ought to be restored."[12] He was not willing to put the owner of funds that had been stolen in competition with the United States Treasury Department as to which one should have a preference to get those funds.

It seems to us that Judge Sibley's argument was then and is now unanswerable. The rightful owner who has entrusted his funds to an employee or agent has troubles enough when those funds are embezzled without having the Federal Government step in with its powerful claim that the embezzlement is a taxable event automatically subjecting part of those funds (still belonging to the owner) to the waiting hands of the Government's tax gatherer. We say part of the *owner's* funds because it is on the supposed "gain" from them that the embezzler is now held to be duty-bound to pay the tax and history probably records few instances of independently wealthy embezzlers who have had non-stolen assets available for payment of taxes.

There has been nothing shown to us on any of the occasions when we have considered this problem to indicate that Congress ever intended its income tax laws to be construed as imposing what is in effect a property or excise tax on the rightful owner's embezzled funds, for which the owner has already once paid income tax when he rightfully acquired them. . . . If Congress ever did manifest an intention to select the mere fact of embezzlement as the basis for imposing a double tax on the owner, we think a serious question of confiscation in violation of the Fifth Amendment would be raised. All of us know that with the strong lien provisions of the federal income tax law an owner of stolen funds would have a very rocky road to travel before he got back, without paying a good slice to the Federal

* 127 F.2d 572 (5th Cir. 1942) — EDS.
10. 127 F.2d, at 573.
12. 127 F.2d, at 574.

Government, such funds as an embezzler who had not paid the tax might, perchance, not have dissipated. An illustration of what this could mean to a defrauded employer is shown in this very case by the employer's loss of some $700,000, upon which the Government claims a tax of $559,000.

It seems to be implied that one reason for overruling *Wilcox* is that a failure to hold embezzled funds taxable would somehow work havoc with the public revenue or discriminate against "honest" taxpayers and force them to pay more taxes. We believe it would be impossible to substantiate either claim. Embezzlers ordinarily are not rich people against whom judgments, even federal tax judgments, can be enforced. Judging from the meager settlements that those defrauded were apparently compelled to make with the embezzlers in this very case, it is hard to imagine that the Treasury will be able to collect the more than $500,000 it claims. . . .

It follows that, except for the possible adverse effect on rightful owners, the only substantial result that one can forsee from today's holding is that the Federal Government will, under the guise of a tax evasion charge, prosecute people for a simple embezzlement. But the Constitution grants power to Congress to get revenue not to prosecute local crimes. And if there is any offense which under our dual system of government is a purely local one which the States should handle, it is embezzlement or theft. . . .

Mr. Justice CLARK, concurring in part and dissenting in part as to the opinion of The Chief Justice. Although I join in the specific overruling of Commissioner v. Wilcox, 327 U.S. 404 (1946), in The Chief Justice's opinion, I would affirm this conviction on either of two grounds. I believe that the court not only devitalized *Wilcox*, by limiting it to its facts in Rutkin v. United States, 343 U.S. 130 (1952), but that in effect the Court overruled that case sub silentio in Commissioner v. Glenshaw Glass Co., 348 U.S. 426 (1955). Even if that not be true, in my view the proof shows conclusively that petitioner, in willfully failing to correctly report his income, placed no bona fide reliance on *Wilcox*.

Mr. Justice HARLAN, whom Mr. Justice FRANKFURTER joins concurring in part and dissenting in part as to the opinion of The Chief Justice. I fully agree with so much of The Chief Justice's opinion as dispatches *Wilcox* to a final demise. But as to the disposition of this case, I think that rather than an outright reversal, which his opinion proposes, the reversal should be for a new trial. . . .

The proper disposition of this case, in my view, is to treat as plain error, Fed. Rules Crim. Proc. 52(b), the failure of the trial court as trier of fact to consider whatever misapprehension may have existed in the mind of the petitioner as to the applicable law, in determining whether the Government had proved that petitioner's conduct had been willful as required by the statute. On that basis I would send the case back for a new trial.

Mr. Justice WHITTAKER, whom Mr. Justice BLACK and Mr. Justice DOUGLAS join, concurring in part and dissenting in part. . . . The Chief Justice's opinion, although it correctly recites *Wilcox*'s holding that "embezzled money does not constitute taxable income to the embezzler *in the year of the embezzlement*" (emphasis added), fails to explain or to answer the true basis of that holding. *Wilcox* did not hold that embezzled funds may never constitute taxable income to the embezzler. To the contrary, it expressly recognized that an embezzler may realize a taxable gain to the full extent of the amount taken, if and when it ever becomes *his*. . . .

. . . *Wilcox* plainly stated that "if the unconditional indebtedness is cancelled or retired taxable income may adhere, under certain circumstances, to the taxpayer." 327 U.S. at 408. More specifically, it recognized that had the embezzler's victim "condoned or forgiven any part of the [indebtedness], the [embezzler] might have been subject to tax liability to that extent," id., at 410, i.e., in the tax year of such forgiveness.

These statements reflect an understanding of, and regard for, substantive tax law concepts solidly entrenched in our prior decisions. Since our landmark case of United States v. Kirby Lumber Co. [Chapter 6A above], it has been settled that, upon a discharge of indebtedness by an event other than full repayment, the debtor realizes a taxable gain in the year of discharge to the extent of the indebtedness thus extinguished. Such gains are commonly referred to as one realized through "bargain cancellations" of indebtedness, and it was in this area, and indeed, in *Kirby Lumber Co.* itself, that the "accession" theory or "economic gain" concept of taxable income, upon which The Chief Justice's opinion today mistakenly relies, found its genesis. . . .

. . . The Chief Justice's opinion quite understandably expresses much concern for "honest taxpayers," but it attempts neither to deny nor justify the manifest injury that its holding will inflict on those honest taxpayers, victimized by embezzlers, who will find their claims for recovery subordinated to federal tax liens. Statutory provisions, by which we are bound, clearly and unequivocally accord priority to federal tax liens over the claims of others, including "judgment creditors."

However, if it later happens that the debtor-creditor relationship between the embezzler and his victim is discharged by something other than full repayment, such as by the running of a Statute of Limitations against the victim's claim, or by a release given for less than the full amount owed, the embezzler at that time, but not before, will have made a clear taxable gain and realized "an accession to income" which he will be required under full penalty of the law to report in his federal income tax return for that year. No honest taxpayer could be harmed by this rule.

The inherent soundness of this rule could not be more clearly demonstrated than as applied to the facts of the case before us. Petitioner, a labor union official, concededly embezzled sums totaling more than $738,000 from the union's funds, over a period extending from 1951 to 1954. When the shortages were discovered in 1956, the union at once filed civil actions against petitioner to compel repayment. For reasons which need not be detailed here, petitioner effected a settlement agreement with the union on July 30, 1958, whereby, in exchange for releases fully discharging his indebtedness, he repaid to the union the sum of $13,568.50. Accordingly, at least so far as the present record discloses, petitioner clearly realized a taxable gain in the year the releases were executed, to the extent of the difference between the amount taken and the sum restored. However, the Government brought the present action against him, not for his failure to report this gain in his 1958 return, but for his failure to report that he had incurred "income" from — actually indebtedness to — the union in each of the years 1951 through 1954. It is true that the Government brought a criminal evasion prosecution rather than a civil deficiency proceeding against petitioner, but this can in no way alter the substantive tax law rules which alone are determinative of liability in either case....

Notes and Questions

1. One of the problems with *Wilcox* was that it encouraged the taxpayer caught with unreported funds to take the position that he had stolen them. In some cases taxpayers claimed to have stolen from closely held corporations in which they were major shareholders. In one celebrated case the Tax Court declined to accept such a defense partly on the ground that the testimony of the taxpayer, who by his own admission was a thief, was not to be believed. Kann v. Commissioner, 18 T.C. 1032 (1952), aff'd 210 F.2d 247 (3d Cir. 1953), cert. denied, 347 U.S. 967 (1954).

How serious was this problem? Did it offer adequate ground for overruling *Wilcox*?

2. How much does *James* leave unclarified? What of Judge Sibley's typical embezzler (described in Justice Black's dissent) who begins his defalcations with the sincere intention of making complete restoration? Is that intention a "consensual recognition, express or implied, of an obligation to repay"? Will there be practical problems about ascertaining when embezzlement income accrues? Are they more or less serious problems than those which arose under *Wilcox*?

3. Is the matter of federal prosecution for state crimes under the guise of income tax evasion a serious problem? Is the criminality of a taxpayer's activity an element in the government's case, or is it only put in issue by the taxpayer's defense?

4. What about the problem of federal tax collector competing unfairly with the victim over the embezzler's few remaining assets? Why did James' victims settle their claims of $738,000 for $13,568.50 (less than 2 percent)?

McKINNEY v. UNITED STATES

76-2 USTC ¶ 9728 (W.D. Tex. 1976), aff'd, 574 F.2d 1240 (5th Cir. 1978)

ROBERTS, District Judge: . . . Plaintiff embezzled $91,702.06 from his employer, Texas Employment Commission, in 1966, culminating a plan originated in 1956, and he reported that amount as miscellaneous income on his 1966 tax return and paid the tax due on it. Subsequently, the embezzlement was discovered, Plaintiff was convicted in state court for the crime, and he repaid the embezzled money to his employer in 1969. Plaintiff claims that he is entitled to special tax treatment as a result of his repayment of the embezzled funds that had been previously included in his income and taxed. Plaintiff claims that he was engaged in the trade or business of embezzling and is therefore entitled to a deduction under §172 of the Internal Revenue Code for a net operating loss carryback to 1966 of the 1969 loss (caused by repayment of the embezzled funds in 1969) incurred in connection with his trade or business of embezzlement. Alternatively, Plaintiff contends that he acquired the embezzled funds under a claim of right so that the repayment of the embezzled funds in 1969 entitles him to the tax benefits of §1341 of the Internal Revenue Code. The Government rejected these claims and allowed plaintiff to deduct the $91,702.06 on his 1969 tax return as a loss incurred in a transaction entered into for profit although not connected with a trade or business, pursuant to §165(c)(2) of the Code. . . .

At the trial, Plaintiff contended that his embezzlement constituted a trade or business. Plaintiff testified that during his high school years, 1924 to 1928, he engaged in a scheme to embezzle money from a high school concession operation and in fact successfully embezzled some amount between $1,000 and $2,000. Plaintiff also testified that he successfully embezzled approximately $58,000 from his employer, Texas Employment Commission, in 1956, and that the embezzlement scheme which is the subject of the instant suit constituted his third embezzlement. Plaintiff contended that he spent approximately fifty percent of all his working time between 1956 and 1966 carrying out the embezzlement scheme that resulted in the embezzlement of the $91,702.06 in 1966. On the strength of these three embezzlements, Plaintiff contended that he was in the trade or business of being an embezzler and as such his repayment of the embezzled money in 1969 constituted an expense connected with his trade or business, and thus, was deductible under §172 net operating loss carryback provisions. On cross examination, the Government brought out the fact that no one knew of these embezzlements prior to the discovery of the last embezzlement in 1969, and that Plaintiff had told no one of any of these schemes. The government also brought out the fact that when Plaintiff reported the embezzled funds as income in 1966, they were reported as miscellaneous income, "windfall," rather than as income from a trade or business.

The Internal Revenue Code does not set out a definition of the term trade or business. . . . Even assuming that embezzlement can theoretically be a trade or business for tax purposes, the Court does not find that Plaintiff's activities were sufficient to constitute a trade or business under §172 of the Internal Revenue Code. Despite Plaintiff's claims, at best, Plaintiff was only an occasional embezzler, and his true trade or business was an employee of the Texas Employment Commission. Plaintiff did not continuously engage in embezzlement as an attempt to earn a livelihood, but as an occasional lark, to see if he could successfully complete the crime. Furthermore, the Court is of the opinion that as a matter of law embezzlement is not a trade or business for §172 purposes. Rev. Rule 65-254, 1965-2 Cum. Bull. 50. There are good policy reasons for not allowing trade or business treatment of repaid embezzled funds. To allow an embezzler to get the benefits of the §172 net operating loss carryback would place him in a much more advantageous position taxwise than he would otherwise be in, and thus it would tend to encourage the commission of this crime. Such a result would be adverse to both policy and comity considerations. See Tank Truck Rentals, Inc. v. Commissioner, 356 U.S. 30 (1958). Thus, the Court holds that as a matter of law an embezzler is not entitled to the benefits of a deduction under §172 when embezzled funds are repaid, and that even if an embezzler were entitled to the benefits of the deduction under §172 for the repayment of the embezzled funds, the plaintiff in the instant suit has not shown that he was in the trade or business of embezzling.

Plaintiff contends that . . . in the alternative, he is entitled to the tax benefits available under §1341 which provide a special tax benefit rule if an item was included in gross income for a prior taxable year because it appeared that the taxpayer had an unrestricted right to such item and it is then determined in a later tax year that the taxpayer did not have an unrestricted right to the item included in income. The crucial issue, for the purpose of this case, is whether Plaintiff had an unrestricted right to the embezzled money in 1966, or as the question is otherwise stated, whether the Plaintiff had a claim of right to the money which he embezzled in 1966. . . .

. . . In Commissioner v. Wilcox, 327 U.S. 404 (1946), the Supreme Court held that an embezzler who had obtained money without any claim of right did not have any taxable income as a result of the embezzlement. The opinion implied that embezzled funds could never be acquired in a manner that would constitute being obtained with a claim of right. In James v. United States, 366 U.S. 213 (1961), the Supreme Court overruled the holding of the *Wilcox* case, holding that embezzled money must be included in gross income whether or not the embezzler held the money under a claim of right. The heart of the argument that an embezzler is entitled to §1341 tax benefits upon the repayment of embezzled money must rest on the contention that when the Supreme Court overruled the *Wilcox* holding that embezzled funds were not gross income, it also reversed the *Wilcox* decision that an embezzler does not hold embezzled funds under a claim of right.

It seems almost too clear for argument that funds received through embezzlement and held by an embezzler are not held under a claim of right or with the appearance that the embezzler has an unrestricted right to the use of the embezzled funds. Furthermore, Plaintiff's argument that he held the embezzled funds under a claim of right and therefore is entitled to §1341 benefits is made more doubtful by the fact that Plaintiff has previously indicated that he did not believe he held the funds in question under a claim of right. In a claim for refund filed with the Internal Revenue service on April 14, 1970 (when Plaintiff apparently believed that it would be to his benefit to so state), the Plaintiff admitted that the embezzled funds "did not belong to me in 1966." (Defendant's exhibit "H".) Furthermore, Plaintiff admitted in a protest filed with the Internal Revenue service on February 24, 1971 (also when he thought the argument would be to his benefit), that "the unlawful earnings acquired by me, if any, and if at any time, were not held by me without restriction as to their disposition." (Defendant's exhibit "I".) Thus, even if it were possible for embezzled funds to be held under a claim of right, the Plaintiff has previously admitted that he did not hold the embezzled funds in question under a claim of right. Plaintiff also admitted in testimony adduced at trial that he included the embezzled funds in income in 1966 not because he believed that he held them under a claim of right, but because he knew of the Supreme Court's holding in the *James* case and therefore included them in income because the Supreme Court had required embezzled funds to be included in income.

... The Internal Revenue service has long interpreted §1341 as not applying to the repayment of embezzled funds. Rev. Rul. 65-254, 1965-2 Cum. Bull. 50. In addition, every court that has faced this issue has denied the embezzler the benefits of §1341. See Hankins v. United States, 36 A.F.T.R. 2d 6008 (N.D. Miss. September 25, 1975). It should also be noted that the same policy and comity considerations that militate against giving the Plaintiff the benefits of §172 also militate against giving him the benefits of §1341. . . .

Accordingly, it is ordered, adjudged and decreed that judgment be, and hereby is, granted for Defendant, and that the relief requested by the Plaintiffs be, and hereby is, denied. This Memorandum Opinion and Order shall constitute findings of facts and conclusions of law.

D.   NONRECOURSE BORROWING

CRANE v. COMMISSIONER
331 U.S. 1 (1947)

Mr. Chief Justice VINSON delivered the opinion of the Court. The question here is how a taxpayer who acquires depreciable property subject to an unassumed mortgage, holds it for a period, and finally sells it still so encumbered, must compute her taxable gain.

Petitioner was the sole beneficiary and the executrix of the will of her husband, who died January 11, 1932. He then owned an apartment building and lot subject to a mortgage,[1] which secured a principal debt of $255,000.00 and interest in default of $7,042.50. As of that date, the property was appraised for federal estate tax purposes at a value exactly equal to the total amount of this encumbrance. Shortly after her husband's death, petitioner entered into an agreement with the mortgagee whereby she was to continue to operate the property — collecting the rents, paying for necessary repairs, labor, and other operating expenses, and reserving $200.00 monthly for taxes — and was to remit the net rentals to the mortgagee. This plan was followed for nearly seven years, during which period petitioner reported the gross rentals as income, and claimed and was allowed deductions for taxes and operating expenses paid on the property, for interest paid on the mortgage, and for the physical exhaustion of the building. Meanwhile, the arrearage of interest increased to $15,857.71. On November 29, 1938, with the mortgagee threatening foreclosure, petitioner sold to a third party for $3,000.00 cash, subject to the mortgage, and paid $500.00 expenses of sale.

Petitioner reported a taxable gain of $1,250.00. Her theory was that the "property" which she had acquired in 1932 and sold in 1938 was only the equity, or the excess in the value of the apartment building and lot over the amount of the mortgage. This equity was of zero value when she acquired it. No depreciation could be taken on a zero value.[2] Neither she nor her vendee ever assumed the mortgage, so, when she sold the equity, the amount she realized on the sale was the net cash received, or $2,500.00. This sum less the zero basis constituted her gain, of which she reported half as taxable on the assumption that the entire property was a "capital asset."

The Commissioner, however, determined that petitioner realized a net taxable gain of $23,767.03. His theory was that the "property" acquired and sold was not the equity, as petitioner claimed, but rather the physical property, itself, or the owner's rights to possess, use, and dispose of it, undiminished by the mortgage. The original basis thereof was $262,042.50, its appraised value in 1932. Of this value $55,000.00 was allocable to land and $207,042.50 to building. During the period that petitioner held the property, there was an allowable depreciation of $28,045.10 on the building, so that the adjusted basis of the building at the time of sale was $178,997.40. The amount realized on the sale was said to include not only the $2,500.00 net cash receipts, but also the principal amount[6] of the mortgage subject to

1. The record does not show whether he was personally liable for the debt.
2. This position is, of course, inconsistent with her practice in claiming such deductions in each of the years the property was held. The deductions so claimed and allowed by the Commissioner were in the total amount of $25,500.00.
6. The Commissioner explains that only the principal amount, rather than the total present debt secured by the mortgage, was deemed to be a measure of the amount realized, because the difference was attributable to interest due, a deductible item.

which the property was sold, both totaling $257,500.00. The selling price was allocable in the proportion, $54,471.15 to the land and $203,028.85 to the building. The Commissioner agreed that the land was a "capital asset," but thought that the building was not. Thus, he determined that petitioner sustained a capital loss of $528.85 on the land, of which 50 percent or $264.42 was taken into account, and an ordinary gain of $24,031.45 on the building, or a net taxable gain as indicated.

The Tax Court agreed with the Commissioner that the building was not a "capital asset." In all other respects it adopted petitioner's contentions, and expunged the deficiency. Petitioner did not appeal from the part of the ruling adverse to her, and these questions are no longer at issue. On the Commissioner's appeal, the Circuit Court of Appeals reversed, one judge dissenting. We granted certiorari because of the importance of the questions raised as to the proper construction of the gain and loss provisions of the Internal Revenue Code.

The 1938 Act, §111(a), defines the gain from "the sale or other disposition of property" as "the excess of the amount realized therefrom over the adjusted basis provided in section 113(b). . . ." It proceeds, §111(b), to define "the amount realized from the sale or other disposition of property" as "the sum of any money received plus the fair market value of the property (other than money) received." Further, in §113(b), the "adjusted basis for determining the gain or loss from the sale or other disposition of property" is declared to be "the basis determined under subsection (a), adjusted . . . [(1)(B)] . . . for exhaustion, wear and tear, obsolescence, amortization . . . to the extent allowed (but not less than the amount allowable). . . ." The basis under subsection (a) "if the property was acquired by . . . devise . . . or by the decedent's estate from the decedent," §113(a)(5), is "the fair market value of such property at the time of such acquisition."

Logically, the first step under this scheme is to determine the unadjusted basis of the property, under §113(a)(5), and the dispute in this case is as to the construction to be given the term "property." If "property," as used in that provision, means the same thing as "equity," it would necessarily follow that the basis of petitioner's property was zero, as she contends. If, on the contrary, it means the land and building themselves, or the owner's legal rights in them, undiminished by the mortgage, the basis was $262,042.50.

We think that the reasons for favoring one of the latter constructions are of overwhelming weight. In the first place, the words of statutes — including revenue acts — should be interpreted where possible in their ordinary, everyday senses. The only relevant definitions of "property" to be found in the principal standard dictionaries[14] are the two favored by the Commissioner, i.e., either that "property" is the physical thing which is a subject of

---

14. See Webster's New International Dictionary, Unabridged, 2d ed.; Funk & Wagnalls' New Standard Dictionary; Oxford English Dictionary.

ownership, or that it is the aggregate of the owner's rights to control and dispose of that thing. "Equity" is not given as a synonym, nor do either of the foregoing definitions suggest that it could be correctly so used. Indeed, "equity" is defined as "the value of a property . . . above the total of the liens. . . ."[15] The contradistinction could hardly be more pointed. Strong countervailing considerations would be required to support a contention that Congress, in using the word "property," meant "equity," or that we should impute to it the intent to convey that meaning.

In the second place, the Commissioner's position has the approval of the administrative construction of §113(a)(5). With respect to the valuation of property under that Section, Reg. 101, Art. 113(a)(5)-1, promulgated under the 1938 Act, provided that "the value of property as of the date of the death of the decedent as appraised for the purpose of the Federal estate tax . . . shall be deemed to be its fair market value. . . ." The land and building here involved were so appraised in 1932, and their appraised value — $262,042.50 — was reported by petitioner as part of the gross estate. This was in accordance with the estate tax law and regulations, which had always required that the value of decedent's property, undiminished by liens, be so appraised and returned, and that mortgages be separately deducted in computing the net estate. As the quoted provision of the Regulations has been in effect since 1918, and as the relevant statutory provision has been repeatedly reenacted since then in substantially the same form, the former may itself now be considered to have the force of law.

Moreover, in the many instances in other parts of the Act in which Congress has used the word "property," or expressed the idea of "property" or "equity," we find no instances of a misuse of either word or of a confusion of the ideas. In some parts of the Act other than the gain and loss sections, we find "property" where it is unmistakably used in its ordinary sense.[24] On the other hand, where either Congress or the Treasury intended to convey the meaning of "equity," it did so by the use of appropriate language.

A further reason why the word "property" in §113(a) should not be construed to mean "equity" is the bearing such construction would have on the allowance of deductions for depreciation and on the collateral adjustments of basis.

Section 23(1) permits deduction from gross income of "a reasonable allowance for the exhaustion, wear and tear of property. . . ." Sections 23(n) and 14(a) declare that the "basis upon which exhaustion, wear and tear . . . are to be allowed" is the basis "provided in Section 113(b) for the purpose of determining the gain upon the sale" of the property, which is the §113(a)

---

15. See Webster's New International Dictionary, supra.

24. Sec. 23(a)(1) permits the deduction from gross income of "rentals . . . required to be made as a condition to the continued use . . . for purposes of the trade or business, of *property* . . . in which he [the taxpayer] has no *equity*." (Italics supplied.)

Sec. 23(1) permits the deduction from gross income of "a reasonable allowance for the exhaustion, wear and tear of *property* used in the trade or business. . . ." (Italics supplied.)

basis "adjusted . . . for exhaustion, wear and tear . . . to the extent allowed (but not less than the amount allowable). . . ."

Under these provisions, if the mortgagor's equity were the §113(a) basis, it would also be the original basis from which depreciation allowances are deducted. If it is, and if the amount of the annual allowances were to be computed on that value, as would then seem to be required,[26] they will represent only a fraction of the cost of the corresponding physical exhaustion, and any recoupment by the mortgagor of the remainder of that cost can be effected only by the reduction of his taxable gain in the year of sale. If, however, the amount of the annual allowances were to be computed on the value of the property, and then deducted from an equity basis, we would in some instances have to accept deductions from a minus basis or deny deductions altogether. The Commissioner also argues that taking the mortgagor's equity as the §113(a) basis would require the basis to be changed with each payment on the mortgage, and that the attendant problem of repeatedly recomputing basis and annual allowances would be a tremendous accounting burden on both the Commissioner and the taxpayer. Moreover, the mortgagor would acquire control over the timing of his depreciation allowances.

Thus it appears that the applicable provisions of the Act expressly preclude an equity basis, and the use of it is contrary to certain implicit principles of income tax depreciation, and entails very great administrative difficulties. It may be added that the Treasury has never furnished a guide through the maze of problems that arise in connection with depreciating an equity basis, but, on the contrary, has consistently permitted the amount of depreciation allowances to be computed on the full value of the property, and subtracted from it as a basis. Surely, Congress' long-continued acceptance of this situation gives it full legislative endorsement.

We conclude that the proper basis under §113(a)(5) is the value of the property, undiminished by mortgages thereon, and that the correct basis here was $262,042.50. The next step is to ascertain what adjustments are required under §113(b). As the depreciation rate was stipulated, the only question at this point is whether the Commissioner was warranted in making any depreciation adjustments whatsoever.

Section 113(b)(1)(B) provides that "proper adjustment in respect of the property *shall in all cases be made* . . . for exhaustion, wear and tear . . . to the extent allowed (but not less than the amount allowable). . . ." (Italics supplied.) The Tax Court found on adequate evidence that the apartment house was property of a kind subject to physical exhaustion, that it was used in taxpayer's trade or business, and consequently that the taxpayer would have been entitled to a depreciation allowance under §23(1), except that, in

---

26. Secs. 23(n) and 114(a), in defining the "basis upon which" depreciation is "to be allowed," do not distinguish between basis as the minuend from which the allowances are to be deducted, and as the dividend from which the amount of the allowance is to be computed. The Regulations indicate that the basis of property is the same for both purposes. Reg. 101, Art. 23(1)-4, 5.

the opinion of that Court, the basis of the property was zero, and it was thought that depreciation could not be taken on a zero basis. As we have just decided that the correct basis of the property was not zero, but $262,042.50, we avoid this difficulty, and conclude that an adjustment should be made as the Commissioner determined.

Petitioner urges to the contrary that she was not entitled to depreciation deductions, whatever the basis of the property, because the law allows them only to one who actually bears the capital loss, and here the loss was not hers but the mortgagee's. We do not see, however, that she has established her factual premise. There was no finding of the Tax Court to that effect, nor to the effect that the value of the property was ever less than the amount of the lien. Nor was there evidence in the record, or any indication that petitioner could produce evidence, that this was so. The facts that the value of the property was only equal to the lien in 1932 and that during the next six and one-half years the physical condition of the building deteriorated and the amount of the lien increased, are entirely inconclusive, particularly in the light of the buyer's willingness in 1938 to take subject to the increased lien and pay a substantial amount of cash to boot. Whatever may be the rule as to allowing depreciation to a mortgagor on property in his possession which is subject to an unassumed mortgage and clearly worth less than the lien, we are not faced with that problem and see no reason to decide it now.

At last we come to the problem of determining the "amount realized" from "the sale . . . of property" as "the sum of any money received plus the fair market value of the property (other than money) received," and §111(a) defines the gain on "the sale . . . of property" as the excess of the amount realized over the basis. Quite obviously, the word "property," used here with reference to a sale, must mean "property" in the same ordinary sense intended by the use of the word with reference to acquisition and depreciation in §113, both for certain of the reasons stated heretofore in discussing its meaning in §113, and also because the functional relation of the two sections requires that the word mean the same in one section that it does in the other. If the "property" to be valued on the date of acquisition is the property free of liens, the "property" to be priced on a subsequent sale must be the same thing.

Starting from this point, we could not accept petitioner's contention that the $2,500.00 net cash was all she realized on the sale except on the absurdity that she sold a quarter-of-a-million dollar property for roughly one percent of its value, and took a 99 percent loss. Actually, petitioner does not urge this. She argues, conversely, that because only $2,500.00 was realized on the sale, the "property" sold must have been the equity only, and that consequently we are forced to accept her contention as to the meaning of "property" in §113. We adhere, however, to what we have already said on the meaning of "property," and we find that the absurdity is avoided by our conclusion that the amount of the mortgage is properly included in the "amount realized" on the sale.

Petitioner concedes that if she had been personally liable on the mortgage and the purchaser had either paid or assumed it, the amount so paid or assumed would be considered a part of the "amount realized" within the meaning of §111(b). The cases so deciding have already repudiated the notion that there must be an actual receipt by the seller himself of "money" or "other property," in their narrowest senses. It was thought to be decisive that one section of the Act must be construed so as not to defeat the intention of another or to frustrate the Act as a whole, and that the taxpayer was the "beneficiary" of the payment in "as real and substantial [a sense] as if the money had been paid it and then paid over by it to its creditors."

Both these points apply to this case. The first has been mentioned already. As for the second, we think that a mortgagor, not personally liable on the debt, who sells the property subject to the mortgage and for additional consideration, realizes a benefit in the amount of the mortgage as well as the boot.[37] If a purchaser pays boot, it is immaterial as to our problem whether the mortgagor is also to receive money from the purchaser to discharge the mortgage prior to sale, or whether he is merely to transfer subject to the mortgage — it may make a difference to the purchaser and to the mortgagee, but not to the mortgagor. Or put in another way, we are no more concerned with whether the mortgagor is, strictly speaking, a debtor on the mortgage, than we are with whether the benefit to him is, strictly speaking, a receipt of money, or property. We are rather concerned with the reality that an owner of property, mortgaged at a figure less than that at which the property will sell, must and will treat the conditions of the mortgage exactly as if they were his personal obligations. If he transfers subject to the mortgage, the benefit to him is as real and substantial as if the mortgage were discharged, or as if a personal debt in an equal amount had been assumed by another.

Therefore we conclude that the Commissioner was right in determining that petitioner realized $257,500.00 on the sale of this property.

The Tax Court's contrary determinations, that "property," as used in §113(a) and related sections, means "equity," and that the amount of a mortgage subject to which property is sold is not the measure of a benefit realized, within the meaning of §111(b), announced rules of general applicability on clear-cut questions of law. The Circuit Court of Appeals therefore had jurisdiction to review them.

Petitioner contends that the result we have reached taxes her on what is not income within the meaning of the Sixteenth Amendment. If this is

---

37. Obviously, if the value of the property is less than the amount of the mortgage, a mortgagor who is not personally liable cannot realize a benefit equal to the mortgage. Consequently, a different problem might be encountered where a mortgagor abandoned the property or transferred it subject to the mortgage without receiving boot. That is not this case.

because only the direct receipt of cash is thought to be income in the constitutional sense, her contention is wholly without merit. If it is because the entire transaction is thought to have been "by all dictates of common sense . . . a ruinous disaster," as it was termed in her brief, we disagree with her premise. She was entitled to depreciation deductions for a period of nearly seven years, and she actually took them in almost the allowable amount. The crux of this case, really, is whether the law permits her to exclude allowable deductions from consideration in computing gain.[42] We have already showed that, if it does, the taxpayer can enjoy a double deduction, in effect, on the same loss of assets. The Sixteenth Amendment does not require that result any more than does the Act itself.

Affirmed.

Mr. Justice JACKSON, dissenting. The Tax Court concluded that this taxpayer acquired only an equity worth nothing. The mortgage was in default, the mortgage debt was equal to the value of the property, any possession by the taxpayer was forfeited and terminable immediately by foreclosure, and perhaps by a receiver pendente lite. Arguments can be advanced to support the theory that the taxpayer received the whole property and thereupon came to owe the whole debt. Likewise it is argued that when she sold she transferred the entire value of the property and received release from the whole debt. But we think these arguments are not so conclusive that it was not within the province of the Tax Court to find that she received an equity which at that time had a zero value. Dobson v. Commissioner, 320 U.S. 489; Commissioner v. Scottish American Investment Co., Ltd., 323 U.S. 119. The taxpayer never became personally liable for the debt, and hence when she sold she was released from no debt. The mortgage debt was simply a subtraction from the value of what she did receive, and from what she sold. The subtraction left her nothing when she acquired it and a small margin when she sold it. She acquired a property right equivalent to an equity of redemption and sold the same thing. It was the "property" bought and sold as the Tax Court considered it to be under the Revenue Laws. We are not required in this case to decide whether depreciation was properly taken, for there is no issue about it here.

We would reverse the Court of Appeals and sustain the decision of the Tax Court.

Mr. Justice FRANKFURTER and Mr. Justice DOUGLAS join in this opinion.

---

42. In the course of the argument some reference was made, as by analogy, to a situation in which a taxpayer acquired by devise property subject to a mortgage in an amount greater than the then value of the property, and later transferred it to a third person, still subject to the mortgage, and for a cash boot. Whether or not the difference between the value of the property on acquisition and the amount of the mortgage would in that situation constitute either statutory or constitutional income is a question which is different from the one before us, and which we need not presently answer.

PARKER v. DELANEY
186 F.2d 455 (1st Cir. 1950), cert. denied, 341 U.S. 926 (1951)

Before Magruder, Chief Judge, and Woodbury and Fahy, Circuit Judges.

FAHY, Circuit Judge. [Taxpayer acquired certain rental real estate by agreement, paying nothing but taking subject to a defaulted mortgage. During his ownership depreciation deductions totalled $45,280.48 and principal payments on the mortgage were $13,989.38. Finally, the mortgage being in default, the taxpayer reconveyed by quit-claim deed to the mortgagee, receiving nothing.

The taxpayer argued that the absence of boot distinguished this case from *Crane*, pointing to footnote 37 in the *Crane* opinion. The court rejected that argument since it had not been shown that the property was worth *less* than the mortgage.]

MAGRUDER, Chief Judge (concurring). I concur. The logic of the court's opinion is inescapable, with Crane v. Commissioner, 331 U.S. 1, as the starting point.

As an original matter, I would have had some difficulty in understanding how the taxpayer in the *Crane* case realized more than $3,000 from her sale of the mortgaged property there involved, in view of the definition of "amount realized" in §111(b) of the Internal Revenue Code. By the same token in the case at bar, under the more natural and obvious reading of §111(b), it would seem that the amount realized by the taxpayer herein was zero, when he caused his straw man to quitclaim to the banks, for no cash consideration, properties then subject to mortgages up to their full value, the taxpayer not being liable on the mortgage debt. To reach the conclusion that the taxpayer thereby "realized" the amount of the outstanding mortgage debt would seem to require a somewhat esoteric interpretation of the statutory language. Also, I do not clearly understand why the Treasury allowed the taxpayer deductions for depreciation, under §§23(*l*) and (n) and §114(a), in the total amount of $45,280.48, taking the taxpayer's original "cost" basis as the amount of the mortgages, though he made no cash investment in the properties upon acquisition, nor did he obligate himself on the mortgage debt. But that matter need not concern us here, because depreciation in the amount of $45,280.48 was in fact "allowed"; and under §113(b), the adjusted basis for determining gain or loss from the sale or other disposition of the property takes account of depreciation "to the extent allowed (but not less than the amount allowable)" under the income tax laws.

Perhaps the net result reached by the court here might be arrived at by another mode of computation with less strain upon the statutory language. Thus, the adjusted basis for determining gain or loss under §113(b) might be computed as follows: Original cost, zero, plus $13,989.38, the total amount which taxpayer paid in reduction of the mortgage debt while he held the properties, minus $45,280.48, the amount of depreciation "allowed," which comes out to an adjusted basis of minus $31,291.10. Now, apply that adjusted basis of minus $31,291.10 to the computation of gain or loss under the formula in §113(a): The "amount realized" upon taxpayer's disposition of the properties, zero (as suggested above), minus the adjusted basis as computed under §113(b), or in other words, minus $31,291.10 subtracted from zero, comes out to a plus figure of $31,291.10, representing the amount of the taxpayer's gain, upon which the tax would be computed.

Notes

1. *Types of debt.* (a) *General unsecured obligations.* If a person borrows money or otherwise incurs a debt by promising to make payment, the resulting obligation is normally enforceable by way of a personal judgment, which can be collected by levying on the debtor's property generally (subject to statutory exemptions for a certain minimum amount and kind of property conceived to be essential to getting along in the world). It can even be enforced against property acquired after the obligation was incurred. If a debtor becomes overburdened there may be contests among the creditors for his assets, and bankruptcy procedures exist in part to provide for more even treatment of creditors than a mere race to the courthouse would accomplish. But so far as the debtor is concerned, substantially all his property is subject to these debts.

(b) *Secured obligations.* A lender may demand a security interest in particular property of a debtor as a condition to extending credit. Such a security interest, particularly in the case of real estate, is commonly called a mortgage. A mortgage usually takes the form of a property conveyance from the debtor to the creditor, but with provisions that it will not take effect so long as the debtor complies with the payment terms and other conditions of his primary obligation. The mortgage is recorded in the registry of deeds as a real estate conveyance so that any purchaser of the mortgaged property, including any subsequent mortgagee, will have notice.

A mortgage enables a creditor to enforce his claim by foreclosing on the mortgaged property. In most situations the creditor can cause the mortgaged property to be sold and the proceeds applied to his loan. If the proceeds of the foreclosure sale exceed the amount due on the mortgage debt, then the excess goes to the debtor; on the other hand, if the foreclosure sale proceeds are less than the amount of the debt, the creditor would ordinarily be entitled to proceed against the debtor personally, and his other property, for the deficiency.

So far as the debtor is directly concerned, giving a mortgage does not generally expand or contract his risk. The mortgaged property would have been among the assets available upon enforcement of his personal obligation anyway, and his other property remains exposed upon enforcement of his personal liability even if it was not included in the mortgage. (The main cost to a debtor of giving a mortgage is the restriction it will impose on his securing credit from other potential creditors.)

So far as the creditor is concerned, the effect of the mortgage is to give him two rights instead of one: a right to foreclose on the mortgaged property and a right to proceed against the debtor personally. He can pursue either or both of these rights until his debt has been collected in full. The most important direct effect of this is between the mortgagee and other creditors of the debtor. In the event of default and foreclosure, the mortgagee will get all the proceeds of sale of the mortgaged property up to the amount of his obligation and will still be able to share equally in any other property until his claim is satisfied in full.

(c) *Nonrecourse obligations.* A nonrecourse obligation is a secured obligation that is not accompanied by a personal obligation to repay because the debtor has somehow avoided or eliminated personal liability. It is a liability with respect to which the creditor has the same rights of foreclosure as any other secured creditor, but cannot proceed against the debtor personally or against the debtor's other property if foreclosure sale proceeds do not cover the full amount of the obligation. In the case of an ordinary secured obligation a creditor is said to have recourse against the debtor personally for any deficiency upon foreclosure; in a nonrecourse loan the creditor bears the risk of deficiency without any such recourse.

Nonrecourse obligations can arise in a variety of ways. *Crane* illustrates what was once perhaps the most common: Property is acquired, by inheritance or gift or even purchase, subject to a preexisting mortgage granted by the transferor (or some other previous owner). In such a case the mortgagee's rights against the property continue unabated by the transfer — otherwise mortgages would not serve their purpose. But the transferee does not incur personal liability just by taking subject to the mortgage, and so the mortgage becomes a nonrecourse liability as to him. The personal obligation of the original mortgagor is also unabated by the mere transfer, and so the creditor can still proceed against the transferor if there is a default. If the transferor paid the liability and the transfer had been subject to the liability, then the transferor would be entitled to proceed against the property for reimbursement. Taking property subject to a mortgage means that the transferee must pay the debt in order to keep the property, even though there is no recourse against him personally or his other assets if the property itself turns out to be insufficient.

Today it is not uncommon to create an obligation that is nonrecourse from the beginning. This is particularly common in the case of income-producing real estate because often the creditor will be relying chiefly on the security value of the property in any event. It is easy to imagine how the added security to a lender from having passive investors personally liable may be worth much less than the added peace of mind to be gained by investors from knowing that while they may lose what they have invested, the rest of their assets (and prospects) are not at risk. If this is the case, then the increase in interest charged by a lender for lending nonrecourse may readily be less than the value to the borrower and one would expect some loans to take this form. Lending and borrowing nonrecourse is similar in many respects to incorporation of a business that might have been conducted in person or through a partnership. Both represent ways in which risks of loss, beyond a certain point, may be carried by creditors rather than borrowers.

There was once some uncertainty about whether a mortgage would itself be valid in the absence of a full recourse loan to be secured, but the imagination of lawyers was sufficient to eliminate this problem through the use of the "dummy" or "straw man."[4] Pursuant to a preexisting plan, these individuals would buy a piece of real estate, giving an ordinary full-recourse note secured by a mortgage in payment of the price, and then either hold the property for the benefit of the real owner or turn around and convey the property to the real purchasers subject to the mortgage. The effect of either of these arrangements would be to make the dummy personally liable for any deficiency that might emerge, but straw men qualified for this line of work by avoiding ownership of anything of value. They were not necessarily poor in living condition, but their wealth was not held in their own names. All this might seem a bit dubious except that it was done with full acquiescence of the creditors whose rights were at issue.

Today, in most jurisdictions at least, one can create a nonrecourse obligation simply by specifying in the note that its obligation is enforceable only against the security without recourse of any kind against the obligor for any deficiency.

In at least one case, nonrecourse liability is today prescribed by law without any indication that the parties intended such an arrangement. That is in California where no suit for a deficiency is permitted in the case of any purchase money residential mortgage.[5] Why do you suppose this provision has not been adopted elsewhere?

2. *Depreciation.* If Mrs. Crane had inherited an apartment building free of any debt or mortgage, she clearly would have been entitled to deduct depreciation on the building in computing her taxable income, even if the building failed to produce any net profit. See §167(a). Depreciation deductions would have been computed by spreading the basis of the building over its estimated useful life and deducting each year's share as the year went by; the basis for determining gain or loss would then be adjusted downward by the amount of depreciation deducted. §1016(a)(2).

In filing her income tax returns for years during which she held the property, Mrs. Crane acted on the assumption that the encumbrance did not impair her ability to deduct depreciation. The government did not contest

---

4. See, e.g., Parker v. Delaney, at p. 464 above, and Woodsam Associates, Inc. v. Commissioner, at pp. 481, 482 below.

5. Cal. Civ. Proc. Code §580b (West 1989); Note, Will Refinancing Your Home Mortgage Risk Your Life Savings?: Refinancing and California Code of Civil Procedure Section 580b, 43 UCLA L. Rev. 2077 (1996).

her right to deduct depreciation; indeed it argued affirmatively, in the principal case, that she was entitled to deduct what she had deducted and even a little more. Under these circumstances, it is perhaps not surprising that the Supreme Court effectively affirmed the propriety of those deductions. Perhaps not surprising, but was it wise? We will return to some of the consequences of that affirmance in Chapters 15 and 16 below.

Once depreciation is allowed in excess of actual investment it is not surprising that the government and courts should find a corresponding amount of gain in excess of actual sale proceeds on disposition of the property. Chief Justice Vinson's opinion in *Crane* and Judge Magruder's concurring opinion in *Parker* illustrate two lines of reasoning by which such gain can be computed. How do they differ, in result or implications? The main substantive difference between them is probably that *Crane* affirms the propriety of the taxpayer's prior depreciation deductions while *Parker* would not.

3. *Negative basis.* Consider carefully the relationship between and relative merits of the analysis in *Crane* and the negative-basis analysis in the *Parker* concurrence. You need to learn and absorb the reasoning in *Crane* because it is the law of the land. You should learn and absorb the negative-basis reasoning in *Parker* too, because it often provides an easier way to compute gain and a check on computations under *Crane*. In complicated transactions the amount of each individual investor's liabilities is often not clear; *Parker* provides a way of computing gain or loss on disposition without finding out. The result should be the same as under a *Crane* computation because whatever gets added to basis on account of indebtedness under *Crane* should also be added to amount realized so that in the end the amount of liabilities makes no difference under either rule. Can you think of any situations in which the two theories would fail to produce the same result?

4. *"Ordinary, everyday senses."* *Crane* is frequently cited for the assertion that "the words of statutes—including revenue acts—should be interpreted where possible in their ordinary, everyday senses." What do you think of that assertion? What do you think of *Crane* as authority for it?

1. Inadequately Secured Nonrecourse Debt

COMMISSIONER v. TUFTS
461 U.S. 300, rehg. denied, 463 U.S. 1215 (1983)

Justice BLACKMUN delivered the opinion of the Court.

Over 35 years ago, in Crane v. Commissioner, 331 U.S. 1 (1947), this Court ruled that a taxpayer, who sold property encumbered by a nonrecourse mortgage (the amount of the mortgage being less than the property's value), must include the unpaid balance of the mortgage in the computation of the amount the taxpayer realized on the sale. The case now before us presents the question whether the same rule applies when the unpaid amount of the nonrecourse mortgage exceeds the fair market value of the property sold.

I

On August 1, 1970, respondent Clark Pelt, a builder, and his wholly owned corporation, respondent Clark, Inc., formed a general partnership. The purpose of the partnership was to construct a 120-unit apartment complex in Duncanville, Tex., a Dallas suburb. Neither Pelt nor Clark, Inc., made any capital contribution to the partnership. Six days later, the partnership entered into a mortgage loan agreement with the Farm & Home Savings Association (F&H). Under the agreement, F&H was committed for a $1,851,500 loan for the complex. In return, the partnership executed a note and a deed of trust in favor of F&H. The partnership obtained the loan on a nonrecourse basis: neither the partnership nor its partners assumed any personal liability for repayment of the loan. Pelt later admitted four friends and relatives, respondents Tufts, Steger, Stephens, and Austin, as general partners. None of them contributed capital upon entering the partnership.

The construction of the complex was completed in August 1971. During 1971, each partner made small capital contributions to the partnership; in 1972, however, only Pelt made a contribution. The total of the partners' capital contributions was $44,212. In each tax year, all partners claimed as income tax deductions their allocable shares of ordinary losses and depreciation. The deductions taken by the partners in 1971 and 1972 totalled $439,972. Due to these contributions and deductions, the partnership's adjusted basis in the property in August 1972 was $1,455,740.

In 1971 and 1972, major employers in the Duncanville area laid off significant numbers of workers. As a result, the partnership's rental income was less than expected, and it was unable to make the payments due on the mortgage. Each partner, on August 28, 1972, sold his partnership interest to an unrelated third party, Fred Bayles. As consideration, Bayles agreed to reimburse each partner's sale expenses up to $250; he also assumed the nonrecourse mortgage.

On the date of transfer, the fair market value of the property did not exceed $1,400,000. Each partner reported the sale on his federal income tax return and indicated that a partnership loss of $55,740 had been sustained.[1] The Commissioner of Internal Revenue, on audit, determined that the sale resulted in a partnership capital gain of approximately $400,000. His theory

---

1. The loss was the difference between the adjusted basis, $1,455,740, and the fair market value of the property, $1,400,000. On their individual tax returns, the partners did not claim deductions for their respective shares of this loss. In their petitions to the Tax Court, however, the partners did claim the loss.

was that the partnership had realized the full amount of the nonrecourse obligation.[2]

Relying on Millar v. Commissioner, 577 F.2d 212, 215 (CA3), cert. denied, 439 U.S. 1046 (1978), the United States Tax Court, in an unreviewed decision, upheld the asserted deficiencies. 70 T.C. 756 (1978). The United States Court of Appeals for the Fifth Circuit reversed. 651 F.2d 1058 (1981). That court expressly disagreed with the *Millar* analysis, and, in limiting Crane v. Commissioner, supra, to its facts, questioned the theoretical underpinnings of the *Crane* decision. We granted certiorari to resolve the conflict. 456 U.S. 960 (1982).

II

Section 752(d) specifically provides that liabilities incurred in the sale or exchange of a partnership interest are to "be treated in the same manner as liabilities in connection with the sale or exchange of property not associated with partnerships." Section 1001 governs the determination of gains and losses on the disposition of property. Under §1001 (a), the gain or loss from a sale or other disposition of property is defined as the difference between "the amount realized" on the disposition and the property's adjusted basis. Subsection (b) of §1001 defines "amount realized": "The amount realized from the sale or other disposition of property shall be the sum of any money received plus the fair market value of the property (other than money) received." At issue is the application of the latter provision to the disposition of property encumbered by a nonrecourse mortgage of an amount in excess of the property's fair market value.

A

In Crane v. Commissioner, supra, this Court took the first and controlling step toward the resolution of this issue. Beulah B. Crane was the sole beneficiary under the will of her deceased husband. At his death in January 1932, he owned an apartment building that was then mortgaged for an amount which proved to be equal to its fair market value, as determined for federal estate tax purposes. The widow, of course, was not personally liable on the mortgage. She operated the building for nearly seven years, hoping to turn it into a profitable venture; during that period, she claimed income tax deductions for depreciation, property taxes, interest, and

---

2. The Commissioner determined the partnership's gain on the sale by subtracting the adjusted basis, $1,455,740, from the liability assumed by Bayles, $1,851,500. Of the resulting figure, $395,760, the Commissioner treated $348,661 as capital gain, pursuant to §741 . . . and $47,099 as ordinary gain under the recapture provisions of §1250 of the Code. The application of §1250 in determining the character of the gain is not at issue here.

operating expenses, but did not make payments upon the mortgage principal. In computing her basis for the depreciation deductions, she included the full amount of the mortgage debt. In November 1938, with her hopes unfulfilled and the mortgagee threatening foreclosure, Mrs. Crane sold the building. The purchaser took the property subject to the mortgage and paid Crane $3,000; of that amount, $500 went for the expenses of the sale.

Crane reported a gain of $2,500 on the transaction. She reasoned that her basis in the property was zero (despite her earlier depreciation deductions based on including the amount of the mortgage) and that the amount she realized from the sale was simply the cash she received. The Commissioner disputed this claim. He asserted that Crane's basis in the property, under [§1014] was the property's fair market value at the time of her husband's death, adjusted for depreciation in the interim, and that the amount realized was the net cash received plus the amount of the outstanding mortgage assumed by the purchaser.

In upholding the Commissioner's interpretation of [§1014] the Court observed that to regard merely the taxpayer's equity in the property as her basis would lead to depreciation deductions less than the actual physical deterioration of the property, and would require the basis to be recomputed with each payment on the mortgage. 331 U.S., at 9-10. The Court rejected Crane's claim that any loss due to depreciation belonged to the mortgagee. The effect of the Court's ruling was that the taxpayer's basis was the value of the property undiminished by the mortgage. Id., at 11.

The court next proceeded to determine the amount realized under [§1001(b)]. In order to avoid the "absurdity," see 331 U.S., at 13, of Crane's realizing only $2,500 on the sale of property worth over a quarter of a million dollars, the Court treated the amount realized as it had treated basis, that is, by including the outstanding value of the mortgage. To do otherwise would have permitted Crane to recognize a tax loss unconnected with any actual economic loss. The Court refused to construe one section of the Revenue Act so as "to frustrate the Act, as a whole." Ibid.

Crane, however, insisted that the nonrecourse nature of the mortgage required different treatment. The Court, for two reasons, disagreed. First, excluding the nonrecourse debt from the amount realized would result in the same absurdity and frustration of the Code. Id., at 13-14. Second, the Court concluded that Crane obtained an economic benefit from the purchaser's assumption of the mortgage identical to the benefit conferred by the cancellation of personal debt. Because the value of the property in that case exceeded the amount of the mortgage, it was in Crane's economic interest to treat the mortgage as a personal obligation; only by so doing could she realize upon sale the appreciation in her equity represented by the $2,500 boot. The purchaser's assumption of the liability thus resulted in a taxable economic benefit to her, just as if she had been given, in addition to the boot, a sum of cash sufficient to satisfy the mortgage.[4]

In a footnote, pertinent to the present case, the Court observed:

> Obviously, if the value of the property is less than the amount of the mortgage, a mortgagor who is not personally liable cannot realize a benefit equal to the mortgage. Consequently, a different problem might be encountered where a mortgagor abandoned the property or transferred it subject to the mortgage without receiving boot. That is not this case. [Id., at 14, n.37.]

B

This case presents that unresolved issue. We are disinclined to overrule *Crane*, and we conclude that the same rule applies when the unpaid amount of the nonrecourse mortgage exceeds the value of the property transferred. *Crane* ultimately does not rest on its limited theory of economic benefit; instead, we read *Crane* to have approved the Commissioner's decision to treat a nonrecourse mortgage in this context as a true loan. This approval underlies *Crane*'s holdings that the amount of the nonrecourse liability is to be included in calculating both the basis and the amount realized on disposition. That the amount of the loan exceeds the fair market value of the property thus becomes irrelevant.

When a taxpayer receives a loan, he incurs an obligation to repay that loan at some future date. Because of this obligation, the loan proceeds do not qualify as income to the taxpayer. When he fulfills the obligation, the repayment of the loan likewise has no effect on his tax liability.

Another consequence to the taxpayer from this obligation occurs when the taxpayer applies the loan proceeds to the purchase price of property used to secure the loan. Because of the obligation to repay, the taxpayer is entitled to include the amount of the loan in computing his basis in the property; the loan, under §1012, is part of the taxpayer's cost of the property. Although a different approach might have been taken with respect to a nonrecourse mortgage loan,[5] the Commissioner has chosen to accord it

---

4. Crane also argued that even if the statute required the inclusion of the amount of the nonrecourse debt, that amount was not Sixteenth Amendment income because the overall transaction had been "by all dictates of common sense . . . a ruinous disaster." Brief for Petitioner in Crane v. Commissioner, O.T. 1946, No. 68, p. 51. The Court noted, however, that Crane had been entitled to and actually took depreciation deductions for nearly seven years. To allow her to exclude sums on which those deductions were based from the calculation of her taxable gain would permit her "a double deduction . . . on the same loss of assets." The Sixteenth Amendment, it was said, did not require that result. 331 U.S., at 15-16.

5. The Commissioner might have adopted the theory, implicit in Crane's contentions, that a nonrecourse mortgage is not true debt, but, instead, is a form of joint investment by the mortgagor and the mortgagee. On this approach, nonrecourse debt would be considered a contingent liability, under which the mortgagor's payments on the debt gradually increase his interest in the property while decreasing that of the mortgagee. Note, Federal Income Tax Treatment of Nonrecourse Debt, 82 Colum. L. Rev. 1498, 1514 (1982); Lurie, Mortgagor's Gain on Mortgaging Property for More than Cost Without Personal Liability, 6 Tax. L. Rev. 319, 323 (1951); cf. Brief for Respondents 16 (nonrecourse debt resembles preferred stock). Because the taxpayer's investment in the property would not include the nonrecourse debt, the taxpayer would not be permitted to include that debt in basis. Note, 82 Colum. L. Rev., at 1515:

the same treatment he gives to a recourse mortgage loan. The Court approved that choice in *Crane*, and the respondents do not challenge it here. The choice and its resultant benefits to the taxpayer are predicated on the assumption that the mortgage will be repaid in full.

When encumbered property is sold or otherwise disposed of and the purchaser assumes the mortgage, the associated extinguishment of the mortgagor's obligation to repay is accounted for in the computation of the amount realized.[6] See United States v. Hendler, 303 U.S. 564, 566-567 (1938). Because no difference between recourse and nonrecourse obligations is recognized in calculating basis,[7] *Crane* teaches that the Commissioner may ignore the nonrecourse nature of the obligation in determining the amount realized upon disposition of the encumbered property. He thus may include in the amount realized the amount of the nonrecourse mortgage assumed by the purchaser. The rationale for this treatment is that the original inclusion of the amount of the mortgage in basis rested on the assumption that the mortgagor incurred an obligation to repay. Moreover, this treatment balances the fact that the mortgagor originally received the proceeds of the nonrecourse loan tax-free on the same assumption. Unless the outstanding amount of the mortgage is deemed to be realized, the mortgagor effectively will have received untaxed income at the time the loan was extended and will have received an unwarranted increase in the basis of his property.[8] The Commissioner's interpretation of §1001(b) in this fashion cannot be said to be unreasonable.

---

cf. Gibson Products Co. v. United States, 637 F.2d 1041, 1047-1048 (CA5 1981) (contingent nature of obligation prevents inclusion in basis of oil and gas leases of nonrecourse debt secured by leases, drilling equipment, and percentage of future production).

6. In this case, respondents received the face value of their note as loan proceeds. If respondents initially had given their note at a discount, the amount realized on the sale of the securing property might be limited to the funds actually received. See Commissioner v. Rail Joint Co., 61 F.2d 751, 752 (CA2 1932) (cancellation of indebtedness); Fashion Park, Inc. v. Commissioner, 21 T.C. 600, 606 (1954) (same). See generally J. Sneed, The Configurations of Gross Income 319 (1967) ("[I]t appears settled that the reacquisition of bonds at a discount by the obligor results in gain only to the extent the issue price, where this is less than par, exceeds the cost of reacquisition").

7. The Commissioner's choice in *Crane* "laid the foundation stone of most tax shelters." Bittker, Tax Shelters, Nonrecourse Debt, and the *Crane* Case, 33 Tax. L. Rev. 277, 283 (1978), by permitting taxpayers who bear no risk to take deductions on depreciable property. Congress recently has acted to curb this avoidance device by forbidding a taxpayer to take depreciation deductions in excess of amounts he has at risk in the investment. §465. Real estate investments, however, are exempt from this prohibition. §465(c)(3)(D). Although this congressional action may foreshadow a day when nonrecourse and recourse debts will be treated differently, neither Congress nor the Commissioner has sought to alter *Crane*'s rule of including nonrecourse liability in both basis and the amount realized.

8. Although the *Crane* rule has some affinity with the tax benefit rule, see Bittker, supra, at 282; Del Cotto, Sales and Other Dispositions of Property Under Section 1001: The Taxable Event, Amount Realized and Related Problems of Basis, 26 Buffalo L. Rev. 219, 323-324 (1977), the analysis we adopt is different. Our analysis applies even in the situation in which no deductions are taken. It focuses on the obligation to repay and its subsequent extinguishment, not on the taking and recovery of deductions. See generally Note, 82 Colum. L. Rev., at 1526-1529.

C

The Commissioner in fact has applied this rule even when the fair market value of the property falls below the amount of the nonrecourse obligation. Treas. Reg. §1.1001-2(b);[9] Rev. Rul. 76-111, 1976-1 Cum. Bull. 214. Because the theory on which the rule is based applies equally in this situation, see Millar v. Commissioner, 67 T.C. 656, 660 (1977), aff'd on this issue, 577 F.2d 212, 215-216 (3d Cir. 1978), cert. denied, 439 U.S. 1046 (1978);[10] Mendham Corp. v. Commissioner, 9 T.C. 320, 323-324 (1947); Lutz & Schramm Co. v. Commissioner, 1 T.C. 682, 688-689 (1943), we have no reason, after *Crane*, to question this treatment.[11]

Respondents received a mortgage loan with the concomitant obligation to repay by the year 2012. The only difference between that mortgage and one on which the borrower is personally liable is that the mortgagee's remedy is limited to foreclosing on the securing property. This difference does not alter the nature of the obligation; its only effect is to shift from the borrower to the lender any potential loss caused by devaluation of the property.[12] If the fair market value of the property falls below the amount of the outstanding obligation, the mortgagee's ability to protect its interests is impaired, for the mortgagor is free to abandon the property to the mortgagee and be relieved of his obligation.

This, however, does not erase the fact that the mortgagor received the loan proceeds tax-free and included them in his basis on the understanding that he had an obligation to repay the full amount. See Woodsam Associates, Inc. v. Commissioner, 198 F.2d 357, 359 (2d Cir. 1952); Bittker, 33 Tax. L. Rev., at 284. . . . When the obligation is canceled, the mortgagor is relieved of his responsibility to repay the sum he originally received and thus realizes value to that extent within the meaning of §1001(b). From the mortgagor's point of view, when his obligation is assumed by a third party who purchases

9. The regulation was promulgated while this case was pending before the Court of Appeals for the Fifth Circuit. T.D. 7741, 45 Fed. Reg. 81743, 1981-1 Cum. Bull. 430 (1980). It merely formalized the Commissioner's prior interpretation, however.

10. The Court of Appeals for the Third Circuit in *Millar* affirmed the Tax Court on the theory that inclusion of nonrecourse liability in the amount realized was necessary to prevent the taxpayer from enjoying a double deduction. 577 F.2d, at 215: cf. n.4, supra. Because we resolve the question on another ground, we do not address the validity of the double deduction rationale.

11. Professor Wayne G. Barnett, as amicus in the present case, argues that the liability and property portions of the transaction should be accounted for separately. Under his view, there was a transfer of the property for $1.4 million, and there was a cancellation of the $1.85 million obligation for a payment of $1.4 million. The former resulted in a capital loss of $50,000, and the latter in the realization of $450,000 of ordinary income. Taxation of the ordinary income might be deferred under §108 by a reduction of respondents' bases in their partnership interests.

12. In his opinion for the Court of Appeals in *Crane*, Judge Learned Hand observed:

[The mortgagor] has all the income from the property; he manages it; he may sell it; any increase in its value goes to him; any decrease falls on him, until the value goes below the amount of the lien. . . . When therefore upon a sale the mortgagor makes an allowance to the vendee of the amount of the lien, he secures a release from a charge upon his property quite as though the vendee had paid him the full price on condition that before he took title the lien should be cleared.

153 F.2d 504, 506 (2d Cir. 1945).

the encumbered property, it is as if the mortgagor first had been paid with cash borrowed by the third party from the mortgagee on a nonrecourse basis, and then had used the cash to satisfy his obligation to the mortgagee.

Moreover, this approach avoids the absurdity the Court recognized in *Crane*. Because of the remedy accompanying the mortgage in the nonrecourse situation, the depreciation in the fair market value of the property is relevant economically only to the mortgagee, who by lending on a nonrecourse basis remains at risk. To permit the taxpayer to limit his realization to the fair market value of the property would be to recognize a tax loss for which he has suffered no corresponding economic loss.[13] Such a result would be to construe "one section of the Act . . . so as . . . to defeat the intention of another or to frustrate the Act as a whole." 331 U.S., at 13.

In the specific circumstances of *Crane*, the economic benefit theory did support the Commissioner's treatment of the nonrecourse mortgage as a personal obligation. The footnote in *Crane* acknowledged the limitations of that theory when applied to a different set of facts. *Crane* also stands for the broader proposition, however, that a nonrecourse loan should be treated as a true loan. We therefore hold that a taxpayer must account for the proceeds of obligations he has received tax-free and included in basis. Nothing in either §1001(b) or in the Court's prior decisions requires the Commissioner to permit a taxpayer to treat a sale of encumbered property asymmetrically, by including the proceeds of the nonrecourse obligation in basis but not accounting for the proceeds upon transfer of the encumbered property. See Estate of Levine v. Commissioner, 634 F.2d 12, 15 (2d Cir. 1980).

III

Relying on the Code's §752(c), however, respondents argue that Congress has provided for precisely this type of asymmetrical treatment in the sale or disposition of partnership property. Section 752 prescribes the Tax treatment of certain partnership transactions, and §752(c) provides that "[f]or purposes of this section, a liability to which property is subject shall, to the extent of the fair market value of such property, be considered as a liability of the owner of the property." Section 752(c) could be read to apply to a sale or disposition of partnership property, and thus to limit the

---

13. In the present case, the Government bore the ultimate loss. The nonrecourse mortgage was extended to respondents only after the planned complex was endorsed for mortgage insurance under §§221(b) and (d)(4) of the National Housing Act, 12 U.S.C. §1715(b) and (d)(4) (1976 ed. and Supp. V). After acquiring the complex from respondents, Bayles operated it for a few years, but was unable to make it profitable. In 1974, F&H foreclosed, and the Department of Housing and Urban Development paid off the lender to obtain title. In 1976, the Department sold the complex to another developer for $1,502,000. The sale was financed by the Department's taking back a note for $1,314,800 and a nonrecourse mortgage. To fail to recognize the value of the nonrecourse loan in the amount realized, therefore, would permit respondents to compound the Government's loss by claiming the tax benefits of that loss for themselves.

amount realized to the fair market value of the property transferred. Inconsistent with this interpretation, however, is the language of §752(d), which specifically mandates that partnership liabilities be treated "in the same manner as liabilities in connection with the sale or exchange of property not associated with partnerships." The apparent conflict of these subsections renders the facial meaning of the statute ambiguous, and therefore we must look to the statute's structure and legislative history.

... In light of the above, we interpret subsection (c) to apply only to §752(a) and (b) transactions, and not to limit the amount realized in a sale or exchange of a partnership interest under §752(d).

IV

When a taxpayer sells or disposes of property encumbered by a nonrecourse obligation, the Commissioner properly requires him to include among the assets realized the outstanding amount of the obligation. The fair market value of the property is irrelevant to this calculation. We find this interpretation to be consistent with Crane v. Commissioner, 331 U.S. 1 (1947), and to implement the statutory mandate in a reasonable manner. National Muffler Dealers Assn. v. United States, 440 U.S. 472, 476 (1979).

The judgment of the Court of Appeals is therefore reversed.

Justice O'CONNOR, concurring. I concur in the opinion of the Court, accepting the view of the Commissioner. I do not, however, endorse the Commissioner's view. Indeed, were we writing on a slate clean except for the *Crane* decision, I would take quite a different approach — that urged upon us by Professor Barnett as *amicus*.

Crane established that a taxpayer could treat property as entirely his own, in spite of the "coinvestment" provided by his mortgagee in the form of a nonrecourse loan. That is, the full basis of the property, with all its tax consequences, belongs to the mortgagor. That rule alone, though, does not in any way tie nonrecourse debt to the cost of property or to the proceeds upon disposition. I see no reason to treat the purchase, ownership, and eventual disposition of property differently because the taxpayer also takes out a mortgage, an independent transaction. In this case, the taxpayer purchased property, using nonrecourse financing, and sold it after it declined in value to a buyer who assumed the mortgage. There is no economic difference between the events in this case and a case in which the taxpayer buys property with cash; later obtains a nonrecourse loan by pledging the property as security; still later, using cash on hand, buys off the mortgage for the market value of the devalued property; and finally sells the property to a third party for its market value.

The logical way to treat both this case and the hypothesized case is to separate the two aspects of these events and to consider, first, the ownership and sale of the property, and second, the arrangement and retirement of the loan. Under *Crane*, the fair market value of the property on the date of acquisition — the purchase price — represents the taxpayer's basis in the property, and the fair market value on the date of disposition represents the proceeds on sale. The benefit received by the taxpayer in return for the property is the cancellation of a mortgage that is worth no more than the fair market value of the property, for that is all the mortgagee can expect to collect on the mortgage. His gain or loss on the disposition of the property equals the difference between the proceeds and the cost of acquisition. Thus, the taxation of the transaction *in property* reflects the economic fate of the *property*. If the property has declined in value, as was the case here, the taxpayer recognizes a loss on the disposition of the property. The new purchaser then takes as his basis the fair market value as of the date of the sale. See, e.g., United States v. Davis, 370 U.S. 65, 72 (1962); Gibson Products Co. v. United States, 637 F.2d 1041, 1045, n.8 (5th Cir. 1981) (dictum); See generally Treas. Reg. §1.1001-2(a)(3) (1982); B. Bittker, 2 Federal Income Taxation of Income, Estates and Gifts, 41.2.2, at 41-10, 41-11 (1981).

In the separate borrowing transaction, the taxpayer acquires cash from the mortgagee. He need not recognize income at that time, of course, because he also incurs an obligation to repay the money. Later, though, when he is able to satisfy the debt by surrendering property that is worth less than the face amount of the debt, we have a classic situation of cancellation of indebtedness, requiring the taxpayer to recognize income in the amount of the difference between the proceeds of the loan and the amount for which he is able to satisfy his creditor. §61(a)(12). The taxation of the financing transaction then reflects the economic fate of the loan.

The reason that separation of the two aspects of the events in this case is important is, of course, that the Code treats different sorts of income differently. A gain on the sale of the property may qualify for capital gains treatment, §§1202, 1221, while the cancellation of indebtedness is ordinary income, but income that the taxpayer may be able to defer. §§108, 1017. Not only does Professor Barnett's theory permit us to accord appropriate treatment to each of the two types of income or loss present in these sorts of transactions, it also restores continuity to the system by making the taxpayer-seller's proceeds on the disposition of property equal to the purchaser's basis in the property. Further, and most important, it allows us to tax the events in this case in the same way that we tax the economically identical hypothesized transaction.

Persuaded though I am by the logical coherence and internal consistency of this approach, I agree with the Court's decision not to adopt it judicially. We do not write on a slate marked only by *Crane*. The Commissioner's longstanding position, Rev. Rul. 76-111, 1976-1 C.B. 214, is now reflected in the regulations. Treas. Reg. §1.1001-2 (1982). In the light of the numerous cases in the lower courts including the amount of the unrepaid proceeds of the mortgage in the proceeds on sale or disposition. See, e.g., Estate of Levine v. Commissioner, 634 F.2d 12, 15 (CA2 1980); Millar v.

Commissioner, 577 F.2d 212 (CA3), cert. denied, 439 U.S. 1046 (1978); Estate of Delman v. Commissioner, 73 T.C. 15, 28-30 (1979), Peninsula Properties Co., Ltd. v. Commissioner, 47 B.T.A. 84, 92 (1942), it is difficult to conclude that the Commissioner's interpretation of the statute exceeds the bounds of his discretion. As the Court's opinion demonstrates, his interpretation is defensible. One can reasonably read §1001(b)'s reference to "the amount realized *from* the sale or other disposition of property" (emphasis added) to permit the Commissioner to collapse the two aspects of the transaction. As long as his view is a reasonable reading of §1001(b), we should defer to the regulations promulgated by the agency charged with interpretation of the statute. National Muffler Dealers Association v. United States, 440 U.S. 472, 488-489 (1979); United States v. Correll, 389 U.S. 299, 307 (1967); see also Fulman v. United States, 434 U.S. 528, 534 (1978). Accordingly, I concur.

Notes

1. What is Bayles' basis for the building after the transaction in *Tufts*?[6]
2. The result in *Tufts* is apparently now codified in §7701(g). What effect does the statutory provision have? Is this form of codification a good idea?

REVENUE RULING 91-31
1991-1 C.B. 19

ISSUE

If the principal amount of an undersecured nonrecourse debt is reduced by the holder of the debt who was not the seller of the property securing the debt, does this debt reduction result in the realization of discharge of indebtedness income for the year of the reduction under section 61(a)(12) of the Internal Revenue Code or in the reduction of the basis in the property securing the debt?

FACTS

In 1988, individual A borrowed $1,000,000 from C and signed a note payable to C for $1,000,000 that bore interest at a fixed market rate payable annually. A had no personal liability with respect to the note, which was secured by an office building valued at $1,000,000 that A acquired from B with the proceeds of the nonrecourse financing. In 1989, when the value of

---

6. Cf. Estate of Franklin, Chapter 16A.

the office building was $800,000 and the outstanding principal on the note was $1,000,000, C agreed to modify the terms of the note by reducing the note's principal amount to $800,000. The modified note bore adequate stated interest within the meaning of section 1274(c)(2).

The facts here do not involve the bankruptcy, insolvency, or qualified farm indebtedness of the taxpayer. Thus, the specific exclusions provided by section 108(a) do not apply.

LAW AND ANALYSIS

Section 61(a)(12) of the Code provides that gross income includes income from the discharge of indebtedness. Section 1.61-12(a) of the Income Tax Regulations provides that the discharge of indebtedness, in whole or in part, may result in the realization of income.

In Rev. Rul. 82-202, 1982-2 C.B. 35, a taxpayer prepaid the mortgage held by a third party lender on the taxpayer's residence for less than the principal balance of the mortgage. At the time of the prepayment, the fair market value of the residence was greater than the principal balance of the mortgage. The revenue ruling holds that the taxpayer realizes discharge of indebtedness income under section 61(a)(12) of the Code, whether the mortgage is recourse or nonrecourse and whether it is partially or fully prepaid. Rev. Rul. 82-202 relies on United States v. Kirby Lumber Co., 284 U.S. 1 (1931), X-2 C.B. 356 (1931), in which the United States Supreme Court held that a taxpayer realized ordinary income upon the purchase of its own bonds in an arm's length transaction at less than their face amount.

In Commissioner v. Tufts, 461 U.S. 300 (1983) the Supreme Court held that when a taxpayer sold property encumbered by a nonrecourse obligation that exceeded the fair market value of the property sold, the amount realized included the amount of the obligation discharged. The Court reasoned that because a nonrecourse note is treated as a true debt upon inception (so that the loan proceeds are not taken into income at that time), a taxpayer is bound to treat the nonrecourse note as a true debt when the taxpayer is discharged from the liability upon disposition of the collateral, notwithstanding the lesser fair market value of the collateral. See section 1.1001-2(c), Example 7, of the Income Tax Regulations.

In Gershkowitz v. Commissioner, 88 T.C. 984 (1987), the Tax Court, in a reviewed opinion, concluded, in part, that the settlement of a nonrecourse debt of $250,000 for a $40,000 cash payment (rather than surrender of the $2,500 collateral) resulted in $210,000 of discharge of indebtedness income. The court, following the *Tufts* holding that income results when a taxpayer is discharged from liability for an undersecured nonrecourse obligation upon the disposition of the collateral, held that the discharge from a portion of the liability for an undersecured nonrecourse obligation through a cash settlement must also result in income.

The Service will follow the holding in *Gershkowitz* where a taxpayer is discharged from all or a portion of a nonrecourse liability when there is no disposition of the collateral. Thus, in the present case, A realizes $200,000 of discharge of indebtedness income in 1989 as a result of the modification of A's note payable to C.

In an earlier Board of Tax Appeals decision, Fulton Gold Corp. v. Commissioner, 31 B.T.A. 519 (1934), a taxpayer purchased property without assuming an outstanding mortgage and subsequently satisfied the mortgage for less than its face amount. In a decision based on unclear facts, the Board of Tax Appeals, for purposes of determining the taxpayer's gain or loss upon the sale of the property in a later year, held that the taxpayer's basis in the property should have been reduced by the amount of the mortgage debt forgiven in the earlier year.

The *Tufts* and *Gershkowitz* decisions implicitly reject any interpretation of *Fulton Gold* that a reduction in the amount of a nonrecourse liability by the holder of the debt who was not the seller of the property securing the liability results in a reduction of the basis in that property, rather than discharge of indebtedness income for the year of the reduction. *Fulton Gold,* interpreted in this manner, is inconsistent with *Tufts* and *Gershkowitz*. Therefore, that interpretation is rejected and will not be followed.

HOLDING

The reduction of the principal amount of an undersecured nonrecourse debt by the holder of a debt who was not the seller of the property securing the debt results in the realization of discharge of indebtedness income under section 61(a)(12) of the Code.

EFFECT ON OTHER REVENUE RULINGS

Rev. Rul. 82-202 is amplified to apply whether the fair market value of the residence is greater or less than the principal balance of the mortgage at the time of the refinancing.

Problems

1. Charlotte inherited a piece of property worth $250,000, subject to a mortgage of $300,000, which she did not assume. After three years, the property having come around somewhat (due to a decrease in the vacancy rate) she sold the property, still subject to the mortgage, for a net cash payment of $25,000. How should this series of events be reflected on Charlotte's income tax returns?

2. Allan owned property subject to a nonrecourse mortgage in default. The mortgagee added defaulted interest to principal and also paid real estate taxes on the property in order to protect its security interest. These, too, were added to the mortgage principal, pursuant to its terms. Allan, an accrual basis taxpayer, took deductions for both the interest and the taxes. Later when the property was disposed of, the government took the position that an amount of the *Crane*-gain equal to the interest and taxes was ordinary income rather than capital gain. What do you think?[7]

2. Mortgaging Out

In the foregoing cases the excess of nonrecourse debt over basis arose from depreciation deductions, which the IRS and the Supreme Court seem to have thought should be allowed. But there is another way such an excess can arise: if a taxpayer owns a piece of property whose value exceeds its basis, a bank or other lender may well lend money in excess of basis (for purposes other than acquisition of the property, since the borrower already owns it). Such a transaction is commonly called "mortgaging out." The word "out" apparently refers to the owner's investment, including gain, and indicates a disinvestment transaction, as compared with an acquisition, which often involves some net investment even if it is subject to a mortgage.

How should mortgaging out be treated for income tax purposes? Consider the following series of events:

1. W buys property for $100x$ in cash.
2. It goes up in value to $250x$.
3. W mortgages out for $175x$ on a nonrecourse basis.
4. The property declines in value to $170x$.
5. W sells, subject to the mortgage for a net cash price of $10x$.[8]

How much gain should be taxed to *W*? When? Why?

WOODSAM ASSOCIATES, INC. v. COMMISSIONER
198 F.2d 357 (2d Cir. 1952)

Before Swan, Chief Judge, and Chase and Clark, Circuit Judges.
CHASE, Circuit Judge. . . . On December 29, 1934, Samuel J. Wood and his wife organized the petitioner and each transferred to it certain property in return for one-half of its capital stock. One piece of property so transferred by Mrs. Wood was the above mentioned parcel of improved real estate

---

7. See Allan v. Commissioner, 856 F.2d 1169 (8th Cir. 1987).
8. Is that a reasonable price for a purchaser to pay? Why?

consisting of land in the City of New York and a brick building thereon divided into units suitable for use, and used, in retail business. The property was subject to a $400,000 mortgage on which Mrs. Wood was not personally liable and on which the petitioner never became personally liable. Having, thus, acquired the property in a tax free exchange, [§351], the petitioner took the basis of Mrs. Wood for tax purposes [§362(a)]. Upon the final disposition of the property at the foreclosure sale there was still due upon the mortgage the principal amount of $381,000 and, as the petitioner concedes,[1] the extent to which the amount of the mortgage exceeds its adjusted basis was income taxable to it even though it was not personally liable upon the mortgage. Crane v. Commissioner [p. 456 above].

Turning now to the one item whose effect upon the calculation of the petitioner's adjusted basis is disputed, the following admitted facts need to be stated. Mrs. Wood bought the property on January 20, 1922 at a total cost of $296,400. She paid $101,400 in cash, took the title subject to an existing mortgage for $120,000 and gave a purchase money bond and second mortgage for $75,000. She had made payments on the first mortgage reducing it to $112,500, when, on December 30, 1925, both of the mortgages were assigned to the Title Guarantee and Trust Company. On January 4, 1926 Mrs. Wood borrowed $137,500 from the Title Guarantee & Trust Company and gave it a bond and mortgage for $325,000 on which she was personally liable, that being the amount of the two existing mortgages, which were consolidated into the new one, plus the amount of the cash borrowed. On June 9, 1931 this consolidated mortgage was assigned to the East River Savings Bank and, shortly thereafter, Mrs. Wood borrowed an additional $75,000 from that bank which she received upon the execution of a second consolidated mortgage for $400,000 comprising the principal amount due on the first consolidated mortgage plus the additional loan. However, this transaction was carried out through the use of a "dummy" so that, under New York law, Mrs. Wood was not personally liable on this bond and mortgage. See In re Childs Co., 2 Cir., 163 F.2d 370. This was the mortgage, reduced as above stated, which was foreclosed.

The contention of the petitioner may now be stated quite simply. It is that, when the borrowings of Mrs. Wood subsequent to her acquisition of the property became charges solely upon the property itself, the cash she received for the repayment of which she was not personally liable was a gain then taxable to her as income to the extent that the mortgage indebtedness exceeded her adjusted basis in the property. That being so, it is argued

---

1. The petitioner requested a finding that the value of the property was less than the principal amount due on the mortgage which, it was apparently urged, prevented it from realizing the full amount due thereon. The authority cited was footnote 37 in Crane v. Commissioner, 331 U.S. 1, where the Court said, "Obviously, if the value of the property is less than the amount of the mortgage, a mortgagor who is not personally liable cannot realize a benefit equal to the mortgage. Consequently, a different problem might be encountered where a mortgagor abandoned the property or transferred it subject to the mortgage without receiving boot. . . ." However, the petitioner has disclaimed reliance upon that and, we think, advisedly so. Cf. Parker v. Delaney [Chapter 7D above].

that her tax basis was, under familiar principles of tax law, increased by the amount of such taxable gain and that this stepped up basis carried over to the petitioner in the tax free exchange by which it acquired the property.

While this conclusion would be sound if the premise on which it is based were correct, we cannot accept the premise. It is that the petitioner's transferor made a taxable disposition of the property, within the meaning of [§1001], when the second consolidated mortgage was executed, because she had, by then, dealt with it in such a way that she had received cash, in excess of her basis, which, at that time, she was freed from any personal obligation to repay. Nevertheless, whether or not personally liable on the mortgage, "The mortgagee is a creditor, and in effect nothing more than a preferred creditor, even though the mortgagor is not liable for the debt. He is not the less a creditor because he has recourse only to the land, unless we are to deny the term to one who may levy upon only a part of his debtor's assets." C.I.R. v. Crane, 2 Cir., 153 F.2d 504, 506. Mrs. Wood merely augmented the existing mortgage indebtedness when she borrowed each time and, far from closing the venture, remained in a position to borrow more if and when circumstances permitted and she so desired. And so, she never "disposed" of the property to create a taxable event which [§1001] makes a condition precedent to the taxation of gain. "Disposition," within the meaning of [§1001], is the "'getting rid, or making over, of anything; relinquishment.'" Herber's Estate v. Commissioner, 3 Cir., 139 F.2d 756, 758, certiorari denied 332 U.S. 752. Nothing of that nature was done here by the mere execution of the second consolidated mortgage; Mrs. Wood was the owner of this property in the same sense after the execution of this mortgage that she was before. As was pointed out in our decision in the Crane case, supra, 153 F.2d at 505-506,

> . . . the lien of a mortgage does not make the mortgagee a cotenant; the mortgagor is the owner for all purposes; indeed that is why the "gage" is "mort," as distinguished from a "vivum vadium." Kortright v. Cady, 21 N.Y. 343, 344, 78 Am. Dec. 145. He has all the income from the property; he manages it; he may sell it; any increase in its value goes to him; any decrease falls on him, until the value goes below the amount of the lien.

Realization of gain was, therefore, postponed for taxation until there was a final disposition of the property at the time of the foreclosure sale. See Lutz & Schramm Co., 1 T.C. 682; Mendham Corp., 9 T.C. 320. Therefore, Mrs. Wood's borrowings did not change the basis for the computation of gain or loss.

Affirmed.

Notes

1. As in *Crane* and *Parker* it is the taxpayer, seeking to avoid tax in a later year, who first asserts that a nonrecourse debt should not have prevented

taxation of income in a prior year. And again one can sympathize a little with a judicial reluctance to accept the argument coming from that quarter in those circumstances. But also again the affirmation of nontaxability in the prior year seems quite unfortunate. Would Judge Magruder's reasoning in *Parker* have provided a good escape from the dilemma posed in this case?

2. Was the court right in *Woodsam* to say that §1001 makes disposition the "taxable event" which is "a condition precedent to the taxation of gain"? Section 1001 does not say that gain can only be realized by disposing of property; it only says that if there is a disposition, gain or loss is to be computed by subtracting adjusted basis from the amount realized. Realization is, as §1001(b) indicates, a matter of what is received, not what is disposed of.

The alleged taxable event in this case is the receipt of mortgage proceeds. The issue is whether mortgage proceeds should be excluded from income, by recognizing the taxpayer's obligation to repay, when there is no personal liability and the obligation is secured only by a piece of property whose basis is less than the amount received. The argument against exclusion is that the obligation should only be recognized to the extent of the tax cost of fulfilling it, which cannot exceed the adjusted basis of the mortgaged property.

3. Does the opportunity to borrow against appreciated property without being taxed on the gain represent a serious inequity? Does it mean that the freedom from tax afforded unrealized capital gains may be allowed to extend to the consumption component of income as well as the savings component?

4. Should *Woodsam* apply if the property in question is worth less than the amount of the nonrecourse debt at the time of mortgaging out? This will not normally occur, of course, in a completely voluntary transaction. But reconsider Allan in Problem 2 following Revenue Ruling 91-31 (p. 478 above). Would it have made sense for the government to deny Allan's deductions in the years the mortgagee paid the taxes and did not receive the interest, or to have required an offsetting inclusion in income, on the ground that at least the right to take tax credit for nonrecourse borrowing should depend on the presence of value sufficient to support that borrowing at the time it is incurred?

3. Gifts of Encumbered Property

ESTATE OF LEVINE v. COMMISSIONER
634 F.2d 12 (2d Cir. 1980)

Before Friendly, Kaufman and Timbers, Circuit Judges.
FRIENDLY, Circuit Judge:
The estate of Aaron Levine and his widow Anna appeal from a part of a decision of the Tax Court, 72 T.C. No. 68 (1979), which found a deficiency of $130,428.42 in Aaron Levine's 1970 income tax. The deficiency resulted from a determination by the Commissioner that the taxpayer had realized

gain upon his gift, on January 1, 1970, of income producing property consisting of land and a building at 20-24 Vesey Street in New York City (the property) to a previously created trust for the benefit of three grandchildren.

The property was originally purchased on November 1, 1944, by a corporation wholly owned by Levine. On August 22, 1957, the corporation, which was in the course of dissolution, made a liquidating distribution of the property to the taxpayer. Thereafter Levine obtained two nonrecourse mortgages secured by the property. One of these, for $500,000, was obtained on March 17, 1966, from the Bowery Savings Bank and represented the consolidation of numerous earlier mortgages. The other, for $300,000, was obtained from the Commercial Trading Company on November 21, 1968; this was later amortized to $280,000.

Levine filed a gift tax return for 1970 reporting the transaction as follows:

2-24 Vesey Street, City, County and State of New York —

Appraisal value	$925,000.00
Mortgages	
Bowery Savings Bank	$500,000.00
Interest accrued 12/1/69 to 12/31/69	2,291.67
Commercial Trading*	280,000.00
Interest accrued 12/1/69 to 12/31/69	3,616.67
Total mortgages and interest	$785,908.34
Expenses incurred by donor in 1969 and assumed and paid by donee:	
Improvements	$117,716.53
Supplies	387.83
Repairs	1,253.93
Paint	63.60
Electricity	1,827.56
Steam	3,324.13
Total expenses	124,573.58
Total mortgages, interest and expenses	910,481.92
Equity	$ 14,518.08

* Between November 1968 and January 1970, $20,000 of the $300,000 principal was amortized.

and paid a gift tax on the equity of $14,518.08. The propriety of this was not challenged. However, the Commissioner assessed a deficiency in income tax on the ground that Levine had realized a gain in the amount of the excess of the total mortgages, interest and expenses aggregating $910,481.34, all of which were assumed by the donee, over Levine's adjusted basis, which, as increased by stipulation between the parties, was $485,429.55. The result was an excess of $425,051.79 and, upon application of capital gains rates, a deficiency of $130,428.42 in income tax. The Tax Court upheld the

Commissioner largely on the authority of Crane v. C.I.R., 331 U.S. 1 . . . (1947), which had affirmed this court's decision, 153 F.2d 504 (1945) (L. Hand, Jr.). This appeal followed.

At first blush the layman and even the lawyer or judge not conditioned by exposure to tax law would find it difficult to understand how a taxpayer can realize $425,051.79 in gain by giving away property in which he possessed an equity of $14,518.08. Doubtless Mrs. Crane experienced a similar difficulty when she was held to have realized $275,500 (for a net taxable gain of $23,031.45), after she netted a mere $2,500 on the sale of an apartment building that she had inherited subject to a $255,000 mortgage and $7,042.50 in over due interest payments, and had sold, under threat of foreclosure, subject to the same mortgage principal and $15,857.71 in defaulted interest payments. However, as stated in the ironic dictum of a distinguished tax practitioner's imaginary Supreme Court opinion,[3] "[e]veryday meanings are only of secondary importance when construing the words of a tax statute and are very seldom given any weight when a more abstruse and technical meaning is available."[4] In any event, *Crane* binds us whatever the yearnings of our untutored intuitions may be. What is more, few scholars quarrel with the wisdom of its holding, as distinguished from some of its language including the famous note 37, 331 U.S. at 14, . . . of which more hereafter.[5]

Instead of addressing himself directly to the ultimately dispositive question, what did Mrs. Crane receive, Chief Justice Vinson stated in his *Crane* opinion, 331 U.S. at 6, . . . that "Logically, the first step . . . is to determine the unadjusted basis of the property. . . ." This must have struck Mrs. Crane as peculiar since she had claimed what would normally be the most favorable stance for the Commissioner in the determination of gain, namely, that her basis was zero. The answer to the Chief Justice's question lay in then §113(a)(5), incorporated as modified in I.R.C. §1014(a), which says that if property is acquired from a decedent the unadjusted basis is "the fair market value of such property at the time of such acquisition." On Mr. Crane's death the property had been appraised—somewhat unscientifically one might guess—as having exactly the value of the encumbrances, $262,042.50. If "property" as used in §113(a) meant simply what the property was worth to Mrs. Crane, i.e., her "equity," her basis was zero, as she contended. However, *Crane* accepted the Commissioner's theory that since the term referred to "the land and buildings themselves, or the owner's rights in

---

3. D. Nelson Adams, Exploring the Outer Boundaries of the Crane Doctrine; an Imaginary Supreme Court Opinion, 21 Tax L. Rev. 159, 164 (1966).

4. The *Crane* opinion insisted that "the words of statutes—including revenue acts—should be interpreted where possible in their ordinary, everyday senses." [Footnote omitted.] 331 U.S. at 6-7, 67 S. Ct. at 1051.

5. In addition to Mr. Adams' article, supra note 3, see, e.g., Bittker, Tax Shelters, Nonrecourse Debt, and the *Crane* Case, 33 Tax L. Rev. 277 (1978); Del Cotto, Basis and Amount Realized under *Crane*: A Current View of Some Tax Effects in Mortgage Financing, 118 U. Pa. L. Rev. 69 (1969). None of these excellent articles was cited in the briefs.

them, undiminished by the mortgage, the basis was the appraised value of $262,042.50."

The next step was to determine whether the unadjusted basis should be adjusted by deducting depreciation "to the extent allowed (but not less than the amount allowable)" as required by §113(b)(1)(B), now incorporated as modified in I.R.C. §1016(a)(2). Here again the parties took unconventional positions. Proceeding from her zero basis theory, Mrs. Crane maintained that no depreciation could be taken, although she had in fact taken depreciation deductions totalling $25,500, 331 U.S. at 3 n.2. . . . The Commissioner, true to his theory of basis, see §§23(n) and 114(a) of the 1938 Act, now I.R.C. §167(g), thought that depreciation deductions of $28,045.10 should have been taken, and the Court agreed.

"At last," said the Chief Justice, 331 U.S. at 12, . . . "we come to the problem of determining the 'amount realized' on the 1938 sale." In fact the Court's answers to the two earlier questions had predetermined the answer to the dispositive one. If non-recourse mortgages contribute to the basis of property, then they must be included in the amount realized on its sale. Any other course would render the concept of basis nonsensical by permitting sellers of mortgaged property to register large tax losses stemming from an inflated basis and a diminished realization of gain. It would also permit depreciation deductions in excess of a property holder's real investment which could never subsequently be recaptured. Although the Court bolstered its holding by explicating the use of the word "property" in §111(a) and (b) of the 1938 Act, now I.R.C. §1001(a) and (b), and with certain other arguments,[6] it was hardly necessary to go beyond the statement that "[i]f the 'property' to be valued on the date of acquisition is the property free of liens, the 'property' to be priced on a subsequent sale must be the same thing." [Footnote omitted.] 331 U.S. at 12.[7]

Taxpayer argues that, be all this as it may, *Crane* is inapplicable because the transaction here was a gift and not a sale.

Apart from the general incongruity in finding that a gift yields a realized gain to the donor, petitioner argues that it is by no means clear how the Code's gross income, realization and recognition provisions apply to a donor's "gain" realized as incidental to a gift. Section 61(a)(3) defines

6. The most notable, 331 U.S. at 13-14, . . . which had been stressed in Judge L. Hand's opinion in this court, 153 F.2d at 505-506, looked to Mrs. Crane's concession that "if she had been personally liable on the mortgage and the purchaser had either paid or assumed it, the amount so paid or assumed would be considered a part of the 'amount realized' within the meaning of §111(b)" — a proposition established by United States v. Hendler, 303 U.S. 564, . . . (1938). The court found no essential distinction between such personal liability and Mrs. Crane's non-recourse mortgage. Bittker, supra, 33 Tax L. Rev. at 281-282, criticizes this portion of the opinion as conceptual sleight-of-hand, although he concludes that the identification of non-recourse and personal obligations was practically necessitated by considerations of administrative simplicity.

7. Had *Crane* begun with the ultimate question, Mrs. Crane's "amount realized," and reached the intuitive answer, $2,500, the need to preserve the Code's depreciation apparatus might well have forced the Court to adopt the concept of "negative basis." For a glimpse at this road not taken, see Parker v. Delaney, 186 F.2d 455, 459-460 (1 Cir. 1950) (Magruder, C.J., concurring), cert. denied, 341 U.S. 926 (1951); Chirelstein, Federal Income Taxation 225-233 (1977).

gross income to include "[g]ains derived from dealings in property"—a term seemingly broad enough to include gains from gifts. The same is true with respect to §1001(a), which provides that "[t]he gain from the sale *or other disposition of property* shall be the excess of the amount realized therefrom over the adjusted basis provided in Section 1011 for determining gain. . . ." (Emphasis supplied.) Apparent difficulty is encountered, however, when we come to the critical provision, §1001(c), entitled "[r]ecognition of gain or loss," which states that "[e]xcept as otherwise provided in this subtitle, the entire amount of the gain or loss, determined under this section, on *the sale or exchange* of property shall be recognized." (Emphasis supplied.)

Taxpayer suggests that the change in language from "other disposition of property" in §1001(a), which seems broad enough to encompass a gift, but see United States v. Davis, 370 U.S. 65, 68-69 & n.5 . . . (1962), to "sale or exchange" in §1001(c), which would appear not to be, postpones recognition of any "gain" realized in the instant transaction. This, he argues, is appropriate because while a sale or exchange results in the transferee's acquisition of a new basis, see §1012, a gift ordinarily transfers the donor's basis plus any gift tax paid to the donee, §1015, and tax on any gain can thus fairly be postponed until the donee engages in a taxable disposition. However, this argument overlooks "[t]he general rule . . . that when property is sold or otherwise disposed of, any gain realized must also be recognized, absent an appropriate nonrecognition provision in the Internal Revenue Code." [Footnote omitted.] King Enterprises v. United States, 418 F.2d 511, 514 (Ct. Cl. 1969). See 3 Mertens, Federal Income Taxation, §20.13 at 50 n.4 (1980). A comparison of the present §1001(c) with its pre-1976 predecessors, which, of course, are here controlling, suggests that §1001(c) merely limits nonrecognition to certain transactions described in detail elsewhere in the Code and does not confer it on all dispositions other than sales or exchanges. However, we need not decide this question in view of our disposition of the case.

Levine relies also on the established principle that a gift of appreciated unmortgaged property does not give rise to a gain, even when deductions have been taken for business expenses which were necessary to the appreciation of the property. Campbell v. Prothro, 209 F.2d 331 (5 Cir. 1954). See also First National Industries, Inc. v. C.I.R., 404 F.2d 1182, 1183 (6 Cir. 1968), cert. denied, 394 U.S. 1014 (1969); The Humacid Company v. C.I.R., 42 T.C. 894, 913 (1964). However, the transaction here in question was not a "pure" gift. The donee assumed not only the $785,908.34 in mortgages and accrued interest for which Levine was not personally liable but also the $124,573.58 of 1969 expenses, not constituting a lien, for which he was. If the donee had paid the latter sum directly to Levine, this case would clearly be governed by *Crane* since the donor would have received "boot." However, the assumption of another's legal obligation or debt is considered income under Old Colony Trust Co. v. C.I.R., 279 U.S. 716, 729 (1929), and United States v. Hendler, supra, 303 U.S. at 566. We can thus see no sound reason for reaching a result differing from that in *Crane* on the facts of this case. We need not decide what the result should be if Levine had merely donated the property subject to non-recourse mortgages without an explicit "sale" element—in this case, the donee's assumption of his 1969 personal liabilities. . . .

. . . This is not to say that we reject the broader analysis urged by the Commissioner and adopted by the Tax Court in this case, to wit, that *Crane* mandates that the transfer of property encumbered by any debt, non-recourse or personal, results in potentially taxable benefits even in the case of a "pure" gift. We simply leave this benefit orientation and the other arguments advanced to another day. It is comforting to note, however, that an analysis of Levine's tax returns indicates his successful conversion of the appreciated value of the Vesey Street property into "benefits" at least as tangible as those in *Crane*. The calculation of Levine's taxable gain, as found by the Tax Court, may be presented as follows:

(1)	Amount realized	
	(a) Expenses assumed by donee	$124,573.00
	(b) Mortgages	780,000.00
	(c) Interest payments assumed by donee	5,908.34
	(d) Total	$910,481.34
(2)	Less: Adjusted basis	
	(a) Unadjusted basis[12]	$385,485.02
	(b) Plus: Capital Improvements	334,452.00
	(c) Improvements paid for by donee	117,716.53
	(d) Subtotal	837,743.55
	(e) Less: Depreciation	352,314.00
	(f) Adjusted basis	$485,429.55
(3)	Gain	$425,051.79

Of the total taxable gain of $425,051.79, the sum of $124,573.00 may be allocated directly to the 1969 expenses which Levine shifted to the donee trust. As was previously noted, these expenses are closely akin to the "boot" of $2,500 received by Mrs. Crane. In addition Levine's mortgage schedule, supra note 2, indicates that of the $780,000 in mortgages on the Vesey Street property at the time of its transfer, at least $235,044.23 derived from an outstanding mortgage which Levine acquired with the property in 1957, while the remaining $544,955.77 represents the net non-recourse indebtedness incurred during the period of Levine's ownership. As the table above indicates, $334,452 of the later amount was reinvested in capital improvements. Since the original mortgage of $235,044.23 must be assumed to have

12. The record does not indicate Levine's unadjusted basis, but this can readily be calculated by subtracting capital improvements from, and adding depreciation deductions to, the stipulated adjusted basis of $485,429.55.

contributed toward Levine's unadjusted basis in the property,[13] and the subsequent capital improvements adjusted Levine's basis upward by the extent of their value, $569,496.23 (or $235,044.23 plus $334,452.00) in basis credit derives solely from the non-recourse mortgages. Yet, upon disposition of the property in 1970 Levine's stipulated basis was merely $485,429.55. The shortfall between this and the aggregate contribution of the non-recourse mortgages, i.e., $84,066.68, can only be explained by depreciation deductions that Levine could not have taken *but for* the mortgages. Finally, there are two additional sources of "benefit" in this case with no analogue in *Crane*. One is the sum of $210,503.77 out of Levine's net borrowings of $544,955.77, see discussion supra, which was apparently not reinvested in capital improvements on the property, and which the taxpayer may thus be considered to have "pocketed." The second is the $5,908.34 in interest payments owed by the taxpayer but assumed by the donee.[14] Together, these four varieties of "benefit" sum exactly to what was found to be the taxpayer's total taxable income:

(a) Expenses assumed by donee	$124,573.00
(b) Depreciation resulting from non-recourse mortgages	84,066.68
(c) Pocketed mortgage funds	210,503.77
(d) Interest assumed by donee	5,908.34
TOTAL	$425,051.79

To tax these "benefits" upon a disposition, at capital gains rates and without interest, is scarcely harsh. Failure to do so would mean, so far as we can see, that the $210,503.77 which the taxpayer obtained for his personal use by non-recourse loans against the appreciation of the property would never be taxed either as ordinary income or as gain (although, unless paid off by the donee, it would diminish any realization on the property), and that the benefits obtained by the depreciation deductions would remain untaxed unless and until the donee sold the property, when they would operate as a reduction of the donee's adjusted basis which was passed on to the donee. In light of the seeming equity of the result reached, an otherwise similar case lacking the element of personal debt assumed by the donee might lead us to look with sympathy on the scant case law suggesting that the *Crane* principle may apply even to "pure" gifts, see Malone v. United States, 326 F. Supp. 106 (N.D. Miss. 1971), aff'd, 455 F.2d 502 (5 Cir. 1972), even though a taxpayer could avoid application of *Crane* by withholding his beneficence until death.

13. Levine acquired his encumbered property at a basis equal to its market value, I.R.C. §334(a). Since any subsequent payments on the principal of the original mortgage would not have increased Levine's basis, see Ford v. United States, 311 F.2d 951, 953-955 (Ct. Cl. 1963), this mortgage must be deemed to be included in the original basis of the property.

14. The Commissioner in *Crane* did not include a similar sum of $15,857.71 in interest payments assumed by the buyer of the mortgaged property, see 331 U.S. at 4 n.6, . . . apparently because interest due was a deductible item. This issue has not been raised before us.

For reasons we have indicated, we simply do not find it necessary to decide that broader question on the facts here before us.

The judgment of the Tax Court is affirmed.

Questions

1. Would the subsequent Supreme Court decision in *Tufts* be enough to overcome Judge Friendly's reluctance to rule on a gift of property subject solely to a nonrecourse debt? Does Judge Friendly's opinion leave any real doubt how that should be resolved?

2. Would a gift of encumbered property to a charity be treated differently from a gift to a relative? Consider Winston F.C. Guest, 77 T.C. 9 (1981) and §1011(b).

DIEDRICH v. COMMISSIONER
457 U.S. 191 (1982)

BURGER, C.J., delivered the opinion of the Court, in which Brennan, White, Marshall, Blackmun, Powell, Stevens, and O'Connor, JJ., joined. Rehnquist, J., filed a dissenting opinion.

Chief Justice BURGER delivered the opinion of the Court: . . . In 1972 petitioners Victor and Frances Diedrich made gifts of approximately 85,000 shares of stock to their three children, using both a direct transfer and a trust arrangement. The gifts were subject to a condition that the donees pay the resulting federal and state gift taxes. . . . The donors' basis in the transferred stock was $51,073; the gift tax paid in 1972 by the donees was $62,992. Petitioners did not include as income on their 1971 federal income tax returns any portion of the gift tax paid by the donees. . . .

The Court of Appeals rejected the Tax Court's conclusion that the taxpayers merely had made a "net gift" of the difference between the fair market value of the transferred property and the gift taxes paid by the donees. The court reasoned that a donor receives a benefit when a donee discharges a donor's legal obligation to pay gift taxes. The Court of Appeals agreed with the Commissioner in rejecting the holding in Turner v. Commissioner, 49 T.C. 356 (1968), aff'd per curiam, 410 F.2d 752 (CA6 1969), and its progeny, and adopted the approach of Johnson v. Commissioner, 59 T.C. 791 (1973), aff'd, 495 F.2d 1079 (CA6), cert. denied, 419 U.S. 1040 (1974), and Estate of Levine v. Commissioner, 72 T.C. 780 (1979), aff'd, 634 F.2d 12 (CA2 1980). We granted certiorari to resolve this conflict, and we affirm. . . .

Pursuant to its Constitutional authority, Congress has defined "gross income" as income "from whatever source derived," including "[i]ncome from discharge of indebtedness." 26 U.S.C. §61 (1976). This Court has recognized that "income" may be realized by a variety of indirect means. In Old Colony Tr. Co. v. Commissioner, 279 U.S. 716 (1929), the Court held that payment of an employee's income taxes by an employer constituted income to the employee. Speaking for the Court, Chief Justice Taft concluded that "[t]he payment of the tax by the employer[] was in consideration of the services rendered by the employee and was a gain derived by the employee from his labor." Id., at 729. The Court made clear that the substance, not the form, of the agreed transaction controls. "The discharge by a third person of an obligation to him is equivalent to receipt by the person taxed." Ibid. The employee, in other words, was placed in a better position as a result of the employer's discharge of the employee's legal obligation to pay the income taxes; the employee thus received a gain subject to income tax.

The holding in *Old Colony* was reaffirmed in Crane v. Commissioner, 331 U.S. 1 (1947). In *Crane* the Court concluded that relief from the obligation of a nonrecourse mortgage in which the value of the property exceeded the value of the mortgage constituted income to the taxpayer. The taxpayer in *Crane* acquired depreciable property, an apartment building, subject to an unassumed mortgage. The taxpayer later sold the apartment building, which was still subject to the nonrecourse mortgage, for cash plus the buyer's assumption of the mortgage. This Court held that the amount of mortgage was properly included in the amount realized on the sale, noting that if the taxpayer transfers subject to the mortgage, "the benefit to him is as real and substantial as if the mortgage were discharged, or as if a personal debt in an equal amount had been assumed by another." Id., at 14. Again, it was the "reality," not the form, of the transaction that governed. Ibid. The Court found it immaterial whether the seller received money prior to the sale in order to discharge the mortgage, or whether the seller merely transferred the property subject to the mortgage. In either case the taxpayer realized an economic benefit.

The principles of *Old Colony* and *Crane* control. A common method of structuring gift transactions is for the donor to make the gift subject to the condition that the donee pay the resulting gift tax, as was done in each of the cases now before us. When a gift is made, the gift tax liability falls on the donor under 26 U.S.C. §2502(d). When a donor makes a gift to a donee, a "debt" to the United States for the amount of the gift tax is incurred by the donor. Those taxes are as much the legal obligation of the donor as the donor's income taxes; for these purposes they are the same kind of debt obligation as the income taxes of the employee in *Old Colony*, supra. Similarly, when a donee agrees to discharge an indebtedness in consideration of the gift, the person relieved of the tax liability realizes an economic benefit. In short, the donor realizes an immediate economic benefit by the donee's assumption of the donor's legal obligation to pay the gift tax.

An examination of the donor's intent does not change the character of this benefit. Although intent is relevant in determining whether a gift has been made, subjective intent has not characteristically been a factor in determining whether an individual has realized income. Even if intent were a factor, the donor's intent with respect to the condition shifting the gift tax obligation from the donor to the donee was plainly to relieve the donor of a debt owed to the United States; the choice was made because the donor would receive a benefit in relief from the obligation to pay the gift tax.

Finally, the benefit realized by the taxpayer is not diminished by the fact that the liability attaches during the course of a donative transfer. It cannot be doubted that the donors were aware that the gift tax obligation would arise immediately upon the transfer of the property; the economic benefit to the donors in the discharge of the gift tax liability is indistinguishable from the benefit arising from discharge of a pre-existing obligation. Nor is there any doubt that had the donors sold a portion of the stock immediately before the gift transfer in order to raise funds to pay the expected gift tax, a taxable gain would have been realized. §1001. The fact that the gift tax obligation was discharged by way of a conditional gift rather than from funds derived from a pregift sale does not alter the underlying benefit to the donors. . . .

We recognize that Congress has structured gift transactions to encourage transfer of property by limiting the tax consequences of a transfer. See, e.g., 26 U.S.C. §102 (gifts excluded from donee's gross income). Congress may obviously provide a similar exclusion for the conditional gift. Should Congress wish to encourage "net gifts," changes in the income tax consequences of such gifts lie within the legislative responsibility. Until such time, we are bound by Congress' mandate that gross income includes income "from whatever source derived." We therefore hold that a donor who makes a gift of property on condition that the donee pay the resulting gift taxes realizes taxable income to the extent that the gift taxes paid by the donee exceed the donor's adjusted basis in the property.[10]

The judgment of the United States Court of Appeals for the Eighth Circuit is

Affirmed.

Justice REHNQUIST, dissenting: It is a well-settled principle today that a taxpayer realizes income when another person relieves the taxpayer of a legal obligation in connection with an otherwise taxable transaction. See Crane v. Commissioner, 331 U.S. 1 (1947) (sale of real property); Old Colony Tr. Co. v. Commissioner, 279 U.S. 716 (1929) (employment compensation). In neither *Old Colony* nor *Crane* was there any question as to the existence of a taxable transaction; the only question concerned the amount of income realized by the taxpayer as a result of the taxable transaction. . . .

---

10. Petitioners argue that even if this Court holds that a donee realizes income on a conditional gift to the extent that the gift tax exceeds the adjusted basis, that holding should be applied prospectively and should not apply to the taxpayers in this case. In this case, however, there was no dispositive Eighth Circuit holding prior to the decision on review. In addition, this Court frequently has applied decisions which have altered the tax law and applied the clarified law to the facts of the case before it. See, e.g., United States v. Estate of Donnelly, 397 U.S. 286, 294-295 (1970).

Unlike *Old Colony* or *Crane*, the question in this case is not the amount of income the taxpayer has realized as a result of a concededly taxable transaction, but whether a taxable transaction has taken place at all. Only *after* one concludes that a partial sale occurs when the donee agrees to pay the gift tax do *Old Colony* and *Crane* become relevant in ascertaining the amount of income realized by the donor as a result of the transaction. Nowhere does the Court explain why a gift becomes a partial sale merely because the donor and donee structure the gift so that the gift tax imposed by Congress on the transaction is paid by the donee rather than the donor.

In my view, the resolution of this case turns upon congressional intent: whether Congress intended to characterize a gift as a partial sale whenever the donee agrees to pay the gift tax. Congress has determined that a gift should not be considered income to the donee. 26 U.S.C. §102. Instead, gift transactions are to be subject to a tax system wholly separate and distinct from the income tax. See id. §2501 et seq. Both the donor and the donee may be held liable for the gift tax. Id. §§2502(d), 6324(b). Although the primary liability for the gift tax is on the donor, the donee is liable to the extent of the value of the gift should the donor fail to pay the tax. I see no evidence in the tax statutes that Congress forbade the parties to agree among themselves as to who would pay the gift tax upon pain of such an agreement being considered a taxable event for the purposes of the income tax. Although Congress could certainly determine that the payment of the gift tax by the donee constitutes income to the donor, the relevant statutes do not affirmatively indicate that Congress has made such a determination.

I dissent.

Questions

Does *Diedrich* really mandate "partial sale" treatment? Or, to pose the question another way, is the Court's result equivalent to the tax consequences that would ensue "had the donors sold a portion of the stock immediately before the gift transfer in order to raise funds to pay the expected gift tax"? Compare Reg. §1.1001-1(e) with §1011(b). See also Reg. §1.1001-2(a)(4)(iii), -2(c) Example (6). Is *Diedrich* subject to the same criticism that Justice O'Connor leveled at the Court's opinion in *Tufts*?

References

A. Cancellation of Indebtedness: Asofsky & Tatlock, Bankruptcy Tax Act Radically Alters Treatment of Bankruptcy and Discharging Debts, 54 J. Taxn. 106 (1981); Bittker, Income from the Cancellation of Indebtedness: A Historical Footnote to the *Kirby Lumber Co.* Case, 4 J. Corp. Taxn. 124 (1977); Gunn, Another Look at the *Zarin* Case, 50 Tax Notes 893 (1991);

Deborah H. Schenk, The Story of *Kirby Lumber:* The Many Faces of Discharge of Indebtedness Income, in Tax Stories 97 (2003); Scranton, Corporate Transactions Under the Bankruptcy Tax Act of 1980, 35 Tax Law. 49 (1981); Theodore P. Seto, Inside *Zarin,* 59 SMU L. Rev. 1761 (2006); Shakow, The Stock-For-Debt De Minimus Exception, 41 Tax Notes 1325 (1988); Shaviro, The Man Who Lost Too Much: *Zarin v. Commissioner* and the Measurement of Taxable Consumption, 45 Tax L. Rev. 215 (1990).

B. Claim of Right: Wooton, The Claim of Right Doctrine and Section 1341, 34 Tax Law. 297 (1981); Emanuel, The Scope of Section 1341, 53 Taxes 644 (1975); Note, Claim of Right: A Tax Doctrine Unjustly Applied to Accrued Income Subject to Litigation, 24 U.C.L.A. L. Rev. (1977).

C. Embezzled Funds: Libin & Haydon, Embezzled Funds as Taxable Income: A Study in Judicial Footwork, 61 Mich. L. Rev. 425 (1963).

D. Nonrecourse Borrowing: Adams, Exploring the Outer Boundaries of the *Crane* Doctrine: An Imaginary Supreme Court Opinion, 21 Tax L. Rev. 159 (1966); Anderson, Federal Income Tax Treatment of Nonrecourse Debt, 82 Colum. L. Rev. 1498 (1982); Andrews, On Beyond *Tufts,* 61 Taxes 949 (1983); Bittker, Tax Shelters, Nonrecourse Debt, and the *Crane* Case, 33 Tax L. Rev. 277 (1978); Blackburn, Important Common Law Developments for Nonrecourse Notes: Tufting It Out, 18 Ga. L. Rev. 1 (1983); Epstein, The Application of the *Crane* Doctrine to Limited Partnerships, 45 S. Cal. L. Rev. 100 (1972); Ginsburg, The Leaky Tax Shelter, 53 Taxes 719 (1975); Handler, Tax Consequences of Mortgage Foreclosures and Transfers of Real Property to the Mortgagee, 31 Tax L. Rev. 193 (1976); Narcisco, Some Reflections on *Commissioner v. Tufts:* Mrs. Crane Shops at Kirby Lumber, 35 Rutgers L. Rev. 929 (1983); Perry, Limited Partnerships and Tax Shelters: The *Crane* Rule Goes Public, 27 Tax L. Rev. 525 (1972); Rosenberg, Better to Burn Out Than Fade Away? The Consequences of the Disposition of a Tax Shelter, 71 Calif. L. Rev. 87 (1983); Weiler, Effect of At-Risk Rules on Nonrecourse Financing and Other Risk-Limiting Devices, 46 J. Taxn. 326 (1977); Whitmire, Bailing Out of Tax Shelters: Selected Techniques, 30 S. Cal. Tax Inst. 503 (1978); George K. Yin, The Story of *Crane:* How a Widow's Misfortune Led to Tax Shelters, in Tax Stories 207 (2003); Note, Income Tax Consequences of Encumbered Gifts: The Advent of *Crane,* 28 U. Fla. L. Rev. 935 (1976).

Chapter 8 — *Tax Expenditures: State and Municipal Bond Interest*

A. *THE EXCLUSION OF INTEREST ON STATE AND LOCAL OBLIGATIONS*

Section 103 has long provided that "gross income does not include interest on any . . . obligations of a State or political subdivision thereof."

From the standpoint of an individual investor this is a relatively simple provision. State and municipal bonds typically pay lower rates of interest than federal and corporate bonds, presumably because of the tax exemption; whether the difference in interest rates is fully offset, or even more than fully offset, by the tax exemption will depend on the marginal tax bracket of each individual investor. Sometimes the matter is put in terms of equivalent taxable yields as indicated in Table 8-1. Figure out and be sure you understand just how the numbers in this table are derived.

There is essentially only one complication about the municipal bond exclusion from the investor's standpoint, and that only arises if the investor is a borrower seeking to deduct interest payments. In that case the investor must determine whether any of his borrowing is incurred or continued to purchase or carry tax-exempt securities, since interest paid on such borrowing is nondeductible. See §265(2); Chapter 10A.2.

From the standpoint of the taxpayer who invests in municipal bonds, the operation of §103 is relatively simple, but quite inexplicable. What possible reason exists for excluding simple interest income from the recipient's taxable income? For those who insist that the individual income tax should be evaluated as a tax on persons according to their income, the municipal bond exclusion has long been considered a glaring loophole.

TABLE 8-1
Yield Equivalents for a 10 Percent Tax-Free Bond

Investor's Tax Bracket	Equivalent Taxable Yield
50% (pre-1986)	20%
35	15.38
33	14.93
28	13.89
25	13.33
15	11.76
10	11.11

To make any sense of the exclusion, one must go beyond its impact on the investor and also consider its impact on the state or municipality issuing tax-exempt obligations.

1.   Constitutional Considerations

Part of the reason the 1894 income tax was held unconstitutional was that a federal tax on the interest on state and local obligations was conceived as an impermissible burden on the sovereign power of the states to borrow money. Pollock v. Farmers' Loan & Trust Co., 157 U.S. 429, 584-586 (1895). That holding was never put to the test under the Sixteenth Amendment since the modern income tax has always contained the statutory exclusion in §103. Nevertheless, clarification of the constitutional issue has come, somewhat surprisingly, without repeal of §103.

SOUTH CAROLINA v. BAKER
485 U.S. 505 (1988)

Justice BRENNAN delivered the opinion of the Court. . . .
Historically, bonds have been issued as either registered bonds or bearer bonds. These two types of bonds differ in the mechanisms used for transferring ownership and making payments. Ownership of a registered bond is recorded on a central list, and a transfer of record ownership requires entering the change on that list. The record owner automatically receives interest payments by check or electronic transfer of funds from the issuer's paying agent. Ownership of a bearer bond, in contrast, is presumed from possession and is transferred by physically handing over the bond. The bondowner obtains interest payments by presenting bond coupons to a bank that in turn presents the coupons to the issuer's paying agent.
In 1982, Congress enacted TEFRA [the Tax Equity and Fiscal Responsibility Act of 1982], which contains a variety of provisions, including §310,

designed to reduce the federal deficit by promoting compliance with the tax laws. Congress had become concerned about the growing magnitude of tax evasion; Internal Revenue Service (IRS) studies indicated that unreported income had grown from an estimated range of $31.1 billion to $32.2 billion in 1973 to a range of $93.3 billion to $97 billion in 1981. Compliance Gap: Hearing before the Subcommittee on Oversight of the Internal Revenue Service of the Senate Committee on Finance, 97th Cong., 2d Sess., 126 (1982). Unregistered bonds apparently became a focus of attention because they left no paper trail and thus facilitated tax evasion. . . .

Because §310 aims to address the tax evasion concerns posed generally by unregistered bonds, it covers not only state bonds but also bonds issued by the United States and private corporations. Section 310(a) requires the United States to issue publicly offered bonds with a maturity of one year or more in registered form. With respect to similar bonds issued by private corporations, §§310(b)(2)-(6) impose a series of tax penalties on nonregistration. Corporations declining to issue the covered bonds in registered form lose tax deductions and adjustments for interest paid on the bonds, §§310(b)(2) and (3), and must pay a special excise tax on the bond principal, §310(b)(4). Holders of these unregistered corporate bonds generally cannot deduct capital losses or claim capital-gain treatment for any losses or gains sustained on the bonds. §§310(b)(5) and (6). Section 310(b)(1) completes this statutory scheme by denying the federal income tax exemption for interest earned on state bonds to owners of long-term publicly offered state bonds that are not issued in registered form.

South Carolina invoked the original jurisdiction of this Court, contending that §310(b)(1) is constitutionally invalid under the Tenth Amendment and the doctrine of intergovernmental tax immunity. . . .

[The Court concluded that nothing in the Tenth Amendment or elsewhere in the constitution would prevent application to state and municipal governments of a general prohibition on the issuance of bonds in bearer form.]

South Carolina contends that even if a statute banning state bearer bonds entirely would be constitutional, §310 unconstitutionally violates the doctrine of intergovernmental tax immunity because it imposes a tax on the interest earned on a state bond. . . .

The Secretary and the Master . . . suggest that we should uphold the constitutionality of §310 without explicitly overruling *Pollock* because §310 does not abolish the tax exemption for state bond interest entirely but rather taxes the interest on state bonds only if the bonds are not issued in the form Congress requires. In our view, however, this suggestion implicitly rests on a rather mischievous proposition of law. . . . The United States cannot convert an unconstitutional tax into a constitutional one simply by making the tax conditional. . . .

Under the intergovernmental tax immunity jurisprudence prevailing at the time, *Pollock* did not represent a unique immunity limited to income derived from state bonds. Rather, *Pollack* merely represented one application of the more general rule that neither the federal nor the state government could tax income an individual directly derived from any contract with another government. Not only was it unconstitutional for the Federal Government to tax a bondowner on the interest she received on any state bond, but it was also unconstitutional to tax a state employee on the income earned from his employment contract, Collector v. Day, 11 Wall. 113 (1871), to tax a lessee on income derived from lands leased from a State, Burnet v. Coronado Oil, 285 U.S. 393 (1932), or to impose a sales tax on proceeds a vendor derived from selling a product to a state agency, Indian Motorcycle Co. v. United States, 283 U.S. 570 (1931). Income derived from the same kinds of contracts with the Federal Government were likewise immune from taxation by the States. . . .

[But t]he rationale underlying *Pollack* and the general immunity for government contract income has been thoroughly repudiated by modern intergovernmental immunity case law. In Graves v. New York ex rel. O'Keefe, 306 U.S. 466 (1939), the Court announced, "The theory . . . that a tax on income is legally or economically a tax on its source is no longer tenable. . . . So much of the burden of a non-discriminatory general tax upon the incomes of employees of a government, state or national, as may be passed on economically to that government, through the effect of the tax on the price level of labor or materials, is but the normal incident of the organization within the same territory of two governments, each possessing the taxing power. The burden, so far as it can be said to exist or to affect the government in any indirect or incidental way, is one which the Constitution presupposes. . . ." Id. at 480, 487.

With the rationale for conferring a tax immunity on parties dealing with another government rejected, the government contract immunities recognized under prior doctrine were, one by one, eliminated. . . . The only premodern tax immunity for parties to government contracts that has so far avoided being explicitly overruled is the immunity for recipients of governmental bond interest. That this court has yet to overrule *Pollock* explicitly, however, is explained not by any distinction between the income derived from government bonds and the income derived from other contracts, but by the historical fact that Congress has always exempted state bond interest from taxation by statute, beginning with the very first federal income tax statute. . . .

We thus confirm that the subsequent case law has overruled the holding in *Pollack* that state bond interest is immune from a nondiscriminatory federal tax. . . . [T]he owners of state bonds have no constitutional entitlement not to pay taxes on income they earn from state bonds, and States have no constitutional entitlement to issue bonds paying lower interest rates than other issuers. . . .

[Concurring and dissenting opinions omitted.]

Note

Another echo of the constitutional concern survives in §115, which codifies one strand of the traditional inter-governmental tax immunity doctrine. Should state or local governments receive a higher (after-tax) interest rate on bank deposits or loans than private investors? A higher return on investments in public utilities? Could Congress constitutionally repeal §115?

2. The Subsidy to Issuers of Tax-Exempt Obligations

The only sensible reason for preserving the statutory exclusion in §103 is a policy reason: to continue federal relief to state and municipal borrowers in the form of lower interest rates. The federal government gives up tax revenue by exempting interest on state and local bonds; those bonds therefore sell at a lower interest rate than if the interest were taxable; and state and local borrowers reap the benefit of lower borrowing costs. In effect the federal government is providing a subsidy to state and municipal borrowers distributed through the income tax system and the bond market, and the benefit of exclusion enjoyed by individual investors in municipal bonds is to be understood as compensation to them for participating in the distribution process.

Consider carefully the advantages and disadvantages of this method of distributing a federal subsidy. In what respects would it be better, or worse, to have the federal government simply reimburse states and municipalities for a specified portion of their interest costs? In particular, consider the legislation described in the following report. Why do you suppose it was not enacted, and has now even disappeared from the agenda?

MUNICIPAL TAXABLE BOND ALTERNATIVE BILL OF 1976

Report of the House Comm. on Ways and Means on H.R. 12,774 H.R.
Rep. No. 94-1016, at 2-7 (1976)

I. SUMMARY

Under present law, State and local governments issue debt obligations whose interest payments are not subject to the Federal income tax. This enables these governments to finance their debt at a considerably lower interest cost than would be the case if they were to use taxable bonds. This bill provides that if State and local governments elect an option to issue bonds the interest on which is taxable, they are to be paid a Federal subsidy of 35 percent of their interest costs.

From the standpoint of the State and local government, the taxable bond option is advantageous for two reasons. First, it will enable them to obtain a lower rate of interest on the tax-exempt bonds which they continue to issue. In no event will the cost of these bonds be more than 65 percent of what the interest rate would be on taxable bonds (otherwise it would be less expensive to issue taxable bonds with the 35 percent Federal subsidy). It is estimated that in the first full year of operation this reduction in the interest rate on tax-exempt bonds will result in an interest saving to the State and local governments of $130 million. By the tenth year of operation, it is estimated that this will result in an annual saving of over $1.6 billion.

Second, the opportunity for State and local governments to issue taxable bonds at no higher, and often lower, interest costs to them than in the case of tax-exempt bonds is advantageous because it will broaden the market for their bonds. Pension funds which have no need for tax exemption on the bonds they hold, banks which believe they already have their quota of tax-exempt funds, and individuals whose tax brackets do not justify purchasing exempt bonds with their lower interest rates, will in many cases find the taxable State and local government bonds desirable investments. It is estimated that the savings to the States and local governments from issuing taxable bonds in the first full year of operation of this provision will be about $30 million and in the tenth year of operation about an annual rate of $340 million.

From the Federal Government's standpoint, the taxable bond option is desirable because, by reducing the tax-exempt interest rate for State and municipal bonds and by reducing the volume of tax-exempt bonds which might otherwise be issued, both the number of persons benefiting from exempt bonds and the amount of their benefit is reduced, thereby increasing the equity of the Federal tax system. Thus, the Federal subsidy will reduce the windfall gain to purchasers of tax-exempt debt issues who are in the higher marginal income tax brackets. Moreover, the revenue generated from the shift from tax-exempt to taxable bonds enables the Federal Government to offset most of the cost of the interest subsidy (about $100 million in the first full year of operation and over $1.2 billion in the tenth year of operation) by additional revenue obtained from the larger volume of taxable bonds (about $80 million of tax revenue in the first year of operation and nearly $1 billion in the 10th year of operation). As a result, at a tax cost to the Federal Government of about $20 million in the first year and about $270 million in the tenth year, the equity of the tax system can be appreciably improved and at the same time interest costs of the States and local governments can be significantly decreased (by nearly $160 million in the first year and by nearly $2 billion in the 10th year).

The Federal subsidy of 35 percent of the interest yield is available under the bill for State and local government general obligation bonds (including government revenue bonds) but not industrial development or arbitrage bonds. State or local governments which elect the subsidy with respect to any issues may do so without any conditions being imposed by the Federal Government on the purposes for, or conditions under, which the obligations are issued. The Federal payments will be made automatically to the local government in time for it to make the periodic payments to the bondholders on behalf of both governments.

Bond interest payable by the Federal Government is provided for through the use of an entitlement, which is the same type of authorization used in the case of social security payments. In the unlikely event that the payment is not made available, suit could be filed in the Court of Claims to obtain the payment.

The Federal subsidy is to be available only in those cases where the State or local government makes its interest payment and the Federal subsidy relates only to 35 percent of the interest yield; the bill does not provide a Federal guarantee of the principal amount of the loan nor does it guarantee the issuing government's liability for its 65 percent of the interest payment where it issues taxable bonds. . . .

II. REASONS FOR THE BILL

Capital outlays by State and local governments, and bond issues to finance them, have increased sixfold since 1950. In addition to traditional expenditures for schools and other public buildings, highway projects and sewer and water projects, substantial capital outlays in recent years have been made for transit systems, public pollution control devices and industrial activity through industrial revenue bonds. . . . State and local government bond issues have increased from about 10 percent to nearly 25 percent of the total funds raised in capital markets since 1947. . . .

From 1960 to 1974 State and local government long-term bond issues have increased from $7.23 billion to $22.95 billion — more than threefold. These capital issues have been used for schools, water and sewer projects, highway projects, veterans aid, public housing, industrial aid, and other uses. The relative importance of these activities has varied during the 15-year period. . . .

Interest yields on both corporate taxable bond issues and on tax-exempt State and local government issues have increased substantially since the end of World War II. Average corporate yields in 1947 were 2.86 percent, and average municipal yields were 1.93 percent. By 1975, average corporate yields had risen to 9.46 percent and average municipal yields to 7.05 percent. Through this period, the ratio of government tax-exempt yields to corporate taxable yields has fluctuated between 64 percent and 80 percent. From 1969 to 1975, the ratio has varied between 67 percent and 79 percent — the lowest level in 1973 and the highest in 1969. The higher ratios have taken place when corporate or government demand for funds has increased or when a tight monetary policy has prevailed. . . .

Notes

1. The President's 1978 Tax Program included a similar taxable bond option, with emphasis on the assertion that nothing should be done to

interfere with the tax exemption or the existing market for exempt bonds. Indeed, it was said that the rate of subsidy should not be too high because of the risk that the market for tax-exempt bonds might wither away.

2. As reported by the Senate Finance Committee, the Revenue Bill of 1978 had an option for *bondholders* to treat *any* municipal bond as taxable, in which case they would be entitled to a grossed-up, refundable credit of 66²⁄₃ percent of interest actually received. The holder of 6 percent municipal bonds, for example, would be entitled to a $40 credit if she included her $60 interest plus the $40 credit in gross income. See S. Rep. No. 95-1263, 95th Cong., at 143-150 (1978). This is apparently the equivalent of a 40 percent subsidy on a 10 percent taxable bond, but with each holder having an option each year to go taxable or tax-exempt. What arguments should be made for and against this proposal?

3. Why do you suppose none of these proposals have been pursued since 1978? (The primary answer to this question is hidden in the next section.)

3.   Tax-Exempt Borrowing to Finance Private Activities

The foregoing discussion assumes that borrowing by state or municipal issuers is to finance public activities or facilities of one sort or another. But what is there to prevent municipalities or other state agencies from borrowing money and then investing it in private enterprise? A municipality could borrow to build an industrial plant, for example, to lease to a privately owned industrial corporation.

Indeed that has happened, beginning a long time ago in Mississippi, where some municipalities determined to combat unemployment by building plants to lease to potential employers. By the 1960s, the practice had spread to major industrial states and had become a fast-growing method of financing industrial expansion generally. Such bonds are referred to as Industrial Development Bonds, or IDBs for short.

Congress has responded with a series of restrictions on this and other practices by which tax-exempt borrowing proceeds have been devoted to private uses. In 1986 these restrictions were put in §§141-150 of the Code. The following excerpt gives some sense of the scope of these restrictions.

TAX-EXEMPT BONDS
Staff of Joint Comm. on Taxation, 100th Cong., General Explanation of the Tax Reform Act of 1986, 1151-1156 (Comm. Print 1987)

REASONS FOR CHANGE

GENERAL CONSIDERATIONS

Congress was concerned with the large and increasing volume of tax-exempt bonds being issued under prior law. The effects of this increasing volume included an inefficient allocation of capital; an increase in the cost of financing traditional governmental activities; the ability of higher-income persons to avoid taxes by means of tax-exempt investments; and mounting revenue losses.

At the same time, Congress recognized the important cost savings that tax-exempt financing could provide for State and local governments, in a period marked by reductions in direct Federal expenditures for such purposes. To the extent possible, Congress desired to restrict tax-exempt financing for private activities without affecting the ability of State and local governments to issue bonds for traditional governmental purposes.

Between 1975 and 1985, the volume of long-term tax-exempt obligations for private activities (including tax-exempt IDBs, student loan bonds, mortgage revenue bonds, and bonds for use by certain nonprofit charitable organizations) increased from $8.9 billion to $116.4 billion. As a share of total State and local government borrowing, financing for these activities increased from 29 percent to 53 percent. Essentially, these bonds provided an indirect Federal subsidy to private activities. This affected the efficiency and equity of the tax system in several ways.

First, the large volume of nongovernmental tax-exempt bonds increased the interest rates that State and local governments were required to pay to finance their activities. As the total volume of tax-exempt bonds increases, the interest rate on the bonds must increase to attract investment from competing sources. The additional bond volume caused by nongovernmental use thus increases the cost of financing essential government services.

Second, tax-exempt financing for certain activities of nongovernmental persons resulted in a misallocation of capital. Efficient allocation of capital requires that the return from a marginal unit of investment be equal across activities. This can result, in turn, only if there is no preferential treatment for investment in certain activities. By restricting the ability of nongovernmental activities to qualify for tax-exempt financing, the Act reduces preferential treatment for certain activities and allows capital to be allocated more efficiently.

Third, the equity of the tax system was harmed as high-income taxpayers and corporations limited their tax liability by investing in tax-exempt securities. Because of the large volume of nongovernmental tax-exempt obligations, tax-exempt yields were often close to taxable yields. Taxpayers with high marginal tax rates accordingly received an after-tax yield on tax-exempt bonds significantly higher than the yield they would have received from taxable investments. A perception of inequity arises when such investors are able to reduce their tax liability and still receive a rate of return nearly as high as that on taxable investments.

Finally, rapid growth in the issuance of nongovernmental tax-exempt bonds resulted in mounting revenue losses.

BONDS FOR GOVERNMENTAL ACTIVITIES

The Act retains the ability of qualified governmental units to issue tax-exempt debt for the financing of traditional governmental activities. These include general government operations and the construction and operation of such governmental facilities as schools, roads, government buildings, and governmentally owned and operated sewage, solid waste, water, and electric facilities.

While retaining the ability to issue bonds for governmental purposes, Congress was concerned that, under prior law, a significant amount of bond proceeds from governmental issues was being used to finance private activities not specifically authorized to receive tax-exempt financing. Abuses were noted whereby governmental bond issues were structured intentionally to maximize private use without violating the 25 percent private use limit of prior law. Other bond issues were intentionally structured to "fail" the prior-law IDB security interest test, when the bonds otherwise would be considered IDBs or would not qualify for tax-exemption. Congress believed that this diversion of governmental bond proceeds to nongovernmental users should be limited, but without setting the threshold amount so low that de minimis or incidental usage of government facilities and services by private users might cause interest on an issue to be taxable.

To accomplish this, the Act generally defines as a private activity (i.e., nongovernmental) bond any bond of which more than 10 percent of the proceeds is to be used in a trade or business of any person or persons other than a governmental unit, and which is to be directly or indirectly repaid from, or secured by, revenues from a private trade or business. (This is similar to the IDB definition of prior law.) Additionally, a bond is a private activity bond if an amount exceeding the lesser of 5 percent or $5 million of the proceeds is to be used for loans to any person or persons other than a governmental unit. Congress believed that these rules provide an appropriate limit for preventing the diversion of governmental bond proceeds for conduit financing for nongovernmental users, without affecting the availability of tax-exempt financing for traditional governmental activities. The Act also modifies the prior-law security interest test to include certain indirect private payments, including payments which may have been structured with the intent of circumventing the test.

Congress recognized that State and local governments can, in certain cases, achieve significant cost efficiencies through joint public-private partnerships that utilize private management skills to assist in the provision of governmental services. Congress believed that properly restricted private management contracts should not prevent qualified governmental units from issuing tax-exempt obligations to finance the provision of these services. The Act accordingly liberalizes prior law by expanding the scope of private management contracts that are permitted in conjunction with governmental tax-exempt financing.

EXCEPTIONS FOR CERTAIN PRIVATE ACTIVITY BONDS

IN GENERAL

The Act continues certain exceptions to the general rule that interest on bonds for persons other than State and local governmental units, referred to collectively as private activity bonds, is taxable. These include many of the exceptions allowing such financing under prior law.[39]

BONDS FOR SECTION 501(C)(3) ORGANIZATIONS

The act generally continues the substantive prior-law treatment of bonds issued for section 501(c)(3) organizations, to the extent the proceeds of those bonds are used to finance activities that are directly related to the exempt purpose of the organization. Congress believed that the services provided to the general public by these organizations warrant continued availability of tax-exempt financing without regard to State volume limitations. Certain restrictions imposed on other private activity bonds, including a public approval requirement and a limit on bond-financed issuance costs, are extended to these bonds.

STATE PRIVATE ACTIVITY BOND VOLUME LIMITATIONS

While continuing tax-exempt financing for certain activities of non-governmental persons, Congress believed it important to control the total volume of tax-exempt bonds issued for such activities. To accomplish this, the Act provides a limitation on the aggregate annual amount of private activity bonds that each State (including local governments therein) may issue. Congress believed that this new private activity bond volume limitation will ensure that the activities for which private activity bonds are issued will be scrutinized more closely by governmental units, and that such bonds will be targeted better to serve those persons and activities for which the exceptions are intended. Imposition of a single volume limitation, in place of the separate limitations imposed under prior law, was intended to allow State and local governments' flexibility in allocating this limited Federal subsidy among qualifying activities.

---

39. The Act permits issuance of tax-exempt private activity bonds if the bonds are exempt-facility bonds (bonds for airports, docks and wharves, mass commuting facilities, water-furnishing facilities, sewage and solid waste disposal facilities, facilities for the local furnishing of electricity or gas, local district heating or cooling facilities, qualified hazardous waste disposal facilities, and multifamily residential rental projects), qualified small issue bonds, certain mortgage revenue bonds, qualified 501(c)(3) bonds, qualified student loan bonds, and qualified redevelopment bonds.

In addition to private activity bonds, Congress intended that the substantial diversion of governmental bond proceeds to nongovernmental persons be scrutinized strictly by State and local government issuers. Therefore, the Act includes in the new State private activity bond volume limitations the portion of governmental bond proceeds, in excess of $15 million, that is to be used by nongovernmental persons. Subjecting this financing to the private activity bond volume limitations provides parity with the treatment accorded other tax-exempt financing nongovernmental persons.

Congress understood the importance of solid waste disposal facilities to many communities, and that such facilities can frequently be operated more efficiently by private contractors. Congress believed that, where solid waste disposal facilities are owned by governmental units, operation by private parties should not cause financing for these facilities to be treated differently from that for comparable governmentally owned and operated facilities. Therefore the Act does not subject tax-exempt financing for governmentally owned solid waste facilities to the new private activity bond volume limitations. Other bonds not subject to the volume limitations include bonds for airports, docks and wharves (facilities which also must be governmentally owned under the Act), and qualified 501(c)(3) bonds. . . .

ARBITRAGE RESTRICTIONS

The lower borrowing cost obtained through tax-exempt bonds provides the potential to earn arbitrage profits by investing tax exempt bond proceeds at higher, taxable yields, unless such transactions are restricted. Arbitrage transactions have no economic substance, but are made profitable solely through the ability to borrow at tax-exempt rates. The ability to earn and retain arbitrage profits provides a substantial incentive for qualified governmental units to issue more bonds, to issue them earlier, and to leave them outstanding longer than they otherwise would. . . .

The Act requires issuers of tax-exempt bonds to rebate to the Federal Government most arbitrage earned from investment of tax-exempt bond proceeds. Congress chose to require rebate of arbitrage profits because it believed that prohibiting earning of any profits (e.g., through elimination of temporary periods and other exceptions to the arbitrage yield restrictions) could prove unduly burdensome administratively. The rebate requirement is more flexible than — but substantively equivalent to — prohibiting the earning of arbitrage profits, a move that Congress initially took on a more limited scale in 1969. . . .

Note

While §103 excludes the interest on qualified private activity bonds from gross income, that interest is classified as an item of tax preference by

§57(a)(5) and is therefore subject to the alternative minimum tax (AMT) by virtue of §55(b)(2). Individuals subject to the AMT may find their "tax-free" bond interest taxed at 26 or 28 percent. If qualified private activity bonds are held in a bond fund offered by a regulated investment company (mutual fund) and the company pays exempt-interest dividends to its shareholders, then both the regular tax exclusion and the AMT taint flow through to the investors.

B. TAX EXPENDITURES IN GENERAL

In 1967, Professor Stanley Surrey, then Assistant Secretary of the Treasury for Tax Policy, coined the expression *tax expenditures* for income tax provisions that might be viewed as functional substitutes for direct government expenditures. He argued that such provisions should be omitted from the tax code and made to stand or fall on their own merits as direct expenditures in competition with other spending programs. The argument is based partly on the distortions that result from intervention of the graduated rate schedule if a tax expenditure takes the form of an exclusion or a deduction in computing taxable income. It is also based in part on institutional considerations that affect both legislation and administration — that tax expenditures should be judged in Congress and administered in the government by the persons responsible for direct expenditures on the same subject and should be subjected to the same process of budgetary evaluation as are direct expenditures. See Surrey, Pathways to Tax Reform (1973).

This mode of analysis is very compelling with respect to the municipal bond exclusion because there is no plausible explanation for the exclusion except as a subsidy for interest costs of state and local governments. Moreover, the distortional effect of graduated individual rates on that subsidy is clear: the tax benefit to individual bondholders will vary according to their marginal rates while the subsidy enjoyed by the borrower on any particular issue can only occur at a single rate. Tax expenditure analysis has been instrumental both in suggesting that a direct subsidy would be more efficient and in generating the proposal for a taxable bond alternative, described in Chapter 8A.2 above.

But when the tax expenditure concept has been more widely applied it presents formidable problems of definition. Tax expenditures are conceived as the revenue losses that result from all special preferences that represent departures from a normal tax system. But there is no consensus on what is special or normal. The municipal bond interest exclusion is an easy case, but other provisions are much more ambiguous because their purposes may be, at least in part, to deal with problems intrinsic to an income tax. The capital gain provisions, for example, can be viewed from one perspective as a subsidy to capital investment, but a substantial part of their purpose has been to mitigate disparities in tax burdens that arise out of the realization requirement, a purpose that might well be viewed as intrinsic to an income tax.

Another example is that of personal deductions. It is easy to see them as subsidies for whatever activity produces the deduction, but some at least can also readily be seen as sensible refinements in the specification of a system of personal income taxation. See, particularly, Chapters 3C.2 (extraordinary medical expenses) and 11 (charitable contributions).

The following excerpts from the Fiscal Year 2009 Budget of the United States Government proceed from the Congressional Budget Act's definition of tax expenditures: "revenue losses due to preferential provisions of the Federal tax laws which allow a special exclusion, exemption, or deductions from gross income or which provide a special credit, a preferential rate of tax, or a deferral of liability." That definition does not overtly distinguish between provisions designed to encourage (subsidize) certain activities, and those enacted to improve fairness, to ease compliance with and administration of the tax system, or to reduce certain tax-induced distortions. The latter purposes, of course, are hardly extraneous to those of an income tax. Absent a clear standard for comparison—which the Congressional Budget Act failed to specify—the notion of a "special" or "preferential" tax provision is at best ambiguous, at worst subject to inconspicuous partisan manipulation. How did the Bush Administration deal with this latitude in the excerpts below? In the end these materials compare tax expenditures with direct outlays and regulations as alternative policy tools, suggesting that for some purposes tax expenditures may be the best choice.

ANALYTICAL PERSPECTIVES, BUDGET OF THE U.S. GOVERNMENT, FISCAL YEAR 2009
287-328 (2008)

TAX EXPENDITURES

The Congressional Budget Act of 1974 (Public Law 93-344) requires that a list of "tax expenditures" be included in the budget. Tax expenditures are defined in the law as "revenue losses attributable to provisions of the Federal tax laws which allow a special exclusion, exemption, or deduction from gross income or which provide a special credit, a preferential rate of tax, or a deferral of liability." These exceptions may be viewed as alternatives to other policy instruments, such as spending or regulatory programs.

Identification and measurement of tax expenditures depends importantly on the baseline tax system against which the actual tax system is compared. In general, the tax expenditure estimates presented in this chapter are patterned on a comprehensive income tax, which defines income as the sum of consumption and the change in net wealth in a given period of time. An alternative approach would be to pattern the tax expenditure estimates on a comprehensive consumption tax. Which approach is used is perhaps the most important factor determining what is included as a tax expenditure. For example, because a consumption tax does not tax the return to saving or investment, using a comprehensive consumption tax as the normative baseline for determining tax expenditures would exclude current tax exemptions related to retirement and education saving accounts. Similarly, business provisions that provide accelerated depreciation or expensing of investment would also be excluded as tax expenditures because investment is generally deducted immediately under a comprehensive consumption tax.

The choice of the baseline — a comprehensive income or a comprehensive consumption tax — is arbitrary when viewed from the perspective of the current so-called income tax system, which includes elements of both income and consumption taxes. According to Treasury Department analysis, roughly 35 percent of household financial assets receive consumption tax treatment because assets are held in tax-preferred accounts such as individual retirement accounts (IRAs), defined-contribution retirement plans (401(k) type plans), defined-benefit pension plans, and tax-preferred annuities and various life insurance products. The balance of household financial assets reflecting most other saving vehicles receive income tax treatment.

The ambiguities in the tax expenditure concept are reviewed in greater detail in Appendix A. This review focuses on defining tax expenditures relative to a comprehensive income tax baseline. . . .

The tax expenditure estimates presented below differ from a comprehensive income tax in a number of other important respects. While under a comprehensive income tax all income is taxed once, the U.S. income tax system generally taxes corporate income twice, first at the corporate level through the corporate income tax and then again when the income is received by investors as dividends or capital gains. This "double tax" is accounted for in some of the tax expenditure estimates, such as those related to retirement savings, but not in the corporate tax expenditures. Indeed, the tax expenditure estimates, in large part, view the individual and corporation income taxes separately, rather than as an integrated system as appropriate under comprehensive income tax principles. Other areas of divergence from a comprehensive income tax are detailed below.

An important assumption underlying each tax expenditure estimate reported below is that other parts of the tax code remain unchanged. The estimates would be different if tax expenditures were changed simultaneously because of potential interactions among provisions. For that reason, this chapter does not present a grand total for the estimated tax expenditures.

Tax expenditures relating to the individual and corporate income taxes are estimated for fiscal years 2007-2013 using two methods of accounting: current revenue effects and present value effects. The present value approach provides estimates of the revenue effects for tax expenditures that generally involve deferrals of tax payments into the future.

. . .

TAX EXPENDITURES IN THE INCOME TAX

Tax Expenditure Estimates

All tax expenditure estimates presented here are based upon current tax law enacted as of December 31, 2007. . . .

Two baseline concepts — the normal tax baseline and the reference tax law baseline — are used to identify and estimate tax expenditures.[1] For the most part, the two concepts coincide. However, items treated as tax expenditures under the normal tax baseline, but not the reference tax law baseline, are indicated by the designation "normal tax method" in the tables. The revenue effects for these items are zero using the reference tax rules. The alternative baseline concepts are discussed in detail following the tables. . . .

Table [8-2] ranks the major tax expenditures by the size of their 2009-2013 revenue effect . . .

Interpreting Tax Expenditure Estimates

The estimates shown for individual tax expenditures in Table [8-2] do not necessarily equal the increase in Federal revenues (or the change in the budget balance) that would result from repealing these special provisions, for the following reasons.

First, eliminating a tax expenditure may have incentive effects that alter economic behavior. These incentives can affect the resulting magnitudes of the activity or of other tax provisions or Government programs. For example, if capital gains were taxed at ordinary rates, capital gain realizations would be expected to decline, potentially resulting in a decline in tax receipts. Such behavioral effects are not reflected in the estimates.

Second, tax expenditures are interdependent even without incentive effects. Repeal of a tax expenditure provision can increase or decrease the tax revenues associated with other provisions. For example, even if behavior does not change, repeal of an itemized deduction could increase the revenue costs from other deductions because some taxpayers would be moved into higher tax brackets. Alternatively, repeal of an itemized deduction could lower the revenue cost from other deductions if taxpayers are led to claim the standard deduction instead of itemizing. Similarly, if two provisions were repealed simultaneously, the increase in tax liability could be greater or less than the sum of the two separate tax

---

1. These baseline concepts are thoroughly discussed in Special Analysis G of the 1985 Budget, where the former is referred to as the pre-1983 method and the latter the post-1982 method.

expenditures, because each is estimated assuming that the other remains in force. . . .

TAX EXPENDITURE BASELINES

A tax expenditure is an exception to baseline provisions of the tax structure that usually results in a reduction in the amount of tax owed. The 1974 Congressional Budget Act, which mandated the tax expenditure budget, did not specify the baseline provisions of the tax law. As noted previously, deciding whether provisions are exceptions, therefore, is a matter of judgment. As in prior years, most of this year's tax expenditure estimates are presented using two baselines: the normal tax baseline and the reference tax law baseline. An exception is provided for the lower tax rate on dividends and capital gains on corporate shares as discussed below.

The normal tax baseline is patterned on a comprehensive income tax, which defines income as the sum of consumption and the change in net wealth in a given period of time. The normal tax baseline allows personal exemptions, a standard deduction, and deduction of expenses incurred in earning income. It is not limited to a particular structure of tax rates, or by a specific definition of the taxpaying unit.

In the case of income taxes, the reference tax law baseline is also patterned on a comprehensive income tax, but it is closer to existing law. Tax expenditures under the reference law baseline are generally tax expenditures under the normal tax baseline, but the reverse is not always true.

Both the normal and reference tax baselines allow several major departures from a pure comprehensive income tax. For example, under the normal and reference tax baselines:

- Income is taxable only when it is realized in exchange. Thus, the deferral of tax on unrealized capital gains is not regarded as tax expenditure. Accrued income would be taxed under a comprehensive income tax.
- A comprehensive income tax would generally not exclude from the tax base amounts for personal exemptions or a standard deduction, except perhaps to ease tax administration.
- A separate corporate income tax is not part of a comprehensive income tax.
- Tax rates vary by level of income. Multiple tax rates exist as a means to facilitate the redistribution of income.
- Tax rates are allowed to vary with marital status.
- Values of assets and debt are not generally adjusted for inflation. A comprehensive income tax would adjust the cost basis of capital assets and debt for changes in the price level during the time the assets or debt are held. Thus, under a comprehensive income tax

baseline, the failure to take account of inflation in measuring depreciation, capital gains, and interest income would be regarded as a negative tax expenditure (i.e., a tax penalty), and failure to take account of inflation in measuring interest costs would be regarded as a positive tax expenditure (i.e., a tax subsidy).

Although the reference law and normal tax baselines are generally similar, areas of difference include:

Tax rates. The separate schedules applying to the various taxpaying units are included in the reference law baseline. Thus, corporate tax rates below the maximum statutory rate do not give rise to a tax expenditure. The normal tax baseline is similar, except that, by convention, it specifies the current maximum rate as the baseline for the corporate income tax. The lower tax rates applied to the first $10 million of corporate income are thus regarded as a tax expenditure. Again, by convention, the Alternative Minimum Tax is treated as part of the baseline rate structure under both the reference and normal tax methods.

Income subject to the tax. Income subject to tax is defined as gross income less the costs of earning that income. The Federal income tax defines gross income to include: (1) consideration received in the exchange of goods and services, including labor services or property; and (2) the taxpayer's share of gross or net income earned and/or reported by another entity (such as a partnership). Under the reference tax rules, therefore, gross income does not include gifts defined as receipts of money or property that are not consideration in an exchange nor does gross income include most transfer payments which can be thought of as gifts from the Government.[3] The normal tax baseline also excludes gifts between individuals from gross income. Under the normal tax baseline, however, all cash transfer payments from the Government to private individuals are counted in gross income, and exemptions of such transfers from tax are identified as tax expenditures. The costs of earning income are generally deductible in determining taxable income under both the reference and normal tax baselines.

Capital recovery. Under the reference tax law baseline no tax expenditures arise from accelerated depreciation. Under the normal tax baseline, the depreciation allowance for property is computed using estimates of economic depreciation. The latter represents a change in the calculation of the tax expenditure under normal law first made in the 2004 Budget. Appendix A provides further details on the new methodology and how it differs from the prior methodology. . . .

In addition to these areas of difference, the Joint Committee on Taxation considers a somewhat broader set of tax expenditures under its normal tax baseline than is considered here.

3. Gross income does, however, include transfer payments associated with past employment, such as Social Security benefits.

TABLE [8-2]
Income Tax Expenditures Ranked by Total
2009-2013 Projected Revenue Effect
(in millions of dollars)

Provision	2009	2009-2013
Exclusion of employer contributions for medical insurance premiums and medical care	168,460	1,051,950
Deductibility of mortgage interest on owner-occupied homes	100,810	576,680
401(k) plans	51,000	325,000
Deductibility of charitable contributions, other than education and health	46,980	273,990
Accelerated depreciation of machinery and equipment (normal tax method)	44,120	270,040
Capital gains (except agriculture, timber, iron ore, and coal)	55,940	257,230
Deductibility of nonbusiness State and local taxes other than on owner-occupied homes	33,200	256,540
Employer plans	45,670	216,310
Step-up basis of capital gains at death	36,750	197,792
Capital gains exclusion on home sales	34,710	191,770
Exclusion of interest on life insurance savings	23,500	140,640
Exclusion of interest on public purpose State and local bonds	25,900	137,490
Deductibility of State and local property tax on owner-occupied homes	16,640	131,660
Deduction for U.S. production activities	15,330	119,270
Child credit	29,950	109,760
Social Security benefits for retired workers	18,640	106,090
Keogh plans	13,000	82,000
Exclusion of net imputed rental income	7,550	80,766
Deferral of income from controlled foreign corporations (normal tax method)	13,780	76,280
Accelerated depreciation on rental housing (normal tax method)	11,760	72,760
Individual Retirement Accounts	11,700	67,400
[Exclusion of interest on non-public purpose (private activity) State and local bonds*]	9,220	48,870
Exception from passive loss rules for $25,000 of rental loss	8,840	47,910
Deductibility of medical expenses	5,920	43,910

(continued)

* Total of all categories of qualified private activity bonds itemized separately in table, including bonds for hospital construction; private nonprofit educational facilities; owner-occupied mortgage subsidy; airport, dock, and similar transportation facilities; qualified rental housing; student loans; water, sewage, and hazardous waste facilities; small issue bonds; highway projects and rail-truck transfer facilities; energy facilities; and veterans housing.–Eds.

Provision	2009	2009-2013
Social Security benefits for disabled	5,810	33,220
Self-employed medical insurance premiums	5,170	33,100
Earned income tax credit	5,440	33,080
Credit for low-income housing investments	5,780	32,440
Deductibility of charitable contributions (health)	5,300	30,900
Deductibility of charitable contributions (education)	5,270	30,660
Exclusion of workers' compensation benefits	5,920	30,540
Graduated corporation income tax rate (normal tax method)	5,290	28,390
Exclusion of veterans death benefits and disability compensation	3,950	22,680
Expensing of research and experimentation expenditures (normal tax method)	4,990	22,600
HOPE tax credit	3,640	21,560
Exclusion of benefits and allowances to armed forces personnel	3,480	18,900
Social Security benefits for dependents and survivors	3,240	17,320
Exclusion of reimbursed employee parking expenses	3,070	16,550
Exclusion of interest on hospital construction bonds	3,040	16,090
Exclusion of income earned abroad by U.S. citizens	2,900	16,040
Inventory property sales source rules exception	2,410	14,210
Lifetime Learning tax credit	2,340	13,800
Parental personal exemption for students age 19 or over	1,760	12,250
Premiums on group term life insurance	2,250	12,130
Additional deduction for the elderly	1,710	12,010
Carryover basis of capital gains on gifts	800	11,510
Exclusion of scholarship and fellowship income (normal tax method)	2,050	11,280
Exclusion of interest on bonds for private nonprofit educational facilities	1,930	10,240
State prepaid tuition plans	1,290	9,620
Special ESOP rules	1,700	9,300
Exemption of credit union income	1,450	8,060
Credit for child and dependent care expenses	1,720	7,680
Medical Savings Accounts/Health Savings Accounts	1,480	7,680
Deferral of income from installment sales	1,250	7,580
Employer provided child care exclusion	1,400	7,470
Deferral of interest on U.S. savings bonds	1,320	6,990
Exclusion of employee meals and lodging (other than military)	1,010	5,580
Exclusion of interest on owner-occupied mortgage subsidy bonds	990	5,280
Exclusion of certain allowances for Federal employees abroad	920	5,100

[About 90 additional items, each under $5 billion over 5-year period]

. . .

DOUBLE TAXATION OF CORPORATE PROFITS

In a gradual transition to a more economically neutral tax system under which all income is taxed no more than once, the lower tax rates on dividends and capital gains on corporate equity under current law have not been considered tax preferences since the 2005 Budget. Thus, the difference between ordinary tax rates and the lower tax rates on dividends, introduced by the Jobs and Growth Tax Relief Reconciliation Act of 2003 (JGTRRA), does not give rise to a tax expenditure. Similarly, the lower capital gains tax rates applied to gains realized from the disposition of corporate equity do not give rise to a tax expenditure. As a consequence, tax expenditure estimates for the lower tax rates on capital, step-up in basis, and the inside build-up on pension assets, 401k plans, IRAs, among others, are limited to capital gains from sources other than corporate equity. Appendix A provides a greater discussion of alternative baselines. . . .

PERFORMANCE MEASURES AND THE ECONOMIC EFFECTS OF TAX EXPENDITURES . . .

Comparison of tax expenditure, spending, and regulatory policies. Tax expenditures by definition work through the tax system and, particularly, the income tax. Thus, they may be relatively advantageous policy approaches when the benefit or incentive is related to income and is intended to be widely available. Because there is an existing public administrative and private compliance structure for the tax system, the incremental administrative and compliance costs for a tax expenditure may be low in many cases. In addition, some tax expenditures actually simplify the operation of the tax system, (for example, the exclusion for up to $500,000 of capital gains on home sales). Tax expenditures also implicitly subsidize certain activities. Spending, regulatory or tax-disincentive policies can also modify behavior, but may have different economic effects. Finally, a variety of tax expenditure tools can be used e.g., deductions, credits, exemptions, deferrals, floors, ceilings; phase-ins; phase-outs; dependent on income, expenses, or demographic characteristics (age, number of family members, etc.). This wide range of policy instruments means that tax expenditures can be flexible and can have very different economic effects.

Tax expenditures also have limitations. In many cases they add to the complexity of the tax system, which raises both administrative and compliance costs. For example, personal exemptions, deductions, credits, and phase-outs can complicate filing and decision-making. The income tax system may have little or no contact with persons who have no or very low incomes, and does not require information on certain characteristics of individuals used in some spending programs, such as wealth. These features may reduce the effectiveness of tax expenditures for addressing certain income-transfer objectives. Tax expenditures also generally do not enable the same degree of agency discretion as an outlay program. For example, grant or direct Federal service delivery programs can prioritize activities to be addressed with specific resources in a way that is difficult to emulate with tax expenditures.

Outlay programs have advantages where direct Government service provision is particularly warranted such as equipping and providing the armed forces or administering the system of justice. Outlay programs may also be specifically designed to meet the needs of low-income families who would not otherwise be subject to income taxes or need to file a tax return. Outlay programs may also receive more year-to-year oversight and fine tuning through the legislative and executive budget process. In addition, many different types of spending programs including direct Government provision; credit programs; and payments to State and local governments, the private sector, or individuals in the form of grants or contracts provide flexibility for policy design. On the other hand, certain outlay programs such as direct Government service provision may rely less directly on economic incentives and private-market provision than tax incentives, which may reduce the relative efficiency of spending programs for some goals. Spending programs also require resources to be raised via taxes, user charges, or Government borrowing, which can impose further costs by diverting resources from their most efficient uses. Finally, spending programs, particularly on the discretionary side, may respond less readily to changing activity levels and economic conditions than tax expenditures.

Regulations have more direct and immediate effects than outlay and tax-expenditure programs because regulations apply directly and immediately to the regulated party (i.e., the intended actor) generally in the private sector. Regulations can also be fine-tuned more quickly than tax expenditures because they can often be changed as needed by the Executive Branch without legislation. Like tax expenditures, regulations often rely largely on voluntary compliance, rather than detailed inspections and policing. As such, the public administrative costs tend to be modest relative to the private resource costs associated with modifying activities. Historically, regulations have tended to rely on proscriptive measures, as opposed to economic incentives. This reliance can diminish their economic efficiency, although this feature can also promote full compliance where (as in certain safety-related cases) policymakers believe that trade-offs with economic considerations are not of paramount importance. Also, regulations generally do not directly affect Federal outlays or receipts. Thus, like tax expenditures, they may escape the degree of scrutiny that outlay programs receive. However, major regulations are subjected to a formal regulatory analysis that goes well beyond the analysis required for outlays and tax-expenditures. . . .

Some policy objectives are achieved using multiple approaches. For example, minimum wage legislation, the earned income tax credit, and the food stamp program are regulatory, tax expenditure, and direct outlay programs, respectively, all having the objective of improving the economic welfare of low-wage workers.

Tax expenditures, like spending and regulatory programs, have a variety of objectives and effects. When measured against a comprehensive income tax, for example, these include: encouraging certain types of activities (e.g., saving for retirement or investing in certain sectors); increasing certain types of after-tax income (e.g., favorable tax treatment of Social Security income); reducing private compliance costs and Government administrative costs (e.g., the exclusion for up to $500,000 of capital gains on home sales); and promoting tax neutrality (e.g., accelerated depreciation in the presence of inflation). Some of these objectives are well suited to quantitative measurement, while others are less well suited. Also, many tax expenditures, including those cited above, may have more than one objective. For example, accelerated depreciation may encourage investment. In addition, the economic effects of particular provisions can extend beyond their intended objectives (e.g., a provision intended to promote an activity or raise certain incomes may have positive or negative effects on tax neutrality).

Performance measurement is generally concerned with inputs, outputs, and outcomes. In the case of tax expenditures, the principal input is usually the revenue effect. Outputs are quantitative or qualitative measures of goods and services, or changes in income and investment, directly produced by these inputs. Outcomes, in turn, represent the changes in the economy, society, or environment that are the ultimate goals of programs.

Thus, for a provision that reduces taxes on certain investment activity, an increase in the amount of investment would likely be a key output. The resulting production from that investment, and, in turn, the associated improvements in national income, welfare, or security, could be the outcomes of interest. For other provisions, such as those designed to address a potential inequity or unintended consequence in the tax code, an important performance measure might be how they change effective tax rates (the discounted present-value of taxes owed on new investments or incremental earnings) or excess burden (an economic measure of the distortions caused by taxes). Effects on the incomes of members of particular groups may be an important measure for certain provisions. . . .

RETHINKING TAX EXPENDITURES

*Address by Edward D. Kleinbard, Chief of Staff, Joint Committee on Taxation,
to the Chicago-Kent College of Law Federal Tax Institute (May 1, 2008)*

A. ORIGINAL GOALS OF TAX EXPENDITURE ANALYSIS

In 1967, Assistant Secretary of the Treasury for Tax Policy Stanley Surrey introduced to U.S. tax policy discussions the phrase "tax expenditures." Surrey used the term to refer to provisions of the Internal Revenue Code that are deliberate departures from generally accepted concepts of net income (usually by way of special exemptions, deductions, credits or exclusions) and that affect the private economy in ways that usually are accomplished by direct government spending. In Surrey's view:

> The federal income tax system consists really of two parts: one part comprises the structural provisions necessary to implement the income tax on individual and corporate net income; the second part comprises a system of tax expenditures under which Governmental financial assistance programs are carried out through special tax provisions rather than through direct Government expenditures. This second system is grafted on to the structure of the income tax proper; it has no basic relation to that structure and is not necessary to its operation. Instead, the system of tax expenditures provides a vast subsidy apparatus that uses the mechanics of the income tax as the method of paying the subsidies.[2]

Surrey believed that a close analysis of tax expenditures could lead to better "expenditure control" by the Congress, through a more complete accounting for government expenditures regardless of their form, and would also be helpful in fashioning "tax reform" policies. Surrey's "expenditure control" theory rested on his belief that tax expenditures escaped the scrutiny applied to actual appropriations programs.

Surrey hoped that the regular publication of a "tax expenditure budget" would induce Congress to abandon narrowly-constructed tax incentives and subsidies. He anticipated that, once tax expenditures were identified and clearly displayed as Government spending substitutes, subsequent dissection would reveal them to be poorly targeted or inefficient, when compared either to an actual government spending program, or (in most cases) when compared to not expending government resources at all. In this way, the "expenditure control" agenda would be advanced.[5]

Surrey also saw tax expenditure analysis as playing a vital role in tax policy debates. In particular, Surrey believed that many tax expenditures violated consensus principles of tax equity, economic efficiency or simplicity. Surrey hoped that, by rephrasing "tax incentive" proposals as "tax expenditures," and then by analyzing the equity, efficiency and simplicity consequences of those proposals as if they were spending requests, policymakers would recognize that many such proposals were inconsistent with the goal of a fair, efficient and simple income tax system.[6]

In the forty years since Surrey introduced the term to U.S. tax policy discourse, policymakers have relied on tax expenditure analysis to judge the policy implications of individual tax proposals, to gauge the overall health of the Federal income tax system, and to measure the aggregate governmental resources devoted to particular policies. Since 1974, Federal law has required

2. Stanley S. Surrey, Pathways to Tax Reform, Cambridge, Mass., Harvard University Press, 1973, at 6.
    5. Stanley S. Surrey and Paul R. McDaniel, Tax Expenditures, Cambridge, Mass., Harvard U. Press, 1985, pp. 32-37.
    6. Id., pp. 25-27, 69-98.

the Congressional Budget Office ("CBO") and the U.S. Treasury annually to publish detailed lists of tax expenditures. (In light of the traditional expertise of the Staff of the Joint Committee on Taxation ("JCT Staff") in respect of revenue matters, and a separate statutory requirement that Congress rely on JCT Staff estimates when considering the revenue effects of proposed legislation, the CBO has always relied on the JCT Staff for the production of this annual tax expenditure publication.) Other Federal organizations (e.g., the Congressional Research Service) also employ the principles of tax expenditure analysis when analyzing Federal income tax policies.

B. HAS THE ENTERPRISE SUCCEEDED?

Surrey's original hope that tax expenditure analysis would have a salutary effect on budget transparency (and through that, on actual budget outlays) has not been realized, for several reasons. First, tax laws and appropriations follow completely different paths through Congress, and in particular are developed by different substantive committees. As a result, in practice one type of legislation does not substitute for the other.[7] Second, many tax expenditures have vaguely similar distributional effects to those achieved through spending programs, but the two delivery systems are so different that in many cases each is a highly imperfect economic substitute for the other. Third, many commentators believe that, as budget and other pressures have made it more difficult to advance policies through the appropriations process, policymakers have wholeheartedly embraced tax expenditures as a second best means of implementing their policy agendas.

In fact, Congress's use of tax expenditures has accelerated over the years. In 1972, for example, the JCT Staff's first description of tax expenditures totaled some 60 items. Our 2007 pamphlet, by contrast, while employing essentially the same methodology as that of our first description 35 years earlier, listed 170 tax expenditures.

The importance of tax expenditures in dollar terms can be seen by comparing actual Federal discretionary outlays to the aggregate amount of tax expenditures. In fiscal 2009, the Federal government projects annual total outlays of more than $3.1 trillion. Of this amount, roughly $1.6 trillion will go to mandatory spending programs including Social Security, Medicare and Medicaid; $730 billion will go to defense and national security programs; and $260 billion will go to service the national debt. This leaves a projected $482 billion for non-defense discretionary spending of all types. . . .

---

7. See Emil Sunley, Tax Expenditures in the United States: Experience and Practice, in Tax Expenditures — Shedding Light on Government Spending Through the Tax System 155, 166 (Hana Pulackova Brixi, Christian M.A. Valenduc, and Zhicheg Li Swift, eds., 2004) ("I can recall only one time when Congress traded off a tax expenditure [tax deduction for adoption expenses] for a direct spending program, and that trade-off was possible only because the tax-writing committees also have jurisdiction over welfare and income support.").

Tax expenditure calculations cannot be compared directly with these projected actual expenditures, because the tax expenditure figure calculates the nominal revenues forgone by the existence of the rule in question, not the revenues that would be raised by repealing the rule; the two are not the same because actual repeal would have behavioral consequences that would affect post-repeal revenue collections. Moreover, tax expenditures are not additive, due to behavioral and other issues. Nonetheless, an indication of the relative magnitude of tax expenditures can be ascertained from the JCT Staff estimates contained in the CBO publication Budget Options.[10]

For fiscal year 2009, implementation of ten of these options, chosen for both quantitative importance and the degree to which they match up with the JCT Staff's most recent tax expenditure list, would increase revenue by about $250 billion (without taking account of potential interactions between the provisions).[11] Some of these options do not represent full repeal; for example, the CBO revenue options list includes converting the home mortgage interest deduction to a tax credit at an effective 15 percent rate for primary residence mortgages below $400,000, but preserves the tax benefits of home mortgage interest payments to that extent. Moreover, while these ten options are among the larger revenue raisers on the CBO list, these options do not correspond strictly to the ten largest tax expenditures contained in our most recent tax expenditure pamphlet. Yet even so, they amount to more than half of all government non-defense discretionary spending. Their magnitude illustrates the enormous importance of tax expenditures today, relative to actual non-defense discretionary appropriations.

Tax expenditure analysis by itself thus has not succeeded in its first mission of "expenditure control." That does not mean, however, that tax expenditure analysis has wholly failed, but rather that its principal utility has been as a tool of tax policy and tax distributional analysis. The rhetoric of tax expenditure analysis in fact can provide a useful mechanism to judge the fairness, efficiency and simplicity consequences of many "incentive" proposals. Policymakers further look to tax expenditure analysis to provide insight into "base broadening" and similar measures.

As a result of contemporary "PAYGO" requirements, policymakers today typically pair tax expenditures against tax revenue-raising measures, rather than proposing them as a direct substitute for spending programs. In light of this reality, and the fact that tax expenditure analysis can provide a successful framework for addressing tax equity, efficiency and simplicity

---

10. Congressional Budget Office Budget Options (February 2007), *http://www.cbo.gov.*

11. . . . These items are, respectively: repeal of the mortgage interest deduction and conversion of the mortgage interest deduction to a credit for primary residence mortgages under $400,000; elimination of the deductions for State and local taxes; limitation on the deductions for charitable giving to amounts exceeding two percent of Adjusted Gross Income; inclusion of employer-paid premiums for income-replacement insurance in employees' taxable income; reduction in the tax exclusion for employer-paid health insurance; elimination of the child tax credit; repeal of the expensing of exploration and development costs for extractive industries; repeal of the deduction for domestic production activities; and elimination of the source rules exception for exports.

issues raised by a new proposal or the tax system as a whole, we believe it appropriate to proceed on the basis that tax expenditure analysis today exists primarily as a tool of tax policy, rather than budget expenditure control.

C. WHY REVISIT TAX EXPENDITURE ANALYSIS NOW?

As currently applied, tax expenditure analysis is less helpful to policy-makers in fashioning tax policy than might otherwise be the case, because the proponents of tax expenditure analysis generally have failed to respond convincingly to the important criticisms leveled against it. Tax expenditure analysis has always been controversial, and there is today a voluminous literature criticizing its premises and implementation as a tool of tax policy.

Many tax academics and policy experts have criticized tax expenditure analysis as resting on insufficiently rigorous foundations. These critics argue that the ideal "normal" tax system from which tax expenditures are identified does not correspond to any generally accepted formal definition of net income. Some observers further view tax expenditure analysis, in the form currently implemented, as a thinly veiled agenda for a specific form of tax reform. Under this view, the normative tax system at the heart of tax expenditure analysis is not simply an analytical tool, but is also an aspirational goal of the process. Others have questioned whether tax expenditure analysis serves any purpose at all, because the doctrine appears to these critics to rest on the unexamined premise that the tax laws should be uniquely "privileged," through not being burdened by the political compromises and policy agendas reflected in appropriations legislation. Finally, some critics question the narrow focus on subsidies that are favorable to taxpayers, noting that there also are narrowly punitive provisions in the Internal Revenue Code. All these criticisms have gone largely unanswered.

The most important of these criticisms is the objection to the "normal" tax system.[12] In current tax expenditure analysis, the "normal" tax plays three roles. First, it serves as the benchmark against which present law tax provisions are measured to determine whether they constitute tax expenditures. Second, the "normal" tax operates, at least in the view of some, as an implicit reproach to the current tax system, through being held up as an aspirational but achievable superior tax system. Third, the "normal" tax serves as the baseline from which to calculate the dollar magnitude of a particular tax expenditure.

The first two of these roles elevate the importance of the "normal" tax to a level it cannot support, because the "normal" tax is largely a common-sense extension (and cleansing) of current tax policies, not a rigorous tax framework developed from first principles. As a result, the "normal" tax

---

12. See, e.g., Boris I. Bittker, Accounting for Federal "Tax Subsidies" in the National Budget, 22 Nat'l. Tax J. 244 (1969).

cannot be defended from criticism as a series of ultimately idiosyncratic or pragmatic choices. If tax expenditure analysis is to enjoy broad support, it must be seen as *neutral* and *principled*; unfortunately, the "normal" tax satisfies these requirements only in the eyes of those who already believe that the "normal" tax accurately captures their personal ideal of an aspirational tax system.

To summarize, tax expenditure analysis can and should serve as an effective and neutral analytical tool for policymakers in their consideration of individual tax proposals or larger tax reforms. Its efficacy has been undercut substantially, however, by the depth and breadth of the criticisms leveled against it. Tax expenditure analysis no longer provides policymakers with credible insights into the equity, efficiency, and simplicity issues raised by a new proposal or by present law, because the premise of the analysis (the validity of the "normal" tax base) is not universally accepted. Driven off track by seemingly endless debates about what should and should not be included in the "normal" tax base, tax expenditure analysis today does not advance either of the two goals that inspired its original proponents: clarifying the aggregate size and application of government expenditures, and improving the Internal Revenue Code. The JCT Staff therefore has begun a project to rethink how best to articulate the principles of tax expenditure analysis, in order to improve the doctrine's utility to policymakers, reemphasize its neutrality, and address the concerns raised by many commentators.

D. PROPOSED NEW APPROACH

In a forthcoming pamphlet we will introduce a new approach to classifying tax provisions as tax expenditures.* Our revised paradigm attempts in particular to respond to what we believe to be the most important consensus objections to the current articulation of tax expenditure analysis. First, in many cases, it is not possible to identify in a neutral manner the terms of the "normal" tax to which present law should be compared. Second, many observers believe that the "normal" tax has been fashioned not simply to serve as the baseline from which to identify tax expenditures but also to advocate the adoption of that "normal" tax into law, by presenting it as an aspirational but achievable tax system that is superior to the current Internal Revenue Code.

To address these concerns, the revised classification of tax expenditures divides the universe of such provisions into two main categories: tax expenditures in a narrow sense (as explained below), which we label "Tax Subsidies," and a new category that we have termed "Tax-Induced Structural Distortions." The two categories together cover much the same ground as

* [Staff of the Joint Comm. on Taxation, 110th Cong., A Reconsideration to Tax Expenditure Analysis (May 12, 2008), *http://www.jct.gov/x-37-08.pdf.*–EDS.]

does the current definition of tax expenditures, and in some cases extends the application of the concept further. The revised approach does so, however, without relying on a hypothetical "normal" tax to determine what constitutes a tax expenditure, and without holding up that "normal" tax as an implicit criticism of present law. The result should be a more principled and neutral approach to the issues.

Our approach to "Tax Subsidies" (that is, tax expenditures in a narrow sense) builds loosely on the work of Seymour Fiekowsky and others, by defining a "Tax Subsidy" as a specific tax provision that is deliberately inconsistent with an identifiable general rule of the present tax law (not a hypothetical "normal" tax), and that collects less revenue than does the general rule. In practice, our conception of the compilation of general rules that together comprise our baseline for identifying Tax Subsidies corresponds closely to the Treasury Department's "reference tax" baseline in its tax expenditure analyses. (We refer to the converse case, of an exception that deliberately overtaxes compared to the general rule, as a "Negative Tax Subsidy.")

The Tax Subsidy tax base is constructed by asking what constitutes the general rule, and what the exception, under actual present law. Our determination of Tax Subsidies in most cases thus is made, not by reference to an alternative and hypothetical normal tax chosen by the JCT Staff, but rather by reference to the face of the Internal Revenue Code itself (along with its legislative history and similar straightforward tools for identifying legislative intent).

Fiekowsky and others would go further than we propose to do, by classifying a tax provision as what we call a Tax Subsidy only if that provision could be replaced by a direct expenditure program in a reasonably administrable manner.[13] The Treasury Department also has adopted this "spending substitute" leg to its definition; we understand, however, that the Treasury Department does not currently exclude any prospective tax expenditure on the grounds that a spending program could not be designed as an effective substitute.

In practice, many Tax Subsidies will satisfy this second test as well, but in the end we believe it better not to add this second test to our definition, for two reasons. First, in some cases the test will lead to new but ultimately fruitless debates about whether a hypothetical spending program could be designed to accomplish the same distributional effects as does a particular tax provision. Second, as explained earlier, we believe that experience has shown that tax expenditure analysis is most successful when applied as a tool of tax policy, rather than budget transparency. In our view, the "spending substitute" leg of the Fiekowsky definition points too much in the direction

---

13. Seymour Fiekowsky, The Relation of Tax Expenditures to the Distribution of the "Fiscal Burden," 2 Can. Tax'n 211, 215 (1980); see also OMB, The Budget of the United States Government, Fiscal Year 1983 — Special Analyses G-5 (1982); Victor Thuronyi, Tax Expenditures: A Reassessment, 1988 Duke L.J. 1155, 1187 (1988) (advocating a two-step classification scheme that (1) identifies a provision's significant purposes and (2) determines whether a nontax program can serve those purposes at least as well).

of the second agenda, by requiring that a Tax Subsidy be convertible into a straightforward spending substitute.

Some important provisions currently identified as tax expenditures cannot easily be described as exceptions to a general rule of present law, because the general rule is not clear from the face of the Internal Revenue Code. In light of this ambiguity, such a provision cannot properly be classified as a tax expenditure (more accurately, a Tax Subsidy) in the proposed narrower sense. If the JCT Staff were to attempt to expand the scope of Tax Subsidies to address these important policy questions by arbitrarily selecting one taxing pattern or another as the general rule, the result would be the same sort of subjective determinations that undermine the utility of a "normal" tax base in the current implementation of tax expenditure analysis.[14]

Present law's "deferral" treatment of the earnings of foreign corporations owned by U.S. persons is one example of a provision that today is treated as a tax expenditure, but that would not be classified as a Tax Subsidy under our proposed definition, because present law is ambiguous as to what constitutes the general rule for taxing foreign earnings. On the one hand, deferral is consistent with the general rules under which the Internal Revenue Code taxes corporations (including its definition of corporate residence). On the other hand, deferral arguably is a departure from the Code's general approach of imposing current tax on business income, wherever earned.[15]

Items like the "deferral" treatment of foreign earnings raise important tax policy issues. Moreover, present law's treatment of these provisions can be criticized on strict economic efficiency grounds. Tax expenditure analysis as currently implemented identifies some of these issues, but does so by reference to the "normal" tax baseline. The result is a sterile debate as to the appropriateness of the choice of that base, which in turn obscures rather than illuminates the important economic efficiency problems that current policies embody.

Our response to the insufficiencies of an inappropriately narrow definition of tax expenditures is to create a second major category of tax expenditures alongside Tax Subsidies, which we have labeled "Tax-Induced Structural Distortions." These we define as structural elements of the Internal Revenue Code (not deviations from any clearly identifiable general tax rule and thus not Tax Subsidies) that materially affect economic decisions in a manner that imposes substantial efficiency costs.

An example of a Tax-Induced Structural Distortion, beyond that already given of the "deferral" of foreign earnings, is the differential taxation of debt and equity. The distinction between debt and equity is a Tax-Induced Structural Distortion, because it encourages business firms to leverage their

---

14. See Thuronyi, *supra* at 1182-1186.

15. See J. Clifton Fleming, Jr. and Robert J. Peroni, Reinvigorating Tax Expenditure Analysis and its International Dimension, 27 Va. Tax Rev. 101, 196-197 (2008).

capital structures, but it is not a tax expenditure (Tax Subsidy) in the narrow sense, because there is no clear consensus as to what general rule of tax law, if any, the debt-equity distinction might violate.

We identify and present Tax-Induced Structural Distortions by considering their economic efficiency costs, not by invoking any normative tax system. For example, we analyze the current "deferral" tax treatment of the earnings of foreign subsidiaries as raising two important efficiency concerns: (i) U.S. firms have an incentive under present law not to repatriate "active" foreign earnings to the United States; and (ii) "deferral" also implies a conditionally different tax rate on foreign active business income than the rate that applies to domestic income, and this difference may affect the type and location of business investment when compared either to a wholly domestic enterprise, or a wholly foreign one.

One possible solution to these efficiency concerns is to adopt a territorial tax regime; another is the first solution's polar opposite, that is, to adopt a "full inclusion" tax regime. Each solution in turn raises issues of its own that policymakers should be aware of. Our tax expenditure presentation of this and similar cases, however, will not prejudge the issue (as current tax expenditure analysis arguably does), by holding up one solution or the other as the "normal" tax system.

While tax expenditure analysis can be helpful in identifying equity and simplicity issues as well as efficiency concerns, our definition of Tax-Induced Structural Distortions looks only to the last of these criteria. There are at least three reasons for this decision. First, efficiency is an inherently more neutral construct than is equity (and possibly simplicity), and our overriding objective in rethinking tax expenditures is to move to a system that most observers can accept as neutral and principled. Second, most tax expenditures that are particularly troubling for equity (or simplicity) reasons will be described as Tax Subsidies. Finally, most of the important structural ambiguities in the Internal Revenue Code today relate to the taxation of capital income (that is, business or investment income); efficiency goals loom largest in this context.

It is instructive to compare the two-pronged definition outlined above to the Treasury Department's current two-layer approach to the issue. The Treasury Department employs two concentric tax bases: a "normal" tax that is similar to that currently employed by the JCT Staff, and a "reference" tax base that (like our proposed tax base for identifying Tax Subsidies) constitutes a compilation of the general rules of the Internal Revenue Code and that can be visualized as a subset of the normal tax base.[16]

The Tax Subsidy component of the two-pronged approach advocated here is determined in a manner generally similar to the Treasury Department's reliance on its reference tax base, except that the definition proposed

---

16. Office of Management and Budget, Analytical Perspective, Budget of the United States Government, Fiscal Year 2009, Chapter 19, at 297.

here does not add an incremental judgment (albeit one that has not figured heavily into the current construction of the Treasury Department's list) as to whether a spending program could substitute for the tax provision in question. The definition of a "Tax-Induced Structural Distortion," by contrast, is very different from our understanding of what the Treasury Department does today, because it does not invoke a "normal" tax base at all. Instead, our definition of "Tax-Induced Structural Distortions" relies entirely on an objective inquiry into efficiency considerations. The two legs of our proposed definition thus are intended to be more transparent and objective than is the alternative.

The above discussion arguably overstates the practical differences among the different definitions. The Treasury Department, for example, lists some 152 items as tax expenditures under its "reference tax" baseline. In the Treasury Department's analysis, employing the "normal" tax as the baseline adds only nine additional items. While the JCT Staff's list of tax expenditures historically has included more items than the Treasury Department's, we nonetheless anticipate that our category of Tax Subsidies will comprise the preponderance of items that today are classified as tax expenditures.

We recognize that a few items that today are classified as tax expenditures may not fit neatly either as Tax Subsidies or as Tax-Induced Structural Distortions. We propose to continue to carry those items on our tax expenditure tables to preserve continuity with all of our prior work in this area. We will reevaluate this decision periodically, in light of the success (or failure) of the new approach proposed here.

Finally, the JCT Staff's revised approach to tax expenditure analysis further expands the traditional definition by identifying special provisions that increase the tax burden (above what the general rule would impose) as "negative" tax expenditures. (As previously noted, we label these provisions "Negative Tax Subsidies.") Limitations directly linked to various positive tax expenditures, the alternative minimum tax, and the phase-out of itemized deductions are not classified as negative tax expenditures but instead are considered reductions in those positive expenditures.

E. ESTIMATING THE MAGNITUDE OF TAX EXPENDITURES

The JCT Staff's current quantification methodologies for tax expenditures are not tantamount to revenue estimates, for two critically important reasons. First, our annual tax expenditure tables do not take into account the many large interactive effects that would be observed if Congress were simultaneously to repeal all the many tax expenditures that appear on our tables. Second, by tradition, tax expenditures are calculated on a static basis: that is, the behavioral consequences that would follow from repeal are ignored. By contrast, the JCT Staff's actual revenue estimates fully reflect anticipated behavioral effects of the proposal under consideration (subject only to the constraint that in the usual case we do not model any macroeconomic growth effects from the proposal).[19]

While the principal thrust of JCT's proposed revised approach to tax expenditure analysis is to deemphasize the relevance of the "normal" tax as much as possible, the new approach must still define a baseline from which to measure the magnitude of tax expenditures. As previously described, current tax expenditure analysis employs the "normal" tax as the baseline from which the JCT Staff can calculate the dollar magnitude of a particular tax expenditure.

By contrast, there is no single objective unit of measurement for determining the magnitude of all the provisions that fall within the two-pronged definition of tax expenditures recommended here. The revenues forgone by Tax Subsidies can be calculated by reference to the general rules of the Internal Revenue Code, but by definition this strategy does not work for Tax-Induced Structural Distortions, which are so classified specifically because there is ambiguity as to what is the present law general rule, and what is the exception.

On balance, we believe that the most feasible approach, and the one most consonant with the original legislative history of the Congressional Budget Act, is to follow general present-law tax rules (what the Treasury Department calls its reference tax base) for Tax Subsidies. We will further supplement that information with data for those Tax-Induced Structural Distortions that today are analyzed as tax expenditures by applying our current definition of the normal tax, as reflected in our recent annual tax expenditure pamphlets, *solely* for purposes of this quantification exercise. The end result is a bit complex, but has several practical benefits.

First, we believe that the most important benefit of tax expenditure analysis is that it provides a useful framework from which to evaluate the equity, efficiency and simplicity issues raised by a new proposal or present law. For this purpose, the *categorization* of the rule in question (as a Tax Subsidy, a Tax-Induced Structural Distortion, or not a tax expenditure at all) is more important than the *quantification* of the revenue foregone by the provision. Second, unless we are to quantify the forgone revenues only of Tax Subsidies, some baseline that is more inclusive than present law is needed, and this one has been developed (and modeled) for many years. Third, as described above, the quantification of tax expenditures is not, and has never been, intended to serve any purpose beyond providing rough rank ordering of the relative importance of different tax expenditures; because the quantification of a tax expenditure has never been presented as tantamount to a revenue estimate, the use of the "normal" tax as the baseline

19. Inside the JCT Revenue Estimating Process, A presentation by the Chief of Staff of the Joint Committee on Taxation to the New York State Bar Association, January 29, 2008. Revised January 30, 2008, *http://www.house.gov/jct/Inside_Revenue_Estimating.pdf.*

does little practical harm. Finally, this approach preserves continuity with our quantitative presentations of tax expenditures in prior years, which we believe to be helpful to policymakers and researchers alike. . . .

F. SUBCATEGORIES OF TAX SUBSIDIES

The JCT Staff believes that it would be helpful to policymakers to divide Tax Subsidies (i.e., tax expenditures in the narrow sense) into three subcategories. We propose these subdivisions with some reservations, because plausible arguments can be made to categorize many items in more than one subcategory, and we would not wish for classification arguments again to rob tax expenditure analysis of its productive power. We therefore emphasize that these subcategories are meant only to help policymakers to compare Tax Subsidies of like kind to one another; regardless of the subcategories to which we have assigned them, all Tax Subsidies rely on the same fundamental definition.

The subcategories of Tax Subsidies are as follows:

1. Tax Transfers

These generally are payments to persons made without regard to their income tax liability, usually because there was no income tax liability to begin with, or because the person's income tax liability was eliminated by another tax subsidy.[20] Unlike Tax Transfers, other Tax Subsidies only reduce (or increase, in the case of Negative Tax Subsidies) a taxpayer's income tax liability.

The subcategory of Tax Transfers today comprises the refundable portions of the earned income tax credit, child tax credit and the 2008 rebate. These provisions usually are based on perceived need as measured by income. The provisions authorizing these payments are the clearest examples of hybrid tax/spending programs, i.e., they are essentially direct government spending programs that use the tax system for distribution.[21]

2. Social Spending

This subcategory of Tax Subsidies includes Tax Subsidies that are unrelated to the production of business income and Tax Subsidies related

---

20. For evaluation purposes, the refundable portion of a tax expenditure is considered separately from the nonrefundable portion.

21. Tax Transfers are also among the tax expenditures that are close substitutes for existing direct government spending programs. For example, the refundable portion of the earned income credit and child tax credit are similar to non-tax-related government programs (both Federal and State and local) that address financial need and encourage employment of low-income persons.

to the supply of labor. These Tax Subsidies often are intended to subsidize or induce behavior (for example, charitable giving) that generally is considered to be unconnected to the production of business income. Examples include the itemized deduction for healthcare expenses, IRA deductions (or exclusions, in the case of Roth IRAs), and the nonrefundable portion of the child care credit. This category also includes the portions of the earned income credit, child tax credit, and 2008 rebate that are not refundable.

In cases where a provision has potentially both business and non-business statutory incidence, we classify the provision based on a judgment about the effect and/or the intent of the provision. Thus, for example, we treat working-condition fringe benefits, which are excludible from employee income (but deductible by businesses), as Tax Subsidies in the Social Spending category rather than in the Business Synthetic Spending category, described below, because this treatment of fringe benefits is generally viewed by analysts as affecting labor supply more than general business decisions. By the same token, IRAs, owing to their role in capital accumulation, are Tax Subsidies that have a link to Business Synthetic Spending. Nevertheless, we classify them as Social Spending, because so much of their design, including their mandatory distribution requirements, is geared toward income support for retirement. . . .

Owner-occupied housing preferences can rationally be categorized either as Social Spending or in the subcategory of Business Synthetic Spending, depending on whether one views home ownership as primarily a consumption activity or a substitute for an income-producing investment. On balance, we believe that they are better described here. Doing so acknowledges that preferences for owner-occupied housing reflect a social policy agenda that transcends the tax law. Moreover, it is more straightforward for non-economists to understand the tax treatment of housing as an exception to the general rule for personal expenditures (no deduction of interest expense or other costs) than it is to see the homeowner as foregoing the rental income that could have been obtained were the housing made available for arm's-length rental.

3. BUSINESS SYNTHETIC SPENDING

This category includes Tax Subsidies intended to subsidize or induce behavior directly related to the production of business or investment income (but excludes any Tax Subsidies related to the supply of labor). Examples of Business Synthetic Spending include the deduction for income attributable to domestic production activities, the completed contract method of accounting rules, various energy subsidies, the last-in-first-out method of accounting and the expensing of soil and water conservation payments. . . .

G. OUTLINE OF SUBSEQUENT WORK

. . . While we hope that our efforts to reduce the relevance of the idiosyncratic "normal" tax are viewed as responsive to the most serious criticisms of current tax expenditure practice, we acknowledge that no effort along the lines of a tax expenditure analysis can ever be entirely value-free. The unavoidable problem is that, by definition, tax expenditure analysis requires comparing actual rules to some hypothetical, whether that hypothetical is entirely exogenous to existing law, as in the case of the "normal" tax, or is inferred from circumstantial evidence and presented as a general rule in the law today, as advocated in our revised approach.

In this regard, we recognize that our specific implementation of tax expenditure analysis is firmly wedded to the view that the current Internal Revenue Code is at heart an income tax, because we employ that perspective when we attempt to identify what are the Code's general rules, and what the exceptions thereto. We believe that this approach is consistent with the language and history of the Code, as well as with the understanding of policymakers today. It of course is possible that subsequent policymakers may embrace a consumption tax as the fundamental starting point for a future Internal Revenue Code, at which point we would need to revisit many of the conclusions reached in [this new approach].

Questions

1. Is the controversy surrounding tax expenditure analysis really grounded in concern that the normal tax baseline is insufficiently neutral and principled, or is the real irritant that the normal tax is an *income* tax? Much of the recent criticism of tax expenditure analysis seems to come from proponents of consumption taxes. Traditional tax expenditure analysis highlights the cost of measures that reduce the tax burden on capital income, such as the expansion of individual retirement accounts and other savings incentives. In contrast, if a consumption tax base were taken as the norm, exemption of capital income would entail no departure from the norm, so saving and investment incentives would go unremarked (and unquantified).

2. How neutral and objective is the "tax subsidy" category? Is the cash receipts and disbursements method of accounting a general rule of present tax law or an exception?

3. Is the category of "tax-induced structural distortions" any more reliable? Is it true that "efficiency is an inherently more neutral construct than is equity"? Consider the "theory of second best," which teaches that, in general, elimination of one Pareto imperfection will be as likely to

increase as to reduce the net effects of the other imperfections in the relevant economy; consequently, there is no general reason to believe that policies that decrease the Pareto-imperfections in an economy without making it Pareto perfect will improve economic efficiency. See Richard S. Markovits, Two Distortion-Analysis Approaches to Economic-Efficiency Analysis: A Third-Best-Economically-Efficient Response to the General Theory of Second Best, U. Texas L. & Econ. Research Paper No. 132 (May 2008). If eliminating an identifiable distortion might actually worsen overall economic efficiency, can the new classification system achieve its "overriding objective . . . to move to a system that most observers can accept as neutral and principled"?

C.   CONCEPTS OF INCOME

As the preceding excerpts indicate, there is a relation of codependency between the concepts of income and tax expenditure. If we had a fixed and definite baseline concept of an income tax, the tax expenditures would all be departures from it. But equally, any agreed upon list of tax expenditures would provide an implicit baseline income concept.

The baseline income concepts all fall short of a comprehensive income tax in important respects: they remain realization-based and therefore do not include imputed income from services or unrealized appreciation in value. (Observe, however, that the Budget does estimate the imputed net rental income on owner-occupied housing.) These omissions are said to reflect difficulties in measurement. But, such difficulties aside, can the idea of a comprehensive income tax be specified in an analytically useful manner?

The best known and most often quoted attempt at such a definition, in our literature, is that of Professor Henry Simons, which was mentioned in Chapter 5 (but should be considered again at this point, and repeatedly hereafter). His definition, in its most explicit form, is as follows.

> Personal income may be defined as the algebraic sum of (1) the market value of rights exercised in consumption and (2) the change in the value of the store of property rights between the beginning and the end of the period in question. [Henry C. Simons, Personal Income Taxation 50 (1938)]

Throughout his book Simons paraphrases this definition repeatedly by asserting that personal income equals consumption plus accumulation. Clearly this is a broader definition than the standard by which tax expenditures are commonly defined, since it includes unrealized appreciation, for example. Can you think of other differences?

What limitations and ambiguities in the concept of personal income, if any, are implied by the Simons definition itself? A reading of Simons' work makes clear that he was primarily concerned with eliminating distinctions among gains attributable to different sources. His principal concrete proposals were to eliminate the municipal bond exemption, the capital gain preference, and the escape of capital appreciation from the tax base at death. His method for eliminating source distinctions, however, was to define income by reference to uses instead. That raises the question whether ambiguities and limitations implicit in the notions of consumption and accumulation are to be considered implicit in the concept of personal income. Some people think not, arguing that the reference to them should be taken as purely formal, a mere accounting identity. But that view would seem to leave the definition itself quite empty and purely formal; to what does it refer in the real world if not consumption and accumulation?

Consider, for example, the question whether theater critics' free tickets are income to them. The Simons definition can be read as suggesting that the answer to this question is uncertain for precisely the reason that it is unclear whether use of such tickets represents consumption that ought to be taxed. Indeed the question is exactly the same, just viewed from the other side.

Or what about the excess of the value over the cost of an education, general or professional, at whatever level? Perhaps one would say that whether this should be taxed is debatable precisely because it is unclear whether education should be accounted for either as consumption or accumulation; is there any "change in the value of the store of property rights" when one completes a course of study? Why did Simons use the word *property*?

On the other hand, interest on a municipal bond, a capital gain, or a cash windfall from whatever source, is no different from any other interest or dividends or cash income of any other kind, in terms of availability to be spent or saved—i.e., used for consumption or accumulation—and so any reason offered for excluding such items must be spurious, or at least extraneous. Or so the argument goes.

An earlier definition of income, by R.M. Haig, went as follows: "Income is the money value of the net accretion to one's economic power between two points in time."[1] Simons concurred in Haig's position but thought clarity was promoted by specifying that accretion consists of consumption plus accumulation, particularly making it explicit that consumption is included.[2] It is customary now to speak of the *Haig-Simons* concept of personal income, implying that Simons' definition is to be taken as a refinement of Haig's, not a new departure.

1. R.M. Haig, "The Concept of Income," in The Federal Income Tax ch. 1 (R.M. Haig, ed. 1921).
2. Henry C. Simons, Personal Income Taxation 61-62 (1938).

References

A. The Exclusion of Interest on State and Local Obligations: S. Surrey, Pathways to Tax Reform 209-222 (1973); Boris I. Bittker, Equity, Efficiency, and Income Tax Theory: Do Misallocations Drive Out Inequities?, 16 San Diego L. Rev. 735 (1979); Marty-Nelson & Blatter, Tax-Exempt Financing in the Aftermath of the Technical and Miscellaneous Revenue Act of 1988, 41 Tax Notes 557 (1988); Michael, State/Local Bond Exemption Is Inefficient, 48 Tax Notes 1671 (1990); Surrey, Federal Income Taxation of State and Local Government Obligations, 36 Tax Policy. Nos. 5-6 (1969); Surrey, The Tax Treatment of State and Local Government Obligations — Some Further Observations, 36 Tax Policy. Nos. 9-10 (1969); Winston, Industrial Development Bonds After TEFRA, 61 Taxes 20 (1983).

B. Tax Expenditures Generally: S. Surrey, Pathways to Tax Reform (1973); Bittker, Income Tax Deductions, Credits, and Subsidies for Personal Expenditures, 16 J.L. & Econ. 193 (1973); Bittker, Accounting for Federal "Tax Subsidies" in the National Budget, 22 Natl. Tax J. 244 (1969); Edrey & Abrams, Equitable Implementation of Tax Expenditures, 9 Va. Tax Rev. 109 (1989); Staff of the Joint Comm. on Taxation, 110th Cong., A Reconsideration to Tax Expenditure Analysis (May 12, 2008), *http://www.jct.gov/x-37-08.pdf;* Surrey & McDaniel, The Tax Expenditure Concept and the Budget Reform Act of 1974, 17 B.C. Indus. & Com. L. Rev. 679 (1976); Surrey & McDaniel, The Tax Expenditure Concept: Current Developments and Emerging Issues, 20 B.C.L. Rev. 225 (1979); Surry & McDaniel, Tax Expenditures (1985); Thuronyi, Tax Expenditures: A Reassessment, 1988 Duke L.J. 1155; Wolfman, Federal Tax Policy and the Support of Science, 114 U. Pa. L. Rev. 171 (1965).

C. Concepts of Income: D. Bradford & U.S. Department of the Treasury Tax Policy Staff, Blueprints for Basic Tax Reform (2d ed. 1984); Joint Comm. on Taxation, 98th Cong., Analysis of Proposals Relating to Comprehensive Tax Reform (1984) (reprinted in 25 Tax Notes 161 (1984)); B. Bittker, C. Galvin, R. Musgrave, & J. Pechman, A Comprehensive Tax Base(1968) (originally published in large part in 80 and 81 Harv. L. Rev. (1967-1968)); Comprehensive Income Taxation (J. Pechman, ed. 1977); Options for Tax Reform: Papers (J. Pechman, ed., Brookings Institution 1984); Henry C. Simons, Personal Income Taxation (1938).

Part II — *Deductions and Credits*

Chapter 9 — *Deductions, Credits, and Computation of Tax*

So far we have focused on the inclusion (or exclusion) of items in *gross income*. But the tax is primarily a function of *taxable income*, which is gross income minus deductions. §§1, 63(a). The time has come to focus on deductions.

There is no catchall provision for deductions like §61 for income; separate particular provisions allow deductions for business expenses (§162), interest (§163), taxes (§164), losses (§165 and 166), depreciation (§§167 and 168), charitable contributions (§170), medical expenses (§213), alimony (§215), moving expenses (§217), and so on. Many of these provisions contain specific and sometimes complicated qualifications and limitations. In addition, there are a variety of separate supervening provisions that disallow particular items. Most generally, for example, §262 disallows deductions for personal, family, and living expenses, "[e]xcept as otherwise expressly provided." For a more specific example, §267(a) disallows losses on sales of property between related parties.

Overlying all that, §§62, 63, and 67 provide different routes by which particular deductions may enter into the computation of taxable income. There are two major stages. Section 62(a) lists deductions that are subtracted from gross income to arrive at *adjusted gross income* (AGI). (These are commonly referred to as "nonitemized deductions" or "above-the-line deductions.") Section 62 does not authorize any deduction; it merely specifies which of the deductions allowed by other provisions are to be taken into account in computing AGI.

Section 63 then describes how to get from adjusted gross income to *taxable income*. Two alternative routes are prescribed. A taxpayer may elect to claim *itemized deductions*; otherwise a *standard deduction* will be allowed. In either case deductions will also be allowed for *personal exemptions*. Itemized deductions are defined to mean all allowable deductions except those already taken in determining AGI and personal exemptions (and the standard deduction itself). §63(a), (d).

So all individual taxpayers are entitled to the deductions specified in §62 and are also entitled to allowable personal exemptions plus an amount equal to the standard deduction. Those with itemized deductions in excess of the amount of the standard deduction can, by electing to itemize, increase their total deductions by the amount of that excess.

Since 1986 the statute has specified a further subcategory: miscellaneous itemized deductions. §67. These are allowed as itemized deductions but only to the extent they exceed 2 percent of a taxpayer's AGI. In 1990 an "overall limitation on personal deductions" was imposed that disallowed most other personal deductions to the extent they fall below 3 percent of the excess of AGI over $100,000 ($166,800 with inflation indexing in 2009), but that overall limit is being phased out and is scheduled to expire in 2010. §68. The medical expense and casualty loss deductions have their own higher floors (now 7.5 percent and 10 percent of AGI).

The most important of the particular provisions allowing and disallowing deductions for specific costs and expenditures are taken up from Chapters 10 through Chapter 15. Here we will deal further with the personal exemptions and standard deduction and the classification of deductions in §§62, 63, and 67, with some general questions about the purposes for which deductions are allowed, followed by a look at the computation of tax and credits.

A.   ADJUSTED GROSS INCOME

1.   Costs Incurred in Carrying on a Business (Other than Employment)

Alice is a lawyer who conducts her own practice. She collects fees of about $400,000 in a year. But that amount is not available to her for personal consumption or accumulation because she has to use much of it to pay rent for her office, salaries of a secretary and a junior associate, bar association dues and fees, the cost of telephone service and mail and services charges to Lexis and Westlaw, subscriptions to legal reporting services, court costs, the cost of traveling out of town to meet with clients and those with whom they do business, and so on; and on a less regular basis she has to buy up-to-date computer and network equipment, books for her library, and office furniture. Her net income, after deducting these costs, is around $85,000. If she were taxed on $400,000 at 2009 rates the tax would be about $115,000 (see Table 1-1) and she would be roughly $30,000 in the hole.

So the first function of deductions is to make taxable income for Alice something like $85,000 rather than $400,000. To that end, most of the items mentioned for Alice would be deductible under §162 as business expenses. For the computer equipment, depreciation would be allowed pursuant to §§167 and 168. If she had borrowing attributable to her business, interest paid on the borrowing would be allowed by §163. Moreover, all these items would be allowed above-the-line, in going from gross income to adjusted gross income, because all are "attributable to a trade or business carried on by the taxpayer" other than performance of services as an employee, as specified in §62(a)(1). In other words, these deductions would be allowed to Alice even if she does not elect to claim itemized deductions; they would be allowable *in addition* to the standard deduction, not just in lieu thereof.

Some people feel that this function of net income measurement is not only the clearest and most important function of deductions but is in some sense the only truly appropriate function. Deductions for expenditures that are not costs of earning income are therefore regularly classified as tax expenditures, whether or not there are other sufficient reasons for allowing them.

Despite their predominant importance for taxpayers like Alice, business cost deductions are not claimed at all by the great majority of taxpayers, primarily because most taxpayers' income is from wages and salaries, and to a lesser extent interest and dividends. These forms of income do not generally involve substantial costs. The activities of an employee may well involve substantial costs, but the normal arrangement between employers and employees will find employers bearing those costs. Salary and wages therefore typically represent something close to net income already.

Alfred, for example, is a law school classmate of Alice, but he works for a law firm as an associate for a salary of $75,000. The costs involved in his practice of law are similar to those born by Alice: office rent, secretarial salaries, travel expenses, and depreciation on computer equipment. (If anything Alfred tends to be more lavish than Alice in incurring some of such costs.) But these are, as is usual, paid by the law firm, not by Alfred, and his $75,000 gross salary income is therefore his to keep (that is, to spend or save for his own benefit). Thus Alfred's $75,000 salary is a sensible measure of his net income as is, without any need for business cost deductions.

Indeed the fact that most individuals' income consists of wages, salaries, interest, and dividends is part of what makes the allowance of deductions in Alice's case essential. To get a figure for Alice that is fairly comparable to Alfred's $75,000, and thus acceptable as a base for the same tax, it is absolutely essential to allow deductions for business costs.

2.   Other Nonitemized (Above-the-Line) Deductions

Look through the list of deductions allowed by §62(a) in computing AGI. These are what Congress has determined should be allowed in addition to the standard deduction even to a taxpayer who does not itemize. Is there any common theme that explains the choice of items for this treatment?

One might try to distinguish among deductions according to whether they represent costs of earning income, and AGI is sometimes talked of as if it reflected that distinction. To some extent it does. For example, while §163 allows a deduction for interest incurred to finance a variety of business or nonbusiness expenditures, §62 only allows a deduction, in computing AGI, of the portion of interest expense incurred in a trade or business. But the distinction is not pursued consistently: Unreimbursed employee business expenses and investment expenses are costs of earning income but are mostly not allowed in computing AGI. Even as to interest, AGI is computed without any deduction for investment interest, although this would seem to be a cost of earning investment income.

The main effect of listing a deduction in §62 is to make it deductible for nonitemizers. One principal effect of the treatment of itemized deductions is to relieve a substantial majority of taxpayers from the burden of recording and reporting deductible expenditures. One criterion for allowing a deduction as an adjustment should therefore be the relative compliance burden involved in keeping track of the particular expense involved. Consider to what extent the choice of what to allow in §62 seems to be influenced by this factor.

If a taxpayer qualifies as an itemizer in any case, then it generally makes no difference for a particular deduction whether it is treated as an adjustment in computing AGI or as an itemized deduction. Yet it may make a difference for other deductions if a taxpayer is affected by a limitation expressed in terms of AGI. The deduction for charitable contributions, for example, is limited to a percentage of AGI, so a taxpayer with excess contributions might prefer to have some other deduction classified as an itemized deduction in order to keep AGI high. See §170(b). Medical expenses and casualty losses, on the other hand, are subject to a floor defined in terms of AGI, so a taxpayer might get more from these deductions if some other deduction were treated as an adjustment to income instead of an itemized deduction. See §§165(h)(2), 213(a).

In discussion of tax policy AGI is sometimes used as a kind of proxy for economic income. It is not a very close substitute, but it does have the advantage of being an available figure in statistics compiled from income tax returns.

Question

Most above-the-line deductions allowed in computing AGI are costs of earning income of some sort. Alimony is not. Are there other adequate reasons for including it on the list?

B.   PERSONAL EXEMPTIONS AND THE STANDARD DEDUCTION

In 2009, Harry has a salary of $30,000, all of which he spends on simple personal consumption: rent, food, and an occasional movie. He does not own a home nor support a church, and he is stingy in relation to his college alumni fund. In short, he hardly spends a nickel on anything for which a tax deduction is allowed. He is unmarried and does not support any relatives (or anyone else).

Nevertheless Harry's taxable income will be only $20,650, since he is entitled to deduct $5,700 ($3,000 plus an inflation adjustment) as a standard deduction and $3,650 ($2,000 plus an inflation adjustment) as a personal exemption. These deductions are available without regard to the manner in which a taxpayer's money is spent. §151.

Personal exemptions are allowed to all taxpayers, whether or not they itemize other deductions, and their amount is substantial. In 2005, 269 million exemptions amounted to $840 billion, which was about 11.3 percent of AGI.[1]

Personal exemptions take the form of deductions but function as part of the rate schedule. The amount deductible for each exemption is specified by statute; it does not reflect any actual expenditure of the amount deductible and does not ordinarily depend on detailed records of expenditures, as do other deductions. In effect, the personal exemptions function in part to specify the amount of income an individual or family can receive without incurring any tax liability at all. They are part of what might be described as a zero-rate bracket in the rate schedule.

While the amount deductible for a personal exemption does not depend on expenditures, the general definition of *dependent* does, because it requires either that the individual claimed as a dependent has not provided more than one-half of his or her own support during the year or that the taxpayer claiming the exemption has provided over half of the individual's support. §152(a), (c)(1)(D), (d)(1)(C). Over the years this has presented very difficult administrative problems in the case of divorced parents in determining which parent, if either, met that requirement. Indeed that was once said to be the most frequently contested factual issue in the administration of the income tax by a considerable margin! There have been a series of statutory modifications of the basic test, of which the most recent now appears in §152(c). Read and evaluate that provision.

Look also at §152(c)(4). Why does that not take adequate care of divorced parents?

---

1. IRS, Individual Income Tax Returns 2005, Table 1.4 at 40, 53 (2007); also available at *http://www.irs.gov/pub/irs-soi/05in01ar.xls* Table 1.

The standard deduction is specified in §63(c); it is currently set for 2009 at $5,700 ($3,000 plus inflation since 1987) for an unmarried individual and double that amount, $11,400, for a married couple filing a joint return. Other amounts are specified for heads of household and married individuals filing separately, and additional amounts are allowed for individuals who are older than 64 years or blind. §63(f).

One function of the standard deduction is administrative: to make itemized deductions irrelevant for a substantial number of taxpayers. Over some period of time the standard deduction has been kept at a level such that only 25-40 percent of returns claim itemized deductions. Indeed the proportion of returns with itemized deductions rose in the early 1980s to nearly 40 percent in 1985, which was one reason for increasing the standard deduction in 1986. By 2005 the number of itemizers had returned to just over 35 percent.[2]

But the primary function of the standard deduction and personal exemptions together is to specify the amount of income that an individual or family can have without incurring any income tax, even if they cannot show any deductible expenditures. The sum of standard deduction and personal exemptions is sometimes referred to as the amount not subject to tax. For a couple with two children that figure is $26,000 in 2009. For an unmarried individual without dependents it is $9,350.

Tax reductions have frequently taken the form, at least in part, of increases in the amount not subject to tax. The 1986 Act involved a near doubling of the personal exemption amount over three years, and a substantial increase in the standard deduction. There has often been an attempt to set exemptions and standard deduction so that the amount not subject to tax will approximate official poverty income levels for various family sizes. In the 1986 Act Congress abandoned that goal for unmarried taxpayers on the ground that many of them share living quarters or live in their parents' homes, with the result that living costs are less than those reflected in the official poverty-level determination.

Look at §63(c)(5)-(6) and figure out what they are about.

Problems

1. *A* is a qualifying child of his parents within the meaning of §152 and has total income of $3,000, consisting of interest on corporate bonds given to him by his grandparents. How should *A* and his income be reported on anyone's income tax returns? Consult §1(g). What is the purpose of that provision?

2. How would your answer differ if *A* had no interest income at all but $5,000 of summer earnings?

---

2. IRS, Individual Income Tax Returns 2005, Tables 1.2, 2.1 at 32, 68 (2007); also available at *http://www.irs.gov/pub/irs-soi/05in01ar.xls* Tables 1 and 3.

C.   ITEMIZED DEDUCTIONS

Itemized deductions are all deductions except those allowed above-the-line in computing AGI and the personal exemptions. Itemized deductions are an elective alternative to the standard deduction. The effect is that itemized deductions only matter to the extent they exceed the amount of the standard deduction.

The magnitude of the major itemized deductions for 2005 is shown in Table 9-1. The major itemized deductions are in substantial part personal deductions — deductions for personal expenditures as compared with costs of earning income. Indeed, one sometimes sees references to "itemized personal deductions," but the categories of itemized and personal are not quite the same. For example, the deduction for alimony, although personal, is allowed above-the-line, while deductions for investment interest and other investment-related expenses, as well as many employee business expenses, are in the category of itemized deductions even though they represent costs of earning income.

Today about 35 percent of individual income tax returns contain claims for itemized deductions, but those returns account for 70 percent of total AGI.[3] The largest itemized deductions are for interest and state and local taxes. Most of the former is home mortgage interest, and the latter includes real estate taxes. These are substantial items for homeowners, and therefore, to a very considerable extent, homeowners are itemizers while others are not. See Chapter 10 below.

TABLE 9-1[4]
Itemized Deductions 2005

	Dollars (in billions)	Percent of AGI
Adjusted Gross Income on 2005 Itemized Returns	$5,185.7	100.0%
Itemized deductions		
Interest	405.7	7.8
Taxes	400.4	7.7
Charitable contributions	183.4	3.5
Medical expenses	67.4	1.3
Casualty or theft losses	15.0	0.3
Miscellaneous deductions (subject to 2% floor)	76.1	1.5
Other miscellaneous deductions	19.1	0.4
Less limitations on itemized deductions	−45.3	−0.9
Net Total	$1,121.8	21.6%

3. Id.
4. *Source:* IRS statistics of income data posted at *http://www.irs.gov/pub/irs-soi/05in01ar.xls* Table 3.

D. MISCELLANEOUS ITEMIZED DEDUCTIONS

Examine §67.

Elmer Employee has his office provided and other major employment expenses paid by his employer, but he does pay for a few items himself: professional association dues, subscriptions to professional journals, and a limited amount of client entertainment. These add up to a little under $1,000. Elmer's only income is his salary of $50,000, and being a homeowner he itemizes deductions. How will his employment expenses be treated?

First, these expenses are probably allowable under §162. Performance of services as an employee is clearly a trade or business within the meaning of §162.

Second, they are not deductible above the line because the trade or business of performing services as an employee is specifically excluded in §62(a)(1), except to the extent that the expenses are reimbursed or are incurred by a qualified performing artist or certain state or local government officials. §62(a)(2). They are therefore itemized deductions, but because Elmer is an itemizer anyway that by itself would probably not make much difference.

In addition, however, these expenses fall within the definition in §67 of *miscellaneous itemized deductions* and are therefore only allowed, even as itemized deductions, to the extent they exceed 2 percent of AGI, which for Elmer is $1,000; so on the facts given nothing is to be allowed. If the items in question added up to a bit more, then Elmer could claim them all in order to deduct the excess over $1,000.

The reduction required by §67 is not an alternative to the requirement of giving up the standard deduction; it is an additional requirement. So one cannot usefully deduct miscellaneous itemized deductions unless they exceed 2 percent of AGI *and* that excess together with other allowable itemized deductions exceeds the standard deduction.

Miscellaneous itemized deductions, like itemized deductions, are defined by exclusion. Section 62(a)(1) lists above-the-line deductions; itemized deductions are what are left. Section 67 lists the principal itemized deductions (and a few more), and miscellaneous itemized deductions are what are still left.

So what *are* the principal miscellaneous deductions? The statute does not answer that question, but committee reports do. The most important are unreimbursed employee business expenses; next are investment expenses; others are tax counsel and assistance fees (§212(3)) and hobby expenses (deductible in any event only to the extent of income from a hobby (§183)).

If one thinks in terms of purposes of deductions, there is something ironic about subjecting employee business expenses to a floor while letting residential mortgage interest be deducted in full. But the legislative history gives some reasons:[5]

> Congress concluded that the prior-law treatment of employee business expenses, investment expenses, and other miscellaneous itemized deductions fostered significant complexity, and that some of these expenses have characteristics of voluntary personal expenditures. For taxpayers who anticipated claiming such itemized deductions, prior law effectively required extensive record-keeping with regard to what commonly are small expenditures. Moreover, the fact that small amounts typically were involved presented significant administrative and enforcement problems for the Internal Revenue Service. These problems were exacerbated by the fact that taxpayers frequently made errors of law regarding what types of expenditures were properly allowable under prior law as miscellaneous itemized deductions.[52]
>
> Since many taxpayers incur some expenses that are allowable as miscellaneous itemized deductions, but these expenses commonly are small in amount, Congress concluded that the complexity created by prior law was undesirable. At the same time, Congress concluded that taxpayers with unusually large employee business or investment expenses should be permitted an itemized deduction reflecting that fact. . . .
>
> The use of a deduction floor also takes into account that some miscellaneous expenses are sufficiently personal in nature that they would be incurred apart from any business or investment activities of the taxpayer. For example, membership dues paid to professional associations may serve both business purposes and also have voluntary and personal aspects; similarly, subscriptions to publications may help taxpayers in conducting a profession and also may convey personal and recreational benefits. Taxpayers presumably would rent safe deposit boxes to hold personal belongings such as jewelry even if the cost, to the extent related to investment assets such as stock certificates, were not deductible.

The term *miscellaneous itemized deductions* was new to the statute in 1986, but it had been used for some time in the income tax return form. Schedule A of form 1040 is a full page titled "Itemized Deductions." The last item in Schedule A used to be titled "Miscellaneous Deductions," and it included everything not already covered under some more specific heading. That was a rather sensible use of the term *miscellaneous*.

Congress then borrowed the term from the form writers importing it in §67, but altered its meaning by excluding the items listed in §67(b)(6)-(12). So what were the form writers to do then? These items had hardly become common enough to take their own independent places on the form, but Congress excluded them from the statutory definition of miscellaneous deductions.

Apparently Congress has authority over meanings of terms as used in the statute, but the form writers remain the masters of their own domain

---

5. Staff of the Joint Committee on Taxation, 100th Cong., General Explanation of the Tax Reform Act of 1986, 78-79 (1987).

52. Common taxpayer errors have included disregarding the restrictions on home office deductions, and on the types of education expenses that are deductible; claiming a deduction for safe deposit expenses even if used only to store personal belongings; and deducting the cost of subscriptions to widely read publications outlining business information without a sufficient business or investment purpose.

(almost).[6] The penultimate item on the current Schedule A is "Job Expenses and Certain Miscellaneous Deductions" and the last is "Other Miscellaneous Deductions." The penultimate item provides for reduction by 2 percent of AGI; the last item consists of the items listed in §67(b)(6)-(12) and is not subject to reduction. In any event, the subject takes up considerably more of the form than it used to.

But if the form is a little more complicated, life under it may indeed have been simplified. Figures for 2005 show $107.8 billion of miscellaneous itemized deductions on 28.6 million returns before the 2 percent reduction and $76.2 billion on 12.4 million returns after reduction. So more than half of the returns on which such deductions are claimed have had them wiped out by the reduction. And many more must have figured it out before they filled it in, so the total reduction in returns whose tax depends on these items must be even greater.[7]

Consider the relation between §67 and the standard deduction in §63(c). Both have the effect of making certain expenditures irrelevant if they fall below a certain level, and both therefore relieve some taxpayers of the need to record certain expenditures. But the floor in §67 is a percentage of AGI while the floor implicit in §63(c) is a flat dollar amount. Years ago the standard deduction was 15 percent of AGI but not more than a specified dollar ceiling. What different effects result from these different formulations?

Section 67 was associated in enactment with §274(n), which simply disallows 50 percent of certain otherwise deductible expenditures for food, drink, and entertainment. The two overlap to some extent, although each applies to many things not covered by the other. We will look harder at them in Chapter 12D.

E. APPLYING THE RATE SCHEDULES

The tax rate schedules of §§1(a)-(e), as modified by §1(i), prescribe individual tax liability as a six-step function of filing status and taxable income, with marginal rates of 10, 15, 25, 28, 33, and 35 percent. Note that the dollar figures that set the break points in the rate schedule vary from subsection to subsection for different sorts of individual taxpayers. These dollar figures are subject to inflation adjustments. §1(f).

---

6. Cf. H. Dumpty, in L. Carroll, Through the Looking Glass 247 (Mod. Lib. Ed.):

"When *I* use a word . . . it means what I choose it to mean — neither more nor less."
"The question is . . . whether you *can* make words mean so many different things."
"The question is . . . which is to be master — that's all."

7. IRS statistics of income data posted at *http://www.irs.gov/pub/irs-soi/05in01ar.xls* Table 3.

Now look at the tax rate schedules prescribed for the current year. What is the relation between the dollar figures in the tax and income columns of each rate schedule? Can either be varied without changing the other? Why?[8] Compare the maximum dollar amount subject to the 10 percent bracket (the first break point) with the minimum dollar amount of tax prescribed for the 15 percent bracket. What is the relationship between these figures, and why? Now, looking at any one of the tables, consider the minimum dollar amount of tax prescribed for the 25 percent bracket. Where does this number come from?

Why are the taxable income dollar break points different in the several subsections? In particular what is the relationship between the figures prescribed for married individuals filing jointly and married individuals filing separately, and why? Now compare the minimum income subject to the 15 percent and 25 percent rates in the schedules applicable to unmarried individuals and married individuals filing separately, and notice that for higher brackets the break points diverge. Why? See §1(f)(8), (i)(1)(B)(iii).

Prior to 1986 the step from taxable income to tax liability before credits was simply a matter of applying a statutory schedule of the same form as those in §1(a)-(e) but with more brackets. There were then 14 or 15 steps ranging from 11 percent to 50 percent. Until 1981, the top rate was 70 percent. This number of rate brackets was prominently identified as an important element of complexity in the pre-1986 law, and reducing the number of brackets was touted as a great simplification. The number of explicit rate brackets in the schedule was indeed drastically reduced to two: 15 and 28 percent. But the claim of significant simplification is very difficult to defend. First, it is hard to think of any sense in which a greater number of rate brackets generated any significant complexity. For any particular level of taxable income the whole tax computation is on one line of the schedule in any event, so the only difficulty involved is that of finding the right line. Moreover, for most taxpayers with taxable income under $100,000, the rate schedules are translated into tax tables in the tax return instructions. These have hundreds of lines, each of which shows a $50 range (or less) of taxable income and a single resulting tax liability (thus avoiding any need to multiply); for these taxpayers the number of rate brackets in the underlying statutory schedule is completely hidden from view. See §3.

Moreover, the matter is more serious than a bogus claim of significant simplification. To achieve a nominal two-bracket rate schedule without an unacceptable loss in revenue Congress added new complications. The overall limitation on itemized deductions, §68, and the phase-out of personal exemptions, §151(d)(3), are two such complications that imposed disguised rate increases on certain high-income taxpayers. Worse still, the phase-out of personal exemptions applies over a limited range of income so that the higher marginal rate it (covertly) imposes on the very rich does not apply

8. Cf. §1(f)(2)(C).

to the extremely rich. See Table 1-1. The impact of these provisions (both §68 and §151(d)(3)) is limited over the period 2006 and 2009, and each of these euphemisms for higher rates is currently scheduled to expire in 2010, but absent further legislation each will reappear with full force in 2011.

F. CREDITS

Some things are allowed as credits against tax instead of deductions. There has been a considerable proliferation of personal credits in the past few years. Credits are set forth for the most part in §§21-54. Many of them are very specific.

A credit is taken into account *after* applying the rate schedules by sub-traction from the *tax* rather than from taxable income. Therefore, a dollar of credit is a dollar of tax reduction; a deduction, on the other hand, generally reduces tax by the same factor as the taxpayer's marginal rate bracket. Many credits are for only a prescribed percentage of the expenditures on which they are based. Look, for example, at §21.

Some credits are only allowable in reduction of taxes due; if credits exceed taxes the excess is lost. Other credits are said to be *refundable*, which is an inelegant way of saying that if the allowable credit exceeds any tax against which it might be applied, then the taxpayer can get payment from the government of the excess just as if getting a refund of an actual overpayment of taxes. At present the statute is arranged to set forth nonre-fundable personal credits first, in §§21-30C, and refundable credits thereaf-ter in §§31-36. The rest are business-related credits.

One credit whose purpose is obvious is the credit for tax withheld on wages. §31. It is also obvious why it is both a dollar-for-dollar (i.e., 100 percent) credit and refundable. The purpose of the credit is to treat taxes withheld from wages by the employer as payments by the employee, so any excess of the credit over the employee's actual tax liability is functionally an overpayment that ought to be returned.

The second refundable personal credit, in §32, is the Earned Income Credit (EIC). In a rather convoluted way this prescribes a negative income tax for earned income up to the "earned income amount" prescribed in §32(b)(2). Both the rate and the earned income amount vary widely depend-ing on whether the taxpayer (credit recipient) has no children, one child, or more than one. For a parent of two or more, the credit is 40 percent of earned income up to $12,570 in 2009 ($8,890 plus inflation adjustments since 1995). And then it stays put, in this case at $5,028, until AGI (with certain modifications) reaches $16,420. From there up the EIC is effectively phased out at the phase-out percentage, which in this case is 21.06 percent. So, assuming AGI consists solely of earned income, in 2009 the EIC imposes a negative marginal rate of 40 percent on income from zero to $12,570, a zero rate from there to $16,420, and a positive rate of tax of 21.06 percent from $16,420 to $40,295, at which point the whole credit will have been recovered.

The EIC is subtracted from any income tax liability a taxpayer might otherwise have, and any excess is paid to the taxpayer. In fact, for 2005 the EIC, which was claimed on 22.8 million returns (17 percent of all individual returns filed), reduced tax receipts by $4.9 billion and increased outlays by $37.5 billion.[9] So the provision is mostly a program for cash disbursements to people in need.

One might be a bit puzzled about why the credit is a positive function of income — more assistance is accorded, up to a point, to those less in need. Traditional negative income tax proposals have been different, providing a lump-sum welfare grant of some sort to people without income and then reducing the grant by a specified percentage of income. The *marginal* rate of tax on income implicit in such a scheme is positive even though the net payment may run in the opposite direction from a normal tax payment.

The negative *marginal* rate in the EIC originated in policies to provide relief from the burden of Social Security taxes, which are payable on an earner's income from the first dollar on. Observe that the credit percentage for an eligible individual with no qualifying children is set at 7.65 percent of earned income, which is the combined Social Security and Medicare tax rate on employee wages. Compare §32(b)(1)(A) with §3101(a), (b). The rate of credit for low-wage workers with children now substantially exceeds that function. Retention and expansion of the EIC reflects considerable political popularity for a scheme whose behavioral effects will be to encourage work, as contrasted with other welfare arrangements that have been thought to discourage it.

G.   ADDITIONAL TAXES

In some instances an additional tax is collected with the income tax (a kind of negative credit?). One is the Alternative Minimum Tax (AMT) for taxpayers with too many tax preferences. §§55-59 (explored in Chapter 16D below). Another is a tax on self-employment income, which is imposed in lieu of the regular Social Security taxes paid by employers and employees in the case of wages and salaries. §§1401-1403.

---

9. IRS statistics of income data posted at *http://www.irs.gov/pub/irs-soi/05in01ar.xls* Table 4.

References

C. Itemized Deductions: Andrews, Personal Deductions in an Ideal Income Tax, 86 Harv. L. Rev. 309 (1972); Koppelman, Personal Deductions Under an Ideal Income Tax, 43 Tax L. Rev. 679 (1988); Turnier, Evaluating Personal Deductions in an Income Tax — The Ideal, 66 Cornell L. Rev. 262 (1981).

D. Miscellaneous Itemized Deductions: Rubin, Tunneling Under the Two Percent Floor, 38 Tax Notes 177 (1988).

F. Credits: Allstott, The Earned Income Tax Credit and the Limitations of Tax-Based Welfare Reform, 108 Harv. L. Rev. 533 (1995).

Chapter 10 — *Interest, Taxes, and Casualty Losses (Home Ownership)*

Interest and state and local taxes account for more than 70 percent of itemized deductions. Both may be costs of earning income. But both may also be expenses of owning a home, and still they are deductible. Indeed, home mortgage interest alone constitutes 34 percent of all itemized deductions, and is claimed by more than 80 percent of all individuals who itemize. Casualty losses are comparatively tiny in magnitude (1.3 percent of itemized deductions) but raise similar issues from a slightly different angle.[1]

A. INTEREST

Read §163(a). This expresses the original rule with respect to interest expense that has been in effect from the beginning of the modern income tax until 1986. Notice that interest expense is deductible according to this provision without any requirement that it be incurred in a trade or business or profit-making activity of any kind. Why?

Next read §265(a)(2). This also has been in the statute for a long, long time. Recent legislation has added other limitations, many in §163 itself, but

---

1. Data in this paragraph are taken from IRS, Individual Income Tax Returns 2005, Table 2.1 (2007), and are also available at the Tax Statistics section of the IRS Web site, *http://www.irs.gov/pub/irs-soi/05in03id.xls.*

cases under the older, simpler statutory formulation provide the most convenient way into the subject.

For one more reference point it may be helpful to know from the outset that interest remains deductible on a mortgage of up to $1,000,000 incurred to purchase, construct, or improve a principal or secondary residence. Home mortgage interest has long been the principal kind of interest deducted on individual income tax returns, and its status has not changed. Moreover, deductions have been preserved on another $100,000 of home mortgage debt, whatever it may have been incurred for (home equity interest). §163(h)(3). Chapter 10C deals generally with the income tax treatment of homeownership.

1. What Is Interest? §163(a)

KNETSCH v. UNITED STATES
364 U.S. 361 (1960)

Mr. Justice BRENNAN delivered the opinion of the Court. This case presents the question of whether deductions from gross income claimed on petitioners' 1953 and 1954 joint federal income tax returns, of $143,465 in 1953 and of $147,105 in 1954, for payments made by petitioner, Karl F. Knetsch, to Sam Houston Life Insurance Company, constituted "interest paid . . . on indebtedness" within the meaning of . . . §163(a) of the Internal Revenue Code of 1954. . . .

On December 11, 1953, the insurance company sold Knetsch ten 30-year maturity deferred annuity savings bonds, each in the face amount of $400,000 and bearing interest at 2½ percent compounded annually. The purchase price was $4,004,000. Knetsch gave the Company his check for $4,000, and signed $4,000,000 of nonrecourse annuity loan notes for the balance. The notes bore 3½ percent interest and were secured by the annuity bonds. The interest was payable in advance, and Knetsch on the same day prepaid the first year's interest, which was $140,000. Under the Table of Cash and Loan Values made part of the bonds, their cash or loan value at December 11, 1954, the end of the first contract year, was to be $4,100,000. The contract terms, however, permitted Knetsch to borrow any excess of this value above his indebtedness without waiting until December 11, 1954. Knetsch took advantage of this provision only five days after the purchase. On December 16, 1953, he received from the company $99,000 of the $100,000 excess over his $4,000,000 indebtedness, for which he gave his notes bearing 3½ percent interest. This interest was also payable in advance and on the same day he prepaid the first year's interest of $3,465. In their joint return for 1953, the petitioners deducted the sum of the two interest payments, that is $143,465, as "interest paid . . . within the taxable year on indebtedness," under [§163(a)].

The second contract year began on December 11, 1954, when interest in advance of $143,465 was payable by Knetsch on his aggregate indebtedness of $4,099,000. Knetsch paid this amount on December 27, 1954. Three days later, on December 30, he received from the company cash in the amount of $104,000, the difference less $1,000 between his then $4,099,000 indebtedness and the cash or loan value of the bonds of $4,204,000 on December 11, 1955. He gave the company appropriate notes and prepaid the interest thereon of $3,640. In their joint return for the taxable year 1954 the petitioners deducted the sum of the two interest payments, that is $147,105, as "interest paid . . . within the taxable year on indebtedness," under §163(a) of the 1954 Code.

The tax years 1955 and 1956 are not involved in this proceeding, but a recital of the events of those years is necessary to complete the story of the transaction. On December 11, 1955, the start of the third contract year, Knetsch became obligated to pay $147,105 as prepaid interest on an indebtedness which now totalled $4,203,000. He paid this interest on December 28, 1955. On the same date he received $104,000 from the company. This was $1,000 less than the difference between his indebtedness and the cash or loan value of the bonds of $4,308,000 at December 11, 1956. Again he gave the company notes upon which he prepaid interest of $3,640. Petitioners claimed a deduction on their 1955 joint return for the aggregate of the payments, or $150,745.

Knetsch did not go on with the transaction for the fourth contract year beginning December 11, 1956, but terminated it on December 27, 1956. His indebtedness at that time totalled $4,307,000. The cash or loan value of the bonds was the $4,308,000 value at December 11, 1956, which had been the basis of the "loan" of December 28, 1955. He surrendered the bonds and his indebtedness was canceled. He received the difference of $1,000 in cash.

The contract called for a monthly annuity of $90,171 at maturity (when Knetsch would be 90 years of age) or for such smaller amount as would be produced by the cash or loan value after deduction of the then existing indebtedness. It was stipulated that if Knetsch had held the bonds to maturity and continued annually to borrow the net cash value less $1,000, the sum available for the annuity at maturity would be $1,000 ($8,388,000 cash or loan value less $8,387,000 of indebtedness), enough to provide an annuity of only $43 per month.

The trial judge made findings that "[t]here was no commercial economic substance to the . . . transaction," that the parties did not intend that Knetsch "become indebted to Sam Houston," that "[n]o indebtedness of [Knetsch] was created by any of the . . . transactions," and that "[n]o economic gain could be achieved from the purchase of these bonds without regard to the tax consequences. . . ." His conclusion of law, based on this Court's decision in Deputy v. du Pont, 308 U.S. 488, was that "[w]hile in form the payments to Sam Houston were compensation for the use or forbearance of money, they were not in substance. As a payment of interest, the transaction was a sham."

We first examine the transaction between Knetsch and the insurance company to determine whether it created an "indebtedness" within the meaning of ... §163(a) of the 1954 Code, or whether, as the trial court found, it was a sham. We put aside a finding by the District Court that Knetsch's "only motive in purchasing these 10 bonds was to attempt to secure an interest deduction."[2] As was said in Gregory v. Helvering, 293 U.S. 465, 469: "The legal right of a taxpayer to decrease the amount of what otherwise would be his taxes, or altogether avoid them, by means which the law permits, cannot be doubted. ... But the question for determination is whether what was done, apart from the tax motive, was the thing which the statute intended."

When we examine "what was done" here, we see that Knetsch paid the insurance company $294,570 during the two taxable years involved and received $203,000 back in the form of "loans." What did Knetsch get for the out-of-pocket difference of $91,570? In form he had an annuity contract with so-called guaranteed cash value at maturity of $8,388,000, which would produce monthly annuity payments of $90,171, or substantial life insurance proceeds in the event of his death before maturity. This, as we have seen was a fiction, because each year, Knetsch's annual borrowings kept the net cash value, on which any annuity or insurance payments would depend, at the relative pittance of $1,000. Plainly, therefore, Knetsch's transaction with the insurance company did "not appreciably affect his beneficial interest except to reduce his tax. ..." Gilbert v. Commissioner, 2 Cir., 248 F.2d 399,411 (dissenting opinion). For it is patent that there was nothing of substance to be realized by Knetsch from this transaction beyond a tax deduction. What he was ostensibly "lent" back was in reality only the rebate of a substantial part of the so-called "interest" payments. The $91,570 difference retained by the company was its fee for providing the facade of "loans" whereby the petitioners sought to reduce their 1953 and 1954 taxes in the total sum of $233,297.68. There may well be single-premium annuity arrangements with nontax substance which create an "indebtedness" for the purposes of ... §163(a) of the 1954 Code. But this one is a sham. The petitioners contend, however, that the Congress in enacting §264 of the 1954 Code, authorized the deductions. They point out that §264(a)(2) denies a deduction for amounts paid on indebtedness incurred to purchase or carry a single-premium annuity contract, but only as to contracts purchased after March 1, 1954. The petitioners thus would attribute to Congress a purpose to allow the deduction of pre-1954 payments under transactions of the kind carried on by Knetsch with the insurance company without regard to

---

2. We likewise put aside Knetsch's argument that, because he received ordinary income when he surrendered the annuities in 1956, he has suffered a net loss even if the contested deductions are allowed, and that therefore his motive in taking out the annuities could not have been tax avoidance.

whether the transactions created a true obligation to pay interest. Unless that meaning plainly appears we will not attribute it to Congress. "To hold otherwise would be to exalt artifice above reality and to deprive the statutory provision in question of all serious purpose." Gregory v. Helvering, supra, p. 470. We, therefore, look to the statute and materials relevant to its construction for evidence that Congress meant in §264(a)(2) to authorize the deduction of payments made under sham transactions entered into before 1954. We look in vain.

Provisions denying deductions for amounts paid on indebtedness incurred to purchase or carry insurance contracts are not new in the revenue acts. A provision applicable to all annuities, but not to life insurance or endowment contracts, was in the statute from 1932 to 1934, 47 Stat. 179. It was added at a time when Congress was developing a policy to deny a deduction for interest allocable to tax-exempt income;[6] the proceeds of annuities were excluded from gross income up to the amount of the consideration paid in by the annuitant. See H.R. Rep. No. 708, 72d Cong., 1st Sess., p. 11. The provision was repealed by the Revenue Act of 1934, 48 Stat. 688, when the method by which annuity payments were taken into gross income was changed in such way that more would be included. 48 Stat. 687. See S. Rep. No. 558, 73d Cong., 2d Sess., p. 24.

Congress then in 1942 denied a deduction for amounts paid on indebtedness incurred to purchase single-premium life insurance and endowment contracts. This provision was enacted by an amendment to the 1939 Code, 56 Stat. 827, "to close a loophole" in respect of interest allocable to partially exempt income. See Hearings before Senate Finance Committee on H.R. 7378, 77th Cong., 2d Sess., p. 54; §22(b)(1) of the 1939 Code (now §101(a)(1) of the 1954 Code).

The 1954 provision extending the denial to amounts paid on indebtedness incurred to purchase or carry single-premium annuities appears to us simply to expand the application of the policy in respect of interest allocable to partially exempt income. The proofs are perhaps not as strong as in the case of life insurance and endowment contracts, but in the absence of any contrary expression of the Congress, their import is clear enough. There is *first* the fact that the provision was incorporated in the section covering life insurance and endowment contracts, which unquestionably was adopted to further that policy. There is *second* the fact that Congress' attention was directed to annuities in 1954; the same 1954 statute again changed the basis for taking part of the proceeds of annuities into gross income. See

---

6. See §23(b) of the Revenue Act of 1932, 47 Stat. 179, which provided:

"(b) Interest — All interest paid or accrued within the taxable year on indebtedness, except (1) on indebtedness incurred or continued to purchase or carry obligations or securities (other than obligations of the United States issued after September 24, 1917, and originally subscribed for by the taxpayer) the interest upon which is wholly exempt from the taxes imposed by this title, or (2) on indebtedness incurred or continued in connection with the purchasing or carrying of an annuity."

§72(b) of the 1954 Code. These are signs that Congress' longstanding concern with the problem of interest allocable to partially exempt income, and not any concern with sham transactions, explains the provision.

Moreover the provision itself negates any suggestion that sham transactions were the congressional concern, for the deduction denied is of certain interest payments on actual "indebtedness." And we see nothing in the Senate Finance and House Ways and Means Committee Reports on §264, H.R. Rep. No. 1337, 83d Cong., 2d Sess., p. 31; S. Rep. No. 1622, 83d Cong., 2d Sess., p. 38, to suggest that Congress in exempting pre-1954 annuities intended to protect sham transactions.[7]

Some point is made in an amicus curiae brief of the fact that Knetsch in entering into these annuity agreements relied on individual ruling letters issued by the Commissioner to other taxpayers. This argument has never been advanced by petitioners in this case. Accordingly, we have no reason to pass upon it.

The judgment of the Court of Appeals is affirmed.

Mr. Justice DOUGLAS, with whom Mr. Justice Whittaker and Mr. Justice Stewart concur, dissenting. I agree with the views expressed by Judge Moore in Diggs v. Commissioner, 2 Cir., 281 F.2d 326, 330-332, and by Judge Brown, writing for himself and Judge Hutcheson, in United States v. Bond, 5 Cir., 258 F.2d 577.

It is true that in this transaction the taxpayer was bound to lose if the annuity contract is taken by itself. At least the taxpayer showed by his conduct that he never intended to come out ahead on that investment apart from this income tax deduction. Yet the same may be true where a taxpayer borrows money at 5 percent or 6 percent interest to purchase securities that pay only nominal interest; or where, with money in the bank earning 3 percent, he borrows from the self same bank at a higher rate. His aim there, as here, may only be to get a tax deduction for interest paid. Yet as long as the transaction itself is not hocus-pocus, the interest charges incident to completing it would seem to be deductible under the Internal Revenue Code as respects annuity contracts made prior to March 1, 1954, the date Congress selected for terminating this class of deductions. 26 U.S.C. §264. The insurance company existed; it operated under Texas law; it was authorized to issue these policies

---

7. The Reports are as follows:

"Under existing law, no interest deduction is allowed in the case of indebtedness incurred, or continued, to purchase a single-premium life-insurance or endowment contract. . . .

"Existing law does not extend the denial of the interest deduction to indebtedness incurred to purchase single-premium annuity contracts. It has come to your committee's attention that a few insurance companies have promoted a plan for selling annuity contracts based on the tax advantage derived from omission of annuities from the treatment accorded single-premium life-insurance or endowment contracts. The annuity is sold for a nominal cash payment with a loan to cover the balance of the single-premium cost of the annuity. Interest on the loan (which may be a nonrecourse loan) is then taken as a deduction annually by the purchaser with a resulting tax saving that reduces the real interest cost below the increment in value produced by the annuity.

"Your committee's bill will deny an interest deduction in such cases but only as to annuities purchased after March 1, 1954."

and to make these annuity loans. While the taxpayer was obligated to pay interest at the rate of 3½ percent per annum, the annuity bonds increased in cash value at the rate of only 2½ percent per annum. The insurance company's profit was in that 1-point spread.

Tax avoidance is a dominating motive behind scores of transactions. It is plainly present here. Will the Service that calls this transaction a "sham" today not press for collection of taxes* arising out of the surrender of the annuity contract? I think it should, for I do not believe any part of the transaction was a "sham." To disallow the "interest" deduction because the annuity device was devoid of commercial substance is to draw a line which will affect a host of situations not now before us and which, with all deference, I do not think we can maintain when other cases reach here. The remedy is legislative. Evils or abuses can be particularized by Congress. We deal only with "interest" as commonly understood and as used across the board in myriad transactions. Since these transactions were real and legitimate in the insurance world and were consummated within the limits allowed by insurance policies, I would recognize them tax-wise.

GOLDSTEIN v. COMMISSIONER
364 F.2d 734 (2d Cir. 1966)

Before Waterman, Moore and Friendly, Circuit Judges.

WATERMAN, Circuit Judge. Tillie Goldstein and her husband petition to review a decision of the Tax Court disallowing as deductions for federal income tax purposes payments totaling $81,396.61 made by petitioner to certain banks, which payments petitioner claimed were payments of interest on indebtedness within Section 163(a) of the 1954 Internal Revenue Code. . . .

During the latter part of 1958 petitioner received the good news that she held a winning Irish Sweepstakes ticket and would shortly receive $140,218.75. This windfall significantly improved petitioner's financial situation, for she was a housewife approximately 70 years old and her husband was a retired garment worker who received a $780 pension each year. In 1958 the couple's only income, aside from this pension and the unexpected Sweepstakes proceeds, was $124.75, which represented interest on several small savings bank accounts. The petitioner received the Sweepstakes proceeds in December 1958 and she deposited the money in a New York bank. She included this amount as gross income in the joint return she and her husband filed for 1958 on the cash receipts and disbursements basis.

---

* Petitioners terminated this transaction in 1956 by allowing the bonds to be cancelled and receiving a check for $1,000. The termination was reflected in their tax return for 1956. It might also be noted that the insurance company reported as gross income the interest payments which it received from petitioners in 1953 and 1954.

Petitioner's son, Bernard Goldstein, was a certified public accountant, practicing in New York in 1958. In November of that year Bernard either volunteered or was enlisted to assist petitioner in investing the Sweepstakes proceeds, and in minimizing the 1958 tax consequences to petitioner of the sudden increase in her income for that year. A series of consultations between Bernard and an attorney resulted in the adoption of a plan, which, as implemented, can be summarized as follows: During the latter part of December 1958 petitioner contacted several brokerage houses that bought and sold securities for clients and also arranged collateral loans. With the assistance of one of these brokerage houses, Garvin, Bantel & Co., petitioner borrowed $465,000 from the First National Bank of Jersey City. With the money thus acquired, and the active assistance of Garvin, Bantel, petitioner purchased $500,000 face amount of United States Treasury 1½ percent notes, due to mature on October 1, 1962. Petitioner promptly pledged the Treasury notes so purchased as collateral to secure the loan with the Jersey City Bank. At approximately the same time in 1958 Bernard secured for petitioner a $480,000 loan from the Royal State Bank of New York. With the assistance of Royal State Bank petitioner purchased a second block of $500,000 face amount of United States Treasury 1½ percent notes, due to mature on October 1, 1961. Again the notes were pledged as collateral with this bank to secure the loan. Bernard testified that the petitioner purchased the Treasury notes because he believed "the time was ripe" to invest in this kind of government obligation. Also, pursuant to the prearranged plan, petitioner prepaid to the First National Bank of Jersey City and to the Royal State Bank the interest that would be due on the loans she had received if they remained outstanding for 1½ to 2½ years. These interest prepayments, made in late December of 1958, totaled $81,396.61. Petitioner then claimed this sum as a Section 163(a) deduction on the 1958 income tax she filed jointly with her husband.

After reviewing these transactions in detail the Tax Court held the $81,396.91 was not deductible as "interest paid or accrued" on "indebtedness" under Section 163(a). In large part this holding rested on the court's conclusion that both loan transactions were "shams" that created "no genuine indebtedness." To support this conclusion the court stressed that, even though petitioner was borrowing approximately one half million dollars from each bank, the banks had agreed to the loans without any of their officers or employees having met petitioner or having investigated her financial position. The court noted that in each of the loan transactions petitioner was not required to commit any of her funds toward the purchase of the Treasury notes in their principal amount. And at several points the court appears to have attached great weight to the fact that most of the relevant transactions were apparently conducted by Garvin, Bantel and the Jersey City Bank, or by Bernard and the Royal State Bank, without petitioner's close supervision. Taking all these factors together, the Tax Court decided that, in fact, each transaction was "... an investment *by the bank* in Treasury obligations; wherein the bank, in consideration for prepayment to it of 'interest' by a customer . . . would carry such Treasury notes in the customer's name as purported collateral for the 'loan.'" 44 T.C. at 299 (italics in original). The court went on to say that ". . . if it is necessary to characterize the customer's payment, we would say that it was a fee to the bank for providing the 'facade' of a loan transaction." Ibid.

There is a certain force to the foregoing analysis. . . .

In our view, however, the facts of the two loan arrangements now before us fail in several significant respects to establish that these transactions were clearly shams. . . .

In the first place, the Jersey City Bank and the Royal State Bank were independent financial institutions; it cannot be said that their sole function was to finance transactions such as those before us. Compare Lynch v. Commissioner, 273 F.2d 867 (2 Cir. 1959); Goodstein v. Commissioner, 267 F.2d 127 (1 Cir. 1959). Second, the two loan transactions here did not within a few days return all the parties to the position from which they had started. Ibid. Here the Royal State Bank loan remained outstanding, and, significantly, that Bank retained the Treasury obligations pledged as security until June 10, 1960, at which time petitioner instructed the bank to sell the notes, apply the proceeds to the loan, and credit any remaining balance to her account. The facts relating to the Jersey City Bank loan are slightly different: this loan was closed in June 1959 when the brokerage house of Gruntal & Co. was substituted for the Jersey City Bank as creditor. . . .

Third, the independent financial institutions from which petitioner borrowed the funds she needed to acquire the Treasury obligations possessed significant control over the future of their respective loan arrangements: for example, the petitioner's promissory note to the Jersey City Bank explicitly gave either party the right to accelerate the maturity of the note after 30 days, and it was the Jersey City Bank's utilization of this clause that necessitated recourse to Gruntal. . . . Fourth, the notes signed by petitioner in favor of both banks were signed with recourse. . . .

In view of this combination of facts we think it was error for the Tax Court to conclude that these two transactions were "shams" which created no genuine indebtedness. Were this the only ground on which the decision reached below could be supported we would be compelled to reverse. . . .

One ground advanced by the Tax Court seems capable of reasoned development to support the result reached in this case by that court. The Tax Court found as an ultimate fact that petitioner's purpose in entering into the Jersey City Bank and Royal State Bank transactions "was not to derive any economic gain or to improve her beneficial interest; but was *solely* an attempt to obtain an interest deduction as an offset to her sweepstake winnings." 44 T.C. at 295 (emphasis added). This finding of ultimate fact was based in part on a set of computations made by Bernard Goldstein shortly after the Jersey City Bank and Royal State Bank loan transactions had been concluded. . . .

562   10. Interest, Taxes, and Casualty Losses (Home Ownership)

Before the Tax Court, and before us, petitioner has argued that she realistically anticipated an economic gain on the loan transactions due to anticipated appreciation in the value of the Treasury obligations, and that this gain would more than offset the loss that was bound to result because of the unfavorable interest rate differential. In support of this position, Bernard testified, and documentary evidence was introduced, to the effect that in December 1958 the market for Treasury obligations was unreasonably depressed, and that many investors at that time were favorably disposed toward their purchase. In short, petitioner argued that she intended a sophisticated, speculative, sortie into the market for government securities.

In holding that petitioner's "sole" purpose in entering into the Jersey City Bank and Royal State Bank transactions was to obtain an interest deduction, the Tax Court rejected this explanation of her purpose in entering into these transactions. For several reasons we hold that this rejection was proper. . . .

We hold, for reasons set forth hereinafter, that Section 163(a) of the 1954 Internal Revenue Code does not permit a deduction for interest paid or accrued in loan arrangements, like those now before us, that cannot with reason be said to have purpose, substance, or utility apart from their anticipated tax consequences. See Knetsch v. United States, 364 U.S. 361, 366. . . .

Admittedly, the underlying purpose of Section 163(a) permitting the deduction of "all interest paid or accrued within the taxable year on indebtedness" is difficult to articulate because this provision is extremely broad: there is no requirement that deductible interest serve a business purpose, that it be ordinary and necessary, or even that it be reasonable. 4 Mertens, Law of Federal Income Taxation §26.01 (1960 ed.). Nevertheless, it is fair to say that Section 163(a) is not entirely unlimited in its application and that such limits as there are stem from the Section's underlying notion that if an individual or corporation desires to engage in purposive activity, there is no reason why a taxpayer who borrows for that purpose should fare worse from an income tax standpoint than one who finances the venture with capital that otherwise would have been yielding income.

In order fully to implement this Congressional policy of encouraging purposive activity to be financed through borrowing, Section 163(a) should be construed to permit the deductibility of interest when a taxpayer has borrowed funds and incurred an obligation to pay interest in order to engage in what with reason can be termed purposive activity, even though he decided to borrow in order to gain an interest deduction rather than to finance the activity in some other way. In other words, the interest deduction should be permitted whenever it can be said that the taxpayer's desire to secure an interest deduction is only one of mixed motives that prompts the taxpayer to borrow funds; or, put a third way, the deduction is proper if there is some substance to the loan arrangement beyond the taxpayer's desire to secure the deduction. After all, we are frequently told that a taxpayer has the right to decrease the amount of what otherwise would be his taxes, or altogether avoid them, by any means the law permits. E.g., Gregory v. Helvering, 293 U.S. 465 (1935).[7] On the other hand, and notwithstanding Section 163(a)'s broad scope, this provision should not be construed to permit an interest deduction when it objectively appears that a taxpayer has borrowed funds in order to engage in a transaction that has no substance or purpose aside from the taxpayer's desire to obtain the tax benefit of an interest deduction: and a good example of such purposeless activity is the borrowing of funds at 4 percent in order to purchase property that returns less than 2 percent and holds out no prospect of appreciation sufficient to counter the unfavorable interest rate differential. . . .

Notes

1. Just what was the taxpayer's objective in *Knetsch*? Even if an interest deduction were allowed, how would Mr. Knetsch have stood to profit in the end?

This question is worth dwelling on, since *Knetsch* provides a simple prototype for tax shelter investments of the kind that became quite common from the late 1960s through the early 1980s. *Tax shelter* refers to the fact that the investment will produce tax losses that may be deducted against unrelated income and so "shelter" that other income from tax. What combination of ingredients is necessary for an investment to function as a tax shelter?

In *Knetsch*, what tax rule(s) besides the deductibility of interest are required to make the shelter work? In the short run? In the long run? Would §72(e) in its present form prevent the game in *Knetsch*, even without any statutory or judicial limitations on the deduction of interest?

2. *Livingstone transactions.* A client (some years ago) received a letter from a broker proposing a transaction as follows:

> We propose to buy for your account certain U.S. government bonds, without interest coupons, at a discount of 5 percent. The bonds will mature in one year. To finance the purchase we have arranged to borrow the purchase price on your note at 6 percent, interest prepaid, the note to be secured by the bonds and without recourse against you personally. The profit to you will arise from the fact that the gain on the government bonds is taxable as a long-term capital gain while the interest paid on your note will be deductible in computing ordinary income.
>
> Thus if you will execute a note for $1,000,000 and send it to us along with your check for $60,000 for interest, we will deliver the note to the lender, use $950,000 to purchase $1,000,000 face amount of government bonds, deliver the bonds to the lender as security for your note, and remit the excess of the loan proceeds over the purchase price of the bonds—$50,000—to you. Upon maturity the bonds will be collected and the proceeds applied to discharge your note.

---

7. This area of the law is particularly full of black-letter maxims that prove singularly unhelpful when it comes to deciding cases.

Since your income is well above $100,000, the $60,000 interest deduction will save you $42,000 in income taxes this year. On the other hand, the $50,000 profit on the government bonds, at capital gain rates, will incur a tax of only $12,500. Thus the net tax saving will be $29,500 for an out-of-pocket cost of $10,000, and you will have realized an after-tax profit of $19,500 without taking any risk at all.

(a) What are the rates of tax implicit in the computation in the last paragraph? (These were actual top rates at the time these transactions arose.) Would the game be worth playing at present top rates?

(b) Advise the client. Would the scheme work? Is it true that the profit is achieved "without taking any risk at all"?

(c) If the interest deduction were disallowed, how would the transaction be taxed? Are there any other bases for deduction?

(d) Would it matter if the broker simply received the $60,000 interest check and sent back $50,000 plus confirmation of the borrowing and bond purchase but in fact tore up the note without ever purchasing the bonds?

(e) There was a plethora of litigation concerning variations on this scheme, many promoted by a Boston broker named Livingstone. In some of the cases it appears that the broker may have carried out the transaction in only a temporary way, if at all. E.g., Goldstein v. Commissioner, 267 F.2d 127 (1st Cir. 1959); Lynch v. Commissioner, 273 F.2d 867 (2d Cir. 1959); Miles v. Livingstone, 301 F.2d 99 (1st Cir. 1962) (suit against broker dismissed since plaintiff knew scheme was a sham); Perry A. Nichols, 43 T.C. 482 (1965) (deduction allowed under §165(c)(3) on theory that broker embezzled from taxpayer by not carrying out transaction).

3. Suppose a taxpayer buys a whole life insurance policy and then systematically borrows against it to the limit of its loan value. The net result is like purchasing term insurance in a declining amount equal to the excess of the original face amount over the amount borrowed. But in form, each year's transaction will include a deductible interest payment, a nondeductible insurance premium, and a nontaxable receipt of additional loan proceeds. Before long the loan proceeds will equal the premium payment so that the taxpayer can claim an interest deduction equal to the full amount of cash outlay.

In 1964, §§264(a)(3) and (d) were added, disallowing an interest deduction in some such cases. But what about contracts purchased prior to 1963? The government has had some success in disallowing deductions in cases involving large prepayments of premiums or of interest, but not much otherwise. Compare Lee v. United States, 571 F.2d 1180 (Ct. Cls. 1978), with Coors v. United States, 572 F.2d 826 (Ct. Cls. 1978) (decisions on same day by same panel).

4. Here are some other problems about what is interest.

(a) *A* purchases an appliance at its listed price of $600 payable in 12 monthly installments. If he had paid cash, the appliance would have been sold to him at a discount of $48. Can he deduct $48 as interest—as if the appliance had been listed for $552 with $48 interest if payment was deferred?

(b) *B* rents a house in which to live. A substantial portion of the rent goes to pay interest on the lessor's mortgage. Can *B* deduct that portion of the rent as interest? Suppose *B*'s lessor let *B* make the mortgage payments directly, reducing the rent correspondingly; could *B* then deduct the interest payments? What if *B* joined on the mortgage note so that she was jointly liable to the mortgagee for payment of the interest — could she then deduct the interest payments? Compare §216 (tenant-shareholders allowed to deduct amounts paid to housing cooperative for mortgage interest and state taxes).

(c) A daughter supports her parents partly by making their mortgage payments; can she deduct the interest component? Can the parents claim the deduction if the daughter cannot? Could the daughter take the interest deduction if she became jointly liable on the mortgage note?

(d) Must indebtedness represent value received in order for interest to be deductible? What if a father simply executes a promise under seal to pay his son $100,000 on demand, with interest at 7 percent per annum? Thereafter he pays his son $7,000 a year. Is the payment deductible as interest? Do you perceive other problems with this arrangement?

2. Debt to Purchase or Carry Tax-Exempt Obligations: §265(a)(2)

REVENUE PROCEDURE 72-18
72-1 C.B. 740

SECTION 1. PURPOSE

The purpose of this Revenue Procedure is to set forth guidelines for taxpayers and field offices of the Internal Revenue Service for the application of section 265[(a)](2) of the Internal Revenue Code of 1954 to certain taxpayers holding state and local obligations the interest on which is wholly exempt from Federal income tax.

SEC. 2. BACKGROUND. . . .

.02 Section 265[(a)](2) of the Code is derived from section 1201(1) of the Revenue Act of 1917 and section 234(a)(2) of the Revenue Act of 1918. It is clear from the legislative history of those sections and of subsequent unsuccessful efforts to amend such sections (or their successors) that Congress intended to disallow interest under section 265[(a)](2) of the Code only upon a showing of a purpose by the taxpayer to use borrowed funds to purchase or carry tax-exempt securities. See, e.g., H. Rept. 767, 65th Cong., 10; S. Rept. 617, 65th Cong., 6, 7 (1918); 65 Cong. Rec. 7541-7542 (1924); and 67 Cong. Rec. 2964 (1925).

.03 Where the required purposive relationship is established, section 265[(a)](2) of the Code will be applicable even though the taxpayer does not receive tax-exempt interest, as for example, where the taxpayer holds defaulted obligations (see Clyde C. Pierce Corp. v. Commissioner, 120 F.2d 206 (1941)), or where the taxpayer holds the obligation for a period before interest begins to accrue (see Illinois Terminal Railroad Co. v. United States, 375 F.2d 1016, 1022 (1967)). Similarly, section 265[(a)](2) of the Code may be applicable even though the taxpayer's purpose in purchasing or carrying the tax-exempt obligations is to produce a taxable profit rather than tax exempt interest. See Denman v. Slayton, 282 U.S. 514 (1931).

SEC. 3. GENERAL RULES

.01 Section 265[(a)](2) of the Code is only applicable where the indebtedness is incurred or continued for the purpose of purchasing or carrying tax-exempt securities. Accordingly, the application of section 265[(a)](2) of the Code requires a determination, based on all the facts and circumstances, as to the taxpayer's purpose in incurring or continuing each item of indebtedness. Such purpose may, however, be established either by direct evidence or by circumstantial evidence.

.02 Direct evidence of a purpose to *purchase* tax-exempt obligations exists where the proceeds of indebtedness are used for, and are directly traceable to, the purchase of tax-exempt obligations. Wynn v. United States, 411 F.2d 614 (1969), certiorari denied 396 U.S. 1008 (1970). Section 265[(a)](2) does not apply, however, where proceeds of a bona fide business indebtedness are temporarily invested in tax-exempt obligations under circumstances similar to those set forth in Revenue Ruling 55-389, C.B. 1955-1, 276.

.03 Direct evidence of a purpose to *carry* tax-exempt obligations exists where tax-exempt obligations are used as collateral for indebtedness. "[O]ne who borrows to buy tax-exempts and one who borrows against tax-exempts already owned are in virtually the same economic position. Section 265[(a)](2) makes no distinction between them." Wisconsin Cheeseman v. United States, 338 F.2d 420, at 422 (1968).

SEC. 4. GUIDELINES FOR INDIVIDUALS

.01 In the absence of direct evidence of the purpose to purchase or carry tax-exempt obligations (as set forth in sections 3.02 and 3.03), the rules set forth in this section shall apply.

.02 An individual taxpayer may incur a variety of indebtedness of a personal nature, ranging from short-term credit for purchases of goods and services for personal consumption to a mortgage incurred to purchase or improve a residence or other real property which is held for personal use. Generally, section 265[(a)](2) of the Code will not apply to indebtedness of this type, because the purpose to purchase or carry tax-exempt obligations cannot reasonably be inferred where a personal purpose unrelated to the tax-exempt obligations ordinarily dominates the transaction. For example, section 265[(a)](2) of the Code generally will not apply to an individual who holds salable municipal bonds and takes out a mortgage to buy a residence instead of selling his municipal bonds to finance the purchase price. Under such circumstances the purpose of incurring the indebtedness is so directly related to the personal purpose of acquiring a residence that no sufficiently direct relationship between the borrowing and the investment in tax-exempt obligations may reasonably be inferred.

.03 The purpose to purchase or carry tax-exempt obligations generally does not exist with respect to indebtedness incurred or continued by an individual in connection with the active conduct of trade or business (other than a dealer in tax-exempt obligations) unless it is determined that the borrowing was in excess of business needs. However, there is a rebuttable presumption that the purpose to *carry* tax-exempt obligations exists where the taxpayer reasonably could have foreseen at the time of purchasing the tax-exempt obligations that indebtedness probably would have to be incurred to meet future economic needs of the business of an ordinary, recurrent variety. See Wisconsin Cheeseman v. United States, [supra p. 459]. The presumption may be rebutted, however, if the taxpayer demonstrates that business reasons, unrelated to the purchase or carrying of tax-exempt obligations, dominated the transaction.

.04 Generally, a purpose to *carry* tax-exempt obligations will be inferred, unless rebutted by other evidence, wherever the taxpayer has outstanding indebtedness which is not directly connected with personal expenditures (see section 4.02) and is not incurred or continued in connection with the active conduct of a trade or business (see section 4.03) and the taxpayer owns tax-exempt obligations. This inference will be made even though the indebtedness is ostensibly incurred or continued to purchase or carry other portfolio investments.

Portfolio investment for the purposes of this Revenue Procedure includes transactions entered into for profit (including investment in real estate) which are not connected with the active conduct of a trade or business. Purchase and sale of securities shall not constitute the active conduct of a trade or business unless the taxpayer is a dealer in securities within the meaning of section 1.471-5 of the Income Tax Regulations. A substantial ownership interest in a corporation will not be considered a portfolio investment. For example, where a taxpayer owns at least 80 percent of the voting stock of a corporation that is engaged in the active conduct of a trade or business, the investment in such controlling interest shall not be considered to be a portfolio investment.

A sufficiently direct relationship between the incurring or continuing of indebtedness and the purchasing or carrying of tax-exempt obligations will generally exist where indebtedness is incurred to finance portfolio investment because the choice of whether to finance a new portfolio investment through borrowing or through the liquidation of an existing investment in tax-exempt obligations typically involves a purpose either to maximize profit or to maintain a diversified portfolio. This purpose necessarily involves a decision, whether articulated by the taxpayer or not, to incur (or continue) the indebtedness, at least in part, to purchase or carry the existing investment in tax-exempt obligations.

A taxpayer may rebut the presumption that section 265[(a)](2) of the Code applies in the above circumstances by establishing that he could not have liquidated his holdings of tax-exempt obligations in order to avoid incurring indebtedness. The presumption may be overcome where, for example, liquidation is not possible because the tax-exempt obligations cannot be sold. The presumption would not be rebutted, however, by a showing that the tax-exempt obligations could only have been liquidated with difficulty or at a loss; or that the taxpayer owned other investment assets such as common stock that could have been liquidated; or that an investment advisor recommended that a prudent man should maintain a particular percentage of assets in tax-exempt obligations. Similarly, the presumption would not be rebutted by a showing that liquidating the holdings of tax-exempt obligations would not have produced sufficient cash to equal the amount borrowed.

The provisions of this paragraph may be illustrated by the following example: Taxpayer A, an individual, owns common stock listed on a national securities exchange, having an adjusted basis of $200,000; he owns rental property having an adjusted basis of $200,000; he has cash of $10,000; and he owns readily marketable municipal bonds having an adjusted basis of $41,000. A borrows $100,000 to invest in a limited partnership interest in a real estate syndicate and pays $8,000 interest on the loan which he claims as an interest deduction for the taxable year. Under these facts and circumstances, there is a presumption that the $100,000 indebtedness which is incurred to finance A's portfolio investment is also incurred to carry A's existing investment in tax-exempt bonds since there are no additional facts or circumstances to rebut the presumption. Accordingly, a portion of the $8,000 interest payment will be disallowed under section 265[(a)](2) of the Code. See section 7 concerning the amount to be disallowed. . . .

SEC. 7. PROCEDURES

.01 When there is direct evidence under sections 3.02 and 3.03 establishing a purpose to purchase or carry tax-exempt obligations (either because tax-exempt obligations were used as collateral for indebtedness or the proceeds of indebtedness were directly traceable to the holding of particular tax-exempt obligations) no part of the interest paid or incurred on such indebtedness may be deducted. However, if only a fractional part of the indebtedness is directly traceable to the holding of particular tax-exempt obligations, the same fractional part of the interest paid or incurred on such indebtedness will be disallowed. For example, if A borrows $100,000 from a bank and invests $75,000 of the proceeds in tax-exempt obligations, 75 percent of the interest paid on the bank borrowing would be disallowed as a deduction.

.02 In any other case where interest is to be disallowed in accordance with this Revenue Procedure, an allocable portion of the interest on such indebtedness will be disallowed. The amount of interest on such indebtedness to be disallowed shall be determined by multiplying the total interest on such indebtedness by a fraction, the numerator of which is the average amount during the taxable year of the taxpayer's tax-exempt obligations (valued at their adjusted basis) and the denominator of which is the average amount during the taxable year of the taxpayer's total assets (valued at their adjusted basis) minus the amount of any indebtedness the interest on which is not subject to disallowance to any extent under this Revenue Procedure.

Questions

1. How does one account for the fact that interest is disallowed on a loan to purchase or carry tax-exempt securities while it is allowed in full on a loan (now only up to $1,000,000) to purchase a home? Isn't the return on an owner-occupied home just as free from tax as interest paid on a municipal bond? And isn't the purpose to subsidize the investment in the latter just as clear?

Does *Knetsch* shed any light on that question?

2. Carefully think through what would be likely to happen if the statute did not contain §265(a)(2) or something like it. What does *Knetsch* suggest about that? But what would be the likely end result for all parties involved, including municipal borrowers?

Some have argued strenuously that §265(a)(2) and other limitations like it are quite misbegotten, undermining the efficient accomplishment of the purposes of §103 and contributing to some of the worst aspects of its operation. How would you argue in favor of that assertion? Would you favor repeal of §265(a)(2)?

3. Jill owns her home free and clear. Recently she has taken out a home equity loan, received an inheritance, purchased some tax-exempt securities, and paid off some student loans. Does §265(a)(2) apply?

Jack owns some tax-exempt securities. He recently borrowed against his brokerage account (in which the tax exempt securities are held) to raise funds with which to make a down payment on the purchase of a home. Does §265(a)(2) apply?

3. Investment Interest

ESTATE OF YAEGER v. COMMISSIONER
889 F.2d 29 (2d Cir. 1989)

Before Feinberg and Newman, Circuit Judges, and Jacob Mishler, Senior District Judge.*

MISHLER, District Judge: . . .

A. BACKGROUND

The facts as stipulated and found by the Tax Court are not in dispute.[3] Yaeger graduated Phi Beta Kappa from Columbia University in 1921 having studied business and finance. Upon graduation he went to work as an accountant and subsequently became employed as an auditing agent for the Internal Revenue Service. He left this employ in 1923 and went to work as a bond salesman in New York City, eventually becoming an investment counselor.

Commencing in the mid-1920s, Yaeger began actively trading stocks and bonds on the stock market on his own account in addition to conducting his investment consulting business. In the 1940s, Yaeger gave up his investment consulting business because the management of his own account had grown so demanding. Thereafter, he devoted himself exclusively to trading on his own account, which was his sole occupation until the day he died.

Prior to 1979, Yaeger maintained accounts with several brokerage firms in New York, including H. Hentz & Co. His account at H. Hentz & Co. was the largest account that firm had maintained for a United States citizen. During the period between 1979 and his death, Yaeger maintained accounts with three brokerage firms and occasionally dealt with two others.

The following chart describes the trading activity in Yaeger's various accounts throughout the years in issue:

Year	Purchase Transactions	Sales Transactions	Number Shares Bought	Number Shares Sold
1979	1,176	86	1,453,555	822,955
1980	1,088	39	1,658,841	173,165

Yaeger maintained an office at H. Hentz & Co. from which he conducted most of his trading activity. For a brief period of time he also

---

* Honorable Jacob Mishler, Senior United States District Judge for the Eastern District of New York, sitting by designation.

3. We follow the Tax Court in noting that we use such words as "speculate," "trade," "invest," and similar terms for convenience and without intending any inference as to the tax characterization or consequences of the facts.

conducted his activity from another brokerage firm. H. Hentz & Co. provided Yaeger with an assistant, a telephone, use of the secretarial pool, and access to the research staff and facilities. Yaeger spent a full day at his office, researching investment opportunities and placing orders, and then returned home to read more financial reports late into the night. He worked every day of the week. When he was out of town, he maintained telephone contact with the brokers who handled his accounts. Yaeger was trading on the stock market the day before he died.

Yaeger subscribed to a distinct investment strategy. His trading strategy was to buy the stock of companies in which the stock prices were extremely undervalued and hold the stock until it reached a price that reflected the underlying value of the company. He rarely purchased "blue chip" stocks and many of the stocks he held did not pay dividends. Instead, Yaeger constantly looked for companies that were experiencing financial distress but whose underlying value was not recognized.

This strategy required thorough research that extended beyond the study of mainstream publications. He also poured over annual reports and brokerage house reports. Once Yaeger determined that the targeted company was experiencing temporary difficulties, he began to accumulate the stock. He would buy stock as it became available, although some of the stock was not frequently or actively traded and was difficult to acquire. He would initially buy small quantities of stock to avoid attracting attention from other investors. Once he obtained a sizeable amount of stock he would let his position be known. Yaeger took whatever steps he thought necessary to improve the position of the companies in which he invested, often supplying unsolicited business advice to the managers and occasionally attempting to arrange mergers or acquisitions.[4]

In addition to selecting financially troubled companies in which to invest, Yaeger increased his gain on his investments by using margin debt. Yaeger financed his purchases by borrowing to the maximum extent allowable under law and the custom of the brokerage houses, which was generally 50 percent. If the value of his stock rose he would use that increased value as equity to support more debt. From time to time Yaeger shifted accounts from one brokerage house to another in order to maximize the volume of margin debt he could carry. Once or twice during his career Yaeger was overleveraged and suffered substantial losses when he was forced to sell enough stock to maintain his margin debt.

During the years 1979 and 1980, the ratio of Yaeger's margin debt to portfolio value was 47 percent and 42 percent, respectively. Yaeger's total

---

4. Yaeger's investment strategy produced some startling successes. For example, in 1980 Yaeger invested in Seton Company upon reading in an annual report footnote that one of its divisions had discovered a material that could be used as artificial skin. Years later, the value of the formerly unprofitable stock rose dramatically as the company shifted to manufacturing artificial skin. Similarly, Yaeger purchased bonds issued by the New York, New Haven and Hartford Railroad while the company was in bankruptcy. After the company was reorganized as Penn Central Corporation, Yeager realized a substantial profit on the bonds.

stock market related debt equalled $42,154,048 in 1979 and $54,968,371 in 1980. When he died, his portfolio was subject to debt in the amount of $70,490,018.

In 1979 and 1980 Yaeger reported income in the following amounts on his federal tax return:

1979	Character of Income	Amount
	Long-term capital gain	$13,839,658
	Short-term capital gain	184,354
	Dividends	2,339,080
	Interest	57,958
		$16,421,050

1980	Character of Income	Amount
	Long-term capital gain	$1,099,921
	Short-term capital gain	728,404
	Dividends	3,648,441
	Interest	91,717
	Director's fees	10,660
		$5,579,083

Of the stock which Yaeger sold in taxable years 1979 and 1980, the percentage of total sales of securities which he had held for twelve months or more was 88 percent and 91 percent, respectively. The purchase dates of the securities sold in 1980 ranged from March 1970 to December 1979. In 1979, Yaeger did not sell any security that had been held for less than three months and, in 1980, did not sell any security that had been held for less than six months. On schedule C of the tax returns, Yaeger deducted interest expense in 1979 and 1980 in the amounts of $5,865,833 and $7,995,010, respectively.

The sole issue considered by the Tax Court was whether the claimed deductions of the interest expenses Yaeger incurred in purchasing securities on margin were subject to the limitation on the deductibility of investment interest set forth in section 163(d).[5] This issue turned on whether Yaeger's stock market activities constituted investment activity or the activity of

---

5. Section 163(d) provided in pertinent part:

(1) In general. — In the case of a taxpayer other than a corporation, the amount of investment interest (as defined in paragraph (3) (D)) otherwise allowable as a deduction under this chapter shall be limited, in the following order, to —

(A) $10,000 . . . , plus

(B) the amount of the net investment income . . . , plus the amount (if any) by which the deductions allowable under this section . . . and sections 162, 164(a)(1) or (2), or 212 attributable to property of the taxpayer subject to a net lease exceeds the rental income produced by such property for the taxable year. . . .

(D) Investment Interest. The term "investment interest" means interest paid or accrued on indebtedness incurred or continued to purchase or carry property held for investment.

trading in securities as a trade or business. According to the Tax Court, the "pivotal inquiry" was "whether Yaeger was interested in deriving income from capital appreciation or from short-term trading." The court determined that Yaeger was an investor, not a trader, because Yaeger held his stocks and bonds for lengthy periods of time anticipating that they would appreciate in value. Thus, the interest expense he incurred was "investment interest" within the meaning of section 163(d) and subject to the deductibility restrictions of that section.

B. DISCUSSION

Section 163 of the Internal Revenue Code generally provides for the deduction of interest incurred on indebtedness. As defined in section 163(d)(3)(D), "investment interest" is "interest paid or accrued on indebtedness incurred or continued to purchase or carry property held for investment." Section 163(d) limits the deductibility of investment interest by a noncorporate taxpayer to the extent of the taxpayer's investment income, plus $10,000. Any amount disallowed is "treated as investment interest paid or accrued in the succeeding taxable year." 26 U.S.C. §163 (d)(2). Section 163(d) does not apply to interest paid to buy property for personal use or property for trade or business use. See H.R. Rep. 413, pt. 1, 91st Cong., 1st Sess. 72, reprinted in 1969 U.S. Code Cong. & Admin. News 1645, 1719 ("interest on funds borrowed in connection with a trade or business would not be affected by the limitation").

The Internal Revenue Code does not define "trade or business." Determining whether a taxpayer's trading activities rise to the level of carrying on a trade or business turns on the facts and circumstances of each case. Higgins v. Commissioner, 312 U.S. 212, 217 (1941). In determining whether taxpayers who manage their own investments are traders, "relevant considerations are the taxpayer's investment intent, the nature of the income to be derived from the activity, and the frequency, extent, and regularity of the taxpayer's securities transactions." Moller v. Commissioner, 721 F.2d 810, 813 (Fed. Cir. 1983), cert. denied, 467 U.S. 1251 (1984).

Investors are engaged in the production of income. Purvis v. Commissioner, 530 F.2d 1332, 1334 (9th Cir. 1976). Traders are those "whose profits are derived from the 'direct management of purchasing and selling.'" Moller, supra, at 813 (quoting Levin v. United States, 597 F.2d 760, 765 (Ct. Cl. 1979)). Investors derive profit from the interest, dividends, and capital appreciation of securities. See Molter, supra, at 813; Purvis, supra, at 1334; Liang v. Commissioner, 23 T.C. 1040, 1043 (1955). They are "primarily interested in the long-term growth potential of their stocks." Id. Traders, however, buy and sell securities "with reasonable frequency in an endeavor to catch the swings in the daily market movements and profit thereby on a short term basis." Purvis, supra, at 1334 (quoting Liang v. Commissioner, 23 T.C. 1040, 1043 (1955)).

Thus, the two fundamental criteria that distinguish traders from investors are the length of the holding period and the source of the profit. These criteria coincide with the congressional purpose behind the enactment of section 163(d), which originated in the Tax Reform Act of 1969, Pub. L. No. 91-172, §221, 83 Stat. 487. Congress was concerned with the prevalent use of borrowed money to purchase investment assets and the distortion of taxable income that often results when the investments produce long-term capital gain rather than ordinary income.[6] As explained in the House Report accompanying the 1969 Act:

> The itemized deduction presently allowed individuals for interest makes it possible for taxpayers to voluntarily incur substantial interest expense on funds borrowed to acquire or carry investment assets. Where the interest expense exceeds the taxpayer's investment income, it, in effect, is used to insulate other income from taxation. For example, a taxpayer may borrow substantial amounts to purchase stocks which have growth potential but which return small dividends currently. Despite the fact that receipt of the income from the investment may be postponed (and may be capital gains), the taxpayer will receive a current deduction for the interest expense even though it is substantially in excess of the income from the investment.

H.R. Rep. 413, supra, at 73. The activity of holding securities for a length of time to produce interest, dividends, and capital gains fits the abuse targeted by section 163(d): investing for postponed income and current interest deduction.

The Tax Court properly concluded that Yaeger was an investor. It is true that Yaeger initiated over 2000 securities transactions in 1979 and 1980 and pursued his security activities vigorously and extensively. And there is no doubt, as the Tax Court stated, that Yaeger "maintained a margin of debt which would have caused a more faint-hearted investor to quail." However, "[n]o matter how large the estate or how continuous or extended the work required may be," the management of securities investments is not the trade or business of a trader. Higgins, supra, at 218.[7]

More importantly, most of his sales were of securities held for over a year. He did not sell any security held for less than three months. He realized a profit on the securities through both dividends and interest. Most of his profit, however, came from holding undervalued stock until its market improved. This emphasis on capital growth and profit from resale indicates an investment motivated activity. See Miller v. Commissioner, 70 T.C. 448, 457 (1978). In addition, since the income came from long-term

---

6. For example, "[a] much publicized study of 154 high income individuals who paid little or no Federal income taxes found that 72 of these individuals benefitted by deducting interest paid on loans taken to acquire growth stock and similar investments the gains on which would constitute capital gains." Miller v. Commissioner, 70 T.C. 448, 453 n.3, (citing H.R. Rep. No. 413, pt. 1 (1969); 115 Cong. Rec. 22,563, 22,760 (Statement of Rep. Mills), 22,573 (Statement of Rep. Byrnes) (1969)).

7. See also Groetzinger v. Commissioner of Internal Revenue, 771 F.2d 269, 275 (7th Cir. 1985) ("The fact that one person has accumulated more wealth than another . . . so that passive investment may command substantially more of the wealthier person's time and attention than that of a poorer counterpart, would not justify allowing the wealthier taxpayer the benefit of trade or business treatment. . . ."), aff'd. 480 U.S. 23 (1987).

appreciation, Yaeger would receive the benefit of favorable capital gains treatment. To disregard the nature of the income and length of his holdings simply because Yaeger was a vigorous investor would defeat the purpose of section 163(d).[8] . . .

[Discussion of procedural issue for tax years 1981 and 1982 omitted.]

Notes

1. Is this case about what constitutes a trade or business for income tax purposes? About the purpose and scope of the investment interest limitation? Or both? What is the relation between the two?

2. As indicated in *Yaeger*, §163(d) dates back to the Tax Reform Act of 1969. In its original form it was pretty much confined to very wealthy people or very abusive situations, since it only disallowed interest exceeding investment income by more than $10,000. In 1986 the $10,000 leeway was repealed and interest expense in excess of investment income was disallowed starting with the first penny, but with a carryforward of nondeductible amounts.

3. In *Yaeger* the issue was characterization of the activity with which the loans were unquestionably associated. But consider a taxpayer who has a trade or business and other investments. The issue then may be which activity is associated with a borrowing. Suppose a taxpayer borrows on the security of his business assets to purchase a private automobile and thus keep other funds available for the purchase of investment assets: How will interest on that borrowing be classified?

Note that the statutory phrase governing this issue, in the statute applied in *Yaeger*, was the same as that in §265(a)(2) — investment interest was interest on debt "incurred or continued to purchase or carry" investment assets. The language has now been changed; the question is whether indebtedness is "properly allocable to property held for investment." Temporary regulations indicate that allocation is to be in accordance with use of loan proceeds. Reg. §1.163-8T(c). What if loan proceeds go into a bank account along with funds from other sources, and the account is used to pay for a variety of different kinds of assets? The regulations have interesting and very detailed provisions for dealing with this and other problems.

4. Other provisions that depend on an allocation of debt to particular properties include §264(a)(2)-(4) (insurance, endowment, and annuity contracts), §1277(c)(1) (market discount bonds), §246A(d)(3)(A) (preferred stock), and §263A(f)(2)(A) (property under construction).

5. Prior to 1986 characterization as investment interest meant subjection to a limitation and was unfavorable for the taxpayer (as in *Yaeger*).

8. Our prior decision in Fuld v. Commissioner, 139 F.2d 465 (2d Cir. 1943), is not to the contrary. In that case we upheld a Tax Court determination that the taxpayers were traders and did so on evidence that the taxpayers had made a large number of sales of securities held for less than two years.

Since 1986 it may often be favorable because personal interest may now be treated even more harshly.

4. Home Mortgage and Other Personal Interest

Prior to 1986 personal interest, including home mortgage interest, was fully deductible by simple operation of §163(a) together with the absence of anything denying a deduction. No separate mention was made of either home mortgage interest or personal interest, and so interest was fully deductible on a range of things, including auto loans, student loans, income tax deficiencies (although not penalties), and credit card loans.

Present §163(h)(1) looks like a simple unconditional reversal of that rule. Henceforth interest that is not allocated to some particular asset or business or investment activity will *not* be deductible. (From now on, therefore, investment interest characterization may sometimes be favorable if the alternative is treatment as personal interest. Consider funds raised by pledging securities to pay for a personal automobile.)

But §163(h)(2) makes a big exception for *qualified residence interest*, which is defined in (h)(3). Qualified residence interest includes interest on up to $1,000,000 of mortgage debt incurred to finance acquisition, construction, or improvement of a qualified residence and up to another $100,000 of mortgage debt incurred for any other purpose — so-called *home equity indebtedness.*

A considerable number of banks offer lines of credit called *home equity loans*, usually under the following pattern: A homeowner gives a mortgage (often a second mortgage) to secure whatever may be advanced under the line of credit; actual borrowing is then done by writing a check against the line of credit. A common limit on such arrangements is $100,000. These arrangements appeared on the banking scene before 1986 and made some sense as a convenient way of borrowing at lower rates than generally available on auto loans or credit card balances without the need of going through a new loan application and approval for each borrowing. The term "home equity indebtedness" in §163(h)(3) is not confined to such arrangements but it clearly includes them.

So now if a homeowner buys an automobile by writing a check against his home equity account, he avoids the paperwork of an auto loan and he gets a better rate of interest. On top of that, he gets a tax deduction for the interest he does pay. First-class service!

Student loans have generally been harder to fit into the mold, since students often are not homeowners, although often their parents are. What would be the effect if a student's parents agree to write a check on their home equity account to pay educational expenses, with the understanding that the student is to pay it off, principal and interest? Compare §221, added in 1998.

The net effect of present law seems to be that for homeowners, personal interest remains fully deductible on debt incurred for purposes other than home ownership, up to $100,000, but only if the borrowing is done through a home equity loan, while for others personal interest is not deductible at all (except as provided in §221). Because many nonhomeowners are not itemizers anyway, the 1986 change may have made very little substantive difference after all (except for the $100,000 cap now contained in the definition of home equity indebtedness).

Policy Evaluation. The deductibility of interest on home acquisition indebtedness is part of the treatment of homeowners in general under the tax law. It is intimately connected in particular with the question of taxing imputed rental value. These questions are taken up in Chapter 10C below.

The deductibility of interest on other personal loans is perhaps more puzzling. Consider the following possible reasons for allowing deductibility.

1. It is too difficult to differentiate personal from business or investment debts.

2. Even if differentiation is easy, it makes no sense. Two taxpayers with identical assets and equal debts are in substantially the same economic situation even if one's debt is on his business assets and the other's is on his personal assets. There is no reason to treat them differently for income tax purposes.

3. A general interest deduction is proper simply because interest reduces what a taxpayer has available to spend on consumption and saving and is therefore negative income in the Haig-Simons sense. Given any two taxpayers in identical circumstances except that one is in debt, the one without debt is wealthier by just that much, and freedom from interest charges is his return on that additional wealth; a general interest deduction causes this difference in circumstances to be reflected in taxable income.

4. How about simply saying that interest expense is negative investment income?

WHITE, PROPER INCOME TAX TREATMENT OF DEDUCTIONS FOR PERSONAL EXPENSE

House Comm. on Ways and Means, 86th Cong., Tax Revision Compendium 365
(Comm. Print 1959)

INTEREST EXPENSE

Often it is the case in applying economic analysis that the subtlest and most elusive — though not necessarily the most significant — aspect of a problem concerns interest and time. This is well exemplified by the question of the deductibility of personal interest expense.

For a convenient point of departure, there is the argument sometimes made in connection with purchases of consumer goods on credit that the interest charge is simply one component of the price of the commodity — the component reflecting impatience of the purchaser — and therefore has no more legitimate claim to deductibility than the rest of the price. This view does correctly recognize the time dimension of consumption as of all economic activity. Consumption of food, or theater tickets, the services of an automobile or a house today is not the same as consumption of the physical equivalent one year from today. It is something more. The existence of a positive rate of interest tells us so. But the interest cost of buying today rather than later is not only paid by the one who goes into debt; it is also paid by the one who finances his purchase by drawing on his assets. The former pays it in the form of an explicit charge, which is negative income; the latter in the form of foregone earnings. The distinction between the two which deductibility of interest expense is intended to reflect is that the former is poorer; that is, he has a lower income, and less taxpaying ability under an income tax. And exactly analogously, the individual who liquidates his earning assets at the beginning of the year to make a consumption purchase will have a lower income for the year than the individual who holds on to his earning assets, since the latter saves relative to the former, thereby earning additional income and increasing his relative taxpaying ability.

What may underlie this interest-is-a-part-of-the-price notion is a disinclination to accept that under the income tax no interest earning is imputed to consumption per se. In choosing to consume rather than save, the individual chooses to reduce his subsequent economic status and taxpaying ability compared to the one who chooses the opposite. "The thrifty may prosper, the spendthrift will not; but each with the Treasury will share his lot."

But even if interest were imputed to consumption, the borrower-buyer would still have a negative element in his income account that the cash buyer would not. The imputation would raise the level of both their incomes (and would equalize the cash buyer with the non-buying saver) but the differential between them would still exist — measured by the interest paid on the borrowed funds.

Thus the role of interest expense in income computation is analytically independent of the use to which the borrowed funds are put. The deductibility of interest expense follows simply from the fact that debt, a negative asset, is a source of negative income. In the logic of income computation, interest expense, however it arises in household or business finance, is properly deductible.

Household debt is associated with the purchase of many of the most popular consumer durables — automobiles, washing machines, television sets—which earn a form of investor's income in kind which is difficult to assess for income tax purposes. If there is a close correlation between the ownership of such durables and the amount of debt outstanding, the disallowance of deductibility of interest expense might be rationalized as a compensating inconsistency for the failure to impute income to the ownership of the durables.

Similarly, in dealing with the problem of imputation of rent for owner-occupied houses, the absence of such imputation in the present law has prompted the suggestion that the deductibility of mortgage interest be disallowed as a practical maneuver to reduce total effective discrimination. The expectation is that the reduced discrimination against the tenant class and among mortgagors as a group would more than offset the increased discrimination in favor of the clear owners.

This is probably not the best approach. It opens up a loophole for operators of business establishments and owners of income-producing property to shift personal interest into the business interest category. It would probably introduce a deprogressive element into the tax base to the extent of interest expense. It would be preferable to adhere to the income concept in allowing deductibility and concentrate on getting more imputation into the tax base. Admittedly the problem of imputation becomes more complicated for durables than housing, since the rental market shrinks and becomes less reliable as a basis for evaluation.

Questions

1. Assuming that some limitations are to be continued on personal interest, how would you respond to a proposal that would eliminate present §§163(h) and (d) and substitute a general limitation on nonbusiness interest, disallowing anything in excess of investment income plus $10,000? One could also exempt interest on home acquisition indebtedness with or without a $1,000,000 cap. Describe exactly how this would differ from present law, and evaluate each point of difference.

2. Look at §§221 and 62(a)(17), added in 1997. Why are these not part of §163?

B. TAXES

Prior to 1964 there was an unlimited deduction for all state and local taxes. In 1964 Congress restricted the deductibility of state taxes to those now enumerated in §164, plus general sales taxes and taxes on gasoline, automobile registration, and drivers' licenses. The following excerpt from the Senate Finance Committee Report explains why deductibility was not further limited.

> Your committee finds no disagreement with the House in the reasons given for the desirability of continuing the deductibility of property taxes, income taxes, and general sales taxes. In the case of property taxes, it was suggested that any denial of the deduction would result in an important shift in the distribution of Federal income taxes between homeowners and nonhomeowners. In the case of State and local income taxes, it was suggested that the continued deductibility of these taxes represents an important means of accommodation to take into account the fact that both State and local governments on one hand and the Federal Government on the other hand tap this same important revenue source. A failure to provide deductions in such a case could mean a combined burden of income taxes which in some cases would be extremely heavy. It was further indicated that, if property and income taxes are to be deductible for Federal income tax purposes, it also is important to allow the deduction of general sales taxes. To deny the deductibility of general sales taxes while allowing deductions for the other major revenue sources would encourage State and local governments to use these other resources in place of the sales tax. Your committee agrees with the House that it is important for the Federal Government to remain neutral as to the relative use made of these three forms of State and local taxation.
>
> Your committee believes that much the same reasons which led to the House continuing the deduction of property, income, and sales taxes also suggest the desirability of continuing the deduction of taxes on gasoline and auto registration and drivers' licenses. Gasoline taxes are also a major source of State revenue and to deny the deduction of this tax while allowing the deduction of property, income, and general sales taxes tends to encourage States to use other than automotive taxes as their more important revenue sources. Moreover, a failure to provide a deduction for these automotive taxes also could result in an important shift in the distribution of Federal income taxes between classes of taxpayers, i.e., between those who own automobiles and those who do not.
>
> Moreover, your committee is inclined to doubt that it is difficult for a taxpayer to make good estimates of the amount of these State and local automotive taxes as is sometimes suggested. The registration and drivers' license taxes are no more than annual taxes and certainly present the taxpayer with no particular recordkeeping problem. For most taxpayers the amount of gasoline taxes paid can be estimated relatively accurately either from credit sales slips or from the mileage added on a car each year. [Report of the Senate Committee on Finance on Revenue Act of 1964, Rep. No. 830, 88th Cong. 54 (1964).]

Notes

1. Are these reasons persuasive? The deductions for automobile registration, drivers' licenses, and gasoline taxes have long since been repealed. Are the reasons given persuasive as to the remaining taxes? Are there other reasons for deductibility?

2. There are a number of similarities between the interest deduction and the deduction for taxes. Both represent expenses that are sometimes business or investment connected and sometimes not, but that are made deductible in either case. Both serve to accentuate tax discrimination between homeowners and renters. Both raise problems when a person

makes a payment that indirectly represents a payment of interest or taxes and when one person discharges another's liability.

(a) *A* rents a house to live in under a lease that requires her to directly pay various expenses. Among the expenses she must pay are the real estate taxes. Can she deduct them?

(b) *B* supports his parents by paying various expenses, including real estate taxes, on their house. Can he deduct the taxes? Can the parents? Can you make any suggestion as to how *B* might arrange to secure a deduction for those taxes?

3. Is there some way a state could redefine its property tax as a tax on tenants instead of owners of residential property in order to give its citizens the benefit of greater federal income tax deductions?

REVENUE RULING 79-180
1979-1 C.B. 95

On July 6, 1978, the State of New York amended the New York Real Property Tax Law (McKinney 1972) to provide that certain renters of residential property have an interest in real property, are personally liable for the real property taxes due on their interest, and are entitled to a federal itemized deduction for those taxes. Laws 1978, chapter 471. The effective date of the amendment is April 1, 1980. Laws 1979, chapter 41.

Section 304 of the New York Real Property Tax Law provides that all assessments shall be against the real property itself which shall be liable to sale pursuant to law for any unpaid taxes or special ad valorem levies.

However, where real property in whole or in part is rented for residential purposes pursuant to a lease or to the same occupant or occupants for twelve consecutive months or longer, or if the dwelling unit is subject to rent controls and regulation, a renter who pays $150 or more a month in rent (or less that $150, if the renter makes an election) is deemed to have an interest in the real property and is subject to state and local laws covering the levy and collection of taxes and the enforcement or collection of delinquent taxes. This provision does not, however, relieve the owner of real property from the obligation of paying all taxes due on the owner's property or vitiate the sale of the real property for unpaid taxes or special ad valorem levies. The owner of real property is obligated to apply the first money received each month from the renter to taxes due on the owner's real property. . . .

Section 926-a of the New York Real Property Tax Law provides that the owner of the real property is deemed an agent of the collecting officer for purposes of collecting taxes due from each renter to whom section 304 applies. The payments by the renter to the owner must be made in two separate amounts, consisting of basic rent (the rental amount less the amount of the real property tax designated for the rental unit) and the real property tax due from the rental unit. The annual real property tax must be paid to the owner in equal monthly installments. Tax payments to the owner discharge the renter's liability for taxes so paid, regardless of any subsequent disposition of the moneys made by the owner. If a renter fails to pay that portion of the rental charges attributable to taxes or is delinquent in payments to the owner so that less than all of the money due for real property taxes is paid to the owner, the owner is deemed to have assumed the renter's interest in the unit. Where a rental unit is vacant all or part of the taxing period, the owner is deemed to hold the renter's interest in that unit for the period of the vacancy and to assume the liability for taxes levied on that unit.

An owner of real property, where a renter who has an interest in real property pursuant to section 304 is an occupant, may not charge such a renter an amount in any rent period in excess of the rent reserved in the lease or the maximum rent permitted under rent controls and regulations, reduced by the renters tax allocated to the renter.

LAW AND ANALYSIS . . .

Rev. Rul. 58-141, 1958-1 C.B. 101, states that the question of whether a particular contribution, charge, or burden is to be regarded as a tax depends on its real nature and, if it is not in its nature a tax, it is not material that it may have been so called.

Thus, the fact that the State of New York treats a portion of the total rental amounts paid by renters to owners of real property as real property tax payments does not establish that those payments are in fact real property tax payments, because the focus is on the nature of the transaction under federal law. See Lyeth v. Hoey, 305 U.S. 188 (1938).

The New York renters tax does not impose on the renter any economic burden that did not exist prior to the enactment of section 304 of the New York Real Property Tax Law. Rather, the renters tax merely divides the separately determined rental amounts into a so-called rental payment and a so-called real property tax payment. The lack of an economic burden on the renter is further evidenced by the fact the owner is not relieved from the obligation of paying all taxes due on the owner's property. Under section 926-a, the owner is deemed to assume the renter's interest in the unit if the renter is delinquent in making payment to the owner. In the event of the renter's nonpayment, section 304 looks to the owner for payment and the taxing authority may enforce payment against the owner's interest in the entire property.

HOLDING

The New York State renters tax paid by renters pursuant to sections 304 and 926-a of the New York Real Property Tax Law is not a tax on the renter for federal income tax purposes, but rather is part of the renter's rental payment. . . .

Notes and Questions

1. Deductibility of state and local taxes was one of the major substantive issues in the debates surrounding enactment of the Tax Reform Act of 1986. The Administration originally sought repeal of the federal tax deduction for all state and local taxes not incurred in a trade or business and for state and local *income* taxes even if they were incurred in a trade or business.[2] (Why this distinction?)

This change would have raised about one-third of the revenue required to pay for individual rate reductions in the original Administration proposal; the rest was to come mostly from increases in taxes on corporations. This proposal attracted strong opposition, especially from governors and other officials in states with relatively high levels of taxation, and the House bill omitted it altogether. The final compromise repealed the federal deduction for state and local sales taxes but preserved it for state and local income and property taxes, even though the Administration had argued against such differentiation. The *General Explanation* points out that only about one-quarter of sales taxes paid were claimed as federal tax deductions, as compared with about half of state income taxes paid.[3] It also asserts that claims for the deduction of sales taxes have not been very accurate.

2. In 2004 a deduction for general sales taxes was reinstated, but it was allowed only to taxpayers who elect to forego the deduction of state and local income taxes. §164(b)(5). The Ways and Means Committee report explained that:

> allowing a deduction for State and local income taxes, but not sales taxes, may create inequities across States and may also create bias in the types of taxes that States and localities choose to impose. The Committee believes that the provision of an itemized deduction for State and local general sales taxes in lieu of the deduction for State and local income taxes provides more equitable Federal tax treatment across states and will cause the Federal tax laws to have a more neutral effect on the types of taxes that State and local governments utilize. [H.R. Rep. No. 108-548, at 241 (2004).]

Do you agree? The sales tax deduction, which is scheduled to expire at the end of 2009, §164(b)(5)(l), allows the taxpayer to compute the deduction either by accumulating receipts showing the total amount of sales taxes paid or by using tables prescribed by the Treasury, which compute the

2. The President's Tax Proposals to the Congress for Fairness, Growth, and Simplicity 62-69 (1985).
3. Staff of the Joint Comm. on Taxation, General Explanation of the Tax Reform Act of 1986, 47.

deduction by applying the appropriate state and local sales tax rate to the average consumption by taxpayers with a given filing status, number of dependents, and adjusted gross income. §164(b)(5)(H).

3. There have been continuing calls for complete repeal of the deduction for state and local taxes or for the imposition of a dollar cap on such deductions, and the arguments deserve careful consideration. It is said that state and local tax payments are essentially a form of consumption expenditure that ought not to be favored over other, nondeductible, forms of consumption expenditure. Furthermore, elimination of the federal deduction would put the full responsibility for state and local tax burdens back on the shoulders of those who impose them, and would thus facilitate a more responsible monitoring of those burdens. And of course total repeal would yield a substantial amount of tax revenue to reduce the federal budget deficit (or to provide for further rate reductions or expenditure increases).

4. Do you agree that state and local tax payments are essentially a form of consumption expenditure not to be favored over others, or are there important differences for this purpose?

In particular, suppose State *X* has a graduated income tax, and that a substantial fraction of its revenues go to support public education. How should these be reflected in the taxable income of each of the following residents of State *X*?

A—high income; children attend private colleges
B—low income; primarily lives in State *X* so his children can have an excellent public education
C—middle income; children have all grown up and left home
D—high-income young investment banker; has not even begun to think about the prospect of children
E—very high income old investment banker; hates children and lives in State *X* solely because that is where the investment banking business is centered; contributes funds and a substantial part of her spare time to the fight against taxes and public expenditures of all sorts, including education

5. In general, is it prudent to expect repeal of all or part of the deduction for state and local taxes to produce an increase in federal revenue? Or would state and local governments be apt to switch their taxes to deductible forms? Note that the Reagan Administration's proposed repeal applied only to individuals; state and local taxes paid by corporations would have remained deductible.

The city of Philadelphia, for example, has a wage tax on persons employed within the city. If the federal deduction were repealed, the city of Philadelphia might change the tax to an excise on employers on the *payment* of wages. In that case each employer could simply reduce his wage payments by the amount of the tax and everyone would come out the same except that the exclusion of the tax payments from employees' income would no longer depend on a deduction.

Are there any persuasive reasons for the city of Philadelphia (and other state and local taxing authorities) not to make this change? (Why hasn't the city of Philadelphia made this change long ago, anyway, for the benefit of employees who do not itemize deductions?)

6. *The Foreign Tax Credit.* Income taxes paid to foreign countries or U.S. possessions may under certain circumstances be taken into account as a credit against U.S. income tax instead of a deduction. §§901-908. What is the difference between a credit and a deduction? Would a credit against federal income tax for state taxes paid be a useful device for dealing with problems of fiscal federalism? Until its repeal in 2005, §2011 granted a credit against the federal estate tax for state death taxes. Why may a credit be sensible for foreign taxes even if state taxes are allowed only as a deduction? Should the United States foreign tax credit extend to Canadian provincial taxes, for instance, as well as Canadian national government taxes?

C. HOMEOWNERS

1. Distortion Produced by the Deductions

The deductions for home mortgage interest and real estate taxes are among the principal itemized deductions. Home mortgage interest deductions in 2005 amounted to $383.7 billion, and real estate taxes to $144.7 billion. Together they accounted for almost half of personal deductions, and 10.2 percent of AGI on itemized returns.[4] Revenue losses from these deductions in 2005 were estimated at $62.2 billion and $19.1 billion,[5] respectively, which amount to about 10.4 percent of total personal income taxes (before credits) on itemizers' returns. The average marginal tax rate implied by these figures is 16.2 percent with respect to mortgage interest and 13.2 percent with respect to real estate taxes. So, to the extent of these expenditures, net costs of owner-occupied housing are being reduced by about 15 percent from what they would be in the absence of the deductions.

This result has been repeatedly criticized (1) for creating an indefensible discrimination between owner-occupiers and renters and (2) for creating

4. IRS, Individual Income Tax Returns 2005, Table 2.1 (2007), *http://www.irs.gov/pub/irs-soi/05in03id.xls.*

5. Analytical Perspectives, Budget of the U.S. Government, Fiscal Year 2007, at 292 (2006) (tax expenditure estimates for 2005).

an undesirable distortion in favor of housing as compared with other capital needs in the economy.

The discrimination between renters and owners may be conceived primarily as one of fairness. But people in serious rate brackets can (and do) respond by switching from renting to owning. Even people who prefer city apartments to suburban houses are likely to purchase condominiums. The income tax advantages of owner occupancy are thought to be a major reason why an apartment building can often be sold for much more as condominiums than as a rental property, and some believe that the tax law has thereby pushed ownership of many urban apartments into relatively inefficient forms.

The distortion in favor of housing over other investments is generally thought of primarily in terms of resource allocation and economic efficiency. There is a fairness problem to the extent that some people spend more of their real income on housing than others do, but the main worry has been that everyone will spend more on housing and less on other forms of investment than they would if all productive investments were taxed alike. Many economists believe that the bias of our income tax in favor of housing has caused the United States to have a serious degree of over-investment in housing and under-investment in other things.

While the itemized deductions for mortgage interest and real estate taxes create an important bias in favor of investment in owner-occupied housing, there is an even more general source of the distortion in question.

2.   Exclusion of Imputed Rental Value

Investment in owner-occupied housing is productive investment just as surely as investment in housing for rent to others. Mortgage interest and real estate taxes are expenses associated with that productive investment, and income tax deduction of expenses associated with productive investment is perfectly normal. What is not normal is to omit the return on productive investment from taxable income.

In the case of owner-occupied housing, that return comes in kind as housing services without payment of rent — commonly referred to as imputed rent or rental value. The distortions discussed in the last section are fundamentally a result of not including imputed rental value of owner-occupied housing in gross income.

Statistics of income do not show the amount of imputed rental value of owner-occupied housing because they are a report of what appears on income tax returns. Traditionally, official lists of tax expenditures did not show how much tax revenue is lost as a result of excluding imputed rent from taxable income due to difficulty of measurement, but the Treasury has recently tried to fill that gap by turning to the aggregate estimates of imputed rent of owner-occupied housing developed by the Bureau of Economic

Analysis of the U.S. Department of Commerce in making up the National Income and Product Accounts (NIPA).

ANALYTICAL PERSPECTIVES, BUDGET
OF THE U.S. GOVERNMENT, FISCAL YEAR 2007
325-326, 328 (2006)

TAX EXPENDITURES

OWNER-OCCUPIED HOUSING

A homeowner receives a flow of housing services equal in gross value to the rent that could have been earned had the owner chosen to rent the house to others. Comprehensive income would include in the homeowner's tax base this gross rental flow, and would allow the homeowner a deduction for expenses such as interest, depreciation, property taxes, and other costs associated with earning the rental income. Thus, a comprehensive tax base would include in its base the homeowner's implicit net rental income (gross income minus deductions) earned on investment in owner-occupied housing.

In contrast to a comprehensive income tax, current law makes no imputation for gross rental income and allows no deduction for depreciation or for other expenses, such as utilities and maintenance. Current law does, however, allow a deduction for home mortgage interest and for property taxes. Consequently, relative to a comprehensive income baseline, the total tax expenditure for owner-occupied housing is the sum of tax on net rental income plus the tax saving from the deduction for property taxes and for home mortgage interest.[31]

Prior to 2006, the official list of tax expenditures did not include the exclusion of net implicit rental income on owner-occupied housing. Instead, it included as tax expenditures deductions for home mortgage interest and for property taxes. While these deductions are legitimately considered tax expenditures, given current law's failure to impute rental income, they are highly flawed as estimates of the total income tax advantage to housing; they overlook the additional exclusion of implicit net rental income. To the extent a homeowner owns his house outright, unencumbered by a mortgage, he would have no home mortgage interest deduction, yet he still would enjoy the benefits of receiving tax free the implicit rental

---

31. The homeowner's tax base under a comprehensive income tax is net rents. Under current law, the homeowner's tax base is $-$ (interest $+$ property taxes). The tax expenditure base is the difference between the comprehensive income base and current law's tax base, which for homeowners is the sum of net rents plus interest plus property taxes.

income earned on his house. On the other hand, a homeowner with a mortgage approximately matching the value of the house might make interest payments that exceed the implicit rental income. The treatment of owner-occupied housing has been revised beginning in the 2006 budget, which now includes an item for the exclusion of net rental income of homeowners. . . .

Appendix Table 3. Revised Tax Expenditure Estimates

	Revenue Loss [in millions of dollars]						
Provision	*2005*	*2006*	*2007*	*2008*	*2009*	*2010*	*2011*
Imputed rent on owner-occupied housing	28,600	29,720	33,210	36,860	40,630	44,785	49,364

Notes and Questions

1. Compare the 2005 revenue loss estimate attributable to imputed net rent, $28.6 billion, with the 2005 tax expenditure estimates for the home mortgage interest and real estate tax deductions, $62.2 billion and $19.1 billion, respectively. Based on these figures, some would assert that about three-quarters of the problem can be cured by eliminating the deductions without getting into the valuation problems involved in estimating imputed rental values of owner-occupied housing. Make a critical evaluation of this suggestion. Think particularly about what might happen to home mortgage debts if this path were pursued.

Another suggestion is to eliminate discrimination between renters and owners by allowing a deduction of 75 percent of rent paid by tenants. What virtues and difficulties do you see with this suggestion? (Residential rent was deductible in full in the United States Civil War income tax.)

2. How do §§119 and 121 enter into your thoughts about income tax distortion with respect to owner-occupied housing?

3. Some have argued that undertaxation of investment in owner-occupied housing under the federal income tax is offset by relative overtaxation of such investment by local property taxes themselves. How would you go about seeking to evaluate this claim?

PRESIDENT'S ADVISORY PANEL ON TAX REFORM, SIMPLE, FAIR AND PRO-GROWTH: PROPOSALS TO FIX AMERICA'S TAX SYSTEM

70-74, 83-84 (2005)

A CLEANER TAX SYSTEM THAT IS SIMPLER, FAIRER, AND MORE EFFICIENT

The Panel began its consideration of options for reform by considering a tax base that was free of exclusions, deductions, and credits. The Panel recommends the retention of some features of the existing tax system, especially those that promote widely shared and valued goals, such as home ownership, charitable giving, and access to health care. However, when the Panel retained a tax preference, it did not simply replicate the current design of these features. Instead, the Panel first determined whether each preference was optimally designed or could be improved. Specifically, the Panel would maintain tax benefits that provide incentives to change behavior in ways that benefit the economy and society, rather than representing a windfall to targeted groups of taxpayers for activity they would be likely to undertake even without a tax subsidy.

A key objective in reforming these tax incentives was making them simpler and more widely available to taxpayers. Under current law, a number of incentives are limited to the 35 percent of taxpayers who itemize deductions instead of claiming the standard deduction. The Panel's recommendations represent a fundamental shift in the way taxpayers compute their taxes — *every* taxpayer would receive a Family Credit that provides a base amount of tax benefits similar to the current law standard deduction and personal exemption. Taxpayers would then be able to claim the following newly-designed tax benefits in addition to the Family Credit.

PROVISIONS AFFECTING HOMEOWNERSHIP

HOUSING TAX BENEFITS UNDER CURRENT LAW

The housing sector is highly favored by the tax code. Taxpayers are allowed to deduct interest paid on up to $1 million of mortgage debt secured by the taxpayer's first or second home. In addition, homeowners may deduct interest on home equity loans of up to $100,000. Other provisions allow taxpayers to deduct state and local property taxes and to exclude some or all of the capital gains on the sale of a primary residence. Together, these benefits provide a generous tax subsidy for taxpayers to invest in housing because the purchase and maintenance of a home is subsidized and a substantial amount of appreciation is not taxed. But there is a question whether the tax code encourages overinvestment in housing at the expense of other productive uses.

Figure [10-1]
Comparison of Effective Tax Rates on Different Types of Investment

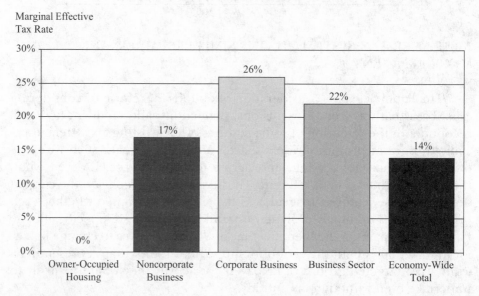

Note: These tax rates were estimated using the Administration's policy baseline, which assumes, among other things, that the 2001 and 2003 tax cuts will be made permanent and that the proposals contained in the President's Budget to create retirement savings accounts and lifetime savings accounts (each with a $5,000 limit) will be enacted.

Source: Department of the Treasury, Office of Tax Analysis.

As Figure [10-1] illustrates, the economy-wide tax rate on housing investment is close to zero, compared with a tax rate of approximately 22 percent on business investment. This may result in too little business investment, meaning businesses purchase less new equipment and fewer new technologies than they otherwise might. Too little investment means lower worker productivity, and ultimately, lower real wages and living standards. While the housing industry does produce jobs and may have other positive effects on the overall economy, it is not clear that it should enjoy such disproportionately favorable treatment under the tax code.

The tax preferences that favor housing exceed what is necessary to encourage home ownership or help more Americans buy their first home. For example, the $1 million mortgage limit may encourage taxpayers to purchase luxury residences and vacation homes. In addition, the deduction for home equity loan interest may encourage taxpayers to use their houses as a source of tax-preferred financing for consumer spending.

The benefits of current tax incentives for housing are not shared equally among all taxpayers. Under current law, the tax benefits for housing, which are larger than the entire budget of the Department of Housing and Urban Development, mostly go to the minority of taxpayers who itemize deductions. These taxpayers typically are drawn from higher-income groups. Over 70 percent of tax filers did not receive any benefit from the home mortgage interest deduction in 2002. According to the Joint Committee on Taxation, more than 55 percent of the estimated tax expenditure for home mortgage interest deductions went to the 12 percent of taxpayers who had cash income of $100,000 or more in 2004. Figure [10-2] demonstrates how households with higher income receive a disproportionate benefit from the home mortgage interest deduction.

Figure [10-2]
Distribution of Tax Benefits from the Home Mortgage
Interest Deduction

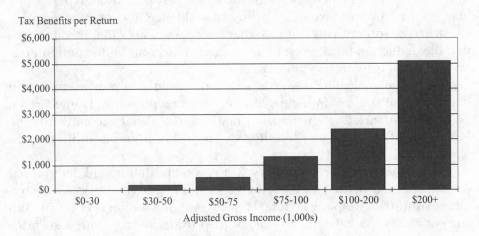

Source: Department of the Treasury, Office of Tax Analysis.

Although the deduction for home mortgage interest is often justified on the grounds that it is necessary for promoting home ownership, it is unclear to what extent rates of home ownership depend on the subsidy. According to the Census Bureau, there are more than 123 million homes in America, with a home ownership rate of 69 percent. There are many countries that do not allow any home mortgage interest deductions for tax purposes, including the United Kingdom, Canada, and Australia. The rate of home ownership in the United States is higher than that in some countries (approximately 66 percent in Canada), lower than that in others (approximately 70 percent in Australia), and comparable to that in still others (the United Kingdom). Thus, it appears that the level of subsidies provided in the United States may not be necessary to ensure high rates of home ownership.

Despite the concerns described above, housing is an important value in our society, and for this reason, the Panel recommends that tax benefits for home mortgage interest be retained, but shared more evenly.

RECOMMENDATIONS

- Replace the deduction for mortgage interest with a Home Credit available to all taxpayers equal to 15 percent of interest paid on a principal residence.
- Establish the amount of mortgage interest eligible for the Home Credit based on average regional housing costs.
- Lengthen the time a taxpayer must own and use a principal residence before gains form the sale of the home can be exempt from tax.

The Panel recommends that the deduction for mortgage interest be replaced with a Home Credit available to all homeowners. The Home Credit would be equal to 15 percent of mortgage interest paid by a taxpayer on a loan secured by the taxpayer's principal residence and used to acquire, construct, or substantially improve that residence. The Panel recommends that the deduction for interest on mortgages on second homes and interest on home-equity loans be eliminated.

To encourage home ownership without subsidizing overinvestment in housing, the Panel recommends limiting the amount of the Home Credit. To adjust for variations in housing markets, the Panel recommends the Home Credit limit be based on the average cost of housing within the tax-payer's area.

The Panel considered various ways to accomplish this, and determined the limit should be based on average area home purchase prices as determined using data from the Federal Housing Administration (FHA). The IRS currently uses a similar methodology to provide average purchase price guidelines for other tax provisions. The FHA insures loans of up to 95 percent of the median home sale price in a given metropolitan area, subject to certain minimum and maximum levels. To estimate average home purchase prices, the Panel considered a mortgage interest cap that was 125 percent of the median sale price for each county (this amount is approximately 31.5 percent higher than the FHA amount after grossing up the FHA median values from 95 to 100 percent). This would result in current limits between approximately $227,147 and $411,704. Estimates suggest that between 85 and 90 percent of mortgages originated in 2004 would have been unaffected by the proposed Home Credit mortgage limit (using the regional limits that would have been applicable for 2004).

The Home Credit would encourage home ownership, not big homes. More Americans would be able to take advantage of tax benefits for owning a home, while the current subsidy for luxury and vacation homes would be curtailed. In addition, the Home Credit would reduce the incentive to take on more debt by eliminating the deduction for interest on home equity loans.

As under current law, mortgage lenders would be required to report the amount of interest eligible for the Home Credit to borrowers on annual information returns. The Home Credit would simplify tax filing because taxpayers would not need to determine whether they are better off claiming the standard deduction or itemizing and claiming the home mortgage interest deduction.

More importantly, under the proposal, millions of Americans would be able to claim a tax benefit for home mortgage interest for the first time, which would make owning a home more affordable. Currently, only 54 percent of taxpayers who pay interest on their mortgages receive a tax benefit. . . . [A]pproximately 88 percent of taxpayers who pay mortgage interest would receive a benefit for home ownership under the Panel's recommendations. Lower-income taxpayers, in particular, would do better under the Panel's recommendations than under the current system. For example, the percentage of taxpayers with adjusted gross income between $40,000 and $50,000 who have mortgages and receive a tax benefit for mortgage interest paid would increase from less than 50 percent to more than 99 percent. Depending on the year, between 77 and 94 percent of taxpayers with adjusted gross income over $100,000 who would receive a lesser subsidy under the Home Credit would have paid higher taxes under the AMT, which would be eliminated under the Panel's options.

The Panel recognizes that limiting the amount of the current tax subsidy for mortgage interest could adversely affect individuals who purchased or refinanced homes assuming they would be able to deduct interest on up to $1.1 million of mortgage debt. To be fair to those who relied on current tax law in making important financial decisions, the options provide for a gradual phase-in of the cap over a five-year period for preexisting home mortgages. Additional information regarding the Home Credit, including the proposed transition relief can be found in the Appendix.

Under current law, up to $500,000 of capital gains on a home that a taxpayer has owned and used as his principal residence for two out of the last five years may be excluded. Although the Panel believes the exemption for gains from the sale of a principal residence should be retained for most homeowners, it also believes that the length of ownership and use required to obtain this benefit is too short. The Panel recommends that the length of time an individual must own and use a home as a principal residence to qualify for the tax exemption be increased from two out of five years to three out of five years. . . .

THE STATE AND LOCAL TAX DEDUCTION

RECOMMENDATION

• Repeal the deduction for state and local taxes.

The Panel recommends eliminating the itemized deduction for state and local taxes. This deduction provides a federal tax subsidy for public services provided by state and local governments. Taxpayers who claim the state and local tax deduction pay for these services with tax-free dollars. These services, which are determined through the political process, represent a substantial personal benefit to the state or local residents who receive them — either by delivering the service directly or by supporting a better quality of life in their community. The Panel concluded that these expenditures should be treated like any other nondeductible personal expense, such as food or clothing, and that the cost of those services should be borne by those who want them — not by every taxpayer in the country.

The state and local tax deduction forces residents of low-tax jurisdictions to subsidize government services received by taxpayers in high-tax jurisdictions. As with many other tax benefits, the state and local tax deduction requires higher tax rates for everyone, but the benefits of the deduction are not shared equally among taxpayers. The deduction is limited to itemizers, and households with higher income and tax rates receive a greater share of the benefit from the deduction. Even among itemizers, the benefits of the deduction are not shared evenly, as the AMT is increasingly erasing the benefit of the state and local tax deduction for many middle-class taxpayers. Depending on the year, between 64 and 70 percent of taxpayers with adjusted gross income over $100,000 who would no longer receive a deduction for state and local taxes also would have paid higher taxes under the AMT, which is repealed under the Panel's options.

Notes and Questions

1. Why tie the proposed Home Credit to the amount of interest paid rather than the price of the home?

2. Are state and local taxes really "like any other nondeductible personal expense"? Do state and local taxpayers receive consumption benefits commensurate with their obligations? What about state-financed health care for the poor (Medicaid), or state-wide baseline support for public education? Would repeal of the federal deduction tend to restrain the growth of state and local government? To shift state and local levies toward less progressive taxes?

3. *Alternative Minimum Tax (AMT)*. State and local (and foreign) taxes are not deductible in computing the base of the alternative minimum tax, §56(b)(1)(A), nor is interest paid on home equity loans, §56(a)(1)(C)(i), (e). Over the past decade the AMT has impacted constantly increasing numbers of upper-income individuals due to the absence of inflation indexing of the AMT rate brackets and exemption amounts. Consequently, many high-income taxpayers have discovered that thanks to the AMT their state and local taxes are already in effect nondeductible, even though they itemize.

4. *First-time Homebuyers' Credit*. New §36, enacted by of the Housing and Economic Recovery Act of 2008, Pub. L. No. 110-289, §3011, 122 Stat. 2654,

2888, grants first-time homebuyers a refundable tax credit of 10 percent of the purchase price of the house, up to a maximum of $8,000. The credit, which is a response to weakness in the housing market caused by the sub-prime mortgage crisis, applies only to principal residences purchased on or after April 9, 2008 and before April 1, 2009. §36(g). The credit is phased out if the taxpayer's modified adjusted gross income falls between $75,000 and $95,000 ($150,000 to $170,000 in the case of a joint return). §36(b)(2). The credit functions as an interest-free loan from the government rather than direct cost sharing, because one-fifteenth of the credit is recaptured each year beginning in the second taxable year after the purchase, and any amounts not previously recaptured become due immediately if the home is sold prior to the end of the recapture period. §36(f).

D.   CASUALTY LOSSES

Section 165(c)(3) authorizes a deduction for casualty losses whether or not incurred in a business or a transaction entered into for profit. In this respect casualty losses are like interest and taxes, and the deduction for nonbusiness casualty losses is generally classified as a personal deduction.

The deduction for casualty losses is in some respects the easiest of the personal deductions to defend, because an unanticipated and unintended loss comes very close to being negative windfall income. (But then interest paid is negative investment income, too.) Consider a taxpayer who is robbed just after cashing his paycheck; is there any substantial reason he should be taxed more heavily than if he had not been paid? The casualty loss deduction, to the extent available, will tend to produce equality of treatment.

But that is hardly the typical case. Most casualty losses involve money brought safely home from the workplace and invested in some personal nonbusiness venture before any loss occurs. And then it is not clear why a casualty loss should be taken into account any more than any other failed consumption expenditure. Economists have occasionally played with the question whether one who buys a lemon for an automobile should get a tax deduction for his loss, but no one has thought that would be a practical arrangement. So maybe the casualty criterion is adopted just because it gives a relatively objective way to isolate at least some cases in which we can have confidence there has actually been a loss. Objective perhaps, but not uncontroversial; the scope of the casualty concept has been the subject of many litigated cases — below we have but one illustration.

Even when the existence of a casualty loss is settled, there are often substantial uncertainties about valuation. It can be persuasively argued that matters of this kind are the last sort of thing to be left for determination by taxpayers on their tax returns, without regular, prompt attention by someone representing the government. Compare the practice of insurance companies handling claims for casualty losses.

Pay particular attention to the limitations in §165(h). Section 165(h)(2)(A), confining the deduction to aggregate losses exceeding 10 percent of adjusted gross income, was adopted in 1982 and has made the casualty loss deduction much less significant than it formerly was. Today for most taxpayers only the uninsured destruction of their personal residence would generate a deduction. That eventuality is not as unlikely as it might seem, however. Homeowners' insurance policies commonly contain exclusions from coverage for damage due to flooding or ground motion (e.g., sinkholes or earthquakes). Widespread flooding in the wake of Hurricane Katrina caused Congress to waive the nondeductible floors ($100 and 10 percent of AGI), but only for losses arising from that disaster. Katrina Emergency Tax Relief Act of 2005, Pub. L. No. 109-73, §402, 119 Stat. 2016, 2027.

WILLIAM H. CARPENTER
T.C. Mem. 1966-228

MEMORANDUM FINDINGS OF FACT AND OPINION

Withey, Judge: A deficiency in the income tax petitioners for the taxable year 1962 has been determined by the Commissioner in the amount of $221.92. The sole issue to be decided is whether respondent has erred in disallowing a claimed casualty loss deduction.

FINDINGS OF FACT

The facts are found which are stipulated.

Petitioners are husband and wife residing at Cleveland Heights, Ohio. They filed their joint Federal income tax return for 1962 with the district director at Cleveland, Ohio.

During 1962 petitioner Nancy Carpenter owned a diamond engagement ring. At an undisclosed time in 1962 she placed the ring in a waterglass of ammonia for the purpose of cleaning it. The glass containing the ring was left "next" to the kitchen sink. While petitioner William Carpenter was washing dishes, he inadvertently "picked up the glass and emptied its contents down the" sink drain, not realizing the ring was part of such contents. He then activated the garbage disposal unit in the sink damaging the ring. The damaged ring was recovered and taken to a jeweler for appraisal. His appraisal was that the ring was a total loss.

The ring consisted of a platinum mounting, one diamond of .76 carat and four small diamonds of undisclosed weight. Immediately before going into the disposal unit the fair market value of the mounting was $235, that of the large diamond $725, and the aggregate of four small diamonds $50, or an aggregate fair market value of $1,010. This amount was deducted on petitioner's income tax return as a casualty loss.

The fair market value of the mounting immediately after being placed in the disposal unit was $5, that of the large diamond zero, and the aggregate of the small diamonds $25, or a total aggregate fair market value of $30.

Following the above event William purchased and gave Nancy a ring at a purchase price of $169.50.

Nancy had a loss as a result of the above facts in the amount of the difference between the fair market value of her original ring immediately before it was damaged and its fair market value immediately after in the resulting amount of $980.

OPINION

Respondent's position here is that Nancy did not suffer a casualty loss within the meaning of section 165(a) and (c)(3) of the Internal Revenue Code of 1954 in that, by applying the principle of ejusdem generis, it cannot be said that the events which gave rise to the ring damage were like or similar to a "fire, storm, [or] shipwreck" and therefore do not amount to "other casualty" under that section. He also takes the position that, should we hold to the contrary on this point, the replacement value of the ring subsequently purchased for Nancy by William and the salvage value of the damaged ring must be offset against the gross loss suffered by Nancy.

Because William's testimony and his demeanor on the witness stand satisfies us that he is not the type of person who would deliberately and knowingly do so, we have concluded that his placing of the original ring in the disposal unit was inadvertent and accidental. We in turn conclude from this that the damage to the ring resulted from the destructive force of the disposal coupled with the accident or mischance of placing it therein; that, because this is so, the damage must be said to have arisen from fortuitous events over which petitioners had no control.

While the application of the principle of ejusdem generis has been consistent in reported cases under this section of the Code and its predecessors, from at least Shearer v. Anderson, 16 F.2d 995 (C.A. 2), the application has been clearly and consistently broadened. Automobile accidental damage has been likened to shipwreck, Shearer v. Anderson, supra; earthslide damage to a building, to fire, storm, and shipwreck, Harry Heyn, 46 T.C. 302; and drought damage to buildings, to storm damage, Maurer v. United States, 178 F. Supp. 223, reversed on other grounds, 284 F.2d 122. Respondent has gone so far as to allow deduction for damage caused by the sonic boom of a speeding airplane as "other casualty." See Rev. Rul. 59-344, 1959-2 C.B. (Part 2) 74, superseded by Rev. Rul. 60-329, 1960-2 C.B. (Part 2) 67, only to clarify the former. This Court has held that "other casualty" includes damage caused by an infestation by termites, E. G. Kilroe, 32 T.C. 1304, in no way departing from the principle in doing so.

We think the principle of ejusdem generis as now applied fulfills congressional intent in the use of the phrase "other casualty" in that it is being generally held that wherever force is applied to property which the owner-taxpayer is either unaware of because of the hidden nature of such application or is powerless to act to prevent the same because of the suddenness thereof or some other disability and damage results, he has suffered a loss which is, in that sense, like or similar to losses arising from the enumerated causes. Of course, we do not mean to say that one may willfully and knowingly sit by and allow himself to be damaged in his property and still come within the statutory ambit of "other casualty."

Nancy sustained a loss here under circumstances which it is true may be due to her or her husband's negligence, but this has no bearing upon the question whether an "other casualty" has occurred absent any willfulness attributable thereto. Harry Heyn, supra.

In the circumstances of this case we do not think that the amount of the loss must be reduced by the value of the "replacement" ring. The husband was not an insurer of the ring and it is difficult to conclude that the wife has any claim or measurable right of reimbursement against him for her loss. What he did was simply make another gift to her as an act of repentance or contrition, and not as a compensatory action.

Decision will be entered under Rule 50.

Notes and Questions

1. In Keenan v. Bowers, 91 F. Supp. 771 (E.D.S.C. 1950), a woman wrapped a ring in tissue and left it on a night stand; her husband flushed the tissue down the toilet. Deduction was disallowed. In John P. White, 48 T.C. 430 (1967), a car door slammed on a taxpayer's hand, springing the diamond out of her ring; the diamond, worth $1,200, was not found. Deduction was allowed.

2. Look at Treas. Reg. §§165-7, 8, 9, and work out the following problems:

(a) *A* bought an automobile for personal use, paying $26,000. She was in an accident in which the car was damaged. The car was worth only $10,000 after the accident. What amount is allowable as a deduction on account of this loss?

(b) *B* bought a house (land and building) for use as his personal residence for $240,000. Later when the property (land and building) was worth $260,000, the house burned down. The land is worth $40,000. How much is allowable as a deduction? What if *B* recovered $180,000 in fire insurance on account of the loss?

(c) *C* owned a piece of property with a basis of $40,000 and a fair market value of $30,000. How much can *C* deduct if this item is stolen?

3. No deduction is allowed for insuring against casualty losses to property not held for the production of income. How does this comport with the treatment of uninsured losses?

References

A. Interest: Asimow, The Interest Deduction, 24 U.C.L.A. L. Rev. 749 (1977); Bedell, The Interest Deduction: Its Current Status, 32 N.Y.U. Inst. on Fed. Tax'n. 1117 (1974); Berger, Simple Interest and Complex Taxes, 81 Colum. L. Rev. 217 (1981); Blum, *Knetsch v. United States:* A Pronouncement on Tax Avoidance, 1961 Sup. Ct. Rev. 135, 40 Taxes 296 (1962); Bossons, Indexing for Inflation and the Interest Deduction, 30 Wayne L. Rev. 945 (1984); Isenbergh, Musings on Form and Substance in Taxation, 49 U. Chi. L. Rev. 859, 874 (1982); McIntyre, An Inquiry into the Special Status of Interest Payments, 1981 Duke L.J. 765 (1981); Port, Tax Avoidance Use of the Interest Deduction, 45 Tex. L. Rev. 1218 (1967); Daniel N. Shaviro, The Story of *Knetsch:* Judicial Doctrines Combating Tax Avoidance in Tax Stories 313 (2003); Steuerle, Tax Arbitrage, Inflation, and the Taxation of Interest Payments and Receipts, 30 Wayne L. Rev. 991 (1984); Warren, The Requirement of Economic Profit in Tax Motivated Transactions, 59 Taxes 985 (1981).

C. Homeowners: H. Aaron, Shelter and Subsidies: Who Benefits from Federal Housing Policies 53-68 (1972); Davies & Hicks, The Itemized Deductions of Homeowners — An Analysis of the Need for Reform, 56 Taxes 22 (1978); Richard Goode, The Individual Income Tax 117-125 (rev. ed. 1976); White & White, Horizontal Inequality in the Federal Income Tax Treatment of Homeowners and Tenants, 18 Natl. Tax J. 225 (1965).

D. Casualty Losses: Epstein, The Consumption and Loss of Personal Property Under The Internal Revenue Code, 23 Stan. L. Rev. 454 (1971).

Chapter 11 — *Charitable Contributions and Tax Exemption*

A. *QUALIFIED ORGANIZATIONS*

REGAN v. TAXATION WITH REPRESENTATION OF WASHINGTON
461 U.S. 540 (1983)

Justice REHNQUIST delivered the opinion of the Court.

Appellee Taxation With Representation of Washington (TWR) is a nonprofit corporation organized to promote what it conceives to be the "public interest" in the area of federal taxation. It proposes to advocate its point of view before Congress, the Executive Branch, and the Judiciary. The case began when TWR applied for tax exempt status under §501(c)(3) of the Internal Revenue Code. The Internal Revenue Service denied the application because it appeared that a substantial part of TWR's activities would consist of attempting to influence legislation, which is not permitted by §501(c)(3)....

TWR was formed to take over the operations of two other non-profit corporations. One, Taxation With Representation Fund, was organized to promote TWR's goals by publishing a journal and engaging in litigation; it had tax-exempt status under §501(c)(3). The other, Taxation With Representation, attempted to promote the same goals by influencing legislation;

it had tax-exempt status under §501(c)(4). Neither predecessor organization was required to pay federal income taxes. For purposes of our analysis, there are two principal differences between §501(c)(3) organizations and §501(c)(4) organizations. Taxpayers who contribute to §501(c)(3) organizations are permitted by §170(c)(2) to deduct the amount of their contributions on their federal income tax returns, while contributions to §501(c)(4) organizations are not deductible. Section 501(c)(4) organizations, but not §501(c)(3) organizations, are permitted to engage in substantial lobbying to advance their exempt purposes.

In this case, TWR is attacking the prohibition against substantial lobbying in §501(c)(3) because it wants to use tax-deductible contributions to support substantial lobbying activities. To evaluate TWR's claims, it is necessary to understand the effect of the tax exemption system enacted by Congress.

Both tax exemptions and tax-deductibility are a form of subsidy that is administered through the tax system. A tax exemption has much the same effect as a cash grant to the organization of the amount of tax it would have to pay on its income. Deductible contributions are similar to cash grants of the amount of a portion of the individual's contributions.[5] The system Congress has enacted provides this kind of subsidy to non-profit civic welfare organizations generally, and an additional subsidy to those charitable organizations that do not engage in substantial lobbying. In short, Congress chose not to subsidize lobbying as extensively as it chose to subsidize other activities that non-profit organizations undertake to promote the public welfare.

It appears that TWR could still qualify for a tax exemption under §501(c)(4). It also appears that TWR can obtain tax deductible contributions for its non-lobbying activity by returning to the dual structure it used in the past, with a §501(c)(3) organization for non-lobbying activities and a §501(c)(4) organization for lobbying. TWR would, of course, have to ensure that the §501(c)(3) organization did not subsidize the §501(c)(4) organization; otherwise, public funds might be spent on an activity Congress chose not to subsidize.[6]

---

5. In stating that exemptions and deductions, on one hand, are like cash subsidies, on the other, we of course do not mean to assert that they are in all respects identical. See, e.g., Walz v. Tax Commission, 397 U.S. 664, 674-676 (1970); id., 690-691 (Brennan, J., concurring); id., at 699 (opinion of Harlan, J.) [exemption of church property from New York City real estate taxes does not violate First and Fourteenth Amendments — Eds.].

6. TWR and some amici are concerned that the IRS may impose stringent requirements that are unrelated to the congressional purpose of ensuring that no tax-deductible contributions are used to pay for substantial lobbying, and effectively make it impossible for a §501(c)(3) organization to establish a §501(c)(4) lobbying affiliate. No such requirement in the code or regulations has been called to our attention, nor have we been able to discover one. The IRS apparently requires only that the two groups be separately incorporated and keep records adequate to show that tax deductible contributions are not used to pay for lobbying. This is not unduly burdensome.

We also note that TWR did not bring this suit because it was unable to operate with the dual structure and seeks a less stringent set of bookkeeping requirements. Rather, TWR seeks to force Congress to subsidize its lobbying activity. See Tr. of Oral Arg. 37-39.

TWR contends that Congress' decision not to subsidize its lobbying violates the First Amendment. It claims, relying on Speiser v. Randall, 357 U.S. 513 (1958), that the prohibition against substantial lobbying by §501(c)(3) organizations imposes an "unconstitutional condition" on the receipt of tax-deductible contributions. In *Speiser*, California established a rule requiring anyone who sought to take advantage of a property tax exemption to sign a declaration stating that he did not advocate the forcible overthrow of the Government of the United States. This Court stated that "[t]o deny an exemption to claimants who engage in speech is in effect to penalize them for the same speech." Id., at 518.

TWR is certainly correct when it states that we have held that the government may not deny a benefit to a person because he exercises a constitutional right. See Perry v Sindermann, 408 U.S. 593, 597 (1972). But TWR is just as certainly incorrect when it claims that this case fits the *Speiser-Perry* model. The Code does not deny TWR the right to receive deductible contributions to support its non-lobbying activity, nor does it deny TWR any independent benefit on account of its intention to lobby. Congress has merely refused to pay for the lobbying out of public monies. This Court has never held that Congress must grant a benefit such as TWR claims here to a person who wishes to exercise a constitutional right.

This aspect of the case is controlled by Cammarano v. United States, 358 U.S. 498 (1959), in which we upheld a Treasury Regulation that denied business expense deductions for lobbying activities. We held that Congress is not required by the First Amendment to subsidize lobbying. Id., at 513. In this case, like in *Cammarano*, Congress has not infringed any First Amendment rights or regulated any First Amendment activity. Congress has simply chosen not to pay for TWR's lobbying. We again reject the "notion that First Amendment rights are somehow not fully realized unless they are subsidized by the State." Id., at 515 (Douglas, J., concurring).

TWR also contends that the equal protection component of the Fifth Amendment renders the prohibition against substantial lobbying invalid. TWR points out that §170(c)(3) permits taxpayers to deduct contributions to veterans' organizations that qualify for tax exemption under §501(c)(19). Qualifying veterans' organizations are permitted to lobby as much as they want in furtherance of their exempt purposes. TWR argues that because Congress has chosen to subsidize the substantial lobbying activities of veterans' organizations, it must also subsidize the lobbying of §501(c)(3) organizations.

Generally, statutory classifications are valid if they bear a rational relation to a legitimate governmental purpose. Statutes are subjected to a higher level of scrutiny if they interfere with the exercise of a fundamental right, such as freedom of speech, or employ a suspect classification, such as race. E.g., Harris v. McRae, 448 U.S. 297, 322 (1980). Legislatures have especially broad latitude in creating classifications and distinctions in tax statutes.

More than forty years ago we addressed these comments to an equal protection challenge to tax legislation:

> The broad discretion as to classification possessed by a legislature in the field of taxation has long been recognized. . . . The passage of time has only served to underscore the wisdom of that recognition of the large area of discretion which is needed by a legislature in formulating sound tax policies. Traditionally classification has been a device for fitting tax programs to local needs and usages in order to achieve an equitable distribution of the tax burden. It has, because of this, been pointed out that in taxation, even more than in other fields, legislatures possess the greatest freedom in classification. Since the members of a legislature necessarily enjoy a familiarity with local conditions which this Court cannot have, the presumption of constitutionality can be overcome only by the most explicit demonstration that a classification is a hostile and oppressive discrimination against particular persons and classes. The burden is on the one attacking the legislative arrangement to negative every conceivable basis which might support it. [Madden v. Kentucky, 309 U.S. 83, 87-88 (1940) (footnotes omitted).]

See also San Antonio School District v. Rodriguez, 411 U.S. 1, 40-41 (1973); Lehnhausen v. Lake Shore Auto Parts Co., 410 U.S. 356, 359-360 (1973).

We have already explained why we conclude that Congress has not violated TWR's First Amendment rights by declining to subsidize its First Amendment activities. The case would be different if Congress were to discriminate invidiously in its subsidies in such a way as to "aim at the suppression of dangerous ideas." *Cammarano*, supra, at 513, quoting *Speiser*, supra, at 519. But the veterans' organizations that qualify under §501(c)(19) are entitled to receive tax-deductible contributions regardless of the content of any speech they may use, including lobbying. . . .

. . . TWR contends that §501(c)(3) organizations could better advance their charitable purposes if they were permitted to engage in substantial lobbying. This may well be true. But Congress — not TWR or this Court — has the authority to determine whether the advantage the public would receive from additional lobbying by charities is worth the money the public would pay to subsidize that lobbying, and other disadvantages that might accompany that lobbying. It appears that Congress was concerned that exempt organizations might use tax-deductible contributions to lobby to promote the private interests of their members. See 78 Cong. Rec. 5861 (1934) (remarks of Senator Reed); Id., at 5959 (remarks of Senator La Follette). It is not irrational for Congress to decide that tax exempt charities such as TWR should not further benefit at the expense of taxpayers at large by obtaining a further subsidy for lobbying.

It is also not irrational for Congress to decide that, even though it will not subsidize substantial lobbying by charities generally, it will subsidize lobbying by veterans' organizations. Veterans have "been obliged to drop their own affairs and take up the burdens of the nation," Boone v. Lightner, 319 U.S. 561, 575 (1943), "subjecting themselves to the mental and physical hazards as well as the economic and family detriments which are peculiar to military service and which do not exist in normal civil life." Johnson v. Robison, 415 U.S. 361, 380 (1974). Our country has a long standing policy of compensating veterans for their past contributions by providing them with numerous advantages. This policy has "always been deemed to be legitimate." Personnel Administrator v. Feeney, 442 U.S. 256, 279, n.25 (1979). . . .

Reversed.

Justice BLACKMUN, with whom Justice Brennan and Justice Marshall join, concurring. . . .

If viewed in isolation, the lobbying restriction contained in §501(c)(3) violates the principle, reaffirmed today, "that the Government may not deny a benefit to a person because he exercises a constitutional right." Section 501(c)(3) does not merely deny a subsidy for lobbying activities, see Cammarano v. United States, 358 U.S. 498 (1959); it deprives an otherwise eligible organization of its tax-exempt status and its eligibility to receive tax-deductible contributions for all its activities, whenever one of those activities is "substantial lobbying." Because lobbying is protected by the First Amendment, Eastern Railroad Presidents Conf. v. Noerr Motor Freight, Inc., 365 U.S. 127, 137-138 (1961), §501(c)(3) therefore denies a significant benefit to organizations choosing to exercise their constitutional rights.

The constitutional defect that would inhere in §501(c)(3) alone is avoided by §501(c)(4). As the Court notes, . . . TWR may use its present §501(c)(3) organization for its nonlobbying activities and may create a §501(c)(4) affiliate to pursue its charitable goals through lobbying. The §501(c)(4) affiliate would not be eligible to receive tax-deductible contributions.

Given this relationship between §501(c)(3) and §501(c)(4), the Court finds that Congress' purpose in imposing the lobbying restriction was merely to ensure that "no tax-deductible contributions are used to pay for substantial lobbying." . . . Consistent with that purpose, "[t]he IRS apparently requires only that the two groups be separately incorporated and keep records adequate to show that tax deductible contributions are not used to pay for lobbying." . . . As long as the IRS goes no further than this, we perhaps can safely say that "[t]he Code does not deny TWR the right to receive deductible contributions to support its nonlobbying activity, nor does it deny TWR any independent benefit on account of its intention to lobby." . . . A §501(c)(3) organization's right to speak is not infringed, because it is free to make known its views on legislation through its §501(c)(4) affiliate without losing tax benefits for its nonlobbying activities.

Any significant restriction on this channel of communication, however, would negate the saving effect of §501(c)(4). It must be remembered that §501(c)(3) organizations retain their constitutional right to speak and to petition the Government. Should the IRS attempt to limit the control these organizations exercise over the lobbying of their §501(c)(4) affiliates, the First Amendment problems would be insurmountable. It hardly answers one person's objection to a restriction on his speech that another person, outside his control, may speak for him. . . .

I must assume that the IRS will continue to administer §§501(c)(3) and 501(c)(4) in keeping with Congress' limited purpose and with the IRS' duty to respect and uphold the Constitution. I therefore agree with the Court that the First Amendment questions in this case are controlled by Cammarano v. United States, 358 U.S. 498, 513 (1959), rather than by Speiser v. Randall, 357 U.S. 513, 518-519 (1958), and Perry v. Sindermann, 408 U.S. 593, 597 (1972).

Notes

1. Section 501(c)(3) provides that "no substantial part of the activities of [the organization] is carrying on propaganda, or otherwise attempting, to influence legislation." The vagueness of the "substantial part" standard became salient and controversial in 1966 when the Sierra Club, which was then accorded tax-exempt status as a §501(c)(3) educational organization, and so was eligible to receive tax-deductible contributions under §170(c)(2), ran full-page advertisements in the New York Times and the Washington Post calling on the public to contribute funds to help the Club fight a bill pending in Congress that would have authorized construction of two dams in the Grand Canyon. The IRS promptly announced that such contributions might not be tax deductible, and subsequently revoked the Sierra Club's exemption. See Sheldon S. Cohen, Letter to the Editor, N.Y. Times, June 27, 1966, at 34 (Commissioner explains agency action); Wallace Turner, Sierra Club Loses Exemption on Tax, N.Y. Times, Dec. 21, 1966, at 27. Mocking the Bureau of Reclamation's claim that the reservoir would make the Grand Canyon more accessible to sightseers, one advertisement published in 1967 famously asked: "Should We Also Flood the Sistine Chapel so Tourists Can Get Nearer the Ceiling?" It closed with the observation:

> Our previous ads, urging that readers exercise a constitutional right of petition to save Grand Canyon from two dams which would have flooded it, produced an unprecedented reaction by the Internal Revenue Service threatening our tax deductible status. IRS called the ads a "substantial" effort to "influence legislations." Undefined, these terms leave organizations like ours at the mercy of administrative whim. (The question has not been raised with organizations that favor Grand Canyon dams.) So we cannot now promise that contributions you send us are tax deductible — pending result of what may be a long legal battle. [N.Y. Times, Mar. 13, 1967, at 41.]

In fact, no such battle was waged. The Sierra Club accepted classification as a social welfare organization under §501(c)(4). As such, it is permitted to engage in substantial lobbying but is barred from receiving tax-deductible contributions; the Club's research and educational functions were segregated into a separate 501(c)(3) organization. For lively profiles of the principal antagonists in the Grand Canyon dam saga, see John McPhee, Encounters with the Archdruid 151 (1971).

2. In 1976 Congress enacted an elective alternative to the substantial part test. Look at §§501(h) and 4911. How do they attempt to deal with the problem of lobbying by tax-exempt organizations? Do they represent an improvement over the formulation involved in *TWR*?

3. In contrast to its toleration of limited lobbying, §501(c)(3) imposes a flat prohibition on participation in "any political campaign on behalf of (or in opposition to) any candidate for public office." But how does one distinguish between nonpartisan voter education or moral teaching and implicit campaign intervention? The IRS investigated the NAACP and several churches based on speeches and sermons critical of President Bush made shortly before the 2004 presidential election. Fred Stokeld, IRS Probe of NAACP Ends; Civil Rights Group Keeps Exemption, 112 Tax Notes 817 (2006); Fred Stokeld, IRS Finds Campaign Intervention by Churches, Charities, 110 Tax Notes 1031 (2006); Fred Stokeld, Sermon at California Church Leads to IRS Probe, 109 Tax Notes 885 (2005); Fred Stokeld, NAACP Refuses IRS Document Request, 106 Tax Notes 1503 (2005). In an effort to offer some clarity, Rev. Rul. 2007-41, 2007-1 C.B. 1421, sets out the Service's position on 21 fact patterns, involving individual activity by organization leaders, candidate appearances, issue advocacy, business activity that aids a candidate, and organization Web sites.

BOB JONES UNIVERSITY v. UNITED STATES
461 U.S. 574 (1983)

Chief Justice BURGER delivered the opinion of the Court. . . .

I

Until 1970, the Internal Revenue Service granted tax-exempt status to private schools, without regard to their racial admissions policies, under §501(c)(3) of the Internal Revenue Code, and granted charitable deductions for contributions to such schools under §170 of the Code.

On January 12, 1970, a three-judge District Court for the District of Columbia issued a preliminary injunction prohibiting the IRS from according tax-exempt status to private schools in Mississippi that discriminated as to admissions on the basis of race. Green v. Kennedy, 309 F. Supp. 1127 (D.D.C.), app. dismissed sub nom. Cannon v. Green, 398 U.S. 956 (1970). Thereafter, in July 1970, the IRS concluded that it could "no longer legally justify allowing tax-exempt status [under §501(c)(3)] to private schools which practice racial discrimination." IRS News Release (7/10/70). At the same time, the IRS announced that it could not "treat gifts to such schools as charitable deductions for income tax purposes [under §170]." Ibid. By letter dated November 30, 1970, the IRS formally notified private schools, including those involved in this case, of this change in policy, "applicable to all private schools in the United States at all levels of education."

On June 30, 1971, the three-judge District Court issued its opinion on the merits of the Mississippi challenge. Green v. Connally, 330 F. Supp. 1150 (D.D.C.), aff'd sub nom. Coit v. Green, 404 U.S. 997 (1971) (per curiam). That court approved the IRS' amended construction of the Tax Code. The court also held that racially discriminatory private schools were not entitled to exemption under §501(c)(3) and that donors were not entitled to deductions for contributions to such schools under §170. The court permanently enjoined the Commissioner of Internal Revenue from approving tax-exempt status for any school in Mississippi that did not publicly maintain a policy of nondiscrimination.

The revised policy on discrimination was formalized in Revenue Ruling 71-447, 1971-2 Cum. Bull. 230:

> Both the courts and the Internal Revenue Service have long recognized that the statutory requirement of being "organized and operated exclusively for religious, charitable, ... or educational purposes" was intended to express the basic common law concept [of "charity"]. . . . All charitable trusts, educational or otherwise, are subject to the requirement that the purpose of the trust may not be illegal or contrary to public policy. [Id., at 230.]

Based on the "national policy to discourage racial discrimination in education," the IRS ruled that "a private school not having a racially nondiscriminatory policy as to students is not " 'charitable' within the common law concepts reflected in sections 170 and 501(c)(3) of the Code." . . .

Bob Jones University is a nonprofit corporation located in Greenville, South Carolina. Its purpose is "to conduct an institution of learning . . . , giving special emphasis to the Christian religion and the ethics revealed in the Holy Scriptures." Certificate of Incorporation, Bob Jones University, Inc., of Greenville, S.C., reprinted in App. in No. 81-3, pp. A118-A119. The corporation operates a school with an enrollment of approximately 5,000 students, from kindergarten through college and graduate school. Bob Jones University is not affiliated with any religious denomination, but is dedicated to the teaching and propagation of its fundamentalist Christian religious beliefs. It is both a religious and educational institution. Its teachers are required to be devout Christians, and all courses at the University are taught according to the Bible. Entering students are screened as to their religious beliefs, and their public and private conduct is strictly regulated by standards promulgated by University authorities.

The sponsors of the University genuinely believe that the Bible forbids interracial dating and marriage. To effectuate these views, Negroes were completely excluded until 1971. From 1971 to May 1975, the University accepted no applications from unmarried Negroes, but did accept applications from Negroes married within their race.

Following the decision of the United States Court of Appeals for the Fourth Circuit in McCrary v. Runyon, 515 F.2d 1082 (CA4 1975), aff'd, 427 U.S. 160 (1976), prohibiting racial exclusion from private schools, the University revised its policy. Since May 29, 1975, the University has permitted unmarried Negroes to enroll; but a disciplinary rule prohibits interracial dating and marriage. . . .

The University continues to deny admission to applicants engaged in an interracial marriage or known to advocate interracial marriage or dating. Id., at A277.

Until 1970, the IRS extended tax-exempt status to Bob Jones University under §501(c)(3). By the letter of November 30, 1970, that followed the injunction issued in Green v. Kennedy, supra, the IRS formally notified the University of the change in IRS policy, and announced its intention to challenge the tax-exempt status of private schools practicing racial discrimination in their admissions policies. . . .

Thereafter, on April 16, 1975, the IRS notified the University of the proposed revocation of its tax-exempt status. On January 19, 1976, the IRS officially revoked the University's tax-exempt status, effective as of December 1, 1970, the day after the University was formally notified of the change in IRS policy. The University subsequently filed returns under the Federal Unemployment Tax Act for the period from December 1, 1970, to December 31, 1975, and paid a tax totalling $21.00 on one employee for the calendar year of 1975. After its request for a refund was denied, the University instituted the present action, seeking to recover the $21.00 it had paid to the IRS. The Government counterclaimed for unpaid federal unemployment taxes for the taxable years 1971 through 1975, in the amount of $489,675.59, plus interest. . . .

II

A

In Revenue Ruling 71-447, the IRS formalized the policy first announced in 1970, that §170 and §501(c)(3) embrace the common law "charity" concept. Under that view, to qualify for a tax exemption pursuant to §501(c)(3), an institution must show, first, that it falls within one of the eight categories expressly set forth in that section, and second, that its activity is not contrary to settled public policy. . . .

It is a well-established canon of statutory construction that a court should go beyond the literal language of a statute if reliance on that language would defeat the plain purpose of the statute. . . .

Section 501(c)(3) therefore must be analyzed and construed within the framework of the Internal Revenue Code and against the background of the Congressional purposes. Such an examination reveals unmistakable evidence that, underlying all relevant parts of the Code, is the intent that entitlement to tax exemption depends on meeting certain common law standards of charity — namely, that an institution seeking tax-exempt status must serve a public purpose and not be contrary to established public policy.

This "charitable" concept appears explicitly in §170 of the Code. That section contains a list of organizations virtually identical to that contained in §501(c)(3). It is apparent that Congress intended that list to have the same meaning in both sections. In §170, Congress used the list of organizations in defining the term "charitable contributions." On its face, therefore, §170 reveals that Congress' intention was to provide tax benefits to organizations serving charitable purposes. The form of §170 simply makes plain what common sense and history tell us: in enacting both §170 and §501(c)(3), Congress sought to provide tax benefits to charitable organizations, to encourage the development of private institutions that serve a useful public purpose or supplement or take the place of public institutions of the same kind.

Tax exemptions for certain institutions thought beneficial to the social order of the country as a whole, or to a particular community, are deeply rooted in our history, as in that of England. The origins of such exemptions lie in the special privileges that have long been extended to charitable trusts.

More than a century ago, this Court announced

the caveat that is critical in this case: [I]t has now become an established principle of American law, that courts of chancery will sustain and protect . . . a gift . . . to public charitable uses, *provided the same is consistent with local laws and public policy.* . . . [Perin v. Carey, 24 How. 465, 501 (1861) (emphasis added).]

Soon after that, in 1878, the Court commented:

A charitable use, *where neither law nor public policy forbids,* may be applied to almost any thing *that tends to promote the well-doing and well-being of social man.* [Ould v. Washington Hospital for Foundlings, 95 U.S. 303, 311 (1878) (emphasis added). See also, e.g., Jackson v. Phillips, 96 Mass. 539, 556 (1867).]

In 1891, in a restatement of the English law of charity which has long been recognized as a leading authority in this country, Lord MacNaghten stated:

"Charity" in its legal sense comprises four principal divisions: trusts for the relief of poverty; *trusts for the advancement of education;* trusts for the advancement of religion; and trusts for *other purposes beneficial to the community,* not falling under any of the preceding heads. [Commissioners v. Pemsel, [1891] A.C. 531, 583 (emphasis added). See., e.g., 4 A. Scott, The Law of Trusts §368, at 2853-2854 (3d ed. 1967) (hereinafter Scott).]

These statements clearly reveal the legal background against which Congress enacted the first charitable exemption statute in 1894: charities were to be given preferential treatment because they provide a benefit to society.

What little floor debate occurred on the charitable exemption provision of the 1894 Act and similar sections of later statutes leaves no doubt that Congress deemed the specified organizations entitled to tax benefits because they served desirable public purposes. See. e.g., 26 Cong. Rec. 585-586 (1894); id., at 1727. In floor debate on a similar provision in 1917, for example, Senator Hollis articulated the rationale: "For every dollar that a man contributes to these public charities, educational, scientific, or otherwise, the public gets 100 percent." 55 id., at 6728 (1917). See also, e.g., 44 id., at 4150 (1909); 50 id., at 1305-1306 (1913). In 1924, this Court restated the common understanding of the charitable exemption provision:

> Evidently the exemption is made in recognition of the benefit which the public derives from corporate activities of the class named, and is intended to aid them when not conducted for private gain. [Trinidad v. Sagrada Orden, 263 U.S. 578, 581 (1924).]

In enacting the Revenue Act of 1938, ch. 289, 52 Stat. 447 (1938), Congress expressly reconfirmed this view with respect to the charitable deduction provision:

> The exemption from taxation of money and property devoted to charitable and other purposes is based on the theory that the Government is compensated for the loss of revenue by its relief from financial burdens which would otherwise have to be met by appropriations from other public funds, and by the benefits resulting from the promotion of the general welfare. [H.R. Rep. No. 1860, 75th Cong., 3d Sess. 19 (1938).]

A corollary to the public benefit principle is the requirement, long recognized in the law of trusts, that the purpose of a charitable trust may not be illegal or violate established public policy. In 1861, this Court stated that a public charitable use must be "consistent with local laws and public policy," Perin v. Carey, supra, 24 How., at 501. Modern commentators and courts have echoed that view. See, e.g., Restatement (Second) of Trusts, §377, comment c (1959); 4 Scott §377, and cases cited therein; Bogert §378, at 191-192.[17]

When the Government grants exemptions or allows deductions all taxpayers are affected; the very fact of the exemption or deduction for the donor means that other taxpayers can be said to be indirect and vicarious "donors." Charitable exemptions are justified on the basis that the exempt entity confers a public benefit—a benefit which the society or the

---

17. Cf. Tank Truck Rentals, Inc. v. Commissioner, 356 U.S. 30, 35 (1958), in which this Court referred to "the presumption against congressional intent to encourage violation of declared public policy" in upholding the Commissioner's disallowance of deductions claimed by a trucking company for fines it paid for violations of state maximum weight laws.

community may not itself choose or be able to provide, or which supplements and advances the work of public institutions already supported by tax revenues.[18] History buttresses logic to make clear that, to warrant exemption under §501(c)(3), an institution must fall within a category specified in that section and must demonstrably serve and be in harmony with the public interest. The institution's purpose must not be so at odds with the common community conscience as to undermine any public benefit that might otherwise be conferred.

B

We are bound to approach these questions with full awareness that determinations of public benefit and public policy are sensitive matters with serious implications for the institutions affected; a declaration that a given institution is not "charitable" should be made only where there can be no doubt that the activity involved is contrary to a fundamental public policy. But there can no longer be any doubt that racial discrimination in education violates deeply and widely accepted views of elementary justice. Prior to 1954, public education in many places still was conducted under the pall of Plessy v. Ferguson, 163 U.S. 537 (1896); racial segregation in primary and secondary education prevailed in many parts of the country. See, e.g., Segregation and the Fourteenth Amendment in the States (B. Reams & P. Wilson, eds. 1975).[20] This Court's decision in Brown v. Board of Education, 347 U.S. 483 (1954), signalled an end to that era. Over the past quarter of a century, every pronouncement of this Court and myriad Acts of Congress

---

18. The dissent acknowledges that "Congress intended . . . to offer a tax benefit to organizations . . . providing a public benefit," post, at 614-615, but suggests that Congress itself fully defined what organizations provide a public benefit, through the list of eight categories of exempt organizations contained in §170 and §501(c)(3). Under that view, any nonprofit organization that falls within one of the specified categories is automatically entitled to the tax benefits, provided it does not engage in expressly prohibited lobbying or political activities. Post, at 617. The dissent thus would have us conclude, for example, that any nonprofit organization that does not engage in prohibited lobbying activities is entitled to tax exemption as an "educational" institution if it is organized for the "instruction or training of the individual for the purpose of improving or developing his capabilities," 26 CFR §1.501(c)(3)-1(d)(3). See post, at 623. As Judge Leventhal noted in Green v. Connally, 330 F. Supp. 1150, 1160 (D.D.C.), aff'd sub nom. Coit v. Green, 404 U.S. 997 (1971) (per curiam), Fagin's school for educating English boys in the art of picking pockets would be an "educational" institution under that definition. Similarly, a band of former military personnel might well set up a school for intensive training of subversives for guerilla warfare and terrorism in other countries; in the abstract, that "school" would qualify as an "educational" institution. Surely Congress had no thought of affording such an unthinking, wooden meaning to §170 and §501(c)(3) as to provide tax benefits to "educational" organizations that do not serve a public, charitable purpose.

20. In 1894, when the first charitable exemption provision was enacted, racially segregated educational institutions would not have been regarded as against public policy. Yet contemporary standards must be considered in determining whether given activities provide a public benefit and are entitled to the charitable tax exemption. In Walz v. Tax Commn., 397 U.S. 664, 672-673 (1970), we observed: "Qualification for tax exemption is not perpetual or immutable; some tax-exempt groups lose that status when their activities take them outside the classification and new entities can come into being and qualify for the exemption."

Charitable trust law also makes clear that the definition of "charity" depends upon contemporary standards. See, e.g., Restatement (Second) of Trusts, §374, comment a (1959); Bogert §369, at 65-67; 4 Scott §368, at 2855-2856.

and Executive Orders attest a firm national policy to prohibit racial segregation and discrimination in public education. . . .

Few social or political issues in our history have been more vigorously debated and more extensively ventilated than the issue of racial discrimination, particularly in education. Given the stress and anguish of the history of efforts to escape from the shackles of the "separate but equal" doctrine of Plessy v. Ferguson, supra, it cannot be said that educational institutions that, for whatever reasons, practice racial discrimination, are institutions exercising "beneficial and stabilizing influences in community life." Walz v. Tax Commn., 397 U.S. 664, 673 (1970), or should be encouraged by having all taxpayers share in their support by way of special tax status.

There can thus be no question that the interpretation of §170 and §501(c)(3) announced by the IRS in 1970 was correct. That it may be seen as belated does not undermine its soundness. It would be wholly incompatible with the concepts underlying tax exemption to grant the benefit of tax-exempt status to racially discriminatory educational entities, which "exer[t] a pervasive influence on the entire educational process." Norwood v. Harrison, supra, 413 U.S., at 469. Whatever may be the rationale for such private schools' policies, and however sincere the rationale may be, racial discrimination in education is contrary to public policy. Racially discriminatory educational institutions cannot be viewed as conferring a public benefit within the "charitable" concept discussed earlier, or within the Congressional intent underlying §170 and §501(c)(3).

C

Petitioners contend that, regardless of whether the IRS properly concluded that racially discriminatory private schools violate public policy, only Congress can alter the scope of §170 and §501(c)(3). Petitioners accordingly argue that the IRS overstepped its lawful bounds in issuing its 1970 and 1971 rulings.

Yet ever since the inception of the tax code, Congress has seen fit to vest in those administering the tax laws very broad authority to interpret those laws. In an area as complex as the tax system, the agency Congress vests with administrative responsibility must be able to exercise its authority to meet changing conditions and new problems. Indeed as early as 1918, Congress expressly authorized the Commissioner "to make all needful rules and regulations for the enforcement" of the tax laws. Revenue Act of 1918, ch. 18, §1309, 40 Stat. 1057, 1143 (1919). The same provision, so essential to efficient and fair administration of the tax laws, has appeared in tax codes ever since, see 26 U.S.C. §7805(a) (1976); and this Court has long recognized the primary authority of the IRS and its predecessors in construing the Internal Revenue Code, see, e.g., Commissioner v. Portland Cement Co., 450 U.S. 156, 169 (1981); United States v. Correll, 389 U.S. 299, 306-307 (1967); Boske v. Comingore, 177 U.S. 459, 469-470 (1900).

Congress, the source of IRS authority, can modify IRS rulings it considers improper; and courts exercise review over IRS actions. In the first instance, however, the responsibility for construing the Code falls to the IRS. Since Congress cannot be expected to anticipate every conceivable problem that can arise or to carry out day-to-day oversight, it relies on the administrators and on the courts to implement the legislative will. Administrators, like judges, are under oath to do so.

In §170 and §501(c)(3), Congress has identified categories of traditionally exempt institutions and has specified certain additional requirements for tax exemption. Yet the need for continuing interpretation of those statutes is unavoidable. For more than 60 years, the IRS and its predecessors have constantly been called upon to interpret these and comparable provisions, and in doing so have referred consistently to principles of charitable trust law. In Treas. Reg. 45, art. 517(1) (1921), for example, the IRS denied charitable exemptions on the basis of proscribed political activity before the Congress itself added such conduct as a disqualifying element. In other instances, the IRS has denied charitable exemptions to otherwise qualified entities because they served too limited a class of people and thus did not provide a truly "public" benefit under the common law test. See, e.g., Crellin v. Commissioner, 46 B.T.A. 1152, 1155-1156 (1942); James Sprunt Benevolent Trust v. Commissioner, 20 B.T.A. 19, 24-25 (1930). See also Treas. Reg. §1.501(c)(3)-1(d)(1)(ii) (1959). Some years before the issuance of the rulings challenged in these cases, the IRS also ruled that contributions to community recreational facilities would not be deductible and that the facilities themselves would not be entitled to tax-exempt status, unless those facilities were open to all on a racially nondiscriminatory basis. See Rev. Rul. 67-325, 1967-2 Cum. Bull. 113. These rulings reflect the Commissioner's continuing duty to interpret and apply the Internal Revenue Code. See also Textile Mills Securities Corp. v. Commissioner, 314 U.S. 326, 337-338 (1941).

Guided, of course, by the Code, the IRS has the responsibility, in the first instance, to determine whether a particular entity is "charitable" for purposes of §170 and §501(c)(3). This in turn may necessitate later determinations of whether given activities so violate public policy that the entities involved cannot be deemed to provide a public benefit worthy of "charitable" status. We emphasize, however, that these sensitive determinations should be made only where there is no doubt that the organization's activities violate fundamental public policy.

On the record before us, there can be no doubt as to the national policy. In 1970, when the IRS first issued the ruling challenged here, the position of all three branches of the Federal Government was unmistakably clear. The correctness of the Commissioner's conclusion that a racially discriminatory private school "is not 'charitable' within the common law concepts reflected in . . . the Code," Rev. Rul. 71-447, 1972-2 Cum. Bull, at 231, is wholly consistent with what Congress, the Executive and the courts had repeatedly declared before 1970. . . . We therefore hold that the IRS did not exceed its authority when it announced its interpretation of §170 and §501(c)(3) in 1970 and 1971.[24]

D

The actions of Congress since 1970 leave no doubt that the IRS reached the correct conclusion in exercising its authority. It is, of course, not unknown for independent agencies or the Executive Branch to misconstrue the intent of a statute; Congress can and often does correct such misconceptions, if the courts have not done so. Yet for a dozen years Congress has been made aware — acutely aware — of the IRS rulings of 1970 and 1971. As we noted earlier, few issues have been the subject of more vigorous and widespread debate and discussion in and out of Congress than those related to racial segregation in education. Sincere adherents advocating contrary views have ventilated the subject for well over three decades. Failure of Congress to modify the IRS rulings of 1970 and 1971, of which Congress was, by its own studies and by public discourse, constantly reminded; and Congress' awareness of the denial of tax-exempt status for racially discriminatory schools when enacting other and related legislation make out an unusually strong case of legislative acquiescence in and ratification by implication of the 1970 and 1971 rulings.

Ordinarily, and quite appropriately, courts are slow to attribute significance to the failure of Congress to act on particular legislation. See, e.g., Aaron v. SEC, 446 U.S. 680, 694 n.11 (1980). We have observed that "unsuccessful attempts at legislation are not the best of guides to legislative intent," Red Lion Broadcasting Co. v. FCC, 395 U.S. 367, 381-382 n.11 (1969). Here, however, we do not have an ordinary claim of legislative acquiescence. Only one month after the IRS announced its position in 1970, Congress held its first hearings on this precise issue. Equal Educational Opportunity: Hearings Before the Senate Select Comm. on Equal Educational Opportunity, 91st Cong., 2d Sess., 1991 (1970). Exhaustive hearings have been held on the issue at various times since then. These include hearings in February 1982, after we granted review in this case. Administration's Change in Federal Policy Regarding the Tax Status of Racially Discriminatory Private Schools: Hearing Before the House Comm. on Ways and Means, 97th Cong., 2d Sess. (1982).

Non-action by Congress is not often a useful guide, but the non-action here is significant. During the past 12 years there have been no fewer than 13 bills introduced to overturn the IRS interpretation of §501(c)(3). Not one of these bills has emerged from any committee, although Congress has enacted

24. Many of the amici curiae, including Amicus William T. Coleman, Jr. (appointed by the Court), argue that denial of tax-exempt status to racially discriminatory schools is independently required by the equal protection component of the Fifth Amendment. In light of our resolution of this case we do not reach that issue. See, e.g., United States v. Clark, 445 U.S. 23, 27 (1980); NLRB v. Catholic Bishop of Chicago, 440 U.S. 490, 504 (1979).

numerous other amendments to §501 during this same period, including an amendment to §501(c)(3) itself. Tax Reform Act of 1976, Pub. L. 94-455, §1313(a), 90 Stat. 1520, 1730 (1976). It is hardly conceivable that Congress—and in this setting, any Member of Congress—was not abundantly aware of what was going on. In view of its prolonged and acute awareness of so important an issue, Congress' failure to act on the bills proposed on this subject provides added support for concluding that Congress acquiesced in the IRS rulings of 1970 and 1971. See., e.g., Merrill, Lynch, Pierce, Fenner & Smith, Inc. v. Curran, 456 U.S. 353, 379-382 (1982); Haig v. Agee, 453 U.S. 280, 300-301 (1981); Herman & MacLean v. Huddleston, 459 U.S. 375, b384-386 (1983); United States v. Rutherford, 442 U.S. 544, 554 n.10 (1979).

The evidence of Congressional approval of the policy embodied in Revenue Ruling 71-447 goes well beyond the failure of Congress to act on legislative proposals. Congress affirmatively manifested its acquiescence in the IRS policy when it enacted the present §501(i) of the Code, Act of October 20, 1976, Pub. L. 94-568, 90 Stat. 2697 (1976). That provision denies tax-exempt status to social clubs whose charters or policy statements provide for "discrimination against any person on the basis of race, color, or religion."[26] Both the House and Senate committee reports on that bill articulated the national policy against granting tax exemptions to racially discriminatory private clubs S. Rep. No. 1318, 94th Cong., 2d Sess., 8 (1976); H.R. Rep. No. 1353, 94th Cong., 2d Sess., 8 (1976).

Even more significant is the fact that both reports focus on this Court's affirmance of Green v. Connally, supra, as having established that "discrimination on account of race is inconsistent with an *educational institution's* tax exempt status." S. Rep. No. 1318, supra, at 7-8 and n.5; H.R. Rep. No. 1353, supra, at 8 and n.5 (emphasis added). These references in Congressional committee reports on an enactment denying tax exemptions to racially discriminatory private social clubs cannot be read other than as indicating approval of the standards applied to racially discriminatory private schools by the IRS subsequent to 1970, and specifically of Revenue Ruling 71-447.

III

Petitioners contend that, even if the Commissioner's policy is valid as to nonreligious private schools, that policy cannot constitutionally be applied to schools that engage in racial discrimination on the basis of sincerely held religious beliefs. As to such schools, it is argued that the IRS construction of §170 and §501(c)(3) violates their free exercise rights under the Religion

---

26. Prior to the introduction of this legislation, a three-judge district court had held that segregated social clubs were entitled to tax exemptions. McGlotten v. Connally, 338 F. Supp. 448 (D.D.C. 1972). Section 501(i) was enacted primarily in response to that decision. See S. Rep. No. 1318, 94th Cong., 2d Sess., 7-8 (1976); H.R. Rep No. 1353, 94th Cong., 2d Sess., 8 (1976).

Clauses of the First Amendment. This contention presents claims not heretofore considered by this Court in precisely this context. . . .

The governmental interest at stake here is compelling. As discussed in Part II(B), supra, the Government has a fundamental, overriding interest in eradicating racial discrimination in education[29] — discrimination that prevailed, with official approval, for the first 165 years of this Nation's history. That governmental interest substantially outweighs whatever burden denial of tax benefits places on petitioners' exercise of their religious beliefs. The interests asserted by petitioners cannot be accommodated with that compelling governmental interest, see United States v. Lee, supra, 455 U.S., at 259-260; and no "less restrictive means," see Thomas v. Review Board, supra, 450 U.S., at 718, are available to achieve the governmental interest.

IV

The remaining issue is whether the IRS properly applied its policy to these petitioners.

Petitioner Bob Jones University . . . contends that it is not racially discriminatory. It emphasizes that it now allows all races to enroll, subject only to its restrictions on the conduct of all students, including its prohibitions of association between men and women of different races, and of interracial marriage. Although a ban on intermarriage or interracial dating applies to all races, decisions of this Court firmly establish that discrimination on the basis of racial affiliation and association is a form of racial discrimination, see, e.g., Loving v. Virginia, 388 U.S. 1 (1967); McLaughlin v. Florida, 379 U.S. 184 (1964); Tillman v. Wheaton-Haven Recreation Assn., 410 U.S. 431 (1973). We therefore find that the IRS properly applied Revenue Ruling 71-447 to Bob Jones University.[32]

The judgments of the Court of Appeals are, accordingly,

Affirmed.

Justice POWELL, concurring in part and concurring in the judgment.

I join the Court's judgment, along with part III of its opinion holding that the denial of tax exemptions to petitioners does not violate the First Amendment. I write separately because I am troubled by the broader implications of the Court's opinion with respect to the authority of the Internal

---

29. We deal here only with religious *schools*—not with churches or other purely religious institutions; here, the governmental interest is in denying public support to racial discrimination in education. As noted earlier, racially discriminatory schools "exer[t] a pervasive influence on the entire educational process," outweighing any public benefit that they might otherwise provide, Norwood v. Harrison, 413 U.S. 455, 469 (1973). See generally Simon 495-496.

32. Bob Jones University also argues that the IRS policy should not apply to it because it is entitled to exemption under §501(c)(3) as a "religious" organization, rather than as an "educational" institution. The record in this case leaves no doubt, however, that Bob Jones University is both an educational institution and a religious institution. As discussed previously, the IRS policy properly extends to all private schools, including religious schools. See n.29, supra. The IRS policy thus was properly applied to Bob Jones University.

Revenue Service (IRS) and its construction of §§170(c) and 501(c)(3) of the Internal Revenue Code. . . .

With all respect, I am unconvinced that the critical question in determining tax-exempt status is whether an individual organization provides a clear "public benefit" as defined by the Court. Over 106,000 organizations filed §501(c)(3) returns in 1981. Internal Revenue Service, 1982 Exempt Organization/Business Master File. I find it impossible to believe that all or even most of those organizations could prove that they "demonstrably serve and [are] in harmony with the public interest" or that they are "beneficial and stabilizing influences in community life." Nor am I prepared to say that petitioners, because of their racially discriminatory policies, necessarily contribute nothing of benefit to the community. It is clear from the substantially secular character of the curricula and degrees offered that petitioners provide educational benefits.

Even more troubling to me is the element of conformity that appears to inform the Court's analysis. The Court asserts that an exempt organization must "demonstrably serve and be in harmony with the public interest," must have a purpose that comports with "the common community conscience," and must not act in a manner "affirmatively at odds with [the] declared position of the whole government." Taken together, these passages suggest that the primary function of a tax-exempt organization is to act on behalf of the Government in carrying out governmentally approved policies. In my opinion, such a view of §501(c)(3) ignores the important role played by tax exemptions in encouraging diverse, indeed often sharply conflicting, activities and viewpoints. As Justice Brennan has observed, private, nonprofit groups receive tax exemptions because "each group contributes to the diversity of association, viewpoint, and enterprise essential to a vigorous, pluralistic society." *Walz*, supra, at 689 (Brennan, J., concurring). Far from representing an effort to reinforce any perceived "common community conscience," the provision of tax exemptions to nonprofit groups is one indispensable means of limiting the influence of governmental orthodoxy on important areas of community life.[3] Given the importance of our tradition of pluralism, "[t]he interest in preserving an area of untrammeled

---

3. Certainly §501(c)(3) has not been applied in the manner suggested by the Court's analysis. The 1,100-page list of exempt organizations includes — among countless examples — such organizations as American Friends Service Committee, Inc., Committee on the Present Danger, Jehovahs Witnesses in the United States, Moral Majority Foundation, Inc., Friends of the Earth Foundation, Inc., Mountain States Legal Foundation, National Right to Life Educational Foundation, Planned Parenthood Federation of America, Scientists and Engineers for Secure Energy, Inc., and Union of Concerned Scientists Fund, Inc. See Internal Revenue Service, Cumulative List of Organizations Described in Section 170(c) of the Internal Revenue Code of 1954, at 31, 221, 376, 518, 670, 677, 694, 795, 880, 1001, 1073 (Revd. Oct. 1981). It would be difficult indeed to argue that each of these organizations reflects the views of the "common community conscience" or "demonstrably . . . [is] in harmony with the public interest." In identifying these organizations, largely taken at random from the tens of thousands on the list, I of course do not imply disapproval of their being exempt from taxation. Rather, they illustrate the commendable tolerance by our Government of even the most strongly held divergent views, including views that at least from time to time *are* "at odds" with the position of our Government. We have consistently recognized that such disparate groups are entitled to share the privilege of tax exemption.

choice for private philanthropy is very great." Jackson v. Statler Foundation, 496 F.2d 623, 639 (CA2 1974) (Friendly, J., dissenting from denial of reconsideration en banc).

I do not suggest that these considerations always are or should be dispositive. Congress, of course, may find that some organizations do not warrant tax-exempt status. In this case I agree with the Court that Congress has determined that the policy against racial discrimination in education should override the countervailing interest in permitting unorthodox private behavior.

I would emphasize, however, that the balancing of these substantial interests is for *Congress* to perform. I am unwilling to join any suggestion that the Internal Revenue Service is invested with authority to decide which public policies are sufficiently "fundamental" to require denial of tax exemptions. Its business is to administer laws designed to produce revenue for the Government, not to promote "public policy." As former IRS Commissioner Kurtz has noted, questions concerning religion and civil rights "are far afield from the more typical tasks of tax administrators — determining taxable income." Kurtz, Difficult Definitional Problems in Tax Administration: Religion and Race, 23 Catholic Lawyer 301 (1978). . . .

The Court's decision upholds IRS Revenue Ruling 71-447, and thus resolves the question whether tax-exempt status is available to private schools that openly maintain racially discriminatory admissions policies. There no longer is any justification for *Congress* to hesitate — as it apparently has — in articulating and codifying its desired policy as to tax exemptions for discriminatory organizations. Many questions remain, such as whether organizations that violate other policies should receive tax-exempt status under §501(c)(3). These should be legislative policy choices. It is not appropriate to leave the IRS "on the cutting edge of developing national policy." Kurtz, supra, at 308. The contours of public policy should be determined by Congress, not by judges or the IRS.

Justice REHNQUIST, dissenting.

The Court points out that there is a strong national policy in this country against racial discrimination. To the extent that the Court states that Congress in furtherance of this policy could deny tax-exempt status to educational institutions that promote racial discrimination, I readily agree. But, unlike the Court, I am convinced that Congress simply has failed to take this action and, as this Court has said over and over again, regardless of our view on the propriety of Congress' failure to legislate we are not constitutionally empowered to act for them. . . .

Questions

1. Justice Rehnquist's opinion in *TWR* starts from the premise that "tax exemptions and tax deductibility are a form of subsidy that is administered

through the tax system." Page 602 above. How would he reconcile that premise with his opinion that exemptions and deductibility should be allowed to Bob Jones University, a religiously established school that practices racial discrimination? Why don't the other opinions in *Bob Jones*, disallowing exemption and deductibility, reason from this premise? Or is Chief Justice Burger's observation that "the very fact of the exemption or deduction for the donor means that other taxpayers can be said to be indirect and vicarious 'donors,'" p. 611, pretty much another way of saying the same thing?

2. In any event, the common rationale for the deduction raises serious questions. Why should the government support all charities on a single formula instead of differentiating according to some sense of priorities among their objectives, as it would surely do in the case of direct expenditures? And what business has the federal government in supporting religious organizations in any event? Finally, even if an undiscriminating matching grant program would make sense in general, why should the rate of matching be graduated according to income so that a poor taxpayer's gift is unmatched, a 15 percent taxpayer's gift is matched at 18 percent, and a 33 percent taxpayer's gift at 49 percent? (The ratio in each case is the ratio of tax saving to after-tax cost of a contribution. The charity gets both.)

Is there any persuasive answer to these questions? What about an argument that the consumption component of taxable income under a graduated, personal income tax may sensibly be defined to mean *preclusive private consumption* of goods and services by the taxpayers themselves and their families? Preclusive consumption is consumption of a sort that precludes consumption of the same goods and services by other persons. Taxpayers may well derive satisfaction from making charitable contributions, but the satisfaction is an incident of giving up some part of their personal consumption or accumulation, and thus is no more fit a subject for taxation than the satisfaction one might derive by performing good deeds in kind. Indeed the effect of the deduction, in the case of cash contributions out of earnings, is precisely to allow taxpayers to assign the fruits of their labor to charity without tax and without the inefficiency of interrupting the performance of what they do best.

Consider, for example, a doctor and a tax lawyer. Both wish to donate a tithe to the poor. The doctor accordingly works half a day a week in a free clinic. The lawyer would do likewise, but the services at which she is most expert are not what the poor need. Accordingly, she works full-time for paying clients and donates one-tenth of her earnings to the poor.

Should the doctor be taxed on what he could have earned by providing his services to paying patients instead of the poor? If he is not taxed, should that result be viewed as a tax expenditure? If not, can the charitable contribution deduction be sensibly viewed as prescribing the same result for the tax lawyer?

None of this is meant to say that Congress has to allow a deduction for charitable contributions and certainly not that qualified recipients have to be specified as broadly as they are. It is only that the deduction *can* be seen as a rational decision about the scope of the tax.

How does the Haig-Simons income definition bear on this rationale?[1]

3. *Bob Jones* affirms the power of the IRS to deny tax benefits to racially discriminatory schools. What if private citizens believe that the government is insufficiently vigorous in identifying racial discrimination and in denying deductions for contributions to schools that practice it? In Allen v. Wright, 468 U.S. 737 (1984), the Supreme Court held that parents of black school children lacked standing to conduct a suit on behalf of all black parents, nationwide, to compel stricter scrutiny by the IRS.

B.   UNRELATED BUSINESS INCOME

UNITED STATES v. AMERICAN BAR ENDOWMENT
477 U.S. 105 (1986)

Justice MARSHALL delivered the opinion of the Court. The first issue in this case is whether income that a tax-exempt charitable organization derives from offering group insurance to its members constitutes "unrelated business income" subject to tax under §§511 through 513 of the Internal Revenue Code (Code), 26 U.S.C. §§511-513. The second issue is whether the organization's members may claim a charitable deduction for the portion of their premium payments that exceeds the actual cost to the organization of providing insurance.

I

Respondent American Bar Endowment (ABE) is a corporation exempt from taxation under §501(c)(3) of the code, which, with certain exceptions not relevant here, exempts organizations "organized and operated exclusively for . . . charitable . . . or educational purposes." ABE's primary purposes are to advance legal research and to promote the administration of justice, and it furthers these goals primarily through the distribution of grants to other charitable and educational groups. All members of the American Bar Association (ABA) are automatically members of ABE. The ABA is exempt from taxation as a "business league" under §501(c)(6).

ABE raises money for its charitable work by providing group insurance policies, underwritten by major insurance companies, to its members. Approximately 20 percent of ABE's members participate in the group insurance program, which offers life, health, accident, and disability policies.

1. See Andrews, Personal Deductions in an Ideal Income Tax, 86 Harv. L. Rev. 309, 344-375 (1972).

ABE negotiates premium rates with insurers and chooses which insurers shall provide the policies. It also compiles a list of its own members and solicits them, collects the premiums paid by its members, transmits those premiums to the insurer, maintains files on each policyholder, answers members' questions concerning insurance policies, and screens claims for benefits.

There are two important benefits of purchasing insurance as a group rather than individually. The first is that ABE's size gives it bargaining power that individuals lack. The second is that group policy is experience-rated. This means that the cost of insurance to the group is based on that group's claims experience, rather than general actuarial tables. Because ABA members have favorable mortality and morbidity rates, experience-rating results in a substantially lower insurance cost. When ABE purchases a group policy for its members, it pays a negotiated premium to the insurance company. If, as is uniformly true, the insurance company's actual cost of providing insurance to the group is lower than the premium paid in a given year, the insurance company pays a refund of the excess, called a "dividend," to ABE. Critical to ABE's fund-raising efforts is the fact that ABE requires its members to agree, as a condition of participating in the group insurance program, that they will permit ABE to keep all of the dividends rather than distributing them pro-rata to the insured members.

It would be possible for ABE to negotiate lower premium rates for its members than the rates it has charged throughout the relevant period, and thus receive a lower dividend. However, ABE prices its policies competitively with other insurance policies offered to the public and to ABE members. 761 F.2d 1573, 1575 (CAFC 1985). In this way ABE is able to generate large dividends to be used for its charitable purposes. In recent years the total amount of dividends has exceeded 40 percent of the members' premium payments. Ibid. ABE advises its insured members that each member's share of the dividends, less ABE's administrative costs, constitutes a tax-deductible contribution from the member to ABE. Thus the after-tax cost of ABE's insurance to its members is less than the cost of a commercial policy with identical coverage and premium rates.

In 1980 the Internal Revenue Service (IRS) advised ABE that it considered ABE's insurance plan an "unrelated trade or business" and that the profits thereon were subject to tax under §§511-513. Subsequently IRS audited ABE's tax returns for 1979 and 1980 and assessed a tax deficiency on ABE's net revenues from the insurance program. ABE paid those taxes, as well as taxes on the 1981 revenues. After exhausting administrative remedies, it brought an action for a refund in the Claims Court, arguing that its revenues from the insurance program were not subject to tax. At approximately the same time, the individual respondents, who were participants in the ABE insurance program but who had not originally deducted any part of the insurance premiums as charitable contributions, brought suit for refunds in the Claims Court as well. The individual respondents argued that they were entitled to charitable deductions for a portion of those premium payments. . . .

II

We recently discussed the history and structure of the unrelated business income provisions of the Code in United States v. American College of Physicians, 475 U.S. 834 (1986). The Code imposes a tax, at ordinary corporate rates, on the income that a tax-exempt organization obtains from an "unrelated trade or business . . . regularly carried on by it." §§512(a)(1), 511(a)(1). An "unrelated trade or business" is "any trade or business the conduct of which is not substantially related . . . to the exercise or performance by such organization of its charitable, educational, or other purpose," §513(a). The Code thus sets up a three-part test. ABE's insurance program is taxable if it (1) constitutes a trade or business; (2) is regularly carried on; and (3) is not substantially related to ABE's tax-exempt purposes. Treas. Reg. §1.513-1(a), 26 CFR §1.513-1(a) (1985); American College of Physicians, supra, at 838-839. ABE concedes that the latter two portions of this test are satisfied. 761 F.2d, at 1576. Its defense is based solely on the proposition that its insurance program does not constitute a trade or business.

A

In the Tax Reform Act of 1969, Pub. L. 91-172, 83 Stat. 487, Congress defined a "trade or business" as "any activity which is carried on for the production of income from the sale of goods or the performance of services." §513(c). The Secretary of the Treasury has provided further clarification of that definition in Treas. Reg. §1.513(b) (1985), which provides: "in general, any activity of [an exempt] organization which is carried on for the production of income and which otherwise possesses the characteristics required to constitute 'trade or business' within the meaning of section 162" is a trade or business for purposes of 26 U.S.C. §§511-513. ABE's insurance program falls within the literal language of these definitions. ABE's activity is both "the sale of goods" and "the performance of services," and possesses the general characteristics of a trade or business. Certainly the assembling of a group of better-than-average insurance risks, negotiating on their behalf with insurance companies, and administering a group policy are activities that can be — and are — provided by private commercial entities in order to make a profit. ABE itself earns considerable income from its program. Nevertheless, the Claims Court and Court of Appeals concluded that ABE does not carry out its insurance program in order to make a profit. The Claims Court relied on the former Court of Claims holding, in Disabled American Veterans v. United States, 650 F.2d 1178, 1187 (1981), that an activity is a trade or business only if "operated in a competitive, commercial manner." See 4 Cl. Ct., at 409. Because ABE does not operate its insurance program in a competitive, commercial manner, the Claims Court decided, that program is not a trade or business. The Court of Appeals adopted this reasoning. 761 F.2d, at 1577.

The Claims Court rested its conclusion on four factors. First, it found that "the program was devised as a means for fundraising and has been so presented and perceived from its inception." 4 Cl. Ct., at 409. Second, the court found that the program's phenomenal success in generating dividends for ABE was evidence of noncommercial behavior. The court noted that ABE's insurance program has provided $81.9 million in dividends in its 28 years of operation, and concluded that such large profits could not be the result of commercial success, but must proceed from the generosity of ABE's members. Third, and most important, in the court's view, was the fact that ABE's members collectively had the power to change ABE's conduct of the insurance program so as to drastically reduce premiums. That the members had not done so was strong evidence that they sought to further ABE's charitable purposes by paying higher insurance rates than necessary. Fourth, because ABE did not underwrite insurance or act as a broker, it was not competing with other commercial entities.

It appears, then, that the Claims Court viewed ABE as engaging in two separate activities — the provision of insurance and the acceptance of contributions in the form of dividends. If so, the unspoken premise of the Claims Court's decision is that ABE's income is not a result of the first activity, but of the second. There is some sense to this reasoning; should ABE sell a product to its members for more than that product's fair market value, it could argue to the IRS that the members intended to pay excessive prices as a form of contribution, and that some formula should be adopted to separate the income received into taxable profits and nontaxable contributions. Even if we viewed it as appropriate for the federal courts to engage in such a quasi-legislative activity, however, there is no factual basis for the Claims Court's attempt to do so in this case.

B

We cannot agree with the Claims Court that the enormous dividends generated by ABE's insurance program demonstrate that those dividends cannot constitute "profits." Were ABE's insurance markedly more expensive than other insurance products available to its members, but ABE nevertheless kept the patronage of those members, we might plausibly conclude that generosity was the reason for the program's success. The Claims Court did not find, however, that this was the case. ABE prices its insurance to remain competitive with the rest of the market. 4 Cl. Ct., at 406. Thus ABE's members never squarely face the decision whether to support ABE or to reduce their own insurance costs.

The Claims Court concluded that "such profit margins [as ABE's] cannot be maintained year after year in a competitive market." Id., at 410. The court apparently reasoned that ABE's staggering success would inevitably induce other firms to offer similar programs to ABA members unless that success is the result of charitable intentions rather than price-sensitive purchasing decisions. It is possible, of course, that ABE's members genuinely intend to support ABE by paying higher premiums than necessary, and would pay those high premiums even if a competing group insurance plan offered very low premiums. But that is by no means the only possible explanation for the market's failure to provide competition for ABE.[2] Lacking a factual basis for concluding that generosity is at the core of ABE's success, we can easily view this case as a standard example of monopoly pricing. ABE has a unique asset—its access to the ABA's members and their highly favorable mortality and morbidity rates—and it has chosen to appropriate for itself all of the profit possible from that asset, rather than sharing any with its members.

The argument that ABE's members could change the insurance program and receive the bulk of the dividends themselves if they so desired is unconvincing.

Were ABE to give each member a choice between retaining his pro-rata share of dividends or assigning them to ABE, the organization would have a strong argument that those dividends constituted a voluntary do nation. That, however, is not the case here. ABE requires its members to assign it all dividends as a condition for participating in the insurance program. It is simply incorrect to characterize the assignment of dividends by each member as "voluntary" simply because the members theoretically could band together and attempt to change the policy.

Again, the Claims Court put too much weight on an unsupported assumption. It found that the program was "operated with the approval and consent of the ABA membership," ibid., observing that the program had met with "surprisingly little dissent," id., at 411, even though there were "ample" opportunities for members to change policies with which they disagree, ibid. We believe that those facts cannot carry the weight that the Claims Court put on them. Perhaps each member that purchases insurance would, given the option, pay excessive premiums in order to support ABE's charitable purposes; however, that is not the only possible explanation for

2. One obvious consideration is that ABE's tax-exempt status would make it difficult for private firms to compete, see infra, at 834, 838. In addition, as the Claims Court recognized, 4 Cl. Ct., at 414, the provision of group insurance coverage to a particular group may have the characteristics of a natural monopoly. The potential savings in insurance costs might decrease rapidly as the group splits into competing components. Finally, if the cost of assembling information about a particular group and maintaining an accurate list of members is high, the provision of group insurance might be economically feasible only if that cost can be shared among a variety of services performed by the group policyholder. In that case pre-existing groups like the ABA or a trade association would obviously have a considerable advantage over new entrants. The record here is barren of facts concerning these hypotheses, and we express no opinion as to their accuracy. We present them, however, to demonstrate that it is incorrect to assume, as did the courts below, that ABE's profitability must result from the generosity of its members.

the members' failure to change the program. Any given member might feel that the potential savings in insurance costs are not sufficient to justify the effort required to mount a challenge to ABE's leadership. Many might not want to "make waves" and upset a program that generates tax-free income for ABE and charitable deductions for their fellow members. The members' theoretical ability to change the program, therefore, is at best inconclusive.

The Claims Court also erred in concluding that ABE's insurance program did not present the potential for unfair competition. The undisputed purpose of the unrelated business income tax was to prevent tax-exempt organizations from competing unfairly with businesses whose earnings were taxed. H.R. Rep. No. 2319, 81st Cong., 2d Sess., 36 (1950); see United States v. American College of Physicians, 475 U.S., at 838. This case presents an example of precisely the sort of unfair competition that Congress intended to prevent. If ABE's members may deduct part of their premium payments as a charitable contribution, the effective cost of ABE's insurance will be lower than the cost of competing policies that do not offer tax benefits. Similarly, if ABE may escape taxes on its earnings, it need not be as profitable as its commercial counterparts in order to receive the same return on its investment. Should a commercial company attempt to displace ABE as the group policyholder, therefore, it would be at a decided disadvantage.

The Claims Court failed to find any taxable entities that compete with ABE, and therefore found no danger of unfair competition. It is likely, however, that many of ABE's members belong to other organizations that offer group insurance policies. Employers, trade associations,[3] and financial services companies frequently offer group insurance policies. Presumably those entities are taxed on their profits, and their policyholders may not deduct any part of the premiums paid. Such entities may therefore find it difficult to compete for the business of any ABE members who are otherwise eligible to participate in these group insurance programs.

The only valid argument in ABE's favor, therefore, is that the insurance program is billed as a fund-raising effort. That fact, standing alone, cannot be determinative, or any exempt organization could engage in a tax-free business by "giving away" its product in return for a "contribution" equal to the market value of the product. ABE further contends that it must prevail because the Claims Court found that ABE's profits represent contributions rather than business income; ABE argues that we may not upset that finding unless it is clearly erroneous. Cf. Carter v. Commissioner, 645 F.2d 784, 786

---

3. The unrelated-business-income cases cited in n.1, supra, all concerned group insurance programs offered by trade associations to their members. In each case the Court of Appeals held that those programs constituted a taxable trade or business. The Claims Court distinguished those cases on the grounds that they involved organizations exempt as business leagues under §501(c)(6) rather than as charities under §501(c)(3). That distinction, however, is insubstantial. Business leagues engage in fund-raising for exempt purposes just as charities do. The taxpayers in those cases could have claimed that the excess dividends constituted tax-exempt membership fees, just as ABE claims that they constitute tax-exempt charitable contributions. Both claims fail for the same reasons.

(CA9 1981) (question of profit motive for purposes of §162 is one of fact). The undisputed facts, however, simply will not support the inference that the dividends ABE receives are charitable contributions from its members rather than profits from its insurance program. Moreover, the Claims Court failed to articulate a legal rule that would permit it to split ABE's activities into the gratuitous provision of a service and the acceptance of voluntary contributions, and we find no such rule in the Code or regulations. . . .

III

Section 170 of the Code provides that a taxpayer may deduct from taxable income any "charitable contribution," defined as "a contribution or gift to or for the use of" qualifying entities, §170(c). The individual respondents contend that the excess of their premium payments over the cost to ABE of providing insurance constitutes a contribution or gift to ABE.

Many of the considerations supporting our holding that ABE's earnings from the insurance program are taxable also bear on the question whether ABE's members may deduct part of their premium payments. The evidence demonstrates, and the Claims Court found, that ABE's insurance is no more costly to its members than other policies — group or individual — available to them. Thus, as we have recognized, ABE's members are never faced with the hard choice of supporting a worthwhile charitable endeavor or reducing their own insurance costs.

A payment of money generally cannot constitute a charitable contribution if the contributor expects a substantial benefit in return. S. Rep. No. 1622, 83rd Cong., 2d Sess., 196 (1954); Singer Co. v. United States, 196 Cl. Ct. 90, 449 F.2d 413 (1971). However, as the Claims Court recognized, a taxpayer may sometimes receive only a nominal benefit in return for his contribution. Where the size of the payment is clearly out of proportion to the benefit received, it would not serve the purposes of §170 to deny a deduction altogether. A taxpayer may therefore claim a deduction for the difference between a payment to a charitable organization and the market value of the benefit received in return, on the theory that the payment has the "dual character" of a purchase and a contribution. See., e.g., Rev. Rul. 67-246, 1967-2 Cum. Bull. 104 (price of ticket to charity ball deductible to extent it exceeds market value of admission); Rev. Rul. 68-432, 1968-2 Cum. Bull. 104, 105 (noting possibility that payment to charitable organization may have "dual character").

In Rev. Rul. 67-246, supra, the IRS set up a two-part test for determining when part of a "dual payment" is deductible. First, the payment is deductible only if and to the extent it exceeds the market value of the benefit received. Second, the excess payment must be "made with the intention of making a gift." 1967-2 Cum. Bull., at 105. The Tax Court has adopted this test, see Murphy v. Commissioner, 54 T.C. 249, 254 (1970), Arceneaux v.

Commissioner, 36 TCM 1461, 1464 (1977); but see Oppewal v. Commissioner, 468 F.2d 1000, 1002 (CA1 1972) (expressing "dissatisfaction with such subjective tests as the taxpayer's motives in making a purported charitable contribution" and relying solely on differential between amount of payment and value of benefit).

The Claims Court applied that test in this case, and held that respondents Broadfoot, Boynton, and Turner had not established that they could have purchased comparable insurance for less money. Therefore, the court held, they had failed to establish that the value of ABE's insurance to these respondents was less than the premiums paid. 4 Cl. Ct., at 415-417. Respondent Sherwood demonstrated that there did exist a group insurance program for which he was eligible and which offered lower premiums than ABE's insurance. However, Sherwood failed to establish that he was aware of that competing program during the years at issue. Sherwood therefore had failed to demonstrate that he met the second part of the above test — that he had intentionally paid more than the market value for ABE's insurance because he wished to make a gift. . . .

We hold that the Claims Court applied the proper standard. The sine quo non of a charitable contribution is a transfer of money or property without adequate consideration. The taxpayer, therefore, must at a minimum demonstrate that he purposely contributed money or property in excess of the value of any benefit he received in return. The most logical test of the value of the insurance respondents received is the cost of similar policies. . . .

Justice Powell and Justice O'Connor took no part in the consideration or decision of this case.

Justice Stevens, dissenting. . . . It is useful to recall the kind of situation that gave rise to the unrelated business tax. Perhaps the best known case involved the C.F. Mueller Company. The Mueller Company was a longstanding macaroni concern. It was acquired and operated for the benefit of the New York University School of Law, and its profits were donated to the University. The Internal Revenue Service claimed that the macaroni company's profits should be taxable, like any other competitive macaroni company, to avoid giving this competitor an unfair advantage. Although longstanding precedent seemed to be against the Commissioner, the Tax Court was sufficiently concerned about the implications that it agreed with the Commissioner. Ultimately, the Court of Appeals reversed, relying on precedent; by that time, however, Congress had acted and imposed a tax on unrelated business income. See C.F. Mueller Co. v. Commissioner, 190 F.2d 120 (3d Cir. 1951).

In considering the ABE insurance fundraising, then, it is appropriate to assume that, if the ABE were funded by operating a normal macaroni company and receiving an unfair competitive advantage from its tax exemption, it would be a "trade or business" within the Act and taxable. On the other hand, it is equally clear that, if the ABE simply provided insurance for

ABA members at very low cost, and sent the insurance dividends with an urgent request that the dividends be assigned to the Endowment, the arrangement would not be a "trade or business," and would not be taxable. The central issue in this case is thus whether the ABE's insurance program should be viewed as akin to the macaroni company, and thus a "trade or business," or as akin to the dividend assignment request, and thus not a "trade or business." . . .

I

. . . There is no evidence in the record, despite more than three weeks of trial and numerous witnesses, to support the notion that the Endowment's provision of insurance to its members has had any competitive impact whatsoever. The Court relies on a parade of hypotheticals to justify its conclusion that there is some effect on competition. The Court is, however, unable to point to a single piece of evidence in the record to justify its conclusion about the effect on competition. "Speculation about hypothetical cases illuminates the discussion in a classroom, but it is evidence and historical fact that provide the most illumination in a courtroom." Brown Forman Distillers Corp. v. New York State Liquor Authority, 476 U.S. 573, (1986) (Stevens, J., dissenting). The trial judge scoured the record for evidence pointing to a harmful effect on competition, and found none.[4] The absence of evidence in the record, rather than the Court's ruminations about possibilities and likelihoods, should control our analysis.

. . . Congress has twice made clear that insurance programs by other nonprofit organizations are not subject to the unrelated business tax. When Congress substantially revised the unrelated business tax in 1969, the accompanying legislative history emphasized that the group insurance policies provided by fraternal organizations were not intended to be subject to the unrelated business tax. Similarly, when a question arose concerning the taxability of income from insurance programs administered by veterans' organizations, Congress enacted legislation to ensure that the insurance income would not be taxed. Indeed, Congress found the taxation of the

---

4. In his oral opinion at the end of trial, the Claims Court emphasized the absence of a "Ronzoni" — the macaroni-selling competitor who had been harmed by New York University's tax-free entry into the business:

The unrelated business income tax was passed to avoid a certain kind of evil. . . . So you go back and look at what evil there is in the market. What was Congress trying to do . . . when the uniform business income tax was passed, and one comes to the frequently-asked question, "Who is Ronzoni[?]"

Now, nobody has really satisfactorily pointed to Ronzoni for me. I have been listening for three weeks of trial and nobody came up and said, ["]Here, this is Ronzoni, this is the competitor that will be adversely affected in the manner in which Congress feared there would be adverse effects when it slapped Mueller Macaroni Company on the wrist, or basically said you cannot do that, you cannot use your . . . tax exempt status to make profits.["]

veterans' insurance operations so contrary to its intent that it took the unusual step of making the 1972 Amendment fully retroactive to 1969.

The Government argues that these developments actually support its position because the need for congressional attention, and the emphasis on the "substantially related" prong for the fraternal societies, reveal that, without such attention, and without such a substantial relationship, the activity should be presumptively taxable. . . .

Ironically, moreover, the tax-exempt alternative suggested by the Government would have a far more obvious effect on competition than the ABE's current fundraising process. For the ABE would then be offering insurance rates dramatically lower than those available elsewhere. If speculation of the kind indulged in by the majority is appropriate, that speculation surely should include the realization that the tax-exempt alternative — in which the ABE would merely recover its actual costs of managing the program and return all of the premium refunds to the individual policyholders — would attract more than the 20 percent of the ABA membership that currently hold ABE policies; it would appeal to those who simply want an insurance bargain rather than those who also want to make a charitable contribution.

Not only does the ABE program completely fail to raise the concerns against which the unrelated business tax is directed, but it is also operated as a charitable fundraising endeavor.

The learned trial judge expressly found, after hearing a good deal of evidence, that the assignment of the dividends was the result of charitable intentions, rather than commercial transaction. First, he found that, since the program's inception, for three decades, the ABE has trumpeted the insurance program as a charitable fundraising activity, and that it has been so understood. . . . Second, the court specifically found that the reason for the Endowment's enormous profits was the charitable intent of the members.[13] . . .

Questions

1. Consider carefully the rationale of the unrelated business income tax as described in these opinions: Does it make sense from an economic standpoint? Would the application of an income tax to one competitor and not to another affect competition between them, or does it only affect the size of the prize when the competition is over?

13. See 4 Cl. Ct., at 411-412 ("The amount of money ABE is permitted to retain far exceeds the value of any service it may be providing through the operation of the insurance programs. It is quite obvious, then, that this money was not earned 'from the sale of goods or the performance of services,' 26 U.S.C. §513(c) (1976), but for some other reason. That reason was the intent of the members to support the Endowment's charitable activities").

2. Are the findings of fact relied on in Justice Stevens' dissenting opinion findings of fact in a narrow sense or general observations and opinions about economic motivation? If the latter, are the trial court's general observations and opinions any better grounded than those of Justice Marshall and the Supreme Court majority who joined in his opinion?

C.   WHAT IS A CONTRIBUTION?

DOWELL v. UNITED STATES
553 F.2d 1233 (10th Cir. 1977)

Before Seth, Barrett, Circuit Judges, and Kerr, District Judge.*

BARRETT Circuit Judge: . . . The issue presented is whether a "sponsorship gift" of $22,500 made by Dowell on February 25, 1971, to Oral Roberts Evangelistic Association, Inc., of Tulsa, Oklahoma, is a charitable contribution deductible under Section 170 of the Internal Revenue Code of 1954, 26 U.S.C.A., §170. The Code allows a deduction from gross income (if deductions are itemized) for any charitable "contribution or gift" to or for the use of a corporation "organized and operated exclusively for religious, charitable, scientific, literary, or educational purposes." 26 U.S.C.A., §170(c). The gift here involved was made to the parent corporation of Oral Roberts University, Inc., and University Village, Inc., also of Tulsa, Oklahoma. Each of the corporations qualifies under §170 of the Code. . . .

Dowell, then 76 years of age with developing cataracts and the prospects of surgery, and her aging, infirm husband, had determined in late 1970 to sell the family home in Tulsa and move into an adequate retirement center. Her husband required personal care and attention. Dowell had heard of University Village and in January, 1971, her daughter drove her to the facility where she visited with one Dan P. White about the accommodations, the financial aspects and the application for admission. White testified that he was sure that he told Dowell of the "sponsorship gift" which was in all such cases requested, although not required, as a condition or requisite for admission or continued residency. Dowell testified that she has no recollection of discussing a "sponsorship gift" with White or anyone else at University Village. She was at no time aware that any gift was required for residency.

On January 26, 1971, Dowell submitted her application for residency to University Village, after thoroughly inspecting the facilities and evaluating the accommodations, care and comfort. Mr. Dowell was to reside in the Health Center. On February 11, 1971, Dowell received a letter advising that she and her husband were accepted as residents of University Village. On February 25, 1971, Dowell submitted a check in amount of $22,500.00

* Of the District of Wyoming, sitting by designation.

payable to Oral Roberts Evangelistic Association, Inc. On March 26, 1971, Dowell moved into Cottage 16D at University Village, Inc. and on April 2 she signed a residency agreement with the Village whereby she agreed to pay a per month rental of $165 and additional amounts for other services. She paid $400 to $600 per month for her husband's health care.

Oral Roberts Association loaned University Village the amount by which construction costs of the Village exceeded the funds obtained from a Tulsa bank, secured by a first mortgage. University Village seeks to repay the funds borrowed for construction by means of the "sponsorship gifts" of the cottage and apartment units. The Village is designed to provide for the needs of those who reach retirement age. The Village prepares and widely distributes a brochure which acknowledges that the monthly rental and other charges are intended simply to cover current operating expenses, while the "sponsorship gifts" program is aimed at repayment of the monies borrowed for construction. The brochure explains: that the monthly charges do not include provisions for amortization of the loans and depreciation; that while a "sponsorship gift" is not a prerequisite for residency, it is requested; that a "sponsorship gift" does not entitle the donor to any "property rights"; that a Standard Agreement for Residency is executed with all residents covering their *lifetime care* "and is entirely separate and apart from any gift consideration." The record reflects that through March 1, 1975, the Village received "sponsorship gifts" totalling $4,844,604.00 and, of this amount, $4,322,712.00 or 89 percent was received from residents and $521,892.00 or 11 percent from relatives and friends of residents and from non-residents. As of March 1, 1975, the Village records revealed that: 40 of the residents made "sponsorship gifts" in whole or in part before their application for residency was accepted; that about 224 residents made the "sponsorship gift" in the full amount suggested for the cottage or apartment they rented; that some 16 residents gave more than that suggested; and that some 63 residents gave nothing or less than the suggested gift. The Village records reflect that relatives of 15 of the residents made the "sponsorship gifts" and that 11 of the residents made "deferred gifts" which, because they are not in cash or its equivalent in value, may be indeterminate and are not treated as "sponsorship gifts" by the Village. Of the 19 residents who moved out of the Village prior to March 1, 1975, 12 received either a full or partial refund of their "sponsorship gift."

Dowell testified that her primary concern, after viewing the Village facilities, was to obtain occupancy for herself and her husband because of the desirable accommodations, the general surroundings in the Village and the care and treatment her husband would receive. She further testified that she made the "sponsorship gift" because she wished to do so; she felt no duress to do so; she does not recall that anyone told her that such a gift was required for admission; she was not promised anything in return for the gift; while she knew of a possible tax deduction for the gift, this was not a consideration on her part and she would have made the gift without any deduction because of the building, the care she would receive and the life she could live in the Village and because of the good works of the Oral Roberts Association; she was never told that a "sponsorship gift" was required as a prerequisite to residency or continuing residency at the Village; not only did she not believe that a "sponsorship gift" was required for residency, but she was unaware of and therefore did not expect to receive lifetime care from the Village in exchange therefor; she made the gift out of charity and generosity knowing that her gift would help others; and she did not anticipate receiving any benefits from the gift nor did she expect that any part of the gift would ever be returned to her.

University Village, Inc. is uniquely designed, planned and managed for the elderly. It maintains five types of facilities to accommodate the residents, varying in design and utility from those for the bedridden to those for the physically mobile and independent. The rental and other charges do not repay the construction costs. The "sponsorship gifts" as suggested in the brochures of University Village, Inc., are essential to such construction cost repayments and are consistent with Oral Roberts' fund raising philosophy; that no applicant for residency is told or required to make a sponsorship gift as a condition for admission; monthly rentals are not reduced or modified for a gift made, and are the same (per unit charge) for all admittees.

The trial court found, inter alia: that although the brochures distributed by the Village to prospective applicants suggest a "sponsorship gift" that it is clear that none is required; that Dowell's testimony aforesaid established a prima facie case, which was not refuted or overcome by IRS; that of the total residents admitted to Village, (a) 13 or 2.5 percent made partial gifts, (b) 46 or 8.98 percent made no gifts, (c) that 16 or 3.1 percent gave more than the suggested gift amount, and 63 or 12.3 percent gave less, (d) that 24.38 percent either made no gifts, gifts of more than the suggested amount, or gifts of less, so that nearly one-fourth of the residents did not give the suggested sponsorship gift. Based upon the totality of its findings and consideration of the legal arguments of the litigants, the trial court concluded that the evidence compelled a conclusion that the "sponsorship gift" of Dowell was a charitable contribution under §170, supra; that the Dowell gift was not made in consideration for lifetime housing, care or any other benefits from the Village; that the Dowell "sponsorship gift" was made out of a detached and disinterested charitable and generous purpose; and that the true nature of Dowell's purpose, considering all of the facts and circumstances, was charitable in nature to the exclusion of any quid pro quo benefits. . . .

On appeal, IRS contends that the trial court erred in holding that the Dowell "sponsorship gift" is deductible as a charitable contribution under §170, supra, in that: (a) the evidence establishes that there was a "quid pro quo" or other significant relationship between the gift and Dowell's receipt of substantial material benefits and, (b) as a matter of law there is a significant relationship between gifts made under University Village's sponsorship gift program and Dowell's receipt of substantial residency benefits.

I

We emphasize, just as did the trial court, that our disposition of this appeal is predicated entirely on the facts in evidence and the circumstances reflected in the record of *this case*. With that in mind, we deem the critical issue to revolve around donative intent.

§170(a), supra, allows a deduction for "charitable contributions." It is firmly established that a gift is a voluntary transfer of property without consideration, and that if a payment or transfer of other thing of value is made in anticipation of a benefit other than the personal satisfaction of having performed the act of generosity, the transaction is not a gift. Commissioner of Internal Revenue v. Duberstein, 363 U.S. 278 (1960). Such a gift has also been said to be out of affection, respect, admiration, charity or like impulses. Commissioner of Internal Revenue v. LoBue, 351 U.S. 243 (1956). A transfer does not, then constitute a gift for deductible purposes if it is made "in expectation of the receipt of certain specific direct economic benefits within the power of the recipient to bestow directly or indirectly, which otherwise might not be forthcoming." Stubbs v. United States, 428 F.2d 885, 887 (9th Cir. 1970), cert. denied, 400 U.S. 1009, (1971). See also: Wardwell's Estate v. Commissioner of Internal Revenue, 301 F.2d 632 (8th Cir. 1962); Johnson v. Commissioner of Internal Revenue, 86 F.2d 710 (2nd Cir. 1936); Jackson v. Commissioner of Internal Revenue, 64 F.2d 359 (4th Cir. 1933).

Motivation and personal expectation do not destroy the reality and genuineness of a given transaction even in a tax case. Gallun v. Commissioner of Internal Revenue, 297 F.2d 455 (7th Cir. 1961). And contributions or gifts to charities "cannot be controverted into a payment for services by inaccurately describing it." Bogardus v. Commissioner of Internal Revenue, 302 U.S. 34, 44 (1937).

Thus, the basic, fundamental consideration in this case, freely recognized by the trial court, involves the determination of Dowell's *intention*. We must be alert to the rule that there is a clear distinction between the motive for entering into a contract and the consideration for the contract. Philpot v. Gruninger, 81 U.S. (14 Wall.) 570 (1871). A decision, then, as to intent or motive is one reserved for the finder of fact and it is not to be disturbed unless held to be "clearly erroneous." Fed. Rules Civ. Proc. rule 52(a), 28 U.S.C.A.; Quarles v. Fuqua Industries, Inc. 504 F.2d 1358 (10th Cir. 1974). The appellate court may not so conclude unless, from a review of the entire evidence, it is convinced that a mistake has been committed. United States v. United States Gypsum Co., 333 U.S. 364 (1948).

The Commissioner (IRS) has consistently introduced parol evidence to show the circumstances which would invalidate a claimed gift, i.e., return of benefit from the gift, direct or indirect, evidenced by an oral understanding or agreement between the donor and donee. Johnson v. Commissioner, supra; Jackson v. Commissioner, supra. Thus, a taxpayer's testimony relative to the circumstances and conditions surrounding a challenged gift transaction is admissible in a fact finding proceeding, to be given such weight as the circumstances from the entire record dictate. King v. United States, 545 F.2d 700 (10th Cir. 1976). We are cognizant that such testimony, subjective in nature and inclined to be self-serving in relation to the issue of intent, is suspect. It is for this very reason that the Court, in Internal Revenue v. Duberstein, supra, stated that in determining a donor's intention the fact finder must predicate his conclusion upon his experience "... with the mainsprings of human conduct as applied to the totality of the facts of each case ...". 363 U.S, at 289. We hold that the trial court did not err in finding that Dowell's purpose, considering all of the facts and circumstances, was charitable in nature qualifying as a charitable contribution under §170, supra.

II

IRS urges that, as a matter of law, there is a significant relationship between gifts made under University Village's sponsorship gift program and Dowell's receipt of substantial residency benefits.

We recognize that this argument "pinpoints" the obvious danger of placing substantial weight upon the subjective intent elicited by testimony of the donor, in light of the self-service urgence. It is precisely because of this motivation that the trial court looked to the totality of all facts and circumstances, together with all reasonable inferences to be drawn therefrom, in finding substantial evidence supporting its legal conclusion that Dowell's "sponsorship gift" qualifies as a charitable contribution.

We hold that there is no justification, from the whole of this record, for reversal of the trial court's findings, conclusions and judgment. There is no evidence of a "quid pro quo" as found in Stubbs v. United States, supra. There the taxpayers entered into an agreement to purchase certain property contingent on rezoning which would permit its use as a trailer court and shopping center. In order to assure access to the property to be developed, the taxpayers conveyed a strip of the property for dedication as a public road, without receipt of payment therefor. The anticipated economic gain to the taxpayers was found to be the dominant factor or intent generating the conveyance, thus disqualifying it as a charitable contribution under §170, supra. We have read those opinions which have held gifts disqualified as charitable contributions for federal income tax purposes. They are based on factual findings that the gift was motivated by an agreed, expected or anticipated (a) direct gain or benefit to the donor such as that found in Sedam v. United States, 518 F.2d 242 (7th Cir. 1975), and Wardwell's

Estate v. Commissioner, supra, (b) indirect economic benefits to the donor, and (c) incidental benefits to the donor. We have further considered those decisions disallowing the deduction because the gift was made under economic stress or duress or because of a legal or moral obligation to give. *In each instance, the donor-taxpayer was found to have expected or anticipated the exchange benefit.* Such is not evidenced in the case at bar.

IRS, in conclusion to its opening brief, states: "... it would be an understatement to say that she [Mrs. Dowell] would have been surprised if, after signing the completed $22,500 check prepared by the village ... , she had been refused entry to the village." [Appellant's Opening Brief, p. 44.] We suggest that the fact that Dowell had been accepted for admission as a resident of the Village facility some two weeks *prior* to the date that she signed the check substantially dispels the possibility of the surprise element. Furthermore, nothing in the record evidences that the Dowell check had been "prepared by the village." While findings and conclusions in cases such as this do involve elements or aspects of surmise and conjecture simply because they cannot be reduced to a quantum of absolute certainty, we nevertheless hold that the IRS is confronted with a trial record which demonstrates that the trial court's judgment is anchored to substantial evidence.

We affirm.

Notes and Questions

1. The problem of distinguishing contributions from payments for services may arise in a variety of contexts. One involves private schools. What problems would you foresee if the trustees of a private school determine not to raise tuition but rather to put on a high-pressure fund-raising effort among parents, pointing out to them how contributions will cost the parents less than an equal number of dollars of tuition increase?

2. Are religious services any different from educational services or others? See Hernandez v. Commissioner, 490 U.S. 680 (1989) (deduction denied for "fixed donation" to Church of Scientology for spiritual "auditing").

3. Another context involves benefits specially conferred on donors. Consider these arrangements.

(a) The cast and producer of a play agree to perform the play free of charge in a charity benefit performance. As a consequence, the $100 per ticket paid by each member of the audience goes to the charitable beneficiary. How much of the cost of a ticket is deductible?

(b) A symphony orchestra conducts a music school for performing musicians in connection with its summer festival in the mountains. Performances by the students — and performances for the students by visiting soloists and chamber groups — are open without charge to Friends of the Symphony. To become a friend all one must do is make a contribution, of any amount, to the symphony orchestra. If a taxpayer makes a contribution of $20 and then attends eight concerts, how much can he deduct?

(c) A state university gives members of its "President's Club" (donors who contribute $10,000 or more during the year) priority in the purchase of season tickets to university football or basketball home games. Home games are generally sold out and many season ticket holders are assigned poor seats. Consult §170(*l*).

D. APPRECIATED PROPERTY

HILLA REBAY
T.C. Mem. 1963-42

MEMORANDUM FINDINGS OF FACT AND OPINION

RAUM, Judge: The Commissioner determined deficiencies in petitioner's income tax for the years 1955-1959 in the respective amounts of $30,417, $28,048, $18,476.75, $22,234.82, and $20,376.42. The principal adjustment, and the only one presently in dispute, is the Commissioner's disallowance in whole or in part of the deductions for charitable contributions by reason of his downward revision of the fair market value of certain paintings contributed by petitioner during the taxable years to several charitable institutions.

The parties have filed two stipulations of fact.

Petitioner resides at Morningside Drive, Green Farms, Connecticut. She filed her individual Federal income tax returns for 1955-1958 with the district director, Upper Manhattan, New York, and for 1959 with the district director, Manhattan, New York.

Petitioner's adjusted gross income during the taxable years, derived primarily from dividends, was as follows:

1955	$143,230.00
1956	159,342.00
1957	148,754.32
1958	134,826.22
1959	140,697.73

During the years 1955-1959 petitioner gave the following non-objective paintings of her own creation to the following charitable organizations, and, in computing the charitable deduction for such gifts claimed the following fair market values for the paintings on her income tax returns:

	1955	*1956*	*1957*	*1958*	*1959*
Arizona State College					
"Con Moto"	$30,000	—	—	—	—
"Andante"	30,000	—	—	—	—
"Allegro"	—	$30,000	—	—	—
Milwaukee-Downer College					
"Cadenza"	—	5,000	—	—	—
"Capriccio"	—	—	$24,000	—	—
Emma Willard School, Troy, N.Y.					
"Rondo No. 1"	—	—	—	$25,000	—
"Scherzo"	—	—	—	1,000	—
"Sonnette"	—	—	—	—	$24,000
Claimed values per returns	$60,000	$35,000	$24,000	$26,000	$24,000

Petitioner was born in Strasbourg, Alsace, in 1890. She has been interested in painting for many years, and particularly in non-objective painting as far back as 1912. She has donated a number of paintings of her own creation to various museums in Europe, and to some in the United States. Her grandfather and her parents had for many years been friends of Solomon R. Guggenheim, and she interested him in non-objective painting in the early 1930's. Guggenheim was a patron of the arts and appears to have been responsible for the establishment of the Solomon R. Guggenheim Museum, New York.

She assisted in the formation of the Solomon R. Guggenheim collection of non-objective paintings and was the first Director of the Solomon R. Guggenheim Museum. She retired as Director in 1952, when she became "Director Emeritus." She has been a trustee of the Solomon R. Guggenheim Foundation since its inception in 1937. A number of her own non-objective paintings have been exhibited in the Solomon R. Guggenheim Museum.

In making the adjustments herein the Commissioner determined that the paintings donated in 1955-1957 did not have fair market value in excess of the following total amounts at the dates the paintings were donated:

	1955	*1956*	*1957*
Arizona State College	$2,000	$1,000	—
Milwaukee-Downer College	—	1,000	$3,000

As to the years 1958 and 1959 the Commissioner determined that the paintings donated in those years did not have any fair market value.

Prior to 1962 petitioner had never sold any non-objective paintings of her own creation. In the spring of 1962 she sold one such painting for $15,000 to a man named Crane, and has not sold any since then. Crane, an engineer, is associated with petitioner's counsel in certain business ventures. He had never previously purchased a non-objective painting. He is not an art collector, nor does he appear to have any training or specialized knowledge in relation to art. He did not consult any expert in buying petitioner's painting. The price of the most expensive painting that he had ever previously purchased did not exceed $50. The evidence surrounding his purchase of petitioner's painting is of such character that we would hardly be justified in according much weight to it in determining the fair market value of petitioner's paintings.

At the trial, the paintings in question were present in the courtroom and we received testimony from an expert in behalf of petitioner and three experts in behalf of the Government as to the fair market value of these paintings. The valuations as of the dates of the gifts testified to by petitioner's expert were substantially less than those claimed in the returns, although they were in turn considerably in excess of those for which the Commissioner contends. The yardstick used by petitioner's expert in making his valuations was the $15,000 sale to Crane, referred to above. The Commissioner's experts in general supported the level of valuation relied upon by him in his determinations for 1955-1957. It would serve no useful purpose to embark upon a discussion of the evidence. Nor are the conclusions reached herein intended to reflect any opinion as to the artistic, aesthetic or intrinsic merits of the paintings in issue. The question is solely one of fair market value at the time of the respective gifts. We have carefully considered the entire record and hereby find as a fact that the paintings in question donated in 1955-1957 did not have a fair market value on the dates of their respective gifts in excess of the amounts determined in respect thereof by the Commissioner, and that the three paintings donated in 1958 and 1959 had a fair market value on the dates of their respective gifts as follows:

	1958	1959
"Rondo No. 1"	$1,000	—
"Scherzo"	300	—
"Sonnette"	—	$1,000

Decisions will be entered under Rule 50.

Notes

1. *Fair market value deduction.* Aside from the valuation question litigated in this case, there is a simple policy question of why a deduction should ever be allowed for more than the basis of contributed property. The rule allowing value rather than basis originated as a matter of administrative interpretation of the statute and was modified in 1969 by enactment of §170(e)(1) and (2), and later by §170(e)(3), (4), (5), and (6). Articulate and criticize the rationale behind these limitations and behind the fair market value rule itself. If *Hilla Rebay* arose today, how much could be deducted? Compare §170(e)(1)(A) with (B)(i), and consult §1221(a)(3).

2. *Recapture.* The rule allowing deduction of the value of tangible personal property contributed to a charity for a use related to its exempt functions was amended in 2006. In most cases §170(e)(1)(B)(i)(II) will deny a deduction in excess of basis if the donee disposes of the property before the end of the taxable year of the donor in which the property was contributed. If the donee sells or disposes of the property after the close of the year of contribution but within three years after the date of contribution, then the donor must ordinarily include in income (for the taxable year in which the donee disposition occurs) the excess of the deduction allowed over the donor's basis in the contributed property. §170(e)(7).

3. *Verification and valuation.* For in-kind contributions of $250 or more, §170(f)(8) now requires written acknowledgment by the donee organization, including a good faith estimate of the value of any goods or services provided by the organization in return for the contribution. See Rev. Proc. 90-12, 1990-1 C.B. 471 (guidelines for insubstantial benefits in other cases); Rev. Proc. 2008-66, §3.25, 2008-45 I.R.B. 1107, 1113 (2009 inflation-indexed amounts). If a deduction of more than $500 is claimed, a description of the property must be included with the return, and a qualified appraisal is required if the claimed deduction exceeds $5,000. §170(f)(11); see IRS Form 8283, Noncash Charitable Contributions (Dec. 2006). Additional requirements are prescribed for commonly abused (over-valued) property contributions: donations of used cars, clothing, and household items. §170(f)(12), (16).

4. *Monetary gifts.* Written confirmation is now required even for contributions by cash or check. No deduction is allowed unless the donor retains either a bank record or written acknowledgment by the donee organization of the amount contributed. §170(f)(17). Why would Congress make money dropped in the church plate during weekly services nondeductible?

5. *Temporal division of ownership.* A special version of the appreciated property problem arises when a taxpayer contributes a limited interest in property to a charity. Before 1969 a taxpayer might contribute an income interest in property, take a deduction for the value of that interest, and then exclude the income itself on the ground it belongs to the charity. That

practice is now substantially eliminated by §170(f)(2)(B) and (C). Indeed the statute also restricts deductions for remainder interests unless they qualify under strict statutory definitions of a charitable remainder annuity trust or unitrust or a pooled income fund. §170(f)(2)(A). The actuarial valuation of simple income interests is not very precise since it does not reflect how different investments may in fact divide total return differently between income and capital appreciation (or depreciation). In the case of annuity trusts and unitrusts, division between income and capital does not depend on investment, and apportionment of value between term and remainder interests is therefore much more accurate than it is in reference to simple income interests.

6. *Fractional interests.* The 1969 restrictions on deductions of partial interests were concerned with the valuation problems associated with temporal divisions of property ownership. The gift of an undivided portion of a taxpayer's entire interest in property remained deductible. §170(f)(3)(B)(ii). More recently, abuses have arisen with respect to gifts of fractional interests in art works. In 2006 Congress added §170(o), which clamps down hard on contributions of fractional interests in tangible personal property. Take a look at that provision. Note that the deduction of a fractional interest is recaptured (with interest) if the taxpayer does not contribute the remainder of her interest in the property to the same donee within 10 years, or by the date of her death if earlier. Why might a wealthy collector want to contribute fractional interests in a valuable object? Will §170(o) eliminate the practice?

7. *Services.* No deduction is allowed for the value of contributed services to a charity, although a taxpayer may deduct unreimbursed expenses incurred in performing them. On the other hand, if compensation from performing services for someone else is contributed to a charity, a deduction will be allowed, but the compensation will be included in income. Thus a lawyer might spend one afternoon a week working for legal aid, in which case the value of the services would never enter into the computation of her taxable income; alternatively, she might perform services for paying clients all week and contribute the proceeds of one afternoon's work a week, in which case compensation for the afternoon in question would be included in her gross income, but the contribution would be deductible. What if an actor in a play agrees that the proceeds from a particular performance are to go to a particular charity and that he will therefore receive no salary for that performance? Has he contributed money or services? Why would it ever make any difference? See §§170(b)(1), 67(a), 213(a).

In 1935 when the deduction for charitable contributions was limited to 15 percent of net income Eleanor Roosevelt gave a series of short weekly radio talks on the "Women of Today" broadcast by CBS. Mrs. Roosevelt received no compensation for her efforts, but she undertook the project pursuant to a contract that obligated a commercial sponsor of the radio program to pay the American Friends Service Committee (a favorite charity)

$3,000 after each broadcast.[2] Did the First Lady underreport her income at a time when the President was attacking tax evaders and "economic royalists"?

Sometimes a question may be raised about whether a person has contributed services or property. What about a blood donor, for example, with a rare and valuable blood type? Can she deduct the value of what she contributes in a Red Cross or hospital blood drive?[3]

References

Andrews, Personal Deductions in an Ideal Income Tax, 86 Harv. L. Rev. 309, 344-375 (1972); Bittker, Charitable Contributions: Tax Deductions or Matching Grants?, 28 Tax L. Rev. 37 (1972); Bittker & Kaufman, Taxes and Civil Rights: "Constitutionalizing" the Internal Revenue Code, 82 Yale L.J. 51 (1972); Feldstein, The Income Tax and Charitable Contributions: Part I—Aggregate & Distributional Effect, 28 Natl. Tax J. 81 (1975), Part II—The Impact on Religious, Educational and Other Organizations, 28 Natl. Tax J. 209 (1975); Gallagher, The Case for the Charitable Tax Exemption, 41 Tax Notes 765 (1988); McDaniel, Federal Matching Grants for Charitable Contributions: A Substitute for the Income Tax Deduction, 27 Tax L. Rev. 377 (1972); Silk, Charitable Deductions and Procedures, 40 Tax Notes 741 (1988); Taggart, The Charitable Deduction, 26 Tax L. Rev. 63 (1970); Young, Donor Restricted Charitable Gifts, 55 Taxes 54 (1977).

B. Unrelated Business Income: Bennett, Unfair Competition and the UBIT, 41 Tax Notes 759 (1988).

D. Appreciated Property: Speiller, The Favored Tax Treatment of Purchasers of Art, 80 Colum. L. Rev. 214 (1980).

2. See Hearings Before the Joint Comm. on Tax Evasion and Avoidance, 75th Cong., 331-333, 336-338, 416-420, 429-440 (1937) (testimony of Congressman Hamilton Fish, correspondence, and testimony of Assistant Attorney General Robert H. Jackson).
3. See Rev. Rul. 162, 1953-2 C.B. 127.

Chapter 12 — *Personal, Living, or Family Expenses*

A. CHILDCARE

HENRY C. SMITH
40 B.T.A. 1038 (1939), aff'd per curiam, 113 F.2d 114 (2d Cir. 1940)

OPINION

OPPER: Respondent determined a deficiency of $23.62 in petitioner's 1937 income tax. This was due to the disallowance of a deduction claimed by petitioners, who are husband and wife, for sums spent by the wife in employing nursemaids to care for petitioner's young child, the wife, as well as the husband, being employed. The facts have all been stipulated and are hereby found accordingly.

Petitioners would have us apply the "but for" test. They propose that but for the nurses the wife could not leave her child; but for the freedom so secured she could not pursue her gainful labors; and but for them there would be no income and no tax. This thought evokes an array of interesting possibilities. The fee to the doctor, but for whose healing service the earner of the family income could not leave his sickbed;[1] the cost of the laborer's raiment, for how can the world proceed about its business unclothed; the very home which gives us shelter and rest and the food which provides energy, might all by an extension of the same proposition be construed as necessary to the operation of business and to the creation of income. Yet these are the very essence of those "personal" expenses the deductibility of which is expressly denied. [§262.]

---

1. Bourne v. Commissioner, 62 Fed.(2d) 648 (C.C.A., 4th Cir.), affirming 23 B.T.A. 1288; certiorari denied, 290 U.S. 650.

We are told that the working wife is a new phenomenon. This is relied on to account for the apparent inconsistency that the expenses in issue are now a commonplace, yet have not been the subject of legislation, ruling, or adjudicated controversy. But if that is true it becomes all the more necessary to apply accepted principles to the novel facts. We are not prepared to say that the care of children, like similar aspects of family and household life, is other than a personal concern. The wife's services as custodian of the home and protector of its children are ordinarily rendered without monetary compensation. There results no taxable income from the performance of this service and the correlative expenditure is personal and not susceptible of deduction. Rosa E. Burkhart, 11 B.T.A. 275. Here the wife has chosen to employ others to discharge her domestic function and the services she performs are rendered outside the home. They are a source of actual income and taxable as such. But that does not deprive the same work performed by others of its personal character nor furnish a reason why its cost should be treated as an offset in the guise of a deductible item.

We are not unmindful that, as petitioners suggest, certain disbursements normally personal may become deductible by reason of their intimate connection with an occupation carried on for profit. In this category fall entertainment, Blackmer v. Commissioner, 70 Fed.(2d) 255 (C.C.A., 2d Cir.), and traveling expenses, Joseph W. Powell, 34 B.T.A. 655; aff'd, 94 Fed.(2d) 483 (C.C.A., 1st Cir.), and the cost of an actor's wardrobe, Charles Hutchison, 13 B.T.A. 1187. The line is not always an easy one to draw nor the test simple to apply. But we think its principle is clear. It may for practical purposes be said to constitute a distinction between those activities which, as a matter of common acceptance and universal experience, are "ordinary" or usual as the direct accompaniment of business pursuits, on the one hand; and those which, though they may in some indirect and tenuous degree relate to the circumstances of a profitable occupation, are nevertheless personal in their nature, of a character applicable to human beings generally, and which exist on that plane regardless of the occupation, though not necessarily of the station in life, of the individuals concerned. See Welch v. Helvering, 290 U.S. 111.

In the latter category, we think, fall payments made to servants or others occupied in looking to the personal wants of their employers. David Sonenblick, 4 B.T.A. 986. And we include in this group nursemaids retained to care for infant children.

Decision will be entered for the respondent.

Notes

1. The opinion here does not indicate what provision Smith was relying on in claiming a deduction. But it is clear that the claim is based on the notion that childcare was a cost of earning the wife's salary. Performance of

services as an employee is a trade or business, and therefore the claim was that childcare was an ordinary and necessary expense incurred in carrying on that business. §162. This is generally regarded as the strongest ground for allowing deductions, and it informs a number of other sections besides §162.

But *Smith* exhibits an important intrinsic problem in income taxation (or income measurement more generally), which is to distinguish between deductible costs and taxable uses of income. Personal consumption is the main thing income is good for. In Henry Simons' formulation personal consumption *is* the major component of personal income. So if an expenditure goes to purchase an item of personal benefit for the owner of a business, it ought *not* to be deducted. That fundamental proposition is embodied in §262.

Many people's personal and business lives do not occur in separate spheres—and then what is to be done with expenditures that have both personal and business aspects? That is what this chapter is about, and *Smith* provides a kind of paradigmatic introduction.

Assuming that a particular expenditure yields both business and personal benefits, how do we sort them out? Should (could?) the payment be treated as partly deductible and partly nondeductible? On what basis might such an allocation be made? Absent allocation, which rule governs, the deduction authorization in §162 or the statutory disallowance, §262? See §§161, 261. Read the introductory language of §162(a) carefully. Did the Commissioner and the Board need to rely on §262 to bar the deduction in *Smith*?

2. Is the classification of childcare as a personal expense a matter of principle or convention? The Board says the "principle is clear," but in what sense is the principle anything more than a matter of convention?

3. Childcare expense may be different from some other personal expenses since it is only incurred as a result of having children *and* working. If a worker with children is compared to one without, the expense of childcare appears to be a cost of having children. If a working parent is compared to a nonworking parent, however, the expense appears as a function of going to work. Childcare in this respect is like commuting: It is the fact of working in X *and* living in Y that necessitates commuting between X and Y. Food, clothing, and housing, on the other hand, are all required whether one works or not (although their cost may vary as a consequence of some sorts of employment).

But which comparison with respect to childcare expense (or commuting) should control classification?

Consider the matter from a different perspective: Suppose there is a welfare program in which benefits are to be reduced for some fraction of income earned (or available to be earned). Should childcare and commuting costs be deducted in determining income for purposes of such a welfare program? Is the income tax different? How?

4. What is the relation between deductibility and individual motivation? Did Lillie Smith hire household help in order to work, or did she work in

order to hire help? Should that issue control deductibility? What if a taxpayer could prove that she ate only to live and lived only to work; should that taxpayer then be allowed a deduction for food?

A great many expenditures are made for mixed motives of profit and pleasure, and the challenge the tax law faces on the deduction side is largely whether these expenditures can be sorted out on a reasonably fair and administrable basis. Common recurring expenditures almost have to be classified on a conventional basis both to be fair and to avoid difficult administrative burdens. But the treatment of unusual expenditures often depends upon a sensitive appraisal of human motivation. Is there any general way to decide when a more or less conventional classification (e.g., nursemaids represent personal or family expenses) should preclude an investigation of motivation in a particular situation? Cf. Ochs v. Commissioner, Chapter 3C.2 above.

5. *Legislation I.* The decision in *Smith* has been partially overruled for some time now by specific statutory provisions authorizing a limited allowance for childcare expenses. The present version is contained in §21, which allows a 35 percent credit (rather than a deduction) for taxpayers with incomes of $15,000 or less; the percentage decreases gradually to 20 percent for taxpayers with higher incomes. The maximum amount of expenses for which a credit is allowed is $3,000 for one child and $6,000 for more than one.

Before 1976, the provision was an itemized deduction. Appraise the substitution of a credit for an itemized deduction. The main reason given when the deduction was changed to a credit was to ensure that the allowance would be available to nonitemizers. But this could have been accomplished just by listing the deduction in §62 as a deduction allowable in computing adjusted gross income. What more does the transformation into a credit do?

6. A two-worker couple may have higher expenses than a one-worker couple for other items than childcare, such as house cleaning, clothing expenses, and eating out more often. It would be impractical to try to measure these incremental costs directly, but one might simply grant a general allowance for two-worker couples to provide some rough compensation for all such items. At the least, a two-worker family (or a family with only one adult member, who is employed) has less time to perform a variety of services for itself; a general allowance would compensate for that difference, leaving it to one-worker couples to determine whether their extra time is to be utilized in childcare or something else. Would such a general allowance be desirable? Should it be allowed as a substitute or a supplement to a childcare deduction or credit? This question is closely related to the question of relative treatment of married couples and single persons. See Chapter 16 below.

7. *Legislation II.* In 1981, §129 was enacted to allow employees to exclude from income amounts paid by an employer for dependent care assistance to an employee, provided the assistance was furnished pursuant to a program

meeting specific requirements. The two major requirements are that the program must be for the exclusive benefit of employees and that the benefits must not discriminate in favor of highly compensated individuals. For married individuals, the exclusion may not exceed the lesser of the earned income of the employee or the earned income of the spouse of the employee and is subject to dollar limitations in any event. Consider how this provision effectively modifies the limitations in §21.

8. *Cafeteria Plans.* Reading §129 alone, one might think it had another implicit limitation, that an employer be willing, in effect, to pay more to employees with qualified dependents than to other employees. But read §125, on "Cafeteria Plans," which permits employees to be given a choice between nontaxable benefits or cash, without the former becoming taxable "solely because, under the plan, the participant may choose among the benefits" offered. How can §§125 and 129 together be sensibly reconciled with the limitations on childcare allowances for high-bracket taxpayers in §21?

9. How do §§21 and 129 interact? Suppose *W* earns $40,000 and *H*, a sculptor, earns $6,000, and *W* receives a childcare allowance of $5,000 from her employer and they spend $10,000 on qualified expenses (for two children). How are these items to be reflected on the income tax return?

B. CLOTHING

PEVSNER v. COMMISSIONER
628 F.2d 467 (5th Cir. 1980)

Before Ainsworth, Garza and Johnson, Circuit Judges.

Johnson, Circuit Judge . . . Since June 1973 Sandra J. Pevsner, taxpayer, has been employed as the manager of the Sakowitz Yves St. Laurent Rive Gauche Boutique located in Dallas, Texas. The boutique sells only women's clothes and accessories designed by Yves St. Laurent (YSL), one of the leading designers of women's apparel. Although the clothing is ready to wear, it is highly fashionable and expensively priced. Some customers of the boutique purchase and wear the YSL apparel for their daily activities and spend as much as $20,000 per year for such apparel.

As manager of the boutique, the taxpayer is expected by her employer to wear YSL clothes while at work. In her appearance, she is expected to project the image of an exclusive lifestyle and to demonstrate to her customers that she is aware of the YSL current fashion trends as well as trends generally. Because the boutique sells YSL clothes exclusively, taxpayer must be able, when a customer compliments her on her clothes, to say that they are designed by YSL. In addition to wearing YSL apparel while at the boutique, she wears them while commuting to and from work, to fashion shows sponsored by the boutique, and to business luncheons at which she represents the boutique. During 1975, the taxpayer bought, at an employee's discount, the following items: four blouses, three skirts, one pair of slacks, one trench coat, two sweaters, one jacket, one tunic, five scarves, six belts, two pairs of shoes and four necklaces. The total cost of this apparel was $1,381.91. In addition, the sum of $240 was expended for maintenance of these items.

Although the clothing and accessories purchased by the taxpayer were the type used for general purposes by the regular customers of the boutique, the taxpayer is not a normal purchaser of these clothes. The taxpayer and her husband, who is partially disabled because of a severe heart attack suffered in 1971, lead a simple life and their social activities are very limited and informal. Although taxpayer's employer has no objection to her wearing the apparel away from work, taxpayer stated that she did not wear the clothes during off-work hours because she felt that they were too expensive for her simple everyday lifestyle. Another reason why she did not wear the YSL clothes apart from work was to make them last longer. Taxpayer did admit at trial, however, that a number of the articles were things she could have worn off the job and in which she would have looked "nice."

On her joint federal income tax return for 1975, taxpayer deducted $990 as an ordinary and necessary business expense with respect to her purchase of the YSL clothing and accessories. However, in the tax court, taxpayer claimed a deduction for the full $1381.91 cost of the apparel and for the $240 cost of maintaining the apparel. The tax court allowed the taxpayer to deduct both expenses in the total amount of $1621.91. The tax court reasoned that the apparel was not suitable to the private lifestyle maintained by the taxpayer. This appeal by the Commissioner followed.

The principal issue on appeal is whether the taxpayer is entitled to deduct as an ordinary and necessary business expense the cost of purchasing and maintaining the YSL clothes and accessories worn by the taxpayer in her employment as the manager of the boutique. This determination requires an examination of the relationship between Section 162(a) of the Internal Revenue Code of 1954, which allows a deduction for ordinary and necessary expenses incurred in the conduct of a trade or business, and Section 262 of the Code, which bars a deduction for all "personal, living, or family expenses." Although many expenses are helpful or essential to one's business activities—such as commuting expenses and the cost of meals while at work—these expenditures are considered inherently personal and are disallowed under Section 262. See, e.g., United States v. Correll, 389 U.S. 299 ... (1967); Commissioner v. Flowers, 326 U.S. 465 ... (1946).

The generally accepted rule governing the deductibility of clothing expenses is that the cost of clothing is deductible as a business expense only if: (1) the clothing is of a type specifically required as a condition of employment, (2) it is not adaptable to general usage as ordinary clothing, and (3) it is not so worn. Donnelly v. Commissioner, 262 F.2d 411, 412 (2d Cir. 1959).

In the present case, the Commissioner stipulated that the taxpayer was required by her employer to wear YSL clothing and that she did not wear such apparel apart from work. The Commissioner maintained, however, that a deduction should be denied because the YSL clothes and accessories purchased by the taxpayer were adaptable for general usage as ordinary clothing and she was not prohibited from using them as such. The tax court, in rejecting the Commissioner's argument for the application of an objective test, recognized that the test for deductibility was whether the clothing was "suitable for general or personal wear" but determined that the matter of suitability was to be judged subjectively, in light of the taxpayer's lifestyle. Although the court recognized that the YSL apparel "might be used by some members of society for general purposes," it felt that because the "wearing of YSL apparel outside work would be inconsistent with . . . [taxpayer's] life-style," sufficient reason was shown for allowing a deduction for the clothing expenditures.

In reaching its decision, the tax court relied heavily upon Yeomans v. Commissioner, 30 T.C. 757 (1958). In *Yeomans*, the taxpayer was employed as fashion coordinator for a shoe manufacturing company. Her employment necessitated her attendance at meetings of fashion experts and at fashion shows sponsored by her employer. On these occasions, she was expected to wear clothing that was new, highly styled, and such as "might be sought after and worn for personal use by women who make it a practice to dress according to the most advanced or extreme fashions." 30 T.C. at 768. However, for her personal wear, Ms. Yeomans preferred a plainer and more conservative style of dress. As a consequence, some of the items she purchased were not suitable for her private and personal wear and were not so worn. The tax court allowed a deduction for the cost of the items that were not suitable for her personal wear. Although the basis for the decision in *Yeomans* is not clearly stated, the tax court in the case *sub judice* determined that

[a] careful reading of *Yeomans* shows that, without a doubt, the Court based its decision on a determination of Ms. Yeomans' lifestyle and that the clothes were not suitable for her use in such lifestyle. Furthermore, the Court recognized that the clothes Ms. Yeomans purchased were suitable for wear by women who customarily wore such highly styled apparel, but such fact did not cause the court to decide the issue against her. Thus, *Yeomans* clearly decides the issue before us in favor of the petitioner. T.C. Memo 1979-311 at 9-10.

Notwithstanding the tax court's decision in *Yeomans*, the Circuits that have addressed the issue have taken an objective, rather than subjective, approach. Stiner v. United States, 524 F.2d 640, 641 (10th Cir. 1975); Donnelly v. Commissioner, 262 F.2d 411, 412 (2d Cir. 1959). An objective approach was also taken by the tax court in Drill v. Commissioner, 8 T.C.

902 (1947). Under an objective test, no reference is made to the individual taxpayer's lifestyle or personal taste. Instead, adaptability for personal or general use depends upon what is generally accepted for ordinary street wear.

The principal argument in support of an objective test is, of course, administrative necessity. The Commissioner argues that, as a practical matter, it is virtually impossible to determine at what point either price or style makes clothing inconsistent with or inappropriate to a taxpayer's lifestyle. Moreover, the Commissioner argues that the price one pays and the styles one selects are inherently personal choices governed by taste, fashion, and other unmeasurable values. Indeed, the tax court has rejected the argument that a taxpayer's personal taste can dictate whether clothing is appropriate for general use. See Drill v. Commissioner, 8 T.C. 902 (1947). An objective test, although not perfect, provides a practical administrative approach that allows a taxpayer or revenue agent to look only to objective facts in determining whether clothing required as a condition of employment is adaptable to general use as ordinary streetwear. Conversely, the tax court's reliance on subjective factors provides no concrete guidelines in determining the deductibility of clothing purchased as a condition of employment.

In addition to achieving a practical administrative result, an objective test also tends to promote substantial fairness among the greatest number of taxpayers. As the Commissioner suggests, it apparently would be the tax court's position that two similarly situated YSL boutique managers with identical wardrobes would be subject to disparate tax consequences depending upon the particular manager's lifestyle and "socio-economic level." This result, however, is not consonant with a reasonable interpretation of Sections 162 and 262.

For the reasons stated above, the decision of the tax court upholding the deduction for taxpayer's purchase of YSL clothing is reversed. Consequently, the portion of the tax court's decision upholding the deduction for maintenance costs for the clothing is also

Reversed.

C.   TRAVELING: §162(a)(2)

1. Away

UNITED STATES v. CORRELL
389 U.S. 299 (1967)

Mr. Justice Stewart delivered the opinion of the Court. The Commissioner of Internal Revenue has long maintained that a taxpayer traveling on business may deduct the cost of his meals only if his trip requires him to stop for sleep or rest. The question presented here is the validity of that rule.

The respondent in this case was a traveling salesman for a wholesale grocery company in Tennessee. He customarily left home early in the morning, ate breakfast and lunch on the road, and returned home in time for dinner. In his income tax returns for 1960 and 1961, he deducted the cost of his morning and noon meals as "traveling expenses" incurred in the pursuit of his business "while away from home" under §162(a)(2) of the Internal Revenue Code of 1954. Because the respondent's daily trips required neither sleep nor rest, the Commissioner disallowed the deductions, ruling that the cost of the respondent's meals was a "personal, living" expense under §262 rather than a travel expense under §162(a)(2). The respondent paid the tax, sued for a refund in the District Court, and there received a favorable jury verdict. The Court of Appeals for the Sixth Circuit affirmed, holding that the Commissioner's sleep or rest rule is not "a valid regulation under the present statute." 369 F.2d 87, 90. In order to resolve a conflict among the circuits on this recurring question of federal income tax administration, we granted certiorari. 388 U.S. 905.

Under §162(a)(2), taxpayers "traveling . . . away from home in the pursuit of a trade or business" may deduct the total amount "expended for meals and lodging."[6] As a result, even the taxpayer who incurs substantial hotel and restaurant expenses because of the special demands of business travel receives something of a windfall, for at least part of what he spends on meals represents a personal living expense that other taxpayers must bear without receiving any deduction at all. Not surprisingly, therefore, Congress did not extend the special benefits of §162(a)(2) to every conceivable situation involving business travel. It made the total cost of meals and lodging deductible only if incurred in the course of travel that takes the taxpayer "away from home." The problem before us involves the meaning of that limiting phrase.

In resolving that problem, the Commissioner has avoided the wasteful litigation and continuing uncertainty that would inevitably accompany any purely case-by-case approach to the question of whether a particular taxpayer was "away from home" on a particular day. Rather than requiring "every meal-purchasing taxpayer to take pot luck in the courts,"[9] the Commissioner has consistently construed travel "away from home" to exclude all trips

---

6. Prior to the enactment in 1921 of what is now §162(a)(2), the Commissioner had promulgated a regulation allowing a deduction for the cost of meals and lodging away from home, but only to the extent that this cost exceeded "any expenditures ordinarily required for such purposes when at home." Treas. Reg. 45 (1920 ed.), Art. 292, 4 Cum. Bull. 209 (1921). Despite its logical appeal, the regulation proved so difficult to administer that the Treasury Department asked Congress to grant a deduction for the "entire amount" of such meal and lodging expenditures. See Statement of Dr. T. S. Adams, Tax Adviser, Treasury Department, in Hearings on H.R. 8245 before the Senate Committee on Finance, 67th Cong., 1st Sess., at 50, 234-235 (1921). Accordingly, §214(a)(1) of the Revenue Act of 1921, c.136, 42 Stat. 239, for the first time included the language that later became §162(a)(2). See n.2, supra. The section was amended in a respect not here relevant by the Revenue Act of 1962, §4(b), 76 Stat. 976.

9. Commissioner v. Bagley, 374 F.2d 204, 207.

requiring neither sleep nor rest, regardless of how many cities a given trip may have touched, how many miles it may have covered, or how many hours it may have consumed. By so interpreting the statutory phrase, the Commissioner has achieved not only ease and certainty of application but also substantial fairness, for the sleep or rest rule places all one-day travelers on a similar tax footing, rather than discriminating against intracity travelers and commuters, who of course cannot deduct the cost of the meals they eat on the road. See Commissioner v. Flowers [Chapter 12C.2 below].

Any rule in this area must make some rather arbitrary distinctions, but at least the sleep or rest rule avoids the obvious inequity of permitting the New Yorker who makes a quick trip to Washington and back, missing neither his breakfast nor his dinner at home, to deduct the cost of his lunch merely because he covers more miles than the salesman who travels locally and must finance all his meals without the help of the Federal Treasury. And the Commissioner's rule surely makes more sense than one which would allow the respondent in this case to deduct the cost of his breakfast and lunch simply because he spends a greater percentage of his time at the wheel than the commuter who eats breakfast on his way to work and lunch a block from his office.

The Court of Appeals nonetheless found in the "plain language of the statute" an insuperable obstacle to the Commissioner's construction. 369 F.2d 87, 89. We disagree. The language of the statute — "meals and lodging . . . away from home" — is obviously not self-defining.[16] And to the extent that the words chosen by Congress cut in either direction, they tend to support rather than defeat the Commissioner's position, for the statute speaks of "meals and lodging" as a unit, suggesting — at least arguably — that Congress contemplated a deduction for the cost of meals only where the travel in question involves lodging as well.[17] Ordinarily, at least, only the taxpayer who finds it necessary to stop for sleep or rest incurs significantly higher living expenses as a direct result of his business travel, and Congress might well have thought that only taxpayers in that category should be permitted to deduct their living expenses while on the road. In any event, Congress certainly recognized, when it promulgated §162(a)(2), that the Commissioner had so understood its statutory predecessor.[20] This case thus comes within the settled

16. The statute applies to the meal and lodging expenses of taxpayers "traveling . . . away from home." The very concept of "traveling" obviously requires a physical separation from one's house. To read the phrase "away from home" as broadly as a completely literal approach might permit would thus render the phrase completely redundant. But of course the words of the statute have never been so woodenly construed. The commuter, for example, has never been regarded as "away from home" within the meaning of §162(a)(2) simply because he has traveled from his residence to his place of business. See Commissioner v. Flowers, 326 U.S. 465, 473. More than a dictionary is thus required to understand the provision here involved, and no appeal to the "plain language" of the section can obviate the need for further statutory construction.

17. See Commissioner v. Bagley, 374 F.2d 204, 207, n.10.

20. In considering the proposed 1954 Code, Congress heard a taxpayer plea for a change in the rule disallowing deductions for meal expenses on one-day trips. Hearings on General Revision of the Internal

principle that "Treasury regulations and interpretations long continued without substantial change, applying to un-amended or substantially reenacted statutes, are deemed to have received congressional approval and have the effect of law." Helvering v. Winmill, 305 U.S. 79, 83; Fribourg Nav. Co. v. Commissioner, 383 U.S. 272, 283.

Alternatives to the Commissioner's sleep or rest rule are of course available. Improvements might be imagined. But we do not sit as a committee of revision to perfect the administration of the tax laws. Congress has delegated to the Commissioner, not to the courts, the task of prescribing "all needful rules and regulations for the enforcement" of the Internal Revenue Code. 26 U.S.C. §7805(a). In this area of limitless factual variations, "it is the province of Congress and the Commissioner, not the courts, to make the appropriate adjustments." Commissioner v. Stidger, 386 U.S. 287, 296. The role of the judiciary in cases of this sort begins and ends with assuring that the Commissioner's regulations fall within his authority to implement the congressional mandate in some reasonable manner. Because the rule challenged here has not been shown deficient on that score, the Court of Appeals should have sustained its validity. The judgment is therefore

Reversed.

Mr. Justice Marshall took no part in the consideration or decision of this case.

Mr. Justice DOUGLAS, with whom Mr. Justice Black and Mr. Justice Fortas concur, dissenting. The statutory words "while away from home," 26 U.S.C. §162(a)(2), may not in my view be shrunken to "overnight" by administrative construction or regulations. "Overnight" injects a time element in testing

---

Revenue Code before the House Committee on Ways and Means, 83d Cong., 1st Sess., pt. 1, at 216-219 (1953); Hearings on H.R. 8300 before the Senate Committee on Finance, 83d Cong., 2d Sess., pt. 4, at 2396 (1954). No such change resulted.

In recommending §62(2) (C) of the 1954 Code, permitting employees to deduct certain transportation expenses in computing adjusted gross income, the Senate Finance Committee stated:

At present, business transportation expenses can be deducted by an employee in arriving at adjusted gross income only if they are reimbursed by the employer or if they are incurred while he was *away from home overnight.* . . .

Because these expenses, when incurred, usually are substantial, it appears desirable to treat employees in this respect like self-employed persons. For this reason both the House and your committee's bill permit employees to deduct business transportation expenses in arriving at adjusted gross income even though the expenses are not incurred in *travel away from home* or not reimbursed by the employer. . . .

S. Rep. No. 1622, 83d Cong., 2d Sess., 9 (1954) (emphasis added). See also H.R. Rep. No. 1337, 83d Cong., 2d Sess., 9 (1954).

And in discussing §120 of the 1954 Code (repealed by 72 Stat. 1607 (1958)), which allowed policemen to exclude from taxable income up to $5 per day in meal allowances, both the House and Senate Reports noted that, under the prevailing rule, police officers could deduct expenses *over* the $5 limit of §120 "for meals while *away from home overnight.*" H.R. Rep. No. 1337, 83d Cong., 2d Sess., A40 (1954) (emphasis added); S. Rep. No. 1622, 83d Cong., 2d Sess., 191 (1954) (emphasis added). Thus Congress was well aware of the Commissioner's rule when it retained in §162(a)(2) the precise terminology it had used in 1921.

deductibility, while the statute speaks only in terms of geography. As stated by the Court of Appeals:

"In an era of supersonic travel, the time factor is hardly relevant to the question of whether or not travel and meal expenses are related to the taxpayer's business and cannot be the basis of a valid regulation under the present statute." Correll v. United States, 369 F.2d 87, 89-90.

I would affirm the judgment below.

Notes

1. Reconsider the rule in §119 about excluding meals furnished on the business premises of the employer. Apparently the cost or value of meals may be omitted from taxable income if they are provided on the business premises or very far away, but not in between. Does this pattern make sense?

2. What if an employer has a policy of reimbursing employees for meals purchased while working away from their regular place of employment, although not overnight. Must the reimbursement be included in income, without any offsetting deduction?

3. Suppose a lawyer goes from Boston to Chicago on a one-day business trip. He has breakfast on the plane to Chicago, lunch in the executive dining room of a Chicago bank (at its expense), and dinner on the plane back to Boston. How should any of those meals be reflected in taxable income?

4. Note that no effort was made to disallow automobile expenses in *Correll*. Why not? If the taxpayer is not away from home, on what ground are those deductible? Sometimes the term *transportation expenses* is used in lieu of *traveling expenses* for items that do not depend on being away from home. See, e.g., §213(d)(1)(B).

2. From Home

COMMISSIONER v. FLOWERS
326 U.S. 465 (1945)

Mr. Justice MURPHY delivered the opinion of the Court. . . . The taxpayer, a lawyer, has resided with his family in Jackson, Mississippi, since 1903. There he has paid taxes, voted, schooled his children and established social and religious connections. He built a house in Jackson nearly thirty years ago and at all times has maintained it for himself and his family. He has been connected with several law firms in Jackson, one of which he formed and which has borne his name since 1922.

In 1906 the taxpayer began to represent the predecessor of the Gulf, Mobile & Ohio Railroad, his present employer. He acted as trial counsel for the railroad throughout Mississippi. From 1918 until 1927 he acted as a special counsel for the railroad in Mississippi. He was elected general solicitor in 1927 and continued to be elected to that position each year until 1930, when he was elected general counsel. Thereafter he was annually elected general counsel until September, 1940, when the properties of the predecessor company and another railroad were merged and he was elected vice president and general counsel of the newly formed Gulf, Mobile & Ohio Railroad.

The main office of the Gulf, Mobile & Ohio Railroad is in Mobile, Alabama, as was also the main office of its predecessor. When offered the position of general solicitor in 1927, the taxpayer was unwilling to accept it if it required him to move from Jackson to Mobile. He had established himself in Jackson both professionally and personally and was not desirous of moving away. As a result, an arrangement was made between him and the railroad whereby he could accept the position and continue to reside in Jackson on condition that he pay his traveling expenses between Mobile and Jackson and pay his living expenses in both places. This arrangement permitted the taxpayer to determine for himself the amount of time he would spend in each of the two cities and was in effect during 1939 and 1940, the taxable years in question.

The railroad company provided an office for the taxpayer in Mobile but not in Jackson. When he worked in Jackson his law firm provided him with office space, although he no longer participated in the firm's business or shared in its profits. He used his own office furniture and fixtures at this office. The railroad, however, furnished telephone service and a typewriter and desk for his secretary. It also paid the secretary's expenses while in Jackson. Most of the legal business of the railroad was centered in or conducted from Jackson, but this business was handled by local counsel for the railroad. The taxpayer's participation was advisory only and was no different from his participation in the railroad's legal business in other areas.

The taxpayer's principal post of business was at the main office in Mobile. However, during the taxable years of 1939 and 1940, he devoted nearly all his time to matters relating to the merger of the railroads. Since it was left to him where he would do his work, he spent most of his time in Jackson during this period. In connection with the merger, one of the companies was involved in certain litigation in the federal court in Jackson and the taxpayer participated in that litigation.

During 1939 he spent 203 days in Jackson and 66 in Mobile, making 33 trips between the two cities. During 1940 he spent 168 days in Jackson and 102 in Mobile, making 40 trips between the two cities. The railroad paid all of his traveling expenses when he went on business trips to points other than Jackson or Mobile. But it paid none of his expenses in traveling between these two points or while he was at either of them.

The taxpayer deducted $900 in his 1939 income tax return and $1,620 in his 1940 return as traveling expenses incurred in making trips from

Jackson to Mobile and as expenditures for meals and hotel accommodations while in Mobile.[2] . . .

Three conditions must thus be satisfied before a traveling expense deduction may be made under [§162(a)(2)]:

(1) The expense must be a reasonable and necessary traveling expense, as that term is generally understood. This includes such items as transportation fares and food and lodging expenses incurred while traveling.

(2) The expense must be incurred "while away from home."

(3) The expense must be incurred in pursuit of business. This means that there must be a direct connection between the expenditure and the carrying on of the trade or business of the taxpayer or of his employer. Moreover, such an expenditure must be necessary or appropriate to the development and pursuit of the business or trade.

Whether particular expenditures fulfill these three conditions so as to entitle a taxpayer to a deduction is purely a question of fact in most instances. . . . And the Tax Court's inferences and conclusions on such a factual matter, under established principles, should not be disturbed by an appellate court. . . .

In this instance, the Tax Court without detailed elaboration concluded that "The situation presented in this proceeding is, in principle, no different from that in which a taxpayer's place of employment is in one city and for reasons satisfactory to himself he resides in another." It accordingly disallowed the deductions on the ground that they represent living and personal expenses rather than traveling expenses incurred while away from home in the pursuit of business. The court below accepted the Tax Court's findings of fact but reversed its judgment on the basis that it had improperly construed the word "home" as used in the second condition precedent to a traveling expense deduction under [§162(a)(2)]. The Tax Court, it was said, erroneously construed the word to mean the post, station or place of business where the taxpayer was employed—in this instance, Mobile—and thus erred in concluding that the expenditures in issue were not incurred "while away from home." The Court below felt that the word was to be given no such "unusual" or "extraordinary" meaning in this statute, that it simply meant "that place where one in fact resides" or "the principal place of abode of one who has the intention to live there permanently." 148 F.2d at 164. Since the taxpayer here admittedly had his home, as thus defined, in Jackson and since the expenses were incurred while he was away from Jackson, the deduction was permissible.

The meaning of the word "home" in [§162(a)(2)] with reference to a taxpayer residing in one city and working in another has engendered much difficulty and litigation. . . . The Tax Court and the administrative rulings

---

2. No claim for deduction was made by the taxpayer for the amounts spent in traveling from Mobile to Jackson. He also took trips during the taxable years to Washington, New York, New Orleans, Baton Rouge, Memphis and Jackson (Tenn.), which were apparently in the nature of business trips for which the taxpayer presumably was reimbursed by the railroad. No claim was made in regard to them.

have consistently defined it as the equivalent of the taxpayer's place of business. . . . On the other hand, the decision below and Wallace v. Commissioner, 144 F.2d 407 (C.C.A. 9) have flatly rejected that view and have confined the term to the taxpayer's actual residence. . . .

We deem it unnecessary here to enter into or to decide this conflict. The Tax Court's opinion, as we read it, was grounded neither solely nor primarily upon that agency's conception of the word "home." Its discussion was directed mainly toward the relation of the expenditures to the railroad's business, a relationship required by the third condition of the deduction. Thus even if the Tax Court's definition of the word "home" was implicit in its decision and even if that definition was erroneous, its judgment must be sustained here if it properly concluded that the necessary relationship between the expenditures and the railroad's business was lacking. Failure to satisfy any one of the three conditions destroys the traveling expense deduction.

Turning our attention to the third condition, this case is disposed of quickly. There is no claim that the Tax Court misconstrued this condition or used improper standards in applying it. And it is readily apparent from the facts that its inferences were supported by evidence and that its conclusion that the expenditures in issue were non-deductible living and personal expenses was fully justified.

The facts demonstrate clearly that the expenses were not incurred in the pursuit of the business of the taxpayer's employer, the railroad. Jackson was his regular home. Had his post of duty been in that city the cost of maintaining his home there and of commuting or driving to work concededly would be non-deductible living and personal expenses lacking the necessary direct relation to the prosecution of the business. The character of such expenses is unaltered by the circumstance that the taxpayer's post of duty was in Mobile, thereby increasing the costs of transportation, food and lodging. Whether he maintained one abode or two, whether he traveled three blocks or three hundred miles to work, the nature of these expenditures remained the same.

The added costs in issue, moreover, were as unnecessary and inappropriate to the development of the railroad's business as were his personal and living costs in Jackson. They were incurred solely as the result of the taxpayer's desire to maintain a home in Jackson while working in Mobile, a factor irrelevant to the maintenance and prosecution of the railroad's legal business. The railroad did not require him to travel on business from Jackson to Mobile or to maintain living quarters in both cities. Nor did it compel him, save in one instance, to perform tasks for it in Jackson. It simply asked him to be at his principal post in Mobile as business demanded and as his personal convenience was served, allowing him to divide his business time between Mobile and Jackson as he saw fit. Except for the federal court litigation, all of the taxpayer's work in Jackson would normally have been performed in the headquarters at Mobile. The fact that he traveled frequently between the two cities and incurred extra living expenses in Mobile, while doing much of his work in Jackson, was occasioned solely by his personal propensities. The railroad gained nothing from this arrangement except the personal satisfaction of the taxpayer.

Travel expenses in pursuit of business within the meaning of [§162(a)(2)] could arise only when the railroad's business forced the taxpayer to travel and to live temporarily at some place other than Mobile, thereby advancing the interests of the railroad. Business trips are to be identified in relation to business demands and the traveler's business headquarters. The exigencies of business rather than the personal conveniences and necessities of the traveler must be the motivating factors. Such was not the case here.

It follows that the court below erred in reversing the judgment of the Tax Court.

Reversed.

Mr. Justice Jackson took no part in the consideration or decision of this case.

Mr. Justice RUTLEDGE, dissenting. I think the judgment of the Court of Appeals should be affirmed. When Congress used the word "home" in [§162] I do not believe it meant "business headquarters." And in my opinion this case presents no other question. . . .

By construing "home" as "business headquarters"; by reading "temporarily" as "very temporarily" into [§162]; by bringing down "ordinary and necessary" from its first sentence into its second; by finding "inequity" where Congress has said none exists; by construing "commuter" to cover long-distance, irregular travel; and by conjuring from the "statutory setting" a meaning at odds with the plain wording of the clause, the Government makes over understandable ordinary English into highly technical tax jargon. There is enough of this in the tax laws inescapably, without adding more in the absence of either compulsion or authority. The arm of the taxgatherer reaches far. In my judgment it should not go the length of this case. Congress has revised [§162] once to overcome niggardly construction.[8] It should not have to do so again.

REVENUE RULING 75-432
1975-2 C.B. 6

The purpose of this Revenue Ruling is to update and restate, under the current statute and regulations, the position set forth in Rev. Rul. 54-497, 1954-2 C.B. 75, at 77-81, with regard to the principles applicable in

---

8. The Treasury Regulations in force in 1920 allowed deduction of only the excess of the cost of meals and lodging away from home over the cost at home; and under earlier regulations none of this expense was allowed. Congress inserted the words "all" and "entire" in the 1921 Act to overcome this ruling.

determining when an employee may deduct expenses for meals and lodging incurred while traveling on business.

The courts in considering questions involving deductions for traveling expenses have frequently stated that each case must be decided on its own particular facts. Furthermore, there appears to be no single rule that will produce the correct result in all situations. . . .

A taxpayer cannot deduct the cost of meals and lodging while performing duties at a principal place of business, even though the tax-payer maintains a permanent residence elsewhere. Congress did not intend to allow as a business expense those outlays that are not caused by the exigencies of the business but by the action of the taxpayer in having a home, for the taxpayer's convenience, at a distance from the business. Such expenditures are not essential for the conduct of the business and were not within the contemplation of Congress, which proceeded on the assumption that a person engaged in business would live within reasonable proximity of the business. See Barnhill v. Commissioner, 148 F.2d 913 (4th Cir. 1945), 1945 C.B. 96; Commissioner v. Stidger, 386 U.S. 237 (1967), 1967-1 C.B. 32.

It is therefore, the long-established position of the Internal Revenue Service that the "home" referred to in section 162(a)(2) of the Code as the place away from which traveling expenses must be incurred to be deductible is, as a general rule, the place at which the taxpayer conducts the trade or business. If the taxpayer is engaged in business at two or more separate locations, the "tax home" for purposes of section 162(a)(2) is located at the principal place of business during the taxable year. Markey v. Commissioner, 490 F.2d 1249 (6th Cir. 1974); Rev. Rul. 60-189, 1960-1 C.B. 60. It should, of course, be emphasized that the location of an employee's tax home is necessarily a question of fact that must be determined on the basis of the particular circumstances of each case.

In the rare case in which the employee has no identifiable principal place of business, but does maintain a regular place of abode in a real or substantial sense in a particular city from which the taxpayer is sent on temporary assignments, the tax home will be regarded as being that place of abode. This should be distinguished from the case of an itinerant worker with neither a regular place of business nor a regular place of abode. In such case, the home is considered to go along with the worker and therefore the worker does not travel away from home for purposes of section 162(a)(2) of the Code, and may not deduct the cost of meals or lodging. Rev. Rul. 73-529, 1973-2 C.B. 37; Rev. Rul. 71-247, 1971-1 C.B. 54.

The tax home rule may be illustrated by its application to railroad employees. The principal or regular post of duty of a member of a train crew is not regarded as being aboard the train, but at the terminal where such member ordinarily, or for an indefinite period (as distinguished from a temporary period, discussed below), begins and ends actual train runs. This terminal is referred to, for tax purposes, as that employee's tax home, the location of which may or may not coincide with the railroad's designation of the home terminal for a particular run.

Whether an employee's current post of duty is that employee's tax home depends on whether that individual is assigned there temporarily or permanently (an assignment for an indefinite period is regarded as a permanent assignment for section 162(a)(2) of the Code purposes). The basic principle is that an employee is considered to maintain a residence at or in the vicinity of that employee's principal place of business. See *Markey.* An employee who is temporarily transferred to a different area is not expected to move to the new area, and is therefore considered away from home and "in a travel status" while at his temporary post. Truman C. Tucker, 55 T.C. 783 (1971); Rev. Rul. 60-189. However, an employee who is permanently transferred to a new area is considered to have shifted the home to the new post, which is the employee's new tax home. See Commissioner v. Mooneyhan, 404 F.2d 522 (6th Cir. 1968), cert. denied, 394 U.S. 1001. The maintenance of the old residence where the taxpayer's family resides, and the taxpayer's travel back and forth, are strictly personal expenses that, under the provisions of section 262, are not deductible. See Commissioner v. Flowers, 326 U.S. 465, 1946-1 C.B. 57.

An exception to this rule exists in those unusual situations when the employee maintains a permanent residence for that employee's family at or near the minor or temporary post of duty, and another residence at or near the principal post of duty. Since the employee is traveling away from the principal post of duty on business where the employee also maintains a residence, the cost of meals and lodging at the minor or temporary post of duty is allowed as a deduction. Of course, the deduction is limited to that portion of the family expenses for meals and lodging that is properly attributable to the employee's presence there in the actual performance of business duties. Rev. Rul. 61-67, 1961-1 C.B. 25; Rev. Rul. 54-147, 1954-1 C.B. 51, 53.

An employee whose assignment away from that employee's principal place of business is strictly temporary (that is, its termination is anticipated within a fixed or reasonably short period of time) is considered to be in a travel status for the entire period during which duties require the employee to remain away from the regular post of duty. For example, if a member of a railroad train crew receives a temporary assignment to a run (whether or not "overnight," a rule discussed below) that begins and ends at a terminal situated at a distance from the tax home, the member may deduct not only the expenses for meals and lodging while making runs from and to that terminal, but all such expenses for the entire time during which duties prevent such member from returning to the regular post of duty. Typical of temporary assignments necessitating such an absence from the employee's regular post of duty are replacement or relief jobs during sick or vacation leave of the employees who regularly perform those duties.

Another kind of temporary assignment away from an employee's regular post of duty is a seasonal job that is not ordinarily filled by the same individual year after year. For example, during seasonal shipping periods for the marketing of crops, an employee may be assigned for several months to one or more places that are located at a distance from the regular place of employment. Such an employee is generally regarded as being in a travel status for the duration of such a temporary assignment.

The same rule would be true even if the seasonal job is not temporary, but a regularly recurring post of duty. A seasonal job to which an employee regularly returns, year after year, is regarded as being permanent rather than temporary employment. For example, a railroad employee might habitually work eight or nine months each year transporting ore from the same terminal, maintaining a residence for the employee's family at or near such work location. During the winter, when the ore-hauling service is suspended, the same employee might also be employed for three or four months each year at another regular seasonal post of duty, taking up residence at or near such employment. The ordinary rule is that when an employee leaves one permanent job to accept another permanent job, such employee is regarded as abandoning the first job for the second, and the principal post of duty shifts from the old to the new place of employment. The employee in the above example, however, is not regarded as having abandoned the ore-hauling assignment during the period in which that service is suspended, since the employee reasonably expects to return to it during the appropriate following season. The employee is conducting a trade or business each year at the same two recurring, seasonal places of employment, and under these circumstances the tax home does not shift during alternate seasons from one business location to the other, but remains stationary at the principal post of duty throughout the taxable year. In each case of this nature, a factual determination must be made in order to establish which of the seasonal posts of duty is the principal post of duty. Of course, the employee may only deduct the cost of the meals and lodging at the minor place of employment while duties there require such employee to remain away from the principal post of duty.

The rule known as the "overnight rule" or the "sleep or rest rule" is used to determine whether an employee whose duties require that employee to leave the principal post of duty during all or part of actual working hours is considered to be in a travel status. An employee may deduct the expenses for meals and lodging on a business trip away from the principal post of duty only when the trip lasts substantially longer than an ordinary day's work, the employee cannot reasonably be expected to make the trip without being released from duty for sufficient time to obtain substantial sleep or rest while away from the principal post of duty, and the release from duty is with the employer's tacit or express acquiescence, or is required by regulations of a governmental agency regulating the activity involved. The overnight rule is discussed in Rev. Rul. 75-170, 1975-19 I.R.B. 14, as are the requirements for substantiating claims for deductions for the cost of meals and lodging under section 274 of the Code.

The portion of Rev. Rul. 54-497 regarding the principles applicable in determining when an employee may deduct expenses for meals and lodging incurred while traveling on business is superseded.

HANTZIS v. COMMISSIONER
638 F.2d 248 (1st Cir.), cert. denied, 452 U.S. 962 (1981)

Before Campbell and Bownes, Circuit Judges, and Keeton.* District Judge.

CAMPBELL, Circuit Judge. . . . In the fall of 1973 Catharine Hantzis (taxpayer), formerly a candidate for an advanced degree in philosophy at the University of California at Berkeley, entered Harvard Law School in Cambridge, Massachusetts, as a full-time student. During her second year of law school she sought unsuccessfully to obtain employment for the summer of 1975 with a Boston law firm. She did, however, find a job as a legal assistant with a law firm in New York City, where she worked for ten weeks beginning in June 1975. Her husband, then a member of the faculty of Northeastern University with a teaching schedule for that summer, remained in Boston and lived at the couple's home there. At the time of the Tax Court's decision in this case, Mr. and Mrs. Hantzis still resided in Boston.

On their joint income tax return for 1975, Mr. and Mrs. Hantzis reported the earnings from taxpayer's summer employment ($3,750) and deducted the cost of transportation between Boston and New York, the cost of a small apartment rented by Mrs. Hantzis in New York and the cost of her meals in New York ($3,204). The deductions were taken under 26 U.S.C. §162(a)(2). . . .

The Commissioner disallowed the deduction on the ground that taxpayer's home for purposes of section 162(a)(2) was her place of employment and the cost of traveling to and living in New York was therefore not "incurred . . . while away from home." The Commissioner also argued that the expenses were not incurred "in the pursuit of a trade or business." Both positions were rejected by the Tax Court, which found that Boston was Mrs. Hantzis' home because her employment in New York was only temporary and that her expenses in New York were "necessitated" by her employment there. The court thus held the expenses to be deductible under section 162(a)(2). . . .

The meaning of the term "home" in the travel expense provision is far from clear. When Congress enacted the travel expense deduction now codified as section 162(a)(2), it apparently was unsure whether, to be deductible, an expense must be incurred away from a person's residence or away from his principal place of business. See Note, A House Is Not a Tax Home,

---

* Of the District of Massachusetts, sitting by designation.

49 Va. L. Rev. 125, 127-28 (1963). This ambiguity persists and courts, sometimes within a single circuit, have divided over the issue. Compare Six v. United States, 450 F.2d 66 (2d Cir. 1971) (home held to be residence) and Rosenspan v. United States, 438 F.2d 905 (2d Cir.), cert. denied, 404 U.S. 864 (1971) and Burns v. Gray, 287 F.2d 698 (6th Cir. 1961) and Wallace v. Commissioner, 144 F.2d 407 (9th Cir. 1944) with Markey v. Commissioner, 490 F.2d 1249 (6th Cir. 1974) (home held to be principal place of business) and Curtis v. Commissioner, 449 F.2d 225 (5th Cir. 1971) and Wills v. Commissioner, 411 F.2d 537 (9th Cir. 1969).[10] It has been suggested that these conflicting definitions are due to the enormous factual variety in the cases. See Bell v. United States, 591 F.2d 647, 649 (Ct. Cl. 1979) ("We believe that much of the problem in differing definitions is the result of attempting to conceptualize the reasons for decisions which are based on widely varying factual situations"); Brandl v. Commissioner, 513 F.2d 697, 699 (6th Cir. 1975) ("Because of the almost infinite variety of the factual situations involved, the courts have not formulated a concrete definition of the term 'home' capable of universal application"). We find this observation instructive, for if the cases that discuss the meaning of the term "home" in section 162(a)(2) are interpreted on the basis of their unique facts as well as the fundamental purposes of the travel expense provision, and not simply pinioned to one of two competing definitions of home, much of the seeming confusion and contradiction on this issue disappears and a functional definition of the term emerges. . . .

We think the critical step in defining "home" in these situations is to recognize that the "while away from home" requirement has to be construed in light of the further requirement that the expense be the result of business exigencies. The traveling expense deduction obviously is not intended to exclude from taxation every expense incurred by a taxpayer who, in the course of business, maintains two homes. Section 162(a) (2) seeks rather "to mitigate the burden of the taxpayer who, *because of the exigencies of his trade or business, must* maintain two places of abode and thereby incur additional and duplicate living expenses." *Kroll,* supra, 49 T.C. at 562 (emphasis added). See *Brandl,* supra, 513 F.2d at 699; *Daly,* supra, 72 T.C. at 195. Consciously or unconsciously, courts have effectuated this policy in part through their interpretation of the term "home" in section 162(a)(2). Whether it is held in a particular decision that a taxpayer's home is his residence or his principal place of business, the ultimate allowance or disallowance of a deduction is a function of the court's assessment of the reason for a taxpayer's maintenance of two homes. If the reason is perceived to be personal, the taxpayer's home will generally be held to be his place of employment rather than his residence and the deduction will be denied. See, e.g., *Markey,*

10. The Tax Court has, with a notable exception, consistently held that a taxpayer's home is his place of business. See Daly v. Commissioner, 72 T.C. 190 (1979); Foote v. Commissioner, 67 T.C. 1 (1976); Montgomery v. Commissioner, 64 T.C. 175 (1975), aff'd. 532 F.2d 1088 (6th Cir. 1976); Blatnick v. Commissioner, 56 T.C. 1344 (1971). The exception, of course, is the present case.

supra, 490 F.2d at 1252-1255; *Wills*, supra, 411 F.2d at 540-541; *Daly*, supra, 72 T.C. at 195-198; Lindsay v. Commissioner, supra, 34 B.T.A. at 843-844. If the reason is felt to be business exigencies, the person's home will usually be held to be his residence and the deduction will be allowed. See, e.g., Frederick v. United States, 603 F.2d 1292 (8th Cir. 1979); Wright v. Hartsell, 305 F.2d 221 (9th Cir. 1962); Harvey v. Commissioner, 283 F.2d 491 (9th Cir. 1960); *LeBlanc*, supra, 278 F.2d 571. We understand the concern of the concurrence that such an operational interpretation of the term "home" is somewhat technical and perhaps untidy, in that it will not always afford bright line answers, but we doubt the ability of either the Commissioner or the courts to invent an unyielding formula that will make sense in all cases. The line between personal and business expenses winds through infinite factual permutations; effectuation of the travel expense provision requires that any principle of decision be flexible and sensitive to statutory policy.

Construing in the manner just described the requirement that an expense be incurred "while away from home," we do not believe this requirement was satisfied in this case. Mrs. Hantzis' *trade or business* did not require that she maintain a home in Boston as well as one in New York. Though she returned to Boston at various times during the period of her employment in New York, her visits were all for personal reasons. It is not contended that she had a business connection in Boston that necessitated her keeping a home there; no professional interest was served by maintenance of the Boston home — as would have been the case, for example, if Mrs. Hantzis had been a lawyer based in Boston with a New York client whom she was temporarily serving. The home in Boston was kept up for reasons involving Mr. Hantzis, but those reasons cannot substitute for a showing by *Mrs.* Hantzis that the exigencies of *her* trade or business required *her* to maintain two homes.[11] Mrs. Hantzis' decision to keep two homes must be seen as a choice dictated by personal, albeit wholly reasonable, considerations and not a business or occupational necessity. We therefore hold that her home for purposes of section 162(a)(2) was New York and that the expenses at issue in this case were not incurred "while away from home."

We are not dissuaded from this conclusion by the temporary nature of Mrs. Hantzis' employment in New York. Mrs. Hantzis argues that the brevity of her stay in New York excepts her from the business exigencies requirement of section 162(a)(2) under a doctrine supposedly enunciated by the Supreme Court in Peurifoy v. Commissioner, 358 U.S. 59 (1958)

---

11. In this respect, Mr. and Mrs. Hantzis' situation is analogous to cases involving spouses with careers in different locations. Each must independently satisfy the requirement that deductions taken for travel expenses incurred in the pursuit of a trade or business arise while he or she is away from home. See Chwalow v. Commissioner, 470 F.2d 475, 477-478 (3d Cir. 1972) ("Where additional expenses are incurred because, for personal reasons, husband and wife maintain separate domiciles, no deduction is allowed."); Hammond v. Commissioner, 213 F.2d 43, 44 (5th Cir. 1954); Foote v. Commissioner, 67 T.C. 1 (1976); Coerver v. Commissioner, 36 T.C. 252 (1961). This is true even though the spouses file a joint return. *Chwalow*, supra, 470 F.2d at 478.

(per curiam).[13] The Tax Court here held that Boston was the taxpayer's home because it would have been unreasonable for her to move her residence to New York for only ten weeks. At first glance these contentions may seem to find support in the court decisions holding that, when a taxpayer works for a limited time away from his usual home, section 162(a)(2) allows a deduction for the expense of maintaining a second home so long as the employment is "temporary" and not "indefinite" or "permanent."

The temporary employment doctrine does not, however, purport to eliminate any requirement that continued maintenance of a first home have a business justification. We think the rule has no application where the taxpayer has no business connection with his usual place of residence. If no business exigency dictates the location of the taxpayer's usual residence, then the mere fact of his taking temporary employment elsewhere cannot supply a compelling business reason for continuing to maintain that residence. Only a taxpayer who lives one place, works another and has business ties to *both* is in the ambiguous situation that the temporary employment doctrine is designed to resolve. . . .

On this reasoning, the temporary nature of Mrs. Hantzis' employment in New York does not affect the outcome of her case. She had no business ties to Boston that would bring her within the temporary employment doctrine. . . .

Reversed.

KEETON, District Judge, concurring in the result. . . . I read the [majority] opinion as indicating that in a dual residence case, the Commissioner must determine whether the exigencies of the taxpayer's trade or business require her to maintain both residences. If so, the Commissioner must decide that the taxpayer's *principal residence* is her "home" and must conclude that expenses associated with the secondary residence were incurred "while away from home," and are deductible. If not, as in the instant case, the Commissioner must find that the taxpayer's *principal place of business* is her "home" and must conclude that the expenses in question were not incurred "while away from home." The conclusory nature of these determinations as to which residence is her "home" reveals the potentially confusing effect of adopting an extraordinary definition of "home."

A word used in a statute can mean, among the cognoscenti, whatever authoritative sources define it to mean. Nevertheless, it is a distinct disadvantage of a body of law that it can be understood only by those who are expert in its terminology. Moreover, needless risks of misunderstanding

13. In *Peurifoy*, the Court stated that the Tax Court had "engrafted an exception" onto the requirement that travel expenses be dictated by business exigencies, allowing "a deduction for expenditures . . . when the taxpayer's employment is 'temporary' as contrasted with 'indefinite' or 'indeterminate.'" 358 U.S. at 59. Because the Commissioner did not challenge this exception, the Court did not rule on its validity. It instead upheld the circuit court's reversal of the Tax Court and disallowance of the deduction on the basis of the adequacy of the appellate court's review. The Supreme Court agreed that the Tax Court's finding as to the temporary nature of taxpayer's employment was clearly erroneous. Id. at 60-61.

and confusion arise, not only among members of the public but also among professionals who must interpret and apply a statute in their day-to-day work, when a word is given an extraordinary meaning that is contrary to its everyday usage. . . .

In analyzing dual residence cases, the majority opinion advances compelling reasons that the first step must be to determine whether the taxpayer has business as opposed to purely personal reasons for maintaining both residences. This must be done in order to determine whether the expenses of maintaining a second residence were "necessitated by business, as opposed to personal, demands," and were in this sense incurred by the taxpayer "while away from home in pursuit of trade or business." Necessarily implicit in this proposition is a more limited corollary that is sufficient to decide the present case: When the taxpayer has a business relationship to only one location, no traveling expenses the taxpayer incurs are "necessitated by business, as opposed to personal demands," regardless of how many residences the taxpayer has, where they are located, or which one is "home."

In the present case, although the taxpayer argues that her employment required her to reside in New York, that contention is insufficient to compel a determination that it was the nature of her trade or business that required her to incur the additional expense of maintaining a second residence, the burden that section 162(a)(2) was intended to mitigate. . . .

In summary, the majority announces a sound principle that, in dual residence cases, deductibility of traveling expenses depends upon a showing that both residences were maintained for business reasons. If that principle is understood to be derived from the language of section 162(a)(2) taken as a whole, "home" retains operative significance for determining *which* of the business-related residences is the one the expense of which can be treated as deductible. In this context, "home" should be given its ordinary meaning to allow a deduction only for expenses relating to an abode that is not the taxpayer's principal place of residence. On the undisputed facts in this case, the Tax Court found that Boston was the taxpayer's "home" in the everyday sense, i.e., her principal place of residence. Were the issue relevant to disposition of the case, I would uphold the Tax Court's quite reasonable determination on the evidence before it. However, because the taxpayer had no business reason for maintaining both residences, her deduction for expenses associated with maintaining a second residence closer than her principal residence to her place of employment must be disallowed without regard to which of her two residences was her "home" under section 162(a)(2).

Notes

1. *Temporary or indefinite?* The most constantly litigated issue in this area seems to be the differentiation of temporary from permanent or indefinite

employment, referred to in the *Hantzis* opinion, in which there is (or has been) some business reason for maintaining the old home. The Commissioner allows that one's tax home does not shift upon commencement of a temporary employment away from home. Some courts may state the matter in terms of whether the prospective duration of employment is sufficient to require an employee to move his or her home or bear the burden of additional expenses as a personal expense. Stated either way, the issue involves continually recurring factual difficulties. The Commissioner tends to apply a rule of thumb that employment realistically expected to last for less than a year is temporary, and longer employment is not. E.g., Rev. Rul. 93-86, 1993-2 C.B. 71.

Employment that is expected to last for less than one year may be extended, however. If the proper inquiry is "When would a reasonable person stop duplicating housing expenses?," then a taxpayer could fairly argue that a distant work assignment lasting longer than one year is temporary because, based on the information available, it was never expected to last more than an additional 12 months. In 1993 Congress added the bright-line rule that "the taxpayer shall not be treated as being temporarily away from home during any period of employment if such period exceeds one year." §162(a) (penultimate sentence). So what happens today if an out-of-town assignment predicted to last 10 months gets extended to 13? If an assignment predicted to last 13 months is actually completed in 10? Assume that in each case the taxpayer spends $1,500 per month on meals and lodging.

2. Suppose a university professor accepts a visiting appointment for a year at another school, moving her own family for the year in question and renting out the home she owns. How is she to be taxed if in fact she returns to her home institution at the end of the year as planned? What if instead she is offered and accepts a permanent appointment at the school she is visiting, and never returns to her old home except briefly to say goodbye to the neighbors and sell the house?

3. *Moving expenses.* Suppose a taxpayer's initial employment at a new location is permanent or indefinite; can he then deduct the one-time cost of moving to that new location? Or is he taxable if the employer reimburses him for moving costs?

Prior to enactment of §217 the IRS position seemed to be that (a) no deduction would be allowed for moving expenses borne by the employee himself; (b) if an employer paid to move an old employee from one location to a new location, and the impetus for the move came from the employer, not the employee, that was not gross income to the employee; but (c) if an employer paid moving expenses for a new employee traveling to his first place of employment, the payment would constitute income. These outcomes appear to have been derived from the "carrying on" requirement of §162(a), which a new employee moving to the job would not satisfy (compare §132(d), the definition of an excludible working condition fringe). As a consequence of the old-employee criterion, some nationwide employers would take on a new employee for a time near his old home before transferring him to an intended new location.

Look at §§217 and 82. How do they vary from the Commissioner's old position, and why? What problems do they raise?

Section 217 was tightened up in various respects in 1993. Previously, among other differences, it allowed (1) the cost of pre-move house hunting trips, (2) the cost of temporary living expenses for up to 30 days in the general location of the new job, (3) the cost of meals while traveling and living in temporary quarters near the new workplace, and (4) costs of selling (or settling an unexpired lease on) the old residence and buying (or acquiring a lease on) the new residence.

4. Suppose an employer — say a California law firm — pays airfare to bring prospective employees and their spouses to California to visit. After employment but before work commences, the employer pays for another round trip for each couple to enable them to look for a home. Do the employees have income on account of either trip? Could they deduct the cost of either if the employer had not paid it? See Rev. Rul. 63-77, 1963-1 C.B. 177, and §195.

5. What is the tax consequence if an employer agrees to reimburse a transferred employee for any loss on the sale of her old home? Commenting on a case requiring the employee to include such a reimbursement in gross income, one tax service said the whole problem could have been avoided if the employer had simply purchased the home from the employee at cost, instead of reimbursing for a loss. What do you think of that advice?

D. TRAVEL AND ENTERTAINMENT

RUDOLPH v. UNITED STATES
370 U.S. 269 (1962)

PER CURIAM. The petition for certiorari in this case was granted because it was thought to present important questions involving the definition of "income" and "ordinary and necessary" business expenses under the Internal Revenue Code. 368 U.S. 913. An insurance company provided a trip from its home office in Dallas, Texas, to New York City for a group of its agents and their wives. Rudolph and his wife were among the beneficiaries of this trip, and the Commissioner assessed its value to them as taxable income. It appears to be agreed between the parties that the tax consequences of the trip turn upon the Rudolphs' "dominant motive and purpose" in taking the trip and the company's in offering it. In this regard the District Court, on a suit for a refund, found that the trip was provided by the company for "the primary purpose of affording a pleasure trip . . . in the nature of a bonus, reward, and compensation for a job well done" and that from the point of view of the Rudolphs it "was primarily a pleasure trip in the nature of a vacation. . . ." 189 F.Supp. 2, 4-5. The Court of Appeals approved these findings. 291 F.2d 841. Such ultimate facts are subject to the "clearly erroneous" rule, cf. Commissioner v. Duberstein, 363 U.S. 278, 289-291 (1960), and their review would be of no importance save to the litigants themselves. The appropriate disposition in such a situation is to dismiss the writ as improvidently granted. See Rice v. Sioux City Memorial Park Cemetery, 349 U.S. 70, 78 n.2 (1955).

Writ of certiorari dismissed.

Mr. Justice Frankfurter took no part in the decision of this case.

Mr. Justice White took no part in the consideration or decision of this case.

Separate opinion of Mr. Justice HARLAN. Although the reasons given by the Court for dismissing the writ as improvidently granted should have been persuasive against granting certiorari, now that the case is here I think it better to decide it, two members of the Court having dissented on the merits.

The courts below concluded (1) that the value of this "all expense" trip to the company-sponsored insurance convention constituted "gross income" to the petitioners within the meaning of §61 of the Internal Revenue Code of 1954, and (2) that the amount reflected was not deductible as an "ordinary and necessary" business expense under §162 of the Code. Both conclusions are, in my opinion, unassailable unless the findings of fact on which they rested are to be impeached by us as clearly erroneous. I do not think they can be on this record. . . .

The basic facts, found by the District Court, are as follows. Petitioners, husband and wife, reside in Dallas, Texas, where the home office of the husband's employer, the Southland Life Insurance Company, is located. By having sold a predetermined amount of insurance, the husband qualified to attend the company's convention in New York City in 1956 and, in line with company policy, to bring his wife with him. The petitioners, together with 150 other employees and officers of the insurance company and 141 wives, traveled to and from New York City on special trains, and were housed in a single hotel during their two-and-one-half-day visit. One morning was devoted to a "business meeting" and group luncheon, the rest of the time in New York City to "travel, sightseeing, entertainment, fellowship or free time." The entire trip lasted one week.

The company paid all the expenses of the convention-trip which amounted to $80,000; petitioners' allocable share being $560. When petitioners did not include the latter amount in their joint income tax return, the Commissioner assessed a deficiency which was sustained by the District Court, 189 F.Supp. 2, and also by the Court of Appeals, one judge dissenting, in a per curiam opinion, 291 F.2d 841, citing its recent decision in Patterson v. Thomas, 289 F.2d 108, where the same result had been reached. The District Court held that the value of the trip being "in the nature of a bonus, reward, and compensation for a job well done," was income to Rudolph, but being "primarily a pleasure trip in the nature of a vacation," the costs were personal and nondeductible.

I.

Under §61 of the 1954 Code was the value of the trip to the taxpayer-husband properly includible in gross income? . . .

In light of the sweeping scope of §61 taxing "all gains except those specifically exempted," Commissioner v. Glenshaw Glass Co., 348 U.S. 426, 430; see Commissioner v. LoBue, 351 U.S. 243, 246; James v. United States, 366 U.S. 213, 219, and its purpose to include as taxable income "any economic or financial benefit conferred on the employee as compensation, whatever the form or mode by which it is effected," Commissioner v. Smith, 324 U.S. 177, 181, it seems clear that the District Court's findings, if sustainable, bring the value of the trip within the reach of the statute.

Petitioners do not claim that the value of the trip is within one of the statutory exclusions from "gross income" . . . ; rather they characterize the amount as a "fringe benefit" not specifically excluded from §61 by other sections of the statute, yet not intended to be encompassed by its reach. Conceding that the statutory exclusions from "gross income" are not exhaustive, as the Government seems to recognize is so under *Glenshaw*, it is not now necessary to explore the extent of any such nonstatutory exclusions.* For it was surely within the Commissioner's competence to consider as "gross income" a "reward, or a bonus given to . . . employees for excellence in service," which the District Court found was the employer's primary purpose in arranging this trip. I cannot say that this finding, confirmed as it has been by the Court of Appeals, is inadequately supported by this record.

II.

There remains the question whether, though income, this outlay for transportation, meals, and lodging was deductible by petitioners as an "ordinary and necessary" business expense under §162.[9] The relevant

---

* [This case arose prior to the 1984 enactment of §132 and the corresponding amendment of §61(a)(1) which expressly included "fringe benefits" within compensation for services. See supra Chapter 2B.2 above. — EDS.]

9. . . . No question is raised in this case as to whether the $80,000 paid by the company for the total convention expense is deductible by the corporation.

There is no need to explore the lack of symmetry in certain "income" and "deductibility" areas in the 1954 Code permitting employers to provide certain "fringe benefits" to employees — such as parking facilities, swimming pools, medical services — which have not generally been considered income to the employee, but which, if paid for by the employee with his own funds, would not be a deductible expense. The practicalities of a tax system do not demand hypothetical or theoretical perfection, and these workaday problems are properly the concern of the Commissioner, not of the Courts.

factors on this branch of the case are found in Treas. Reg. §1.162-2. In summary, the regulation in pertinent part provides:

Traveling expenses, including meals, lodgings and other incidentals, reasonable and necessary in the conduct of the taxpayer's business and directly attributable to it are deductible, but expenses of a trip "undertaken for other than business purposes" are "personal expenses" and the meals and lodgings are "living expenses." Treas. Reg. §1.162-2(a).

If a taxpayer who travels to a destination engages in both "business and personal activities," the traveling expenses are deductible only if the trip is "related primarily" to the taxpayer's business; if "primarily personal," the traveling expenses are not deductible even though the taxpayer engages in some business there; yet expenses allocable to the taxpayer's trade or business there are deductible even though the travel expenses to and fro are not. Id., §1.162-2(b)(1).

Whether a trip is related primarily to the taxpayer's business or is primarily personal in nature "depends on the facts and circumstances in each case." Id., §1.162-2(b)(2); so too with expenses paid or incurred in attending a convention. Id., §1.162-2(d).

Finally, the deductibility of the expenses of a taxpayer's wife who accompanies her husband depends, first, on whether his trip is a "business trip." Id., §1.162-2(c); if so, it must further be shown that the wife's presence on the trip also had a bona fide business purpose.*

Whereas here, it may be arguable that the trip was both for business and personal reasons, the crucial question is whether, under all the facts and circumstances of the case, the purpose of the trip was "related primarily to business" or was, rather, "primarily personal in nature." That other trips to other conventions or meetings by other taxpayers were held to be primarily related to business is of no relevance here; that certain doctors, lawyers, clergymen, insurance agents or others have or have not been permitted similar deductions only shows that in the circumstances of those cases, the courts thought that the expenses were or were not deductible as "related primarily to business."

The husband places great emphasis on the fact that he is an entrapped "organization man," required to attend such conventions, and that his future promotions depend on his presence. Suffice it to say that the District Court did not find any element of compulsion; to the contrary, it found that the petitioners regarded the convention in New York City as a pleasure trip in the nature of a vacation. Again, I cannot say that these findings are without adequate evidentiary support. . . .

The trip not having been primarily a business trip, the wife's expenses are not deductible. It is not necessary, therefore, to examine whether they

---

* [This standard for the deductibility of spousal expenses has since been superseded by §274(m)(3). —EDS.]

would or would not be deductible if, to the contrary, the husband's trip was related primarily to business.

Where, as here, two courts below have resolved the determinative factual issues against the taxpayers, according to the rules of law set forth in the statute and regulations, it is not for this Court to re-examine the evidence, and disturb their findings, unless "clearly erroneous." That is not the situation here.

I would affirm.

[Dissenting opinion of Justice Douglas omitted.]

SANITARY FARMS DAIRY, INC.
25 T.C. 463 (1955), acq., 1956-2 C.B. 8

The Commissioner determined a deficiency of $7,304.96 in income tax for 1950 against Sanitary Farms Dairy, Inc., and, for the same year against O. Carlyle Brock and Emily A. Brock, a deficiency of $7,290.72. . . .

FINDINGS OF FACT

Sanitary Farms Dairy, Inc., called herein the Dairy, was organized under the laws of Pennsylvania in 1934. . . .

The outstanding stock of the Dairy at the beginning of 1950 consisted of 5,531 shares, of which O. Carlyle Brock owned 3,608 shares, his wife owned 408 shares, his father and mother owned 460 shares, his son Omar C. Brock, owned 400 shares and his daughter Carolyn owned 400 shares. The remaining 255 shares were owned by 26 employees, none of whom was related to the Brocks. Brock was president, treasurer, and a director of the Dairy. His wife was a director. There were 5 other directors, 2 of whom were also officers but none of whom was related to the Brocks.

Brock was born and raised in Canada where he learned to fish and hunt. He was trained and experienced in the milk business and built up the business of the Dairy to be the largest in Erie. The Dairy purchases milk, processes some of it, and distributes milk and milk products, including butter and ice cream, throughout Erie, Pennsylvania, and the surrounding territory.

Brock began an advertising practice in 1938 of inviting wholesale customers and prospective customers to the plant where he and his wife served them dinners of game which he had shot at various places on the North American continent. Later groups such as associations and clubs were invited. Those dinners became so frequent and so large that Brock sent out other employees of the Dairy to assist in killing game for the purpose of the dinners. Motion pictures taken on the hunts were shown at the dinners. The expenses of the dinners were borne by the Dairy.

Some of the mounted heads and cured skins of the game killed for meat for the dinners were assembled in a room in the plant which gradually became a museum for the display of such trophies. The public was invited to see the museum and the plant. A guide was in attendance. The museum attracted groups from the local schools, clubs, and other organizations to the plant, and the Dairy made use of such visits to bring its products to the attention of the visitors as a part of its method of advertising. Many thousands of people have visited the museum.

The advertising manager of the Dairy called to Brock's attention in 1948 or 1949 the publicity which had been given to an individual from a nearby city who had gone to Africa on a brief big game hunting expedition. Discussions ensued involving the advertising manager, Brock, and others in the employ of the Dairy as well as a representative of an outside advertising agency and the board of directors. The decision was reached that it would be good advertising for the Dairy to send Brock and his wife, both experienced hunters, to Africa on an extended big game hunting expedition on which they would obtain additional specimens for the museum, write letters for publication during the period of the trip, and take motion pictures of the expedition which could later be shown to audiences throughout the area served by the Dairy.

Plans for the trip were made in 1949 and early 1950 and carried out in 1950. Brock and his wife flew to Africa by way of London, Paris, and Rome, stopping briefly and taking motion pictures in each city. They left Erie on May 28 and returned in November. They and the Dairy received considerable publicity when they left and when they returned. They wrote letters and took still and motion pictures during the course of their trip. The letters and still pictures, when received in Erie, were given as much publicity as possible, not only in a publication of the Dairy but also in local newspapers. The Brocks killed in Africa and eventually displayed in the museum many animals, always taking extra time, where necessary, to get the finest specimens available. For example, they refrained from killing any elephants except so-called "hundred pounders," which meant that each tusk of the animal weighed at least 100 pounds. The Dairy gave 2 leopards and a tiger, brought back alive, to the Erie zoo and conducted a "Name-the-Tiger" contest through the Erie newspapers.

Emily edited the films after the completion of the trip, and the Dairy began showing the films in auditoriums throughout the Erie district early in 1951. Brock explained the films as they were shown by Emily. He invited the audience to visit the museum. A showing would last over 2 hours.

Every person in each audience had to have a ticket. Tickets were distributed free by drivers on retail routes to their customers and to others who might be prospective customers. Persons in the vicinity where it was proposed to show the films would be advised by handbills and otherwise that they could obtain free tickets by contacting one of the drivers or by a call to the office of the Dairy, in which latter case the tickets would be delivered by the driver who would make personal contact with the recipient. About 180,000 tickets were distributed, and most of them were used.

The Dairy later prepared and distributed a pamphlet containing pictures and descriptive matter pertaining to the safari. The name of the Dairy was prominent in all publicity obtained as a result of the safari.

The net sales, total advertising expenses and net income reported by the Dairy were approximately as follows:

Year	Net sales	Advertising expenses	Income
1947	$2,112,000	$60,200	$29,600
1948	2,302,800	52,400	56,100
1949	2,470,100	58,000	54,300
1950	2,448,700	69,400	49,100
1951	2,784,400	73,800	35,900
1952	2,886,100	57,600	13,300
1953	2,865,600	61,800	26,000
1954	2,720,300	46,200	38,400

Expenses of the African trip in the amount of $16,818.16 were paid by the Dairy in 1950. The value to the Dairy of the advertising obtained as a result of the trip, the showing of the films and, in later years, the display of the trophies in the museum was far in excess of the entire cost of the expedition.

The Dairy, on its return for 1950, claimed as a part of its advertising expenses $16,818.16 of the amount paid in that year as expenses of the African safari. The Commissioner, in determining the deficiency against the Dairy, disallowed $15,618.16 of the expenses of the safari but allowed $1,200 thereof designated "portion of cost of film deducted." He also "disallowed another item of $375 with respect to which the corporation is taking no issue" and as to which there is no further evidence.

The Commissioner, in determining the deficiency against the Brocks, included in their income the $15,993.16 which he had disallowed as a deduction of the Dairy. $15,618.16 of that amount was not taxable income to the individual taxpayers.

The portion of the cost of the safari paid in 1950 was an ordinary and necessary expense of the Dairy for advertising. . . .

OPINION

MURDOCK, Judge: The cost of a big game hunt in Africa does not sound like an ordinary and necessary expense of a dairy business in Erie, Pennsylvania, but the evidence in this case shows clearly that it was and was so intended. Rodgers Dairy Co., 14 T.C. 66. It provided extremely good advertising at a relatively low cost. The planning of the trip, the departure, news of the progress of the hunt, the return of the hunters, and the presentation and naming of the live animals was reported free by the newspapers as news, to the advantage of the Dairy which was recognized throughout as the sponsor. An advertising agent expressed it as follows:

> To a newspaper looking for copy, a big game hunter would get top billing. It appeals to the imagination. There is a little bit of the hunter in all of us, a little of the adventurer, I should say, a little hunting for adventure. When that big game hunter is a prominent member of the newspaper's community, taking a very active and prominent part in the business, civic, fraternal life of the community, then his desirability as copy has increased considerably. It is my opinion that Mr. and Mrs. Brock fill that requirement admirably.

The films were exploited successfully by the Dairy. Credit was given to it at each showing. "The people were invited and greeted as customers and friends of the Dairy. The film was presented to them as a dividend for their good will and their patronage. The Brocks [there in person] were presented as executive officers of the Dairy." "Any facility that can hold the attention of an audience for an hour and a half, to two hours, sometimes three, and impress them favorably [with] the product and the makers of that product, is a highly valuable advertising property." The quotes are from the testimony of the advertising agent who favored the trip and introduced the Brocks at the showing of the films. The trophies came into the museum in later years, because it took time to process, ship, and mount them, but when they arrived they too provided good advertising for the Dairy. Costs incident to the preparation, shipping, and mounting of the trophies were paid in later years and are not involved herein.

The evidence shows that advertising of equal value to that here involved could not have been obtained for the same amount of money in any more normal way. The Commissioner allowed $1,200 of the safari expense of 1950 and does not seek to have that changed but contends, as an alternative to complete disallowance, that the remainder of the 1950 expenditures, if legitimate advertising expense, should be spread over later years. There is no pleading to support any amortizing of the amount. Advertising expense is normally deductible in the year paid or accrued. . . . The portion of the cost of the safari accrued and paid in 1950 was deductible in whole in that year as a relatively small part of the advertising program carried on by the Dairy.

No part of that cost is taxable to the Brocks as personal travel and pleasure expense of theirs. They admittedly enjoyed hunting, but enjoyment of one's work does not make that work a mere personal hobby or the cost of a hunting trip income to the hunter. There is evidence that this trip represented hard work on the part of the Brocks, undertaken for the benefit of the Dairy, rather than as frolic of their own. . . .

Decisions will be entered under Rule 50.

Question

In *Sanitary Farms Dairy*, deficiencies were asserted both against the corporation and against the Brocks individually. Is that "double taxation" of the travel benefit justified?

What if the Brocks had not been shareholders of the Dairy but the facts were otherwise the same? Against whom should the IRS then assert a deficiency? (On review, consider the effect of §274(e)(2), which we take up below.)

MOSS v. COMMISSIONER
758 F.2d 211 (7th Cir. 1985)

Before Cummings, Chief Judge, Bauer and Posner, Circuit Judges.

Posner, Circuit Judge, delivered the opinion of the court. The taxpayers, a lawyer named Moss and his wife, appeal from a decision of the Tax Court disallowing federal income tax deductions of a little more than $1,000 in each of two years, representing Moss's share of his law firm's lunch expense at the Cafe Angelo in Chicago. The Tax Court's decision in this case has attracted some attention in tax circles because of its implications for the general problem of the deductibility of business meals. See, e.g., McNally, Vulnerability of Entertainment and Meal Deductions Under the Sutter Rule, 62 Taxes 184 (1984).

Moss was a partner in a small trial firm specializing in defense work, mostly for one insurance company. Each of the firm's lawyers carried a tremendous litigation caseload, averaging more than 300 cases, and spent most of every working day in courts in Chicago and its suburbs. The members of the firm met for lunch daily at the Cafe Angelo near their office. At lunch the lawyers would discuss their cases with the head of the firm, whose approval was required for most settlements, and they would decide which lawyer would meet which court call that afternoon or the next morning. Lunchtime was chosen for the daily meeting because the courts were in recess then. The alternatives were to meet at 7:00 a.m. or 6:00 p.m., and these were less convenient times. There is no suggestion that the lawyers dawdled over lunch, or that the Cafe Angelo is luxurious.

The framework of statutes and regulations for deciding this case is simple, but not clear. . . .

The problem is that many expenses are simultaneously business expenses in the sense that they conduce to the production of business income and personal expenses in the sense that they raise personal welfare. This is plain enough with regard to lunch; most people would eat lunch even if they didn't work. Commuting may seem a pure business expense, but is not; it reflects the choice of where to live, as well as where to work. Read literally, section 262 would make irrelevant whether a business expense is also a personal expense*; so long as it is ordinary and necessary in the taxpayer's business, thus bringing section 162(a) into play, an expense is (the statute seems to say) deductible from his income tax. But the statute has not been read literally. There is a natural reluctance, most clearly manifested in the regulation disallowing deduction of the expense of commuting, to lighten the tax burden of people who have the good fortune to interweave work with consumption. To allow a deduction for commuting would confer a windfall on people who live in the suburbs and commute to work in the cities; to allow a deduction for all business-related meals would confer a windfall on people who can arrange their work schedules so they do some of their work at lunch.

Although an argument can thus be made for disallowing any deduction for business meals, on the theory that people have to eat whether they work or not, the result would be excessive taxation of people who spend more money on business meals because they are business meals than they would spend on their meals if they were not working. Suppose a theatrical agent takes his clients out to lunch at the expensive restaurants that the clients demand. Of course he can deduct the expense of their meals, from which he derives no pleasure or sustenance, but can he also deduct the expense of his own? He can, because he cannot eat more cheaply; he cannot munch surreptitiously on a peanut butter and jelly sandwich brought from home while his client is wolfing down tournedos Rossini followed by souffle au grand marnier. No doubt our theatrical agent, unless concerned for his longevity, derives personal utility from his fancy meal, but probably less than the price of the meal. He would not pay for it if it were not for the business benefit; he would get more value from using the same money to buy something else; hence the meal confers on him less utility than the cash equivalent would. The law could require him to pay tax on the fair value of the meal to him; this would be (were it not for costs of administration) the economically correct solution. But the government does not attempt this difficult measurement; it once did, but gave up the attempt as not worth the cost, see United States v. Correll, supra, 389 U.S. at 301 n.6. The taxpayer is permitted to deduct the whole price, provided the expense is "different from or in excess of that which would have been made for the taxpayer's personal purposes." Sutter v. Commissioner, 21 T.C. 170, 173 (1953).

Because the law allows this generous deduction, which tempts people to have more (and costlier) business meals than are necessary, the Internal Revenue Service has every right to insist that the meal be shown to be a

---

   * [Judge Posner is apparently referring to the introductory clause of §262(a), which seems to limit disallowance to circumstances that don't satisfy statutory deduction criteria: "Except as otherwise expressly provided in this chapter, no deduction shall be allowed for personal, living, or family expenses." The introductory clause has never been read that way, presumably because that approach would deprive §262 of independent force, interpreting it as merely a limited codification of the long-settled doctrine that a deduction is allowed only if authorized by statute. To avoid that result while still giving effect to the introductory clause, much depends on the meaning of "expressly provided." —Eds.]

real business necessity. This condition is most easily satisfied when a client or customer or supplier or other outsider to the business is a guest. Even if Sydney Smith was wrong that "soup and fish explain half the emotions of life," it is undeniable that eating together fosters camaraderie and makes business dealings friendlier and easier. It thus reduces the costs of transacting business, for these costs include the frictions and the failures of communication that are produced by suspicion and mutual misunderstanding, by differences in tastes and manners, and by lack of rapport. A meeting with a client or customer in an office is therefore not a perfect substitute for a lunch with him in a restaurant. But it is different when all the participants in the meal are coworkers, as essentially was the case here (clients occasionally were invited to the firm's daily luncheon, but Moss has made no attempt to identify the occasions). They know each other well already; they don't need the social lubrication that a meal with an outsider provides — at least don't need it daily. If a large firm had a monthly lunch to allow partners to get to know associates, the expense of the meal might well be necessary, and would be allowed by the Internal Revenue Service. See Wells v. Commissioner, 36 T.C.M. 1698, 1699 (1977), aff'd without opinion, 626 F.2d 868 (9th Cir. 1980). But Moss's firm never had more than eight lawyers (partners and associates), and did not need a daily lunch to cement relationships among them.

It is all a matter of degree and circumstance (the expense of a testimonial dinner, for example, would be deductible on a morale-building rationale); and particularly of frequency. Daily — for a full year — is too often, perhaps even for entertainment of clients, as implied by Hankenson v. Commissioner, 47 T.C.M. 1567, 1569 (1984), where the Tax Court held nondeductible the cost of lunches consumed three or four days a week, 52 weeks a year, by a doctor who entertained other doctors who he hoped would refer patients to him, and other medical personnel.

We may assume it was necessary for Moss's firm to meet daily to coordinate the work of the firm, and also, as the Tax Court found, that lunch was the most convenient time. But it does not follow that the expense of the lunch was a necessary business expense. The members of the firm had to eat somewhere, and the Cafe Angelo was both convenient and not too expensive. They do not claim to have incurred a greater daily lunch expense than they would have incurred if there had been no lunch meetings. Although it saved time to combine lunch with work, the meal itself was not an organic part of the meeting, as in the examples we gave earlier where the business objective, to be fully achieved, required sharing a meal.

The case might be different if the location of the courts required the firm's members to eat each day either in a disagreeable restaurant, so that they derived less value from the meal than it cost them to buy it, cf. Sibla v. Commissioner [Chapter 2B.1 above]; or in a restaurant too expensive for their personal tastes, so that, again, they would have gotten less value than the cash equivalent. But so far as appears, they picked the restaurant they liked most. Although it must be pretty monotonous to eat lunch the same place every working day of the year, not all the lawyers attended all the lunch meetings and there was nothing to stop the firm from meeting occasionally at another restaurant proximate to their office in downtown Chicago; there are hundreds.

An argument can be made that the price of lunch at the Cafe Angelo included rental of the space that the lawyers used for what was a meeting as well as a meal. There was evidence that the firm's conference room was otherwise occupied throughout the working day, so as a matter of logic Moss might be able to claim a part of the price of lunch as an ordinary and necessary expense for work space. But this is cutting things awfully fine; in any event Moss made no effort to apportion his lunch expense in this way.

Affirmed.

Notes and Questions

1. Moss likened his situation to Sibla v. Commissioner, 611 F.2d 1260 (9th Cir. 1980), Chapter 2B.1 above, the case of the Los Angeles firemen who were required to contribute to a communal meal fund each day they were on duty, regardless of whether or how much they ate. *Sibla* held payments to the common mess either deductible under §162 or excludible under §119, emphasizing that restrictions imposed by the employer's requirements limited the benefit to the employee. The Tax Court responded at length to this argument.

> Petitioner relies on this notion of restriction in contending that the cost of the lunches, like the cost of the firehouse mess in *Sibla* and *Cooper*, should be deductible. He argues that the attorneys "considered the luncheon meetings as a part of their regular work day," and that the firm incurred the expense "solely for the benefit of its practice and not for the personal convenience of its attorneys."
>
> Petitioner has not explained, however, how this "restriction" is any different than that imposed on an attorney who must spend his lunch hour boning up on the Rules of Civil Procedure in preparation for trial or reading an evidence book to clarify a point that may arise during an afternoon session. In all these cases, the lawyer spends an extra hour at work. The mere fact that this time is given over the noon hour does not convert the cost of daily meals into a business expense to be shared by the Government.

80 T.C. 1073, 1079-80 (1983). Moreover, discussing business over lunch "does not make his lunch deductible any more than riding to work together each morning to discuss partnership affairs would make his share of the commuting costs deductible." Id. at 1081. Could nondeductibility of the meal expenses in *Moss* be predicated on the language of §162, without regard to §262?

2. It was reported in the press sometime after this decision that Moss's law firm installed a lunchroom inside its own offices and hired the chef from Cafe Angelo to run it. How should that be treated for income tax purposes?

3. Are you convinced by Judge Posner's assertion that the theatrical agent will find the fancy restaurant meal worth less than its price? How about his clients? If the personal utility derived from the meal is less than its price all around, why don't agent and clients seek (and the market provide) a more modest place to dine? Of course, under present tax rules (and even more under pre-1986 rates) the fancy business meal *costs* less than its *price* by the amount of the tax saving, but it would be circular to justify the deduction by reference to that.

COHAN v. COMMISSIONER
39 F.2d 540 (2d Cir. 1930)

Before L. Hand, Swan, and Mack, Circuit Judges.

L. HAND, Circuit Judge. . . . In the production of his plays Cohan was obliged to be free-handed in entertaining actors, employees, and, as he naively adds, dramatic critics. He had also to travel much, at times with his attorney. These expenses amounted to substantial sums, but he kept no account and probably could not have done so. At the trial before the Board he estimated that he had spent eleven thousand dollars in this fashion during the first six months of 1921, twenty-two thousand dollars, between July first, 1921, and June thirtieth, 1922, and as much for his following fiscal year, fifty-five thousand dollars in all. The Board refused to allow him any part of this, on the ground that it was impossible to tell how much he had in fact spent, in the absence of any items or details. The question is how far this refusal is justified, in view of the finding that he had spent much and that the sums were allowable expenses. Absolute certainty in such matters is usually impossible and is not necessary; the Board should make as close an approximation as it can, bearing heavily if it chooses upon the taxpayer whose inexactitude is of his own making. But to allow nothing at all appears to us inconsistent with saying that something was spent. True, we do not know how many trips Cohan made, nor how large his entertainments were; yet there was obviously some basis for computation, if necessary by drawing upon the Board's personal estimates of the minimum of such expenses. The amount may be trivial and unsatisfactory, but there was basis for some allowance, and it was wrong to refuse any, even though it were the traveling expenses of a single trip. It is not fatal that the result will inevitably be speculative; many important decisions must be such. We think that the Board was in error as to this and must reconsider the evidence. . . .

1. The 1962 Legislation

In 1961, President Kennedy called for a broad rewriting of the law governing travel and entertainment expenses. The theory of the legislative request was that entertainment was essentially personal, and that deductions for entertainment should be disallowed in full because of the personal consumption elements involved, whether or not a business purpose was also served. Expenses for entertainment facilities would have likewise been disallowed, with narrow exceptions, and business travel expenses would have been subjected to ceilings on meals and lodging (at 200 percent of the federal government per diem rate for the place involved) and proration of transportation expense whenever a vacation and business trip were combined.

In support of the proposal, the government presented extensive evidence of abuses and of administrative difficulties in dealing with them under existing law. *Sanitary Farms* was cited: "... when judicial decisions permit the cost of a safari to Africa undertaken by a hunting enthusiast and his wife to be deducted as an expense for advertising dairy milk, one cannot expect revenue agents to question successfully the business necessity for duck hunting or nightclubbing with business associates." Hearings on Tax Revision Before the House Committee on Ways and Means, 87th Cong., at 43 (1961).

As not infrequently happens, Congress responded by trying to curb abuses without much changing the underlying rules. The compromise is in §274. Entertainment is not generally disallowed, but subjected to limitations expressed in a kind of code language distinguishing between items that are "directly related to" and only "associated with" the conduct of business. §274(a)(1). Section 274(d) generally requires more substantiation than did the *Cohan* rule.

Section 274(a) imposes a set of objective disallowance rules. In situations involving mixed business and pleasure, Congress considered the primary purpose test too lax. See *Rudolph*, p. 668 above. Instead of looking to the taxpayer's subjective motivation, these rules apply to any activity "which is of a type *generally considered to constitute* entertainment, amusement, or recreation" (emphasis added). The restrictions on deductibility apply even if the taxpayer's motivations are entirely mercenary, and even in the face of convincing proof that the taxpayer's participation in some event (attending the opera, for example) was pure drudgery or personally distasteful.

Once triggered by objective (conventional) standards, three general rules apply to entertainment-related deductions. With respect to activities, items that are "*directly related* to ... the *active* conduct of the taxpayer's trade or business" remain deductible. This test was intended to bar deduction of amounts spent solely for business promotion, customer relations, or to develop a favorable reputation — generally, to maintain or improve goodwill. Berkley Machine Works & Foundry Co. v. Commissioner, 623 F.2d 898, 902 (4th Cir.), cert. denied, 449 U.S. 919 (1980). The expectancy of increased patronage (or reduced expenses) at some indefinite future time contributes to business success, but it does not do so directly or immediately.

In contrast, an expenditure *is* "directly related to . . . the active conduct" of business if it relates to a meeting, discussion or negotiation at which some specific deal or business transaction is discussed. See Reg. §1.274-2(c)(3); *Berkley Machine Works*, 623 F.2d at 903-905.

While marking entertainment aimed at producing goodwill as suspect, Congress wasn't willing to entirely rule out deductions for schmoozing with existing or potential customers, suppliers or clients. (Why not?) Amounts spent entertaining individuals with whom one is currently conducting business are considered "associated with" the active conduct of business and are deductible provided that the entertainment occurs "directly preceding or following a substantial and bona fide business discussion." So, if the entertainment occurs near in time to the active conduct of business, the cost of taking a customer to a ball game or the ballet can be deducted even if you don't talk business during the event. The IRS applies the temporal standard, "directly preceding or following" a substantial business discussion, quite liberally, interpreting it to mean, in general, the same day, and in some circumstances the day before or the day after. Reg. §1.274-2(c)(3)(ii).

Finally, deductions related to entertainment facilities are barred. Entertainment facilities include yachts, hunting lodges, swimming pools, and tennis courts. This rule disallows items such as depreciation, maintenance, utilities, and other operating costs of property owned by the taxpayer (Congress had in mind corporate-owned yachts and hunting lodges), as well as rent charges for the use of entertainment facilities owned by someone else. Membership dues to country clubs and other social, recreational, or athletic organizations are also within the prohibition. §274(a)(1)(B), (a)(2)(A), (a)(3).[1] Expenses relating to eating and recreational facilities for employees, such as a company cafeteria or gym, may be deducted if the facilities satisfy certain conditions. §274(e)(1), (4).

Notes and Questions

1. *Activity or facility?* Is the cost of box seats at the stadium or the opera house the rental of space (a facility charge) or the purchase of entertainment (an activity)? (Compare Judge Posner's suggestion in *Moss*, p. 679 above.) Apparently the activity rules apply to the full cost of attending public entertainment events. However, a special rule provides that the amount deductible for an entertainment event is limited to the face value of the ticket, and if a private luxury box is leased for more than one event, the maximum deduction is pegged to the cost of a regular box seat. §274(*l*).

---

1. As enacted in 1962, §274(a)(1)(B) allowed some costs related to entertainment facilities to be deducted if very stringent conditions were met. Amendments in 1978 disallowed items related to owned and most rented facilities, but continued a narrow exception for clubs. Further amendments in 1993 seem to have closed the door on the deduction of costs related to clubs, but a vestige of the prior rule survives in §274(a)(2)(C), which Congress failed to repeal. See Reg. §1.274-2(e).

2. *Scope of disallowance.* The activity rules appear to permit a deduction only if the entertainment has a proximate connection to the active conduct of a trade or business. Is any deduction available if following an afternoon meeting you take your financial planner or stock broker to a ball game? Entertainment having a sufficient nexus with investment activities can also support a deduction, §274(a)(2)(B), but the deduction remains subject to the 2 percent floor on miscellaneous itemized deductions, §67. If the taxpayer sometimes uses her second home located in a seaside resort area for weekend retreats with important customers, will the facility rule cause her to forfeit part of her mortgage interest and real property tax deductions? Consult §274(f).

3. *Substantiation.* Section 274(d), which demands more specificity than the sort of rough and ready approximation accepted under the *Cohan* rule, is no doubt the government's most important defense against abusive business expense deductions. In addition to entertainment-related expenses, the substantiation rules also apply to travel expenses, business gifts, and listed property (including automobiles, computer equipment, cell phones, and other items that, because they are commonly used in both business and personal activities, are subject to special restrictions on depreciation). Notwithstanding popular notions to the contrary, adequate substantiation does not always require written records much less receipts. Generally, sufficient evidence corroborating the taxpayer's own statement will suffice, but since 1998 the IRS has by regulation insisted on documentary evidence to support deductions for lodging while traveling away from home, and for other expenditures of $75 or more. Reg. §1.274-5(c)(2)(iii). On the other hand, the Treasury is authorized to relax substantiation requirements in appropriate circumstances, §274(d) (penultimate sentence), and has issued regulations doing so. Per diem allowances may be accepted in lieu of evidence of the amount actually expended for meal and incidental expenses while traveling away from home and a standard mileage rate can substitute for the actual cost of business use of automobiles. Absent such dispensation, however, the taxpayer must adequately substantiate *each* element that §274(d) requires in support the deduction claim. *Berkley Machine Works*, 623 F.2d at 906-907 (entertainment deduction denied where taxpayer established amount, time, and place of entertainment, but failed to adequately support business purpose or business relationship of individuals entertained; identification of only the company whose employees were entertained insufficient to show business relationship).

4. *Foreign travel.* Section 274(c) provides that the costs of travel outside the United States may be partially disallowed if the trip is undertaken for both business and personal reasons (tacking a week of sightseeing and vacation onto a 10-day business trip to China, for example). The rule does not apply if the overall trip lasts less than one week or the time devoted to personal pursuits is less than 25 percent of the total. The regulations provide rules for counting days as either business or personal, addressing such issues

as travel days, weekends, or holidays that intervene between required business meetings, and partial work days. Treas. Reg. §1.274-4(d).

5. *Foreign conventions.* Section 274(h)(1) has additional special requirements to justify deductions for foreign conventions. These rules might entirely disallow meeting-related travel expenses that survive foreign travel business allocation under §274(c). Do these make sense? If the American Bar Association holds part of its annual meeting in London, would travel to that meeting qualify under §274(h)? How about Australia? What if an association of ski instructors held its annual convention in Hawaii?

6. *Allocation or apportionment?* The costs of combined business and pleasure are either deductible in full or entirely disallowed under the primary purpose test of §162. See *Rudolph*, p. 668 above. If the expense relates to an entertainment activity, §274(a) imposes more stringent and objective requirements for deductibility, but still the item is ordinarily deductible in full or not at all. What explains this all-or-nothing approach, allocating individual expenditures between allowed and disallowed categories? Wouldn't we come closer to an accurate measure of individual enrichment by treating a mixed or dual-benefit expenditure as a deductible business expense to the extent that the cost of the item exceeds the expected value of its personal consumption benefits? Why not apportionment rather than allocation? Note that the foreign travel rule, §274(c), may treat a single item, such as the cost of a round-trip airline ticket to Europe, as nondeductible in part. Why is apportionment applied here and not more generally? Also consult the last sentence of §274(a)(1), which purports to mandate apportionment but rarely applies in practice.

2. The 1986 Legislation

PERCENTAGE REDUCTION FOR MEALS & ENTERTAINMENT

Staff of Joint Comm. on Taxation, 100th Cong., General Explanation of the Tax Reform Act of 1986, 60-61, 63-65 (1987) (Comm. Print 1987)

REASONS FOR CHANGE

Since the 1960s the Congress has sought to address various aspects of deductions for meals, entertainment, and travel expenses that the Congress and the public have viewed as unfairly benefiting those taxpayers who were able to take advantage of the tax benefit of deductibility. In his 1961 Tax Message, President Kennedy reported that "too many firms and individuals have devised means of deducting too many personal living expenses as business expenses, thereby charging a large part of their cost to the Federal Government." He stated: "This is a matter of national concern, affecting not only our public revenues, our sense of fairness, and our respect for the tax system, but our moral and business practices as well."

After careful review during consideration of the Act, the Congress concluded that these concerns were not addressed adequately by prior law. In general, prior law required some heightened showing of a business purpose for travel and entertainment costs, as well as stricter substantiation requirements than those applying generally to all business deductions; this approach is retained under the Act. However, the prior-law approach failed to address a basic issue inherent in allowing deductions for many travel and entertainment expenditures — the fact that, even if reported accurately and having some connection with the taxpayer's business, such expenditures also convey substantial personal benefits to the recipients.

The Congress believed that prior law, by not focusing sufficiently on the personal-consumption element of deductible meal and entertainment expenses, unfairly permitted taxpayers who could arrange business settings for personal consumption to receive, in effect, a Federal tax subsidy for such consumption that was not available to other taxpayers. The taxpayers who benefit from deductibility tend to have relatively high incomes, and in some cases the consumption may bear only a loose relationship to business necessity. For example, when executives have dinner at an expensive restaurant following business discussions and then deduct the cost of the meal, the fact that there may be some bona fide business connection does not alter the imbalance between the treatment of those persons, who have effectively transferred a portion of the cost of their meal to the Federal Government, and other individuals, who cannot deduct the cost of their meals.

The significance of this imbalance is heightened by the fact that business travel and entertainment often may be more lavish than comparable activities in a nonbusiness setting. For example, meals at expensive restaurants and the most desirable tickets at sports events and the theatre are purchased to a significant degree by taxpayers who claim business deductions for these expenses. This disparity is highly visible, and has contributed to public perceptions that the tax system under prior law was unfair. Polls indicated that the public identified the full deductibility of normal personal expenses such as meals and entertainment tickets to be one of the most significant elements of disrespect for and dissatisfaction with the tax system.

In light of these considerations, the Act generally reduces to 80 percent [reduced to 50 percent in 1993] the amount of otherwise allowable deductions for business meals, including meals while on a business trip away from home, meals furnished on an employer's premises to its employees, and meal expense at a business luncheon club or a convention, and business entertainment expenses, including sports and theatre tickets and club dues. This reduction rule reflects the fact that all meals and entertainment inherently involve an element of personal living expenses, but still allows [a 50] percent deduction where such expenses also have an identifiable business relationship. The Act also tightens the requirements for establishing a bona fide business reason for claiming food and beverage expenses as deductions. The Act includes specified exceptions to the general percentage reduction rule.

In certain respects, more liberal deduction rules were provided under prior law with respect to business meals than other entertainment expenses, both as to the underlying legal requirements for deductibility and as to substantiation requirements. The Congress concluded that more uniform deduction rules should apply; thus, deductions for meals are subject to the same business-connection requirement as applies for deducting other entertainment expenses.

EXPLANATION OF PROVISIONS

Under the Act, any amount otherwise allowable as a deduction under chapter 1 of the Code for any expenses for food or beverages, or for any item with respect to an entertainment, amusement, or recreation activity or facility used in connection with such activity, is reduced by [50] percent (new Code sec. 274(n)). Thus, if a taxpayer spends $100 for a business meal or an entertainment expense that, but for this rule, would be fully deductible, the amount of the allowable deduction is $[50].

This reduction rule applies, for example, to food or beverage costs incurred in the course of travel away from home (whether eating alone or with others), in entertaining business customers at the taxpayer's place of business or a restaurant, or in attending a business convention or reception, business meeting, or business luncheon at a luncheon club. Similarly, the cost of a meal furnished by an employer to employees on the employer's premises is subject to the reduction rule, whether or not the value of the meal is excludable from the employee's gross income under section 119. . . . However, as discussed below, the Act provides certain exceptions to the percentage reduction rule.

In determining the amount of any otherwise allowable deduction that is subject to reduction under this rule, expenses for taxes and tips relating to a meal or entertainment activity are included. For example, in the case of a business meal for which the taxpayer pays $50, plus $4 in tax and $10 in tips, the amount of the deduction cannot exceed $[32] ([50] percent of $64). Expenses such as cover charges for admission to a nightclub, the amount paid for a room which the taxpayer rents for a dinner or cocktail party, or the amount paid for parking at a sports arena in order to attend an entertainment event there, likewise are deductible (if otherwise allowable) only to the extent of [50] percent under the rule. However, an otherwise allowable deduction for the cost of transportation to and from a business meal (e.g., cab fare to a restaurant) is not reduced pursuant to the rule.

The percentage reduction rule is applied only after determining the amount of the otherwise allowable deduction under section 162 (or section

212) and under other provisions of section 274. Meal and entertainment expenses first are limited to the extent (if any) required pursuant to other applicable rules set forth in section 162, 212, or section 274, and then are reduced by [50] percent.

For example, if a meal costs $100, but, under section 162(a)(2) or new section 274(k)(1), $40 of that amount is disallowed as lavish and extravagant, then the remaining $60 is reduced by [50] percent, leaving a deduction of $[30]. Similarly, when a taxpayer buys a ticket to an entertainment event for more than the ticket's face value, the deduction cannot exceed [50] percent of the face value of the ticket.

Following application of the percentage reduction rules as described above, the deductibility of an expense next is subject to the new two-percent floor under the total of unreimbursed employee business expenses and other miscellaneous itemized deductions, if applicable to such expense, and then to any deduction limitation that is specifically expressed in dollars. . . .

The effect of the percentage reduction rule cannot be avoided by reason of the absence of separate charges for, payments for, or allocations as between meal and entertainment expenses subject to the rule, and business expenses that are deductible in full. For example, assume that a hotel charges $200 per night for a room, that it provides dinner and breakfast free of any separately stated charge, and that the amount properly allocable to the meals (or the right to the meals) is $50 of the taxpayer's $200 payment to the hotel; assuming all other requirements for a business deduction are met, only $[175] ($150 for the room, plus 50 percent of the $50 allocable to the meals) is deductible. Similarly, if a business provides its employees with a fixed per diem amount to cover lodging and meal expenses incurred in business travel, an allocation on a reasonable basis must be made between the meal expenses and the lodging or other expenses, and the percentage reduction rule applies to the amount so allocated to meal expenses. . . .

Note

The limitation in §67 is called a *floor*. Some floors are stated in dollar amounts; more are percentages of adjusted gross income. Amounts that fall below a floor are wholly disallowed.

Limitations of the sort in §274(j)(2) are often called *ceilings*. Amounts expended above a ceiling are wholly disallowed (although sometimes with a carryover to other years). See, e.g., §170(b) (and (d)).

The limitation in §274(n) is neither a floor nor a ceiling. What is it?

In its first attempt to reflect the consumption component of business meals, the Treasury imposed a floor. See United States v. Correll, Chapter 12C.1 above, note 6. Is §274(n) superior? Could we do better?

E.   ACTIVITIES NOT FOR PROFIT (HOBBIES)

In the foregoing cases there was a trade or business; the problem was one of allocation of multipurpose costs between that activity and the personal pursuits of the taxpayer. Sometimes the issue is whether there is any business to be connected to. Or stated differently, the taxpayer's claim is that the activity producing the disputed deductions is itself a trade or business.

BESSENYEY v. COMMISSIONER
379 F.2d 252 (2d Cir.), cert. denied, 389 U.S. 931 (1967)

Before Watermann, Friendly and Anderson, Circuit Judges.

FRIENDLY, Circuit Judge: Mrs. Margit Sigray Bessenyey seeks review of a decision of the Tax Court, 45 T.C. 261 (1965), insofar as it denied the deduction of losses[1] incurred in the tax years 1955-1959 in the breeding and raising of horses.[2] The facts are quite fully stated in Judge Raum's opinion and a summary will suffice to expose the issue.

Mrs. Bessenyey, a woman in her fifties, resides in New York City. She is the daughter of a Hungarian count and his American wife and the granddaughter of Marcus Daly, the "copper king" of Montana. She was born and raised on her father's large Hungarian estate, a family farm devoted to forestry production and crop and livestock cultivation. The latter included horse breeding and training — heavy horses for agricultural work, and riding and carriage horses, known as Hungarians or Hungarian Half-Breds, primarily for use on the estate but also occasionally for sale. Under her father's guidance she obtained substantial knowledge of this subject and from about 1930 to 1946 had principal responsibility for the breeding and training of the Hungarian Half-Breds. After the end of World War II the family emigrated to the United States.

---

1. The relevant provisions are I.R.C. §§162, 165 and 212.
2. The deductions were:

1955	$6,028
1956	9,142
1957	18,162
1958	35,393
1959	56,231

In later returns the taxpayer claimed similar deductions as follows:

1960	$64,133
1961	75,550
1962	63,708

Some time thereafter Mrs. Bessenyey learned that the Army had brought some Hungarian Half-Breds back to this country and placed them in the Remount Service of the Cavalry and, later, in 1948, that the horses were to be sold. Thinking it would be a pity if these good blood lines were "to get scattered amongst people who did not know what they were" and hoping "in the future to be able to breed them and continue," she decided to buy some. Since illness prevented her attending the sale, she commissioned a Hungarian veterinarian who had formerly worked for the Hungarian Department of Agriculture in connection with the state farms which raised these horses to purchase mares with "the best blood lines" for her; he bought nine brood mares for about $150 each. She first had the horses sent to a ranch in Montana which had been owned by Marcus Daly, and had passed to his descendants. Then, hearing that the horses were not receiving proper care, Mrs. Bessenyey journeyed to Montana, placed them at an adjacent family property known as the Montana Farm, and returned to New York because of her illness and that of her parents.

No breeding was done until 1954 when Mrs. Bessenyey leased a Hungarian stallion, Hompolgar IV, also known as Humphrey, who had been brought from Europe by the Army and later sold. As the result of his service, both immediate and mediate, the initial herd increased to 31 by 1959. Prior to 1955 Mrs. Bessenyey had purchased a 510-acre farm in Charles County, Maryland, because of uncertainty whether her relations with the other Daly heirs would permit continued maintenance of the horses at the Montana Farm. Although she acquired the full interest in both the Montana Farm and the adjacent ranch in 1962, she has kept the Maryland Farm and used it for the boarding and training of some of the horses especially during months when the cold Montana winter impedes training there. Since 1955 she has spent between five and six months of each year at the Montana Farm, living in what had formerly been the chauffeur's cottage and devoting most of her time to the horses; during the rest of the year she has spent considerable time visiting her trainers, comparing notes with other horse breeders, viewing competitions and shows, and attending horse management courses.

Total expenses of the Montana Farm rose from $2,546 in 1955 to $46,037 in 1959, and of the Maryland Farm from $3,482 to $10,195. Combined income during the tax years here in question ranged from a low of $683 in 1958 for tobacco sales from the Maryland Farm to a high of $4,034 the following year for tobacco and hay sales from the Maryland Farm and Agricultural Program Payments to the Montana Farm. Mrs. Bessenyey has sold only one Hungarian, a seven year old gelding for $3,000 in 1964. Successful sales depend in some measure on the establishment of a registry for Hungarians in the United States. Before doing this it would be preferable to await the existence of 100 brood mares, whereas in 1964 Mrs. Bessenyey had only 28 mares and fillies and the only other breeder, a Mrs. Gyurky, had 12.

As this recital of her expenses and losses makes evident, Mrs. Bessenyey is a woman of independent means. For example, in 1956 she received $129,587 in dividends and $18,743 in tax exempt income; the corresponding figures for 1959 were $139,504 and $10,417. In 1962 she made sales of securities, evidently in anticipation of that year's stock market drop which produced capital gains of $1,844,102, and contributed securities with a fair market value of $2,959,401 to a wholly owned corporation that had become sole owner of the Montana ranch.

Mrs. Bessenyey testified that the expectation of selling the horses at a good price was on her mind before 1955, when she began to devote full attention to their breeding and training. She later discovered that until the breed had acquired public acceptance, she would have to sell the horses as trained animals. Thus she began to incur heavy expenses for training and exhibiting her geldings. In a protest filed in September, 1961, she estimated that sales would first produce a profit in 1970, that by 1975 she would have an annual income of $25,000, and that by that time her herd would be worth at least $254,000 — slightly less than the expenses incurred for the four years, 1959-1962. This projection, though was based on the assumption that by 1970 training needs would be diminished so that annual expenses could be reduced from the 1959-1962 average of about $65,000 to $36,420, an assumption which the Tax Court regarded with a "dim view" and did not deem to be sincerely entertained.

Judge Raum began his discussion by stating that "Under any of the possibly pertinent provisions of the 1954 Code, it is necessary that the operation be conducted for the purpose of making a profit" if a deduction was to be allowed. While such a purpose may exist even in the face of a history of unrelieved losses, such losses and the likelihood of achieving a profitable operation have an important "bearing on the taxpayer's true intention." He found that "although petitioner's horse enterprise has some of the trappings of a business, . . . she did not in fact have a bona fide intention to conduct her activities for a profit" and that her rewards from her work with the horses and the expenditures upon them "consisted of personal satisfaction in the activity." He based this conclusion in part on "the impression from observation of her during his testimony that figures and financial matters even bored her," an attitude which led him to believe "that she gave little or no thought to whether her horse enterprise would ever be profitable, or whether the large losses that were being sustained annually would ever be recouped."

The exceedingly able argument of taxpayer's counsel challenged the Tax Court's conclusion on many fronts. He stressed such undisputed facts as Mrs. Bessenyey's expert qualifications in the breeding and training of Hungarian horses, the time and effort devoted to the task, the practical and nonrecreational character of her farms, the keeping of detailed accounts, the rapid development of the light horse industry in America, and the Spartan conditions of her life in Montana. He cited her testimony that although she knew it would be expensive to build up the herd, she expected to end with a new and different luxury item for which rich people would pay well, and that she would not continue the operation if she would never make a profit but "that is not going to occur because I have a good product" — a view confirmed by an expert witness. He discounted the conclusions the judge drew from observations of Mrs. Bessenyey as having stemmed from a belief, erroneous although not unnatural in one whose daily concern is with figures, that a taxpayer who relies on books and accountants for detailed information thereby displays a lack of profit motive. He pointed to the large amount of the losses in relation to Mrs. Bessenyey's investment income, e.g., $56,231 of losses for 1959 as compared with $139,504 in dividends and $10,417 in tax exempt income — rather a high proportion for a hobby, even though the same year produced capital gains of $73,531. He further argued that the large losses taken as deductions are attributable in part to the liberality of the Internal Revenue Service in ruling that "A farmer who operates a farm for profit is entitled to deduct from gross income as necessary expenses all amounts actually expended in the carrying on of the business of farming," Reg. §1.162-12, such expenses including many amounts, e.g., feed and training costs, that might be considered to be capital expenditures under ordinary accounting principles. In summary he asked us to rule that the finding as to Mrs. Bessenyey's lack of profit motive is clearly erroneous within the formulation of United States v. United States Gypsum Co., 333 U.S. 364, 395 (1948), and urges that reversal is necessary in the interest of achieving consistency and avoiding results "as variable as the Chancellor's foot," citing Selden, Table Talk, c. 38, p. 44 (1689).

If the matter were res nova, question could well be raised whether Congress intended that when certain productive activity is generally regarded as a business for which taxpayers can deduct expenses or losses, a particular taxpayer engaged in precisely the same physical acts should be refused a deduction because of lack of the profit motivation the others had.[3] Certainly the lack of profit motivation does not affect how the activity will contribute to the overall economic welfare. On the other hand, under high tax rates such a test would put the government in the presumably undesired position of subsidizing activities in which wealthy persons engage primarily for pleasure, see Reg. §1.212-1(c) denying deductions for transactions "carried on primarily as a sport, hobby, or recreation . . ." and Surrey & Warren, Federal Income Taxation, Cases and Materials 344-345 (1960 ed.). However, we are not writing on a clean slate. Although "horse breeding and racing, though the sport of kings, have been held in a surprising number of cases to be the business of taxpayers," Bittker, Federal Income, Estate and Gift Taxation 207

---

3. As counsel for the taxpayer has argued, extravagance in operations could be handled by disallowing excessive expenses. Although this approach would involve administrative difficulties, they might not exceed those of the profit motive test.

(3d ed. 1964) — and even of rich ones . . . — the courts found a profit motive in all these cases.[4] The established rule, approved by this circuit and others, is that deductibility of "business-like" expenses or losses is denied unless the taxpayer can show an intention to seek profit. . . . Indeed, counsel for Mrs. Bessenyey does not urge us to reject the profit motive test but rather asks us to hold the Tax Court to have been in clear error in finding that she failed to meet it.

If our objective were to stay as close as possible to a curve plotted through the irreconcilable body of cases in this general area, we would reverse. Speaking about deductions for losses on country estates and racing stables, Randolph Paul noted long ago that "The American businessman has never appeared so indefatigably optimistic as in some of the cases on this point; taxpayers have earnestly contended (sometimes successfully) that they expected to reap an ultimate profit even though operating losses exceeded receipts with depressing regularity over a long period of years." Motive and Intent in Federal Tax Law, in Selected Studies in Federal Taxation 281-282 (2d Series, 1938). The degree of taxpayers' success is attested by the many decisions cited in 5 Mertens, Law of Federal Income Taxation, §28.74 notes 42-49 (1963 rev.), which also notes the occasional failures. Again, if the case were to be decided by a nose-count of the recognized "Factors Indicating Operation as Business or Transaction Entered Into for Profit," see 5 Mertens, supra, §28.73, we think the taxpayer would win. But we have been instructed that these are not the proper criteria for an appellate court when a tax case turns on an issue of intent. C.I.R. v. Duberstein, [Chapter 3C.3 above]. The Supreme Court's decision rested on the belief that where a court must apply a statutory tax standard of a "non-technical nature," decision necessarily turns on "the close relationship of it to the data of practical human experience, and the multiplicity of relevant factual elements, and their various combinations, creating the necessity of ascribing the proper force to each,"; determination "must be based ultimately on the application of the fact-finding tribunal's experience with the mainsprings of human conduct to the totality of the facts of each case," [p. 184 above]; and appellate efforts to set guidelines within the broad standard would elevate mere "maxims of experience" into rules of law [p. 183 above]. Thus "appellate review of determinations in this field must be quite restricted," and the findings of a trial judge, including "factual inferences from undisputed basic facts . . . as will on many occasions be presented in this area," are not to be upset unless "clearly erroneous," C.I.R. v. Duberstein, [Chapter 3C.3 above, at p. 185], citing F.R. Civ. P. 52(a), made applicable to the Tax Court by I.R.C. §7482(a).

---

4. See also John S. Ellsworth, 21 T.C.M. 145 (1962), where a wealthy taxpayer whose prime source of income was dividends and interest was held to have been engaged in business in conducting "Folly Farm" despite 13 years of uninterrupted losses aggregating almost $700,000, his own acknowledgement of the fact that when he entered the "business" at age 65, he realized that he would not make a profit before attaining 75 or 80, and evidence that his interest in breeding was scientific.

We cannot conscientiously say Judge Raum's conclusion that Mrs. Bessenyey "did not in fact have a bona fide intention to conduct her activities for a profit" leaves us with a "definite and firm conviction that a mistake has been committed." . . . A composite of such facts as her professed interest in the breed's fate, her mounting expenses, the long period before any expected initial profit, the meagerness of this profit in relation to the sums expended, her somewhat casual attitude on the subject, and her economic independence permit a reasonable conclusion, which the judge's observation fortified, that she started her activity primarily to preserve the breed with which she had worked as a young noblewoman and continued without much caring whether she made a profit or not although naturally hoping that she might. It is immaterial that the record would also have supported a contrary view. While we do have "a definite and firm conviction" that the judge here did not make good on the Court's prophecy of "a natural tendency of professional triers of fact to follow one another's determinations, even as to factual matters," [p. 185 above], as we read *Duberstein* such a failure is not enough for reversal. If the judge thought, as he might well have, that other courts had been overly credulous regarding the profit motivation of wealthy taxpayers who have viewed long years of equine losses with an equanimity not manifested in true business ventures, he was free to follow his bent. The mandate of *Duberstein*, to an appellate court is to give "primary weight . . . to the conclusions of the trier of fact" as against "an academic desire for tidiness, symmetry and precision," [p. 184 above], even though this may have the unfortunate consequence of lessening the predictability peculiarly essential in tax matters.

Judgment affirmed.

WATERMAN, Circuit Judge (concurring): I concur with my brothers in affirming the Tax Court. . . .

I must point out, however, that I am disturbed by the slant the Tax Court has adopted when it determines whether a very wealthy taxpayer's activity in the production of economic goods has been motivated by a "profit motive." See Schley v. Commissioner, [375 F.2d 747 (2d Cir. 1967)] (dissenting opinion). It would seem that it has become the Tax Court's practice to emphasize by an emphasis which I believe to be out of proportion to a "close relationship to the data of practical human experience and the multiplicity of relevant factual elements"[1] the factors of a taxpayer's great wealth and income, his love of his work, and the losses he incurs in prosecuting that work. And as to the losses, even though they, as in *Schley*, may have been occasioned by a forward-looking somewhat expensive temporary program adopted in the relevant taxable years so as to make future farming operations profitable, or, as here, may have been occasioned by Bessenyey's firm belief that her horse enterprise would assuredly make profits for her in the future, the fact that the taxpayer is wealthy enough to absorb the losses appears

---

1. Commissioner v. Duberstein [Chapter 3C.3 above, at p. 184].

694   12. *Personal, Living, or Family Expenses*

automatically to result in having findings found below such as those here: "Her rewards consisted of personal satisfaction in the activity." It would seem that, as to a wealthy taxpayer, inasmuch as losses taxpayer incurs may be comfortably absorbed by him he could not have had a profit motive in engaging in the business activity that resulted in the losses.

Of course an independently wealthy person will naturally be less concerned about temporarily making ends meet in the business activity in which he is engaged than one who, as taxpayer's parallel horse-breeder here, is "in the serious business of making a living." But this no more indicates that the activity is conducted primarily for pleasure, see Treas. Reg. §1.212-1(c), than does a large corporation's expenditure of huge sums for new product development and marketing indicate it. Also, nobody would deny that if one enjoys one's primary business activity financial losses suffered thereby are more happily endured than such losses would be if suffered in an activity one detests. But should one's happiness or unhappiness be conclusive on whether one is or is not in a business for profit? Moreover, it seems inequitable that a well-capitalized corporation may undertake a long-range project despite that necessity of enduring continuous early losses in the launching of the project, but an affluent individual taxpayer may not. For example, here the Tax Court apparently disregarded the testimony of taxpayer's expert to the effect that "the enterprise should show a profit in proper time" and that taxpayer was "proceeding as expeditiously as possible" in her long-range plan of developing a new breed of luxury horses. While in this case I cannot term the Tax Court's inferences fallacious or its ultimate finding "clearly erroneous," I would suggest that the court in adjudicating cases of this kind could well give more serious consideration to such factors as whether the expectation of an ultimate profit is reasonable, how the operation is conducted, to what extent the taxpayer personally participates therein, and the likelihood that the activity taxpayer is engaged in is encompassed within the normal activities that occupy the time of other wealthy taxpayers. Surely such factors are as relevant to the question of a taxpayer's intent as the single factor of enjoyment of one's work. My views may be caused by "an academic desire for tidiness, symmetry and precision," but see Commissioner v. Duberstein, [p. 184 above], and the thought that in tax matters the Tax Court's approach to a study of the motives of the very rich would seem to be materially different from the approach to a study of the motives of the rest of us.

Notes and Questions

1. Why did the Commissioner seek only to disallow the excess of expenses over income in *Bessenyey*? If the activity was not a trade or business, what authority was there for deducting any expenses incurred? Whatever the authority, the Commissioner has consistently allowed expenses to the extent

of income from nonprofit activities, and a deduction so limited is now explicitly allowed by §183, which was enacted in 1969.

2. Take a look at the Treasury's attempt to capture the meaning of "activity not engaged in for profit." Reg. §1.183-2. Is this an improvement on the judiciary's approach (i.e., *Bessenyey* and *Rudolph*)?

3. What if a transaction were entered into purely for financial gain as compared with pleasure (or principle), but the anticipated financial gain was completely and solely attributable to tax reductions; that is, there was no bona fide purpose to make a pretax profit? See Chapter 16.

F. HOUSING

Owner-occupied housing is treated very favorably under the income tax in any event. See Chapter 10C above. Sometimes taxpayers have claimed business or investment deductions also — or, if they are renters, instead.

1. Loss on Sale

WEIR v. COMMISSIONER
109 F.2d 996 (3d Cir.), cert. denied, 310 U.S. 637 (1940)

Before Maris, Clark, and Biddle, Circuit Judges.

CLARK, Circuit Judge. The first issue at bar concerns the disallowance of a loss deduction from petitioner's net income for the year 1932. The loss asserted is on a transaction involving the purchase and sale of preferred stock in the Bellefield Company, a corporation which owned hotels and apartment houses in Pittsburgh. Petitioner bought the stock in lots at various times in 1925 and 1926, and sold it on December 16, 1932. He repurchased it three and one-half months later, on March 1, 1933. We say "it" because, as it happened, the identical shares were reacquired on repurchase. One Falk, an acquaintance, had held them in the three and one-half months' interval. The Commissioner, not unnaturally, denied the deduction and attacked the good faith of the sale before the Board. But that attack failed utterly. The purchase, sale, and repurchase were made in due course through petitioner's brokers, and in such wise as to establish petitioner's complete ignorance of Falk's connection with the stock. This assurance was made doubly sure by other undisputed facts. Petitioner was, as he explained, a tenant in an apartment owned by the Bellefield Company. His motive in acquiring the stock was to have a voice in the management in order to "maintain certain standards." He sold the stock because he had decided to move out, the rent, in his opinion, being too high; he repurchased it because he changed his mind and decided to remain inasmuch as the rent had been reduced. The Board, however, stressed the motive for the purchase and held, sua sponte that the transaction was not "entered into for profit" within the meaning of the statute [§165(c)(2)].

The limitation of deductible losses, outside the sphere of the taxpayer's trade or business, to those incurred in "transactions entered into for profit," first appeared on the statute books as §5(a) (5th) of the Revenue Act of 1916, 39 Stat. 759. It has been construed ever since in terms of the taxpayer's state of mind, see, Paul, Motive and Intent in Federal Tax Law, Selected Studies in Federal Taxation, Second Series, p. 280. The myriad cases and rulings are collected and discussed in the article above cited, in 3 Paul & Mertens, The Law of Federal Income Taxation §26.49, and in 401 C.C.H. para. 195. There are no apt precedents among them. Some are complicated by the rather technical circumstance of a shift in ownership through gift, bequest or devise. Some are concerned with the narrow and often elusive connection between profit and real estate holdings. Others reflect the dreary financial lot of guarantors, or entrepreneurs acting under the suasion of moral obligation. Still others (with, we think, greater pertinence) involve a more sportive segment of the citizenry and their characteristic exploits, such, for example, as the breeding of polo ponies, Farish v. Comm., 36 B.T.A. 1114; Id., 5 Cir., 103 F.2d 63; the maintenance of racing stables, Whitney v. Comm., 3 Cir., 73 F.2d 589; Comm. v. Widener, 3 Cir., 33 F.2d 833; the equipment of expeditions to find the quasi-mythical Central American "white Indian," Du Pont v. Comm., 36 B.T.A. 223; the purchase of cabin cruisers, Lihme v. Anderson, D.C., 18 Supp. 566; the culture of trees, Montgomery v. Comm., 37 B.T.A. 232; or the pursuit of gentleman farming, Thacher v. Lowe, D.C., 288 F. 994. Generally speaking, the Board and the courts have been liberal in finding the requisite greed. As the author cited above puts it: "The American business man has never appeared so indefatigably optimistic as in some of the cases on this point."[1]

When stock is the subject matter of the transaction, the taxpayer's optimism stands on much firmer footing. More than twenty years ago a terse Office Decision ruled that the "profit" which must be intended on the purchase of property might relate to income flowing from the tenure of that property, as well as gains realized from its resale, O.D. 138, 1 C.B. 124, and see L.O. 1061, 4 C.B. 160, A.R.R. 604, 5 C.B. 136. This construction is of course an eminently reasonable, indeed necessary, one — otherwise it would be virtually impossible to buy bonds at a premium "for profit" — and it has been consistently followed, see Lewis v. Comm., 34 B.T.A. 996; Tanzer v. Comm., 37 B.T.A. 244; Heiner v. Tindle, 276 U.S. 382. By hypothesis, the purchase of stock carries with it in the form of dividends a share in the earnings and profits of the corporation. Again, by hypothesis, although profits are not always forthcoming, the corporation, at least, is trying to earn them, and generally does. Of course if the corporation cannot earn them, and the

---

1. Paul, Motive and Intent in Federal Tax Law, Selected Studies in Federal Taxation, Second Series, p. 281.

taxpayer knows that its stock is worthless, his acquisition of that stock is surely not for profit, Dresser v. United States, Ct. Cl. 55 F.2d 499, certiorari denied, 287 U.S. 635. The simpler case is where the corporation is not even trying to earn profits, and the taxpayer has been instrumental in its organization, see Paine v. Comm., 37 B.T.A. 427, affirmed 1 Cir., 102 F.2d 110. So, the intention to purchase stock must from the very nature of the thing purchased include the intention to receive profits (dividends or accretion in value) unless the purchaser knows at the time of purchase that such profits are an impossibility.

Before proceeding further, it is appropriate to notice a timeworn but salient distinction and corresponding difference in terminology. We quote:

> . . . "Intent" may be used in at least three distinct legal meanings. It may designate simply the exercise of will power necessary to cause muscular or physical movement. This concept is, of course, irrelevant in the field of tax law. Secondly, it may denote the immediate result desired by the actor. Thirdly, it may signify the ultimate reason for aiming at that immediate objective. At this point, however, intent shades into motive, which is really the *ulterior* intent or the *cause* of the intent. Intent, in other words, is the object of the act; motive, in turn, is the object or spring of the intent. Using the terms in these senses, intent is frequently material to tax questions; whereas motive — properly enough — is of importance only in comparatively rare instances. [Paul, Motive and Intent in Federal Tax Law, Selected Studies in Federal Taxation, Second Series, pp. 257, 258.]

Petitioner's profit intention must, we think, be taken for granted. His purchase of preferred stock is of course conceded, and that is sufficient to establish prima facie his intent to profit. The deduction has been allowed on similar showings, Tanzer v. Comm., above cited, Lewis v. Comm., above cited, Terry v. United States, D.C., 10 F. Supp. 183, and see T.B.R. 35, 1 C.B. 122, 123. Nothing in the record tends to disprove the intention so established. It is not suggested that petitioner knew, or had any cause to know, that his purchase would be profitless. Furthermore, petitioner's intention and motive of influencing the "standards" of the corporation through his stock ownership presents no repugnancy. One does not exhibit an intention to bid farewell to profits by signing a proxy. This last, it will be noted, serves to distinguish the decisions dealing with non-income producing property. If, for instance, the taxpayer has purchased a yacht, his cruising about in it presupposes a state of mind inconsistent with making a profit out of it by chartering. Hence that inconsistency must be resolved by ascertaining whether the intention or motive of pleasure or that of profit is the "prime thing," Lihme v. Anderson, above cited, and see Helvering v. National Grocery Co., 304 U.S. 282, footnote 5. In the instant case, on the other hand no such resolution is necessary. We have a profit intention, side by side with a non-profit motive.

We are brought, then, to the final question: Is the requirement "for profit" satisfied by the petitioner's intention or by his motive? The answer, of course, does not lie in the language used. Nor is the legislative history of the statute of any assistance. The similarly worded provision governing the losses of non-residents was debated at some length in the Senate with the result that the words "for profit" were deleted, 53 Cong. Rec. 13263, 13266; Seidman, Legislative History of Federal Income Tax Laws pp. 964 et seq. But the phrase was reinserted by the conference committee, and became law without further discussion, see 53 Cong. Rec. 14110. Nevertheless, the fundamental object of the statute is discernible. As stated by Mr. Justice Stone speaking for a unanimous court: "Section 214, read as a whole, discloses plainly a general purpose to permit deductions of capital losses wherever the capital investment is used to produce taxable income." Heiner v. Tindle, 276 U.S. 582, 585. See also, Dresser v. United States, above cited, and excerpts there quoted. In other words, the government says to the taxpayer with shrewd benevolence, "If you intend to benefit us by producing taxable profits, you may take your loss,[3] but if you don't intend to so benefit us, you cannot deduct your losses and we, furthermore will tax you on your windfalls." The benefit of increased revenue is certainly not assured when there is no intention to profit. But the profit intention and profit motive each assure that benefit with equal force. The public coffers are weighted with the same amount from taxes on Bellefield Company dividends, whether the stock is held with the motive of voting or with the motive of profit. That portion of petitioner's capital was "used to produce taxable income." That being so, petitioner is entitled to his deduction. We need hardly add that a contrary position would only serve to embroil the administrators of the taxing statute in a hectic and ridiculous search for non-profit motives. . . .

Questions

1. If a person purchases a house in which to live, she will ordinarily hope for gain in value as well as a place to live, but the investment would not be regarded as a transaction entered into for profit and a loss on sale would routinely be classed as nondeductible. Reg. §1.212-1(h) (no deduction while property held by the taxpayer for use as a residence); see also id. -1(c) (primary purpose test). Is that consonant with the reasoning in *Weir*? There is no correspondingly general tax exemption for gain on sale of a home, although §§121 and 1014 operate in fact to eliminate tax on much of such gain.

2. Some special problems arise when the purpose for holding property changes. *F* bought a house for $60,000 in 1983; in 1984 when it was worth $50,000, he moved out and listed it for sale or rent; in 1985 when it was worth $40,000 he succeeded in renting it; in 1986 he sold it for $30,000. For which periods, if any, can he deduct depreciation? On what basis? How much of an allowable loss does he realize in 1986 on the sale? Reg. §§1.167(g)-1, 1.165-9.

3. What about rental pending sale at a gain? If depreciation, maintenance, and insurance, together with mortgage interest and taxes, come to

---

3. The 1916 Act drove a harder but more logical bargain by restricting losses on transactions "entered into for profit" to "an amount not exceeding the profits arising therefrom," Revenue Act of 1916, §5(a) (5th). The restriction was eliminated by §214(a)(5) of the Revenue Act of 1918, 40 Stat. 1067.

more than the rental income, is the excess deductible? Is the §121 exclusion compatible with a profit motive, or does §183 necessarily apply? See Technical Advice Memorandum 8132017 (April 30, 1981).

4. If a taxpayer sells municipal bonds for less than cost the loss is deductible under §165(c)(2); the purchase and holding of the bonds constitute a transaction entered into for profit even if the interest is tax free. Contrast the municipal bondholder, who can deduct losses but not interest, §265(a)(2), with the homeowner, who can deduct interest but not a loss on sale. Is there any convincing explanation for the difference?

Extending the comparison, neither can deduct expenses other than interest and both are potentially taxable on any gains they may realize on sale, although homeowners' gains are to a large extent exempted by §121.

5. Weir was a tenant and so presumably he was not enjoying the benefit of mortgage interest or tax deductions or tax-free imputed rent; does this make the allowance of a deduction for his loss more acceptable?

2. Rental Losses

If a family owns a vacation home solely for its own use, the tax treatment is relatively simple and favorable. The rental value of the family use of the property is not imputed for income tax purposes. State and local property taxes are allowable in full as itemized deductions, and interest on a mortgage is allowable as home mortgage interest (but only on one such nonprincipal residence). §163(h)(4)(A)(i)(II).

Sometimes a vacation home is rented to other vacationers during some or all of the time it is not in use by its owners. How is that to be treated for income tax purposes?

The Boltons had figures like these (at 1976 prices):[2]

Income and Use	Time	Money
by tenants	91 days	$2,700
by owners	30 days	
vacant	244 days	

Expenses		
mortgage interest		$2,800
property taxes		600
maintenance		2,600

The rental income is clearly includible in gross income, and the mortgage interest and taxes are deductible, as itemized deductions if not otherwise. But should the Boltons be able to deduct all or part of the maintenance expenses or anything else?

2. Bolton v. Commissioner, 694 F.2d 556 (9th Cir. 1982).

Before any special legislation on the subject, aggressive taxpayers might have taken the position that the whole investment was *intended* to make a profit and would have if they had only succeeded in renting it for some of those vacant days; therefore, deductions should be allowed for all three listed expenses, plus any other deductible costs, like insurance and depreciation, that are not included in maintenance. The result would be a net loss of $3,300 plus those other costs. The government would not readily have accepted this claim, but it does not have the resources to audit every return.

Suppose a public-spirited taxpayer did not claim a profit motivation for his investment but rather conceded that rental activities were undertaken merely to defray the cost of maintaining a vacation home for personal use; what then? Following the rationale in *Bessenyey* and §183, maintenance should be allowed as a deduction only to the extent that it is allocable to rental use and only to the extent it does not produce a net loss. That is, the maintenance deduction should be limited to rental income minus the interest and tax deductions that would be allowable even in the absence of any rental income. But what is that limitation on the figures given?

The applicable statutory provision is §280A. Look particularly at §280A(e) with respect to the allocation of the maintenance expense. Does that make good sense?

The limitation prohibiting a net loss is in §280A(c)(5), which at the time did not contain (B)(ii). So computation of the limitation, under what is now (B)(i), depended on how much of deductions "allowable . . . whether or not such unit . . . was [rented]" were "allocable to [the rental] use."

The parties' positions were summarized as follows:

Taxpayer's Position:

Gross rental income		$2,700
Total interest and property taxes	$3,400	
Allocation fraction 91/365 = 25% (attributable to rental use)		(850)
Rental income in excess of interest and property taxes		$1,850
Total maintenance expenses	2,600	
Allocation fraction 91/121 = 75%		1,950
Maximum allowable (lesser of above)		1,850

Commissioner's Position:

Gross rental income		$2,700
Total interest and property taxes	$3,400	
Allocation fraction 91/121 = 75% (attributable to rental use)		(2,550)
Rental income in excess of interest and property taxes		$150
Total maintenance expenses	2,600	
Allocation fraction 91/121 = 75%		1,950
Maximum allowable (lesser of above)		150

Which of these positions should prevail? The Commissioner's position was (and still is) reflected in a proposed regulation, Prop. Reg. §1.280A-3(d)(3), (4). As a matter of policy, is there some other position superior to either of these?

The Tax Court and Court of Appeals both held for the taxpayer despite the proposed regulation. The reasons included the following.

(1) *Statutory language:* The IRS seeks to allocate interest and taxes through use of the fraction prescribed for the maintenance expenses pursuant to §280A(e)(1). But §280A(e)(2) says "This subsection shall not apply with respect to deductions which would be allowable under this chapter for the taxable year whether or not such unit . . . was rented."

(2) *Theory:* A computation based on the period of time a unit was actually used is useful with respect to maintenance expenses since they are ordinarily associated with actual use. But interest and taxes accrue ratably over the whole year whether the property is in use or not.

Is either of these reasons convincing?

Section 280A(c)(5)(B) was amended in 1986 by the addition of clause (ii) and the language following. Does the new version specify whether the denominator of the allocation fraction is the number of days the dwelling unit is used during the year or the total number of days in the year? What is the purpose of the amendment?

3. Home Offices

DRUCKER v. COMMISSIONER
715 F.2d 67 (2d Cir. 1983)

Before Kaufman, Van Graafeiland and Pratt, Circuit Judges.

VAN GRAAFEILAND, Circuit Judge: An oft-repeated, perhaps apocryphal, story tells of the musician who, when asked the best way to get to Carnegie Hall, replied, "Practice! Practice!" Whether the story is truth or fiction, the fact remains that, for a performing musician, practice is not simply the best way to get to Carnegie Hall, it is the only way. It is the only way to get there, and it is the only way to ensure that, having arrived, one stays there. Ignace Paderewski, the famous pianist, once said:

> If I don't practice for one day, I know it; if I don't practice for two days, the critics know it; if I don't practice for three days, the audience knows it. [Elyse Mach, Great Pianists Speak for Themselves (Introduction by Sir George Solti XIV) (1980).]

Since a musician must practice, he must have a place in which he can practice. This appeal concerns the tax treatment of portions of residential areas which are set aside and used solely for such purpose.

Ernest Drucker, Patricia Rogers, and Philip Cherry are concert musicians employed by the Metropolitan Opera Association, Inc. (the Met). During the period relevant to this appeal, each of them lived in a New York City apartment in which one room or a portion of a room was set aside and used exclusively for musical study and practice. Appellants spent approximately thirty to thirty-two hours per week studying and practicing in the areas reserved for such use, and this appears to be about average for musical artists. See e.g., Mach, supra, at 9, 14, 63. On their tax returns, appellants deducted from gross income the rent, electricity, and maintenance costs allocable to the practice areas.

The Commissioner disallowed these deductions and assessed deficiencies against Drucker for the tax years 1976 and 1977, against Rogers for 1977, and against the Cherrys, on their joint return, for 1976. The taxpayers petitioned the Tax Court for redetermination of the deficiencies. With six judges dissenting, the Tax Court first denied Drucker his claimed deduction. Drucker v. CIR, 79 T.C. 605 (1982). The other two petitions then were disposed of by memoranda on the authority of the *Drucker* opinion. Rogers v. CIR, 44 T.C.M. (CCH) 1312 (1982); Cherry v. CIR, 44 T.C.M. (CCH) 1316 (1982). The three cases are now before us on a consolidated appeal. We reverse.

Section 280A(a) of the Internal Revenue Code of 1954, as amended, 26 U.S.C. §280A(a) (1976 & Supp. V 1981), generally disallows any deduction for individuals "with respect to the use of a dwelling unit which is used by the taxpayer during the taxable year as a residence." Section 280A(c)(1)(A), however, permits the deduction of the expenses "allocable to a portion of the dwelling unit which is exclusively used on a regular basis" as the "principal place of business for any trade or business of the taxpayer." In the case of an employee, the deduction is available "only if the exclusive use . . . is for the convenience of his employer." Section 280A(c)(5) contains the further limitation that any deductions must be limited to the excess of gross income derived from such use for the taxable year over those deductions allocable to such use, such as mortgage interest, which are permitted by the tax laws without reference to the business use concerned.

Unfortunately, terms such as "trade," "business," and "principal place of business" do not fit comfortably into a discussion of the manner in which a professional musician earns his living. Harry Ellis Dickson, a long-time member of the Boston Symphony Orchestra, wrote of his colleagues:

> A musician's life is different from that of most people. We don't go to an office every day, or to a factory, or a bank. We go to an empty hall. We don't deal in anything tangible, nor do we produce anything except sounds. We saw away, or blow, or pound for a few hours and then we go home. It is a strange way to make a living! [Dickson, Gentlemen, More Dolce Please (Preface) (1969).]

It is indeed a "strange way to make a living," and we believe that the Tax Court failed to come to grips with that fact. Although the taxpayer musicians worked for portions of the tax years in question for employers other than the Met, the Tax Court held that they were in the "trade or business" of being Met employees. Applying its rule that the "focal point" of a taxpayer's activities determines his "principal place of business," Baie v. CIR, 74 T.C. 105, 109 (1980), the Tax Court held that appellant musicians' principal place of business was the same as that of their employer, i.e. Lincoln Center. In reaching this conclusion, the Tax Court majority made a number of findings which we are unable to reconcile. They said that, although individual practice by appellants was a necessity, and although appellants were expected to practice individually off the employer's premises because the Met did not provide facilities for such practice, off-premise practice was not "requested" by their employer and was not a "requirement" of employment. We are unable to comprehend how something can be "necessary" and "essential" and yet not be a "requirement." We do not understand how the Tax Court majority can say in one breath that "[a]s a professional musician [Drucker] was required to practice numerous hours in order to maintain, refine, and perfect his skill" and to perfect his "parts ... prior to a rehearsal or performance," 79 T.C. at 607-608, while denying in a second breath that practice was a "condition of employment," 79 T.C. at 608. In short, we conclude that the Tax Court's finding that individual home practice was not a "requirement or condition of employment" was clearly erroneous and that it was this error which led the Tax Court to the equally erroneous holding that petitioner's principal place of business was at Lincoln Center.

We believe that appellant musicians' "principal place[s] of business" were their home practice studios. In so holding, we see no need to disturb the Tax Court's ruling that the taxpayers are in the business of being employees of the Met. Rather, we find this the rare situation in which an employee's principal place of business is not that of his employer. Both in time and in importance, home practice was the "focal point" of the appellant musicians' employment-related activities. See Wisconsin Psychiatric Servs., Ltd. v. CIR, 76 T.C. 839, 848-849 & n.9 (1981); Moller v. United States, 553 F. Supp. 1071, 1078 (Cl. Ct. 1982); Huges v. CIR, 41 T.C.M. 1153, 1159 (1981). Less than half of appellants' working time was spent at Lincoln Center. The work they did perform there, i.e. rehearsals and performances, was made possible only by their solo practice at home. Moreover, the Met also performed in the City parks and on tour. The place of performance was immaterial so long as the musicians were prepared, and most of the preparation occurred at home. The home practice areas were appellants' principal places of business within the meaning of section 280A.

This holding is in accord with the legislative history of section 280A. Prior to the enactment of this section as part of the Tax Reform Act of 1976, Pub. L. No. 94-455, §601, courts sometimes allowed deductions for the business use of residences if such use was "appropriate and helpful" to the taxpayer's business. This construction of the law might permit an employee to take deductions for a home office even though his employer provided him with an adequate office at the employer's place of business. It also permitted business use deductions because of the performance of "appropriate and helpful" activities, "even though only minor incremental expenses were incurred in order to perform these activities." S. Rep. No. 938, 94th Cong., 2d Sess. 147, reprinted in 1976 U.S. Code Cong. & Ad. News 3439, 3580; H.R. Rep. No. 658, 94th Cong., 2d Sess. 160, reprinted in 1976 U.S. Code Cong. & Ad. News 2897, 3054; Joint Comm. on Taxation, General Explanation of the Tax Reform Act of 1976, 94th Cong., 2d Sess. 139 (Comm. Print 1976), reprinted in 1976-3 C.B. (Vol. 2) 1, 151. In enacting section 280A, Congress intended to provide clearer standards for deductions and to prevent the conversion of nondeductible personal, living, and family expenses into deductible business expenses. Id. The changes were not directed at taxpayers such as appellants.

Because the Met provided appellants with no space for the essential task of private practice, the maintenance of residential space exclusively for such purpose was an expense almost entirely additional to nondeductible personal living expenses. The appellant musicians' use of home studios "was not 'purely a matter of personal convenience, comfort, or economy,' Sharon v. Commissioner, 66 T.C. 515, 523 (1976). Rather, it was a business necessity." Gestrich v. CIR, 74 T.C. 525, 530 (1980). As such, as a requirement of appellants' employment, home practice by appellants was for the "convenience of [their] employer," as the meaning of those words of art has developed over a period of time. See CIR v. Kowalski, [supra Chapter 2B.1]; Adams v. United States, 585 F.2d 1060, 1064-65 (Ct. Cl. 1978); United States Junior Chamber of Commerce v. United States, 334 F.2d 660, 663 (Ct. Cl. 1964).

The judgments of the Tax Court are reversed and the matters are remanded for further proceedings in accordance with his opinion.

COMMISSIONER v. SOLIMAN
506 U.S. 168 (1993)

Justice KENNEDY delivered the opinion of the Court. . . .

I

Respondent Nader E. Soliman, an anesthesiologist, practiced his profession in Maryland and Virginia during 1983, the tax year in question. Soliman spent 30 to 35 hours per week with patients, dividing that time among three hospitals. About 80 percent of the hospital time was spent at Suburban Hospital in Bethesda, Maryland. At the hospitals, Soliman administered the anesthesia, cared for patients after surgery, and treated patients for pain. None of the three hospitals provided him with an office.

Soliman lived in a condominium in McLean, Virginia. His residence had a spare bedroom which he used exclusively as an office. Although he did not meet patients in the home office, Soliman spent two to three hours per day there on a variety of tasks such as contacting patients, surgeons, and hospitals by telephone; maintaining billing records and patient logs; preparing for treatments and presentations; satisfying continuing medical education requirements; and reading medical journals and books.

On his 1983 federal income tax return, Soliman claimed deductions for the portion of condominium fees, utilities, and depreciation attributable to the home office. . . .

The Tax Court, with six of its judges dissenting, ruled that Soliman's home office was his principal place of business. 94 T.C. 20 (1990). After noting that in its earlier decisions it identified the place where services are performed and income is generated in order to determine the principal place of business, the so-called "focal point test," the Tax Court abandoned that test, citing criticism by two Courts of Appeals. Id., at 24-25 (noting Meiers v. Commissioner, 782 F.2d 75 (CA7 1986); Weissman v. Commissioner, 751 F.2d 512 (CA2 1984); and Drucker v. Commissioner, 715 F.2d 67 (CA2 1983)]). . . .

The Commissioner appealed to the Court of Appeals for the Fourth Circuit. A divided panel of that court affirmed. 935 F.2d 52 (1991). It adopted the test used in the Tax Court and explained it as follows:

> [The] test . . . provides that where management or administrative activities are essential to the taxpayer's trade or business and the only available office space is in the taxpayer's home, the "home office" can be his "principal place of business," with the existence of the following factors weighing heavily in favor of a finding that the taxpayer's "home office" is his "principal place of business": (1) the office in the home is essential to the taxpayer's business; (2) he spends a substantial amount of time there; and (3) there is no other location available for performance of the office functions of the business." Id., at 54.

For further support, the Court of Appeals relied upon a proposed IRS regulation related to home office deductions for salespersons. Under the proposed regulation, salespersons would be entitled to home office deductions "even though they spend most of their time on the road as long as they spend 'a substantial amount of time on paperwork at home.'" Ibid. (quoting Proposed Income Tax Reg. §1.280A-2(b)(3), 45 Fed. Reg. 52399 (1980), as amended, 48 Fed. Reg. 33320 (1983)). While recognizing that the proposed regulation was not binding on it, the court suggested that it "evinced a policy to allow 'home office' deductions for taxpayers who maintain 'legitimate' home offices, even if the taxpayer does not spend a majority of his time in the office." 935 F.2d, at 55. The court concluded that the Tax Court's test would lead to identification of the "true headquarters of the business." Ibid.

Like the dissenters in the Tax Court, Judge Phillips in his dissent argued that the plain language of §280A(c)(l)(A) requires a comparative analysis of the places of business to assess which one is principal, an analysis that was not undertaken by the majority. Ibid.

Although other Courts of Appeals have criticized the focal point test, their approaches for determining the principal place of business differ in significant ways from the approach employed by the Court of Appeals in this case, see Pomarantz v. Commissioner, 867 F.2d 495, 497 (CA9 1988); Meiers v. Commissioner, supra, at 79; Weissman v. Commissioner, supra, at 514-516; Drucker v. Commissioner, supra, at 69. Those other courts undertake a comparative analysis of the functions performed at each location. We granted certiorari to resolve the conflict. 503 U.S. (1992).

II

A

... Congress adopted §280A as part of the Tax Reform Act of 1976. Pub. L. No. 94-455, 94th Cong., 2d Sess. Before its adoption, expenses attributable to the business use of a residence were deductible whenever they were "appropriate and helpful" to the taxpayer's business. See, e.g., Newi v. Commissioner, 432 F.2d 998 (CA2 1970). This generous standard allowed many taxpayers to treat what otherwise would have been nondeductible living and family expenses as business expenses, even though the limited business tasks performed in the dwelling resulted in few, if any, additional or incremental costs to the taxpayer. H. R. Rep. No. 94-658, p. 160 (1975); S. Rep. No. 94-938, p. 147 (1976). Comparing the newly enacted section with the previous one, the apparent purpose of §280A is to provide a narrower scope for the deduction, but Congress has provided no definition of "principal place of business." ...

Contrary to the Court of Appeals' suggestion, the statute does not allow for a deduction whenever a home office may be characterized as legitimate. See 935 F.2d, at 55. That approach is not far removed from the "appropriate and helpful" test that led to the adoption of §280A. Under the Court of Appeals' test, a home office may qualify as the principal place of business whenever the office is essential to the taxpayer's business, no alternative office space is available, and the taxpayer spends a substantial amount of time there. See id., at 54. This approach ignores the question whether the home office is more significant in the taxpayer's business than every other place of business. The statute does not refer to the "principal office" of the business. If it had used that phrase, the taxpayer's deduction claim would turn on other considerations. The statute refers instead to the "principal place" of business. It follows that the most important or significant place for the business must be determined.

B

In determining the proper test for deciding whether a home office is the principal place of business, we cannot develop an objective formula that yields a clear answer in every case. The inquiry is more subtle, with the ultimate determination of the principal place of business being dependent upon the particular facts of each case. There are, however, two primary considerations in deciding whether a home office is a taxpayer's principal place of business: the relative importance of the activities performed at each business location and the time spent at each place.

Analysis of the relative importance of the functions performed at each business location depends upon an objective description of the business in question. This preliminary step is undertaken so that the decision maker can evaluate the activities conducted at the various business locations in light of the particular characteristics of the specific business or trade at issue. Although variations are inevitable in case-by-case determinations, any particular business is likely to have a pattern in which certain activities are of most significance. If the nature of the trade or profession requires the taxpayer to meet or confer with a client or patient or to deliver goods or services to a customer, the place where that contact occurs is often an important indicator of the principal place of business. A business location where these contacts occur has sometimes been called the "focal point" of the business and has been previously regarded by the Tax Court as conclusive in ascertaining the principal place of business. See 94 T.C., at 24-25. We think that phrase has a metaphorical quality that can be misleading, and, as we have said, no one test is determinative in every case. We decide, however, that the point where goods and services are delivered must be given great weight in determining the place where the most important functions are performed.

Section 280A itself recognizes that the home office gives rise to a deduction whenever the office is regularly and exclusively used "by patients, clients, or customers in meeting or dealing with the taxpayer in the normal course of his trade or business." §280A(c)(1)(B). In that circumstance, the deduction is allowed whether or not the home office is also the principal place of business. The taxpayer argues that because the point of delivery of goods and services is addressed in this provision, it follows that the availability of the principal place of business exception does not depend in any way upon whether the home office is the point of delivery. We agree with the ultimate conclusion that visits by patients, clients, and customers are not a required characteristic of a principal place of business, but we disagree with the implication that whether those visits occur is irrelevant. That Congress allowed the deduction where those visits occur in the normal course even when some other location is the principal place of business indicates their importance in determining the nature and functions of any enterprise. . . .

Unlike the Court of Appeals, we do not regard the necessity of the functions performed at home as having much weight in determining entitlement to the deduction. In many instances, planning and initial preparation for performing a service or delivering goods are essential to the ultimate performance of the service or delivery of the goods, just as accounting and billing are often essential at the final stages of the process. But that is simply because, in integrated transactions, all steps are essential. . . .

We reject the Court of Appeals' reliance on the availability of alternative office space as an additional consideration in determining a taxpayer's principal place of business. . . . [A]ny taxpayer's home office that meets the criteria here set forth is the principal place of business regardless of whether a different office exists or might have been established elsewhere.

In addition to measuring the relative importance of the activities undertaken at each business location, the decisionmaker should also compare the amount of time spent at home with the time spent at other places where business activities occur. This factor assumes particular significance when comparison of the importance of the functions performed at various places yields no definitive answer to the principal place of business inquiry. This may be the case when a taxpayer performs income-generating tasks at both his home office and some other location.

The comparative analysis of business locations required by the statute may not result in every case in the specification of which location is the principal place of business; the only question that must be answered is whether the home office so qualifies. There may be cases when there is no principal place of business, and the courts and the Commissioner should not strain to conclude that a home office qualifies for the deduction simply because no other location seems to be the principal place. The taxpayer's house does not become a principal place of business by default. . . .

III

Under the principles we have discussed, the taxpayer was not entitled to a deduction for home office expenses. The practice of anesthesiology requires the medical doctor to treat patients under conditions demanding immediate, personal observation. So exacting were these requirements that all of respondent's patients were treated at hospitals, facilities with special characteristics designed to accommodate the demands of the profession. The actual treatment was the essence of the professional service. We can assume that careful planning and study were required in advance of performing the treatment, and all acknowledge that this was done in the home office. But the actual treatment was the most significant event in the professional transaction. The home office activities, from an objective standpoint, must be regarded as less important to the business of the taxpayer than the tasks he performed at the hospital.

A comparison of the time spent by the taxpayer further supports a determination that the home office was not the principal place of business. The 10 to 15 hours per week spent in the home office measured against the 30 to 35 hours per week at the three hospitals are insufficient to render the home office the principal place of business in light of all of the circumstances of this case. That the office may have been essential is not controlling.

The judgment of the Court of Appeals is reversed.

It is so ordered.

[Concurring opinion of Justice BLACKMUN omitted.]

Justice THOMAS, with whom Justice SCALIA joins, concurring in the judgment. . . . I write separately because I believe that in the overwhelming majority of cases (including the one before us), the "focal point" test — which emphasizes the place where the taxpayer renders the services for which he is paid or sells his goods — provides a clear, reliable method for determining whether a taxpayer's home office is his "principal place of business." I would employ the totality-of-the-circumstances inquiry, guided by the two factors discussed by the Court, only in the small minority of cases where the home office is one of several locations where goods or services are delivered, and thus also one of the multiple locations where income is generated.

I certainly agree that the word "principal" connotes "'most important,'" ante, at 5, but I do not agree that this definition requires courts in every case to resort to a totality-of-the-circumstances analysis when determining whether the taxpayer is entitled to a home office deduction under §280A(c)(l)(A). Rather, I think it is logical to assume that the single location where the taxpayer's business income is generated — i.e., where he provides goods or services to clients or customers — will be his principal place of business. This focal point standard was first enunciated in Baie v. Commissioner, 74 T.C. 105 (1980),[1] and has been consistently applied by the Tax Court (until the present case) in determining whether a taxpayer's home office is his principal place of business. . . .

We granted certiorari to clarify a recurring question of tax law that has been the subject of considerable disagreement. Unfortunately, this issue is no clearer today than it was before we granted certiorari. I therefore concur only in the Court's judgment.

---

1. In *Baie*, the taxpayer operated a hot dog stand. She prepared all the food in the kitchen at her home and transferred it daily to the stand for sale. She also used another room in her house exclusively for the stand's bookkeeping. The Tax Court denied the taxpayer a home office deduction under §280A(c)(1)(A), recognizing that although "preliminary preparation may have been beneficial to the efficient operation of petitioner's business, both the final packaging for consumption and sales occurred on the premises of the [hot dog stand]." 74 T.C., at 109-110. Thus, the Court concluded that the hot dog stand was the "focal point of [the taxpayer's] activities." Id., at 109.

Justice STEVENS, dissenting. Respondent is self-employed. He pays the ordinary and necessary expenses associated with the operation of his office in McLean, Virginia; it is the only place of business that he maintains. . . .

Before 1976, home office deductions were allowed whenever the use of the office was "appropriate and helpful" to the taxpayer. That generous standard was subject to both abuse and criticism; it allowed homeowners to take deductions for personal expenses that would have been incurred even if no office were maintained at home and its vagueness made it difficult to administer. It was particularly favorable to employees who worked at home on evenings and weekends even though they had adequate office facilities at their employer's place of business.[6] In response to these criticisms, Congress enacted §280A to prohibit deductions for business uses of dwelling units unless certain specific conditions are satisfied.

The most stringent conditions in §280A, enacted to prevent abuse by those who wanted to deduct purely residential costs, apply to deductions claimed by employees.[7] This provision alone prevents improper deduction for any second office located at home and used merely for the taxpayer's convenience. It thus responds to the major concern of the Commissioner identified in the legislative history.[8]

Self-employed persons, such as respondent, must satisfy three conditions. Each is more strict and more definite than the "appropriate and helpful" standard that Congress rejected.

First, a portion of the dwelling unit must be used "exclusively" for a business purpose. . . .

Second, the portion of the dwelling unit that is set aside for exclusive business use must be so "used on a regular basis." . . .

Third, the use of the space must be . . . :

"(A) as the principal place of business for any trade or business of the taxpayer,

"(B) as a place of business which is used by patients, clients, or customers in meeting or dealing with the taxpayer in the normal course of his trade or business, *or*

---

6. Congress may have been particularly offended by the home office deductions claimed by employees of the Internal Revenue Service. See Bodzin v. Commissioner, 60 T.C. 820 (1973), rev'd, 509 F.2d 679 (CA4), cert. denied, 423 U.S. 825 (1975); Sharon v. Commissioner, 66 T.C. 515 (1976), aff'd, 591 F.2d 1273 (CA9 1978), cert. denied, 442 U.S. 941 (1979). The Senate Report also used a common example of potential abuse:

"For example, if a university professor, who is provided an office by his employer, uses a den or some other room in his residence for the purpose of grading papers, preparing examinations or preparing classroom notes, an allocable portion of certain expenses . . . were incurred in order to perform these activities." S. Rep. No. 94-938, pt. 1, at 147.

7. In addition to the conditions applicable to self-employed taxpayers, an employee must demonstrate that his office is maintained "for the convenience of his employer." See 26 U.S.C. §280A(c)(1).

8. "With respect to the maintenance of an office in an employee's home, the position of the Internal Revenue Service is that the office must be required by the employer as a condition of employment and regularly used for the performance of the employee's duties. . . .

"Certain courts have held that a more liberal standard than that applied by the Internal Revenue Service is appropriate. Under these decisions, the expenses attributable to an office maintained in an employee's residence are deductible if the maintenance of the office is 'appropriate and helpful' to the employee's business." S. Rep. No. 94-938, pt. 1, at 144-145 (citations omitted); see also n.6, supra.

"(C) in the case of a separate structure which is not attached to the dwelling unit, in connection with the taxpayer's trade or business." 26 U.S.C. 280A(c)(1) (emphasis added)

Subsection (C) is obviously irrelevant in this case, as is subsection (B). The office itself is not a separate structure, and respondent does not meet his patients there. Each of the three alternatives, however, has individual significance, and it is clear that subsection (A) was included to describe places where the taxpayer does not normally meet with patients, clients, or customers. Nevertheless, the Court suggests that Soliman's failure to meet patients in his home office supports its holding. It does not. By injecting a requirement of subsection (B) into subsection (A) the Court renders the latter alternative entirely superfluous. Moreover, it sets the three subsections on unequal footing: subsection (A) will rarely apply unless it includes subsection (B); subsection (B) is preeminent; and the logic of the Court's analysis would allow a future court to discover that, under subsection (C), a separate structure is not truly "separate" (as a principal place of business is not truly "principal") unless it is also the site of meetings with patients or clients. . . .

By conflating subsections (A) and (B) the Court makes the same mistake the courts of appeal refused to make when they rejected the Tax Court's "focal point" test, which proved both unworkable and unfaithful to the statute. In this case the Tax Court itself rejected that test because it "merges the 'principal place of business' exception with the 'meeting clients' exception . . . from section 280A." 94 T.C. 20, 25 (1990). The Court today steps blithely into territory in which several courts of appeal and the Tax Court, whose experience in these matters is much greater than ours, have learned not to tread; in so doing it reads into the statute a limitation Congress never meant to impose.

The principal office of a self-employed person's business would seem to me to be the most typical example of a "principal place of business." It is, indeed, the precise example used in the Commissioner's proposed regulations of deductible home offices for taxpayers like respondent, who have no office space at the "focal point" of their work.[13] Moreover, it is a mistake to focus attention entirely on the adjective "principal" and to overlook the significance of the term "place of business." When the term "principal place of business" is used in other statutes that establish the jurisdiction or venue in which a corporate defendant may be sued, it commonly identifies the headquarters of the business. The only place where a business is managed is fairly described as its "principal" place of business.

---

13. The proposed regulations stated that "if an outside salesperson has no office space except at home and spends a substantial amount of time on paperwork at home, the office in the home may qualify as the salesperson's principal place of business." 45 Fed. Reg. 52403 (1980), 48 Fed. Reg. 33324 (1983).

The Court suggests that Congress would have used the term "principal office" if it had intended to describe a home office like respondent's. Ante, at [p. 706]. It is probable, however, that Congress did not select the narrower term because it did not want to exclude some business uses of dwelling units that should qualify for the deduction even though they are not offices. Because some examples that do not constitute offices come readily to mind—an artist's studio, or a cabinet-maker's basement—it is easy to understand why Congress did not limit this category that narrowly.

The test applied by the Tax Court, and adopted by the Court of Appeals, is both true to the statute and practically incapable of abuse. In addition to the requirements of exclusive and regular use, those courts would require that the taxpayer's home office be essential to his business and be the only office space available to him. 935 F.2d 52, 54 (CA4 1991); 94 T.C., at 29. Respondent's home office is the only place where he can perform the administrative functions essential to his business. . . . As I would construe the statute in this context, respondent's office is not just the "principal" place of his trade or business; it is the only place of his trade or business. . . .

I respectfully dissent.

Notes and Questions

1. In response to the Court's decision, the IRS withdrew proposed regulations addressing the determination of principal place of business, including the language quoted in footnote 13 of the dissenting opinion. Notice 94-62, 1994-1 C.B. 373. In place thereof it obediently issued a revenue ruling implementing *Soliman.* Revenue Ruling 94-24, 1994-1 C.B. 87, dealt with a self-employed plumber working 48 hours a week at customer locations and 18 hours a week in a home office talking with customers on the telephone, deciding what supplies to order, and reviewing the books of the business. He had a full-time employee keeping books and records for the business in that office. Since "[t]he essence of *A*'s trade or business as a plumber requires *A* to perform services and deliver goods at the homes or offices of *A*'s customers" and he spent most of his time at that, the home office was held not to qualify as his principal place of business. The full-time employee did not change that result.

2. Revenue Ruling 94-24 also dealt with these cases:

> *Situation 2. B* is employed as a teacher. *B* is required to teach and meet with students at the school and to grade papers and tests. In addition to a small shared office at the school, *B* maintains a home office for use in class preparation and for grading papers and tests. *B* spends approximately 25 hours per week of *B*'s work time at the school, with an additional 30 to 35 hours of *B*'s work time per week spent in *B*'s home office.
>
> *Situation 3. C* is a self-employed author who uses a home office to write. *C* spends 30 to 35 hours of *C*'s work time per week in the home office writing. *C* also spends another

10 to 15 hours of *C*'s work time per week at other locations conducting research, meeting with *C*'s publishers, and attending promotional events.

Situation 4. D is a self-employed retailer of costume jewelry. *D* orders the jewelry from wholesalers and sells it at craft shows, on consignment, and through mail orders. *D* spends approximately 25 hours of *D*'s work time per week in *D*'s home filling and shipping mail orders, ordering supplies, and keeping the books of *D*'s business. *D* also spends approximately 15 hours of *D*'s work time per week at craft shows and consignment sale locations. *D* generates a substantial amount of income from each type of sales activity.

How should they be treated?

3. Now look at the last sentence in §280A(c)(1), enacted in 1997. Does that overrule *Soliman* and take care of the plumber and the salesman? Where does it leave the other situations in Revenue Ruling 94-24 and *Drucker*?

4. Feldman was an employee, director, and shareholder of an accounting firm. Since the firm had an "open door" policy toward other employees, Feldman needed an office away from the main firm office to get his work done. (His work included personnel matters that needed to be discussed in private.) Feldman and the firm concluded that certain space in his home would best serve this need, and accordingly the firm agreed to rent certain space in Feldman's home, for use by Feldman as an office, and thereafter Feldman received $5,400 a year from the firm as rent. How should this arrangement be treated for federal income tax purposes?[3] After thinking about how the problem ought to be handled, look at §280A(c)(6), added in response to the *Feldman* decision. The precursor of this provision in the House bill was brought to the attention of the court of appeals in *Feldman;* the court responded "[w]e are content to await the action of Congress. Moreover, we decline to treat the actions of the present Congress as indicative of the purposes motivating a Congress ten years past. . . . Indeed, one could easily interpret the House's action as a tacit admission that the statute as enacted contains an undesirable loophole." 791 F.2d at 784.

What's up? Were the "purposes motivating a Congress ten years past" to enact "an undesirable loophole"? Why? And wouldn't a sensible interpretation be one that avoided such nonsense? Who do you think "created" the "undesirable loophole"?[4]

5. Home office questions have created an unusual number of conflicting opinions and reversals, judicial and congressional, over something that is not typically a very big item. Can you think of any particular reason why?

---

3. Feldman v. Commissioner, 791 F.2d 781 (9th cir. 1986), aff'g. 84 T.C. 1 (1985).

4. A baseball umpire received fulsome introductions at a dinner in his honor. The first speaker said "He always called 'em as he saw 'em." The next speaker inflated the compliment: "He always called 'em *as they were.*" The umpire demurred: "You're both wrong: they aint nothin' *'til* I calls 'em."

6. Consider other kinds of property whose business usefulness may be incidental to the personal pleasure or convenience they generate. During 1984 there was much talk about luxury automobiles and personal computers. Take a critical look at the outcome in §280F.

G. MARITAL LITIGATION

UNITED STATES v. GILMORE
372 U.S. 39 (1963)

Mr. Justice HARLAN delivered the opinion of the Court. In 1955 the California Supreme Court confirmed the award to the respondent taxpayer of a decree of absolute divorce, without alimony, against his wife Dixie Gilmore. . . . The case before us involves the deductibility for federal income tax purposes of that part of the husband's legal expense incurred in such proceedings as is attributable to his successful resistance of his wife's claims to certain of his assets asserted by her to be community property under California law. . . .

At the time of the divorce proceedings instituted by the wife but in which the husband also cross-claimed for divorce, respondent's property consisted primarily of controlling stock interests in three corporations, each of which was a franchised General Motors automobile dealer. As president and principal managing officer of the three corporations, he received salaries from them aggregating about $66,800 annually, and in recent years his total annual dividends had averaged about $83,000. His total annual income derived from the corporations was thus approximately $150,000. His income from other sources was negligible.

As found by the Court of Claims, the husband's overriding concern in the divorce litigation was to protect these assets against the claims of his wife. Those claims had two aspects: *first,* that the earnings accumulated and retained by these three corporations during the Gilmores' marriage (representing an aggregate increase in corporate net worth of some $600,000) were the product of respondent's personal services, and not the result of accretion in capital values, thus rendering respondent's stockholdings in the enterprises pro tanto community property under California law; *second,* that to the extent that such stockholdings were community property, the wife, allegedly the innocent party in the divorce proceeding, was entitled under California law to more than a one-half interest in such property.

The respondent wished to defeat those claims for two important reasons. *First,* the loss of his controlling stock interests, particularly in the event of their transfer in substantial part to hostile wife, might well cost him the loss of his corporate positions, his principal means of livelihood. *Second,* there was also danger that if he were found guilty of his wife's sensational and reputation-damaging charges of marital infidelity, General Motors Corporation might find it expedient to exercise its right to cancel these dealer franchises.

The end result of this bitterly fought divorce case was a complete victory for the husband. He, not the wife, was granted a divorce on his crossclaim; the wife's community property claims were denied in their entirety; and she was held entitled to no alimony. 45 Cal. 2d 142, 287 P.2d 769.

Respondent's legal expenses in connection with this litigation amounted to $32,537.15 in 1953 and $8,074.21 in 1954—a total of $40,611.36 for the two taxable years in question. The Commissioner found all of these expenditures "personal" or "family" expenses and as such none of them deductible. [§262.] In the ensuing refund suit, however, the Court of Claims held that 80 percent of such expense (some $32,500) was attributable to respondent's defense against his wife's community property claims respecting his stockholdings and hence deductible under [§212] as an expense "incurred . . . for the . . . conservation . . . of property held for the production of income." In so holding the Court of Claims stated:

> Of course it is true that in every divorce case a certain amount of the legal expenses are incurred for the purpose of obtaining the divorce and a certain amount are incurred in an effort to conserve the estate and are not necessarily deductible under [§212], but when the facts of a particular case clearly indicate [as here] that the property, around which the controversy evolves, is held for the production of income and without this property the litigant might be denied not only the property itself but the means of earning a livelihood, then it must come under the provisions of [§212]. . . . The only question then is the allocation of the expenses of this phase of the proceedings. 290 F.2d, at 947.

The Government does not question the amount or formula for the expense allocation made by the Court of Claims. Its sole contention here is that the court below misconceived the test governing [§212] deductions, in that the deductibility of these expenses turns, so it is argued, not upon the *consequences* to respondent of a failure to defeat his wife's community property claims but upon the *origin* and *nature* of the claims themselves. So viewing Dixie Gilmore's claims whether relating to the existence or division of community property, it is contended that the expense of resisting them must be deemed nondeductible "personal" or "family" expense under [§262], not deductible expense under [§212]. For reasons given hereafter we think the Government's position is sound and that it must be sustained.

I

For income tax purposes Congress has seen fit to regard an individual as having two personalities: "one is [as] a seeker after profit who can deduct the expenses incurred in that search; the other is [as] a creature satisfying his needs as a human and those of his family but who cannot deduct such consumption and related expenditures."[11] The Government regards [§212] as embodying a category of the expenses embraced in the first of these roles.

Initially, it may be observed that the wording of [§212] more readily fits the Government's view of the provision than that of the Court of Claims. For in context "conservation of property" seems to refer to operations performed with respect to the property itself, such as safeguarding or upkeep, rather than to a taxpayer's retention of ownership in it. But more illuminating than the mere language of [§212] is the history of the provision.

Prior to 1942 §23 allowed deductions only for expenses incurred "in carrying on any trade or business," the deduction presently authorized by [§162]. In Higgins v. Commissioner, 312 U.S. 212, this Court gave that provision a narrow construction, holding that the activities of an individual in supervising his own securities investments did not constitute the "carrying on of trade or business," and hence that expenses incurred in connection with such activities were not tax deductible. . . . The Revenue Act of 1942 (56 Stat. 798, §121), by adding what is now [§212], sought to remedy the inequity inherent in the disallowance of expense deductions in respect of such profit-seeking activities, the income from which was nonetheless taxable.

As noted in McDonald v. Commissioner, 323 U.S. 57, 62, the purpose of the 1942 amendment was merely to enlarge "the category of incomes with reference to which expenses were deductible." And committee reports make clear that deductions under the new section were subject to the same limitations and restrictions that are applicable to those allowable under [§162].[14] Further, this Court has said that [§212] "is comparable and in pari materia with [§162]," providing for a class of deductions "coextensive with the business deductions allowed by [§162], except for" the requirement that the income-producing activity qualify as a trade or business. Trust of Bingham v. Commissioner, 325 U.S. 365, 373, 374.

A basic restriction upon the availability of a [§162] deduction is that the expense item involved must be one that has a business origin. That restriction not only inheres in the language of [§162] itself, confining such deductions to "expenses . . . incurred . . . in carrying on any trade or business," but also follows from [§262], expressly rendering nondeductible "in any case . . . [p]ersonal, living, or family expenses." . . . In light of what has already been said with respect to the advent and thrust of [§212], it is clear that the "[p]ersonal . . . or family expenses" restriction of [§262] must impose the same limitation upon the reach of [§212] — in other words that the only kind of expenses deductible under [§212] are those

---

11. Surrey and Warren, Cases on Federal Income Taxation, 272 (1960).

14. H.R. Rep. No. 2333, 77th Cong., 2d Sess. 75: "A deduction under this section is subject, except for the requirement of being incurred in connection with a trade or business, to all the restrictions and limitations that apply in the case of the deduction under section 23(a)(1)(A) of an expense paid or incurred in carrying on any trade or business." See also S. Rep. No. 1631, 77th Cong., 2d Sess. 88.

that relate to a "business," that is, profit-seeking, purpose. The pivotal issue in this case then becomes: was this part of respondent's litigation costs a "business" rather than a "personal" or "family" expense?

The answer to this question has already been indicated in prior cases. In Lykes v. United States, 343 U.S. 118, the Court rejected the contention that legal expenses incurred in contesting the assessment of a gift tax liability were deductible. The taxpayer argued that if he had been required to pay the original deficiency he would have been forced to liquidate his stockholdings, which were his main source of income, and that his legal expenses were therefore incurred in the "conservation" of income-producing property and hence deductible under [§212]. The Court first noted that the "deductibility [of the expenses] turns wholly upon the nature of the activities to which they relate" (343 U.S., at 123), and then stated:

> Legal expenses do not become deductible merely because they are paid for services which relieve a taxpayer of liability. That argument would carry us too far. It would mean that the expense of defending almost any claim would be deductible by a taxpayer on the ground that such defense was made to help him keep clear of liens whatever income-producing property he might have. For example, it suggests that the expense of defending an action based upon personal injuries caused by a taxpayer's negligence while driving an automobile for pleasure should be deductible. Section [212] never has been so interpreted by us. . . .
>
> While the threatened deficiency assessment . . . added urgency to petitioner's resistance of it, neither its size nor its urgency determined its character. It related to the tax payable on petitioner's gifts. . . . The expense of contesting the amount of the deficiency was thus at all times attributable to the gifts, as such, and accordingly was not deductible.
>
> If, as suggested, the relative size of each claim, in proportion to the income-producing resources of a defendant, were to be a touchstone of the deductibility of the expense of resisting the claim, substantial uncertainty and inequity would inhere in the rule. . . . It is not a ground for [deduction] that the claim, if justified, will consume income-producing property of the defendant. 343 U.S., at 125-126.

In Kornhauser v. United States, 276 U.S. 145, this Court considered the deductibility of legal expenses incurred by a taxpayer in defending against a claim by a former business partner that fees paid to the taxpayer were for services rendered during the existence of the partnership. In holding that these expenses were deductible even though the taxpayer was no longer a partner at the time of suit, the Court formulated the rule that "where a suit or action against a taxpayer is directly connected with, or . . . proximately resulted from, his business, the expense incurred is a business expense. . . ." 276 U.S., at 153. Similarly, in a case involving an expense incurred in satisfying an obligation (though not a litigation expense), it was said that "it is the origin of the liability out of which the expense accrues" or "the kind of transaction out of which the obligation arose . . . which [is] crucial and controlling." Deputy v. du Pont, 308 U.S. 488, 494, 496.

The principle we derive from these cases is that the characterization, as "business" or "personal," of the litigation costs of resisting a claim depends on whether or not the claim *arises in connection with* the taxpayer's profit-seeking activities. It does not depend on the *consequences* that might result to a taxpayer's income-producing property from a failure to defeat the claim, for, as Lykes teaches, that "would carry us too far" and would not be compatible with the basic lines of expense deductibility drawn by Congress. Moreover, such a rule would lead to capricious results. If two taxpayers are each sued for an automobile accident while driving for pleasure, deductibility of their litigation costs would turn on the mere circumstance of the character of the assets each happened to possess, that is, whether the judgments against them stood to be satisfied out of income or non-income-producing property. We should be slow to attribute to Congress a purpose producing such unequal treatment among taxpayers, resting on no rational foundation.

Confirmation of these conclusions is found in the incongruities that would follow from acceptance of the Court of Claim's reasoning in this case. Had this respondent taxpayer conducted his automobile-dealer business as a sole proprietorship, rather than in corporate form, and claimed a deduction under [§162][17] the potential impact of his wife's claims would have been no different than in the present situation. Yet it cannot well be supposed that [§162] would have afforded him a deduction since his expenditures, made in connection with a marital litigation, could hardly be deemed "expenses . . . incurred . . . in carrying on any trade or business." Thus, under the Court of Claims' view expenses may be even less deductible if the taxpayer is carrying on a trade or business instead of some other income-producing activity. But it was manifestly Congress' purpose with respect to deductibility to place all income-producing activities on an equal footing. And it would surely be a surprising result were it now to turn out that a change designed to achieve equality of treatment in fact had served only to reverse the inequality of treatment.

For these reasons, we resolve the conflict among the lower courts on the question before us . . . in favor of the view that the origin and character of the claim with respect to which an expense was incurred, rather than its potential consequences upon the fortunes of the taxpayer, is the controlling basic test of whether the expense was "business" or "personal" and hence whether it is deductible or not under [§212]. We find the reasoning underlying the cases taking the "consequences" view unpersuasive.

Baer v. Commissioner, 8 Cir., 196 F.2d 646, upon which the Court of Claims relied in the present case, is the leading authority on that side of the question. There the Court of Appeals for the Eighth Circuit allowed a [§212] expense deduction to a taxpayer husband with respect to attorney's fees paid in a divorce proceeding in connection with an alimony settlement which had the effect of preserving intact for the husband his controlling stock interest in a corporation, his principal source of livelihood. The court reasoned that

---

17. We find no indication that Congress intended [§212] to include such expenses.

since the evidence showed that the taxpayer was relatively unconcerned about the divorce itself "[t]he controversy did not go to the question of . . . [his] liability [for alimony] but to the manner in which [that liability] might be met . . . without greatly disturbing his financial structure"; therefore the legal services were "for the purpose of conserving and maintaining" his income-producing property. 196 F.2d, at 649-650, 651.

It is difficult to perceive any significant difference between the "question of liability" and "the manner" of its discharge, for in both instances the husband's purpose is to avoid losing valuable property. Indeed most of the cases which have followed *Baer* have placed little reliance on that distinction, and have tended to confine the deduction to situations where the wife's alimony claims, if successful, might have completely destroyed the husband's capacity to earn a living. Such may be the situation where loss of control of a particular corporation is threatened, in contrast to instances where the impact of a wife's support claims is only upon diversified holdings of income-producing securities. But that rationale too is unsatisfactory. For diversified security holdings are no less "property held for the production of income" than a large block of stock in a single company. And as was pointed out in *Lykes*, supra, 343 U.S. at 126, if the relative impact of a claim on the income-producing resources of a taxpayer were to determine deductibility, substantial "uncertainty and inequity would inhere in the rule."

We turn then to the determinative question in this case: did the wife's claims respecting respondent's stockholdings arise in connection with his profit-seeking activities?

II

In classifying respondent's legal expenses the court below did not distinguish between those relating to the claims of the wife with respect to the *existence* of community property and those involving the *division* of any such property. . . . Nor is such a break-down necessary for a disposition of the present case. It is enough to say that in both aspects the wife's claims stemmed entirely from the marital relationship, and not, under any tenable view of things, from income-producing activity. This is obviously so as regards the claim to more than an equal division of any community property found to exist. For any such right depended entirely on the wife's making good her charges of marital infidelity on the part of the husband. The same conclusion is no less true respecting the claim relating to the existence of community property. For no such property could have existed but for the marriage relationship.[22] Thus none of respondent's expenditures in resisting these

---

22. The respondent's attempted analogy of a marital "partnership" to the business partnership involved in the *Kornhauser* case, supra, is of course unavailing. The marriage relationship can hardly be deemed an income-producing activity.

claims can be deemed "business" expenses, and they are therefore not deductible under [§212].

In view of this conclusion it is unnecessary to consider the further question suggested by the Government: whether that portion of respondent's payments attributable to litigating the issue of the existence of community property was a capital expenditure or a personal expense. In neither event would these payments be deductible from gross income.

The judgment of the Court of Claims is reversed and the case is remanded to that court for further proceedings consistent with this opinion. It is so ordered.

Mr. Justice BLACK and Mr. Justice DOUGLAS believe that the Court reverses this case because of an unjustifiably narrow interpretation of [§212] and would accordingly affirm the judgment of the Court of Claims.

UNITED STATES v. PATRICK
372 U.S. 53 (1963)

Mr. Justice HARLAN delivered the opinion of the Court. This case presents the question, similar to that decided today in No. 21, United States v. Gilmore, 372 U.S. 39, as to the deductibility of certain legal fees paid by the respondent to his attorneys and attorneys representing his wife in connection with divorce proceedings instituted by the wife. . . .

In 1955 respondent's wife sued for divorce, alleging adultery on the part of her husband. Extended negotiations by the attorneys for both parties resulted in a property settlement agreement, and thereafter respondent filed his answer to the complaint neither admitting nor denying the allegations of adultery. Respondent did not testify at the trial. The South Carolina divorce court granted the wife an absolute divorce, approved the property settlement agreement, and in accordance therewith ordered respondent to pay the attorneys' fees for both parties.

At the time of these proceedings, respondent was president of the Herald Publishing Company in Rock Hill, South Carolina, and editor of the newspaper published by it. He owned 28% of the corporation's outstanding stock, his wife owned 28%, their oldest son, Hugh Patrick, owned 9%, and the remaining 35% was held in trusts for Hugh and the parties' two minor children. The real property on which the Herald Company was situated was owned by respondent and his wife, the former having an 80% undivided interest and the latter a 20% undivided interest. The couple also owned two houses. In addition, each independently owned diversified securities and other assets of substantial value.

The property settlement agreement recited that "by virtue of this agreement a final and lump settlement has been made of any and all rights whatsoever . . . concerning the matter of support, separate maintenance, alimony or any financial obligation of whatsoever sort due to [the wife] . . . on account of and growing out of the marital relationship of the parties. . . ." Besides provisions of the custody and support of the minor children and a provision giving one of the two houses to each of the parties, certain arrangements were made concerning the respective interests in the newspaper properties. Respondent delivered to his wife high-quality securities worth $112,000, the agreed value of her 28% of the publishing company stock, which she transferred to him subject to the condition that such stock should go to their three children in the event of his death or a sale of the entire business. A new long-term lease of the real property housing the newspaper was entered into with the corporation, and both parties then transferred their interests in this property to a trust, the income therefrom being payable to the wife for life and the remainder to pass in equal shares to the children. Finally, respondent agreed to pay all of his wife's attorneys' fees for services rendered in connection with the divorce and property settlement arrangements.

These fees, paid by respondent in 1956, amounted to $24,000— $12,000 to his attorneys and $12,000 to his wife's attorneys. The $24,000 total was allocated by agreement of counsel and the parties as follows: $4,000 for handling the divorce itself; $16,000 for rearranging the stock interests in the publishing company; and $4,000 for leasing the real property and transferring it to a trust. Respondent claimed a deduction for the $16,000 item and for 80% of the $4,000 ($3,200) item relating to the business real estate. . . .

The situation, in short, is comparable to that in United States v. Gilmore, supra. The principles held governing in that case are equally applicable here. It is evident that the claims asserted by the wife in the divorce action arose from respondent's marital relationship with her and were thus the product of respondent's personal or family life, not profit-seeking activity. As we have held in *Gilmore*, payments made for the purpose of discharging such claims are not deductible as "business" expenses.

We find no significant distinction in the fact that the legal fees for which deduction is claimed were paid for arranging a transfer of stock interests, leasing real property, and creating a trust rather than for conducting litigation. These matters were incidental to litigation brought by respondent's wife, whose claims arising from respondent's personal and family life were the origin of the property arrangements. The property settlement agreement itself recited that it settled rights "growing out of the marital relationship," . . . and both courts below found that, although nominally an agreement for the purchase of the wife's property, it served ultimately to protect respondent's income-producing property from an assertion of his wife's latent marital rights. It would be unsound to make deductibility turn on the nature of the measures taken to forestall a claim rather than the source of the claim itself. . . .

Mr. Justice BLACK and Mr. Justice DOUGLAS dissent.

HUNTER v. UNITED STATES
219 F.2d 69 (2d Cir. 1955)

Before Clark, Chief Judge, and Frank and Hincks, Circuit Judges.

FRANK, Circuit Judge. Taxpayer contends that [attorney's fees incurred in securing a reduction in alimony] are deductible under [§212] as "ordinary and necessary expenses . . . for the production . . . of income. . . ." He argues that, as the settlement reduced the amount of his liability for alimony and thus increased his taxable net income, it constituted the "production of income." We cannot agree. We think the "production" of income means the creation of increased gross income, not a reduction of liabilities or an increase of net taxable income by a reduction of allowable deductions in computing net income. Lykes v. United States, 343 U.S. 118; Howard v. Commissioner, 9 Cir., 202 F.2d 28.

Affirmed.

RUTH K. WILD
42 T.C. 706 (1964), acq., 1967-2 C.B. 4

OPINION

KERN, Judge. . . . In 1959 petitioner sued her husband for a legal separation. Subsequently her action was changed to one of divorce. In 1960 a divorce was granted to the petitioner and a stipulation relative to child custody and support and property was made a part of the divorce decree. . . .

On her individual income tax return for 1960 petitioner claimed a deduction of $6,000 under "Other Deductions" for "Atty. fees re negotiating alimony payments and Court hearings." In schedule H of her individual income tax return for 1960 petitioner included in her gross income $9,850 as "Alimony payments from Norman R. Wild."

Respondent disallowed the claimed deduction for legal fees in the amount of $6,000 with the following explanation:

"The claimed legal fees have not been demonstrated to be expenses ordinary and closely related to the production, maintenance, or protection of taxable income as required under section 212 of the Internal Revenue Code."

Petitioner contends that the amount of the legal fees claimed as a deduction was an ordinary and necessary expense incurred for the production of income which is deductible under section 212(1). Respondent contends that such expense is not deductible pursuant to section 262 because it was a personal expense arising from the marital relationship and was thus "the product of her [petitioner's] personal and family life and not a profit-seeking activity." Respondent relies on United States v. Gilmore, 372 U.S. 39, and United States v. Patrick, 372 U.S. 53. . . .

Section 1.262-1 (b)(7), Income Tax Regulations, which has never been withdrawn or modified by respondent, provides as follows:

Sec. 1.262-1 Personal, living, and family expenses.

   (b) *Examples of personal, living, and family expenses.* Personal, living, and family expenses are illustrated in the following examples: . . .
   (7) Generally, attorney's fees and other costs paid in connection with a divorce, separation, or decree for support are not deductible by either the husband or the wife. However, the part of an attorney's fee and the part of other costs paid in connection with a divorce, legal separation, written separation agreement, or a decree for support, which are properly attributable to the production or collection of amounts includible in gross income under section 71 are deductible by the wife under section 212.

In Jane U. Elliott, 40 T.C. 304 (filed May 15, 1963), acq. 1964-1 C.B. (Part 1) 4, we held that legal fees paid for the collection of alimony from the taxpayer's former husband were deductible under section 212(1). See also Estate of Daniel Buckley, 37 T.C. 664, 674; Barbara B. LeMond, 13 T.C. 670: and Elsie B. Gale, 13 T.C. 661, affirmed on other grounds 191 F.2d 79.

Respondent argues that these cases are no longer applicable in view of the Supreme Court's decisions in United States v. Gilmore, supra, and United States v. Patrick, supra (both decided on February 18, 1963). . . . In those cases it was held that expenses of husbands in connection with resisting money demands of their wives in divorce actions could not be deducted under section 212(2) as expenses paid for the management, conservation, or maintenance of property held for the production of income. In the instant case the deduction is claimed under section 212(1), which expressly provides for the deduction of expenses "paid or incurred . . . for the production or collection of income." Here the expenses were paid "for the production or collection" of alimony which was reported, when paid to petitioner, as her taxable income in conformity with the provisions of the Internal Revenue Code.

In view of the fact that respondent has never changed or modified his regulation as above quoted since the Supreme Court's decisions in the *Gilmore* and *Patrick* cases were handed down on February 18, 1963, the fact that we decided the case of Jane U. Elliott, supra, some 3 months after February 18, 1963, and the fact that respondent noted his acquiescence in that case on March 16, 1964, and has never withdrawn it, we would be disinclined to overrule our holding in the *Elliott* case and to disapprove respondent's pertinent and outstanding regulation unless we were compelled to do so by the decisions of the Supreme Court in the *Gilmore* and *Patrick* cases. Since those cases dealt with another subsection of the Internal Revenue Code in the context of another factual background, it is our opinion that we are not compelled by them to reach such a result. . . .

Reviewed by the Court.

Decision will be entered for the petitioner.

RAUM, J., dissenting: I think that a fair reading of United States v. Gilmore, 372 U.S. 39, and United States v. Patrick, 372 U.S. 53, calls for a result contrary to that reached in the prevailing opinion, and that the distinction between sections 212(1) and (2) relied upon by the majority is spurious.

Sections 212(1) and (2) of the 1954 Code, here involved, are merely fragmented parts of what was formerly section 23(a)(2) of the 1939 Code, the history of which was outlined in *Gilmore.* At one time section 23(a) provided merely for the deduction of expenses in carrying on a trade or business. It was then amended so as to add deductions for like expenses not connected with trade or business. The old trade or business deductions were continued in section 23(a)(1), and the new deductions were contained in section 23(a)(2). These new deductions were spelled out in section 23(a)(2) as follows:

> (2) Non-trade or Non-business Expenses. — In the case of an individual, all the ordinary and necessary expenses paid or incurred during the taxable year for the production or collection of income, or for the management, conservation, or mainte-nance of property held for the production of income.

The Supreme Court in *Gilmore* held that section 24(a)(1), which specif-ically denied any deduction for "personal" or "family" expenses, was a lim-itation upon section 23(a)(2), and that, accordingly, expenses incurred by a husband in a divorce action to protect his income-producing property were not deductible even though the situation were otherwise literally covered by section 23(a)(2). The theory of the decision in that case and in *Patrick* was that the claims in respect of which the expenses were incurred arose from the taxpayer's "marital relationship . . . and were thus the product of [his] . . . personal or family life. . . ." 372 U.S. at 56.

That theory was plainly applicable to all parts of section 23(a)(2), which had the *identical* legislative history, and I can conceive of no justification for reaching a different result in respect of that portion of section 23(a)(2) that became section 212(1) of the 1954 Code from that portion which became section 212(2). . . .

Gilmore and *Patrick* make it clear that such limitations are operative when the claim arises out of the marital relationship in a divorce proceeding, and I think it quixotic to reach a different result here. The mere fact that the Treasury has not withdrawn the regulation upon which the majority rely is of no con-trolling significance. The *Gilmore* and *Patrick* cases were decided only last year, and it is notorious that the wheels of administration often turn slowly.

TIETJENS and PIERCE, JJ., agree with this dissent.

PIERCE, J., dissenting: I agree with the dissenting opinion of Judge Raum, but I wish to add a word about Jane U. Elliott, 40 T.C. 304, upon which the majority relies in part. I regard it as distinguishable. In the instant case, expenses were incurred in order to *establish* petitioner's right to alimony, plainly a "personal" or "family" right. In *Elliott,* on the other hand, the right to alimony had already been established, and the expenses were incurred merely in order to effect *collection* of a fixed obligation, just as they might have been incurred by a noteholder seeking to collect interest on his note or a lessor seeking to collect rent from his lessee. Since *Elliott* is distinguishable I see no reason to extend it to reach an unsound result.

TIETJENS and RAUM, JJ., agree with this dissent.

Notes and Questions

1. Was the Court right to treat *Patrick* as governed by *Gilmore*, or are there important differences?

Assume that a businesswoman enters into an agreement entitling her divorced husband, among other things, to 30 percent of the profits of her business. Subsequently a dispute develops about the computation of earnings and the wife hires counsel to defend the claim. Can she deduct the counsel fees she pays?

Does *Gilmore* work the other way? Suppose a movie actor and actress meet performing in a film together. Can they deduct the expenses arising out of their subsequent marriage and divorce as having had their origin in a business relationship? Why not?

2. Is the reasoning in *Hunter* sound? What if a taxpayer incurs legal expenses in a controversy over the fee charged her by a doctor? Does *Hunter* indicate it would be nondeductible?

Suppose a taxpayer disputes and refuses to pay the bill submitted by her investment advisor. Does *Hunter* indicate that expenses incurred defending against the investment advisor's claim would be nondeductible?

Can the result in *Hunter* be satisfactorily reconciled with that in *Wild*?

3. An Army Reserve officer was tried before a general court martial on a charge of conduct unbecoming an officer in that he had dishonorably refused payment of alimony to his divorced wife. Can he deduct his legal expenses defending himself before the court martial? Howard v. Commissioner, 202 F.2d 28 (9th Cir. 1953).

4. An author's wife brought a proceeding to have him declared an incompetent and committed to an asylum. Can he deduct the cost of resisting that proceeding? What if his primary motivation is to avoid an adverse impact on the sale of his books? What if the attempted proof of his incompetence rests heavily on the contents of his books? Lewis v. Commissioner, 253 F.2d 821 (2d Cir. 1958).

5. A lawyer was having marital difficulties and her husband began calling her clients to complain to them about her treatment of him. The lawyer brought proceedings to restrain her husband's interference with her client relationships. Would her litigation expenses be deductible?

6. *Lykes*, on which the Court relied in *Gilmore*, was effectively overruled by enactment of §212(3) in 1954. What is the implication of that? Does §212(3) provide a ground for deducting divorce litigation and settlement expenses besides those covered in *Wild*?

7. Does the Court in *Gilmore* explain satisfactorily *why* deductibility is to be determined by reference to the origin of the claim rather than purpose of defense? Is the definition of the issue in these terms oversimplified in any event? Consider the following dissenting opinion in Lykes v. United States, 343 U.S. 118, 127 (1951):

> Mr. Justice JACKSON, whom Mr. Justice FRANKFURTER joins, dissenting.
>
> Lykes made a gift of corporate stock to his children. It was a legitimate transaction, duly reported for gift-tax purposes and a tax of over $13,000 paid thereon. By overvaluing the stock which had been given, the Commissioner asserted a gift-tax deficiency of $145,276.50, of which about $130,000 was found by the Tax Court to be unjustified. But, to protect himself against the Government's unjustified claim, Lykes spent $7,263.83 for legal services.
>
> I am unable to understand why this payment was not deductible as being an expense incurred "for the management, conservation, or maintenance of property held for the production of income." Had the taxpayer yielded to the Government's unjustified demand, it would have depleted his capital by about $130,000 and thenceforward he could not have enjoyed income from it. Of course, it is not the amount but the principle that is significant. Indeed, the burden of legal expense is likely to be in inverse proportion to the amount of the deficiency asserted. Here the expense was only about 5 percent of the saving. In small cases of small taxpayers the percentage will be far greater and in many may exceed 100 percent. Certainly contest against unwarranted exaction, regardless of its amount or outcome, is for the conservation of property and its reasonable cost is deductible.
>
> A majority of my brethren seem to think they can escape this conclusion by going further back in the chain of causation. They say the cause of this legal expense was the gift. Of course one can reason, as my brethren do, that if there had been no gifts there would have been no tax, if there had been no tax there would have been no deficiency, if there were no deficiency there would have been no contest, if there were no contest there would have been no expense. And so the gifts caused the expense. The fallacy of such logic is that it would be just as possible to employ it to prove that the lawyer's fees were caused by having children. If there had been no children there would have been no gift, and if no gift no tax, and if no tax no deficiency, and if no deficiency no contest, and if no contest no expense. Hence, the lawyer's fee was not due to the contest at all but was a part of the cost of having babies. If this reasoning were presented by a taxpayer to avoid a tax, what would we say of it? So treacherous is this kind of reasoning that in most fields the law rests its conclusion only on proximate cause and declines to follow the winding trail of remote and multiple causations. . . .

8. When Gilmore later sold his stock, should he have added the divorce litigation costs to his basis in computing gain or loss? See Gilmore v. United States, 245 F. Supp. 383 (N.D. Calif. 1965) (addition to basis permitted).

9. *Liability payments.* Is *Gilmore* limited to legal expenses? What considerations determine whether or not damages or settlement payments are deductible? Suppose that *W*, a wealthy individual, is involved in an automobile accident as a result of which he is required to pay the other driver $500,000 in personal injury damages from *W*'s own funds (because the liability exceeds his insurance policy limits, for example). Is the payment deductible? Does it matter whether the accident occurred:

(a) When *W* was driving home from the office?

(b) When *W* was driving from his office to a meeting with an important customer?

(c) When *W* was driving to a meeting with his personal investment advisor?

(d) When *W* was driving to the closing of his purchase of investment real estate?

(e) When *W* was driving his daughter to her weekend soccer practice?

(f) In each of the foregoing situations, while *W*, a repeat offender, was intoxicated? See Oden v. Commissioner, T.C. Memo. 1988-567 (sole proprietor's legal expenses and damage payments nondeductible where taxpayer gave maliciously defamatory reference on former employee); see also Kelly v. Commissioner, T.C. Memo. 1999-69 (costs of defending sexual assault charges nondeductible despite employment setting).

H.   EDUCATION AND TRAINING

1.   Business Expense Deduction

JORGENSEN v. COMMISSIONER
T.C. Memo 2000-138; 79 T.C.M. (CCH) 1926 (2000)

Memorandum Opinion

DEAN, Special Trial Judge: Respondent determined deficiencies in petitioner's Federal income taxes of $1,596 and $2,282 for taxable years 1995 and 1996, respectively.

The issue for decision is whether petitioner incurred nondeductible expenses for travel as a form of education within the meaning of section 274(m)(2) or whether she had ordinary and necessary employee business expenses for travel and education under section 162.

Some of the facts have been stipulated and are so found. The stipulation of facts and the attached exhibits are incorporated herein by reference. Petitioner resided in San Francisco, California, at the time she filed her petition.

BACKGROUND

Petitioner teaches English at Abraham Lincoln High School, a culturally diverse San Francisco public high school with a predominantly Asian student population. During 1995 and 1996, petitioner also was the chair of the high school's English department. Most of petitioner's students are immigrants or have parents who are immigrants.

As a teacher in the San Francisco Unified School District, petitioner has a mission to promote both intellectual growth and cultural and linguistic sensitivity to enable students from all cultural backgrounds to succeed. Petitioner's duties as a teacher include, among others, to be competent in her subject field, to be involved in the development and implementation of curriculum, to demonstrate a repertoire of teaching strategies and techniques, and to participate in professional growth activities. Some of petitioner's additional duties and responsibilities as English department chair were to assist in establishing department curriculum objectives and develop a plan for the implementation and evaluation of these objectives, to develop innovative or experimental work and articulate instruction with various grade levels, to assist department teachers with day-to-day problems of instruction, to act as a resource person for department teachers on curriculum questions, and to be able to relate successfully with diverse groups of students and adults.

In 1995 petitioner enrolled in a summer course sponsored by the University of California, Berkeley Extension Program (U.C. Extension) entitled "Legendary Greece: Minoans, Mycenaeans, and Classical Athens" (Legendary Greece) in order to study how legend grew out of historical events. The course took place in Greece from June 20 to July 8, 1995. Petitioner paid the following amounts for the Legendary Greece course and deducted the total amount on her 1995 Federal income tax return as an employee business expense:

U.C. Extension:	
Tuition, lodging, meals	$4,140
Airfare	1,117
Miscellaneous:	
Two extra nights at hotel	240
Books and airport shuttle	77
Total	$5,574

In 1996, petitioner attended a U.C. Extension course entitled "Southeast Asia: Sacred Places" (Southeast Asia) to study how the religious traditions of Buddhism and Hinduism have shaped and continue to shape the culture of Southeast Asia. The course took place in Thailand, Cambodia, and Indonesia from December 27, 1996, to January 11, 1997. Petitioner paid the following amounts in connection with the Southeast Asia course and deducted the total amount on her 1996 Federal income tax return as an employee business expense:

U.C. Extension:	
Tuition, meals, lodging	$4,500
Airfare	2,335
Visas, transfers, taxes, misc.	1,070
Total	$7,805

Both of these courses were taught by university professors and qualified for upper division, undergraduate U.C. Extension credit. In both courses, credit requirements included the completion of a research paper. Petitioner did not seek or obtain credit for the courses.

Both courses had focused academic purposes and consisted of a series of formal lectures and visits to historical and cultural sites. The Legendary Greece course had a required reading list for all attendees, and the Southeast Asia course required reading only for attendees seeking credit. Petitioner completed all credit requirements for the courses with the exception of the research papers. Petitioner's employer did not require her to take these courses as a condition to retaining her employment as a high school English teacher.

Petitioner has applied what she learned in the Legendary Greece course to develop additional curriculum for her English classes. This curriculum includes the study of methods Homer used to "compose" the "Odyssey" and of the historical Mycenaean palace culture, in which ancient Greek tragedies were set. In addition, petitioner has added a "strand" explaining the historical and cultural roots of certain myths and legends.

Petitioner has applied what she learned in the Southeast Asia course to understand better her Asian students' responses in class and to work more effectively with them. Petitioner's experiences in Asia serve as a basis for further intelligent and respectful discussion with her students about their cultures. Petitioner also has used the knowledge she gained in the Southeast Asia course to enhance her curriculum: Introducing works written by Americans of Southeast Asian origin, discussing novels with an Asian immigrant theme, and working to bring the Indian epic "Ramayana" into her high school's world literature curriculum.

In the notice of deficiency, respondent disallowed $5,676 and $8,125 of the deductions petitioner claimed as employee business expenses on her Federal income tax returns for taxable years 1995 and 1996, respectively. Respondent concedes that petitioner is entitled to $103 of the disallowed deductions for 1995 and $320 of the disallowed deductions for 1996. The remaining disallowed deductions are for the expenditures associated with petitioner's participation in the Legendary Greece and Southeast Asia courses. Respondent maintains that these expenses were incurred for travel as a form of education and that such expenses are nondeductible under section 274(m)(2). In the alternative, respondent argues that even if the expenses are for education other than that which resulted from the travel itself, the expenses are nevertheless not deductible under section 162 because they are not ordinary and necessary business expenses.

DISCUSSION

Section 162(a) permits a deduction for all ordinary and necessary expenses paid or incurred during the taxable year in carrying on a trade or business. Such expenses generally include expenditures for travel, including amounts expended on meals and lodging, while away from home in the pursuit of a trade or business. See sec. 162(a)(2).

In contrast, no deductions are allowed for personal, living, or family expenses unless otherwise expressly provided by the Internal Revenue Code. See sec. 262(a). Expenditures made by a taxpayer in obtaining or furthering education are considered personal expenses and are not deductible unless they qualify under section 162 and section 1.162-5, Income Tax Regs., as business expenses. See sec. 1.262-1(b)(9), Income Tax Regs. Objective criteria for distinguishing between business expenses and personal expenses are set forth in section 1.162-5, Income Tax Regs. See Boser v. Commissioner, 77 T.C. 1124, 1128-1129 (1981), revised 79 T.C. II (1982), affd. without published opinion (9th Cir., Dec. 22, 1983); McCulloch v. Commissioner, T.C. Memo 1988-84.

Before 1987, section 1.162-5(d), Income Tax Regs., specifically provided that expenditures for travel as a form of education could properly be deducted under section 162 to the extent the travel was directly related to the duties of the individual in his or her employment or other trade or business. This regulation, however, was expressly overruled for years beginning after 1986 by the enactment of section 274(m)(2). See Tax Reform Act of 1986, Pub. L. 99-514, sec. 142(b), 100 Stat. 2118. Section 274(m)(2) provides that "No deduction shall be allowed under this chapter for expenses for travel as a form of education."

Although no regulations have yet been promulgated under section 274(m), its legislative history offers insight into congressional intent in enacting section 274(m)(2). In H. Conf. Rept. 99-841 (Vol. 2), at II-30 (1986), 1986-3 C.B. (Vol. 4) 1, 30, the legislation was explained as follows:

> Educational travel. — No deduction is allowed for costs of travel that would be deductible only on the ground that the travel itself constitutes a form of education (e.g., where a teacher of French travels to France to maintain general familiarity with the French language and culture, or where a social studies teacher travels to another State to learn about or photograph its people, customs, geography, etc.). This provision overrules Treas. Reg. sec. 1.162-5(d) to the extent that such regulation allows deductions for travel as a form of education.

While the statute expressly overrules section 1.162-5(d), Income Tax Regs., the report makes no mention of section 1.162-5(e), Income Tax Regs., which provides, in part, for the deductibility of a taxpayer's travel expenses if the primary purpose of the travel is to engage in activities that themselves represent deductible education expenses. A report from the House of Representatives Committee on Ways and Means provides additional insight into the rationale underlying section 274(m)(2) and further indicates that Congress intended to leave intact the provisions for deductibility under section 1.162-5(e), Income Tax Regs.:

> The committee is concerned about deductions claimed for travel as a form of "education". The committee believes that any business purpose served by traveling for general educational purposes, in the absence of a specific need such as engaging in research

which can only be performed at a particular facility, is at most indirect and insubstantial. By contrast, travel as a form of education may provide substantial personal benefits by permitting some individuals in particular professions to deduct the cost of a vacation, while most individuals must pay for vacation trips out of after-tax dollars, no matter how educationally stimulating the travel may be. Accordingly, the committee bill disallows deductions for travel that can be claimed only on the ground that the travel itself is "educational", but permits deductions for travel that is a necessary adjunct to engaging in an activity that gives rise to a business deduction relating to education. [H.Rep. 99-426, at 122 (1985), 1986-3 C.B. (Vol. 2) 1, 122.]

Petitioner argues that her travel was not travel as a form of education within the meaning of section 274(m)(2) because she traveled to participate in academic courses, and thus, the travel was "a necessary adjunct to engaging in an activity that gives rise to a business deduction relating to education." Respondent, on the other hand, contends that petitioner's travel does not differ materially from any organized group tour with a knowledgeable group leader. We agree with petitioner that the U.C. Extension courses fall outside the scope of section 274(m)(2).

Both of the courses had focused educational purposes beyond mere travel as evidenced by the fact that university credit was available for the courses. Unlike the example of a French teacher improving her familiarity with the French language and culture simply through traveling in France, the U.C. Extension courses were conducted on an organized basis with regular lectures from university professors and planned tours of historically and culturally significant sites directly related to the course of study. Petitioner's participation in the courses involved following structured syllabi and completing significant reading assignments. Both U.C. Extension courses and instructors who teach them are reviewed and approved by the appropriate academic department on the University of California, Berkeley campus, and the Committee on Courses of the Academic Senate. Although petitioner did not complete the credit requirements, we are satisfied that her participation in the courses was not within the ambit of section 274(m)(2).

Having determined that the U.C. Extension courses were educational activities beyond mere travel, we nevertheless must determine whether petitioner's expenses meet the requirements for deductibility under section 162. Expenditures made by a taxpayer for education are deductible, with certain exceptions not relevant here,[2] if the education either: (1) Maintains or improves skills required in an individual's employment or other trade or business; or (2) meets the express requirements of the individual's

---

2. The parties agree that the U.C. Extension courses do not meet the minimum educational requirements of petitioner's employment. They further agree that the courses do not qualify petitioner for a new trade or business. Thus, deductions associated with the courses are not prohibited under sec. 1.162-5(b), Income Tax Regs.

employer, or meets the requirements of applicable law or regulations, imposed as a condition to the retention of employment, status, or rate of compensation. See sec. 1.162-5(a), Income Tax Regs. Petitioner's employer did not expressly require her to take the courses at issue. We therefore assess whether these course[s] maintained or improved petitioner's skills as a high school English teacher.

Whether education maintains or improves skills required by the taxpayer's employment is a question of fact. See Boser v. Commissioner, 77 T.C. at 1131; Schwartz v. Commissioner, 69 T.C. 877, 889 (1978); Baker v. Commissioner, 51 T.C. 243, 247 (1968). The burden of proof is on the taxpayer. See Rule 142(a); Welch v. Helvering, 290 U.S. 111 (1933); Boser v. Commissioner, supra at 1131; cf. sec. 7491.[3] The fact that petitioner's education is helpful to her in the performance of her employment does not establish that its cost is deductible as a business expense. See Carroll v. Commissioner, 51 T.C. 213, 215 (1968), aff'd. 418 F.2d 91 (7th Cir. 1969). Petitioner must establish that there is a direct and proximate relationship between the U.C. Extension courses and the skills required in her employment as a high school English teacher. See Kornhauser v. United States, 276 U.S. 145, 153 (1928); Boser v. Commissioner, supra at 1131. A precise correlation is not necessary, but the expenditure must enhance existing employment skills. See Boser v. Commissioner, supra.

We believe that petitioner's participation in the U.C. Extension courses improved her teaching skills in a direct and proximate manner. Petitioner is able to provide specific examples of how her teaching skills were enhanced by both courses.

Petitioner's duties as an English teacher and as chair of the English department entailed more than simply providing instruction in English reading and writing skills. The mission of the San Francisco Unified School District (school district) is in part "to provide each student with an equal opportunity to succeed by promoting intellectual growth, creativity, self discipline, [and] cultural and linguistic sensitivity". In promoting this mission, petitioner's duties and responsibilities as a teacher required her to be competent in her subject field, to be involved in the development and implementation of curriculum, and to demonstrate a repertoire of teaching strategies and techniques. A 1998 resolution of the school district provides in part that the English/language arts curriculum of the school district must "reflect the diversity of culture, race, and class of the students of the San Francisco Unified School District", and the required reading in high schools shall include those works of literature which are referenced on

---

3. Sec. 7491, as effective for court proceedings arising in connection with examinations commencing after July 22, 1998, shifts the burden of proof to the Commissioner, subject to certain limitations, where a taxpayer introduces credible evidence with respect to factual issues relevant to ascertaining the taxpayer's liability for tax. Petitioner does not contend that her examination commenced after July 22, 1998, or that sec. 7491 is applicable to her.

college entrance examinations. Petitioner testified that as an English teacher, she spends 9 to 12 weeks out of a 36-week school year teaching Greek mythology to ninth graders and that she teaches a minimum of 6 weeks of Greek drama to students in the 12th grade. Petitioner did not provide any materials as evidence of the specific content of English courses at Abraham Lincoln High School, nor did she explain why her ninth grade English class includes the study of mythology. Petitioner's testimony, however, explaining why she chose to enroll in the Legendary Greece course, illuminates the need to teach mythology as part of an English class. Petitioner testified that as an undergraduate English major, she took a course in mythology so that she could become familiar with Greek myths and understand the mythical allusions prevalent in literature, but she further explained that the course neglected to relate the mythology to the culture or the civilization in Greece. Turning to the study of Greek drama, we understand such material to be among the great works of Western literature and a fundamental component in the study of world literature. On these bases and with our observations of petitioner, we find petitioner's testimony regarding the curriculum of her English classes credible.

As a result of the Legendary Greece course, petitioner now is able to explain the historical and cultural roots of certain myths and legends which helps her to capture her students' interest and impart greater understanding of the literature her students read for class. The Legendary Greece course also helped petitioner develop additional curriculum for her English classes, including study of the methods Homer used to "compose" the "Odyssey" and study of the historical Mycenaean palace culture, in which ancient Greek tragedies were set.

With regard to the Southeast Asia course, petitioner testified that she is now able to understand better her students from Southeast Asian countries and modify her teaching approaches appropriately. Her understanding also helps petitioner introduce literature written by Southeast Asian writers and enables her to help students understand the themes. Petitioner is also seeking to make the "Ramayana", an ancient Indian epic poem pervasive in Southeast Asia that she discovered through the course, part of the world literature curriculum at her high school.

In contrast to the situation in Takahashi v. Commissioner, 87 T.C. 126 (1986), in which we found that the taxpayers failed to demonstrate a connection between their attendance at a seminar in Hawaii on "Hawaiian Cultural Transition in a Diverse Society" and their jobs as science teachers, petitioner is able to point to tangible ways in which the Southeast Asia course improved her teaching skills. Petitioner testified that, before taking the course, she sometimes had difficulty determining when an Asian student's response to a piece of literature signified a problem with reading comprehension or was a cultural response to a theme the student had difficulty understanding. Petitioner testified that the course has improved her ability to assess students' responses and help them understand themes in literature.

Petitioner's study in Southeast Asia enhanced her skills beyond merely helping her to increase rapport with her Asian students. See Dollins v. Commissioner, T.C. Memo 1982-394. But see Gino v. Commissioner, 60 T.C. 304,
310-311 (1973), revd. on other issue 538 F.2d 833 (9th Cir. 1976). Petitioner
has incorporated much of the knowledge she gained and many of the skills
she acquired in the Southeast Asia course into her English classes. See
Dollins v. Commissioner, supra.

Respondent acknowledges that petitioner's participation in the U.C.
Extension courses has improved her skills by helping her relate to her students and develop curriculum for both her classes and the English department, but respondent maintains that petitioner's skills improved as a result
of her travel and not as a result of the courses. Although petitioner was
required to travel to participate in the courses, it was the content of the
courses that directed petitioner's attention to materials that enhanced her
teaching. Through the course lectures and readings, petitioner was able to
gain more from her travel experience. In light of the classes petitioner
taught, her role in developing curriculum for the English department,
the racial and cultural background of many of her students, and petitioner's
incorporation of tangible knowledge and skills learned in the U.C. Extension courses into the classes she teaches, we find the courses had a direct and
proximate relationship in maintaining and improving petitioner's skills as a
high school English teacher and as chair of the English department.

In addition to proving that the U.C. Extension courses maintained or
improved her teaching skills, petitioners must prove that such expenses were
"ordinary and necessary" within the meaning of section 162(a). See Boser v.
Commissioner, 77 T.C. at 1132; Ford v. Commissioner, 56 T.C. 1300, 1305-
1307 (1971), aff'd per curiam 487 F.2d 1025 (9th Cir. 1973); Stricker v.
Commissioner, T.C. Memo 1995-530; McCulloch v. Commissioner, T.C.
Memo 1988-84; Raines v. Commissioner, T.C. Memo 1983-125; sec. 1.262-
1(b)(9), Income Tax Regs.

"Ordinary" has been defined in the context of section 162(a) as that
which is "normal, usual, or customary" in the taxpayer's trade or business.
Deputy v. du Pont, 308 U.S. 488, 495 (1940). The activity which gives rise to
the expense must not be one that is rare in the taxpayer's business. See
Welch v. Helvering, 290 U.S. at 114; Stricker v. Commissioner, supra. An
activity that is not required by the taxpayer's employer may still be ordinary.
See Boser v. Commissioner, supra at 1132; Carlucci v. Commissioner, 37 T.C.
695 (1962).

Respondent acknowledges that it is a customary practice of teachers to
travel for the sake of professional development, but respondent argues that
petitioner has not established that it is normal, usual, or customary for teachers to take U.C. Extension courses involving travel to foreign countries for
professional development. It is not necessary that petitioner establish that
teachers customarily enroll in U.C. Extension courses. See Hill v. Commissioner, 181 F.2d 906, 908 (4th Cir. 1950), revg. 13 T.C. 291 (1949). In *Hill*,

the Court of Appeals for the Fourth Circuit found that it was unreasonable to require the taxpayer to show that the course she pursued in obtaining further education was the usual method followed by teachers in obtaining renewal of their teaching certificates. See id. The court found it sufficient to establish that an expense is ordinary if the "particular course adopted by the taxpayer is a response that a reasonable person would normally and naturally make under the specific circumstances". Id.; see also Sanders v. Commissioner, T.C. Memo 1960-61.

Petitioner is expected, as a teacher in the San Francisco Unified School District, to pursue a program of professional growth. One of the accepted means of pursuing such a program is to complete college or university courses. Petitioner enrolled in the U.C. Extension courses with specific educational objectives. She testified that she has not seen classes available elsewhere offering similar courses of study. As evidenced by several Tax Court cases involving teachers enrolling in university courses and studying abroad in order to improve teaching skills, such an expenditure is "normal" for a high school teacher. See, e.g., Ford v. Commissioner, supra; Weiman v. Commissioner, T.C. Memo 1971-92. Professional educators act on the assumption that further education improves their ability to use their knowledge effectively. See Ford v. Commissioner, supra at 1306. Under the particular facts of this case, petitioner's participation in the U.C. Extension courses resulted in ordinary business expenditures.

"Necessary" has been construed to mean "appropriate" or "helpful", not "indispensable" or "required". 56 T.C. at 1305-1307. If there are "reasonably evident business ends to be served, and the intention to serve them appears adequately from the record", expenses satisfy the "necessary" requirement. Manischewitz Co. v. Commissioner, 10 T.C. 1139, 1145 (1948). As discussed, the U.C. Extension courses improved petitioner's teaching skills. The expenses associated with a teacher's pursuing further education that develops her understanding of topics which are part of the curriculum she teaches in her classroom, helps her incorporate new materials into her curriculum, and increases her ability to reach out to her students are "appropriate" and "helpful" for a high school teacher.

Inherent in the concept of necessary, however, is that an expenditure must be reasonable in relation to its purpose. See Boser v. Commissioner, supra at 1133; Stricker v. Commissioner, supra; McCulloch v. Commissioner, supra. To the extent that an expense is unreasonable, it is not necessary. See McCulloch v. Commissioner, supra; Raines v. Commissioner, T.C. Memo 1983-125. In such case, only the portion which is reasonable is deductible under section 162. See United States v. Haskel Engg. & Supply Co., 380 F.2d 786, 788-789 (9th Cir. 1967); Boser v. Commissioner, supra at 1133; McCulloch v. Commissioner, supra. An expenditure may be ordinary and necessary, but at the same time it may be unreasonable in amount. See United States v. Haskel Engg. & Supply Co., supra at 788; Stricker v. Commissioner, supra.

Respondent contends that because petitioner did not isolate the tuition cost for the courses, it is impossible to determine whether the cost petitioner incurred for the education itself is reasonable.[4] In the case at hand, isolation of the expense is not necessary to determine the reasonableness of the expense. Whether an expenditure is reasonable is a question of fact. See Commissioner v. Heininger, 320 U.S. 467, 475 (1943); Boser v. Commissioner, supra at 1133; Voigt v. Commissioner, 74 T.C. 82, 89 (1980). The focus of our inquiry is on "the primary purpose of the expenditure as it may be inferred from the totality of the facts concerning the benefits to be achieved, the direct relationship of those benefits to petitioner's business, and the reasonableness of the expenses." Stricker v. Commissioner, supra (citing Love Box Co. v. Commissioner, T.C. Memo 1985-13, aff'd 842 F.2d 1213 (10th Cir. 1988)).

As discussed, the course improved petitioner's teaching skills. Given the important purpose served by the skills petitioner developed and the benefit derived from her participation in the courses, the expenses associated with the courses appear to be reasonable. See McCulloch v. Commissioner, supra. None of the expenses incurred appear to be lavish, and the particular courses selected by petitioner served important educational purposes. See id.

In order for petitioner to be able to deduct the travel expenses associated with the U.C. Extension courses, she also must establish that her travel was undertaken primarily to obtain education which maintains and improves the skills required in her employment. See sec. 1.162-5(e), Income Tax Regs. If a taxpayer travels to a destination and engages in both business and personal activities while at that destination, the expenses attributable to the personal activity constitute nondeductible personal or living expenses. See id.

Whether a trip is related primarily to the taxpayer's trade or business or is primarily personal in nature depends on the facts and circumstances of each case. See McCulloch v. Commissioner, supra; sec. 1.162-5(e), Income Tax Regs. The amount of time during the trip which is spent on activities directly relating to the taxpayer's trade or business relative to the amount of time devoted to personal activity is an important factor in determining the trip's primary purpose. See McCulloch v. Commissioner, supra; sec. 1.162-5(e), Income Tax Regs. Petitioner's travel to Greece and Southeast Asia undoubtedly involved significant elements of personal pleasure; however, we are satisfied that petitioner's primary purpose in undertaking the travel was to maintain and improve her skills as an English teacher.

In petitioner's case, the U.C. Extension courses involved significant travel and tours. Although a number of the sites petitioner visited while she participated in the courses were places many tourists would visit while

---

4. Petitioner paid $4,140 for the Legendary Greece course and $4,500 for the Southeast Asia course. These amounts include course tuition, lodging, and meals. Petitioner contends that respondent assured her that no breakdown of expenses was necessary. Petitioner, therefore, objects to respondent's raising this issue in brief.

sightseeing in the respective countries, each site visit served an educational purpose as part of an organized course of study.

While traveling in Greece and in Southeast Asia, petitioner spent the majority of her time involved in course activity. The record indicates she was primarily engaged in course activity on all but one of the 18 days that the Legendary Greece course was in session. During these 17 days, a course itinerary indicates petitioner spent a minimum of 5 hours a day engaged in course activity. Although a detailed itinerary with the time allocated to specific activities is not available for the Southeast Asia course, petitioner testified that during the Southeast Asia course most of her time during the day was spent either en route to sites, observing sites, or hearing lectures at the sites. She further testified that she had minimal free time during the course which might consist of up to 3 hours on some days.

Given the nature of the educational programs petitioner pursued, it is impossible to separate definitively the personal aspects of petitioner's travel during the time she participated in the U.C. Extension courses from the business aspects. The fact that she undoubtedly derived personal benefit from her travels does not subvert their business purpose. On the basis of the record, we find that petitioner spent most of her time in Greece and in Southeast Asia participating in the U.C. Extension courses.[5]

Petitioner, however, has not established that the $240 expense she incurred for hotel accommodations before the Legendary Greece course began is attributable to business activity. Petitioner testified that she arrived 2 days early in Greece so that she would have an opportunity to recover from jet lag before the course began. We find this expense to be attributable to personal activity.

We thus hold that petitioner's education and travel expenses, with the exception of the $240, are ordinary and necessary business expenses within the meaning of section 162.

In addition to being subject to the requirements of section 162 and the provisions under section 274 already discussed, a taxpayer's deductions for certain travel expenditures are subject to other provisions of section 274. Respondent, however, has not challenged petitioner's travel expenses under the substantiation requirements of section 274(d) or under the limitation on meal and entertainment expenses under section 274(n). We consequently do not address the extent to which these provisions may limit petitioner's deductions.

Accordingly, we find petitioner is entitled to deduct all but $240 of her education and travel expenses.

To reflect the foregoing,

Decision will be entered under Rule 155.

---

5. Although respondent does not contend that petitioner's travel expenses are subject to the provisions of sec. 274(c), the regulations issued under this section tend to support our determination that petitioner was primarily engaged in business activity during the time she spent in Greece and in Southeast Asia. See sec. 1.274-4(d)(2), Income Tax Regs.

Notes and Questions

1. *Business, personal, or capital?* Depending on the circumstances, the costs of education can be in the nature of current business expenses (skills maintenance, such as continuing professional education seminars), might partake of consumption (recreation or entertainment, such as evening pottery or yoga classes), or could amount to the acquisition of a long-lived income-producing skill set (capital expenditure, such as medical or law school tuition). As in Welch v. Helvering, Chapter 13A below, the issue is whether the business expense deduction, §162(a), is trumped by the disallowance of personal, living, or family expenses, §262(a), or the capitalization requirement, §§263(a), 263A.

2. *Capital cost recovery.* Deduction of educational costs as business expenses has long been primarily dealt with by Reg. §1.162-5. Read through that regulation. Why does paragraph (b)(1) of the regulation assert that nondeductible education expenditures "are personal expenditures or constitute an inseparable aggregate of personal and capital expenditures"? Would it be easier to justify nondeductibility of a law school education by simply classifying it as a capital expenditure? One implication of that would be that a later deduction by way of loss or amortization would be appropriate. In Denman v. Commissioner, 48 T.C. 439 (1967) (acq.), a taxpayer sought to amortize the cost of his engineering education. The Tax Court said:

> It is well established that the cost of education undertaken to qualify or establish oneself in a trade or business, or to meet the minimum requirements of a particular employment, constitutes a personal expense and is therefore not deductible. Welch v. Helvering, 290 U.S. 111; Laurie S. Robertson, 37 T.C. 1153, 1158; T. F. Driscoll, 4 B.T.A. 1008. . . .
>
> Neither is petitioner's case improved by the contention that the expenditures for his education should be capitalized rather than treated as expense items for the year or years in which they were incurred. Expenditures which are not deductible because personal are not made any less personal or transformed into business expenditures through the mechanics of capitalizing them as cost of an engineering degree so as to supply a basis for claiming a deduction therefor as depreciation. See and compare Huene v. United States, 257 F. Supp. 564.

See also Sharon v. Commissioner, 78-2 USTC ¶9834 (9th Cir. 1978) (amortization of costs of college, law school and bar review precluded by §262).

Is the permanent disallowance of professional education costs really attributable to the operation of §§262 or 263? The function of the capitalization rules, after all, is to defer deduction so as to better match the expense with the income it produces. Deferred expense recognition is accomplished by creating or increasing basis in property, §§1012, 1016(a)(1), which is later recovered either by depreciation deductions, in the case of property subject to exhaustion, wear and tear, or obsolescence, §167(a), or via the basis offset on disposition, §1001, perhaps operating in conjunction with the loss deduction, §165(a), (c). See Chapter 6A.2 above. Shouldn't the cost of your law license, including law school tuition and fees, bar review course charges, and the cost of the bar exam, be amortized over the 30- or 40-year anticipated duration of your professional career? Applying a plain meaning reading of §167(a), what's the obstacle to that approach? Is cost recovery on retirement from the practice of law an alternative (return-of-capital last)? One's professional skill set (knowledge and experience) is inalienable, so there will be no sale or exchange to generate disposition proceeds against which adjusted basis can be offset. But isn't retirement equivalent to abandonment and hence an "other disposition" of income-earning skills? As a technical matter, is such a "loss" allowable? See §165 and Reg. §1.165-2(a). See also Reg. §1.263(a)-4(b)(3)(i) ("separate and distinct intangible asset" means legally protected property interest of ascertainable value which is "intrinsically capable of being sold, transferred or pledged" separate from a trade or business).

3. *Line drawing.* If amortization of professional education costs were authorized, should undergraduate education costs also be recoverable? Should the answer depend on whether the student's baccalaureate is in engineering or business, as opposed to, say, a B.A. in English or History? What about tuition at a private prep school that's a feeder to the Ivy League? While a primary purpose rule ordinarily governs the treatment of mixed-motive expenditures under §162, the objective disallowance rules of Reg. §1.162-5(b) forestall such nice questions.

4. *"Carrying on" business.* One reason professional and general education expenses are ordinarily nondeductible is because they are not "incurred in carrying on" a trade or business, §162(a), but rather in preparation for it. But then it may seem unfair to allow a deduction just because particular taxpayers commence business activity before completing their education. The Tax Court disallowed a deduction for costs of going to college while serving as a police officer, even though the police department encouraged such study and set duty hours to accommodate it:

> Millions of people must secure a general college education before they commence their life's employment, and it is generally accepted that obtaining such education is a personal responsibility in preparing for one's career. Should the result be any different for the man who goes to college after commencing work? Though his perseverance is to be admired, we do not believe that he should receive tax deductions not available to those who complete their general college preparation before beginning their career. [Carroll v. Commissioner, 51 T.C. 213, 216 (1968), aff'd. 418 F.2d 91 (7th Cir. 1969).]

If a law student accepts a permanent position with a law firm after serving as a summer associate and works for the firm part-time during her final year of law school, does her third-year tuition become deductible? See Reg. §1.162-5(b)(2). The effect of the regulations on education expenses is to deny any deduction for expenses that are normally incurred prior to commencement of a particular business.

There are other instances in which preparatory expenses have been disallowed. In Frank v. Commissioner, 20 T.C. 511 (1953), a taxpayer was denied any deduction for costs incurred in hunting for a newspaper to buy and operate, since the taxpayer was not engaged in any business at the time the expenses were incurred. How does §195 affect this situation? And fees paid to an employment agency have created continuing controversy. See generally Chapter 13E below.

5. *Additional limits of §274.* As *Jorgensen* illustrates, education costs that pass muster under §162 and Reg. §1.162-5 may still have to contend with the objective disallowance rules of §274. Why didn't the Commissioner invoke §274(a)(1) or (n)(1)(B) as grounds for disallowance? Travel expenses (foreign or domestic) bring into play substantiation rules and 50 percent meal disallowance, §274(d), (n), while foreign travel may trigger allocation rules and special nexus requirements, §274(c), (h). On the meaning of travel as a form of education, §274(m)(2), did Jorgensen have "a specific need such as engaging in research which can only be performed at a particular facility," or were her courses in Greece and Southeast Asia more akin to the social studies teacher traveling to another state "to learn about or photograph its people, customs, geography"? Would the result differ if Jorgensen were employed in rural Wyoming rather than San Francisco? If she had not been chair of the English department?

6. *Employee business expenses.* When paid by an employee, the cost of education that maintains or improves skills or meets requirements for maintaining the taxpayer's current position or pay level is an itemized deduction, §§62(a)(1), 63(d), and is also categorized as a miscellaneous itemized deduction subject to the nondeductible floor of 2 percent of adjusted gross income. §67. If paid or reimbursed by the employer, however, those restrictions do not apply. §62(a)(2). Why the difference?

7. *Educational assistance programs.* If paid by the employer, education costs that do not satisfy the strict requirements for allowance of a business expense deduction (perhaps because the education meets minimum educational requirements for a position, or qualifies the employee for a new trade or business) may be received tax free. Up to $5,250 per year of employer-provided educational assistance (tuition, fees, books, supplies and equipment) may be excluded from gross income if the eligibility rules of the educational assistance program (not actual utilization of the benefit) do not discriminate in favor of highly compensated employees. §127. The employer's involvement in setting the terms and bearing the costs of an educational assistance program offers independent assurance that the education is expected to produce important job-related benefits. Unlike the tax benefits for education discussed below, the exclusion is available for education provided to the employee alone; education benefits given to the worker's spouse or dependents are not excludible under §127.

2. Tax Benefits for Education

Accelerated depreciation offers a deliberate tax-based incentive (i.e., deferral) for business investment. Maximal acceleration, in the form of expensing (return-of-capital first) is sometimes available (see §179) and has the effect of exempting the return on the investment from tax. See generally Chapter 15C below. In stark contrast to such investments in depreciable property, investments in income-producing skills (human capital) are *never* deductible despite their limited duration. Is this disparity between the treatment of labor and capital troublesome? Is it mitigated by public investments in higher education, such as state-supported public universities and federal financial aid and research funding? Is shrinking state support for public higher education exacerbating economic neutrality violations at the dawning of a service-based information economy?

Fueled by middle-class angst about escalating college costs, recent legislation has spawned a raft of new tax benefits for education. The proliferation is daunting; the 2007 version of IRS Publication 970, Tax Benefits for Education, describes 12 distinct benefits and requires 80 pages to do it! It is probably fair to say that recent legislative attention has more to do with practical politics than abstract concerns about economic neutrality, but as you study the nature of these allowances it would be well to consider why Congress chose the tax route instead of increased direct expenditures. Is any (only?) federal spending that can be characterized as middle-class tax relief politically viable?

Putting aside the longstanding business expense deduction for work-related education (skills maintenance, Chapter 12E.1 above), tax allowances for education fall into four broad categories. These categories concern the federal income tax treatment of (1) scholarships, (2) direct payment of tuition and fees, (3) borrowing costs, and (4) education savings programs. Without delving into all the nasty details, each category is briefly described in the paragraphs below.

Scholarships. Amounts "received as a qualified scholarship by an individual who is a candidate for a degree at [a qualified] educational organization" are excluded from gross income by §117. The Treasury has defined "candidate for a degree" very broadly to comprehend any primary or secondary school student, any undergraduate or graduate student at a college or university who is pursuing studies or conducting research to meet the requirements of an academic or professional degree, and any student at an educational organization that offers a program of training to prepare students for employment in a recognized occupation (i.e., trade schools). Prop. Reg. §1.117-6(b)(4). To be a "qualified scholarship" the grant must be used to pay tuition, fees required to enroll, or expenses required of all students in a course, such as special course fees, books, supplies, and equipment. Insofar as the grant is applied to pay for other expenses, such as room and board, it must be included in gross income. Importantly, the definition of scholarship is not tied to the source of funding. It applies to tuition remission granted by the educational organization at which the student is enrolled, whether such aid is based on academic or athletic merit or financial need. (Absent §117, would such scholarships be characterized for tax purposes as rebates or price reductions as opposed to gross income?) It applies as well to educational grants from funders unrelated to the student or school, like National Merit scholarships or scholarships sponsored by fraternal organizations, businesses, or foundations. (Presumably, such third-party grants would be categorized as taxable prizes or awards absent §117.) Furthermore, tuition reduction granted by an educational organization to its employees or their spouses or dependent children, or paid by the employer educational organization to another educational organization, may also be excludible despite its compensatory nature. The exclusion is generally limited to reductions in tuition for education at the undergraduate level and below, but graduate students engaged in teaching or research can also receive (be paid with) tax-free tuition remission. The exclusion applies even if the tuition assistance would not satisfy the general exclusions for fringe benefits as a "no-additional-cost service" or a "qualified employee discount," but in the case of a highly compensated employee the exclusion is allowed only if the program is nondiscriminatory. Compare §132(a), (b), (c), and (j) with §117(d).

In certain circumstances student loan cancellations, which would otherwise generate income from the discharge of indebtedness, may be tax free. Under §108(f) student loans made by an agency of the United States, a state or political subdivision, certain tax-exempt charitable organizations controlling public hospitals, or by an educational organization under a program designed to encourage students to fulfill unmet needs in community service work, may be forgiven without giving rise to income if the loan conditions such forgiveness on working for a certain period in specified professions for any of a broad class of employers. This exclusion covers loan forgiveness to encourage students to pursue certain occupations (e.g., teaching), to practice a profession in an underserved geographic area (e.g., medical care in rural areas of Indian country) or to perform community service work for a governmental unit or charitable organization. Some professional schools at high-tuition universities have established loan repayment assistance programs to permit their students to pursue careers in public service without being deterred by the combination of high debt burden and relatively low pay for community service work. Such loan cancellation programs amount, in substance, to post-paid merit scholarships, but unlike the scholarship exclusion, the debt forgiveness is excluded even if the loan proceeds were used to pay room and board expenses. H.R. Rep. 105-148, at 324-325 (1997); see Rev. Rul. 2008-34, 2008-28 I.R.B. 76.

Direct payment of tuition and fees. An individual who pays tuition and fees for herself, her spouse, or her dependent to attend a college, university, vocational school, or other postsecondary educational institution may be eligible to claim one of two tax credits or (at least through 2009) a deduction. The alternatives, which are mutually exclusive, are the Hope Scholarship Credit, the Lifetime Learning Credit (both in §25A), and the tuition and fees deduction (§222). The choice between them can be complicated because they are subject to different conditions and limitations and provide different amounts of tax relief.

The Hope Scholarship Credit, if available, is the most generous because it grants a nonrefundable tax credit of 100 percent of the first $1,000 of qualified tuition and related expenses (full reimbursement by the federal government) and 50 percent of the next $1,000 (dollar-for-dollar cost sharing). The $1,000 amounts are inflation indexed (to $1,200 in 2009, for a maximum tax reduction of $1,800). Creditable expenses are generally limited to tuition and mandatory charges (activity fees and course related expenses that must be paid to the institution as a condition of enrollment) for a student enrolled at least half time in one academic period in a postsecondary educational program that leads to a degree, certificate, or other recognized educational credential. The Hope Credit is only available for expenses arising from the first two years of postsecondary education and may only be claimed with respect to a particular student in two taxable years. §25A(b), (f); 20 U.S.C. §1091(a)(1).

The Lifetime Learning Credit also applies to postsecondary education costs (tuition and mandatory charges), but it covers more expenses at a lower credit rate: 20 percent of up to $10,000 in qualified tuition and related expenses. The Lifetime Learning Credit, as the name implies, is more capacious than the Hope Credit in several important respects: It is available for an unlimited number of years; the student does not need to be pursuing a degree or recognized educational credential; it is available for courses to acquire or improve job skills; and it is available for one or more courses (the student need not be enrolled at least half time). §25A(c), (f). Unlike the Hope Credit, which may be claimed for each eligible student, the Lifetime Learning Credit is limited to $2,000 per return regardless of the number of eligible students for whom tuition payments are made.

If the Hope Credit is allowed for a particular student, the Lifetime Learning Credit cannot be claimed in the same year to cover education expenses that exceed the limits of the Hope Credit. In addition, both the Hope Credit and the Lifetime Learning Credit are subject to an income phase-out: The credit amount is reduced if the taxpayer's modified adjusted gross income falls in the range between $40,000 and $50,000 ($80,000 to $100,000 in the case of a joint return), and is entirely unavailable at higher income levels. The phase-out range is inflation adjusted (for 2009 the range is $50,000-$60,000, or in the case of a joint return $100,000-$120,000), and modified adjusted gross income ordinarily is simply adjusted gross income. (The modifications add back amounts excluded as foreign earned income or foreign housing benefits, and income exclusions applicable to certain residents of Puerto Rico or American Samoa.) Neither credit can be claimed with respect to higher education costs that get special tax treatment under other rules. Under this no-double-benefit rule, a credit is barred if a deduction is allowed for the tuition, if the expenses are paid with a tax-free scholarship, grant, or employer-provided educational assistance, or if the expenses were funded with certain tax-advantaged educational savings devices (discussed below). §25A(g)(2), (5).

A deduction is more valuable to high-income taxpayers than a 20 percent credit, and under current rate schedules the education credits would ordinarily be phased out before the 25 percent tax bracket kicks in. (The phase-out is tied to adjusted gross income [AGI], while tax rates depend on taxable income, which is AGI reduced by personal exemptions and itemized or standard deductions.) At least temporarily, Congress authorized a nonitemized deduction for up to $4,000 of qualified tuition and related expenses in lieu of the credits. §§222, 62(a)(18). The deduction, however, is also subject to an AGI-based limit. The limit steps the maximum deductible amount down from $4,000 to $2,000 for AGI above $65,000, and to zero if AGI exceeds $80,000 (the step-down is at $130,000 and $160,000 in the case of a joint return).[5] This limit is set slightly higher than the inflation-adjusted phase-out range for the Lifetime Learning Credit. Consequently, some taxpayers whose income is too high for the credit may take a deduction, but the step-down virtually assures that the deduction is unavailable to taxpayers in the 28 percent or higher brackets. For a particular student's tuition expenses in a given year, either a credit or a deduction may be claimed, but not both. Hence, if a student attends a high-cost private college, the taxpayer cannot claim a Lifetime Learning Credit for $10,000 of the tuition and also deduct another $4,000. As with the credits, rules coordinate the tuition deduction with other education tax allowances to prevent double tax benefits based on the same expenses. §222(c).

Borrowing costs. With the exception of certain home mortgage interest, interest on borrowing that is unrelated to the taxpayer's trade or business or investment activities (so-called personal interest) is ordinarily nondeductible. Interest on some student loans gets special treatment, however. §§163(h)(2), 221. A taxpayer may deduct up to $2,500 of interest paid on a loan used to pay higher education expenses as a nonitemized deduction so that tax savings may be had even if the taxpayer takes the standard deduction. §§221, 62(a)(17). For interest to be deductible, (1) the loan must be taken out solely to pay qualified higher education expenses for the taxpayer or his spouse or dependent who was enrolled at least half time in a higher education program leading to a degree, certificate, or other recognized

---

5. Observe that under the step-down approach, an additional dollar of AGI can trigger the complete loss of a $2,000 deduction. Assuming that the taxpayer subject to the step down is in the 15 percent tax bracket, the step down creates an effective marginal tax rate of . . . ?

educational credential, (2) the taxpayer must be legally obligated to pay interest on the loan (e.g., signed the note or loan agreement), and (3) the expenses must be paid or incurred within a reasonable time before or after the loan is taken out. For this purpose, "qualified higher education expenses" means the total costs of attendance, including room and board, books, supplies, and equipment, in addition to tuition, but the amount of the allowable loan proceeds must be reduced to the extent that the educational costs were funded by a tax-free scholarship or gave rise to excluded income under a tax-favored education savings program (below). §221(d)(2); Reg. §1.221-1(e)(2)(ii). The loan is not eligible for interest deductions if the lender is related to the taxpayer or comes from a qualified retirement plan, but a refinancing of a qualified loan is also qualified. §221(d)(1). Assuming all these conditions are satisfied, up to $2,500 of interest may be deducted each year, but the maximum deduction is subject to an income phase-out if the taxpayer's modified AGI falls in the range of $50,000-$65,000, or for joint returns $100,000-$130,000, inflation adjusted (in 2009 the phase-out range is $60,000-$75,000, or for joint filers $120,000-$150,000). For most taxpayers, modified AGI is usually AGI computed without the qualified tuition deduction or the student loan interest deduction itself. §221(b).

It is worthwhile to step back from the infuriating details and to consider why the core higher education tax allowances were cast as credits rather than deductions, and why the credits and deductions are all subject to income limits. The answer, it seems clear, is that middle-income taxpayers are the target of these tax incentives. Instead of matching grants (tax credits) or borrowing, high-income families are apparently expected to save for the costs of education. But will they save adequately to meet escalating college costs? And is tax assistance for education politically viable if limited to the middle-class?

Education savings programs. Higher-education saving tax incentives began in 1990 with §135. Traditional (paper) Series EE U.S. savings bonds do not pay periodic interest but are instead issued at a 50 percent discount (i.e., a bond's issue price is one-half of its face amount, which is its redemption value at maturity) and they are exempt from the periodic accrual requirement imposed by the original issue discount rules. §1272(a)(2)(B). In the 1980s the yield on newly issued U.S. savings bonds was changed from fixed to floating, as rates were made subject to periodic adjustment for increases in consumer prices. As a result, savings bonds became popular as a no-risk (but low yield) inflation-protected tax-deferred savings vehicle. With §135, Congress permitted some taxpayers to redeem U.S. savings bonds entirely tax free (i.e., interest excluded, not just deferred) if the taxpayer spends an amount at least equal to the bond proceeds on qualified higher education expenses for himself, his spouse, or a dependent during the year of redemption. The exclusion applies only to series EE and I savings bonds issued after 1989 to an individual who was at least 24 years old, and qualified higher education expenses are limited to tuition and fees required for enrollment at a college, university, vocational school, or other postsecondary educational institution eligible to participate in student aid programs administered by the Department of Education. Should bond proceeds exceed qualified higher education expenses for the year of redemption, the exclusion is reduced proportionately. §135(b)(1). Like the education tax preferences discussed earlier, the savings bond interest exclusion is also subject to an income phase-out. For 2009 the phase-out occurs between $69,950 and $84,950 of modified AGI for single taxpayers; the range is $104,900-$134,900 for joint returns. In addition, the exclusion cannot be claimed based on educational expenses that generated other education tax benefits (e.g., scholarships, Hope or Lifetime Learning Credits, exclusions under qualified tuition programs, or Coverdell education savings accounts). §135(d).

The savings bond interest exclusion exempts from tax investment earnings devoted to education but eligible expenses are limited to higher education tuition, the exclusion is restricted to income from a particular source (U.S. savings bonds), and the benefit is withdrawn from high-income individuals. Recently, Congress has created three additional education savings vehicles that offer exempt earnings with few restrictions on permissible investments (i.e., regardless of source), but these programs differ with respect to eligible education expenses and income limitations. As described below, tax-exempt education savings may be accumulated under a Coverdell education savings account (ESA), a qualified tuition program (also known as a "529 plan"), or under an individual retirement account (IRA).

A Coverdell ESA is exempt from income tax on its investments earnings; contributions to the account are nondeductible but distributions are entirely tax free so long as aggregate distributions do not exceed the beneficiary's qualified education expenses for the year. §530(a), (b)(2). Under this provision "qualified education expenses" are not limited to tuition and mandatory fees for higher education. Instead, eligible education costs under a Coverdell ESA are broadly defined to include tuition and fees, books, supplies and equipment, and room and board, whether these expenses are for higher education or elementary or secondary school. Hence room and board at a private prep school is a qualified education expense. Contributions to an ESA are strictly limited, however — contributions must be in cash, are limited to $2,000 per year and must (in general) be made before the ESA beneficiary attains age 18. The $2,000 limit applies to the total of all contributions from all contributors to all Coverdell ESAs set up for a particular beneficiary. S. Rep. No. 107-84, at 150 (2001) (Conf. Rep.). Therefore, maximum total contributions for the education of any individual ordinarily cannot exceed $36,000, and the annual limit is reduced if the contributor's modified AGI is too high. §530(c).

A qualified tuition program or 529 plan may be established either by a state or by a college, university, vocational school, or other postsecondary educational institution eligible to participate in student aid programs administered by the Department of Education. State-sponsored plans may be defined contribution programs that credit contributions to an account established for the purpose of meeting the higher education expenses of a designated beneficiary. The account is invested by the program administrator to accumulate funds to that end, and many plans allow the account owner typically the parent or other contributor) to choose between a variety of investment vehicles (stock or bond mutual funds).[6] Like a Coverdell ESA, a 529 plan is exempt from income tax on its investments earnings, contributions to the plan are nondeductible, but distributions can be entirely tax free. §529(a), (c)(3). Compared with an ESA, however, far greater contributions are allowed under a 529 plan, and unlike most other education tax benefits, §529 is *not subject to an income phase-out.* There is also no annual limit on contributions. Instead, a 529 plan must merely provide "adequate safeguards to prevent contributions on behalf of a designated beneficiary in excess of those necessary to provide for the qualified higher education expenses of the beneficiary." §529(b)(6). (Missouri's 529 plan, for example, allows contributions so long as the aggregate balance of all accounts established under all Missouri-sponsored 529 plans for the designated beneficiary does not exceed $235,000.) Although contributions are not deductible for federal income tax purposes, some states allow a state income tax deduction for contributions made under that state's 529 plan. Qualified higher education expenses are broadly defined by §529(e)(3) to include tuition, fees, books, supplies and equipment, and room and board for students enrolled at least half time at an eligible postsecondary institution. While elementary and secondary education costs are not covered (in contrast to a Coverdell ESA), the benefits of a 529 plan are not restricted to undergraduate or vocational training—graduate and professional education costs are also eligible. Another advantage of higher education saving through a 529 plan lies in its coordination with other education tax allowances. A taxpayer may contribute to a 529 plan and a Coverdell ESA in the same year for the same designated beneficiary, and a Hope or Lifetime Learning Credit can be claimed in the same year that the beneficiary takes a tax-free distribution from a 529 plan if each tax benefit relates to different expenses. §529(c)(3)(B)(v). If $2,400 of college tuition is taken into account for purposes of the Hope Credit, for example, the remainder of the tuition, along with fees, books, and room and board, would count as qualified higher education expenses and support tax-free distributions from a 529 plan account.

In operation, both the Coverdell ESA and 529 plans operate like the Roth IRA (see §408A): Contributions are nondeductible (i.e., are made from

6. Plans maintained by educational institutions (or consortia thereof) must be defined benefit programs that allow the advance purchase of tuition credits that will entitle the beneficiary to the later waiver or payment of college tuition or other higher education expenses regardless of any intervening escalation in tuition or college costs. States may also establish such tuition credit advance purchase programs. §529(b)(1)(A)(i). These defined-benefit-style 529 plans have become less popular with the advent of State-sponsored individual college savings accounts, and will not be discussed further.

after-tax income), but qualified distributions are tax free. In both cases, moreover, nonqualified distributions are both taxable and discouraged by imposition of a 10 percent surtax. §§530(d)(4), 529(c)(6).

Provided certain conditions are satisfied, deferral of tax on an investment is equivalent to tax exemption of the investment's yield during the period of deferral. The latter treatment, yield exemption, is available to education savings under a Coverdell ESA or a 529 plan. Perhaps not surprisingly, Congress has also authorized the former treatment, tax deferral. That was accomplished not by creating some new education-dedicated savings arrangement but by the simple expedient of permitting early withdrawal from an individual retirement account (IRA) for education purposes. Contributions to a regular IRA are deductible (within limits), §219, and the IRA is exempt from tax, §408(e), but distributions are ordinarily taxable in full, §408(d)(1). A 10 percent additional tax on early withdrawals ordinarily limits this tax deferral incentive to retirement savings, §72(t), but a special exception allows ordinary income tax treatment of distributions that do not exceed the taxpayer's qualified higher-education expenses for the taxable year. §72(t)(2)(E). Qualified higher-education expenses are defined as under §529 to comprehend pretty much any postsecondary education costs of the taxpayer, her spouse, or a child, step-child, or grandchild of the taxpayer or the taxpayer's spouse, including room and board and the costs of graduate or professional education. §§72(t)(7), 152(f)(1).

Notes and Questions

1. *IRA contribution limits.* Deductible contributions to a traditional IRA are generally limited to $5,000 per year, §219(b)(1), (5). Furthermore, if the taxpayer or his spouse is an active participant in an employer-sponsored qualified retirement plan during the year, then the dollar limit is also subject to an income phase-out. For joint filers, if either is covered by an employer plan the limit on deductible IRA contributions is reduced to zero as the couple's AGI (with certain adjustments) increases from $80,000 to $90,000. (The phase-out range is $50,000-$60,000 for single individuals.) §219(g). Consequently, among the whole array of tax benefits for education, only the exclusion for qualified scholarships and savings under a 529 plan are generally available without regard to income.

2. *Coverdell ESA v. 529 plan.* Why was Congress so much more restrictive of accumulations under a Coverdell education savings account than under a 529 plan? In addition to amount, more stringent limitations also apply to the period of deferral under an ESA. Generally, all assets remaining in a Coverdell ESA must be distributed within 30 days after the designated beneficiary attains age 30 (or earlier dies). §530(b)(1)(E). In contrast, assets in a 529 plan can be used to fund graduate or professional education regardless of age and may be transferred tax free to the credit of another designated

beneficiary under the same or another 529 plan (a "rollover") if the new beneficiary is a member of the family of the former beneficiary. §529(c)(3)(C).

References

R. Goode, The Individual Income Tax 75-96 (rev. ed. 1976); Hanlon, Job-Related Expenses: New Opportunities for Employee Deductions, 23 Tul. Tax Inst. 386 (1974); Malloy & Bratton, Unreimbursed Expenses — A Problem Area, 55 Taxes 257 (1977); Misiewicz, A Contemporary Look at Reimbursed Employee Business Expenses, 55 Taxes 401 (1977); C. Kahn, Personal Deductions in the Federal Income Tax, ch. 8 (1960); Halperin, Business Deduction for Personal Living Expenses: A Uniform Approach to an Unsolved Problem, 122 U. Pa. L. Rev. 859 (1974).

A. Childcare: Blumberg, Sexism in the Code: A Comparative Study of Income Taxation of Working Wives and Mothers, 21 Buffalo L. Rev. 49 (1971); Feld, Deductibility of Expenses for Childcare and Household Services: New Section 214, 27 Tax L. Rev. 415 (1972); Schaffer & Berman, The Child Care Deduction and the Progressivity of the Income Tax: A Reply to Professor Feld, 28 Tax L. Rev. 549 (1973); Feld, Another Word on Child Care, 28 Tax L. Rev. 546 (1973); Schaffer & Berman, Two Cheers for the Child Care Deduction, 28 Tax L. Rev. 535 (1973); Hjorth, A Tax Subsidy for Childcare: Sec. 210 of the Revenue Act of 1971, 50 Taxes 133 (1972); Parr, Section 504 of the Tax Reform Act of 1976: The New Credit for Child Care Expenses, 30 Tax Law. 456 (1977); Popkin, Household Services and Child Care in the Income Tax and Social Security Laws, 50 Ind. L.J. 238 (1975); Shreiber & Young, Childcare Expenses: A Proposal for a More Equitable and Efficient Tax Treatment, 54 Taxes 345 (1976); Brian Wolfman, Child Care, Work, and the Federal Income Tax, 3 Am. J. Tax Policy 153 (1984).

C. Traveling: Huffaker, "Away from Home" As a Tax Concept, 22 N.Y.U. Inst. on Fed. Taxn. 869 (1954); Klein, Income Taxation and Commuting Expenses: Tax Policy and the Need for Nonsimplistic Analysis of "Simple Problems", 54 Cornell L. Rev. 871 (1969); Kohl, The Outlook for Deducting a Law Student's Summer Travel Expenses After *Hantzis:* "Never Say Die!," 59 Taxes 598 (1981); Maples, When Is a Job Temporary for Tax Purposes?, 49 J. Taxn. 292 (1978); Note, Away from Home Traveling Expense Deductions: How Fair Are They to the Homeless Traveling Salesman?, 39 Alb. L. Rev. 119 (1974); Note, A House Is Not a Tax Home, 39 Va. L. Rev. 125 (1963).

D. Travel and Entertainment: Axelrad, An Evaluation of the New Rules Relating to the Deductibility of Entertainment, Travel, and Gifts: A Critical Look at Section 274, 16 S. Cal. Tax Inst. 345 (1964); Emmanuel & Lipoff,

Travel and Entertainment: The New World of Section 274, 18 Tax L. Rev. 487 (1963); Heffernan & Terr, Tax Planning for Foreign Conventions After the Tax Reform Act of 1976, 32 Tax L. Rev. 273 (1977); Klein, The Deductibility of Transportation Expenses of a Combination Business and Pleasure Trip — A Conceptual Analysis, 18 Stan. L. Rev. 1099 (1966); Shnee & Bates, Entertainment Expenses Under the Revenue Act of 1978, 57 Taxes 435 (1979); Wolfman, Silver & Silver, Dissent Without Opinion: The Behavior of Justice William O. Douglas in Federal Tax Cases 54-59 (1975), 122 U. Pa. L. Rev. 235, 272-276 (1973).

E. *Home Offices:* Zimmerman, Abandonment of the Focal Point Test for Office-in-Home Deductions, 68 Tax Notes 434 (1990).

F. *Activities Not for Profit:* Lang, Vacation Homes Revisited: *Bolton* Mistakenly Unbolts Door to Extra Deductions, 37 Tax Law. 323 (1984); Lee, A Blend of Old Wines in a New Wineskin: Section 183 and Beyond, 29 Tax L. Rev. 347 (1974); Swanson, Loss on Sale of Residential Property, 33 Taxes 589 (1955).

G. *Marital Litigation:* Grishman, Deductibility of Legal Expenses for Federal Income Tax Purposes, 26 S. Cal. Tax Inst. 875 (1974); Joel S. Newman, *Gilmore v. United States:* The Divorce, 116 Tax Notes 493 (2007) (recounting the sensational facts surrounding the Gilmore's marriage and divorce).

H. *Education and Training:* Kerry A. Ryan, Access Assured: Restoring Progressivity in the Tax and Spending Programs for Higher Education, 38 Seton Hall L. Rev. 1 (2008); Deborah H. Schenk & Andrew L. Grossman, The Failure of Tax Incentives for Education, 61 Tax L. Rev. 295 (2008); IRS, Tax Benefits for Education (Pub. 970) (2007); Wolfman, The Cost of Education and the Federal Income Tax, 42 F.R.D. 535 (1966); Wolfman, Professors and the "Ordinary and Necessary" Business Expense, 112 U. Pa. L. Rev. 1089 (1964).

Chapter 13 — *Business and Investment Expenses*

The last chapter focused on the crucial problem of distinguishing between personal and business expenditures. This chapter focuses on the other issues that arise if an expenditure is not personal. Yet as we have already seen, the division between personal and business is not clear-cut.

A.   ORDINARY AND NECESSARY

WELCH v. HELVERING
290 U.S. 111 (1933)

Mr. Justice CARDOZO delivered the opinion of the Court. . . . In 1922 petitioner was the secretary of the E. L. Welch Company, a Minnesota corporation, engaged in the grain business. The company was adjudged an involuntary bankrupt, and had a discharge from its debts. Thereafter the petitioner made a contract with the Kellogg Company to purchase grain for it on a commission. In order to reestablish his relations with customers whom he had known when acting for the Welch Company and to solidify his credit and standing, he decided to pay the debts of the Welch business so far as he was able. In fulfillment of that resolve, he made payments of substantial amounts during five successive years. In 1924, the commissions were $18,028.20, the payments $3,975.97; in 1923, the commissions $31,377.07, the payments $11,968.20; in 1926, the commissions $20,925.25, the payments $12,815.72; in 1927, the commissions $22,119.61, the payments $7,379.72;

and in 1928, the commissions $26,177.56, the payments $11,068.25. The Commissioner ruled that these payments were not deductible from income as ordinary and necessary expenses, but were rather in the nature of capital expenditures, an outlay for the development of reputation and good will. The Board of Tax Appeals sustained the action of the Commissioner (25 B.T.A. 117), and the Court of Appeals for the Eighth Circuit affirmed. 63 F.(2d) 976. The case is here in certiorari.

"In computing net income there shall be allowed as deductions . . . all the ordinary and necessary expenses paid or incurred during the taxable year in carrying on any trade or business." [§162.]

We may assume that the payments to creditors of the Welch Company were necessary for the development of the petitioner's business, at least in the sense that they were appropriate and helpful. McCulloch v. Maryland, 4 Wheat. 316. He certainly thought they were, and we should be slow to override his judgment. But the problem is not solved when the payments are characterized as necessary. Many necessary payments are charges upon capital. There is need to determine whether they are both necessary and ordinary. Now, what is ordinary, though there must always be a strain of constancy within it, is none the less a variable affected by time and place and circumstance. Ordinary in this context does not mean that the payments must be habitual or normal in the sense that the same taxpayer will have to make them often. A lawsuit affecting the safety of a business may happen once in a lifetime. The counsel fees may be so heavy that repetition is unlikely. None the less, the expense is an ordinary one because we know from experience that payments for such a purpose, whether the amount is large or small, are the common and accepted means of defense against attack. Cf. Kornhauser v. United States, 276 U.S. 145. The situation is unique in the life of the individual affected, but not in the life of the group, the community, of which he is a part. At such times there are norms of conduct that help to stabilize our judgment, and make it certain and objective. The instance is not erratic, but is brought within a known type.

The line of demarcation is now visible between the case that is here and the one supposed for illustration. We try to classify this act as ordinary or the opposite, and the norms of conduct fail us. No longer can we have recourse to any fund of business experience, to any known business practice. Men do at times pay the debts of others without legal obligation or the lighter obligation imposed by the usages of trade or by neighborly amenities, but they do not do so ordinarily, not even though the result might be to heighten their reputation for generosity and opulence. Indeed, if language is to be read in its natural and common meaning (Old Colony R. Co. v. Commissioner, 284 U.S. 552, 560; Woolford Realty Co. v. Rose, 286 U.S. 319, 327), we should have to say that payment in such circumstances, instead of being ordinary is in a high degree extraordinary. There is nothing ordinary in the stimulus evoking it, and none in the response. Here, indeed, as so often in other branches of the law, the decisive distinctions are those of degree and not of kind. One struggles in vain for any verbal formula that will supply a ready touchstone. The standard set up by the statute is not a rule of law; it is rather a way of life. Life in all its fullness must supply the answer to the riddle.

The Commissioner of Internal Revenue resorted to that standard in assessing the petitioner's income, and found that the payments in controversy came closer to capital outlays than to ordinary and necessary expenses in the operation of a business. His ruling has the support of a presumption of correctness, and the petitioner has the burden of proving it to be wrong. Wickwire v. Reinecke, 275 U.S. 101; Jones v. Commissioner, 38 F.(2d) 550, 552. Unless we can say from facts within our knowledge that these are ordinary and necessary expenses according to the ways of conduct and the forms of speech prevailing in the business world, the tax must be confirmed. But nothing told us by this record or within the sphere of our judicial notice permits us to give that extension to what is ordinary and necessary. Indeed, to do so would open the door to many bizarre analogies. One man has a family name that is clouded by thefts committed by an ancestor. To add to his own standing he repays the stolen money, wiping off, it may be, his income for the year. The payments figure in his tax return as ordinary expenses. Another man conceives the notion that he will be able to practice his vocation with greater ease and profit if he has an opportunity to enrich his culture. Forthwith the price of his education becomes an expense of the business, reducing the income subject to taxation. There is little difference between these expenses and those in controversy here. Reputation and learning are akin to capital assets, like the good will of an old partnership. Cf. Colony Coal & Coke Corp. v. Commissioner, 52 F.(2d) 923. For many, they are the only tools with which to hew a pathway to success. The money spent in acquiring them is well and wisely spent. It is not an ordinary expense of the operation of a business.

Many cases in the federal courts deal with phases of the problem presented in the case at bar. To attempt to harmonize them would be a futile task. They involve the appreciation of particular situations, at times with borderline conclusions. Typical illustrations are cited in the margin.*

---

* Ordinary expenses: Commissioner v. People's-Pittsburgh Trust Co., 60 F.2d 187, expenses incurred in the defense of a criminal charge growing out of the business of the taxpayer; American Rolling Mill Co. v. Commissioner, 41 F.(2d) 314, contributions to a civic improvement fund by a corporation employing half of the wage earning population of the city, the payments being made, not for charity, but to add to the skill and productivity of the workmen (cf. the decisions collated in 30 Columbia Law Review 1211, 1212, and the distinctions there drawn); Corning Glass Works v. Lucas, 59 App. D.C. 168; 37 F.(2d) 798, donations to a hospital by a corporation whose employees with their dependents made up two-thirds of the population of the city; Harris v. Lucas, 48 F.(2d) 187, payments of debts discharged in bankruptcy, but subject to be revived by force of a new promise. Cf. Lucas v. Ox Fibre Brush Co., 281 U.S. 115, where additional compensation, reasonable in amount, was allowed to the officers of a corporation for services previously rendered.

Not ordinary expenses: Hubinger v. Commissioner, 36 F.(2d) 724, payments by the taxpayer for the repair of fire damage, such payments being distinguished from those for wear and tear; Lloyd v. Commissioner, 55 F.(2d) 842, counsel fees incurred by the taxpayer, the president of a corporation, in prosecuting a slander suit to protect his reputation and that of his business; 105 West

The decree should be
Affirmed.

Questions

What is the ground for disallowance in *Welch*? The government argued
that the payments were capital expenditures akin to a purchase of goodwill. The Court mostly focuses on the statutory phrase "ordinary and
necessary" without much indication of any reason for that requirement.
Welch is frequently cited for the assertion that "necessary" means appropriate and useful, as in the Constitution's necessary and proper clause. It
has also been cited as establishing that the statutory requirement of ordi-
nariness is meant to separate current expenses from capital expenditures.[1]
Indeed, the opinion even says, "[r]eputation and learning are akin to
capital assets."

Is there any suggestion that the payments in *Welch* ought to be thought
of as personal? Does that make sense as a reason for denying deduction of
very unusual (extraordinary) payments? In *Welch*? In general? Would it be
useful to know more than the Court tells about the relation between the
taxpayer and the Welch Company, for which he previously "act[ed]"?

The operational distinction between a capital expenditure and a
personal expense is whether it gives rise to a basis that might be set off against
some future receipts either as a deduction or in computing gain on a disposition. In *Welch*, the taxpayer might subsequently sell his business, including goodwill, and then seek to treat the payments to the predecessor's
creditors as his cost basis in computing gain or loss. Would that be allowed,
or could he be met with a claim that the payments were for personal reputation or family good name, which cannot be disposed of, rather than business goodwill? If it were personal nontransferable reputation that he paid to
protect, should he get a deduction by way of amortization over his
professional life expectancy?

What about tuition, fees, books, and other costs of education? Are
such expenses personal, business, or capital? Does (should) it depend on
the level of education (primary, secondary, college, graduate, etc.) or its
relationship to the taxpayer's income-producing activities? See Chapter
12H.1 above.

55th Street v. Commissioner, 42 F.(2d) 849, and Blackwell Oil & Gas Co. v. Commissioner, 60 F.(2d) 257,
gratuitous payments to stockholders in settlement of disputes between them, or to assume the expense of
a lawsuit in which they had been made defendants; White v. Commissioner, 61 F.(2d) 726, payments in
settlement of a lawsuit against a member of a partnership, the effect being to enable him to devote his
undivided efforts to the partnership business and also to protect its credit.

1. See Commissioner v. Tellier, infra, next case.

B. PUBLIC POLICY LIMITATIONS

COMMISSIONER v. TELLIER
383 U.S. 687 (1966)

Mr. Justice STEWART delivered the opinion of the Court. The question presented in this case is whether expenses incurred by a taxpayer in the unsuccessful defense of a criminal prosecution may qualify for deduction from taxable income under §162(a) of the Internal Revenue Code of 1954, which allows a deduction of "all the ordinary and necessary expenses paid or incurred during the taxable year in carrying on any trade or business. . . ." The respondent Walter F. Tellier was engaged in the business of underwriting the public sale of stock offerings and purchasing securities for resale to customers. In 1956 he was brought to trial upon a 36-count indictment that charged him with violating the fraud section of the Securities Act of 1933 and the mail fraud statute, and with conspiring to violate those statutes. He was found guilty on all counts and was sentenced to pay an $18,000 fine and to serve four and a half years in prison. The judgment of conviction was affirmed on appeal. In his unsuccessful defense of this criminal prosecution, the respondent incurred and paid $22,964.20 in legal expenses in 1956. He claimed a deduction for that amount on his federal income tax return for that year. The Commissioner disallowed the deduction. . . .

There can be no serious question that the payments deducted by the respondent were expenses of his securities business under the decisions of this Court, and the Commissioner does not contend otherwise. In United States v. Gilmore [Chapter 12G above], we held that "the origin and character of the claim with respect to which an expense was incurred, rather than its potential consequences upon the fortunes of the taxpayer, is the controlling basic test of whether the expense was 'business' or 'personal'" within the meaning of §162(a). 372 U.S., at 49. Cf. Kornhauser v. United States, 276 U.S. 145, 153; Deputy v. du Pont, 308 U.S. 488, 494, 496. The criminal charges against the respondent found their source in his business activities as a securities dealer. The respondent's legal fees, paid in defense against those charges, therefore clearly qualify under Gilmore as "expenses paid or incurred . . . in carrying on any trade or business" within the meaning of §162(a).

The Commissioner also concedes that the respondent's legal expenses were "ordinary" and "necessary" expenses within the meaning of §162(a). Our decisions have consistently construed the term "necessary" as imposing only the minimal requirement that the expense be "appropriate and helpful" for "the development of the [taxpayer's] business." Welch v. Helvering [Chapter 13A above, at p. 752]. . . . The principal function of the term "ordinary" in §162(a) is to clarify the distinction, often difficult, between those expenses that are currently deductible and those that are in the nature of capital expenditures, which, if deductible at all, must be amortized over the useful life of the asset. Welch v. Helvering, supra.[6] The legal expenses deducted by the respondent were not capital expenditures. They were incurred in his defense against charges of past criminal conduct, not in the acquisition of a capital asset. Our decisions establish that counsel fees comparable to those here involved are ordinary business expenses, even though a "lawsuit affecting the safety of a business may happen once in a lifetime." Welch v. Helvering, supra, at [p. 752]. . . .

It is therefore clear that the respondent's legal fees were deductible under §162(a) if the provisions of that section are to be given their normal effect in this case. The Commissioner and the Tax Court determined, however, that even though the expenditures meet the literal requirements of §162(a), their deduction must nevertheless be disallowed on the ground of public policy. That view finds considerable support in other administrative and judicial decisions. It finds no support, however, in any regulation or statute or in any decision of this Court, and we believe no such "public policy" exception to the plain provisions of §162(a) is warranted in the circumstances presented by this case.

We start with the proposition that the federal income tax is a tax on net income, not a sanction against wrongdoing. That principle has been firmly imbedded in the tax statute from the beginning. One familiar facet of the principle is the truism that the statute does not concern itself with the lawfulness of the income that it taxes. Income from a criminal enterprise is taxed at a rate no higher and no lower than income from more conventional sources. "[T]he fact that a business is unlawful [does not] exempt it from paying the taxes that if lawful it would have to pay." United States v. Sullivan, 274 U.S. 259, 263. See James v. United States, 366 U.S. 213.

With respect to deductions, the basic rule, with only a few limited and well-defined exceptions, is the same. During the Senate debate in 1913 on the bill that became the first modern income tax law, amendments were rejected that would have limited deductions for losses to those incurred in a "legitimate" or "lawful" trade or business. Senator Williams, who was in charge of the bill, stated on the floor of the Senate that

> [T]he object of this bill is to tax a man's net income; that is to say, what he has at the end of the year after deducting from his receipts his expenditures or losses. It is not to reform men's moral characters; that is not the object of the bill at all. The tax is not levied for the purpose of restraining people from betting on horse races or upon "futures," but the tax is framed for the purpose of making a man pay upon his net income, his actual profit during the year. The law does not care where he got it from, so far as the tax is concerned, although the law may very properly care in another way. 50 Cong. Rec. 3849.

---

6. See Griswold, An Argument Against the Doctrine that Deductions Should be Narrowly Construed as a Matter of Legislative Grace, 56 Harv. L. Rev. 1142, 1145; Wolfman, Professors and the "Ordinary and Necessary" Business Expense, 112 U. Pa. L. Rev. 1089, 1111-1112.

The application of this principle is reflected in several decisions of this Court. As recently as Commissioner v. Sullivan, 356 U.S. 27, we sustained the allowance of a deduction for rent and wages paid by the operators of a gambling enterprise, even though both the business itself and the specific rent and wage payments there in question were illegal under state law. In rejecting the Commissioner's contention that the illegality of the enterprise required disallowance of the deduction, we held that, were we to "enforce as federal policy the rule espoused by the Commissioner in this case, we would come close to making this type of business taxable on the basis of its gross receipts, while all other business would be taxable on the basis of net income. If that choice is to be made, Congress should do it." Id., at 29. In Lilly v. Commissioner, 343 U.S. 90, the Court upheld deductions claimed by opticians for amounts paid to doctors who prescribed the eyeglasses that the opticians sold, although the Court was careful to disavow "approval of the business ethics or public policy involved in the payments. . . ." 343 U.S., at 97. And in Commissioner v. Heininger, 320 U.S. 467, a case akin to the one before us, the Court upheld deductions claimed by a dentist for lawyer's fees and other expenses incurred in unsuccessfully defending against an administrative fraud order issued by the Postmaster General.

Deduction of expenses falling within the general definition of §162(a) may, to be sure, be disallowed by specific legislation, since deductions "are a matter of grace and Congress can, of course, disallow them as it chooses." Commissioner v. Sullivan, 356 U.S., at 28. The Court has also given effect to a precise and longstanding Treasury Regulation prohibiting the deduction of a specified category of expenditures; an example is lobbying expenses, whose nondeductibility was supported by considerations not here present. Textile Mills Corp. v. Commissioner, 314 U.S. 326; Cammarano v. United States, 358 U.S. 498. But where Congress has been wholly silent, it is only in extremely limited circumstances that the Court has countenanced exceptions to the general principle reflected in the *Sullivan, Lilly* and *Heininger* decisions. Only where the allowance of a deduction would "frustrate sharply defined national or state policies proscribing particular types of conduct" have we upheld its disallowance. Commissioner v. Heininger, 320 U.S., at 473. Further, the "policies frustrated must be national or state policies evidenced by some *governmental* declaration of them." Lilly v. Commissioner, 343 U.S., at 97. (Emphasis added.) Finally, the "test of nondeductibility always is the severity and immediacy of the frustration resulting from allowance of the deduction." Tank Truck Rentals v. Commissioner, 356 U.S. 30, 35. In that case, as in Hoover Motor Express Co. v. United States, 356 U.S. 38, we upheld the disallowance of deductions claimed by taxpayers for fines and penalties imposed upon them for violating state penal statutes; to allow a deduction in those circumstances would have directly and substantially diluted the actual punishment imposed.

The present case falls far outside that sharply limited and carefully defined category. No public policy is offended when a man faced with serious criminal charges employs a lawyer to help in his defense. That is not "proscribed conduct." It is his constitutional right. Chandler v. Fretag, 348 U.S. 3. See Gideon v. Wainwright, 372 U.S. 335. In an adversary system of criminal justice, it is a basic of our public policy that a defendant in a criminal case have counsel to represent him.

Congress has authorized the imposition of severe punishment upon those found guilty of the serious criminal offenses with which the respondent was charged and of which he was convicted. But we can find no warrant for attaching to that punishment an additional financial burden that Congress has neither expressly nor implicitly directed. To deny a deduction for expenses incurred in the unsuccessful defense of a criminal prosecution would impose such a burden in a measure dependent not on the seriousness of the offense or the actual sentence imposed by the court, but on the cost of the defense and the defendant's particular tax bracket. We decline to distort the income tax laws to serve a purpose for which they were neither intended nor designed by Congress.

The judgment is affirmed.

Affirmed.

RAYMOND MAZZEI
61 T.C. 497 (1974)

QUEALY, Judge: . . . . During the year at issue, and for some time prior thereto, petitioner operated a sheet metal company in Hopewell, Va., in partnership with his brother. Vernon Blick was an employee of the company in 1965 and had been an employee for four or five years.

In March 1965, Blick was told by a man named Cousins of a scheme for reproducing money. Blick accompanied Cousins to a hotel in Washington, D.C., where Cousins introduced Blick to two other men named Collins and Joe. At that time, Collins and Joe showed Blick a black box which they asserted was capable of reproducing money. The black box was approximately 15 inches long, 8 or 10 inches wide, and 6 inches deep, about the size of a shoebox. It was made of metal and had a handle on it.

Blick gave Collins a $10 bill which Collins took and placed between two pieces of white paper of about the same size. Collins put the money and the paper into the box and connected the box to an electric outlet. The black box began a buzzing sound which continued for about ten minutes. Then Collins reached into the box and pulled out Blick's $10 bill and what appeared to be a new $10 bill. Collins then told Blick that they could not reproduce any more money at that time because they did not have enough of the type of paper required. In addition, Collins indicated that they would rather not use small denomination bills, but instead they wanted larger denominations such as $100 bills. Blick then returned to Hopewell.

Blick having told Cousins about petitioner, Cousins requested Blick to have petitioner meet with Cousins. In April or May of 1965, Blick recounted the events of the demonstration to petitioner. Thereafter, petitioner and Blick went to see Cousins in Hopewell and discussed a "deal" to reproduce money with Cousins, Collins, and Joe in Washington, D.C., and New York City. Petitioner was to provide money which Cousins, Collins, and Joe would reproduce and then return to petitioner.

After his first meeting with Cousins, petitioner was contacted several times concerning further arrangements for reproducing money.

In May 1965, Cousins took petitioner and Blick to New York City. Petitioner carried $10,000 in cash with him at Cousins' request. They went to a hotel in Brooklyn where Cousins telephoned Collins and Joe who then came over with the black box. Petitioner gave Collins a $100 bill in order to demonstrate the reproduction box. Collins went through the "reproduction" process and returned to petitioner his bill and a new $100 bill. Petitioner requested that they reproduce more money, but was told that there was not enough of the right kind of paper, which was supposed to be a special type used by the Federal Government and obtained through a "friend" in Washington, D.C. Cousins then took petitioner and Blick back to Hopewell that afternoon.

Petitioner continued to inquire of Cousins about reproducing more money but again was told that the difficulty in obtaining the right kind of reproducing paper was holding things up. However, petitioner did give $700 to Cousins who supposedly went to New York and reproduced it. Cousins returned petitioner's $700 plus $300 more, supposedly reproduced. Once again, Cousins said that the reason he did not reproduce more was because of the lack of sufficient paper.

Approximately a week later, Joe telephoned petitioner from New York and stated that they would be ready in a few days to proceed with the deal. Joe requested petitioner to obtain $20,000 in large denominations, preferably $100 bills.

On June 1, 1965, petitioner cashed a check for $20,000 on his company's account at a local bank, taking the proceeds in $100 bills. Blick obtained $5,000, borrowed from petitioner's brother, also through a check on the company account. Several days later, Joe called petitioner, confirmed that petitioner had acquired the cash and requested petitioner and Blick to meet him in New York.

On June 3, 1965, petitioner and Blick flew to New York City with the money. Once in New York, petitioner and Blick went to a designated hotel to meet Cousins, Collins, and Joe. Joe came by the hotel and met petitioner, confirming that petitioner and Blick had the money. The three then went outside where Collins was waiting with a taxicab. They proceeded to an apartment in Brooklyn, stopping on the way for Collins or Joe to purchase some liquor.

Once at the apartment, petitioner and Blick were again shown the black box. Collins then asked petitioner for the money. Petitioner handed Collins a packet of money containing $5,000. Collins removed the wrapper and placed the money into a pan of water. Collins then removed the money from the water and placed each $100 bill between two pieces of white paper which he then set aside. Collins continued the process until he finished with the series of bills in the $5,000 packet. Petitioner then handed Collins another $5,000 packet, and Collins repeated the same process. This continued until petitioner had given Collins the entire $20,000. Petitioner then informed Collins that Blick had $5,000, which Blick then gave to petitioner who in turn gave it to Collins.

Collins then informed petitioner and Blick that the black box was broken and would not work. Collins told them that they would have to use an oven, apparently to complete the reproduction process. Collins then turned on an ordinary electric oven which was in the apartment and put all of the money in the oven. At this point, two armed men broke into the room impersonating law enforcement officers making a counterfeiting raid. Petitioner and Blick were held at gunpoint while one of the men placed handcuffs on Joe. The two men representing themselves to be officers then removed the money from the oven. As the two intruders proceeded to the door of the apartment, petitioner broke away and ran up the street to seek the assistance of a police officer whom he saw. Petitioner reported the incident to the police officer, who told petitioner to wait until a squad car could arrive.

Meanwhile, Blick, who had remained with Collins, Joe, and the two intruders, requested them to return the money. Blick was told he would be shot if he attempted to retrieve the money. Then Collins, Joe and the two intruders went out of the apartment, got into a taxicab and left with the money.

Petitioner returned with the police and found Blick alone. The black box was examined and found to be nothing more than a tin box with a buzzer. It could not have reproduced any money. Petitioner and Blick accompanied the police to the police station and filed a report of the incident. The next day, petitioner and Blick returned to Hopewell and reported the incident to the police there. The incident was also discussed with the Federal Bureau of Investigation.

On his Federal income tax return for the calendar year 1965, petitioner claimed a theft loss in the amount of $20,000 and took a deduction therefore in the amount of $19,900.

In his statutory notice of deficiency, respondent disallowed the deduction for the loss under section 165(c)(2) or (3) on the grounds of lack of adequate substantiation of the loss and, further, that allowance of the deduction would be contrary to public policy.

OPINION

Petitioner contends that the fact that he incurred a loss is substantiated by the evidence and that such loss is deductible under section 165(c)(2) or section 165(c)(3). Respondent contends initially that petitioner has failed to prove that a loss was in fact suffered, and, further, that even if a loss were proven in fact, a deduction for such loss would not be allowed under section 165(c)(2) or section 165(c)(3) on the grounds that allowance of such a deduction would be contrary to public policy. As our findings of fact indicate, the Court is convinced that petitioner, in fact, incurred a loss in the sum of $20,000, as the result of being defrauded. However, the deductibility of such loss is precluded by our decision in Luther M. Richey, Jr., 33 T.C. 272 (1959).

In the *Richey* case, the taxpayer became involved with two other men in a scheme to counterfeit United States currency. The taxpayer observed a reproduction process involving the bleaching out of $1 bills and the transferring of the excess ink from $100 bills onto the bleached-out bills. Upon observing this demonstration, the taxpayer became convinced that the process could reproduce money. When the taxpayer later met with the other men in a hotel room to carry out the scheme, the taxpayer turned over to one of the other men $15,000 which was to be used in the duplication process. Before the process was completed, one of the other men to whom the taxpayer had given the $15,000 left the room under the pretext of going to get something and never returned. . . .

Petitioner would distinguish the *Richey* case on the grounds that there the taxpayer was involved in an actual scheme to duplicate money where the process was actually begun, only to have the taxpayer swindled when his cohorts made off with his money, whereas in the instant case there never was any real plan to counterfeit money, it being impossible to duplicate currency with the black box. Petitioner contends that, from the inception, the only actual illegal scheme was the scheme to relieve petitioner of his money, and petitioner was a victim and not a perpetrator of the scheme.

In our opinion, the fact that the petitioner was victimized in what he thought was a plan or conspiracy to produce counterfeit currency does not make his participation in what he considered to be a criminal act any less violative of a clearly declared public policy. Not only was the result sought by the petitioner contrary to such policy, but the conspiracy itself constituted a violation of law. The petitioner conspired with his covictim to commit a criminal act, namely, the counterfeiting of United States currency and his theft loss was directly related to that act. If there was a transaction entered into for profit, as petitioner argues, it was a conspiracy to counterfeit.

While it is also recognized that the Supreme Court in Commissioner v. Tellier, 383 U.S. 687 (1966), may have redefined the criteria for the disallowance on grounds of public policy of an otherwise deductible business expense under section 162(a), we do not have that type of case. The loss claimed by the petitioner here had a direct relationship to the purported illegal act which the petitioner conspired to commit. Compare Commissioner v. Heininger, 320 U.S. 467 (1943).

We also do not feel constrained to follow Edwards v. Bromberg, 232 F.2d 107 (C.A. 5, 1956), wherein the court allowed a deduction for a loss incurred by the taxpayer when money, which he thought was being bet on a "fixed" race, was stolen from him. The taxpayer never intended to participate in "fixing" the race.

The ultimate question for decision in this case is whether considerations of public policy should enter into the allowance of a theft loss under section 165(c)(3). Where there is a "theft" — and the loss by the petitioner of his money would certainly qualify as such — the statute imposes no limitation on the deductibility of the loss. Nevertheless, in Luther M. Richey, Jr., supra, this Court held that the deduction of an admitted theft was properly disallowed on grounds of public policy in a factual situation which we find indistinguishable. We would follow that case.

Reviewed by the Court.

Decision will be entered for the respondent.

Dawson, J., concurring: . . . The claimed theft loss here was connected with an intended initiation of the criminal enterprise of counterfeiting. We are not confronted with income from the criminal enterprise, but only with a loss of capital invested in the scheme to counterfeit. And we are not dealing with any gross income from the "business" of counterfeiting, nor are we faced with a claimed "business expense." This is purely and simply a situation in which the test of nondeductibility is the severity and immediacy of the frustration resulting from the allowance of the deduction. Tank Truck Rentals v. Commissioner, 356 U.S. 30, 35 (1958). There is a sharply defined national policy proscribing counterfeiting. It would be utterly senseless to frustrate this policy.

Drennen, J., agrees with this concurring opinion.

Tannenwald, J., concurring: I wholeheartedly agree with the result reached by the majority. It is inconceivable to me that Congress intended that a taxpayer should be allowed to deduct a payment *voluntarily made*, which is part and parcel of the very act believed by him to constitute a crime and involving a type of conduct proscribed by sharply defined "national or state policies evidenced by some governmental declaration" (See Commissioner v. Tellier, [Chapter 13B above, at p. 757] (1966)). To put a more extreme case, could there be any doubt that no deduction would be allowable where the taxpayer, desiring to have a particular person murdered, pays a sum of money for that purpose to a thug who pockets the cash without intending to carry out the deed?

There is a sharp distinction between such payments, so interwoven with the purported criminal act, and payments of an inherently innocent character, like rent or utility charges, which Commissioner v. Sullivan, 356 U.S. 27 (1958), held might appropriately be taken into account in determining the taxable income of an illegal enterprise because they bore only "a remote relation to an illegal act." See 356 U.S. at 29. The fact that the particular mechanism chosen in this case would not have resulted in the successful consummation of the contemplated crime seems to me to be irrelevant — petitioner was unaware of such incapability of the mechanism.

Clearly, *Tellier* did not preclude the application of public policy considerations under any and all circumstances. Similarly, in enacting the amendments to section 162, dealing with the deduction of various items involving such considerations, Congress left the door open by recognizing that "public policy, in other circumstances, *generally* is not sufficiently clearly defined to justify the disallowance of deductions." See S. Rept. No. 91-552, 91st Cong., 1st Sess., p. 274 (1969) (emphasis added). The reference to legislative retention of control over deductions in the Senate committee report accompanying the Revenue Act of 1971 was limited to situations involving bribes and kickbacks. See S. Rept. No. 92-137, 92d Cong., 1st Sess., p. 72 (1971).

I would apply the "narrow delineation of the standard of nondeductibility" set forth in *Tellier* (see James B. Carey, 56 T.C. 477 (1971), affirmed per curiam 460 F.2d 1259 (C.A. 4, 1972)) in terms of the seriousness of the purported crime involved. That counterfeiting is a serious crime within the contemplation of declared national policy is beyond question. United States Constitution, art. 1, sec. 8, cl. 6 (18 U.S.C. sec. 471 (1970)).

The obvious reply to the contention that my approach may involve "the task of grading criminal activity" is that, to the extent that this may be the result, the courts will simply be dealing with another instance of line-drawing which is part of the daily grist of judicial life. See Harrison v. Schaffner, 312 U.S. 579, 583 (1941).

DAWSON and RAUM, JJ., agree with this concurring opinion.

FEATHERSTON, J., dissenting: I have joined in Judge STERRETT's dissenting opinion, but I add that I do not think the facts show that petitioner was a party to any conspiracy to counterfeit United States currency. He and his covictim knew they could not counterfeit currency. The other parties pretended that they could and would use their black box for currency reproduction purposes, but they knew the box could not be so used. Thus, there was no conspiratorial agreement between petitioner and anyone who actually intended to do any counterfeiting. The whole scheme was designed to defraud petitioner of his money, and that is what happened. His intentions may have been evil, but that is no ground for denying him a tax deduction. In my opinion, the case is controlled by Edwards v. Bromberg, 232 F.2d 107, 111 (C.A. 5, 1956), now deeply imbedded in the tax law and heavily reinforced by the subsequent Supreme Court decisions cited in Judge STERRETT's dissent. I do not think the Court should decline to follow that precedent.

FORRESTER, STERRETT, and HALL, JJ., agree with this dissent.

STERRETT, J., I respectfully dissent from the majority opinion for the following reasons:

In Tank Truck Rentals v. Commissioner, 356 U.S. 30, 33, 35 (1958), the Supreme Court laid down the test for denying a deduction on the grounds of public policy. An otherwise allowable deduction may be denied if allowance would "severely and immediately" frustrate "sharply defined national or

State policies proscribing particular types of conduct, evidenced by some governmental declaration thereof." Frustration of a particular State policy "is most complete and direct when the expenditure for which deduction is sought is itself prohibited by statute." Tank Truck Rentals v. Commissioner, supra at 35. If the expenditure is payment of a penalty imposed by the State because of an illegal act, allowance of a deduction would clearly frustrate State policy by reducing the "sting" of the penalty imposed. Accordingly, the Supreme Court disallowed the deduction of fines the taxpayer had paid during the course of its trucking operations. The Court said, "To allow the deduction sought here would but encourage continued violations of State law by increasing the odds in favor of non-compliance." Tank Truck Rentals v. Commissioner, supra at 35.

In Commissioner v. Sullivan, 356 U.S. 27 (1958), decided the same day as *Tank Truck Rentals,* the Court refused to disallow the deduction of rent and wage expenses in operating an illegal bookmaking establishment. The Court stated, "The fact that an expenditure bears a remote relation to an illegal act does not make it nondeductible." Commissioner v. Sullivan, supra at 29. See also Commissioner v. Heininger, 320 U.S. 467 (1943); Lilly v. Commissioner, 343 U.S. 90 (1952). Once again in Commissioner v. Tellier, 383 U.S. 687, 694 (1966), the Supreme Court reiterated and emphasized its position that an otherwise allowable deduction should only be disallowed when in violation of a public policy that is sharply limited and carefully defined.

Against this background, Congress as part of the Tax Reform Acts of 1969 and 1971 attempted to set forth categories of expenditures within the purview of section 162 which were to be denied on the grounds of public policy. The Senate Finance Committee report for the 1969 Tax Reform Act states "The provision for the denial of the deduction for payments in these situations[1] which are deemed to violate public policy is intended to be *all inclusive.* Public policy, in other circumstances, generally is not sufficiently clearly defined to justify the disallowance of deductions." (Emphasis added.) S. Rept. No. 91-552, 91st Cong., 1st Sess. (1969), 1969-3 C.B. 597. In expanding the category of nondeductible expenditures, the legislative history of the 1971 Tax Reform Act states, "The committee continues to believe that the determination of when a *deduction* should be *denied* should remain under the *control* of *Congress.*" (Emphasis added.) S. Rept. No. 92-437, 92d Cong., 1st Sess. (1971), 1972-1 C.B. 599.

While the above statements have direct effect under section 162, where most of the public policy decisions have arisen, it does seem to call for judicial restraint in other areas where Congress has not specifically limited deductions. Moreover, such statements may have been a reaction to widely varied decisions such as those in Edwards v. Bromberg, 232 F.2d 107 (C.A. 5, 1956), and Luther M. Richey, Jr., 33 T.C. 272 (1959), which we think are not

---

1. Fines, a portion of treble damages under antitrust laws, bribes to public officials, and other unlawful bribes and kickbacks.

fairly distinguishable, and have led to the disparate results so inimical to the uniform administration of the tax laws.[2]

Despite the above, the majority seeks to invoke public policy as the tool to deny the petitioner an otherwise allowable theft loss. While congressional intent could logically be read to remove public policy considerations from the Internal Revenue Code where not specifically included,[3] at a minimum the strict test laid down by the Supreme Court must be met.

In the majority opinion, as in *Richey*, we apparently pay lip service to the Supreme Court by stating "that to allow the loss deduction would constitute an immediate and severe frustration of the clearly defined policy against counterfeiting obligations of the United States." Unfortunately in both cases we fail to discuss precisely how that frustration will occur. In the case of illegal payments such as bribes and kickbacks and the payments of fines, we are able to see a direct relationship between the allowance of the deduction and encouragement of continued violations of the law. In essence, the Government underwrites a portion of the expenses. However in the instant case we cannot see how counterfeiting will be encouraged in any manner by allowing the petitioner a theft loss deduction arising out of a distinctly different act. At best, the relationship is more remote than that in *Sullivan*, for the term "theft" presupposes that the victim has not voluntarily parted with his property.[4]

The majority seems to indicate that a deduction can be denied where there is *any* relationship between the loss or expense and the illegal activity, a position specifically rejected by *Sullivan*. Such reasoning does not readily lend itself to being "sharply limited" or "carefully defined." Had petitioner contracted pneumonia on his New York excursion, would the majority also deny him a medical expense deduction?

Or assume that customers on the premises of the bookmaking establishment involved in *Sullivan* were robbed by an outside intruder. Would the majority deny them a theft loss because they were engaged in an illegal activity? Or would the majority have this Court of special jurisdiction add to its assigned duties of interpreting the Internal Revenue Code the task of grading criminal activity, a task for which we obviously have no particular expertise. The authority for undertaking such additional duties remains obscure to me and would also be, I suspect, obscure to Congress.

Congress has authorized the imposition of severe punishment upon those found guilty of counterfeiting United States currency. It is designed to repress such criminal conduct. In the interest of uniform application of

2. We note that our decision in *Richey* did not mention or discuss Edwards v. Bromberg, 232 F.2d 107 (C.A. 5, 1956), decided $3^{1}/_{2}$ years earlier.

3. Sec. 902, Tax Reform Act of 1969 had retroactive effect with respect to fines, penalties, and bribes and kickbacks to Government officials. See sec. 902(c), Pub. L. 91-172 (Dec. 30, 1969), 1969-3 C.B. 147.

4. This should be contrasted with the situation where a counterfeiter has money and equipment confiscated during a legal search by police. Allowance of a casualty loss would frustrate public policy by lessening the adverse effect of proper governmental action directly related to the counterfeiting. Cf. Hopka v. United States, 195 F. Supp. 474 (N.D. Iowa 1961).

the Internal Revenue Code, where the frustration of State or national policy is neither severe nor immediate, we must not be tempted to impose a "clean hands doctrine" as a prerequisite to deductibility. To hold otherwise, especially in light of the broad brushstroke of public policy applied by the majority opinion, makes the taxing statute an unwarranted instrument of further punishment.

FORRESTER, FEATHERSTON, HALL, and WILES, JJ., agree with this dissent.

Notes

1. The question of disallowing deductions for public policy reasons has been one of continuing controversy over a long period of time. Congressional responses to judicial and administrative decisions on this subject are now contained in §§162(c), (e), (f), and (g). Do these make a sensible pattern? As indicated in *Mazzei*, Congress's formulation was supposed to be exclusive, but it is not clear whether the issue is susceptible of such formulation.

2. What if a taxpayer violated wartime price ceilings in purchasing goods for resale? In computing taxable income, a seller of goods will of course normally subtract the price paid from her sales proceeds, but formally this is part of the computation of gross income, not a deduction from gross income. It has been held that such a taxpayer can subtract her full purchase price, including the illegal portion exceeding the legal ceiling, since to hold otherwise would be to tax her on more than her gross income from her sales. Does this make sense? Lela Sullenger, 11 T.C. 1076 (1948); cf. Weather-Seal Manufacturing Co., 16 T.C. 1312 (1951), aff'd per curiam, 199 F.2d 376 (6th Cir. 1952). Compare §280E, enacted in 1982, on the expenses of illegal drug trafficking.

3. Reconsider McKinney v. United States, Chapter 7C above, in connection with these materials.

C. *CAPITAL EXPENDITURES*

MT. MORRIS DRIVE-IN THEATRE CO.
25 T.C. 272 (1955)

FINDINGS OF FACT. . . .

In 1947 petitioner purchased 13 acres of farm land located on the outskirts of Flint, Michigan, upon which it proceeded to construct a drivein or outdoor theatre. Prior to its purchase by the petitioner the land on which the theatre was built was farm land and contained vegetation. The slope of the land was such that the natural drainage of water was from the southerly line to the northerly boundary of the property and thence onto the adjacent land, owned by David and Mary D. Nickola, which was used both for farming and as a trailer park. The petitioner's land sloped sharply from south to north and also sloped from the east downward towards the west so that most of the drainage from the petitioner's property was onto the southwest corner of the Nickolas' land. The topography of the land purchased by petitioner was well known to petitioner at the time it was purchased and developed. The petitioner did not change the general slope of its land in constructing the drive-in theatre, but it removed the covering vegetation from the land, slightly increased the grade, and built aisles or ramps which were covered with gravel and were somewhat raised so that the passengers in the automobiles would be able to view the picture on the large outdoor screen.

As a result of petitioner's construction on and use of this land rain water falling upon it drained with an increased flow into and upon the adjacent property of the Nickolas. This result should reasonably have been anticipated by petitioner at the time when the construction work was done.

The Nickolas complained to the petitioner at various times after petitioner began the construction of the theatre that the work resulted in an acceleration and concentration of the flow of water which drained from the petitioner's property onto the Nickolas' land causing damage to their crops and roadways. On or about October 11, 1948, the Nickolas filed a suit against the petitioner in the Circuit Court for the County of Genesee, State of Michigan, asking for an award for damages done to their property by the accelerated and concentrated drainage of the water and for a permanent injunction restraining the defendant from permitting such drainage to continue. Following the filing of an answer by the petitioner and of a reply thereto by the Nickolas, the suit was settled by an agreement dated June 27, 1950. This agreement provided for the construction by the petitioner of a drainage system to carry water from its northern boundary across the Nickolas' property and thence to a public drain. The cost of maintaining the system was to be shared by the petitioner and the Nickolas, and the latter granted the petitioner and its successors an easement across their land for the purpose of constructing and maintaining the drainage system. The construction of the drain was completed in October 1950 under the supervision of engineers employed by the petitioner and the Nickolas at a cost to the petitioner of $8,224, which amount was paid by it in November 1950. The performance by the petitioner on its part of the agreement to construct the drainage system and to maintain the portion for which it was responsible constituted a full release of the Nickolas' claims against it. The petitioner chose to settle the dispute by constructing the drainage system because it did not wish to risk the possibility that continued litigation might result in a permanent injunction against its use of the drive-in theatre and because it wished to eliminate the cause of the friction between it and the adjacent landowners, who were in a position to seriously interfere with the petitioner's use of its property for outdoor theatre purposes. A settlement based on a monetary payment for past damages, the petitioner believed, would not remove the threat of claims for future damages.

On its 1950 income and excess profits tax return the petitioner claimed a deduction of $822.40 for depreciation of the drainage system for the period July 1, 1950, to December 31, 1950. The Commissioner disallowed without itemization $5,514.60 of a total depreciation expense deduction of $19,326.41 claimed by the petitioner. In its petition the petitioner asserted that the entire amount spent to construct the drainage system was fully deductible in 1950 as an ordinary and necessary business expense incurred in the settlement of a lawsuit, or, in the alternative, as a loss, and claimed a refund of part of the $10,591.56 of income and excess profits tax paid by it for that year.

The drainage system was a permanent improvement to the petitioner's property, and the cost thereof constituted a capital expenditure.

The stipulation of facts and the exhibits annexed thereto are incorporated herein by this reference.

OPINION

KERN, Judge: When petitioner purchased, in 1947, the land which it intended to use for a drive-in theatre, its president was thoroughly familiar with the topography of this land which was such that when the covering vegetation was removed and graveled ramps were constructed and used by its patrons, the flow of natural precipitation on the lands of abutting property owners would be materially accelerated. Some provision should have been made to solve this drainage problem in order to avoid annoyance and harassment to its neighbors. If petitioner had included in its original construction plans an expenditure for a proper drainage system no one could doubt that such an expenditure would have been capital in nature.

Within a year after petitioner had finished its inadequate construction of the drive-in theatre, the need of a proper drainage system was forcibly called to its attention by one of the neighboring property owners, and under the threat of a lawsuit filed approximately a year after the theatre was constructed, the drainage system was built by petitioner who now seeks to deduct its cost as an ordinary and necessary business expense, or as a loss.

We agree with respondent that the cost to petitioner of acquiring and constructing a drainage system in connection with its drive-in theatre was a capital expenditure.

Here was no sudden catastrophic loss caused by a "physical fault" undetected by the taxpayer in spite of due precautions taken by it at the time of its original construction work as in American Bemberg Corporation, 10 T.C. 361; no unforeseeable external factor as in Midland Empire Packing Co., 14

T.C. 635; and no change in the cultivation of farm property caused by improvements in technique and made many years after the property in question was put to productive use as in J.H. Collingwood, 20 T.C. 937. In the instant case it was obvious at the time when the drive-in theatre was constructed, that a drainage system would be required to properly dispose of the natural precipitation normally to be expected, and that until this was accomplished, petitioner's capital investment was incomplete. In addition, it should be emphasized that here there was no mere restoration or rearrangement of the original capital asset, but there was the acquisition and construction of a capital asset which petitioner had not previously had, namely, a new drainage system.

That this drainage system was acquired and constructed and that payments therefor were made in compromise of a lawsuit is not determinative of whether such payments were ordinary and necessary business expenses or capital expenditures. "The decisive test is still the character of the transaction which gives rise to the payment." Hales-Mullaly v. Commissioner, 131 F.2d 509, 511, 512.

In our opinion the character of the transaction in the instant case indicates that the transaction was a capital expenditure.

Reviewed by the Court.

Decision will be entered for the respondent.

RAUM, J., concurring: The expenditure herein was plainly capital in nature, and as the majority opinion points out, if provision had been made in the original plans for the construction of a drainage system there could hardly be any question that its cost would have been treated as a capital outlay. The character of the expenditure is not changed merely because it is made at a subsequent time, and I think it wholly irrelevant whether the necessity for the drainage system could have been foreseen, or whether the payment therefor was made as a result of the pressure of a law suit.

FISHER, J., agrees with this concurring opinion.

RICE, J., dissenting: It seems to me that J.H. Collingwood, 20 T.C. 937 (1953), Midland Empire Packing Co., 14 T.C. 635 (1950), American Bemberg Corporation, 10 T.C. 361 (1948), aff'd, 177 F.2d 200 (C.A. 1949), and Illinois Merchants Trust Co., Executor, 4 B.T.A. 103 (1926), are ample authority for the conclusion that the expenditure which petitioner made was an ordinary and necessary business expense, which did not improve, better, extend, increase, or prolong the useful life of its property. The expenditure did not cure the original geological defect of the natural drainage onto the Nickolas' land, but only dealt with the intermediate consequence thereof. The majority opinion does not distinguish those cases adequately. And since those cases and the result reached herein do not seem to me to be able to "live together," I cannot agree with the majority that the expenditure here was capital in nature.

OPPER, JOHNSON, BRUCE, and MULRONEY, JJ., agree with this dissent.

MT. MORRIS DRIVE-IN THEATRE CO. v. COMMISSIONER
238 F.2d 85 (6th Cir. 1956)

Before Simons, Chief Judge, and Allen and McAllister, Circuit Judges.

PER CURIAM. The above cause is affirmed for the reasons given in the memorandum opinion of the Tax Court. The drainage system there involved we think was a capital improvement. There is substantial evidence that it added to the value of the petitioner's land for the use to which it had been put; that it is immaterial that that increase in value was not by evidence measured in dollars, and that the inferences of the Tax Court could be and were drawn from the physical configuration of the land and what it had been necessary to do to establish thereon the Drive-In Theatre which the petitioner erected thereon.

The decision of the Tax Court is affirmed.

McALLISTER, Circuit Judge (dissenting). It appears clear to me that the finding of the Tax Court that the drainage system in question was a permanent improvement to petitioner's property was unsupported by the evidence. If it had not been for the action brought against petitioner by the Nickolas for damages to their property because of the alleged conduct of petitioner in increasing the drainage of rainfall upon their land, petitioner would never have thought of constructing a drain; and if it had paid $8,224 to the Nickolas in settlement of their suit or claims for past, present, and future damages resulting from such increased drainage of water, such payment could not be considered as an expenditure for a permanent improvement to increase the value of its property, or, as the Tax Court found, "a permanent improvement to petitioner's property." There is no difference between the construction of the drain by petitioner and the payment to the Nickolas of the account required for its construction. I therefore concur with the minority opinion of the Tax Court and accordingly am of the view that the decision should be reversed.

COMMISSIONER v. IDAHO POWER CO.
418 U.S. 1 (1974)

Mr. Justice BLACKMUN delivered the opinion of the Court. . . .

I

. . . The taxpayer-respondent, Idaho Power Company, is a Maine corporation organized in 1915, with its principal place of business at Boise, Idaho. It is a public utility engaged in the production, transmission, distribution, and sale of electric energy. . . .

For many years, the taxpayer has used its own equipment and employees in the construction of improvements and additions to its capital facilities. The major work has consisted of transmission lines, transmission switching stations, distribution lines, distribution stations, and connecting facilities.

During 1962 and 1963, the tax years in question, taxpayer owned and used in its business a wide variety of automotive transportation equipment, including passenger cars, trucks of all descriptions, power operated equipment and trailers. Radio communication devices were affixed to the equipment and were used in its daily operations. The transportation equipment was used in part for operation and maintenance and in part for the construction of capital facilities having a useful life of more than one year.

On its books, the taxpayer used various methods of charging costs incurred in connection with its transportation equipment either to current expense or to capital accounts. To the extent the equipment was used in construction, the taxpayer charged depreciation of the equipment, as well as all operating and maintenance costs (other than pension contributions, social security and motor vehicle taxes) to the capital assets so constructed. This was done either directly or through clearing accounts in accordance with procedures prescribed by the Federal Power Commission and adopted by the Idaho Public Utilities Commission.

For federal income tax purposes, however, the taxpayer treated the depreciation on transportation equipment differently. It claimed as a deduction from gross income *all* the year's depreciation on such equipment, including that portion attributable to its use in constructing capital facilities. The depreciation was computed on a composite life of 10 years and under straight-line and declining balance methods. The other operating and maintenance costs the taxpayer had charged on its books to capital were not claimed as current expenses and were not deducted. . . .

Upon audit, the Commissioner of Internal Revenue disallowed the deduction for the construction-related depreciation. He ruled that that depreciation was a nondeductible capital expenditure to which §263(a) had application. He added the amount of the depreciation so disallowed to the taxpayer's adjusted basis in its capital facilities, and then allowed a deduction for an appropriate amount of depreciation on the addition, computed over the useful life (30 years or more) of the property constructed. A deduction for depreciation of the transportation equipment to the extent of its use in day-to-day operation and maintenance was also allowed. . . .

II

Our primary concern is with the necessity to treat construction-related depreciation in a manner that comports with accounting and taxation realities. Over a period of time a capital asset is consumed and, correspondingly over that period, its theoretical value and utility are thereby reduced.

Depreciation is an accounting device which recognizes that the physical consumption of a capital asset is a true cost, since the asset is being depleted.[7] As the process of consumption continues, and depreciation is claimed and allowed, the asset's adjusted income tax basis is reduced to reflect the distribution of its cost over the accounting periods affected. . . .

When the asset is used to further the taxpayer's day-to-day business operations, the periods of benefit usually correlate to the production of income. Thus, to the extent that equipment is used in such operations, a current depreciation deduction is an appropriate offset to gross income currently produced. It is clear, however, that different principles are implicated when the consumption of the asset takes place in the construction of other assets that, in the future, will produce income themselves. In this latter situation, the cost represented by depreciation does not correlate with production of current income. Rather, the cost, although certainly presently incurred, is related to the future and is appropriately allocated as part of the cost of acquiring an income-producing capital asset.

The Court of Appeals opined that the purpose of the depreciation allowance under the Code was to provide a means of cost recovery, Knoxville v. Knoxville Water Co., 212 U.S. 1, 13-14 (1909), and that this Court's decisions, e.g., Detroit Edison Co. v. Commissioner, 319 U.S. 98, 101 (1943), endorse a theory of replacement through "a fund to restore the property." 477 F.2d, at 691. Although tax-free replacement of a depreciating investment is one purpose of depreciation accounting, it alone does not require the result claimed by the taxpayer here. Only last Term, in United States v. Chicago, Burlington & Quincy R. Co., 412 U.S. 401 (1973), we rejected replacement as the strict and sole purpose of depreciation:

"Whatever may be the desirability of creating a depreciation reserve under these circumstances, as a matter of good business and accounting practice, the answer is . . . 'Depreciation reflects the cost of an existing capital asset, not the cost of a potential replacement.'" Id., at 415.

Even were we to look to replacement, it is the replacement of the constructed facilities, not the equipment used to build them, with which we would be concerned. If the taxpayer now were to decide not to construct any more capital facilities with its own equipment and employees, it, in theory, would have no occasion to replace its equipment to the extent that it was consumed in prior construction. . . .

---

7. The Committee on Terminology of the American Institute of Certified Public Accountants has discussed various definitions and concluded that:

These definitions view depreciation, broadly speaking, as describing not downward changes of value regardless of their causes but a money cost incident to exhaustion of usefulness. The term is sometimes applied to the exhaustion itself, but the committee considers it desirable to emphasize the cost concept as the primary if not the sole accounting meaning of the term: thus, *depreciation* means the cost of such exhaustion, as *wages* means the cost of labor (emphasis in original). 2 APB Accounting Principles, Accounting Terminology Bulletin No. 1 — Review and Resume ¶48, p. 9512 (1973).

There can be little question that other construction-related expense items, such as tools, materials, and wages paid construction workers, are to be treated as part of the cost of acquisition of a capital asset. The taxpayer does not dispute this. Of course, reasonable wages paid in the carrying on of a trade or business qualify as a deduction from gross income. §162(a)(1) of the 1954 Code, 26 U.S.C. §162(a)(1). But when wages are paid in connection with the construction or acquisition of a capital asset, they must be capitalized and are then entitled to be amortized over the life of the capital asset so acquired. . . .

Construction-related depreciation is not unlike expenditures for wages for construction workers. The significant fact is that the exhaustion of construction equipment does not represent the final disposition of the taxpayer's investment in that equipment; rather, the investment in the equipment is assimilated into the cost of the capital asset constructed. Construction-related depreciation on the equipment is not an expense to the taxpayer of its day-to-day business. It is, however, appropriately recognized as a part of the taxpayer's cost or investment in the capital asset. The taxpayer's own accounting procedure reflects this treatment, for on its books the construction-related depreciation was capitalized by a credit to the equipment account and a debit to the capital facility account. By the same token, this capitalization prevents the distortion of income that would otherwise occur if depreciation properly allocable to asset acquisition were deducted from gross income currently realized. See, e.g., Coors v. Commissioner, 60 T.C., at 398; Southern Natural Gas Co. v. United States, 412 F.2d, at 1265.

An additional pertinent factor is that capitalization of construction-related depreciation by the taxpayer who does its own construction work maintains tax parity with the taxpayer who has its construction work done by an independent contractor. The depreciation on the contractor's equipment incurred during the performance of the job will be an element of cost charged by the contractor for his construction services, and the entire cost, of course, must be capitalized by the taxpayer having the construction work performed. The Court of Appeals holding would lead to disparate treatment among taxpayers because it would allow the firm with sufficient resources to construct its own facilities and to obtain a current deduction, whereas another firm without such resources would be required to capitalize its entire cost including depreciation charged to it by the contractor.

Some, although not controlling, weight must be given to the fact that the Federal Power Commission and the Idaho Public Utilities Commission required the taxpayer to use accounting procedures that capitalized construction-related depreciation. . . .

The presence of §263(a) in the Code is of significance. Its literal language denies a deduction for "[a]ny amount paid out" for construction or permanent improvement of facilities. The taxpayer contends, and the Court of Appeals held, that depreciation of construction equipment represents merely a decrease in value and is not an amount "paid out," within the meaning of §263(a). We disagree. . . .

There is no question that the cost of the transportation equipment was "paid out" in the same manner as the cost of supplies, materials, and other equipment, and the wages of construction workers.[11] The taxpayer does not question the capitalization of these other items as elements of cost of acquiring a capital asset. We see no reason to treat construction-related depreciation differently. In acquiring the transportation equipment, taxpayer "paid out" the equipment's purchase price; depreciation is simply the means of allocating the payment over the various accounting periods affected. As the Tax Court stated in Brooks v. Commissioner, 50 T.C., at 935, "depreciation — inasmuch as it represents a using up of capital — is as much an 'expenditure' as the using up of labor or other items of direct cost."

Finally, the priority-ordering directive of §161 — or, for that matter, §261 of the Code, 26 U.S.C. §261 — requires that the capitalization provision of §263(a) take precedence, on the facts here, over §167(a). . . .

The Court of Appeals concluded, without reference to §161, that §263 did not apply to a deduction, such as that for depreciation of property used in a trade or business, allowed by the Code even though incurred in the construction of capital assets.[13] We think that the court erred in espousing so absolute a rule, and it obviously overlooked the contrary direction of §161. . . .

We hold that the equipment depreciation allocable to taxpayer's construction of capital facilities is to be capitalized. . . .

Mr. Justice DOUGLAS, dissenting. . . . A company truck has, let us say, a life of 10 years. If it cost $10,000, one would expect that "a reasonable allowance for the exhaustion, wear, and tear" of the truck would be $1,000 a year within the meaning of 26 U.S.C. §167(a). . . .

Not so, says the Government. Since the truck was used to build a plant for the taxpayer and the plant has a useful life of 40 years, a lower rate of

---

11. The taxpayer contends that depreciation has been held not to be an expenditure or payment for purposes of a charitable contribution under §170 of the Code, 26 U.S.C. §170, e.g., Orr v. United States, 343 F.2d 553 (CA5 1965); Mitchell v. Commissioner, 42 T.C. 953, 973-974 (1964), or for purposes of a medical expense deduction under §213, 26 U.S.C. §213, e.g., Gordon v. Commissioner, 37 T.C. 986 (1962). Section 263 is concerned, however, with the capital nature of an expenditure and not with its timing, as are the phrases "payment . . . within the taxable year" or "paid during the taxable year," respectively used in §§170 and 213. The treatment of depreciation under those sections has no relevance to the issue of capitalization here. See, e.g., Producers Chemical Co. v. Commissioner, 50 T.C., at 959.

13. The Court of Appeals relied on All-Steel Equipment, Inc. v. Commissioner, 54 T.C. 1749 (1970), reversed in part, 467 F.2d at 1184 (CA7 1972), in holding that §263 was inapplicable to deductions specifically allowed by the Code. 477 F.2d, at 693. In *All-Steel*, the Tax Court faced the question whether taxes, losses, and research and experimental expenses incurred in manufacturing inventory items were currently deductible and need not be capitalized. The Tax Court held that these items were deductible, and that the taxpayer's method of accounting did not clearly reflect income. The Court of Appeals, in contrast, held that certain repair expenses incurred in producing inventory could be deducted "only in the taxable year in which the manufactured goods to which the repairs relate are sold." 467 F.2d, at 1186. We need not decide this issue, but we note that §263(a)(1)(B) excepts research and experimental expenditures from capitalization treatment, see Snow v. Commissioner 416 U.S. 500, 94 S. Ct. 1876 (1974), and that §266 of the Code, 26 U.S.C. §266, creates a further exception by providing taxpayers with an election between capitalization and deduction of certain taxes and carrying charges. The Tax Court, in discussing deductions for taxes, losses, and research and experimental expenditures, observed that "deductions expressly granted by statute are not to be deferred even though they relate to inventory or capital items." 54 T.C., at 1759. This statement, when out of context, is subject to overbroad interpretation and, as is evident from our holding in the present case, has decided limitations in application.

depreciation must be used—a rate that would spread out the life of the truck for 40 years even though it would not last more than 10. Section 167 provides for a depreciation deduction with respect to property "used in the (taxpayer's) trade or business" or "held for the production of income" by the taxpayer. There is no intimation that §167 is not satisfied. The argument is rested upon §161 which allows the deductions specified in §167(a) "subject to the exceptions" in §263(a). . . .

I agree with the Court of Appeals that depreciation claimed on a truck whose useful life is 10 years is not an amount "paid out" within the meaning of §263(a). . . .

I suspect that if the life of the vehicle were 40 years and the life of the building were 10 years IRS would be here arguing persuasively that depreciation of the vehicle should be taken over a 40 year period. That is not to impugn the integrity of IRS. It is only an illustration of the capricious character of how law is construed to get from the taxpayer the greatest possible return that is permissible under the Code. . . .

Depreciation on an automobile is not allowed as a charitable deduction, Orr v. United States, 343 F.2d 553, since it is not a "payment" within the meaning of §170(a)(1). Likewise depreciation on an automobile used to transport the taxpayer's son to a doctor is not deductible as a medical expense under §213 because it is not an expense "paid" within the meaning of the section. Maurice S. Gordon, 37 T.C. 986; Calafut v. Commissioner, 23 T.C.M. 1431 (1964). . . .

If the test under §263(a) were the cost of capital improvements, the result would be different. But, as noted, the test is "any amount paid out," which certainly does not describe depreciation deductions unless words are to acquire esoteric meanings merely to accommodate IRS. Congress is the lawmaker: and taking the law from it, we should affirm the Court of Appeals.

Notes

1. Just as §262 operates to protect the personal consumption component of taxable income, §263 operates to conserve the accumulation component. It says there is to be no deduction for savings since accumulation is part of what is to be taxed. In this case that is not the end of the matter, since capital expenditures may be deductible as depreciation over time or as basis in computing gain or loss on the occurrence of further events. We will take up loss and depreciation deductions in the next two chapters.

2. The cases here are a mere sampling of the myriad of contexts in which the issue of capitalization arises. Do they suggest any general principles for resolution of this issue, or only recurrent arguments and continual conflict?

Look at §263A. Added in 1986 to impose "uniform capitalization rules," it deals quite specifically with a few items like interest and taxes during construction but is also understood to represent a directive to the IRS to take stricter positions and to try generally to achieve greater uniformity in application of the capitalization requirement.

3. *Improvements and repairs.* The distinction between improvements and ordinary repairs has been continuously troublesome. What factors should control this issue? The longevity of the item in question? Anything else? Is increase in value a useful criterion? Why would one perform a repair unless it increases the value of the repaired property by an amount at least equal to the cost of repair? See Reg. §1.162-4.

Consider a new safety regulation that requires the installation of sprinkler systems in nursing homes. If an existing home were to install sprinklers in order to comply with the ordinance, would the cost be deductible? Is that case essentially different from *Mt. Morris?*

For some taxpayers, the issue of repair or improvement may now be ameliorated by application of elective expensing under §179. Recently proposed regulations try to clarify the distinction between repairs and improvements of tangible property. In an effort to reduce controversies, the proposal includes a safe harbor for routine maintenance and would authorize the establishment of industry-specific repair allowances. Prop. Reg. §1.263(a)-3, 2008-18 I.R.B. 871.

4. *Cash method accounting.* The nondeductibility of capital expenditures is clearly not a mere matter of accounting method. Even cash method taxpayers are precluded from deducting the cost of buildings or machinery or corporate stock. But what about prepayment of items more in the nature of expenses? Suppose a taxpayer on the cash receipts and disbursements method of accounting buys insurance in three-year policies, making payment for each policy at inception. The business has scores of insurance policies with different inception dates, so deduction of premiums on payment does not cause big fluctuations in insurance expense. Should each premium be required to be capitalized and amortized accurately over the tax years for which it is in effect?[2]

Prepaid rent has apparently been a clearer case for requiring capitalization. Why? Is it because the prepayment can be conceived as the purchase price for a possessory interest in the leased property? Compare treatment of the lessee, who is required to defer deduction of prepaid rent even if he is on a cash method, with the treatment of the lessor, who is not permitted to defer recognition of income even if he uses an accrual method. Reg. §1.61-8(b); see Rev. Proc. 2004-34, §4.02(1), Chapter 6D.1 above.

There are some items, however, for which a cash method of accounting has operated to permit immediate deduction. For many years a cash method taxpayer was allowed to deduct prepaid interest on indebtedness. The matter became one of abuse, and §461(g) now requires deferral. Farmers who utilize cash receipts and disbursements accounting have long been allowed to

---

2. See, e.g., Commissioner v. Boylston Market Assn., 131 F.2d 966 (1st Cir. 1942); Reg. §1.263(a)-4(d)(3).

deduct expenditures that would be classified as capital under other circumstances. See §263A(d)(1), Reg. §§1.61-4, 1.162-12.

5. *Further accounting considerations.* Even passing the question of simple cash accounting, there are enormous differences in the sophistication of accounting techniques applied in different business situations. *Idaho Power* illustrates the relatively refined accounting that is typically required of public utilities, in which an effort is made to trace all sorts of costs through to current expense or increase in total plant. To what extent should tax accounting be influenced or controlled by differences in financial accounting practice between industry groups?

Consider executive salaries, for example. A utility company will be required by regulatory authorities to charge part of those salaries to plant instead of to current expense, for executives who spend time and take responsibility for plant expansion. In *Idaho Power* it seems to have been agreed that such salary costs were not currently deductible for income tax purposes.

But then what about a private company not subject to utility regulation whose officers and shareholders are satisfied to treat executive salaries as current expense without making precise allocations? Will such a company be forced to adopt a more refined system of accounting for income tax purposes? Cf., e.g., William K. Coors, 60 T.C. 368 (1973), aff'd sub nom. Adolf Coors Co. v. Commissioner, 519 F.2d 1280 (10th Cir.), cert. denied, 423 U.S. 1087 (1975).

In *Idaho Power* itself the Court indicates that "pension contributions, social security, and motor vehicle taxes" were not capitalized as construction costs. Why not? Should this qualification in the taxpayer's method of accounting be accepted for income tax purposes? Why?

For more on accrual accounting for income tax purposes and on relations between accrual accounting for financial and tax purposes, see Chapter 6D above.

6. *Interest and taxes during construction.* Construction of real estate and other substantial capital items takes time and money. One of the costs of construction, therefore, is the cost of money — that is, interest on money borrowed to finance construction. Furthermore, one is apt to incur real estate taxes on property under construction and sales taxes on materials used in construction, which are also part of the cost of construction activity. How should these items be treated in financial and income tax accounting?

In any kind of careful financial accounting these items would quite commonly be capitalized as part of the cost of plant construction. Utility accounting regularly requires such treatment. Would it follow, under *Idaho Power*, that interest and taxes during construction should be treated as nondeductible capital expenditures for tax purposes?

For whatever reason, until 1976 interest and taxes were generally allowed as a current deduction for income tax purposes notwithstanding their functional tie-in to construction activity. Perhaps the reason relates somehow to the allowance of personal deductions for interest and taxes: If such items are deductible without any business connection at all, surely the presence of a deferred business connection should not preclude or delay deductibility. Or should it?

In practice, the immediate deductibility of interest and taxes during construction was a major factor in allowing utility companies and real estate developers to pay tax on much less than their financial income. The deduction was also a key item in certain forms of real estate tax shelters.

In 1976 Congress enacted §189, which required interest during construction of real estate to be capitalized and amortized over a ten-year period. Ten years later §189 was repealed and the matter of interest and taxes during construction was put under the new uniform capitalization rules prescribed by §263A. See §263A(f). The effect of this provision was to cause capitalized interest and taxes to be added to the basis of the constructed property, and deducted accordingly.

There are problems in ascertaining what portion of what debts should be associated with a particular property under construction. The Treasury was to have issued regulations dealing with this question under §189, but they never appeared. Does §263A(f) provide useful guidance on this issue?

7. *Ground rent.* Suppose a taxpayer, already in business, leases land on which to construct and operate a new plant: Should a deduction be allowed for rent paid during the construction period, or should this be capitalized as part of the cost of construction?[3]

8. *Other statutory provisions.* There are a number of specific statutory provisions that authorize an immediate deduction for particular costs that perhaps ought to be classed as capital expenditures. The purpose of these provisions is in part to avoid accounting difficulties in determining when else to allow a deduction. In some cases, at least, the purpose is also to encourage the expenditure in question by increasing after-tax rate of return through tax deferral. See, e.g., §174 (research and experimental expenditures), §175 (soil and water conservation expenditures), §173 (periodical circulation expenditures), §180 (expenditures by farmers for fertilizer, etc.), §181 (film and television production costs if at least 75 percent of compensation costs are for services performed inside the United States), and §263(c) (intangible drilling and development costs for oil and gas wells).

Another set of statutory provisions allow amortization of certain capital costs over a prescribed period much shorter than probable useful life, often five years. See, e.g., §169 (pollution control facilities) and §248 (corporate organizational expenditures).

---

3. The IRS has disallowed rental deductions during construction of a property for use in a *new* business, before the business has commenced, on the ground that they are not incurred *in carrying on* the business. See Chapter 13E below; Herschel H. Hoopengarner, 80 T.C. 538 (1983), aff'd (9th Cir. 1984, unpublished opinion); Arthur H. Hardy, 93 T.C. 684 (1989). See also Keller, The Capitalization of Construction Costs: Expanding the Scope of *Idaho Power,* 62 Taxes 618 (1984).

9. *Capital gain implications.* In general, costs associated with the acquisition or sale of a capital asset are required to be capitalized. Brokers' commissions for the purchase and sale of securities must be capitalized, for example, even by a taxpayer who incurs such expenses on a frequently recurring basis. A major effect of capitalization in this case is to make such commissions ultimately a charge against capital gains (or a source of capital loss) rather than a charge against ordinary income.

But the question of what costs are sufficiently associated with acquisition may be rather conventionally determined. An investment advisor's fees, for example, are commonly deducted as ordinary expenses, even though her advice relates primarily to purchasing and selling securities. As a result, some investors may secure a return that consists entirely of capital gains and may still get an ordinary deduction for investment advice, while other investors may secure their return all in the form of interest and dividends and get only a capital loss for their brokerage commissions. Should these results be changed? How? (Don't forget §67.)

10. *T* borrowed $1 million in 2004 to purchase some scotch whiskey, which he held until 2009 when he sold the whiskey and repaid the loan. He prepaid the interest for five years in 2004. Should the interest be deducted in 2004, deducted ratably over the period of the loan, deducted in 2009, or added to basis for determining gain or loss on sale of the whiskey? See §§461(g), 163(d); cf. §263A(f).

11. Often the corollary of disallowing an expense deduction will be the allowance of capital cost recovery deductions in subsequent years. If that is the case, does the issue of capitalization matter? How much? We will return to that question in the next chapter.

INDOPCO, INC. v. COMMISSIONER
503 U.S. 79 (1992)

Justice BLACKMUN delivered the opinion of the Court. . . .

I

. . . Petitioner INDOPCO, Inc., formerly named National Starch and Chemical Corporation and hereinafter referred to as National Starch, is a Delaware corporation that manufactures and sells adhesives, starches, and specialty chemical products. In October 1977, representatives of Unilever United States, Inc., also a Delaware corporation (Unilever), expressed interest in acquiring National Starch, which was one of its suppliers, through a friendly transaction. National Starch at the time had outstanding over 6,563,000 common shares held by approximately 3700 shareholders. The stock was listed on the New York Stock Exchange. Frank and Anna Greenwall were the corporation's largest shareholders and owned approximately 14.5% of the common. The Greenwalls, getting along in years and concerned about their estate plans, indicated that they would transfer their shares to Unilever only if a transaction tax-free for them could be arranged.

Lawyers representing both sides devised a "reverse subsidiary cash merger" that they felt would satisfy the Greenwalls' concerns. . . .

In November 1977, National Starch's directors were formally advised of Unilever's interest and the proposed transaction. At that time, Debevoise, Plimpton, Lyons & Gates, National Starch's counsel, told the directors that under Delaware law they had a fiduciary duty to ensure that the proposed transaction would be fair to the shareholders. National Starch thereupon engaged the investment banking firm of Morgan Stanley & Co., Inc. to evaluate its shares, to render a fairness opinion, and generally to assist in the event of the emergence of a hostile tender offer.

Although Unilever originally had suggested a price between $65 and $70 per share, negotiations resulted in a final offer of $73.50 per share, a figure Morgan Stanley found to be fair. Following approval by National Starch's board and the issuance of a favorable private ruling from the Internal Revenue Service that the transaction would be tax-free under §351 for those National Starch shareholders who exchanged their stock for Holding preferred, the transaction was consummated in August 1978.[2]

Morgan Stanley charged National Starch a fee of $2,200,000, along with $7,586 for out-of-pocket expenses and $18,000 for legal fees. The Debevoise firm charged National Starch $490,000, along with $15,069 for out-of-pocket expenses. National Starch also incurred expenses aggregating $150,962 for miscellaneous items—such as accounting, printing, proxy solicitation, and Securities and Exchange Commission fees—in connection with the transaction. No issue is raised as to the propriety or reasonableness of these charges.

On its federal income tax return for its short taxable year ended August 15, 1978, National Starch claimed a deduction for the $2,225,586 paid to Morgan Stanley, but did not deduct the $505,069 paid to Debevoise or the other expenses. Upon audit, the Commissioner of Internal Revenue disallowed the claimed deduction and issued a notice of deficiency. Petitioner sought redetermination in the United States Tax Court, asserting, however, not only the right to deduct the investment banking fees and expenses but, as well, the legal and miscellaneous expenses incurred.

The Tax Court, in an unreviewed decision, ruled that the expenditures were capital in nature and therefore not deductible under §162(a) in the 1978 return as "ordinary and necessary expenses." National Starch and Chemical Corp. v. Commissioner, 93 T.C. 67 (1989). The court based its

---

2. Approximately 21% of National Starch common was exchanged for Holding preferred. The remaining 79% was exchanged for cash. App. 14.

holding primarily on the long-term benefits that accrued to National Starch from the Unilever acquisition. Id., at 75. The United States Court of Appeals for the Third Circuit affirmed, upholding the Tax Court's findings that "both Unilever's enormous resources and the possibility of synergy arising from the transaction served the long-term betterment of National Starch." National Starch and Chemical Corp. v. Commissioner, 918 F.2d 426, 432-433 (1990). In so doing, the Court of Appeals rejected National Starch's contention that, because the disputed expenses did not "create or enhance . . . a separate and distinct additional asset," see Commissioner v. Lincoln Savings & Loan Assn., 403 U.S. 345, 354 (1971), they could not be capitalized and therefore were deductible under §162(a). 918 F.2d, at 428-431. We granted certiorari to resolve a perceived conflict on the issue among the Courts of Appeals.[3] 500 U.S. 914 (1991).

II

Section 162(a) of the Internal Revenue Code allows the deduction of "all the ordinary and necessary expenses paid or incurred during the taxable year in carrying on any trade or business." 26 U.S.C. §162(a). In contrast, §263 of the Code allows no deduction for a capital expenditure — an "amount paid out for new buildings or for permanent improvements or betterments made to increase the value of any property or estate." 26 U.S.C. §263(a)(1). The primary effect of characterizing a payment as either a business expense or a capital expenditure concerns the timing of the taxpayer's cost recovery: While business expenses are currently deductible, a capital expenditure usually is amortized and depreciated over the life of the relevant asset, or, where no specific asset or useful life can be ascertained, is deducted upon dissolution of the enterprise. See 26 U.S.C. §§167(a) and 336(a); Treas. Reg. §1.167(a), 26 CFR §1.167(a) (1991). Through provisions such as these, the Code endeavors to match expenses with the revenues of the taxable period to which they are properly attributable, thereby resulting in a more accurate calculation of net income for tax purposes. See, e.g., Commissioner v. Idaho Power Co., 418 U.S. 1, 16 (1974); Ellis Banking Corp. v. Commissioner, 688 F.2d 1376, 1379 (CA11 1982), cert. denied, 463 U.S. 1207 (1983).

---

3. Compare the Third Circuit's opinion, 918 F.2d, at 430, with NCNB Corp. v. United States, 684 F.2d 285, 293-294 (CA4 1982) (bank expenditures for expansion-related planning reports, feasibility studies, and regulatory applications did not "create or enhance separate and identifiable assets," and therefore were ordinary and necessary expenses under §162(a)), and Briarcliff Candy Corp. v. Commissioner, 475 F.2d 775, 782 (CA2 1973) (suggesting that *Lincoln Savings* "brought about a radical shift in emphasis," making capitalization dependent on whether the expenditure creates or enhances a separate and distinct additional asset). See also Central Texas Savings & Loan Assn. v. United States, 731 F.2d 1181, 1184 (CA5 1984) (inquiring whether establishment of new branches "creates a separate and distinct additional asset" so that capitalization is the proper tax treatment).

In exploring the relationship between deductions and capital expenditures, this Court has noted the "familiar rule" that "an income tax deduction is a matter of legislative grace and that the burden of clearly showing the right to the claimed deduction is on the taxpayer." Interstate Transit Lines v. Commissioner, 319 U.S. 590, 593 (1943); Deputy v. Du Pont, 308 U.S. 488, 493 (1940); New Colonial Ice Co. v. Helvering, 292 U.S. 435, 440 (1934). The notion that deductions are exceptions to the norm of capitalization finds support in various aspects of the Code. Deductions are specifically enumerated and thus are subject to disallowance in favor of capitalization. See §§161 and 261. Nondeductible capital expenditures, by contrast, are not exhaustively enumerated in the Code; rather than providing a "complete list of nondeductible expenditures," *Lincoln Savings,* 403 U.S., at 358, §263 serves as a general means of distinguishing capital expenditures from current expenses. See Commissioner v. Idaho Power Co., 418 U.S., at 16. For these reasons, deductions are strictly construed and allowed "as there is a clear provision therefor." New Colonial Ice Co. v. Helvering, 292 U.S., at 440; Deputy v. Du Pont, 308 U.S., at 493.[4]

The Court also has examined the interrelationship between the Code's business expense and capital expenditure provisions.[5] In so doing, it has had occasion to parse §162(a) and explore certain of its requirements. For example, in *Lincoln Savings,* we determined that, to qualify for deduction under §162(a), "an item must (1) be 'paid or incurred during the taxable year,' (2) be for 'carrying on any trade or business,' (3) be an 'expense,' (4) be a 'necessary' expense, and (5) be an 'ordinary' expense." 403 U.S., at 352. See also Commissioner v. Tellier, 383 U.S. 687, 689 (1966) (the term "necessary" imposes "only the minimal requirement that the expense be 'appropriate and helpful' for the development of the [taxpayer's] business," quoting Welch v. Helvering, 290 U.S. 111, 113 (1933)); Deputy v. Du Pont, 308 U.S. 488, 495 (1940) (to qualify as "ordinary," the expense must relate to

4. See also Johnson, The Expenditures Incurred by the Target Corporation in an Acquisitive Reorganization are Dividends to the Shareholders, 53 Tax Notes 463, 478 (1991) (noting the importance of a "strong law of capitalization" to the tax system).

5. See, e.g., Commissioner v. Idaho Power Co., 418 U.S. 1 (1974) (equipment depreciation allocable to construction of capital facilities is to be capitalized); United States v. Mississippi Chemical Corp., 405 U.S. 298 (1972) (cooperatives' required purchases of stock in Bank for Cooperative are not currently deductible); Commissioner v. Lincoln Savings & Loan Assn., 403 U.S. 345 (1971) (additional premiums paid by bank to federal insurers are capital expenditures); Woodward v. Commissioner, 397 U.S. 572 (1970) (legal, accounting, and appraisal expenses incurred in purchasing minority stock interest are capital expenditures); United States v. Hilton Hotels Corp. 397 U.S. 580 (1970) (consulting, legal, and other professional fees incurred by acquiring firm in minority stock appraisal proceeding are capital expenditures); Commissioner v. Tellier, 383 U.S. 687 (1966) (legal expenses incurred in defending against securities fraud charges are deductible under §162(a)); Commissioner v. Heininger, 320 U.S. 467 (1943) (legal expenses incurred in disputing adverse postal designation are deductible as ordinary and necessary expenses); Interstate Transit Lines v. Commissioner, 319 U.S. 590 (1943) (payment by parent company to cover subsidiary's operating deficit is not deductible as a business expense); Deputy v. Du Pont, 308 U.S. 488 (1940) (expenses incurred by shareholder in helping executives of company acquire stock are not deductible); Helvering v. Winmill, 305 U.S. 79 (1938) (brokerage commissions are capital expenditures); Welch v. Helvering, 290 U.S. 111 (1933) (payments of former employer's debts are capital expenditures).

a transaction "of common or frequent occurrence in the type of business involved"). The Court has recognized, however, that the "decisive distinctions" between current expenses and capital expenditures "are those of degree and not of kind," Welch v. Helvering, 290 U.S., at 114, and that because each case "turns on its special facts," Deputy v. Du Pont, 308 U.S., at 496, the cases sometimes appear difficult to harmonize. See Welch v. Helvering, 290 U.S., at 116.

National Starch contends that the decision in *Lincoln Savings* changed these familiar backdrops and announced an exclusive test for identifying capital expenditures, a test in which "creation or enhancement of an asset" is a prerequisite to capitalization, and deductibility under §162(a) is the rule rather than the exception. Brief for Petitioner 16. We do not agree, for we conclude that National Starch has overread *Lincoln Savings*.

In *Lincoln Savings*, we were asked to decide whether certain premiums, required by federal statute to be paid by a savings and loan association to the Federal Savings and Loan Insurance Corporation (FSLIC), were ordinary and necessary expenses under §162(a), as *Lincoln Savings* argued and the Court of Appeals had held, or capital expenditures under §263, as the Commissioner contended. We found that the "additional" premiums, the purpose of which was to provide FSLIC with a secondary reserve fund in which each insured institution retained a pro rata interest recoverable in certain situations, "serv[e] to create or enhance for Lincoln what is essentially a separate and distinct additional asset." 403 U.S., at 354. "As an inevitable consequence," we concluded, "the payment is capital in nature and not an expense, let alone an ordinary expense, deductible under §162(a)." Ibid.

Lincoln Savings stands for the simple proposition that a taxpayer's expenditure that "serves to create or enhance . . . a separate and distinct" asset should be capitalized under §263. It by no means follows, however, that *only* expenditures that create or enhance separate and distinct assets are to be capitalized under §263. We had no occasion in *Lincoln Savings* to consider the tax treatment of expenditures that, unlike the additional premiums at issue there, did not create or enhance a specific asset, and thus the case cannot be read to preclude capitalization in other circumstances. In short, *Lincoln Savings* holds that the creation of a separate and distinct asset well may be a sufficient but not a necessary condition to classification as a capital expenditure. See General Bancshares Corp. v. Commissioner, 326 F.2d 712, 716 (CA8) (although expenditures may not "result[] in the acquisition or increase of a corporate asset, . . . these expenditures are not, because of that fact, deductible as ordinary and necessary business expenses"), cert. denied, 379 U.S. 832 (1964).

Nor does our statement in *Lincoln Savings*, 405 U.S., at 354, that "the presence of an ensuing benefit that may have some future aspect is not controlling" prohibit reliance on future benefit as a means of distinguishing an ordinary business expense from a capital expenditure.[6] Although the mere presence of an incidental future benefit — "*some* future aspect" — may not warrant capitalization, a taxpayer's realization of benefits beyond the year in which the expenditure is incurred is undeniably important in determining whether the appropriate tax treatment is immediate deduction or capitalization. See United States v. Mississippi Chemical Corp., 405 U.S. 298, 310 (1972) (expense that "is of value in more than one taxable year" is a nondeductible capital expenditure); Central Texas Savings & Loan Assn. v. United States, 731 F.2d 1181, 1183 (CA5 1984) ("While the period of the benefits may not be controlling in all cases, it nonetheless remains a prominent, if not predominant, characteristic of a capital item."). Indeed, the text of the Code's capitalization provision, §263(a)(1), which refers to "permanent improvements or betterments," itself envisions an inquiry into the duration and extent of the benefits realized by the taxpayer.

III

In applying the foregoing principles to the specific expenditures at issue in this case, we conclude that National Starch has not demonstrated that the investment banking, legal, and other costs it incurred in connection with Unilever's acquisition of its shares are deductible as ordinary and necessary business expenses under §162(a).

Although petitioner attempts to dismiss the benefits that accrued to National Starch from the Unilever acquisition as "entirely speculative" or "merely incidental," Brief for Petitioner 39-40, the Tax Court's and the Court of Appeals' findings that the transaction produced significant benefits to National Starch that extended beyond the tax year in question are amply supported by the record. For example, in commenting on the merger with Unilever, National Starch's 1978 "Progress Report" observed that the company would "benefit greatly from the availability of Unilever's enormous resources, especially in the area of basic technology." App. 43. See also id., at 46 (Unilever "provides new opportunities and resources"). Morgan Stanley's report to the National Starch board concerning the fairness to shareholders of a possible business combination with Unilever noted that National Starch management "feels that some synergy may exist with the Unilever organization given a) the nature of the Unilever chemical, paper, plastics and packaging operations . . . and b) the strong consumer products orientation of Unilever United States, Inc." Id., at 77-78.

---

6. Petitioner contends that, absent a separate-and-distinct-asset requirement for capitalization, a taxpayer will have no "principled basis" upon which to differentiate business expenses from capital expenditures. Brief for Petitioner 37-41. We note, however, that grounding tax status on the existence of an asset would be unlikely to produce the bright-line rule that petitioner desires, given that the notion of an "asset" is itself flexible and amorphous. See Johnson, 53 Tax Notes, at 477-478.

In addition to these anticipated resource-related benefits, National Starch obtained benefits through its transformation from a publicly held, freestanding corporation into a wholly owned subsidiary of Unilever. The Court of Appeals noted that National Starch management viewed the transaction as "swapping approximately 3500 shareholders for one." 918 F.2d, at 427; see also App. 223. Following Unilever's acquisition of National Starch's outstanding shares, National Starch was no longer subject to what even it terms the "substantial" shareholder-relations expenses a publicly traded corporation incurs, including reporting and disclosure obligations, proxy battles, and derivative suits. Brief for Petitioner 24. The acquisition also allowed National Starch, in the interests of administrative convenience and simplicity, to eliminate previously authorized but unissued shares of preferred and to reduce the total number of authorized shares of common from 8,000,000 to 1,000. See 93 T.C., at 74.

Courts long have recognized that expenses such as these, " 'incurred for the purpose of changing the corporate structure for the benefit of future operations are not ordinary and necessary business expenses.' " General Bancshares Corp. v. Commissioner, 326 F.2d, at 715 (quoting Farmers Union Corp. v. Commissioner, 300 F.2d 197, 200 (CA9), cert, denied, 371 U.S. 861 (1962)). See also B. Bittker & J. Eustice, Federal Income Taxation of Corporations and Shareholders, pp. 5-33 to 5-36 (5th ed. 1987) (describing "well-established rule" that expenses incurred in reorganizing or restructuring corporate entity are not deductible under §162(a)). Deductions for professional expenses thus have been disallowed in a wide variety of cases concerning changes in corporate structure.[7] Although support for these decisions can be found in the specific terms of §162(a), which require that deductible expenses be "ordinary and necessary" and incurred "in carrying on any trade or business,"[8] courts more frequently have characterized an expenditure as capital in nature because "the purpose for which the expenditure is made has to do with the corporation's operations and betterment, sometimes with a continuing capital asset, for the duration of its existence or for the indefinite future or for a time somewhat longer than the current taxable year." General Bancshares Corp. v. Commissioner, 326 F.2d, at 715. See also Mills Estate, Inc. v. Commissioner, 206 F.2d 244, 246

7. See, e.g., McCrory Corp. v. United States, 651 F.2d 828 (CA2 1981) (statutory merger under 26 U.S.C. §368(a) (1) (A)); Bilar Tool & Die Corp. v. Commissioner, 530 F.2d 708 (CA6 1976) (division of corporation into two parts); E.I. du Pont de Nemours & Co. v. United States, 432 F.2d 1052 (CA3 1970) (creation of new subsidiary to hold assets of prior joint venture); General Bancshares Corp. v. Commissioner, 326 F.2d 712, 715 (CA8) (stock dividends), cert. denied, 379 U.S. 832 (1964); Mills Estate, Inc. v. Commissioner, 206 F.2d 244 (CA2 1953) (recapitalization).

8. See, e.g., Motion Picture Capital Corp. v. Commissioner, 80 F.2d 872, 873-874 (CA2 1936) (recognizing that expenses may be "ordinary and necessary" to corporate merger, and that mergers may be "ordinary and necessary business occurrences," but declining to find that merger is part of "ordinary and necessary business activities," and concluding that expenses are therefore not deductible); Greenstein, The Deductibility of Takeover Costs After National Starch, 69 Taxes 48, 49 (1991) (expenses incurred to facilitate transfer of business ownership do not satisfy the "carrying on [a] trade or business" requirement of §162(a)).

(CA2 1953). The rationale behind these decisions applies equally to the professional charges at issue in this case.

IV

The expenses that National Starch incurred in Unilever's friendly takeover do not qualify for deduction as "ordinary and necessary" business expenses under §162(a). The fact that the expenditures do not create or enhance a separate and distinct additional asset is not controlling; the acquisition-related expenses bear the indicia of capital expenditures and are to be treated as such.

The judgment of the Court of Appeals is affirmed.

It is so ordered.

Notes

1. In *Lincoln Savings* the Court required capitalization of a payment required by federal bank regulators because it created or enhanced "what is essentially a separate and distinct additional asset." Unfortunately it added that "the presence of an ensuing benefit that may have some future aspect is not controlling." So taxpayers, including INDOPCO, sought to deduct things long held capital by pointing to the absence of any "separate and distinct additional asset."

2. In *INDOPCO* it might have been enough just to say that creation of a separate and distinct additional asset was sufficient to require capitalization, but not necessary; and to affirm that *Lincoln Savings* had not "changed the familiar backdrops" of prior decisions as claimed by the taxpayer. But *INDOPCO* is itself full of unnecessary additional language, announcing a presumption in favor of capitalization and suggesting that anything beyond "the mere presence of an incidental future benefit" may warrant disallowance of a current deduction.

3. *Lower court reception.* In the immediate aftermath of *INDOPCO*, it was the IRS's turn to argue that familiar backdrops had changed. IRS field agents took the position that expenditures relating to the acquisition, creation, or enhancement of intangible assets must be capitalized if they yield a "significant future benefit," and the Tax Court usually agreed, even where capitalization was contrary to longstanding industry practice. The Courts of Appeals, however, were far less sympathetic to wholesale expansion of capitalization requirements and tended to tolerate immediate deduction under conventional categorical approaches. E.g., FMR Corp. v. Commissioner, 110 T.C. 402 (1998) (mutual fund management company required to capitalize the cost of organizing new mutual funds since this activity provides significant future benefits); PNC Bancorp, Inc. v. Commissioner, 110 T.C. (1998) (bank loan origination costs were required to be capitalized and amortized

over the life of the associated loans as now required for financial accounting purposes), rev'd, 212 F.3d 822 (3d Cir. 2000); RJR Nabisco Inc., T.C. Memo 1998-252 (expenditures relating to the graphic design of cigarette packaging materials and cigarette papers, tips, and other components not required to be capitalized), nonacq., 1999-2 C.B. xvi, action on dec., 1999-012 (Oct. 4, 1999) (nonacquiescence based on distinction between ordinary advertising and graphic design costs that generate brand identity); Norwest Corp. v. Commissioner, 112 T.C. 89 (1999) (officers' salaries and legal fees paid by state bank investigating friendly acquisition by bank holding company must "be capitalized [under *INDOPCO*] when it produces a significant long-term benefit, even when, as is the case here, the expense does not produce a separate and distinct asset"), rev'd sub nom., Wells Fargo & Co. v. Commissioner, 224 F.3d 874 (8th Cir. 2000).

4. INDOPCO *regulations.* After ten years of uncertainty and intense industry pressure, the Treasury proposed and adopted new regulations that disavow a broad reading of *INDOPCO.* Reg. §§1.263(a)-4, -5. According to the notice of proposed rulemaking, "The IRS and Treasury Department note that the separate and distinct asset standard has not historically yielded the same level of controversy as the significant future benefit standard. . . . A 'significant future benefit' standard . . . does not provide the certainty and clarity necessary for compliance with, and sound administration of, the law." 2003-1 C.B. 373, 374. The regulations identify specific categories of expenditures which must be capitalized; other amounts that produce significant future benefits are not required to be capitalized. 2004-1 C.B. 447, 448. So much for a presumption in favor of capitalization.

5. *One-year rule.* Must expenditures that yield benefits extending substantially beyond the end of the current taxable year be capitalized if the benefits will expire within one year from the date of the outlay? What are the competing arguments? See U.S. Freightways Corp. v. Commissioner, 270 F.3d 1137 (7th Cir. 2001); Reg. 1.263(a)-4(f)(1).

D.   A REASONABLE ALLOWANCE FOR SALARIES

PATTON v. COMMISSIONER
168 F.2d 28 (6th Cir. 1948)

Before Hicks, McAllister and Miller, Circuit Judges.

Hicks, Circuit Judge. . . . During the calendar year 1943 petitioners were partners doing a general jobbing business under the firm name of "Patton Company, Cleveland, Ohio," and one William Kirk was an employee of the firm. The partnership claimed deductions for 1943 for compensation of $46,049.41 paid to Kirk. The Commissioner determined that $13,000.00 constituted reasonable compensation for him for that year and disallowed the deductions claimed above that amount. The Tax Court sustained the Commissioner. . . .

The Tax Court found the following facts: Prior to July 1, 1940, petitioner, James F. Patton, operated the machine shop as an individual, during which time his business was small. At times he had no employees and did all the work himself. At other times the work required additional help. At times his son, Vincent, assisted him, although Vincent had full time employment elsewhere. About 1937 James F. Patton employed Kirk to do his office work. Kirk had a grammar school education and a two years' commercial course in high school. From 1893 to 1919 he engaged in clerical work and following that, he operated a small trucking business until 1929. From then, until his employment by James F. Patton he had no regular employment. From 1919 to 1941 his earnings were not sufficient to require the filing of tax returns. From 1937 to 1940 Kirk's compensation was approximately as follows: For 1937, $939.00; for 1938, $1,230.00; for 1939, $1,385.00; for 1940, $1,855.00.

On July 1, 1940, James F. Patton and his son Vincent formed a partnership and shortly thereafter James F. turned over the affairs of the partnership to Vincent. Up to December 17, 1940, the partnership, called The Patton Company, did job work for general customers, but on that date The General Motors Corporation began sending work to the Company in such volume that its productive capacity was absorbed by the new customer.

On January 2, 1941, petitioners contracted in writing with Kirk whereby he was to receive a minimum salary of $2,400.00 a year until such time as 22½ percent of the net profits exceeded $2,400.00. In such event the contract provided that Kirk was to receive 10 percent of the net sales for as long as that percentage, plus the $2,400.00 basic salary, did not exceed 22½ percent of the net profits.

The gross sales from 1941 to 1943 were, for 1941, $179,050.00; for 1942, $365,609.53; for 1943 [the year involved here] $460,494.06. Kirk kept the books on a cash basis in a simple way. He recorded in a cash book all receipts and disbursements and at the end of each month prepared two summary sheets, one showing total receipts and disbursements of each class and the other showing materials purchased. At the end of each year the summary sheets showing totals for each month and year were used by an accountant who translated them to an accrual basis in preparing income tax returns. Kirk kept a ledger and did the billing, which required little effort because substantially all of the Company's work was for General Motors. He prepared the payrolls, kept social security records and made quarterly social security reports. He kept petitioner Vincent Patton informed of the bank balances and transmitted to shop foremen information from General Motors as to the orders it desired to be finished first. He spoke to insurance salesmen before purchases of insurance were approved by Vincent. About five times in 1942-1943 he called the appropriate agents for approval of wage increases for employees. Kirk was not a partner in the Patton Company nor related to either of the partners.

The case strips to one question: whether, as determined by the Commissioner, $13,000.00 was reasonable compensation to Kirk for 1943. We are dealing with a pure question of fact. Wilmington Co. v. Helvering, 316 U.S. 164. In the Wilmington case, supra, the court said:

> It is the function of the Board, not the Circuit Court of Appeals, to weigh the evidence, to draw inferences from the facts, and to choose between conflicting inferences. The court may not substitute its view of the facts for that of the Board. Where the findings of the Board are supported by substantial evidence they are conclusive.

. . . We think that petitioners have failed to carry the burden, which the law imposes upon them, to make out their case by clear and convincing evidence. . . . Probably one of the most important factors in determining the reasonableness of compensation is the amount paid to similar employees by similar concerns engaged in similar industries. The petitioner introduced no evidence upon this subject. Moreover, it occurs to us that the books of the partnership kept by Kirk would have disclosed to a great extent the nature and volume of his work and his capabilities to perform it, but neither the books nor any verified entries therefrom were introduced by petitioners. There is of course a presumption that as between the parties to the contract the compensation agreed to be paid was reasonable. But, as between petitioners and the Commissioner, such a presumption is not controlling in a controversy of this nature before the Tax Court. Botany Worsted Mills v. United States, 278 U.S. 282, 292.

Affirmed.

Mr. ALLISTER, Circuit Judge (dissenting). . . . It does not seem to me that the *Botany Mills* case controls the controversy before us. There the stockholders of a corporation adopted a bylaw providing for the payment of more than 50 percent of the annual net profits to the members of the board of directors, for their services, in addition to their regular annual salaries of $9,000 each. In 1917, the tax year there in controversy, the amount paid out of net profits to the board of directors was $1,565,739.39, or a payment to each director of $156,573.93, in addition to his salary. Under a statute, similar in phrasing to the one before us, providing for deductions of all "the ordinary and necessary expenses paid within the year in the maintenance and operation of its business," 39 Stat. 756, the court held that this amount so greatly exceeded the amounts which are usually paid to directors for their attendance at meetings of the board and the discharge of their customary duties, as to raise a strong inference that the "amount paid to the directors was *not in fact compensation for their services, but merely a distribution of a fixed percentage of the net profits* that had no relation to the services rendered." (Emphasis supplied.) The *Botany Mills* case cites three other cases, hereinafter briefly discussed, that seem to me to elucidate the reason for the court's decision. . . .

In all of these cases, the amounts were paid to officers who were really beneficial owners of the corporation and who controlled its action in contracting for and paying them the unusually high salaries based upon net profits. The reasons the courts have held such salaries were not deductible as "ordinary and necessary expenses," were because they were not, in fact, compensation, but merely a distribution of profits; that such profits, divided on the basis of stock holdings, were not payments of compensation; that the claimed salaries were not salaries at all, but profits diverted to stock holding officers under the guise of salaries; and that a distribution of profits "under the guise of salaries" to officers who held the stock of a company and controlled its affairs, is not an ordinary and necessary expense, within the meaning of the statute.

In this case, Kirk was not an owner or part owner of the company, directly or indirectly. His contract of employment, providing for a salary, based on profits, was not a distribution of profits under the guise of a salary. There is no question that the contract of employment was bona fide. . . .

Although much importance is seemingly attached by the Government to the fact that, before the contract of employment was entered into between Kirk and petitioners, his salary for the preceding four years was only $939, $1,230, $1,385, and $1,855, the Commissioner finally allowed a deduction on the basis of a salary to Kirk in the amount of $13,000. It can easily be perceived from the evidence that this was a purely arbitrary allowance on the part of the Commissioner. If it was based on the previous earnings of Kirk or upon what he actually did, it was obviously excessive. If it was arrived at by taking the contract for his services into consideration, it was clearly inadequate. It is impossible to escape the conclusion that the Commissioner based his allowance on the ground that the amount of compensation provided by the contract eventually turned out to be too high, merely because the profits during the years in question were so great. No such arbitrary determinations are valid, either in administrative decisions or in court adjudications. The decision that the amount provided by the contract of employment was too high was, as has been stated by the courts, no business or concern of the Government. The decisive question is whether the amount paid to Kirk was salary or a distribution of profits paid under the guise of salary. It was not a distribution of profits, for Kirk has no interest in the company.

It is admitted in this case that the amount paid to Kirk was salary, and there is nothing in the case to overcome the presumption that such compensation was reasonable. In my opinion, the partners were entitled to deduct the payment of such salary as an ordinary and necessary expense incurred during the taxable year, and the decision of the Tax Court to the contrary should be reversed.

Notes

1. "*A reasonable allowance for salaries.*" (a) What language in §162 (or elsewhere) operates to disallow the deduction in this case? Would the result

be different if the language "including a reasonable allowance for salaries or other compensation for personal services actually rendered" were not in the statute? What is the purpose of that language?

(b) Might the language "including a reasonable allowance for salaries or other compensation for personal services actually rendered" be construed to authorize a deduction for an allowance for salaries where none have been paid? Consider a closely held corporation whose officers, being large stockholders, do not charge for their services: Might the quoted language be held to authorize a deduction for the reasonable value of their services? Or might it be held to authorize deduction of an "allowance for salaries" to partners by a partnership?

(c) During several wartime periods we have had an excess profits tax based on the excess of wartime earnings over some peacetime norm, computed either as a set rate of return on invested capital or as an average of actual earnings in prewar years. In the context of this sort of tax, would there be some argument in favor of a deduction for an allowance for salaries even where salaries were not in fact paid?

(d) If it were shown that the language "including a reasonable allowance for salaries . . ." was introduced into the tax law for the purpose of authorizing a deduction for excess profits tax purposes in excess of salaries actually paid, what implication would that have for a case like *Patton*? See Griswold, New Light on "A Reasonable Allowance for Salaries," 59 Harv. L. Rev. 286 (1945).

2. *Partners.* What would have been the result, so far as the Pattons were concerned, if Mr. Kirk had been made a partner of the Patton Company with a share of profits equal to $22^1/2$ percent of profits or 10 percent of net sales? Is there any reason why the employment in this case should have any different income tax effect from a partnership agreement?

3. *Shareholder employees.* The reasonable compensation issue arises most frequently in the context of a closely held corporation paying salaries to its shareholders. Why? What function does the disallowance of unreasonable salary payments perform in this context?

4. The figures in *Patton* are rather extraordinary. Why do you suppose the Patton brothers gave such a substantial share of prospective revenues, in 1941, to an employee with Mr. Kirk's background? See M. Chirelstein, Federal Income Taxation 146-147 (10th ed. 2005).

5. In 1993 Congress imposed a cap on deductions for compensation paid by a publicly traded corporation to its chief executive and to each of the four other highest-paid officers. Total compensation exceeding $1 million to any such employee is nondeductible, but compensation paid on account of attainment of pre-established objective performance goals set by a committee of outside directors and approved by vote of the shareholders is not subject to the limitation. §162(m); Reg. §1.162-27(e). What explains (justifies?) this disallowance? Under a regime that taxes dividends at the lower rates applicable to long-term capital gains, see §1(h), should any nondeductible compensation be taxed to the recipient officer at 15 percent?

E. CARRYING ON ANY TRADE OR BUSINESS

ESTATE OF ROCKEFELLER v. COMMISSIONER
762 F.2d 264 (2d Cir. 1985), cert. denied 474 U.S. 1037 (1986)

Before: Feinberg, Chief Judge, and Friendly and Newman, Circuit Judges.

FRIENDLY, Circuit Judge: This appeal by the Estate of Nelson A. Rockefeller and his widow from a decision of the Tax Court, 83 T.C. 368 (1984), Featherston, J., presents a new variation on the old theme of what constitutes "ordinary and necessary expenses paid or incurred . . . in carrying on any trade or business," I.R.C. §162(a), which are deductible in determining net income. Appellants contended that expenses incurred by Mr. Rockefeller in connection with the confirmation by the Senate and the House of Representatives, pursuant to the Twenty-Fifth Amendment, of his nomination to be Vice President of the United States were such expenses. The Commissioner denied this, the Tax Court agreed, and this appeal followed. We affirm.

The case arises as follows: Mr. Rockefeller incurred expenses of $550,159.78 in connection with the confirmation hearings in 1974, primarily for legal and other professional services. The Commissioner does not contend that the expenses were excessive or unreasonable in relation to the services rendered. In their joint income tax return for 1974, which showed a gross income of $4,479,437, Mr. and Mrs. Rockefeller claimed a deduction of $63,275—an amount of these expenses equal to his salary as Vice President during the year. When the Commissioner disallowed this deduction, Mr. Rockefeller's estate and Mrs. Rockefeller petitioned for review by the Tax Court and asserted that the entire amount of $550,159.78 was deductible as expenses of the trade or business of "performing the functions of public office."

The case was submitted on a rather meagre stipulation of facts which cited only Mr. Rockefeller's tenure as Governor of New York State between January 1959 and December 1973, when he resigned to devote his full time to the Commission on Critical Choices for Americans (1973-1974) and the National Commission on Water Quality (1973-1974), as showing the trade or business in which Mr. Rockefeller had engaged. However, copies of the hearings before and the reports of the Senate and House Committees on his nomination as Vice President were attached to the stipulation, and the Tax Court's opinion lists other positions held by Mr. Rockefeller referred to in these hearings, as follows: Coordinator of Inter-American Affairs (1940-1944), Assistant Secretary of State for American Republic Affairs (1944-1945), Chairman of the Presidential Advisory Board on International Development (1950-1951), Undersecretary of Health, Education and Welfare (1953-1954), and Special Assistant to the President for International Affairs (1954-1955). 83 T.C. at 374-375.

DISCUSSION

Decision turns on the interpretation of the familiar provision of I.R.C. §162(a), going back to the Revenue Act of 1918, which allows as a deduction

all the ordinary and necessary expenses paid or incurred during the taxable year in carrying on any trade or business.

Also relevant is I.R.C. §7701(a)(26), adopted as §48(d) of the Revenue Act of 1934, 48 Stat. 680, 696, ch. 277, which says:

The term "trade or business" includes the performance of the functions of a public office.[2]

Almost all discussions of the problem here at issue begin, and many of them end, with McDonald v. Commissioner, 323 U.S. 57 (1944), although in fact it sheds a most uncertain light. McDonald had been appointed to serve an unexpired term as judge on a Pennsylvania court, carrying an annual salary of $12,000, with the understanding that he would be a contestant in the ensuing primary and general elections for a full term often years. To obtain the support of his party organization, he was forced to pay an "assessment" of $8,000, which was to be used for the support of the entire ticket; he spent an additional $5,017.27 for expenses of his own campaign. The Commissioner disallowed the deduction of both amounts. The Tax Court affirmed, 1 T.C. 738 (1943), as did a sharply divided Supreme Court.[3] The bases for the decision are not altogether clear. At one point Justice Frankfurter emphasized that McDonald's "campaign contributions were not expenses incurred in being a judge but in trying to be a judge for the next ten years." 323 U.S.

2. The Senate and Conference Committee Reports describe this addition as "clerical" and "declaratory of existing law," S. Rep. No. 558, 73d Cong., 2d Sess. at 29; H.R. Rep. No. 1385, 73d Cong., 2d Sess. at 17 (Conference Report) (1934). A discussion before the Senate Committee on Finance suggests that the primary reason for the provision was to overcome doubts whether Senators were engaged in a "trade or business" so as to permit deduction for extra staff and telephone expenses. 1 Hearings Before Committee on Finance on H.R. 7835, 73d Cong., 2d Sess. (March 6, 1934), pp. 29-30. The Ninth Circuit has said that §48(d) was adopted to modify the general rule that "in order for an activity to be considered a trade or business under Section 162 it must be engaged in for profit." Frank v. United States, 577 F.2d 93, 95 (9 Cir. 1978). The court cited Jackling v. Commissioner, 9 B.T.A. 312, 320 (1927), as the "best statement of the [existing] law" with respect to public officers, which the amendment was said to have codified. In Jackling, the Board of Tax Appeals allowed business deductions by a wartime government employee whose salary was only one dollar a year and rejected the Commissioner's argument that the expenses were not deductible because the taxpayer's employment was not profit motivated. Further support for this reading of §48(d) can be found in Revenue Ruling 55-109, 155-1 Cum. Bul. 262 (1955), in which the Commissioner interpreted the section as allowing a public office to be treated as a trade or business "even though the incumbent thereof may serve without compensation, a factor which is ordinarily regarded as a prerequisite to the pursuit of a trade or business."

3. Justice Frankfurter delivered a plurality opinion for himself, Chief Justice Stone and Justices Roberts and Jackson. Justice Rutledge concurred in the result. Justice Black dissented for himself and Justices Reed, Douglas and Murphy. It may not be altogether accidental that three of the dissenters had held elective office, an experience not shared by any member of the plurality.

at 60. Perhaps fearing that this being-becoming distinction would cut too widely, Justice Frankfurter elaborated other factors. One was that allowance of a deduction for the assessments paid by McDonald would lead to deductions by persons who were not candidates but paid "such 'assessments' out of party allegiance mixed or unmixed by a lively sense of future favors," id., a proposition which would not necessarily follow and which in any event would not explain the disallowance of McDonald's own campaign expenses. This was followed by a sentence, again emphasizing the being-becoming distinction but with a different thought added for good measure, 323 U.S. at 60-61:

> To determine allowable deductions by the different internal party arrangements for bearing the cost of political campaigns in the forty-eight states would disregard the explicit restrictions of §23 confining deductible expenses solely to outlays in the efforts or services — here the business of judging — from which the income flows. Compare Welch v. Helvering, 290 U.S. 111, 115-116.

After disposing of arguments based on what are now I.R.C. §165 and §212(1), he continued with some observations concerning the increased public hostility to campaign contributions by "prospective officeholders, especially judges," and then concluded on two notes. One was that, 323 U.S. at 63-64:

> To find sanction in existing tax legislation for deduction of petitioner's campaign expenditures would necessarily require allowance of deduction for campaign expenditures by all candidates, whether incumbents seeking reelection or new contenders. To draw a distinction between outlays for reelection and those for election — to allow the former and disallow the latter — is unsupportable in reason. It is even more unsupportable in public policy to derive from what Congress has thus far enacted a handicap against candidates challenging existing officer holders. And so we cannot recognize petitioner's claim on the score that he was a candidate for reelection. (footnote omitted).

The other was the desirability of according special deference to the Tax Court's determination on a matter of the sort sub judice, id. at 64-65. The Supreme Court has not had subsequent occasion to revisit the field plowed in *McDonald*. . . .

   The courts have echoed the various themes sounded in *McDonald*. Some decisions have stressed the being-becoming distinction; see, e.g., Diggs v. Commissioner, 715 F.2d 245, 250 (6 Cir. 1983). Others have emphasized the policy argument against deduction of campaign expenses, namely, that allowing such deductions would involve the whole community in partial subsidization of the electoral expenses of a particular candidate — a subsidy that would pay a larger amount of the campaign expenses of high than of low bracket candidates. See, e.g., James B. Carey, 56 T.C. 477, 479-481 (1971), aff'd per curiam, 460 F.2d 1259 (4 Cir.), cert. denied, 409 U.S. 990 (1972). The appellants distinguish the latter cases, stressing that the expenses here at issue were not incurred in an election in which Mr. Rockefeller was pitted against another citizen but in a confirmation in which he was the only candidate.[4] However, the policy argument in *McDonald* is only dubiously applicable to Campbell v. Davenport, 362 F.2d 624, 626 (5 Cir. 1966), Nichols v. Commissioner, 511 F.2d 618 (5 Cir.) (en banc), cert. denied, 423 U.S. 912 (1975), and Levy v. United States, 535 F.2d 47 (Ct. Cl.), cert. denied, 429 U.S. 885 (1976), disallowing the deduction of small qualification fees payable by any candidate to his party to help to defray the costs of conducting the primary election and of which "[n]o part . . . was used to espouse the causes of party candidates in the general election." Nichols, supra, 511 F.2d at 619. Further support for the Commissioner's position can be found in Joseph W. Martino, 62 T.C. 840, 844 (1974), disallowing deduction of legal fees incurred by a successful primary candidate in defending his victory against an election contest suit filed by his opponent; Martino, like Mr. Rockefeller, was not seeking the suffrage of the people as against another candidate.

Appellants' principal argument is that a post-*McDonald* decision of the Tax Court, in which the Commissioner has acquiesced, David J. Primuth, 54 T.C. 374 (1970), has undermined the being-becoming distinction. Primuth, the secretary-treasurer of a small corporation, Foundry Allied Industries, enlisted the aid of a "head-hunter" organization to find him a better job. This work resulted in his employment as "secretary-controller" of a company with greater geographical scope. The Tax Court held that the fees and expenses paid to the head-hunter organization were deductible under I.R.C. §162.

Judge Sterrett's opinion for a plurality took off from the proposition that "a taxpayer may be in the trade or business of being an employee, such as a corporate executive or manager," 54 T.C. at 377, rather than or in addition to the trade or business of holding a particular job, citing numerous cases including our own Hochschild v. Commissioner, 161 F.2d 817 (1947). With that established, Judge Sterrett believed that "the problem presented . . . virtually dissolve[d] for it is difficult to think of a purer business expense than one incurred to permit such an individual to continue to carry on that very trade or business—albeit with a different corporate employer." 54 T.C. at 379. However, he proceeded to emphasize the relatively narrow scope of the decision, id.:

> Furthermore, the expense had no personal overtones, led to no position requiring greater or different qualifications than the one given up, and did not result in the

---

4. The force of this distinction between election and confirmation expenses is debatable. Mr. Rockefeller's expenses included not simply amounts incurred in preparing answers to questions of Senators and Representatives but also amounts incurred, with entire propriety, in convincing Congress that he was a good selection for Vice President. Nomination of Nelson A. Rockefeller to be Vice President of the United States: Hearings before the House Comm. on the Judiciary, 93d Cong., 2d Sess., pp. 1-3 (1974). While Mr. Rockefeller was not in direct contest with anyone, others were waiting in the wings if Congress was not so convinced. For reasons developed below, we are not required to pass on the force of the distinction.

acquisition of any asset as that term has been used in our income tax laws. It was expended for the narrowest and most limited purpose. It was an expense which must be deemed ordinary and necessary from every realistic point of view in today's marketplace where corporate executives change employers with a noticeable degree of frequency. We have said before, and we say again, that the business expenses which an employee can incur in his own business are rare indeed. Virtually all his expenses will be incurred on behalf of, and in furtherance of, his corporate employer's business. What we have here, however, is an exception to that rule. (footnote omitted).

Judge Tannenwald, joined by three other judges, concurred: they were concerned over the "subtle distinctions" which they saw developing in the deduction of employment agency fees and suggested that "everyday meaning" should be the touchstone in interpreting §162. 54 T.C. at 382. In a separate concurring opinion, Judge Simpson took issue with language in the plurality opinion which he feared might confine the decision to cases where the taxpayer actually secured a new job. Id. at 383. Judge Featherston's concurrence placed greater weight on a Revenue Ruling that explicitly "allow[ed] deductions for fees paid to employment agencies for securing employment." Id. at 384. Six judges dissented. The Department of Justice rejected the Commissioner's request for an appeal and the Commissioner acquiesced in the result, 1972-2 Cum. Bul. 2 (1972).

In Leonard F. Cremona, 58 T.C. 219 (1972), a majority of the Tax Court rejected an attempt by the Commissioner to contain *Primuth* to cases where the employee had in fact obtained a new position. Again the Department of Justice declined a request to appeal and the Commissioner acquiesced, 1975-1 Cum. Bul. 1 (1975).

However, the erosion of the being-becoming distinction effected by *Primuth* and *Cremona* and the Commissioner's acquiescence in these decisions was partial only. The Tax Court, with the approval of the courts of appeals, has limited deductibility to cases where the taxpayer was seeking employment in the same trade or business. Moreover, the courts have insisted on a high degree of identity in deciding the issue of sameness. Thus, in William D. Glenn, 62 T.C. 270 (1974), the court found that the broader scope of activities permitted in Tennessee to certified public accountants as compared with public accountants made the former a new trade or business and, in consequence, that the expense of taking a review course designed to assist the taxpayer in qualifying for certification was not deductible. Similarly, being a registered pharmacist constitutes a different trade or business than being an intern pharmacist, so that expenses of attending courses on pharmacology were not deductible, Gary Antzoulatos, T.C. Memo. 1975-327 (1975). In Joel A. Sharon, 66 T.C. 515 (1976), aff'd, 591 F.2d 1273 (9 Cir. 1978), cert. denied, 442 U.S. 941 (1979), the Tax Court disallowed an IRS attorney's deductions for expenses related to taking the California bar examination. The court found that these expenditures would permit the taxpayer to engage in the new "trade or business" of the general practice of law in the State of California. The Ninth Circuit agreed with the

Tax Court's reasoning that private practice involved "significantly different tasks and activities" from those required of an IRS lawyer, 591 F.2d at 1275. . . . Joseph Sorin Schnieder, supra, T.C. Memo. 1983-753 (1983), denied a deduction sought by a taxpayer who had resigned from the U.S. Army with a captain's commission and who later, after graduation, entered the business world as a consultant, for amounts spent in applying to graduate schools, in getting the graduate degrees of M.B.A. and M.P.A. at Harvard, and in seeking a summer job in Europe. The court said that the taxpayer's business had been that of an Army officer and rejected his claim that he had been in the business of being a "manager" — a claim strongly resembling the one made here that Mr. Rockefeller was in the business of being "a governmental executive." . . .

. . . In fact, the only public posts Mr. Rockefeller held at the time of his nomination were the chairmanships of two commissions, posts in which he had no executive duties. One of these, the National Commission on Water Quality was created by the Federal Water Pollution Control Act Amendments of 1972, 86 Stat. 816, to review water pollution control methods and issue a report to Congress recommending modifications. Although Mr. Rockefeller was elected chairman by the other members when he joined the Commission while still Governor of New York, the record reveals almost nothing about his activities there. The Commission on Critical Choices for Americans was an idea of Mr. Rockefeller's. It was not a governmental body, although its membership included some members of Congress and of the executive branch. Since federal funding was denied, the Commission was funded from private sources and foundation grants. If only these two activities were to be considered, it would be plain beyond all argument that holding the chairmanship of these Commissions and being Vice President are not the same trade or business but rather separate trades or businesses, if indeed membership on the commissions, particularly the Commission on Critical Choices, was a trade or business at all.

However, a taxpayer who is unemployed when the expenses are incurred is "viewed as still engaged in the business of providing the type of services performed for [his] prior employer, unless 'there is a substantial lack of continuity between the time of [the employee's] past employment and the seeking of the new employment.'" 1 Bittker, Federal Taxation of Income, Estates and Gifts §20.4.6, at 20-85 to 20-86 (1981), quoting Rev. Rul. 75-120, 1975-1 Cum. Bul. 55, at 56; see, 4A Mertens, The Law of Federal Income Taxation §25.08, at 33 (1985) (taxpayer's "trade or business [does] not cease to exist during a reasonable period of transition"). See also Stephen G. Sherman, supra, T.C. Memo. 1977-301. Appellants urge that this principle allows us to look to Mr. Rockefeller's fifteen years of service as Governor of New York in considering whether the confirmation expenses on his nomination to be Vice President were in connection with the continuation of the same trade or business. We disagree, for two reasons. In order to take advantage of what is called the "hiatus" principle, a taxpayer must at least show that during the hiatus he intended to resume the same trade or business. See *Sherman,* supra, T.C. Memo. 1977-301. There is no such showing here. Mr. Rockefeller clearly did not intend to run again for Governor after having resigned that office after holding it for fifteen years. . . . We also cannot fault the Tax Court's holding that being governor of the second most populous state in the union and being Vice President of the United States are not the same trade or business in the narrow sense in which sameness has been consistently characterized. While there are certain areas of overlap, the governorship entails many duties — enforcement of the laws of the state, developing and promoting new laws, supervising a multitude of departments and agencies having thousands of employees and spending billions of dollars, proposing and securing the passage of a budget and the revenues needed to meet it, making appointments, and lobbying for the interests of the state with the Federal Government — which either find no counterparts in the Vice Presidency or find them only to the extent, usually quite limited, which the President had directed. On the other hand, the Vice Presidency involves many duties not found in the governorship of New York — presiding over the Senate, acting on behalf of the President on ceremonial occasions both within and without the United States, and executing special assignments by the President — not to speak of the Vice President's most important task, readying himself for the possibility of assuming the Presidency on a moment's notice. Although positions with somewhat different duties and responsibilities may be found to be within the same trade or business, whether in public or private employment, the Tax Court's finding that the Vice Presidency involved a trade or business for Mr. Rockefeller different from any in which he was engaged at the time of his nomination is not one that we are free to disturb, see I.R.C. §7482(a).

Appellants ask us to take a still broader view and consider Mr. Rockefeller as having been engaged in the same trade or business since his appointment as Coordinator of Inter-American Affairs in 1940. But the cases do not recognize a definition of "trade or business" wide enough to bring all Mr. Rockefeller's various posts within it. While there might be sufficient resemblance and continuity between the posts of Coordinator of Inter-American Affairs which Mr. Rockefeller held between 1940 and 1944 and that of Assistant Secretary of State for American Republic Affairs which he held between 1944 and 1945 to have qualified him as being in the business of being a public servant with special interest and expertise in Latin America, we see little resemblance between these positions and his service as Undersecretary of Health, Education and Welfare in 1953 and 1954 or as Governor of New York between 1959 and 1973. Furthermore there are substantial gaps between Mr. Rockefeller's various posts — five years between 1945 and 1950, one and one-half years between 1951 and 1953, three years between 1955 and 1958 — far longer than the "hiatus" theory would recognize. See, e.g., Canter v. United States, 354 F.2d 352 (Ct. Cl. 1965) (taxpayer who discontinued nursing activities for more than four years held not to retain status of being in the trade or business of nursing); Peter G. Corbett, 55 T.C. 884 (1971). See also Rev. Rul. 68-591, 1968-2 Cum. Bul. 73 (1968) ("Ordinarily, a suspension [of employment] for a period of a year or less, after which the taxpayer resumes the same . . . trade or business, will be considered temporary"). Our reading of the record shows Mr. Rockefeller as a distinguished and public-spirited citizen, ready, for a third of a century, to put his great abilities at the disposal of the government in both appointive and elective office. While he was, of course, entitled to deduct unreimbursed expenses incurred in performing the functions of any of the many offices he held, I.R.C. §7701(a)(26), the Tax Court was warranted in holding that he had not engaged in any trade or business comparable to the Vice Presidency, within the rather narrow sense which the courts have reasonably given to the concept of identity. We therefore have no occasion to decide whether the "policy" reasons underlying the decisions disallowing expenses incurred in elections apply to expenses incurred in seeking confirmation to an appointive office which would seem to be properly regarded as the same trade or business,[9] or whether if they generally do not, there are special considerations for applying them to the unusual bicameral confirmation required by the Twenty-Fifth Amendment which the Commissioner characterizes as the equivalent of an election.

The judgment of the Tax Court is affirmed.

Notes

1. Nelson Rockefeller obviously wasn't in this for the money. Could these expenses have been deducted as a contribution "to or for the use of . . . the United States"? §170(c)(1). If instead of retaining his own counsel, Justice Department or White House attorneys had been assigned to investigate and prepare Mr. Rockefeller for the confirmation hearings, would such public representation give rise to gross income? Cf. §132(d), enacted in 1984. Look at §195, which was enacted in 1980 and amended in 1984 and 2004. Would it operate to allow amortization of the expenses in *Rockefeller*?

2. The rule disallowing expenses incurred before commencement of a trade or business has a variety of applications. One concerns professional education, the costs of which are disallowed at least partly on the ground that the professional business to which they relate has not begun when educational expenses are normally incurred. See Chapter 12H.1 above.

3. What is the reason, if any, for the rule? To what extent is it simply derived from the language of §162 referring to expenses incurred "in carrying on" a trade or business? The Tax Court first held that a taxpayer paying

---

9. E.g., a judge of a federal district court nominated to a court of appeals, a judge of a state court nominated to a federal court, or a foreign service officer nominated to be an ambassador.

rent for land during the construction of property to be used in a new leasing business could not deduct the rent under §162 because the business had not commenced, but that a deduction was allowable under §212 since that provision has no requirement that an expense be "incurred in carrying on" any kind of activity. Herschel H. Hoopengarner, 80 T.C. 538 (1983), aff'd in unpublished opinion, 745 F.2d 66 (9th Cir. 1984). Is that holding consistent with the relation between §§162 and 212 as described in *Gilmore*, Chapter 12G above? Other courts thought not, and finally the Tax Court itself overruled *Hoopengarner*. Arthur H. Hardy, 93 T.C. 684 (1989).

4. *McDonald* and other reelection cases are not strictly pre-opening cases, since the taxpayers in those cases were engaged in the business of holding the offices in question when the expenses were incurred. Is the law in those cases peculiar to the business of holding public or political office? For more on the special problems of adapting the business expense deduction to public officials look at §162(h) and compare the second sentence (flush language) of §162(a), which concerns members of Congress.

References

C. Capital Expenditures: Daugherty & Biebl, The Preproductive Period Expense Question for Farmers: Deduct or Capitalize?, 38 Tax Notes 727 (1988); Gunn, The Requirement That a Capital Expenditure Create or Enhance an Asset, 15 B.C. Indus. & Com. L. Rev. 443 (1974); Lennon, Does Supreme Court's *Idaho Power* Decision Endanger Other Capital-Related Deductions?, 41 J. Taxn. 146 (1974); Schapiro, Prepayments and Distortion of Income Under Cash Basis Tax Accounting, 30 Tax L. Rev. 117 (1975); Travostino, *Idaho Power*: The Capitalization of Depreciation, 28 Tax Law. 149 (1974); Ethan Yale, When Are Capitalization Exceptions Justified?, 57 Tax L. Rev. 549 (2004); Note, Legal Fees Incurred in Litigation Involving Title to Assets, 126 U. Pa. L. Rev. 1100 (1978).

Chapter 14 — *Losses*

The cost of acquiring or improving business or investment property is not ordinarily deductible as such. §§263, 263A; Chapter 13C above. But often a deduction is later allowed on account of what happens to such property.

If the property is expected to wear out or to be used up over time, then a deduction is likely to be allowed for exhaustion, wear, and tear — that is, depreciation — by way of amortization of cost over the anticipated useful life of the asset. Depreciation deductions and related matters are taken up at some length in Chapters 15 and 16.

Whether or not depreciation is allowed, the property may be disposed of for less than its adjusted basis, in which case the statute generally allows a deduction for the loss, but it is subject to a battery of limitations. Sometimes a loss is even allowed without a sale if there is some other sufficient event of realization. Mere unrealized decline in value is not deductible, however, any more than unrealized appreciation is taxable.

This chapter deals with deductions for losses and limitations on those deductions.

A. IN GENERAL: §165

UNITED STATES v. S.S. WHITE DENTAL MANUFACTURING CO.
274 U.S. 398 (1927)

Mr. Justice STONE delivered the opinion of the Court. . . . Respondent is a Pennsylvania corporation, engaged in the manufacture and sale of dental supplies. Before 1918 it had organized and controlled, by ownership of all the capital stock, the S.S. White Dental Manufacturing Company, m.b.h. of

Berlin, Germany, a German corporation. Its investment in the German corporation in 1918, as carried on its books, aggregated more than $130,000.

The agreed statement of facts adopted as findings by the court below are so vague as to leave it uncertain whether this investment was represented on the books of respondent by the capital stock alone, or in part by the capital stock and in part by an open account between it and the German corporation. The case was argued on the assumption, which we make, that the investment was represented by both the capital stock and an open account, due to respondent from the German company. The total is conceded to be no more than the fair value of the net assets of the German corporation.

In March, 1918, the sequestrator appointed by the German government took over the property of the German corporation and the management of its business. It is inferable from the findings, as the government concedes, that the sequestration was similar in purpose and legal effect to that authorized under the Trading with the Enemy Act of the United States, Oct. 6 1917, . . . and we shall deal with the case on that basis.

In March, 1920, the possession of the seized assets and business was relinquished to the German corporation by the sequestrator. As a result of the mismanagement of its affairs while in his custody, and investments of its funds by him in German war loans, the value of its assets was seriously impaired. In 1922 its tangible assets and its lease were sold for $6,000. This sum was included in respondent's income tax return for that year. Later respondent filed a claim with the Mixed Claims Commission which was allowed in 1924 to the extent of $70,000. What if anything may ultimately be realized from this award remains uncertain.

In 1918 the respondent charged off as a loss the entire amount of its investment in the German corporation as shown by its books, and in July of that year passed a resolution authorizing the establishment of a reserve against this loss at the rate of $15,000 quarterly, beginning March, 1918. In making its income tax return for 1918 respondent deducted from gross income the amount of its investment in the German corporation. The deduction was disallowed by the Commissioner . . . on the sole ground that the loss was not evidenced by a closed and completed transaction in the year for which it was deducted. The tax so assessed was paid under protest and this suit followed.

Section 234 of the Revenue Act of 1918, c. 18, 40 Stat. 1057, 1077, 1078, authorizes the deduction in the computation of income taxes of "Losses sustained during the taxable year and not compensated for by insurance or otherwise." In explaining this section, Article 141 of Treasury Regulations, 45, provides that losses incurred in the taxpayer's trade or business or in any transaction entered into for profit may be deducted but such losses "must usually be evidenced by closed and completed transactions." Article 151 provides in part: "Where all the surrounding and attendant circumstances indicate that a debt is worthless and uncollectible and that legal action to enforce payment would in all probability not result in the satisfaction of execution on a judgment, a showing of these facts will be sufficient evidence of the worthlessness of the debt for the purpose of deduction." And Art. 144 reads in part: "if stock of a corporation becomes worthless, its cost or its fair market value as of March 1, 1913, if acquired prior thereto, may be deducted by the owner in the taxable year in which the stock became worthless, provided a satisfactory showing of its worthlessness be made as in the case of bad debts." See Art. 561, making these provisions applicable to corporations.

The case turns upon the question whether the loss, concededly sustained by the respondent through the seizure of the assets of the German company in 1918, was so evidenced by a closed transaction within the meaning of the quoted statute and treasury regulations as to authorize its deduction from gross income of that year. The statute obviously does not contemplate and the regulations (Art. 144) forbid the deduction of losses resulting from the mere fluctuation in value of property owned by the taxpayer. New York Ins. Co. v. Edwards, 271 U.S. 109, 116; cf. Miles v. Safe Deposit Co., 259 U.S. 247. But with equal certainty they do contemplate the deduction from gross income of losses, which are fixed by identifiable events, such as the sale of property (Art. 141, 144), or caused by its destruction or physical injury (Art. 141, 142, 143) or, in the case of debts, by the occurrence of such events as prevent their collection (Art. 151).

The transaction evidencing the loss here was the seizure of the property of the German company. The loss resulted to the respondent because it was a creditor and stockholder of that company which, as a result of the sequestration, was left without property or assets of any kind. The sequestration of enemy property was within the rights of the German government as a belligerent power and when effected left the corporation without right to demand its release or compensation for its seizure, at least until the declaration of peace. . . . What would ultimately come back to it, as the event proved, might be secured not as a matter of right, but as a matter either of grace to the vanquished or exaction by the victor. In any case the amount realized would be dependent upon the hazards of the war then in progress.

That legal action by respondent upon its open accounts against a corporation thus despoiled would have been fruitless within the meaning of Art. 151 seems not open to question. No distinction is urged by the government between respondent's investment in the stock of the German company and in its open accounts. It is equally apparent that the stock after the seizure was as worthless as the obligations of the German company and was deductible under Art. 144 on the same basis as bad debts.

If the seized assets are viewed as the property of respondent, ignoring the entity of the German company, the result is the same. The quoted regulations, consistently with the statute, contemplate that a loss may become complete enough for deduction without the taxpayer's establishing that there is no possibility of an eventual recoupment. It would require a high degree of optimism to discern in the seizure of enemy property by the

German government in 1918 more than a remote hope of ultimate salvage from the wreck of the war. The Taxing Act does not require the taxpayer to be an incorrigible optimist.

We need not attempt to say what constitutes a closed transaction evidencing loss in other situations. It is enough to justify the deduction here that the transaction causing the loss was completed when the seizure was made. It was none the less a deductible loss then, although later the German government bound itself to repay and an award was made by the Mixed Claims Commission which may result in a recovery.

Judgment affirmed.

Notes

1. Sometimes the line between losses and expenses is not clear, but often the distinction is not important. Consider, for example, the payment of a tort judgment for a liability incurred in the course of conducting business operations: Is that a loss or an expense? Courts have generally found it unnecessary to answer this question because the conditions on which a deduction is allowed and the consequences of the deduction if allowed are essentially the same either way. See, e.g., Bessenyey v. Commissioner, Chapter 12E above. There are special limitations on the deductibility of particular kinds of losses, as we shall see, but the basic requirements of §165(c)(1) and (2) are quite like those of §§162 and 212.

The provision for deducting losses is essential in cases like *S.S. White* since there is no current outlay that could be claimed as a deductible expense. Even in such cases there must have been some prior expenditure to provide a basis for computing a loss; but that expenditure, when made, was a nondeductible capital expenditure. The provision for deducting losses is one of the ways an originally nondeductible capital expenditure may ultimately produce a deduction after all.

2. Securities losses are most commonly realized by selling or otherwise disposing of securities whose value has declined. In the case of a sale, there is no need for the securities to have become worthless; any sale for less than adjusted basis will produce a potentially deductible loss. In *S.S. White*, the taxpayer sought and ultimately secured a deduction without any sale or disposition of the securities in question, but often the requirement of a sale operates to give taxpayers considerable control over the timing of loss recognition and deduction. The rule that worthlessness produces a deductible loss may then operate to restrict or limit the taxpayer's freedom to choose his time for deduction. What if a taxpayer seeks to deduct a loss on a sale of securities and the government then argues that the securities became worthless in a prior year for which the statute of limitations on tax refunds has now run? See §6511(d). What if an embezzlement loss is

not discovered until many years after the guilty employee absconded with the money? See Reg. §1.165-8(a)(2), -8(d).

3. For some cautions about what constitutes a realization of loss by sale or exchange, reread or review *Cottage Savings Assn.* and materials following it, Chapter 5C.2 above.

4. *Abandonment versus sale or exchange.* Suppose that property has gone way down in value but perhaps has not become worthless. Can a taxpayer then secure a loss deduction by abandoning the property? Why might abandonment be preferred to sale? See §1211; compare §165(g). How does one go about abandoning a piece of property (other than an automobile)? Compare §1234A, which provides that gain or loss "attributable to the cancellation, lapse, expiration or other termination" of a property right that is a capital asset in the hands of the taxpayer is treated as gain or loss from the sale of a capital asset.

5. *Outstanding compensation claims.* To be deductible, a loss must be both "sustained during the taxable year and not compensated for by insurance or otherwise." §165(a). Why was a loss deduction allowed in *S.S. White* for 1918, the year the subsidiary was seized, when the parent company filed a claim for reparations which, we are told, was allowed in 1924 to the extent of $70,000? Consult Reg. §1.165-1(d)(2). Assuming S.S. White eventually collected some of the allowed claim, how should that development be reported?

6. Sometimes a determination of worthlessness depends on just what the relevant property interest is defined to be. Consider a taxpayer who owns commercial fishing rights on a river whose fish are destroyed by pollution. Then compare a taxpayer who owns land adjacent to the river with fishing rights appurtenant thereto. Under what conditions, if any, could the latter taxpayer secure a deduction for worthlessness of his fishing rights? Compare Inaja Land Co. v. Commissioner, 9 T.C. 727 (1947) and Chapter 6A.1 above.

7. Is worthlessness solely a way of realizing losses, or might it also be the occasion for recognizing gain? Think about this a bit before looking at §1233(h), added in 1997.

B. WASH SALES AND TRANSACTIONS AMONG RELATED PARTIES

McWILLIAMS v. COMMISSIONER
331 U.S. 695 (1947)

Mr. Chief Justice VINSON delivered the opinion of the Court. The facts of these cases are not in dispute. John P. McWilliams, petitioner in No. 945, had for a number of years managed the large independent estate of his wife, petitioner in No. 947, as well as his own. On several occasions in 1940 and 1941 he ordered his broker to sell certain stock for the account of one of the two, and to buy the same number of shares of the same stock for the other, at as nearly the same price as possible. He told the broker that his purpose was to establish tax losses. On each occasion the sale and purchase were promptly negotiated through the Stock Exchange, and the identity of the persons buying from the selling spouse and of the persons selling to the buying spouse was never known. Invariably, however, the buying spouse received stock certificates different from those which the other had sold. Petitioners filed separate income tax returns for these years, and claimed the losses which he or she sustained on the sales as deductions from gross income.

The Commissioner disallowed these deductions on the authority of [§267] which prohibits deductions for losses from "sales or exchanges of property, directly or indirectly . . . between members of a family," and between certain other closely related individuals and corporations. . . .

Petitioners contend that Congress could not have intended to disallow losses on transactions like those described above, which, having been made through a public market, were undoubtedly bona fide sales, both in the sense that title to property was actually transferred, and also in the sense that a fair consideration was paid in exchange. They contend that the disallowance of such losses would amount, pro tanto, to treating husband and wife as a single individual for tax purposes.

In support of this contention, they call our attention to the pre-1934 rule, which applied to all sales regardless of the relationship of seller and buyer, and made the deductibility of the resultant loss turn on the "good faith" of the sale, i.e., whether the seller actually parted with title and control. They point out that in the case of the usual intra-family sale, the evidence material to this issue was peculiarly within the knowledge and even the control of the taxpayer and those amenable to his wishes, and inaccessible to the Government. They maintain that the only purpose of the provisions of the 1934 and 1937 Revenue Acts—the forerunners of [§267]—was to overcome these evidentiary difficulties by disallowing losses on such sales irrespective of good faith. It seems to be petitioners' belief that the evidentiary difficulties so contemplated were only those relating to proof of the parties' observance of the formalities of a sale and of the fairness of the price, and consequently that the legislative remedy applied only to sales made immediately from one member of a family to another, or mediately through a controlled intermediary.

We are not persuaded that Congress had so limited an appreciation of this type of tax avoidance problem. Even assuming that the problem was thought to arise solely out of the taxpayer's inherent advantage in a contest concerning the good or bad faith of an intra-family sale, deception could obviously be practiced by a buying spouse's agreement or tacit readiness to hold the property sold at the disposal of a selling spouse, rather more easily than by a pretense of a sale where none actually occurred, or by an unfair price. The difficulty of determining the finality of an intra-family transfer was one with which the courts wrestled under the pre-1934 law, and which Congress undoubtedly meant to overcome by enacting the provisions of [§267].

It is clear, however, that this difficulty is one which arises out of the close relationship of the parties, and would be met whenever, by prearrangement, one spouse sells and another buys the same property at a common price regardless of the mechanics of the transaction. Indeed, if the property is fungible, the possibility that a sale and purchase may be rendered nugatory by the buying spouse's agreement to hold for the benefit of the selling spouse, and the difficulty of proving that fact against the taxpayer, are equally great when the units of the property which the one buys are not the identical units which the other sells. . . .

Moreover, we think the evidentiary problem was not the only one which Congress intended to meet. Section [267] states an absolute prohibition — not a presumption — against the allowance of losses on any sales between the members of certain designated groups. The one common characteristic of these groups is that their members, although distinct legal entities, generally have a near-identity of economic interests. It is a fair inference that even legally genuine intra-group transfers were not thought to result, usually, in economically genuine realizations of loss, and accordingly that Congress did not deem them to be appropriate occasions for the allowance of deductions.

The pertinent legislative history lends support to this inference. The Congressional Committees, in reporting the provisions enacted in 1934, merely stated that "the practice of creating losses through transactions between members of a family and close corporations has been frequently utilized for avoiding the income tax," and that these provisions were proposed to "deny losses to be taken in the case of [such] sales" and "to close this loophole of tax avoidance." Similar language was used in reporting the 1937 provisions. Chairman Doughton of the Ways and Means Committee, in explaining the 1937 provisions to the House, spoke of "the artificial taking and establishment of losses where property was shuffled back and forth between various legal entities owned by the same persons or person," and stated that "these transactions seem to occur at moments remarkably opportune to the real party in interest in reducing his tax liability but, at the same time allowing him to keep substantial control of the assets being traded or exchanged."

We conclude that the purpose of [§267] was to put an end to the right of taxpayers to choose, by intra-family transfers and other designated devices, their own time for realizing tax losses on investments which, for most practical purposes, are continued uninterrupted.

We are clear as to this purpose, too, that its effectuation obviously had to be made independent of the manner in which an intra-group transfer was accomplished. Congress, with such purpose in mind, could not have intended to include within the scope of [§267] only simple transfers made directly or through a dummy, or to exclude transfers of securities effected through the medium of the Stock Exchange, unless it wanted to leave a loophole almost as large as the one it had set out to close.

Petitioners suggest that Congress, if it truly intended to disallow losses on intra-family transactions through the market, would probably have done so by an amendment to the wash sales provisions [§1091], making them applicable where the seller and buyer were members of the same family, as well as where they were one and the same individual. This extension of the wash sales provisions, however, would bar only one particular means of accomplishing the evil at which [§267] was aimed, and the necessity for a comprehensive remedy would have remained.

Nor can we agree that Congress' omission from [§267] of any prescribed time interval, comparable in function to that in the wash sales provisions, indicates that [§267] was not intended to apply to intra-family transfers through the Exchange. Petitioners' argument is predicated on the difficulty which courts may have in determining whether the elapse of certain periods of time between one spouse's sale and the other's purchase of like securities on the Exchange is of great enough importance in itself to break the continuity of the investment and make [§267] inapplicable.

Precisely the same difficulty may arise, however, in the case of an intra-family transfer through an individual intermediary, who, by pre-arrangement, buys from one spouse at the market price and a short time later sells the identical certificates to the other at the price prevailing at the time of sale. The omission of a prescribed time interval negates the applicability of [§267] to the former type of transfer no more than it does to the latter. But if we should hold that it negated both, we would have converted the section into a mere trap for the unwary.

Petitioners also urge that, whatever may have been Congress' intent, its designation in [§267] of sales "between" members of a family is not adequate to comprehend the transactions in this case, which consisted only of a sale of stock by one of the petitioners to an unknown stranger, and the purchase of different certificates of stock by the other petitioner, presumably from another stranger.

We can understand how this phraseology, if construed literally and out of context, might be thought to mean only direct intrafamily transfers. But petitioners concede that the express statutory reference to sales made "directly or indirectly" precludes that construction. Moreover, we can discover in this language no implication whatsoever that an indirect intra-family sale of fungibles is outside the statute unless the units sold by one spouse and those bought by the other are identical. Indeed, if we accepted petitioners' construction of the statute, we think we would be reading into it a crippling exception which is not there.

Finally, we must reject petitioners' assertion that the Dobson rule[18] controls this case. The Tax Court found the facts as we stated them, and then overruled the Commissioner's determination because it thought that [§267] had no application to a taxpayer's sale of securities on the Exchange

---

18. Dobson v. Commissioner, 320 U.S. 489.

to an unknown purchaser, regardless of what other circumstances accompanied the sale. We have decided otherwise, and on our construction of the statute, and the conceded facts, the Tax Court could not have reached a result contrary to our own.

Affirmed.

Mr. Justice Burton took no part in the consideration or decision of these cases.

Questions

1. What is the basis for computing future gain and loss on the shares acquired in the transactions in *McWilliams*? See §267(d).

2. Explain the difference between the basis rule in §1091(d) and that in §267(d).

3. (a) *A* owns TQ with a basis of 100. On June 1 he sells ten shares at 90, and on June 15 buys ten shares at 85. What will his allowable loss and basis be?

(b) *B* owns TQ with a basis of 100. On June 1 she buys ten shares at 90, and on June 15 she sells ten shares at 85. What will her allowable loss and basis be?

(c) *C* owned no TQ. On June 1 he buys at 90, and on June 15 he sells at 85. Does he have an allowable loss?

4. *D* owns 10,000 shares of GRX with a basis of 80 and a current market value of 50. She does not want to dispose of this stock, even for 30 days, but is willing to increase or reduce her holdings by 10 percent. Her accountant, therefore, devises this scheme: Buy 1,000 shares; 31 days later sell 2,000 shares — being careful these are among the old shares, not the newly acquired ones; 31 days later buy 2,000; 31 days later sell 2,000 more old shares, and so forth. By this method the whole loss can be taken within a year's time.

(a) Will this scheme work?

(b) How does *D* establish that it is the old shares and not the newly acquired shares that she is selling? See Reg. §1.1012-1(c).

(c) Should *D* be able to establish her loss on GRX stock in this manner?

5. *Indirect wash sales. E*, an individual, owns 100 shares of *X* Company stock with a basis of $1,000. On December 20, 2007, *E* sells the 100 shares on the open market for $600. The next day *E* causes an individual retirement account (IRA), as defined by §408, which was previously established for the exclusive benefit of *E* and *E*'s beneficiaries, to purchase 100 shares of *X* Company stock from an unrelated market participant for $590, the stock's then fair market value. The IRS ruled that the $400 loss is nondeductible because the purchase of substantially identical shares by the IRA should be treated as the acquisition by *E* for purposes of §1091(a). The ruling also states that the disallowed loss does not increase *E*'s basis in the IRA under

§1091(d), presumably because the wash sale basis adjustment applies only to the substantially identical stock or securities. Rev. Rul. 2008-5, 2008-1 C.B. 272. IRAs are generally exempt from taxation under §408(e)(1), and so the basis of shares purchased for the IRA is largely irrelevant. What is the effect of this ruling? Why doesn't §267 disallow the loss? (Or does it?)

6. *LIFO inventories.* (a) When goods or merchandise are acquired at varying costs, one method of computing gross profit on sale is always to treat the Last goods In as the First to go Out (LIFO). §472; see Chapter 6D.3 above. This has the effects of matching current costs against current revenues, and excluding from income changes in value of any basic stock of inventory that is kept on hand from year to year (although it may be turned over so that no individual item is retained from year to year).

(b) Would it be advisable to apply the LIFO rule to securities sales? As so applied, the rule would require that in any sale of securities in which a taxpayer retains any other securities of the same class, he shall be treated as having sold the most recently acquired and having retained the earliest acquired of those securities.

(c) Could the LIFO rule be extended to cover wash sales? As so extended, the rule might simply require that if within 30 days after any sale of securities a taxpayer acquires substantially identical securities at a cost lower than that of the securities sold, then the gain or loss on the securities sold shall be recomputed as if the subsequently acquired securities were the ones sold and the old ones had been retained.

(d) How would the cases in 3 and 4 come out under a LIFO rule as stated in (b) and (c)?

(e) Would a LIFO rule as stated in (b) and (c) deal adequately with the wash sale problem? Would it deal effectively with any other problems? Would it be a good rule to have?

7. (a) Section 16(b) of the Securities Exchange Act of 1934 requires corporate insiders to pay over to their corporations any profit from the purchase and sale or sale and purchase of equity securities of the corporation within any six-month period. The rule for computing recoverable profit under this provision is to match the highest-priced sale against the lowest-cost purchase within six months before or after the sale. Smolowe v. Delendo Corp., 136 F.2d 231 (2d Cir. 1943), cert. denied, 320 U.S. 751 (1943). Sometimes a corporate insider has recoverable profits under §16(b) while having nothing but losses for tax purposes. How?

(b) Would the lowest-in-highest-out rule of §16(b) be a good one for income tax purposes?

(c) What should be the income tax treatment of a corporate insider who incurs liability under §16(b)?

8. How would the holding in *McWilliams* be affected today by §1041?

9. *Straddles.* Commodities markets make it possible for investors to buy or sell commodities for future delivery at a price fixed when the contract is entered into. If an investor buys silver for delivery in eight months, he is said

to be long in silver for the date eight months ahead; if he sells, he is short. If the underlying commodity goes up in price, then long contracts will also go up in value, although not necessarily by exactly the same amount since there might be small differences due to different dates; and short contracts will become losers; and vice versa. Typically a futures contract can be settled or closed out at any time by paying or receiving cash in the amount of the loss or gain that has occurred.

Suppose an investor bought silver for delivery eight months hence and contemporaneously sold silver for ten months hence. In this case there will be a strong tendency for gains or losses on either of these contracts to be offset by losses or gains on the other. So if silver in fact goes up, the short position would suffer a loss in value but the long position would enjoy a closely corresponding gain. A pair of positions like this is commonly referred to as a *straddle*, and each of the contracts singly is referred to as a *leg of the straddle*.

Now what if an investor acquires a silver straddle, and then when the price of silver moves enough to suit his taste he closes out the loss leg, hanging onto the gain leg. Should he be able to deduct his loss in this situation?

Section 1092 is entitled *Straddles*. It is not an easy provision to understand or even to read in full, but the facts above make an easy case and the deduction would be disallowed. The problems that make §1092 difficult arise from the fact that offsetting positions may be much harder to find and to evaluate. Should the IRS be required or authorized to go through a taxpayer's various investment accounts looking for offsetting positions? What about accounts of his close relations? And how closely must one position offset another to have the pair treated as a straddle? These are questions without easy answers.

C.   CAPITAL LOSSES: §1211

When an ordinary investor sells securities at a loss, even to a wholly unrelated party, §165 will allow a deduction, but §1211 will impose a limitation on that deduction. Read §§1211(b) and 1212(b) to figure out just what that limitation is. Then try to think why the limitation is imposed.

Think particularly about the relation between the capital loss limitation in §1211 and any favorable rate of tax on net capital gains that has been or might be provided by any other section. One effect of the capital loss limitation through most of its history was to prevent deduction of large capital losses against ordinary income in one year followed by favorable treatment of large net capital gains in a subsequent year. The limitation requires the losses to be carried over and set off against the subsequent capital gains. People who advocate repeal of the special treatment of capital gains used to offer repeal of the capital loss limitation as a natural corollary.

But when the capital gain preference *was* repealed in 1986, the capital loss limitation was retained substantially unchanged. Why?

Clearly, the capital loss limitation has always done much more than limit capital gain treatment to net capital gains. For a taxpayer who has no subsequent capital gains — even if she had had substantially taxed capital gains in prior years — the capital loss limitation may have the effect of disallowing deductions altogether for a substantial part of her losses. Why?

Be very clear that §1211 does not authorize deductions at all: It operates only as a limitation on losses otherwise allowable by reason of some other provision, usually §165. If one sells one's home, for example, for less than its adjusted basis, no deduction is allowed because the loss does not fit within the limitation in §165(c) or any alternative allowance provision. The transaction fits within the language of §1211, but that section simply has no effect in the absence of some other provision authorizing a deduction.

Section 1211 applies by its own terms only if there has been a loss from the sale or exchange of a capital asset. What if an investor realizes a loss without a sale or exchange? Would that avoid the limitation? How might the loss be realized without a sale or exchange?

In this connection take careful note of §165(g) and read §1234A, which was broadened to its current form in 1997 (previously its application had been limited to actively traded personal property).

The present discussion is only intended as a rudimentary introduction to the capital loss limitation. We will return to the subject in greater detail later in the context of a fuller examination of the capital gain and loss provisions. The following case, even at this point, however, may help to illuminate the intent and scope of the limitation.

O. L. BURNETT
40 B.T.A. 605 (1939), aff'd in part and rev'd in part,
118 F.2d 659 (5th Cir. 1941)

BLACK. . . . It has been stipulated that during the taxable year 1934, the petitioner sustained a loss of $18,964.21 in the purchase and sale of stocks and commodities. Petitioner claimed this loss on her income tax return for 1934 as an ordinary loss, deductible in full from her income in that year. In his deficiency notice the Commissioner limited this loss to $2,000 and gave the following reason therefor:

> The amount claimed as a business loss from trading in stocks and commodities has been disallowed as a loss from business, and the limited amount of $2,000 allowable under section 117(d) of the Revenue Act of 1934 has been allowed as a capital net loss. The agent's investigations covering 1934 and prior years have indicated that your method of conducting your trading transactions is not such as would entitle you to be classed as carrying on a business.

The facts with reference to petitioner's trading on margin through brokers in corporate stocks and in wheat and cotton, during the year 1934, have been stipulated in great detail. It is not necessary to incorporate these details in this report. Suffice it to say that the stipulation shows that during the taxable year 1934 the activities of the petitioner in the purchase and sale of stocks and commodities on margin compares with the annual average of her like activities during the 10-year period ended December 31, 1936, as follows:

Items	Year 1934	10-year Averages
Number of contracts	646	584
Property values	$3,830,036.15	$10,831,466.07

It seems manifest from the facts which have been stipulated that during the taxable year and several years prior thereto petitioner was engaged in the business of trader in securities and commodities on her own account and we so find. Her business consisted of buying and selling stocks and commodities on her own account, primarily for the profit to be derived from selling for a price in excess of the cost of the stocks and commodities to her. Therefore, if deciding that petitioner was a trader in stocks and commodities on her own account during 1934 and that stocks and commodities held in her margin accounts were held primarily for sale in her business were all that is necessary, we would decide issue (1) for petitioner. Such would have been sufficient under the Revenue Act of 1932 and the loss which petitioner incurred in these trading accounts would have been an ordinary loss and deductible in full. . . .

In the 1934 Act the definition of "capital assets" was changed so as to drop the requirement that the property should have been held for more than two years and to narrow the provision that capital assets should not include "property held by the taxpayer primarily for sale in the course of his business" to a provision that capital assets shall not include "property held by the taxpayer primarily for sale *to customers* in *the ordinary course of* his trade or business." (Italics ours.) The words in italics are those which were added in the Revenue Act of 1934.

Section 117(b) of the Revenue Act of 1934 reads as follows:

(b) *Definition of Capital Assets.* For the purposes of this title, "capital assets" means property held by the taxpayer (whether or not connected with his trade or business), but does not include stock in trade of the taxpayer or other property of a kind which would properly be included in the inventory of the taxpayer if on hand at the close of the taxable year, or property held by the taxpayer primarily for sale to customers in the ordinary course of his trade or business.

Under the above definition any property is a "capital asset" unless it may properly be included in an inventory or is held for sale to customers.

Petitioner being a trader in securities and commodities for her own account, as distinguished from a "dealer" in securities and commodities, was not entitled to use inventories in determining her net income. . . . [See Reg. §1.471-5.]

It being clear the petitioner is not one who is entitled to use inventories in determining her net income, we next inquire whether the stocks and commodities purchased and sold by petitioner through brokers for her own account in 1934 constituted property held by the taxpayer primarily for sale to customers in the ordinary course of her trade or business.

The Board has held that a taxpayer who trades for his own account does not sell to "customers." Oil Shares, Inc., 29 B.T.A. 664. It seems plain that the very purpose of the change in the Revenue Act of 1934 defining "capital assets" to which we have just referred was to see to it that the limitation on deductible capital losses provided by section 117 (d) should apply to speculative traders who purchase and sell securities and commodities for their own account and not for resale to customers.

Under the Revenue Act of 1932 the definition of "capital assets" was as follows:

> Sec. 101(c)(8). "Capital assets" means property held by the taxpayer for more than two years . . . but does not include . . . property held by the taxpayer primarily for sale in the course of his trade or business.

In the Revenue Act of 1934 this definition was changed in the manner we have already indicated. The reason for the changes made is shown in the report of the Senate Finance Committee and in the conference report of the two houses. The remarks of the Senate Finance Committee regarding the matter are found at page 12 of the report, and in part are as follows:

> Second, the definition of capital assets has been slightly revised to prevent tax avoidance by excluding from the category of a capital asset "property held by the taxpayer primarily for sale to customers in the ordinary course of his trade or business," instead of merely "property held by the taxpayer primarily for sale in the course of his trade or business."

The observations by the committee on conference are found in its report at page 22, being in part as follows:

> Amendment no. 66: The house bill excluded from the definition of "capital assets" property held primarily for sale in the course of taxpayer's trade or business. The Senate amendment confines the exclusion to property held primarily for sale to customers in the ordinary course of the taxpayer's trade or business, thus making it impossible to contend that a stock speculator trading on his own account is not subject to the provisions of section 117. The House recedes. . . .

Petitioner's stocks and commodities held in her margin accounts with brokers were not held primarily for sale "to customers in the ordinary course" of the taxpayer's trade or business within the meaning of the Revenue Act of 1934. We, therefore, hold against the petitioner on this point and sustain the Commissioner in his application of the $2,000 limitation on capital losses provided by section 117(d) of the Revenue Act of 1934. . . .

D.   SECTION 1231

1.   Property Used in a Trade or Business

Suppose a taxpayer suffers a loss on sale of a piece of real estate held directly, not through a corporation, for use in his trade or business: Will that loss be subject to the capital loss limitation?

Look first at §1221(a)(2). It excludes depreciable business property and business realty generally from the capital asset category so the loss is apparently not subject to the capital loss limitation. This provision, as it applies to depreciable property, was enacted in 1938 for the avowed purpose of getting rid of the capital loss limitation. The trouble was that taxpayers were hanging on to assets they ought to have sold, even at a loss, because they could get depreciation deductions by hanging on, while the capital loss limitation would effectively bar deductions if they sold.

But what about a sale at a gain? Section 1221(a)(2) by itself would prevent capital gain treatment and did from 1938 to 1942. But in 1942 prices had gone up and many sales would have been at a gain; the imposition of ordinary income tax on such gains was locking in the owners of business properties that might otherwise have found their ways into the hands of others who could make better use of them. The demands of war made it especially important that the economy operate as efficiently as possible, so capital *gain* treatment was reinstated by enacting §1231.

Look at §1231 and ponder. In general it seems intended to preserve capital gain treatment for gain on dispositions of property used in a trade or business and ordinary loss treatment for loss on such dispositions, but only on a net basis. If there are gains and losses, then all are to be treated as capital or ordinary according to whether they all together produce a gain or loss. It is easy to understand Congress's reluctance to allow simultaneous capital gain treatment of gains and ordinary loss treatment of losses, but the consequence of netting is that the original objectives with respect to a particular property may well be frustrated. In a §1231-loss period, a taxpayer considering sale of one more §1231 item, at a gain, will indeed face tax at an ordinary income rate, and in a year in which §1231 gains predominate, a §1231 loss will have the same tax effect as a simple capital loss.

Prior to 1984 it was rather standard tax planning practice to try to isolate §1231 gains and losses in separate (perhaps alternating) years. Section 1231(c) was enacted in 1984 to control that practice. Was it done soundly?

2. Involuntary Conversions

Involuntary conversions of business property and capital assets are another problem dealt with in the hotchpot of §1231. Suppose a tract of land held for investment is taken by eminent domain. Or suppose a farmer's barn burns to the ground, insurance proceeds exceed the adjusted basis, and there is no reinvestment of proceeds that qualifies the gain for non-recognition under §1033. Is the gain in either case capital gain?

However the asset is characterized, the gain has been held not to be from a sale or exchange. Helvering v. Flaccus Leather Co., 313 U.S. 247 (1941). To alter that harsh result, §1231 embraces gains and losses from involuntary conversions of §1231 assets and certain capital assets. §1231(a)(3)(A)(ii) and (B). Thus a gain from an involuntary conversion, standing alone, will be treated as capital gain while such a loss will be fully deductible from ordinary income. If such a gain or loss does not stand alone it will be combined with similar gains and losses and capital gain or ordinary loss treatment effectively applied to the net amount.

Again one can readily understand impulses (1) to treat an involuntary conversion gain no worse than gain on sale, (2) to relieve the victim of an involuntary conversion loss of the burden of the capital loss limitation, and (3) to confine capital gain treatment to net gains from similar transactions. But again these impulses conflict. Why such transactions should be netted with sales of property used in a trade or business is not at all clear. Indeed §1231(a)(4)(C) undoes that netting to some degree. Try to figure out its operation and rationale.

Problem

Suppose a person's uninsured vacation house burns down. How is the loss treated for income tax purposes?

What if there had been insurance proceeds in excess of basis? How is the gain treated under the present statute? (Read very carefully.) The language that requires capital assets to be held in connection with a trade or business or a transaction entered into for profit was introduced in 1984; before that this fire gain would have been covered by §1231.

Now go back to §165 to be sure you are right about the loss. Do not ignore §165(h). What is it doing there? What were they up to in 1984 anyway?

All this should be read as confirming any skepticism one may have had about the capital loss limitation being (just) a natural corollary of the favorable treatment of capital gains.

3. Statutory Structure and Interpretation

Note the technique of §1231. Specified transactions, under specified conditions, "shall be treated as long-term capital gains or . . . losses." A significant number of provisions talk this way, indicating that something will be "treated" or "considered" as meeting or not meeting some or all of the requirements for capital gain treatment.

One might think of these provisions as borrowing the operative provisions that govern capital gains and losses for application to a variety of rather dissimilar situations. Sometimes that is probably a sensible view.

But another interpretation is that they are extending the initial definition of capital gains to embrace or exclude a variety of other more or less similar transactions. That view invites an attempt to generalize about the common idea or ideas that underlie various statutory manifestations. See, e.g., Commissioner v. Gillette Motor Transport, Inc., Chapter 19B.2 below, at 1071, 1072 ("Section [1231] . . . is an integral part of the statute's comprehensive treatment of capital gains and losses. . . . [It] effects no change in the nature of a capital asset. . . . '[P]roperty used in the trade or business,' to be eligible for capital-gains treatment, must satisfy the same general criteria as govern the definition of capital assets. . . .").

How does this interpretation apply on the loss side?

E. BAD DEBTS

WHIPPLE v. COMMISSIONER
373 U.S. 193 (1963)

Mr. Justice WHITE delivered the opinion of the Court. Section [166(a)] provides for the deduction in full of worthless debts other than nonbusiness bad debts while [§166(d)] restricts nonbusiness bad debts to the treatment accorded losses on the sale of short-term capital assets. The statute defines a nonbusiness bad debt in part as "a debt . . . other than a debt the loss from the worthlessness of which is incurred in the taxpayer's trade or business." The question before us is whether petitioner's activities in connection with several corporations in which he holds controlling interests can themselves be characterized as a trade or business so as to permit a debt owed by one of the corporations to him to be treated within the general rule of [§166(a)] as a "business" rather than a "nonbusiness" bad debt.

   Prior to 1941 petitioner was a construction superintendent and an estimator for a lumber company but during that year and over the next several ones he was instrumental in forming and was a member of a series of partnerships engaged in the construction or construction supply business. In 1949 and 1950 he was an original incorporator of seven corporations, some of which were successors to the partnerships, and in 1951 he sold his interest in the corporations along with his equity in five others in the rental and construction business, the profit on the sales being reported as long-term capital gains. In 1951 and 1952 he formed eight new corporations, one of which was Mission Orange Bottling Co. of Lubbock, Inc., bought the stock of a corporation known as Mason Root Beer and acquired an interest in a related vending machine business. From 1951 to 1953 he also bought and sold land, acquired and disposed of a restaurant and participated in several oil ventures.

   On April 25, 1951, petitioner secured a franchise from Mission Dry Corporation entitling him to produce, bottle, distribute and sell Mission beverages in various counties in Texas. Two days later he purchased the assets of a sole proprietorship in the bottling business and conducted that business pursuant to his franchise as a sole proprietorship. On July 1, 1951, though retaining the franchise in his own name, he sold the bottling equipment to Mission Orange Bottling Co. of Lubbock, Inc., a corporation organized by petitioner as mentioned, of which he owned approximately 80 percent of the shares outstanding. In 1952 he purchased land in Lubbock and erected a bottling plant thereon at a cost of $43,601 and then leased the plant to Mission Orange for a 10-year term at a prescribed rental. Depreciation was taken on the new bottling plant on petitioner's individual tax returns for 1952 and 1953.

   Petitioner made sizable cash advances to Mission Orange in 1952 and 1953, and on December 1, 1953, the balance due him, including $25,502.50 still owing from his sale of the bottling assets to the corporation in July 1951, totaled $79,489.76. On December 15, 1953, petitioner advanced to Mission Orange an additional $48,000 to pay general creditors and on the same day received a transfer of the assets of the corporation with a book value of $70,414.66. The net amount owing to petitioner ultimately totaled $56,975.10, which debt became worthless in 1953 and is in issue here. During 1951, 1952 and 1953 Mission Orange made no payments of interest, rent or salary to petitioner although he did receive such income from some of his other corporations.

   Petitioner deducted the $56,975.10 debt due from Mission Orange as a business bad debt in computing his 1953 taxable income. The Commissioner, claiming the debt was a nonbusiness bad debt, assessed deficiencies. The Tax Court, after determining that petitioner in 1953 was not in the business of organizing, promoting, managing or financing corporations, of bottling soft drinks or of general financing and money lending, sustained the deficiencies. A divided Court of Appeals affirmed, 5 Cir., 301 F.2d 108, and upon a claim of conflict among the Courts of Appeals, we granted certiorari. 371 U.S. 875.

I

The concept of engaging in a trade or business as distinguished from other activities pursued for profit is not new to the tax laws. As early as 1916, Congress, by providing for the deduction of losses incurred in a trade or business separately from those sustained in other transactions entered into for profit, §5, Revenue Act of 1916, c. 463, 39 Stat. 756, distinguished the broad range of income or profit producing activities from those satisfying the narrow category of trade or business. This pattern has been followed elsewhere in the Code. See, e.g., [§§162 and 212] (ordinary and necessary expenses); [§165(c)(1) and (2)] (losses); [§167(a)(1) and (2)] (depreciation); [§172(d)(4)] (net operating loss deduction). It is not surprising, therefore, that we approach the problem of applying that term here with much writing upon the slate.

In Burnet v. Clark, 287 U.S. 410 (1932), the long-time president and principal stockholder of a corporation in the dredging business endorsed notes for the company which he was forced to pay. These amounts were deductible by him in the current year under the then existing law, but to carry over the loss to later years it was necessary for it to have resulted from the operation of a trade or business regularly carried on by the taxpayer. The Board of Tax Appeals denied the carry-over but the Court of Appeals for the District of Columbia held otherwise on the grounds that the taxpayer devoted all of his time and energies to carrying on the business of dredging and that he was compelled by circumstances to endorse the company's notes in order to supply it with operating funds. This Court in turn reversed and reinstated the judgment of the Board of Tax Appeals, since "[t]he respondent was employed as an officer of the corporation; the business which he conducted for it was not his own. . . . The unfortunate endorsements were no part of his ordinary business, but occasional transactions intended to preserve the value of his investment in capital shares. . . . A corporation and its stockholders are generally to be treated as separate entities." A similar case, Dalton v. Bowers, 287 U.S. 404, decided the same day, applied the same principles.

A few years later the same problem arose in another context. A taxpayer with large and diversified holdings, including a substantial but not controlling interest in the du Pont Company, obtained a block of stock of that corporation for distribution to its officers in order to increase their management efficiency. The taxpayer, as a result, became obligated to refund the annual dividends and taxes thereon and these amounts he sought to deduct as ordinary and necessary expenses paid or incurred in the carrying on of a trade or business pursuant to [§162]. The Court, Deputy v. du Pont, 308 U.S. 488 (1940), assuming arguendo that the taxpayer's activities in investing and managing his estate were a trade or business, nevertheless denied the deduction because the transactions "had their origin in an effort by that company to increase the efficiency of its management" and "arose out of transactions which were intended to preserve his investment in the corporation. . . . The well established decisions of this Court do not permit any such blending of the corporation's business with the business of its stockholders." 308 U.S., at 494. Reliance was placed upon Burnet v. Clark and Dalton v. Bowers, supra.

The question assumed in *du Pont* was squarely up for decision in Higgins v. Commissioner, 312 U.S. 212 (1941). Here the taxpayer devoted his time and energies to managing a sizable portfolio of securities and sought to deduct his expenses incident thereto as incurred in a trade or business under [§162]. The Board of Tax Appeals, the Court of Appeals for the Second Circuit and this Court held that the evidence was insufficient to establish taxpayer's activities as those of carrying on a trade or business. "The petitioner merely kept records and collected interest and dividends from his securities, through managerial attention for his investments. No matter how large the estate or how continuous or extended the work required may be, such facts are not sufficient as a matter of law to permit the courts to reverse the decision of the Board." 312 U.S., at 218.

Such was the state of the cases in this Court when Congress, in 1942, amended the Internal Revenue Code in respects crucial to this case. In response to the *Higgins* case and to give relief to Higgins-type taxpayers, see H.R. Rep. No. 2333, 77th Cong., 2d Sess. 46, [§162] was amended not by disturbing the Court's definition of "trade or business" but by following the pattern that had been established since 1916 of "[enlarging] the category of incomes with reference to which expenses were deductible," McDonald v. Commissioner, 323 U.S. 57, 62; United States v. Gilmore, [supra Chapter 12G] to include expenses incurred in the production of income. [§212.]

At the same time to remedy what it deemed the abuses of permitting any worthless debt to be fully deducted, as was the case prior to this time, see H.R. Rep. No. 2333, 77th Cong., 2d Sess. 45, Congress restricted the full deduction under [§166] to bad debts incurred in the taxpayer's trade or business and provided that "nonbusiness" bad debts were to be deducted as short-term capital losses. Congress deliberately used the words "trade or business," terminology familiar to the tax laws, and the respective committees made it clear that the test of whether a debt is incurred in a trade or business "is substantially the same as that which is made for the purpose of ascertaining whether a loss from the type of transaction covered by [§165] is 'incurred in trade or business' under paragraph [(c)(1)] of that section." H.R. Rep. No. 2333, 77th Cong., 2d Sess. 76-77; S. Rep. No. 1631, 77th Cong., 2d Sess. 90. Section [165], of course, was a successor to the old §5 of the Revenue Act of 1916 under which it had long been the rule to distinguish between activities in a trade or business and those undertaken for profit. The upshot was that Congress broadened [§§162 and 212] to reach income producing activities not amounting to a trade or business and conversely narrowed [§166] to exclude bad debts arising from these same sources.

The 1942 amendment of [§166], therefore, as the Court has already noted, Putnam v. Commissioner, 352 U.S. 82, 90-92, was intended to accomplish far more than to deny full deductibility to the worthless debts of family and friends. It was designed to make full deductibility of a bad debt turn upon its proximate connection with activities which the tax laws recognized as a trade or business, a concept which falls far short of reaching every income or profit making activity.

II

Petitioner, therefore, must demonstrate that he is engaged in a trade or business, and lying at the heart of his claim is the issue upon which the lower courts have divided and which brought the case here: That where a taxpayer furnishes regular services to one or many corporations, an independent trade or business of the taxpayer has been shown. But against the background of the 1942 amendments and the decisions of this Court in the *Dalton, Burnet, du Pont* and *Higgins* cases, petitioner's claim must be rejected.

Devoting one's time and energies to the affairs of a corporation is not of itself, and without more, a trade or business of the person so engaged. Though such activities may produce income, profit or gain in the form of dividends or enhancement in the value of an investment, this return is distinctive to the process of investing and is generated by the successful operation of the corporation's business as distinguished from the trade or business of the taxpayer himself. When the only return is that of an investor, the taxpayer has not satisfied his burden of demonstrating that he is engaged in a trade or business since investing is not a trade or business and the return to the taxpayer, though substantially the product of his services, legally arises not from his own trade or business but from that of the corporation. Even if the taxpayer demonstrates an independent trade or business of his own, care must be taken to distinguish bad debt losses arising from his own business and those actually arising from activities peculiar to an investor concerned with, and participating in, the conduct of the corporate business.

If full-time service to one corporation does not alone amount to a trade or business, which it does not, it is difficult to understand how the same service to many corporations would suffice. To be sure, the presence of more than one corporation might lend support to a finding that the taxpayer was engaged in a regular course of promoting corporations for a fee or commission, see Ballantine, Corporations (rev. ed. 1946), 102, or for a profit on their sale, see Giblin v. Commissioner, 227 F.2d 692 (C.A. 5th Cir.), but in such cases there is compensation other than the normal investor's return, income received directly for his own services rather than indirectly through the corporate enterprise, and the principles of *Burnet, Dalton, du Pont* and

Higgins are therefore not offended. On the other hand, since the Tax Court found, and the petitioner does not dispute, that there was no intention here of developing the corporations as going businesses for sale to customers in the ordinary course, the case before us inexorably rests upon the claim that one who actively engages in serving his own corporations for the purpose of creating future income through those enterprises is in a trade or business. That argument is untenable in light of *Burnet, Dalton, du Pont* and *Higgins*, and we reject it. Absent substantial additional evidence, furnishing management and other services to corporations for a reward not different from that flowing to an investor in those corporations is not a trade or business under [§166]. We are therefore, fully in agreement with this aspect of the decision below.

III

With respect to the other claims by petitioner, we are unwilling to disturb the determinations of the Tax Court, affirmed by the Court of Appeals, that petitioner was not engaged in the business of money lending, of financing corporations, of bottling soft drinks or of any combination of these since we cannot say they are clearly erroneous. See Commissioner v. Duberstein [supra Chapter 4C.3]. Nor need we consider or deal with those cases which hold that working as a corporate executive for a salary may be a trade or business. E.g., Trent v. Commissioner, 291 F.2d 669 (C.A. 2d Cir.). Petitioner made no such claim in either the Tax Court or the Court of Appeals and, in any event, the contention would be groundless on this record since it was not shown that he has collected a salary from Mission Orange or that he was owed one. Moreover, there is no proof (which might be difficult to furnish where the taxpayer is the sole or dominant stockholder) that the loan was necessary to keep his job or was otherwise proximately related to maintaining his trade or business as an employee. Compare Trent v. Commissioner, supra.

We are more concerned, however, with the evidence as to petitioner's position as the owner and lessor of the real estate and bottling plant in which Mission Orange did business. The United States does not dispute the fact that in this regard petitioner was engaged in a trade or business but argues that the loss from the worthless debt was not proximately related to petitioner's real estate business. While the Tax Court and the Court of Appeals dealt separately with assertions relating to other phases of petitioner's case, we do not find that either court disposed of the possibility that the loan to Mission Orange, a tenant of petitioner, was incurred in petitioner's business of being a landlord. We take no position whatsoever on the merits of this matter but remand the case for further proceedings in the Tax Court.

Vacated and remanded.

Mr. Justice DOUGLAS dissents.

Notes

1. *Trade or business.* It is at least ironic that the Court in *Whipple* relies on the separate references to trade or business and other profit-oriented activities in §§162, 212, 165, and 167, since the intended effect in those sections is to extend deductibility to expenses incurred in those other profit-oriented activities, thus treating them the same as a trade or business. Congress in 1942 must have been aware that "trade or business" did not embrace all money-making activities, but it misses the point of those provisions to say they evidence a congressional intention to keep trade or business separate from other income-producing activities. In the long run, however, Congress came around to the view that investment expenses should in some respects be treated less favorably than the costs of carrying on an active business. The 2 percent floor on miscellaneous itemized deductions can be seen in this light, §67. What about the passive activity loss limitation, §469, Chapter 16C below?

2. *Special treatment of bad debts.* How would bad debt losses be treated if §166 simply were not in the statute? State as precisely as you can how §166 modifies the treatment that would otherwise be accorded under §§165 and 1211. Is there any reason why debts should be treated differently from other assets?

3. *Personal debts.* (a) A taxpayer advances money to his brother, who fails to pay it back. Can he deduct the amount of the advance? When? Subject to what conditions?

(b) A taxpayer sells her personal automobile on credit to a purchaser who subsequently fails to pay. Can she deduct the unpaid note as a bad debt loss?

(c) Is there anything about a bad debt loss that justifies a deduction of any kind when the loss was not incurred in a trade or business or a transaction entered into for profit?

4. *Partial worthlessness.* Note §166(a)(2) which provides for the deduction of partially worthless bad debts; is that the same thing as allowing a deduction for mere decline in value?

5. *Bad debt reserves.* In normal accounting for business operations, bad debts are accounted for through a reserve. This means that a charge is made against earnings for estimated bad debt losses, with a corresponding credit to a bad debt reserve. Periodically outstanding accounts are examined to see how much is in default and for how long and the reserve is evaluated to see if it covers estimated losses on present accounts. If the reserve is either too high or too low, the charge to earnings can be adjusted up or down to bring it back in line. The process thus depends on estimation at two points in the process, with one estimation serving as a check on the other.

At some point individual accounts become so far in default that it is not worthwhile to continue accounting for them, and so they are charged off. Charging off means removing from the accounts receivable asset account and reducing the reserve by the same amount, and it has no immediate effect on income or net worth. Moreover, it is hard to think of any other real effect it has. Charging off a bad debt does not discharge the debtor from liability or prevent further efforts at collection. It is purely an accounting matter, and is essentially a matter of tidying up accounts rather than making an important determination.

Charging off debts will cause the reserve to be a smaller percentage of accounts receivable, and that by itself might seem to call for an increase in charges to earnings. But charging off the worst debts — generally those most in default — will also cause the remaining accounts to present a better profile for which a smaller reserve will be quite adequate. In the case of commercial accounts receivable, the hard fact would seem to be an array of accounts in various stages of default — days or months of nonpayment — with respect to which it is possible to make reasonable estimates in the aggregate of what will not be collected, although *which* bills will ultimately be paid may remain quite uncertain.

Section 166 used to have a provision for deducting additions to a reserve for bad debts. But the government apparently concluded that the reserve method of accounting for bad debts was too flexible for income tax purposes,[1] particularly in the case of banks for whom possible bad debt losses are obviously very large in relation to income.[2] Section 166(c) was repealed in 1986, and §585 was made inapplicable to large banks, as defined, by §585(c). As a result, most tax deductions for bad debt losses now depend on determinations of worthlessness of particular debts, the timing of which is often not very important for any other purpose.[3] Is this an advance?

6. *Guaranties.* What if Mission Orange had borrowed from a bank and Whipple had guaranteed the loan? Then Whipple would not have advanced anything until Mission Orange proved unable to pay the bank. Would Whipple's payment at that point be free of the nonbusiness bad debt loss restriction?

In Putnam v. Commissioner, 352 U.S. 82 (1956), the Supreme Court held that such a guarantor's loss was a nonbusiness bad debt loss.

---

1. "The Congress believed that the use of the reserve method for determining losses from bad debts resulted in the deductions being allowed for tax purposes for losses that statistically occur in the future. Thus, the Congress believed that the use of the reserve method for determining losses from bad debts allowed a deduction to be taken prior to the time that the loss actually occurred. . . . If a deduction is allowed prior to the taxable year in which the loss actually occurs, the value of the deduction to the taxpayer is overstated and the overall tax liability of the taxpayer understated." Staff of the Joint Committee on Taxation, 100th Cong., 1st Sess. General Explanation of the Tax Reform Act of 1986, 531 (Comm. Print 1987).

2. "Finally, the Congress is concerned that many banks, particularly those who are members of large banking organizations, have used the reserve method of determining losses from bad debts to lower substantially their Federal income tax liabilities." Id. at 550. What does that mean?

3. "The Congress has directed the Secretary of the Treasury to study and to issue a report regarding appropriate criteria to be used to determine if a debt is worthless for Federal income tax purposes. It is anticipated that the report will consider under what circumstances a rule providing for a conclusive or rebuttable presumption of the worthlessness of an indebtedness is appropriate.

"The final report is to be submitted, by January 1, 1988, . . ." Id. at 532.

Its reasoning was that upon payment of a guarantee the guarantor is subrogated to the creditor's rights against the debtor, and the debtor thus becomes the guarantor's debtor, and the guarantor's loss is due to the worthlessness of those rights and thus constitutes a bad debt loss itself. Is this a sound result? Sound reasoning? Suppose a taxpayer had a fire loss and his insurer became insolvent before paying his claim: Is the taxpayer's loss an unreimbursed fire loss or a bad debt loss? How is that any different?

7. *Business or investment.* The effect of §166 as construed in *Whipple* is to draw a distinction between investment activities and conduct of a trade or business, and to impose the capital loss limitation with respect to the former but not the latter. Section 1231 draws a broadly similar distinction with respect to losses on property used in a trade or business.

Is the distinction between an investor and a direct participant in business activity something fundamental that underlies these disparate manifestations? Is it an intelligible and viable distinction? Are there good reasons why investor losses should be able to be offset only against capital gains, while losses incurred in a trade or business should not be so limited?

8. *Debt or equity.* Another ground on which the Commissioner has sometimes sought to impose the capital loss limitation is that a purported debt is actually an equity investment. Recharacterization of debt as equity has other consequences, too, such as turning deductible interest into nondeductible dividends and subjecting repayment to the risk of dividend treatment under §302(d). Distinguishing debt from equity has proved a continuously troublesome question, particularly in the context of a close corporation. In 1969, Congress enacted §385 to try to strengthen the Commissioner's hand in dealing with the problem, but no one has yet prepared acceptable regulations thereunder. (Regulations were in fact adopted in 1980 but were not to take effect until 1982; their effective date was later postponed and the regulations were revoked before the postponed effective date. No further revision has been proposed. Cf. Rev. Rul. 83-98, 1983-2, C.B. 40.)

9. What if Whipple had drawn a salary from Mission Orange? Would that have provided a viable basis for treating his losses as business bad debt losses? The Supreme Court soon had this issue in United States v. Generes, 405 U.S. 93 (1971).

Generes and his son-in-law Kelly each owned 44 percent of a corporation's outstanding capital stock. Generes's original investment in his shares was $38,900. The remaining 12 percent of the stock was owned by a son of Generes and by another son-in-law. Generes was president of the corporation and received from it an annual salary of $12,000. Kelly was executive vice president and received an annual salary of $15,000. Generes's employment was part-time; he was also president of a savings and loan association he had founded, for which he received an annual salary of $19,000. Kelly worked full-time for the construction company.

Generes from time to time advanced personal funds to the corporation to enable it to complete construction jobs. He also guaranteed loans made to the corporation by banks. In addition, the construction company was required to submit bid and performance bonds in connection with its public contracts. The insurance company that issued these bonds required Generes and Kelly to sign contracts indemnifying it against loss.

In 1962 the corporation seriously underbid two contracts, and as a result it subsequently went into receivership and Generes was required to make good on his indemnity agreement and guarantees. He ultimately lost most of what he had lent to the corporation. In his federal income tax return Generes claimed the indemnification loss as a business bad debt.

At trial Generes testified that his sole motive in signing the indemnification agreement was to protect his $12,000 salary. The jury, by special interrogatory, was asked to determine whether Generes's signing the indemnification agreement "was proximately related to his trade or business of being an employee" of the corporation. The District Court charged the jury, over the Government's objection, that *significant* motivation satisfies the Regulations' requirement of proximate relationship, and refused the Government's request for an instruction that the applicable standard was that of *dominant* rather than significant motivation.

The Supreme Court held that significant motivation was not enough — there must be a dominant business motivation to qualify the losses as business bad debts. Moreover, the Court declined to return the matter to the trial court for redetermination with a correct instruction, but rather concluded that on this record a jury finding of dominant motivation could not be upheld. The Court pointed out that $12,000 salary, after a 40 percent tax, would be only about $7,000, which is less than 20 percent of Generes's original investment in the corporation, and concluded that saving the salary could not on these numbers provide a dominant motivation as compared with that of saving the investment. Mention was also made of saving his son-in-law's job and other family members' investments as likely further sources of nonbusiness motivation.

10. *Noncorporate business activity.* What if *Whipple* had conducted the business of his several corporations directly in his own name? Or through partnerships, if other investors were also involved? In that case he would simply have deducted business expenses himself as they were incurred, and since they undoubtedly exceeded income he would have recognized an ordinary business loss directly without either waiting for securities to become worthless or having to face the capital loss limitation.

It is quite common for businesses starting up from scratch to lose money for some initial period; so many new businesses are conducted in noncorporate form until they turn profitable. Sometimes tax rules cause businesses to show losses even when in economic terms they are breaking even or better, which also creates an incentive to operate in noncorporate form. Some of the reasons for this phenomenon and some of the limitations that have now been imposed on deduction of such net losses are taken up in the next two chapters.

References

A. *Realization:* Judd & Kramer, An Empirical Analysis of How the Tax Court Determines When Stock Becomes Worthless for Purposes of Loss Recognition, 66 Taxes 518 (1988).

E. *Bad Debts:* Crane, Refining the Time Value Approach to Bad Debts, 44 Tax Notes 803 (1989).

Chapter 15 — *Capital Cost Recovery*

Section 167(a) has long allowed "as a depreciation deduction a reasonable allowance for the exhaustion, wear and tear (including a reasonable allowance for obsolescence) . . . of property used in the trade or business, or . . . held for the production of income." The cost of machinery and equipment and buildings and a variety of other things has been regularly amortized under this provision. There are also special provisions for depletion of mineral deposits. Other provisions are just exceptions to the prohibition of §263(a), allowing immediate deduction of specified capital expenditures. For most of the period between 1962 and 1986 there was also a general investment credit; this was a direct reduction of tax liability in the amount of a specified percentage of qualifying investments in tangible business assets.

Whether an asset is depreciable or not, its cost may eventually be recovered in the computation of gain or loss on sale or other disposition. §§165, 1001; Chapters 6A and 14. Basis for determining gain or loss is adjusted downward for depreciation allowed or allowable. §1016(a)(2). The issues surrounding depreciation are therefore primarily issues of timing, but as usual timing issues are often of immense importance. Sometimes matters of timing have ripened into matters of rate reduction or effective exemption through the capital gain provisions or otherwise. Even if they do not, long-term tax deferral is tantamount to significant partial exemption. See Chapter 5B.

Before 1986 there was a marked proliferation of so-called tax shelters, which are investments intended to produce tax losses to be set off against other taxable income. Capital cost allowances played a central role in most such shelters. Some of the transactions that created tax shelters and limitations that have now been imposed are taken up in Chapter 16.

A.   *WHAT IS DEPRECIABLE*

No depreciation is allowed for assets whose useful life is indefinite or unlimited. Land, for instance, is nondepreciable, although even this rule has its exceptions. In one case depreciation was allowed for the space contained in an abandoned clay pit; the parcel was used as a dump, and its usefulness as such would end when the excavation was filled. J.J. Sexton, 42 T.C. 1094 (1964) (acq.).

Buildings and other improvements to real estate and tangible business personalty like machinery and equipment are almost always presumed to have a limited useful life, and thus are depreciable even if in fact their value goes up rather than down.

For intangibles, the rule historically was stricter: Depreciation was allowed only if an item had a limited useful life whose length could be ascertained with reasonable certainty. Reg. §1.167(a)-3(a). Thus patents and copyrights are depreciable over their statutory lives because the monopoly rights wear out over that period. A bond is not depreciable even though its useful life is definite and limited because full repayment of principal on maturity means that the investment is not diminished by exhaustion, wear and tear, or obsolescence. There has been considerable litigation over such things as liquor licenses, television affiliation contracts, and other franchises that confer rights of limited duration but also carry expectations of successive renewals over an indefinitely extended period of time. The enactment of §197, Chapter 15B.4 below, and new regulations relaxing capitalization requirements for intangibles, Reg. §§1.263(a)-4, -5, Chapter 13C above, have largely alleviated this source of controversy. Section 197 allows 15-year straight-line amortization of most *purchased* intangibles that lack an ascertainable useful life, and in conjunction with the intangible capitalization regulations, the Treasury amended the depreciation regulations to allow 15-year straight-line amortization of most intangibles *created* after 2003 that lack an ascertainable useful life. Reg. §1.167-3(b).

Many controversies arise upon the purchase of a going business, in which case it is often not clear how the total purchase price should be allocated, or even just what are the elements of value among which it should be allocated.

1.   Antique Musical Instruments

RICHARD L. SIMON

103 T.C. 247 (1994), aff'd 68 F.3d 41 (2d Cir. 1995), nonacq. 1996-2 C.B.2

LARO, Judge: . . . During the year in issue, petitioners were both fulltime performers with the [New York] Philharmonic, playing locally, nationally, and internationally in the finest concert halls in the world. In 1989, petitioners performed four concerts per week with the Philharmonic, playing over 200 different works, and attended many rehearsals with the Philharmonic that were more demanding and more time-consuming than the concerts. Petitioners also carried out the busy schedules connected with their second careers. . . .

A violin bow consists of a flexible wooden stick, horsehair, a frog, and a ferrule (screw). The stick, which varies in thickness, weight, and balance, is the working part of the bow and is an integral part in the production of sound through vibration. It is designed so that horsehair can be stretched between its ends.

The horsehair is a group of single strands of hair that come from the tails of Siberian horses. A hatchet-shaped head holds one end of the horsehair, and the other end is attached to a frog. The frog, which is inserted into the stick, is a movable hollow piece by which the bow is held. The frog has an eyepiece on the end that catches the screw. The screw is the small knob at the end of the bow that is adjusted to tighten or loosen the horsehair in order to change the tension on the horsehair. The horsehair is the part of the bow that touches the violin strings. Rosin is applied to the horsehair to supply the frictional element that is necessary to make the violin strings vibrate.

Old violins played with old bows produce exceptional sounds that are superior to sounds produced by newer violins played with newer bows. The two violin bows in issue were made in the 19th century by Francois Xavier Tourte (1747-1835). Francois Tourte is considered the premier violin bow maker. . . .

On November 13, 1985, petitioners purchased bow 1 for $30,000; the bow was purchased from Moes & Moes, Ltd., a dealer and restorer of violins and violin bows. On December 3, 1985, petitioners purchased bow 2 from this dealer for $21,500. The sticks, frogs, and screws were originals of Francois Tourte at the time of each purchase. No cracks or other defects were apparent in the sticks at the time of each purchase. The frogs and screws, however, were not in playable condition. Therefore, petitioners replaced them.

Petitioners acquired the Tourte bows for regular use in their full-time professional employment as violinists. Petitioners purchased the Tourte bows for their tonal quality, not for their monetary value. In the year of acquisition, petitioners began using the Tourte bows with the original sticks in their trade or business as full-time professional violinists. . . .

On their 1989 Form 1040, petitioners claimed a depreciation deduction of $6,300 with respect to bow 1 and $4,515 with respect to bow 2; these amounts were in accordance with the appropriate ACRS provisions that applied to 5-year property. See sec. 168(b)(1). Respondent disallowed petitioners' depreciation deduction in full and reflected her disallowance in the notice of deficiency at issue here. . . .

Playing with a bow adversely affects the bow's condition; when a musician plays with a bow, the bow vibrates up, down, sideways, and at different angles. In addition, perspiration from a player's hands enters the wood of a bow and ultimately destroys the bow's utility for playing. Cracks and heavy-handed bearing down while playing certain pieces of music also create wear and tear to a bow. . . .

Frequent use of a violin bow will cause it to be "played out," meaning that the wood loses its ability to vibrate and produce quality sound from the instrument. From the point of view of a professional musician, a "played out" bow is inferior and of limited use. The Tourte bows were purchased by petitioners, and were playable by them during the year in issue, only because the Tourte bows were relatively unused prior to petitioners' purchase of them; the Tourte bows had been preserved in pristine condition in collections. . . .

On November 21, 1985, bow 1 was appraised for insurance purposes as having a fair market value of $35,000. On December 3, 1985, bow 2 was appraised for insurance purposes as having a fair market value of $25,000. Petitioners obtained both appraisals from Moes & Moes, Ltd.

In 1994, at the time of trial, the Tourte bows were insured with the Philharmonic for $45,000 and $35,000, respectively. These amounts are based on an appraisal dated May 14, 1990, from Yung Chin Bowmaker, a restorer and dealer of fine bows. . . .

An independent market exists for the Tourte bows and other antique bows. . . .

One factor that adds value to the Tourte bows is the fact that Pernambuco wood, the wood that was used to make the sticks, is now very scarce. The wood that is currently used to make the sticks of violin bows is inferior to Pernambuco wood.

OPINION

Taxpayers have long been allowed asset depreciation deductions in order to allow them to allocate their expense of using an income-producing asset to the periods that are benefited by that asset. The primary purpose of allocating depreciation to more than 1 year is to provide a more meaningful matching of the cost of an income-producing asset with the income resulting therefrom; this meaningful match, in turn, bolsters the accounting integrity for tax purposes of the taxpayer's periodic income statements. Hertz Corp. v. United States, 364 U.S. 122, 126 (1960); Massey Motors, Inc. v. United States, 364 U.S. 92, 104 (1960). Such a system of accounting for depreciation for Federal income tax purposes has been recognized with the approval of the Supreme Court for over 65 years; as the Court observed in 1927: "The theory underlying this allowance for depreciation is that by using up the plant, a gradual sale is made of it." United States v. Ludey, 274 U.S. 295, 301 (1927);

see also Massey Motors, Inc. v. United States, supra at 104. In this sense, an allocation of depreciation to a given year represents that year's reduction of the underlying asset through wear and tear. United States v. Ludey, supra at 300-301. Depreciation allocations also represent a return to the taxpayer of his or her investment in the income-producing property over the years in which depreciation is allowed. Virginian Hotel Corp. v. Helvering, 319 U.S. 523, 528 (1943); Detroit Edison Co. v. Commissioner, 319 U.S. 98, 101 (1943).

Prior to the Economic Recovery Tax Act of 1981 (ERTA), Pub.L. 97-34, 95 Stat. 172, personal property was depreciated pursuant to section 167 of the Internal Revenue Code of 1954 (1954 Code). . . . The regulations under this section expanded on the text of section 167 by providing that personal property was only depreciable before ERTA if the taxpayer established the useful life of the property. See sec. 1.167(a)-1(a) and (b), Income Tax Regs.

The "useful life" of property under pre-ERTA law was the period over which the asset could reasonably be expected to be useful to the taxpayer in his or her trade or business, or in the production of his or her income. Fribourg Navigation Co. v. Commissioner, 383 U.S. 272, 277 (1966); Massey Motors, Inc. v. United States, supra; sec. 1.167(a)-1(b), Income Tax Regs. This useful life period was not always the physical life or maximum useful life inherent in the asset. Massey Motors, Inc. v. United States, supra; sec. 1.167(a)-1(b), Income Tax Regs. A primary factor to consider in determining an asset's useful life was any "wear and tear and decay or decline from natural causes" that was inflicted upon the asset. Sec. 1.167(a)-1(b), Income Tax Regs.

Before ERTA, the primary method that was utilized to ascertain the useful life for personal property was the asset depreciation range (ADR) system. Under the ADR system, which was generally effective for assets placed in service after 1970 and before 1981, property was grouped into broad classes of industry assets, and each class was assigned a guideline life. See, e.g., sec. 1.167(a)-11, Income Tax Regs.; Rev. Proc. 83-35, 1983-1 C.B. 745, superseded by Rev. Proc. 87-56, 1987-2 C.B. 674; see also ERTA sec. 209(a), 95 Stat. 226. A range of years, i.e., the ADR, was then provided for each class of personal property; the ADR extended from 20 percent below to 20 percent above the guideline class life. For each asset account in the class, the taxpayer selected either a class life or an ADR that was utilized as the useful life for computing depreciation. See, e.g., sec. 1.167(a)-11(a), Income Tax Regs.; Rev. Proc. 83-35, supra. If an asset was not eligible for ADR treatment, or if the taxpayer did not elect to use the ADR system, the useful life of that asset was generally determined based on either the particular facts and circumstances that applied thereto, or by agreement between the taxpayer and the Commissioner. Massey Motors, Inc. v. United States, supra; sec. 1.167(a)-1(b), Income Tax Regs. See generally Staff of Joint Comm. on Taxation, General Explanation of the Economic Recovery Tax Act of 1981, at 67 (J. Comm. Print 1981) (hereinafter referred to as the 1981 Bluebook).

In enacting ERTA, the Congress found that the pre-ERTA rules for determining depreciation allowances were unnecessarily complicated and did not generate the investment incentive that was critical for economic expansion. The Congress believed that the high inflation rates prevailing at that time undervalued the true worth of depreciation deductions and, hence, discouraged investment and economic competition. The Congress also believed that the determination of useful lives was "complex" and "inherently uncertain," and "frequently [resulted] in unproductive disagreements between taxpayers and the Internal Revenue Service." S. Rept. 97-144, at 47 (1981), 1981-2 C.B. 412, 425. See generally 1981 Bluebook, at 75. Accordingly, the Congress decided that a new capital cost recovery system would have to be structured which, among other things, lessened the importance of the concept of useful life for depreciation purposes. S. Rept. 97-144, supra at 47, 1981-2 C.B. at 425. See generally 1981 Bluebook, at 75. This new system is ACRS. ACRS is mandatory and applies to most tangible depreciable assets placed in service after 1980 and before 1987. ERTA sec. 209(a), 95 Stat. 172; see also Tax Reform Act of 1986, Pub.L. 99-514, secs. 201(a), 203(a)(1), 100 Stat. 2085, 2121, 2143.

The rules implementing ACRS were prescribed in section 168. . . . [T]hrough ERTA, the Congress minimized the importance of useful life by: (1) Reducing the number of periods of years over which a taxpayer could depreciate his or her property from the multitudinous far-reaching periods of time listed for the ADR system to the four short periods of time listed in ERTA (i.e., the 3-year, 5-year, 10-year, and 15-year ACRS periods), and (2) basing depreciation on an arbitrary statutory period of years that was unrelated to, and shorter than, an asset's estimated useful life. This minimization of the useful life concept through a deemed useful life was in spirit with the two main issues that ERTA was designed to address, namely: (1) Alleviating the income tax problems that resulted mainly from complex depreciation computations and useful life litigation, and (2) responding to economic policy concerns that the pre-ERTA depreciation systems spread the depreciation deductions over such a long period of time that investment in income-producing assets was discouraged through the income tax system. S. Rept. 97-144, supra at 47, 1981-2 C.B. at 425. See generally 1981 Bluebook, at 75.

With respect to the pre-ERTA requirement of useful life, the Commissioner had initially taken the position that a taxpayer generally could not deduct depreciation on expensive works of art and curios that he purchased as office furniture. See A.R.R. 4530, II-2 C.B. 145 (1923). This position was superseded by a similar position that was reflected in Rev. Rul. 68-232, 1968-1 C.B. 79. That ruling states:

> A valuable and treasured art piece does not have a determinable useful life. While the actual physical condition of the property may influence the value placed on the object, it will not ordinarily *limit or determine* the useful life. Accordingly, depreciation of works of art generally is not allowable. [Emphasis added.]

. . .

Inasmuch as section 168(a) allows a taxpayer to deduct depreciation with respect to "recovery property," petitioners may deduct depreciation on the Tourte bows if the bows fall within the meaning of that term. The term "recovery property" is defined broadly under ERTA to mean tangible property of a character subject to the allowance for depreciation and placed in service after 1980. Accordingly, property is "recovery property" if it is: (1) Tangible, (2) placed in service after 1980, (3) of a character subject to the allowance for depreciation, and (4) used in the trade or business, or held for the production of income. Sec. 168(c)(1); Noyce v. Commissioner, 97 T.C. 670, 689 (1991); see also ERTA sec. 209(a), 95 Stat. 172.

The Tourte bows fit snugly within the definition of recovery property. First, it is indisputable that the Tourte bows are tangible property, and that they were placed in service after 1980. Thus, the first two prerequisites for ACRS depreciation are met. Second, petitioners regularly used the Tourte bows in their trade or business as professional violinists during the year in issue. . . .

The last prerequisite for depreciating personal property under section 168 is that the property must be "of a character subject to the allowance for depreciation." The term "of a character subject to the allowance for depreciation" is undefined in the 1954 Code. Comparing the language that the Congress used in section 167(a) of the 1954 Code immediately before its amendment by ERTA, with the language that it used in section 168(a) and (c)(1) as added to the 1954 Code by ERTA, we believe that the Congress used the term "depreciation" in section 168(c)(1) to refer to the term "exhaustion, wear and tear (including a reasonable allowance for obsolescence)" that is contained in section 167(a). See Noyce v. Commissioner, supra at 689. Accordingly, we conclude that the term "of a character subject to the allowance for depreciation" means that property must suffer exhaustion, wear and tear, or obsolescence in order to be depreciated. Accordingly, petitioners will meet the final requirement under section 168 if the Tourte bows are subject to exhaustion, wear and tear, or obsolescence.

We are convinced that petitioners' frequent use of the Tourte bows subjected them to substantial wear and tear during the year in issue. Petitioners actively played their violins using the Tourte bows, and this active use resulted in substantial wear and tear to the bows.[11] Indeed, respondent's expert witness even acknowledged at trial that the Tourte bows suffered wear and tear stemming from petitioners' business; the witness testified that the Tourte bows had eroded since he had examined them 3 years before, and

11. In this regard, we do not believe that the Tourte bows are so-called works of art. We define a "work of art" as a passive object, such as a painting, sculpture, or carving, that is displayed for admiration of its aesthetic qualities. See Webster's New World Dictionary 1539 (3d coll. ed. 1988). The Tourte bows, by contrast, functioned actively, regularly, and routinely to produce income in petitioners' trade or business. Although a computer utilized by a child to play games is not a depreciable asset, the same computer becomes a depreciable asset if it is used actively, regularly, and routinely by a data processor in his or her trade or business. By the same token, the Tourte bows could have been collector's items except for the fact that petitioners used them actively, regularly, and routinely in their full-time business.

that wood had come off them. Thus, we conclude that petitioners have satisfied the final prerequisite for depreciating personal property under section 168, and, accordingly, hold that petitioners may depreciate the Tourte bows during the year in issue. . . .

With respect to respondent's arguments in support of a contrary holding, we believe that respondent places too much reliance on the fact that the Tourte bows are old and have appreciated in value since petitioners acquired them. Indeed, respondent believes that this appreciation, in and of itself, serves to prevent petitioners from claiming any depreciation on the Tourte bows. We disagree; section 168 does not support her proposition that a taxpayer may not depreciate a business asset due to its age, or due to the fact that the asset may have appreciated in value over time. Noyce v. Commissioner, supra at 675, 691 (taxpayer allowed to deduct depreciation under section 168 on an airplane that had appreciated in economic value). Respondent incorrectly mixes two well-established, independent concepts of tax accounting, namely, accounting for the physical depreciation of an asset and accounting for changes in the asset's value on account of price fluctuations in the market. Accord Fribourg Navigation Co. v. Commissioner, 383 U.S. at 277; Macabe Co. v. Commissioner, 42 T.C. 1105, 1109 (1964). . . .

We also reject respondent's contention that the Tourte bows are non-depreciable because they have value as collectibles independent of their use in playing musical instruments, and that this value prolongs the Tourte bows' useful life forever. First, it is firmly established that the term "useful life" under pre-ERTA law refers to the period of time in which a particular asset is useful to the taxpayer in his or her trade or business. Fribourg Navigation Co. v. Commissioner, supra at 277; Massey Motors, Inc. v. United States, 364 U.S. 92 (1960); sec. 1.167(a)-1(b), Income Tax Regs. Thus, the fact that an asset such as the Tourte bows may outlive a taxpayer is not dispositive of the issue of whether that asset has a useful life for depreciation purposes under pre-ERTA law. Second, the same argument concerning a separate, nonbusiness value can be made of many other assets. Such types of assets could include, for example, automobiles, patented property, highly sophisticated machinery, and real property. For the Court to delve into the determination of whether a particular asset has a separate, nonbusiness value would make the concept of depreciation a subjective issue and would be contrary to the Congress' intent to simplify the concept and computation of depreciation.

With respect to respondent's contention that petitioners must prove a definite useful life of the Tourte bows, we acknowledge that the concept of useful life was critical under pre-ERTA law. Indeed, the concept of useful life was necessary and indispensable to the computation of depreciation because taxpayers were required to recover their investments in personal property over the estimated useful life of the property. Sec. 1.167(a)-1(a), Income Tax Regs. However, the Congress enacted ERTA, in part, to avoid constant disagreements over the useful lives of assets, to shorten the writeoff periods for assets, and to encourage investment by providing for accelerated cost recovery through the tax law. . . . Respondent's argument that a taxpayer must first prove the useful life of personal property before he or she may depreciate it over the 3-year or 5-year period would bring the Court back to pre-ERTA law and reintroduce the disagreements that the Congress intended to eliminate by its enactment of ERTA. This the Court will not do. . . .

We have considered all other arguments made by respondent and find them to be without merit.

To reflect concessions by the parties,

Decision will be entered under Rule 155.

Parker, Swift, Wright, Parr, Wells, Ruwe, and Colvin, JJ., agree with this majority opinion.

Chiechi, J., dissents.

RUWE, J., concurring: In this case, section 168 is being applied to violin bows used by professional violinists. Everyone would ordinarily agree that such an asset is the "type" of asset that would be subject to an allowance for depreciation.

Under section 167, depreciation was allowed over the useful life of the asset in order to allow taxpayers to deduct the anticipated loss in value attributable to wear and tear. This, in turn, required the often difficult task of proving the useful life and salvage or residual value of the asset. In a significant step in the direction of tax simplification, both of these requirements were eliminated by section 168, which specifies the number of years over which the cost of certain types of assets may be deducted and eliminates the need to calculate salvage or residual value in order to determine the expected economic loss.

Everyone seems to favor tax simplification until the simplified law is actually applied to a real set of facts and produces a less-than-perfect result. The dissenting opinions would resurrect the obligation to establish an asset's actual expected useful life and the actual expected decrease in value over that life, in order to qualify for a section 168 deduction. It is unclear whether the dissenters intend to limit their analyses to assets that are "works of art," whatever that term may mean. However, their legal theories would seem to apply to any case where the Commissioner raises the useful life and value issues.

I can understand the dissenters' concern that section 168 might allow an asset to be written off over a period much shorter than its actual useful life and that the entire cost might be deducted despite the fact that there might be no actual economic decrease in value. However, that is the price of the tax simplification implicit in section 168.

Parker, Cohen, Swift, Wright, Parr, Wells, and Beghe, JJ., agree with this concurring opinion.

[Separate concurrence of BEGHE, J, and dissenting opinions of HAMBLEN, C.J., GERBER, J. and HALPERN, J., omitted.]

Note and Questions

1. A similar result was reached in a companion case involving a bass viol built by Francesco Ruggeri (c. 1620-1695) a luthier active in Cremona, Italy. It was purchased in 1984 for $28,000 by a player in the Philadelphia Orchestra. Brian P. Liddle, 103 T.C. 285 (1994), aff'd, 65 F.3d 329 (3d Cir. 1995).

2. Would a law firm be allowed to deduct depreciation on office furniture consisting of fine paintings? How about usable antiques? The court of appeals opinion in *Simon* says "We acknowledge that the result of our holding may give favorable treatment to past investment decisions that some regard as wasteful, such as a law firm's purchase of expensive antique desks, the cost of which could have been quickly depreciated under our current ruling." 68 F.3d at 46. Does the Tax Court opinion imply that result?

3. In explanation of its refusal to acquiesce in *Simon* the IRS said: "It is the Service's position that the enactment of ACRS merely shortened the recovery period over which an asset is depreciated to stimulate economic growth but did not convert assets that formerly were not depreciable into assets that are depreciable." Action on Dec. 1996-009 (July 15, 1996). Contrary the Second Circuit's attempt to limit its holding to property placed in service between 1981 and 1986,[1] the IRS also observed that the current version of §168 is susceptible to the same interpretation despite extensive statutory revisions. Therefore, "the issue should be pursued in other circuits" to create a conflict and potential for certiorari. Action on Dec. 1996-009.

2.   Land and Improvements

WORLD PUBLISHING CO. v. COMMISSIONER
299 F.2d 614 (8th Cir. 1962)

Before Vogel, Van Oosterhout and Blackmun, Circuit Judges.

BLACKMUN, Circuit Judge. . . . The issue before us concerns the taxpayer's right to a deduction for depreciation of a portion of the price it paid when it purchased improved real estate subject to an outstanding lease to the tenant who had built the building on the property.

The facts are not in dispute: On June 29, 1928, George Warren Smith, Inc., was the owner of two mid-block lots in downtown Omaha. On that date Smith leased those lots to Farnam Realty Corporation. The lease was for a

---

1. The court of appeals opinion contains this disclaimer:

We note that our decision today is limited to "recovery property," a concept that was deleted from the statute in the Tax Reform Act of 1986, Pub.L. No. 99-514, 100 Stat. 2085. Moreover, ACRS' depreciation deductions first became available in 1981. Therefore, this opinion applies only to property placed in service between January 1, 1981 and January 1, 1987.

68 F.3d at 47, n.7.

term of fifty years from July 1, 1928, and called for annual rentals averaging $28,500 but varying between $25,000 and $32,500 for specified decades. It required Farnam immediately to construct a "six (6) story, or more, and basement building" on the property at a cost of not less than $250,000. Farnam complied with this requirement.

On January 4, 1950, the taxpayer purchased as an investment Smith's entire interest in the property, including the lease, for $700,000. The deed recited that it was subject to the lease to Farnam. The parties have stipulated that "the remaining useful life of the building in January, 1950, was not greater than the unexpired term of the lease."

In its income tax return of the years in question the taxpayer asserted a deduction of $10,547.92 for "Depreciation and Amortization." This amount was determined by spreading $300,000 (constituting that part of its purchase price which the taxpayer claimed was allocable to the building) over the remaining years of the still outstanding lease. The Commissioner disallowed this deduction.[3] . . .

There is substantial, and uncontradicted, evidence in the record to support the $300,000 figure. A qualified appraiser testified that at the time of purchase the fair and reasonable value of the ground alone was $400,000 and the fair and reasonable value of the building alone was around $300,000. These valuation allocations correspond, too, with the full valuations thereof used for real estate assessment purposes at the time of the purchase. The witness also testified that in his opinion the probable value of the land alone at the expiration of the lease in 1978 would be approximately $400,000.

On these facts, uninfluenced by any decided lease cases, it would seem clearly to follow that the taxpayer is entitled to a deduction, under §167(a) and under the parallel §23(l) of the 1939 Code, respectively applicable to the tax years in question, for depreciation of the $300,000 portion of its 1950 purchase price allocable to the improvements on the real estate in question. See Detroit Edison Co. v. Commissioner, 1943, 319 U.S. 98, 101. The building, as well as the land, was acquired and held by the taxpayer "for the production of income." The taxpayer's interest was one acquired by purchase and was not in any sense a derivative right acquired without investment on its part. By the stipulation, the building is a wasting asset and its complete exhaustion will have been effected before the end of the lease term. The taxpayer's spreading of the wasting portion of its purchase price over the entire remaining lease term by the straight-line method approximated the minimal deduction for the taxpayer.

Furthermore, for what it may be worth, the lessor, and consequently the taxpayer, in spite of a contrary suggestion at the trial by the Commissioner's

3. In the 90-day letter the Commissioner said, "It is held that no part of the amount of $700,000 paid by you in 1950 to acquire real estate which was subject to a lease granted by the previous owner may be allocated to the building constructed by the lessee under the terms of the lease, and, further, that no part of said purchase price may be allocated as a basis for annual amortization deductions."

counsel, clearly owned the building in more than a bare-legal-title sense. The lease recites that all buildings erected on the premises "shall, *at and upon the construction thereof, be and become* a part of the realty and upon the termination of this lease . . . shall pass to and *remain* the property of the Lessor." (Emphasis supplied.) Consistent with this are other provisions of the lease: the reference in the tax clause to the lessor's interest in the "land or improvements"; the lessor's right to amend and even reject plans and specifications for the building; the insurance protection afforded the lessor and its being named as insured; the lessor's right to subject the improvements as well as the ground to a mortgage lien; and the lessee's inability to alter the completed building beyond a $10,000 cost without the lessor's approval. . . . This is consistent, too, with the general law, evidently recognized in Nebraska, to the effect that, unless provided otherwise by contract, a building permanently affixed to the land becomes a part of it. . . .

But the Commissioner — and the Tax Court has agreed with him — has taken the position that the taxpayer here acquired no depreciable interest in the property; that what it acquired was the land, not a wasting asset, for which it received ground rental income; that the taxpayer has not shown that it held any interest in the building for the production of income; that it acquired only such interest as its grantor Smith had; and that Smith had no depreciable interest in the lessee-constructed building. He strenuously urges, as supporting authority, a line of cases, including one of our own, concerning the situation where a taxpayer, through *inheritance* or *devise* from a deceased lessor, comes into the ownership of tenant improved property subject to an outstanding lease. . . .

The theories which find expression in these cases are (a) that the decedent had — and his successor has — no investment in the wasting asset and (b) that the heir or devisee could acquire no different interest than was possessed by the decedent. "The major thrust of the statute is toward an allowance for recovery of investment in a wasting asset." *Goelet* (District Court), p. 307 of 161 F. Supp. "Appellants fail to show how a depreciable interest in the building was supplied to them. . . ." *Goelet* (2 Cir.), p. 882 of 266 F.2d. "All she [the taxpayer] could acquire by inheritance from her mother, the testatrix, was such interest as her mother had to devise." *Schubert*, p. 579 of 286 F.2d.

Are these inheritance-or-devise cases cited by the Commissioner proper or helpful precedent for a situation involving acquisition by purchase? In determining this, some comments about the death cases are perhaps in order:

A. They have provoked substantial criticism. . . .

B. The facts of certain of these cases possess some significance. In *Goelet* the district court emphasized that, although the taxpayer by the terms of the lease may have had "technical legal title to the building," this was not determinative but "beneficial ownership" was. In *Schubert* it appears from the majority opinion of the Tax Court, p. 1049 of 33 T.C., that under the lease the improvement was to become the property of the lessor only "upon the termination of the lease." In *Friend*, too, it is clear from the Board's opinion, p. 771 of 40 B.T.A., that the taxpayers "did not own the buildings" and did not "even claim that they are entitled to an allowance for depreciation in respect of the buildings." In *Pearson*, *Moore*, and *Nee* the appellate courts all concluded that no part of the estate tax valuation, which constituted basis, was attributable to the improvements and that the taxpayer's case, depending, as it did, on a basis to depreciate, consequently failed. And in our *Nee* case we concluded that the rentals were attributable solely to the land; that the building was not held by the testamentary trustee for the production of income; that the tenant had the right to remove the building and replace it; and that because of this right the title to the building may have been in the lessee (the trial court had held specifically that under the terms of the lease title to the building was in the lessee: D.C., 85 F. Supp. 840, 843; D.C., 92 F. Supp. 328, 329).

C. An alternative and forceful argument made by the taxpayer in some of these cases is that he is entitled to claim a deduction for amortization of the "premium value" of the lease. The argument was rejected in *Schubert* (4 Cir. and Tax Court), *Friend* (Tax Court) and *Moore* (Tax Court); see Martha R. Peters, 1945, 4 T.C. 1236, 1241-1242. It prevailed, however, in *Moore* [207 F.2d 265 (9th Cir. 1953)] and necessarily by the Tax Court on remand in that case. T.C. Memo. 1955-219. It was avoided in *Goelet*, on the ground the point was not preserved below or in the administrative proceedings, and in Frieda Bernstein, 1954, 22 T.C. 1146, 1151-1152, affirmed, 2 Cir., 230 F.2d 603, on the ground of failure of proof. *Moore* demonstrates, however, that one circuit has afforded relief to a taxpayer who found himself with a newly acquired interest in property with a newly acquired basis which had no rational relationship to land value alone. This alternative argument was mentioned by the Tax Court in the present case and was again rejected; it is not particularly urged by the taxpayer on this appeal.

D. The cases themselves intimate, though perhaps by indirection, that the purchase situation is distinguishable. Thus, in *Friend*, the Seventh Circuit, at p. 960 of 119 F.2d, describes the testamentary trustees' position there as though "they have the same right to amortize such cost as if the purchase had been made for cash" and, on p. 961 of 119 F.2d, denies a construction of the statute that would "place the petitioners in the position of a purchaser of the leaseholds [together with the reversions] for a valuable consideration." . . .

E. Finally, as a collateral comment on the cases, we cannot fail to observe that the depreciation provisions of the Internal Revenue Codes draw no distinction between death-acquired property and purchased property. The basis they establish for depreciation is the same as the basis for determining gain. §167[(g)]. . . .

So much for these death cases. The situation before us, however, is that of a purchaser of the lessor's interest and is not that of the lessor's heir or devisee.

No purchase case precisely in point has been found. We therefore start with three established propositions:

1. Where an owner of land erects a building on it and then leases it he is still entitled to recover the cost of the improvement by depreciation deductions. . . .

2. Where a lessee makes a capital improvement on leased property he is entitled to recover its cost by appropriate deductions for depreciation or for amortization. . . .

3. Conversely, in the situation just described, the lessor, having no investment in the lessee's improvements, is not entitled to a deduction with respect to them. 4 Mertens, §23.90, where possible exceptions to this rule are noted.

To these may be added the result reached by the death cases cited above. We think, however, that the death cases do not govern the purchase situation. We reach this result because:

A. The taxpayer-purchaser by his purchase of the property has made an investment. He is not concerned with the identity, as between his vendor-lessor and the tenant, of the builder of the building. From this point of view, if he is entitled to the deduction where his vendor-lessor was the builder, he is entitled to a deduction where the tenant was the builder.

B. To allow the purchaser to depreciate in the one situation and to deny him depreciation in the other, especially where, as here, title to the building is in the lessor and then in the purchaser, seems to be illogical, to emphasize a historical fact not participated in or caused by the purchaser and not of any other considered economic consequence to him, and to exhalt form over substance. This would be illustrated by identical buildings, one constructed by the lessor and one by the lessee, on adjoining identical lots, subject to otherwise identical leases, when both improved properties are sold to the taxpayer-purchaser. There seems to be no merit in allowing the taxpayer, as distinguished from the lessor, depreciation on the one but not on the other.

C. It is no answer to say that the lease rentals, averaging $28,500, constitute only ground rent. We are concerned here not with depreciation of rentals, but with depreciation of a portion of this taxpayer's investment in the income producing property he purchased.

D. Whatever may be the proper result in the inheritance or devise situation, as exemplified by our 1951 holding in the *Nee* case, and by the other cases cited above, we are not now willing to extend the philosophy of those cases to the purchase situation of the present litigation.

We regard Millinery Center Building Corporation v. Commissioner, 2 Cir., 1955, 221 F.2d 322, as of particular and helpful significance here. That taxpayer had leased land with an option to renew and, in accordance with the lease, had erected a substantial building on it. Title to the building was in the taxpayer but under the lease it would vest in the lessor at the end of the lease term or the lessor could then compel the taxpayer to remove it.

During the lease period the taxpayer fully depreciated the cost of the building. Then it exercised its option to renew. When this was done, it bought the fee. The taxpayer sought to deduct the difference between its purchase price and the then value of the land, as unimproved, as a business expense. The Tax Court disallowed this; it also refused to accept the taxpayer's alternative contentions (a) that the difference should be amortized over the lease term and (b) that it should be depreciated over the remaining useful life of the building. 21 T.C. 817. Six judges dissented on the ground that some part of the purchase price should be allocated to the additional rights the taxpayer acquired in the building and should be recovered through depreciation. On petition for review the Second Circuit reversed on the depreciation issue. It said, p. 324 of 221 F.2d, "A third-party purchaser of such a fee would be entitled to allocate part of its cost to the building and to depreciate it as such." On the taxpayer's petition for certiorari the Supreme Court affirmed. 350 U.S. 456. The Commissioner did not seek review of the allowance of depreciation.

The taxpayer there occupied a position similar to that of the taxpayer here. The only fact differences were the taxpayer's additional posture as lessee and the lease's consequent extinguishment upon the purchase. These differences seem to us, however, of minor import.

That Farnam may have been taking depreciation with respect to its cost in the building need not concern us. Its right so to do is not here at issue. Despite the Ninth Circuit's observation, by way of dictum in the *Moore* case, p. 272 of 207 F.2d, that "A construction of the law to permit not only the lessee (who has a real economic interest) but also the taxpayer here to take depreciation on the same building would be somewhat anomalous," we fail to see the anomaly. What is significant is that each taxpayer has a separate wasting investment which meets the statutory requirements for depreciation. To allow each to recover his own, and separate, investment is not, as is suggested, to permit duplication at the expense of the revenues and is not to permit one taxpayer to depreciate another's investment. That each is concerned with the same building is of no relevance. Farnam has its lessee's cost of the structure and the present taxpayer has the portion of its purchase price attributable to the building. If two taxpayers own undivided interests in improved real estate, each may be entitled to depreciation. The situation here is not dissimilar.

This leaves only the question of proof. We could remand the case with instructions to the Tax Court to take further evidence as to that portion of the taxpayer's purchase price which was properly allocable to the building as distinguished from the land. We feel, however, that on this record the taxpayer has sufficiently established his $300,000 allocation. The Commissioner had his opportunity in the proceedings which have already taken place in the Tax Court to controvert the taxpayer's evidence. This he did not do but chose, instead, to rely on his basic thesis that the taxpayer had no investment which was entitled to depreciation.

The decision of the Tax Court is reversed with directions to recompute the taxpayer's deficiencies in accord with the views herein expressed.

Notes and Questions

1. *Unleased realty.* If the land and building in *World Publishing* had not been subject to a lease, then the purchase price would be allocated between land and building on the basis of current fair market value. In that case it would be irrelevant what the seller's basis was or how it was allocated between land and building. Indeed, with rising values and accelerated depreciation, many sales are encouraged by the prospect that the buyer will get a higher depreciation basis than the seller had. Is this any different from *World Publishing*?

2. *Leases.* What is the effect of the lease in *World Publishing*?

(a) The government argument is that the lease keeps the purchaser from acquiring any depreciable investment in the building: Since the seller had no depreciable interest to sell and all the purchaser can receive is ground rent during the remaining term of the lease, the building will (according to the useful life on which depreciation is being claimed) be gone when the lease expires.

(b) *L* leases land to *T* for 50 years for $28,000 per year (plus all expenses, including real estate taxes); *T* constructs a building on it; *L* then sells his whole interest to *P* for $700,000. The prevailing net rental rate on unimproved land (interest for this sort of investment) is 4 percent, there has been no change in values throughout, the fair value of the land is $700,000, and the fair rental value is $28,000. Can *P* deduct depreciation? Is this any different from *World Publishing*?

3. *Premium leases.* On the other hand, a lease will enhance the value of the lessor's interest in a piece of real estate if the rental is more than current fair rental value, and that increment in value has a limited useful life since it cannot outlast the term of the lease. The increment might arise in a variety of ways.

(a) *L* owned a piece of land worth $100,000. When prevailing interest rates were 6 percent she leased it for 20 years at an annual rental of $6,000. Fifteen years later the land is still worth $100,000, but interest rates have fallen to 4 percent, and the land would now rent for only $4,000. *A* now purchases the land for $107,000, $7,000 representing the value to him of receiving the extra $2,000 per year for the remaining term of the lease. Can *A* amortize the $7,000 premium?

(b) Is *A*'s case any different from that of *B* who pays a 7 percent premium to buy a 6 percent bond when prevailing interest rates have dropped to 4 percent? How should *B* treat that premium? §171.

(c) *L* owned a piece of land worth $150,000. She rented it for $6,000 a year (4 percent). At the end of 15 years the land is worth only $100,000 and would rent for $4,000 a year (still 4 percent). *C* then purchases it for $107,000. Can *C* amortize the $7,000 premium? Is *C*'s case any different from *A*'s?

(d) *L* owned land and a building worth $200,000. She leased them to *T* for 20 years for $20,000 a year. At the end of 15 years the building burns down, neither party rebuilds, *T* remains obligated (and able) to pay the full rent for the remaining term. Without the building the land is worth $50,000 and would rent for $3,000 a year. *D* purchases *L*'s interest for $100,000, figuring the value roughly as follows:

1st year's rent:	$20,000 discounted at 10% for 1 year	$ 18,180
2nd year's rent:	$20,000 discounted at 10% for 2 years	16,520
3rd year's rent:	$20,000 discounted at 10% for 3 years	15,020
4th year's rent:	$20,000 discounted at 10% for 4 years	13,660
5th year's rent:	$20,000 discounted at 10% for 5 years	12,420
Land:	$50,000 discounted at 10% for 5 years	31,050
		$106,850

Can *D* deduct any part of his purchase price over the remaining term of the lease? How much?

(e) State precisely what facts as to values and changes in value would have to be established to show the existence of a premium lease in *World Publishing*. Do you think (or suspect) these facts could have been established if the case had been thoroughly investigated and tried on this sort of theory?

3. Goodwill and Other Intangibles

NEWARK MORNING LEDGER CO. v. UNITED STATES
507 U.S. 546 (1993)

Justice BLACKMUN delivered the opinion of the Court.

This case presents the issue whether, under section 167 of the Internal Revenue Code, 26 U.S.C. section 167, the Internal Revenue Service (IRS) may treat as nondepreciable an intangible asset proved to have an ascertainable value and a limited useful life, the duration of which can be ascertained with reasonable accuracy, solely because the IRS considers the asset to be goodwill as a matter of law.[1]

Petitioner Newark Morning Ledger Co., a New Jersey corporation, is a newspaper publisher. It is the successor to The Herald Company with which it merged in 1987. Eleven years earlier, in 1976, Herald had purchased substantially all the outstanding shares of Booth Newspapers, Inc., the publisher of daily and Sunday newspapers in eight Michigan communities. Herald and Booth merged on May 31, 1977, and Herald continued to publish the eight papers under their old names. Tax code provisions in effect in 1977 required that Herald allocate its adjusted income tax basis in the Booth shares among the assets acquired in proportion to their respective fair market values at the time of the merger. See 26 U.S.C. sections 332 and 334(b)(2) (1976 ed.).

Prior to the merger, Herald's adjusted basis in the Booth shares was approximately $328 million. Herald allocated $234 million of this to various financial assets (cash, securities, accounts and notes receivable, the shares of its wholly owned subsidiary that published Parade Magazine, etc.) and tangible assets (land, buildings, inventories, production equipment, computer hardware, etc.). Herald also allocated $67.8 million to an intangible asset denominated "paid subscribers."[4] This consisted of 460,000 identified subscribers to the eight Booth newspapers as of May 31, 1977, the date of merger. These subscribers were customers each of whom had requested that the paper be delivered regularly to a specified address in return for payment of the subscription price. The $67.8 million figure was petitioner's estimate of future profits to be derived from these at-will subscribers, all or most of whom were expected to continue to subscribe after the Herald acquisition. The number of "paid subscribers" was apparently an important factor in Herald's decision to purchase Booth and in its determination of the appropriate purchase price for the Booth shares. See Brief for Petitioner 4-5. After these allocations, the approximately $26.2 million remaining was allocated to going-concern value and goodwill.

On its federal income tax returns for the calendar years 1977-1980, inclusive, Herald claimed depreciation deductions on a straight-line basis for the $67.8 million allocated to "paid subscribers." The IRS disallowed these deductions on the ground that the concept of "paid subscribers"

---

1. . . . Treasury Regulations section 1.167(a)-(3) interprets section 167(a) and states:

"If an intangible asset is known from experience or other factors to be of use in the business or in the production of income for only a limited period, the length of which can be estimated with reasonable accuracy, such an intangible asset may be the subject of a depreciation allowance. Examples are patents and copyrights. An intangible asset, the useful life of which is not limited, is not subject to the allowance for depreciation. No allowance will be permitted merely because, in the unsupported opinion of the taxpayer, the intangible asset has a limited useful life. No deduction for depreciation is allowable with respect to goodwill." 26 CFR section 1.167(a)-3 (1992).

4. According to petitioner, the term "'paid subscribers' is intended to reflect the fact that the customers in question paid for their newspapers, rather than receiving them for free, and that they subscribed to the newspaper, requesting regular delivery, rather than purchasing it on a single copy basis." Brief for Petitioner 4, n.5. The term does not connote subscription payments in advance; indeed, the customer relationship was terminable at will.

was indistinguishable from goodwill and, therefore, was nondepreciable under the applicable Regulations. Herald paid the resulting additional taxes. After the 1987 merger, petitioner filed timely claims for refund. . . .

. . . Petitioner presented financial and statistical experts who testified that, using generally accepted statistical techniques, they were able to estimate how long the average at-will subscriber of each Booth newspaper as of May 31, 1977 would continue to subscribe. The estimates ranged from 14.7 years for a daily subscriber to *The Ann Arbor News* to 23.4 years for a subscriber to the Sunday edition of *The Bay City Times*. This was so despite the fact that the total number of subscribers remained almost constant during the tax years in question. The experts based their estimates on actuarial factors such as death, relocation, changing tastes, and competition from other media. The experts also testified that the value of "paid subscribers" was appropriately calculated using the "income approach." Under this, petitioner's experts first calculated the present value of the gross-revenue stream that would be generated by these subscriptions over their estimated useful lives. From that amount they subtracted projected costs of collecting the subscription revenue. Petitioner contended that the resulting estimated net-revenue stream — calculated as $67,773,000 by one of its experts — was a reasonable estimate of the value of "paid subscribers."

The Government did not contest petitioner's expert evidence at all. In fact, it stipulated to the estimates of the useful life of "paid subscribers" for each newspaper. Also, on valuation, the Government presented little or no evidence challenging petitioner's calculations. Instead, it argued that the only value attributable to the asset in question was the cost of generating 460,000 new subscribers through a subscription drive. Under this "cost approach," the Government estimated the value of the asset to be approximately $3 million.

The Government's principal argument throughout the litigation has been that "paid subscribers" represents an asset indistinguishable from the goodwill of the Booth newspapers. . . .

"Goodwill" is not defined in the Code or in any Treasury Department Regulations. There have been attempts, however, to devise workable definitions of the term. In Metropolitan Bank v. St. Louis Dispatch Co., 149 U.S. 436 (1893), for example, this Court considered whether a newspaper's goodwill survived after it was purchased and ceased publishing under its old name. It ruled that the goodwill did not survive, relying on Justice Story's notable description of "goodwill" as

> the advantage or benefit, which is acquired by an establishment, beyond the mere value of the capital, stock, funds, or property employed therein, in consequence of the general public patronage and encouragement which it receives from constant or habitual customers, on account of its local position, or common celebrity, or reputation for skill or affluence, or punctuality, or from other accidental circumstances or necessities, or even from ancient partialities, or prejudices.

Id., at 446, quoting J. Story, Partnerships sections 99 (1841). . . .

Although the definition of goodwill has taken different forms over the years, the short-hand description of goodwill as "the expectancy of continued patronage," Boe v. Commissioner, 307 F.2d 339, 343 (CA9 1962), provides a useful label with which to identify the total of all the imponderable qualities that attract customers to the business. See Houston Chronicle Publishing Co. v. United States, 481 F.2d, at 1248, n.5. This definition, however, is of little assistance to a taxpayer trying to evaluate which of its intangible assets is subject to a depreciation allowance. The value of every intangible asset is related, to a greater or lesser degree, to the expectation that customers will continue their patronage. But since 1918, at least some intangible assets have been depreciable. Because intangible assets do not exhaust or waste away in the same manner as tangible assets, taxpayers must establish that public taste or other socioeconomic forces will cause the intangible asset to be retired from service, and they must estimate a reasonable date by which this event will occur. See B. Bittker & M. McMahon, Federal Income Taxation of Individuals paragraph 12.4, p. 12-10 (1988). Intangibles such as patents and copyrights are depreciable over their "legal lives," which are specified by statute. Covenants not to compete, leaseholds, and life estates, for example, are depreciable over their useful lives that are expressly limited by contract.

The category of intangibles that has given the IRS and the courts difficulty is that group of assets sometimes denominated "customer-based intangibles." This group includes customer lists, insurance expirations, subscriber lists, bank deposits, cleaning-service accounts, drugstore-prescription files, and any other identifiable asset the value of which obviously depends on the continued and voluntary patronage of customers. The question has been whether these intangibles can be depreciated notwithstanding their relationship to "the expectancy of continued patronage."

When considering whether a particular customer-based intangible asset may be depreciated, courts often have turned to a "mass asset" or "indivisible asset" rule. The rule provides that certain kinds of intangible assets are properly grouped and considered as a single entity; even though the individual components of the asset may expire or terminate over time, they are replaced by new components, thereby causing only minimal fluctuations and no measurable loss in the value of the whole. The following is the usually accepted description of a mass-asset:

> [A] purchased terminable-at-will type of customer list is an indivisible business property with an indefinite, nondepreciable life, indistinguishable from — and the principal element of — goodwill, whose ultimate value lies in the expectancy of continued patronage through public acceptance. It is subject to temporary attrition as well as expansion through departure of some customers, acquisition of others, and increase or decrease in the requirements of individual customers. A normal turnover of customers represents merely the ebb and flow of a continuing property status in this species, and does not within ordinary limits give rise to the right to deduct for tax purposes the loss of individual customers. The whole is equal to the sum of its fluctuating parts at any

given time, but each individual part enjoys no separate capital standing independent of the whole, for its disappearance affects but does not interrupt or destroy the continued existence of the whole.

Golden State Towel & Linen Service, Ltd. v. United States, 179 Ct. Cl. 300, 310, 373 F.2d 938, 944 (1967).

The mass-asset rule prohibits the depreciation of certain customer-based intangibles because they constitute self-regenerating assets that may change but never waste. Although there may have been some doubt prior to 1973 as to whether the mass-asset rule required that any asset related to the expectancy of continued patronage always be treated as nondepreciable goodwill as a matter of law, that doubt was put to rest by the Fifth Circuit in the Houston Chronicle case. The court there considered whether subscription lists, acquired as part of the taxpayer's purchase of The Houston Press, were depreciable. The taxpayer had no intention of continuing publication of the purchased paper, so there was no question of the lists' being self-regenerating; they had value only to the extent that they furnished names and addresses of prospective subscribers to the taxpayer's newspaper. After reviewing the history of the mass-asset rule, the court concluded that there was no per se rule that an intangible asset is nondepreciable whenever it is related to goodwill. On the contrary, the rule does not prevent taking a depreciation allowance "if the taxpayer properly carries his dual burden of proving that the intangible asset involved (1) has an ascertainable value separate and distinct from goodwill, and (2) has a limited useful life, the duration of which can be ascertained with reasonable accuracy." Id., at 1250. . . .

Despite the suggestion by the Court of Appeals in this case that the mass-asset rule is "now outdated," 945 F.2d, at 561, it continues to guide the decisions of the Tax Court with respect to certain intangible assets. In Ithaca Industries, Inc. v. Commissioner, 97 T.C. 253 (1991), for example, the Tax Court recently considered whether a taxpayer could depreciate the value allocated to the trained work force of a purchased going concern over the length of time each employee remained with the purchasing company. The court acknowledged that "whether the assembled work force is an intangible asset with an ascertainable value and a limited useful life separate from goodwill or going-concern value is a question of fact." Id., at 263-264. After reviewing the record, it concluded that the mass-asset rule applied to prohibit the depreciation of the cost of acquiring the assembled work force:

> Although the assembled work force is used to produce income, this record fails to show that its value diminishes as a result of the passing of time or through use. As an employee terminated his or her employment, another would be hired and trained to take his or her place. While the assembled work force might be subject to temporary attrition as well as expansion through departure of some employees and the hiring of others, it would not be depleted due to the passage of time or as a result of use. The turnover rate of employees represents merely the ebb and flow of a continuing work

force. An employee's leaving does not interrupt or destroy the continued existence of the whole.

Id., at 267. . . .

Since 1973, when *Houston Chronicle* clarified that the allowability of the depreciation allowance was primarily a question of fact, taxpayers have sought to depreciate a wide variety of customer-based intangibles. The courts that have found these assets depreciable have based their conclusions on carefully developed factual records. In Richard S. Miller & Sons, Inc. v. United States, 210 Ct. Cl. 431, 537 F.2d 446 (1976), for example, the court considered whether a taxpayer was entitled to a depreciation deduction for 1,383 insurance expirations that it had purchased from another insurer.[10] The court concluded that the taxpayer had carried its heavy burden of proving that the expirations had an ascertainable value separate and distinct from goodwill and had a limited useful life, the duration of which could be ascertained with reasonable accuracy. The court acknowledged that the insurance expirations constituted a "mass asset" the useful life of which had to be "determined from facts relative to the whole, and not from experience with any particular policy or account involved." Id., at 443, 537 F.2d, at 454. The court also noted, however, that the mass-asset rule does not prevent a depreciation deduction "where the expirations as a single asset can be valued separately and the requisite showing made that the useful life of the information contained in the intangible asset as a whole is of limited duration." Id., at 439, 537 F.2d, at 452. All the policies were scheduled to expire within three years, but their continuing value lay in their being renewable. Based on statistics gathered over a 5-year period, the taxpayer was able to estimate that the mass asset had a useful life of not more than 10 years from the date of purchase. Any renewals after that time would be attributable to the skill, integrity, and reputation of the taxpayer rather than to the value of the original expirations. "The package of expirations demonstrably was a wasting asset." Id., at 444, 537 F.2d, at 455. The court ruled that the taxpayer could depreciate the cost of the collection of insurance expirations over the useful life of the mass asset.

In Citizens & Southern Corp. v. Commissioner, 91 T.C. 463 (1988), aff'd, 919 F.2d 1492 (CA11 1990), the taxpayer argued that it was entitled to depreciate the bank-deposit base acquired in the purchase of nine separate banks.[11] The taxpayer sought to depreciate the present value of the

10. An "expiration" is a copy of the face of an insurance policy made when the policy is issued. It shows the name of the insured, the type of insurance, the premium, the covered property, and the expiration date. "Its principal value in the insurance business is its indication of the most advantageous time to solicit a renewal." Richard S. Miller & Sons, Inc. v. United States, 210 Ct. Cl., at 436, 537 F.2d, at 450.

11. The term "deposit base" describes "the intangible asset that arises in a purchase transaction representing the present value of the future stream of income to be derived from employing the purchased core deposits of a bank." Citizens & Southern Corp. v. Commissioner, 91 T.C., at 465. The value of the deposit base rests upon the "ascertainable probability that inertia will cause depositors to leave their funds on deposit for predictable periods of time." Id., at 500.

income it expected to derive from the use of the balances of deposit accounts existing at the time of the bank purchases. The Commissioner argued that the value of the core deposits was inextricably related to the value of the overall customer relationship, that is, to goodwill. The Commissioner also argued that the deposit base consisted of purchased, terminable-at-will customer relationships that are equivalent to goodwill as a matter of law. The Tax Court rejected the Commissioner's position, concluding that the taxpayer had demonstrated with sufficient evidence that the economic value attributable to the opportunity to invest the core deposits could be (and, indeed, was) valued and that the fact that new accounts were opened as old accounts closed did not make the original purchased deposit base self-regenerating. Id., at 499.

The court also concluded that, based on "lifing studies" estimating the percentage of accounts that would close over a given period of time, the taxpayer established that the deposit base had a limited useful life, the duration of which could be ascertained with reasonable accuracy. The taxpayer had established the value of the intangible asset using the cost-savings method, entitling it to depreciate that portion of the purchase price attributable to the present value of the difference between the ongoing costs associated with maintaining the core deposits and the cost of the market alternative for funding its loans and other investments. Id., at 510. . . .

The Eighth Circuit has considered a factual situation nearly identical to the case now before us. In Donrey, Inc. v. United States, 809 F.2d 534 (1987), the taxpayer sought to depreciate the subscription list of a newspaper it had purchased as a going concern. The taxpayer asserted that the subscription list was not simply a list of customers but "a machine to generate advertising revenue." Id., at 536. There was expert testimony that the value of the subscription list was "the present value of the difference in advertising revenues generated by the subscription list as compared to the revenues of an equivalent paper without a subscription list." Ibid. A jury found that the list had a limited useful life, the duration of which could be ascertained with reasonable accuracy; that the useful life was 23 years; and that it had an ascertainable value of $559,406 separate and distinct from goodwill. The District Court denied a motion for judgment notwithstanding the verdict after concluding that, although reasonable minds could have differed as to the correct result, there was evidence from which the jury could properly find for the taxpayer. The Court of Appeals implicitly rejected the Government's argument that the subscription list was necessarily inseparable from the value of goodwill when it deferred to the jury's finding that the subscription list was depreciable because it had a determinable useful life and an ascertainable value. . . .

The Government concedes: "The premise of the regulatory prohibition against the depreciation of goodwill is that, like stock in a corporation, a work of art, or raw land, goodwill has no determinate useful life of specific duration." Brief for United States 13. See also Richard S. Miller & Sons,

Inc. v. United States, 210 Ct. Cl., at 437, 537 F.2d, at 450 ("Goodwill is a concept that embraces many intangible elements and is presumed to have a useful life of indefinite duration"). The entire justification for refusing to permit the depreciation of goodwill evaporates, however, when the taxpayer demonstrates that the asset in question wastes over an ascertainable period of time. . . .

Although we now hold that a taxpayer able to prove that a particular asset can be valued and that it has a limited useful life may depreciate its value over its useful life regardless of how much the asset appears to reflect the expectancy of continued patronage, we do not mean to imply that the taxpayer's burden of proof is insignificant. On the contrary, that burden often will prove too great to bear. See, e.g., Brief for Coopers & Lybrand as Amicus Curiae 11 ("For example, customer relationships arising from newsstand sales *cannot* be specifically identified. In [our] experience, customers were identified but their purchases were too sporadic and unpredictable to reasonably ascertain either the duration of the relationships or the value of the relationships (based on their net income stream)" (emphasis in original)).

Petitioner's burden in this case was made significantly lighter by virtue of the Government's litigation strategy. . . .

Petitioner estimated the fair market value of the "paid subscribers" at approximately $67.8 million. This figure was found by computing the present value of the after-tax subscription revenues to be derived from the "paid subscribers," less the cost of collecting those revenues, and adding the present value of the tax savings resulting from the depreciation of the "paid subscribers." As the District Court explained, the taxpayer's experts "utilized this method because they each independently concluded that this method best determined the additional value of the Booth newspapers attributable to the existence of the paid subscribers as of May 31, 1977, and, thus, the fair market value of those subscribers." Id., at 183. The Government presented no evidence challenging the accuracy of this methodology. It took the view that the only value attributable to the "paid subscribers" was equivalent to the cost of generating a similar list of new subscribers, and it estimated that cost to be approximately $3 million. The Court of Appeals agreed with the Government that this "cost approach" was the only appropriate method for valuing the list of subscribers. "The fact is that, when employed in the context of the sale of an ongoing concern, the income approach to valuing a list of customers inherently includes much or all of the value of the expectancy that those customers will continue their patronage — i.e., the goodwill of the acquired concern." 945 F.2d, at 568.

Both the Government and the Court of Appeals mischaracterized the asset at issue as a mere list of names and addresses. The uncontroverted evidence presented at trial revealed that the "paid subscribers" had substantial value over and above that of a mere list of customers. App. 67 (Price Waterhouse's Fair Market Value Study of Paid Newspaper Subscribers to Booth Newspapers as of May 31, 1977); id., at 108-111 (testimony of Roger J. Grabowski, Principal and National Director, Price Waterhouse Valuation Services). These subscribers were "seasoned"; they had subscribed to the paper for lengthy periods of time and represented a reliable and measurable source of revenue. In contrast to new subscribers, who have no subscription history and who might not last beyond the expiration of some promotional incentive, the "paid subscribers" at issue here provided a regular and predictable source of income over an estimable period of time. . . .

Petitioner has borne successfully its substantial burden of proving that "paid subscribers" constitutes an intangible asset with an ascertainable value and a limited useful life, the duration of which can be ascertained with reasonable accuracy. It has proved that the asset is not self-regenerating but rather wastes as the finite number of component subscriptions are canceled over a reasonably predictable period of time. The relationship this asset may have to the expectancy of continued patronage is irrelevant, for it satisfies all the necessary conditions to qualify for the depreciation allowance under section 167 of the Code.

The judgment of the Court of Appeals is reversed, and the case is remanded for further proceedings consistent with this opinion.

It is so ordered.

Justice SOUTER, with whom the Chief Justice, Justice WHITE, and Justice SCALIA join, dissenting. . . . Ledger would have us scrap the accepted and substantive definition of "goodwill" as an expectation of continued patronage, in favor of a concept of "goodwill" as a residual asset of ineffable quality, whose existence and value would be represented by any portion of a business's purchase price not attributable to identifiable assets with determinate lives. Goodwill would shrink to an accounting leftover. See id., at 19, 29-30 (relying on accounting standards).

In accommodating Ledger on this point, see ante, at 18-19, n. 13, the Court abandons the settled construction of a regulation more than 65 years old, see T.D. 4055, VI-2 Cum. Bull. 63 (1927), and repudiates the equally settled interpretation of the corresponding section of the tax code itself. We are, after all, dealing with a statute reenacted without substantial change not less than six times since 1919. . . .

Even under Ledger's revision of the regulation, a depreciation deduction would depend on showing the Booth newspapers' goodwill to have a useful life both limited and measurable with some reasonable degree of certainty. The further step needed for victory is thus evidentiary in nature, and Ledger's success or failure is solely a function of the evidentiary record. Ledger has failed.

Here, it is helpful to recall one defining characteristic of the only kind of asset Ledger claims to be entitled to depreciate: it must be an asset acquired from Booth Newspapers, Inc. upon the sale of its stock to Ledger's predecessor, Herald. If the goodwill is to be depreciated at all, in other words, it must be goodwill purchased, not goodwill attributable to anything occurring after the purchase date. It must be an expectation of continued patronage as it existed when the old Booth newspapers changed hands.

Assuming that there is a variety of goodwill that may be separately identified as an asset on the date of sale, some limitation on its useful life may be presumed. Whatever may be the force of habit, or inertia, that is valued as goodwill attributable to events occurring before the date of sale, the influence of those events wanes over time, and so must the habit or inertia by which that influence is made manifest and valued as goodwill. On the outside, the economically inert subscribers will prove to be physically mortal.

What the Government does not concede, however, and what Ledger has not proven, is the duration of that date-of-sale influence and consequent goodwill. Ledger, indeed, has not even purported to show that. Instead, its expert has estimated the quite different periods over which subscribers on the date of sale will continue to subscribe to the various papers. In the District Court, Ledger offered a single witness for its claim to have estimated the useful life of each newspaper's "subscriber relationships" with reasonable accuracy. Herald had originally hired that witness, Dr. Gerald Glasser, to predict the average remaining lives of existing subscriptions to the eight Booth newspapers. See App. in No. 90-5637 (CA3), p. 1010. Dr. Glasser testified that he first compiled statistics on the length of time existing subscribers had received each newspaper, by directing a survey that asked a selection of those subscribers one central question: "For how long has the [newspaper] been delivered to your present address?" Id., at 157, 166, 182-183, 1012. He then made a crucial assumption, that the total number of subscriptions to each newspaper would remain stable over time. Id., at 170-172, 187, 194-195. Finally, by subjecting the survey results to techniques of statistical analysis based on this crucial assumption, Dr. Glasser produced a series of figures that, he said, represented the average remaining life of existing subscriptions to each newspaper. Solely on the basis of Dr. Glasser's testimony, the District Court held that "the remaining useful lives of the paid subscribers of the Booth newspapers as of May 31, 1977, could be estimated with reasonable accuracy." 734 F. Supp. 176, 181 (NJ 1990).

Dr. Glasser's assumption is the key not only to the results he derived, but to the irrelevance of those results to the predictable life on the date of sale of the goodwill (or "paid subscribers") actually purchased from Booth. The key, in turn, to that irrelevance lies not in Dr. Glasser's explicit statement of his assumption, but in what the assumption itself presupposes. Since the District Court was not concerned with predicting the value that any given Booth newspaper might have in the future (as distinct from predicting the useful life of pre-existing subscriber goodwill), an assumption that the level of a paper's subscriptions would remain constant was useful only insofar as it had a bearing on predicting the behavior of the old subscribers. For this purpose, assuming a constant subscription level was a way of supposing that a given newspaper would remain as attractive to subscribers in the future as it had been during the period prior to the newspaper's sale. The assumption was thus a surrogate for the supposition that the new owners would not rock the boat and would succeed in acting intelligently to keep the paper, if not exactly as it had always been, at least as relatively attractive as it had been in relation to its various competitors on the date of sale.

What is significant about this assumption for present purposes is not its doubtful validity, but the very fact of its being an assumption about the behavior of the paper's management after the date of sale. And since this assumption is the basis for a prediction about the life of subscriptions existing on the date of sale, that prediction is by definition not simply about the duration of subscriber goodwill (or habit or inertia) as it existed on the date the paper changed hands. On the contrary, it is a prediction about the combined effect of pre-sale goodwill and post-sale satisfaction with the paper as Ledger presumably continues to produce it. Nowhere in Dr. Glasser's testimony do we find an opinion that the pre-sale goodwill has a life coextensive with the predicted life of the subscriptions, and nowhere do we find an opinion about the point at which the old goodwill finally peters out as a measurable, and hence valuable, influence on the old subscribers' behavior. It is not, of course, important for present purposes whether such an opinion would be possible, though I am skeptical that it would be.[9] But it is important that no such evidence exists in this case. In place of evidence showing the depreciable lifespan of date-of-sale goodwill with a reasonable degree of accuracy, Ledger has presented evidence of how long an old subscriber will remain one, on the assumption that the subscriber's prior satisfaction is confirmed, and (for all we know) replaced, with satisfaction resulting from Ledger's publishing performance over the years following its acquisition of a given newspaper.

This, of course, misses the point entirely. In telling us merely how long a subscriber is likely to subscribe, Ledger tells us nothing about how long date-of-sale subscriber habit or inertia will remain a cause of predicted subscriber faithfulness. Since, however, only the date-of-sale probability of faithfulness could be entitled to depreciation as a purchased asset, Ledger's expert on his own terms has not even claimed to make the showing of definite duration necessary to depreciate an asset under section 167(a). Indeed, once duration of subscriptions and purchased goodwill are seen to be conceptually different, Ledger's claim to have satisfied the requirements for depreciating an intangible asset simply vanishes. Ledger's entire case thus rests on the confusion of subscription duration with goodwill on the date of sale, and only that confusion could suggest that Ledger has shouldered its burden of estimating the lifespan of the asset purchased from Booth. It is not surprising, then, that the Commissioner has stood by her categorical judgment that

9. Goodwill results from such a mix of influences over time that it seems unlikely that the skein of them all could be untangled to identify the degree to which even present custom results from the goodwill purchased, as distinct from goodwill subsequently cultivated. Ledger has not even attempted such a disentanglement.

goodwill is not depreciable, that Congress has not disturbed this judgment,[10] and that lower courts have consistently agreed that goodwill is nondepreciable as a matter of law. . . . I respectfully dissent.

Questions

1. What, if anything, does Justice Blackmun's opinion here have in common with his Court of Appeals opinion in *World Publishing*?

2. Is it right to say that the underlying problem in this case is whether a taxpayer may account separately for the customers of a business at the time of acquisition and customers acquired thereafter? Or whether he must treat the latter as replacing the former so that the customer base is self-renewing? If so, is that a question of fact for business and financial experts or a question of law to be determined by interpretation of the applicable legislation?

3. The opinion, like many others on this (and many other) topic(s), makes much depend on classification as goodwill versus other customer-based intangibles. Is the definition of categories for the purpose of this classification a matter of fact or of law?

4. Much is made of the experts' ability to estimate the rate at which pre-acquisition "paid subscribers" will leave the fold, and their appearance of expertise is enhanced by the emergence of different estimates for different newspapers based on factual differences among them and among the areas they serve. But if the objective were to allow a deduction that matches the rate of exhaustion of the pre-acquisition subscriber base, why not just let deductions follow actual events by taking a loss each year for the number of such subscribers who in fact do terminate? Would such a deduction be allowed? Some of the cases that allow depreciation of customer-based intangibles, as described in *Newark Morning Ledger*, have described the intangibles in question as mass assets, which seems to have meant that deductions could not be taken for the defection of particular customers as such. Cf. Skilken v. Commissioner, 420 F.2d 266 (6th Cir. 1969) (purchaser of cigarette vending machine business allocated part of purchase price to each at-will machine location on the basis of sales, and then deducted as losses the allocated amounts for locations terminated each year thereafter; deductions disallowed). But then why allow depreciation, which comes down to an estimate of the same thing?

5. Do Justice Souter's criticisms of the taxpayer's proof imply that the true useful life of purchased goodwill would be shorter or longer than the taxpayer's expert indicated? Would that produce more or less valuable

---

10. The majority claims its approach to be "more faithful to the purposes of the Code," in allowing taxpayers to make a better match of expenses with revenues. . . . Such policy initiatives are properly left to Congress, which can modify the per se ban on depreciating goodwill at any time. Despite several recent opportunities to do so, Congress has so far refused to alter the tax treatment of goodwill and other intangibles. . . .

depreciation deductions? Or does that depend on value and hence allocated cost? Presumably Justice Souter felt it was enough to show that the taxpayer had not presented convincing proof of any useful life, without going into what the result might have been if his expert had gone at the question properly.

6. *Houston Chronicle.* The Court makes clear that *Houston Chronicle* was a pivotal case in the development of this topic. It also states clearly that *Houston Chronicle* involved acquisition of a customer list from a defunct business, a context in which it was reasonable to argue there was no transfer of business and goodwill of which the list was just a part. The Court does not appear to understand how big a step it was, conceptually and practically, to extend the ruling to active business acquisitions.

The Court does not make clear how the customer list in *Houston Chronicle* was evaluated. In fact it was evaluated by estimating the cost of an advertising campaign to get the customers without buying the list. That is the valuation method that the government advanced in *Newark Morning Ledger,* estimating that it would produce a value of $3 million — less than 5 percent of the value claimed by the taxpayer and approved by the Court.

The valuation and deductibility issues are not unrelated. The *Houston Chronicle* valuation effectively characterizes the customer list purchase as a simple alternative to a deductible advertising expense to be incurred over a relatively short period of time. The taxpayer's much larger valuation in this case effectively characterizes what was acquired as much, much more, and something much more like goodwill. The Court pays no significant attention to this 20-fold expansion of *Houston Chronicle.*

7. Would you favor legislation to make goodwill itself depreciable? Why? On what terms?

4. Section 197

AMORTIZATION OF GOODWILL AND CERTAIN OTHER INTANGIBLES

1994 Budget Reconciliation Recommendation of the House Committee on Ways and Means, 103d Cong., 1st Sess. (Comm. Print 103-11)

PRESENT LAW

In determining taxable income for Federal income tax purposes, a taxpayer is allowed depreciation or amortization deductions for the cost or other basis of intangible property that is used in a trade or business or held for the production of income if the property has a limited useful life that may be determined with reasonable accuracy. Treas. Reg. sec. 1.167(a)-(3). These Treasury Regulations also state that no depreciation deductions are allowed with respect to goodwill.

The U.S. Supreme Court recently held that a taxpayer able to prove that a particular asset can be valued, and that the asset has a limited useful life which can be ascertained with reasonable accuracy, may depreciate the value over the useful life regardless of how much the asset appears to reflect the expectancy of continued patronage. However, the Supreme Court also characterized the taxpayer's burden of proof as "substantial" and stated that it "often will prove too great to bear." Newark Morning Ledger Co. v. United States, [507 U.S. 546 (1993)].

REASONS FOR CHANGE

The Federal income tax treatment of the costs of acquiring intangible assets is a source of considerable controversy between taxpayers and the Internal Revenue Service. Disputes arise concerning (1) whether an amortizable intangible asset exists; (2) in the case of an acquisition of a trade or business, the portion of the purchase price that is allocable to an amortizable intangible asset; and (3) the proper method and period for recovering the cost of an amortizable intangible asset. These types of disputes can be expected to continue to arise, even after the decision of the U.S. Supreme Court in Newark Morning Ledger Co. v. United States, supra.

It is believed that much of the controversy that arises under present law with respect to acquired intangible assets could be eliminated by specifying a single method and period for recovering the cost of most acquired intangible assets and by treating acquired goodwill and going concern value as amortizable intangible assets. It is also believed that there is no need at this time to change the Federal income tax treatment of self-created intangible assets, such as goodwill that is created through advertising and other similar expenditures.

Accordingly, the bill requires the cost of most acquired intangible assets, including goodwill and going concern value, to be amortized ratably over a 14-year* period. It is recognized that the useful lives of certain acquired intangible assets to which the bill applies may be shorter than [15] years, while the useful lives of other acquired intangible assets to which the bill applies may be longer than [15] years.

EXPLANATION OF PROVISION

The bill allows an amortization deduction with respect to the capitalized costs of certain intangible property (defined as a section 197 intangible) that is acquired by a taxpayer and that is held by the taxpayer in connection with the conduct of a trade or business or an activity engaged in for the

---

* [The amortization period was increased from 14 to 15 years in conference. Accordingly, "14" is replaced with "[15]" throughout the remainder of these excerpts. — Eds.]

production of income. The amount of the deduction is determined by amortizing the adjusted basis (for purposes of determining gain) of the intangible ratably over a [15]-year period that begins with the month that the intangible is acquired. No other depreciation or amortization deduction is allowed with respect to a section 197 intangible that is acquired by a taxpayer.

In general, the bill applies to a section 197 intangible acquired by a taxpayer regardless of whether it is acquired as part of a trade or business. . . . The bill generally does not apply to a section 197 intangible that is created by the taxpayer if the intangible is not created in connection with a transaction (or series of related transactions) that involves the acquisition of a trade or business or a substantial portion thereof.

Except in the case of amounts paid or incurred under certain covenants not to compete (or under certain other arrangements that have substantially the same effect as covenants not to compete) and certain amounts paid or incurred on account of the transfer of a franchise, trademark, or trade name, the bill generally does not apply to any amount that is otherwise currently deductible (i.e., not capitalized) under present law. . . .

DEFINITION OF SECTION 197 INTANGIBLE

The term "section 197 intangible" is defined as any property that is included in any one or more of the following categories: (1) goodwill and going concern value; (2) certain specified types of intangible property that generally relate to workforce, information base, know-how, customers, suppliers, or other similar items; (3) any license, permit, or other right granted by a governmental unit or an agency or instrumentality thereof; (4) any covenant not to compete (or other arrangement to the extent that the arrangement has substantially the same effect as a covenant not to compete) entered into in connection with the direct or indirect acquisition of an interest in a trade or business (or a substantial portion thereof); and (5) any franchise, trademark, or trade name.

Certain types of property, however, are specifically excluded . . . The term "section 197 intangible" does not include: (1) any interest in a corporation, partnership, trust, or estate; (2) any interest under an existing futures contract, foreign currency contract, notional principal contract, interest rate swap, or other similar financial contract; (3) any interest in land; (4) certain computer software; (5) certain interests in films, sound recordings, video tapes, books, or other similar property; (6) certain rights to receive tangible property or services; (7) certain interests in patents or copyrights; (8) any interest under an existing lease of tangible property; (9) any interest under an existing indebtedness (except for the deposit base and similar items of a financial institution); (10) a franchise to engage in any professional sport, and any item acquired in connection with such a franchise; and (11) certain transaction costs.

In addition, the Treasury Department is authorized to issue regulations that exclude certain rights of fixed duration or amount from the definition of a section 197 intangible. . . .

Notes and Questions

1. The principal effect of §197 is to allow 15-year straight-line amortization of goodwill and going concern value and the like, things for which formerly no amortization was allowed at all. §197(a). The prescribed deduction is allowed for any "amortizable section 197 intangible." Section 197(d) defines "section 197 intangible" to include a variety of things. Section 197(c) indicates which section 197 intangibles are amortizable.

For goodwill the effect of being dubbed an amortizable section 197 intangible is clearly favorable, since it provides a deduction where otherwise there would be none.

But §197 also applies to some things that previously had more favorable treatment: the cost of a patent, for example, that expires in five years, will be subject to 15-year amortization instead of 5-year if it is an amortizable section 197 intangible. Such classification is therefore likely to be unfavorable.

Part of the difficulty in reading the section is that while it has a variety of subcategories for reaching a decision about whether different sorts of intangibles are amortizable section 197 intangibles, it does not have subcategories for things outside that definition that would help us to keep in mind the different consequences that result from excluding different sorts of assets. Indeed those different treatments of different excluded items are generally not dealt with by §197 at all; one needs to know something of the prior law for that.

2. *Noncompetition agreements.* A very common strategy prior to 1993, upon acquisition of a going business, was to allocate part of the consideration to a covenant not to compete. Typically such a covenant would be limited in duration to five years. In many situations a covenant for any longer than that might have been invalid as a restraint on trade. In any event, sellers were reluctant to tie their hands for longer than that, and buyers could be convinced that they ought to be able to meet competition after five years. Buyers also liked five-year amortization of that part of their purchase price.

During much of our tax history, the tax advantage of amortization to the buyer was offset to a considerable degree by the fact that money assigned to a covenant not to compete would be ordinary income to the seller, while gain on the sale of goodwill would be capital gain. To a considerable extent, therefore, the tension over this allocation was between buyer and seller, with the government in the position of a relatively disinterested stakeholder. As a result, many cases gave the parties considerable leeway in allocating consideration to such a covenant if both parties agreed to the allocation. Moreover parties tended to be held to their bargain for tax purposes, although the IRS could disallow unreasonable taxpayer allocations.

Noncompetition agreements entered into in connection with a business acquisition are §197 assets. The intended effect of that for the purchaser is that it will make no substantial difference whether money is allocated to the purchase of goodwill or to a noncompetition agreement. Prior to 1993 it also did not make much difference to the seller whether part of the proceeds were taxed as ordinary income rather than capital gain. Somewhat ironically, the 1993 legislation that eliminated the difference in treatment on the buyer side also restored a substantial difference in rates between ordinary income and capital gain on the seller side. Subsequent legislation has made that differential even greater. So now allocation of price to a noncompetition agreement appears to be an undesirable move from an income tax standpoint.

3. *Residual valuation.* If a business is purchased as a going concern, how is the price paid to be allocated among assets? In particular, how much is to be allocated to goodwill as compared with tangible assets and other intangibles?

The original simple rule was that price paid should be allocated in proportion to fair market value. Under that rule, taxpayers were tempted to assert a low value for goodwill, with the result that total value of all other (identifiable) assets acquired was less than price paid, and everything would get a purchase-cost basis of more than fair market value. The portion of the excess allocated to inventory and depreciable machinery and equipment would produce a rather prompt reduction of taxable income.

The IRS on the other hand was likely to assert that the excess of price paid over value was itself very strong evidence, or virtual proof, that goodwill was worth more than the taxpayer reported. The IRS assertion could take the form of declaring that the best way to value goodwill was by residual valuation: allocate to other assets not more than their fair market value, and the residue, if any, of price paid should be allocated to goodwill. The IRS position has been approved by Congress, in §§338(b)(5) and 1060. Take a look at the regulations to see how the concept of residual allocation has been elaborated. Reg. §§1.1060-1(c), 1.338-6, -7.

B.   RATES AND METHODS

Most depreciation is claimed for tangible business or investment assets with respect to which there is no question of eligibility for depreciation. The main question is how fast the cost can be written off: over what period of time (*useful life*) and how distributed over that period (*depreciation method*). For property put into service since 1981, those questions are governed by §168 of the statute itself, which dictates what will be considered a reasonable allowance under §167(a). But the statute incorporates administrative developments prior to 1981, and so some history is unavoidable.

1.   The Straight-Line Method

The simplest and oldest way of calculating depreciation is the *straight-line* method. This is simply adjusted basis minus estimated *salvage value* spread in equal increments over the estimated *useful life*. If an automobile purchased for use in a business cost $14,000 and was anticipated to be used for five years and to sell for $2,000, then straight-line depreciation would be $2,400 per year for five years. See Reg. §1.167(b)-1.

The straight-line method is the only clearly authorized method for depreciation of intangibles. Straight-line depreciation (with no adjustment for salvage) is also currently the prescribed method for real estate and an available elective method for other property. §168(b)(3)(A), (B), and (D).

2.   Declining Balance Methods

Today the most common method of depreciation for income tax purposes is a *declining balance* method. Declining balance depreciation goes at a faster initial rate than straight-line depreciation, but applies that rate each year to the remaining unrecovered cost, not the whole original cost. Declining balance depreciation is commonly authorized at 150 or 200 percent of the straight-line rate, figured without salvage. So, for example, property with a 20-year estimated useful life would have a straight-line depreciation rate of 5 percent. Double declining balance depreciation would therefore go at a 10 percent rate as follows.

Year	Adjusted Basis	Rate	Depreciation Allowance
1	1,000	10	100
2	900	10	90
3	810	10	81
4	729	10	73
5	656	10	66
6	590	10	59
7	531	10	53
8	478	10	48
9	430	10	43
10	387	10	39
11-20	348	10	35^2

2. It is customary to switch to straight-line recovery of the remaining cost over the remaining useful life at the point where that becomes greater than continued declining balance. The switch to straight line is currently authorized by §168(b)(1)(B). The crossover point will normally be at about the midpoint for double declining balance. The switch would come later if there were any salvage value to take into account.

Double declining balance depreciation has been specifically authorized by statute since 1954, and apparently had some recognition for tax purposes before that time. It is the method currently prescribed for most short-lived property in §168(b)(1). For some property the current statute prescribes 150 percent declining balance depreciation. §168(b)(2).

3.   Useful Lives

Under any of these methods, the rate of depreciation allowable in any particular year depends on an estimate of useful life and sometimes salvage value. How are these estimates to be made, and by whom?

In the first 20 years after 1913, this matter seems to have been left largely to taxpayers, in part because it was recognized that in most cases differences in these estimates would only affect the timing of deductions, and in part because there was not a widespread appreciation of the time value of money in relation to taxes. (Or perhaps the time value was not so great because interest rates were low.)

Then for nearly 50 years it was primarily a matter of administrative action. In the 1930s, the IRS, under prodding by Congress, began auditing depreciation deductions. In 1942, the IRS published Bulletin F, which prescribed depreciation lives for each of thousands of asset classifications. In 1962, Bulletin F was replaced by Guidelines Lives, which spoke in terms of about 75 broad industrial and general asset categories and authorized lives approximately 30 to 40 percent shorter than those in Bulletin F. In 1971, the IRS adopted Asset Depreciation Ranges (ADR), which were Guidelines plus or minus up to 20 percent, at the option of taxpayers. This struck many as a euphemism for an unjustified 20 percent across-the-board acceleration of depreciation deductions. Litigation followed but was rendered moot by legislation explicitly approving the change.

In 1981 the matter was taken over by Congress itself by the adoption of the Accelerated Cost Recovery System (ACRS) prescribed in §168. The sorting of assets into classes is still mostly a matter of administration. §168(i)(1); but cf. §§168(e)(3), (i)(2)(C), (D). However, what constitutes a reasonable allowance for each class is prescribed in the statute itself and is sometimes more generous than the very name of the class would imply. §168(e)(1). For example, seven-year property is property that has a class life of 10 years or more but less than 16. On an administrative determination of a class life of 15 years, therefore, the statute now authorizes double declining balance depreciation at a 28.6 percent rate. (Straight-line rate is 1/7, which equals 14.3 percent; 200 percent of 14.3 is 28.6.)

ACRS, as adopted in 1981, was in some respects even more generous than the present version. Then, buildings in general were depreciable over 15 years instead of the present 27.5 and 31.5. Machinery and equipment were not much different than at present, but there was in place a general investment credit of 10 percent: The combined effect of the credit plus ACRS was much more generous than ACRS alone. The investment credit was repealed in 1986. (See Chapter 15.D below.)

4.   Optional Expensing

Another 1981 innovation is in §179. Although not doing much for large corporations, it takes small businesses almost out of the depreciation system altogether by making the purchase cost of depreciable property immediately deductible. There is a cap on this deduction of $25,000, but the limit is $125,000 for taxable years beginning in 2007, 2009, and 2010, and for 2008 it was temporarily raised to $250,000 as an economic stimulus measure. §179(b)(1), (7). Look critically at the "reduction in limitation" in §179(b)(2).

Deductions under §179 are subject to depreciation recapture, affirming that they are thought of as very fast depreciation. §1245(a)(2)(C). The deduction is computed and claimed on a depreciation schedule to the return. Note also the possibility of recapture on conversion to personal use. §179(d)(10).

5.   Alternative Depreciation — §168(g)

Look at §168(g), added in 1986. How close does this come to economic depreciation? What do you make of the purposes for which it is prescribed?

6.   Purposes for Setting Rates and Methods

What are the purposes pursued in setting depreciation rates and methods? At least three have persisted, with varying emphases through much of this history.

(a) *Income measurement.* Some deduction for depreciation is an essential element in measuring net income, and so one aim in setting useful lives has been accuracy of income measurement. Of course that is easier to say than to achieve. It is sometimes apparently assumed that accurate income measurement would depend primarily on actual useful lives: how long taxpayers in fact keep using equipment before retiring it. But older equipment may be less productive than newer equipment even though it is kept in service. Sometimes older equipment is actually used less than newer equipment but it is kept in service to meet peak period demands. So acceleration of depreciation may well have some basis in income measurement, and actual retirement of some assets may be a poor measurement of when their utility is mostly exhausted.

One special problem in income measurement is inflation. Income may be overstated, it is said, because capital equipment costs are constantly being measured by reference to outdated, unindexed prices for capital equipment.

It is not easy to think of a fix for this concern short of general indexing, but accelerated depreciation has sometimes been defended as a rough offset to the capital cost understatement produced by inflation.

(b) *Ease of administration.* Prior to 1981 taxpayers always had the option to show by facts and circumstances that their own business had shorter useful lives than those prescribed in Bulletin F or Guidelines.[3] It has been repeatedly asserted that the IRS does not have adequate personnel to audit individualized claims of faster depreciation. When lives have been shortened it has been routinely asserted that the shorter lives should reduce conflicts arising out of facts and circumstances claims. But conflict did not disappear following any of the administrative revisions; whether it was reduced is hard to say.

The current legislation eliminates the facts and circumstances test and makes the statutory prescription exclusive. This presumably will reduce the administrative burden of dealing with taxpayers on audit (adjudication?), but this whole evolution has likely increased the administrative burden associated with taxpayer efforts to get changes in the rules.

Besides disputes about actual useful lives, predicted salvage value was another fact-based source of controversy. To forestall unproductive disputes, starting in 1962 Congress permitted taxpayers to reduce the estimated salvage value required to be taken into account in computing depreciation allowances by 10 percent of the initial cost of the property, or to ignore salvage altogether if the property was expected to be worth less than 10 percent of its original cost upon retirement. See Reg. §1.167(f)-1. With the enactment of ACRS in 1981, salvage value was removed from any role in computing depreciation. §168(b)(4).

Section 179 shows another way to eliminate administrative burdens in determining rates and methods of depreciation.

(c) *Investment stimulus.* It is now well understood that faster depreciation — shorter lives and accelerated methods — may stimulate investment in depreciable assets, and this effect has been repeatedly cited as a reason for making depreciation more generous. Economic stimulus was cited in 1962 as a supporting reason for the replacement of Bulletin F by Guideline Lives, and in 1971 as a prominent reason for adopting ADR. Indeed it was the main ground for challenging ADR: Tax reduction for economic stimulus was asserted to be a matter for legislation, not administration. And ACRS, the dramatic shortening of lives in 1981, was adopted by legislation, in a statute entitled the "Economic Recovery Tax Act of 1981" (ERTA), and was clearly intended to stimulate investment.

The next section is an introduction to the economics of investment stimulus through capital cost allowances.

---

3. In 1962, a mathematical test, called the *Reserve Ratio Test*, was proposed, to test whether a particular taxpayer's depreciation had been excessive or deficient in relation to his actual practice concerning property retirements over some extended period of time. The test was not simple and was criticized on other grounds and never went into effect.

C.   *THE ECONOMICS OF CAPITAL COST ALLOWANCES*

Depreciation, in the oldest view of the matter, is a function of investment: The more often one replaces equipment the faster it should be depreciated, just as a matter of sensible income measurement.

But investment is partially a function of tax depreciation and other capital cost allowances. Levels of investment will be affected by capital cost allowances whether we like it or not. In recent years, as indicated above, tax legislators and administrators have come more and more to assert investment stimulus as a legitimate tax policy objective to be pursued in setting depreciation rates.

How does tax depreciation affect levels of investment? One answer that used to be given some prominence pointed simply to current cash flow. Depreciation is not a cash flow item, but income taxes are. If tax depreciation is increased, taxes will be reduced, businesses will have more cash left after payment of taxes, and some of that cash may get used for investment that otherwise would not have occurred.

The main answer today goes a little deeper. A successful business person contemplating a capital investment must ask what the rate of return will be on that investment, so that it can be evaluated in relation to borrowing and other capital costs and other competing uses for the funds (including government bonds). The relevant rate of return for this purpose is after-tax return: If more can be made from one investment than another, but the taxes will be higher by even more, then clearly it is in his interest to make the other investment. For purposes of sensible investment appraisal income taxes have to be taken into account just like any other cost.

Rate of return will be a function of all the benefits derived from a particular investment minus costs incurred over all time. In a business setting, the benefits will be entered into income, the costs deducted, and income tax liability will be a function of the excess of the former over the latter. The cost of capital equipment will eventually get taken into account through depreciation deductions, whatever the applicable rates and methods.

In evaluating rate of return, not all dollars of income or expense are equal. The present value of a future deduction is less than that of a present deduction by an amount that is a function of interest rates and the period of time involved. Accelerated depreciation means deferred taxes, which means accelerated after-tax cash flow and therefore a higher rate of return than the same amount of depreciation allowed at a slower rate. So shorter depreciation lives may well *induce* more rapid capital replacement, even if it is hard to show they are *reflecting* it.

Rather sophisticated calculations of the effects of depreciation on rates of return are now commonplace because computers and even electronic calculators have helped to make it that way. Although most tax lawyers still get along without being able to do such calculations, one must get comfortable with reading the results. And one will be much better off if she can develop some reasonably accurate intuitions about the general results that are apt to emerge from careful calculations.

Two benchmarks worth knowing well are described below.

1.   Complete Acceleration, or Expensing

The first benchmark is as follows:

At any constant rate of income tax, allowing an immediate deduction for an investment has the same effect as exempting the return on that investment from the burden of the tax. The after-tax rate of return, in other words, will be fully equal to the rate of return if there had been no tax.

Consider, for example, a taxpayer in a 33 percent bracket who buys a perpetual 12 percent bond. She will receive $120 each year, of which $40 will go in taxes leaving her $80 to spend or save. An annual return of $80 on an investment of $1,000 is 8 percent, which is 12 percent reduced by 33 percent.

But suppose she were able to deduct the cost of the bond. The interest income, before and after tax, would remain the same, but deduction of the purchase price would produce a $330 tax saving in the year of purchase, which would reduce the after-tax cost of the bond from $1,000 to $670. An after-tax return of $80 on an after-tax investment of $670 is 12 percent, which is precisely the *pretax rate* of return on the bond.

When the bond is paid off, the taxpayer who deducted its cost will have to pay tax on the proceeds, since she will have no basis to subtract. But that just means, at constant rates, that her after-tax recovery of principal will be $670, just equal to her after-tax cost for purchasing the bond. The payment of the bond is therefore a no-gain-or-loss transaction, before and after tax, whether or not a deduction is allowed for its purchase.

In effect the government will have shifted its role from tax collector to co-investor. By allowing the initial deduction the government suffered a loss or deferral of tax in the amount of $330. It subsequently collected income taxes of $40 per year while the bond was outstanding and $330 when it was paid off. Its position is precisely the same as if it had collected the $330 in the first place and then invested it in a fixed principal 12 percent interest-paying obligation of $330. And from this perspective, nothing it collects can be seen as tax on the taxpayer's investment.

The matter can be generalized to get away from the format of a fixed principal investment. Just suppose a taxpayer spends $100 on an improvement to a machine that will increase revenues (or decrease expenses) by $400 in some one subsequent year. The before-tax profit on this particular investment then, over the period involved, is 300 percent.

Now consider income taxes. If the expenditure is nondeductible, there will be a taxable gain of $300 in the later year. At 33 percent this would produce a tax of $99, which would reduce the proceeds in the later year from $400 to $301, and the rate of profit from 300 percent to 201 percent. Reducing the rate of profit from 300 percent to 201 percent is just what one would expect from a 33 percent tax.

On the other hand, if the $100 expenditure were deductible when made, then the whole $400 return would be taxable in the subsequent year. At 33 percent, the tax would be $132 and the net after-tax proceeds only $268. But the deduction reduced the after-tax cost of the expenditure itself from $100 to $67. An after-tax return of $268 from an after-tax investment of $67 represents a dollar profit of $201 just as if the original expenditure were nondeductible. But $201 profit on an after-tax investment of $67 is a 300 percent profit after all. The *rate* of return on investment is just the same as if there had been no tax in effect.

No Immediate Deduction

	Investment	Return	Profit	
Before Tax	$100	$400	$300	300%
Tax	0	99	99	
After Tax	$100	$301	$201	201%

Immediate Deduction

	Investment	Return	Profit	
Before Tax	$100	$400	$300	300%
Tax	33	132	99	
After Tax	$ 67	$268	$201	300%

This relationship has not always been obvious to everyone. According to Professor Shoup,[4] "The fact that completely accelerated depreciation, when coupled with complete loss offset, is equivalent to exemption of net return from the asset, under an income tax, was discovered by E. Cary Brown [in 1948]. . . ."[5] Professor Surrey quotes Shoup, notes his use of the term "discovered," and observes: "Perhaps a Congressman can be pardoned for not appreciating the benefit of deferral if its ramifications apparently eluded public finance specialists for 35 years of our income tax history."[6]

---

4. Public Finance 302 n.20 (1969).

5. E.C. Brown, Business-Income Taxation and Investment Incentives, in Income, Employment and Public Policy: Essays in Honor of Alvin H. Hansen 309-310 (New York: Norton, 1948), reprinted in Musgrave and Shoup, Readings in the Economics of Taxation.

6. S. Surrey, Pathways to Tax Reform 123 (1973).

2. No Acceleration — Economic Depreciation

In the prior examples, when deduction for an investment is deferred until return of the investment, an income tax has the effect of reducing the investor's return by the expected amount: The after-tax return for a 33 percent taxpayer is only two-thirds of the return for an exempt investor. A depreciation scheme that produces that result is often called *economic depreciation.*

In the two examples above it is easy to judge when a deduction should be allowed to achieve economic depreciation. In the bond case it is when principal is repaid; in the return-in-a-single-year case it is that single year. But what if an investment were expected to return value to a business over a series of years — that, after all, is the general case with depreciable assets. What if, for example, a $100,000 machine is expected to produce services worth $20,000 a year for 20 years, and then be worthless? To make that hypothesis concrete, suppose that a taxpayer buys a machine and leases it to a high-credit lessee for $20,000 a year for 20 years and expects it to have no value beyond the term of the lease. How should return of investment be allocated among years to produce economic depreciation?

Straight-line depreciation would be $5,000 per year. Thus taxable income would be $15,000, tax would be $4,950, and net cash flow after tax would be $15,050. By use of a spreadsheet program or a hand-held calculator with simple financial functions, one can quickly ascertain that 20 annual payments of $15,050 for a lump sum of $100,000 represents a rate of return of 13.944 percent; so this is the after-tax rate of return. But 20 annual payments of $20,000, the pretax return, represents a rate of return of 19.426 percent. The former is 71.78 percent of the latter, so the effective rate of tax is only 28.21, not 33. What's wrong?

Consider the matter from the standpoint of the income. A pretax rate of return of 19.426 implies there should have been $19,426 of income in the first year, so that only $574 (instead of $5,000) should have been allowed as amortization of investment. In the second year, since only $99,426 of unamortized investment remains, a rate of return of 19.426 percent would imply income of $19,314 and return of capital of $686. Since income becomes a smaller portion of each payment, return of capital will be a larger portion each year. (But still less than the straight-line amount of $5,000 through the 13th year.)

Computation of the after-tax rate of return in this case is somewhat tedious, since the after-tax cash flow is not a fixed annual amount. (Since the income portion of payments goes down, tax liability goes down, and total payment minus tax goes up from period to period.) But doing it will confirm that the after-tax return is related to the pretax return, by a ratio of one minus the tax rate, for whatever pretax rate of return and rate of tax may be chosen. Indeed this conclusion is implicit in the method of computing return of capital stated in the last paragraph.

Another way to view the logic of this method of amortization is by considering the value of remaining benefits still to be received after each year goes by. At the beginning of year one there were 20 years of benefits to look forward to. At the beginning of year two there are only 19 years of benefits left, but they are the next 19 years. What has changed is that there is no longer a benefit anticipated for the 20th year out. The present value of 19 annual payments of $20,000, at 19.426 percent interest, is $99,426, which is $574 less than $100,000. And the present value of 18 remaining payments is $98,740, a further reduction of $685. And so on.

Present values at 19.4258 percent of remaining annual payments

	Value	Change
20 payments of $20,000	$100,000	—
19 payments of $20,000	99,426	574
18 payments of $20,000	98,740	686
17 payments of $20,000	97,921	819
16 payments of $20,000	96,943	978
15 payments of $20,000	95,775	1,168
14 payments of $20,000	94,380	1,495
13 payments of $20,000	92,714	1,666
12 payments of $20,000	90,725	1,989
11 payments of $20,000	88,349	2,396
10 payments of $20,000	85,511	2,838
9 payments of $20,000	82,122	3,389
8 payments of $20,000	78,075	4,047
7 payments of $20,000	73,242	4,833
6 payments of $20,000	67,469	5,773
5 payments of $20,000	60,576	6,893
4 payments of $20,000	52,343	8,233
3 payments of $20,000	42,511	9,832
2 payments of $20,000	30,770	11,741
1 payments of $20,000	16,747	14,023
No remaining payments	-0-	16,747

This method of amortization corresponds exactly with the calculations of remaining principal due on a level payment mortgage, on which early payments are likely to be almost all interest while later payments are substantially return of capital. It is commonly called *sinking fund depreciation.*[7]

---

7. Individual bonds are commonly for a fixed principal amount, none of which is due until maturity, because that is thought to be what some investors want. But a prudent underwriter may require the issuer to make provision for payment of the bonds by contributing periodically to a sinking fund. Sinking fund depreciation matches the amount that would have to be contributed to such a sinking fund to provide for full payment at maturity, with interest earned on the fund equal to that payable on the bonds. Often that rate of return is assured by arranging to invest the sinking fund in the bonds themselves.

This analysis, or something like it, has led some to conclude that straight-line depreciation is generally a species of accelerated depreciation and that economic depreciation should generally follow a sinking fund type of curve. See, e.g., Marvin A. Chirelstein, Federal Income Taxation: A Law Student's Guide to the Leading Cases and Concepts 170-172 (10th ed. 2005). But that is much too sweeping a conclusion, since the analysis depends upon the current utility of the asset being constant from year to year throughout the useful life, like "the wonderful one-hoss-shay . . . that . . . ran a hundred years to a day [and] went to pieces all at once — all at once, and nothing first, just as bubbles . . . when they burst."[8] That condition is probably only met in practice by certain financial assets such as annuities, fixed payment loan contracts, and property subject to long-term fixed rental leases.[9]

The above calculations do not indicate that sinking fund depreciation is correct or that straight-line or even accelerated depreciation is wrong for ordinary business assets, because we have no reason for supposing that the utility of a machine is constant from year to year. But the analysis suggests what economic depreciation would be in other circumstances. Economic depreciation is the anticipated decline in present value of remaining benefits from the investment, or in other words, decline in value. Well, maybe not quite, since actual value may reflect unanticipated developments like changes in the discount rate, changes in demand for a company's product, or in the supply of machines, or the development of cheaper alternative technology (obsolescence?), or whatnot. How should all those things be treated?

The above calculations do show that even straight-line depreciation is only correct if benefits produced — net utility of the machine in business operations — goes down from year to year. And for declining balance depreciation to match economic depreciation, annual utility would have to go down even more.[10]

Despite these warnings, considerable evidence suggests that economic depreciation for most machinery and equipment and other depreciable property except real estate would follow a declining balance sort of

8. O.W. Holmes, The Deacon's Masterpiece, or, The Wonderful "One-Hoss Shay," in The Poetical Works of Oliver Wendell Holmes 158 (E. Tilton ed. 1975).

9. If the property subject to the lease has a declining annual utility, then fixed rental payments are themselves a distorted reflection of underlying economic reality. G. Mundstock, Taxation of Business Rent, 11 Va. L. Rev. 683 (1992). One wonders to what extent that distortion is commonly tolerated because it tends to be offset by inflation.

10. For pure declining balance depreciation (ignoring the switch to straight-line at the end), 20 percent declining balance depreciation would represent economic depreciation if and only if current utility itself declines by 20 percent per year. This results from the fact that remaining future utility at the beginning of year two will look just the same as at the beginning of year one except 20 percent smaller. This works equally for rates other than 20 percent, and is also independent of the interest rate chosen for discounting future benefits (provided that rate does not change from period to period), since the future seen from the beginning of the second year will be an accurate reduction of the pattern seen a year earlier, whatever its shape (so long as the shape does not change).

Students of calculus will recognize that this has something to do with the formula $\frac{de^x}{dx} = e^x$. (Most others should put this suggestion out of mind.)

curve.[11] An old machine is very apt to contribute less or to cost more to operate than a new one.

3. Other Cases

Economic depreciation and expensing are the benchmark cases. Something can be inferred about others by comparison with these.

If depreciation is allowed at a rate slower than expensing but faster than economic depreciation, the effective rate of tax will be somewhere between zero and the nominal marginal tax rate, and the after-tax rate of return will be in between the pretax rate of return and the pretax rate of return times one minus the marginal tax rate. And the nearer the depreciation is to either benchmark, the closer the results will be to that conclusion.

In some cases depreciation may be beyond one of the benchmarks. If no depreciation is allowed for an asset which does in fact exhibit economic depreciation, or even if depreciation is allowed but in an amount less than economic depreciation, then the effective rate of tax will be *greater than the nominal rate*. And on the other hand if capital allowances are granted at a rate in excess of expensing, the effective rate of tax will be *less than zero*. Examples of the latter may not be immediately obvious, but they have arisen in effect from the presence of additional capital allowances like the investment credit (Chapter 15D below), and from our treatment of borrowing (Chapter 7D above and Chapter 16A below), as we shall see shortly.

D. OTHER INVESTMENT STIMULI

In 1962, in addition to adopting Guideline Lives, the administration proposed and Congress enacted a general credit against income tax for investment in depreciable property, initially 7 percent of the amount of qualified investment. Between 1962 and 1986 the credit was suspended and reinstated, terminated and restored, and modified in rate and various other respects. At the end, the maximum credit was 10 percent of investment for most qualifying property. Higher percentages applied to investment in certain types of energy property and rehabilitation expenditures. Lower rates applied to very short-lived property. And there was an investment credit recapture requirement for property actually disposed of sooner than had been anticipated when the original credit was computed.

---

11. Hulten & Wykoff, Depreciation, Inflation, and the Taxation of Income from Capital 81, 112 (C. Hulten ed. 1981).

The purpose of the investment credit was purely to stimulate business capital spending for the general good of the economy. Changes in the rate of the credit were made, and the credit was even suspended and reinstated, in response to economic conditions calling for increased or decreased stimulation. At one time there was considerable confidence that the investment credit, with other devices, could be used effectively for fine-tuning the economy; later events dispelled that optimism.[12]

The investment credit was generally unavailable for buildings and their structural components, except elevators and escalators, certain special buildings and certain expenditures for rehabilitation of older buildings.

When ACRS (the Accelerated Cost Recovery System) was adopted in 1981 with a frank exposition of purpose to stimulate investment, the general investment credit was left in place. It was perhaps not fully anticipated how powerful the combination of ACRS and investment credit would be, but it was immediately apparent after it was done. In 1982 the congressional Joint Committee on Taxation explained that the effect was to generate tax benefits with a present value more generous than would have resulted from expensing, and that this produced an incentive for uneconomic investment.[13] To bring the benefits back to parity with expensing, some of the scheduled accelerations of depreciation enacted in 1981 were repealed, and a provision was adopted requiring a reduction in basis of depreciable property by half the amount of the investment credit. Assuming this did reduce the present value of tax benefits to that of expensing, did that eliminate the incentive for uneconomic investment? And if expensing was to be the benchmark, why not just adopt expensing as such?

In 1986, the concern with benefits in excess of expensing continued, but more broadly there was considerable criticism of highly accelerated capital cost allowances in general on the ground that they discriminate against businesses whose capital is tied up in inventories or other non-depreciable assets. Most of all, there was a fascination with lower marginal rates as the predominant tax policy objective to be pursued. So the investment credit was repealed, and lives were substantially lengthened for real estate (which had never had the investment credit), and the resulting predicted increases in corporate income tax revenues were used to pay a substantial part of the cost of rate reductions for both corporations and individuals. Substitution of lower rates for some of the acceleration in our depreciation deductions has been hailed as creating something closer to a level playing field.

12. One problem was that if investors began to anticipate an increase in the rate of investment credit because the economy needed stimulus, they would have an inducement to put off investment until the increase occurred, thus aggravating the very condition which generated the anticipation.

13. See Staff of Joint Comm. on Taxation, 97th Cong., General Explanation of the Revenue Provisions of the Tax Equity and Fiscal Responsibility Act of 1982, 35-36, 40 (Comm. Print 1982).

On the other hand, the 1986 law provides a new investment credit for real estate, which had not had it before. But it is only for one particular kind of real estate: low-income housing, which has long enjoyed special tax or borrowing benefits of other kinds. §42.

As part of an economic stimulus package Congress enacted a temporary increase in first-year depreciation that permits an immediate 50 percent write-off for property placed in service in 2008, §168(k), and also increased the limit of expensing under §179 during 2008 to $250,000, §179(b)(7). Are temporary tax allowances a sensible way to "jump start" the economy? Concerns have been expressed that these incentives will stimulate uneconomic investments.[14] And what about labor-intensive businesses? Should we be concerned that special cost recovery allowances favor investments in machinery over investments in people?

Take a look at §199, enacted in 2004, which allows businesses to deduct a portion (9 percent) of their income attributable to domestic manufacturing and production activities. How does this fit in?

E.   *DISPOSITION OF DEPRECIABLE PROPERTY: RECAPTURE OR CONVERSION*

What happens if a taxpayer takes depreciation on a machine and then sells it at a price indicating that it did not depreciate by that much after all? Suppose the machine cost $100x$; depreciation taken is $60x$; and resale price is $75x$.

First, look at §1016(a)(2), which prescribes an adjustment to basis for depreciation allowed or allowable.[15] The adjusted basis in the example would therefore be $40x$, and sale for $75x$ would produce a gain of $35x$. A gain of $35x$ combined with depreciation deductions of $60x$ represents a net loss or cost over the course of the investment of $25x$, which just matches the excess of original cost over eventual sale proceeds.

But what about the character of gain (or loss)? If the gain on disposition of the property is treated as capital gain, then the net tax effect of the transaction would be a deduction against ordinary income of $60x$ together with $35x$ of capital gain. That would amount to a net deduction of $25x$, plus a *conversion* of $35x$ of ordinary income (offset by the rest of the depreciation deduction) into capital gain.

14. Calvin H. Johnson, Pretty Cruddy Investments Brought to You by Stimulus Depreciation, 118 Tax Notes 731 (2008).

15. As to the possibility of a greater adjustment (and consequent lower basis and higher gain on subsequent sale) for depreciation allowable though not taken, see Crane v. Commissioner, Chapter 7D above.

But §1245, enacted in 1962 (along with the investment credit, and at the time of Guideline Lives), says in effect that an amount of gain, if any, equal to the amount of depreciation taken on the machine will be treated as ordinary income and taxed as such, anything elsewhere in the statute to the contrary notwithstanding. So in our example the whole gain of $35x$ would be taxed as ordinary income. Gain so treated is commonly called *depreciation recapture,* which carries the suggestion that somehow it represents a correction of depreciation deductions now shown to have been excessive, rather than a separate item of gain.

Section 1245 does not apply to buildings and other real property improvements §1245(a)(3). Section 1250, which was enacted two years after §1245, provides for a more limited form of depreciation recapture on real estate: Its main limitation is that it only recaptures *additional depreciation,* which means, for property held more than a year, depreciation in excess of what would have been allowed on a straight-line basis. §§1250(a)(1)(A), (b)(1). In some years, too, it only applied to a diminishing percentage of that excess, so that after a specified period of years recapture would disappear. (Such a reduction still occurs for special categories of property. §1250(a)(1)(B).) In any event a substantial part of real estate depreciation has always remained free of the recapture provisions, and therefore, since real estate frequently sells for more than adjusted basis, conversion of ordinary income (from the real estate or from other activities and invest-ments) into capital gain on sale remained as a substantial tax benefit for real estate investors right up until repeal of the capital gain rate preference itself in 1986. When ordinary income tax rates rose above 28 percent, gains on depreciable real estate, above the recaptured amount, stayed at 28 percent. But when a big capital gain rate differential was restored in 1997, there was a compromise: The rate of tax on "unrecaptured section 1250 capital gain" is now set at 25 percent—lower than 28 but considerably higher than the new general top rate of 15 percent. Unrecaptured section 1250 capital gain is defined as the additional amount of gain that would have been recaptured under §1250 if it recaptured all depreciation. §1(h)(1)(D), (h)(6).

What is the treatment of gain in excess of all depreciation taken on a property that is disposed of? Suppose, for example, that the Simons sell their violin bows for more than original cost; how will their gains be treated?

Or suppose depreciable property sells for less than its adjusted basis: What is the character of the loss on sale? Those questions are now dealt with primarily by §1231, which tends to produce capital gain in the first case or ordinary loss in the second. But it gets quite complicated if there are gains *and* losses. See Chapter 14D above.

The foregoing discussion assumes that depreciable assets are recorded in individual asset accounts. Large businesses are apt to utilize multiple asset accounts, however, in which case no effort is usually made to ascertain the basis of individual assets on disposition. See §168(i)(4), General Asset Accounts.

F. *DEPLETION OF MINERAL DEPOSITS*

DEPLETION ALLOWANCES[16]

Capital sums invested in the development of natural resource properties may be recovered through depletion allowances. These, like depreciation allowances, are deducted over the productive life of the property. In the case of mineral properties, depletion allowances are computed by either the cost depletion or percentage depletion method, whichever provides greater deductions. §§611-613. Under the cost depletion method, which must be used with respect to timber, the adjusted basis of the property is divided by the total number of units estimated to remain in the deposit or property (i.e., barrels of oil, tons of ore, board feet of lumber, etc.) and the result is multiplied by the number of units sold during the year. Reg. §1.611-2. Cost depletion deductions cease when the adjusted basis of the property is reduced to zero.

Under the percentage method, depletion is computed as a specific percentage of the annual gross income from the property, but cannot exceed 50 percent of the net income therefrom. §613. Although allowable percentage depletion serves to reduce the basis of the property for the purpose of determining gain or loss at the time of sale, exhaustion of basis or the absence of any original basis does not preclude further percentage depletion allowances since these are related to the income from the property rather than to actual investment costs. Accordingly, percentage depletion allowances may be claimed with respect to the income from a property the basis of which has been completely written off through prior depletion allowances.

For many years the statutory rate for oil and gas was $27\frac{1}{2}$ percent; percentage depletion rates for other minerals were lower. Percentage depletion for oil and gas was widely criticized as a major, unjustified tax preference, but both the concept and the rate proved very resistant to change. Finally, during the early 1970s, and largely in response to public criticism of the oil companies for gasoline shortages, percentage depletion for oil was first reduced and then effectively eliminated, except for relatively small producers. §§613(d), 613A(a). Even for them, the rate was scheduled to go down, in steps, to the level of 15 percent by 1984. Similar restrictions apply to natural gas unless it is regulated, sold under a fixed contract, or derived from geopressured brine. §613A.

Depletion allowances are generally available to every person who has an economic interest in and receives income from the exhaustion of a natural resource, the total allowances being apportioned among the various parties

---

16. Adapted from U.S. Congress, Joint Economic Committee, The Federal Tax System: Facts and Problems 107-110 (1964).

in interest. Such allowances, however, may not be claimed by taxpayers whose economic interests in depletable properties are indirect, such as shareholders or creditors of a corporation which owns the mineral properties.

The 1913 income tax legislation provided a reasonable allowance for depletion, not to exceed 5 percent of gross income, for wasting mineral assets. This was later changed to a more specific allowance for depletion based on the cost or 1913 value of the property. Allowances in excess of cost depletion were granted, in the form of discovery depletion, in 1918 to stimulate mineral exploration for war purposes and to lessen tax burdens on small-scale prospectors who made discoveries after years of fruitless search. Discovery depletion deductions allowed the discoverer of any new mineral deposit to recoup not only his costs but also the materially larger appreciated value of the property at the time its profitability was established. In 1921, disturbed by the extent to which large discovery depletion deductions were being used to offset other income, Congress limited annual discovery depletion to the amount of net income from the mineral property. In 1924, it further lowered this limitation to 50 percent of net income.

Discovery depletion was eliminated for oil and gas properties in 1926, and for metals, sulfur, and coal in 1932, by substituting allowances based on a percentage of gross income. The 50 percent of net income limitation was retained. Percentage depletion was gradually substituted for discovery depletion on other minerals, until, in 1954, discovery depletion was eliminated altogether. The original percentage depletion rates for oil and gas and metals were, in general, fixed at levels designed to afford these industries approximately the same total annual depletion which they had been allowed under discovery depletion. The percentage depletion rates on coal, sulfur, and other nonmetallics were not based on industry experience under prior discovery depletion allowances but were selected to provide tax relief and incentives deemed suitable by Congress in view of the rates accorded oil and gas and metals. Subsequent legislation increased these rates in numerous cases.

EXPLORATION AND DEVELOPMENT COSTS

In addition to depletion allowances, the tax law also provides special treatment for certain capital expenditures incurred in bringing mineral properties into production. Section 617 of the Internal Revenue Code permits a taxpayer to write off as incurred the costs of exploring to ascertain the existence, location, extent, or quality of mineral deposits (except oil and gas wells). Deductions for such expenditures are subject to recapture when a mine reaches production or is disposed of.

Section 616 of the Internal Revenue Code permits a taxpayer either to write off as incurred the costs of developing a mineral deposit (except oil and gas wells) or to set these up as deferred expenses to be deducted ratably as the deposit is exhausted. Development expenses include expenditures for mine shafts, tunnels, and stripping which are incurred after the presence of minerals in sufficient quantity and quality to justify commercial exploitation has been ascertained. If the expenditures are incurred during the development stage of a mine, the election to treat the expenditures as a deferred expense only applies to the excess of the expenditures over the net proceeds from the mine during the year the expenses were incurred; if the expenditures are incurred during the production stage of a mine, the full amount of the expenditure may be treated as a deferred expense.

Section 263(c) of the Revenue Code grants oil and gas operators the option of either capitalizing or charging as a current expense so-called intangible drilling and development costs of wells. The expenses currently deductible include those for labor, fuel and power, materials and supplies, tool rental, repairs of drilling equipment, and nonrecoverable materials used in drilling, if incurred while drilling a well or preparing it for production. There is no ceiling on the amount of such outlays which may be deducted.

The privilege of expensing the intangible drilling and development costs of oil and gas wells has existed since an administrative ruling under the Revenue Act of 1916; a concurrent resolution of Congress in 1945 assured its continuance, and finally an express statutory provision was incorporated in the Internal Revenue Code of 1954.

To some extent, exploration costs of oil and gas wells are also currently expensed through loss deductions which are allowed by the regulations governing the treatment of the cost of exploration projects that prove unsuccessful and are dropped (such as dry wells and surrendered leases).

When currently expensed, the capital costs incurred in the development of mineral properties are not included in the adjusted basis of the properties, which determines the sum to be recovered through cost depletion. Broadly speaking, these deductions are in lieu of cost-depletion deductions. On the other hand, the expensing of such costs does not serve to reduce percentage-depletion allowances, which are based on the income from the property.

OTHER SPECIAL TAX PROVISIONS

A number of other specific provisions afford special tax treatment to taxpayers in the extractive industries. For example, special treatment is accorded income arising from certain types of timber cutting and iron and coal mining operations. A taxpayer owning timber or the contract right to cut timber for more than one year may elect to treat cutting the timber as a realization event that gives rise to §1231 gain or loss, rather than ordinary income. §§631(a), 1231(b)(2).[17] The election to treat income from timber as a capital gain extends to producers of Christmas trees which are more than six years old when cut. §631(a) (last sentence). A taxpayer owning timber or coal or iron ore for more than one year before its disposal who retains an economic interest following such a disposal is also permitted to treat the royalties received under §1231. §§631(b)-(c), 1231(b)(2). Recall that the hotchpot characterization approach of §1231, Chapter 14D above, provides that net section 1231 gain for the taxable year may be treated as long-term capital gain, but if the result of all transactions subject to §1231 for the year is a net loss it is treated as an ordinary loss.

References

A. *What Is Depreciable:* Beghe, Income Tax Treatment of Covenants Not to Compete, Consulting Agreements and Transfer of Goodwill, 30 Tax Law. 587 (1977); Blum, Valuing Intangibles: Choices for Valuing Professional Sports Teams, 45 J. Taxn. 286 (1976); Gregorich, Amortization of Intangibles: A Reassessment of the Tax Treatment of Purchased Intangibles, 28 Tax Law. 251 (1975); Lurie, Depreciating Structures Bought Under Long Leases: An Adventure in Blunderland, 18 N.Y.U. Inst. on Fed. Taxn. 43 (1960). Note, Amortization of Intangibles: An Examination of the Tax Treatment of Purchased Goodwill, 81 Harv. L. Rev. 859 (1968).

B. *Rates and Methods:* Auerbach & Jorgenson, The First Year Capital Recovery System, 10 Tax Notes 515 (1980); Blum, Accelerated Depreciation: A Proper Allowance for Measuring Net Income?!!, 78 Mich. L. Rev. 1172 (1980); Kahn, Accelerated Depreciation Revisited—A Reply to Professor Blum, 78 Mich. L. Rev. 1185 (1980); McCabe, ACRS—After the First Year, 41 N.Y.U. Inst. on Fed. Taxn. 9 (1983).

C. *The Economics of Capital Cost Allowances:* Hall & Jorgenson, Tax Policy and Investment Behavior, 57 Am. Econ. Rev. 391 (1967).

D. *Other Investment Stimuli:* Chevis, An Analysis of the Effects of TEFRA on ACRS and Investment Credit Allowances, 58 J. Taxn. 42 (1983); Harney, The Investment Credit: Experiences to Date, 22 N.Y.U. Inst. on Fed. Taxn. 519 (1964).

E. *Disposition of Depreciable Property: Recapture or Conversion:* Schapiro, Recapture of Depreciation and Section 1245 of the Internal Revenue

---

17. The purpose of this provision is to give the taxpayer the benefit of the capital gain rate which he would get if he sold the timber for cutting rather than cutting it himself.

Code, 72 Yale L.J. 1483 (1963); Horvitz, Sections 1250 and 1245: The Puddle and the Lake, 20 Tax L. Rev. 285 (1965).

F. Depletion of Mineral Deposits: Baker & Griswold, Percentage Depletion — A Correspondence, 64 Harv. L. Rev. 361 (1951); Galvin, The "Ought" and "Is" of Oil-and-Gas Taxation, 73 Harv. L. Rev. 1441 (1960).

Chapter 16 — *Leverage, Leasing, and Tax Shelter Limitations*

A. LEVERAGE

1. Overvaluation

ESTATE OF FRANKLIN v. COMMISSIONER
544 F.2d 1045 (9th Cir. 1976)

Before Barnes, Trask and Sneed, Circuit Judges.

SNEED, Circuit Judge: This case involves another effort on the part of the Commissioner to curb the use of real estate tax shelters.[1] In this instance he seeks to disallow deductions for the taxpayers' distributive share of losses reported by a limited partnership with respect to its acquisition of motel and related property. These "losses" have their origin in deductions for depreciation and interest claimed with respect to the motel and related property. These deductions were disallowed by the Commissioner on the ground

---

1. An early skirmish in this particular effort appears in Manual D. Mayerson, 47 T.C. 340 (1966), which the Commissioner lost. The Commissioner attacked the substance of a nonrecourse sale, but based his attack on the nonrecourse and long-term nature of the purchase money note, without focusing on whether the sale was made at an unrealistically high price. In his acquiescence to Mayerson, 1969-2 Cum. Bull. xxiv, the Commissioner recognized that the fundamental issue in these cases generally will be whether the property has been "acquired" at an artificially high price, having little relation to its fair market value. "The Service emphasizes that its acquiescence in Mayerson is based on the particular facts in the case and will not be relied upon in the disposition of other cases except where it is clear that the property has been acquired at its fair market value in an arm's length transaction creating a bona fide purchase and a bona fide debt obligation." Rev. Rul. 69-77, 1969-1 Cum. Bull. 59.

either that the acquisition was a sham or that the entire acquisition transaction was in substance the purchase by the partnership of an option to acquire the motel and related property on January 15, 1979. The Tax Court held that the transaction constituted an option exercisable in 1979 and disallowed the taxpayers' deductions. Estate of Charles T. Franklin, 64 T.C. 752 (1975). We affirm this disallowance although our approach differs somewhat from that of the Tax Court.

The interest and depreciation deductions were taken by Twenty-Fourth Property Associates (hereinafter referred to as Associates), a California limited partnership of which Charles T. Franklin and seven other doctors were the limited partners. The deductions flowed from the purported "purchase" by Associates of the Thunderbird Inn, an Arizona motel, from Wayne L. Romney and Joan E. Romney (hereinafter referred to as the Romneys) on November 15, 1968.

Under a document entitled "Sales Agreement," the Romneys agreed to "sell" the Thunderbird Inn to Associates for $1,224,000. The property would be paid for over a period of ten years, with interest on any unpaid balance of seven and one-half percent per annum. "Prepaid interest" in the amount of $75,000 was payable immediately; monthly principal and interest installments of $9,045.36 would be paid for approximately the first ten years, with Associates required to make a balloon payment at the end of the ten years of the difference between the remaining purchase price, forecast as $975,000, and any mortgages then outstanding against the property.

The purchase obligation of Associates to the Romneys was nonrecourse; the Romneys' only remedy in the event of default would be forfeiture of the partnership's interest. The sales agreement was recorded in the local county. A warranty deed was placed in an escrow account, along with a quitclaim deed from Associates to the Romneys, both documents to be delivered either to Associates upon full payment of the purchase price, or to the Romneys upon default.

The sale was combined with a leaseback of the property by Associates to the Romneys; Associates therefore never took physical possession. The lease payments were designed to approximate closely the principal and interest payments with the consequence that with the exception of the $75,000 prepaid interest payment no cash would cross between Associates and Romneys until the balloon payment. The lease was on a net basis; thus, the Romneys were responsible for all of the typical expenses of owning the motel property including all utility costs, taxes, assessments, rents, charges, and levies of "every name, nature and kind whatsoever." The Romneys also were to continue to be responsible for the first and second mortgages until the final purchase installment was made; the Romneys could, and indeed did, place additional mortgages on the property without the permission of Associates. Finally, the Romneys were allowed to propose new capital improvements which Associates would be required to either build themselves or allow the Romneys to construct with compensating modifications in rent or purchase price.

In holding that the transaction between Associates and the Romneys more nearly resembled an option than a sale, the Tax Court emphasized that Associates had the power at the end of ten years to walk away from the transaction and merely lose its $75,000 "prepaid interest payment." It also pointed out that a *deed* was never recorded and that the "benefits and burdens of ownership" appeared to remain with the Romneys. Thus, the sale was combined with a leaseback in which no cash would pass; the Romneys remained responsible under the mortgages, which they could increase; and the Romneys could make capital improvements.[2] The Tax Court further justified its "option" characterization by reference to the nonrecourse nature of the purchase money debt and the nice balance between the rental and purchase money payments.

Our emphasis is different from that of the Tax Court. We believe the characteristics set out above can exist in a situation in which the sale imposes upon the purchaser a genuine indebtedness within the meaning of section 167(a), Internal Revenue Code of 1954, which will support both interest and depreciation deductions. They substantially so existed in Hudspeth v. Commissioner, 509 F.2d 1224 (9th Cir. 1975) in which parents entered into sale-leaseback transactions with their children. The children paid for the property by executing nonnegotiable notes and mortgages equal to the fair market value of the property; state law proscribed deficiency judgments in case of default, limiting the parents' remedy to foreclosure of the property. The children had no funds with which to make mortgage payments; instead, the payments were offset in part by the rental payments, with the difference met by gifts from the parents to their children. Despite these characteristics this court held that there was a bona fide indebtedness on which the children, to the extent of the rental payments, could base interest deductions. See also American Realty Trust v. United States, 498 F.2d 1194 (4th Cir. 1974); Manuel D. Mayerson, 47 T.C. 340 (1966).

In none of these cases, however, did the taxpayer fail to demonstrate that the purchase price was at least approximately equivalent to the fair market value of the property. Just such a failure occurred here. The Tax Court explicitly found that on the basis of the facts before it the value of the property could not be estimated. 64 T.C. at 767-768.[4] In our view this defect in the taxpayers' proof is fatal.

---

2. There was evidence that not all of the benefits and burdens of ownership remained with the Romneys. Thus, for example, the leaseback agreement appears to provide that any condemnation award will go to Associates, Exhibit 6-F, at p. 5.

4. The Tax Court found that appellants had "not shown that the purported sales price of $1,224,000 (or any other price) had any relationship to the actual market value of the motel property. . . ." 64 T.C. at 767.

Petitioners spent a substantial amount of time at trial attempting to establish that, whatever the actual market value of the property, Associates acted in the good faith belief that the market value of the property approximated the selling price. However, this evidence only goes to the issue of sham and

Reason supports our perception. An acquisition such as that of Associates if at a price approximately equal to the fair market value of the property under ordinary circumstances would rather quickly yield an equity in the property which the purchaser could not prudently abandon. This is the stuff of substance. It meshes with the form of the transaction and constitutes a sale.

No such meshing occurs when the purchase price exceeds a demonstrably reasonable estimate of the fair market value. Payments on the principal of the purchase price yield no equity so long as the unpaid balance of the purchase price exceeds the then existing fair market value. Under these circumstances the purchaser by abandoning the transaction can lose no more than a mere chance to acquire an equity in the future should the value of the acquired property increase. While this chance undoubtedly influenced the Tax Court's determination that the transaction before us constitutes an option, we need only point out that its existence fails to supply the substance necessary to justify treating the transaction as a sale ab initio. It is not necessary to the disposition of this case to decide the tax consequences of a transaction such as that before us if in a subsequent year the fair market value of the property increases to an extent that permits the purchaser to acquire an equity.[5]

Authority also supports our perception. It is fundamental that "depreciation is not predicated upon ownership of property *but rather upon an investment in property.* Gladding Dry Goods Co., 2 BTA 336 (1925)." Mayerson, supra at 350 (italics added). No such investment exists when payments of the purchase price in accordance with the design of the parties yield no equity to the purchaser. Cf. Decon Corp., 65 T.C. 829 (1976); David F. Bolger, 59 T.C. 760 (1973); Edna Morris, 59 T.C. 21 (1972). In the transaction before us and during the taxable years in question the purchase price payments by Associates have not been shown to constitute an *investment in the property.*

---

does not supply substance to this transaction. "Save in those instances where the statute itself turns on intent, a matter so real as taxation must depend on objective realities, not on the varying subjective beliefs of individual taxpayers." Lynch v. Commissioner, 273 F.2d 867, 872 (2d Cir. 1959). See also Bornstein v. Commissioner, 334 F.2d 779 (1st Cir. 1964); MacRae v. Commissioner, 294 F.2d 56 (9th Cir. 1961).

In oral argument it was suggested by the appellants that neither the Tax Court nor they recognized the importance of fair market value during the presentation of evidence and that this hampered the full and open development of this issue. However, upon an examination of the record, we are satisfied that the taxpayers recognized the importance of presenting objective evidence of the fair market value and were awarded ample opportunity to present their proof; appellants merely failed to present clear and admissible evidence that fair market value did indeed approximate the purchase price. Such evidence of fair market value as was relied upon by the appellants, viz. two appraisals, one completed in 1968 and a second in 1971, even if fully admissible as evidence of the truth of the estimates of value appearing therein, does not require us to set aside the Tax Court's finding. As the Tax Court found, the 1968 appraisal was "error-filled, sketchy" and "obviously suspect." 64 T.C. at 767 n.13. The 1971 appraisal had little relevancy as to 1968 values. On the other side, there existed cogent evidence indicating that the fair market value was substantially less than the purchase price. This evidence included (i) the Romneys' purchase of the stock of the two corporations, one of which wholly-owned the motel, for approximately $800,000 in the year preceding the "sale" to Associates ($660,000 of which was allocable to the sale property, according to Mr. Romneys estimate), and (ii) insurance policies on the property from 1967 through 1974 of only $583,200, $700,000, and $614,000. 64 T.C. at 767-768.

Given that it was the appellants' burden to present evidence showing that the purchase price did not exceed the fair market value and that he had a fair opportunity to do so, we see no reason to remand this case for further proceedings.

5. These consequences would include a determination of the proper basis of the acquired property at the date the increments to the purchaser's equity commenced.

Depreciation was properly disallowed. Only the Romneys had an investment in the property.

Authority also supports disallowance of the interest deductions. This is said even though it has long been recognized that the absence of personal liability for the purchase money debt secured by a mortgage on the acquired property does not deprive the debt of its character as a bona fide debt obligation able to support an interest deduction. *Mayerson*, supra at 352. However, this is no longer true when it appears that the debt has economic significance only if the property substantially appreciates in value prior to the date at which a very large portion of the purchase price is to be discharged. Under these circumstances the purchaser has not secured "the use or forbearance of money." See Norton v. Commissioner, 474 F.2d 608, 610 (9th Cir. 1973). Nor has the seller advanced money or forborne its use. See Bornstein v. Commissioner, 334 F.2d 779, 780 (1st Cir. 1964); Lynch v. Commissioner, 273 F.2d 867, 871-872 (2d Cir. 1959). Prior to the date at which the balloon payment on the purchase price is required, and assuming no substantial increase in the fair market value of the property, the absence of personal liability on the debt reduces the transaction in economic terms to a mere chance that a genuine debt obligation may arise. This is not enough to justify an interest deduction. To justify the deduction the debt must exist; potential existence will not do. For debt to exist, the purchaser, in the absence of personal liability, must confront a situation in which it is presently reasonable from an economic point of view for him to make a capital investment in the amount of the unpaid purchase price. See *Mayerson*, supra at 352.[6] Associates, during the taxable years in question, confronted no such situation. Compare Crane v. Commissioner, 331 U.S. 1, 11-12 (1947).

Our focus on the relationship of the fair market value of the property to the unpaid purchase price should not be read as premised upon the belief that a sale is not a sale if the purchaser pays too much. Bad bargains from the buyer's point of view—as well as sensible bargains from buyer's, but exceptionally good from the seller's point of view—do not thereby cease to be sales. See Commissioner v. Brown, 380 U.S. 563 (1965); Union Bank v. United States, 285 F.2d 126, 128, 152 Ct. Cl. 126 (1961). We intend our holding and explanation thereof to be understood as limited to transactions substantially similar to that now before us.

Affirmed.

Question

The taxpayer in *Estate of Franklin* failed to prove any particular value for the Thunderbird Inn and was therefore not allowed any deductions for

---

6. Emphasis on the fair market value of the property in relation to the apparent purchase price animates the spirit, if not the letter, of Rev. Rul. 69-77, 1969-1 Cum. Bull. 59.

depreciation (or interest). But suppose the taxpayer had offered to show that the property was in fact worth half the amount of the nonrecourse loan and argued that it would be unconstitutional not to allow him depreciation and interest deductions to that extent. Should the case then have been remanded for a more specific finding on value?

PLEASANT SUMMIT LAND CORP. v. COMMISSIONER
863 F.2d 263 (3d Cir.), cert. denied sub nom. Commissioner v. Prussin,
493 U.S. 901 (1989)

Before: Higginbotham, Mansmann, and Greenberg, Circuit Judges.

GREENBERG, Circuit Judge. . . . On May 3, 1978, in an arm's length transaction, PSLC entered into an agreement to purchase the Summit House, a property on Summit Street, West Orange, New Jersey, containing two apartment buildings and a small separate resident manager's apartment for $4,200,000. The purchase was closed on or about June 1, 1978 and the consideration was paid by $250,000 in cash, by delivery of a $1,350,000 note secured by a purchase money mortgage, and by PSLC taking title subject to a previously existing $2,600,000 nonrecourse mortgage.

Contemporaneously with the purchase, PSLC created a wholly owned subsidiary, Mount Orange Realty Corp. (MORC), to which it then sold the Summit House buildings while retaining the land beneath them. The sale price to MORC was $5,200,000, consisting of $500,000 in cash which MORC borrowed or owed and a $4,700,000 nonrecourse mortgage which wrapped around and was subject to the prior two mortgages. . . .

PSLC then sold its MORC stock to the newly created PSA, which was organized to acquire the Summit House, for $2,559,200, paid in the form of a nonrecourse note secured by the MORC shares, for which a mortgage of Summit House to PSLC was immediately substituted. . . . PSA then dissolved MORC, took direct ownership of the Summit House buildings and took over MORC's obligations including the $500,000 due on the purchase of the Summit House and the $4,700,000 nonrecourse wraparound mortgage. Thus, the cost to PSA for acquisition of Summit House was the $2,559,200 indebtedness for the purchase of the MORC shares, assumption of MORC's $500,000 obligation, and assumption of MORC's $4,700,000 nonrecourse wraparound mortgage for a total of $7,759,200. . . . The consequence of these transactions was to leave PSA with large debts with interest charges and a substantial depreciable asset, a situation setting up the possibility for it to claim large tax deductions. . . .

PSA sold thirty limited partnership units to a group of investors including George Prussin for a total of $1,980,000 paid with down payments and subsequent installments. . . .

PSA reported losses on its income tax returns for 1978 and 1979, and later years, largely attributable to interest deductions and depreciation.

These losses were passed through to the limited partners who used them to offset income on their individual tax returns. On December 19, 1985 an unrelated third party purchased the Summit House land from PSLC and the buildings and lease from PSA for a total of $7,000,000. . . .

Given her consideration of many different bases for finding fair market value and the Prussins' failure to present expert testimony on value, we conclude that Judge Cohen's findings as to the maximum fair market value were not clearly erroneous. Accordingly, we will not disturb her finding that the nonrecourse financing exceeded the fair market value of Summit House. . . .

Of the cases decided by other courts of appeals, that most similar to this case is Odend'hal v. Commissioner, 748 F.2d 908. *Odend'hal* stands for the proposition that if the fair market value of property is less than its nonrecourse financing, the principal of the nonrecourse financing in excess of fair market value is not included in the basis for the purpose of claiming depreciation. Moreover, *Odend'hal* holds this excess nonrecourse debt does not sustain a deduction for interest payments. . . .

While we regard *Odend'hal* and *Estate of Franklin* as the appropriate precedents, we do not consider them as authority to eliminate all deductions for interest and depreciation. While we realize that a taxpayer holding property subject to a nonrecourse debt in excess of the market value of the property may have no incentive to pay off any portion of the debt, including the amount not exceeding the fair market value of the property, it is equally logical to recognize that the creditor holding the debt has no incentive to take back the property if the taxpayer offers to pay the debt up to the value of the property. For example, if a creditor held a nonrecourse debt for $1,500,000 on a property with a fair market value of $1,000,000, he would have a disincentive to foreclose if his defaulting debtor offered to settle the debt for not less than $1,000,000. Thus, it is appropriate to disregard only the portion of nonrecourse debt in excess of the fair market value of the property when it was acquired for purposes of calculations of the depreciation and interest deductions and to regard the nonrecourse debt as genuine indebtedness to the extent it is not disregarded. Moreover, there is precedent for disallowing deductions based on nonrecourse debt only insofar as attributable to the excess of debt over the fair market value. See *Odend'hal*, 748 F.2d at 912-914.

Unquestionably the record compels the conclusion that Summit House, though not exceeding $4,200,000 in fair market value, had a substantial value. Thus, under our analysis the Tax Court's determination that the deductions should be disallowed in full cannot be sustained. Accordingly, we will remand the case to the Tax Court for a determination of fair market value of Summit House at the time of PSA's acquisition. . . .

ON PETITION FOR REHEARING

GREENBERG, Circuit Judge. . . . While the Commissioner dismisses the compromise possibility as "entirely speculative" and "wholly unpredictable at the time the borrower acquires the property subject to the nonrecourse note" his argument proves too much because the concept of disallowance of the deductions in excess non-recourse financing situations is based on the theoretical economic disincentive to the borrower to pay the debt rather than upon what ultimately happens. It is no more speculative to assume that the lender will act rationally in compromising than it is to assume that the borrower will not foolishly pay the entire nonrecourse debt. We said as much in our original opinion and we see no reason to change our conclusion in this regard.

The Commissioner's Petition for Rehearing will be denied.

Notes and Questions

1. *Incentives.* Do you find edification in the argument between the Third Circuit and the government concerning debtors' and creditors' incentives to pay or to compromise?

Many people concerned with curbing abusive tax shelters talked about incentives at an earlier stage in the transaction: The holding in *Franklin* would give promoters and taxpayers an incentive not to overvalue, while under *Pleasant Summit* they have nothing to lose by giving it a try. Should those incentives have been given more explicit attention in the court's opinions?

2. In March 1991 the IRS formally and forcefully rejected the Third Circuit decision in *Pleasant Summit* (despite the Supreme Court's denial of certiorari): It asserted that "the issue has currently demonstrable administrative importance," and announced that it would continue to litigate this issue based on the rationale of *Estate of Franklin*. IRS, Action on Decision 1991-09 (March 29, 1991). For one court's rejection of *Pleasant Summit*, citing other rejections, see Bergstrom v. United States, 37 Fed. Cl. 164 (1996).

3. Reexamine the Supreme Court decision in Commissioner v. Tufts, Chapter 7D above. What is its relation to the decision in *Estate of Franklin?* See, e.g., Odend'hal v. Commissioner, 748 F.2d 908 (4th Cir. 1984); Andrews, On Beyond *Tufts*, 61 Taxes 949 (1983).

4. What is the effect of *Estate of Franklin* on the tax treatment of Fred Bayles, who purchased Tufts' and his partners' interests? In other words, is *Estate of Franklin* applicable to a preexisting mortgage debt payable to some one other than the seller? Under what circumstances?

5. Nonrecourse purchase-money debt has sometimes been used to pay inflated prices for more speculative property than rental real estate — motion picture films, for example, or lithographic plates, or master recordings, sometimes by quite unknown artists. For clear and sensible opinions dealing with nonrecourse debt in an oil and gas drilling partnership and a motion picture partnership, see, respectively, Brountas v. Commissioner,

692 F.2d 152 (1st Cir. 1982), cert. denied, 462 U.S. 1106 (1983) and Brannen v. Commissioner, 722 F.2d 695 (11th Cir. 1984).

6. Congress has addressed the problem of overvaluation by imposing special penalties on taxpayers, appraisers, and tax-shelter promoters. See §§6662(b)(3), (e), (h), 6695A, and 6700.

Problem

Titus Tufts constructed an apartment building for $2,000,000, borrowing $1,800,000 of the construction cost on a nonrecourse note. Titus held the building for several years but it did not rent successfully, and no payments were ever made on the principal of the loan. Titus has received nothing from his investment in the property except depreciation deductions of $600,000. The nonrecourse lender has recently had the property examined by an appraiser who says that its value cannot possibly exceed $1,400,000.

The nonrecourse lender was about to foreclose when Felicia Franklin, an experienced real estate developer and promoter, came along with the suggestion that she purchase the property from Titus, subject to the nonrecourse mortgage. This she would only do on the condition that the nonrecourse loan be renegotiated to provide a lower interest rate and deferral of all principal payments until five years after her acquisition of the property. The lender and Titus agreed happily to this proposal; indeed, Titus seemed anxious to convey his interest to Felicia for nothing, but Felicia insisted, successfully, that she pay him $2,000.

(a) What are the federal income tax consequences of this transaction for all the parties (Titus, Felicia, and the nonrecourse lender)?

(b) Under Felicia's management the apartment building soon became a great success. After four years she sold it back to Titus, still subject to the $1,800,000 nonrecourse loan, for a cash payment of $200,000. How will Felicia's gain be computed and taxed on this sale?

2. The At-Risk Limitation

Read §465, and try to get some sense of its import.

Originally, in 1976, the at-risk limitation applied only to the activities listed in §465(b). It was soon extended to all activities except that of owning real estate. In 1986 the general exclusion for real estate was replaced by the qualified nonrecourse debt provision in §465(b)(6).

Amount at risk is apparently something like basis but without the benefit of the *Crane* rule: basis but *not* including nonrecourse debt. Be clear, however, that §465 does not change the basis rules themselves. And those are still important because the at-risk limitation applies only to *losses* (that is, an excess of deductions over income from the relevant activity).

Amount at risk excludes some fully recourse loans (loans that may represent a very real economic risk for the taxpayer) if they are from persons with some interest in the activity other than that of creditor or if some other person bears the primary liability with respect to them.

Questions

1. How would §465 now apply to *Estate of Franklin* and *Pleasant Summit?*
2. What is the need for §465, given decisions like that in *Franklin* and *Pleasant Summit?* What additional ground, if any, does it cover?
3. Conversely, given §465, what is the continuing significance, if any, of decisions like those in *Estate of Franklin* and *Pleasant Summit?*

3. The Economics of Leverage and Taxes

A conservatively financed, residential real estate venture might show an initial balance sheet something like this.

Building	$1,000,000	Mortgage	$800,000
		Partners' equity	200,000

The mortgage requires $105,000 level annual payments to be applied first to interest at 12 percent on the outstanding principal, with the remainder to principal reduction. This mortgage will pay off in less than 22 years. Rents are estimated at $150,000 and current expenses for taxes, repairs, and the like at $26,000. Depreciation will be charged using the straight-line method over 27.5 years.

The results of operations for the first year are therefore projected as follows.

Cash Flow		*Taxable Income*	
Rent	$150,000	Rent	$150,000
Current expenses	(26,000)	Current expenses	(26,000)
Interest	(96,000)	Interest	(96,000)
Principal reduction	(9,000)	Depreciation	(36,364)
Net left for investors	$19,000	Net Loss	($8,364)
Tax savings (@ 35%)	2,927		
Total return	$21,927		

How would you advise a client considering an investment on the basis of these figures? How should an arrangement like this be taxed? If you want to explore these questions in simple quantitative terms, see the Appendix in the back of the book.

In Chapter 15C it was shown how the effect of allowing an immediate deduction for any investment is to exempt the return on that investment from the burden of the tax. Illustrations there show how the after-tax and pretax *rates* of return are equal — the effective rate of tax is zero — if a taxpayer's investment is immediately deductible.

The effect of leverage — borrowing to pay all or part of the cost of the investment — may be to enable a taxpayer to deduct more than net investment, and the effect of that will be to make the after-tax rate of return on after-tax investment *greater than* the pretax rate of return.

The point can be illustrated by extending the illustrations in Chapter 15C.1.

The first case in 15C.1 was a 33 percent taxpayer who bought a 12 percent perpetual $1,000 bond on a deductible basis. The discussion there showed that the effect of immediate deductibility was to enable that taxpayer to make an after-tax return of $80 a year on an after-tax investment of $670, which amounts to the same *rate* of return (12 percent) as in the absence of tax.

Suppose purchase of the bond is financed, in part, by borrowing $500 at 11 percent interest. Net income from the investment, before tax, is then $65 ($120 interest received minus $55 interest paid) on a net investment of $500, for a rate of return of 13 percent. In effect there is a 12 percent return on the investor's own funds, plus a profit of 1 percent on investment of the borrowed funds. This is an illustration of the normal effect of leverage without regard to taxes: If money can be borrowed at a lower rate than that at which it is invested, the net rate of return will be even higher than the gross return on investment. If, on the other hand, the interest rate on borrowing were more than 12 percent, the net return to the borrower would drop below 12 percent to reflect the net loss on the borrowed funds.

Now again consider income taxes. The income tax on net income from this arrangement will be 33 percent of $65, or $21, since the interest received is fully taxable and interest paid is fully deductible. This leaves $44 of net income after tax.

But the taxpayer's net, after-tax investment is now only $170: $1,000 for the bond minus $500 borrowed and $330 of tax savings from deducting the $1,000 cost of the bond. A net after-tax annual return of $44 on a net after-tax investment of $170 is a rate of return of 25.9 percent, almost twice the pretax rate of return. The effective rate of tax is thus *minus* 99 percent! A negative income tax indeed!

This illustration is worth playing with. What will happen when the taxpayer disposes of the bond and pays off the borrowing? What would happen if the taxpayer borrowed a higher portion of the purchase price of the bond? (80, 90, and even 100 percent financing is not uncommon in real estate transactions.) What would happen to the pretax and after-tax rates of return if the interest rate on the taxpayer's borrowing were higher than on the bond? Would it ever pay to borrow at 13 percent in order to buy a 12 percent bond? (Sure; but how and why?)

Another way to analyze this illustration is to consider the tax effect on the unleveraged investment and on the cost of borrowing separately. Immediate deduction of an investment makes the effective rate of tax zero; hence our 12 percent bond yields 12 percent, even after tax, since the cost is deductible. On the other hand, if borrowing is treated in the normal manner,[1] the tax lowers the effective cost of borrowing by its full nominal amount. Hence the after-tax cost of borrowing in our case is only 7.4 percent $(11 \times (1 - .33))$. Of course there is a big profit to be made with a differential of 4.6 points between cost of funds and return on investment!

This perspective suggests that a 33 percent taxpayer can make some net after-tax return on a 12 percent investment whose cost is immediately deductible if the after-tax purchase price can be borrowed at any pretax interest rate below 17.9 percent.

Check this suggestion carefully. What does it imply about tax policy if it is true? Cf. §265(2), and materials in Chapter 10A.2 above.

The second illustration in Chapter 15C.1 above postulated an expenditure of $100 in one period that returns $400 in some subsequent period; it showed that the ratio of return to expenditure is the same after tax as before if the expenditure is currently deductible.

Now suppose the taxpayer's $100 expenditure is the net result of borrowing $50 and expending $150, and that the whole $150 is deductible. Then the net after-tax outlay, for the 33 percent taxpayer in the illustration, would be $50.50, calculated as follows: $150 expended minus $50 borrowed and $49.50 saved in taxes. Now the $400 return is the net pretax return after repaying interest and principal on the loan. Interest on the loan would be deductible, but principal would not, so the amount taxable would be $450 and the tax would be $148.50 leaving an after-tax return of $251.50. A net after-tax return of $251.50 from an investment of $50.50 represents a profit of $201, just as in Chapter 15C.1; but $201 profit on an investment of $50 represents a *rate* of return[2] of 402 percent, considerably *more* than the rate of return in absence of tax. For a higher rate of tax or leverage the after-tax return would be even higher.

Here is a tabulation of these calculations, together with calculations for higher degrees of leverage.

---

1. Deduction allowed for interest paid, but proceeds not taxable and principal repayments not deductible.
2. Over the period of the investment, not annually.

$50 Borrowed, $150 Gross Investment Deducted

	Net Investment	Net Return	Profit	
Before Tax	$100	$400	$300	300%
Tax (@ 33%)	50	149	99	
After Tax	$ 50	$251	$201	402%

$100 Borrowed, $200 Gross Investment Deducted

	Net Investment	Net Return	Profit	
Before Tax	$100	$400	$300	300%
Tax (@ 33%)	66	165	99	
After Tax	$ 34	$235	$201	591%

$200 Borrowed, $300 Gross Investment Deducted

	Net Investment	Net Return	Profit	
Before Tax	$100	$400	$300	300%
Tax (@ 33%)	99	198	99	
After Tax	$ 1	$202	$201	20,100%!!

Questions

1. Would either of the limitations considered so far — *Estate of Franklin* or §465 — prevent the emergence of a negative effective tax rate as described in this section (and illustrated at greater length in the Appendix)?

2. What is the best argument to be made in favor of allowing a negative effective tax as described here? Do you find even the best argument convincing?

3. What would be needed to prevent negative income taxes for the wealthy as here described? Is such a general preventative warranted?

B. LEASING

1. Real Estate

The transaction in *Estate of Franklin* involved both a nonrecourse loan and a lease, but the decision turns entirely on the former. *Franklin* is applicable to a purchase of property for a nonrecourse obligation substantially in excess of fair market value whether or not there is also a lease back to the seller-lender party.

On the other hand, leases can raise problems in the absence of any overvaluation or nonrecourse liability. The simplest case arises if a taxpayer simply leases property from its owner, instead of purchasing it. Who then gets the depreciation deductions? The owner, of course. But what if the lease is for 99 years, and the lessee has an option to purchase the property for $1 at the end of the term, and the rent has been calculated to equal interest and principal, at current long-term rates, on the price at which the property would sell, and the lease is "net, net, net ..." meaning that the lessee is to pay every conceivable cost, like real estate taxes and assessments, and insurance, that he would have incurred as a purchaser of the property. A lease contract is essentially a transfer of some of the most important aspects of ownership — present possession and rights appurtenant thereto — in exchange for a stream of cash payments, and is thus similar to a sale of property on secured credit. It can be written to include more. A good property lawyer can presumably make it include just about everything of any significance, and thus virtually identical in effect to a sale. And if so, then the tax law will treat it as a sale and the purported "lessee" will be the owner entitled to the depreciation deductions. Helvering v. Lazarus & Co., 308 U.S. 252, 255 (1939).

Just how much of which incidents of ownership have to be retained by a lessor to prevent the lease being recharacterized as a sale is very hard to specify.

One subsidiary question is whether it matters that the lease is part of a sale and leaseback transaction, or that the price paid by the buyer-lessor in such a transaction is borrowed (from an independent, bona fide financing party like an insurance company). One might have thought that the answer to both these questions should be no, except that perhaps if most of the money comes from the lender and flows through to the seller-lessee, that would support an inference that the borrower-buyer-lessor was something of an accomodation party, which might somehow weaken his claim to ownership status. In Frank Lyon Co. v. United States, 435 U.S. 561 (1978), however, the Supreme Court got talked into exactly the opposite conclusion.

Here is a summary of *Frank Lyon* by the Tax Court, Nims, J., in Carol W. Hilton, 74 T.C. 305, 361-362, aff'd per curiam, 671 F.2d 316 (9th Cir.) cert. denied, 459 U.S. 907 (1982):

"... The facts of the *Frank Lyon* case are rather complicated but are pointedly significant. Initially, Worthen Bank & Trust Co. (Worthen) planned to construct a bank and office building. Its plans ran afoul of legal and regulatory restrictions and, as an alternative, Worthen proposed a sale and leaseback transaction. Bank regulatory authorities approved the plan as long as Worthen retained a repurchase option after the 15th year of the lease and obtained an independent third-party buyer-lessor. Frank Lyon Co. (Frank Lyon) became interested in the transaction and, after negotiating with several other equally interested entities, Worthen selected Frank Lyon to be the buyer-lessor. Meanwhile, Worthen had already arranged for the financing and the financiers approved Frank Lyon as the buyer-lessor.

"Frank Lyon, the purchaser, was a substantial corporate entity which participated actively in negotiating the terms and conditions of the sale and leaseback, was personally liable for the payment of the principal and paid, in addition to the mortgage financing, $500,000 out of its own funds to Worthen.

"The terms of the agreement called for Worthen to lease the land to Frank Lyon for 76 years and to sell the building and lease it back for a 25-year primary term and eight 5-year option terms. The sale and leaseback were effected simultaneously. The lease was a net lease, with Frank Lyon's only current financial obligation being the quarterly mortgage payments. Rent payments for the 25-year primary term were calculated to exactly equal the mortgage payments: $582,224 annually for the first 11 years and $613,156 annually for the succeeding 14 years. Thereafter, the amount of rent decreased to $300,000 per year during the option periods totaling 40 years. Worthen had options to repurchase the building at periodic intervals for the amount of the outstanding mortgage plus Frank Lyon's original $500,000 investment, with 6-percent interest compounded thereon.

"The District Court held that Frank Lyon was entitled to the depreciation and mortgage interest deductions. The court based its finding that the substance comported with the form on the facts that the rent payments were reasonable, the option prices represented the fair market value of the properties, and the unlikelihood that Worthen would exercise the repurchase option. It refused to draw any negative inference from the fact that rentals combined with the options were sufficient to amortize the loan and pay Frank Lyon a fixed 6-percent return on its equity or that the lease was a net lease.

"The Court of Appeals reversed. Analogizing property rights to "a bundle of sticks," the court concluded that Frank Lyon did not have sufficient sticks to allow it to be treated as the owner.

"The Supreme Court reversed the Court of Appeals, sustaining the form of the transaction, and held that Frank Lyon was indeed the owner of the property for tax purposes, holding that "so long as the lessor retains significant and genuine attributes of the traditional lessor status, the form of the transaction adopted by the parties governs for tax purposes." The Court was very careful to circumscribe the scope of its imprimatur: "we emphasize that we are not condoning manipulation by a taxpayer through arbitrary labels and dealings that have no economic significance," Frank Lyon Co. v. United States, supra at 584."

And now in the words of the Supreme Court itself, 435 U.S. at 574-576 Blackmun, J.:

The Government places great reliance on Helvering v. Lazarus & Co., supra, and claims it to be precedent that controls this case. The taxpayer there was a department store. The legal title of its three buildings was in a bank as trustee for land-trust certificate holders. When the transfer to the trustee was made, the trustee at the same time leased the buildings back to the taxpayer for 99 years, with option to renew and purchase. The Commissioner, in stark contrast to his posture in the present case, took the position that the statutory right to depreciation followed legal title. The Board of Tax Appeals, however, concluded that the transaction between the taxpayer and the bank in reality was a mortgage loan and allowed the taxpayer depreciation on the buildings. This Court, as had the Court of Appeals, agreed with that conclusion and affirmed. It regarded the "rent" stipulated in the leaseback as a promise to pay interest on the loan, and a "depreciation fund" required by the lease as an amortization fund designed to pay off the loan in the stated period. Thus, said the Court, the Board justifiably concluded that the transaction, although in written form a transfer of ownership with a leaseback, was actually a loan secured by the property involved.

The *Lazarus* case, we feel, is to be distinguished from the present one and is not controlling here. Its transaction was one involving only two (and not multiple) parties, the taxpayer-department store and the trustee-bank. The Court looked closely at the substance of the agreement between those two parties and rightly concluded that depreciation was deductible by the taxpayer despite the nomenclature of the instrument of conveyance and the leaseback. See also Sun Oil Co. v. Commissioner, 562 F.2d 258 (CA3 1977) (a two-party case with the added feature that the second party was a tax-exempt pension trust). The present case, in contrast, involves three parties, Worthen, Lyon, and the finance agency. The usual simple two-party arrangement was legally unavailable to Worthen. Independent investors were interested in participating in the alternative available to Worthen, and Lyon itself (also independent from Worthen) won the privilege. Despite Frank Lyon's presence on Worthen's board of directors, the transaction, as it ultimately developed, was not a familial one arranged by Worthen, but one compelled by the realities of the restrictions imposed upon the bank. Had Lyon not appeared, another interested investor would have been selected. The ultimate solution would have been essentially the same. Thus, the presence of the third party, in our view, significantly distinguishes this case from *Lazarus* and removes the latter as controlling authority.

Notes and Questions

1. Does the Court's focus on the presence of three parties instead of two, as a reason for not following the ruling in *Lazarus*, make any sense at all? Some New York lawyers were quoted as saying, with disdain (or glee), that in New York they had never seen a real estate tax shelter with less than seven parties.

2. The taxpayer's advocate in the Supreme Court was a distinguished former Solicitor General of the United States who had argued often before the Court on behalf of the government. He was also a distinguished tax lawyer and teacher and had argued other important tax cases in the Supreme Court, often for the government. The decision has been described as a failure of judicial process, resulting in part from the present government's failure to come up with an advocate or argument of sufficient stature or force to make the Court take a properly skeptical attitude toward some of the things said on the taxpayer's behalf. Wolfman, The Supreme Court in the Lyon's Den: A Failure of Judicial Process, 66 Cornell L. Rev. 1075 (1981). (In a coda to his article, Wolfman reports that Worthen Bank in fact did exercise its option to buy back the property at its earliest opportunity.)

3. Part of the taxpayer's argument in the Supreme Court was that the *Lyon* transaction could not have been significantly tax-motivated since both Worthen and Lyon were corporations subject to tax at the regular, top corporate income tax rate, and therefore any tax advantage to *Lyon* from the transaction would just offset an equal tax detriment to *Worthen*. These considerations were said to show that the motivation for the transaction was something else—overcoming banking regulatory obstacles—and also that the government will not suffer any net loss of revenue from the transaction. Wolfman's research reveals that Worthen, like many other banks at that time, was just barely into the top corporate rate and was able to maintain that position by adjusting its relative holdings of taxable and tax-exempt obligations, with the net result that its effective rate of tax on any substantial additional item of taxable income or deduction was the implicit rate of tax on tax-exempt obligations, which was lower than the top corporate rate.

4. Whatever the facts about tax avoidance in *Frank Lyon*, multi-party leveraged leases were a widespread way of generating net losses for syndication to tax shelter investors with other income to offset. What are the implications of the *Lyon* decision for them? What follows is a severely truncated version of an excellent Tax Court opinion dealing with that problem.

CAROL W. HILTON
74 T.C. 305, aff'd per curiam 671 F.2d 316 (9th Cir.),
cert. denied, 459 U.S. 907 (1982)

NIMS, Judge: . . . This case involves (1) a sale-leaseback transaction between Broadway-Hale Stores, Inc. (Broadway), as seller-lessee, and Fourth Cavendish Properties, Inc. (Fourth Cavendish), as buyer-lessor; (2) the transfer by Fourth Cavendish of its interest, if any, in the property, located in Bakersfield, Calif., which is the subject of the sale-leaseback transaction (the property) to Medway Associates, a New York general partnership (Medway); (3) the acquisition of various interests in Medway by a series of "tier" partnerships: Grenada Associates (Grenada), Fourteenth Property Associates (14th P.A.), and Thirty-Seventh Property Associates (37th P.A.); and (4) the investment by petitioners as limited partners in two of the tier partnerships: 14th P.A. and 37th P.A. . . .

The terms of this sale and leaseback transaction are fairly traditional. In 1964, Broadway, a large department store chain, decided to build a retail department store in a proposed shopping center in Bakersfield, Calif. Although Broadway would provide immediate financing for construction through internal sources, its intention from the start was to obtain long-term financing for the building once it had been completed.

It had been decided that the store would be financed by making use of what has come to be known in the trade as a single-purpose financing corporation, formed and availed of for, and limited to, the sole purpose of facilitating this one transaction. Under this plan, the single-purpose corporation, Fourth Cavendish, would sell its corporate notes to certain insurance company lenders. Broadway would then sell the property to Fourth Cavendish and funds derived from the sale of the notes would be paid to Broadway as the purchase price for the property. Simultaneously with the sale, Fourth Cavendish would lease the property back to Broadway. In February 1965, commitments were obtained from the insurance companies to provide the financing once the building was completed.

Construction of the store by Broadway was completed in January 1967, and the store was occupied and opened for business in February 1967. Fourth Cavendish was formed on January 17, 1967. The stock of Fourth Cavendish was held in the name of Wood, Struthers, a New York investment firm that served as the intermediary in negotiating the transaction between Broadway and the insurance companies. On December 20, 1967, Fourth Cavendish sold its mortgage notes to the lenders and turned the proceeds over to Broadway as the purchase price for the property.

The entire cost of the purchase was raised by the sale of mortgage notes. Broadway paid the commitment fees and commissions for arranging the sale of the mortgage notes. Fourth Cavendish then transferred the property back to Broadway as lessee under a net lease (the lease) for a 30-year term with options for Broadway to extend for another 68 years.

The mortgage notes were secured by an indenture of mortgage and deed of trust which conveyed Fourth Cavendish's interest in the property to trustees (the trustee) for the insurance companies and by an assignment of the lease and the rentals to the trustee.

The transaction and the lease were structured so that Broadway's relationship vis-a-vis the property remained virtually unchanged. The lease is of the type known in the trade as a "triple net" lease; it absolved Fourth Cavendish and its assignees of any financial obligation relating to the property except the obligation to make monthly principal and interest payments. Even this obligation was structured so that it would place no burden on Fourth Cavendish. Rent payments were calculated to provide the lessor with just enough money to meet the periodic principal and interest payments and expenses incident thereto for the 30-year term that the third-party financing was outstanding. Fourth Cavendish was not required to take the formal step of making the payments. The rent flowed directly to the insurance companies from Broadway.

The transaction was further structured so that when Fourth Cavendish or its assignee completes paying off the financing, rental payments (assuming renewal options are exercised by Broadway) will be reduced to $1\frac{1}{2}$ percent of the purchase price for the first renewal term of 23 years and to 1 percent of the purchase price for the second and third renewal terms.

At approximately the time that the sale and leaseback was effected in December 1967, Fourth Cavendish transferred its interest in the property to Medway, a general partnership that had just been formed to receive such interest. The partners in Medway were Cushman, holding a 50-percent partnership interest, MacGill, holding a 1-percent interest (both were partners in the Wood, Struthers investment firm), and a limited partnership that had just been formed, 14th P.A., which held a 49-percent interest.

It was to 14th P.A. that some of the petitioners in this case belonged as limited partners. The general partner in 14th P.A. was Jack R. Young & Associates (JRYA). The only contributions to 14th P.A. were made by the limited partners, who also held a 100-percent interest in the profits and losses of that partnership. Of the $180,000 contributed by the limited partners to the partnership, $70,000 was paid by the partnership to the general partner, JRYA, for "services," and the remainder $110,000 was paid to Medway as a capital contribution. Medway in turn paid the $110,000 to Cushman for services.

Fourteenth P.A. had only a 49-percent interest in Medway and thus a 49-percent interest in the property. A 51-percent interest in Medway (and thus the property) continued to be held by Cushman.

In 1969, Cushman and his colleagues [disposed of most of the remaining 51 percent interest through a similar set of partnership transactions]. . . . *

BACKGROUND

Broadway has used sale and leaseback transactions rather than conventional mortgage financing as a method of financing since 1947. This technique has enabled Broadway to carry an obligation on its books as rent rather than debt service, thus enabling Broadway to sidestep contractual limits on the amount of debt it could incur.

As sale and leaseback transactions were originally conceived in 1947, Broadway would simultaneously sell property directly to an insurance company and lease it back. Around 1964, the form of the transaction changed, and Broadway began to sell the property to a single-purpose financing corporation, which corporation (rather than an insurance company) would lease the property back to Broadway. The single-purpose financing corporation, which is established in each instance exclusively to effect a particular sale and leaseback transaction, would raise money to satisfy the purchase price by selling its newly issued bonds to insurance companies. The terms and conditions of and interest rates set by the insurance companies for the bonds would be governed by the going cost of money and the credit rating of Broadway.

Sale and leasebacks effected through single-purpose financing corporations were more advantageous to Broadway than a straight sale and leaseback

---

* [The foregoing synopsis of facts (beginning with the second excerpted paragraph) is inserted here from a later portion of the opinion, 74 T.C. at 343-345. — Eds.]

with an insurance company because the insurance companies treated the bond purchase in the same manner as they treated the purchase of any other security, even to the point that the insurance company's bond department, rather than its real estate department, conducted the transaction. The bond department generally charges a lower interest rate, provides 100-percent financing (as opposed to the 66⅔- to 75-percent limit for mortgage financing), and repayment terms such that less than the face amount of the financing has to be amortized over the term of the note. It also usually allows more self-insurance on the part of the seller-lessee.

Wood, Struthers & Winthrop (Wood, Struthers), a Wall Street brokerage firm which has dealt in the sale of securities on the various exchanges, was involved with Broadway in the modified form of sale and leasebacks from the inception. Robert Winthrop, a "name" partner at Wood, Struthers, made the firm's connection with Broadway through two of Broadway's top executives. Subsequently, Roderick Cushman (Cushman), the head of the Wood, Struthers real estate department, was the Wood, Struthers individual primarily concerned with negotiating various terms of the individual transactions. The Wood, Struthers real estate department would handle a transaction from beginning to end; it would negotiate the sale and leaseback with the lessee principals, establish the limited-purpose financing corporation, obtain permanent financing, and, ultimately, find investors. . . .

Jack R. Young (Young) promoted many Wood, Struthers transactions and he and his corporation, Jack R. Young & Associates, Inc. (JRYA), participated in the syndication of 50 to 60 limited partnerships during the years of 1967 to 1970. JRYA was a California corporation incorporated on May 11, 1966. Young owned approximately 75 percent of the stock and served as its president through 1967. Prior to embarking on a real estate career, Young was a life insurance salesman and a major portion of his clients were medical doctors, described by him as "relatively unsophisticated . . . investors . . . with [a] very limited knowledge in economics and finance," who looked to Young for advice concerning various investments which they were considering. Young found himself acting as a financial adviser, searching for good investments for his clients and for cures for financial woes brought on by the poor advice of others. Young considered himself a better financial adviser than many of those whom his clients were using, which point of view led him into the business of finding real estate investments for his clients. . . .

THE LEASE

. . . The lease, commonly known as a bond-type lease, is prior in right to the mortgage lien. The insurance companies lent money to Fourth Cavendish on the strength and security of the lease. The interest rate of 5⅛ percent charged by the insurance companies on the mortgage notes was tied to the credit rating of Broadway.

Annual rentals were calculated without regard to a fair market value rental. Annual rentals for the initial 30-year term were $198,603.75, or 6.33 percent of the purchase price of $3,137,500 paid by Fourth Cavendish to Broadway. This figure was calculated to provide that amount of cash flow necessary to satisfy interest and principal payments, when due (90 percent of the principal was to be amortized over the initial 30 years) and minor expenses (essentially the trustee's commission) amounting to approximately $200 to $300 per year. As to the first renewal term of 23 years, the lease provides annual rentals of $47,062.50, or 1^{1}/$_{2}$ percent of the purchase price, and for the second and third renewal periods of 23 and 22 years, respectively, the lease provides for annual rentals of $31,375, which is 1 percent of the purchase price. All the parties expected that the 10-percent balloon payment due at the end of the initial 30-year term would be financed, and future rentals would be about the amount necessary to pay off this financing.

Rents are to be paid directly to the trustee and are applied to the extent required to service the loan.

The terms of the lease and the simultaneous nature of the sale and leaseback are such that Broadway's status vis-a-vis the land and building underwent no appreciable change after the sale-leaseback was effected. Possession of the property was never actually transferred to Fourth Cavendish or the partnerships. The 30-year lease, with renewable options of up to an additional 68 years, executed contemporaneously with the sales agreement, left Broadway in possession of the property, with the right to use the property for virtually any lawful purpose. To the same extent as any owner would be, Broadway continues to be liable under the lease for the payment of taxes, assessments, charges, and levies of all kinds. Broadway is required, at its own expense, to keep and maintain the premises in good order, condition, and repair, waiving "the right to perform such construction, or to make repairs at the expense of Lessor which may be provided for in any law now in effect or hereafter enacted." It is also required at its own expense to maintain casualty and liability insurance and to save the lessor "harmless from and against all liabilities, losses, obligations, claims, damages, penalties, causes of action, suits, costs and expenses," related to the property, which may arise or become due during the term of the lease. . . .

ECONOMICS OF THE TRANSACTION AND EXPERT WITNESSES

Both the petitioners and the respondent retained experts to analyze and testify regarding the economics of the transactions in question.

Respondent's expert, C. Everett Steichen, . . . reached the following conclusion regarding petitioners' involvement with the property: "An analysis of this transaction including suitable alternative comparable investment alternatives indicates that with the exception of losses which could be transferred to other income to obtain tax benefits there was no economic foundation for the investments of the limited partners in Fourteenth Property Associates and Thirty-Seventh Property Associates."

Petitioners' expert, Robert J. Lichter, . . . analyzed the economic viability of petitioners' investments in 14th P.A. and 37th P.A. using the discounted yield or internal rate of return method. His instructions were to ignore tax considerations and to look at the entire transaction as if it were a nontaxable event. He concluded: "this transaction under all reasonable assumptions, both pre-tax and after-tax, would have reasonable economic justification." . . .

OPINION . . .

INTEREST AND DEPRECIATION DEDUCTIONS

Notwithstanding the intricacies of the above-described tier partnership labyrinth, the central issue in this case is the bona fides of the sale-lease-back. This is essentially an exercise in substance versus form, and as earlier stated by the Supreme Court, "In the field of taxation, administrators of the law, and the courts, are concerned with substance and realities, and formal written documents are not rigidly binding." Helvering v. Lazarus & Co., 308 U.S. 252, 255 (1939). Notwithstanding the approval of the sale-leaseback in the *Frank Lyon* case, we do not understand the teaching of the Supreme Court's decision in that case to be that we are to accept *every* putative sale-leaseback transaction at face value, but rather that our precept is to determine whether there is, in the words of the Supreme Court, "a genuine multiple-party transaction with economic substance which is compelled or encouraged by business or regulatory realities, is imbued with tax-independent considerations, and is not shaped solely by tax-avoidance features that have meaningless labels attached." Frank Lyon Co. v. United States, 435 U.S. 561, 583-584. . . .

One key element of the above test is the phrase "genuinely multiple-party" for, obviously, when looked at only from the viewpoint of Broadway, as seller-lessee, the transaction had economic substance and was encouraged by business realities. Petitioners have claimed in their brief and we have no reason to gainsay them that, had conventional mortgage financing been used, the insurance companies would have lent only 75 percent of the value of the property. The insurance companies, furthermore, had limitations on the total amounts and proportions of their funds that could be committed to direct real estate mortgages. Under the sale-leaseback approach Broadway was, in effect, able to finance 100 percent of the acquisition cost of the property. In addition, the purchase of corporate notes, which were secured by a lease between the corporation and a well-rated tenant, avoided certain other insurance company lending restrictions.

Similarly, Broadway had limitations in its loan and credit agreements with its banks which put a ceiling on the total amount of debt it could incur and also limited the total value of its property which could be mortgaged. At the same time, Broadway expected to be able to deduct as rent, during the initial 30-year term of the lease, an amount equal to 90 percent of the principal amortization and 100 percent of the interest costs of the underlying mortgage on the property. The mortgage contained a 10-percent balloon at the end of the 30-year term.

It is thus apparent that, viewed broadly from the vantage point of Broadway and the insurance companies, the sale-leaseback transaction followed what is essentially a widely used and acceptable business practice embracing substantial business as well as tax purposes and which had significant economic, nontaxable substance. In this context, we do not deem the existence of a net lease, a nonrecourse mortgage or rent during the initial lease term geared to the cost of interest and mortgage amortization to be, in and of themselves, much more than neutral commercial realities. Furthermore, the fact that the transaction was put together by an "orchestrator" (to use petitioner's term) would not alone prove fatal to the buyer-lessor's cause provided the result is economically meaningful on both sides of the equation. For even before the enactment of the at-risk rules of section 465, equipment-leveraged leases, often "packaged" by brokers, were acceptable to the Commissioner where substantial nontax economic interests were acquired by the buyer-lessor. Rev. Proc. 75-21, 1975-1 C.B. 715.

Overall, considering the involvement of Broadway and the insurance companies, there was at least a two-party aspect to the transaction. . . .

But what Broadway sees is a reflection from only one polygon of the prism. In the *Frank Lyon* case, the Supreme Court appraised not only the substance of the seller-lessee's interest, but also that of the buyer-lessor and the legal and economic substance of the contractual relationship between the two.

We, therefore, turn now to a consideration of the substance of the buyer-lessor's (i.e., the petitioners') interest, and here the substantiality of that interest, aside from tax considerations, is far less apparent. We must thus inquire: does the buyer-lessor's interest have substantial legal and economic significance aside from tax considerations, or is that interest simply the purchased tax byproduct of Broadway's economically impelled arrangement with the insurance companies? . . .

Under the *Frank Lyon* test, petitioners must show not only that their participation in the sale-leaseback was not motivated or shaped solely by tax avoidance features that have meaningless labels attached, but also that there is economic substance to the transaction independent of the apparent tax shelter potential. Another way of stating the test is suggested by the Ninth Circuit's opinion in Estate of Franklin v. Commissioner, 544 F.2d 1045 (9th Cir. 1976), affg. 64 T.C. 752 (1975), to wit: Could the buyer-lessor's method of payment for the property be expected at the outset to rather quickly yield an equity which buyer-lessor could not prudently abandon? An affirmative answer would produce, in the words of the Circuit Court, "the stuff of

substance. It meshes with the form of the transaction and constitutes a sale."
(544 F.2d at 1098.) Consequently, if the test is not met, the buyer-lessor will
not have made an investment in the property, regardless of the form of
ownership. And it is fundamental that depreciation is not predicated
upon ownership of property but rather upon an investment in property.
Estate of Franklin v. Commissioner, supra at 1049; Mayerson v. Commissioner, 47 T.C. 340, 350 (1966).

We recognize that the result in *Estate of Franklin* was predicated upon a
finding that the purchase price of the property in question exceeded a
demonstrably reasonable estimate of the fair market value. Nevertheless,
we consider the imprudent abandonment test to be equally applicable to
other fact patterns. For example, we find it appropriate to inquire, as we do
in the instant case, whether the foreseeable value of the property *to the buyer-
lessor* would ever make abandonment imprudent. This then requires an
examination of the economics of the buyer-lessor's position to determine
whether there has been, in fact, an investment in the property.

Petitioners and respondent each relied substantially upon the testimony of expert witnesses to show the presence or absence of economic
motivation on the part of petitioners. In our findings of fact, we have recited
in detail the qualifications of the respective experts and the conclusions they
reached. We now explore the rationale behind their respective conclusions.

We begin by noting that Lichter, petitioners' expert, placed substantially his entire emphasis upon the making of assumptions about the value of
the property, alternatively, 30, 53, or 76 years from 1967, determining the
result of those assumptions in terms of the economic return to the petitioners, and then testing the reasonableness of the underlying assumptions.
Lichter assumed that the property (land and building) would be worth its
purchase price of $3,150,000 (rounded off from $3,144,337) on the date
Broadway decided not to extend the lease, whether it be 30, 53, or 76 years
from the commencement of the lease. He then calculated the discounted
rate of return to be 7.08 percent, 4.81 percent, and 3.95 percent, depending
upon whether Broadway terminated the lease after 30, 53, or 76 years.

Lichter asserted that the 100-percent residual value theory is a reasonable and neutral assumption and one that is employed by a number of
institutional lenders or purchasers in evaluating potential investments,
although he did concede that the assumption might be considered "slightly
positive" in this case. To illustrate the reasonableness of the assumption as
applied in this case, Lichter employed several tests. Using the assessed value
of $812,690 assigned to the land in 1967, Lichter concluded that the land
value would have to appreciate only 4.7 percent per year for the land alone to
be worth, in 1997, what the total land and improvements were worth in
1967. . . .

The weakness in Lichter's approach is that it assumes a priori one of the
very points in issue, namely, the residual value of the property at such time
when it is no longer subject to the lease. Lichter's attempt to establish this

assumed value, the 100-percent residual value, fails because neither the 100-percent residual value theory nor the two tests employed to check the reasonableness of the theory are tied to the facts. . . .

. . . Lichter might have been able to lay a foundation for this evidence by undertaking his own analysis of the property and economic trends to determine independently the known values or even to check the assessor's valuation. But he did not do that. Although Lichter did examine the Bakersfield store, he did not inspect the surrounding neighborhood or the city of Bakersfield, and there is no evidence that he examined the rest of the shopping center or that he looked at the 1965 agreement between Sears and Broadway restricting use of the property. In short, he did not consider many of the factors which would normally be considered by a qualified appraiser.

This does not mean that Lichter was careless in his work; he chose the assessed values with great care to justify the result he desired. . . .

In short, Lichter did not establish the necessary factual link between the instant property and his assumptions. It might have been gratifying for petitioners to know that they could expect to realize a certain return on their investment if the property will be worth a certain amount when the lease expires, but that knowledge has little utility if it cannot reasonably be demonstrated that the property will actually have that value. Lichter's failure to lay the proper foundation for that conclusion means that his analysis is fatally defective for purposes of this case.

The knowledge and experience of Steichen (respondent's expert witness) in real estate development and investment generally, and especially with regard to retail properties, were impressive. We find his analyses, opinions, and conclusions to be generally persuasive. His report and testimony, unlike that of petitioners' expert, were based upon a thorough investigation of the property and the details of the actual transaction before us, and we find the underlying premises of his analysis to be valid. . . .

Assuming refinancing at $5\frac{1}{8}$-percent interest (the rate in the original mortgage) over the 23-year period of the first lease extension, the annual financing cost would be approximately $23,000, to be paid out of the fixed rental of $47,062.50; thus leaving a total pre-tax cash flow for division among and distribution to all of the petitioners of approximately $23,000 per annum. It goes without saying that the opportunity to earn $23,000 annually, commencing 30 years from the inception of the transaction, would not in and of itself appear to justify the $334,000 original investment by the petitioners in the 14th P.A. and 37th P.A. partnerships.

The foregoing analysis assumes, of course, that Broadway would exercise its renewal option for the first 23-year period. Given the extremely favorable terms on which Broadway could renew, however, the only conceivable reason why it (or any corporate successor) would not renew would be that the property had lost its economic viability, in which event the property would also be worthless to the petitioners. . . .

In concluding the part of his report dealing with cash flow, Steichen stated that "an analysis of the cash flow from the rentals to be received when adjusted to reflect the financing costs indicates that there would be no cash available for distribution to the partners until the 31st year of the lease term and that where tax considerations are not taken into account the return at that time is too small to justify the wait." We agree.

The other possibilities for economic gain foreseeable at the inception of the transaction were sale, condemnation, or destruction or mortgage refinancing of the property. Section 21 of the lease deals with a sale or transfer of the property, and provides, in effect, that if the lessor receives a bona fide offer for the purchase of the property and decides to accept such offer, the lessee would have the right to purchase the interest of the lessor for $50,000. The property would still remain subject to the nonrecourse debt. Of this purchase price, the limited partners of both partnerships would be entitled to receive, as a group, 49 percent or $24,500. The limited partners of 14th Property Associates would thus suffer a loss of $155,500, and the limited partners of 37th Property Associates would lose $130,500. If the offering price were greater than $50,000, Broadway, as lessee, would merely exercise its option and pocket the gain. . . .

Another possible source of economic gain would be through receipt of the proceeds of condemnation. However, since the act of condemnation lies wholly beyond the control of the owner or the lessee of property, and since the amounts of awards cannot even be speculated in advance, a prospective investor would not ordinarily look to condemnation as a likely source of economic gain. . . .

A final potential source of economic gain is through mortgage refinancing. . . .

Respondent's expert, Steichen, testified at the trial that since the stated rate of interest of the mortgage notes was below the prevailing commercial lending rates at the time the financing was obtained, and since there was already in evidence continuing upward pressure on interest rates in general, the likelihood of a substantial reduction in interest payments which would lead to an economic gain through mortgage refinancing was quite remote. We find Steichen's testimony on this point convincing.

Finally, in considering whether petitioners made an investment in the property, we consider it to be significant that none of the petitioners' cash outlays went to Broadway. Petitioners' entire investment in 14th P.A. and 37th P.A. went to Cushman and others, but not to Broadway. Such payments constituted, in one sense, brokers' commissions which customarily (and absent a special agreement for shifting the burden of commissions) are paid by the seller. We do not intend to infer that the cost of brokers' commissions is not ordinarily taken into consideration by sellers of real estate in fixing the asking price for property, and, if the asking price is obtained, thereby passed on to the buyer. In such cases, the commissions become indirectly part of the cost of the property and one would normally expect that the purchasers of property would negotiate a return on this cash outlay in the form of increased rent. By contrast, Broadway's rent only covered that part of the investment represented by the mortgage.

Indeed, the petitioners do not pretend that the amounts paid to Cushman and others are part of the cost of the property. Rather, they seek to deduct the payments as the cost of services rendered to the partnerships. Thus, by petitioners' own admission, none of their payments went to the seller, directly or indirectly, so their investment in the property, absent the principal payments on the note, assuming arguendo they may be attributed to petitioners, was zero. . . .

We are, in summary, persuaded that an objective economic analysis of this transaction from the point of view of the buyer-lessor, and therefore the petitioners, should focus on the value of the cash flow derived from the rental payments and the little or no weight should be placed on the speculative possibility that the property will have a substantial residual value at such time, if ever, that Broadway abandons the lease. The low rents and almost nominal cash flow leave little room for doubt that, apart from tax benefits, the value of the interest acquired by the petitioners is substantially less than the amount they paid for it. In terms discussed above, the buyer-lessor would not at any time find it imprudent from an economic point of view to abandon the property. Estate of Franklin v. Commissioner, 544 F.2d 1045 (9th Cir. 1976), aff'g 64 T.C. 752 (1975). There is no justification for the petitioners' participation in this transaction apart from its tax consequences.

Having so analyzed petitioners' lack of potential for economic gain, we must nevertheless confront the question of how petitioners' position differs, if it does, from that of the buyer-lessor in the *Frank Lyon* case. . . .

Among the facts in the *Frank Lyon* case which distinguish it significantly from those in the case before us are the following:

(1) The rent during the initial lease term was sufficient to completely amortize the underlying mortgage principal, whereas in the case before us, the rent will amortize only 90 percent of the note principal, leaving a sizable balloon at the end.

(2) The rent in *Frank Lyon* was fair rental value for the property and after the initial lease term was substantial and free and clear to the buyer-lessor. In the case before us, the rent is not based on fair rental value. In the first renewal option period, the rent is relatively insignificant and, if applied to amortize the refinanced balloon, will provide an insignificant, if any, cash flow to petitioners.

(3) The buyer-lessor in *Frank Lyon* paid $500,000 of its own funds to the seller-lessee; in the case before us none of petitioners' funds went to Broadway.

(4) In *Frank Lyon*, the buyer-lessor stood to realize a substantial gain in the event the seller-lessee exercised its repurchase option; in the case before us, the petitioners cannot dispose of the property at a profit.

(5) In *Frank Lyon*, the buyer-lessor was a substantial corporate entity which participated actively in negotiating the terms and conditions of the sale and leaseback, while in the instant case the entire "deal" was packaged as a financing transaction by the orchestrator, Cushman, and then marketed by him and his colleagues as a tax shelter. While, as we have indicated previously, this factor, alone, might not be fatal to petitioners' cause, considered in concert with the other negative factors outlined above, it lends no credence to any contention that there is here present any "genuine multi-party transaction with economic substance," as mandated by the Supreme Court in *Frank Lyon*. Furthermore, the extremely casual, not to say careless, way in which the various tier partnerships were fabricated, financed, and managed gives them an aura of mechanical contrivance which does not inspire confidence in the genuineness of the requisite multiparty transaction.

We recently applied the rule in *Frank Lyon* to uphold the validity of a sale-leaseback transaction in a case where the totality of facts and circumstances convinced us that the substance of the transaction was a bona fide sale-leaseback which should be given effect for tax purposes. Belz Investment Co. v. Commissioner, 72 T.C. 1209 (1979). In that case, the lessee and lessor were both substantial business entities and those two parties, as in *Frank Lyon*, negotiated the terms of the transaction at arm's length. Such cannot be said for the case before us. Fourth Cavendish, the putative buyer-lessor, was organized and put into place only after the financing was negotiated and finalized.

(6) The fact that the buyer-lessor in *Frank Lyon* was personally liable on the mortgage was, of course, a significant factor supporting the bona fides of the sale-leaseback transaction in that case. Nevertheless, we regard personal liability on the mortgage as atypical in modern real estate transactions and, consequently, we consider the absence of personal liability as a neutral factor in the case before us.

In summary, after considering all of the facts and circumstances in the case before us, we find that the petitioners have failed to show a genuine multiparty transaction with economic substance, compelled or encouraged by business realities and imbued with tax-independent considerations and not shaped solely by tax-avoidance features that have meaningless labels attached. Frank Lyon Co. v. United States, supra at 583-584. We further find that Medway, the limited partnership from which petitioners seek to derive their deductible losses, is a mere conduit through which Broadway's debt payments pass on their way to the insurance companies. It follows that petitioners have no "investment" in the property upon which depreciation can be predicated; it also follows that the debt in question has no economic significance to the petitioners and thus they have not, in this case, secured "the use or forbearance of money." Estate of Franklin v. Commissioner, 544 F.2d at 1049. We therefore conclude that petitioners, as members of 14th P.A. or 37th P.A., are not entitled to deduct partnership losses resulting from depreciation allowances and interest payments.

PAYMENTS TO PROMOTERS

Our determination that the buyer-lessors served as nothing more than a conduit still leaves for consideration the question of the deductibility of the payments to the promoters.

The limited partners of 14th P.A. paid $180,000 for their interests. Seventy thousand dollars of this amount was allocated to the capital account of JRYA and then withdrawn by JRYA in 1967 as compensation for services. Young and his salesmen each received a 12½-percent commission from JRYA for each sale. The remaining $110,000 of the capital contributions made to 14th P.A. by its limited partners was paid by 14th P.A. as its capital contribution to Medway. Medway, in turn, paid the entire $110,000 to Cushman in 1967. Of that amount, $105,350 was treated as a salary payment to Cushman. The difference in the amount of $4,650 was treated as a withdrawal from Cushman's capital account, leaving a balance in that account of $5,097.71. The withdrawal of capital was made without any prior unanimous agreement of the partners as required by the partnership agreement. . . .

It is clear that Cushman and JRYA, through its president, Young, and its salesmen, performed substantial services in organizing the partnership and in selling partnership shares. Similarly, it is clear that Cushman performed substantial services in putting together the sale and leaseback transaction. While expenses incurred in organizing a partnership are non-deductible expenses (Cagle v. Commissioner, 539 F.2d at 415), as are expenses incurred in connection with the sale and leaseback,[27] petitioners adhere to their assertion that the entire amount of the promoters' fees are deductible. The reason for this devotion to their argument: petitioners take the position that none of the promoters' fees is attributable to these past services.

Instead, petitioners ask the Court to believe the frivolous argument that the entire amount of the fees of the promoters is attributable to future services that JRYA is expected to render to 14th P.A. and 37th P.A. and that Cushman is expected to render to Medway and Grenada. Not only were these services nominal at most, as will be seen below, but petitioners' plaint in effect asks the Court to overlook the 12½-percent commissions paid by JRYA to its employees for selling these partnership shares. . . .

Having decided that the principal issue and the payments to general partners issue in favor of respondent, it is unnecessary for us to consider the alternative issues raised by respondent. Decisions will be entered for the respondent . . .

---

27. The latter are capital in nature because they are expenses incurred in connection with the acquisition of a capital asset. Sec. 263(a).

2. Machinery and Equipment

The tax treatment of machinery and equipment leases is governed by the same general principles as real estate, but there have been additional authorities applicable only to them.

(a) Safe-Harbor Leasing

When ACRS was enacted in its original 1981 form, Congress foresaw that a substantial number of taxpayers would not have sufficient income to take advantage of all the accelerated deductions being offered. The corporations so limited would include some, like the Chrysler Corporation, that were then in deep financial difficulty, but also some apparently healthy corporations with a very high ratio of depreciable property to other costs and income, like the airlines.

Leasing was one natural way to deal with this problem. Permit General Electric (GE), which seems consistently to have a comfortable excess of income over deductions, to become owner of the automobile manufacturing equipment and airplanes and to lease them to Chrysler and the airlines. It may be argued that there is no particular reason to give expensive tax benefits to GE for equipment not to be used in its regular business; the response was that GE could be expected to pass through the benefit of accelerated deductions and credits in the form of a lower rent than it would otherwise charge: The intended stimulating effects would be accomplished with respect to the users of the property after all.

However, because the buyer-lessor (GE) might be adjudged not to be the owner for tax purposes, the resulting doubts about the tax benefits to be realized would tend to increase the rent and thus block the effective shifting of economic benefit to the lessee (Chrysler or the airlines). And this problem would be magnified by the very provisions of ERTA itself: If the rent were set low enough to effect a complete shifting of tax benefits to the lessee, the lessor would often be unable to show any chance of pretax profit.

To deal with these problems the statute created a new category of transactions, called *safe harbor leasing*. If one complied with the rather formal statutory requirements for safe-harbor leasing, the transaction was to be treated as a lease without any inquiry into its economic reality or into who was really the owner of the property.

The authors understood and intended that this would have the effect of stimulating lots of safe harbor leasing transactions with no purpose or effect except to reduce the taxes of buyer-lessors and pass the benefits of such reductions through to seller lessees in the form of below-market rent. See Staff of the Joint Comm. on Taxation, 97th Cong., General Explanation of the Economic Recovery Tax Act of 1981 102-107 (1981). But the public did not fully understand, and the press made something of a scandal of the unseemly process and the resulting tax elimination by vigorous buyer-lessors. Safe harbor leasing was repealed in 1982. A milder substitute called *finance leasing* was enacted to go into effect a couple of years later; but it was postponed and finally repealed, in 1986, before taking effect.

(b) Objective Guidelines

Repeal of the safe harbor and finance leasing provisions had the effect of restoring the "pre-safe harbor lease rules." These consist of the same underlying principles as apply to real estate leasing, but also include some administrative guidelines described in the following excerpt from the General Explanation of the 1984 Act.

OBJECTIVE GUIDELINES USED IN STRUCTURING TRANSACTIONS

Staff of Joint Comm. on Taxation, 98th Cong., General Explanation of the Revenue Provisions of the Deficit Reduction Act of 1984, 16-17 (Comm. Print 1984)

The question of exactly what burdens and benefits of ownership have to be retained by the lessor under pre-safe harbor lease rules created some confusion and difficulty for people trying to structure leases that, at least in part, were motivated by tax considerations. To give taxpayers guidance in structuring leveraged leases (i.e., where the property is financed by a loan from a third party), the Internal Revenue Service in 1975 issued Revenue Procedure 75-21, 1975-1 C.B. 715, and a companion document, Revenue Procedure 75-28, 1975-1 C.B. 752 (the guidelines).* If the requirements of the guidelines are met and if the facts and circumstances do not indicate a contrary result, the Service will issue an advance letter ruling that the transaction is a lease and that the lessor is the owner for Federal income tax purposes.

The guidelines generally apply only to leveraged leases of equipment. The general principles described above continue to govern nonleveraged leases and leases of real property. The guidelines are not a definitive statement of legal principles and are not intended for audit purposes. If less than all requirements of the guidelines are met, a transaction might still be considered a lease if, under all the facts and circumstances, the transaction is a lease under the general principles discussed previously. However, in practice, many taxpayers have taken into account the guidelines' requirements in structuring transactions. The guidelines may be viewed as a type of safe harbor.

The specific requirements for obtaining a ruling under the guidelines are as follows:

(1) *Minimum investment.* — The lessor must have a minimum 20 percent unconditional at-risk investment in the property. This rule represents an

---

* [The current guidelines are set forth in Rev. Proc. 2001-28, 2001-1 C.B. 1156, which supersedes Rev. Proc. 75-21 but contains the same six basic requirements and closely follows the prior approach. — EDS.]

attempt to ensure that the lessor experiences some significant loss if the property declines in value. By limiting the degree of nonrecourse leverage, this guideline also limits the pool of potentially transferable tax benefits from such transactions.

(2) *Purchase options.* — In general, the lessee may not have an option to purchase the property at the end of the lease term unless, under the lease agreement, the option can be exercised only at fair market value (determined at the time of exercise). This rule precludes fixed price purchase options, even at a bona fide estimate of the projected fair market value of the property at the option date. In addition, when the property is first placed in service by the lessee, the lessor cannot have a contractual right to require the lessee or any other party to purchase the property, even at fair market value.

The fair market value purchase option requirement fulfills three purposes related to the determination of the economic substance of the transaction. First, it ensures that the lessor bears the risk implicit in ownership that no market or an unfavorable market will exist at the end of the lease. Second, it ensures that the lessor has retained an equity interest in the property. Any fixed price option represents a limitation on the lessor's right to full enjoyment of the property's value. Third, it limits the ability of the parties to establish an artificial rent structure to avoid the cash flow test (described below). However, several courts have held that the mere existence of a fixed price purchase option does not prevent lease treatment so long as the lessor retains other significant burdens and benefits of ownership.[8]

(3) *Lessee investment precluded.* — Neither the lessee nor a party related to the lessee may furnish any part of the cost of the property. The rationale is that a lessee investment may suggest that the lessee is in substance a co-owner of the property.

(4) *No lessee loans or guarantees.* — As a corollary to the prior rule, the lessee must not loan to the lessor any of the funds necessary to acquire the property. In addition, the lessee must not guarantee any lessor loan.

(5) *Profit and cash flow requirements.* — The lessor must expect to receive a profit from the transaction and have a positive cash flow from the transaction independent of tax benefits. These guidelines are based on the requirement, as previously mentioned, that lease transactions must have a business purpose independent of tax benefits.

(6) *Limited use property.* — Under Revenue Procedure 76-30, 1976-2 C.B. 647, property that can be used only by the lessee (limited use property) is not eligible for lease treatment. The rationale is that if the lessee is the only person who could realistically use the property, the lessor has not retained any significant ownership interest. . . .

---

8. See, e.g., Northwest Acceptance Corp. v. Commissioner, 58 T.C. 836 (1972), aff'd 500 F.2d 1222 (9th Cir. 1974).

3. Leasing to Tax-Exempt Entities

If a taxable corporation leases property, the tax benefits enjoyed by the lessor are in general just what the lessee would have enjoyed if it had purchased the property. The lease transaction is therefore said to accomplish a tax benefit transfer from lessee to lessor. But what if the lessee is a tax-exempt entity that would not have enjoyed any tax benefits beyond its general tax exemption if it had owned the property outright? Suppose a college were to sell and lease back its dormitories and classroom buildings?

Section 168(g) prescribes an alternative depreciation system, slower than ACRS (the straight-line method is applied over longer recovery periods), for various categories of property, one of which is tax-exempt use property. §168(g)(1)(B). "Tax-exempt use property" is defined in §168(h) in a manner that includes most tangible property leased to a tax-exempt entity, but with exceptions for real estate leases that meet certain minimum standards. How should the lines be drawn? If longer than the period prescribed by the alternative depreciation system, the recovery period for tax-exempt use property is set at 125 percent of the lease term, in which the lease term is defined broadly to include any optional renewal periods as well as the duration of any follow-on service contract or successive lease that is part of the same transaction. §168(g)(3)(A), (i)(3).

REFORM OF TAX TREATMENT OF CERTAIN LEASING ARRANGEMENTS AND LIMITATION ON DEDUCTIONS ALLOCABLE TO PROPERTY USED BY GOVERNMENTS OR OTHER TAX-EXEMPT ENTITIES

Staff of the Joint Comm. on Taxation, General Explanation of Tax Legislation Enacted in the 108th Congress 418, 420-421 (2005)

The special rules applicable to the depreciation of tax-exempt use property were enacted to prevent tax-exempt entities from using leasing arrangements to transfer the tax benefits of accelerated depreciation on property they used to a taxable entity. The Congress was concerned that some taxpayers were attempting to circumvent this policy through the creative use of service contracts with the tax-exempt entities.

More generally, the Congress believed that certain ongoing leasing activity with tax-exempt entities and foreign governments indicated that the prior-law tax rules were not effective in curtailing the ability of a tax-exempt entity to transfer certain tax benefits to a taxable entity. The Congress was concerned about this activity and the continual development of new structures that purported to minimize or neutralize the effect of these rules. In addition, the Congress also was concerned about the increasing use of certain leasing structures involving property purported to be qualified technological equipment. Although the Congress recognized that leasing plays an important role in ensuring the availability of capital to businesses, it believed that certain transactions of which it recently had become aware did not serve this role. These transactions resulted in little or no accumulation of capital for financing or refinancing but, instead, essentially involved an accommodation fee paid by a U.S. taxpayer to a tax indifferent party.

In discussing the reasons for the enactment of rules in 1984 that were intended to limit the transfer of tax benefits to taxable entities with respect to property used by tax-exempt entities, Congress at the time stated that: (1) the Federal budget was in no condition to sustain substantial and growing revenue losses by making additional tax benefits (in excess of tax exemption itself) available to tax-exempt entities through leasing transactions; (2) there were concerns about possible problems of accountability of governments to their citizens, and of tax-exempt organizations to their clientele, if substantial amounts of their property came under the control of outside parties solely because the Federal tax system made leasing more favorable than owning; (3) the tax system should not encourage tax-exempt entities to dispose of assets they own or to forego control over the assets they use; (4) there were concerns about waste of Federal revenues because in some cases a substantial portion of the tax savings was retained by lawyers, investment bankers, lessors, and investors and, thus, the Federal revenue loss became more of a gain to financial entities than to tax-exempt entities; (5) providing aid to tax-exempt entities through direct appropriations was more efficient and appropriate than providing such aid through the Code; and (6) popular confidence in the tax system must be sustained by ensuring that the system generally is working correctly and fairly.[803]

The Congress believed that the reasons stated above for the enactment in 1984 of the present-law rules are as important today as they were in 1984. Unfortunately, the prior-law rules did not adequately deter taxpayers from engaging in transactions that attempted to circumvent the rules enacted in 1984. Therefore, the Congress believed that changes to prior law were essential to ensure the attainment of the aforementioned Congressional intentions, provided such changes did not inhibit legitimate commercial leasing transactions that involve a significant and genuine transfer of the benefits and burdens of tax ownership between the taxpayer and the tax-exempt lessee.

Prompted by these anti-abuse concerns, in 2004 Congress enacted §470, which limits deductions relating to property leased to a tax-exempt entity to

---

803. See H.R. Rep. No. 98-432, Pt 2, pp. 1140-1141 (1984) and S. Prt. No. 98-169, Vol. I, pp. 115-127 (1984).

the income produced by the property unless the lease satisfies certain conditions. Disallowed excess deductions (the "tax-exempt use loss") may be carried forward to offset future lease income, and may be deducted when the taxpayer disposes of its entire interest in the property. §470(b), (e)(2). Deductibility of a tax-exempt use loss is not restricted if the lease satisfies four safe-harbor conditions: (1) the taxpayer-lessor must at all times maintain a minimum at-risk investment of 20 percent of its adjusted basis in the property; (2) the lessee must not bear too large a share of a loss resulting from decline in value of the leased property; (3) the lessee must not be required to advance more than a specified amount of funds to secure its obligations (generally, the limit is 20 percent of the adjusted basis of the property at the time of leasing); and (4) the price of any lessee purchase option must be set at fair market value of the property determined at the time of exercise (but property with a class life of seven years or less, ships and fixed-wing aircraft are excepted from this final requirement).

Section 470 was modeled on §469, the passive activity loss limitation, examined immediately below. Why was additional legislation necessary? See §469(a)(2) and Chapter 16E below.

C.   THE PASSIVE ACTIVITY LOSS LIMITATION

As illustrated by the cases on nonbusiness bad debts in Chapter 14E, individuals who conduct business in corporate form and suffer losses are likely to find deductibility of those losses severely limited: no deduction until losses are realized by sale or worthlessness and even then only a capital loss. By contrast, as illustrated by the leasing cases in this chapter, individuals conducting business in proprietorship or partnership form were once able to deduct business expenses and capital costs directly against any income they had from whatever sources. Net losses were once thus fully and immediately deductible, generally without regard to the capital loss limitation. Moreover, tax losses might exceed real, economic losses, because of over-generous capital recovery allowances or laxity in the application of the prohibition on deductions for capital expenditures. Farmers, for example, have traditionally been allowed to deduct costs, like feed for animals being raised for sale, which would be required to be capitalized under general accounting standards.

As also illustrated by the cases in this chapter, these possibilities led to the promotion of *tax shelter* investments, whose chief source of return was tax deductions against other income. Holding of property for leasing to others has perhaps been the most important and pervasive form of tax shelter, but others were important, too. Limited partnership interests have been created and sold in farming, oil and gas drilling, other mineral extraction activities, raising of rosebushes, production or importation of motion pictures, and ownership of lithographic plates with the advertised possibility of using them to produce such products as bed sheets imprinted with pictures of beautiful people.

One of the major structural revisions in the 1986 tax law was a sweeping new limitation on the deduction of losses from all such investments. It is in §469, titled, *Passive activity losses and credits limited.* This section is long and complicated, but an effort should be made to understand its general outlines.

Put credits aside. Then the main operative rule is in §469(a)(1)(A), which simply disallows any passive activity loss. *Passive activity loss* (PAL) is defined as the excess of losses over income from passive activities. §469(d)(1). The effect, therefore, is to limit the deductibility of losses from passive activities to the amount of income from such activities. Passive activity income thus becomes a conditionally preferred income item: not preferred at all if it stands alone, but effectively exempt from tax to the extent of any otherwise nondeductible passive losses a taxpayer may have.

Like the capital loss limitation, the PAL limitation is essentially a deferral provision, since the losses disallowed are carried over into subsequent years. §469(b). Accordingly, PALs will be deductible after all in any subsequent year in which there is net income from passive activities sufficient to absorb them.

1. Passive Activities

The charming oxymoron *passive activity* does not carry its meaning unaided (how could it?); it is defined prosaically and at some length in §469(c). In general it is a trade or business *activity* in which the taxpayer is a *passive* investor, not a material participant. §469(c)(1). *Material participation* is defined in §469(h)(1) to mean "involve[ment] in the operations of the activity on a basis that is — (A) regular, (B) continuous, and (C) substantial." Section 469(h)(2) indicates that a limited partner will generally not be regarded as a material participant in partnership activities.

So if a law professor invests in an ethnic restaurant that loses money, the deductibility of those losses against her other income would depend first on whether she was involved in the restaurant activity on a regular, continuous, and substantial basis. What would that take? Cooking? Tasting? Letting her name and picture be used in advertising? Talking in the media about how great the restaurant is (and about the inferiority of others)? Calling on her friends in the community for financing?

Or, for another example, if one purchases a limited partnership interest in a cattle farm, that will be a passive activity. If deductions exceed income from that activity, the excess will not be allowed as a deduction (except against net income from other passive activities). On the other hand, one personally involved in the cattle business, for whom this farm was his main activity, would be able to take excess deductions arising from the business against any other income he might have. If one simply bought a cattle farm as outright owner but continued to practice accounting as his main business and hired others to work the farm, then §469 would require a judgment about whether his involvement in the cattle business was regular, continuous, and substantial. What amount of involvement would satisfy these requirements?

Regulations under §469 flesh out the meaning of *material participation*, defining it mostly in terms of hours spent in an activity (or a number of activities). Reg. §1.469-5T. That method of measurement will be familiar to lawyers and other professionals, although the new regulations specify that taxpayers are not required to keep diaries or timesheets in order to claim deductions.

2.   Disposition of Interests

If a passive activity is sold or otherwise disposed of in a taxable transaction, then losses from that activity become deductible in the year of disposition against any other income. §469(g). In this respect the PAL provision is quite unlike the capital loss limitation, which by its terms generally applies to the liquidation of an investment. All or part of the loss that is allowed on disposition of a passive activity, whether incurred in the disposition or earlier, may be capital loss, and if so it is subject to the capital loss limitation as such. In general, capital losses incurred in a passive activity are not taken into account in determining net capital gains or losses until such time as they get by the passive activity loss limitation.

What if a taxpayer dies holding an interest in a passive activity with undeducted PALs? The statute then allows the deductions but only to the extent they exceed step-up of basis at death. §469(g)(2). Is this limitation well conceived?

3.   Activities

The general rule of §469(a) applies to income and deductions from passive activities in the aggregate, and so does not require any differentiation among particular passive activities. But the disposition rule in §469(g) does require such differentiation, and so does application of the test of material participation, since participation in one activity will not prevent another activity from being passive. One of the complexities involved in the limitation, therefore, is that of differentiating among and keeping separate accounts for particular activities. (The at-risk limitation also requires an identification and separation of activities for its application; is *activity* the same for the two provisions? Why?)

4.   Portfolio and Earned Income

Section 469(e)(1) specifies that interest, dividends, annuities and royalties not derived in the ordinary course of business, and associated expenses (including interest) should not be taken into account in determining the income or loss from an activity. As a result such income, commonly called "portfolio" income, cannot be passive activity income. (It is certainly passive enough; the trouble is that it is so passive it is not even considered to come from an activity.)

Thus if a limited partnership holds stock or bonds, its net dividend and interest income must be separately determined and reported as taxable portfolio income by limited partners even if the partnership is otherwise producing a net loss from business activities subject to the PAL limitation.

Section 469(e)(3) similarly excludes earned income in computing income or loss from a passive activity, so if a limited partner performs professional services for the partnership, her fee will not be income from a passive activity and may not be offset by her share of partnership losses. (The trouble with earned income is indeed that it is *not* passive, even if the earner's investment is classified as passive.)

These exclusions in computing passive activity income and loss directly illuminate the rationale of the whole limitation. Most of the revenue raised by the income tax, by far, comes from salaries and wages and other compensation for services. The rest comes mostly from dividends and interest and annuities. The idea behind the PAL limitation was to protect these revenues from the incursions of tax shelter deductions, whatever might happen to the computation of income and collection of tax on account of the rest of the investments and business activities individuals might engage in. As to the rest, the statute in effect lets income from one be offset by losses, real or artificial, from others. Passive activity income is thus a conditionally favored category of income under the 1986 law, in a similar way to capital gain income; that is, it is the only sort of income that can be absorbed by passive activity losses, except on disposition of an activity.

5.   Rental and Oil and Gas Activities

Rental activity is specially dealt with under §469 in several ways. First any rental activity is considered a passive activity, without regard to material participation. §469(c)(2) and (4). But then there is a special "$25,000 offset for rental real estate activities" in which a taxpayer "actively participates." §469(i). This "exemption" is subject to "phase-out" — that is, reduction — by

50 percent of the amount by which an individual's adjusted gross income exceeds $100,000 (or $200,000 in the case of certain subsidized low-income housing). Another blow for simplification!

Another quite different exception to the rental rule was added in 1993, in §469(c)(7). This is designed for real estate professionals and is without income limits or phase-out. The critical limitations are in §469(c)(7)(B), which requires that more than half the personal services performed in trades or business during the year be in real property trades or businesses in which the taxpayer materially participates, and that such services be more than 750 hours. Should this provision be viewed as special legislation for the real estate industry or can it be justified as bringing the treatment of real estate professionals more nearly in line with professional farmers and others who are exempted from the passive loss limitation on the basis of material participation?

Look at §469(c)(3), which generally excludes working interests in oil and gas properties from the passive activity category unless they are held in a limited partnership. What is the rationale for that?

Questions

1. Consider an unmarried taxpayer with rental real estate activities producing tax losses in excess of $25,000 a year, and income from other sources of $110,000. What would be the effect on taxable income and tax liability of receiving an additional $10,000 of compensation for services? Would it be accurate to say that the marginal rate of tax on such additional compensation income is around 42 percent? Is such a marginal rate consistent with the central objectives of the 1986 Code? Is anything else about the phase-out worth incurring this effect to achieve?

2. Compare the PAL limitation with the at-risk limitation in §465. In particular:

(a) Given the at-risk limitation, why was the PAL limitation needed?

(b) Does *activity* have the same function and meaning under the two provisions? Should it?

(c) What is the relevance of leverage, if any, under §469?

3. Reexamine *Estate of Franklin, Pleasant Summit*, and *Hilton.* How would §469 apply to them?

What is the need for §469, as it applies to leasing, given decisions like that in *Hilton?* What additional ground, if any, does it cover?

Conversely, given §469, do decisions like those in *Estate of Franklin* and *Hilton* have any continuing significance? What is it? And how about the at-risk limitation in §465?

4. What is the significance of leverage in relation to §469? Clearly one possible response to the at-risk limitation might often be to increase the

amount at risk by making a larger equity investment, thus reducing leverage. Will such a response have any efficacy in relation to §469? Should it?

5. Suppose X owns commercial real estate subject to a mortgage, on which tax losses of $20,000 are realized, and stocks and securities producing interest and dividends of $20,000. What will the income tax effect be if X sells the stocks and securities and uses the proceeds to pay down the mortgage on his commercial real estate? Why?

What if X borrowed against the stock and securities and used the proceeds to pay down the mortgage? Why?

D.   THE ALTERNATIVE MINIMUM TAX

An older and even more general attack on tax shelters, preferences, and tax benefits is the Alternative Minimum Tax, prescribed in §55. This section requires taxpayers to compute a Tentative Minimum Tax (TMT) by applying somewhat lower rates to a broader base entitled Alternative Minimum Taxable Income (AMTI), and then to pay tax in the amount of TMT or regular tax, whichever is more.[3]

PRESENT LAW AND BACKGROUND RELATING TO THE INDIVIDUAL ALTERNATIVE MINIMUM TAX

Staff of the Joint Committee on Taxation, 110th Cong. (2007)

I. INDIVIDUAL ALTERNATIVE MINIMUM TAX

A.   PRESENT LAW AND LEGISLATIVE BACKGROUND

IN GENERAL

An alternative minimum tax ("AMT") is imposed on an individual, estate, or trust in an amount by which the tentative minimum tax exceeds the regular income tax for the taxable year.[2] The tentative minimum tax is the sum of (1) 26 percent of so much of the taxable excess as does not exceed $175,000 ($87,500 in the case of a married individual filing a separate return) and (2) 28 percent of the remaining taxable excess. The taxable excess is so much of the alternative minimum taxable income ("AMTI") as exceeds the exemption amount. [§55(b).] The maximum tax rates on

---

3. If TMT is more than the regular tax for the taxable year, then §55(a) requires payment of the excess in addition to the regular tax itself, so the effect is to require a total payment equal to TMT instead of the regular tax. The statute apparently uses the term Alternative Minimum Tax to refer to this excess; others often use the term to refer to TMT.

2. There is also a corporate alternative minimum tax, which is not the subject of this document.

net capital gain and dividends used in computing the regular tax are used in computing the tentative minimum tax. [§55(b)(3).]

The exemption amounts are: (1) $62,550 for taxable years beginning in 2006 [$69,950 for taxable years beginning in 2008] and $45,000 for taxable years beginning thereafter in the case of married individuals filing a joint return and surviving spouses; (2) $42,500 for taxable years beginning in 2006 [$46,200 for taxable years beginning in 2008] and $33,750 for taxable years beginning thereafter in the case of other unmarried individuals; (3) $31,275 for taxable years beginning in 2006 [$34,975 for taxable years beginning in 2008] and $22,500 in taxable years beginning thereafter in the case of married individuals filing separate returns; and (4) $22,500 in the case of an estate or trust. [§55(d)(1).] The exemption amounts are phased out by an amount equal to 25 percent of the amount by which the individual's AMTI exceeds (1) $150,000 in the case of married individuals filing a joint return and surviving spouses, (2) $112,500 in the case of other unmarried individuals, and (3) $75,000 in the case of married individuals filing separate returns or an estate or a trust. [§55(d)(3).] These amounts are not indexed for inflation.

Alternative minimum taxable income is the individual's regular taxable income increased by certain adjustments and preference items. [§55(b)(2).] In the case of items that involve the timing of deductions, the AMTI treatment negates the deferral of income resulting from the regular tax treatment of these items.

ADJUSTMENTS AND PREFERENCES

The adjustments and preferences[3] that individuals must take into account to compute AMTI are:

1. Depreciation on property placed in service after 1986 and before January 1, 1999, is computed by using the generally longer class lives prescribed by the alternative depreciation system of section 168(g) and either (a) the straight-line method in the case of property subject to the straight-line method under the regular tax or (b) the 150-percent declining balance method in the case of other property. [§56(a)(1)(A).] Depreciation on property placed in service after December 31, 1998, is computed by using the regular tax recovery periods and the AMT methods described in the previous sentence. Depreciation on property acquired after September 10, 2001, and before January 1, 2005 . . . which is allowed an additional allowance under section 168(k) for the regular tax, is computed without regard to any AMT adjustments. [§168(k)(2)(G).]

---

3. "Adjustments" is the term used for those items listed in section 56 of the Code and "preferences" is the term used for those listed in section 57 of the Code.

2. Mining exploration and development costs are capitalized and amortized over a 10-year period. [§56(a)(2).]

3. Taxable income from a long-term contract (other than a home construction contract) is computed using the percentage of completion method of accounting. [§56(a)(3).]

4. The amortization deduction allowed for pollution control facilities placed in service before January 1, 1999 (generally determined using 60-month amortization for a portion of the cost of the facility under the regular tax), is calculated under the alternative depreciation system (generally, using longer class lives and the straight-line method). The amortization deduction allowed for pollution control facilities placed in service after December 31, 1998, is calculated using the regular tax recovery periods and the straight-line method. [§56(a)(5).]

5. Miscellaneous itemized deductions are not allowed. [§56(b)(1)(A)(i).]

6. [Itemized] Deductions for State, local, and foreign real property taxes; State and local personal property taxes; State, local, and foreign income, war profits, and excess profits taxes; and State and local sales taxes are not allowed. [§56(b)(1)(A)(ii).]

7. Medical expenses are allowed only to the extent they exceed ten percent of the taxpayer's adjusted gross income. [§56(b)(1)(B).]

8. The standard deduction and personal exemptions are not allowed. [§56(b)(1)(E).]

9. The amount allowable as a deduction for circulation expenditures are capitalized and amortized over a three-year period. [§56(b)(2)(A)(i).]

10. The amount allowable as a deduction for research and experimentation expenditures from passive activities are capitalized and amortized over a 10-year period. [§56(b)(2)(A)(ii), (b)(2)(D).]

11. The regular tax rules relating to incentive stock options do not apply. [§56(b)(3).]

12. The excess of the deduction for percentage depletion over the adjusted basis of each mineral property (other than oil and gas properties) at the end of the taxable year is not allowed. [§57(a)(1).]

13. The amount by which excess intangible drilling costs (i.e., expenses in excess of the amount that would have been allowable if amortized over a 10-year period) exceed 65 percent of the net income from oil, gas, and geothermal properties is not allowed. This preference applies to independent producers only to the extent it reduces the producer's AMTI (determined without regard to this preference and the net operating loss deduction) by more than 40 percent). [§57(a)(2).]

14. Tax-exempt interest income on private activity bonds (other than qualified 501(c)(3) bonds) issued after August 7, 1986, is included in AMTI. [§57(a)(5).]

15. Accelerated depreciation or amortization on certain property placed in service before January 1, 1987, is not allowed. [§57(a)(6).]

16. Seven percent of the amount excluded from income under section 1202 (relating to gains on the sale of certain small business stock) is included in AMTI. [§57(a)(7).]

17. Losses from any tax shelter farm activity or passive activities are not taken into account in computing AMTI. [§58(a), (b).]

OTHER RULES

Net Operating Loss Deduction

The taxpayer's net operating loss deduction cannot reduce the taxpayer's AMTI by more than 90 percent of the AMTI (determined without the net operating loss deduction). [§56(a)(4), d)(1).]

Nonrefundable Tax Credits

Except as otherwise described below, nonrefundable tax credits may not exceed the excess of the individual's regular tax liability over the tentative minimum tax, meaning they are not allowed against the alternative minimum tax. [§26(a)(1).] [C]redits such as the general business credit, the alternative motor vehicle credit, and the alternative fuel vehicle refueling credit generally are not allowed against the AMT. [§§38(c)(1), 30B(g)(2), 30C(d)(2).]

Several exceptions apply to the general rule denying credits against the AMT.

The alternative minimum tax foreign tax credit reduces the tentative minimum tax. [§55(b)(1)(A)(i) (final sentence), 59(a).]

For taxable years beginning before [2009], the nonrefundable personal credits (i.e., the dependent care credit, the credit for the elderly and disabled, the adoption credit, the child tax credit, the credit for interest on certain home mortgages, the HOPE Scholarship and Lifetime Learning credits, the saver's credit, the D.C. homebuyer's credit, the nonbusiness energy credit, and the residential energy efficient property credit) are allowed to the extent of the entire amount of the individual's regular tax and alternative minimum tax. [§26(a)(2).]

For taxable years beginning after [2008], the nonrefundable personal credits (other than the adoption credit, child credit and saver's credit) are allowed only to the extent that the individual's regular income tax liability exceeds the individual's tentative minimum tax (determined without regard to the minimum tax foreign tax credit). The adoption credit, child credit, and saver's credit are allowed to the full extent of the individual's regular tax (reduced by the other nonrefundable personal credits) and alternative minimum tax.[6] [§26(a)(1).]

---

6. The rule applicable to the adoption credit and child credit is subject to the sunset provision of the Economic Growth and Tax Relief Reconciliation Act of 2001.

If an individual is subject to AMT in any year, the amount of tax exceeding the taxpayer's regular tax liability is allowed as a credit (the "AMT credit") in any subsequent taxable year to the extent the taxpayer's regular tax liability exceeds his or her tentative minimum tax liability in such subsequent year. [§53(a), (b), (c).] For individuals, the AMT credit is allowed only to the extent that the taxpayer's AMT liability is the result of adjustments that are timing in nature. [§53(d)(1)(B).] The individual AMT adjustments relating to itemized deductions and personal exemptions are not timing in nature, and no minimum tax credit is allowed with respect to these items. . . .

LEGISLATIVE BACKGROUND

The Tax Equity and Fiscal Responsibility Act of 1982 enacted the first comprehensive individual AMT.[7] According to the legislative history of that Act, "the committee has amended the present minimum tax provisions applying to individuals with one overriding objective: no taxpayer with substantial economic income should be able to avoid all tax liability by using exclusions, deductions, and credits."[8] The AMT provisions enacted in 1982 are the foundation for the present law individual AMT. Under the 1982 Act, in computing AMTI, the deduction for State and local taxes, the deduction for personal exemptions, the standard deduction, and the deduction for interest on home equity loans were not allowed. Incentive stock option gain was included in AMTI. These remain the principal preferences and adjustments under present law. A rate of 20 percent applied to AMTI in excess of an exemption amount of $40,000 ($30,000 for unmarried taxpayers). The exemption amounts were not indexed for inflation, even though the regular rates were scheduled to be indexed for inflation in future years. Nonrefundable credits (other than the foreign tax credit) were not allowed against the AMT.

The Tax Reform Act of 1986 largely retained the structure of the prior-law AMT, except that deferral preferences were properly adjusted over time and a minimum tax credit was added. Preferences were added for interest on private activity bonds and for appreciation on charitable contributions (later repealed). The tax rate was increased from 20 to 21 percent, and the exemption amount was phased-out for individuals with AMTI in excess of $150,000 (112,500 for unmarried taxpayers). The prior-law preferences were retained. Net operating losses were allowed to offset only 90 percent of AMTI and the foreign tax credit was not allowed to reduce the tentative minimum tax by more than 90 percent.

7. An add-on minimum tax was first enacted by the Tax Reform Act of 1969. The add-on minimum tax was repealed by the 1982 Act. The add-on minimum tax, as originally enacted, generally was a tax at a 10-percent rate on the sum of the specified tax preferences in excess of the sum of $30,000 plus the taxpayer's regular tax.

8. Tax Equity and Fiscal Responsibility Act of 1982, S. Rpt. No. 97-494 Vol. 1, at 108 (July 12, 1982).

Since 1986, several changes have been made to the computation of the individual AMT. The principal changes are set forth below:

Adjustments and Preferences. — The principal changes made in the determination of AMTI were to repeal the preference for charitable contributions of appreciated property; repeal the preference for percentage depletion on oil and gas wells; substantially reduce the amount of the preference for intangible drilling expenses; and repeal the requirement that alternative depreciation lives be used in computing the deduction for ACRS depreciation.

Rates. — The Omnibus Budget Reconciliation Act of 1990 increased the individual AMT tax rate from 21 percent to 24 percent (when the maximum regular tax rate was increased from 28 percent to 31 percent) and the rate was further increased by the Omnibus Budget Reconciliation Act of 1993 to the 26- and 28-percent rate structure of present law (when the maximum regular tax rate was increased from 31 percent to 39.6 percent).

The Revenue Reconciliation Act of 1997 conformed the AMT capital gain rates to the lower capital gain rates adopted for the regular tax. The Jobs and Growth Tax Relief Reconciliation Act of 2003 conformed the AMT rates for dividends to the lower rates adopted for the regular tax.

Exemption amounts. — The Omnibus Budget Reconciliation Act of 1993 increased the AMT exemption amounts to $45,000 ($33,750 for unmarried taxpayers). The AMT exemption amounts were temporarily increased to $49,000 ($35,750 for unmarried individuals) for 2001 and 2002, further increased to $58,000 ($40,250 for unmarried individuals) for 2003, 2004, and 2005, and further increased to $62,550 ($42,500 for unmarried individuals) for 2006 [and in 2007 and 2008 Congress again enacted annual extensions of the temporary increases in the exemption amounts, raising them about 5 percent each year].

Credits. — For 1998 and subsequent years, the nonrefundable personal credits have been allowed on a temporary basis to offset the AMT. The last extension, through [2008], was enacted by the [Tax Extenders and Alternative Minimum Tax Relief Act of 2008, §101, Pub. L. No. 110-343 (Division C), 122 Stat. 3861, 3863]. The Economic Growth and Tax Relief Reconciliation Act of 2001 ("EGTRRA") provided that the child tax credit, the adoption credit, and the saver's credit may offset the AMT (subject to the sunset provisions of that Act). . . .

II. DATA AND DISCUSSION OF ISSUES

A. DATA

DATA ON TAXPAYERS AFFECTED BY THE AMT

A taxpayer has an alternative minimum tax liability only when his tentative minimum tax exceeds his regular tax liability. However, under present law, for taxable years after [2008], nonrefundable personal credits (with certain exceptions as described above) may not reduce regular tax liability below the tentative minimum tax. Thus, a taxpayer may be affected by the AMT without technically having an AMT liability if the taxpayer's regular tax exceeds the tentative minimum tax by an amount that is less than the credits. In this case, the taxpayer may reduce his or her regular tax liability to the tentative minimum tax amount, but cannot use the full amount of credits because the credits cannot be used to reduce tax liability below that of the tentative minimum tax. Because the number of taxpayers affected by the AMT through lost credits or with actual AMT liability is determined by an interaction with the regular tax system, in general reductions in regular tax liability, whether from decreases in regular tax rates or from expansions of credits and deductions, will increase the number of taxpayers impacted by the AMT. Similarly, increases in regular tax liability will decrease the number of taxpayers impacted by the AMT.

Figure 16-1, below, shows the number of taxpayers with AMT liability and the aggregate amount of such liabilities from 1987 through 2004, together with projections for 2006 through 2017. Figure 16-2 presents projected data on individual taxpayers affected by the individual AMT for 2006 through 2017.[10] These data show that there will be a sharp increase in the number of taxpayers affected by the AMT in 2007. The principal reason for this increase is that, beginning in 2007, the AMT exemption levels revert to the levels in effect prior to 2001 and certain nonrefundable personal credits are no longer allowed against the AMT.* The number of taxpayers affected by the AMT continues to rise through 2010 as a result of the fact that the AMT exemption levels are not indexed for inflation while the regular income tax is indexed for inflation. By 2010, almost 31 million individual income tax returns will have AMT liability and/or restricted use of credits totaling approximately $119 billion. The number of taxpayers affected by the AMT declines in 2011 as a result of the expiration of the provisions of EGTRRA.[11] The expiration of EGTRRA raises regular income tax liability and thus causes fewer taxpayers to be affected by the AMT. After a one-time decline in the number of taxpayers affected by the AMT in 2011, the number

10. The figures and tables in this pamphlet define taxpayers affected by the AMT as those who have an AMT liability or who have restricted use of credits as a result of the AMT. There are some other ways in which taxpayers can be affected by the AMT that do not show up in this definition. For example, some taxpayers may choose to itemize deductions, even when the standard deduction would be higher, because certain itemized deductions are allowed on the AMT while the standard deduction is not. Such a taxpayer could then have a regular tax liability in excess of their AMT liability and not show up in the tables as a return "affected by the AMT," even though in the absence of the AMT they would have chosen to take the standard deduction in order to further reduce their tax liability.

* [As indicated above, after the release of this document Congress enacted two one-year extensions of the higher AMT exemption levels and continued through 2008 the permission to apply of certain nonrefundable personal credits against the AMT. Consequently the projected sharp rise in the number of taxpayers affected by the AMT and the amount of AMT liability shown in Figures 16-1 and 16-2 has been postponed at least until 2009. — EDS.]

11. The principal provisions that expire and reduce the number of taxpayers affected by the AMT include the expiration of the reduced regular income tax rates, the elimination of the phaseouts of personal exemptions and itemized deductions, and the marriage penalty relief for the standard deduction and the 15-percent bracket.

will resume rising because the AMT exemption amounts are not indexed for inflation. . . .

Figure 16-1
Individual Alternative Minimum Tax 1987-2017

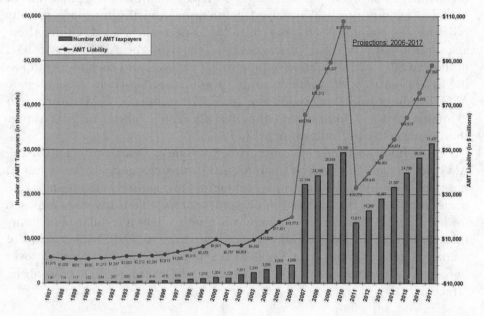

Source: SOI Historical data and JCT projections.

Figure 16-2
Taxpayers Affected by the AMT Projections: 2006-2017

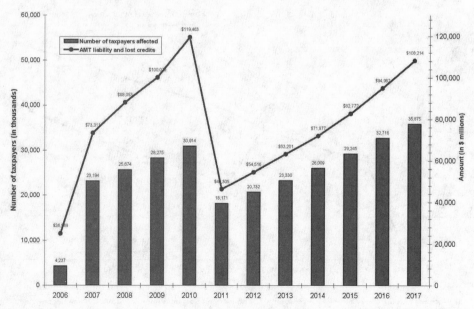

Source: Joint Committee on Taxation

Figure 16-3, below, shows the projected number of taxpayers affected by the AMT under the assumption that the principal tax rate provisions of EGTRRA are extended beyond their expiration under current law. These include the extension of the lower regular income tax rates including the establishment of the 10 percent bracket, the elimination of the phaseouts of personal exemptions and itemized deductions, and the marriage penalty relief for the standard deduction and the 15-percent bracket. Under these assumptions, the number of taxpayers affected by the AMT rises to 35.3 million in 2011 rather than dropping to 8.2 million, and rises to 51 million in 2017 rather than 35.9 million under present law. Similarly, . . . aggregate AMT liabilities and lost credits rise to $136.9 billion in 2011 rather than dropping to $46.3 billion, and they rise to $256.9 billion in 2017 rather than rising to $108.2 billion in 2017.

. . . While the upper income groups are most heavily affected by the AMT, those with the highest incomes within this category are less likely to be affected by the AMT since most of their income is taxed at the highest rate under the regular income tax, 35 percent, which exceeds the rates imposed under the AMT and thus such taxpayers tend to have a regular tax liability that exceeds their AMT liability. Note that while, in 2010, 31.5 percent of taxpayers with incomes over $1,000,000 will be affected by the AMT, over 98 percent of those with incomes between $200,000 and $500,000 will be affected.

Figure 16-3
Projected Number of Taxpayers Affected by the AMT
Under Present Law and with the Extension of EGTRRA Rates[1]

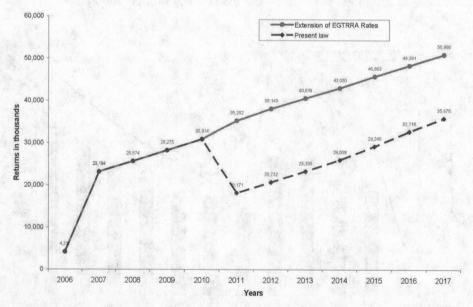

[1] This includes the extension of regular income tax rates, the elimination of the personal exemption and itemized deduction phaseouts, and the marriage penalty relief for the standard deduction and the 15-percent bracket.
Source: Joint Committee on Taxation.

. . . Also, while the initial decline in the AMT exemption levels will cause a substantial spike in the numbers of taxpayers affected by the AMT, more taxpayers at ever lower income levels will gradually be affected by the AMT with each passing year because the AMT exemption levels are not indexed for inflation while the regular income tax generally is indexed for inflation. . . .

. . . [The data show that] State and local taxes and personal exemptions are the largest preferences by a substantial margin. They also show that while the State and local tax deduction preference is nearly three times as large as the personal exemptions preference in 2006, after 2006 the personal exemptions become equally important and grow to become more important by 2017. The reason for the increased importance of personal exemptions is that the decline in the real value of the AMT exemption over time causes the AMT to extend further down the income distribution. At lower income levels the amount of State and local tax deductions tend to be less than the value of personal exemptions, because State and local taxes are highly correlated with income, while personal exemptions are not.

B.   DISCUSSION OF ISSUES

The individual AMT is in some sense a separate tax system within the individual income tax system that applies a more compressed rate structure to a broader base of income. However, the AMT should be analyzed in terms of equity, efficiency, and growth by how it interacts with the regular tax system in determining overall Federal income tax liabilities and how it affects individuals' marginal tax rates. In terms of its affect on the simplicity of the tax system, it is unambiguous that a separate calculation of tax liability under alternative rules is a complication to the individual complying with his tax obligation and the IRS in administering it.

EQUITY

In practice, the AMT has the effect of requiring more taxpayers to remit at least some funds to the Federal Treasury every year than would be the case if only the regular income taxes applied. This occurs if (1) the taxpayer's tentative minimum tax exceeds his or her regular tax liability, or (2) the use of tax credits allowed under the regular tax is limited by the taxpayer's tentative minimum tax. To the extent that taxpayers who outwardly appear to have the ability to pay taxes indeed do pay taxes, some observers conclude that the AMT increases the perceived fairness of the income tax system.

Indeed, the rationale for enacting the original individual minimum tax in 1969 and revising it later was that some taxpayers were able to avoid paying tax on relatively large incomes. Minimum tax legislation targeted those deductions, exemptions, exclusions, accounting methods, and tax credits that were considered to have contributed to such results. Some of the enacted AMT preferences and adjustments relate to business or investment income (e.g., the depreciation adjustment and the private activity tax-free bond preference) while others relate to regular-tax items that are more personal in nature (e.g., the denial of personal exemptions and certain itemized deductions).

The AMT raises particular equity issues with respect to preference items that are personal in nature. For example, some believe that it is fair that families with many dependents pay less tax than families with fewer dependents and support the regular-tax allowance of personal exemptions and child credits to further this goal. Additionally, many believe that the regular tax permits a deduction for State and local taxes because such payments impact ability to pay Federal income tax, and therefore they believe a similar deduction for AMT purposes should be allowed.[12] The AMT, in disallowing these exemptions, deductions, and credits, may frustrate this view of fairness. Also, under present law, as a result of the lack of indexing the AMT exemption levels, the reach of the AMT will increasingly extend further down the income distribution and thus make the tax system less progressive. . . .

To assess whether the AMT promotes the overall equity of the tax system, it is necessary to look beyond who remits tax payments to the Federal Treasury to who bears the burden of the AMT. Regarding the individual income tax, while economists generally believe that income taxes on wages are borne by taxpayers who supply labor, there is disagreement concerning the incidence of taxes that affect the returns earned by capital such as the taxation of interest, dividends, capital gains, and business income from pass-through entities. Economists generally believe that businesses do not bear the burden of the tax (including the individual AMT), but rather individuals bear the burden of the tax. There is disagreement, however, over which individuals bear the burden of a business income tax, whether it is customers in the form of higher prices, workers in the form of reduced wages, owners of all capital in the form of lower after-tax returns on investment, or some combination of these individuals.

The uncertainty regarding the incidence of income taxes on the returns to capital makes it difficult to assess the effect the AMT has on the equity of the burden of the income tax system. The AMT raises average tax rates for affected taxpayers. That is, the AMT increases the amount of the affected taxpayer's tax liability as a percentage of his or her income. At the individual level, higher-income taxpayers are more likely to be AMT taxpayers than are lower-income taxpayers. . . . If the burden of the taxes were to rest with the affected taxpayers, the individual AMT might increase the overall progressivity of the income tax system.

12. Others believe that the deduction for State and local taxes should not be permitted under either the regular tax or the AMT, as they believe such a deduction subsidizes public expenditure at the State and local level.

Some analysts argue that certain of the business and capital income related aspects of the AMT promote horizontal equity by taxing more equally taxpayers who have the same economic capacity but choose to engage in different patterns of tax-favored activities. Other analysts note that in a market economy, investment by taxpayers would be expected to equilibrate risk-adjusted, after-tax returns. As a consequence, the prices of tax-favored investments would be bid up (or their quantity increase) and the prices of tax-disfavored investments would fall (or their quantity decrease). In equilibrium, the pre-tax returns of tax-favored and tax-disfavored investments would differ, but their after-tax returns would be the same. For example, tax-exempt private activity bonds trade at interest rates lower than otherwise comparable taxable bonds. This is because the tax-exempt borrower does not have to offer as great an interest rate to the lender to provide the lender with a competitive after-tax return. If after-tax returns equilibrate, analysts may question whether a horizontal inequity even exists for the AMT to correct.

EFFICIENCY AND GROWTH

A tax system is efficient if it does not distort the choices that would be made in the absence of the tax system. No tax system can be fully efficient. Whether the AMT contributes to the efficiency of the United States tax system depends on the extent to which it reduces other inefficiencies in the tax system and the extent to which it creates new inefficiencies. As an income tax, the AMT reduces the return to work (labor income is taxed) and saving (investment income is taxed). As such, the AMT may distort decisions to supply labor and capital. The size of the marginal tax rate is one of the primary determinants of the size of any distortion created.[13] However, the degree of additional distortion, if any, created by the AMT depends upon the tax rates of the AMT compared to those of the regular income tax. In this regard, it is useful to distinguish the effect on labor income from the effect on investment income.

The measurement of labor income is nearly identical under the regular income tax and the AMT. The two differences arise in the measurement of income from certain incentive stock options and the measurement of net labor income when the taxpayer incurs expenses categorized as miscellaneous itemized expenses. If labor income is measured identically under the regular income tax and the AMT, then any distortions in labor supply are altered if a taxpayer subject to the AMT has a different marginal tax rate under the AMT than he or she would have under the regular tax. The AMT

13. For a more detailed discussion of marginal tax rates and possible distortions of labor supply and saving under an income tax see Joint Committee on Taxation, Overview of Present Law and Economic Analysis Relating to Marginal Tax Rates and the President's Individual Income Tax Rate Proposal (JCX-6-01), March 6, 2001.

has statutory marginal tax rates of 26 and 28 percent. However, those with alternative minimum taxable income in the phaseout range of the exemption level ($150,000 to $400,200 for married taxpayers filing jointly and $112,500 to $282,500 for unmarried individuals, in 2006)[14] will have an effective marginal tax rate of 32.5 and 35 percent, respectively.[15] In general, for 2006, taxpayers affected by the AMT are likely to have statutory regular tax rates in the 25 to 35 percent range,[16] and thus in general it may be the case that taxpayers affected by the AMT do not experience a marginal tax rate that is much different than they would have faced on the regular tax. To the extent this is true, the AMT is not likely to have a significant impact on labor supply distortions relative to the regular income tax. Under present law, however, over time many more taxpayers with regular income tax rates of 15 percent will be affected by the AMT, causing their marginal tax rate to rise to at least 26 percent, thus likely exacerbating labor supply distortions. . . . [W]hile in 2006 less than one percent of taxpayers with a regular marginal tax rate of 15 percent or less were affected by the AMT, by 2010 over 18 percent of taxpayers with a marginal income tax rate of 15 percent or less under the regular tax will face the significantly higher marginal tax rates of the AMT. . . .

A caveat to this discussion is warranted. For the AMT to mitigate or exacerbate a distortion under the regular tax, the taxpayer must know that he or she will be subject to the AMT. If a taxpayer is uncertain whether the tax rates of the AMT or the regular tax will apply it is difficult to assess the taxpayer's behavioral response. In general, if a taxpayer subject to the AMT views himself or herself as only temporarily subject to the AMT, he or she is less likely to view the AMT tax rates as the relevant tax rates upon which to plan labor supply decisions.

The same general analysis of comparing the possible distorting effects of the difference in marginal tax rates under the regular income tax and the AMT applies to taxpayer's decisions to save (to supply capital) in response to tax rates on investment income. There are several more cases where investment income is measured differently under the AMT than under the regular income tax than was the case with the measurement of labor income. By discouraging some taxpayers from undertaking what are otherwise tax-favored investments, efficiency may be increased to the extent that inefficient investment distortions that would otherwise have been

14. The length of the phaseout range is four times the size of the exemption level. . . .

15. For a taxpayer in the phaseout range, a dollar of additional AMTI causes the taxpayer to lose $0.25 in exemptions. Hence a dollar in additional AMTI causes the tax base of the AMT to rise by $1.25. Thus a taxpayer in the phaseout range with a statutory rate of 26 percent has an effective marginal rate of 26 times 1.25, or 32.5 percent. Similarly, a taxpayer in the 28 percent statutory bracket would face an effective rate of 1.25 times 28, or 35 percent.

16. Taxpayers paying under the regular tax are also often subject to various phaseouts of credits, deductions, and other benefits that raise effective marginal tax rates above these statutory rates. See, for example, Joint Committee on Taxation, Present Law and Analysis Relating to Individual Effective Marginal Tax Rates (JCS-3-98), February 3, 1998.

caused by the tax-favored treatment under the regular tax are reversed. However, the AMT generally does not eliminate tax-favored treatment of certain activities or investments, but rather limits which taxpayers may take full advantage of the tax-favored treatment provided by the regular income tax. . . . Moreover, some tax-favored activities may be permitted as part of the regular income tax as a way to reduce some other inefficiency in the economy. These arguments might suggest that efficiency could be better improved by changes in the regular income taxes. The aggregate effect of the AMT on the efficient allocation of capital across various investment opportunities may be modest. Since the Taxpayer Relief Act of 1997 conformed depreciation recovery periods for both the regular income tax and the AMT, the number of investment opportunities on which the income might subject a taxpayer to the AMT rather than the regular tax has been modest in comparison to aggregate investment in the United States. . . .

Some specific preferences and adjustments within the AMT seem inconsistent with other parts of the AMT and thus may lead to inefficiencies. For example, it is often presumed that one goal of the AMT is to apply tax to a better measure of economic income, relative to the regular tax. It is generally conceded that in measuring economic income, deductions should be allowed for expenses incurred in the production of income. However, the AMT disallows the deduction of miscellaneous itemized deductions — including unreimbursed employee business expenses and investment expenses that relate to the production of income. The disallowance of such deductions may lead to inefficiencies as taxpayers may be discouraged from certain otherwise profitable investments or activities, or encouraged to rearrange their affairs to secure AMT deductions for such costs (e.g., by attempting to move such deductions "above-the-line").

SIMPLICITY AND COMPLIANCE

The AMT requires a calculation of a second income tax base and computation of a tax on that base, so the present tax system, with an AMT, is not as simple to administer or comply with as would be the same system without an AMT. However, some might argue that the availability and widespread use of tax preparation software substantially reduces the compliance costs of the AMT.

As detailed above, relatively few taxpayers currently are subject to the AMT. . . . However, this observation understates the extent to which the AMT imposes a compliance burden on taxpayers. Many taxpayers must undertake the AMT calculation to determine whether, in fact, they are liable or whether the utilization of certain credits is limited. There are no studies that specifically measure compliance costs arising from the individual AMT. Figure [16-2], above, indicates that many more individuals will become affected by the AMT in the future.

SELECTED REFORM OPTIONS

In order to reduce the burden of the individual AMT, the tax could be amended in a number of ways. The exemption amounts could be indexed or increased so as to reduce the number of individuals subject to the AMT; the deduction for personal exemptions and the standard deduction could be allowed in computing AMTI; State and local taxes could be permitted against AMTI; the minimum tax rates could be reduced; the phaseout of the minimum tax exemption could be eliminated; all nonrefundable personal credits could be allowed to offset the minimum tax after 2006; or the AMT could be repealed.

... [A]llowing the personal exemptions against AMTI removes more taxpayers from being affected by the AMT than does allowing the deduction for state and local taxes against AMTI, and it does so at a lower revenue cost. ... [W]ith respect to reducing the number of taxpayers affected by the AMT and AMT liability and lost credits, the State and local tax option has a relatively greater effect at the upper ends of the income distribution, while the personal exemption option has the relatively greater effect at the middle and lower end of the distribution. ...

Notes and Questions

1. More and more individuals with incomes between $200,000 and $300,000 are finding to their dismay that they owe AMT, although substantially all of their income is salary and they are not involved in tax shelters. Disallowance of the deductions for state and local taxes, personal exemptions, and interest on home equity loans can easily cause AMTI to exceed taxable income by $40,000 or more, while a married couple with income of $250,000 loses $25,000 of the AMT exemption to the phase-out. For 2008 the remaining exemption may be roughly equal to the deductions lost in figuring AMTI ($45,000 or so), but while the tax bases (taxable income and AMTI) are comparable, the 10, 15, and 25 percent brackets are not available in computing AMT.

2. To avoid massive expansion in the number of taxpayers affected by the AMT, see Figure [16-1], Congress has been enacting one-year extensions of higher AMT exemption levels and continuing the temporary permission to apply nonrefundable credits against the AMT. This stop-gap approach was used in 2006, 2007, and again in 2008. The need for a long-term AMT fix (repeal?), and the looming expiration (at the end of 2010) of the Bush tax cuts may provide political impetus for wide-ranging tax reform in 2009.

3. The AMT retains the lower tax rates applicable to capital gains and qualified dividends, §55(b)(3), but taxpayers with income in the AMT exemption phase-out range find that an additional dollar of capital gain or dividend income causes their "taxable excess" that is subject to the

regular AMT rates (26 or 28 percent) to go up by 25 cents. Consequently, within the AMT exemption phase-out range, the marginal tax rate on capital gains and dividends is the statutory rate of 15 percent plus one-quarter of the applicable AMT rate. In 2007 almost half of all AMT taxpayers — 46.5 percent — faced marginal rates of 21.5 or 22 percent on capital gains and dividends. Benjamin H. Harris & Christopher Geisser, Tax Rates on Capital Gains and Dividends under the AMT, 118 Tax Notes 1031 (2008).

4. Consider charitable contributions of appreciated property. In general, these produce deductions under §170 in the amount of the fair market value of the property, without realization of the unrealized gain. In 1986 such contributions were listed as tax preferences in the AMT. One consequence was, as reported by museum directors, a total cessation of private donations of works of art to museums. In response to this behavioral reaction, Congress made a temporary exception to the rule for tangible property contributed to a charity to whose charitable purpose the property was germane. The suspension was extended and finally expanded into a permanent repeal of this as a preference item.

This history might be taken to confirm the predictions of critics who said there was no reason to think AMTI would be any more resistant than regular taxable income to the effects of intensive lobbying.

5. Alex, an unmarried individual, was discharged from his job at age 64, even though he had a contract to work to age 70. He sued for breach of contract, including restoration of pension rights and for age discrimination. The suit was settled for payments totaling $350,000 in the year of settlement and $70,000 a year thereafter for the rest of his life. His attorney's fee, taken out of the original payment, was $250,000.

Alex paid ordinary income tax of about $19,000 on the net recovery of $100,000 in the year of settlement. The IRS has asserted a deficiency of more than $60,000. They assert that the attorney's fee is a miscellaneous itemized deduction that is deductible only to the extent it exceeds 2 percent of AGI. This would increase Alex's taxable income by $7,000 (2 percent of $350,000) and raise his tax by $1,960 (28 percent of $7,000). But the more serious consequence is that miscellaneous itemized deductions are disallowed entirely in the calculation of AMTI. So Alex has AMTI of $350,000, on which the TMT is $94,500, which he thinks is outrageous on a net recovery of only $100,000.

How would you advise Alex? See Commissioner v. Banks, 543 U.S. 426, 430 (2005) ("as a general rule, when a litigant's recovery constitutes income, the litigant's [gross] income includes the portion of the recovery paid to the attorney as a contingent fee" despite the adverse impact of the AMT). In 2004 (one week before oral argument in *Banks*) Congress enacted §62(a)(20) and (e), which make attorney's fees and court costs paid in connection with certain discrimination suits nonitemized (i.e., above-the-line) deductions. Is this a sensible solution? What if Alex's claim was founded on intentional infliction of emotional distress?

6. *The Corporate AMT.* Corporate AMTI is said to be somewhat broader than individual AMTI. Partly this results from the inclusion in preferences or adjustments of some specific business accounting matters. Partly it is because depreciation, which is a bigger item in corporate income, on average, than in individual income, has long been a major adjustment in the computation of AMTI. See §56(a)(1)(A).

And partly it results from the presence of a quite general alternative standard in §56(g). Or at least it started out being quite general. In its original temporary form this preference was 50 percent of the difference between AMTI as computed without this provision and adjusted book income. (This amounted to setting corporate AMTI at the arithmetic mean of AMTI as otherwise defined and adjusted book income.) Since 1990 this has been 75 percent of the difference between AMTI as computed without this provision and "adjusted current earnings." Adjusted current earnings is defined to a large extent by reference to earnings and profits, which is the corporate income figure used to determine whether a corporate distribution is to be taxed as a dividend or return of capital. §316(a)(2).

One of several 1997 and 1998 amendments to the AMT is in §55(e), which simply exempts small corporations, as defined.

E.   CORPORATE TAX SHELTERS

Section 469 substantially wiped out the syndicated individual tax shelter business as it existed prior to 1986, but a new phenomenon has emerged, commonly referred to as Corporate Tax Shelters. These often involve exploitation of not-well-known imperfections in specialized parts of the tax law to produce results that everyone knows would not have been intended if they had been foreseen, and which are likely to be corrected soon after they are discovered. Often they involve modern, sophisticated financial products, and they frequently involve participation by foreigners not subject to U.S. taxation. The big accounting firms are currently said to be the leading inventors and promoters of these devices, although investment bankers and law firms have also been involved.

Most of these shelters are not publicly syndicated, partly to keep them secret from competitors, but largely to keep them secret from the government as long as possible. Indeed many of these schemes have been shown to prospective customers subject to confidentiality agreements committing the prospects not to reveal anything about the shelter to anyone else. Sometimes the prospect is not even permitted to show the deal to his lawyer for legal advice unless the lawyer subscribes to the confidentiality agreement. Congress responded to that aspect of the phenomenon with an array of new disclosure and penalty provisions in 2004. Take a look at §§6111 (required disclosure of reportable transactions by material advisers, including tax shelter organizers and promoters), 6707 (penalty on material advisors for failure to disclose), 6707A (penalty on shelter investors for failure to disclose reportable or listed transaction on return), and 6662A (penalty on investors for understatements attributable to reportable or listed transactions). In addition, material advisors are required to maintain lists identifying each person to whom they provided advice about reportable transactions and make that information available to the IRS on request, §§6112, 6708 (penalty for failure to maintain required lists). The §6707A definitions of "reportable transaction" and "listed transaction" supply the tripwire for this arsenal. A reportable transaction is an arrangement of "a type which the Secretary determines as having a potential for tax avoidance or evasion" determined in according to regulations prescribed under §6011, while a listed transaction is a nefarious subset, a reportable transaction specifically identified as a tax avoidance transaction. §6707A(c). Transactions offered under confidentiality conditions, transactions in which there is a right to a refund of fees if the intended tax benefits are not sustained, large loss transactions, and patented tax planning strategies are some of the categories of reportable transactions. Reg. §1.6011-4(b), Prop. Reg. §1.6011-4(b)(7). A number of procedural devices reinforce these new shelter obligations. §§6501(c)(10) (statute of limitation on assessment extended if undisclosed listed transaction), 7408 (injunctions), 7525(b) (confidentiality exception). Observe that the new disclosure and penalty regime, while responsive to the corporate tax shelter epidemic of the 1990s, is not so limited — the rules apply with equal force to individual tax shelters.

One widely discussed corporate tax shelter has been the subject of successful IRS challenge in ACM Partnership v. Commissioner, T.C. Memo 1997-115, aff'd, 157 F.3d 231 (3d Cir. 1998). The opinion in the Tax Court is long, and the transaction is complicated, but reading the opinion is rewarding if one wants to see what some of corporate America was up to in the way of "sophisticated" tax avoidance. Also illuminating is the recent government victory in a test case involving the so-called "lease-in, lease-out" (LILO) transaction, in which a U.S. corporation leases property (in this case wood pulp manufacturing equipment) from a tax exempt entity (here, a Swedish cooperative) and simultaneously subleases it back to the owner-operator together with the grant of an option to acquire the remaining term of the prime lease. BB&T Corp. v. United States, 523 F.3d 461 (4th Cir. 2008).

References

A. Leverage: Anderson, Federal Income Tax Treatment of Nonrecourse Debt, 82 Colum. L. Rev. 1498 (1982); Andrews, On Beyond *Tufts*, 61 Taxes 949 (1983); Berger, Simple Interest and Complex Taxes, 81 Colum. L. Rev.

217 (1981); Blackburn, Important Common Law Developments for Nonrecourse Notes: Tufting It Out, 18 Ga. L. Rev. 1 (1983); Halpern, Liabilities
and Cost Basis: Some Fundamental Considerations, 7 J. Real Est. Taxn. 334
(1980); Johnson, Tax Shelter Gain: The Mismatch of Debt and Supply Side
Depreciation, 61 Tex. L. Rev. 1013 (1983).

  B. Leasing: DelCotto, Sale and Leaseback: A Hollow Sound When
Tapped?, 37 Tax L. Rev. 1 (1982); Edward K. Dennehy et al., Whose Asset
Is It? An Overview of True Lease Characterization, 118 Tax Notes 627 (2008);
Faber, Determining the Owner of an Asset for Tax Purposes, 61 Taxes 795
(1983); Alex Raskolnikov, Contextual Analysis of Tax Ownership, 85 B.U. L.
Rev. 431 (2005); Warren & Auerbach, Tax Policy and Equipment Leasing
After TEFRA, 96 Harv. L. Rev. 1579 (1983); Warren & Auerbach, Transfer-
ability of Tax Incentives and the Fiction of Safe Harbor Leasing, 95 Harv.
L. Rev. 1752 (1982); Wolfman, The Supreme Court in the *Lyon*'s Den: A
Failure of Judicial Process, 66 Cornell L. Rev. 1075 (1981).

  C. The Passive Activity Loss Limitation: How, Passive Loss Relief for Real
Estate Entrepreneurs, 48 Tax Notes 1527 (1990); Lipton, PALS at Four:
Living with the Regulations, 68 Tax Notes 779 (1990).

  D. The Alternative Minimum Tax: Shaviro, Perception, Reality and Strategy: The New Alternative Minimum Tax, 66 Tax Notes 91 (1988).

  E. Corporate Tax Shelters: Karen C. Burke & Grayson M.P. McCouch,
COBRA Strikes Back: Anatomy of a Tax Shelter [SSRN abstract 1148371
(Aug. 7, 2008)]; James S. Eustice, Abusive Corporate Tax Shelters: Old
"Brine" in New Bottles, 55 Tax L. Rev. 135 (2002) (and see the other con-
tributions to the symposium on Corporate Tax Shelters published in volume
55 of the Tax Law Review); Mark P. Gergen, How Corporate Integration
Could Kill the Market for Corporate Tax Shelters, 61 Tax L. Rev. 145
(2008); Lee A. Sheppard, More Bad Law From LILO Cases?, 119 Tax
Notes 557 (2008); George K. Yin, Getting Serious About Corporate Tax
Shelters: Taking a Lesson from History, 54 S.M.U. L. Rev. 209 (2001)
(and see the other contributions to the symposium on Business Purpose,
Economic Substance, and Corporate Tax Shelters published in volume 54 of
the S.M.U. Law Review).

Part III — *Attribution of Income Among Taxpayers*

Chapter 17 — *Taxation and the Family*

A. *INTERSPOUSAL INCOME ATTRIBUTION*

1. First Principles

LUCAS v. EARL
281 U.S. 111 (1930)

Mr. Justice HOLMES delivered the opinion of the Court. This case presents the question whether the respondent, Earl, could be taxed for the whole of the salary and attorney's fees earned by him in the years 1920 and 1921, or should be taxed for only a half of them in view of a contract with his wife which we shall mention. The Commissioner of Internal Revenue and the Board of Tax Appeals imposed a tax upon the whole, but their decision was reversed by the Circuit Court of Appeals, 30 F.(2d) 909. A writ of certiorari was granted by this Court.

By the contract, made in 1901, Earl and his wife agreed

> that any property either of us now has or may hereafter acquire . . . in any way, either by earnings (including salaries, fees, etc.), or any rights by contract or otherwise, during the existence of our marriage, or which we or either of us may receive by gift, bequest, devise, or inheritance, and all the proceeds, issues, and profits of any and all such property shall be treated and considered and hereby is declared to be received, held, taken, and owned by us as joint tenants, and not otherwise, with the right of survivorship.

The validity of the contract is not questioned, and we assume it to be unquestionable under the law of the State of California, in which the parties lived.

Nevertheless we are of opinion that the Commissioner and Board of Tax Appeals were right.

The Revenue Act of 1918 ... imposes a tax upon the net income of every individual including "income derived from salaries, wages, or compensation for personal service ... of whatever kind and in whatever form paid," §213(a). The provisions of the Revenue Act of 1921 ... are similar to those of the above. A very forcible argument is presented to the effect that the statute seeks to tax only income beneficially received, and that taking the question more technically the salary and fees became the joint property of Earl and his wife on the very first instant on which they were received. We well might hesitate upon the latter proposition, because however the matter might stand between husband and wife he was the only party to the contracts by which the salary and fees were earned, and it is somewhat hard to say that the last step in the performance of those contracts could be taken by anyone but himself alone. But this case is not to be decided by attenuated subtleties. It turns on the import and reasonable construction of the taxing act. There is no doubt that the statute could tax salaries to those who earned them and provide that the tax could not be escaped by anticipatory arrangements and contracts however skillfully devised to prevent the salary when paid from vesting even for a second in the man who earned it. That seems to us the import of the statute before us and we think that no distinction can be taken according to the motives leading to the arrangement by which the fruits are attributed to a different tree from that on which they grew.

Judgment reversed.

The Chief Justice took no part in this case.

POE v. SEABORN
282 U.S. 101 (1930)

Mr. Justice ROBERTS delivered the opinion of the Court. Seaborn and his wife, citizens and residents of the State of Washington, made for the year 1927 separate income tax returns as permitted by the Revenue Act of 1926 c.27, §223.

During and prior to 1927 they accumulated property comprising real estate, stocks, bonds and other personal property. While the real estate stood in his name alone, it is undisputed that all of the property real and personal constituted community property and that neither owned any separate property or had any separate income.

The income comprised Seaborn's salary, interest on bank deposits and on bonds, dividends, and profits on sales of real and personal property. He and his wife each returned one-half of the total community income as gross income and each deducted one-half of the community expenses to arrive at the net income returned.

The Commissioner of Internal Revenue determined that all of the income should have been reported in the husband's return, and made an additional assessment against him. Seaborn paid under protest, claimed a refund, and on its rejection, brought this suit. . . .

The case requires us to construe Sections 210(a) and 211(a) of the Revenue Act of 1926, and apply them, as construed, to the interests of husband and wife in community property under the law of Washington. These sections lay a tax upon the net income of every individual. The Act goes no farther, and furnishes no other standard or definition of what constitutes an individual's income. The use of the word "of" denotes ownership. It would be a strained construction, which, in the absence of further definition by Congress, should impute a broader significance to the phrase.

The Commissioner concedes that the answer to the question involved in the case must be found in the provisions of the law of the State, as to a wife's ownership of or interest in community property. What, then, is the law of Washington as to the ownership of community property and of community income, including the earnings of the husband's and wife's labor?

The answer is found in the statutes of the State, and the decisions interpreting them.

These statutes provide that, save for property acquired by gift, bequest, devise or inheritance, all property however acquired after marriage, by either husband or wife, or by both, is community property. On the death of either spouse his or her interest is subject to testamentary disposition, and failing that, it passes to the issue of the decedent and not to the surviving spouse. While the husband has the management and control of community personal property and like power of disposition thereof as of his separate personal property, this power is subject to restrictions which are inconsistent with denial of the wife's interest as co-owner. The wife may borrow for community purposes and bind the community property. . . . Since the husband may not discharge his separate obligation out of community property, she may, suing alone, enjoin collection of his separate debt out of community property. . . . She may prevent his making substantial gifts out of community property without her consent. . . . The community property is not liable for the husband's torts not committed in carrying on the business of the community. . . .

The books are full of expressions such as "the personal property is just as much hers as his." . . . ; "her property right in it [an automobile] is as great as his." . . . ; "the title of one spouse . . . was a legal title as well as that of the other." . . .

Without further extending this opinion it must suffice to say that it is clear the wife has, in Washington, a vested property right in the community property, equal with that of her husband; and in the income of the community, including salaries or wages of either husband or wife, or both. A description of the community system of Washington and of the rights of the spouses, and of the powers of the husband as manager, will be found in Warburton v. White, 176 U.S. 484.

The taxpayer contends that if the test of taxability under Sections 210 and 211 is ownership, it is clear that income of community property is owned by the community and that husband and wife have each a present vested one-half interest therein.

The Commissioner contends, however, that we are here concerned not with mere names, nor even with mere technical legal titles; that calling the wife's interest vested is nothing to the purpose, because the husband has such broad powers of control and alienation, that while the community lasts, he is essentially the owner of the whole community property, and ought so to be considered for the purposes of Sections 210 and 211. He points out that as to personal property the husband may convey it, may make contracts affecting it, may do anything with it short of committing a fraud on his wife's rights. And though the wife must join in any sale of real estate, he asserts that the same is true, by virtue of statutes, in most States which do not have the community system. He asserts that control without accountability is indistinguishable from ownership, and that since the husband has this, quoad community property and income, the income is that "of" the husband under Sections 210-211 of the income tax law.

We think, in view of the law of Washington above stated, this contention is unsound. The community must act through an agent. This Court has said with respect to the community property system (Warburton v. White, 176 U.S. 494) that "property acquired during marriage with community funds became an acquêt of the community and not the sole property of the one in whose name the property was bought, although by the law existing at the time the husband was given the management, control and power of sale of such property. This right being vested in him, not because he was the exclusive owner, but because by law he was created the agent of the community."

In that case, it was held that such agency of the husband was neither a contract nor a property right vested in him, and that it was competent to the legislature which created the relation to alter it, to confer the agency on the wife alone, or to confer a joint agency on both spouses, if it saw fit, — all without infringing any property right of the husband. . . .

The obligations of the husband as agent of the community are no less real because the policy of the State limits the wife's right to call him to account in a court. Power is not synonymous with right. Nor is obligation coterminous with legal remedy. The law's investiture of the husband with broad powers, by no means negatives the wife's present interest as a co-owner.

We are of opinion that under the law of Washington the entire property and income of the community can no more be said to be that of the husband, than it could rightly be termed that of the wife.

We should be content to rest our decision on these considerations. Both parties have, however, relied on executive construction and the history of the income tax legislation as supporting their respective views. We shall, therefore, deal with these matters.

The taxpayer points out that, following certain opinions of the Attorney General, the Decisions and Regulations of the Treasury have uniformly made the distinction that while under California law the wife's interest in community property amounts to a mere expectancy contingent on her husband's death and does not rise to the level of a present interest, her interest under the laws of Washington, Arizona, Texas and some other states is a present vested one. They have accordingly denied husband and wife the privilege of making separate returns of one-half the community income in California, but accorded that privilege to residents of such other states. . . .

On the whole, we feel that, were the matter less clear than we think it is, on the words of the income tax law as applied to the situation in Washington, we should be constrained to follow the long and unbroken line of executive construction, applicable to words which Congress repeatedly reemployed in acts passed subsequent to such construction, . . . reenforced, as it is, by Congress' refusal to change the wording of the Acts to make community income in states whose law is like that of Washington returnable as the husband's income.

The Commissioner urges that we have, in principal, decided the instant question in favor of the Government. He relies on United States v. Robbins, 269 U.S. 315; Corliss v. Bowers, 281 U.S. 376, and Lucas v. Earl, 281 U.S. 111.

In the *Robbins* case, we found that the law of California, as construed by her own courts, gave the wife a mere expectancy and that the property rights of the husband during the life of the community were so complete that he was in fact the owner. Moreover, we there pointed out that this accorded with the executive construction of the Act as to California.

The *Corliss* case raised no issue as to the intent of Congress, but as to its power. We held that where a donor retains the power at any time to revest himself with the principal of the gift, Congress may declare that he still owns the income. While he has technically parted with title, yet he in fact retains ownership, and all its incidents. But here the husband never has ownership. That is in the community at the moment of acquisition.

In the *Earl* case a husband and wife contracted that any property they had or might thereafter acquire in any way, either by earnings (including salaries, fees, etc.) or any rights by contract or otherwise, "shall be treated and considered and hereby is declared to be received held taken and owned by us as joint tenants. . . ." We held that, assuming the validity of the contract under local law, it still remained true that the husband's professional fees, earned in years subsequent to the date of the contract, were his individual income, "derived from salaries, wages, or compensation for personal services" under §§210, 211, 212(a) and 213 of the Revenue Act of 1918. The very assignment in that case was bottomed on the fact that the earnings would be the husband's property, else there would have been nothing on which it could operate. That case presents quite a different question from this, because here, by law, the earnings are never the property of the husband, but that of the community.

Finally the argument is pressed upon us that the commissioner's ruling will work uniformity of incidence and operation of the tax in the various states, while the view urged by the taxpayer will make the tax fall unevenly upon married people. This argument cuts both ways. When it is remembered that a wife's earnings are a part of the community property equally with her husband's, it may well seem to those who live in states where a wife's earnings are her own, that it would not tend to promote uniformity to tax the husband on her earnings as part of his income. The answer to such argument, however, is, that the constitutional requirement of uniformity is not intrinsic, but geographic. . . . And differences of state law, which may bring a person within or without the category designated by Congress as taxable, may not be read into the Revenue Act to spell out a lack of uniformity. . . .

The District Court was right in holding that the husband and wife were entitled to file separate returns, each treating one-half of the community income as his or her respective income, and its judgment is

Affirmed.

The Chief Justice and Mr. Justice Stone took no part in the consideration or decision of this case.

Notes and Questions

1. (a) What is the issue in these cases? Is the government seeking to tax both Mr. and Mrs. Earl on the same income? Should it? If not, what is all the shouting about?

(b) Would it be accurate to say that the issue in these cases is simply one of rate graduation? Does that help in resolving the problems presented?

(c) Can the results and reasoning in these two cases be reconciled? Or does the difference in style between Justice Holmes and Justice Roberts reflect a more fundamental inconsistency? Note the absence of dissent in both cases and the short time between them.

(d) Can the difference in result between these two cases be tolerated? How long? If not, what should be done about it?

2. Does tax avoidance, or the possibility of tax avoidance, make a significant difference between these cases?

Earl can hardly be thought of as a tax avoidance case itself, in view of the date of the contract involved. But if the case had gone the other way the door might have been opened to tax avoidance in a rather easy manner. The Court did not think that was "the import of the statute before us."

But does this provide a satisfactory ground for distinguishing *Seaborn*? Perhaps the community property system is to be given greater weight than the Earls' contract because it is something already there, not of the parties' making, and therefore not subject to easy (ab)use for the sake of tax avoidance.

Not easy, perhaps, but not impossible either. The California community property law, for example, was long ago amended to make it effective for federal income tax splitting. And at least two common-law states, Pennsylvania and Massachusetts, adopted community property laws, in the 1940s, for the purpose of reducing their citizens' federal income tax burdens. One might still conclude that tax avoidance at this level is best left to Congress itself to deal with.

3. *Horizontal equity*, or the proposition that taxpayers in like circumstances should be taxed alike, is another perspective from which to view these cases. Justice Holmes' opinion seems to say that the arrangement involved in *Earl* does not produce enough difference in circumstances to justify a substantial change in tax burdens. Is this a sounder perspective than that of tax avoidance?

But if this is the rationale for *Earl*, what of *Seaborn*? Is the discrimination between taxpayers approved in *Seaborn* any less objectionable than that which was avoided in *Earl*?

Indeed, given *Seaborn*, could not a persuasive argument be made for deciding *Earl* in favor of the taxpayer to ameliorate the discrimination implicit in *Seaborn*?

Even if *Seaborn* had gone the other way, why should a taxpayer like Earl — who earns his living — be denied the tax advantage which a rentier can achieve by giving property to his spouse?

On the whole, does *Earl* promote horizontal equity or not?

What is the purpose of §66? Does it promote horizontal equity or not?

4. We have seen that monetary gifts to friends or family are taxed to the *donor* only, in that no deduction is allowed for noncharitable gifts given, while §102(a) excludes gifts received from the income of the donee. See generally Chapter 4 above. In contrast to current law, under a theoretical construct known as the *material consumption* definition of income, gifts would be taxable to the *donee* only; this would be accomplished by allowing the donor a deduction for all gifts given (not just gifts to charity) and by requiring gifts received to be included in the donee's income (which would necessitate repeal of §102(a)). If Congress adopted the material consumption definition of income would it affect the result in cases like *Earl*? What if Earl had instructed his clients to pay half their bills to his independent adult daughter, who was not his law partner?

5. *Nonspousal assignees.* Although *Earl* involved spouses, it states a principle that is fully applicable outside the marital context as well. Indeed it has been called "the first principle of income taxation: that income must be taxed to him who earns it." Commissioner v. Culbertson, 337 U.S. 733 (1949). Is that generally a sound proposition?

(a) *A*, a famous actress, agreed to donate her services on a particular day to a charity. The charity then contracted for *A* to appear on a television program for a fee which would be paid, pursuant to the agreement, to the charity. Is the fee includible in *A*'s gross income? Does it make any significant difference whether it is? Reconsider in this regard note 7 on p. 641.

(b) *B*, a well-known film actor, formed a corporation. The stock is owned by *B*, his wife, his agent, his attorney, and his tax advisor. *B* enters into a contract to provide his services as an actor solely and exclusively to the corporation. His salary under this contract is adequate but not really competitive for a man of *B*'s reputation.

The corporation then enters into a variety of arrangements for the production of motion pictures featuring *B*. In some cases the corporation simply provides *B*'s services to another producer for a fee or for a percentage of the gross profit from a film.

Is *B* taxable on anything more than his salary from the corporation? Is this case essentially any different from any other case of a closely held corporation whose owners work harder to build it up than would an outsider at the same salary?

(c) *Earl* and the foregoing examples all involve an assignment preceding the earning of the assigned income. Would the case for taxing the assignor be stronger or weaker if the assignment occurred after performance of all services, so that the assignment would operate to confer an unconditional right on the assignee? Consider, for example, a life insurance salesperson entitled to receive renewal commissions upon the renewal of policies previously sold by him. If he assigns that right, would *Earl* indicate that he should remain taxable nevertheless?[1]

(d) Both *Earl* and *Seaborn* involve compensation for services. What application do they have to other sorts of income?

2.   Split Income and Joint Returns

Efforts were made to ameliorate discrepancies between common law and community property states by taxing community income entirely to the person whose services earned it, but the objections of community property state representatives proved very difficult to overcome. In 1948, with the end of wartime revenue requirements, an opportunity arose to deal with the problem the other way around, by letting common law couples compute income taxes as if they were in community property states.

Married taxpayers had long been allowed to file joint returns, so that excess deductions of one spouse could be taken against income of the other. See Edward H. Clark, Chapter 3A above. But if both spouses had positive income this was generally disadvantageous, since the income would be piled up and taxed as if it all accrued to a single individual. There was at that time only a single graduated rate schedule in the individual income tax, and it applied to a joint return in the same way as to any other return.

---

1. See Helvering v. Eubank, Chapter 18A below.

In 1948 the method of computing tax on a joint return was changed. Under the new, split-income method, one computed joint taxable income by including all income and deductions of both spouses, divided that joint taxable income by two, looked up the tax on (either) half, and multiplied that tax by two — exactly as if the joint income were divided equally between spouses and reported half on the individual return of each.

The split income computation was eliminated as such in 1969, when a separate rate schedule was adopted for married couples filing joint returns. But the computation is incorporated in that schedule as compared with the schedule for married individuals filing separate returns. (Study §§1(a) and (d) to confirm that assertion.) So the substance of the split income provision has been retained down to the present day, and it has had the effect of virtually eliminating any general difference in income tax burdens between common law and community property states as such, and of eliminating the problem of determining attribution of income as between spouses. The result of Lucas v. Earl has thus been rejected in the marital context in which it arose.

Notes and Questions

1. After 1948 no state adopted community property laws, and those that had adopted them in the 1940s abandoned them. Pennsylvania accomplished the abandonment in the most elegant manner, retroactively, by declaring the community property law unconstitutional. Wilcox v. Pennsylvania Mutual Life Ins. Co., 357 Pa. 581, 55 A.2d 521 (1947). Where the community property law was only repealed, conveyancers have had to be concerned about possible continuing effects on property titles of transactions during the period the community property law was in effect.

2. The split income provision of 1948 has been applauded for treating all couples with the same total income alike, regardless of how the earning of the income is distributed between spouses. This has undoubtedly solved or avoided many vexing questions of income attribution. But is this effect basically sound? Are there compelling reasons for taxing some couples differently because of the source of their income as between spouses even though the total income is the same?

Consider first the question of imputed income. It is sometimes argued that a two-earner couple ought to be taxed less than a one-earner couple with the same money income because the latter has the same money income plus the imputed income from services (or leisure) of the nonworking spouse. Is that a convincing argument? If so, what should be done about it?

Second, consider a nonworking spouse contemplating employment: What will be the marginal rate of tax on earnings from that employment? Are there persuasive reasons why it ought to be something less? If so, how could that best be achieved?

3. *Same-sex marriage.* Traditionally, state law was taken as the starting point for the tax law's determination of marital status. See §7703. Massachusetts has recognized same-sex marriage since 2004, see Goodridge v. Department of Public Health, 798 N.E.2d 941(2003), and a number of other states (including California, Connecticut, New Hampshire, New Jersey, and Vermont) allow gay couples to enter into "domestic partnerships" or "civil unions" that while not called marriages are defined to provide all the rights and responsibilities of marriage under state law. Despite state sanction, the benefits (or burdens) of married tax status are not available to same-sax couples by operation of 1 U.S.C. §7, enacted in 1996 as part of the Defense of Marriage Act.

> In determining the meaning of any Act of Congress, or of any ruling, regulation, or interpretation of the various administrative bureaus and agencies of the United States, the word "marriage" means only a legal union between one man and one woman as husband and wife, and the word "spouse" refers only to a person of the opposite sex who is a husband or a wife.

B. THE MARRIAGE BONUS AND THE MARRIAGE PENALTY

Whatever one thinks of the split-income provision as it affects relative tax burdens of married taxpayers, it created a radical difference in tax liability in some cases between two individuals earning the same salary if one was unmarried while the other was married to a spouse without income. In some cases, the tax on the unmarried earner was as much as 48 percent higher than that on his married counterpart.

This discrepancy was perhaps particularly burdensome when an unmarried person was supporting dependents other than a spouse; and so we have a special rate schedule for heads of households. That schedule is now in §1(b). It was originally designed to impose a tax about midway between that of a married couple and that of an unmarried taxpayer on the same total income. The definition of head of household has varied but it has always included a widow or widower with dependent children.

In 1969, Congress acted in favor of unmarried individuals more generally, by enacting the rate schedule in §1(c). This was constructed to ensure that the tax on an unmarried individual would never exceed 120 percent of the tax on a married couple filing jointly with the same total income. By its terms, therefore, this change did not eliminate the tax advantage that might result from marriage, but only cut it back by about half.

But what then about married couples in which both spouses have substantial incomes? The rates in §1(c) are available only to unmarried taxpayers, not to married taxpayers filing separately. The result is that two persons with equal individual incomes will now find that marriage produces an increase in tax over that they would pay if unmarried. This increase is the so-called *marriage penalty*, and it has been the subject of considerable controversy.

1. Constitutionality of the Marriage Penalty

MAPES v. UNITED STATES
576 F.2d 896 (Ct. Cl.), cert. denied, 439 U.S. 1046 (1978)

Before Davis, Nichols, and Kashiwa, Judges.

NICHOLS, Judge, delivered the opinion of the court. . . . At issue is the constitutionality of what plaintiffs characterize the federal tax system's "marriage penalty." Under existing provisions of the Internal Revenue Code, some married couples incur substantially greater personal income tax liabilities than they would if unmarried and filing as single persons. . . .

Plaintiffs seek a refund of $1,220.10 for tax year 1976, which is the additional amount they paid to IRS as a consequence of being married and thereby precluded from filing separately under the tax schedule applicable to single taxpayers. Plaintiff Mapes' taxable income for 1976 was $16,763.20. Plaintiff Bryson's taxable income was $15,890.17. Prior to filing their claim for a refund, plaintiffs calculated that under section 1 of the Code, if unmarried in 1976, Mr. Mapes would have incurred a total tax liability of $3,701 and Ms. Bryson's total tax liability would have been $3,611. The difference, which constituted their claim for refund, between the combined tax liability if unmarried ($7,312) and that incurred because they were married ($8,532.10) is $1,220.10. Plaintiffs are to be congratulated for the able way in which they have put a serious and important issue before this court.

It should be noted at the outset that not all married couples are penalized taxwise by reason of their status. To the contrary, many, if not most, married couples achieve considerable tax savings through income-splitting on a joint return. [Tables 17-1 and 17-2] are taken from plaintiffs' brief and reflect their calculation of the variable impact of the penalty or reward offered for marriage. It is when both spouses generate somewhat comparable incomes that the benefits of income-splitting cease to exist. As a general rule, two-income couples would benefit from filing separately and using the tax rates applicable to single persons. They are not, however, eligible to use these schedules, but are restricted to filing jointly under Code section 1(a) or separately under section 1(d). As plaintiffs observe, of course, the option to file under section 1(d) is of marginal value to the typical couple, even those with dual-incomes, because the total tax liability of married couples filing separately nearly always equals or exceeds the combined tax liability on a joint return.

TABLE [17-1]
1976 Marriage Penalty by Income Combinations*

Husband's Adjusted Gross Income	Wife's Adjusted Gross Income										
	Zero	2,000	4,000	6,000	8,000	10,000	12,000	14,000	16,000	18,000	20,000
Zero	Zero	Zero	-177	-248	-319	-405	-458	-486	-625	-787	-932
2,000	Zero	54	121	91	61	-13	-40	-123	-190	-287	-328
4,000	-177	121	229	240	222	174	92	81	79	32	-53
6,000	-248	91	240	263	271	168	158	212	260	213	213
8,000	-319	61	222	271	224	193	248	352	410	448	443
10,000	-405	-13	174	168	193	227	332	446	579	622	685
12,000	-458	-40	92	158	248	332	447	636	774	885	960
14,000	-486	-123	81	212	352	446	636	830	1,036	1,159	1,285
16,000	-625	-190	79	260	410	579	774	1,036	1,254	1,428	1,563
18,000	-787	-287	32	223	448	622	885	1,159	1,428	1,611	1,797
20,000	-932	-382	-53	213	443	685	960	1,285	1,563	1,797	1,992

* All calculations assume each taxpayer elects the standard deduction. Computations do not include the 1976 General Tax Credit. A minus sign indicates a tax reduction.

TABLE [17-2]

Difference Between the Tax of a Married Couple Filing Joint Return and the
Combined Tax of Two Single Persons with the Same Income Combination as the
Married Couple — 1976*

Joint adjusted gross income	Tax liability	Amount of Marriage Penalty by the Ratio of the Spouses' Separate Incomes in Dollars and as a Percent of the Joint Tax Liability		
		100/zero	75/25	50/50
$ 4,000	$ 54	−177/−327%	−22/−40%	54/100%
8,000	691	−319/−46	91/13	229/33
12,000	1,463	−458/−31	151/10	263/18
16,000	2,244	−625/−27	91/4	224/10
20,000	3,179	−932/−29	184/5	227/10
24,000	4,289	−1,264/−29	213/5	447/10
32,000	6,992	−1,881/−26	429/6	1,254/18

* All calculations assume each taxpayer elects the standard deduction. Computations do not include the 1976 General Tax Credit. A minus sign indicates a tax reduction.

While the Code provisions involved are loosely called a "marriage penalty," their effects are thus more complex in reality. We expect all persons to make all important decisions in life in light of their tax effect. For the tax-minded young man or woman, with a substantial income, the Code adds to the attractiveness of a prospective spouse without taxable income, and detracts from one with it. Thus the provisions may have an income-levelling effect. But we have no data showing that as yet they operate in that manner. Love and marriage defy economic analysis. As one of Gilbert and Sullivan's heroines sang many years ago:

> True love must single-hearted be —
>   *Bunthorne:* Exactly so!
> From every selfish fancy free —
>   *Bunthorne:* Exactly so!
> No idle thought of gain or joy,
> A maiden's fancy should employ —
> True love must without alloy,
>
>   *   *   *
>
> It follows then, a maiden who
> Devotes herself to loving *you*
> Is prompted by no selfish view!
>   *Men:* Exactly so!

The humor of this was in the unattractiveness of the love object. But our Internal Revenue Code provides an opportunity to the young to demonstrate the depth of their unselfishness, however kind and beautiful the beloved may be.

Formerly society frowned upon cohabitation without marriage, assessing various punitive sanctions by law and custom against the partners themselves, and their innocent offspring. Most of these have now been eliminated in our more "enlightened" society. Cohabitation without marriage, and illegitimacy, or whatever it is now called, are said to be rapidly increasing. Certainly the tax-minded young man and woman, whose relative incomes place them in the disfavored group, will seriously consider cohabitation without marriage. Thereby they can enjoy the blessings of love while minimizing their forced contribution to the federal fisc. They can synthesize the forces of love and selfishness.

It is easier, however, to point out these effects, than it is to show how the Constitution forbids Congress from achieving them in its revenue laws. The Supreme Court is not easily astonished by anything it finds therein. In Commissioner v. Kowalski [Chapter 2B.1 above, p. 50, at 59] (1977), Justice Brennan said: "[A]rguments of equity have little force in construing the boundaries of exclusions and deductions from income many of which, to be administrable, must be arbitrary." . . .

In reviewing the evolution of the tax rates in section 1 of the Code it appears that the pendulum at different times has swung to favor both married and single taxpayers, without ever quite reaching equilibrium. In fact, the perplexities of shaping a legislative scheme which distributes the incidence of the personal income tax equitably between married and single taxpayers have confounded Congress for many years. Before 1948, income was taxed on an individual basis, without regard to marital status. The loophole inherent in this set-up was that married couples, fortunate enough to reside in community property states were able to split, on a 50-50 basis, the marital community's income, thereby enjoying lower graduated tax rates and reaping considerable tax savings relative to their counterparts in non-community property states. Income-splitting in community property states was upheld in Poe v. Seaborn [Chapter 17A above] (1930). The issue now before the court had its roots in the Revenue Act of 1948, which sought to neutralize the effect of income-splitting in community property states vis-a-vis other married couples, and to equalize geographically taxes paid by couples. The Act amended the Code to allow all married couples to file joint returns, treating the couples as if they consisted of two single individuals each of whom had one-half the couple's combined income. The net result was that married couples paid a tax equal to twice what a single taxpayer would pay on one-half of their total income.

One of the consequences of the 1948 amendment was that single taxpayers paid substantially higher taxes than did married couples with the same income. Under the prior rates a single person's tax could be as much as 40.9 percent higher than the tax paid by couples filing a joint return on the same amount of taxable income. See S. Rep. No. 552, 91st Cong., 2d Sess. 260 (1969), reprinted in Internal Revenue Acts: Text and Legislative

History 1966-1970, 1639, 1909. Convinced that this disparity in tax burden was excessive, Congress enacted a new single person rate schedule designed to provide a tax liability for single persons ranging from 17 to 20 percent above that of married couples with taxable incomes between $14,000 and $100,000. See id. At the same time Congress repealed the previous arrangement wherein couples had the option of filing jointly or of choosing the schedule applicable to single taxpayers. The 1969 Act substituted four schedules: sections 1(a), applicable to married individuals filing joint returns; 1(b), applicable to heads of households; 1(c), applicable to unmarried individuals; and 1(d), applicable to married individuals not filing joint returns. The rates in section 1(d) are considerably higher than those in subsection (c). Apparently Congress precluded use of the lower rates for single individuals in order to discourage married taxpayers from rearranging their finances and shifting income so as to avoid or lower their tax liabilities. See Staff of the Joint Committee on Internal Revenue Taxation, General Explanation of the Tax Reform Act of 1969 at 223 (1970).

Although the Tax Reform Act succeeded in removing the disparity in tax burden between married and unmarried individuals, it also created the marriage penalty, by preventing married couples from taking advantage of the lower combined rates applicable to unmarried taxpayers. While this creates some inequalities, perhaps, for two-income couples, we are persuaded that overall the legislation is constitutionally acceptable. . . .

Plaintiffs first advocate that the penalty on marriage, because it burdens the fundamental right to marry, should be subjected to a strict scrutiny for purposes of equal protection and due process analysis. . . .

. . . Califano v. Jobst, 434 U.S. 47 (1977) concerned a challenge to sections of the Social Security Act providing that benefits to a dependent child would terminate upon marriage to an individual not eligible for social security benefits. In upholding the termination of benefits upon marriage, the Court stated that the "general rule is not rendered invalid simply because some persons who might otherwise have married were deterred by the rule or because some who did marry were burdened thereby." 434 U.S. at 54. . . .

. . . The effect of the rates in Code section 1 is somewhat analogous to the effect of the termination of social security benefits in *Jobst:* the elevated tax burden might in fact dissuade some couples from entering into matrimony, but does not present an insuperable barrier to marriage. More often it changes the relative attraction of different prospective spouses for the tax-minded individual wishing to marry. For many it provides an incentive to marry. . . . This does not rise to the level of an "impermissible" interference with the enjoyment of a fundamental right. . . .

In addition to the fundamental interest argument, plaintiffs assert a second ground for rigorously scrutinizing the challenged provisions. They contend that because the marriage penalty has a discriminatory impact on women it is based on suspect criteria, and cannot be upheld in the absence of a showing of governmental interests. It is plaintiffs' position that the Code implicitly treats wives as secondary earners and husbands as primary earn-ers. . . . The net outcome, it is urged, is that the tax rates discriminate on the basis of sex, a result which is prohibited under the rationales of such cases as Weinberger v. Wisenfeld, 420 U.S. 636 (1975), and Frontiero v. Richardson, 411 U.S. 677 (1973).

. . . The essence of the discrimination argument is that the wife's "secondary" income is taxed at higher graduated rates when that income is aggregated with the income of the husband. This is said to burden the wife's constitutional right to pursue a career, contrary to Truax v. Raich, 239 U.S. 33, 41 (1915). It seems to us that the fatal flaw in this analysis is that the Code does not label either spouse's income as primary or secondary, but simply provides for its aggregation on the joint return. It is as easy to argue that if the wife should earn a higher salary than her husband his right to pursue an occupation is burdened by the higher marginal tax rates imposed once the income is aggre-gated. The Code simply does not differentiate on this basis, and its failure to do so is likewise not per se invidious discrimination on the basis of sex.

Even assuming *arguendo*, that the rates might reasonably be attacked as founded on discriminatory stereotypes, the joint return system does not operate to the financial detriment of all women. . . . Whenever statutes have been invalidated for invidious discrimination on the basis of sex, it has been the case that all members of the class were burdened, and not simply a portion of the class. . . .

A third contention offered by plaintiffs is that the tax rates in question are invalidated by Hoeper v. Tax Commission of Wisconsin, 284 U.S. 206 (1931). *Hoeper* adjudicated the constitutionality of a Wisconsin law requiring the aggregation of the separate incomes of spouses. The combined incomes were then taxed at rates higher than would apply if the taxpayers were single and filing separately. . . . The Court majority concluded that the Wisconsin law was arbitrary and a denial of due process under the fourteenth amend-ment because it measured "the tax on one person's property or income by reference to the property or income of another." 284 U.S. at 215. . . .

We find, however, that there are sufficient distinctions between the present system and that in *Hoeper* to justify upholding the current rates and filing elections. Principally, we rest on the fact that the Wisconsin law provided no alternative to that of taxation of combined income. The federal scheme, on the other hand, offers married couples the opportunity to file separately and each be taxed individually on his or her own income. Thus, the present provision does not altogether mandate that the tax on one spouse's income be measured by reference to the earnings of the other. . . .

Eliminating, then, issues of fundamental rights and of sex, not here applicable, the standard for testing the challenged provisions is whether they are reasonable, not arbitrary, and whether they "rest upon some ground of difference having a fair and substantial relation to the object of the leg-islation, so that all persons similarly circumstanced shall be treated alike." Royster Guano Co. v. Virginia, 253 U.S. 412, 415 (1920). . . .

In San Antonio School district v. Rodriguez, supra, the Court eloquently discussed the difficulties of invalidating tax legislation:

> Thus, we stand on familiar ground when we continue to acknowledge that the Justices of this Court lack both the expertise and the familiarity with local problems so necessary to the making of wise decisions with respect to the raising and disposition of public revenues. . . . *No scheme of taxation*, whether the tax is imposed on property, income, or purchases of goods and services, *has yet been devised which is free of all discriminatory impact.* In such a complex arena in which no perfect alternatives exist, the Court does well not to impose too rigorous a standard of scrutiny lest all . . . fiscal schemes become subjects of criticism under the Equal Protection Clause. [(Footnote omitted — Emphasis supplied) 411 U.S. at 41.]

The Court further noted that "within the limits of rationality, 'the legislature's efforts to tackle the problems' should be entitled to respect." Id. at 42.

In this setting, we examine the respective claims of the parties about the rationality and reasonability of the present taxation schedules and elections. A major criticism plaintiffs voice is that the legislative policy of taxing all married couples equally, regardless of whether their income is derived from the efforts of one spouse or of both, conflicts with the fundamental principle of progressive taxation, that of ability to pay. It is argued accordingly that there is no relation to a legitimate purpose, a point amply demonstrated by the uneven impact of the marriage penalty. For example, married taxpayers with one income save as much as $1,881 a year over two single taxpayers while dual income taxpayers with the same income may pay as much as $1,264 a year more than they would if they were single. Plaintiffs contend that this situation is hardly a rational reflection of Congress' desire to tax household economies stemming from marriage. Rather, to serve due process purposes, plaintiffs would have us require that all similarly-situated married couples incur tax obligations not greater than the tax burden imposed on two single individuals with comparable incomes.

Plaintiffs offer considerable support for the argument that the marriage penalty does not reflect taxation based on ability to pay, or an allocation of tax burden designed to tax fairly the household economies achieved by marriage. They directed us to one study actually showing an inverse relationship between living expenses and the disparity between the incomes of each spouse:

> The tax provisions applying to one- and two-earner couples are identical; hence, if they have the same money income, the same number of exemptions, and the same deductions, they pay the same tax. This gives the wrong tax result, because the married couple with one spouse working has more taxpaying ability than the married couple with two spouses working. [G. Break and J. Pechman, Federal Tax Reform, The Impossible Dream? 34 (1975).]

Working couples have less financial ability to pay taxes than do single-income couples, principally because of the significant expenses of earning the second income, such as transportation, lunches, and clothing, which are not tax deductible. In reality, the two job couple is economically worse off. See generally Bittker, Federal Income Taxation and the Family, 27 Stan. L. Rev. 1389 (1975). The essence of plaintiffs' argument then, is that the challenged provisions fail even the minimum scrutiny test.

Again, we cannot agree. Plaintiffs have demonstrated that the tax classifications used by Congress are imperfect and imprecise, at least to some degree. This, however, is not sufficient to justify invalidating the legislation. . . .

As defendant properly asserts, there cannot be a "marriage-neutral" tax system. The policy of taxing all couples with equal incomes equally, a major factor in the 1948 income-splitting provision, is not unreasonable. Nor is it unreasonable to attempt to tax the household economies enjoyed by married people. In certain instances these assumptions fail. See Hearings Before the House Ways and Means Committee on Tax Treatment of Single Persons and Married Persons Where Both Spouses are Working, 92d Cong., 2d Sess. 76-77 (1972). This does not invalidate the overall scheme. . . . Finally, we note that the legislature is entitled to make reforms on a piecemeal basis, and solve one inequity at a time, as it did in 1969, by providing relief for unmarried taxpayers. See, e.g., Williamson v. Lee Optical Co., supra, 348 U.S. at 489. . . .

In short, the foregoing serves to illustrate that tax disparities will exist no matter how the rates are structured. This is simply the nature of the beast. The tax law is complicated enough already without the added complexity a full solution to this problem would apparently require. We in the judiciary, are neither equipped nor inclined to second guess the legislature in its determination of appropriate tax policies. See San Antonio School Board v. Rodriguez, supra. Like the court in Johnson v. United States, 422 F. Supp. 958 (N.D. Ind. 1976), aff'd sub nom. Barter v. United States, 550 F.2d 1239 (7th Cir. 1977), cert. denied, 434 U.S. 1012 (1978), we are satisfied that the present provisions pass a minimum rationality test, and should be upheld as constitutional.

One final point — plaintiffs have argued to us that their case is distinguishable from *Johnson* because of the existence of the oral antenuptial agreement entered into by them before their marriage in 1976. The terms of the agreement are that each spouse will manage his or her own income separately, each contributing equally to the expenses of maintaining their common home. Plaintiffs argue that the existence of this arrangement provides an even better reason for finding the statute unconstitutional, at least as applied to them. The difficulty is that even if this unusual situation creates an additional burden for these plaintiffs, there is certainly not the massive discrimination here that is envisioned in cases such as Reed v. Reed, supra, and Frontiero v. Richardson, supra. Plaintiffs admit they cannot describe the disfavored class as those who have made agreements like theirs. In fact, the plaintiffs' extra burden appears self-inflicted.

Accordingly, we hold that the section 1 rates . . . are constitutional. Plaintiffs motion for summary judgment is denied and defendant's cross-motion for summary judgment is granted. The petition is dismissed.

Note

To the same effect, see Druker v. Commissioner, 697 F.2d 46 (2d Cir. 1983) cert. denied, 461 U.S. 957 (1983), affirming the Tax Court on the issue of constitutionality, but also upholding the Commissioner's imposition of a 5 percent penalty under §6653 for "intentional though honest disregard of the statute." 697 F.2d at 56.

Some constitutional courts in Europe have gone the other way, however, under constitutional provisions requiring taxation to be in accordance with ability to pay.

2. Legislative Relief

In 1981 Congress provided limited relief from the marriage penalty by allowing married couples a deduction of 10 percent of the amount of the qualified earned income of the spouse with smaller earned income, up to $30,000. The maximum deduction allowable was thus $3,000. This provision (§221) was repealed in 1986 on the grounds suggested in the excerpts which follow.

REPEAL TWO-EARNER DEDUCTION

*United States Treasury Department, 2 Tax Reform for Fairness,
Simplicity, and Economic Growth 13-14, (1984) (Treasury I)*

The current deduction for two-earner married couples is poorly designed to offset the increased tax liabilities that some couples face as a result of marriage. The deduction does not eliminate the marriage penalty for many couples, and for some it provides a benefit that exceeds any increase in tax liability caused by marriage. For still others, the deduction merely increases the marriage bonus. Moreover, because the deduction applies only to earned income, it has no effect when the marriage penalty arises from investment income. . . .

The Treasury Department proposals include flatter tax rate schedules and lower marginal tax rates. In general, these changes would reduce the significance of tax consequences in individual decisions and improve incentives for taxpayers to work and invest. Since the tax structure would retain a degree of progressivity, as well as joint return treatment for married couples, the Treasury Department proposals would not eliminate the possibility of a marriage penalty, nor, for that matter, of a marriage bonus. They represent, however, a more direct and consistent attempt to minimize the impact of marriage on tax liabilities than the current two-earner deduction.

Repeal of the two-earner deduction would eliminate Schedule W and one line from Form 1040 and seven lines from Form 1040A. It may also increase the number of taxpayers eligible to file Form 1040EZ. . . .

Notes and Questions

1. *Current magnitude of the marriage penalty: comparing the rate schedules.* One can compute taxes for a variety of income combinations and produce a table for current law akin to Table [17-1] for prior law. It is less tedious to take the matter up more analytically, beginning with the current rate schedules. Locating the current rate schedules in itself requires a little digging because the schedules set forth in §1(a)-(e) have both their rates and bracket endpoints adjusted elsewhere. Rate reductions in 2001 added an initial 10 percent bracket and reduced by 3 percentage points each tax rate above 15 percent except for the top rate, which was cut from 39.6 to 35 percent. §1(i). Bracket endpoints are now adjusted annually to account for increases in the cost of living so that inflation does not trigger tax increases. §1(f), (i)(1)(C). The IRS publishes a document each year that sets forth the adjusted rate tables. The tables for 2009 are set forth in Rev. Proc. 2008-66, 2008-45 I.R.B. 1107, 1109 (Nov. 10, 2008).

Compare the schedules prescribed for 2009 for single[2] taxpayers and married taxpayers filing separate returns[3]: In each case there are six brackets (taxable income ranges) to which the same sequence of progressive rates (10, 15, 25, 28, 33, and 35 percent) is applied. The width of the brackets sometimes differs, however. Observe that the first two brackets (10 percent and 15 percent) are the same for single individuals and for married individuals filing separately. By virtue of this equivalence a single individual with an income of up to $67,900 [2009] could marry without experiencing a tax increase. While the 25 percent bracket begins at $33,950 for both single individuals and married individuals filing separately, the bracket is wider for single individuals; that is, the 28 percent rate starts to apply at a lower taxable income level for married individuals filing separately ($68,525), than for single individuals ($82,250). Consequently, a single individual can have as much as $13,725 (= $82,250 − $68,525) more income taxed at the 25 percent rate than a married individual filing separately, who would pay a 28 percent rate of tax on this additional income. Thus if two individuals each have taxable income of $82,250 or more, marriage will cause $13,725 for each of them to be shifted from the 25 percent bracket into the 28 percent bracket. A 3 percentage point difference in tax on $13,725 is $411.75. For the newly married couple the additional tax from marrying will be twice that, or $823.50. To put this dollar figure in perspective, it is one-half of 1 percent of the minimum taxable income necessary to produce it, and 2.5 percent of the tax the couple would have paid but for the

---

2. The word *single* is used here as a shorthand for the statutory phrase "unmarried individuals (other than surviving spouses and heads of households)."

3. The usual comparison is between the rate schedules for married couples and for single individuals. But for comparability one must either double the brackets in the latter (to compare couples) or halve the brackets in the former (to compare individuals). The latter adjustment is already reflected in the schedule for married taxpayers filing separately, so it is marginally easier to make the comparisons on an individual basis.

marriage. These percentages decline as one moves from the bottom to the top of the 25 percent bracket because the dollar amount of the penalty remains constant.

A similar computation for the breakpoints between the 28 and 33 percent brackets shows marriage pushing $67,125 (= $171,550 − $104,425) of taxable income into the higher rate for each individual. The 5 percent rate differential produces a marriage penalty of $6,712.50 for the couple. This is in addition to the penalty produced at the 25/28 line, so the total is $7,536, or 2.2 percent of the minimum taxable income necessary to produce it. The breakpoints between the 33 and 35 percent brackets differ by $186,475 (= $372,950 − $186,475), to which a 2 percent rate differential applies, producing a penalty of $3,729.50 each, or $7,459 for the couple. This yields a total maximum marriage penalty in 2009 of $14,995, on a minimum combined taxable income of $745,900, or 2.0 percent.

These results are depicted graphically in Figure 17-1. Observe that there is no penalty associated with the first two steps in the rate schedule and that penalty becomes significant only for high income couples. According to the Census Bureau, in 2005 median household income was $46,326, and 71 percent of all American households had total money income of less than $75,000. U.S. Census Bureau, Statistical Abstract of the United States: 2008, Table 668 (127th ed. 2007).

2. *Marriage bonuses.* Maximum marriage bonuses can be computed in a similar manner, except that the comparison is between a single taxpayer and a couple filing jointly with only one income, so the computations

Figure 17-1
Federal Income Tax Rates, 2009: The Marriage Penalty

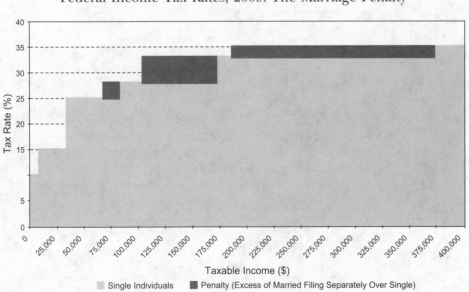

should be done with the rate schedule for couples filing joint returns instead of separate returns. A single individual with a taxable income of $16,700 [2009] would have half of it taxed at 10 percent and the other half at 15 percent, but if he or she marries a spouse with no income and they file jointly, all $16,700 would fall in the lower bracket, for a tax saving (marriage bonus) of $417.50 (= 5% of $8,350). Similarly, a single individual is subject to a 25 percent rate on income over $33,950 [2009], but joint filers reach the 25 percent bracket only at $67,900, producing an additional marriage bonus at this rate step of $3,395 (= 10% of ($67,900 – $33,950)). The differences in relative bracket size that produce larger marriage penalties as taxpayers reach the 33 and 35 percent brackets produce smaller marriage bonuses. As the brackets for a single taxpayer get farther from those for a married individual, they get closer to those for a married couple. Indeed, for the 35 percent bracket there is no difference between the bracket boundary for a couple filing jointly and for a single taxpayer, and therefore no marriage bonus can result from this step in the schedule. The total maximum dollar amount of the marriage bonus in 2009 is $7,321.50 on taxable income of $208,850; a single individual with this income would experience a 13.5 percent tax reduction by marrying a spouse without income. See Figure 17-2.

As a percentage of tax, the marriage bonus is much larger at lower incomes — the 2001 legislation that eliminated the marriage penalty in the 10 percent and 15 percent brackets (by making the brackets for married

Figure 17-2
Federal Income Tax Rates, 2009: The Marriage Bonus

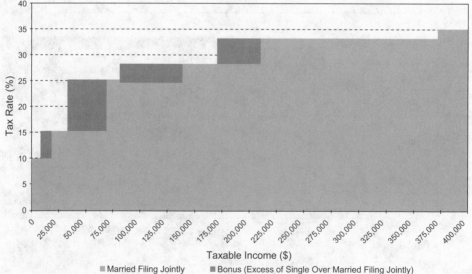

taxpayers filing jointly double the width of the brackets applicable to single individuals) exacerbated marriage bonuses for low- and middle-income taxpayers. A single individual with taxable income of $67,900 [2009] could experience a tax reduction of $3,812.50 by wedding a spouse without income, a 29.0 percent reduction in her $13,162.50 single tax liability! Is that fair? Does it matter that this tax reduction is not equally available to all? (Same-sex couples, even if married under state law, cannot file jointly for federal income tax purposes. 1 U.S.C. §7.) Is there a strong economic or social policy reason for subsidizing stay-at-home spouses?

3. *Unequal incomes.* For a couple with two unequal incomes, one can think of the rate schedules for married individuals as producing penalties up to the level of the smaller income and bonuses on the excess of the larger income over the smaller. The computation does not generally reduce to fixed dollar amounts for each step in the schedule, however, because the tax for two singles in different brackets varies with each dollar shifted from one to the other.

4. *The standard deduction.* Historically, the standard deduction also contributed to the marriage penalty because the amount of the standard deduction for a single taxpayer was more than half the standard deduction for a married couple filing jointly. Consequently, marriage would cause each individual to forfeit part of his or her standard deduction, making some income subject to tax that, absent the marriage, would have been exempt. The 2001 legislation eliminated this component of the marriage penalty by equalizing the standard deductions for single taxpayers and married individuals filing separately. §63(c)(2).

5. *Other provisions.* Numerous other provisions contribute to the marriage penalty. One way to find them is to look for references to married individuals filing separate returns, since Congress has been quite thorough about preventing married taxpayers from avoiding their "penalties" by that route. Among the other provisions are phase-outs of various deductions and credits that start at different income levels for married and single individuals.

6. *Policy questions.* Are the reasons given in 1986 for repeal of the two-earner deduction persuasive? If the deduction was "poorly designed" perhaps it should have been redesigned rather than repealed. Can you suggest a better designed deduction for two-earner couples?

What about the criticism that the two-earner deduction had "no effect when the marriage penalty arises from investment income"? Are there good reasons for focusing relief on two-earner couples as contrasted with couples in which either or both spouses have investment income?

7. *Distortions, assuming marriage.* Assume two individuals are happily married and are not tempted to change that status. Does the present system of taxing married couples create serious inequities or behavioral distortions other than the one for or against marriage, and if so what could usefully be done about them?

The most obvious beginning of an answer is the assertion that the joint return system causes the income of the second earner to be effectively taxed at a beginning marginal rate equal to the top marginal rate achieved by the primary earner. This might be called the *second-earner penalty*. Is it right to think of a couple's highest marginal rates applying all to the income of one spouse?

If there is a second-earner penalty, is that something that ought to be eliminated, or at least mitigated? How?

Problem

Alice and Jack are both single and are subject to the Alternative Minimum Tax in §55. What will be the effect of marriage on their income tax liabilities?

3.   Self-Help

BOYTER v. COMMISSIONER
668 F.2d 1382 (4th Cir. 1981)

Before Winter, Chief Judge, Russell and Widner, Circuit Judges.
Winter, Chief Judge: . . .

I

Taxpayers were married in Maryland in 1966 and were domiciled in Maryland during the tax years in issue, 1975 and 1976. Both are employed as federal civil service employees and have not insubstantial earnings. They filed joint federal income tax returns and reported their income as married individuals filing separately from 1966 to 1974.

Probably as a result of dinner table conversation with a friend who had been recently divorced, taxpayers came to the realization that their combined federal income tax liability would be lower if they were able to report their respective incomes as unmarried individuals. They were also aware that the Internal Revenue Code provides that the determination of whether an individual is married shall be made as of the close of the taxable year. 26 U.S.C. §143(a)(1). . . .

Late in 1975 taxpayers traveled to Haiti. Through an attorney, whose name they had obtained from a Baltimore public library and who in correspondence had quoted them an attractive estimate of his fee and expenses, they obtained a decree of divorce. The action was instituted by Angela Boyter and the divorce decree was granted on the ground of incompatibility of character notwithstanding that the parties occupied the same hotel room prior to and immediately after the granting of the decree. Moreover, Angela Boyter testified before the Tax Court that her character was not incompatible to that of David Boyter. She testified also that the sole reason for her obtaining the divorce was "because the tax laws, as currently written, caused us to pay a penalty for being married." Indeed she testified that she advised her Haitian counsel "that we got along quite well and planned to continue to live together...."[2] Shortly after the Haitian court granted the divorce, taxpayers returned to their matrimonial domicile in Maryland and were remarried in Howard County, Maryland on January 9, 1976. For the calendar year 1975 taxpayers filed separate income tax returns claiming the rates applicable to unmarried individuals.

In November of 1976 taxpayers traveled to the Dominican Republic where David Boyter, as the moving party, obtained a divorce decree on November 22, 1976.... The taxpayers returned to Maryland to their matrimonial domicile and they were remarried on February 10, 1977....

The Commissioner determined a deficiency in income taxes for each of the taxpayers for 1975 and 1976 and taxpayers sought review in the Tax Court. The Tax Court sustained the deficiencies. Although the government argued that the divorce decrees should be disregarded for federal income tax purposes because a year-end divorce whereby the parties intend to and do in fact remarry early in the next year is a sham transaction, the Tax Court expressed no view of this argument. Rather, it undertook an elaborate analysis of Maryland law with respect to the validity of the divorce decrees and concluded that Maryland would not recognize the foreign divorces as valid to terminate the marriage. On this basis, the Tax Court entered judgment for the government.

---

2. The perspective in which the Boyters viewed their purported divorce further appears in the following testimony of Angela Boyter:

Q. You testified that you intended to be divorced, I think I understood you as saying, for all purposes of divorce even though your motivation was for purposes of tax reduction. Is that correct?
A. For all legal purposes, yes.
Q. Did you intend to physically separate from your spouse?
A. No.
Q. Did you continue to cohabit with your spouse throughout the period?
A. To what?
Q. Cohabit. Live together.
A. I suppose so, yes.
Q. You suppose so? You did? Is that correct?
A. Yes.
Q. Okay. Did you intend to separate your finances with respect to savings and checking accounts?
A. No.
Q. Investments?
A. Only in the kinds of property separations that automatically happen when you get divorced.

II

We agree with the government's argument that under the Internal Revenue Code a federal court is bound by state law rather than federal law when attempting to construe marital status. Eccles v. Commissioner, 19 T.C. 1049, aff'd, 208 F.2d 796 (4 Cir. 1953). The difficulty with this approach in this case, however, is that the Maryland authorities do not establish beyond peradventure of doubt that the two divorces with which we are concerned are invalid under Maryland law. As the Tax Court stated, "the law in Maryland with regard to the recognition of migratory divorces obtained in a foreign country by Maryland domiciliaries has not been explicitly declared by either the legislature or the highest court of that state," although, as the taxpayers have demonstrated, a number of Maryland trial courts, explicitly and implicitly, have recognized the validity of migratory foreign divorces.

In this ambiguous state of the Maryland law, we would ordinarily be disposed to invoke the certification procedure authorized by Ann. Code of Md., Cts. & Jud. Proc. §12-601 (1980), and ask the Maryland Court of Appeals for a definitive pronouncement on the validity of these bilateral foreign migratory divorces.[3]

But there are other factors which must be considered. The Commissioner has made it clear to us both in his brief and in oral argument that he intends to press the contention, advanced in the Tax Court but not decided by it, that under the sham transaction doctrine taxpayers must be treated as husband and wife in computing their federal income taxes for the years 1975 and 1976 even if Maryland recognizes the validity of their migratory foreign divorces. Of course, if the issue of their validity were certified to the Maryland Court of Appeals and that court ruled them invalid, that decision would decide this case. Significantly, however, if the Maryland Court of Appeals ruled them valid, further proceedings would still be necessary in a federal tribunal and those proceedings might result in an adjudication which would render the certification and the opinion of the Maryland court a futile, academic exercise with respect to final disposition of this case.

We think that certification is inappropriate here. Considerations of comity lead us to conclude that we ought not to request the Maryland Court of Appeals to answer a question of law unless and until it appears that the answer is dispositive of the federal litigation or is a necessary and inescapable ruling in the course of the litigation. . . .

---

3. This option was not available to the Tax Court because the Maryland statute does not permit a certification from that tribunal.

III. . . .

The sham transaction doctrine has its genesis in Gregory v. Helvering, 293 U.S. 465 (1935). There, a taxpayer wished to effect the distribution to herself of stock of Monitor Securities Corporation, which was owned by United Mortgage Corporation of which she was the sole stockholder, without paying the tax which would apply to a direct transfer of Monitor's stock as a dividend from United. Strictly in accordance with the letter of the law, she sought to effect a tax-free reorganization of United whereby United transferred the Monitor stock to a new corporation, owned solely by taxpayer, and promptly liquidated the new corporation, distributing the stock to her. She then sold the stock, contending that she owed taxes only for the capital gain that she had realized.

The Court conceded that the reorganization was conducted in technical compliance with applicable statutes and that taxpayers are entitled to arrange their affairs so as to decrease their tax liability. It held nonetheless that the "whole undertaking . . . was in fact an elaborate and devious form of conveyance masquerading as a corporate reorganization" and should be disregarded for income tax purposes. 293 U.S. at 470. The Court relied on the fact that the transaction had no business or corporate purpose—that it was "a mere device which put on the form of a corporate reorganization as a disguise for concealing its real character, . . . the sole object of which was the consummation of a preconceived plan, not to reorganize a business, or any part of a business, but to transfer a parcel of corporate shares to [taxpayer]." Id. at 469. The Court concluded: "The rule which excludes from consideration the motive of tax avoidance is not pertinent to this situation, because the transaction upon its face lies outside the plain intent of the statute. To hold otherwise would be to exalt artifice above reality and to deprive the statutory provision in question of all serious purpose." Id. at 470.

Gregory has been subsequently invoked by the courts to disregard the form of a variety of business transactions and to apply the tax laws on the basis of the substance or economic reality of the transactions. . . .

In evaluating the substance of a transaction, the courts take care to examine the transaction as a whole, not as the sum of its component parts. Accordingly, the liquidation of a corporation will be disregarded when it reincorporates subsequently and the business enterprise remains in substantially continuous operation. Atlas Tool Co. v. Commissioner, 614 F.2d 860, 866-867 (3 Cir. 1980); accord, Rose v. United States, 640 F.2d 1030 (9 Cir. 1981); cf. Pridemark, Inc. v. Commissioner, 345 F.2d 35, 41 (4 Cir. 1965) (enterprise not continuous where business suspended for a year), overruled in different part, Of Course, Inc. v. Commissioner, 499 F.2d 754 (4 Cir. 1974). In addition, as the Supreme Court has stated, "Tax consequences follow what has taken place, not what might have taken place." Central Tablet Mfg. Co. v. United States, 417 U.S. 673 790 (1974). Benefits

under the tax laws are thus not available on the basis of hypothetical contingencies. See Knetsch v. United States, 364 U.S. 361, 365-368 (1960)
[Chapter 10A.1 above].

Although the sham transaction doctrine has been applied primarily
with respect to the tax consequences of commercial transactions, personal
tax consequences have often served as the motive for those transactions. E.g.,
Tower, 327 U.S. at 289. *Clifford*, 309 U.S. at 333-336. The principles involved,
moreover, are fundamental to the system of income taxation in the United
States and should be applicable generally. As Judge Learned Hand, the
author of the *Gregory* opinion in the Court of Appeals, noted:

> The question always is whether the transaction under scrutiny is in fact what it appears
> to be in form; a marriage may be a joke; a contract may be intended only to deceive
> others; an agreement may have a collateral defeasance. In such cases the transaction as
> a whole is different from its appearance. True, it is always the intent that controls; and
> we need not for this occasion press the difference between intent and purpose. We may
> assume that purpose may be the touchstone, but the purpose which counts is one which
> defeats or contradicts the apparent transaction, not the purpose to escape taxation
> which the apparent, but not the whole, transaction would realize. In Gregory v. Helver-
> ing . . . , the incorporators adopted the usual from for creating business corporations;
> but their intent, or purpose, was merely to draught the papers, in fact not to create
> corporations as the court understood that word. That was the purpose which defeated
> their exemption, not the accompanying purpose to escape taxation; that purpose was
> legally neutral. Had they really meant to conduct a business by means of two reorga-
> nized companies, they would have escaped whatever other aim they might have had,
> whether to avoid taxes, or to regenerate the world. [Chisholm v. Commissioner, 79 F.2d
> 14, 15 (2 Cir. 1935) (citation omitted).]

Thus Revenue Ruling 76-255 applies the sham transaction doctrine to the
divorce of taxpayers who promptly remarry. The underlying purpose of the
transaction, viewed as a whole, is for the taxpayers to remain effectively
married while avoiding the marriage penalty in the tax laws. It is the prompt
remarriage that defeats the apparent divorce when assessing the taxpayers'
liability, just as the prompt reincorporation of a business enterprise in continuous operation defeats the apparent liquidation of the predecessor corporation. Atlas Tool Co., 614 F.2d at 866-867. Thus, the sham transaction
doctrine may apply in this case if, as the record suggests, the parties intended
merely to procure divorce papers rather than actually to effect a real dissolution of their marriage contract.[7]

Having decided in principle that the sham transaction doctrine may
apply to the conduct of the parties, we make no finding that the conduct
in fact constituted a sham. In our view, the Tax Court as the trier of fact is
the only body competent to make that determination in the first
instance. . . .

---

7. Relevant to their intentions is the evidence suggesting that they may have practiced fraud upon the
tribunals granting the divorces.

Accordingly we remand the case to the Tax Court to determine whether the divorces, even if valid under Maryland law, are nonetheless shams and should be disregarded for federal income tax purposes for the years in question.

Remanded.

WIDENER, Circuit Judge, dissenting: . . . I think the Tax Court had the proper thought in mind when it treated the case as one under Maryland law. I express no opinion on the correctness of the Tax Court's decision that the divorces in question were invalid under Maryland law, but note, as does the majority, that various inferior Maryland courts have held similar divorces obtained in foreign countries to be valid.

I think the case should be certified to the Maryland courts under the applicable statutes of that State. This case presents a classic opportunity to take advantage of the certification procedure permitted by the statutes of various states, including Maryland, so that we may actually decide a case at hand instead of deciding as we are bound to do what the opinion of a State court of last resort would be, Commissioner v. Estate of Bosch, 387 U.S. 456 (1967), or upon an assumption as we do here. . . .

Questions

1. Suppose a man secures a foreign migratory divorce and then returns and marries another woman. Suppose further that his former spouse probably could, if so disposed, secure a decree annulling the foreign divorce for lack of jurisdiction in the court granting it, but that she shows no signs of doing any such thing. How should the foreign divorce and the remarriage be treated for income tax purposes?

What if the woman in the last paragraph also remarried; how should her marital status be adjudged for income tax purposes?

Would it matter if it is the practice in the community where these parties live to deal with divorce and remarriage in this manner, without attention to legal niceties? Should federal income taxes still be left to turn on state law for a determination of marital status?

Suppose, as a further complication, that state welfare law, as administered, would treat these divorces and remarriages as valid unless challenged by one of the parties. Should federal tax law then follow the state welfare law or family law in determining marital status? See Borax v. Commissioner, 349 F.2d 666 (2d Cir.), cert. denied, 383 U.S. 935 (1965) and Currie, Suitcase Divorce in the Conflict of Law, *Simons, Rosenthal,* and *Borax,* 34 U. Chi. L. Rev. 26 (1966).

2. Now that the tables have turned and a large marriage bonus has reappeared for many one-earner couples, are cases like *Boyter* mere curiosities?

C. *SUPPORT, GIFT, OR COMPENSATION?*

UNITED STATES v. HARRIS
942 F.2d 1125 (7th Cir. 1991)

Before Cudahy and Flaum, Circuit Judges, and Eschbach, Senior Circuit Judge.

ESCHBACH, Senior Circuit Judge: David Kritzik, now deceased, was a wealthy widower partial to the company of young women. Two of these women were Leigh Ann Conley and Lynnette Harris, twin sisters. Directly or indirectly, Kritzik gave Conley and Harris each more than half a million dollars over the course of several years. For our purposes, either Kritzik had to pay gift tax on this money or Harris and Conley had to pay income tax. The United States alleges that, beyond reasonable doubt, the obligation was Harris and Conley's. In separate criminal trials, Harris and Conley were convicted of willfully evading their income tax obligations regarding the money,[1] and they now appeal.

Under Commissioner v. Duberstein, 363 U.S. 278, 285 (1960), the donor's intent is the "critical consideration" in distinguishing between gifts and income. We reverse Conley's conviction and remand with instructions to dismiss the indictment against her because the government failed to present sufficient evidence of Kritzik's intent regarding the money he gave her. . . .

THE ADMISSIBILITY OF KRITZIK'S LETTERS

Harris was convicted of two counts of willfully failing to file federal income tax returns under 26 U.S.C. §7203 (the same offense for which Conley was convicted) and two counts of willful tax evasion under 26 U.S.C. §7201.[4] At trial, Harris tried to introduce as evidence three letters that Kritzik wrote, but the District Court excluded the letters as hearsay. . . .

The first of the letters at issue was a four page, handwritten letter from Kritzik to Harris, dated April 4, 1981. In it, Kritzik wrote that he loved and trusted Harris and that, "so far as the things I give you are concerned—let me say that I get as great if not even greater pleasure in giving than you get in receiving." Def. Ex. 201, p. 2. He continued, "I love giving things to you and to see you happy and enjoying them." Id. In a second letter to Harris of the

---

1. Harris was sentenced to ten months in prison, to be followed by two months in a halfway house and two years of supervised release. She was also fined $12,500.00 and ordered to pay a $150.00 special assessment. Conley was sentenced to five months in prison, followed by five months in a halfway house and one year supervised release. She was also fined $10,000.00 and ordered to pay a $100.00 assessment.

4. 26 U.S.C. §7201 provides:

Any person who willfully attempts in any manner to evade or defeat any tax imposed by this title or the payment thereof shall, in addition to other penalties provided by law, be guilty of a felony. . . .

same date, Kritzik again wrote, "I . . . love you very much and will do all that I can to make you happy," and said that he would arrange for Harris' financial security. Def. Ex. 202, p. 3. In a third letter, dated some six years later on May 28, 1987, Kritzik wrote to his insurance company regarding the value of certain jewelry that he had "given to Ms. Lynette Harris as a gift." Kritzik forwarded a copy of the letter to Harris.

These letters were hearsay if offered for the truth of the matters asserted — that Kritzik did in fact love Harris, enjoyed giving her things, wanted to take care of her financial security, and gave her the jewelry at issue as a gift. But the letters were not hearsay for the purpose of showing what Harris believed, because her belief does not depend on the actual truth of the matters asserted in the letters. Even if Kritzik were lying, the letters could have caused Harris to believe in good faith that the things he gave her were intended as gifts. . . .

In general, hearsay problems like this — evidence being admissible for one purpose but not for another — still leave the District Court discretion. . . . [W]e will usually defer to a trial judge's conclusion that, under Fed. R. Evid. 403, otherwise admissible evidence is likely to do more harm than good. . . .

In this case, however, the letters were too important to Harris' defense to be excluded. Her belief about Kritzik's intent decides the issue of willfulness, which is an element of the offense, and she had no other objective means of proving that belief. . . .

THE TAX TREATMENT OF PAYMENTS TO MISTRESSES

Our conclusion that Harris should have been allowed to present the letters at issue as evidence would ordinarily lead us to remand her case for retrial. We further conclude, however, that current law on the tax treatment of payments to mistresses provided Harris no fair warning that her conduct was criminal. Indeed, current authorities favor Harris' position that the money she received from Kritzik was a gift. We emphasize that we do not necessarily agree with these authorities, and that the government is free to urge departure from them in a noncriminal context. But new points of tax law may not be the basis of criminal convictions. . . .

Again, the definitive statement of the distinction between gifts and income is in the Supreme Court's *Duberstein* decision, which applies and interprets the definition of income contained in 26 U.S.C. §§61. But as the Supreme Court described, the *Duberstein* principles are "necessarily general." It stated, " 'One struggles in vain for any verbal formula that will supply a ready touchstone. The standard set up . . . is not a rule of law; it is rather a way of life. Life in all its fullness must supply the answer to the riddle.' " Id., quoting Welch v. Helvering, 290 U.S. 111, 115 (1933). Along these lines, Judge Flaum's concurrence properly characterizes *Duberstein* as "eschew[ing] ... [any] categorical, rule-bound analysis" in favor of a "case-by-case" approach.

   Duberstein was a civil case, and its approach is appropriate for civil cases. But criminal prosecutions are a different story. These must rest on a violation of a clear rule of law, not on conflict with a "way of life." If "defendants [in a tax case] ... could not have ascertained the legal standards applicable to their conduct, criminal proceedings may not be used to define and punish an alleged failure to conform to those standards." United States v. Mallas, 762 F.2d 361, 361 (4th Cir. 1985). This rule is based on the Constitution's requirement of due process and its prohibition on ex post facto laws. ... The rule is also statutory in tax cases, because only "willful" violations are subject to criminal punishment. *Mallas*, 762 F.2d at 363; see Cheek v. United States, 498 U.S. 192 (1991). In the tax area, "willful" wrongdoing means the "voluntary, intentional violation of a known" — and therefore knowable — "legal duty." *Cheek*, 111 S. Ct. at 610, quoting United States v. Bishop, 412 U.S. 346 (1973). If the obligation to pay a tax is sufficiently in doubt, willfulness is impossible as a matter of law, and the "defendant's actual intent is irrelevant." United States v. Garber, 607 F.2d 92, 98 (5th Cir. 1979) (en banc), quoting United States v. Critzer, 498 F.2d 1160, 1162 (4th Cir. 1974).

   We do not doubt that *Duberstein*'s principles, though general, provide a clear answer to many cases involving the gift versus income distinction and can be the basis for civil as well as criminal prosecutions in such cases. We are equally certain, however, that *Duberstein* provides no ready answer to the taxability of transfers of money to a mistress in the context of a long term relationship. The motivations of the parties in such cases will always be mixed. The relationship would not be long term were it not for some respect or affection. Yet, it may be equally clear that the relationship would not continue were it not for financial support or payments.

   Usually, a tax decision by the Supreme Court does not stand by itself. Treasury Regulations add specifics to broad principles, and federal cases apply the broad principles and prevailing regulations to the facts of particular cases. But these usual sources of authority are silent when it comes to the tax treatment of money transferred in the course of long term, personal relationships. No regulations cover the subject, and we have found no appellate or district court cases on the issue.

   The most pertinent authority lies in several civil cases from the Tax Court, but these cases favor Harris' position. At its strongest, the government's case against Harris follows the assertions that Harris made, but now repudiates, in a lawsuit she filed against Kritzik's estate. According to her sworn pleadings in that suit, "all sums of money paid by David Kritzik to Lynette Harris ... were made ... in pursuance with the parties' express oral agreement." Government Exhibit 22, p. 4. As Harris' former lawyer testified at her trial, the point of this pleading was to make out a "palimony" claim under the California Supreme Court's decision in Marvin v. Marvin, 18 Cal. 3d 660 (1976). Yet, the Tax Court has likened *Marvin*-type claims to amounts paid under antenuptial agreements. Under this analysis, these claims are not taxable income to the recipient:

> In an antenuptial agreement the parties agree, through private contract, on an arrangement for the disposition of their property in the event of death or separation. Occasionally, however, the relinquishment of marital rights is not involved. These contracts are generally enforceable under state contract law. See Marvin v. Marvin, 18 Cal. 3d 660 (1976). Nonetheless, transfers pursuant to an antenuptial agreement *are generally treated as gifts* between the parties, because under the gift tax law the exchanged promises are not supported by full and adequate consideration, in money or money's worth.

Green v. Commissioner, T.C. Memo 1987-503 (emphasis added). We do not decide whether Marvin-type awards or settlements are or are not taxable to the recipient. The only point is that the Tax Court has suggested they are not. Until contrary authority emerges, no taxpayer could form a willful, criminal intent to violate the tax laws by failing to report *Marvin*-type payments. Reasonable inquiry does not yield a clear answer to the taxability of such payments.

Other cases only reinforce this conclusion. Reis v. Commissioner, T.C. Memo 1974-287 is a colorful example. The case concerned the tax liability of Lillian Reis, who had her start as a 16 year old nightclub dancer. At 21, she met Clyde "Bing" Miller when he treated the performers in the nightclub show to a steak and champagne dinner. As the Tax Court described it, Bing passed out $50 bills to each person at the table, on the condition that they leave, until he was alone with Reis. Bing then offered to write a check to Reis for any amount she asked. She asked for $1,200 for a mink stole and for another check in the same amount so her sister could have a coat too.

The next day the checks proved good; Bing returned to the club with more gifts; and "a lasting friendship developed" between Reis and Bing. For the next five years, she saw Bing "every Tuesday night at the [nightclub] and Wednesday afternoons from approximately 1:00 p.m. to 3:00 p.m. . . . at various places including . . . a girl friend's apartment and hotels where [Bing] was staying." He paid all of her living expenses, plus $200 a week, and provided money for her to invest, decorate her apartment, buy a car, and so on. The total over the five years was more than $100,000. The Tax Court held that this money was a gift, not income, despite Reis' statement that she "earned every penny" of the money. Similarly, in Libby v. Commissioner, T.C. Memo 1969-184 (1969), the Tax Court accorded gift treatment to thousands of dollars in cash and property that a young mistress received from her older paramour. And in Starks v. Commissioner, T.C. Memo 1966-134, the Tax Court did the same for another young woman who received cash and other property from an older, married man as part of "a very personal relationship."

The Tax Court did find that payments were income to the women who received them in Blevins v. Commissioner. T.C. Memo 1955-211, and in Jones v. Commissioner, T.C. Memo 1977-329. But in *Blevins*, the taxpayer was a woman who practiced prostitution and "used her home to operate a house of prostitution" in which six other women worked. Nothing suggested that the money at issue in that case was anything other than payments in the normal course of her business. Similarly in *Jones*, a woman had frequent hotel meetings with a married man, and on "each occasion" he gave her cash (emphasis added). Here too, the Tax Court found that the relationship was one of prostitution, a point that was supported by the woman's similar relationships with other men.

If these cases make a rule of law, it is that a person is entitled to treat cash and property received from a lover as gifts, as long as the relationship consists of something more than specific payments for specific sessions of sex. What's more, even in *Blevins*, in which the relationship was one of raw prostitution, the Tax Court rejected the IRS claim that a civil fraud penalty should be imposed. Nor was a fraud penalty applied in Jones, the other prostitution case, although there the issue apparently was not raised. The United States does not allege that Harris received specific payments for specific sessions of sex, so *Reis*, *Libby*, and *Starks* support Harris' position.

Judge Flaum argues in his concurrence that these cases turn on their particular facts and do not make a rule of law. Fair enough (although the cases do cite each other in a manner that suggests otherwise). We need not decide this issue. We only conclude that a reasonably diligent taxpayer is entitled to look at the reported cases with the most closely analogous fact patterns when trying to determine his or her liability. When, as here, a series of such cases favors the taxpayer's position, the taxpayer has not been put on notice that he or she is in danger of crossing the line into criminality by adhering to that position. These Tax Court cases can turn entirely on their facts, yet together show that the law provided no warning to Harris that she was committing a criminal act in failing to report the money that she received. It is also worth noting that Judge Flaum's argument has no application to the case of Green v. Commissioner, T.C. Memo 1987-503, which, as discussed at the start of this section, suggests that *Marvin*-type palimony payments are not taxable income as a matter of law.

Besides Harris' prior suit, the United States also presented evidence regarding the overall relationship between Harris and Kritzik. Testimony showed that Harris described her relationship with Kritzik as "a job" and "just making a living." . . . [T]his evidence tells us only what Harris thought of the relationship. Again, the Supreme Court in *Duberstein* held that the donor's intent is the "critical consideration" in determining whether a transfer of money is a gift or income. Commissioner v. Duberstein, 363 U.S. 278, 285 (1960). If Kritzik viewed the money he gave Harris as a gift, or if the dearth of contrary evidence leaves doubt on the subject, does it matter how mercenary Harris' motives were? *Duberstein* suggests that Harris' motives may not matter, but the ultimate answer makes no difference here. As long as the answer is at least a close call, and we are confident that it is, the prevailing law is too uncertain to support Harris' criminal conviction. . . .

For the reasons stated, we reverse Harris and Conley's convictions and remand with instructions to dismiss the indictments against them.

FLAUM Circuit Judge, concurring: . . . I part company with the majority when it distills from our gift/income jurisprudence a rule that would tax only the most base type of cash-for-sex exchange and categorically exempt from tax liability all other transfers of money and property to so-called mistresses or companions. . . . In Commissioner v. Duberstein, 363 U.S. 278 (1960), the font of our analysis of the gift/income distinction, the Supreme Court expressly eschewed the type of categorical, rule-bound analysis propounded by the majority. . . . After reading *Duberstein*, a reasonable taxpayer would conclude that payments from a lover were taxable as income if they were made "in return for services rendered" rather than "out of affection, respect, admiration, charity or like impulses." Id. at 285 (quoting Robertson v. United States, 343 U.S. 711, 714 (1952)).

Viewed in this light, I suggest that the bulk of the tax court cases cited by the majority offer no more than that the transferors in those particular cases harbored a donative intent. In my view, one cannot convincingly fashion a rule of law of general application from such a series of necessarily fact-intensive inquiries. . . .

Consider the following example. A approaches B and offers to spend time with him, accompany him to social events, and provide him with sexual favors for the next year if B gives her an apartment, a car, and a stipend of $5,000 a month. B agrees to A's terms. According to the majority, because this example involves a transfer of money to a "mistress in the context of a long-term relationship," A could never be charged with criminal tax evasion if she chose not to pay taxes on B's stipend. I find this hard to accept; what A receives from B is clearly income as it is "in return for services rendered." 363 U.S. at 285. . . .

I am thus prompted to find Harris' conviction infirm because of the relative scantiness of the record before us, not because mistresses are categorically exempt from taxation on the largess they receive. Simply put, the record before us does not establish beyond a reasonable doubt that Kritzik's intent was to pay Harris for her services, rather than out of affection or charitable impulse. . . .

Notes and Questions

1. Is this a case about income attribution and tax rates, or something else? If the payments to Harris are deemed compensatory, then how should they have been reported by Kritzik? How do the very rich treat amounts paid to household staff, be they cooks, maids, gardeners, chauffeurs, or pool boys? §262(a).

2. What does this decision indicate about Harris's civil liability for income tax on the money she received from Kritzik? Perhaps that depends solely on his intentions because it does not require, like criminal liability, that her nonpayment of tax be willful. But does that make good sense?

3. Suppose Harris' motives had been entirely mercenary and that she put on a show of affection solely to accomplish her mercenary objective. Should she escape income tax if she succeeded in duping Kritzik?

4. From Kritzik's viewpoint, wasn't this most likely a mixed motive situation? How do the courts deal with this real-world messiness? Returning to *Duberstein*, Chapter 4C.3, p. 179, above, observe the Court's touchstone is "the *dominant* reason that explains his action in making the transfer" and whether "the payment proceeds *primarily* from 'the constraining force of moral or legal duty,' or from 'the incentive of anticipated benefit.'" Id. at 183, 182 (emphasis added). Is this all-or-nothing approach workable? Is it fair? Why do we put up with this state of affairs? See Chapter 12D above (primary purpose test used to categorize mixed business and consumption expenses).

D. CHILDREN AND DEPENDENTS

Problems relating to income attribution, the definition of the taxable unit, and the distinction between compensation and gifts or support, are not confined to marital or sexual relationships. Resource sharing with children or other members of the household present analogous difficulties.

ADJUST TAX RATE ON UNEARNED INCOME OF MINOR CHILDREN

The President's Tax Proposals to the Congress for Fairness, Growth and Simplicity 85-88 (1985) (Treasury II)

CURRENT LAW

Minor children generally are subject to the same Federal income tax rules as adults. If a child is claimed as a dependent on another taxpayer's return, however, the child's [standard deduction] is limited to the amount of the child's earned income. Accordingly, the child must pay tax on any unearned income in excess of the personal exemption ($1,040 in 1985).

Under current law, when parents or other persons transfer investment assets to a child, the income from such assets generally is taxed thereafter to the child, even if the transferor retains significant control over the assets. For example, under the Uniform Gifts to Minors Act ("UGMA"), a person may give stock, a security (such as a bond), a life insurance policy, an annuity contract, or money to a custodian, who generally may be the donor, for the child. As a result of the gift, legal title to the property is vested in the child. During the child's minority, however, the custodian has the power to sell and reinvest the property; to pay over amounts for the support, maintenance, and benefit of the minor; or to accumulate income. Results similar to those achieved by a transfer under the UGMA may be obtained by transferring property to a trust or to a court-appointed guardian.

Parents also may shift income-producing assets to a child, without relinquishing control over the assets, by contributing such assets to a partnership or S corporation and giving the child an interest in the partnership or corporation.

REASONS FOR CHANGE

Under current law, a family may reduce its aggregate tax liability by shifting income-producing assets among family members. Such "income shifting" is a common tax-planning technique, typically accomplished by the parents transferring assets to their children so that a portion of the family income will be taxed at the child's lower marginal tax rate.

Income shifting undermines the progressive rate structure, and results in unequal treatment of taxpayers with the same ability to pay tax. A family whose income consists largely of wages earned by one or both parents pays tax on that income at the marginal rate of the parents. Even though such wage income is used in part for the living expenses of the children, parents may not allocate any portion of their salary to their children in order that it be taxed at the children's lower tax rates. Families with investment income, however, may be financially able to transfer some of it to the children, thereby shifting the income to lower tax brackets. Typically, this ability is most prevalent among wealthy taxpayers. Moreover, use of a trust or a gift under the UGMA allows the parents to achieve this result without relinquishing control over the property until the children come of age.

The opportunity for income shifting also complicates the financial affairs of persons who take advantage of it, and causes some persons to make transfers they would not make absent tax considerations. Disputes with the Internal Revenue Service are created in the case of transfers that arguably are ineffective in shifting the incidence of taxation to the transferee, such as when a parent nominally transfers property to children but in reality retains the power to revoke the transfer.

PROPOSAL

Unearned income of children under 14 years of age that is attributable to property received from their parents would be taxed at the marginal tax rate of their parents. This rule would apply only to the extent that the child's unearned income exceeded [a specified de minimis amount]. The child's tax liability on such unearned income would be equal to the additional tax that his or her parents would owe if such income were added to the parents' taxable income and reported on their return. If the parents report a net loss on their return, the proposed rule would not apply, and the child's unearned income would be taxed along with his or her earned income. If more than one child has unearned income which is taxable at the parents' rate, such income would be aggregated and added to the parents' taxable income. Each child would then be liable for a proportionate part of the incremental tax. . . .

ANALYSIS

The proposal would help to ensure the integrity of the progressive tax rate structure, which is designed to impose tax burdens in accordance with each taxpayer's ability to pay. Families would be taxed at the rate applicable to the total earned and unearned income of the parents, including income from property that the parents have transferred to the children's names. The current Federal income tax incentive for transferring substantial amounts of investment property to minor children would be eliminated.

Under the proposal, the unearned income of a minor child under 14 years of age would be taxed at his or her parents' rate. This is the age at which children may work in certain employment under the Fair Labor Standards Act. Because most children under 14 have little or no earned income, . . . preparation of their returns under the proposal should not be complex.

In most cases the income tax return of a child under 14 years of age is prepared by or on behalf of the parent and signed by the parent as guardian of the child. In such cases, the requirement that a child's income be aggregated with that of his or her parents would not create a problem of confidentiality with respect to the parents' return information, since there would be no need to divulge this information to the child. Although the return generally would be filed by a parent on behalf of a child, liability for the tax would rest, as under current law, on the child.

Only children required to file a return under current law would be required to do so under the proposal. In 1981, only 612,000 persons who filed returns reporting unearned income were claimed as dependents on another taxpayer's return. This represents less than one percent of the number of children claimed as dependents in that year. . . .

Notes and Questions

1. *Scope.* The reach of the "kiddie tax" was broadened in 2006 to a child who has not attained age 18 before the close of the taxable year, and for tax years beginning after May 25, 2007, the tax was expanded again to encompass a student who has not attained age 24 by the end of the year and whose earned income does not exceed one-half of his support. §1(g)(2)(A).

2. *Policy.* As originally proposed, the parents' marginal tax rate would have applied only to income from property received from the parents, not to all unearned income of the child. Why was this source limitation dropped? Should §1(g) be amended to tax the net unearned income of any individual, regardless of age, who is a dependent of another taxpayer (see §152) at the marginal rate of that other taxpayer?

3. *Interest-free loans.* Father (*F*) transfers $100,000 to his 30-year-old son (*S*) in exchange for a promissory note that obligates *S* to repay the principal in a lump sum five years hence without interest. Assume that prevailing interest rates on similar loans are 6 percent. *S* invests the money and earns $11,000 annually, which he dutifully reports on his return. If the form of the transaction is respected, *S* deducts no interest expense and *F* reports no interest income. Should it be respected? How would the tax results compare if *F* had loaned money at arms length to an unrelated borrower, while *S* had obtained a bank loan to finance his investments? Read §7872(a), (e), and (f). What are the actual tax consequences? Would the results differ if instead *F* conveys to *S* a five-year term interest in a parcel of crop land that *F* owns in fee, and *S* leases the land to a tenant for annual rent of $11,000? See Chapter 18D below.

4. *Personal exemptions.* In computing taxable income each taxpayer is ordinarily allowed a "personal exemption" deduction for himself, for his spouse, and for every individual who is a dependent of the taxpayer. §§151, 152. Dependent status requires that the taxpayer provide more than one-half the individual's support for the year, §152(c)(1)(D), (d)(1)(C) (query, why the difference in these tests?), where support "includes food, shelter, clothing, medical and dental care, education, and the like," whether furnished by the payment of expenses or provided in kind. Reg. §1.152-1(a)(2)(i). The amount of the deduction is $3,650 per person in 2009 ($2,000 plus inflation since 1988, §151(f)(4)). Rev. Proc. 2008-66, §3.19, 2008-45 I.R.B. 1107, 1112. Unlike other deductions, personal exemptions are available without regard to how the taxpayer's money is spent, provided that the overall majority support standard is met. Personal exemptions, in combination with the standard deduction and child tax credits, assure that a minimum amount of income, sufficient to meet subsistence or baseline-level consumption needs, is free from tax. The income tax ought not to force people into homelessness or malnutrition, and the personal exemptions recognize that individuals with very little income have no "ability to pay." As such, the personal exemption and child tax credits can be seen as the counterpart to §262, which disallows deductions for personal, living, or family expenses. And in keeping with this policy, where a taxpayer is entitled to a personal exemption deduction for a child or other dependent, the dependent cannot claim an exemption for himself even if he has income of his own (no double-dipping). §151(d)(2).

5. *Standard deduction.* In computing taxable income an unmarried individual who does not elect to claim itemized deductions is entitled to

take a "standard deduction" of $5,700 in 2009 ($3,000 plus inflation since 1987, §63(c)(4)). The amount of the standard deduction depends on filing status, but to alleviate the marriage penalty the standard deduction for a married couple filing a joint return is double the amount for a single individual or a married taxpayer filing separately. See Chapter 17B above. An intermediate amount is specified for heads of households, and additional amounts are allowed for individuals who are older than 64 years or who are blind §63(f).

One function of the standard deduction is administrative: to make itemized deductions irrelevant for a substantial number of taxpayers. Over an extended period of time the standard deduction has been kept at a level such that only 25 to 40 percent of returns claim itemized deductions. After the proportion of returns with itemized deductions rose in the early 1980s to nearly 40 percent in 1985, Congress substantially increased the standard deduction in 1986. In 2005 the number of itemizers was 35.5 percent.

But the primary function of the standard deduction and personal exemptions together is to specify the amount of income an individual or family can have without incurring any income tax, even if they cannot show any deductible expenditures. The sum of standard deduction and personal exemptions is sometimes referred to as the *amount not subject to tax*. For a couple with two children that figure is $26,000 in 2009. For an unmarried individual without dependents it is $9,350 in 2009.

Tax reductions have frequently taken the form, at least in part, of increases in the amount not subject to tax. The 1986 Act involved a near doubling of the personal exemption amount, over three years, and a substantial increase in the standard deduction. There has often been an attempt to set exemptions and standard deduction so that the amount not subject to tax will match official poverty income levels for various family sizes. In the 1986 Act, Congress rejiggered the numbers to make the income tax thresholds track poverty levels quite closely for most taxpayers, with the glaring exception of single individuals (other than heads of households), for whom the amount not subject to tax was set about $1,100 below the poverty level. The goal of matching poverty and income tax thresholds was abandoned for unmarried taxpayers on two grounds. First, many of them share living quarters or live in their parents' homes with the result that living costs are less than those reflected in the official poverty-level determination, and second, because a further increase in the tax-free baseline for singles would have significantly increased the marriage penalty. Staff of the Joint Comm. on Taxation, 100th Cong., General Explanation of the Tax Reform Act of 1986 15-16 (1987). See Chapter 17B above.

6. *Child tax credits.* In 1997 Congress enacted a Child Tax Credit, which is now set at $1,000 per qualifying child. §24.

The Congress believed that the individual income tax structure does not reduce tax liability by enough to reflect a family's reduced ability to pay taxes as family size increases. In part, this is because over the last 50 years the value of the dependent personal exemption has declined in real terms by over one-third. [Staff of the Joint Comm. on Taxation, 105th Cong., General Explanation of Tax Legislation Enacted in 1997 6-7 (1997).]

The definition of qualifying child is similar to that for personal exemptions but with an age limit of 16 years. This credit is given in addition to the deduction for personal exemptions. Taking account of this credit, the amount of gross income that a couple with two qualifying children can receive free of tax in 2009 is $44,900 ($14,600 for four personal exemptions plus $11,400 standard deduction, while two child credits eliminate tax on the first $18,900 of taxable income). See Chapter 1A and Table 1-1. If the goal was to reduce the tax burden on low-income families, why didn't Congress simply increase the size of the personal exemption?

7. *Labor income.* Thanks to the kiddie tax, a child with substantial unearned income is taxed on that investment income at her parents' rate. What about a teenager or college student with an after-school or summer job? What is the purpose of §73? Cf. Poe v. Seaborn, Chapter 17A above. Where a child can be claimed as a dependent on another taxpayer's return, the child cannot shelter any of her own income from tax by means of the personal exemption. Shouldn't the standard deduction likewise be disallowed? §151(d)(2). Now read §63(c)(5). What do you make of this? For 2009, the inflation-adjusted limit is the greater of (1) $950, or (2) the sum of $300 and the individual's earned income. Does this rule reflect some deep administrative or cultural reality?

E. SEPARATION AND DIVORCE

1. Support Payments

Alimony may be conceived as damages for the failure to provide support according to the primary obligations of the marital contract. As such, its taxability should depend on the tax treatment of such support if it had been supplied in normal course. There is no income tax on the support one receives from a spouse, parent, child, or other family member. (Why not?) Therefore alimony, taking the tax character of the item it replaces, should be free of tax too. Gould v. Gould, 245 U.S. 151 (1917).

And so it was until 1942, when §71 was enacted. One might think §71 reflected the needs of war to include in taxable income whatever might serve as a source of tax revenue: But in truth §71 was a companion to §215, and together they undoubtedly operated to reduce taxes. (Why?) Yet §215 was itself enacted as relief from the burdens of new high wartime rates (why?), so the taxation of alimony is an indirect offspring of wartime revenue needs after all.

What should be the normal treatment of alimony? When must alimony be distinguished from other payments made in similar contexts? How is the distinction to be drawn, and why?

BERNATSCHKE v. UNITED STATES
364 F.2d 400 (Ct. Cl. 1966)

Before Cowen, Chief Judge, Laramore, Durfee, Davis, and Collins, Judges. . . . Since the court agrees with the trial commissioner's opinion, findings and recommended conclusion of law, as hereinafter set forth, it hereby adopts the same as the basis for its judgment in this case without oral arguments. . . .

MALETZ, Commissioner: This is a suit for refund of income taxes and assessed interest thereon paid by plaintiff for the years 1956 through 1959 and 1961, together with statutory interest. The sole issue is whether Section 72 or Section 71(a)(1) of the Internal Revenue Code of 1954 governs the taxability of the sum of $25,000 received each year by plaintiff under certain annuity contracts for which the consideration was paid by her former husband, Cornelius Crane, pursuant to an Agreement of February 20, 1940 incident to a divorce.[2]

In general, annuity payments are taxable under the rules of Section 72 of the Code, with Section 72(b) providing for the exclusion from gross income of a portion of amounts received as an annuity, based on the ratio of the "investment in the contract" to the "expected return." These rules, however, are not applicable to payments under an annuity contract which are includible in the income of the wife under Section 71; such payments are

---

2. The Agreement recites that plaintiff had instituted a divorce action against Cornelius Crane; that each of the parties was possessed of separate property and estate; that each of the parties was fully appraised of the financial position of the other; that the parties were "desirous of making a complete adjustment and final settlement of all property rights and the respective interests of each of the parties in the properties of the other by virtue of their marital relation, and of releasing to the other all interest in the other's property"; and that Cornelius Crane was desirous of "satisfying and discharging his obligation to pay alimony to . . . [plaintiff]." The Agreement provides that in the event plaintiff was found by the court entitled to a divorce, Cornelius Crane agreed "in lieu of alimony, to deposit with one or more life insurance companies . . . a sum or sums of money sufficient to purchase annuity contracts which shall yield the sum of . . . $25,000 per year payable to . . . [plaintiff] during her lifetime, which sum of money is estimated to be approximately . . . $647,000. . . ." The Agreement states that the annuity contracts were to provide in substance that there was to be no power to revoke the annuities therein provided, nor any power to change the beneficiaries without the consent of both parties; that upon the death of plaintiff, any refund due under the policies was to be divided equally between the daughter of plaintiff (who had been adopted by Cornelius Crane) and Cornelius Crane; and that in the event of the prior decease of Cornelius Crane, any refund was to be distributed to plaintiff's daughter. The Agreement provides that plaintiff agreed to accept the payments "in lieu of all claims of alimony which she may by virtue of said decree have against him." It also provided that Cornelius Crane "does hereby waive, release, quitclaim, relinquish, sell, assign and convey" to plaintiff "all rights of dower, as well as all rights and claims as husband, widower or otherwise" in and to "all property and estate" of plaintiff, "both real, personal and mixed." In addition, plaintiff gave, in the same language, a release and conveyance to Cornelius Crane of "all rights of dower, as well as all rights and claims as wife, widow, or otherwise."

wholly includible in the wife's gross income.[3] Thus, Section 72 of the Code provides in part:

§72. ANNUITIES; CERTAIN PROCEEDS OF ENDOWMENT AND LIFE INSURANCE CONTRACTS. . . .

(k) *Payments in discharge of alimony.* —
(1) In general. — This section shall not apply to so much of any payment under an annuity . . . contract (or any interest therein) as is includible in the gross income of the wife under section 71. . . .

Section 71(a)(1) (the portion of Section 71 which is pertinent here) provides:

§71. ALIMONY AND SEPARATE MAINTENANCE PAYMENTS.

(a) *General rule.* —
(1) Decree of divorce or separate maintenance. — If a wife is divorced or legally separated from her husband under a decree of divorce of or separate maintenance, the wife's gross income includes periodic payments (whether or not made at regular intervals) received after such decree in discharge of (or attributable to property transferred, in trust or otherwise, in discharge of) a legal obligation which, because of the marital or family relationship, is imposed on or incurred by the husband under the decree or under a written instrument incident to such a divorce or separation.

The substance of Section 71 was first enacted in 1942 to allow the husband to deduct "payments in the nature of or in lieu of alimony or an allowance for support" and to tax such payments to the wife who receives them.[5] In conformity with this legislative purpose, Section 1.71-1 of the Treasury Regulations on Income Tax (1954) specifies that "Section 71 provides rules for treatment in certain cases of payments in the nature of or in lieu of alimony or allowance for support as between spouses who are divorced or separated. . . ." In addition, Section 1.71-1(b)(4) of the Regulations states that "Section 71(a) applies only to payments made because of the family or marital relationship in recognition of the general obligation to support which is made specific by the decree, instrument, or agreement. . . ."

The nub of the problem is thus to determine whether or not plaintiff's former husband, Cornelius Crane, paid the consideration for the annuities by virtue of an obligation to support plaintiff which was imposed on him by their marital relationship. This is a question that depends upon the substance of the transaction and the true intent of the parties, rather than on the labels or formal provisions of the written contract or divorce decree. . . .

---

3. The parties have stipulated that if the annuity amount of $25,000 received by plaintiff is taxable under Section 72 rather than under Section 71, then the sum of $7,199.05 (rather than $25,000) was properly included in her gross income for each of the years in issue.

5. Though the 1942 Act was adopted some two years after plaintiff's divorce from Cornelius Crane, the Act made these provisions applicable, in general, to amounts received in taxable years beginning after December 31, 1941, regardless of the date of the divorce or written instrument. . . .

Plaintiff who was born in 1906 is a housewife and has never been gain-fully employed. Her father was a naval medical officer who came from a family of well-to-do professional people; her mother also had considerable means in her own right due largely to her skill as an investor. In 1922 plaintiff was married to a naval flier but the marriage ended in divorce some seven years later. They had one child, a daughter.

In 1929 plaintiff married Cornelius Crane (hereafter referred to as "Cornelius"), the grandson of the founder of the Crane Company (a man-ufacturer of plumbing equipment and valves) and the only son of R. T. Crane, Jr., the president and controlling stockholder of that company. The Crane family was possessed of great wealth and its members — including Cornelius and plaintiff — lived on a lavish scale in family mansions in Chicago (their primary residence), Massachusetts and Georgia, and a family apartment at the Ritz in New York. Cornelius, who himself possessed substantial wealth through gifts and inheritance, and also received income from trusts established by his father, was not interested in the family business and at no time in his life held a position for which he received a salary. As a young man he decided he did not want to go to college, but would like to go around the world on a yacht and explore parts of the world which others had not reached. Accordingly, his father bought him a sailing ship which was about 140 feet in length and carried a crew of 26. From this trip he developed an interest in archeology and anthropology, and financed and conducted several expeditions in his vessel to the South Seas. His other interests con-sisted of hunting, fishing, walking through the woods and reading.

Cornelius' personal budget (as well as that of the entire Crane family) was managed by J. K. Prentice, who had been his father's private secretary, who served as a confidant to the entire family and who stood in place of a father to Cornelius after R. T. Crane, Jr. died. Cornelius had a different attitude toward money than most people. For example, very early in his marriage to plaintiff he became "sick" of Bermuda and suddenly sold for the extraordinarily low price of $25,000 a 26-acre island he owned at the entrance to the harbor in Bermuda, together with a restored house thereon and four boats. He pur-chased property in Tahiti without even having seen it. Withal, Cornelius and plaintiff were more alike than different in various aspects. Neither had ever been gainfully employed. While Cornelius occupied himself with his interests in archeology and anthropology, plaintiff occupied herself with giving singing concerts (which were artistic successes rather than profitable ven-tures) and with charitable endeavors. Both were unconcerned with, and uninterested in, finances and property. Thus, until her marriage to Cornelius, plaintiff relied on her mother completely to manage stocks and bonds which her mother and grandmother had given her; after the marriage she turned her investments over to the Crane family to manage. During her marriage to Cornelius, her stock and bond holdings were augmented by gifts from Cornelius and his father, and as of February 1940 had a market value of about $347,000, which produced a yield of about $13,000 in that year.

Throughout his marriage to plaintiff, Cornelius continued his sailing expeditions and was away for extended periods of time; plaintiff did not accompany him on these trips. After February 1936, Cornelius and plaintiff did not live together as man and wife, although he continued to support her and her daughter by her first marriage. By 1939, plaintiff was considering getting a divorce and retained an attorney, but did not pursue the matter further at that time. In the latter part of that year, Cornelius adopted plaintiff's daughter, the adoption being prompted at least in part by his desire to effect a reconciliation with plaintiff. (Plaintiff and Cornelius had no children of their own.) Thereafter, upon the happening of some incident, plaintiff finally reached a firm decision to go ahead with the divorce and filed a divorce action in the Circuit Court of Cook County, Illinois, on February 19, 1940. The divorce was granted on the ground of desertion on February 23, 1940. Up to the final day of the divorce, Cornelius tried to dissuade plaintiff from going through with it. Plaintiff and Cornelius remained friendly at all times during, before and after the divorce proceedings.

At the time that she finally decided to proceed with the divorce, plaintiff's attorney indicated to her that she had a dower right and that such right was a third of an estate. Plaintiff told her attorney that she wanted a lump-sum settlement and asked him to find out from Cornelius what would be fair. She felt that having been a good wife something was due her and she wanted any settlement in a lump sum so that she would never again have to go back to Cornelius and ask for anything — for household money and things like that in the future; she wanted all ties cut.

Meanwhile, Cornelius discussed the matter with his advisers and stated that he would be willing to make a reasonable property settlement, based on his assets, to take care of plaintiff and that he wanted to be, if anything, liberal in the amount of such settlement. He requested one of his advisers to ascertain the amount of income-producing assets he had under his control and it was determined that they were worth about $2,000,000. Cornelius thereupon indicated to his attorney that if he died without a will, plaintiff would get one-third of that amount. The attorney said that that would probably be right by virtue of her dower rights.[6] Cornelius then stated to his advisers that he and plaintiff had been married for ten years; that he thought he should make a property settlement which substantially represented her dower rights in his assets; and that he would give her $650,000, approximately one-third of his assets of $2,000,000. After having so decided (and also determining what he would give to plaintiff's daughter whom he had adopted), he told his advisers to work out the details.

J. K. Prentice (who, as previously indicated, managed Cornelius' personal budget) approved of Cornelius' decision to make a liberal

6. Under Chapter 3, Section 11 of the Illinois Code, effective January 1, 1940 (Ill. Rev. Stat. 1941, Ch. 3, §162), the surviving spouse of a resident intestate decedent was entitled to one-third of his real and personal property when there was also a surviving descendant of the decedent; under Chapter 3, Section 14, a lawfully adopted child was deemed a descendant for this purpose (Ill. Rev. Stat. 1941, Ch. 3, §165).

settlement for the plaintiff, but opposed turning over liquid assets to her since he was afraid she might give them away or that someone might take them from her. Consequently, he felt strongly that the sum to be paid should be so invested that she could not dissipate her principal, and he urged that annuities be used for that purpose. He mentioned the subject to plaintiff; she respected and trusted Prentice and when he recommended annuities to her, she accepted this recommendation and asked Cornelius to take care of buying the annuities for her, insisting, however, that Cornelius be given contingent right to receive refunds under the annuity contracts in the event of her death. The actual arrangements for the purchase of annuities were handled by Cornelius' advisers who made inquiries of insurance companies to ascertain how much of an annuity for a person of plaintiff's age and description could be bought for $650,000 and were informed by such insurance companies that approximately $647,000 would buy an exact or round amount of $25,000 per year. The amount of the income to be paid was the result of the determination of the approximate amount of the principal to be paid, not the cause of such amount.

In the discussions Cornelius had with his advisers there was no mention of alimony; Cornelius simply determined that he would give plaintiff part of his assets. Nor did anyone at any time mention alimony in the discussions in which plaintiff participated with her attorney, Cornelius or any of his advisers. During the course of the negotiations, Cornelius told her she would receive a lump sum and plaintiff understood that she would get a "one-time payment."

At the time of the divorce, plaintiff did not transfer any of her property to Cornelius, except for such items as primitive artifacts that had no great intrinsic value. Nor, with the exception of some household items, did Cornelius transfer any property to plaintiff at the time of the divorce other than the amount provided in the Agreement of February 20, 1940.

Following the divorce, plaintiff in March 1940 married her present husband, a portrait painter, who has been successful artistically though not financially.

Subsequently, in accordance with the Agreement of February 20, 1940, plaintiff (and her present husband) granted to Cornelius quitclaim deeds and released to him all rights in property Cornelius owned in Massachusetts and Tahiti. Cornelius fulfilled his obligations under the Agreement by liquidating a substantial portion of his income-producing assets and having one his advisers in the months following the divorce purchase 13 annuity policies from various insurance companies to provide total annual payments of $25,000 to plaintiff.

Plaintiff's standard of living changed markedly after her divorce from Cornelius since she could no longer live in the kind of lavish luxury produced by the Crane family's great wealth. In the tax years here involved, plaintiff has received dividend and interest income from her stocks and bonds (which are now worth about $1,000,000) of from $23,000 to

$30,000 a year, which income is over and above the $25,000 each year received under the annuity contracts. The $25,000 annuity is commingled with her dividend income and is used for normal living expenses, taxes, investments, savings, etc.

In summary, the record shows that at no time during the negotiations of the Agreement of February 20, 1940 was there any mention of alimony. Plaintiff did not request it and Cornelius did not mention it. Nor was there any attempt to determine the extent or the dollar value of Cornelius' obligation to support plaintiff or to pay alimony. The record shows, rather, that the amount which plaintiff received pursuant to the Agreement was derived solely on the basis of the income-producing property then owned outright by Cornelius and what the parties understood to be plaintiff's intestate share in his estate or "dower" right; and that such amount was determined without reference to any obligation to support or pay alimony. Thus, it seems evident that the amounts paid by Cornelius for the annuity contracts were not based on the marital obligation to support and were not intended to be payments in discharge of such an obligation but rather were intended to be in the nature of a property settlement[7] under which plaintiff's inchoate interests in Cornelius' property under Illinois law were extinguished.[8]

In addition to these considerations, other factors present here provide further indication that the annuity payments to plaintiff do not have the usual characteristics of alimony or support. See generally 5 Mertens, Law of Federal Income Taxation. §31A.02, pp. 20-21. First, the fact that the payments were to continue for the lifetime of the plaintiff, without regard to her remarriage or the death of her ex-husband, tends to show that they were not intended as alimony or in discharge of a marital obligation to support. It is relevant, also, that plaintiff received and exercised the right to determine the beneficiary of refunds that might be payable after her death. It would appear that if the annuity payments had been intended as support payments for plaintiff, Cornelius, rather than plaintiff, would have retained and exercised the power to determine the recipient of any part of the sum not needed for that purpose.

In addition, it is customary for support payments to be related to the husband's income and, frequently, to vary if there is a substantial change in such income. The wife is ordinarily entitled to be supported in the same style of living to which she was accustomed during the marriage.

---

7. It is not necessary that there be an exact, mathematical division of property in order for a divorce agreement to constitute a property settlement. In Scott v. United States, 225 F. Supp. 257 (D. Ore. 1963), it was held that payments received by the wife were pursuant to a property settlement and not taxable under Section 71, even though neither the wife nor the husband knew what property stood in their individual names and what property stood in their joint names.

8. Even under the somewhat unusual facts of the present case, it would be unrealistic to regard the transaction here as a gift. "Property transferred pursuant to a negotiated settlement in return for the release of admittedly valuable [inchoate marital] rights is not a gift in any sense of the term." United States v. Davis [Chapter 17E.2 belwo (next case)].

The amount of the wife's own income is, obviously, also a factor in determining her need for support. Here the payments were not related in any way to Cornelius' substantial income. The parties agreed on a lump sum based entirely on assets which he owned outright, without reference to the trust income he received, and then fixed the amount of the annual payments on the basis of what annuities the lump sum would buy. There could be no variation, of course, because of changes in Cornelius' income (or because of any property which he might later inherit). Nor was plaintiff's income considered in any way as a factor in determining the amount to be paid. Furthermore, the amount of the annuity payments, even when combined with plaintiff's income from her stocks and bonds, could not possibly allow her to live in a style which would in any way approach that to which she had been accustomed as Cornelius' wife, and the record in fact shows that her standard of living changed markedly after the divorce.

Another factor of significance is whether or not there is a fixed sum the husband is required to pay; the absence of such a fixed sum is considered to indicate that support was intended. Here the contract itself specifically provided the amount which the husband was required to pay and the record shows that the settlement was determined on the basis of his paying such amount.

In conclusion, the record establishes that Cornelius Crane did not pay the consideration for the annuity contracts because of any marital obligation to support plaintiff and, accordingly, the annuity payments are not taxable under Section 71.[10] Plaintiffs are entitled to a refund of income tax for the years involved based on the application of the rules of Section 72 to the annuity payments received in each year.

Notes and Questions

1. *Nondeductible alimony. Bernatschke* reflects the happy intersection of two unfortunate pre-1984 rules concerning alimony. The first was the nondeductible alimony rule, under which the Cranes' arrangement would have generated taxable income to Bernatschke without any offsetting deduction to Cornelius Crane or anyone else if the annuity payments had been alimony. This rule was apparently the logical, though harsh, outcome of the general notion that alimony includes periodic payments but not lump sum transfers: The annuity payments received by Ms. Bernatschke were clearly periodic, while Mr. Crane's premium payment to the insurance company was clearly a lump sum.

---

10. In view of this conclusion, it is unnecessary to pass upon plaintiff's alternative contention that she in substance purchased the annuities with her own money, with Cornelius acting, in effect, as her agent for that purpose.

The general notion that alimony includes periodic payments but not lump sums usually favors taxpayers if applied consistently to direct payments, since periodic payments are apt to be deducted from a higher income and added to a lower income. Lump sum settlements, if treated as alimony, might give the payor excessive deductions in a single year and also throw the recipient into an unrepresentatively high tax bracket for a single year. Of course, treating a transfer as taxable periodic payments to the recipient *and* a nondeductible lump sum transfer to the payor was inconsistent with the general pattern that taxes the alimony recipient only on income that would otherwise have been taxed to the payor.

This rule created a trap into which the unwary Bernatschke and Crane almost fell. Could the threatened result have been readily avoided? How?

Section 72(k) was repealed in 1984 in connection with a general revision of the alimony rules designed among other things to eliminate the nondeductible alimony rule.[4]

2. *Distinguishing between support and property rights.* The other unfortunate rule illustrated in *Bernatschke* was that even a payment that has all the formal aspects of a periodic income payment would not be treated as alimony if the reason for the payment was to compensate for marital property rights rather than support. That rule had the happy effect in *Bernatschke* of providing an escape from the nondeductible alimony trap, but in cases of direct payments it merely created a rather pointless and very cloudy factual issue for many cases. That is why we learn so much about the Cranes' unusual marital and financial relationships: because all these things are relevant to the question of why the payments were provided. And if taxpayers can succeed in getting payments like those in *Bernatschke* out of the alimony category, many other recipients will be tempted to give it a try. In normal cases, however, payors will take the opposite position, often causing the government to get caught in the middle struggling to achieve consistency one way or the other.

Look at the present §71(a) and compare it with the statute cited in *Bernatschke.* The change was made in 1984. Do you see how this second rule was repealed?

The 1984 amendments to §§71 and 215 (and the repeal of §72(k)) followed long study by lawyers, in and out of the government, who concluded that limitations like those reflected in *Bernatschke* were senseless and should be eliminated. They reasoned in part that well-advised parties could usually arrange to have payments qualify or not qualify as alimony, and that such arrangements were unobjectionable from the government's standpoint so long as the parties' treatment was consistent. The generally recommended fix was to simplify §71 to read much as it does now, but without subsections (c)(2) and (f). Those two limitations

---

4. A similar rule used to apply to trusts as well as annuities. A payor's contribution of funds to an alimony trust was nondeductible, while periodic payments out of the trust were taxed as alimony even if they exceeded the income of the trust.

were added in executive committee session without published reasons, reportedly at the urging of one or a few congressional committee members. Why?

How would *Bernatschke* now be decided, and why?

3. *Form over substance?* Carefully examine the definition of alimony in §71(b). Today alimony tax status depends only on five readily-determinable objective criteria. This bright-line approach avoids the difficulties of prior law, under which the distinction between alimony and property settlement payments required examination of the intention of the parties and state law, and was therefore virtually unworkable on a mass scale. Yet mechanical (i.e., formalistic) rules permit taxpayers, with proper planning, to select the most advantageous tax consequences without fundamentally altering the substance of their relationship. Whatever became of substance over form as a fundamental tenet of tax policy? Why doesn't *Old Colony Trust Co.* (Chapter 2A above) govern here?

4. *Alimony planning.* Observe that alimony tax treatment is overtly elective, §71(b)(1)(B). Did Congress get the default rule right? Suppose that Anne is better endowed with wealth and talent than her husband Henry, and that they have therefore agreed that upon their divorce she should pay him a regular sum for his support for the rest of his life. Henry wants his stipend to be "free and clear of income taxes, state or federal." Can that demand be met? How? Should Henry's lawyer try to talk him out of insisting on this condition? Should Anne's attorney urge her to resist it? What particular problems need to be addressed in drafting a provision to meet Henry's demand?

5. *Front-loading.* Look at §71(f), sometimes called the *alimony recapture* rule. What is its function? Could you structure a deductible cash property settlement? How would §71(f) apply in these cases:

(a) alimony is paid in the amount of $50,000 in the first year, and none thereafter (*Hint:* When working with §71(f), always *start* by calculating the "excess payments for the 2nd post-separation year" because that quantity is needed to compute the "excess payments for the 1st post-separation year.");

(b) alimony is paid in the amount of $40,000 in the first year, $10,000 in the second year, and none thereafter;

(c) alimony is paid in the amount of $60,000 in the first year, none in years two and three, and $20,000 per year thereafter for the life of the payee.

6. *Nonitemized deduction.* The deduction for alimony payments is not classified as an itemized deduction. §62(a)(10). Why? What about alimony recapture? §71(f)(1)(B). What happens if the recapture deduction is very large? Cf. §172(d)(4).

7. *Child support.* Payments for the support of children are typically made to a former spouse with custody of the children (whether sole or shared), not to the children directly. Consequently, cash transfers intended to benefit children can readily be structured to satisfy the (formal) statutory definition of alimony, §71(b), thereby rendering child support deductible by the payor, §215. This treatment also appears to be fundamentally elective, by virtue of

§71(c)(1). But what does it mean for an amount to be "fixed" as child support?

Suppose a wife is to receive payments of a specified amount but which will be reduced by one-sixth on the majority, death, or marriage of any of her three children. In Commissioner v. Lester, 366 U.S. 299 (1961), the Court rejected an argument that one-half (three-sixths) of the payments in such a case were child support rather than alimony, reasoning that the provision excluding from alimony payments "fix[ed] . . . as . . . support of minor children" was intended to give the parties negotiating an alimony arrangement flexibility to determine tax consequences as between themselves. That purpose would be fostered by interpreting the phrase to require an explicit designation of part of a payment as child support.

Lester was overturned by the enactment of §71(c)(2) in 1984, although it is not at all clear *why.* Are payments relating to children now necessarily taxable to the payor rather than the payee? In particular, what does it mean for a time to be "clearly associated with a contingency" relating to a child? §71(c)(2)(B). Read Reg. §1.71-1T, Q&A-18. Assume that *W* is divorced when her only child is seven years old. The divorce decree provides that *W*'s former husband, *H*, will pay *W* (provided that she is then living) $2,000 per month for 15 years and $1,000 monthly thereafter. How would these payments be taxed?

8. *Personal exemptions in case of divorced parents.* While the amount deductible for a personal exemption does not depend on expenditures, the general definition of *dependent* does, since it requires provision of over half of a dependent's support. §152. Over the years this has presented very difficult administrative problems in the case of divorced parents in determining which parent, if either, met that requirement. Indeed that was once said to be the most frequently contested factual issue in the administration of the income tax by a considerable margin! There have been a series of statutory modifications of the basic test, which now appears in §152(e). Read and evaluate that provision.

Look also at §152(c)(4) and (d)(3). Why don't those provisions take adequate care of divorced parents?

2. Property Transfers

UNITED STATES v. DAVIS
370 U.S. 65 (1962)

Mr. Justice CLARK delivered the opinion of the Court. These cases involve the tax consequences of a transfer of appreciated property by Thomas Crawley Davis to his former wife pursuant to a property settlement agreement executed prior to divorce. . . .

In 1954 the taxpayer and his then wife made a voluntary property settlement and separation agreement calling for support payments to the wife
and minor child in addition to the transfer to certain personal property to
the wife. Under Delaware law all the property transferred was that of the
taxpayer, subject to certain statutory marital rights of the wife including a
right of intestate succession and a right upon divorce to a share of the husband's property. Specifically as a "division in settlement of their property"
the taxpayer agreed to transfer to his wife, inter alia, 1,000 shares of stock in
the E. I. du Pont de Nemours & Co. The then Mrs. Davis agreed to accept this
division "in full settlement and satisfaction of any and all claims and rights
against the husband whatsoever (including but not by way of limitation,
dower and all rights under the laws of testacy and intestacy). . . ." Pursuant
to the above agreement which had been incorporated into the divorce,
decree, one-half of this stock was delivered in the tax year involved, 1955,
and the balance thereafter. Davis' cost basis for the 1955 transfer was
$74,775.37, and the fair market value of the 500 shares there transferred
was $82,250. . . .

I

The determination of the income tax consequences of the stock transfer
described above is basically a two-step analysis: (1) Was the transaction a
taxable event? (2) If so, how much taxable gain resulted therefrom? Originally the Tax Court (at that time the Board of Tax Appeals) held that the
accretion to property transferred pursuant to a divorce settlement could not
be taxed as capital gain to the transferor because the amount realized by the
satisfaction of the husband's marital obligations was indeterminable and
because, even if such benefit were ascertainable, the transaction was a nontaxable division of property. Mesta v. Commissioner, 42 B.T.A. 933 (1940);
Halliwell v. Commissioner, 44 B.T.A. 740 (1941). However, upon being
reversed in quick succession by the Courts of Appeals of the Third and
Second Circuits, Commissioner v. Mesta, 123 F.2d 986 (C.A.3d Cir. 1941);
Commissioner v. Halliwell, 131 F.2d 642 (C.A.2d Cir. 1942), the Tax Court
accepted the position of these courts and has continued to apply these views
in appropriate cases since that time. . . . In *Mesta* and *Halliwell* the Courts of
Appeals reasoned that the accretion of the property was "realized" by the
transfer and that this gain could be measured on the assumption that the
relinquished marital rights were equal in value to the property transferred.
The matter was considered settled until the Court of Appeals for the Sixth
Circuit, in reversing the Tax Court, ruled that, although such a transfer
might be a taxable event, the gain realized thereby could not be determined
because of the impossibility of evaluating the fair market value of the wife's
marital rights. Commissioner v. Marshman, 279 F.2d 27 (1960). In so
holding that court specifically rejected the argument that these rights

could be presumed to be equal in value to the property transferred for their release. This is essentially the position taken by the Court of Claims in the instant case.

II

We now turn to the threshold question of whether the transfer in issue was an appropriate occasion for taxing the accretion to the stock. There can be no doubt that Congress, as evidenced by its inclusive definition of income subject to taxation, i.e., "all income from whatever source derived, including . . . [g]ains derived from dealings in property," intended that the economic growth of this stock be taxed. The problem confronting us is simply *when* is such accretion to be taxed. Should the economic gain be presently assessed against taxpayer, or should this assessment await a subsequent transfer of the property by the wife? The controlling statutory language, which provides that gains from dealings in property are to be taxed upon "sale or other disposition,"[5] is too general to include or exclude conclusively the transaction presently in issue. Recognizing this, the Government and the taxpayer argue by analogy with transactions more easily classified as within or without the ambient of taxable events. The taxpayer asserts that the present disposition is comparable to a nontaxable division of property between two co-owners,[6] while the Government contends it more resembles a taxable transfer of property in exchange for the release of an independent legal obligation. Neither disputes the validity of the other's stating point.

In support of his analogy the taxpayer argues that to draw a distinction between a wife's interest in the property of her husband in a common-law jurisdiction such as Delaware and the property interest of a wife in a typical community property jurisdiction would commit a double sin; for such differentiation would depend upon "elusive and subtle casuistries which . . . possess no relevance for tax purposes," Helvering v. Hallock, 309 U.S. 106, 118 (1940), and would create disparities between common-law and community property jurisdictions in contradiction to Congress' general policy of equality between the two. The taxpayer's analogy, however, stumbles on its

5. Internal Revenue Code of 1954, §1001. . . .
6. Any suggestion that the transaction in question was a gift is completely unrealistic. Property transferred pursuant to a negotiated settlement in return for the release of admittedly valuable rights is not a gift in any sense of the term. To intimate that there was a gift to the extent the value of the property exceeded that of the rights released not only invokes the erroneous premise that every exchange not precisely equal involves a gift but merely raises the measurement problem discussed in Part III, infra. . . . - Cases in which this Court has held transfers of property in exchange for the release of marital right subject to gift taxes are based not on the premise that such transaction are inherently gifts but on the concept that in the contemplation of the gift tax statute they are to be taxed as gifts. . . . In interpreting the particular income tax provisions here involved, we find ourselves unfettered by the language and considerations ingrained in the gift and estate tax statutes. See Farid-Es-Sultaneh v. Commissioner, [Chapter 17E.2 below (next case)].

own premise, for the inchoate rights granted a wife in her husband's property by the Delaware law do not even remotely reach the dignity of co-ownership. The wife has no interest — passive or active — over the management or disposition of her husband's personal property. Her rights are not descendible, and she must survive him to share in his intestate estate. Upon dissolution of the marriage she shares in the property only to such extent as the court deems "reasonable." 13 Del. Code Ann. §1531(a). What is "reasonable" might be ascertained independently of the extent of the husband's property by such criteria as the wife's financial condition, her needs in relation to her accustomed station in life, her age and health, the number of children and their ages, and the earning capacity of the husband. See, e.g., Beres v. Beres, 2 Storey 133, 52 Del. 133, 154 A.2d 384 (1959).

This is not to say it would be completely illogical to consider the shearing off of the wife's rights in her husband's property as a division of that property, but we believe the contrary to be the more reasonable construction. Regardless of the tags, Delaware seems only to place a burden on the husband's property rather than to make the wife a part owner thereof. In the present context the rights of succession and reasonable share do not differ significantly from the husband's obligations of support and alimony. They all partake more of a personal liability of the husband than a property interest of the wife. The effectuation of these marital rights may ultimately result in the ownership of some of the husband's property as it did here, but certainly this happenstance does not equate the transaction with a division of property by co-owners. Although admittedly such a view may permit different tax treatment among the several States, this Court in the past has not ignored the differing effects on the federal taxing scheme of substantive differences between community property and common-law systems. E.g., Poe v. Seaborn, 282 U.S. 101 (1930). To be sure Congress has seen fit to alleviate this disparity in many areas, e.g., Revenue Act of 1948, 62 Stat. 110, but in other areas the facts of life are still with us.

Our interpretation of the general statutory language is fortified by the longstanding administrative practice as sounded and formalized by the settled state of law in the lower courts. The Commissioner's position was adopted in the early 40s by the Second and Third Circuits and by 1947 the Tax Court had acquiesced in this view. This settled rule was not disturbed by the Court of Appeals for the Sixth Circuit in 1960 or the Court of Claims in the instant case, for these latter courts in holding the gain indeterminable assumed that the transaction was otherwise a taxable event. Such unanimity of views in support of a position representing a reasonable construction of an ambiguous statute will not lightly be put aside. It is quite possible that this notorious construction was relied upon by numerous taxpayers as well as the Congress itself, which not only refrained from making any changes in the statutory language during more than a score of years but re-enacted this same language in 1954.

III

Having determined that the transaction was a taxable event, we now turn to the point on which the Court of Claims balked, viz., the measurement of the taxable gain realized by the taxpayer. The Code defines the taxable gain from the sale or disposition of property as being the "excess of the amount realized therefrom over the adjusted basis. . . ." I.R.C. (1954) §1001(a). The "amount realized" is further defined as "the sum of any money received plus the fair market value of the property (other than money) received." I.R.C. (1954) §1001(b). In the instant case the "property received" was the release of the wife's inchoate marital rights. The Court of Claims, following the Court of Appeals for the Sixth Circuit, found that there was no way to compute the fair market value of these marital rights and that it was thus impossible to determine the taxable gain realized by the taxpayer. We believe this conclusion was erroneous.

It must be assumed, we think, that the parties acted at arm's length and that they judged the martial rights to be equal in value to the property for which they were exchanged. There was no evidence to the contrary here. Absent a readily ascertainable value it is accepted practice where property is exchanged to hold, as did the Court of Claims in Philadelphia Park Amusement Co. v. United States, 130 Ct. Cl. 166, 172, 126 F. Supp. 184, 189 (1954), that the values "of the two properties exchanged in an arm's-length transaction are either equal in fact or are presumed to be equal." . . . To be sure there is much to be said of the argument that such an assumption is weakened by the emotion, tension and practical necessities involved in divorce negotiation and the property settlements arising therefrom. However, once it is recognized that the transfer was a taxable event, it is more consistent with the general purpose and scheme of the taxing statutes to make a rough approximation of the gain realized thereby than to ignore altogether its tax consequences. . . .

Moreover, if the transaction is to be considered a taxable event as to the husband, the Court of Claims' position leaves up in the air the wife's basis for the property received. In the context of a taxable transfer by the husband,[7] all indicia point to a "cost" basis for this property in the hands of the wife. Yet under the Court of Claims' position her cost for this property, i.e., the value of the marital rights relinquished therefor, would be indeterminable, and on subsequent disposition of the property she might suffer inordinately over the Commissioner's assessment which she would she would have the burden of proving erroneous. . . . Our present holding that the value of these rights is ascertainable eliminates this problem; for the same calculation that

7. Under the present administrative practice, the release of marital rights in exchange for property or other consideration is not considered a taxable event as to the wife. For a discussion of the difficulties confronting a wife under a contrary approach, see Taylor and Schwartz, Tax Aspects of Martial Property Agreements, 7 Tax L. Rev. 19,30 (1951); Comment, The Lump Sum Divorce Settlement as a Taxable Exchange, 8 U.C.L.A. L. Rev. 593, 601-602 (1961).

determines the amount received by the husband fixes the amount given up by the wife, and this figure, i.e., the market value of the property transferred by the husband, will be taken by her as her tax basis for the property received.

Finally, it must be noted that here, as well as in relation to the question of whether the event is taxable, we draw support from the prior administrative practice and judicial approval of that practice. . . . We therefore conclude that the Commissioner's assessment of a taxable gain based upon the value of the stock at the date of its transfer has not been shown erroneous. . . .

Reversed in part and affirmed in part.

Mr. Justice Frankfurter took no part in the decision of these cases.

Mr. Justice White took no part in the consideration or decision of these cases.

Notes and Questions

1. Is this also a taxable exchange for Mrs. Davis? The Court observes that the IRS does not attempt to tax the recipient (note 7). But is that theoretically correct or just matter of prosecutorial discretion? Is a divorce property settlement a market transaction? Could she have gotten such a payment from anyone else?

2. The taxpayer and Mrs. Davis made a voluntary property settlement. What would have happened had they failed to come to terms? Try to state, as precisely as possible, the nature of the claims that Mrs. Davis might have asserted. If she prevailed, how would the proceeds of such claims be taxed? See Raytheon Production Co. v. Commissioner, Chapter 3A above.

3. From the standpoint of tax administration, does *Davis* establish a workable rule? Do you suppose that most people who are compelled to transfer appreciated property to exit a bad marriage feel that they are thereby enriched? What do you predict would come of the common law versus community property divide that the Court endorses?

FARID-ES-SULTANEH v. COMMISSIONER
160 F.2d 812 (2d Cir. 1947)

Before Swan, Chase, and Clark, Circuit Judges.

CHASE, Circuit Judge. . . . The petitioner is an American citizen who filed her income tax return for the calendar year 1938 with the Collector of Internal Revenue for the Third District of New York and in it reported sales during that year of 12,000 shares of the common stock of the S.S. Kresge Company at varying prices per share, for the total sum of $230,802.36 which admittedly was in excess of their cost to her. How much this excess amounted to for tax purposes depends upon the legal significance of the facts now to be stated.

In December 1923 when the petitioner, then unmarried, and S.S. Kresge, then married, were contemplating their future marriage, he delivered to her 700 shares of the common stock of the S.S. Kresge Company which then had a fair market value of $290 per share. The shares were all in street form and were to be held by the petitioner "for her benefit and protection in the event that the said Kresge should die prior to the contemplated marriage between the petitioner and said Kresge." The latter was divorced from his wife on January 9, 1924, and on or about January 23, 1924 he delivered to the petitioner 1800 additional common shares of S.S. Kresge Company which were also in street form and were to be held by the petitioner for the same purposes as were the first 700 shares he had delivered to her. On April 24, 1924, and when the petitioner still retained the possession of the stock so delivered to her, she and Mr. Kresge executed a written ante-nuptial agreement wherein she acknowl-edged the receipt of the shares "as a gift made by the said Sebastian S. Kresge, pursuant to this indenture, and as an ante-nuptial settlement, and in consid-eration of said gift and said ante-nuptial settlement, in consideration of the promise of said Sebastian S. Kresge to marry her, and in further consideration of the consummation of said promised marriage" she released all dower and other marital rights, including the right to her support to which she otherwise would have been entitled as a matter of law when she became his wife. They were married in New York immediately after the ante-nuptial agreement was executed and continued to be husband and wife until the petitioner obtained a final decree of absolute divorce from him on, or about, May 18, 1928. No alimony was claimed by, or awarded to, her.

The stock so obtained by the petitioner from Mr. Kresge had a fair market value of $315 per share on April 24, 1924, and of $330 per share on, or about May 6, 1924, when it was transferred to her on the books of the corporation. She held all of it for about three years, but how much she continued to hold thereafter is not disclosed except as that may be shown by her sales in 1938. Meanwhile her holdings had been increased by a stock dividend of 50 percent, declared on April 1, 1925; one of 10 to 1 declared on January 19, 1926; and one of 50 percent, declared on March 1, 1929. Her adjusted basis for the stock she sold in 1938 was $10.661/2 per share com-puted on the basis of the fair market value of the shares which she obtained from Mr. Kresge at the time of her acquisition. His adjusted basis for the shares she sold in 1938 would have been $0.159091.

When the petitioner and Mr. Kresge were married he was 57 years old with a life expectancy of 16 1/2 years. She was then 32 years of age with a life expectancy of 33 1/2 years. He was then worth approximately $375,000,000 and owned real estate of the approximate value of $100,000,000.

The Commissioner determined the deficiency on the ground that the petitioner's stock obtained as above stated was acquired by gift within the meaning of that word as used in [§1015] and, as the transfer to her was after

December 31, 1920, used as the basis for determining the gain on her sale of it the basis it would have had in the hands of the donor. This was correct if the just mentioned statute is applicable, and the Tax Court held it was on the authority of Wemyss v. Commissioner, 324 U.S. 303, and Merrill v. Fahs, 324 U.S. 308.

The issue here presented cannot, however, be adequately dealt with quite so summarily. The *Wemyss* case determined the taxability to the transferor as a gift, under §§501 and 503 of the Revenue Act of 1932, and the applicable regulations, of property transferred in trust for the benefit of the prospective wife of the transferor pursuant to the terms of an ante-nuptial agreement. It was held that the transfer, being solely in consideration of her promise of marriage, and to compensate her for loss of trust income which would cease upon her marriage, was not for an adequate and full consideration in money or money's worth within the meaning of §503 of the statute, the Tax Court having found that the transfer was not one at arm's length made in the ordinary course of business. But we find nothing in this decision to show that a transfer, taxable as a gift under the gift tax, is ipso facto to be treated as a gift in construing the income tax law.

In Merrill v. Fahs, supra, it was pointed out that the estate and gift tax statutes are in pari materia and are to be so construed. . . . The estate tax provisions in the Revenue Act of 1916 required the inclusion in a decedent's gross estate of transfers made in contemplation of death, or intended to take effect in possession and enjoyment at or after death except when a transfer was the result of "a bona fide sale for a fair consideration in money or money's worth." . . . The first gift tax became effective in 1924, and provided inter alia, that where an exchange or sale of property was for less than a fair consideration in money or money's worth the excess should be taxed as a gift. . . . While both taxing statutes thus provided, it was held that a release of dower rights was a fair consideration in money or money's worth. . . . Following that, Congress in 1926 replaced the words "fair consideration" in the 1924 Act limiting the deductibility of claims against an estate with the words "adequate and full consideration in money or money's worth" and in 1932 the gift tax statute as enacted limited consideration in the same way. . . . Although Congress in 1932 also expressly provided that the release of marital rights should not be treated as a consideration in money or money's worth in administering the estate tax law, . . . and failed to include such a provision in the gift tax statute, it was held that the gift tax law should be construed to the same effect. Merrill v. Fahs, supra.

We find in this decision no indication, however, that the term "gift" as used in the income tax statute should be construed to include a transfer which, if made when the gift tax were effective, would be taxable to the transferor as a gift merely because of the special provisions in the gift tax statute defining and restricting consideration for gift tax purposes. A fortiori, it would seem that limitations found in the estate tax law upon according the usual legal effect to proof that a transfer was made for a fair consideration should not be imported into the income tax law except by action of Congress.

In our opinion the income tax provisions are not to be construed as though they were in pari materia with either the estate tax law or the gift tax statutes. They are aimed at the gathering of revenue by taking for public use given percentages of what the statute fixes as net taxable income. Capital gains and losses are, to the required or permitted extent, factors in determining net taxable income. What is known as the basis for computing gain or loss on transfers of property is established by statute in those instances when the resulting gain or loss is recognized for income tax purposes and the basis for succeeding sales or exchanges will, theoretically at least, level off taxwise any hills and valleys in the consideration passing either way on previous sales or exchanges. When Congress provided that gifts should not be treated as taxable income to the donee there was, without any correlative provisions fixing the basis of the gift to the donee, a loophole which enabled the donee to make a subsequent transfer of the property and take as the basis for computing gain or loss its value when the gift was made. Thus it was possible to exclude from taxation any increment in value during the donor's holding and the donee might take advantage of any shrinkage in such increment after the acquisition by gift in computing gain or loss upon a subsequent sale or exchange. It was to close this loophole that Congress provided that the donee should take the donor's basis when property was transferred by gift. Report of Ways and Means Committee (No. 350, P. 9, 67th Cong., 1st Sess.). This change in the statute affected only the statutory net taxable income. The altered statute prevented a transfer by gift from creating any change in the basis of the property in computing gain or loss on any future transfer. In any individual instance the change in the statute would but postpone taxation and presumably would have little effect on the total volume of income tax revenue derived over a long period of time and from many taxpayers. Because of this we think that a transfer which should be classed as a gift under the gift tax law is not necessarily to be treated as a gift income-tax-wise. Though such a consideration as this petitioner gave for the shares of stock she acquired from Mr. Kresge might not have relieved him from liability for a gift tax, had the present gift tax then been in effect, it was nevertheless a fair consideration which prevented her taking the shares as a gift under the income tax law since it precluded the existence of a donative intent.

Although the transfers of the stock made both in December 1923, and in the following January by Mr. Kresge to this taxpayer are called a gift in the ante-nuptial agreement later executed and were to be for the protection of his prospective bride if he died before the marriage was consummated, the "gift" was contingent upon his death before such marriage, an event that did not occur. Consequently, it would appear that no absolute gift was made before the ante-nuptial contract was executed and that she took title to the stock under its terms, viz: in consideration for her promise to marry him coupled with her promise to relinquish all rights in and to his property which she would otherwise acquire by the marriage. Her inchoate interest in the property of her affianced husband greatly exceeded the value of the stock transferred to her. It was a fair consideration under ordinary legal concepts of that term for the transfers of the stock by him. . . . She performed the contract under the terms of which the stock was transferred to her and held the shares not as a donee but as a purchaser for a fair consideration.

As the decisive issue is one of law only, the decision of the Tax Court interpreting the applicable statutory provisions has no peculiar finality and is reviewable. . . .

Decision reversed.

CLARK, Circuit Judge (dissenting). The opinion accepts two assumptions, both necessary to the result. The first is that definitions of gift under the gift and estate tax statutes are not useful, in fact are directly opposed to, definitions of gift under the capital-gains provision of the income tax statute. The second is that the circumstances here of a transfer of the stock some months before the marriage showed, contrary to the conclusions of the Tax Court, a purchase of dower rights, rather than a gift. The first I regard as doubtful; the second, as untenable.

It is true that Commissioner v. Wemyss, 324 U.S. 303, and Merrill v. Fahs, 324 U.S. 308, which would require the transactions here to be considered a gift, dealt with estate and gift taxes. But no strong reason has been advanced why what is a gift under certain sections of the Revenue Code should not be a gift under yet another section. As a matter of fact these two cases indicate that the donative intent of the common law is not an essential ingredient of a gift for tax purposes. Conversely love, affection, and promise of future marriage will not be consideration adequate to avoid the gift tax. If that is so, it would seem that these should not be sufficient to furnish new and higher cost bases for computing capital gains on ultimate sale. The Congressional purpose would seem substantially identical — to prevent a gap in the law whereby taxes on gifts or on capital gains could be avoided or reduced by judicious transfers within the family or intimate group.

But decision on that point might well be postponed, since, to my mind, the other point should be decisive. Kresge transferred the stock to petitioner more than three months before their marriage. Part was given when Kresge was married to another woman. At these times petitioner had no dower or other rights in his property. If Kresge died before the wedding, she could never secure dower rights in his lands. Yet she would nevertheless keep the stock. Indeed the specifically stated purpose of the transfer was to protect her against his death prior to marriage. It is therefore difficult to perceive how her not yet acquired rights could be consideration for the stock. Apparently the parties themselves shared this difficulty, for in their subsequent instrument releasing dower rights they referred to the stock transfer as a gift and an antenuptial settlement.

If the transfer be thus considered a sale, as the majority hold, it would seem to follow necessarily that this valuable consideration (equivalent to one-third for life in land valued at one hundred million dollars) should have yielded sizable taxable capital gains to Kresge, as well as a capital loss to petitioner when eventually she sold. I suggest these considerations as pointing to the unreality of holding as a sale what seems clearly only intended as a stimulating cause to eventual matrimony.

Since Judge Murdock in the Tax Court found this to be a gift, not a sale, and since this decision is based in part at least upon factual considerations, it would seem binding upon us. At any rate, it should be persuasive of the result we ought to reach.

Notes and Questions

1. In 1899 Sebastion S. Kresge opened a store in downtown Detroit that sold all items for five or ten cents. By 1912 he had stores in 85 locations, and the S.S. Kresge Company rapidly expanded to become the nation's first mass-market discount retail chain. In the 1960s and 1970s Kresge stores morphed into larger discount department stores, Kmart. Why do you suppose Kresge had such a low basis in his stock?

2. The court in *Farid-es-Sultaneh* gives a fairly good account of the purpose of §1015 and the possibilities of tax avoidance it was designed to curb, but stops short of explicitly considering the implication of that account for the case at hand. What of it? Does the court's holding open the door to the very sort of avoidance §1015 was designed to prevent? Or does that depend on something else? Does *Farid-es-Sultaneh* have any unstated implications with respect to the income tax liability of S.S. Kresge? Cf. United States v. Davis, Chapter 17E.2 above (previous case).

3. (a) Assuming Farid-es-Sultaneh's stock was *not* a gift, what follows? Was it income to her when she received it? Why not?

What statutory provision determines her basis for the stock if it was not a gift? Section 1012 prescribes the ordinary rule that basis equals cost. What was Farid-es-Sultaneh's cost for the stock in this case? Why not the value of the dower and other rights she gave up? Or the value of her service as Kresge's wife? Or why not zero, since whatever she gave up had no basis and she did not have any taxable income on the exchange? On what ground can her cost be said to be the fair market value of the stock when she received it?

(b) "Cost," as used in §1012, is a term of art whose meaning has been shaped by its function: to assure that income or gain gets taken into account once but only once. If a taxpayer, for example, received stock in connection with her employment, her cost would be whatever amount was properly includible in her income on receipt of the stock, since that will assure that when she sells, the sale proceeds will all have been taxed at one time or the other but not both. How does that reasoning apply in *Farid-es-Sultaneh?*

TRANSFER OF PROPERTY BETWEEN SPOUSES OR INCIDENT TO DIVORCE [§1041]

Staff of Joint Comm. on Taxation, 98th Cong., General Explanation of the Revenue Provisions of the Deficit Reduction Act of 1984, 710-712 (Comm. Print 1984)

PRIOR LAW

The Supreme Court had ruled that a transfer of appreciated property to a spouse (or former spouse) in exchange for the release of martial claims resulted in the recognition of gain to the transferor (United States v. Davis 370 U.S. 65 (1962)). The spouse receiving the property received a basis in the asset transferred equal to its fair market value. These rules did not apply in the case of equal division of community property, and the IRS had ruled that this rule did not apply to the partition of jointly held property.[7] The Tax treatment of divisions of property between spouses involving other various types of ownership under the different State laws was often unclear and had resulted in must litigation.[8] Several states had amended their property law in an attempt to avoid the result in the *Davis* case.

In addition, under prior law, losses were not allowed with respect to the transfer of property between spouses (sec. 267), and capital gains treatment and installment sales reporting were not allowed on the sale or exchange of depreciable property between spouses (secs. 1239 and 453 (g)). These limitations did not apply to transfers of property between former spouses.

REASONS FOR CHANGE

The Congress believes that, in general, it is inappropriate to tax transfers between spouses. This policy is already reflected in the Code rule that exempts marital gifts from the gift tax, and reflects the fact that a husband and wife are a single economic unit.

The current rules governing transfers of property between spouses or former spouses incident to divorce have not worked well and have led to much controversy and litigation. Often the rules have proved a trap for the unwary as, for example, where the parties view property acquired during marriage

---

7. See Rev. Rul. 74-347, 1974-2 C.B. 26.

8. See e.g., Commissioner v. Collins, 412 F.2d 211 (10th Cir. 1969); U.S. v. Wallace, 439 F.2d 757 (8th Cir. 1971); Commissioner v. Wiles, 499 F.2d 255 (10th Cir. 1974); U.S. v. Imel, 523 F.2d 853 (10th Cir. 1975); W. W. McKinney, 64 T.C. 262 (1975); U.S. v. Bosch, 590 F.2d 165 (5th Cir. 1979).

(even though held in one spouse's name) as jointly owned, only to find that the equal division of the property upon divorce triggers recognition of gain.

Furthermore, in divorce cases, the government often gets whipsawed. The transferor will not report any gain on the transfer, while the recipient spouse, when he or she sells, is entitled under the *Davis* rule to compute his or her gain or loss by reference to a basis equal to the fair market value of the property at the time received.

The Congress believes that to correct these problems, and make the tax laws as unintrusive as possible with respect to relations between spouses, the tax laws governing transfers between spouses and former spouses should be changed.

EXPLANATION OF PROVISION

The Act provides that the transfer of property to a spouse incident to a divorce[9] will be treated, for income tax purposes, in the same manner as gift. Gain (including recapture income) or loss will not be recognized to the transferor, and the transferee will receive the property at the transferor's basis (whether the property has appreciated or depreciated in value). Because any transfer of property, including money, is treated as if made by (and acquired by) gift, the recapture rules of sections 1245, 1250, 1254, etc. will not apply, and the limitation on amortizing certain term interests under section 273 will apply.

A transfer will be treated as incident to a divorce if the transfer occurs within one year after the parties cease to be married or is related to the divorce. This nonrecognition rule applies whether the transfer is for the relinquishment of marital rights, for cash or other property, for the assumption of liabilities in excess of basis,[10] or for other consideration and is intended to apply to any indebtedness which is discharged. Thus, uniform Federal income consequences will apply to these transfers notwithstanding that the property may be subject to differing state property laws.

In addition, this nonrecognition rule applies in the case of transfers of property between spouses during marriage (except where the transferee spouse is a non-resident alien).

Where an annuity is transferred, or a beneficial interest in a trust is transferred or created, incident to divorce or separation, the transferee will be entitled to the usual annuity treatment, including recovery of the transferor's investment in the contract (under sec. 72), or the usual treatment as the beneficiary of a trust (by reason of sec. 682), notwithstanding that the annuity payments or payments by the trust qualify as alimony or otherwise discharge a

---

9. For purposes of this provision, an annulment is to be treated as a divorce.

10. It is intended that no gain is to be recognized on the transfer of property for the assumption of (or subject to) liabilities in excess of basis only if the spouse (and not a trust) owns the property after the transfer is made.

1004   *17. Taxation and the Family*

support obligation.[11] The transfer of a life insurance contract to spouse incident to a divorce or separation generally will no longer result in the proceeds of the policy later being includible in income, since the policy will have a carryover basis and therefore the transfer for value rules (sec. 101(a)(2)) will not apply. Also, the transfer of an installment obligation will not trigger gain and the transfer of investment credit property will not result in recapture if the property continues to be used in the trade or business. . . .

REVENUE EFFECT

This provision will reduce revenues by less than $5 million annually.

Notes and Questions

1. Section 1041, a nonrecognition rule, grants tax deferral to gains realized under *Davis.* Nevertheless, the Treasury strongly supported the legislation. Why?

2. Ordinarily, the recipient of property transferred incident to divorce is in tighter economic circumstances than the transferor. Assume that the transferor owns a large portfolio of investment assets (stocks, bonds, real estate, etc.), some of which have appreciated while others have declined in value. How should divorcing parties select assets to be transferred under the property settlement?

3. Were it then in effect, would §1041 protect S.S. Kresge from tax on the stock transfers pursuant to the antenuptial agreement in *Farid-es-Sultaneh?* How would you advise a client in similar circumstances? More generally, with §1041 now the governing standard, does *Davis* have much (any?) continuing relevance?

4. *Legal expenses.* For the tax treatment of attorney's fees and other expenses incurred in connection with separation and divorce, see Gilmore v. United States, Chapter 12G above.

5. John and Michael are a same-sex couple. They live in a state that recognizes domestic partnerships, and several years ago they registered their relationship so that they were accorded all the rights and responsibilities of spouses under state law. During the course of their relationship John and Michael accumulated two investment properties, Blackacre, a tract of land held in joint tenancy, which cost $60,000, and shares of stock in Xerox Corporation, which John bought for $40,000 and held as separate property (i.e., sole registered owner). This year the couple takes steps to dissolve their domestic partnership, and in settlement of all obligations relating thereto Michael takes title to the Xerox stock and John obtains sole ownership of Blackacre.

---

11. This rule relates, in part, to amendments made to Code section 71 by section 422 of the Act.

Assume that the land and stock are each worth $100,000 when ownership interests are rearranged. What are the tax consequences for each party?

6. *A* owns stock in Corporation *A* worth $1 million with an adjusted basis of only $200,000. *B* owns a large block of stock in Corporation *B* worth $1 million that she purchased for $1.8 million. Neither taxpayer owns substantial investment assets apart from these stock interests, and they would both like to liquidate their holdings at minimum tax cost (each is in the 35 percent tax bracket). At the suggestion of an accountant, *A* and *B* get married and briefly live in the same house. The next year they separate and obtain a divorce. Their written property settlement provides that *A* will transfer half of his stock in Corporation *A* to *B*, who will transfer half of her holdings in Corporation *B* to *A*. In addition, *A* agrees to pay *B* $20,000 each year for three years if *B* is then living. After the stock transfers are finalized, *A* sells his stock in both companies, reporting a $400,000 loss on the Corporation *B* stock and a $400,000 gain from his remaining interest in Corporation *A*. Shortly thereafter *B* does likewise. How should these transactions be treated for tax purposes?

References

B. The Marriage Bonus and the Marriage Penalty. Bittker, Federal Income Taxation and the Family, 27 Stan. L. Rev. 1389 (1975); Blumberg, Sexism in the Code: A Comparative Study of Income Taxation of Working Wives and Mothers, 21 Buffalo L. Rev. 49 (1971); Currie, Suitcase Divorce in the Conflict of Laws: *Simons, Rosenstiel,* and *Borax,* 34 U. Chi. L. Rev. 26 (1966). Feld, Divorce, Tax-Style, 54 Taxes 608 (1976); Jensen, The Historical Discrimination of the Federal Income Tax Rates, 54 Taxes 445 (1976); McIntyre & Oldman, Taxation of the Family in a Comprehensive and Simplified Income Tax, 90 Harv. L. Rev. 1573 (1977); Surrey, Federal Taxation of the Family — The Revenue Act of 1948, 61 Harv. L. Rev. 1097, 1103 (1948).

C. Support, Gift, or Compensation? Viviana A. Zelizer, The Purchase of Intimacy, 25 Law & Soc. Inquiry 817 (2000); Carol Rose, Giving, Trading, Thieving, and Trusting: How and Why Gifts Becomes Exchanges, and (More Importantly) Vice Versa, 44 Fla. L. Rev. 295 (1992); Randall, Tax Status of Friendly, but Unmarried, Taxpayers, 57 Taxes 27 (1979).

E. Separation and Divorce. Asimow, The Assault on Tax-Free Divorce: Carryover Basis and Assignment of Income, 44 Tax L. Rev. 65, (1988); Hagan, Policy Analysis of Alimony, 41 Tax Notes 971 (1988); Hjorth, Divorce, Taxes, and the 1984 Tax Reform Act: An Inadequate Response to an Old Problem, 61 Wash. L. Rev. 151 (1986); Moran, Welcome to the Funhouse: The Incredible Maze of Modern Divorce Taxation, 26 Harv. J. Leg. 117 (1989).

Chapter 18 — *Investment Income*

Income from personal services is generally to "be taxed to him who earns it."[1] But what about income from investments (sometimes called *unearned income*)? In simple cases, investment income is taxable to the investor — the one who owns the investment. However, ownership is a bundle of rights that can readily be separated among a number of people, and then the question of who should be taxed may be of some difficulty.

One important way of dividing ownership of investment property is by putting it in trust. Control is thus vested in a trustee or trustees, while beneficial ownership is vested in beneficiaries. Trusts are wondrously flexible devices. Beneficial ownership may be divided among different individuals, born and unborn, in a variety of ways, and the trustee (or one or more of several trustees) may or may not be among the beneficiaries. The grantor may or may not be a trustee or a beneficiary, and particular powers may be conferred on trustees or on beneficiaries or retained by the grantor as such.

The taxation of trust income has long been the subject of specific statutory provisions that have long provided that trust income is taxable to trust beneficiaries to whom it is distributed or distributable; that the trust will itself be taxed on income which is not either distributable or distributed; and further, in some circumstances, that trust income is taxable to the grantor who is not a beneficiary.

Very detailed statutory provisions governing trust income were enacted in 1954 and appear in subchapter J (§§641 et seq.), which we will look at a little more closely in section B of this chapter. These provisions generally preserve the pattern described in the last paragraph, but with some important qualifications and elaborations.

---

1. Commissioner v. Culbertson, 337 U.S. 733 (1949), citing Lucas v. Earl, Chapter 17A above.

We will first examine Supreme Court cases decided in the decade from 1930 to 1940, dealing mostly with trusts but also with simple assignments of investment income. The trust cases are important, despite the later more detailed legislation in 1954, for several reasons: they are part of the pattern of judicial decisions that still governs simple income assignments without any special statute; they introduce the statutory provisions governing trust income in an earlier, simpler, form; and, as will appear, they provide the origin and reason for some of the more complicated present statutory provisions.

A.   THE BASIC SUPREME COURT CASES

CORLISS v. BOWERS
281 U.S. 376 (1930)

Mr. Justice HOLMES delivered the opinion of the Court. This is a suit to recover the amount of an income tax paid by the plaintiff, the petitioner, under the Revenue Act of 1924, June 2, 1924, c. 234, §219, (g)(h), 43 Stat. 253, 277. . . .

The question raised by the petitioner is whether the above section of the Revenue Act can be applied constitutionally to him upon the following facts. In 1922 he transferred the fund from which arose the income in respect to which the petitioner was taxed, to trustees, in trust to pay the income to his wife for life with remainder over to their children. By the instrument creating the trust the petitioner reserved power "to modify or alter in any manner, or revoke in whole or in part, this indenture and the trusts then existing, and the estates and interests in property hereby created" etc. It is not necessary to quote more words because there can be no doubt that the petitioner fully reserved the power at any moment to abolish or change the trust at his will. The statute referred to provides that "when the grantor of a trust has, at any time during the taxable year, . . . the power to revest in himself title to any part of the corpus of the trust, then the income of such part of the trust for such taxable year shall be included in computing the net income of the grantor." §219(g) with other similar provisions as to income in §219(h). There can be no doubt either that the statute purports to tax the plaintiff in this case. But the net income for 1924 was paid over to the petitioner's wife and the petitioner's argument is that however it might have been in different circumstances the income never was his and he cannot be taxed for it. The legal estate was in the trustee and the equitable interest in the wife.

But taxation is not so much concerned with the refinements of title as it is with actual command over the property taxed — the actual benefit for which the tax is paid. If a man directed his bank to pay over income as received to a servant or friend, until further orders, no one would doubt that he could be taxed upon the amounts so paid. It is answered that in that case he would have a title, whereas here he did not. But from the point of view of taxation there would be no difference. The title would merely mean a right to stop the payment before it took place. The same right existed here although it is not called a title but is called a power. The acquisition by the wife of the income became complete only when the plaintiff failed to exercise the power that he reserved. . . . Still speaking with reference to taxation, if a man disposes of a fund in such a way that another is allowed to enjoy the income which it is in the power of the first to appropriate it does not matter whether the permission is given by assent or by failure to express dissent. The income that is subject to a man's unfettered command and that he is free to enjoy at his own option may be taxed to him as his income, whether he sees fit to enjoy it or not. We consider the case too clear to need help from the local law of New York or from arguments based on the power of Congress to prevent escape from taxes or surtaxes by devices that easily might be applied to that end.

Judgment affirmed.

The Chief Justice took no part in this case.

Questions

1. This is a constitutional case; the holding is only that a statute taxing the grantor on income of a revocable trust is not unconstitutional.

But how important is the statutory provision here? What if there had been no specific statute on the matter? Would the Court that decided Lucas v. Earl have decided this case for the government, too? Reread the last full paragraph in the opinion.

To put the matter in less hypothetical terms, who is taxable on the income of a revocable trust for years prior to 1924 under this decision?

2. The statute involved in this case applied "when the grantor of a trust has, *at any time during the taxable year,* . . . the power to revest in himself title to any part of the corpus of the trust . . ." (emphasis added).

What if the grantor retained the power to revoke but only after giving two years' advance notice of intention to revoke? Then as long as the notice was not given he could argue that he did not have the power during any particular year to revoke. Would he nevertheless be taxable? What if only one year's advance notice were required?

3. The statute was amended in 1934 by deleting the words "during the taxable year." Under the amended statute, how should the following cases be treated?

(a) *A* created a trust for his children, retaining a power to revoke after three years.

(b) *B* created a trust for his children, retaining a power to revoke after all his children finished their college educations. His youngest child is presently *in utero.*

(c) *C* created a trust for his children, retaining a reversion after three years. The trust instrument contains a simple procedure by which *C* can extend it for additional years.

4. These questions are dealt with further in the *Clifford* case, below; but think now how they ought to be resolved under the opinion in *Corliss*.

DOUGLAS v. WILLCUTS
296 U.S. 1 (1935)

Mr. Chief Justice HUGHES delivered the opinion of the Court. On September 12, 1923, petitioner, Edward B. Douglas, entered into an agreement with his wife and the Minneapolis Trust Company, by which he transferred securities in trust for his wife's benefit. Out of the income of the trust estate the trustee was to pay Mrs. Douglas annually the sum of $15,000, up to November 6, 1927, and thereafter $21,000. Deficiencies were to be made up in a prescribed manner. Excess income (in case the principal was not impaired) was to be paid to petitioner. On the death of his wife, he was to receive the property free of the trust. Petitioner reserved the right to designate securities for investment, subject however, to the approval of the trustee acting in that respect on behalf of Mrs. Douglas.

The parties stipulated that the provisions for Mrs. Douglas were "in lieu of, and in full settlement of alimony, and of any and all dower rights or statutory interests in the estate" of her husband, and "in lieu of any and all claims for separate maintenance and allowance for her support."

Three days later, Mrs. Douglas obtained a decree of absolute divorce in a district court of the State of Minnesota. The decree provided:

> It Is Further Adjudged and Decreed that the defendant provide and create the trust fund as set out in that certain agreement between said parties and the Minneapolis Trust Company as trustee now on file with said trustee, and that the plaintiff have the provision therein made in lieu of all other alimony or interest in the property or estate of the defendant and that neither party have any costs or disbursements herein.

The question in this case relates to the net income of the trust which was distributed to Mrs. Douglas in the years 1927 and 1928. The Commissioner of Internal Revenue determined that these amounts were income to the petitioner. . . .

The authority of the district court is defined by statute. Mason's Minnesota Statutes, 1927, §§8601-8604. The court is empowered upon divorce for any cause, except that of the wife's adultery, to decree to the wife "such part of the personal and real estate of the husband, not exceeding in value one-third thereof, as it deems just and reasonable, having regard to the ability of the husband, the character and situation of the parties, and all other circumstances of the case." The court may also decree "such alimony out of the estate, earnings and income of the husband as it may deem just and reasonable," but "the aggregate award and allowance made to the wife from the estate of the husband" is not "to exceed in present value one-third of the personal estate, earnings, and income of the husband, and one-third in value of his real estate." Id. §8602. The court "may appoint trustees, whenever it is deemed expedient, to receive any money ordered to be paid to the wife, upon trust to invest the same, and pay over the income for the support of the wife, or of the wife and minor children of the parties, or any of them, in such manner as the court shall direct, or to pay over to the wife the principal sum in such proportions and at such times as the court shall order." Id. §8601. After a decree "for alimony, or other allowance for the wife and children," or "for the appointment of trustees to receive and hold any property for the use of the wife or children," the court may from time to time "revise and alter" the decree, with respect to the amount "of such alimony or allowance" and also with respect to "the appropriation and payment of the principal and income of the property so held in trust, and may make any order respecting any of the said matters which it might have made in the original action." Id. §8603. . . .

In the instant case, the trust agreement was made on the day that the suit for divorce was brought. The agreement was manifestly made in contemplation of that suit. When the district court was shortly called upon to determine what provision should be made for the wife, the court was not bound by the trust agreement. . . . While the terms of the trust as set up in the trust agreement were approved, the court made those terms its own. It was from this action of the court that the trust derived its force.

Amounts paid to a divorced wife under a decree for alimony are not regarded as income of the wife but as paid in discharge of the general obligation to support, which is made specific by the decree. Gould v. Gould, 245 U.S. 151, 153; Audubon v. Shufeldt, 181 U.S. 575, 577. Petitioner's contention that the district court did not award alimony is not supported by the terms of the decree. It described the provision as made "in lieu of all *other* alimony or interest in the property or estate of the defendant." However designated, it was a provision for annual payments to serve the purpose of alimony, that is, to assure to the wife suitable support. The fact that the provision was to be in lieu of any other interest in the husband's property did not affect the essential quality of these payments. Upon the preexisting duty of the husband the decree placed a particular and adequate sanction, and imposed upon petitioner the obligation to devote the income in question, through the medium of the trust, to the use of his divorced wife.

No question is raised as to the constitutional power of the Congress to attribute to petitioner the income thus segregated and paid in discharge of his obligation, and that authority could not be challenged successfully.

Burnet v. Wells, 289 U.S. 670, 677, 682, 684. The question is one of statutory construction. We think that the definitions of gross income (Revenue Acts, 1926, §213; 1928; §22) are broad enough to cover income of that description. They are to be considered in the light of the evident intent of the Congress "to use its power to the full extent." . . . In the present case, the net income of the trust fund, which was paid to the wife under the decree, stands substantially on the same footing as though he had received the income personally and has been required by the decree to make the payment directly.

We do not regard the provisions of the statutes as to the taxation of trusts, fiduciaries and beneficiaries (Revenue Acts, 1926, §§2, 219; 1928, §§161, 162) as intended to apply to cases where the income of the trust would otherwise remain, by virtue of the nature and purpose of the trust, attributable to the creator of the trust and accordingly taxable to him. These provisions have appropriate reference to cases where the income of the trust is no longer to be regarded as that of the settlor, and we find no warrant for a construction which would preclude the laying of the tax against the one who through the discharge of his obligation enjoys the benefit of the income as though he had personally received it.

The decision in Helvering v. Butterworth, 290 U.S. 365, is not opposed. There the trust was testamentary and the only question was with respect to the liability for the tax as between the trustee and the beneficiary. The Court observed that "the evident general purpose of the statute was to tax in some way the whole income of all trust estates." The decision has no application to a case where the income is still taxable to the grantor. Nor are the provisions of the statutes (Revenue Acts, 1926, §219(h); 1928, §167) defining instances in which the grantor remains taxable, as in case of certain reservations for his benefit or provisions for the payment of premiums upon policies of insurance on his life, to be regarded as excluding instances not specified, where in contemplation of law the income remains in substance that of the grantor. No such exclusion is expressed and we see no ground for implying it.

The decree of the Circuit Court of Appeals is
Affirmed.

Notes and Questions

1. Under *Douglas*, as construed, if a trust property settlement had operated to discharge the husband from any continuing obligation with respect to his wife, fixed or contingent, then the income would have been taxed to her, not him. The resulting confusion, uncertainty, and dependence on the variety of state laws on the subject were part of what led to the statutory reform respecting alimony generally, reflected in §§71, 215, and 682. See Chapter 17E.1.

2. What are the implications of *Douglas* outside the marital context?

(a) *A* transfers securities in trust for her minor daughter, directing the trustee first to apply the income to payment of the gift tax payable on the transfer, then to accumulate the income until the daughter's majority, then to pay over the whole trust property to her. To whom is the income taxable?

(b) *B* owns a piece of rental real estate subject to a level-payment, purchase-money mortgage. He transfers it to a trustee for the benefit of *S*, his son, directing that the trustee collect the rent, pay all current expenses and make the current mortgage payments, and distribute the balance to *S*. The figures are:

Rental income		$20,000
Fire insurance	$ 600	
Maintenance	1,400	
Real estate taxes	6,000	
Mortgage (interest, $4,000; principal, $5,000)	9,000	17,000
Distributed to *S*		$3,000

Who has how much taxable income on account of this investment? Assume in this question that *B* has no reversion and the property is ultimately to be distributed to his son. Should the answer be different if *B* had a reversionary interest?

(c) *C* created a trust for his minor children. The trustee has power and discretion to use the income of the trust to pay tuition bills for *C*'s children at any secondary school or undergraduate college, and in fact he makes substantial payments for just that purpose. See §677(b).

BURNET v. WELLS
289 U.S. 670 (1933)

Mr. Justice CARDOZO delivered the opinion of the Court. Income of a trust has been reckoned by the taxing officers of the Government as income to be attributed to the creator of the trust in so far as it has been applied to the maintenance of insurance on his life. Section 219(h) of the Revenue Acts of 1924 and 1926 permits this to be done. The question is whether as applied to this case the acts are constitutional.

On December 30, 1922, the respondent Frederick B. Wells, created three trusts, referred to in the record as numbers 1, 2 and 3, and on August 6, 1923, two additional ones, numbers 4 and 5, all five being irrevocable.

By trust number 1, he assigned certain shares of stock of the par value of $100,000 to the Minneapolis Trust Company as trustee. The income of the trust was used to pay the annual premiums upon a policy of insurance for

$100,000 on the life of the grantor. After the payment of the premiums, the excess income, if any, was to be accumulated until an amount sufficient to pay an additional annual premium had been reserved. Any additional income was, in the discretion of the trustee, to be paid to a daughter. Upon the death of the grantor, the trustee was to collect the policy, and with the proceeds was to buy securities belonging to the Wells estate amounting to $100,000 at their appraised value. The securities so purchased, which were a substitute for the cash proceeds of the policy, were to be held as part of the trust during the life of the daughter, who was to receive the income. On her death the trust was to end, and the corpus was to be divided as she might appoint by her will, and, in default of appointment or issue, to the grantor's sons.

The other trusts carried out very similar plans, though for the use of other beneficiaries. . . .

The grantor in making the returns of his own income for the years 1924, 1925, and 1926, did not include any part of the income belonging to the trusts. Upon an audit of the returns the Commissioner of Internal Revenue assessed a deficiency to the extent that the income of the trusts had been applied to the payment of premiums on the policies of insurance. There was no attempt to charge against the taxpayer the whole income of the trusts, to charge him with the excess applied to other uses than the preservation of the policies. The deficiency assessment was limited to that part of the income which had kept the policies alive. . . .

The meaning of the statute is not doubtful, whatever may be said of its validity.

> Where any part of the income of a trust is or may be applied to the payment of premiums upon policies of the life of the grantor (except policies of insurance irrevocably payable for the purposes and in the manner specified in paragraph (10) of subdivision (a) of Section 214 [the exception having relation to trusts for charities]), such part of the income of the trust shall be included in computing the net income of the grantor.

One can read in the revisions of the revenue acts the record of the Government's endeavor to keep pace with the fertility of invention whereby taxpayers had contrived to keep the larger benefits of ownership and be relieved of the attendant burdens. . . .

A method, much in vogue until an amendment made it worthless, was the creation of a trust with a power of revocation. This device was adopted to escape the burdens of the tax upon incomes and the tax upon estates. To neutralize the effect of the device in its application to incomes, Congress made provision by §219(g) of the Revenue Act of 1924 that "where the grantor of a trust has, at any time during the taxable year, either alone or in conjunction with any person not a beneficiary of the trust, the power to revest in himself title to any part of the corpus of the trust, then the income of such part of the trust for such taxable year shall be included in computing the net income of the grantor." The validity of this provision was assailed by taxpayers. It was upheld by this court in Corliss v. Bowers, 281 U.S. 376, as applied to a trust in existence at the enactment of the statute, the power of revocation in that case being reserved to the grantor alone, and recently, at the present term, was upheld where the power of revocation had been reserved to the grantor in conjunction with someone else. Reinecke v. Smith, ante, p. 172. Cf. Burnet v. Guggenheim, 288 U.S. 280. Other amendments of the statute were directed to the trust as an instrument for the avoidance of the tax upon estates. By §302(d) of the Revenue Act of 1924, the gross estate of a decedent is to be taken as including the subject of any trust which he has created during life "where the enjoyment thereof was subject at the date of his death to any change through the exercise of a power, either by the decedent alone or in conjunction with any person, to alter, amend or revoke, or where the decedent relinquished any such power in contemplation of his death, except in case of a bona fide sale for a fair consideration in money or money's worth." The validity of this provision as to trusts both past and future is no longer open to debate. . . . Through the devices thus neutralized as well as through many others there runs a common thread of purpose. The solidarity of the family is to make it possible for the taxpayer to surrender title to another and to keep dominion for himself, or if not technical dominion, at least the substance of enjoyment. At times escape has been blocked by the resources of the judicial process without the aid of legislation. Thus, Lucas v. Earl, 281 U.S. 111, held that the salary earned by a husband was taxable to him, though he had bound himself by a valid contract to assign it to his wife. Burnet v. Leininger, 285 U.S. 136, laid down a like rule where there had been an assignment by a partner of his interest in the future profits of a partnership. Old Colony Trust Co. v. Commissioner, [Chapter 2A above] and United States v. Boston & Maine R. Co., 279 U.S. 732, held that income was received by a taxpayer when pursuant to a contract, debt or other obligation was discharged by another for his benefit, the transaction being the same in substance as if the money had been paid to the debtor and then transmitted to the creditor. Cf. United States v. Mahoning Coal R. Co., 51 F.(2d) 208. In these and other cases there has been a progressive endeavor by the Congress and the courts to bring about a correspondence between the legal concept of ownership and the economic realities of enjoyment or fruition. Of a piece with that endeavor is the statute now assailed.

   The controversy is one as to the boundaries of legislative power. It must be dealt with in a large way, as questions of due process always are, not narrowly or pedantically, in slavery to forms or phrases. "Taxation is not so much concerned with the refinements of title as it is with the actual command over the property taxed — the actual benefit for which the tax is paid." Corliss v. Bowers, supra, p. 378. Cf. Burnet v. Guggenheim, supra, p. 283. Refinements of title have at times supplied the rule when the question has been one of construction and nothing more, a question as to the meaning of a taxing act to be read in favor of the taxpayer. Refinements of title are without controlling force when a statute, unmistakable in meaning, is assailed by a taxpayer as overpassing the bounds of reason, an exercise by the lawmakers of arbitrary power. In such circumstances the question is no longer whether the concept of ownership reflected in the statute is to be squared with the concept embodied, more or less vaguely, in common law traditions. The question is whether it is one that an enlightened legislator might act upon without affront to justice. . . .

Wells, by the creation of these trusts, did more than devote his income to the benefit of relatives. He devoted it at the same time to the preservation of his own contracts, to the protection of an interest which he wished to keep alive. The ends to be attained must be viewed in combination. True he would have been at liberty, if the trusts had not been made, to put an end to his interest in the policies through nonpayment of the premiums, to stamp the contracts out. The chance that economic changes might force him to that choice was a motive, along with others, for the foundation of the trusts. In effect he said to the trustee that for the rest of his life he would dedicate a part of his income to the preservation of these contracts, so much did they mean for his peace of mind and happiness. Income permanently applied by the act of the taxpayer to the maintenance of contracts of insurance made in his name for the support of his dependents is income used for his benefit in such a sense and to such a degree that there is nothing arbitrary or tyrannical in taxing it as his.

Insurance for dependents is today in the thought of many a pressing social duty. Even if not a duty, it is a common item in the family budget, kept up very often at the cost of painful sacrifice, and abandoned only under dire compulsion. It will be a vain effort at persuasion to argue to the average man that a trust created by a father to pay premiums on life policies for the use of sons and daughters is not a benefit to the one who will have to pay the premiums if the policies are not to lapse. Only by closing our minds to common modes of thought, to everyday realities, shall we find it in our power to form another judgment. . . .

Trusts for the preservation of policies of insurance involve a continuing exercise by the settlor of a power to direct the application of the income along predetermined channels. In this they are to be distinguished from trusts where the income of a fund, though payable to wife or kin, may be expended by the beneficiaries without restraint, may be given away or squandered, the founder of the trust doing nothing to impose his will upon the use. There is no occasion at this time to mark the applicable principle for those and other cases. The relation between the parties, the tendency of the transfer to give relief from obligations that are recognized as binding by normal men and women, will be facts to be considered. . . . We do not go into their bearing now. Here the use to be made of the income of the trust was subject, from first to last, to the will of the grantor announced at the beginning. A particular expense, which for millions of men and women has become a fixed charge, as it doubtless was for Wells, an expense which would have to be continued if he was to preserve a contract right, was to be met in a particular way. He might have created a blanket trust for the payment of all the items of his own and the family budget, classifying the proposed expenses by adequate description. If the transaction had taken such a form, one can hardly doubt the validity of a legislative declaration that income so applied should be deemed to be devoted to his use. Instead of shaping the transaction thus, he picked out of the total budget an item or class of items, the cost of continuing his contracts of insurance, and created a source of income to preserve them against lapse.

Congress does not play the despot in ordaining that trusts for such uses, if created in the future, shall be treated for the purpose of taxation as if the income of the trust had been retained by the grantor.

It does not play the despot in ordaining a like rule as to trusts created in the past, at all events when in so doing it does not cast the burden backward beyond the income of the current year. . . .

The judgment is

Reversed.

Mr. Justice SUTHERLAND, dissenting. Mr. Justice VAN DEVANTER, Mr. Justice McREYNOLDS, Mr. Justice BUTLER and I think otherwise.

The powers of taxation are broad, but the distinction between taxation and confiscation must still be observed. So long as the Fifth Amendment remains unrepealed and is permitted to control, Congress may not tax the property of *A* as the property of *B*, or the income of A as the income of B.

The facts here show that Wells created certain irrevocable trusts. He retained no vestige of title to, interest in, or control over, the property transferred to the trustee. The result was a present, executed, outright gift, which could then have been taxed to the settlor. Burnet v. Guggenheim, 288 U.S. 280. That the property which was the subject of the gift could never thereafter, without a change of title, be taxed to the settlor is, of course, too plain for argument. To establish the contention that the income from such property, the application of which for the benefit of others had been irrevocably fixed, is nevertheless the income of the settlor and may lawfully be taxed as his property, requires something more tangible than a purpose to perform a social duty, or the recognition of a moral claim as distinguished from a legal obligation, which, we think is not supplied by an assumption of his desire thereby to secure his own peace of mind and happiness or relieve himself from further concern in the matter. If the trusts in question had irrevocably devoted the income to charitable purposes, to the cause of scientific research, or to the promotion of the spread of religion among the heathen, and the statute had authorized its taxation, probably no thoughtful person would have insisted that the relation of the settlor to the benefaction was such as constitutionally to justify the tax against him. And yet in each of these supposed cases it would not be hard to find a purpose to discharge a social duty, or unreasonable to assume the desire of the settlor thereby to enjoy the mental comfort which is supposed to follow the voluntary performance of righteous deeds.

If there be any difference between the cases supposed and the present one, it is a difference without real substance. In each the motive of the taxpayer is immaterial. The material question is, what has he done? — not, why has he done it? — however pertinent the latter query might be in a different case. Obviously, as it seems to us, the distinction to be observed is between the devotion of income to payments which the settlor is bound to make, and to those which he is free to make or not make, as he may see fit. In the former case the payments have the substantial elements of income to the settlor. In the latter, whatever may be said of the moral influence which induced the settlor to direct the payments, they are income of the trustee for the benefit of others than the settlor.

It is not accurate, we think, to say that these trusts involve the continuing exercise by the settlor of a power to direct the application of the income along predetermined channels. The exertion of power on the part of the settlor to direct such application begins and ends with the creation of the irrevocable trusts. Thereafter, the power is to be exercised automatically by the trustee under a grant which neither he nor the settlor can recall or abridge. The income, of course, is taxable, but to the trustee, not to the settlor. The well reasoned opinion of the court below, which fully sustains respondent's contention here, renders it unnecessary to discuss the matter at greater length. We think that opinion should be sustained. It finds ample support in Hoeper v. Tax Commission, 284 U.S. 206, 215; Heiner v. Donnan, 285 U.S. 312, 326; and other decisions of this court.

Questions

1. The provision involved in *Wells* is now contained in §677(a)(3) (when read together with §671).

(a) Is this a sound continuing provision?

(b) What if a woman creates an irrevocable trust for her son, giving the trustee authority to distribute or accumulate income and to invest in "any and every sort of property whatsoever, productive or nonproductive"? Would the trust income be taxable to the grantor if under the controlling state law the trustee could purchase an insurance policy on the grantor's life and use the trust income to pay the premiums?

(c) What if a trust is created for the benefit of a child of the grantor, with directions to accumulate during the grantor's lifetime? Why should the trust income be treated differently if used to purchase life insurance than if invested any other way?

(d) What if a man transfers life insurance policies and securities outright to his daughter, suggesting that she use the income from the securities to pay premiums on the policies? Who would be taxed on the income from the securities? Is there any reason why the result should be different in case of a transfer to a trustee for the benefit of the daughter? What if the daughter is the trustee?

2. (a) What about the retroactivity problem in this case? Does it deserve more analysis than it is given in the final paragraph of the Court's opinion? Would the dissenters have assented if the Court's holding had been confined to trusts created after enactment of the 1924 act?

(b) Should Congress, as a matter of policy, have made the rule in *Wells* applicable only in the case of trusts created after enactment (or proposal) of the 1924 act?

(c) Suppose that because of the Court's decision Congress could not tax to the grantor the income of a pre-existing irrevocable trust, but that it remained anxious not to give a permanent boon to those who had created trusts prior to the new statute. Can you suggest another legislative formulation that would achieve the Congressional objective? Cf. §1(g).

BLAIR v. COMMISSIONER
300 U.S. 5 (1937)

Mr. Chief Justice HUGHES delivered the opinion of the Court. This case presents the question of the liability of a beneficiary of a testamentary trust for a tax upon the income which he had assigned to his children prior to the tax years and which the trustees had paid to them accordingly.

The trust was created by the will of William Blair, a resident of Illinois who died in 1899, and was of property located in that State. One-half of the net income was to be paid to the donor's widow during her life. His son, the petitioner Edward Tyler Blair, was to receive the other one-half and, after the death of the widow, the whole of the net income during his life. In 1923, after the widow's death, petitioner assigned to his daughter, Lucy Blair Linn, an interest amounting to $6,000 for the remainder of that calendar year, and to $9,000 in each calendar year thereafter, in the net income which the petitioner was then or might thereafter be entitled to receive during his life. At about the same time, he made like assignments of interests, amounting to $9,000 in each calendar year, in the net income of the trust to his daughter Edith Blair and to his son, Edward Seymour Blair, respectively. In later years, by similar instruments, he assigned to these children additional interests, and to his son William McCormick Blair other specified interests, in the net income. The trustees accepted the assignments and distributed the income directly to the assignees.

The question first arose with respect to the tax year 1923 and the Commissioner of Internal Revenue ruled that the income was taxable to the petitioner. The Board of Tax Appeals held the contrary. 18 B.T.A. 60. The Circuit Court of Appeals reversed the Board, holding that under the law of

Illinois the trust was a spendthrift trust and the assignments were invalid. Commissioner v. Blair, 60 F.2d 340. We denied certiorari. 288 U.S. 602.

Thereupon the trustees brought suit in the Superior Court of Cook County, Illinois, to obtain a construction of the will with respect to the power of the beneficiary of the trust to assign a part of his equitable interest and to determine the validity of the assignments he had made. The petitioner and the assignees were made defendants. The Appellate Court of Illinois, First District, after a review of the Illinois decisions, decided that the trust was not a spendthrift trust and upheld the assignments. Blair v. Linn, 274 Ill. App. 23. Under the mandate of the appellate court, the Superior Court of Cook County entered its decree which found the assignments to be "voluntary assignments of a part of the interest of said Edward Tyler Blair in said trust estate" and as such adjudged them to be valid.

At that time there were pending before the Board of Tax Appeals proceedings involving the income of the trust for the years 1924, 1925, 1926, and 1929. The Board received in evidence the record in the suit in the state court and, applying the decision of that court, the Board overruled the Commissioner's determination as to the petitioner's liability. 31 B.T.A. 1192. The Circuit Court of Appeals again reversed the Board. That court recognized the binding effect of the decision of the state court as to the validity of the assignments but decided that the income was still taxable to the petitioner upon the ground that his interest was not attached to the corpus of the estate and that the income was not subject to his disposition until he received it. Commissioner v. Blair, 83 F.2d 655, 662.

Because of an asserted conflict with the decision of the state court, and also with decisions of circuit courts of appeals, we granted certiorari. October 12, 1936.

First. The Government contends that the judgment relating to the income for 1923 is conclusive in this proceeding as res judicata. Tait v. Western Maryland Ry. Co., 289 U.S. 620. Petitioner insists that this question was not raised before the Board of Tax Appeals and hence was not available before the Circuit Court of Appeals. . . .

It is not necessary to review the respective contentions upon this point, as we think that the ruling in the *Tait* case is not applicable. That ruling and the reasoning which underlies it apply where in the subsequent proceeding, although relating to a different tax year, the questions presented upon the facts and the law are essentially the same. Tait v. Western Maryland Ry. Co., supra, pp. 624, 626. Here, after the decision in the first proceeding, the opinion and decree of the state court created a new situation. The determination of petitioner's liability for the year 1923 had been rested entirely upon the local law. Commissioner v. Blair, 60 F.2d 340, 342, 344. The supervening decision of the state court interpreting that law in direct relation to this trust cannot justly be ignored in the present proceeding so far as it is found that the local law is determinative of any material point in controversy. . . .

Second. The question of the validity of the assignments is a question of local law. The donor was a resident of Illinois and his disposition of the property in that State was subject to its law. By that law the character of the trust, the nature and extent of the interest of the beneficiary, and the power of the beneficiary to assign that interest in whole or in part, are to be determined. The decision of the state court upon these questions is final. . . . It matters not that the decision was by an intermediate appellate court. . . . In this instance, it is not necessary to go beyond the obvious point that the decision was in a suit between the trustees and the beneficiary and his assignees, and the decree which was entered in pursuance of the decision determined as between these parties the validity of the particular assignments. Nor is there any basis for a charge that the suit was collusive and the decree inoperative. . . . The trustees were entitled to seek the instructions of the court having supervision of the trust. That court entertained the suit and the appellate court, with the first decision of the Circuit Court of Appeals before it, reviewed the decisions of the Supreme Court of the State and reached a deliberate conclusion. To derogate from the authority of that conclusion and of the decree it commanded, so far as the question is one of state law, would be wholly unwarranted in the exercise of federal jurisdiction.

In the face of this ruling of the state court it is not open to the Government to argue that the trust "was, under the Illinois law, a spendthrift trust." The point of the argument is that, the trust being of that character, the state law barred the voluntary alienation by the beneficiary of his interest. The state court held precisely the contrary. The ruling also determines the validity of the assignment by the beneficiary of parts of his interest. That question was necessarily presented and expressly decided.

Third. The question remains whether, treating the assignments as valid, the assignor was still taxable upon the income under the federal income tax act. That is a federal question.

Our decisions in Lucas v. Earl, 281 U.S. 111, and Burnet v. Leininger, 285 U.S. 136, are cited. In the *Lucas* case the question was whether an attorney was taxable for the whole of his salary and fees earned by him in the tax years or only upon one-half by reason of an agreement with his wife by which his earnings were to be received and owned by them jointly. We were of the opinion that the case turned upon the construction of the taxing act. We said that "the statute could tax salaries to those who earned them and provide that the tax could not be escaped by anticipatory arrangements and contracts however skillfully devised to prevent the same when paid from vesting even for a second in the man who earned it." That was deemed to be the meaning of the statute as to compensation for personal service, and the one who earned the income was held to be subject to the tax. In Burnet v. Leininger, supra, a husband, a member of a firm, assigned future partnership income to his wife. We found that the revenue act dealt explicitly with the liability of partners as such. The wife did not become a member of the firm; the act specifically taxed the distributive share of each partner in the net income of the firm; and the husband by the fair import of the act remained taxable upon his distributive share. These cases are not in point. The tax here is not upon earnings which are taxed to the one who earns them. Nor is it a case of income attributable to a taxpayer by reason of application of the income to the discharge of his obligation. Old Colony Trust Co. v. Commissioner, 279 U.S. 716; Douglas v. Willcuts, 296 U.S. 1, 9. . . . See also, Burnet v. Wells, 289 U.S. 670, 677. There is here no question of evasion or of giving effect to statutory provisions designed to forestall evasion; or of the taxpayer's retention of control. Corliss v. Bowers, 281 U.S. 376. . . .

In the instant case, the tax is upon income as to which, in the general application of the revenue acts, the tax liability attaches to ownership. See Poe v. Seaborn, supra. . . .

The Government points to the provisions of the revenue acts imposing upon the beneficiary of a trust the liability for the tax upon the income distributable to the beneficiary.[1] But the term is merely descriptive of the one entitled to the beneficial interest. These provisions cannot be taken to preclude valid assignments of the beneficial interest, or to affect the duty of the trustee to distribute income to the owner of the beneficial interest, whether he was such initially or becomes such by valid assignment. The one who is to receive the income as the owner of the beneficial interest is to pay the tax. If under the law governing the trust the beneficial interest is assignable, and if it has been assigned without reservation, the assignee thus becomes the beneficiary and is entitled to rights and remedies accordingly. We find nothing in the revenue acts which denies him that status.

The decision of the Circuit Court of Appeals turned upon the effect to be ascribed to the assignments. The court held that the petitioner had no interest in the corpus of the estate and could not dispose of the income until he received it. Hence it was said that "the income was *his*" and his assignment was merely a direction to pay over to others what was due to himself. The question was considered to involve "the date when the income became transferable." 83 F.(2d), p. 662. The Government refers to the terms of the assignment — that it was of the interest in the income "which the said party of the first part now is, or may hereafter be, entitled to receive during his life from the trustees." From this it is urged that the assignments "dealt only with a right to receive the income" and that "no attempt was made to assign any equitable right, title or interest in the trust itself." This construction seems to us to be a strained one. We think it apparent that the convey-ancer was not seeking to limit the assignment so as to make it anything less than a complete transfer of the specified interest of the petitioner as the life beneficiary of the trust, but that with ample caution he was using words to effect such a transfer. That the state court so construed the assignments appears from the final decree which described them as voluntary

1. [§§652(a), 662(a)(1)].

assignments of interests of the petitioner "in said trust estate," and it was in that aspect that petitioner's rights to make the assignments was sustained.

The will creating the trust entitled the petitioner during his life to the net income of the property held in trust. He thus became the owner of an equitable interest in the corpus of the property. . . . Irwin v. Gavit [Chapter 4A above]. . . . By virtue of that interest he was entitled to enforce the trust, to have a breach of trust enjoined and to obtain redress in case of breach. The interest was present property alienable like any other, in the absence of a valid restraint upon alienation. . . . The beneficiary may thus transfer a part of his interest as well as the whole. . . .

We conclude that the assignments were valid, that the assignees thereby became the owners of the specified beneficial interests in the income, and that as to these interests they and not the petitioner were taxable for the tax years in question. The judgment of the Circuit Court of Appeals is reversed and the cause is remanded with direction to affirm the decision of the Board of Tax Appeals.

Reversed.

Notes

1. *Collateral estoppel and res judicata.* How should a judgment with respect to one taxable year affect litigation over taxes in subsequent years when similar issues are involved? The matter is strictly one of collateral estoppel rather than res judicata, is it not?

Was the Supreme Court correct in concluding that the state court proceeding in *Blair* "created a new situation"? Would a supervening federal decision reinterpreting the relevant tax law create a new situation?

Should a judgment in one year create a collateral estoppel for subsequent years if it was an unreviewed trial court judgment? What if the amount involved in the first year was small and represented only one minor issue in a controversy that focused on other things?

2. *State court judgments.* Does the court in *Blair* say the state court judgment forecloses any inquiry into the state law question of assignability? Should it? What does the Court mean when it says there was no "basis for a charge that the suit was collusive and the decree inoperative"? What if the government had offered to show simply that all the parties to the state court proceeding wanted it to come out the way it did (in order to hold federal income taxes to a minimum) and that none of them presented the strongest authority or argument against assignability?

Could the IRS have made those arguments in the state court proceeding? Should it have to? Should the IRS appear in state court proceedings in cases of this kind?

Should the state court decree have any different effect in tax years after the state decree is entered than it does with respect to prior years? Why?

Would it make any difference whether the state court judgment is by an appellate court or a trial court? Which appellate court? Whether or not an opinion is written and published? See Commissioner v. Estate of Bosch, 387 U.S. 456 (1967) (estate tax); Wolfman, *Bosch,* Its Implications and Aftermath: The Effect of State Court Adjudications on Federal Tax Litigation, Univ. of Miami Law Center, 3d Annual Institute on Estate Planning, ch. 69-2 (1969).

3. On the merits, what does *Blair* stand for? Is the holding itself sound? Why? Are problems likely to arise in other cases from the Court's opinion here?

HELVERING v. CLIFFORD
309 U.S. 331 (1940)

Mr. Justice Douglas delivered the opinion of the Court. In 1934 respondent declared himself trustee of certain securities which he owned. All net income from the trust was to be held for the "exclusive benefit" of respondent's wife. The trust was for a term of five years, except that it would terminate earlier on the death of either respondent or his wife. On termination of the trust the entire corpus was to go to respondent, while all "accrued or undistributed net income" and "any proceeds from the investment of such net income" was to be treated as property owned absolutely by the wife. During the continuance of the trust respondent was to pay over to his wife the whole or such part of the net income as he in his "absolute discretion" might determine. And during that period he had full power (a) to exercise all voting powers incident to the trusteed shares of stock; (b) to "sell, exchange, mortgage, or pledge" any of the securities under the declaration of trust "whether as part of the corpus or principal thereof or as investments or proceeds and any income therefrom, upon such terms and for such consideration" as respondent in his "absolute discretion may deem fitting"; (c) to invest "any cash or money in the trust estate or any income therefrom" by loans, secured or unsecured, by deposits in banks, or by purchase of securities or other personal property "without restriction" because of their "speculative character" of "rate of return" or any "laws pertaining to the investment of trust funds"; (d) to collect all income; (e) to compromise, etc., any claims held by him as trustee; (f) to hold any property in the trust estate in the names of "other persons or in my own name as an individual" except as otherwise provided. Extraordinary cash dividends, stock dividends, proceeds from the sale of unexercised subscription rights, or any enhancement, realized or not, in the value of the securities were to be treated as principal, not income. An exculpatory clause purported to protect him from all losses except those occasioned by his "own wilful and deliberate" breach of duties as trustee. And finally it was provided that neither the principal nor any future or accrued income should be liable for the debts of the wife; and that the wife could not transfer, encumber, or anticipate any interest in the trust or any income therefrom prior to actual payment thereof to her.

It was stipulated that while the "tax effects" of this trust were considered by respondent they were not the "sole consideration" involved in his decision to set it up, as by this and other gifts he intended to give "security and economic independence" to his wife and children. It was also stipulated that respondent's wife had substantial income of her own from other sources; that there was no restriction on her use of the trust income, all of which income was placed in her personal checking account, intermingled with her other funds, and expended by her on herself, her children and relatives; that the trust was not designed to relieve respondent from liability for family or household expenses and that after execution of the trust he paid large sums from his personal funds for such purposes.

Respondent paid a federal gift tax on this transfer. During the year 1934 all income from the trust was distributed to the wife who included it in her individual return for that year. The Commissioner, however, determined a deficiency in respondent's return for that year on the theory that income from the trust was taxable to him. The Board of Tax Appeals sustained that redetermination. 38 B.T.A. 1532. The Circuit Court of Appeals reversed. 105 F.2d 586. We granted certiorari because of the importance to the revenue of the use of such short term trusts in the reduction of surtaxes.

Sec. 22(a) of the Revenue Act of 1934, 48 Stat. 680, includes among "gross income" all "gains, profits, and income derived . . . from professions, vocations, trades, businesses, commerce, or sales, or dealings in property, whether real or personal, growing out of the ownership or use of or interest in such property; also from interest, rent, dividends, securities, or the transaction of any business carried on for gain or profit, or gains or profits and income derived from any source whatever." The broad sweep of this language indicates the purpose of Congress to use the full measure of its taxing power within those definable categories. Cf. Helvering v. Midland Mutual Life Insurance Co., 300 U.S. 216. Hence our construction of the statute should be consonant with that purpose. Technical considerations, niceties of the law of trusts or conveyances, or the legal paraphernalia which inventive genius may construct as a refuge from surtaxes should not obscure the basic issue. That issue is whether the grantor after the trust has been established may still be treated, under this statutory scheme, as the owner of the corpus. See Blair v. Commissioner, 300 U.S. 5, 12. In absence of more precise standards or guides supplied by statute or appropriate regulations, the answer to that question must depend on an analysis of the terms of the trust and all the circumstances attendant on its creation and operation. And where the grantor is the trustee and the beneficiaries are members of his family group, special scrutiny of the arrangement is necessary lest what is in reality but one economic unit be multiplied into two or more by devices which, though valid under state law, are not conclusive so far as §22(a) is concerned.

In this case we cannot conclude as a matter of law that respondent ceased to be the owner of the corpus after the trust was created. Rather, the short duration of the trust, the fact that the wife was the beneficiary, and the retention of control over the corpus by respondent all lead irresistibly to the conclusion that respondent continued to be the owner for purposes of §22(a).

So far as his dominion and control were concerned it seems clear that the trust did not effect any substantial change. In substance his control over the corpus was in all essential respects the same after the trust was created, as before. The wide powers which he retained included for all practical purposes most of the control which he as an individual would have. There were, we may assume, exceptions, such as his disability to make a gift of the corpus to others during the term of the trust and to make loans to himself. But this dilution in his control would seem to be insignificant and immaterial, since control over investment remained. If it be said that such control is the type of dominion exercised by any trustee, the answer is simple. We have at best a temporary reallocation of income within an intimate family group. Since the income remains in the family and since the husband retains control over the investment, he has rather complete assurance that the trust will not effect any substantial change in his economic position. It is hard to imagine that respondent felt himself the poorer after this trust had been executed or, if he did, that it had any rational foundation in fact. For as a result of the terms of the trust and the intimacy of the familial relationship respondent retained the substance of full enjoyment of all the rights which previously he had in the property. That might not be true if only strictly legal rights were considered. But when the benefits flowing to him indirectly through the wife are added to the legal rights he retained, the aggregate may be said to be a fair equivalent of what he previously had. To exclude from the aggregate those indirect benefits would be to deprive §22(a) of considerable vitality and to treat as immaterial what may be highly relevant considerations in the creation of such family trusts. For where the head of the household has income in excess of normal needs, it may well make but little difference to him (except income-tax-wise) where portions of that income are routed — so long as it stays in the family group. In those circumstances the all-important factor might be retention by him of control over the principal. With that control in his hands he would keep direct command over all that he needed to remain in substantially the same financial situation as before. Our point here is that no one fact is normally decisive but that all considerations and circumstances of the kind we have mentioned are relevant to the question of ownership and are appropriate foundations for findings on that issue. Thus, where, as in this case, the benefits directly or indirectly retained blend so imperceptibly with the normal concepts of full ownership, we cannot say that the triers of fact committed reversible error when they found that the husband was the owner of the corpus for the purposes of §22(a). To hold otherwise would be to treat the wife as a complete stranger; to let mere formalism obscure the normal consequences of family solidarity; and to force concepts of ownership to be fashioned out of legal niceties which may have little or no significance in such household arrangements.

The bundle of rights which he retained was so substantial that respondent cannot be heard to complain that he is the "victim of despotic power when for the purpose of taxation he is treated as owner altogether." See DuPont v. Commissioner, 289 U.S. 685, 689.

We should add that liability under §22(a) is not foreclosed by reason of the fact that Congress made specific provision in §166 for revocable trusts, but failed to adopt the Treasury recommendation in 1934, Helvering v. Wood, post, p. 344, that similar specific treatment should be accorded income from short term trusts. Such choice, while relevant to the scope of §166, Helvering v. Wood, supra, cannot be said to have subtracted from §22(a) what was already there. Rather, on this evidence it must be assumed that the choice was between a generalized treatment under §22(a) or specific treatment under a separate provision (such as was accorded revocable trusts under §166); not between taxing or not taxing grantors of short term trusts. In view of the broad and sweeping language of §22(a), a specific provision covering short term trusts might well do no more than to carve out of §22(a) a defined group of cases to which a rule of thumb would be applied. The failure of Congress to adopt any such rule of thumb for that type of trust must be taken to do no more than to leave to the triers of fact the initial determination of whether or not on the facts of each case the grantor remains the owner for purposes of §22(a).

In view of this result we need not examine the contention that the trust device falls within the rule of Lucas v. Earl, 281 U.S. 111 and Burnet v. Leininger, 285 U.S. 136, relating to the assignment of future income; or that respondent is liable under §166, taxing grantors on the income of revocable trusts.

The judgment of the Circuit Court of Appeals is reversed and that of the Board of Tax Appeals is affirmed.

Reversed.

Mr. Justice ROBERTS, dissenting: I think the judgment should be affirmed.

The decision of the court disregards the fundamental principle that legislation is not the function of the judiciary but of Congress.

In every revenue act from that of 1916 to the one now in force a distinction has been made between income of individuals and income from property held in trust. It has been the practice to define income of individuals, and, in separate sections, under the heading "Estates and Trusts," to provide that the tax imposed upon individuals shall apply to the income of estates or of any kind of property held in trust. A trust is a separate taxable entity. The trust here in question is a true trust.

While the earlier acts were in force creators of trusts reserved power to repossess the trust corpus. It became common also to establish trusts under which, at the grantor's discretion, all or part of the income might be paid to him, and to set up trusts to pay life insurance premiums upon policies on the grantor's life. The situation was analogous to that now presented. The Treasury, instead of asking this court, under the guise of construction, to amend the act, went to Congress for new legislation. Congress provided, by §219(g)(h) of the Revenue Act of 1924, that if the grantor set up such a life insurance trust, or one under which he could direct the payment of the trust income to himself, or had the power to revest the principal in himself *during any taxable year,* the income of the trust, for the taxable year, was to be treated as his.

After the adoption of these amendments taxpayers resorted to the creation of revocable trusts with a provision that more than a year's notice of revocation should be necessary to termination. Such a trust was held not to be within the terms of §219(g) of the Revenue Act of 1924, because not revocable within the taxable year.

Again, without seeking amendment in the guise of construction from this court, the Treasury applied to Congress, which met the situation by adopting §166 of the Revenue Act of 1934, which provided that, in the case of a trust under which the grantor reserved the power *at any time* to revest the corpus in himself, the income of the trust should be considered that of the grantor.

The Treasury had asked that there should also be included in that act a provision taxing to the grantor income from short term trusts. After the House Ways and Means Committee had rendered a report on the proposed bill, the Treasury, upon examination of the report, submitted a statement to the Committee containing recommendations for additional provisions; amongst others, the following: "(6) The income from short-term trust and trusts which are revocable by the creator at the expiration of a short period after notice by him should be made taxable to the creator of the trust." Congress adopted an amendment to cover the one situation but did not accept the Treasury's recommendation as to the other. The statute, as before, clearly provided that the income from a short term irrevocable trust was taxable to the trust, or the beneficiary, and not to the grantor. . . .

The fact that the petitioner is in truth asking us to legislate in this case is evident from the form of the existing regulation and from the argument presented. The important portion of the regulation reads as follows:

> In determining whether the grantor is in substance the owner of the corpus, the Act has its own standard, which is a substantial one, dependent neither on the niceties of the particular conveyancing device used, nor on the technical description which the law of property gives to the estate or interest transferred to the trustees or beneficiaries of the trust. In that determination, among the material factors are: The fact that the corpus is to be returned to the grantor after a specific term; the fact that the corpus is or may be administered in the interest of the grantor; the fact that the anticipated income is being appropriated in advance for the customary expenditures of the grantor or those which he would ordinarily and naturally make; and any other circumstances bearing on the

impermanence and indefiniteness with which the grantor has parted with the substantial incidents of ownership in the corpus.

In his brief the petitioner says:

> On the other hand, the income of a long term irrevocable trust which committed the possession and control of the corpus to an independent trustee *would not likely* be taxed to the settlor merely because of a reversionary interest. The question here, as in many other tax problems, *is simply one of degree.* The grantor's liability to tax must depend upon whether he retains so many of the attributes of ownership as to require that he be treated as the owner for tax purposes, or whether he has given up the substance of his dominion and control over the trust property.
>
> Under these circumstances, the question of *precisely where the line should be drawn* between those irrevocable trusts which deprive the grantor of command over the trust property and those which leave in him the practical equivalent of ownership is, in our view, *a matter peculiarly for the judgment of the agency charged with the administration of the tax law.* (Italics supplied.)

It is not our function to draw any such line as the argument suggests. That is the prerogative of Congress. As far back as 1922, Parliament amended the British Income Tax Act, so that there would be no dispute as to what short term trust income should be taxable to the grantor, by making taxable to him any income which, by virtue of any disposition, is payable to, or applicable for the benefit of, any other person for a period which cannot exceed six years.

If some short term trusts are to be treated as nonexistent for income tax purposes, it is for Congress to specify them.

Mr. Justice MCREYNOLDS joins in this opinion.

Notes

1. In a companion case, Helvering v. Wood, 309 U.S. 344 (1940), the government had sought to tax the grantor of a short-term trust under §166, but neglected to base its argument on §22(a) before either the Board or the court of appeals. The Supreme Court held it was too late to rely on §22(a) for the first time in the Supreme Court, and that §166 would not permit taxation of a grantor on the basis of a reversion as compared with a power of revocation.

2. *Fidelity to law* in the matter of statutory interpretation is the most important issue in these cases. The issue had been brought before Congress, and Congress had, in a manner, responded.

(a) Under these circumstances do the courts and the Commissioner remain free to deal with the matter under the general language of the statute or should they be constrained to work with the specific Congressional response?

(b) Would it have shown greater or lesser fidelity to the statute to have accepted the government's argument under §166 and rejected its argument under §22(a)?

(c) Note the last sentence of §671 of the present statute. Would that prevent a holding like *Clifford* today? Is that sentence necessary, or is its import implicit in the statutory structure anyway?

(d) As a matter of fact §4 of the Revenue Act of 1934 was something like the last sentence in §671:

> The application of the General Provisions . . . [including the predecessor of §61] to each of the following special classes of taxpayers, shall be subject to the exceptions and additional provisions found in the Supplement applicable to each class, as follows:
> (a) Estates and trusts and the beneficiaries thereof — Supplement E.

Why is this provision not cited in the opinions?

(e) Compare Justice Roberts' dissent in *Clifford*, with that of Justice Douglas in *Knetsch*, Chapter 10A.1 above, at p. 558.

3. What of *Clifford* as a substantive matter?

(a) Does the *Clifford* holding leave the law in a settled and satisfactory state? What about the Treasury regulation quoted in the *Clifford* dissent?

(b) The Treasury, apparently convinced that the resulting law was insufficiently settled, issued in 1945 the so-called *Clifford* regulations, which undertook to spell out the reach of the *Clifford* doctrine. Reg. 111, §§29.22(a)-21, 22, T.D. 5488, 1946-1 C.B. 19, amended, T.D. 5567, 1947-2 C.B. 9. These apparently gave a definite answer to some cases, but rivaled the common law rule against perpetuities in complexity. In addition there was uncertainty about whether it was within the authority of regulations to reduce a doctrine like *Clifford* into such a highly articulated set of rules. One court of appeals rejected the *Clifford* regulations as unconstitutionally arbitrary, saying they were beyond the power of Congress, let alone the Treasury, to enact. Commissioner v. Clark, 202 F.2d 94 (7th Cir. 1953).

(c) In 1954 Congress removed some of the uncertainty by enacting §§673-675 of the present statute. We shall return to these provisions shortly, after a brief consideration of the statutory scheme governing trusts generally.

HELVERING v. HORST
311 U.S. 112 (1940)

Mr. Justice STONE delivered the opinion of the Court. The sole question for decision is whether the gift, during the donor's taxable year, of interest coupons detached from the bonds, delivered to the donee and later in the year paid at maturity, is the realization of income taxable to the donor.

In 1934 and 1935 respondent, the owner of negotiable bonds, detached from them negotiable interest coupons shortly before their due date and delivered them as a gift to his son who in the same year collected them at maturity. The Commissioner ruled that under the applicable §22 of the Revenue Act of 1934, 48 Stat. 680, 686, the interest payments were taxable, in the years when paid, to the respondent donor who reported his income on the cash receipts basis. The Circuit Court of Appeals reversed the order of the Board of Tax Appeals sustaining the tax. 107 F.2d 906; 39 B.T.A. 757. We granted certiorari, 309 U.S. 650, because of the importance of the question in the administration of the revenue laws and because of an asserted conflict in principle of the decision below with that of Lucas v. Earl, 281 U.S. 111, and with that of decisions by other circuit courts of appeals. See Bishop v. Commissioner, 54 F.2d 298; Dickey v. Burnet, 56 F.2d 917, 921; Van Meter v. Commissioner, 61 F.2d 817.

The court below thought that as the consideration for the coupons had passed to the obligor, the donor had, by the gift, parted with all control over them and their payment, and for that reason the case was distinguishable from Lucas v. Earl, supra, and Burnet v. Leininger, 285 U.S. 136, where the assignment of compensation for services had preceded the rendition of the services, and where the income was held taxable to the donor.

The holder of a coupon bond is the owner of two independent and separable kinds of right. One is the right to demand and receive at maturity the principal amount of the bond representing capital investment. The other is the right to demand and receive interim payments of interest on the investment in the amounts and on the dates specified by the coupons. Together they are an obligation to pay principal and interest given in exchange for money or property which was presumably the consideration for the obligation of the bond. Here respondent, as owner of the bonds, had acquired the legal right to demand payment at maturity of the interest specified by the coupons and the power to command its payment to others, which constituted an economic gain to him.

Admittedly not all economic gain of the taxpayer is taxable income. From the beginning the revenue laws have been interpreted as defining "realization" of income as the taxable event, rather than the acquisition of the right to receive it. And "realization" is not deemed to occur until the income is paid. But the decisions and regulations have consistently recognized that receipt in cash or property is not the only characteristic of realization of income to a taxpayer on the cash receipts basis. Where the taxpayer does not receive payment of income in money or property realization may occur when the last step is taken by which he obtains the fruition of the economic gain which has already accrued to him. Old Colony Trust Co. v. Commissioner, 279 U.S. 716; Corliss v. Bowers, 281 U.S. 376, 378. Cf. Burnet v. Wells, 289 U.S. 670.

In the ordinary case the taxpayer who acquires the right to receive income is taxed when he receives it, regardless of the time when his right to receive payment accrued. But the rule that income is not taxable until realized has never been taken to mean that the taxpayer, even on the cash

receipts basis, who has fully enjoyed the benefit of the economic gain represented by his right to receive income, can escape taxation because he has not
himself received payment of it from his obligor. The rule, founded on
administrative convenience, is only one of postponement of the tax to the
final event of enjoyment of the income, usually the receipt of it by the taxpayer, and not one of exemption from taxation where the enjoyment is
consummated by some event other than the taxpayer's personal receipt of
money or property. Cf. Aluminum Castings Co. v. Routzahn, 282 U.S. 92, 98.
This may occur when he has made such use or disposition of his power to
receive or control the income as to procure in its place other satisfactions
which are of economic worth. The question here is, whether because one
who in fact receives payment for services or interest payments is taxable
only on his receipt of the payments, he can escape all tax by giving away
his right to income in advance of payment. If the taxpayer procures payment
directly to his creditors of the items of interest or earnings due him, see Old
Colony Trust Co. v. Commissioner, supra; Bowers v. Kerbaugh-Empire Co.,
271 U.S. 170; United States v. Kirby Lumber Co., 284 U.S. 1, or if he sets up
a revocable trust with income payable to the objects of his bounty, §§166,
167, Revenue Act of 1934, Corliss v. Bowers, supra; cf. Dickey v. Burnet, 56
F.2d 917, 921, he does not escape taxation because he did not actually
receive the money. Cf. Douglas v. Willcuts, 296 U.S. 1; Helvering v. Clifford,
309 U.S. 331.

Underlying the reasoning in these cases is the thought that income is
"realized" by the assignor because he, who owns or controls the source of the
income, also controls the disposition of that which he could have received
himself and diverts the payment from himself to others as the means of
procuring the satisfaction of his wants. The taxpayer has equally enjoyed
the fruits of his labor or investment and obtained the satisfaction of his
desires whether he collects and uses the income to procure those satisfactions, or whether he disposes of his right to collect it as the means of procuring them. Cf. Burnet v. Wells, supra.

Although the donor here, by the transfer of the coupons, has precluded
any possibility of his collecting them himself, he has nevertheless, by his act,
procured payment of the interest as a valuable gift to a member of his family.
Such a use of his economic gain, the right to receive income, to procure a
satisfaction which can be obtained only by the expenditure of money or
property, would seem to be the enjoyment of the income whether the satisfaction is the purchase of goods at the corner grocery, the payment of his
debt there, or such nonmaterial satisfactions as may result from the payment
of a campaign or community chest contribution, or a gift to his favorite son.
Even though he never receives the money, he derives money's worth from
the disposition of the coupons which he has used as money or money's worth
in the procuring of a satisfaction which is procurable only by the expenditure
of money or money's worth. The enjoyment of the economic benefit accruing to him by virtue of his acquisition of the coupons is realized as completely

as it would have been if he had collected the interest in dollars and expended them for any of the purposes named. Burnet v. Wells, supra.

In a real sense he has enjoyed compensation for money loaned or services rendered, and not any the less so because it is his only reward for them. To say that one who has made a gift thus derived from interest or earnings paid to his donee has never enjoyed or realized the fruits of his investment or labor, because he has assigned them instead of collecting them himself and then paying them over to the donee, is to affront common understanding and to deny the facts of common experience. Common understanding and experience are the touchstones for the interpretation of the revenue laws.

The power to dispose of income is the equivalent of ownership of it. The exercise of that power to procure the payment of income to another is the enjoyment, and hence the realization, of the income by him who exercises it. We have had no difficulty in applying that proposition where the assignment preceded the rendition of the services, Lucas v. Earl, supra; Burnet v. Leininger, supra, for it was recognized in the Leininger case that in such a case the rendition of the service by the assignor was the means by which the income was controlled by the donor and of making his assignment effective. But it is the assignment by which the disposition of income is controlled when the service precedes the assignment, and in both cases it is the exercise of the power of disposition of the interest or compensation, with the resulting payment to the donee, which is the enjoyment by the donor of income derived from them.

This was emphasized in Blair v. Commissioner, 300 U.S. 5, on which respondent relies, where the distinction was taken between a gift of income derived from an obligation to pay compensation and a gift of income-producing property. In the circumstances of that case, the right to income from the trust property was thought to be so identified with the equitable ownership of the property, from which alone the beneficiary derived his right to receive the income and his power to command disposition of it, that a gift of the income by the beneficiary became effective only as a gift of his ownership of the property producing it. Since the gift was deemed to be a gift of the property, the income from it was held to be the income of the owner of the property, who was the donee, not the donor — a refinement which was unnecessary if respondent's contention here is right, but one clearly inapplicable to gifts of interest or wages. Unlike income thus derived from an obligation to pay interest or compensation, the income of the trust was regarded as no more the income of the donor than would be the rent from a lease or a crop raised on a farm after the leasehold or the farm had been given away. Blair v. Commissioner, supra, 12, 13 and cases cited. See also Reinecke v. Smith, 289 U.S. 172, 177. We have held without deviation that where the donor retains control of the trust property the income is taxable to him although paid to the donee. Corliss v. Bowers, supra. Cf. Helvering v. Clifford, supra.

The dominant purpose of the revenue laws is the taxation of income to those who earn or otherwise create the right to receive it and enjoy the benefit of it when paid. See, Corliss v. Bowers, supra, 378; Burnet v. Guggenheim, 288 U.S. 280, 283. The tax laid by the 1934 Revenue Act upon income "derived from . . . wages, or compensation for personal service, of whatever kind and in whatever form paid . . . ; also from interest . . ." therefore cannot fairly be interpreted as not applying to income derived from interest or compensation when he who is entitled to receive it makes use of his power to dispose of it in procuring satisfactions which he would otherwise procure only by the use of the money when received.

It is the statute which taxes the income to the donor although paid to his donee. Lucas v. Earl, supra; Burnet v. Leininger, supra. True, in those cases the service which created the right to income followed the assignment, and it was arguable that in point of legal theory the right to the compensation vested instantaneously in the assignor when paid, although he never received it; while here the right of the assignor to receive the income antedated the assignment which transferred the right and thus precluded such an instantaneous vesting. But the statue affords no basis for such "attenuated subtleties." The distinction was explicitly rejected as the basis of decision in Lucas v. Earl. It should be rejected here; for no more than in the *Earl* case can the purpose of the statute to tax the income to him who earns, or creates and enjoys it be escaped by "anticipatory arrangements however skilfully devised" to prevent the income from vesting even for a second in the donor.

Nor is it perceived that there is any adequate basis for distinguishing between the gift of interest coupons here and a gift of salary or commissions. The owner of a negotiable bond and of the investment which it represents, if not the lender, stands in the place of the lender. When, by the gift of the coupons, he has separated his right to interest payments from his investment and procured the payment of the interest to his donee, he has enjoyed the economic benefits of the income in the same manner and to the same extent as though the transfer were of earnings, and in both cases the import of the statute is that the fruit is not to be attributed to a different tree from that on which it grew. See Lucas v. Earl, supra, 115.

Reversed.

The separate opinion of Mr. Justice McREYNOLDS. The facts were stipulated. In the opinion of the court below the issues are thus adequately stated —

The petitioner owned a number of coupon bonds. The coupons represented the interest on the bonds and were payable to bearer. In 1934 he detached unmatured coupons of face value of $25,182.50 and transferred them by manual delivery to his son as a gift. The coupons matured later on in the same year, and the son collected the face amount, $25,182.50, as his own property. There was a similar transaction in 1935. The petitioner kept his books on a cash basis. He did not include any part of the moneys collected on the coupons in his income tax returns for these two years. The son included them in his returns. The Commissioner added the moneys collected on the coupons to the petitioner's taxable income and determined a tax deficiency for each year. The Board of Tax Appeals, three members dissenting, sustained the Commissioner, holding that the amounts collected on the coupons were taxable as income to the petitioner.

The decision of the Board of Tax Appeals was reversed and properly so, I think.

The unmatured coupons given to the son were independent negotiable instruments, complete in themselves. Through the gift they became at once the absolute property of the donee, free from the donor's control and in no way dependent upon ownership of the bonds. No question of actual fraud or purpose to defraud the revenue is presented.

Neither Lucas v. Earl, 281 U.S. 111, nor Burnet v. Leininger, 285 U.S. 136, support petitioner's view. Blair v. Commissioner, 300 U.S. 5, 11, 12, shows that neither involved an unrestricted completed transfer of property.

Helvering v. Clifford, 309 U.S. 331, 335, 336, decided after the opinion below, is much relied upon by petitioner, but involves facts very different from those now before us. There no separate thing was absolutely transferred and put beyond possible control by the transferror. The Court affirmed that Clifford, both conveyor and trustee, "retained the substance of full enjoyment of all the rights which previously he had in the property." "In substance his control over the corpus was in all essential respects the same after the trust was created, as before." "With that control in his hands he would keep direct command over all that he needed to remain in substantially the same financial situation as before."

The general principles approved in Blair v. Commissioner, 300 U.S. 5, are applicable and controlling. The challenged judgment should be affirmed.

The Chief Justice and Mr. Justice ROBERTS concur in this opinion.

HELVERING v. EUBANK
311 U.S. 122 (1940)

Mr. Justice STONE delivered the opinion of the Court. This is a companion case to Helvering v. Horst, [311 U.S. 112 (1940), preceding case], and presents issues not distinguishable from those in that case.

Respondent, a general life insurance agent, after the termination of his agency contracts and services as agent, made assignments in 1924 and 1928 respectively of renewal commissions to become payable to him for services which had been rendered in writing policies of insurance under two of his agency contracts. The Commissioner assessed the renewal commissions paid by the companies to the assignees in 1933 as income taxable to the assignor in that year under the provisions of the 1932 Revenue Act, 47 Stat. 169, §22 of which does not differ in any respect now material from §22 of the 1934 Revenue Act involved in the *Horst* case. The Court of Appeals for the Second Circuit reversed the order of the Board of Tax Appeals sustaining the assessment. 110 F.2d 737; 39 B.T.A. 583. We granted certiorari October 14, 1940.

No purpose of the assignments appears other than to confer on the assignees the power to collect the commissions, which they did in the taxable year. The Government and respondent have briefed and argued the case here on the assumption that the assignments were voluntary transfers to the assignees of the right to collect the commissions as and when they became payable, and the record affords no basis for any other.

For the reasons stated at length in the opinion in the *Horst* case, we hold that the commissions were taxable as income of the assignor in the year when paid. The judgment below is

Reversed.

The separate opinion of Mr. Justice McREYNOLDS. The cause was decided upon stipulated facts. The following statement taken from the court's opinion discloses the issues.

> The question presented is whether renewal commissions payable to a general agent of a life insurance company after the termination of his agency and by him assigned prior to the taxable year, must be included in his income despite the assignment.
>
> During part of the year 1924 the petitioner was employed by the Canada Life Assurance Company as its branch manager for the state of Michigan. His compensation consisted of a salary plus certain commissions. His employment terminated on September 1, 1924. Under the terms of his contract he was entitled to renewal commissions on premiums thereafter collected by the company on policies written prior to the termination of his agency, without the obligation to perform any further services. In November 1924 he assigned his right, title, and interest in the contract as well as the renewal commissions to a corporate trustee. From September 1, 1924, to June 30, 1927, the petitioner and another, constituting the firm of Hart & Eubank, were general agents in New York City for the Aetna Life Insurance Company, and from July 1, 1927 to August 31, 1927, the petitioner individually was general agent for said Aetna Company. The Aetna contracts likewise contained terms entitling the agent to commissions on renewal premiums paid after termination of the agency, without the performance of any further services. On March 28, 1928, the petitioner assigned to the corporate trustee all commissions to become due him under the Aetna contracts. During the year 1933 the trustee collected by virtue of the assignments renewal commissions payable under the three agency contracts above mentioned, amounting to some $15,600. These commissions were taxed to the petitioner by the Commissioner, and the Board has sustained the deficiency resulting therefrom. 110 F.2d 738.

The court below declared—

> In the case at bar the petitioner owned a right to receive money for past services; no further services were required. Such a right is assignable. At the time of assignment there was nothing contingent in the petitioner's right, although the amount collectible

in future years was still uncertain and contingent. But this may be equally true where the assignment transfers a right to income from investments, as in Blair v. Commissioner, 300 U.S. 5, and Horst v. Commissioner, 107 F.2d 906 (C.C.A. 2), or a right to patent royalties, as in Nelson v. Ferguson, 56 F.2d 121 (C.C.A. 3), certiorari denied, 286 U.S. 565. By an assignment of future earnings a taxpayer may not escape taxation upon his compensation in the year when he earns it. But when a taxpayer who makes his income tax return on a cash basis assigns a right to money payable in the future for work already performed, we believe that he transfers a property right, and the money, when received by the assignee, is not income taxable to the assignor.

Accordingly, the Board of Tax Appeals was reversed; and this, I think, is in accord with the statute and our opinions.

The assignment in question denuded the assignor of all right to commissions thereafter to accrue under the contract with the insurance company. He could do nothing further in respect of them; they were entirely beyond his control. In no proper sense were they something either earned or received by him during the taxable year. The right to collect became the absolute property of the assignee without relation to future action by the assignor.

A mere right to collect future payments, for services already performed, is not presently taxable as "income derived" from such services. It is property which may be assigned. Whatever the assignor receives as consideration may be his income; but the statute does not undertake to impose liability upon him because of payments to another under a contract which he had transferred in good faith, under circumstances like those here disclosed.

As in Helvering v. Horst, just decided, the petitioner relies upon opinions here; but obviously they arose upon facts essentially different from those now presented. They do not support his contention. The general principles approved in Blair v. Commissioner, 300 U.S. 5, and applied in Helvering v. Horst, are controlling and call for affirmation of the judgment under review.

The Chief Justice and Mr. Justice ROBERTS concur in this opinion.

Questions

1. Does *Horst* overrule *Blair*? If not, how are the cases to be reconciled?

2. What would the result be if Horst had clipped all the coupons off his bond and delivered them to his son who then collected them as they fell due? Income to him? When? How much? Any income to his son? When and how much?

3. Does *Horst* involve taxing the nonmaterial satisfactions derived by a taxpayer from making a gift to his son? Why does the opinion talk of such matters? What is to be made of that part of the opinion?

4. The assignment in *Eubank* apparently included all the taxpayer had: Why is it not therefore governed by *Blair* instead of *Horst*?

5. What does *Eubank* indicate about when Horst would be taxed, and on how much, if he had assigned all his coupons?

6. Examine the dissent in *Eubank* with care. Does it suggest an explanation for why the majority opinion in *Horst* goes on the way it does about realization of income by giving away the right to receive it? Note that *Horst* and *Eubank* were companion cases in the Supreme Court, decided the same day with opinions by the same justices.

7. How does *Eubank* relate to Lucas v. Earl, Chapter 17A above?

8. Consider the following problems:

(a) *A*, a farmer, contributed wheat to a charity, claiming a deduction for a charitable contribution in the amount of its value. The government allowed the deduction but also proposed to include the value of the wheat in *A*'s gross income, relying on *Horst*. What results? How else might the government go at the problem? Notice how §170(e)(1)(A) would now bear on this problem. Cf. Haverly v. United States, Chapter 2A above.

(b) *B* owns all the stock of a corporation, which he proposes to sell to *P*. He intends to distribute part of the sale proceeds among his children. Just before the sale is consummated *B* consults a lawyer who points out that his children are in lower tax brackets and that the tax would be less if he distributed the stock to the children and had them sell to *P*. How should *B* proceed?

(c) *C* is a farm landlord who leases her farm land for a share of the crop. The crop is sold and *C* reports her share of the sale proceeds as income when she receives it.

C gives her farm land to her son, *S*, along with all crop rents and shares presently due, unsold or uncollected. At the time of the gift there are (1) rents due with respect to which the tenant has delivered nothing; (2) crop shares due for crops still unsold for which the tenant has delivered title documents; and (3) crop shares due for crops which have been sold but for which payment has not yet been received. Which, if any, of these items will be taxed to *C* when collected?

(d) *D*, a college professor, is writing a basic economics textbook. He has talked with a publisher who has agreed to publish the book and to pay *D* a royalty on a standard scale. *D* wishes to use the royalties for the education and welfare of his children. Since he is in a high income tax bracket, he wants to assign his royalties in advance so that they will be taxed to his children, or to a trust for his children, but not to him. Advise *D*.

(e) *E* has a life income interest in a trust. She assigns to her daughter all her right, title, and interest in the income for the next five years. Does *E* remain taxable on the income paid to her daughter? Harrison v. Schaffner, 312 U.S. 579 (1941).

(f) *F* has a right to receive a specified share of the income from a trust for a 12-year term. Near the end of the term he assigns to his son all his right, title, and interest in the income for the last three years of the term. Will *F* remain taxable on that income? Would it matter whether *F* were also to receive some part of the trust corpus at the end of the 12-year term? At some later date?

(g) *G* owned a piece of real estate. He rented it to *L* for a five-year term and then proceeded to "assign all [his] right, title and interest in [the] leasehold" to *X*. (1) Is *G* taxable on the rent that is thereafter paid to *X*? (2) Would the result be different if *G* had leased the parcel to *X* for five years at an annual rental of a peppercorn, and *X* had proceeded to sublet to *L* for a substantial rental? (3) What would you be careful of if you were setting up the transaction this way?

(h) *H* has a son a couple of years out of school who has decided to go to college. *H* wants to help him financially. Accordingly, *H* gives her son appreciated securities from time to time, and the son sells them, using the proceeds to pay tuition and other expenses. Who is taxable on the gain from selling the securities?

B.   *STATUTORY RULES FOR NONGRANTOR TRUSTS*

The rules for attributing trust income among beneficiaries and the trust itself, when it is not taxed to the grantor, are contained in §§641-668. These provisions date from 1954, although the general pattern is older and there have been some modifications since.

The general pattern is the one adopted in the beginning and reflected in Irwin v. Gavit, Chapter 4A above. Trust income currently distributed or required to be distributed to a trust beneficiary is taxed to that beneficiary, in full, without diminution to reflect depletion of the beneficiary's interest in the trust. If trust income is not currently distributed, on the other hand, it is normally taxed to the trust itself. The rates of tax for income left in the trust are graduated rates similar to those for individual taxpayers, except that the rate brackets are much narrower, so that trust income reaches the top individual rate faster. §1(e).

This general pattern is relatively simple, but its implementation is subject to a host of technical qualifications and refinements, only some of which are suggested in the following discussion.

1.   Simple Trusts and Distributable Net Income

If a trust is required to distribute all income currently and if it makes no distributions of corpus during a particular year, then it is classified as a simple trust, and taxation of its distributions is governed by §§651 and 652. Section 651 allows the trust to deduct what it is required to distribute, and §652 requires inclusion of the same amount in the taxable income of the beneficiaries. These provisions apply even if the trust does not in fact distribute the distributable amount. Together these provisions have the effect of shifting tax liability on the distributable amount from the trust itself to the beneficiaries, and making the trust itself a conduit.

Income may be defined differently for trust accounting purposes than for tax purposes, and then a problem arises about how much should be subject to §§651 and 652. Suppose, for example, that the trust receives a tax-free stock dividend that is nevertheless treated as income for trust accounting purposes and therefore required to be distributed to the income beneficiary. If the beneficiary were taxed on all trust income distributable to him, without limit, the result would be to impose a tax even though none would have been due if the beneficiary had owned the trust assets and received the stock dividend directly. The offsetting deduction to the trust might not make up for this burden since there might not be enough taxable income, from any source, to absorb the deduction.

In order to avoid this result the statute limits the amount deductible and includible under §§651 and 652 to something called *distributable net income* (DNI). This is defined in §643(a). The definition begins with taxable income (so that the tax-free stock dividend in the last paragraph, for example, would not be included), but then it contains a bewildering array of modifications that ultimately make DNI a hybrid between taxable and trust accounting income.

One important modification is that DNI does not include capital gains, unless under the terms of a particular trust instrument such gains are required to be distributed to income beneficiaries. §643(a)(3). As a result, capital gains are normally taxed to the trust, even if beneficiaries are receiving income distributions partially free of tax because of the DNI limitation.

Another modification is that tax-exempt interest is *included* in DNI. §643(a)(5). But taxation of the trust beneficiary is avoided by another technique: Section 652(b) provides that the tax-exempt character of the interest is to flow through to the beneficiary on the distribution, and the last sentence of §651(b) denies the trust any deduction.

It is easier to accept the end results in these cases than to understand why they are reached in such different ways. If you want to pursue the complexities of DNI further, a good starting place is the example in Reg. §1.652(c)-4.

2. Complex Trusts and the Tier System

If a trust is not required to distribute all income currently, or if it makes distributions out of corpus, then it is classified as a complex trust and treatment of distributions is governed by §§661-664. These are similar in operation to §§651 and 652, but somewhat more elaborate in order to deal with the further potential complexities of such distributions.

One complication arises when total distributions exceed DNI. Taxable distributions (that is, distributions deductible by the trust and taxable to the beneficiary) are limited to DNI. §§661(a), 651(b). But which distributions are to be considered taxable and which are not? The statute resolves this problem for complex trusts by adopting a so-called tier system, which as a general rule attributes taxable income first pro rata among required distributions and then among discretionary distributions. §§661(a), 661(b).

There are also special rules for a variety of transactions. Distributions to charities are effectively treated as falling in between the first and second tiers. §§642(c), 662(a)(1) (parenthetical expression referring to §642(c)). Some distributions may be treated as nontaxable gifts or bequests even in the presence of excess DNI. §663(a)(1). Distributions in the first 65 days of a taxable year may be treated as made in the previous taxable year. §663(b). And so forth.

For more on these complications, if you wish, take a look at the example in Reg. §1.662(c)-4 and the other examples throughout the regulations under §§661-663.

3. Accumulation Distributions

Once upon a time there was no separate rate schedule for trusts; undistributed trust income was taxed on one of the rate schedules applicable to natural persons. Significant current taxes could therefore be saved by accumulating taxable income in a trust (or trusts). In response, the statute provided specially that when accumulated trust income was later distributed there would be a further tax on the *accumulation distribution,* reflecting the difference between what the beneficiary would have paid and what the trust did pay in tax as the money was accumulated. There were shortcut modes of calculation or estimation, which were still devilishly complicated. And the remedy remained inadequate in many cases since no interest was charged or imputed to compensate for the delay in paying the full amount of tax.

In 1986 Congress adopted a very compressed rate schedule for trusts and estates under which they reach the top rate much sooner than any natural person. As a result, even with inflation and the addition of new rate brackets, the tax on trust income is within $1,000 of simply applying the 35 percent top rate to all undistributed trust income.

In 1997 the accumulation distribution provisions were repealed except as they apply to foreign trusts (including domestic trusts that were once foreign) and certain trusts organized prior to 1985. §665(c).

4. Fiscal Years

A trust or estate might have a taxable year different from that of one or more beneficiaries, and the question then arises of when to include trust income in the beneficiary's return. The general rule in §662(c) is to include it in the taxable year of the beneficiary that includes the *end* of the taxable year of the trust. So if an estate had a January 31 taxable year and calendar year beneficiaries, income received in February 2010 and distributed in March 2010 would be reported by the beneficiary in April 2012 as income for 2011. This deferral opportunity led many trusts and estates to adopt noncalendar taxable years. Section 644, enacted in 1986, now prescribes the calendar year as taxable year for all trusts.

C.   GRANTOR TRUSTS

The circumstances under which trust income is taxed to the grantor of a trust are now specified in subpart E, §§671-677. These provisions were enacted in 1954 to provide relief from the uncertainty created by the *Clifford* decision in particular, and others like it.

From 1954 until 1986, §673 treated the grantor as owner of any trust in which he retained a reversionary interest "if, as of the inception of . . . the trust, the interest will or may reasonably be expected to take effect in possession or enjoyment within 10 years . . ." Other sections treating the grantor as owner because of retained powers had exceptions, then as now, for a "power, the exercise of which can only affect the beneficial enjoyment of the income for a period commencing after the occurrence of an event such that a grantor would not be treated as the owner under section 673 if the power were a reversionary interest . . ." §§674(b)(2), 676(b). As a result, many viewed the grantor trust provisions as primarily an affirmation that an irrevocable assignment of ten years' income or more, at least by way of a trust, would be effective for tax purposes. This provided a means by which upper middle class families whose income was going to go in substantial part for their children's higher education anyway could get some of that income taxed at the children's rates.

The 1986 version of §673 is much stricter, taxing the grantor on income of any inter vivos trust with a reversionary interest actuarially worth 5 percent or more of the value of the trust. At interest rates prevailing around 1986, a term of years would have had to run for over 30 years for the remainder to be worth less than 5 percent. At the interest rate in effect for this purpose in mid-2008 (4.2 percent), see §7520, a term of years would have to run 73 years to achieve this effect. If one is going to give the property away for that long, it almost always makes more sense to give it away completely than to retain any reversionary interest at all.

One may be prepared to give up all beneficial interest in property placed in trust but still wish to retain some powers over enjoyment by others or over management of the property. The terms of §§674 and 675 then may be quite important.

In addition to making it harder to have a nongrantor trust, the 1986 Act also made it less worthwhile by reason of changes in §1 of the statute. The reduction of the top rate makes it less worthwhile to avoid tax in any event, even if the person to whom income is attributed is at a nontaxable income level, and more specifically, under §1(g), unearned income (i.e., dividends or interest income, as compared with wages and salaries) of a child under age 18 (or a student under age 24 whose earned income does not exceed half of the cost of his support) is taxed at the parents' applicable rate, even in the case of securities owned outright by the child and obtained from sources other than the parents' beneficence.

As a way to dig into these materials, consider and work out each of the following problems. What do the statute and regulations say with respect to each? What ought to be said?

Problems

1. *D* transfers property in trust to pay the income in equal shares to her children during *D*'s life, then to distribute the property as *D* may by deed or will appoint. What are the income tax consequences for *D*?

2. *E* transfers property in trust, all the income to be paid to his children in equal shares. *E* retains power to distribute corpus to his wife for her reasonable comfort and support. Is *E* taxable on any of the trust income?

3. *F* transfers property in trust to pay the income to her children in equal shares during her lifetime. *F* retains power to withhold income from any child, however, and add it to corpus. On *F*'s death the corpus is to be distributed in equal shares to *F*'s surviving children.

4. *G* transfers property in trust for her life to pay the income each year to *G*'s children in such shares as the trustees may determine. The trustees are the vice president of *G*'s corporation and *G*'s lawyer. *G* retains power to remove and replace either or both of the trustees.

5. *H* borrows $100,000 from the *X* Bank on a 12 percent unsecured demand note. *H* then creates a trust to pay income to her oldest daughter and contributes $100,000 to the trust. The trustees are *H*'s brother and the *X* Bank, and they are given broad investment discretion. In fact, after three months, the trustees purchase *H*'s note for the trust. What are the income tax consequences for *H*?

Sections 673-677 all prescribe that the grantor shall be treated as the owner of any portion of a trust meeting the specified conditions. Section 671 indicates that the main consequence of being treated as the owner is being taxed on the income, and getting the benefit of any correlative deductions and credits as if one were the owner. But are there other tax consequences? In particular, can there be recognition of gain or loss on a sale between a grantor and a grantor trust? And should gain accrue as on a sale if the conditions that cause a trust to be treated as owned by the grantor cease to exist?[2]

D.   INTEREST-FREE LOANS

What would be the tax result if a wealthy parent were simply to lend money to her low-bracket son on an interest-free basis, letting the son invest the loan proceeds and keep the return from the investment? Would the term of the loan matter, or whether the loan were payable on demand? Would this be a good way to avoid the limitations imposed by §§673-676 on the use of short-term or revocable trusts?

Or what would be the result if an employer lent money to an employee on an interest-free basis? Is there any net avoidance of income tax if the employee is not taxed on this income in kind?

Prior to 1984 the government repeatedly asserted income tax liability against the employee in the second case, for the most part without success. In the leading case, J. Simpson Dean, 35 T.C. 1083, 1090 (1961), the Tax Court concluded that the transactions did not result in income to the borrowers since "had petitioners borrowed the funds in question on interest-bearing notes, their payment of interest would have been fully deductible by them under section 163, I.R.C. 1954." Cases imposing tax on rent-free, personal use of property are different because the rent would not be deductible if it had been paid.

As to the family case, the government asserted gift tax liability against the lender-parent until at last it prevailed in Dickman v. Commissioner, 465 U.S. 330 (1984). So far as income tax liability is concerned, however, the government hardly even tried. A Technical Advice Memorandum in 1982 explained that

> [i]n order to apply the assignment of income doctrine to the interest-free loans in this case, such loans would have to be viewed as two-step transactions in which [the lender] made interest-bearing loans to the borrowers followed by a transfer from [the lender] to the borrowers of the right to receive the interest paid by the borrowers for the loan. That is not what happened in this case: no right to receive interest income by [the lender] was ever created. Therefore, we would not extend the assignment of income doctrine to cover the interest-free loans in this case. [National Office Technical Advice Memorandum, IRS Letter Ruling 8309002, November 2, 1982, withdrawn, IRS Letter Ruling 8403012, October 4, 1983.]

---

2. See Rev. Rul. 77-402, 1977-2 C.B. 222; Rothstein v. United States, 735 F.2d 704 (2d Cir. 1984) (three opinions); Rev. Rul. 85-13, 1985-1 C.B. 184 (refusing to follow *Rothstein*). The position of Revenue Ruling 77-402 was incorporated in Reg. §1.1002-2(c), Example 5, the validity of which was upheld in Madorin v. Commissioner, 84 T.C. 667 1985) (distinguishing *Rothstein*).

Did this position make sense?

All these questions are now dealt with by §7872, enacted in 1984. Look at that section and at the following explanatory excerpts. Does this statute do a better job?

BELOW-MARKET AND INTEREST-FREE LOANS [§7872]

Staff of Joint Comm. on Taxation, 98th Cong., General Explanation of the Revenue Provisions of the Deficit Reduction Act of 1984, 527-530 (Comm. Print 1984)

REASONS FOR CHANGE

A below-market loan is the economic equivalent of a loan bearing a market rate of interest, and a payment by the lender to the borrower to fund the payment of interest by the borrower. The Congress believed that, in many instances, the failure of the tax laws to treat these transactions in accordance with their economic substance provided taxpayers with opportunities to circumvent well-established tax rules.

Under prior law, loans between family members (and other similar loans) were being used to avoid the assignment of income rules and the grantor trust rules. A below-market loan to a family member, for example, generally involves a gratuitous transfer of the right to use the proceeds of the borrowing until repayment is demanded (in the case of a demand loan) or until the end of the term of the loan (in the case of a term loan). If the lender had assigned the income from the proceeds to the borrower instead of lending the proceeds to the borrower, the assignment of income doctrine would have taxed the lender (and not the borrower) on the income. If the lender had transferred the principal amount to a trust established for the benefit of the borrower that was revocable at will (similar to a demand loan), or that would terminate at the end of a period of not more than 10 years (similar to a term loan with a term of not more than 10 years), the income earned on trust assets would have been taxed to the lender under the grantor trust provisions set forth in Code secs. 671-679.

In addition, loans from corporations to shareholders were being used to avoid rules requiring the taxation of corporate income at the corporate level. A below-market loan from a corporation to a shareholder is the economic equivalent of a loan by the corporation to the shareholder requiring the payment of interest at a market rate, and a distribution by the corporation to the shareholder with respect to its stock equal to the amount of interest required to be paid under the terms of the loan. If a transaction were structured as a distribution and a loan, the borrower would have dividend income and an offsetting interest deduction. The lender would have interest income. Under prior law, if the transaction was structured as a below-market loan, the lender avoided including in income the interest that would have been paid by the borrower. As a result, the lender was in the same economic position as it would have been if it had deducted amounts distributed as dividends to shareholders.

Finally, loans to persons providing services were being used to avoid rules requiring the payment of employment taxes and rules restricting the deductibility of interest in certain situations by the person providing the services. A below-market loan to a person providing services is the economic equivalent of a loan requiring the payment of interest at a market rate, and a payment in the nature of compensation equal to the amount of interest required to be paid under the terms of the loan. Under prior law, a transaction structured as a loan and a payment in the nature of compensation often did not result in any tax consequences for either the lender or the borrower because each would have offsetting income and deductions. However, there were a number of situations in which the payment of compensation and a loan requiring the payment of interest at a market rate did not offset. For example, if a taxpayer used the proceeds of an arm's-length loan to invest in tax-exempt obligations, the deduction for interest paid on the loan would be disallowed under section 265. Similarly, if a term loan extended beyond the taxable year in which it was made, income and deductions did not offset because the compensation income was includible in the year the loan was made. In such circumstances, substantial tax advantages could have been derived by structuring the transaction as a below-market loan.

EXPLANATION OF PROVISION

OVERVIEW

The Act adds to the Code new section 7872 (relating to the tax treatment of loans that, in substance, result in a gift, payment of compensation, dividend, capital contribution, or other similar payment from the lender to the borrower). Loans that are subject to the provision and that do not require payment of interest, or require payment at a rate below the statutory rate (referred to as the "applicable Federal rate"), are recharacterized as an arm's-length transaction in which the lender made a loan to the borrower in exchange for a note requiring the payment of interest at the applicable Federal rate. This rule results in the parties being treated as if:

(1) The borrower paid interest to the lender that may be deductible to the borrower and is included in income by the lender; and

(2) The lender (a) made a gift subject to the gift tax (in the case of a gratuitous transaction), or (b) paid a dividend or made a capital contribution (in the case of a loan between a corporation and a shareholder), or (c) paid compensation (in the case of a loan to a person providing services), or (d) made some other payment characterized in accordance with the substance of the transaction.

The Congress intended that, in general, in the case of a loan subject to this provision, the amount of the deemed payment from the lender to the borrower is to be determined solely under this provision. Thus, in the case of a below-market loan from a parent to a child, the amount of the gift is to be determined under section 7872, and not under the decision in the *Dickman* case, supra, even if the applicable Federal rate is less than a fair market interest rate. Further, in the case of a loan from an employer to an employee, the amount of the compensation is to be determined under section 7872, and not under section 83, even if the applicable Federal rate is less than a fair market interest rate.

Payments deemed made under this provision are, in general, treated as actually made for all purposes of the Code. . . .

LOANS SUBJECT TO THE PROVISION

The provision applies to term or demand loans that are gift loans, compensation-related loans, corporation-shareholder loans, and tax avoidance loans. In addition, the Congress intended that, under regulations to be prescribed by the Treasury, the provision is to apply to other similar transactions (i.e., loan transactions that in substance affect a transfer from the lender to the borrower other than the transfer of the principal amount of the loan) if the interest arrangements have a significant effect on the tax liability of either the borrower or the lender.

Generally, it was intended that the term "loan" be interpreted broadly in light of the purposes of the provision. Thus, any transfer of money that provides the transferor with a right to repayment is a loan. For example, advances and deposits of all kinds are treated as loans.

Demand loans and term loans. — A demand loan is any loan which is payable in full at any time upon the demand of the lender. A term loan is any loan which is not a demand loan.

Gift loans. — A gift loan is any below-market loan where the foregone interest is in the nature of a gift. In general, there is a gift if property (including foregone interest) is transferred for less than full and adequate consideration under circumstances where the transfer is a gift for gift tax purposes. A sale, exchange, or other transfer made in the ordinary course of business (i.e., a transaction which is bona fide, at arm's length and free from any donative intent) generally is considered as made for and full and adequate consideration. A loan between unrelated persons can qualify as a gift loan.

It was intended that if a taxpayer makes a below-market demand loan to a trust and the loan is treated as a revocable transfer of property for purposes of Subpart E, the provisions of Subpart E govern.[8] Further, the Congress

---

8. This result is required because it would be anomalous to give effect for tax purposes to a loan made by a taxpayer to himself or herself.

anticipated that regulations may be prescribed by the Treasury describing the circumstances under which a loan to a trust will be treated as a revocable transfer. . . .

Note

The 1986 Act did not change §7872 itself, but it radically altered its implications by disallowing any deduction for personal interest, limiting investment interest deductions to investment income, and taxing investment income of children at their parents' rates. §§1(g), 163(d), (h). Should §7872, or the regulations under it, be altered in view of these changes? How? In connection with the following problems consider particularly how the 1986 changes affect the operation of §7872.

Problems

1. *A*'s employer lends her $100,000 interest free to purchase a home. What are the tax consequences? What if the purpose were to pay for *A*'s children's college tuition? To purchase municipal bonds?

2. *B*'s mother lends him $100,000 interest free to purchase a home. What are the tax consequences? What if the purpose were to pay for *B*'s children's college tuition? To purchase municipal bonds?

3. What difference would it make in either of the above cases whether the loan were a demand loan or a fixed-term loan? What if the employer loan, in particular, were a 15-year term loan, but with a provision requiring payment sooner upon termination of employment?

4. Are there relationships other than those specified in §7872 in which an interest-free or below-market interest loan may represent a disguise for something else passing the other way between the parties, and where interest ought to be imputed to prevent a distortion of tax treatment? What about a seller of property who extends credit without adequate interest but makes it up by charging a higher price? How might that result in a distorted reflection of taxable income? Whose taxable income? As we have seen, Congress addressed this problem with a provision that is quite akin to §7872. See §§1274 and 483; Chapter 6C.2 above.

5. Geraldine's parents are retired and live on a modest pension together with a small amount of investment income. They have lived for some time in a rent-controlled apartment, with a monthly rental of $500 which has been paid by Geraldine. Recently the parents have been notified that their apartment building is to be converted into condominiums, and they have been offered a chance to purchase the apartment they live in for $200,000. Financing is available for 80 percent of the purchase price ($160,000) at 12 percent per annum interest. Geraldine's parents would very much like to stay where

they are, but the costs will be much higher. Annual costs of owning their apartment are estimated as follows:

Interest (12% of $160,000)	$19,200
Taxes	1,500
Condominium association dues and other expenses	1,000
Total	$21,700

Geraldine is a successful professional with funds to spare and wants to enable her parents to stay in their home. Several particular ways of helping have been suggested:

(a) Geraldine could simply make her parents a $40,000 interest-free loan to enable them to purchase the condominium and then increase her annual contributions from $6,000 to $21,700 to enable them to meet the resulting annual costs.

(b) Geraldine could seek to borrow $160,000 on her own credit and then lend her parents $200,000 with no interest to enable them to buy the condominium without a mortgage. In this case Geraldine would only have to advance $2,500 a year thereafter to enable them to pay taxes and other expenses.

(c) Geraldine might simply purchase the condominium herself and then let her parents live in it rent free. She would pay all the expenses of ownership, including mortgage interest and principal, directly.

(d) Geraldine could purchase the condominium herself and then let her parents live in it charging them the existing ceiling rental of $6,000 ($500/month). In this case Geraldine would plan to treat her investment in the condominium as an income-producing investment. She would in this case also plan to give her parents about $6,000 a year in some other form to meet other expenses, so that their total budget would not be upset by the necessity of paying rent.

Evaluate these four plans, and any others you think should be considered, from an income tax standpoint.

References

A. *Attribution in the Supreme Court:* Lyon & Eustice, Assignment of Income: Fruit and Tree as Irrigated by the *P. G. Lake* Case, 17 Tax L. Rev. 295 (1962); Miller, Gifts of Income and of Property: What the *Horst* Case Decides, 5 Tax L. Rev. 1 (1949); Soll, Intra-Family Assignments: Attribution and Realization of Income, 6 Tax L. Rev. 435, 7 Tax L. Rev. 61 (1951); Surrey, The Supreme Court and the Federal Income Tax: Some Implications of the Recent Decisions, 35 Ill. L. Rev. 779, 784-791 (1941).

B. Statutory Rules for Nongrantor Trusts: M. Carr Ferguson, James J. Freeland, & Mark L. Ascher, Federal Income Taxation of Estates, Trusts and Beneficiaries (3d ed. 1998); Elting, New Income Tax Rules for Accumulation Trusts with Some Drafting Suggestions, 24 Tax Law. 453 (1971); Estes, Using Trusts in Family Tax Planning, 23 Tul. Tax Inst. 367 (1974); Joyce, The Income Taxation of the Capital Gains of a Trust, 23 Tax L. Rev. 361 (1968); Kamin, Surrey, & Warren, The Internal Revenue Code of 1954: Trusts, Estates and Beneficiaries, 54 Colum. L. Rev. 1237 (1954); Jeffrey G. Sherman, All You Really Need to Know about Subchapter J You Learned from This Article, 63 Mo. L. Rev. 1 (1998); Stevens, The Income Taxation of Trusts and Estates, 1955 U. Ill. L.F. 406 (1955).

C. Grantor Trusts: Mark L. Ascher, When to Ignore a Grantor Trust: The Precedents, a Proposal, and a Prediction, 41 Tax L. Rev. 253 (1986); Brown, The Growing "Common Law" of Taxation, 34 S. Cal. L. Rev. 235 (1961); Casner, The Internal Revenue Code of 1954: Estate Planning, 68 Harv. L. Rev. 222 (1954); Jay A. Soled, Reforming the Grantor Trust Rules, 76 Notre Dame L. Rev. 375 (2001); Westfall, Trust Grantors and Section 674: Adventures in Income Tax Avoidance, 60 Colum. L. Rev. 326 (1960); Note, Federal Tax Aspects of the Obligations to Support, 74 Harv. L. Rev. 1191 (1961).

D. Interest-free Loans: Jacobs, Of No Interest: Truth, Substance, and Bargain Borrowing, 9 Fla. St. U.L. Rev. 261 (1981); Joyce & DelCotto, Interest-Free Loans: The Odyssey of a Misnomer, 35 Tax L. Rev. 459 (1980); McCue & Brosterhous, Interest-Free and Below-Market Loans After *Dickman* and the Tax Reform Act of 1984, 62 Taxes 1010 (1984); Note, The Income Tax Treatment of Interest Free Loans, 1 Va. Tax Rev. 137 (1981).

Part IV — *Capital Gains and Losses*

Chapter 19 — *Capital Gains*

Read or review the introduction to capital gains in Chapter 5F. The idea of taxing net capital gains at a substantially lower rate than ordinary income persisted from 1921 to 1986. The differential was repealed in 1986 in connection with a reduction of the top nominal rate on all income to 28 percent. At the same time Congress announced that if rates later increased beyond that level, the maximum tax rate on capital gains would remain at 28 percent. The top rate on ordinary income was raised by 3 percentage points in 1990 and again by 8.6 points in 1993, thus permitting reappearance of an 11.6 point differential. In 1997 the top rate on most capital gains was reduced to 20 percent (where it was prior to 1986). Tax cut legislation enacted during the Bush Administration has (for the time being) lowered the top rate on ordinary income to 35 percent and set the maximum rate of tax on most capital gains at 15 percent. §1(h)(1)(C), (i).

Prior to 1986 virtually all the complications in the capital gain provisions were in arriving at the amount of *net capital gain*. Once that amount was arrived at, the application to it of a lower rate of tax was relatively straightforward. But in 1997 Congress was more discriminating and determined to treat some components of net capital gain more favorably than others. This differentiation introduces awesome new computational complexities. Unfortunately, none of the old complexities have been removed since the statute still provides relief only for net capital gain.

The new complexities are in significant ways an echo of the old, and so it makes sense to work through the latter first.

A. THE STATUTORY SCHEME

Our courts concluded early that "profit gained through a sale or conversion of capital assets" was within the constitutional and statutory concept of income. See Eisner v. Macomber, Chapter 5A above. Such profit is presently within the general statutory notion of income in §61(a) (whether or not within the more specific language of §61(a)(3)), and the profit on a sale is usually recognized under the default rule of §1001(c).

But the full statutory answer to the question whether such profits are to be taxed as income has mostly been more complex, amounting to a kind of compromise. In the case of the sale or exchange of a capital asset held for more than some minimum period (usually six months or a year) the statute long provided, in effect, for a substantially lower rate — generally less than half the rate applied to ordinary income. Indeed, the income tax imposed on such profits is sometimes referred to as the capital gains tax as if it were a different and separate imposition.

The basic provisions granting favorable tax treatment to long-term capital gains and restricting deduction of capital losses are now in §1(h) and §§1201-1223. There are a great many other statutory provisions that assimilate other transactions to those described in these sections. Many of these appear right after the basic provisions, beginning at §1231.

1.   The Deduction for Capital Gains

Prior to 1986, §1202(a) provided as follows:

SECTION 1202 — DEDUCTION FOR CAPITAL GAINS

(a) In General. — If for any taxable year a taxpayer other than a corporation has a net capital gain, 60 percent of the amount of the net capital gain shall be a deduction from gross income.

This deduction was allowed above the line, so adjusted gross income only included 40 percent of net capital gain. The deduction was often referred to as a partial *exclusion* of capital gains. However it was referred to, its *function* was to reduce the rate of tax on net capital gain to 40 percent of what it would otherwise have been. If, for example, a taxpayer in the 70 percent rate bracket had $100x$ of net capital gain, her gross income would include the whole $100x$, but the capital gain deduction of $60x$ would reduce her taxable income from the gain to $40x$. The tax at 70 percent on $40x$ would be $28x$, for an effective rate of tax on the whole gain of 28 percent. Section 1202 was thus the principal provision for implementing a preferential rate of tax on capital gain income.

For a taxpayer in the 20 percent rate bracket, the capital gain deduction would produce an effective rate of tax of 8 percent. Indeed the deduction would produce an effective rate of 8 percent if $40x$ would fit into the taxpayer's 20 percent rate bracket even if the next $60x$ would have been taxed at a higher rate. For very large capital gains and limited ordinary income this could sometimes make the rate of tax considerably less than 40 percent of what it would have been without the deduction.

Questions

1. An unmarried taxpayer has ordinary income just equal to total deductions and net capital gain of $100,000. Suppose §1202, as quoted above, were in effect. What would be the rate of tax on the capital gain?

2. Same as above, but with deductions $30,000 in excess of ordinary income: What would be the rate of tax on the capital gain?

Section 1202 was simply repealed in 1986. The present version was enacted in 1993. This is like capital gain relief in the past in that it takes the form of a 50 percent exclusion, which helps taxpayers more or less proportionately in every rate bracket. But it is limited to gains on stock of certain small business corporations. The stock must have been purchased from the corporation on original issue, and it must have been held for at least five years to qualify for partial exclusion. There are also dollar limits on the amount that a particular taxpayer can exclude on account of investments in any single company. The five-year holding requirement is said to be to encourage long-term investments as compared with mere speculation. It has another interesting effect as well: Because budget deficit accounting only looks forward five years, the exclusion was not treated as a revenue loser whose cost must be made up through some other provision. And when its effect does come in view it is treated as part of the baseline from which further deficit reduction is measured.

We already have had special relief for some time for certain small business corporations, in the form of an exemption from the capital loss limitation. §1244. That provision should be compared with the new §1202 in terms of coverage and likely incentive effects as well as general tax equity.

2. Maximum Rates for Capital Gains

Another form of relief for capital gains is a maximum or ceiling rate to be applied to net capital gain even if a taxpayer's ordinary income reaches higher rates. The mechanics are to compute a partial tax on ordinary income by excluding net capital gain, and then add to that a tax on the excluded capital gain at the ceiling rate.

The principal form of capital gain relief since 1986 has been a ceiling rate (or now rates) in §1(h). In 1986 there was a provision that if the rate on ordinary income were ever raised about 28 percent, net capital gain would have a ceiling rate of 28 percent. When the 31 percent ordinary income rate was added in 1990, the promise was kept and §1(h) became a simple 28 percent ceiling provision. The present multirate version of §1(h) (explained below) was enacted in 1997 and revised and complicated frequently thereafter.

The capital gain rate preference for corporations has long taken the form of a ceiling rate. Look at §1201, which effectively prescribes a top rate of 35 percent for net capital gain of a corporate taxpayer. Since 1986 this provision has provided no relief because the rate prescribed for capital gains has been the same as the top rate on ordinary income in §11. Before that the top ordinary income rate for corporations was 46 percent, while §1201 set 28 percent as the maximum for capital gains.

Think carefully about differences between a ceiling rate mechanism and the deduction mechanism for implementing a capital gain preference. Most obviously, a deduction provides proportionate relief for taxpayers in all brackets, while a ceiling rate only benefits taxpayers with a regular rate above the ceiling. Which makes more sense in light of this difference? Is there any difference between individuals and corporations that explains the use of a deduction for the former and a ceiling rate for the latter? Prior to 1969, individuals had the benefit of a 50 percent exclusion or a 25 percent ceiling rate, whichever was better.

Notice that this provision has only to do with getting from taxable income to tax liability, not with the computation of taxable income. Taxable income still includes capital gains in full. Capital gains are thus still fully subject to the effective rate add-ons created by the limitation on personal deductions in §68 and the phase-out of personal exemptions for high-income taxpayers. §151(d)(3). See Chapter 1A, Table 1-1 and Chapter 9E.

Questions

1. An unmarried taxpayer has ordinary income just equal to total deductions and net capital gain of $100,000. What will be the rate of tax on the capital gain?

2. Same case as above, but with deductions $30,000 in excess of ordinary income. What would be the rate of tax on the capital gain?

3. Capital Losses

Section 1211 limits deduction of capital losses to capital gains plus $3,000. Or, in effect, net capital loss is deductible only to the extent of $3,000. We have looked at this provision in Chapter 14C, and we will focus on it again in Chapter 20, but right here we need to consider its interaction with the treatment of capital gains.

First note that §1211 cannot apply in the same year as any of the capital gain preference provisions, since one cannot have a net capital gain if capital losses exceed capital gains. So for any particular tax year a taxpayer may be in net capital gain mode or in capital loss limitation mode but not both.

Then consider the effective tax treatment of capital gains in a capital loss limitation year — a year in which capital losses exceed gains by more than $3,000. In the year in question such gains are wholly free of tax. Whether a particular gain qualifies as capital gain, therefore, makes a considerably *bigger* immediate difference in tax liability than if the capital gain preference provisions were in play.

Disallowed capital losses carry over to future years. §1212. Accordingly a capital gain in a capital loss limitation year may eventually bear some tax burden after all, by way of reducing the capital loss carryover into a future year. That will only occur if the carryover would eventually be absorbed, either by future capital gains or the $3,000 annual allowance against ordinary income. A taxpayer with a large capital loss carryover may be in capital loss limitation mode for the whole foreseeable future.

This aspect of the treatment of capital gains — being able to be offset by otherwise nondeductible capital losses — was not eliminated in 1986. For most taxpayers it was relatively unimportant. For the few to whom it applied it fully preserved the most preferred status of capital gains.

Just as capital gains may fall in a capital loss limitation year, capital losses may fall in a net capital gain year. In that case §1211 will not apply, and they will be fully deductible. But occurrence of a capital loss will reduce the amount of net capital gain, and therefore it will reduce any capital gain deduction or the amount of income entitled to the benefit of any rate ceiling, and so the total tax effect is likely to be less than that of an ordinary deduction. Even a capital loss currently disallowed under §1211 may be allowed in a future year pursuant to §1212, but then only by way of reducing capital gains which themselves might otherwise be taxed at some preferential rate. Permanent complete disallowance is reserved for those who suffer capital losses in excess of current and future capital gains.

4. Short-term Capital Gains (and Losses)

The discussion so far has assumed that capital gains were realized on assets held long enough to qualify as long-term capital gains.[1] Preferential rate treatment is denied for short-term gains, which do not meet that condition. These results are prescribed in the statute in §1222, in the definition of *net capital gain* as the excess of net long-term capital gain over net short-term capital loss. (In reading that provision, remember that the excess of one over five, for example, is *zero*, not negative four, and that a net

---

1. In that case the holding period for capital losses would be irrelevant.

short-term capital gain is therefore *not* a negative net short-term capital loss. If there are net gains in both the long- and short-term categories, the net short-term capital loss is zero, and net capital gain equals net long-term capital gain.) An alternative (and equivalent) formulation would define net capital gain as the excess of all capital gains over all capital losses, or the excess of long-term capital gains over long-term capital losses, whichever is less.

A short-term gain is defined as a gain realized on an asset held for not more than one year. The line has often been drawn at six months; long ago it was two years. It has sometimes been suggested that there should be a sliding scale along which the capital gain preference would be phased in as the holding period increased, so that fully preferential treatment would only accrue after five years. Section 1223 has a number of rules for tacking holding periods of other property or other owners in cases of nonrecognition exchanges and carryover-basis transfers (and some other transactions). Property received in a like-kind exchange, for example, starts with the holding period of the property exchanged (provided that the property exchanged was a capital asset or property used in a trade or business), §§1223(1), 1031(d), and property acquired by gift starts with the donor's holding period, §§1223(2), 1015.

The reason for excluding short-term capital gains is not clear. The holding period has never been long enough to isolate transactions that represent a bunching in one year of gain that accrued over an extended period. The holding period is sometimes said to separate investment gains from mere speculative gains, but it is not clear how speculative gains differ from investment gains, or why they should be excluded.

The capital loss limitation draws no distinction between short- and long-term losses (or gains). See O. L. Burnett, Chapter 14C above. But the statute still draws a distinction between short- and long-term losses, which may be important if capital losses are deducted in a year that still ends up with an excess of capital gains over capital losses, since long-term losses are deducted first against long-term gains, while short-term losses are deducted first against short-term gains. If there is an excess of losses in either category and an excess of gains in the other, these are offset against one another as the last step. All of this is in the definitions in §1222.

Short-term capital gains as such are ineligible for the preferential rates afforded capital gains, but this does not mean they are taxed the same as ordinary income. In a capital loss year, since the capital loss limitation draws no distinction between short- and long-term capital losses, short-term gains will enjoy the benefit of being fully offset by otherwise nondeductible losses, and thus enjoy an effective marginal tax rate of zero (the same as long-term gains). Even in a capital gain year, if there is otherwise an excess of short-term capital losses over gains (and a larger excess of long-term capital gains over losses), then a short-term capital gain will have the effect of absorbing short-term capital loss and leaving more long-term capital gain subject to tax as such at preferential rates.

In summary, the choice between ordinary, capital gain, and zero marginal tax rates applicable to any particular item depends on the balance of all items for the taxable year, not just on the character of the item in question. If a taxpayer is in excess capital loss mode, then all capital gains and losses, short- and long-term alike, are effectively taxed at a zero rate. If the mode is net short-term capital loss and net long-term capital gain and the latter is larger than the former, then all capital gains and losses are effectively taxed at the preferential capital gains rate. If the mode is net short-term capital gain and net long-term capital loss, then all gains and losses are effectively taxed at full ordinary income rates. Otherwise — chiefly if gains exceed losses in both term categories — long-term gains and losses will be taxed at the capital gain rate while short-term will be taxed at ordinary income rates.

5. Section 1231

The complications of netting gains and losses within limited categories are amplified by §1231. Read or reread the discussion of this provision in Chapter 14D above.

6. Definitional Problems — Sale or Exchange

Long- and short-term capital gain (or loss) are defined in §1222 as gain (or loss) "from the sale or exchange of a capital asset. . . ." Clearly capital gains do not include gains in the form of recurring payments of interest, rent, or the like even if the underlying loan or rental property is a capital asset, and the sale or exchange requirement functions to exclude such returns. Traditionally, dividends on corporate stock were also excluded by this requirement, but a special rule (described below) now taxes most dividends at favorable capital gains rates. (This temporary provision is scheduled to expire for taxable years beginning after 2010.)

Are there transactions that have the effect of liquidating a taxpayer's investment but nevertheless do not constitute sales or exchanges? What if a building burns down, for example, and the owner receives insurance proceeds in excess basis? Or what if a taxpayer buys corporate bonds at a discount and the corporation later redeems them at par or at a premium? Is the profit in either situation gain from a "sale or exchange"?

The slight difference in terminology between "sale or exchange" in §1222 and "sale or other disposition" in §1001(b) has sometimes been taken to indicate that there are dispositions outside the scope of "sale or exchange" and capital gains treatment. Moreover, some of the reasons for favorable treatment of capital gains (and limited deductibility of capital losses) may have less application to involuntary liquidation of an investment than to a voluntary sale.

Many problems concerning the sale or exchange requirement are now resolved, at least partially, by other sections of the statute providing that specified sorts of gains or losses shall be considered as gains or losses from the sale or exchange of the property disposed of. For example, §1231 provides, among other things, that a gain from insurance proceeds received on destruction of a capital asset may be "treated as" a gain from the sale or exchange of a capital asset. Section 1271(a)(1) provides that amounts received on retirement of bonds and other corporate debt instruments "shall be considered as amounts received in exchange therefor." Both §§1231 and 1271 have a host of other conditions on ultimate capital gain or loss treatment. Since 1997, §1234A has generally equated "cancellation, lapse, expiration or other termination" of a right or obligation with respect to a capital asset with the sale of the asset.[2]

Several of the special sections feeding into the capital gain provisions are found in Subchapter C, dealing with corporate transactions. For example, §331(a) provides, "[a]mounts received by a shareholder in a distribution in complete liquidation of a corporation shall be treated as in full payment in exchange for the stock." Section 302(a) provides that a corporate redemption of stock that meets certain tests "shall be treated as a distribution in part or full payment in exchange for the stock"; §302(d) indicates that under other circumstances a redemption may be treated as a dividend. The tax advantage of treating liquidations and certain redemptions as deemed sales of stock is greatly reduced so long as dividends are taxed like long-term capital gains rather than ordinary income, but it's not eliminated because deemed sale treatment triggers basis recovery under §1001.

7. Definitional Problems — Capital Assets

"Capital assets" are defined in §1221 to mean "property held by the taxpayer," but with five specified exceptions. The affirmative aspect of the definition — "property held by the taxpayer" — is both broad and vague in its limits. In our legal tradition almost any right may be conceived as "property" for some purposes so there have been innumerable taxpayer attempts to characterize all sorts of payments as receipts from the sale or exchange of an underlying property right. The courts have responded in a variety of ways, sometimes by just ignoring the statutory definition and announcing that a particular transaction was not intended to be treated as producing capital gain or loss.

---

2. S. Rep. 105-33, 132-136 (2007) describes the history of the issue and contains an excellent discussion of the case law.

On the exclusion side the most important and troublesome clause is §1221(1). Property excluded from the capital asset definition by §1221(1) is also excluded from §1231 by the language of §1231(b)(1)(A) and (B).

Section 1221(2) is less important than it would seem because §1231 operates to give capital gain treatment to the sales of assets described in §1221(2) after all, if the total of gains described in §1231 exceeds losses. Such assets are, therefore, sometimes called *quasi-capital assets*. The exclusions in clauses (3) through (8) are narrower.

Section 1221(1) is clear enough in its application to a merchant's inventory. It is usually clear, on the other hand, that §1221(1) does not embrace corporate securities, except in the case of a regular securities dealer. But there is a large intermediate zone, particularly involving real estate, in which §1221(1) has provided a source of seemingly interminable controversy and uncertainty. The application of §1221(1) is probably the most frequently controverted issue in the whole area of capital gains treatment.

8. Depreciation Recapture

Look at §1245(a) and read or review Chapter 15E. To the extent it applies, §1245 cuts across and supersedes §1231 and other applicable provisions. See also §1250.

9. Qualified Dividends

The rate reduction traditionally accorded long-term capital gains was extended to "qualified dividend income" in 2003. Qualified dividend income includes most dividends received from domestic corporations and from many foreign corporations. §1(h)(11). Mechanically, qualified dividends are included in "adjusted net capital gain" and so are taxed at either the 15 percent or zero rate. §1(h)(3), (h)(1)(B), (C). At this writing, the reduced tax rates for dividends are a temporary provision, scheduled to expire for taxable years beginning on or after January 1, 2011.

Dividends on corporate stock, as recurring returns to equity, are not gains from a "sale or exchange" even though the shares on which they are paid typically qualify as a capital asset. Consequently dividends cannot qualify as a capital gain (short- or long-term) under the definitions of §1222, and have historically been taxed at the rates applicable to ordinary income.

The current (experimental?) taxation of dividends at capital gain rates can be viewed as a modern attempt at partial integration of the corporate and individual income taxes. See Chapter 5A above. Reducing the shareholder-level tax on distributed profits reduces the "double tax" on corporate-source income (recall that profits are taxed when earned by the corporation, but the corporation is not allowed a dividends-paid deduction) and to that extent mitigates the tax-based distortion in the choice between forms of business organization (e.g., regular corporation versus partnership or sole proprietorship). It also reduces the bias in favor of leverage or debt financing (interest paid is deductible while dividends are not). Perhaps most importantly, taxing dividends at capital gains rates greatly alleviates the tax bias in the choice between distributing and retaining corporate earnings. Under the traditional approach dividends were taxed as ordinary income, but if the profits were instead retained in corporate solution, then the shareholder-level tax would be at capital gains rates. That's because retained earnings increase corporate assets and hence share values, leading to an increase in amount realized and gain on the eventual sale of stock.

> [P]resent law, by taxing dividend income at a higher rate than income from capital gains, encourages corporations to retain earnings rather than to distribute them as taxable dividends. If dividends are discouraged, shareholders may prefer that corporate management retain and reinvest earnings rather than pay out dividends, even if the shareholder might have an alternative use for the funds that could offer a higher rate of return than that earned on the retained earnings. This is another source of inefficiency as the opportunity to earn higher pre-tax returns is bypassed in favor of lower pre-tax returns. [H.R. Rep. No. 108-94, at 31 (2003).]

In addition to improving economic neutrality, taxing dividends at capital gains rates should reduce administrative costs. Historically, many of the most hotly contested issues in corporate taxation involved the classification of a distribution as a dividend because the tax stakes were so high.

10. The Multiple Rate Ceilings in §1(h)

In 1997 Congress brought the top rate on adjusted net capital gains back down to 20 percent, where it was immediately prior to 1986, and in 2003 that rate was further reduced to 15 percent. (At present the 15 percent rate is scheduled to expire for taxable years beginning after 2010.) These reductions were accomplished by modification of the rate ceiling in §1(h). But a host of new complications were introduced.

First, capital gain relief was extended to low-income taxpayers. A 15 percent ceiling is no relief for a taxpayer who is in the 10 or 15 percent bracket anyway. So to the extent that capital gain would have been taxed at or below 15 percent, it now has a ceiling rate of zero. §1(h)(1)(B).

Second, the rate ceilings (currently 15 percent and zero) are applied only to *adjusted* net capital gain. The adjustments are to exclude from the privileged category (A) unrecaptured section 1250 gain and (B) 28-percent rate gain. §1(h)(1)(B), (C), (h)(3).

Unrecaptured section 1250 gain is basically the depreciation on real estate that is not recaptured by §1250 itself. §1(h)(6)(A)(i). For that the statute prescribes a ceiling rate of 25 percent. §1(h)(1)(D). So gain on the sale of depreciable real estate is now taxed as ordinary income to the extent provided in §1250 itself, at a top rate of 25 percent for the remainder of depreciation taken, and at a top rate of 15 (or zero) percent to the extent of gain over original cost.

Gain and loss on collectibles is included in 28-percent rate gain. Collectibles include art, antiques, metals and gems, stamps and coins, and alcoholic beverages. §§1(h)(5), 408(m). These continue to enjoy a ceiling rate of 28 percent but not the new lower ceiling rates. As you study the matter of capital gains, consider whether the reasons for special rates apply less persuasively to collectibles than to other capital assets.

The second item in 28-percent rate gain is section 1202 gain, which is an amount equal to the gain excluded from gross income by §1202. The effect of the 50 percent exclusion in §1202, together with a 28 percent ceiling rate is to create an effective top rate of 14 percent for the narrow category of gains described in §1202. The effect of excluding this item from the new lower ceilings in §1(h) is to hold the effective rate at 14 percent instead of reducing it to 7.5 percent or zero.

These modifications, stated separately, are complicated enough. Fitting them together raises more problems.

Some but not all of the new categories include the possibility of loss as well as gain. In general, as in combining short- and long-term capital gains and losses to determine net capital gain, losses will be offset first against gains of the same category. Beyond that it is hard to generalize.

Look for example at the treatment of collectibles in §§1(h)(4) and (5); collectibles losses are set off against collectibles gains and other items in the computation of 28-percent rate gain. But suppose there is a net loss in the 28 percent rate category. In that case §1(h)(4) itself has no application — it applies only to an excess of gains over losses. But §1(h)(6)(A)(ii) effectively allows a deduction of net 28 percent rate losses in the computation of unrecaptured section 1250 gain. If there are no gains in the section 1250 gain category, then adjusted net capital gain will not differ from unadjusted net capital gain, in which the net collectibles loss is fully reflected. So effectively, collectibles losses, if deductible at all, are applied first against 28-percent rate gain, second against 25 percent rate gain, and last against 15(zeros) percent rate gain.

Now consider an ordinary long-term capital loss from sale of corporate securities. Nothing provides for its subtraction in the computation of 28 percent or 25 percent gain, so apparently it will only affect adjusted net capital gain, the 15(zero) percent category. But suppose there were no gains in that category.

Consider, for example, a taxpayer with $100x$ of net collectibles gain and $80x$ of net long-term securities losses. This makes 28-percent rate gain of $100x$; there is no provision in the definition for subtracting securities losses.

Does that mean there will be a 28 percent tax on the collectibles gain with no offset for the securities loss?

The answer to this question is apparently not in the definition of 28-percent rate gain, but the operative language in §1(h)(1)(E). The 28 percent tax is not applied to 28-percent rate gain as such, but to taxable income not taxed under the prior provisions. The increment to taxable income from the collectibles gain and the securities loss is determined by provisions outside §1, and is only $20x$ (net capital gain per §1222), while the *adjusted* net capital gain is zero according to §1(h)(3), and so effectively a net loss in the 15(zero) percent rate category will be offset against a net gain in the 28 percent rate category.

What about a net short-term loss, which is not within any of the §1(h) categories? Or a long-term loss carryover from a prior year? Both of these are effectively applied first against 28-percent rate gain, next against §1250 gain, and last against adjusted net capital gain. §1(h)(4)(B)(ii) & (iii), (6)(A)(ii), (3).

Questions

1. A client has $100x$ of net long-term losses from sale of securities this year. He is expecting to realize $100x$ of collectibles gains and $100x$ of securities gains next year. He could accelerate the securities gains into the current year and asks your advice about whether that would be a good idea from a tax standpoint.

2. Apart from losses, for a taxpayer whose ordinary income does not exhaust the 15 percent bracket, there is a question of ordering to determine how much 15 percent gain should go untaxed. Consider a taxpayer with ordinary income of $32x$, collectibles gain of $10x$, and securities gain of $7x$. Suppose the 15 percent ordinary income bracket ends at $42x$. How much, if any, of the securities gain will be eligible for the zero rate instead of 15 percent? The answer appears to be none, since the amount taxed under §1(h)(1)(A) in this case is $42x$. In effect, the collectibles gain uses up $10x$ of space on the regular rate schedule that might otherwise have permitted a zero ceiling rate for the securities. Can you think of any reason for this disadvantageous result? Or is it disadvantageous? Work out the full consequences if the securities gain had been stacked ahead of the collectibles gain, before concluding which stacking order is preferable.

If you find all this bewilderingly complicated, you have important company. The IRS found it impossible to implement the §1(h) as it was enacted in 1997. The IRS proposed amendments that congressional leaders promised to get enacted retroactively to cover 1997, and 1997 returns were prepared on that basis. We have only tried to deal here with the corrected version! Even that produces 37 lines of computations on the Schedule D tax worksheet, which most taxpayers and many professionals can only follow by rote with little sense of the significance of or reasons for what they are doing.

It has now been predicted by some that simplification would be too complicated for anyone to understand! And there is something of an attitude of: Who cares anymore? Few taxpayers with capital gains do their own returns, and perhaps most of those who do use computer software that does these computations in uncomplaining silence.

Is this a desirable state of affairs?

B.   THE QUEST FOR A CONCEPT

1.   Sale of a Business

WILLIAMS v. McGOWAN
152 F.2d 570 (2d Cir. 1945)

Before L. Hand, Swan, and Frank, Circuit Judges.

L. HAND, Circuit Judge. Williams, the taxpayer, and one, Reynolds, had for many years been engaged in the hardware business in the City of Corning, New York. On the 20th of January, 1926, they formed a partnership, of which Williams was entitled to two-thirds of the profits, and Reynolds, one-third. They agreed that on February 1, 1925, the capital invested in the business had been $118,082.05, of which Reynolds had a credit of $29,029.03, and Williams, the balance [of] $89,053.02. At the end of every business year, on February 1st, Reynolds was to pay to Williams, interest upon the amount of the difference between his share of the capital and one-third of the total as shown by the inventory; and upon withdrawal of one partner the other was to have the privilege of buying the other's interest as it appeared on the books. The business was carried on through the firm's fiscal year, ending January 31, 1940, in accordance with this agreement, and thereafter until Reynolds' death on July 18th of that year. Williams settled with Reynolds' executrix on September 6th in an agreement by which he promised to pay her $12,187.98, and to assume all liabilities of the business; and he did pay her $2,187.98 in cash at once, and $10,000 on the 10th of the following October. On September 17th of the same year, Williams sold the business as a whole to the Corning Building Company for $63,926.28 — its agreed value as of February 1, 1940 — "plus an amount to be computed by multiplying the gross sales of the business from the first day of February, 1940 to the 28th day of September, 1940," by an agreed fraction. This value was made up of cash of about $8,100, receivables of about $7,000, fixtures of about $800, and a merchandise inventory of about $49,000, less some $1,000 for bills payable. To this was added about $6,000 credited to Williams for profits under the language just quoted, making a total of nearly $70,000. Upon this sale Williams suffered a loss upon his original two-thirds of the business, but he made a small gain upon the one-third which he had bought from Reynolds' executrix; and in his income tax return he entered both as items of "ordinary income," and not as transactions in "capital assets." This the Commissioner disallowed and recomputed the tax accordingly; Williams paid the deficiency and sued to recover it in this action. The only question is whether the business was "capital assets" under §117(a)(1) of the Internal Revenue Code, 26 U.S.C.A. Int. Rev. Code, §117(a)(1).

It has been held that a partner's interest in a going firm is for tax purposes to be regarded as a "capital asset." Stilgenbaur v. United States, 9 Cir., 115 F.2d 283; Commissioner v. Shapiro, 6 Cir., 125 F.2d 532, 144 A.L.R. 349. We too accepted the doctrine in McClellan v. Commissioner, 2 Cir., 90 F.2d 988, although we had held the opposite in Helvering v. Smith, 2 Cir., 90 F.2d 590, 591, where the partnership articles had provided that a retiring partner should receive as his share only his percentage of the sums "actually collected" and "of all earnings . . . for services performed." Such a payment, we thought, was income; and we expressly repudiated the notion that the Uniform Partnership Act had, generally speaking, changed the firm into a juristic entity. See also Doyle v. Commissioner, 4 Cir., 102 F.2d 86. If a partner's interest is the same. New York Partnership Law §§61, 62(4), Consol. Laws N.Y. c.39. We need not say. When Williams bought out Reynolds' interest, he became the sole owner of the business, the firm had ended upon any theory, and the situation for tax purposes was no other than if Reynolds had never been a partner at all, except that to the extent of one-third of the "amount realized" on Williams' sale to the Corning Company, his "basis" was different. The judge thought that, because upon that sale both parties fixed the price at the liquidation value of the business while Reynolds was alive, "plus" its estimated earnings thereafter, it was as though Williams had sold his interest in the firm during its existence. But the method by which the parties agreed upon the price was irrelevant to the computation of Williams' income. The Treasury, if that served its interest, need not heed any fiction which the parties found it convenient to adopt; nor need Williams do the same in his dealings with the Treasury. We have to decide only whether upon the sale of a going business it is to be comminuted into fragments, and these are to be separately matched against the definition in §117(a)(1), or whether the whole business is to be treated as if it were a single piece of property.

Our law has been sparing in the creation of juristic entities; it has never, for example, taken over the Roman "universitas facti";[1] and indeed for many years it fumbled uncertainly with the concept of a corporation.[2] One might

---

1. "By universitas facti is meant a number of things of the same kind which are regarded as a whole; e.g., a herd, a stock of wares." Mackeldey, Roman Law §162.

2. "To the 'church' modern law owes its conception of a juristic person, and the clear line that it draws between 'the corporation aggregate' and the sum of its members." Pollack & Maitland, Vol. 1, p. 489.

have supposed that partnership would have been an especially promising field in which to raise up an entity, particularly since merchants have always kept their accounts upon that basis. Yet there too our law resisted at the price of great and continuing confusion; and, even when it might be thought that a statute admitted, if it did not demand, recognition of the firm as an entity, the old concepts prevailed. Francis v. McNeal, 228 U.S. 695. And so, even though we might agree that under the influence of the Uniform Partnership Act a partner's interest in the firm should be treated as indivisible, and for that reason a "capital asset" within §117(a)(1), we should be chary about extending further so exotic a jural concept. Be that as it may, in this instance the section itself furnishes the answer. It starts in the broadest way by declaring that all "property" is "capital assets," and then makes three exceptions. The first is "stock in trade . . . or other property of a kind which would properly be included in the inventory"; next comes "property held . . . primarily for sale to customers"; and finally, property "used in the trade or business of a character which is subject to . . . allowance for depreciation." In the face of this language, although it may be true that a "stock in trade," taken by itself, should be treated as a "universitas facti," by no possibility can a whole business be so treated; and the same is true as to any property within the other exceptions. Congress plainly did mean to comminute the elements of a business; plainly it did not regard the whole as "capital assets."

As has already appeared, Williams transferred to the Corning Company "cash," "receivables," "fixtures" and a "merchandise inventory." "Fixtures" are not capital because they are subject to a depreciation allowance; the inventory, as we have just seen, is expressly excluded. So far as appears, no allowance was made for "good-will"; but, even if there had been, we held in Haberle Crystal Springs Brewing Company v. Clarke, Collector, 2 Cir., 30 F.2d 219, that "good-will" was a depreciable intangible. It is true that the Supreme Court reversed that judgment — 280 U.S. 384 — but it based its decision only upon the fact that there could be no allowance for the depreciation of "good-will" in a brewery, a business condemned by the Eighteenth Amendment. There can of course be no gain or loss in the transfer of cash; and, although Williams does appear to have made a gain of $1,072.71 upon the "receivables," the point has not been argued that they are not subject to a depreciation allowance. That we leave open for decision by the district court, if the parties cannot agree. The gain or loss upon every other item should be computed as an item in ordinary income.

Judgment reversed.

FRANK, Circuit Judge (dissenting in part). I agree that it is irrelevant that the business was once owned by a partnership. For when the sale to the Corning Company occurred, the partnership was dead, had become merely a memory, a ghost. To say that the sale was of the partnership's assets would, then, be to indulge in animism.

But I do not agree that we should ignore what the parties to the sale, Williams and the Corning Company, actually did. They did not arrange for a transfer to the buyer, as if in separate bundles, of the several ingredients of the business. They contracted for the sale of the entire business as a going concern. Here is what they said in their agreement:

> The party of the first part agrees to sell and the party of the second part agrees to buy, *all of the right, title and interest* of the said party of the first part *in and to the hardware business* now being conducted by the said party of the first part, *including* cash on hand and on deposit in the First National Bank & Trust Company of Corning in the A. F. Williams Hardware Store account, in accounts receivable, bills receivable, notes receivable, merchandise and fixtures, including two G.M. trucks, good will and all other assets of every kind and description used in and about said business.[3] . . . Said party of the first part agrees not to engage in the hardware business within a radius of twenty-five miles from the City of Corning, New York, for a period of ten years from the 1st day of October 1940.

To carve up this transaction into distinct sales — of cash, receivables, fixtures, trucks, merchandise, and good will — is to do violence to the realities. I do not think Congress intended any such artificial result. In the Senate Committee Report on the 1942 amendment to §117, it was said:

> It is believed that this Senate amendment will be of material benefit to businesses which, due to depressed conditions, have been compelled to dispose of their plant or equipment at a loss. The bill defines property used in a trade or business as property used in the trade or business of a character which is subject to the allowance for depreciation, and real property held for more than six months which is not properly includible in the inventory of the taxpayer if on hand at the close of the taxable year or property held by the taxpayer primarily for sale to customers in the ordinary course of his trade or business. If a newspaper purchased the plant and equipment of a rival newspaper and later sold such plant and equipment at a loss, such plant and equipment, being subject to depreciation, would constitute property used in the trade or business within the meaning of this section.

These remarks show that what Congress contemplated was not the sale of a going business but of its dismembered parts. Where a business is sold as a unit, the whole is greater than its parts. Businessmen so recognize; so too, I think, did Congress. Interpretation of our complicated tax statutes is seldom aided by saying that taxation is an eminently practical matter (or the like). But this is one instance where, it seems to me, the practical aspects of the matter should guide our guess as to what Congress meant. I believe Congress had those aspects in mind and was not thinking of the nice distinctions between Roman and Anglo-American legal theories about legal entities.

---

3. Emphasis added — Eds.

Notes

1. (a) Is this decision sound? Is it implicit in the capital gain definition that the sale of a business should be comminuted into a sale of separate assets? Or could the definition be read to show an intent only to except sales in the ordinary course of business? Cf. Corn Products Refining Co. v. Commissioner, Chapter 20B below.

(b) Is it useful in answering the problem in this case to refer to the failure of the common law to take over the Roman *universitas facti*?

(c) How far will the idea of comminution of sale proceeds go? What about the sale of land with growing crops on it? Should a portion of the sale price be allocated to the crops and taxed as ordinary income? In Watson v. Commissioner, 345 U.S. 544 (1953) the Supreme Court so held as to a crop of oranges, citing and approving *Williams*. The Congress responded with §§1231(b)(4) and 268.

2. *Present statutory provisions.* The applicable statutory provisions are now somewhat different from those in force at the time *Williams* was decided. Today §1231 regrants quasi-capital asset status to depreciable property, but subject to the prior application of §§1245 and 1250. Furthermore, goodwill came to be held nondepreciable, and therefore a pure capital asset, until enactment of §197. On the other hand, §1221(4) excludes accounts receivable from capital asset status.

3. *Sale of a corporate business or partnership interest.* The sale of a corporate business will be subject to the rule in *Williams* if the corporation makes the sale and remains in existence thereafter. On the other hand, if the sale is accomplished by shareholders selling their shares, there may be no tax on the corporation and shareholders' gain will usually be taxed at capital gain rates without comminution. Are these results inconsistent with *Williams*?

Sale of a partnership interest is now governed by §§741 and 751.

4. *Allocation of sale proceeds.* The allocation of sale proceeds required by the rule in *Williams* has been a longstanding source of controversy. The old rule was simple to state: total price paid is to be allocated among assets in proportion to their fair market values. But not all fair market value determinations are equally firm or accurate. So now we have a system of allocating successively to the following classes of assets:

Class I—cash and general deposit accounts (but not certificates of deposit);

Class II—certificates of deposit, foreign currency, and actively traded personal property (including government securities and publicly traded stock);

Class III—other debt instruments, and financial positions that the taxpayer marks to market for federal tax purposes (that is, the taxpayer accounts annually for unrealized changes in value);

Class IV — stock in trade, inventory, or property held primarily for sale to
   customers in the ordinary course of the taxpayer's trade or business;
Class V — any property that does not fit into one of the other six classes;
Class VI — §197 intangibles other than goodwill and going concern
   value; and
Class VII — goodwill and going concern value.

Allocations go proportionately up to fair market value in each class in
turn until Class VII; the amount allocated to goodwill and going concern
value is the excess of total basis over fair market value of assets in Classes I
through VI. This method is sometimes referred to as *residual valuation of
goodwill or going concern value.* See §§1060 and 338(b)(5); Reg. §§1.1060-
1(c)(2); 1.338-6(b).

The purchaser also is concerned about allocation of the purchase price
among assets acquired. The buyer's interest is frequently but not always
adverse to that of the seller. For example, the purchaser will often prefer
a greater allocation to inventory, since inventory costs can be recovered
relatively fast, while the seller, under *Williams,* will want a smaller allocation
to inventory because inventory profits are taxable as ordinary income.

Would it be advisable to try to fix the allocation of price among items
sold in the sale contract? Why? When? How? Would the government be
bound by any such contractual allocation? Would the taxpayers be
bound? Look at the last sentence in §1060(a).

2. A Temporary Taking

COMMISSIONER v. GILLETTE MOTOR TRANSPORT, INC.
364 U.S. 130 (1960)

Mr. Justice HARLAN delivered the opinion of the Court. The question in
this case is whether a sum received by respondent from the United States as
compensation for the temporary taking by the Government of its business
facilities during World War II represented ordinary income or a capital gain.
The issue involves the construction and application of §117(j) of the Internal
Revenue Code of 1939.

In 1944, respondent was a common carrier of commodities by motor
vehicle. On August 4, 1944, respondent's drivers struck, and it completely
ceased to operate. Shortly thereafter, because of the need for respondent's
facilities in the transportation of war materiel, the President ordered the
Director of the Office of Defense Transportation to "take possession and
assume control of" them. The Director assumed possession and control as of
August 12, and appointed a Federal Manager, who ordered respondent to
resume normal operations. The Federal Manager also announced his intention to leave title to the properties in respondent and to interfere as little as

possible in the management of them. Subject to certain orders given by the Federal Manager from time to time, respondent resumed normal operations and continued so to function until the termination of all possession and control by the Government on June 16, 1945.

Pursuant to an Act of Congress creating a Motor Carrier Claims Commission, 62 Stat. 1222, respondent presented its claim for just compensation. The Government contended that there had been no "taking" of respondent's property but only a regulation of it. The Commission, however, determined that by assuming actual possession and control of respondent's facilities, the United States had deprived respondent of the valuable right to determine freely what use was to be made of them. In ascertaining the fair market value of that right, the Commission found that one use to which respondent's facilities could have been put was to rent them out, and that therefore their rental value represented a fair measure of respondent's pecuniary loss. The Commission noted that in other cases of temporary takings, it has typically been held that the market value of what is taken is the sum which would be arrived at by a willing lessor and a willing lessee. Accordingly, it awarded, and the respondent received in 1952, the sum of $122,926.21, representing the fair rental value of its facilities from August 12, 1944, until June 16, 1945, plus $34,917.78, representing interest on the former sum, or a total of $157,843.99.

The Commissioner of Internal Revenue asserted that the total compensation award represented ordinary income to respondent in 1952. Respondent contended that it constituted an amount received upon an "involuntary conversion" of property used in its trade or business and was therefore taxable as long-term capital gain pursuant to §117(j) of the Internal Revenue Code of 1939. . . .

Respondent stresses that the Motor Carrier Claims Commission, rejecting the Government's contention that only a regulation, rather than a taking, of its facilities had occurred, found that respondent had been deprived of *property*, and awarded compensation therefor. That is indeed true. But the fact that something taken by the Government is property compensable under the Fifth Amendment does not answer the entirely different question whether that thing comes within the capital gains provisions of the Internal Revenue Code. Rather, it is necessary to determine the precise nature of the property taken. Here the Commission determined that what respondent had been deprived of, and what the Government was obligated to pay for, was the right to determine freely what use to make of its transportation facilities. The measure of compensation adopted reflected the nature of that property right. Given these facts, we turn to the statute.

Section 117(j), under which respondent claims, is an integral part of the statute's comprehensive treatment of capital gains and losses. Long-established principles govern the application of the more favorable tax rates to long-term capital gains: (1) There must be first, a "capital asset," and second, a "sale or exchange" of that asset (§117(a)); (2) "capital asset" is defined as "property held by the taxpayer," with certain exceptions not here relevant (§117(a) (1)); and (3) for purposes of calculating gain, the cost or other basis of the property (§113(b)) must be subtracted from the amount realized on the sale or exchange (§111(a)).

Section 117(j), added by the Revenue Act of 1942, effects no change in the nature of a capital asset. It accomplishes only two main objectives. First, it extends capital gains treatment to real and depreciable personal property used in the trade or business, the type of property involved in this case. Second, it accords such treatment to involuntary conversions of both capital assets, strictly defined, and property used in the trade or business. Since the net effect of the first change is merely to remove one of the exclusions made to the definition of capital assets in §117(a)(1), it seems evident that "property used in the trade or business," to be eligible for capital-gains treatment, must satisfy the same general criteria as govern the definition of capital assets. The second change was apparently required by the fact that this Court had given a narrow construction to the term "sale or exchange." See Helvering v. Flaccus Leather Co., 313 U.S. 247. But that change similarly had no effect on the basic notion of what constitutes a capital asset.

While a capital asset is defined in §117(a)(1) as "property held by the taxpayer," it is evident that not everything which can be called property in the ordinary sense and which is outside the statutory exclusions qualifies as a capital asset. This Court has long held that the term "capital asset" is to be construed narrowly in accordance with the purpose of Congress to afford capital-gains treatment only in situations typically involving the realization of appreciation in value accrued over a substantial period of time, and thus to ameliorate the hardship of taxation of the entire gain in one year. Burnet v. Harmel, 287 U.S. 103, 106. Thus the Court has held that an unexpired lease, Hort v. Commissioner [Chapter 21A below], corn futures, Corn Products Co. v. Commissioner [Chapter 20B below], and oil payment rights, Commissioner v. P. G. Lake, Inc. [Chapter 21A below], are not capital assets even though they are concededly "property" interests in the ordinary sense. And see Surrey, Definitional Problems in Capital Gains Taxation, 69 Harv. L. Rev. 985, 987-989 and Note 7.

In the present case, respondent's right to use its transportation facilities was held to be a valuable property right compensable under the requirements of the Fifth Amendment. However, that right was not a capital asset within the meaning of §§117(a)(1) and 117(j). To be sure, respondent's facilities were themselves property embraceable as capital assets under §117(j). Had the Government taken a fee in those facilities, or damaged them physically beyond the ordinary wear and tear incident to normal use, the resulting compensation would no doubt have been treated as gain from the involuntary conversion of capital assets. See, e.g., *Waggoner*, 15 T.C. 496; *Henshaw*, 23 T.C. 176. But here the Government took only the right to determine the use to which those facilities were to be put.

That right is not something in which respondent had any investment, separate and apart from its investment in the physical assets themselves. Respondent suggests no method by which a cost basis could be assigned to the right; yet it is necessary, in determining the amount of gain realized for purposes of §117, to deduct the basis of the property sold, exchanged, or involuntarily converted from the amount received. §111(a). Further, the right is manifestly not of the type which gives rise to the hardship of the realization in one year of an advance in value over cost built up in several years, which is what Congress sought to ameliorate by the capital-gains provisions. . . . In short, the right to use is not a capital asset, but is simply an incident of the underlying physical property, the recompense for which is commonly regarded as rent. That is precisely the situation here, and the fact that the transaction was involuntary on respondent's part does not change the nature of the case.

Respondent lays stress on the use of the terms "seizure" and "requisition" in §117(j). More specifically, the section refers to the "involuntary conversion (as a result of destruction in whole or in part, theft or seizure, or an exercise of the power of requisition or condemnation or the threat or imminence thereof) *of property used in the trade or business and capital assets.* . . ." (Emphasis added.) It is contended that the Government's action in the present case is perhaps the most typical example of a seizure or requisition, and that, therefore, Congress must have intended to treat it as a capital transaction. This argument, however, overlooks the fact that the seizure or requisition must be "of property used in the trade or business [or] capital assets." We have already shown that §117(j) does not change the long-standing meaning of those terms and that the property taken by the Government in the present case does not come within them. The words "seizure" and "requisition" are not thereby deprived of effect, since they equally cover instances in which the Government takes a fee or damages or otherwise impairs the value of physical property.

We conclude that the amount paid to respondent as the fair rental value of its facilities from August 12, 1944, to June 16, 1945, represented ordinary income to it. A fortiori, the interest on that sum is ordinary income. Kieselbach v. Commissioner, 317 U.S. 399.

Reversed.

Mr. Justice DOUGLAS dissents.

Notes

1. *The nature of a capital asset.* Note carefully what the Court says about §117(j) (now §1231): that it "effects no change in the nature of a capital asset." What does that mean?

2. *The nature of a capital conversion.* Note also the Court's description of the "statute's comprehensive treatment of capital gains and losses,"

beginning with the proposition that "there must be first, a 'capital asset,' and second, a 'sale or exchange' of that asset." As the Court indicates, "sale or exchange" was once given a narrow reading, excluding involuntary conversions along with various other dispositive transactions; part of the purpose of §1231 is to alter that result, at least on the gain side. This case is typical of more recent cases in shifting the focus of inquiry from the "sale or exchange" requirement to the "capital asset" requirement.

But is the shift overdone? The Court says the temporary use of the taxpayer's facilities is not a capital asset, but the taxpayer's argument was that the facilities themselves were subjected to "seizure" or "requisition." The response to that is that the facilities themselves were seized only temporarily, not "converted"; while §1231 makes it clear that capital gain treatment is not restricted to voluntary sales and exchanges, the statute requires some change of circumstances answering to the idea of a conversion or liquidation of an investment. Just as §1231 effects no change in the nature of a capital asset, it also effects no change in the fundamental nature of the sale or exchange requirement.

Would it be better if the requirements of "capital asset" and "sale or exchange" (and their respective statutory transformations) were not stated separately? Would it be possible and preferable to take whole the expression "sale or exchange of a capital asset" (transformed in this case by §1231 to the expression "involuntary conversion . . . of . . . property used in the trade or business, of a character which is subject to the allowance for depreciation") and then inquire whether there is a transaction that answers to the description? Might the Court have said that §1231 effects no change in the nature of a capital conversion, meaning that the underlying invariant is not in either "capital asset" or "sale and exchange" but in the nature of the transaction in which they are melded?

3. *Purpose.* Note carefully and critically the Court's identification of "the purpose of Congress to afford capital-gains treatment only in situations typically involving the realization of appreciation in value accrued over a substantial period of time, and thus to ameliorate the hardship of taxation of the entire gain in one year." This is a widely accepted statement of the reason for capital gain treatment. In what ways is it an inadequate rationale for the present statutory treatment? Can you offer a better rationale?

3. Discounted Notes and Bonds

UNITED STATES v. MIDLAND-ROSS CORP.
381 U.S. 54 (1965)

Mr. Justice BRENNAN delivered the opinion of the Court. The question for decision is whether, under the Internal Revenue Code of 1939, certain gains realized by the taxpayer are taxable as capital gains or as ordinary income. The taxpayer bought noninterest-bearing promissory notes from the issuers at prices discounted below the face amounts. With one exception, each of the notes was held for more than six months, and, before maturity and in the year of purchase, was sold for less than its face amount but more than its issue price.[1] It is conceded that the gain in each case was the economic equivalent of interest for the use of the money to the date of sale but the taxpayer reported the gains as capital gains. The Commissioner of Internal Revenue determined that the gains attributable to original issue discount were but interest in another form and therefore were taxable as ordinary income. . . .

The more favorable capital gains treatment applied only to gain on "the sale or exchange of a capital asset." §117(a)(4). Although original issue discount becomes property when the obligation falls due or is liquidated prior to maturity and §117(a)(1) defined a capital asset as "property held by the taxpayer," we have held that

> not everything which can be called property in the ordinary sense and which is outside the statutory exclusions qualifies as a capital asset. This Court has long held that the term "capital asset" is to be construed narrowly in accordance with the purpose of Congress to afford capital-gains treatment only in situations typically involving the realization of appreciation in value accrued over a substantial period of time, and thus to ameliorate the hardship of taxation of the entire gain in one year. Commissioner v. Gillette Motor Co., 364 U.S. 130, 134. See also Corn Products Co. v. Commissioner, 350 U.S. 46, 52.

In applying this principle, this Court has consistently construed "capital asset" to exclude property representing income items or accretions to the value of a capital asset themselves properly attributable to income. Thus the Court has held that "capital asset" does not include compensation awarded a taxpayer as representing the fair rental value of its facilities during the period of their operation under government control. Commissioner v. Gillette Motor Co., supra; the amount of the proceeds of the sale of an orange grove attributable to the value of an unmatured annual crop, Watson v. Commissioner, 345 U.S. 544; an unexpired lease, Hort v. Commissioner [Chapter 21A below]; and oil payment rights, Commissioner v. P. G. Lake, Inc. [Chapter 21A below]. Similarly, earned original issue discount cannot be regarded as "typically involving the realization of appreciation in value accrued over a substantial period of time . . . [given capital gains treatment] to ameliorate the hardship of taxation of the entire gain in one year."

---

1. The original plaintiff, Industrial Rayon Corporation, was merged into respondent Midland-Ross Corporation in 1961. During 1952, 1953, and 1954, Industrial's idle funds were used to purchase 13 noninterest-bearing notes, varying in face amount from $500,000 to $2,000,000, from General Motors Acceptance Corporation, Commercial Investment Trust Company and Commercial Credit Company. The original issue discount in most instances was calculated to yield the equivalent of 2% to 2½% on an annual basis if the note were held to maturity, and the gains on sale approximated the discount earned to date. It is not contended that any part of the gain was attributable to market fluctuations as opposed to the passage of time.

Earned original issue discount serves the same function as stated interest, concededly ordinary income and not a capital asset; it is simply "compensation for the use or forbearance of money." Deputy v. du Pont, 308 U.S. 488, 498; cf. Lubin v. Commissioner, 335 F.2d 209 (C.A. 2d Cir.). Unlike the typical case of capital appreciation, the earning of discount to maturity is predictable and measurable, and is "essentially a substitute for . . . payments which §22(a) expressly characterizes as gross income [; thus] it must be regarded as ordinary income, and it is immaterial that for some purposes the contract creating the right to such payments may be treated as 'property' or 'capital.' " Hort v. Commissioner, supra, at 31. The $6 earned on a one-year note for $106 issued for $100 is precisely like the $6 earned on a one-year loan of $100 at 6% stated interest. The application of general principles would indicate, therefore, that earned original issue discount, like stated interest, should be taxed under §22(a) as ordinary income.[4]

The taxpayer argues, however, that administrative practice and congressional treatment of original issue discount under the 1939 Code establish that such discount is to be accounted for as capital gain when realized. [Former §1232(a)(2)(A) of the Internal Revenue Code of 1954] provides that "upon sale or exchange of . . . evidences of indebtedness issued after December 31, 1954, held by the taxpayer more than 6 months, any gain realized . . . [up to the prorated amount of original issue discount] shall be considered as gain from the sale or exchange of property which is not a capital asset," that is, it is to be taxed at ordinary income rates. From this the taxpayer would infer that Congress understood prior administrative and legislative history as extending capital gains treatment to realized original issue discount. If administrative practice and legislative history before 1954 did in fact ignore economic reality and treat stated interest and original issue discount differently for tax purposes, the taxpayer should prevail. See Hanover Bank v. Commissioner, 369 U.S. 672; Deputy v. du Pont, supra; cf. Helvering v. R.J. Reynolds Tobacco Co., 306 U.S. 110. But the taxpayer must persuade us that this was clearly the case, see Watson v. Commissioner, supra, at 551, and has not done so. . . .

The taxpayer premises . . . part of his argument primarily upon the case of Caulkins v. Commissioner, 1 T.C. 656, acq., 1944 Cum. Bull. 5, aff'd, 144 F.2d 482 (C.A. 6th Cir.), acq. withdrawn, 1955-1 Cum. Bull. 7. The taxpayer there purchased an "Accumulative Installment Certificate" providing for

---

4. Our disposition makes it unnecessary to decide certain questions raised at argument, as to which we intimate no view: (1) Since each note was sold in the year of purchase, we do not reach the question whether an accrual-basis taxpayer is required to report discount earned before the final disposition of an obligation; (2) Since no argument is made that the gain on the sale of each note varied significantly from the portion of the original issue discount earned during the holding period, we do not reach the question of the tax treatment under the 1939 Code of "market discount" arising from post-issue purchases at prices varying from issue price plus a ratable portion of the original issue discount, or the tax treatment of gains properly attributable to fluctuations in the interest rate and market price of obligations as distinguished from the anticipated increase resulting from mere passage of time.

ten annual payments of $1,500 in return for $20,000 at the end of ten years. The certificate provided for gradually increasing cash surrender and loan values. In 1939 the taxpayer received $20,000 as agreed and, relying on the long-term capital gains provisions of the Revenue Act of 1938, c. 289, 52 Stat. 447, reported only half the profit as taxable income. Acting primarily on the theory that the certificate was not in registered form as required by §117(f), the Commissioner sought to treat the increment as interest or as income arising out of a transaction entered into for profit. The Tax Court upheld the taxpayer, finding that the certificate was in registered form within the meaning of §117(f) of the Revenue Act of 1938, a provision identical to §117(f) of the 1939 Code,[11] but its discussion of the capital gains question is at best opaque. The Court of Appeals acknowledged that "the transaction presents no true aspect of capital gain" and that "Congress might well have made the differentiation urged by the Commissioner, since it is difficult to perceive any practical reason for taxing increments of the type involved here differently from ordinary income . . . [as] consideration paid for the use of the amounts paid in. . . ." 144 F.2d, at 484. Nevertheless it construed the words "amounts received by the holder upon . . . retirement" in §117(f) as unsusceptible of partition, and therefore as including the increment attributable to interest, which, with the principal amount, was thus taxable only as capital gain.

Caulkins did not unambiguously establish that original issue discount was itself a "capital asset" entitled to capital gains treatment. It held only that under §117(f) Congress had not provided that the "amount" received on retirement might be broken down into its component parts. This was inconsistent with the view expressed in Williams v. McGowan [Chapter 19B.1 above], and approved by this Court in Watson v. Commissioner, supra, at 552, that "Congress plainly did mean to comminute the elements of a business; plainly it did not regard the whole as 'capital assets.' " 152 F.2d, at 572. The Tax Court has consistently regarded *Caulkins* as having erroneously read §117(f) to preclude differentiation of the sources of proceeds on redemption. Paine v. Commissioner, 23 T.C. 391, 401, reversed on other grounds, 236 F.2d 398 (C.A. 8th Cir.); Stanton v. Commissioner, 34 T.C. 1; see 3B Mertens, The Law of Federal Income Taxation 184-186, 378-381 (Zimet rev.). The Commissioner, in addition to withdrawing his acquiescence in *Caulkins*, has also rejected the interpretation of "amount" under §117(f) as not subject to apportionment under general principles. Rev. Rul. 119, 1953-2 Cum. Bull. 95; Rev. Rul. 55-136, 1955-1 Cum. Bull. 213; Rev. Rul. 56-299, 1956-1 Cum. Bull. 603. To the extent the Tax Court's decision in *Caulkins* rested, as its opinion indicates, on a reading of §117(f) to require more favorable treatment on redemption than on sale, it is clearly at odds with the legislative purpose, which was merely to treat alike redemptions and

11. "*Retirement of Bonds, Etc.*—For the purposes of this chapter, amounts received by the holder upon the retirement of bonds, debentures, notes, or certificates or other evidences of indebtedness issued by any corporation (including those issued by a government or political subdivision thereof), with interest coupons or in registered form, shall be considered as amounts received in exchange therefor."

sales or exchanges of securities in registered form or with coupons attached, and not to extend the class of capital assets. Rev. Rul. 56-299, supra. Such an interpretation, which would not benefit the taxpayer in the sale transactions here involved, may underlie the Tax Court's decision but it has no justification in logic or in the legislative history, and even the taxpayer would reject such a meaning, however well supported by the *Caulkins* acquiescence. Finally, notwithstanding the acquiescence, what little other administrative practice we are referred to seems contrary to *Caulkins.* See I.T. 1684, II-1 Cum. Bull. 60 (1923).

The concept of discount or premium as altering the effective rate of interest is not to be rejected as an "esoteric concept derived from subtle and theoretic analysis." Old Colony R. Co. v. Commissioner, 284 U.S. 552, 561. For, despite some expressions indicating a contrary view,[13] this Court has often recognized the economic function of discount as interest. In Old Mission Co. v. Helvering, 293 U.S. 289, 290, for example, the Court regarded it as "no longer open to question that amortized bond discount may be deducted in the separate return of a single taxpayer." The radical changes since *Caulkins* in the concept of treatment of accumulated interest under the 1939 Code are consistent with this. For example, accrued bond interest on stated interest bonds sold between interest dates has long been taxable to the seller of the bonds. See I.T. 3175, 1938-1 Cum. Bull. 200. But on "flat" sales of defaulted notes at prices in excess of face amount, with no attribution of interest arrearages in the sale price, the requirement of allocation to treat a portion of the proceeds as ordinary income dates only from 1954. Fisher v. Commissioner, 209 F.2d 513 (C.A. 6th Cir.); see Jaglom v. Commissioner, 303 F.2d 847 (C.A. 2d Cir.). The propriety of such allocation in the present case is even more evident; unlike defaulted bond interest, there is no suggestion that full payment of the original issue discount will not be made at maturity.

For these reasons we hold that earned original issue discount is not entitled to capital gains treatment under the 1939 Code.

Reversed.

Notes

1. This case again illustrates the early narrow construction of "sale or exchange" and the congressional response broadening the term to include other transactions — this time retirement of bonds — that terminate a taxpayer's investment. The statutory provision is now §1271(a)(1).

But it soon appeared that gain realized on the payment of notes or bonds — or indeed on the sale of notes or bonds prior to payment — might

---

13. See, e.g., New York Life Ins. Co. v. Edwards, 271 U.S. 109, 116; Old Colony R. Co. v. Commissioner, supra. Though these bond premium cases are said to be inconsistent with the view taken here, they are equally inconsistent with the treatment of discount to the borrower.

represent interest. The Congress responded with §§1271(c)(2) and 1272. See Chapter 6C.2 above. The early judicial response (for years before §1271(c)(2) was effective) is in *Caulkins*, discussed in *Midland-Ross*. The final (?) judicial response is in *Midland-Ross* itself.

The whole development poses a number of questions. Do §§1271 and 1272 succeed in separating interest income from capital gain? Does *Midland-Ross* exhibit any greater success? How is it different?

Is it possible to define any noninterest element in the gain from investments in debt securities? What is it? Can you suggest any ideal formula for separating interest from other gain? In particular, if an investor buys a bond at a discount because current interest rates are higher than the stated interest on the bond, does it make any difference whether there was an original issue discount? Or does the discount represent interest to him in any event? See §§1276-1278.

2. Suppose *A* buys a 10 percent bond at par. Interest rates rise and the price of the bond drops to $95. *A* sells to *B* at $95. *B* holds the bond until maturity when it is paid in full.

(a) How would *A* be treated under present law? In a perfect world?

(b) How would *B* be treated under present law? In a perfect world?

(c) How would each be treated if interest rates had fallen and *A* had sold to *B* at $105? Read §171.

(d) How would each be treated if *A* had sold to *B* at $45 because the issuing company was in trouble and doubt had arisen whether the bonds would be paid?

(e) Would it be accurate to say that retirement should not be treated differently from sale or exchange, but that neither should be given capital gain treatment at or near maturity? On what ground?

3. *Endowment insurance policies.* A taxpayer holds an endowment insurance policy that is about to mature. The proceeds will exceed his total premium payments. If he holds the policy until payment, the excess will be taxable to him under §72(e) and nothing would provide capital gain treatment. What if the taxpayer sells the endowment policy for slightly less than its face amount shortly prior to maturity? Is the profit then taxable as capital gain? E.g., Commissioner v. Phillips, 275 F.2d 33 (4th Cir. 1960).

4. *Section 61.* The Court says in *Midland-Ross* that "earned original issue discount, like stated interest, should be taxed under [§61(a)] as ordinary income." But aren't capital gains also taxed under §61(a) as "gains derived from dealings in property"? The issue is not one of includibility in gross income but of the availability of the capital gains deduction under §1202. What does §61(a) have to do with that?

5. *Corporate stock.* A taxpayer bought stock in a corporation on original issue at par, which was $100 a share. Several years later she sold at book value, which was $220 a share (earned surplus amounting now to $120 a share). Does *Midland-Ross* provide any basis for comminuting the sale proceeds into $100 for the original investment and $120 for the surplus and taxing the latter as ordinary income? Why not?

4.   Purchased Remainder Interests

JONES v. COMMISSIONER
330 F.2d 302 (3d Cir. 1964)

Before McLaughlin and Forman, Circuit Judges, and Leahy, District Judge.

PER CURIAM. Taxpayer, inter alia, purchases remainder interests in trusts. In the two interests before us in this review, as is his practice, after the deaths of the life tenants but prior to the distribution of the estate remainders of the trusts, he transferred his interests therein. His motivation is to obtain capital gains treatment for income tax purposes. The Tax Court held that the taxpayer could not transmute gain which would be ordinary income to him into capital gain by the device of a sale, notwithstanding that the sale was the bona fide sale of a capital asset. The Commissioner argues for the sustaining of the decision on the theory that the taxpayer's gain upon the sales of the remainders represents an increase in value attributable to interest income, in the form of an interest discount in his original purchase price for the remainders. We are impressed with this and in connection therewith consider it necessary to remand the case to the Tax Court for further proceedings to determine what part, if any, of the gain received upon the taxpayer's sale of the remainders was in fact the realization of interest discount and, if the latter is established, to make an allocation of the proceeds between its ordinary income and capital gain components.

The decision will be vacated and the case remanded to the Tax Court for further proceedings in line with this opinion.

Question

Donated remainder interests. Why does the problem in this case not arise in the case of remainder interests acquired by gift or devise?

C.   *PROPERTY HELD PRIMARILY FOR SALE TO CUSTOMERS*

CURTIS CO. v. COMMISSIONER
232 F.2d 167 (3d Cir. 1956)

Before Goodrich, McLaughlin and Kalodner, Circuit Judges.

GOODRICH, Circuit Judge. . . . There are two chapters to the taxpayer's story. One has to do with the sale of houses; the other has to do with the sale of unimproved land.

I. SALE OF HOUSES

The house question will be considered first. The taxpayer during the years 1942 through 1944 built 1,098 units of housing for rental purposes. 858 units of these were single family homes; 240 were duplex apartments. Petitioner, prior to this, had bought land, divided it, built houses thereon and sold them. This was an established division of its business and through the years ordinary income tax was paid on the profits resulting. Likewise, ordinary income tax was paid on profits derived from the rental of the houses just described.

In 1946 the restrictions on the prices at which these houses could be sold were removed.[5] Restrictions were still retained upon the price at which the property could be rented, however. The taxpayer decided to sell the houses and put its capital into the development of shopping centers, for rental purposes. It doubted whether the market value of the houses would continue to appreciate. The taxpayer thereupon made efforts to sell the houses. 851 units were sold in its tax year ending in 1947; 2 in 1948; 76 in 1949 and 45 in 1950. A gross profit of $2,829,742.81 was realized in 1947; $8,560.08 in 1948; $638,043.98 in 1949 and $377,626.31 in 1950.

The method adopted by the taxpayer was as follows: Sales were made by taxpayer's own staff. This saved the taxpayer money; its commissions were much less than if it had employed real estate brokers at the established 5 percent commission price. Some advertising was used, more in the case of the single residences than in the case of the duplex apartments. The sales were for cash. No inspection of the properties was permitted. They were all sold in the condition in which they then were; no effort was made to improve their appearance or to make them more saleable. No additional properties of similar nature were bought by the taxpayer nor were any properties not owned by it sold in this fashion. When the rental properties were all sold the rental part of the taxpayer's business was wound up. Upon these facts, is a conclusion justified to the effect that these rental properties which were to be sold were held by the taxpayer primarily for sale to customers in the ordinary course of its trade or business?

We find helpful language used by Judge Tuttle for the court in Goldberg v. Commissioner, 5 Cir., 1955, 223 F.2d 709, 712. The court says:

> (2) In the typical case it is clear that the property owner did not intend to engage in the business of buying and selling real estate when he acquired or developed it, but on the contrary intended only to rent it. At the time he may have been restrained from selling by wartime legislation or the terms of a government loan. But years later, his intention changes or the government restrictions are removed, and he proceeds to sell the property. The test as to whether the capital gain provisions apply in such event is, at bottom, whether the purpose of the sales is primarily making money by carrying on a substantial

---

5. National Housing Agency Regulation 60-17, 10 Fed. Reg. 12762 (1945). These restrictions were imposed when priorities for building materials were obtained.

part of the activities of a person engaged in the business of selling houses, or to dispose of or liquidate the rental business. If the latter is the case, the owner obtains capital gain benefits.

There is no doubt in this particular case that prior to the decision to sell these houses the properties were being held for investment purposes. The Tax Court so states and explicitly says that "up until the decisions to sell its rental houses and apartments, petitioner had [not] done anything which would disqualify these rental units for capital gains treatment under section [1231] upon their sale."

The court, however, did conclude that because of the manner in which the sales were made they were conducted in the ordinary course of business of selling real property. It was expressly pointed out, however, that the court did not rely merely on the large number of sales involved but upon the various actions by the taxpayer.

It was conceded by counsel for the Commissioner at the argument that if the taxpayer had sold all these properties to one buyer at one time there would be no basis for holding that they were sold in the ordinary course of the taxpayer's business. It was also conceded that had taxpayer employed a firm of brokers to sell the properties for it the sales then would not be in the ordinary course of the taxpayer's business.

Is the taxpayer any worse off because it did the selling itself and by single parcels instead of job lots? We do not see how it can be fairly said so. With the concession that up to the very minute of decision to get out of the housing rental business the property was held for investment and with the undisputed fact that after the rental properties were sold the taxpayer turned its attention to other activities, we do not see that there is a basis for saying that the regular course of its business, as to these houses, was real estate selling. We think it a case of one having an investment property on hand which he wants to turn into another form of investment.[8] By the very nature of the case he had to sell the properties a piece at a time. Surely that does not make him a "dealer" in these parcels of land any more than it would make a man a dealer if he wanted to liquidate his holdings in a corporate stock for which the market was weak so that he had to sell by small parcels instead of by one sale. That is the taxpayer's situation here.

There is no dispute as to the evidentiary facts. The only question is whether on these facts the conclusion is supportable that petitioner went ad hoc into the ordinary course of business when it sold these rental properties. We think not.

A legislative attempt to draw a distinction between the tax on capital gain and ordinary income must necessarily produce a puzzling line of

---

8. It is precisely this sort of thing which prompted the passage of the capital gains provisions. Capital gains were taxed at lower rates to relieve the taxpayer from "excessive tax burdens on gains resulting from a conversion of capital investments, and to remove the deterrent effect of those burdens on such conversions." Burnet v. Harmel, 1932, 287 U.S. 103, 106.

decisions for the facts are as variable as human activities. Variations of the fact situation of this case are found in a number of decisions. They indicate some disagreement not unnaturally. We think on the whole the conclusion we reach in this case is in the pattern which the majority of the Courts of Appeals have followed.

II. SALES OF THE UNIMPROVED LAND

Petitioner bought from time to time undeveloped land. With regard to one block of it, he has had the advantage of the capital gains provisions upon its sale. This was a piece of land which was bought for the development of a shopping center but the plan failed because of zoning restrictions which could not be met. The major portion of the land was sold off in two pieces at a profit. The taxpayer had the advantage of the capital gains provisions.

With regard to the other pieces the Commissioner insists that the taxpayer is not entitled to the benefit of the capital gains provisions. There were seventeen pieces held by the taxpayer during the taxable years. The taxpayer made a total of eighteen sales of undeveloped land during this period. Six of them the taxpayer conceded resulted in ordinary income.

Here, too, the evidentiary facts are not in dispute. The question is whether the taxpayer was holding this undeveloped land for sale in the ordinary course of its trade or business. The Tax Court believed the "essential fact seems to be that these properties were acquired for the purpose of re-sale whenever a satisfactory profit could be made . . ." and "primarily for sale to its customers in the ordinary course of its business. . . ."

We do not profess to know precisely what makes one a dealer in undeveloped land. There were, as those things go, quite a number of parcels and the sales were comparatively rapid. There was no such showing of a change in purpose of the taxpayer's activities to induce the sale as we had in the case of the rental properties. We cannot say under these circumstances that the Tax Court was wrong in reaching the conclusion that it did.

The judgment of the Tax Court will be reversed and the case remanded for further proceedings consistent with this opinion.

McLAUGHLIN, Circuit Judge (dissenting). Section [1231] accords capital gain treatment to "property used in the trade or business" unless the property is inventory or "held . . . for sale to customers." The Supreme Court recently in construing this section stated "Since this section is an exception from the normal tax . . . [it] must be narrowly applied and its exclusions interpreted broadly."[1] Our Saltzman v. Commissioner, 3 Cir., 1955, 227 F.2d 49 is very much in point and does, I think, govern here. By any and

1. Corn Products Refining Co. v. Commissioner [Chapter 20B below].

all of the established criteria, i.e. purpose of acquisition, improvements made on the land, number of sales, advertising and selling efforts, the "busyness" test, reinvestment of proceeds, related activities, this income was ordinary profit of the taxpayer's building and real estate business.

Such conclusion has the solid support of the pertinent decisional law. . . . In Goldberg v. Commissioner, 5 Cir., 1955, 223 F.2d 709, 713, "[t]here was absolutely no evidence of any promotional activity . . . ;" there was no advertising; no salesmen; no commissions paid; though price ceilings had been removed, the houses were sold to tenants at the F.H.A. prices; neither the taxpayer nor any of the transferees there had ever before or since been in the business of building and holding houses for sale. . . .

The circumstance that these properties were not readily salable as investment real estate, reflects back on the purpose for which taxpayer built them. An apartment house is typical investment housing. It is salable as such and capital gain results. But suppose it is divided into 1,000 cooperative apartments, should not the "sale to customers" exclusion deny the favored treatment?

The analogy to a trader in securities is inapposite. Trading in securities for one's own account, no matter how extensive, is not a business for tax purposes. Real estate operations, however, are taxable as a business. Higgins v. Commissioner, 1941, 312 U.S. 212. This taxpayer's regular business is buying land, subdividing, building, and selling real estate to consumers or investors. If analogy to the securities field is to be used it is the "underwriter" or "dealer" operation which is comparable to the taxpayer. The "dealer" or "underwriter" may have an investment account and thereby obtain capital gains, but he must conform closely to [§1236] and the regulations thereunder. Even after designation . . . of [the] acquisition as an investment, if the security is thereafter ever held for sale to the firm's customers the favored treatment . . . is lost. A "dealer" cannot buy or underwrite a large block of securities, and, after holding more than six months, sell them piece-meal to his customers and still qualify under [§§1201 et seq.].

In Section 1237 of the Internal Revenue Code of 1954, Congress sharply outlined the sale of realty area. Taxpayer's facts patently would not qualify for favored treatment under that section. And ". . . 'subsequent legislation may be considered to assist in the interpretation of prior legislation upon the same subject.' . . ." Great Northern Railway Co. v. United States, 1942, 315 U.S. 262, 277.

The basis of the majority thesis is that property once "used in a trade or business" retains that character regardless of whether it is subsequently inventoried or held for sale to customers. Section [1231] has not been and cannot be so construed but is the sound source of the well established principle that manner and purpose of holding property may change or be twofold. . . .

In selling the houses taxpayer was engaged in business. It should be so taxed. I would therefore affirm the Tax Court on this point also.

MALAT v. RIDDELL
383 U.S. 569 (1966)

PER CURIAM. Petitioner was a participant in a joint venture which acquired a 45-acre parcel of land the intended use for which is somewhat in dispute. Petitioner contends that the venturers' intention was to develop and operate an apartment project on the land; the respondent's position is that there was a "dual purpose" of developing the property for rental purposes or selling, whichever proved to be the more profitable. In any event, difficulties in obtaining the necessary financing were encountered, and the interior lots of the tract were subdivided and sold. The profit from those sales was reported and taxed as ordinary income.

The joint venturers continued to explore the possibility of commercially developing the remaining exterior parcels. Additional frustrations in the form of zoning restrictions were encountered. These difficulties persuaded petitioner and another of the joint venturers of the desirability of terminating the venture; accordingly, they sold out their interests in the remaining property. Petitioner contends that he is entitled to treat the profits from this last sale as capital gains; the respondent takes the position that this was "property held by the taxpayer primarily for sale to customers in the ordinary course of his trade or business," and thus subject to taxation as ordinary income.

The District Court made the following finding:

> The members of [the joint venture], as of the date the 44.901 acres were acquired, intended either to sell the property or develop it for rental, depending upon which course appeared to be most profitable. The venturers realized that they had made a good purchase price-wise and, if they were unable to obtain acceptable construction financing or rezoning . . . which would be prerequisite to commercial development, they would sell the property in bulk so they wouldn't get hurt. The purpose of either selling or developing the property continued during the period in which [the joint venture] held the property.

The District Court ruled that petitioner had failed to establish that the property was not held *primarily* for sale to customers in the ordinary course of business, and thus rejected petitioner's claim to capital gain treatment for the profits derived from the property's resale. The Court of Appeals affirmed, 347 F.2d 23. We granted certiorari (382 U.S. 900) to resolve a conflict among the courts of appeals[3] with regard to the meaning of the term "primarily" as it is used in §1221(1) of the Internal Revenue Code of 1954.

---

3. Compare Rollingwood Corp. v. Commissioner, 190 F.2d 263, 266 (C.A. 9th Cir.); American Can Co. v. Commissioner, 317 F.2d 604, 605 (C.A. 2d Cir.), with United States v. Bennett, 186 F.2d 407, 410-411 (C.A. 5th Cir.); Municipal Bond Corp. v. Commissioner, 341 F.2d 683, 688-689 (C.A. 8th Cir.). Cf. Recordak Corp. v. United States, 163 Ct. Cl. 294, 300-301, 325 F.2d 460, 463-464.

The statute denies capital gain treatment to profits reaped from the sale of "property held by the taxpayer *primarily* for sale to customers in the ordinary course of his trade or business." (Emphasis added.) The respondent urges upon us a construction of "primarily" as meaning that a purpose may be "primary" if it is a "substantial" one.

As we have often said, "the words of statutes — including revenue acts — should be interpreted where possible in their ordinary, everyday senses." Crane v. Commissioner [Chapter 7D.1 above]. . . . Departure from a literal reading of statutory language may, on occasion, be indicated by relevant internal evidence of the statute itself and necessary in order to effect the legislative purpose. . . . But this is not such an occasion. The purpose of the statutory provision with which we deal is to differentiate between the "profits and losses arising from the everyday operation of a business" on the one hand (Corn Products Co. v. Commissioner) and "the realization of appreciation in value accrued over a substantial period of time" on the other. (Commissioner v. Gillette Motor Co.) A literal reading of the statute is consistent with this legislative purpose. We hold that, as used in §1221(1), "primarily" means "of first importance" or "principally."

Since the courts below applied an incorrect legal standard, we do not consider whether the result would be supportable on the facts of this case had the correct one been applied. We believe, moreover, that the appropriate disposition is to remand the case to the District Court for fresh fact-findings, addressed to the statute as we have now construed it.

Vacated and remanded.

Mr. Justice BLACK would affirm the judgments of the District Court and the Court of Appeals.

Mr. Justice White took no part in the decision of this case.

Notes and Questions

1. *Ambiguities.* Whether property is held primarily for sale to customers in the ordinary course of trade or business is clear enough in lots of cases, but it turns out to bristle with ambiguities on and near the borderline. For example, what constitutes a trade or business? Who are customers? What is to be done about dual purposes, alternative purposes, or conditional purposes? What sort of evidence of purpose is to be entertained and how should it be weighed? When is purpose to be tested? Are there differences in the acceptability of different alternative purposes to show that property is not held primarily for sale to customers? And so forth.

Does *Malat* help with this morass? Or would it be fair to say that *Malat* deals with words instead of the underlying problem? Could the Supreme Court have given more useful guidance in dealing with the problem here? Should it at least have discussed the problem instead of only the verbal formula?

2. *Improved and unimproved realty.* Does *Curtis* indicate that different standards will be applied to improved and unimproved realty? Should different standards be applied? Why? Is it because improved realty presumably yields ordinary income from rent or use, and that capital gain on sale is a reward for paying ordinary income rates on the rent? Or is it just because improvement provides a credible basis for urging some purpose other than sale? Or, put the other way around, is it because unimproved real estate can only yield a return by being sold—putting aside cases of an abandoned original intention to improve—and, therefore, is considered to be held for sale?

3. *Securities.* As intimated in *Curtis,* securities are capital assets even in the hands of a busy trader. A trader is said not to sell "to customers"; only a dealer has customers. See O. L. Burnett, Chapter 14C above.

It is sometimes said that if real estate is held primarily for sale, then any purchaser is a customer, so that the statutory phrase "to customers" is redundant. Is this difference in treatment between securities and real estate justified? How?

Is it persuasive to say that the phrase "to customers" was specifically inserted to limit the deductibility of securities losses during the depression? Are securities more apt to show a loss than are real estate investments? If they were, would that justify a difference in treatment, either under the present statute or as an original proposition?

A securities dealer may be distinguished from a trader on economic grounds as follows: A dealer makes a profit by promoting the largest possible turnover maintaining a spread between bid and asked prices, and seeking to avoid taking significant long and short positions except temporarily. A trader, on the other hand, seeks to profit by taking a long position when the price is rising (and perhaps a short position on falling markets), and thus seeks to capitalize on price changes whose effect the dealer seeks to avoid.

Are there good reasons for distinguishing between dealers and traders this way and giving capital gain and loss treatment to traders? Why are similar distinctions not drawn with respect to real estate?

4. *Other sorts of property.* While real estate has created the most litigation, there have been cases involving other sorts of property. What about a collector's paintings, for example? Or an inherited collection of jewelry which the legatee seeks to dispose of by individual sales? Or an inherited business inventory? Or machines owned by a manufacturer who prefers to lease them, but will sell if asked to? Or moving pictures held first for rental and later sold? And so on and so forth. Are the criteria for classifying real estate adequate for these other sorts of property? Are they any less adequate for these others than for real estate itself?

5. *Special statutory provisions.* Look at §§1236 and 1237, which establish rather special procedures for dealing with little bits of the securities and real estate problems, respectively.

D. REASONS FOR PREFERENTIAL TREATMENT OF CAPITAL GAINS

There is no consensus about the reasons for taxing long-term capital gains at a lower rate than other income, and there is a substantial body of opinion that none of the reasons offered is sufficient to justify the present statutory provisions. It is important, however, to have a critical look at some of the reasons offered.

(a) The most commonly given reason for taxing long-term capital gains at lower rates is to alleviate the burden on a taxpayer whose property has increased in value over a long period of time from having the profits from sales taxed at graduated tax rates designed for a single year's income. Will this reason hold up?

The first difficulty is that long-term capital gain treatment has often been provided for assets held only six months, so that many long-term capital gains occur mostly within a single year. (The current period is one year; it has sometimes been as long as two years.)

A second difficulty is that most capital gains are realized by wealthy taxpayers whose annual income puts them in a rate bracket well over 15 percent year after year, in any event. Indeed, some substantial capital gain taxpayers are probably in or near the top income tax bracket year after year. For them, having a gain fall all in one year cannot cause it to be taxed at a higher rate.

A third difficulty is that for many substantial capital gain taxpayers such gains in fact occur more or less regularly year after year. Indeed, one of the things about securities profits is that a taxpayer may have a good deal of choice as to when to take them, so that he may be more able to prevent bunching of such profits in a single year than in the case of other income items.

The right remedy for the problem of bunching under a scheme of graduated rates is general averaging, letting a taxpayer compute his tax by reference to his income level over several years. Cf. §1301. A general provision for income averaging was repealed in 1986, to make things simple.

(b) A second reason for lower rates is suggested in the language from *Burnet v. Harmel*, 287 U.S. 103, 106 (1932), quoted in footnote 8 of *Curtis Co.*: "Capital gains were taxed at lower rates to relieve the taxpayer from "excessive tax burdens on gains resulting from a conversion of capital investments, and to remove the deterrent effect of those burdens on such conversions." The deterrent effect of tax burdens on capital investment conversions arises from the alternative possibility of deferring the tax for a substantial period by putting off conversion and holding onto the present investment. The Court does not spell out explicitly why a tax at ordinary rates would put an "excessive burden" on capital conversions, but presumably the reason is the same: Such tax burdens are excessive in relation to the complete freedom from tax of unrealized capital appreciation. The capital gains rates would thus be seen as alleviating the discrimination between realized and unrealized gains resulting from nontaxation of the latter.

This purpose provides a reason for allowing capital gains rates on property held less than a year, if the property is of a kind that could be held for a substantial future period in lieu of being sold. It does not require that appreciation have occurred over a long period, but that taxable gain could have been deferred over a substantial future period. Furthermore, this statement of purpose would provide a reason for favorable treatment in cases where capital gains do not in fact put a taxpayer in a higher rate bracket than usual.

But this statement of purpose has its own difficulties. First, some would say that if the problem arises from failure to tax unrealized gain, the solution lies in the direction of correcting that failure, not relieving realized gains of tax.

Second, even if the discrimination between realized and unrealized gains were to be mitigated by reducing the tax burden on the former, relief should be confined to cases that do represent a conversion of capital investments. There is nothing in the present statute requiring reinvestment. Taxpayers can and do live off capital gains just as well as ordinary dividends and interest income.

Finally, as they presently operate, the capital gain provisions sometimes aggravate rather than mitigate the discrimination between realized and unrealized gains. Under what circumstances is this the case? *Macomber* presents one example: The gain deferred in that case would be likely to be taxed ultimately as capital gain on a sale of shares; if the stock dividend were taxable, it would be taxed sooner *and* at higher, ordinary-income rates.

If the purpose is to reduce the burdens on conversions of capital investments, then the statute should have some sort of more general nonrecognition provisions, akin to §§1031 and 1033, under which tax would be deferred rather than reduced.

(c) Another popular justification for capital gain rates has to do with inflation. If a person has invested a dollar of after-tax income in an asset that has grown in value, and later sells the asset, the proceeds should be regarded as tax-paid to the full extent of the real value of his or her original tax-paid investment, undiluted by inflation. In a very rough way, if capital gains were in fact about half due to inflation, the capital gain provisions would serve on average to accomplish this objective. At least, some would say, the capital gain provisions should not be repealed until something else is done about inflation.

This explanation is still, of course, much too rough, even though inflation is a very real problem. The capital gain provisions exempt a share of the realized gain from tax; the more one gains, the more relief one will be granted. There is no very high correlation, however, between the amount of gain one enjoys and the burden of inflation one bears, except insofar as both are functions of wealth and time. For any two taxpayers with similar amounts of wealth held over the same period of time, the burden of inflation will be just as heavy for the one with no gains as for the one with large gains, and if relief is to be provided for the latter it should be provided for the former, too. Justification of the existing capital gain provisions because *on average* they may compensate for inflation is essentially no justification at all, since the essence of justice in taxation is to treat individuals fairly in relation to one another, according to their relevant individual circumstances, without having one taxpayer bear another's share of the burden to make the average come out right.

If inflation is the problem, then the right remedy would be basis adjustments to reflect increases in general price levels for all assets held, say, for more than two years. A basis adjustment would be proportional to original investment, not gain, and would produce a loss for holders of fixed principal securities as well as reducing gains for equity holders. Under this approach some adjustment also should be made to reflect a taxpayer's gain for having debts of significant amount and duration outstanding during a period of inflation.

The Revenue Bill of 1978, as it passed the House of Representatives, had a general indexing provision for property other than debt instruments. The theory was that omission of creditors' inflation losses would compensate for omission of debtors' inflation gains. Is that a sound theory? The provision was dropped in the Senate and not revived.

(d) Capital gain sometimes results from a change in capitalization rates. Consider, for example, the holder of a long-term bond paying 9 percent interest. If general interest rates drop, the value of the bond will go up — but is the holder really any better off than if market interest rates had risen or remained steady? Even if he sells at a gain, he will only be able to reinvest at the new lower interest rate. Insofar as he measures his well being in terms of the level of income he can maintain indefinitely, therefore, the rise in capital value does not represent a substantial change, and full taxation of capital gains would cause a diminution of welfare for those who realize such gains.

(e) The capital gain provisions are sometimes defended just as a desirable incentive for investment; or an offset of some sort to the general disincentive effect of an income tax on saving and productive investment. But such a defense offers no reason for discriminating between capital gains and other investment returns. A more general way of reducing tax burdens on saving and investment would be either to reduce the rate of tax on investment income generally, as compared with personal service income, or to rely more than we do on consumption taxes.

References

B. *The Quest for a Concept:* Miller, The "Capital Asset" Concept: A Critique of Capital Gains Taxation, 59 Yale L.J. 837, 1057 (1950); Surrey, Definitional

Problems in Capital Gains Taxation, 69 Harv. L. Rev. 985 (1956); Note, A Spreading of Receipts Formula For Creating a Capital Gains/Ordinary Income Brightline, 87 Yale L.J. 729 (1978); Note, The Troubled Distinction Between Capital Gain and Ordinary Income, 73 Yale L.J. 693 (1964).

   1. Sale of a Business: Beghe, Income Tax Treatment of Covenants Not to Compete, Consulting Agreements and Transfers of Goodwill, 30 Tax Law. 587 (1977); Stansbury, Advising Clients on Tax Treatment of Goodwill v. Covenant-Not-to-Compete Issue, 45 J. Taxn. 208 (1976).

   C. Property Held Primarily for Sale to Customers: Bernstein, Primarily for Sale: A Semantic Snare, 20 Stan. L. Rev. 1093 (1968).

   D. Reasons for Preferential Treatment of Capital Gains: Blum, A Handy Summary of the Capital Gains Argument, 35 Taxes 247 (1957); Clark, The Paradox of Capital Gains: Taxable Income That Ought Not to Be Currently Taxed, 2 House Comm. on Ways and Means Tax Revision Compendium 1243 (1959); Noël B. Cunninghan & Deborah H. Schenck, The Case for a Capital Gains Preference, 48 Tax L. Rev. 319 (1993) (with commentary by Daniel Halperin and Daniel N. Shaviro); McDonald, Inflation: Concepts of Income, Tax Reform, 28 Tax Law. 533 (1975); Popkin, The Deep Structure of Capital Gain, 33 Case W. Res. L. Rev. 153 (1983); Robert H. Scarborough, Risk, Diversification and the Design of Loss Limitations Under a Realization-Based Income Tax, 48 Tax L. Rev. 677 (1993) (with commentary by Calvin H. Johnson); Reed Shuldiner, Indexing the Tax Code, 48 Tax L. Rev. 537 (1993) (with commentary by Charles O. Galvin and Lewis R. Steinberg); Surrey, Definitional Problems in Capital Gains Taxation, 69 Harv. L. Rev. 985 (1956); George R. Zodrow, Economic Analyses of Capital Gains Taxation: Realizations, Revenues, Efficiency and Equity, 48 Tax L. Rev. 419 (1993) (with commentary by Alan J. Auerbach and David F. Bradford); Note, Inflation and the Federal Income Tax, 82 Yale L.J. 716 (1973).

Chapter 20 — *Capital Losses*

Review or read Chapter 14C. Reconsider critically the relationship between the capital loss limitation and the favorable treatment of capital gains. To what extent is either required or justified by the other? Do the materials in this chapter have a bearing on that question?

A. *THE ARROWSMITH DOCTRINE*

ARROWSMITH v. COMMISSIONER
344 U.S. 6 (1952)

Mr. Justice BLACK delivered the opinion of the Court. . . . In 1937 two taxpayers, petitioners here, decided to liquidate and divide the proceeds of a corporation in which they had equal stock ownership. Partial distributions made in 1937, 1938, and 1939 were followed by a final one in 1940. Petitioners reported the profits obtained from this transaction, classifying them as capital gains. They thereby paid less income tax than would have been required had the income been attributed to ordinary business transactions for profit. About the propriety of these 1937-1940 returns, there is no dispute. But in 1944 a judgment was rendered against the old corporation and against Frederick R. Bauer, individually. The two taxpayers were required to and did pay the judgment for the corporation, of whose assets they were transferees. . . . Classifying the loss as an ordinary business one, each took a tax deduction for 100 percent of the amount paid. Treatment of the loss as a capital one would have allowed deduction of a much smaller amount. . . .

[Section 165(f)] treats losses from sales or exchanges of capital assets as "capital losses" and I.R.C. [§331] requires that liquidation distributions be treated as exchanges. The losses here fall squarely within the definition of "capital losses" contained in these sections. Taxpayers were required to pay the judgment because of liability imposed on them as transferees of liquidation distribution assets. And it is plain that their liability as transferees was not based on any ordinary business transaction of theirs apart from the liquidation proceedings. It is not even denied that had this judgment been paid after liquidation, but during the year 1940, the losses would have been properly treated as capital ones. For payment during 1940 would simply have reduced the amount of capital gains taxpayers received during that year.

It is contended, however, that this payment which would have been a capital transaction in 1940 was transformed into an ordinary business transaction in 1944 because of the well-established principle that each taxable year is a separate unit for tax accounting purposes. . . . But this principle is not breached by considering all the 1937-1944 liquidation transaction events in order properly to classify the nature of the 1944 loss for tax purposes. Such an examination is not an attempt to reopen and readjust the 1937 to 1940 tax returns, an action that would be inconsistent with the annual tax accounting principle.

The petitioner Bauer's executor presents an argument for reversal which applies to Bauer alone. He was liable not only by reason of being a transferee of the corporate assets. He was also held liable jointly with the original corporation, on findings that he had secretly profited because of a breach of his fiduciary relationship to the judgment creditor. . . . The judgment was against both Bauer and the corporation. For this reason it is contended that the nature of Bauer's tax deduction should be considered on the basis of his liability as an individual who sustained a loss in an ordinary business transaction for profit. We agree with the Court of Appeals that this contention should not be sustained. While there was a liability against him in both capacities, the individual judgment against him was for the whole amount. His payment of only half the judgment indicates that both he and the other transferee were paying in their capacities as such. We see no reason for giving Bauer a preferred tax position.

Affirmed.

Mr. Justice DOUGLAS, dissenting. I agree with Mr. Justice JACKSON that these losses should be treated as ordinary, not capital, losses. There were no capital transactions in the year in which the losses were suffered. Those transactions occurred and were accounted for in earlier years in accord with the established principle that each year is a separate unit for tax accounting purposes. See United States v. Lewis [Chapter 7B above]. I have not felt, as my dissent in the *Lewis* case indicates, that the law made that an inexorable principle. But if it is the law, we should require observance of it — not merely by taxpayers but by the government as well. We should force each year to stand on its own footing, whoever may gain or lose from it in a particular case. We impeach that principle when we treat this year's losses as if they diminished last year's gains.

Mr. Justice JACKSON, whom Mr. Justice FRANKFURTER joins, dissenting. This problem arises only because the judgment was rendered in a taxable year subsequent to the liquidation.

Had the liability of the transferor-corporation been reduced to judgment during the taxable year in which liquidation occurred, or prior thereto, this problem, under the tax laws, would not arise. The amount of the judgment rendered against the corporation would have decreased the amount it had available for distribution which would have reduced the liquidating dividends proportionately and diminished the capital gains taxes assessed against the stockholders. Probably it would also have decreased the corporation's own taxable income.

Congress might have allowed, under such circumstances, tax returns of the prior year to be reopened or readjusted so as to give the same tax results as would have obtained had the liability become known prior to liquidation. Such a solution is foreclosed to us and the alternatives left are to regard the judgment liability fastened by operation of law on the transferee as an ordinary loss for the year of adjudication or to regard it as a capital loss for such year.

This Court simplifies the choice to one of reading the English language, and declares that the losses here come "squarely within" the definition of capital losses contained within two sections of the Internal Revenue Code. What seems so clear to this Court was not seen at all by the Tax Court, in this case or in earlier consideration of the same issue; nor was it grasped by the Court of Appeals for the Third Circuit. Commissioner v. Switlik, 184 F.2d 299 (1950).

I find little aid in the choice of alternatives from arguments based on equities. One enables the taxpayer to deduct the amount of the judgment against his ordinary income which might be taxed as high as 87%, while if the liability had been assessed against the corporation prior to liquidation it would have reduced his capital gain which was taxable at only 25% (now 26%). The consequence may readily be characterized as a windfall (regarding a windfall as anything that is left to a taxpayer after the collector has finished with him).

On the other hand, adoption of the contrary alternative may penalize the taxpayer because of two factors: (1) since capital losses are deductible only against capital gains, plus $1,000, a taxpayer having no net capital gains in the ensuing five years would have no opportunity to deduct anything beyond $5,000; and (2) had the liability been discharged by the corporation, a portion of it would probably in effect have been paid by the Government, since the corporation could have taken it as a deduction, while here the total liability comes out of the pockets of the stockholders.

Solicitude for the revenues is a plausible but treacherous basis upon which to decide a particular tax case. A victory may have implications which in future cases will cost the Treasury more than a defeat. This might be such a case, for anything I know. Suppose that subsequent to liquidation it is found that a corporation has undisclosed claims instead of liabilities and that under applicable state law they may be prosecuted for the benefit of the stock-holders. The logic of the Court's decision here, if adhered to, would result in a lesser return to the Government than if the recoveries were considered ordinary income. Would it be so clear that this is a capital loss if the shoe were on the other foot?

Where the statute is so indecisive and the importance of a particular holding lies in its rational and harmonious relation to the general scheme of the tax law, I think great deference is due the twice-expressed judgment of the Tax Court. In spite of the gelding of Dobson v. Commissioner [Chapter 3D.2 above], by the recent revision of the Judicial Code, Act of June 25, 1948, §36, 62 Stat. 991-992, 26 U.S.C.A. §1141(a), I still think the Tax Court is a more competent and steady influence toward a systematic body of tax law than our sporadic omnipotence in a field beset with invisible boomerangs. I should reverse, in reliance upon the Tax Court's judgment more, perhaps, than my own.

B.   *THE CORN PRODUCTS DOCTRINE*

CORN PRODUCTS REFINING CO. v. COMMISSIONER
350 U.S. 46 (1955)

Mr. Justice CLARK delivered the opinion of the Court. This case concerns the tax treatment to be accorded certain transactions in commodity futures.[1] In the Tax Court, petitioner Corn Products Refining Company contended that its purchases and sales of corn futures in 1940 and 1942 were capital-asset transactions under §117(a) of the Internal Revenue Code of 1939. . . .

Petitioner is a nationally known manufacturer of products made from grain corn. It manufactures starch, syrup, sugar, and their byproducts, feeds and oil. Its average yearly grind of raw corn during the period 1937 through 1942 varied from thirty-five to sixty million bushels. Most of its products were sold under contracts requiring shipment in thirty days at a set price or at market price on the date of delivery, whichever was lower. It permitted cancellation of such contracts, but from experience it could calculate with some accuracy future orders that would remain firm. While it also sold to a few customers on long-term contracts involving substantial orders, these had little effect on the transactions here involved.[4]

---

1. A commodity future is a contract to purchase some fixed amount of a commodity at a future date for a fixed price. Corn futures, involved in the present case, are in terms of some multiple of five thousand bushels to be delivered eleven months or less after the contract. Cf. Hoffman, Future Trading (1932), 118.

4. Petitioner had contracts with three consumers to furnish, for a period of ten years or more, large quantities of starch or feed. In January 1940, petitioner had sold 2,000,000 bags of corn sugar, delivery to be made several months in the future. Also, members of the canning industry on the Pacific Coast had contracts to purchase corn sugar for delivery in more than thirty days.

In 1934 and again in 1936 droughts in the corn belt caused a sharp increase in the price of spot corn. With a storage capacity of only 2,300,000 bushels of corn, a bare three weeks' supply, Corn Products found itself unable to buy at a price which would permit its refined corn sugar, cerelose, to compete successfully with cane and beet sugar. To avoid a recurrence of this situation, petitioner, in 1937, began to establish a long position in corn futures "as a part of its corn buying program" and "as the most economical method of obtaining an adequate supply of raw corn" without entailing the expenditure of large sums for additional storage facilities. At harvest time each year it would buy futures when the price appeared favorable. It would take delivery on such contracts as it found necessary to its manufacturing operations and sell the remainder in early summer if no shortage was imminent. If shortages appeared, however, it sold futures only as it bought spot corn for grinding. In this manner it reached a balanced position with reference to any increase in spot corn prices. It made no effort to protect itself against a decline in prices.

In 1940 it netted a profit of $680,587.39 in corn futures, but in 1942 it suffered a loss of $109,969.38. In computing its tax liability Corn Products reported these figures as ordinary profit and loss from its manufacturing operations for the respective years. It now contends that its futures were "capital assets" under §117 and that gains and losses therefrom should have been treated as arising from the sale of a capital asset. In support of this position it claims that its futures trading was separate and apart from its manufacturing operations and that in its futures transactions it was acting as a "legitimate capitalist." United States v. New York Coffee & Sugar Exchange, 263 U.S. 611, 619. It denies that its futures transactions were "hedges" or "speculative" dealings as covered by the ruling of General Counsel's Memorandum 17322, XV-2 Cum. Bull. 151, and claims that it is in truth "the forgotten man" of that administrative interpretation.

Both the Tax Court and the Court of Appeals found petitioner's futures transactions to be an integral part of its business designed to protect its manufacturing operations against a price increase in its principal raw material and to assure a ready supply for future manufacturing requirements. Corn Products does not level a direct attack on these two-court findings but insists that its futures were "property" entitled to capital-asset treatment under §117 and as such were distinct from its manufacturing business. We cannot agree.

We find nothing in this record to support the contention that Corn Products' futures activity was separate and apart from its manufacturing operation. On the contrary, it appears that the transactions were vitally important to the company's business as a form of insurance against increases in the price of raw corn. Not only were the purchases initiated for just this reason, but the petitioner's sales policy, selling in the future at a fixed price or less, continued to leave it exceedingly vulnerable to rises in the price of corn. Further, the purchase of corn futures assured the company a source of supply which was admittedly cheaper than constructing additional storage facilities for raw corn. Under these facts it is difficult to imagine a program more closely geared to a company's manufacturing enterprise or more important to its successful operation.

Likewise the claim of Corn Products that it was dealing in the market as a "legitimate capitalist" lacks support in the record. There can be no quarrel with a manufacturer's desire to protect itself against increasing costs of raw materials. Transactions which provide such protection are considered a legitimate form of insurance. United States v. New York Coffee & Sugar Exchange, 263 U.S., at 619; Browne v. Thorn, 260 U.S. 137, 139-140. However, in labeling its activity as that of a "legitimate capitalist" exercising "good judgment" in the futures market, petitioner ignores the testimony of its own officers that in entering the market the company was "trying to protect a part of [its] manufacturing costs"; that its entry was not for the purpose of "speculating and buying and selling corn futures" but to fill an actual "need for the quantity of corn [bought] . . . in order to cover . . . what [products] we expected to market over a period of fifteen or eighteen months." It matters not whether the label be that of "legitimate capitalist" or "speculator"; this is not the talk of the capital investor but of the far-sighted manufacturer. For tax purposes petitioner's purchases have been found to "constitute an integral part of its manufacturing business" by both the Tax Court and the Court of Appeals, and on essentially factual questions the findings of two courts should not ordinarily be disturbed. Comstock v. Group of Investors, 335 U.S. 211, 214.

Petitioner also makes much of the conclusion by both the Tax Court and the Court of Appeals that its transactions did not constitute "true hedging." It is true that Corn Products did not secure complete protection from its market operations. Under its sales policy petitioner could not guard against a fall in prices. It is clear, however, that petitioner feared the possibility of a price rise more than that of a price decline. It therefore purchased partial insurance against its principal risk, and hoped to retain sufficient flexibility to avoid serious losses on a declining market.

Nor can we find support for petitioner's contention that hedging is not within the exclusions of §117(a). Admittedly, petitioner's corn futures do not come within the literal language of the exclusions set out in that section. They were not stock in trade, actual inventory, property held for sale to customers or depreciable property used in a trade or business. But the capital-asset provision of §117 must not be so broadly applied as to defeat rather than further the purpose of Congress. Burnet v. Harmel, 287 U.S. 103, 108. Congress intended that profits and losses arising from the everyday operation of a business be considered as ordinary income or loss rather than capital gain or loss. The preferential treatment provided by §117 applies to transactions in property which are not the normal source of business income. It was intended "to relieve the taxpayer from . . . excessive tax burdens on gains resulting from a conversion of capital investments, and to remove the deterrent effect of those burdens on such conversions." Burnet v. Harmel, 287 U.S., at 106. Since this section is an exception from the normal tax requirements of the Internal Revenue Code, the definition of a capital asset must be narrowly applied and its exclusions interpreted broadly. This is necessary to effectuate the basic congressional purpose. This Court has always construed narrowly the term "capital assets" in §117. See Hort v. Commissioner, 313 U.S. 28, 31; Kieselbach v. Commissioner, 317 U.S. 399, 403.

The problem of the appropriate tax treatment of hedging transactions first arose under the 1934 Tax Code revision.[7] Thereafter the Treasury issued G.C.M. 17322, supra, distinguishing speculative transactions in commodity futures from hedging transactions. It held that hedging transactions were essentially to be regarded as insurance rather than a dealing in capital assets and that gains and losses therefrom were ordinary business gains and losses. The interpretation outlined in this memorandum has been consistently followed by the courts as well as by the Commissioner. While it is true that this Court has not passed on its validity, it has been well recognized for 20 years; and Congress has made no change in it though the Code has been re-enacted on three subsequent occasions. This bespeaks congressional approval. Helvering v. Winmill, 305 U.S. 79, 83. Furthermore, Congress has since specifically recognized the hedging exception here under consideration in the short-sale rule of §1233(a) of the 1954 Code.

We believe that the statute clearly refutes the contention of Corn Products. Moreover, it is significant to note that practical considerations lead to the same conclusion. To hold otherwise would permit those engaged in hedging transactions to transmute ordinary income into capital gain at will. The hedger may either sell the future and purchase in the spot market or take delivery under the future contract itself. But if a sale of the future created a capital transaction while delivery of the commodity under the same future did not, a loophole in the statute would be created and the purpose of Congress frustrated.

The judgment is
Affirmed.

Mr. Justice Harlan took no part in the consideration or decision of this case.

---

7. Section 208(8) of the Revenue Act of 1924 limited "capital assets" to property held more than two years. This definition was retained until the Act of 1934. Since the rules of the various commodity exchanges required that futures contracts be closed out in periods shorter than two years, these contracts could not qualify as capital assets.

Questions

1. *Inventory.* Why did the Supreme Court not affirm on the ground offered by the courts below—that corn futures for this company come within §1221(1)? Is the Court being true to the statute by giving §1221(1) a narrow and literal interpretation that excludes corn futures, while simultaneously concluding that the futures are not capital assets on another ground that has no statutory foundation? In what other situations will this choice of grounds make a critical difference in the outcome? See Arkansas Best Corporation v. Commissioner, immediately following.

2. The rulings on futures discussed in the opinion involved losses on which taxpayers were seeking to avoid the capital loss limitation. This is partly because favorable treatment of capital gains still required a holding period of over a year, even after 1934, and commercial futures contracts are not ordinarily written for more than 11 months. The rulings, therefore, represent an allowance of losses where futures contracts are tied closely enough to inventory operations, and the references to true hedging have their origin in that context. The holding period for long-term capital gains has often been only six months, which would make long-term holding of an 11-month contract quite possible. It is now back up to a year; but when it was raised to a year in 1976 the flush language at the end of §1222 was added preserving the six-month holding period for "futures transactions in any commodity subject to the rules of a board of trade or commodity exchange."

3. *Electivity.* Note carefully what the Court says in the last paragraph of its opinion about the electivity of capital asset treatment if futures were held to be capital assets.

4. *Speculators.* Is there any reason why profits from futures transactions should be given long-term capital gain treatment even in the case of a pure speculator or "legitimate capitalist" (whatever that means)?

What about the argument that "sale or exchange of a capital asset" contemplates some change in position through liquidation of an investment that might otherwise have been continued? Section 1221(1) then operates to exclude sales that do not represent such a liquidation of investment or change in position, because the only way to earn a return on inventory is by sales. Section 1221(1) would then be interpreted to include any asset on which a profit is only to be made by current sale or exchange—any asset which fails to offer a choice between long-term investment and immediate liquidation. Commodity futures, by that standard, would come within §1221(1) in any taxpayer's hands.

What about losses? Are there reasons why a speculator's losses on future contracts should be disallowed or limited? If so, is favorable treatment of net gains required? Compare §165(d).

5. The *Corn Products* decision has been extensively cited in favor of taxpayers seeking to avoid the limitation on deduction of capital losses in connection with business-motivated investments in the stock of other corporations.

ARKANSAS BEST CORPORATION v. COMMISSIONER
485 U.S. 212 (1988)

Justice MARSHALL delivered the opinion of the Court. The issue presented in this case is whether capital stock held by petitioner Arkansas Best Corporation (Arkansas Best) is a "capital asset" as defined in section 1221 of the Internal Revenue Code regardless of whether the stock was purchased and held for a business purpose or for an investment purpose.

I

Arkansas Best is a diversified holding company. In 1968 it acquired approximately 65% of the stock of the National Bank of Commerce (Bank) in Dallas, Texas. Between 1969 and 1974, Arkansas Best more than tripled the number of shares it owned in the Bank, although its percentage interest in the Bank remained relatively stable. These acquisitions were prompted principally by the Bank's need for added capital. Until 1972, the Bank appeared to be prosperous and growing, and the added capital was necessary to accommodate this growth. As the Dallas real estate market declined, however, so too did the financial health of the Bank, which had a heavy concentration of loans in the local real estate industry. In 1972, federal examiners classified the Bank as a problem bank. The infusion of capital after 1972 was prompted by the loan portfolio problems of the bank.

Petitioner sold the bulk of its Bank stock on June 30, 1975, leaving it with only a 14.7% stake in the Bank. On its federal income tax return for 1975, petitioner claimed a deduction for an ordinary loss of $9,995,688 resulting from the sale of the stock. The Commissioner of Internal Revenue disallowed the deduction, finding that the loss from the sale of stock was a capital loss, rather than an ordinary loss, and that it therefore was subject to the capital loss limitations in the Internal Revenue Code.[1]

Arkansas Best challenged the Commissioner's determination in the United States Tax Court. The Tax Court, relying on cases interpreting Corn Products Refining Co. v. Commissioner, 350 U.S. 46 (1955), held that stock purchased with a substantial investment purpose is a capital asset which, when sold, gives rise to a capital gain or loss, whereas stock purchased and held for a business purpose, without any substantial investment motive, is an ordinary asset whose sale gives rise to ordinary gains or losses. See 83 T.C. 640, 653-654 (1984). The court characterized Arkansas Best's acquisitions through 1972 as occurring during the Bank's "'growth' phase," and found that these acquisitions "were motivated

---

1. Title 26 U.S.C. section 1211(a) states that "[i]n the case of a corporation, losses from sales or exchanges of capital assets shall be allowed only to the extent of gains from such sales or exchanges," Section 1212(a) establishes rules governing carrybacks and carryovers of capital losses, permitting such losses to offset capital gains in certain earlier or later years.

primarily by investment purpose and only incidentally by some business purpose." Id., at 654. The stock acquired during this period therefore constituted a capital asset, which gave rise to a capital loss when sold in 1975. The court determined, however, that the acquisition after 1972 occurred during the Bank's "'problem' phase," ibid., and, except for certain minor exceptions, "were made exclusively for business purposes and subsequently held for the same reason." Id., at 656. These acquisitions, the court found, were designed to preserve petitioner's business reputation, because without the added capital the Bank probably would have failed. Id., at 656-657. The loss realized on the sale of this stock was thus held to be an ordinary loss.

The Court of Appeals for the Eighth Circuit reversed the Tax Court's determination that the loss realized on stock purchased after 1972 was subject to ordinary-loss treatment, holding that all of the Bank stock sold in 1975 was subject to capital-loss treatment. 800 F.2d 215 (1986). The court reasoned that the Bank stock clearly fell within the general definition of "capital asset" in Internal Revenue Code section 1221, and that the stock did not fall within any of the specific statutory exceptions to this definition. The court concluded that Arkansas Best's purpose in acquiring and holding the stock was irrelevant to the determination whether the stock was a capital asset. We granted certiorari, 480 U.S. 930, and now affirm.

II

Section 1221 of the Internal Revenue Code defines "capital asset" broadly, as "property held by the taxpayer (whether or not connected with his trade or business)," and then excludes five specific classes of property from capital-asset status. In the statute's present form,[2] the classes of property exempted from the broad definition are (1) "property of a kind which would properly be included in the inventory of the taxpayer"; (2) real property or other depreciable property used in the taxpayer's trade or business; (3) "a copyright, a literary, musical, or artistic composition," or similar property; (4) "accounts or notes receivable acquired in the ordinary course of trade or business for services rendered" or from the sale of inventory; and (5) publications of the Federal Government. Arkansas Best acknowledges that the Bank stock falls within the literal definition of capital asset in section 1221, and is outside of the statutory exclusions. It asserts, however, that this determination does not end the inquiry. Petitioner argues that in Corn Products Refining Co. v. Commissioner, supra, this Court rejected a literal reading of section 1221, and concluded that assets acquired and sold for

2. In 1975, when petitioner sold its Bank stock, section 1221 contained a different exception (5), which excluded certain federal and state debt obligations. See 26 U.S.C. section 1221 (5) (1970 ed.). That exception was repealed by the Economic Recovery Tax Act of 1981, Pub. L. 97-34, section 505(a), 95 Stat. 331. The present exception (5) was added by the Tax Refund Act of 1976, Pub. L. 94-455, section 2132(a), 90 Stat. 1925. These changes have no bearing on this case.

ordinary business purposes rather than for investment purposes should be given ordinary-asset treatment. Petitioner's reading of *Corn Products* finds much support in the academic literature[3] and in the courts.[4] Unfortunately for petitioner, this broad reading finds no support in the language of section 1221.

In essence, petitioner argues that "property held by the taxpayer (whether or not connected with his trade or business)" does not include property that is acquired and held for a business purpose. In petitioner's view an asset's status as "property" thus turns on the motivation behind its acquisition. This motive test, however, is not only nowhere mentioned in section 1221, but it is also in direct conflict with the parenthetical phrase "whether or not connected with his trade or business." The broad definition of the term "capital asset" explicitly makes irrelevant any consideration of the property's connection with the taxpayer's business, whereas petitioner's rule would make this factor dispositive.[5]

In a related argument, petitioner contends that the five exceptions listed in section 1221 for certain kinds of property are illustrative, rather than exhaustive, and that courts are therefore free to fashion additional exceptions in order to further the general purposes of the capital-asset provisions. The language of the statute refutes petitioner's construction. Section 1221 provides that "capital asset" means "property held by the taxpayer[,] . . . but does not include" the five classes of property listed as exceptions. We believe this locution signifies that the listed exceptions are exclusive. The body of section 1221 establishes a general definition of the term "capital asset," and the phrase "does not include" takes out of that broad definition only the classes of property that are specifically mentioned. The legislative history of the capital asset definition supports this interpretation, see H.R. Rep. 704, 73d Cong., 2d Sess., 31 (1934) ("[T]he definition includes all property, except as specifically excluded"); H.R. Rep. 1337, 83d

---

3. See, e.g., 2 B. Bittker, Federal Taxation of Income, Estates and Gifts paragraph 51.10.3, p. 51-62 (1981); Chirelstein, Capital Gain and the Sale of a Business Opportunity: The Income Tax Treatment of Contract Termination Payments, 49 Minn. L. Rev. 1, 41 (1964); Troxell & Noall, Judicial Erosion of the Concept of Securities as Capital Assets, 19 Tax L. Rev. 185, 187 (1964); Note, The Corn Products Doctrine and Its Application to Partnership Interests, 79 Colum. L. Rev. 341, and n.3 (1979).

4. See, e.g., Campbell Taggart, Inc. v. United States, 744 F.2d 442, 456-458 (CA5 1984); Steadman v. Commissioner, 424 F.2d 1, 5 (CA6), cert. denied, 400 U.S. 869 (1970); Booth Newspapers, Inc. v. United States, 157 Ct. Cl. 886, 893-896, 303 F.2d 916. 920-921 (1962); W. W. Windle Co. v. Commissioner, 65 T.C. 694, 707-713 (1976).

5. Petitioner mistakenly relies on cases in which this Court, in narrowly applying the general definition of capital asset, has "construed 'capital asset' to exclude property representing income items or accretions to the value of a capital asset themselves properly attributable to income," even though these items are property in the broad sense of the word. United States v. Midland-Ross Corp., 381 U.S. 54, 57 (1965). See, e.g., Commissioner v. Gillette Motor Co., 364 U.S. 130 (1960) ("capital asset" does not include compensation awarded taxpayer that represented fair rental value of its facilities); Commissioner v. P. G. Lake, Inc., 356 U.S. 260 (1958) ("capital asset" does not include proceeds from sale of oil payment rights); Hort v. Commissioner, 313 U.S. 28 (1941) ("capital asset" does not include payment to lessor for cancellation of unexpired portion of a lease). This line of cases, based on the premise that section 1221 "property" does not include claims or rights to ordinary income, has no application in the present context. Petitioner sold capital stock, not a claim to ordinary income.

Cong., 2d Sess., A273 (1954) ("[A] capital asset is property held by the taxpayer with certain exceptions"), as does the applicable Treasury regulation, see 26 CFR section 1.1221-1(a) (1987) ("The term 'capital assets' includes all classes of property not specifically excluded by section 1221").

Petitioner's reading of the statute is also in tension with the exceptions listed in section 1221. These exclusions would be largely superfluous if assets acquired primarily or exclusively for business purposes were not capital assets. Inventory, real or depreciable property used in the taxpayer's trade or business, and accounts or notes receivable acquired in the ordinary course of business, would undoubtedly satisfy such a business-motive test. Yet these exceptions were created by Congress in separate enactments spanning 30 years.[6] Without any express direction from Congress, we are unwilling to read section 1221 in a manner that makes surplusage of these statutory exclusions.

In the end, petitioner places all reliance on its reading of Corn Products Refining Co. v. Commissioner, 350 U.S. 46 (1955) — a reading we believe is too expansive. In *Corn Products*, the Court considered whether income arising from a taxpayer's dealings in corn futures was entitled to capital gains treatment. The taxpayer was a company that converted corn into starches, sugars, and other products. After droughts in the 1930s caused sharp increases in corn prices, the company began a program of buying corn futures to assure itself an adequate supply of corn and protect against price increases. See id., at 48. The company "would take delivery on such contracts as it found necessary to its manufacturing operations and sell the remainder in early summer if no shortage was imminent. If shortages appeared, however, it sold futures only as it bought spot corn for grinding." Id., at 48-49. The Court characterized the company's dealing in corn futures as "hedging." Id., at 51. As explained by the Court of Appeals in *Corn Products*, "[h]edging is a method of dealing in commodity futures whereby a person or business protects itself against price fluctuations at the time of delivery of the product which it sells or buys." 215 F.2d 513, 515 (CA2 1954). In evaluating the company's claim that the sales of corn futures resulted in capital gains and losses, this Court stated:

> Nor can we find support for petitioner's contention that hedging is not within the exclusions of [section 1221]. Admittedly, petitioner's corn futures do not come within the literal language of the exclusions set out in that section. They were not stock in trade, actual inventory, property held for sale to customers or depreciable property used in a trade or business but the capital-asset provision of [section 1221] must not be so broadly applied as to defeat rather than further the purpose of Congress. Congress

6. The inventory exception was part of the original enactment of the capital-asset provision in 1924. See Revenue Act of 1924, ch. 234, section 208(a)(8), 43 Stat. 263. Depreciable property used in a trade or business was excluded in 1938, see Revenue Act of 1988, ch. 289, section 117(a)(1), 52 Stat. 500, and real property used in a trade or business was excluded in 1942, see Revenue Act of 1942, ch. 619, section 151(a), 56 Stat. 846. The exception for accounts and notes receivable acquired in the ordinary course of trade or business was added in 1954. Internal Revenue Code of 1954, section 1221(4), 68A Stat. 322.

intended that profits and losses arising from the everyday operation of a business be considered as ordinary income or loss rather than capital gain or loss. . . . Since this section is an exception from the normal tax requirements of the Internal Revenue Code, the definition of a capital asset must be narrowly applied and its exclusions interpreted broadly. 350 U.S., at 51-52. (citations omitted.)

The Court went on to note that hedging transactions consistently had been considered to give rise to ordinary gains and losses, and then concluded that the corn futures were subject to ordinary-asset treatment. Id., at 52-53.

The Court in *Corn Products* proffered the oft-quoted rule of construction that the definition of capital asset must be narrowly applied and its exclusions interpreted broadly, but it did not state explicitly whether the holding was based on a narrow reading of the phrase "property held by the taxpayer," or on a broad reading of the inventory exclusion of section 1221. In light of the stark language of section 1221, however, we believe that *Corn Products* is properly interpreted as involving an application of section 1221's inventory exception. Such a reading is consistent both with the Court's reasoning in that case and with section 1221. The Court stated in *Corn Products* that the company's futures transactions were "an integral part of its business designed to protect its manufacturing operations against a price increase in its principal raw material and to assure a ready supply for future manufacturing requirements." 350 U.S., at 50. The company bought, sold, and took delivery under the futures contracts as required by the company's manufacturing needs. As Professor Bittker notes, under these circumstances, the futures can "easily be viewed as surrogates for the raw material itself." 2 B. Bittker, Federal Taxation of Income, Estates and Gifts paragraph 51.10.3, p. 51-62 (1981). The Court of Appeals for the Second Circuit in *Corn Products* clearly took this approach. That court stated that when commodity futures are "utilized solely for the purpose of stabilizing inventory cost[,] . . . [they] cannot reasonably be separated from the inventory items," and concluded that "property used in hedging transactions properly comes within the exclusions of [section 1221]." 215 F.2d. at 516. This Court indicated its acceptance of the Second Circuit's reasoning when it began the central paragraph of its opinion, "Nor can we find support for petitioner's contention that hedging is not within the exclusions of [section 1221]." 350 U.S., at 51. In the following paragraph, the Court argued that the Treasury had consistently viewed such hedging transactions as a form of insurance to stabilize the cost of inventory, and cited a Treasury ruling which concluded that the value of a manufacturer's raw-material inventory should be adjusted to take into account hedging transactions in futures contracts. See id., at 52-53 (citing G.C.M. 17322, XV-2 Cum. Bull. 151 (1936)). This discussion, read in light of the Second Circuit's holding and the plain language of section 1221, convinces us that although the corn futures were not "actual inventory," their use as an integral part of the taxpayer's inventory-purchase system led the Court to treat them as substitutes for the corn inventory such that they came within a broad reading of "property of a kind which would properly be included in the inventory of the taxpayer" in section 1221.

Petitioner argues that by focusing attention on whether the asset was acquired and sold as an integral part of the taxpayer's everyday business operations, the Court in *Corn Products* intended to create a general exemption from capital-asset status for assets acquired for business purposes. We believe petitioner misunderstands the relevance of the Court's inquiry. A business connection, although irrelevant to the initial determination of whether an item is a capital asset, is relevant in determining the applicability of certain of the statutory exceptions, including the inventory exception. The close connection between the futures transactions and the taxpayer's business in *Corn Products* was crucial to whether the corn futures could be considered surrogates for the stored inventory of raw corn. For if the futures dealings were not part of the company's inventory-purchase system, and instead amounted simply to speculation in corn futures, they could not be considered substitutes for the company's corn inventory, and would fall outside even a broad reading of the inventory exclusion. We conclude that *Corn Products* is properly interpreted as standing for the narrow proposition that hedging transactions that are an integral part of a business' inventory-purchase system fall within the inventory exclusion of section 1221.[7] Arkansas Best, which is not a dealer in securities, has never suggested that the Bank stock falls within the inventory exclusion. *Corn Products* thus has no application to this case.

It is also important to note that the business-motive test advocated by petitioner is subject to the same kind of abuse that the Court condemned in *Corn Products*. The Court explained in *Corn Products* that unless hedging transactions were subject to ordinary gain and loss treatment, taxpayers engaged in such transactions could "transmute ordinary income into capital gain at will." 350 U.S., at 53-54. The hedger could garner capital-asset treatment by selling the future and purchasing the commodity on the spot market, or ordinary-asset treatment by taking delivery under the future contract. In a similar vein, if capital stock purchased and held for a business purpose is an ordinary asset, whereas the same stock purchased and held with an investment motive is a capital asset, a taxpayer such as Arkansas Best could have significant influence over whether the asset would receive capital or ordinary treatment. Because stock is most naturally viewed as a capital asset, the Internal Revenue Service would be hard pressed to challenge a taxpayer's claim that stock was acquired as an investment, and that a gain

---

7. Although congressional inaction is generally a poor measure of congressional intent, we are given some pause by the fact that over 25 years have passed since Corn Products Refining Co. v. Commissioner, 350 U.S. 46 (1955), was initially interpreted as excluding assets acquired for business purposes from the definition of capital asset, see Booth Newspapers, Inc. v. United States, 157 Ct. Cl. 886, 303 F.2d 916 (1962), without any sign of disfavor from Congress. We cannot ignore the unambiguous language of section 1221, however, no matter how reticent Congress has been. If a broad exclusion from capital-asset status is to be created for assets acquired for business purposes, it must come from congressional action, not silence.

arising from the sale of such stock was therefore a capital gain. Indeed, we are unaware of a single decision that has applied the business-motive test so as to require a taxpayer to report a gain from the sale of stock as an ordinary gain. If the same stock is sold at a loss, however, the taxpayer may be able to garner ordinary-loss treatment by emphasizing the business purpose behind the stock's acquisition. The potential for such abuse was evidenced in this case by the fact that as late as 1974, when Arkansas Best still hoped to sell the Bank stock at a profit, Arkansas Best apparently expected to report the gain as a capital gain. See 83 T.C. at 647-648.

III

We conclude that a taxpayer's motivation in purchasing an asset is irrelevant to the question whether the asset is "property held by a taxpayer (whether or not connected with his business)" and is thus within section 1221's general definition of "capital asset." Because the capital stock held by petitioner falls within the broad definition of the term "capital asset" in section 1221 and is outside the classes of property excluded from capital-asset status, the loss arising from the sale of the stock is a capital loss. Corn Products Refining Co. v. Commissioner, supra, which we interpret as involving a broad reading of the inventory exclusion of section 1221, has no application in the present context. Accordingly, the judgment of the Court of Appeals is affirmed.

It is so ordered.

Justice Kennedy took no part in the consideration or decision of this case.

References

Warren, The Deductibility by Individuals of Capital Losses Under the Federal Income Tax, 40 U. Chi. L. Rev. 291 (1973); Young, Income Tax Consequences of Investment Losses of Individuals, 27 Tax L. Rev. 1 (1971).

A. *The Arrowsmith Doctrine:* Englebrecht, The *Arrowsmith* Doctrine, 52 Taxes 686 (1974); Lokken, Tax Significance of Payments in Satisfaction of Liabilities Arising Under Section 16(b) of the Securities Exchange Act of 1934, 4 Ga. L. Rev. 298 (1970); Schenk, *Arrowsmith* and Its Progeny: Tax Characterization by Reference to Past Events, 33 Rutgers L. Rev. 317 (1981).

B. *The Corn Products Doctrine:* Sheila C. Bair, Susan M. Milligan, & Elizabeth L.R. Fox, The Worst of *Arkansas Best*, 41 U. Kan. L. Rev. 535 (1993); Brown, The Growing "Common Law" of Taxation, 34 S. Cal. L. Rev. 235 (1961); Edward D. Kleinbard & Suzanne F. Greenberg, Business Hedges After *Arkansas Best*, 43 Tax L. Rev. 393 (1988); Troxell & Noall, Judicial Erosion of the Concept of Securities as Capital Assets, 19 Tax L. Rev. 185 (1964).

Chapter 21 — *Future Income Streams*

A. RECEIPT OF A LUMP-SUM PAYMENT FOR A FUTURE INCOME STREAM

HORT v. COMMISSIONER
313 U.S. 28 (1941)

Mr. Justice MURPHY delivered the opinion of the Court. We must determine whether the amount petitioner received as consideration for cancellation of a lease of realty in New York City was ordinary gross income as defined in §22(a) of the Revenue Act of 1932 (47 Stat. 169, 178), and whether, in any event, petitioner sustained a loss through cancellation of the lease which is recognized in §23(e) of the same Act (47 Stat. 169, 180).

Petitioner acquired the property, a lot and ten-story office building, by devise from his father in 1928. At the time he became owner, the premises were leased to a firm which had sublet the main floor to the Irving Trust Co. In 1927, five years before the head lease expired, the Irving Trust Co. and petitioner's father executed a contract in which the latter agreed to lease the main floor and basement to the former for a term of fifteen years at an annual rental of $25,000, the term to commence at the expiration of the head lease.

In 1933, the Irving Trust Co. found it unprofitable to maintain a branch in petitioner's building. After some negotiations, petitioner and the Trust Co. agreed to cancel the lease in consideration of a payment to petitioner of $140,000. Petitioner did not include this amount in gross income in his income tax return for 1933. On the contrary, he reported a loss of $21,494.75 on the theory that the amount he received as consideration for the cancellation was $21,494.75 less than the difference between the present value of the unmatured rental payments and the fair rental value of the main floor and basement for the unexpired term of the lease. He did not deduct this figure, however, because he reported other losses in excess of gross income.

The Commissioner included the entire $140,000 in gross income, disallowed the asserted loss, made certain other adjustments not material here, and assessed a deficiency. The Board of Tax Appeals affirmed. 39 B.T.A. 922. The Circuit Court of Appeals affirmed per curiam on the authority of Warren Service Corp. v. Commissioner, 110 F.2d 723. 112 F.2d 167. Because of the conflict with Commissioner v. Langwell Real Estate Corp., 47 F.2d 841, we granted certiorari limited to the question whether, "in computing net gain or loss for income tax purposes, a taxpayer [can] offset the value of the lease canceled against the consideration received by him for the cancellation." 311 U.S. 641.

Petitioner apparently contends that the amount received for cancellation of the lease was capital rather than ordinary income and that it was therefore subject to §§101, 111-113 and 117 (47 Stat. 169, 191, 195-202, 207) which govern capital gains and losses. Further, he argues that even if that amount must be reported as ordinary gross income he sustained a loss which §23(e) authorizes him to deduct. We cannot agree.

The amount received by petitioner for cancellation of the lease must be included in his gross income in its entirety. Section 22(a) ... expressly defines gross income to include "gains, profits, and income derived from rent, ... or gains or profits and income derived from any source whatever." Plainly this definition reached the rent paid prior to cancellation just as it would have embraced subsequent payments if the lease had never been canceled. It would have included a prepayment of the discounted value of unmatured rental payments whether received at the inception of the lease or at any time thereafter. Similarly, it would have extended to the proceeds of a suit to recover damages had the Irving Trust Co. breached the lease instead of concluding a settlement. Compare United States v. Safety Car Heating Co., 297 U.S. 88; Burnet v. Sanford, 282 U.S. 359. That the amount petitioner received resulted from negotiations ending in cancellation of the lease rather than from a suit to enforce it cannot alter the fact that basically the payment was merely a substitute for the rent reserved in the lease. So far as the application of §22(a) is concerned, it is immaterial that petitioner chose to accept an amount less than the strict present value of the unmatured rental payments rather than to engage in litigation, possibly uncertain and expensive.

The consideration received for cancellation of the lease was not a return of capital. We assume that the lease was "property," whatever that signifies abstractly. Presumably the bond in Helvering v. Horst [Chapter 18A above] and the lease in Helvering v. Bruun [Chapter 5C.1 above] were also "property," but the interest coupon in *Horst* and the building in *Bruun* nevertheless were held to constitute items of gross income. Simply because the lease was "property" the amount received for its cancellation was not a return of capital, quite apart from the fact that "property" and "capital" are not necessarily synonymous in the Revenue Act of 1932 or in common usage. Where, as in this case, the disputed amount was essentially a substitute for rental payments which §22(a) expressly characterizes as gross income, it must be regarded as ordinary income, and it is immaterial that for some purposes the contract creating the right to such payments may be treated as "property" or "capital."

For the same reasons, that amount was not a return of capital because petitioner acquired the lease as an incident of the realty devised to him by his father. Theoretically, it might have been possible in such a case to value realty and lease separately and to label each a capital asset. Compare Maass v. Higgins, 312 U.S. 443; Appeal of Farmer, 1 B.T.A. 711. But that would not have converted into capital the amount petitioner received from the Trust Co., since [§102] would have required him to include in gross income the rent derived from the property, and that section, like §22(a), does not distinguish rental payments and a payment which is clearly a substitute for rental payments.

We conclude that petitioner must report as gross income the entire amount received for cancellation of the lease, without regard to the claimed disparity between that amount and the difference between the present value of the unmatured rental payments and the fair rental value of the property for the unexpired period of the lease. The cancellation of the lease involved nothing more than relinquishment of the right to future rental payments in return for a present substitute payment and possession of the leased premises. Undoubtedly it diminished the amount of gross income petitioner expected to realize, but to that extent he was relieved of the duty to pay income tax. Nothing in [§165] indicates that Congress intended to allow petitioner to reduce ordinary income actually received and reported by the amount of income he failed to realize. See Warren Service Corp. v. Commissioner, supra; Josey v. Commissioner, 104 F.2d 453; Tiscornia v. Commissioner, 95 F.2d 678; Farrelly-Wasch, Inc. v. Commissioner, 13 B.T.A. 923; Goerke Co. v. Commissioner, 7 B.T.A. 860; Merckens v. Commissioner, 7 B.T.A. 32. Compare, United States v. Safety Car Heating Co., supra; Voliva v. Commissioner, 36 F.2d 212; Appeal of Denholm & McKay Co. 2 B.T.A. 444. We may assume that petitioner was injured insofar as the cancellation of the lease affected the value of the realty. But that would become a deductible loss only when its extent had been fixed by a closed transaction. Regulations No. 77, Art. 171, p. 46; United States v. White Dental Mfg. Co. [Chapter 14A above].

The judgment of the Circuit Court of Appeals is
    . . . Affirmed.

McALLISTER v. COMMISSIONER
157 F.2d 235 (2d Cir. 1946), cert. denied, 330 U.S. 826 (1947)

Before Swan, Clark, and Frank, Circuit Judges.

CLARK, Circuit Judge. This petition for review presents the question whether the sum of $55,000 received by petitioner on "transfer" or "surrender" of her life interest in a trust to the remainderman constitutes gross income under I.R.C. §22(a), or receipts from the sale of capital assets as defined in I.R.C. §117(a)(1). As we shall see, some significance seemingly is attached to a choice between the two words set in quotation marks as a description of the transaction. Petitioner contends that the life estate was a capital asset, the transfer of which resulted in a deductible capital loss, leaving her with no taxable income for the year. A majority of the Tax Court agreed with the Commissioner that the receipt in question was merely an advance payment of income, while four judges dissented, Judges Opper and Disney writing the opposing opinions. 5 T.C. 714.

The will of Richard McAllister established a trust fund of $100,000, the income of which was to be paid to his son John McAllister for life, and, on the latter's death without children, to John's wife, the petitioner herein. On her death, the trust was to terminate, the residue going to the testator's wife and his son Richard. The testator died in 1926, his widow in 1935, and John in 1937. Except for stock in the R. McAllister corporation, not immediately salable at a fair price, John left assets insufficient to meet his debts; and in order to obtain immediate funds and to terminate extended family litigation according to an agreed plan, petitioner brought suit in the Court of Chancery of New Jersey to end the trust. The parties then agreed upon, and the court in its final decree ordered, a settlement by which the remainderman Richard, in addition to taking over the stock for $50,000, was to pay petitioner $55,000, with accumulated income and interest to the date of payment, in consideration of her release of all interest in the trust and consent to its termination and cancellation. Receiving payment on July 19, 1940, petitioner, in accordance with the court order, executed a release, providing: "I do further consent and agree that my estate in the aforesaid trust, created under the third paragraph of the . . . will . . . shall be and the same is hereby terminated absolutely, and I do decline to accept further any benefits therefrom or interest therein." For the year 1940, she reported a capital loss on the transaction of $8,790.20, the difference between the amount received and the value of the estate computed under I.T. 2076. The Commissioner disallowed the loss and made the deficiency assessment which was upheld by the majority below.

The issue, as stated by the Tax Court and presented by the parties, reduces itself to the question whether the case is within the rule of Blair v. Commissioner [Chapter 18A above], or that of Hort v. Commissioner [previous case]. In the *Blair* case, the life beneficiary of a trust assigned to his children specified sums to be paid each year for the duration of the estate.

The Supreme Court held that each transfer was the assignment of a property right in the trust and that, since the tax liability attached to ownership of the property, the assignee, and not the assignor, was liable for the income taxes in the years in question. The continued authority of the case was recognized in Helvering v. Horst [Chapter 18A above] although a majority of the Court thought it not applicable on the facts, and in Harrison v. Schaffner, 312 U.S. 579, 582, where the Court very properly distinguished it from the situation where an assignor transferred a portion of his income for a single year. It has been relied upon by other cases cited below which we find indistinguishable from the present case.

Petitioner's right to income for life from the trust estate was a right in the estate itself. Had she held a fee interest, the assignment would unquestionably have been regarded as the transfer of a capital asset; we see no reason why a different result should follow the transfer of the lesser, but still substantial, life interest. As the Court pointed out in the *Blair* case, the life tenant was entitled to enforce the trust, to enjoin a breach of trust, and to obtain redress in case of breach. The proceedings in the state chancery court completely divested her of these rights and of any possible control over the property. The case is therefore distinguishable from that of Hort v. Commissioner, supra, where a landlord for a consideration cancelled a lease for a term of years, having still some nine years to run. There the taxpayer surrendered his contractual right to the future yearly payments in return for an immediate payment of a lump sum. The statute expressly taxed income derived from rent, Revenue Act of 1932, §22(a); and the consideration received was held a substitute for the rent as it fell due. It was therefore taxed as income.

What we regard as the precise question here presented has been determined in the taxpayer's favor on the authority of the *Blair* case by the Eighth Circuit in Bell's Estate v. Commissioner, 8 Cir., 137 F.2d 454, reversing 46 B.T.A. 484. This case, in turn, has been followed by the Tax Court in Harman v. Commissioner, 4 T.C. 335 acquiesced in by the Commissioner, 1945-6 Int. Rev. Bull. No. 6 p. 1, and by the District Court in First Nat. Bank & Trust Co. in Macon v. Allen, D.C.M.D. Ga., 65 F. Supp. 128. . . .

The Tax Court and the government have attempted to distinguish both the *Bell* and the *Blair* cases on grounds which seem to us to lack either substance or reality. The principal ground seems to be the form the transaction assumed between the parties. Thus the Court says that petitioner received the payment for "surrendering" her rights to income payments, and "she did not assign her interest in the trust, as did petitioners in the *Bell* case." But what is this more than a distinction in words? Both were cases where at the conclusion of the transaction the remaindermen had the entire estate and the life tenants had a substantial sum of money. There surely cannot be that efficacy in lawyers' jargon that termination or cancellation or surrender carries some peculiar significance vastly penalizing laymen whose counsel have chanced to use them. And the fact that the whole affair was embodied in a court decree can add nothing more than a seal of legal validity to it. What was practically accomplished remained the same. And that here, as in the *Bell* case, there was a "surrender" to the remainderman, rather than a "transfer" to third persons as in the *Blair* case, does not change the essentially dispositive nature of the transaction so far as the former property owner is concerned.

Other suggestions seem equally dubious. Thus it is said that the transfer in the *Blair* case was without consideration. But it is hard to see how this affects either the fact or the validity of the transfer; if anything, the odds should favor the conveyance for a consideration — the income of which will yield taxes in the future. Naturally, since there were no capital gains or losses, the *Blair* case does not discuss them. (Actually it cites neither the gross income nor the capital assets statutes.) But its holding that the assignment leaves no taxable income with the assignor is just as potent here on the like point, even though we do have the further problem posited by the claim of a capital loss. And there was very definitely a consideration paid in the *Bell* case. Next it is urged that there could be no assignment because this was a spendthrift trust where the creator had forbidden assignment or anticipation by a beneficiary. (The form of prohibition here was an express command as to a vested equitable interest; there was no grant of discretionary power to the trustees to withhold income.) But the answer is that it was done by a series of transactions affirmed by the state court. That is, the trust provisions made passing of the interest somewhat more difficult, but not beyond the ingenuity of lawyers, when the parties were agreed. So in the *Blair* case the government argued that the trust was a spendthrift trust under Illinois law. Said the Court, 300 U.S. 5, 10:

> The point of the argument is that, the trust being of that character, the state law barred the voluntary alienation by the beneficiary of his interest. The state court held precisely the contrary. The ruling also determines the validity of the assignment by the beneficiary of parts of his interest. That question was necessarily presented and expressly decided.

Setting the bounds to the area of tax incidence involves the drawing of lines which may often be of an arbitrary nature. But they should not be more unreal than the circumstances necessitate. Here the line of demarcation between the *Blair* and the *Hort* principles is obviously one of some difficulty to define explicitly or to establish in borderline cases. Doubtless all would agree that there is some distinction between selling a life estate in property and anticipating income for a few years in advance. It is the kind of distinction stressed in Harrison v. Schaffner, supra, 312 U.S. 579, 583, where the Court said: "Nor are we troubled by the logical difficulties of drawing the line between a gift of an equitable interest in property for life effected by a gift for life of a share of the income of the trust and the gift of the income or a part of it for the period of a year as in this case." The distinction seems logically and practically to turn upon anticipation of income payments over a reasonably short period of time and an out-and-out transfer of a substantial and durable property interest, such as a life estate at least is. See 57 Harv. L. Rev. 382; 54 Harv. L. Rev. 1405; 50 Yale L.J. 512, 515. Where the line should be finally placed we need not try to anticipate here. But we are clear that distinctions attempted on the basis of the various legal names given a transaction, rather than on its actual results between the parties, do not afford a sound basis for its delimitation. More rationally, to accept the respondent's contention we ought frankly to consider the *Blair* case as overruled, 50 Yale L.J. 512, 518, a position which, as we have seen, the Supreme Court itself has declined to take.

The parties are in conflict as to the valuation of the life estate; and we are returning the case to the Tax Court for computation, without, of course, assuming that there will necessarily be some tax.

Reversed and remanded.

FRANK, Circuit Judge (dissenting). Taxpayer's father-in-law, by his will, created a trust by which taxpayer during her life was to receive the income from a fund of $100,000; the will provided that she was not to dispose of her interest or otherwise to anticipate the income. She joined with others interested in the trust to demolish it; in consideration of her doing so, she received a lump sum of $55,000. The question is whether, with respect to that $55,000, resulting from the frustration of the testator's purpose through the destruction of the trust, she is entitled to the exceptional advantage of the capital gains provisions.

We must, then, ascertain the intention of Congress expressed in those provisions — especially §117(a)(1) — in the light of the language it employed and the policy there embodied, i.e., we must determine whether Congress intended that a taxpayer who receives income in those circumstances should come within that exception.

My colleagues avoid a direct discussion of that problem. Instead, they rely on Blair v. Commissioner [Chapter 18A above] which they hold to be controlling. But the court in the *Blair* case had no occasion to, and did not, consider §117; it considered solely the interpretation of §22(a). . . .

Since the Court in the *Blair* case was not called on to say (as we are here) whether the taxpayer was liable under either §22(a) or under §117, but only whether taxpayer was liable, if at all, under §22(a), the *Blair* case sheds no light on the construction of §117. Surely it does not follow merely (1) because one who makes a gift of a life estate does not retain such "nonmaterial satisfactions" as to be liable under §22(a), that (2) one who disposes of a life estate for a valuable consideration is to be treated as having disposed of a "capital asset" under §117(a)(1) and is therefore entitled to the peculiar, exceptional, treatment accorded by the capital gains provisions. So, when it was argued that an interest which, pursuant to the *Horst* case, was "property" for purposes of §22(a) must be "capital" for purposes of the capital gains provisions, the Supreme Court answered that " 'property' and 'capital' are not necessarily synonymous in the Revenue Act of 1932 or in common usage." Hort v. Commissioner, 313 U.S. 28.

In interpreting the capital gains provisions, we ought to have in mind that they have a legislative history and embody a legislative policy distinct, respectively, from the history and the policy embodied in §22(a)....

The policy of the capital gains provisions is not in doubt: Congress believed that the exaction of income tax on the usual basis on gains resulting from dispositions of capital investments would undesirably deter such dispositions. To put it differently, Congress made an exception to §22(a), in order to give an incentive to the making of such transfers. Having regard to that purpose, the courts have been cautious in interpreting the clauses creating that exception. They have refused to regard as "capital" transactions for that purpose divers sorts of transfers of "property," especially those by which transferors have procured advance payments of future income.

Those cases and Hort v. Commissioner, 313 U.S. 28, seem to me to render it somewhat doubtful whether any transfer of a life estate for a valuable consideration is within §117. The consideration paid for such a transfer is a substitute for future payments which would be taxable as ordinary income, and resembles the advance payment of dividends, interest or salaries. I am, therefore, not at all sure that Bell's Estate v. Commissioner, 8 Cir., 137 F.2d 454, is correct (although, for reasons noted below, I think it is not apposite here). It may well be that, had Congress specifically thought of the problem, it would explicitly so have defined "capital assets" as to exclude such an interest. I do not say that Hort v. Commissioner conclusively fixes that interpretation, but it does so suggest.

It suggests far more strongly that we cannot reasonably extrapolate the language of §117 to include the transaction before us in the instant case. In the *Hort* case, the Supreme Court held that the "prepayment of the discounted value of unmatured rental payments" to a landlord on the cancellation of a lease constituted "ordinary income," coming within §22(a), and not within the capital gains clauses. The Court said, "Simply because the lease was 'property' the amount received for its cancellation was not a return of capital"; and it also said that "it is immaterial that for some purposes the contract creating the right to such payments may be treated as 'property' or 'capital.' . . . The cancellation of the lease involved nothing more than the relinquishment of the right to future rental payments in return for a present substitute payment and possession of the leased premises . . ."; and it added that §22(a) "does not distinguish rental payments and a payment which is clearly a substitute for rental payments."

That ruling is indeed suggestive here. For here we have these facts: The creator of the trust did everything he could to keep the taxpayer from disposing of her life interest. Aided by what my colleagues described as "the ingenuity of counsel," she succeeded in frustrating his effort to prevent such alienation, by joining with the other persons interested in the trust to "extinguish" and "cancel" it; the instruments she executed in that connection recited that the payment to her was "to represent the value of her life interest" and that the "settlement is based to a large extent upon her life expectancy." In that way, what the testator intended should be given to her only in instalments, she procured, in effect, in a lump sum payment.

I think it most unlikely that Congress intended by §117 to relieve such a taxpayer of the ordinary tax burdens, to supply an incentive for the demolition of such a trust. That the life tenant in the *Blair* case in somewhat similar manner avoided the intent of the trust's creator is, I think, of no moment; for that conduct was not relevant to the issue of Congressional purpose there before the Court, i.e., whether §22(a) made her taxable on the income subsequently paid her donee. But here the question is whether Congress meant that the exceptional benefits of §117 should be accorded a taxpayer who, in disposing of her life interest, circumvented the avowed purpose of the creator of the trust. I think not.

Perhaps Bell's Estate v. Commissioner, 8 Cir., 137 F.2d 454, is distinguishable from the instant case. For there the creator of the trust had not sought to prevent alienation of the life interests, and it is arguable that furtherance of sales of such interests falls within the intention of §117. But, since that question is not present here, I think we should leave it unanswered.

For the foregoing reasons, I think the Tax Court's decision should be affirmed.

COMMISSIONER v. P.G. LAKE, INC.
356 U.S. 260 (1958)

Mr. Justice DOUGLAS delivered the opinion of the Court. We have here, consolidated for argument, five cases involving an identical question of law. Four are from the Tax Court whose rulings may be found in 24 T.C. 1016 (the *Lake* case); 24 T.C. 818 (the *Fleming* case); 24 T.C. 1025 (the *Weed* case). (Its findings and opinion in the *Wrather* case are not officially reported.) Those four cases involved income tax deficiencies. The fifth, the *O'Connor* case, is a suit for a refund originating in the District Court. 143 F.Supp. 240. All five are from the same Court of Appeals, 241 F.2d 71, 65, 78, 84, 69. The cases are here on writs of certiorari which we granted because of the public importance of the question presented. 353 U.S. 982.

The facts of the *Lake* case are closely similar to those in the *Wrather* and *O'Connor* cases. Lake is a corporation engaged in the business of producing oil and gas. It has a seven-eighths working interest[1] in two commercial oil and

---

1. An oil and gas lease ordinarily conveys the entire mineral interest less any royalty interest retained by the lessor. The owner of the lease is said to own the "working interest" because he has the right to develop and produce the minerals.

In Anderson v. Helvering, 310 U.S. 404, we described an oil payment as "the right to a specified sum of money, payable out of a specified percentage of the oil, or the proceeds received from the sale of such oil, if, as and when produced." Id., at 410. A royalty interest is "a right to receive a specified percentage of all oil and gas produced" but, unlike the oil payment, is not limited to a specified sum of money. The royalty interest lasts during the entire term of the lease. Id. at 409.

gas leases. In 1950 it was indebted to its president in the sum of $600,000 and in consideration of his cancellation of the debt assigned him an oil payment right in the amount of $600,000, plus an amount equal to interest at 3 percent a year on the unpaid balance remaining from month to month, payable out of 25 percent of the oil attributable to the taxpayer's working interest in the two leases. At the time of the assignment it could have been estimated with reasonable accuracy that the assigned oil payment right would pay out in three or more years. It did in fact pay out in a little over three years.

In its 1950 tax return Lake reported the oil payment assignment as a sale of property producing a profit of $600,000 and taxable as a long-term capital gain under §117 of the Internal Revenue Code of 1939. The Commissioner determined a deficiency, ruling that the purchase price (less deductions not material here) was taxable as ordinary income, subject to depletion. The *Wrather* case has some variations in its facts. In the *O'Connor* case the assignors of the oil payments owned royalty interests[2] rather than working interests. But these differences are not material to the question we have for decision.

The *Weed* case is different only because it involves sulphur rights, rather than oil rights. The taxpayer was the owner of a pooled overriding royalty in a deposit known as Boiling Dome.[3] The royalty interest entitled the taxpayer to receive $0.00966133 per long ton of sulphur produced from Boling Dome, irrespective of the market price. Royalty payments were made each month, based on the previous month's production.

In 1947, the taxpayer, in order to obtain a sure source of funds to pay his individual income taxes, agreed with one Munro, his tax adviser, on a sulphur payment assignment. The taxpayer assigned to Munro a sulphur payment totaling $50,000 and consisting of 86.254514 percent of his pooled royalty interest, which represented the royalty interest on 6,000,000 long tons of the estimated remaining 21,000,000 long tons still in place. The purchase price was paid in three installments over a three-year period. Most of the purchase price was borrowed by Munro from a bank with the sulphur payment assignment as security. The assigned sulphur payment right paid out within 28 months. The amounts received by the taxpayer in 1948 and 1949 were returned by him as capital gains. The Commissioner determined that these amounts were taxable as ordinary income, subject to depletion.

The *Fleming* case is a bit more complicated and presents an additional question not in the other cases. Here oil payment assignments were made, not for cash but for real estate. Two transactions are involved. Fleming and others with whom he was associated made oil payment assignments, the

---

2. See note 1, supra.

3. Boling Dome is a tract composed of various parcels of land. The owners of the royalty interests in sulphur produced from the separate parcels entered into a pooling agreement by which royalties from sulphur produced anywhere in Boling Dome were distributed pro rata among all the royalty interest holders. In that sense was the interest of each "pooled."

rights and interests involved being held by them for productive use in their respective businesses of producing oil. Each oil payment was assigned for an interest in a ranch. Each was in an amount which represented the uncontested fair value of the undivided interest in the ranch received by the assignor, plus an amount equal to the interest per annum on the balance remaining unpaid from time to time. The other transaction consisted of an oil payment assignment by an owner of oil and gas leases, held for productive use in the assignor's business, for the fee simple title to business real estate. This oil payment assignment, like the ones mentioned above, was in the amount of the uncontested fair market value of the real estate received, plus interest on the unpaid balance remaining from time to time.

First, as to whether the proceeds were taxable as long-term capital gains under §117 or as ordinary income subject to depletion. The Court of Appeals started from the premise, laid down in Texas decisions, see especially Tennant v. Dunn, 130 Tex. 285, 110 S.W.2d. 53, that oil payments are interests in land. We too proceed on that basis; and yet we conclude that the consideration received for these oil payment rights (and the sulphur payment right) was taxable as ordinary income, subject to depletion.

The purpose of §117 was "to relieve the taxpayer from . . . excessive tax burdens on gains resulting from a conversion of capital investments, and to remove the deterrent effect of those burdens on such conversions." See Burnet v. Harmel, 287 U.S. 103, 106. And this exception has always been narrowly construed so as to protect the revenue against artful devices. See Corn Products Refining Co. v. Commissioner, 350 U.S. 46, 52.

We do not see here any conversion of a capital investment. The lump sum consideration seems essentially a substitute for what would otherwise be received at a future time as ordinary income. The pay-out of these particular assigned oil payment rights could be ascertained with considerable accuracy. Such are the stipulations, findings, or clear inferences. In the O'Connor case, the pay-out of the assigned oil payment right was so assured that the purchaser obtained a $9,990,350 purchase money loan at $3^{1}/_{2}$ percent interest without any security other than a deed of trust of the $10,000,000 oil payment right, he receiving 4 percent from the taxpayer. Only a fraction of the oil or sulphur rights were transferred, the balance being retained.[5]

5. Until 1946 the Commissioner agreed with the contention of the taxpayers in these cases that the assignment of an oil payment right was productive of a long-term capital gain. In 1946 he changed his mind and ruled that "consideration (not pledged for development) received for the assignment of a short-lived in-oil payment right carved out of any type of depletable interest in oil and gas in place (including a larger in-oil payment right) is ordinary income subject to the depletion allowance in the assignor's hands." G.C.M. 24849, 1946-1 Cum. Bull. 66, 69. This ruling was made applicable "only to such assignments made on or after April 1, 1946," I.T. 3895, 1948-1 Cum. Bull. 39. In 1950 a further ruling was made that represents the present view of the Commissioner. I.T. 4003, 1950-1 Cum. Bull. 10, 11, reads in relevant part as follows:

"After careful study and considerable experience with the application of G.C.M. 24849, supra, it is now concluded that there is no legal or practical basis for distinguishing between short-lived and long-lived in-oil payment rights. It is, therefore, the present position of the Bureau that the assignment of any in-oil payment right (not pledged for development, which extends over a period less than the life of the depletable property interest from which it is carved, is essentially the assignment of expected income from

Except in the *Fleming* case, which we will discuss later, cash was received which was equal to the amount of the income to accrue during the term of the assignment, the assignee being compensated by interest on his advance. The substance of what was assigned was the right to receive future income. The substance of what was received was the present value of income which the recipient would otherwise obtain in the future. In short, consideration was paid for the right to receive future income, not for an increase in the value of the income-producing property.

These arrangements seem to us transparent devices. Their forms do not control. Their essence is determined not by subtleties of draftsmanship but by their total effect. See Helvering v. Clifford, 309 U.S. 331; Harrison v. Schaffner, 312 U.S. 579. We have held that if one, entitled to receive at a future date interest on a bond or compensation for services, makes a grant of it by anticipatory assignment, he realizes taxable income as if he had collected the interest or received the salary and then paid it over. That is the teaching of Helvering v. Horst, 311 U.S. 112, and Harrison v. Schaffner, supra; and it is applicable here. As we stated in Helvering v. Horst, supra, at 117, "The taxpayer has equally enjoyed the fruits of his labor or investment and obtained the satisfaction of his desires whether he collects and uses the income to procure those satisfactions, or whether he disposes of his right to collect it as the means of procuring them." There the taxpayer detached interest coupons from negotiable bonds and presented them as a gift to his son. The interest when paid was held taxable to the father. Here, even more clearly than there, the taxpayer is converting future income into present income.

Second, as to the *Fleming* case. The Court of Appeals in the *Fleming* case held that the transactions were tax-free under §112(b)(1) which provides:

> No gain or loss shall be recognized if property held for productive use in trade or business or for investment (not including stock in trade or other property held primarily for sale, nor stocks, bonds, notes, choses in action, certificates of trust or beneficial interest, or other securities or evidences of indebtedness or interest) is exchanged solely for property of a like kind to be held either for productive use in trade or business or for investment. 53 Stat. 37.

In the alternative and as a second ground, it held that this case, too, was governed by §117.

We agree with the Tax Court, 24 T.C. 818, that this is not a tax-free exchange under §112(b)(1). Treasury Regulations 111, promulgated

---

such property interest. Therefore, the assignment for a consideration of any such in-oil payment right results in the receipt of ordinary income by the assignor which is taxable to him when received or accrued, depending upon the method of accounting employed by him. Where the assignment of the in-oil payment right is donative, the transaction is considered as an assignment of future income which is taxable to the donor at such time as the income from the assigned payment right arises.

"Notwithstanding the foregoing, G.C.M. 24849, supra, and I.T. 3935, supra, do not apply where the assigned in-oil payment right constitutes the entire depletable interest of the assignor in the property or a fraction extending over the entire life of the property."

under the 1939 Act, provide in §29.112(b)(1)-1 as respects the words "like kind," as used in §112(b)(1), that "One kind or class of property may not ... be exchanged for property of a different kind or class." The exchange cannot satisfy that test where the effect under the tax laws is a transfer of future income from oil leases for real estate. As we have seen, these oil payment assignments were merely arrangements for delayed cash payment of the purchase price of real estate, plus interest. Moreover, §39.112(a)-1 states that the "underlying assumption of these exceptions is that the new property is substantially a continuation of the old investment still unliquidated." Yet the oil payment assignments were not conversions of capital investments, as we have seen.

Reversed.

Notes

1. Do these three cases exhibit an intelligible pattern? Describe the pattern, its rationale, and the questions it poses as determinative of capital gain treatment.

2. The opinions in *Hort* and *McAllister* set up and apply a dichotomy between capital gains and ordinary income as described in §61. Which of the following criticisms of that approach are valid?

(a) Section 61 is no help in identifying capital gains because it describes all income from all sources, including capital gains. It refers just as explicitly to gains from dealings in property as to rent, or interest, or dividends, or any other form of income. Capital gains are a kind of gross income, not something different.

(b) Apart from statutory semantics, the suggestion that an item is not capital gain if it is a substitute for future ordinary income is erroneous as a matter of economic analysis. The price of any income-producing asset is principally a reflection of the present discounted value of its estimated future earnings (plus liquidation value); and most capital gains, therefore, are a substitute for the increased future earnings that would have been received if the asset had not been sold.

(c) In any event the reference to the capital gain provisions in these two cases is erroneous because the primary issue in each case is whether there was a gain or loss, not whether it was ordinary or capital. The statutory provisions governing basis and computation of gain or loss (§§1001 et seq.) are applicable to all gains and losses without regard to the capital gain criteria. The issue of gain or loss should, therefore, be determined first without reference to capital gain criteria, and the latter should only be looked to for the purpose of determining whether §§1(h), 1201, and 1202, or §1211, is applicable to the gain or loss so determined.

3. What is the issue in *Hort*? Certiorari was "limited to the question" whether, "in computing net gain or loss for income tax purposes, a taxpayer

[can] offset the value of the lease canceled against the consideration received by him for the cancellation." Why would it not be an adequate answer to that question to say that it is never value, but rather basis, that is set off against sale proceeds, citing §1001? In any event, what do the capital gain provisions have to do with it?

4. Suppose that Hort had proven that the fair rental value of the property in 1928 when he inherited it was $10,000 a year, that the fair market value of the property in 1928 without the lease would have been $200,000, and that the fair market value of the property with the lease, which was to run until 1947 at an annual rental of $25,000, was $400,000. Suppose that he had also proven that the latter was the value at which the property was included in Hort's father's estate in computing his federal estate tax.

What would have been the correct income tax treatment on these facts? Do you suspect that the taxpayer could have made out a claim along these lines? What facts in the case suggest that he could not? Cf. World Publishing Co. v. Commissioner, Chapter 15A.2 above.

5. But what of the capital gain issue?

(a) Suppose Hort had admitted that no part of his basis was separately allocable to a premium lease, and, therefore, had conceded $140,000 of gross income; could he nevertheless have made a persuasive argument for taxing the $140,000 as long-term capital gain?

(b) Is there any significant difference between a lessor and a lender? Consider a lender who lends money to a corporation taking bonds with an interest rate of 10 percent; interest rates then drop and the value of the bonds goes up; the corporation then buys the bonds back at a premium. That premium would presumably be capital gain to the lender. How is Mr. Hort's position any different? He gave the lessee the use of a piece of real estate rather than a sum of money, but why should that matter?

(c) Sometimes rents rise and then lessors have to pay lessees to cancel leases, or interest rates rise causing bond prices to fall. In that case can a borrower claim capital gain treatment for the discount at which he re-acquires his bonds? Can the lessee obtain capital gain treatment for the cancellation payment he receives? See Commissioner v. Ferrer, Chapter 21B below. How do the lessor and lender treat their payment and loss?

6. Again in *McAllister* the primary issue is whether there is gain or loss, not whether it is capital or ordinary. Again, both parties and the court seem to have assumed that the gain-or-loss issue depends on whether there was a sale of a capital asset. Is that assumption sound?

7. The court does not dwell on how the taxpayer computed a loss. The basis for her computation is that contained in Reg. §§1.1014-4 and 1.1014-5(a), which provide essentially that a seller of a limited actuarial interest in property—a life interest, a fixed-term interest, or a remainder interest—can use as her basis her actuarial share of the total basis for the whole property. If a trust contains property with an aggregate basis of $100,000, for example, and a life tenant's actuarial share of the trust,

based on her age and sex, is 43 percent, then her basis for determining gain or loss on a sale of her interest would be $43,000. In such a case, if there are only two beneficiaries, the remainderman's basis would be $57,000. Actuarial shares, under the regulation, are to be determined at the time of a disposition, and so they shift in favor of the remainderman with the passage of time.

Suppose property is left in trust for L for life with remainder to R. Now suppose L sells her interest to T, an unrelated third party. (There are people who make a business of purchasing life estates; McAllister presumably helped to stimulate demand for such a service!) Figure out how L, T, and R should then compute their income from the transaction. Does something go wrong?

In 1969, Congress responded to the problem of selling life estates by enacting §1001(e). Examine it together with Reg. §§1.1001-1(f) and 1.1014-5(b) and (c). Do these provisions represent a sensible resolution of the problem of computing gain or loss from sale of an income interest?

8. But then what about the capital gain issue? If a life tenant sells her interest today the whole sale proceeds are taxable gain, but are they taxable as capital gain? Should they be? The IRS has announced it will follow McAllister, "which held that the proceeds received by the life tenant of a testamentary trust in consideration for the transfer of her entire interest in the trust to the remainderman, are to be treated as an amount realized from the sale or exchange of a capital asset under section 1222. . . ." The announcement points out that for transfers after 1969 the basis will be zero, pursuant to §1001(e). Rev. Rul. 72-243, 1972-1 C.B. 233.

Consider a 65-year-old life tenant of a trust containing $100,000 of 10 percent securities. She sells her life estate, pays her tax, if any, on the sale, and then reinvests the proceeds net of tax in a life annuity. Assume that she sells her life estate at the valuation figure given in Reg. §20.2031-7 under the estate tax, using a §7520 interest rate of 10 percent (i.e., the discount rate for valuation equals the yield on the securities), or $72,860. See Reg. §20.2031-7(d)(2)(iii) and (d)(7), Table S. Assume she also purchases her annuity at that price, and that her marginal tax rate is 35 percent for ordinary income and 15 percent for capital gain.

Then under McAllister there would be no tax on sale of the life estate; the taxpayer would have the full proceeds, $72,860, available to invest in an annuity; and the annuity she could buy would pay $10,000 a year, just what she was receiving as life tenant. But she will have improved her position with respect to taxes because now she can exclude part of her annuity payments pursuant to §72. In fact, Reg. §1.72-9, Table V, gives an expected return multiple of 20.0 for a 65-year-old annuitant. The exclusion ratio would therefore be calculated as follows:

$$\$72,860 \div (\$10,000 \times 20.0) = 36.430\%$$

Hence, the annual tax after the sale and reinvestment would be $10,000 ×
63.570 percent × 35 percent = $2,225, as compared with $10,000 ×
35 percent = $3,500 before, and her after-tax income will have risen from
$6,500 to $7,775. See Table 21-1, columns (a) and (b). That produces a
19.6 percent increase in after-tax income and a 12.8 percentage point reduction
in effective rate of tax, as shown. It clearly will not do to give taxpayers a substantial partial exclusion grounded on a step-up in basis from zero to 72.9 percent of fair market value without any tax on the gain that increase represents.

TABLE 21-1
Sale of a Life Estate

	(a) No Sale of Life Estate	(b) Sale Proceeds Treated as in McAllister	(c) Sale Proceeds Taxed as Ordinary Income (35.0%)	(d) Sale Proceeds Taxed as Capital Gain (15.0%)
(1) Proceeds of sale	—	$72,860	$72,860	$72,860
(2) Tax on proceeds	—	—	25,501	10,929
(3) Proceeds of sale net of tax	—	72,860	47,359	61,931
(4) Annuity from reinvesting net sale proceeds	$10,000	10,000	6,500	8,500
(5) Amount excluded under §72	0	3,643	2,368	3,097
(6) Amount subject to tax	10,000	6,357	4,132	5,403
(7) Annual tax at 35%	3,500	2,225	1,446	1,891
(8) Net after-tax annuity	6,500	7,775	5,054	6,609
(9) Ratio to after-tax life income with no sale	1.000	1.196	0.778	1.017
(10) Effective total rate of tax on pmts received	35.0%	22.2%	49.5%	33.9%

Where:
(1) = life estate value from Reg. §20.2031-7(d)(7), Table S;
(2) = 35.0% of (1) in column (c); 15% of (1) in column (d);
(3) = (1) minus (2);
(4) = 10,000 times the ratio of (3) to 71,213 in columns (c) and (d);
(5) = 36.43% of (4) in columns (b), (c), and (d);
(6) = (4) minus (5);
(7) = 35% of (6);
(8) = (4) minus (7);
(9) = (8)/6,500; and
(10) = 100% times the ratio of 10,000 minus (8) to 10,000.

Under the government's theory in *McAllister*, on the other hand, the $72,860 would be subject to tax as ordinary income in the year of sale. At a 35 percent rate the tax would be $25,501, leaving $47,359 to reinvest. This would purchase only 65 percent as much annuity as in column (b), $6,500 a year; this is just what the taxpayer would have had left after tax if she had retained her life estate. But the annuity proceeds are themselves partially taxable under §72. The tax would be $6,500 × 63.570 percent × 35 percent = $1,446, and the taxpayer would, therefore, have only $5,054 left after tax, with the result that after-tax income is diminished by 22 percent and the effective rate of tax has gone up by 14.5 percentage points.

Notice in this case that whatever amount is taxed in the year of sale of the life estate will be excluded from income over a normal lifetime pursuant to the annuity rules; the aggregate amount of taxable income and of taxes paid will thus be the same. The very substantial extra burden on the taxpayer in column (c) results solely from acceleration.

Column (d) is like column (c) except that the rate of tax on sale proceeds—the part of the income that is accelerated—is cut by more than half due to capital gain treatment. As a result, the effective rate of tax decreases slightly (a little more than 1 percentage point) and the after-tax return goes up by 1.7 percent as a net result of the sale. On these facts the capital gain rate preference provides relief almost exactly equal to the additional burden produced by acceleration in both columns (c) and (d).

The computations in Table 21-1 are for a 65-year-old life tenant in the 35 percent rate bracket. Similar computation for other ages and rate brackets would yield different results. At any age the relief is smaller or greater depending on the ratio of the applicable capital gain rate to the taxpayer's marginal tax rate on ordinary income. So, for example, a 65-year-old taxpayer in the 25 percent bracket (and so subject to a 15 percent rate on capital gains) would have an effective total tax rate of 28.5 percent (incomplete relief). If this taxpayer were in the 15 percent bracket so that no tax was due on her capital gains, then she would pay an effective total tax rate of only 9.5 percent (overcorrection). Near neutrality would be achieved if a taxpayer in the 25 percent bracket were taxed on capital gains at a rate of 10 percent, and a taxpayer in the 15 percent bracket paid capital gains tax at a 5 percent rate.

9. Does this line of analysis for sale of a life estate suggest any definitional criteria for capital gains more generally? How about this:

Capital gains treatment is appropriate when a taxpayer, through any kind of exchange or termination of an income-producing investment or relationship, recognizes a gain which otherwise could have been deferred over a substantial period — like a lifetime.

Capital gain rate relief is compensation for the acceleration of tax liability and consequent loss of part of the future income in such a case. Thus, in general, a lump sum payment for a future income stream should be treated as capital gain, but only if the income stream would otherwise have continued long enough into the future to make the acceleration of tax liability important.

Recall the problem of the investor with appreciated stock who is considering switching to another stock. A tax which is imposed only if his gain is realized means that he will have less to invest in the new stock than what he could keep invested in the old. Capital gain rates are quite clearly intended to mitigate this difference. Does the rationale suggested above cover the case of the stock investor?

This rationale may be the best there is for long-term capital gain treatment, but is it enough to justify the statutory provision? In particular doesn't the whole argument depend on reinvestment, while capital gain treatment is available in many instances for recurring profits that are not reinvested? Should capital gain treatment be restricted to profits that are reinvested? Extended to all reinvested profits? How? Is the difference between capital gain and ordinary income really more one of use or application of funds than of source?

10. In *Lake* the only issue is over the applicability of capital gain rates; the taxpayer admits the whole sale proceeds are includible in gross income.

(a) Why?

(b) Is it important in *Lake* that the pay-out period is relatively short?

(c) See §636(a), added by the Tax Reform Act of 1969, which apparently would postpone taxation in a case like *Lake*. Prior to 1969, production payments were sometimes sold in order to accelerate income and thereby avoid the limitation of percentage depreciation to 50 percent of net income in §613(a). For example, if a well produces gross income of $100 with expenses of $70, the 50 percent limitation would permit a depletion deduction of only $15. If the taxpayer can get $200 of gross income in one year, however, against expenses of $70, the 50 percent limit would not come into play and he would succeed in deducting the full gross income percentage.

11. *ABC transactions.* (a) Can the holding in *Lake* be avoided if the taxpayer simultaneously or previously conveys the rest of his interest? Consider this typical ABC transaction:

A owned a fully depleted oil lease which was estimated to have remaining net profit capacity of $200,000 a year for ten years. She was willing to sell for $1 million.

B wanted to buy the oil lease and was willing to pay $1 million, but he only had $350,000 of his own money to invest.

C had $650,000 which he would advance at 7 percent interest to finance the transaction. *C* was willing to look only to the lease for payment.

To accommodate all three parties, *A* sold the lease to *B* for $350,000, reserving an oil payment of $650,000 plus 7 percent interest, payable out of 80 percent of the net income from the lease. Then *A* sold the retained oil payment to *C* for $650,000.

Prior to 1969, *A* would have had capital gain since he disposed of everything; *C* would have been allowed to amortize his investment as cost depletion, thus being taxed only on the interest component in his return; and *B* would have reported income only when it began to flow to him.

Section 636(b) was enacted in 1969 to change this treatment. How? And why? Is this statutory provision sound?

(b) For analytical purposes consider an ABC transaction with a coupon bond. *A*, who owns the bond, cuts off ten years' coupons; she delivers the bond without those coupons to *B*, and the coupons themselves to *C*. On a 10 percent bond *B* would pay a little over one-third the present value of the whole bond, *C* a little less than two-thirds. How should each party be taxed?

Consider the effect of §1286 on this transaction. Is this a sound provision?

(c) Would it be an accurate general description to say that the effect of an ABC transaction was to enable a purchaser, *B*, to finance acquisition of an asset out of earnings from that asset without being taxed on those earnings until he liquidates his investment? Why is this of particular value with respect to oil interests?

B.   RECEIPT OF PAYMENTS OUT OF A FUTURE INCOME STREAM

COMMISSIONER v. CARTER
170 F.2d 911 (2d Cir. 1948)

Before L. Hand, Chief Judge, and Swan and Chase, Circuit Judges.

SWAN, Circuit Judge. This appeal presents the question whether income received by the taxpayer in 1943 is taxable as long-term capital gain, as the Tax Court ruled, or as ordinary income as the Commissioner contends. The facts are not in dispute. The taxpayer, Mrs. Carter, had owned for ten years all the stock of a corporation which was dissolved on December 31, 1942. Upon its dissolution all of its assets were distributed to her in kind, subject to all its liabilities which she assumed. In the distribution she received property having a fair market value exceeding by about $20,000 the cost basis of her stock, and she reported such excess as a capital gain in her 1942 return and paid the tax thereon. In the corporate liquidation she also received thirty-two oil brokerage contracts which the parties stipulated had no ascertainable fair market value when distributed. Each contract provided for payment to the corporation of commissions on future deliveries of oil by a named seller to a named buyer. The contracts required no additional services to be performed by the corporation or its distributee, and the future commissions were conditioned on contingencies which made uncertain the amount and time of payment. In 1943 the taxpayer collected commissions of $34,992.20 under these contracts. She reported this sum as a long-term capital gain; the Commissioner determined it to be ordinary income. The Tax Court held it taxable as capital gain. The correctness of this decision is the sole question presented by the Commissioner's appeal.

Mrs. Carter's stock was a "capital asset" as defined by section 117(a) of the Internal Revenue Code. In exchange for her stock, she received the assets of the corporation upon its dissolution. The tax consequences of such a transaction are controlled by section 115(c), which provides that "the gain or loss to the distributee resulting from such exchange" shall be determined under section 111, but recognized only to the extent provided in section 112. Turning to section 111(a): the "gain from the sale or other disposition of property" is the excess of "the amount realized therefrom" over the adjusted cost basis provided in section 113(b). Paragraph (b) of section 111 defines the "amount realized from the sale or other disposition of property" to be the sum of money received "plus the fair market value of the property (other than money) received." Paragraph (c) of the same section provides that "In the case of a sale or exchange, the extent to which the gain or loss determined under this section shall be recognized for the purposes of this chapter, shall be determined under the provisions of section 112." That section lays down the general rule, subject to exceptions not pertinent to the case at bar, that "upon the sale or exchange of property" the entire amount of the gain or loss, determined under section 111, shall be recognized. From the foregoing statutory provisions, it is obvious that if the oil brokerage contracts distributed to the taxpayer had then had a "fair market value," such value would have increased correspondingly the "amount realized" by her in exchange for her stock and would have been taxable as long-term capital gain, not as ordinary income. Boudreau v. Commissioner, 5 Cir., 134 F.2d 360; Fleming v. Commissioner, 5 Cir. 153 F.2d 361. The question presented by the present appeal is whether a different result is required when contract obligations having no ascertainable fair market value are distributed in liquidation of a corporation and collections thereunder are made by the distributee in later years.

In answering this question in the negative, the Tax Court relied primarily upon Burnet v. Logan, 283 U.S. 404 (1931). That involved a sale of stock, not a distribution in liquidation, under which the seller received cash and the buyer's promise to make future payments conditioned on contingencies. The cash received did not equal the seller's cost basis for the stock, and the contingencies affecting future payments precluded ascribing a fair market value to the buyer's promise. In later years payments were made which the seller did not return as income. The decision held that she was not required to do so. With respect to such payments, the court said, 283 U.S. at pages 412, 413:

> As annual payments on account of extracted ore come in, they can be readily apportioned first as return of capital and later as profit. . . . When the profit, if any, is actually realized, the taxpayer will be required to respond. The consideration for the sale was $2,200,000 in cash and the promise of future money payments wholly contingent upon facts and circumstances not possible to foretell with anything like fair certainty. The promise was in no proper sense equivalent to cash. It had no ascertainable fair market value. The transaction was not a closed one. Respondent might never recoup her

capital investment from payments only conditionally promised. . . . She properly demanded the return of her capital investment before assessment of any taxable profit based on conjecture.

The Commissioner argues that the *Logan* case is inapplicable because there the taxpayer had not recovered the cost basis of her stock while here she had. The Tax Court thought the distinction immaterial. We agree. The Supreme Court spoke of the annual payments as constituting "profit" after the seller's capital investment should be returned. Until such return it cannot be known whether gain or loss will result from a sale; thereafter it becomes certain that future payments will result in gain. No reason is apparent for taxing them as ordinary income. As this court said in Commissioner v. Hopkinson, 2 Cir., 126 F.2d 406, 410, "payments received by the seller after his basis had been extinguished would have been taxable to him as capital gains from the sale of the property," citing Burnet v. Logan as authority.

The Commissioner also urges that the *Logan* case is distinguishable because it dealt with a sale of stock rather than exchange of stock for assets distributed in a corporate liquidation. This contention is answered by White v. United States, 305 U.S. 281, 288, and Helvering v. Chester N. Weaver Co., 305 U.S. 293, 295, where the court held that the recognition required by section 115(c) of gains and losses on liquidations must for purposes of computation of the tax, be taken to be the same as that accorded to gains and losses on sales of property. Consequently we agree with the Tax Court's ruling that the principle of the *Logan* case is applicable to a corporate liquidation where stock is exchanged in part for contracts having no ascertainable market value, and that future collections under such contracts are taxable as capital gain in the year when received if the distributee has previously recovered the cost basis for the stock.

The Commissioner's argument that such collections are analogous to the receipt of interest or rent upon bonds or real estate distributed in a corporate liquidation overlooks a significant distinction. Payment of interest or rent does not impair the value of the bond or real estate since each remains as a capital asset regardless of the number of payments. See Helvering v. Manhattan Life Ins. Co., 2 Cir., 71 F.2d 292, 293. But with respect to the oil brokerage contracts, under which no additional services were to be rendered by the payee, each payment decreases their value until, with the final payment it will be completely exhausted; and, if the payments be treated as income, the distributee has no way to recoup his capital investment, since concededly he has no economic interest in the oil producing properties and therefore no right to depletion deductions.[2] Hence to consider the brokerage payments as ordinary income would produce a most

---

2. It is true, in the case at bar, the taxpayer had no capital investment in the brokerage contracts because from other assets distributed she had already recovered the cost basis of her stock and the oil brokerage contracts had no ascertainable fair market value. But the Commissioner's analogy argument would be equally applicable if the brokerage contracts had been the only corporate assets distributed and

unjust result and one quite unlike the result which follows the distribution of bonds or real estate in a corporate liquidation.

For the foregoing reasons we think the decision of the Tax Court correct. It is affirmed.

Notes

1. Review Bernice Patton Testamentary Trust v. United States and the notes following concerning Burnet v. Logan, Chapter 5E above. What is the "principle of the *Logan* case," which the Tax Court and the court of appeals found applicable in *Carter*? Note that *Logan* involved tax years prior to the adoption of special provisions for capital gains. What precisely were the issues and the stakes in *Logan*? Would it be accurate to say it had solely to do with computing gross income and not with the availability of the special rates for capital gains? The government, as paraphrased by the Court, does not seem to have made this point, but rather to have argued that *Logan* itself would have been somehow inapplicable on the facts of *Carter*.

2. (a) Suppose that in *Carter* a court had concluded, on the facts, that the right to royalties did have a readily ascertainable fair market value of $21,000. Then gain (or loss) on receipt of the royalty right would presumably be computed by assigning that value to the royalty right (§1001), and $21,000 would become the taxpayer's basis for the royalty right. Suppose the royalties to be received were estimated at $5,000 a year for seven years after receipt of the royalty right. How then would the taxpayer compute his gain in each subsequent year? Would it be taxable as ordinary income or capital gain?

(b) One way to compute gain would be to amortize the basis of $21,000 ratably over the seven-year estimated life of the royalty right. That would produce a net gain of $2,000 a year if the royalties received correspond to the estimate. The total amount ultimately taken into income — $21,000 on the liquidation plus $2,000 a year for seven years thereafter — will, of course, equal $35,000, the amount of royalties received.

(c) If this computation of gain is correct, and if the $2,000 net income in each subsequent year would be taxable as ordinary income, then the stakes riding on the question whether the royalty right has an ascertainable market value are high indeed. A total of $35,000 — the total amount of royalties received — is ultimately includible in computing gross income in either case. But open transaction treatment will let it all be deferred and all

---

it had been possible to ascribe to them a fair market value of $21,000. In that case, the distributee's capital investment in the brokerage contracts would have been $20,000, the cost basis of her stock being $1,000. She would be entitled to recover her capital investment before she could be charged with receiving either gain or ordinary income, and the only source of recovery would be the payments which would ultimately exhaust the value of the contracts. Hence the answer given above to the analogy argument is apposite.

taxed at capital gain rates, while closed transaction treatment would accelerate the tax on $21,000 and require the rest to be taxed as ordinary income.

(d) Once closed transaction treatment is agreed to there is a certain trade-off between deferral and capital gain treatment in fixing the value of the royalty right: Any decrease in the fair market value assigned will decrease the capital gain tax payable immediately but will increase the portion of the gain ultimately taxable as ordinary rates. Open transaction treatment destroys this trade-off by producing deferral *and* capital gain treatment for the whole amount in question.

(e) Can persuasive arguments be made for the proposition that only the gain recognized at the time of liquidation or sale should be taxed at capital gain rates — that in effect an open transaction should be treated like a closed transaction in which the royalty right is assigned, as a matter of convenience, a value equal to any excess of the taxpayer's basis for the property given up over the value of the other property received, or zero if there is no such excess? Can any such arguments be brought within the present statutory language?

(f) What is the relevance here of the rationale for capital gain treatment suggested in Table 21-1 and notes 8 and 9, pp. 1123-1126 above.

3. What about the installment method of reporting pursuant to §453? See Chapter 5E above. Are the reduced rates applicable to capital gains appropriate if gain is deferred beyond the year of disposition? See Calvin H. Johnson, Deferred Payment Sales: Change the Basis and Character Rules, 120 Tax Notes 157 (2008).

COMMISSIONER v. BROWN
380 U.S. 563 (1965)

Mr. Justice WHITE delivered the opinion of the Court. . . . Clay Brown, members of his family and three other persons owned substantially all of the stock in Clay Brown & Company, with sawmills and lumber interests near Fortuna, California. Clay Brown, the president of the company and spokesman for the group, was approached by a representative of California Institute for Cancer Research in 1952, and after considerable negotiation the stockholders agreed to sell their stock to the Institute for $1,300,000, payable $5,000 down from the assets of the company and the balance within ten years from the earnings of the company's assets. It was provided that simultaneously with the transfer of the stock, the Institute would liquidate the company and lease its assets for five years to a new corporation, Fortuna Sawmills, Inc., formed and wholly owned by the attorneys for the sellers.[4]

---

4. The net current assets subject to liabilities were sold by the Institute to Fortuna for a promissory note which was assigned to sellers. The lease covered the remaining assets of Clay Brown & Company. Fortuna was capitalized at $25,000, its capital being paid in by its stockholders from their own funds.

Fortuna would pay to the Institute 80% of its operating profit without allowance for depreciation or taxes, and 90% of such payments would be paid over by the Institute to the selling stockholders to apply on the $1,300,000 note. This note was noninterest bearing, the Institute had no obligation to pay it except from the rental income and it was secured by mortgages and assignments of the assets transferred or leased to Fortuna. If the payments on the note failed to total $250,000 over any two consecutive years, the sellers could declare the entire balance of the note due and payable. The sellers were neither stockholders nor directors of Fortuna but it was provided that Clay Brown was to have a management contract with Fortuna at an annual salary and the right to name any successor manager if he himself resigned.[5]

The transaction was closed on February 4, 1953. Fortuna immediately took over operations of the business under its lease, on the same premises and with practically the same personnel which had been employed by Clay Brown & Company. Effective October 31, 1954, Clay Brown resigned as general manager of Fortuna and waived his right to name his successor. In 1957, because of a rapidly declining lumber market, Fortuna suffered severe reverses and its operations were terminated. Respondent sellers did not repossess the properties under their mortgages but agreed they should be sold by the Institute with the latter retaining 10% of the proceeds. Accordingly, the property was sold by the Institute for $300,000. The payments on the note from rentals and from the sale of the properties totaled $936,131.85. Respondents returned the payments received from rentals as the gain from the sale of capital assets. The Commissioner, however, asserted the payments were taxable as ordinary income and were not capital gain within the meaning of I.R.C. 1939, §117(a)(4) and I.R.C. 1954, §1222(3). These sections provide that "[t]he term 'long-term capital gain' means gain from the sale or exchange of a capital asset held for more than 6 months. . . ."

In the Tax Court, the Commissioner asserted that the transaction was a sham and that in any event respondents retained such an economic interest in and control over the property sold that the transaction could not be treated as a sale resulting in a long-term capital gain. A divided Tax Court, 37 T.C. 461, found that there had been considerable good-faith bargaining at arm's length between the Brown family and the Institute, that the price agreed upon was within a reasonable range in the light of the earnings history of the corporation and the adjusted net worth of its assets, that the primary motivation for the Institute was the prospect of ending up with the assets of the business free and clear after the purchase price had been fully paid, which would then permit the Institute to convert the property and the

---

5. Clay Brown's personal liability for some of the indebtedness of Clay Brown & Company, assumed by Fortuna, was continued. He also personally guaranteed some additional indebtedness incurred by Fortuna.

money for use in cancer research, and that there had been a real change of economic benefit in the transaction.[6] Its conclusion was that the transfer of respondents' stock in Clay Brown & Company to the Institute was a bona fide sale arrived at in an arm's-length transaction and that the amounts received by respondents were proceeds from the sale of stock and entitled to long-term capital gains treatment under the Internal Revenue Code. The Court of Appeals affirmed, 325 F.2d 313, and we granted certiorari, 377 U.S. 962.

Having abandoned in the Court of Appeals the argument that this transaction was a sham, the Commissioner now admits that there was real substance in what occurred between the Institute and the Brown family. The transaction was a sale under local law. The Institute acquired title to the stock of Clay Brown & Company and, by liquidation, to all of the assets of that company, in return for its promise to pay over money from the operating profits of the company. If the stipulated price was paid, the Brown family would forever lose all rights to the income and properties of the company. Prior to the transfer, these respondents had access to all of the income of the company; after the transfer, 28% of the income remained with Fortuna and the Institute. Respondents had no interest in the Institute nor were they stockholders or directors of the operating company. Any rights to control the management were limited to the management contract between Clay Brown and Fortuna, which was relinquished in 1954.

Whatever substance the transaction might have had, however, the Commissioner claims that it did not have the substance of a sale within the meaning of §1222(3). His argument is that since the Institute invested nothing, assumed no independent liability for the purchase price and promised only to pay over a percentage of the earnings of the company, the entire risk of the transaction remained on the sellers. Apparently, to qualify as a sale, a transfer of property for money or the promise of money must be to a financially responsible buyer who undertakes to pay the purchase price other than from the earnings or the assets themselves or there must be a substantial down payment which shifts at least part of the risk to the buyer and furnishes some cushion against loss to the seller.

To say that there is no sale because there is no risk-shifting and that there is no risk-shifting because the price to be paid is payable only from the income produced by the business sold, is very little different from saying that because business earnings are usually taxable as ordinary income, they are subject to the same tax when paid over as the purchase price of property. This argument has rationality but it places an unwarranted construction on the term "sale," is contrary to the policy of the capital gains provisions of the Internal Revenue Code, and has no support in the cases. We reject it.

"Capital gain" and "capital asset" are creatures of the tax law and the Court has been inclined to give these terms a narrow, rather than a broad, construction. Corn Products Co. v. Commissioner, 350 U.S. 46, 52. A "sale," however, is a common event in the non-tax world; and since it is used in the Code without limiting definition and without legislative history indicating a contrary result, its common and ordinary meaning should at least be persuasive of its meaning as used in the Internal Revenue Code. "Generally speaking, the language in the Revenue Act, just as in any statute, is to be given its ordinary meaning, and the words 'sale' and 'exchange' are not to be read any differently." Helvering v. Flaccus Leather Co., 313 U.S. 247, 249; Hanover Bank v. Commissioner, 369 U.S. 672, 687; Commissioner v. Korell, 339 U.S. 619, 627-628; Crane v. Commissioner, 331 U.S. 1, 6; Lang v. Commissioner, 289 U.S. 109, 111; Old Colony R. Co. v. Commissioner, 284 U.S. 552, 560.

"A sale, in the ordinary sense of the word, is a transfer of property for a fixed price in money or its equivalent." Iowa v. McFarland, 110 U.S. 471, 478; it is a contract "to pass rights of property for money, — which the buyer pays or promises to pay to the seller . . ." Williamson v. Berry, 8 How. 495, 544. Compare the definition of "sale" in §1(2) of the Uniform Sales Act and in §2-106(1) of the Uniform Commercial Code. The transaction which occurred in this case was obviously a transfer of property for a fixed price payable in money.

Unquestionably the courts, in interpreting a statute, have some "scope for adopting a restricted rather than a literal or usual meaning of its words where acceptance of the meaning would lead to absurd results . . . or would thwart the obvious purpose of the statute." Helvering v. Hammel, 311 U.S. 504, 510-511; cf. Commissioner v. Gillette Motor Co., 364 U.S. 130, 134, and Commissioner v. P.G. Lake, Inc., 356 U.S. 260, 265. But it is otherwise "where no such consequences would follow and where . . . it appears to be consonant with the purposes of the Act. . . ." Helvering v. Hammel, supra, at 511; Ozawa v. United States, 260 U.S. 178, 194. We find nothing in this case indicating that the Tax Court or the Court of Appeals construed the term "sale" too broadly or in a manner contrary to the purpose or policy of capital gains provisions of the Code.

Congress intended to afford capital gains treatment only in situations "typically involving the realization of appreciation in value accrued over a substantial period of time, and thus to ameliorate the hardship of taxation of the entire gain in one year." Commissioner v. Gillette Motor Co., 364 U.S. 130, 134. It was to "relieve the taxpayer from . . . excessive tax burdens on gains resulting from a conversion of capital investments" that capital gains were taxed differently by Congress. Burnet v. Harmel, 287 U.S. 103, 106; Commissioner v. P.G. Lake, Inc., 356 U.S. 260, 265.

As of January 31, 1953, the adjusted net worth of Clay Brown & Company as revealed by its books was $619,457.63. This figure included accumulated earnings of $448,471.63, paid in surplus, capital stock and notes payable to the Brown family. The appraised value as of that date, however, relied upon by the Institute and the sellers, was $1,064,877, without figuring interest on deferred balances. Under a deferred payment plan with a 6% interest figure, the sale value was placed at $1,301,989. The Tax Court found the sale price agreed upon was arrived at in an arm's-length transaction, was the result of real negotiating and was "within a reasonable range in light of the earnings history of the corporation and the adjusted net worth of the corporate assets." 37 T.C. 461, 486.

Obviously, on these facts, there had been an appreciation in value accruing over a period of years, Commissioner v. Gillette Motor Co., supra, and an "increase in the value of the income-producing property." Commissioner v. P.G. Lake, Inc., supra, at 266. This increase taxpayers were entitled to realize at capital gains rates on a cash sale of their stock; and likewise if they sold on a deferred payment plan taking an installment note and a mortgage as security. Further, if the down payment was less than 30% (the 1954 Code requires no down payment at all) and the transaction otherwise satisfied I.R.C. 1939, §44, the gain itself could be reported on the installment basis.

In the actual transaction, the stock was transferred for a price payable on the installment basis but payable from the earnings of the company. Eventually $936,131.85 was realized by respondents. This transaction, we think, is a sale, and so treating it is wholly consistent with the purposes of the Code to allow capital gains treatment for realization upon the enhanced value of a capital asset.

The Commissioner, however, embellishes his risk-shifting argument. Purporting to probe the economic realities of the transaction, he reasons that if the seller continues to bear all the risk and the buyer none, the seller must be collecting a price for his risk-bearing in the form of an interest in future earnings over and above what would be a fair market value of the property. Since the seller bears the risk, the so-called purchase price *must* be excessive and *must* be simply a device to collect future earnings at capital gains rates.

We would hesitate to discount unduly the power of pure reason and the argument is not without force. But it does present difficulties. In the first place, it denies what the Tax Court expressly found—that the price paid was within reasonable limits based on the earnings and net worth of the company; and there is evidence in the record to support this finding. We do not have, therefore, a case where the price has been found excessive.

Secondly, if an excessive price is such an inevitable result of the lack of risk-shifting, it would seem that it would not be an impossible task for the Commissioner to demonstrate the fact. However, in this case he offered no evidence whatsoever to this effect; and in a good many other cases involving similar transactions, in some of which the reasonableness of the price paid by a charity was actually contested, the Tax Court has found the sale price to be within reasonable limits, as it did in this case.

Thirdly, the Commissioner ignores as well the fact that if the rents payable by Fortuna were deductible by it and not taxable to the Institute, the Institute could pay off the purchase price at a considerably faster rate than the ordinary corporate buyer subject to income taxes, a matter of considerable importance to a seller who wants the balance of his purchase price paid as rapidly as he can get it. The fact is that by April 30, 1955, a little over two years after closing this transaction, $412,595.77 had been paid on the note and within another year the sellers had collected another $238,498.80, for a total of $651,094.57.

Furthermore, risk-shifting of the kind insisted on by the Commissioner has not heretofore been considered an essential ingredient of a sale for tax purposes. In LeTulle v. Scofield, 308 U.S. 415, one corporation transferred properties to another for cash and bonds secured by the properties transferred. The Court held that there was "a sale or exchange upon which gain or loss must be reckoned in accordance with the provisions of the revenue act dealing with the recognition of gain or loss upon a sale or exchange," id., at 421, since the seller retained only a creditor's interest rather than a proprietary one. "[T]hat the bonds were secured solely by the assets transferred and that, upon default, the bondholder would retake only the property sold, [did not change] his status from that of a creditor to one having a proprietary stake." Ibid. Compare Marr v. United States, 268 U.S. 536. To require a sale for tax purposes to be to a financially responsible buyer who undertakes to pay the purchase price from sources other than the earnings of the assets sold or to make a substantial down payment seems to us at odds with commercial practice and common understanding of what constitutes a sale. The term "sale" is used a great many times in the Internal Revenue Code and a wide variety of tax results hinge on the occurrence of a "sale." To accept the Commissioner's definition of sale would have wide ramifications which we are not prepared to visit upon taxpayers, absent congressional guidance in this direction.

The Commissioner relies heavily upon the cases involving a transfer of mineral interests, the transferor receiving a bonus and retaining a royalty or other interest in the mineral production. Burnet v. Harmel, 287 U.S. 103; Palmer v. Bender, 287 U.S. 551; Thomas v. Perkins, 301 U.S. 655; Kirby Petroleum Co. v. Commissioner, 326 U.S. 599; Burton-Sutton Oil Co. v. Commissioner, 328 U.S. 25; Commissioner v. Southwest Exploration Co., 350 U.S. 308. Thomas v. Perkins is deemed particularly pertinent. There a leasehold interest was transferred for a sum certain payable in oil as produced, and it was held that the amounts paid to the transferor were not includable in the income of the transferee but were income of the transferor. We do not, however, deem either Thomas v. Perkins or the other cases controlling.

First, "Congress . . . has recognized the peculiar character of the business of extracting natural resources," Burton-Sutton Oil Co. v. Commissioner, 328 U.S. 25, 33; see Stratton's Independence, Ltd. v. Howbert, 231 U.S. 399, 413-414, which is viewed as an income-producing operation and not as a conversion of capital investment, Anderson v. Helvering, 310 U.S. 404, at 407, but one which has its own built-in method of allowing through depletion "a tax-free return of the capital consumed in the production of gross income through severance," Anderson v. Helvering, supra, at 408, which is independent of cost and depends solely on production, *Burton-Sutton*, at 34. Percentage depletion allows an arbitrary deduction to compensate for exhaustion of the asset, regardless of cost incurred or any investment which the taxpayer may have made. The Commissioner, however, would assess to respondents as ordinary income the entire amount of all rental payments made by the Institute, regardless of the accumulated values in the corporation which the payments reflected and without regard for the present policy of the tax law to allow the taxpayer to realize on appreciated values at the capital gains rates.

Second, Thomas v. Perkins does not have unlimited sweep. The Court in Anderson v. Helvering, supra, pointed out that it was still possible for the owner of a working interest to divest himself finally and completely of his mineral interest by effecting a sale. In that case the owner of royalty interest, fee interest and deferred oil payments contracted to convey them for $160,000 payable $50,000 down and the balance from one-half the proceeds which might be derived from the oil and gas produced and from the sale of the fee title to any of the lands conveyed. The Court refused to extend Thomas v. Perkins beyond the oil payment transaction involved in that case. Since the transferor in *Anderson* had provided for payment of the purchase price from the sale of fee interest as well as from the production of oil and gas, "the reservation of this additional type of security for the deferred payments serve[d] to distinguish this case from Thomas v. Perkins. It is similar to the reservation in a lease of oil payment rights together with a personal guarantee by the lessee that such payments shall at all events equal the specified sum." Anderson v. Helvering, supra, at 412-413. Hence, there was held to be an outright sale of the properties, all of the oil income therefrom being taxable to the transferee notwithstanding the fact of payment of part of it to the seller. The respondents in this case, of course, not only had rights against income, but if the income failed to amount to $250,000 in any two consecutive years, the entire amount could be declared due, which was secured by a lien on the real and personal properties of the company.[8]

8. Respondents place considerable reliance on the rule applicable where patents are sold or assigned, the seller or assignor reserving an income interest. In Rev. Rul. 58-353, 1958-2 Cum. Bull. 408, the Service announced its acquiescence in various Tax Court cases holding that the consideration received by the owner of a patent for the assignment of a patent or the granting of an exclusive license to such patent may be treated as the proceeds of a sale of property for income tax purposes, even though the consideration received by the transferor is measured by production, use, or sale of the patented article. The Government now says that the Revenue Ruling amounts only to a decision to cease litigating the question, at least temporarily, and that the cases on which the rule is based are wrong in principle and inconsistent with the cases dealing with the taxation of mineral interests. We note, however, that in Rev. Rul. 60-226, 1960-1 Cum. Bull. 26, the Service extended the same treatment to the copyright field. Furthermore, the Secretary of the Treasury in 1963 recognized the present law to be that "the sale of a patent by the inventor may be treated as the sale of a capital asset," Hearings before the House Committee on Ways and Means, 88th Cong., 1st Sess., Feb. 6, 7, 8 and 18, 1963, Pt. I (rev.), on the president's

There is another reason for us not to disturb the ruling of the Tax Court and the Court of Appeals. In 1963, the Treasury Department, in the course of hearings before the Congress, noted the availability of capital gains treatment on the sale of capital assets even though the seller retained an interest in the income produced by the assets. The Department proposed a change in the law which would have taxed as ordinary income the payments on the sale of a capital asset which were deferred over more than five years and were contingent on future income. Payments, though contingent on income, required to be made within five years would not have lost capital gains status nor would payments not contingent on income even though accompanied by payments which were. Hearings before the House Committee on Ways and Means, 88th Cong., 1st Sess., Feb. 6, 7, 8 and 18, 1963, Pt. I (rev.), on the President's 1963 Tax Message, pp. 154-156.

Congress did not adopt the suggested change[9] but it is significant for our purposes that the proposed amendment did not deny the fact or occurrence of a sale but would have taxed as ordinary income those income-contingent payments deferred for more than five years. If a purchaser could pay the purchase price out of earnings within five years, the seller would have capital gain rather than ordinary income. The approach was consistent with allowing appreciated values to be treated as capital gain but with appropriate safeguards against reserving additional rights to future income. In comparison, the Commissioner's position here is a clear case of "overkill" if aimed at preventing the involvement of tax-exempt entities in the purchase and operation of business enterprises. There are more precise approaches to this problem as well as to the question of the possibly excessive price paid by the charity or foundation. And if the Commissioner's approach is intended as a limitation upon the tax treatment of sales generally, it represents a considerable invasion of current capital gains policy, a matter which we think is the business of Congress, not ours.

The problems involved in the purchase of a going business by a tax-exempt organization have been considered and dealt with by the Congress. Likewise, it has given its attention to various kinds of transactions involving

---

1963 Tax Message, p. 150, and the Congress failed to enact the changes in the law which the Department recommended.

These developments in the patent field obviously do not help the position of the Commissioner. Nor does I.R.C. 1954, §1235, which expressly permits specified patent sales to be treated as sales of capital assets entitled to capital gains treatment. We need not, however, decide here whether the extraction and patent cases are irreconcilable or whether, instead, each situation has its own peculiar characteristics justifying discrete treatment under the sale and exchange language of §1222. Whether the patent cases are correct or not, absent §1235, the fact remains that this case involves the transfer of corporate stock which has substantially appreciated in value and a purchase price payable from income which has been held to reflect the fair market value of the assets which the stock represents.

9. It did, however, accept and enact another suggestion made by the Treasury Department. Section 483, which was added to the Code, provided for treating a part of the purchase price as interest in installment sales transactions where no interest was specified. The provision was to apply as well when the payments provided for were indefinite as to their size, as for example "where the payments are in part at least dependent upon future income derived from the property." S. Rep. No. 830, 88th Cong., 2d Sess., p. 103. This section would apparently now apply to a transaction such as occurred in this case.

the payment of the agreed purchase price for property from the future earnings of the property itself. In both situations it has responded, if at all, with precise provisions of narrow application. We consequently deem it wise to "leave to the Congress the fashioning of a rule which, in any event, must have wide ramifications." American Automobile Assn. v. United States, 367 U.S. 687, 697.

Affirmed.

Mr. Justice HARLAN, concurring. Were it not for the tax laws, the respondents' transaction with the Institute would make no sense, except as one arising from a charitable impulse. However the tax laws exist as an economic reality in the businessman's world, much like the existence of a competitor. Businessmen plan their affairs around both, and a tax dollar is just as real as one derived from any other source. The Code gives the Institute a tax exemption which makes it capable of taking a greater after-tax return from a business than could a nontax-exempt individual or corporation. Respondents traded a residual interest in their business for a faster payout apparently made possible by the Institute's exemption. The respondents gave something up; they received something substantially different in return. If words are to have meaning, there was a "sale or exchange."

Obviously the Institute traded on its tax exemption. The Government would deny that there was an exchange, essentially on the theory that the Institute did not put anything at risk; since its exemption is unlimited, like the magic purse that always contains another penny, the Institute gave up nothing by trading on it.

One may observe preliminarily that the Government's remedy for the so-called "bootstrap" sale — defining sale or exchange so as to require the shifting of some business risks — would accomplish little by way of closing off such sales in the future. It would be neither difficult nor burdensome for future users of the bootstrap technique to arrange for some shift of risks. If such sales are considered a serious abuse, ineffective judicial correctives will only postpone the day when Congress is moved to deal with the problem comprehensively. Furthermore, one may ask why, if the Government does not like the tax consequences of such sales, the proper course is not to attack the exemption rather than to deny the existence of a "real" sale or exchange.

The force underlying the Government's position is that the respondents did clearly retain some risk-bearing interest in the business. Instead of leaping from this premise to the conclusion that there was no sale or exchange, the Government might more profitably have broken the transaction into components and attempted to distinguish between the interest which respondents retained and the interest which they exchanged. The worth of a business depends upon its ability to produce income over time. What respondents gave up was not the entire business, but only their interest in the business' ability to produce income in excess of that which was necessary to pay them off under the terms of the transaction. The value of such a residual interest is a function of the risk element of the business and the amount of income it is capable of producing per year, and will necessarily be substantially less than the value of the total business. Had the Government argued that it was that interest which respondents exchanged, and only to that extent should they have received capital gains treatment, we would perhaps have had a different case.

I mean neither to accept nor reject this approach, or any other which falls short of the all-or-nothing theory specifically argued by the petitioner, specifically opposed by the respondents, and accepted by the Court as the premise for its decision. On a highly complex issue with as wide ramifications as the one before us, it is vitally important to have had the illumination provided by briefing and argument directly on point before any particular path is irrevocably taken. Where the definition of "sale or exchange" is concerned, the court can afford to proceed slowly and by stages. The illumination which has been provided in the present case convinces me that the position taken by the Government is unsound and does not warrant reversal of the judgment below. Therefore I concur in the judgement to affirm.

Mr. Justice GOLDBERG, with whom The Chief Justice and Mr. Justice Black join, dissenting. The essential facts of this case which are undisputed illuminate the basic nature of the transaction at issue. Respondents conveyed their stock in Clay Brown & Co., a corporation owned almost entirely by Clay Brown and the members of his immediate family, to the California Institute for Cancer Research, a tax-exempt foundation. The Institute liquidated the corporation and transferred its assets under a five-year lease to a new corporation, Fortuna, which was managed by respondent Clay Brown, and the shares of which were in the name of Clay Brown's attorneys, who also served as Fortuna's directors. The business thus continued under a new name with no essential change in control of its operations. Fortuna agreed to pay 80% of its pretax profits to the Institute as rent under the lease, and the Institute agreed to pay 90% of this amount to respondents in payment for their shares until the respondents received $1,300,000, at which time their interest would terminate and the Institute would own the complete beneficial interest as well as all legal interest in the business. If remittances to respondents were less than $250,000 in any two consecutive years or any other provision in the agreements was violated, they could recover the property. The Institute had no personal liability. In essence respondents conveyed their interest in the business to the Institute in return for 72% of the profits of the business and the right to recover the business assets if payments fell behind schedule.

At first glance it might appear odd that the sellers would enter into this transaction, for prior to the sale they had a right to 100% of the corporation's income, but after the sale they had a right to only 72% of that income and would lose the business after 10 years to boot. This transaction, however, afforded the sellers several advantages. The principal advantage sought by the sellers was capital gain, rather than ordinary income, treatment for that share of the business profits which they received. Further, because of the Tax Code's charitable exemption[1] and the lease arrangement with Fortuna,[2] the Institute believed that neither it nor Fortuna would have to pay income tax on the earnings of the business. Thus the sellers would receive free of corporate taxation, and subject only to personal taxation at capital gains rates, 72% of the business earnings until they were paid $1,300,000. Without the sale they would receive only 48% of the business earnings, the rest going to the Government in corporate taxes, and this 48% would be subject to personal taxation at ordinary rates. In effect the Institute sold the respondents the use of its tax exemption, enabling the respondents to collect $1,300,000 from the business more quickly than they otherwise could and to pay taxes on this amount at capital gains rates. In return, the Institute received a nominal amount of the profits while the $1,300,000 was being paid, and it was to receive the whole business after this debt had been paid off. In any realistic sense the Government's grant of a tax exemption was used by the Institute as part of an arrangement that allowed it to buy a business that in fact cost it nothing. I cannot believe that Congress intended such a result.

The Court today legitimates this bootstrap transaction and permits respondents the tax advantage which the parties sought. The fact that respondent Brown, as a result of the Court's holding, escapes payment of about $60,000 in taxes may not seem intrinsically important—although every failure to pay the proper amount of taxes under a progressive income tax system impairs the integrity of that system. But this case in fact has very broad implications. We are told by the parties and by interested amici that this is a test case. The outcome of this case will determine whether this bootstrap scheme for the conversion of ordinary income into capital gain, which has already been employed on a number of occasions, will become even more widespread. It is quite clear that the Court's decision approving this tax device will give additional momentum to its speedy proliferation. In my view Congress did not sanction the use of this scheme under the present revenue laws to obtain the tax advantages which the Court authorizes. Moreover, I believe that the Court's holding not only deviates from the intent of Congress but also departs from this Court's prior decisions.

The purpose of the capital gains provisions of the Internal Revenue Code of 1954, §1201 et. seq., is to prevent gains which accrue over a long

---

1. See I.R.C. 1954, §501(c)(3).

2. This lease arrangement was designed to permit the Institute to take advantage of its charitable exemption to avoid taxes on payment of Fortuna's profits to it, with Fortuna receiving a deduction for the rental payments as an ordinary and necessary business expense, thus avoiding taxes to both. Though unrelated business income is usually taxable when received by charities, an exception is made for income received from the lease of real and personal property of less than five years. See I.R.C. §514; Lanning, Tax Erosion and the "Bootstrap Sale" of a Business—I, 108 Pa. L. Rev. 623, 684-689. Though denial of the charity's tax exemption on rent received from Fortuna would also remove the economic incentive underlying this bootstrap transaction, there is no indication in the Court's opinion that such income is not tax exempt. See the Court's opinion, ante, at 565-566.

period of time from being taxed in the year of their realization through a sale at high rates resulting from their inclusion in the higher tax brackets. Burnet v. Harmel, 287 U.S. 103, 106. These provisions are not designed, however, to allow capital gains treatment for the recurrent receipt of commercial or business income. In light of these purposes this Court has held that a "sale" for capital gains purposes is not produced by the mere transfer of legal title. Burnet v. Harmel, supra; Palmer v. Bender, 287 U.S. 551. Rather, at the very least, there must be a meaningful economic transfer in addition to a change in legal title. See Corliss v. Bowers, 281 U.S. 376. Thus the question posed here is not whether this transaction constitutes a sale within the terms of the Uniform Commercial Code or the Uniform Sales Act—we may assume it does—but, rather, the question is whether, at the time legal title was transferred, there was also an economic transfer sufficient to convert ordinary income into capital gain by treating this transaction as a "sale" within the terms of I.R.C. §1222(3). . . .

To hold as the Court does that this transaction constitutes a "sale" within the terms of I.R.C. §1222(3), thereby giving rise to capital gain for the income received, legitimates considerable tax evasion. Even if the Court restricts its holding, allowing only those transactions to be §1222(3) sales in which the price is not excessive, its decision allows considerable latitude for the unwarranted conversion of ordinary income into capital gain. Valuation of a closed corporation is notoriously difficult. The Tax Court in the present case did not determine that the price for which the corporation was sold represented its true value; it simply stated that the price "was the result of real negotiating" and "within a reasonable range in light of the earnings history of the corporation and the adjusted net worth of the corporate assets." 37 T.C., at 486. The Tax Court, however, also said that "[i]t may be . . . that petitioner [Clay Brown] would have been unable to sell the stock at as favorable a price to anyone other than a tax-exempt organization." 37 T.C., at 485. Indeed, this latter supposition is highly likely, for the Institute was selling its tax exemption, and this is not the sort of asset which is limited in quantity. Though the Institute might have negotiated in order to receive beneficial ownership of the corporation as soon as possible, the Institute, at no cost to itself, could increase the price to produce an offer too attractive for the seller to decline. Thus it is natural to anticipate sales such as this taking place at prices on the upper boundary of what courts will hold to be a reasonable price—at prices which will often be considerably greater than what the owners of a closed corporation could have received in a sale to buyers who were not selling their tax exemptions. Unless Congress repairs the damage done by the Court's holding, I should think that charities will soon own a considerable number of closed corporations, the owners of which will see no good reason to continue paying taxes at ordinary income rates. It should not be necessary, however, for Congress to address itself to this loophole, for I believe that under the present laws it is clear that Congress did not intend to accord capital gains treatment to the proceeds of the type of sale present here.

Although the Court implies that it will hold to be "sales" only those transactions in which the price is reasonable, I do not believe that the logic of the Court's opinion will justify so restricting its holding. If this transaction is a sale under the Internal Revenue Code, entitling its proceeds to capital gains treatment because it was arrived at after hard negotiating, title in a conveyancing sense passed, and the beneficial ownership was expected to pass at a later date, then the question recurs, which the Court does not answer, why a similar transaction would cease to be a sale if hard negotiating produced a purchase price much greater than actual value. . . .

Further, a bootstrap tax avoidance scheme can easily be structured under which the holder of any income-earning asset "sells" his asset to a tax-exempt buyer for a promise to pay him the income produced for a period of years. The buyer in such a transaction would do nothing whatsoever; the seller would be delighted to lose his asset at the end of, say, 30 years in return for capital gains treatment of all income earned during that period. It is difficult to see, on the Court's rationale, why such a scheme is not a sale. And, if I am wrong in my reading of the Court's opinion, and if the Court would strike down such a scheme on the ground that there is no economic shifting of risk or control, it is difficult to see why the Court upholds the sale presently before it in which control does not change and any shifting of risk is nominal.

I believe that the Court's overly conceptual approach has led to a holding which will produce serious erosion of our progressive taxing system, resulting in greater tax burdens upon all taxpayers. The tax avoidance routes opened by the Court's opinion will surely be used to advantage by the owners of closed corporations and other income-producing assets in order to evade ordinary income taxes and pay at capital gains rates, with a resultant large-scale ownership of private businesses by tax-exempt organizations.[5] While the Court justifies its result in the name of conceptual purity,[6] it simultaneously violates long-standing congressional tax policies that capital gains treatment is to be given to significant economic transfers of investment-type assets but not to ordinary commercial or business income and that transactions are to be judged on their entire substance rather than their naked form. Though turning tax consequences on form alone might produce greater certainty of the tax results of any transaction, this stability exacts as its price the certainty that tax evasion will be

5. Attorneys for amici have pointed out that tax-exempt charities which they represent have bought numerous closed corporations.

6. It should be noted, however, that the Court's holding produces some rather unusual conceptual results. For example, after the payout is complete the Institute presumably would have a basis of $1,300,000 in a business that in reality cost it nothing. If anyone deserves such a basis, it is the Government, whose grant of tax exemption is being used by the Institute to acquire the business.

produced. In Commissioner v. P.G. Lake, Inc., 356 U.S. 260, 265, this Court recognized that the purpose of the capital gains provisions of the Internal Revenue Code is " 'to relieve the taxpayer from . . . excessive tax burdens on gains resulting from a conversion of capital investments, and to remove the deterrent effect of those burdens on such conversions.' . . . And this exception has always been narrowly construed so as to protect the revenue against artful devices." I would hold in keeping with this purpose and in order to prevent serious erosion of the ordinary income tax provisions of the Code, that the bootstrap transaction revealed by the facts here considered is not a "sale" within the meaning of the capital gains provisions of the Code, but that it obviously is an "artful device," which this Court ought not to legitimate. The Court justifies the untoward result of this case as permitted tax avoidance; I believe it to be a plain and simple case of unwarranted tax evasion.

Notes

1. As the Court indicates, after the transaction here, all Mr. Brown had was the right to 72 percent of the income, limited to $1.3 million, instead of all the income without limit. Be sure you understand why the transaction was nevertheless advantageous. Does the advantage depend on the capital gain provisions, or the charitable exemption, or both? Would either alone be sufficient to make the transaction attractive? What other purchasers besides tax-exempt charities could make attractive purchase offers of the kind involved here?

Careful analysis of these questions would require separate consideration of corporate and individual taxes. Exemption from corporate tax may not be a prerequisite, but apparently the purchaser must be in a more favorable tax posture than the seller to be able to pay over more than what the seller could have had in after-tax income.

2. For analytical purposes consider a taxpayer with a 6 percent coupon bond. (a) Under what circumstances might it pay her to "sell" the bond to a charity in return for payment over to her of the interest as installment payments? (b) Would there be some abuse even if the charity made a substantial down payment? (c) How would the taxpayer be treated if she simply tore off eight years' coupons, sold the bond without them, and then collected the coupons herself? (d) Should she be treated differently if a charity collects the coupons and then pays the money over to her?

3. What does the Court's opinion in *Brown* contribute to general understanding of the capital gain provisions? The opinion seems to focus on value, on the fact that there has been a gradual increase in value over a period of time, which the taxpayer is entitled to realize at capital gain rates. Is that a sound line of analysis? Was it soundly applied in this case?

4. What would be the effect of §§1274 and 483 on the transaction in *Brown*? Are they enough, or is further legislation needed? What sort of further legislation? See Chapter 6C.2.

5. Look at §§512(b)(4) and 514, which were added to deal with *Brown* from the charity's end. Evaluate this response.

6. How would you have argued *Brown* for the government? Was it a mistake to urge that the price logically must have been excessive?

STERN v. UNITED STATES

164 F. Supp. 847 (E.D. La. 1958), aff'd per curiam, 262 F.2d 957 (5th Cir. 1959), cert. denied, 359 U.S. 969 (1959)

J. S. WRIGHT, District Judge. This case concerns "Francis," the talking mule. Francis is a product of World War II. It was created by a lonely second lieutenant in the Pacific theater of operations who sometimes wondered whether there was anything in the Army lower than a second lieutenant. Francis convinced him there was. Now, seven motion pictures later, that second lieutenant, the taxpayer here, is claiming that the income from "Francis" is entitled to capital gains treatment under the Internal Revenue laws.

In 1933, after attending Harvard University, David Stern, III, was employed as a dramatic critic for the Philadelphia Record, a newspaper owned by his father. Beginning four months later, he became successively comptroller of the Record, classified advertising salesman, assistant classified manager, classified manager, promotion manager, and general manager. During the time that Stern was learning the business, he continued to serve the Record as part-time dramatic critic. In 1938 he became publisher of the Courier-Post newspapers in Camden, New Jersey. Throughout the prewar years, when Stern was a newspaper business executive, his hobby was writing. He wrote some stories and articles in his spare time, but he was unable to sell any of them.

In the spring of 1943, Stern enlisted as a private in the United States Army. He was later commissioned as a second lieutenant, and subsequently became co-officer in charge of the Central Pacific Edition of Stars and Stripes. While in the Pacific, Stern wrote some imaginary dialogue between a second lieutenant and an old Army mule, some of which he sold to Esquire for approximately $200. He also wrote several short stories while in the Army which he sold to magazines for $50 to $250.

After his release from the Army in 1946, Stern returned to Camden as publisher of the Courier-Post newspapers. In 1947 Stern's connection with the Courier-post newspapers was terminated. He immediately entered negotiations to purchase a newspaper. While so doing and at the suggestion of a book publisher, he rewrote in book form all of the episodes about the talking mule, Francis. During this period he also wrote a sequel to "Francis," called "Francis Goes to Washington." It, too, was published by Farrar-Strauss, publisher of "Francis." In July 1949 Stern completed negotiations for the purchase of The New Orleans Item and took over the controlling interest and active management of the newspaper as its publisher. Since that date, he has devoted virtually his full time to the newspaper business as publisher.

On June 2, 1950 Stern sold to Universal Pictures Co., Inc., all of his "right, title and interest . . . in and to . . . that certain character known as 'Francis' conceived and created by" him, together with all of his rights to the two novels mentioned above and all of his rights to any contracts with respect to the properties conveyed. In consideration of this transfer, Universal agreed to pay him $50,000 plus 5% of the net profits from photoplays based on the character Francis, and 75% of all sums received by Universal under contracts for the use of licensing of the property. Payment of the $50,000 entitled Universal to a "commitment period" of two years within which to make a motion picture. Thereafter, and following release of each picture, Universal was entitled to additional commitment periods by paying a similar fixed consideration of $50,000 as to each picture or period. The contract further provided that "if purchaser shall elect not to pay fixed consideration with respect to any next succeeding commitment period . . . the property shall revert to the seller," all rights in motion pictures produced to remain in Universal. Under this agreement, Universal produced six additional motion pictures[1] in which the character Francis was used. Stern prepared the screen play for the first of these pictures but has had no connection whatever with the writing or production of subsequent pictures except occasionally and incidentally as a consultant. The novel, "Francis Goes to Washington," was not used for screen material.

Plaintiffs have reported as ordinary income for tax purposes all amounts received by them from the sale of the motion picture and publishing rights to the novel "Francis," for preparing a short screen treatment of the book, "Rhubarb," and income received under the agreement for writing screen plays. Only those amounts received from Universal for the character Francis have been treated by plaintiffs as capital gains, accrued during the years received. For the year 1950, the Internal Revenue Service originally accepted plaintiffs' treatment of this income as capital gains from the sale of the character Francis. In considering subsequent years, the Appellate Division of the Internal Revenue reopened the return for the year 1950 and ruled that income from the character Francis was not subject to capital gains treatment for the reason that the contract with Universal was not a sale of the character Francis, that if it were, Francis was property held by the taxpayer primarily for sale to customers in the ordinary course of his business and, further, under the provision of [§1221 (3)] the character Francis was similar to a copyright, a literary or artistic composition and, therefore, not a capital asset. . . .

The question as to whether the taxpayer's contract with Universal Pictures is a sale will be considered first because if it is not a sale, it will be

---

1. In 1949 the first Francis movie was produced. It was based on the novel, "Francis," and the taxpayer here wrote the screen play. Its production, of course, was not pursuant to the June 2, 1950 contract in suit.

unnecessary to consider the other objections to capital gains treatment of the income made by the Government. It will be noted in the contract that Stern sold all of his interest in the books, "Francis," and "Francis Goes to Washington," the character Francis, and all rights and pending contracts concerning them. The agreement makes reference to "the full and complete ownership in the property sold, transferred and granted to (Universal) hereunder." It declares that Stern "hereby sells, transfers and conveys . . . all right, title and interest" in the property to Universal and guarantees "the full benefit of (Universal's) full and complete ownership in the property." . . .

The Government's suggestion, without citation of authority, that the contract in suit is not a sale because it provided for contingent payments of indeterminate sums similar to royalties, and because the property reverted back to Stern if the fixed consideration for any period is not paid, cannot convert this contract of sale into a licensing agreement. Perhaps a sale which provides for contingent payments of indeterminate sums and reversion does violence to the doctrinaire concepts of what a sale should be. But the tax cases interpreting Section 117 of the Code have so long and so consistently held such contracts to be sales that the Internal Revenue Service itself in a recent ruling is now indicating its acquiescence in this classification.

The Government next contends that if the contract in suit is a sale, then the income therefrom is still not entitled to capital gains treatment because it was a sale of "property held by the taxpayer primarily for sale to customers in the ordinary course of his trade or business." Section 117(a)(1)(A), Internal Revenue Code of 1939. The resolution of this question depends on appraisal of the total factual situation. Smith v. Commissioner, 5 Cir., 232 F.2d 142; Consolidated Naval Stores Company v. Fahs, 5 Cir., 227 F.2d 923. Unquestionably, under Section 117(a) of the Code, a taxpayer may have more than one business. Snell v. Commissioner, 5 Cir., 97 F.2d 891. Before any business can come within Section 117(a), however, it must be an "occupational undertaking which required the habitual devotion of time, attention or effort with substantial regularity." Thomas v. Commissioner, 5 Cir., 254 F.2d 233, 237. The criteria in making this determination are fully set forth in opinions by the Fifth Circuit so it would serve no useful purpose to repeat them here. Those cases do show that a court should not be quick to put a man in business under Section 117(a) simply because he has been successful in earning extra income through a hobby or some other endeavor which takes a relatively small part of his time.

Here the taxpayer is a newspaper publisher and has been, with the exclusion of the war years, actively directing newspapers since 1938. Virtually his entire time has been given to that endeavor. As a hobby he has written a few short stories, some of which have been productive of small amounts of income. On two occasions he has written screen plays. He has created the character Francis and written two novels about it. This literary work has taken relatively little of his time. It was more or less a relaxation from his principal employment. Under the circumstances, it can hardly be said that the taxpayer created "Francis" to hold as "property held by the taxpayer primarily for sale to customers in the ordinary course of his trade or business." Section 117(a)(1)(A), I.R.C., 1939.

The Government makes much of the fact that in one of the schedules attached to taxpayer's return, he professes to be a writer. Even if the taxpayer were responsible for this statement, his literary license in this regard should not be allowed to affect the tax treatment accorded his income. Actually, the indication of Stern as a writer was the work of the accountant who prepared the return. It is further noted that the schedule on which the profession appears relates to income and expenses attendant his writing. On the first page of each return in the space provided for "Occupation," the word "Publisher" appears.

Finally, and unfortunately for the taxpayer, the government's position on the 1950 amendment to the 1939 Code is well taken. That amendment excludes from capital gains treatment income from the sale of "a copyright; a literary, musical, or artistic composition; or similar property," held by "a taxpayer, whose personal efforts created such property." The purpose of this amendment is obvious. It is intended to deny capital gains treatment to income from the sale, by their creator, of literary, musical, or artistic compositions, or similar property. Prior to 1950, various rulings of the Internal Revenue Service had approved capital gains treatment of various literary, musical and artistic compositions, including books and radio programs. Congress determined to eliminate such treatment for such compositions. Hence the amendment.

The taxpayer contends that the character "Francis" is not covered by the amendment, that it is not subject to copyright, that it is not a literary, musical or artistic composition or similar property. He argues that he has paid his taxes at the regular rates on all of his income from his writings. He states that the character "Francis" is an "intellectual conception" and that as such the income from the sale thereof is entitled to capital gains treatment.

The taxpayer cites several cases in support of his position that the character Francis is not subject to being copyrighted. And he spends much time in his brief arguing that the Internal Revenue Service itself has limited the words of the statute "or similar property" to property capable of being copyrighted.[10] It is not necessary for this Court to appraise the taxpayer's citations, his argument on this point, or the counter citations and

---

10. The taxpayer refers to that portion of the Treasury Regulations (Treas. Reg. 118, Secs. 39.117(a)-1 which reads as follows:

"The phrase 'similar property' includes, for example, such property as a theatrical production, a radio program, a newspaper cartoon strip, or any other property eligible for copyright protection (whether under state or common law)."

But see Section 3797(b) of the Internal Revenue Code, which reads:

"The terms 'includes' and 'including' when used in a definition contained in this title shall not be deemed to exclude other things otherwise within the meaning of the term defined."

argument of the Government. It is this Court's view that the character Francis, irrespective of its susceptibility to copyright, is a "literary composition" and as such the income from the sale thereof is not entitled to capital gains treatment. The taxpayer concedes, as he must, that the novel, "Francis," in which the character Francis is the leading figure, is a literary composition, but he argues that Francis, the principal characterization in the book, is not. In this he is mistaken. The character Francis gets its definition and its delineation from the book. The literary description in the book composes the character. How can it be said that the book is a literary composition yet the main character delineated therein is not? A slice of the loaf is still bread. It would be absurd to attribute to Congress the intention, under the 1950 amendment, of covering whole literary compositions but not parts thereof, particularly in view of the catchall, "or similar property," which appears at the end of the amendment.

Without the literary description of Francis, his mannerisms and his manifestations, Francis would cease to exist. In any event, an amorphous Francis could hardly be called "property held by the taxpayer," the sale of which is entitled to capital gains treatment. Section 117(a)(1), I.R.C., 1939. If Francis is, as taxpayer suggests, an "intellectual conception," sans form and substance, existing in the mind alone, it is incapable of ownership and, therefore, of being "property held by the taxpayer." See Holmes v. Hurst, 174 U.S. 82, 86; Nichols v. Universal Pictures Corporation, 2 Cir., 45 F.2d 119, 121. If Francis has sufficient form and substance to be considered property capable of ownership, this is so because of its literary composition. Compare Warner Bros. Pictures v. Columbia Broadcasting System, 9 Cir., 216 F.2d 945.

The taxpayer is entitled to capital gains treatment on the income from the contract in suit for the year 1950 because the 1950 amendment to the Code does not apply to income received during that year. As to subsequent years, however, capital gains treatment of the income from the contract must be denied as proscribed by that amendment.

Judgment accordingly.

Note

The 1950 amendment is now in §1221(a)(3), but by §1221(b)(3) (added in 2006) self-created musical works have again become eligible for capital gain treatment even if the taxpayer is in the business of composing and selling such works. What's the distinction here? That the country music industry leans Republican, but not so the film industry?

Letters and memoranda prepared by *or for* the taxpayer were later included in §1221(a)(3) in order to curb charitable contribution deductions for donation of official papers to presidential libraries. Exclusion from the capital asset category interacts with §170(e)(1)(A) to produce the desired limitation. In a footnote to the Watergate scandal, an attempt to beat the 1969 effective date of this rule on his donation of vice-presidential papers came back to haunt President Nixon. See Staff of the Joint Comm. on Internal Revenue Taxation, Examination of President Nixon's Tax Returns for 1969 Through 1972, H.R. Rep. No. 93-966, at 39-41, A-85 to A-151 (1974).

BUSSE v. COMMISSIONER
479 F.2d 1147 (7th Cir. 1973)

Before Hastings, Senior Circuit Judge, Cummings, Circuit Judge, and Campbell, Senior District Judge.*

Hastings, Senior Circuit Judge. Sometime before March 20, 1958, taxpayer invented a method and machine for stacking cans on pallets. On that date, he assigned an undivided one-half interest in the invention to his brother. A patent covering the invention issued to taxpayer on August 16, 1960. By reason of the assignment, taxpayer and his brother each owned one-half of the patent. When the brother died on July 10, 1962, his interest passed to his widow. Taxpayer and the widow organized Busse Bros., Inc., a Wisconsin corporation, on January 2, 1966, in which at all relevant times each owned 50 percent of the issued and outstanding stock. On the same day the corporation was organized, taxpayer, his sister-in-law and the corporation entered into an oral agreement by which each shareholder sold his entire interest in the patent to the corporation. In return, the corporation agreed to pay taxpayer and his sister-in-law quarterly installments, during the life of the patent, equal to five percent of the corporation's net selling price (as that term was defined in the agreement) of devices covered by the patent claims.

During 1967 the corporation paid taxpayer $36,029.01 as his one-half share of the payments required under the agreement. Although taxpayer's 1966 assignment to the corporation was plainly "[a] transfer . . . of property consisting of . . . an undivided interest [in all substantial rights to a patent] which includes a part of all such rights, by any holder,"[3] as described in §1235(a) of the Code, taxpayer was not able to treat the 1967 payments as long-term capital gain under §1235. Such treatment was precluded by the operation of §1235(d), because taxpayer's assignment to the corporation was a transfer between related persons, specifically, in the words of §267(b)(2) as modified by §1235(d)(1), between "[a]n individual and a corporation 25 percent or more in value of the outstanding stock of

---

* Senior District Judge William J. Campbell of the Northern District of Illinois is sitting by designation.

3. As an "individual whose efforts created such property," taxpayer comes within the definition of "holder" for purposes of §1235. Code, §1235(b)(l).

which is owned . . . by . . . such individual." However, taxpayer was able to and did report the entire amount of the 1967 payments as long-term gain received upon the sale of a capital asset, under the general provisions of §§1221 and 1222.[4] The Commissioner, pursuant to the appropriate regulations under §483, nevertheless concluded that only $33,011.81 of the 1967 payments constituted capital gain, while the remaining $3,017.20 was unstated interest on an installment sale, taxable at ordinary income rates. In line with this analysis, the Commissioner determined an income tax deficiency for 1967 of $1,659.47. He rejected taxpayer's contention that §483[(d)](4) protected the 1967 payments from unstated interest treatment. Taxpayer petitioned the Tax Court for a redetermination, and that court determined that there was no 1967 deficiency. This appeal followed.

The Tax Court's decision was of a narrow legal question: Given a patent transfer which is described in §1235(a) of the Code but which does not receive its capital gain treatment under §1235, should some part of the payment received pursuant thereto be treated as unstated interest under §483, or is such treatment precluded by the exception contained in §483[(d)](4)? We agree with the Tax Court that such payments do qualify for the statutory exception[5] and, accordingly, affirm the decision and order. . . .

On brief, the Commissioner agrees that the payments made pursuant to the 1966 assignment "appear to fall within the literal language of Section 1235(a)." It would seem, then, that taxpayer is entitled to be excepted from the operation of §483 by the "plain, unambiguous and understandable" words of the statue. United States v. Chused, 8 Cir., 209 F.2d 548, 550 (1954). . . .

Nevertheless, the Commissioner seeks to avoid the consequences of strict construction by invoking the judicially developed rule which justifies "a departure from the letter of the law" when adherence to the letter would cause an absurdity "so gross as to shock the general moral or common sense" and when it is plain that Congress intended "that the letter of the statute is not to prevail." Crooks v. Harrelson, 282 U.S. 55, 60 (1930).

The best indication of the intent of Congress is, of course, the literal wording of the statute itself, which we have held is not ambiguous. Discussion of subsection [(d)](4) in the congressional committee reports is minimal and perfunctory, shedding no light on the intent the Commissioner purports to see of avoiding the result the Tax Court decision dictates. Contemporaneous agency interpretation of the statute, as represented by Treas. Reg. §1.483-2(b)(4), is largely a restatement of the statute and, when considered in the light most favorable to the Commissioner's position, is ambiguous in a way that the statute is not. To turn from a

---

4. Rev. Rul. 69-482, 1969-2 Cum. Bull. 164.
5. In so holding, the Tax Court specifically adhered to its prior decision in Floyd G. Paxton, 53 T.C. 202 (1969). Although the Commissioner did not elect to appeal *Paxton*, he expressed his disagreement with the result by means of a nonacquiescence, 1971-2 Cum. Bull, 4.

clear statute to an unclear regulation for guidance is hardly an accepted method of interpretation.

To support his contention that the plain language of the statute leads to absurd results, the Commissioner cites two examples of what he terms "anomalous situation[s]." The first of these examples proceeds from the Commissioner's assumption that Congress created a favored class of tax-payers in enacting §1235, a class of which the present taxpayer is not a member. Characterizing the exception of §483[(d)](4) as "a benefit essentially ancillary to the benefits provided by Section 1235," the Commissioner is disturbed by the spectre of the present taxpayer obtaining some of the benefits of class membership without qualifying for actual membership in the class.

The second example springs from the interrelationship of words and phrases within the various subsections of §1235. The word "holder" in subsection (a) is defined in subsection (b). As we have noted previously, taxpayer qualifies as a holder under subsection (b)(1) because he "created" the property transferred. The Commissioner points out, however, that subsection (b)(2)(B) makes eligibility for holder status by persons other than "creators" turn on their not being related to the creator within the meaning of subsection (d). Thus, for example, should Busse Bros., Inc., assign the patent rights to a third party at some future time, it may not claim the benefit of the §483[(d)](4) exception even if, like taxpayer, it can qualify the transfer for capital gain treatment under §§1221 and 1222. Or, as the Commissioner states the situation in his brief:

> Put another way, Section 1235-type transactions disqualified because of an unauthorized "transfer" would not be subject to imputed interest, but Section 1235-type transactions disqualified because of failure to meet the definition of "holder" would be so subject. The proper distinction should lie, in our view, not in *how* the transaction became disqualified, but rather in *whether* the transaction was disqualified under Section 1235. (Emphasis in original.)

However much the statute, in operation, may offend the Commissioner's sense of symmetry and propriety, we cannot say that the results it causes are either absurd or unintended by Congress. Courts have no power (just as the Commissioner has no power in his capacity as an administrative official) "to rewrite legislative enactments to give effect to" their "ideas of policy and fitness or the desirability of symmetry in statutes." United States v. Shirah, 4 Cir., 253 F.2d 798,800 (1958). . . .

In sum, taxpayer's 1966 assignment to the corporation was "a transfer described in section 1235(a)." Payments received pursuant to the assignment thereby qualified for the exception from unstated interest treatment contained in §483[(d)](4). Since there is every reason to give effect to the plain language of the latter statute, the Commissioner erred in determining a deficiency in taxpayer's 1967 income tax. The United States Tax Court was correct in so holding, and we affirm its decision and order.

Affirmed.

Notes

1. What is the effect if a taxpayer fails to qualify as a holder, as defined in §1235(b)? In Busse v. United States, 543 F.2d 1321 (Ct. Cl. 1976), the present taxpayer's sister-in-law was denied the benefit of §483(d)(4) on the ground that, not being a holder, her transfer was not described in §1235(a).

2. The exclusion of patents from the imputed interest rules is now contained in §§483(d)(4) and 1274(c)(3)(E). In connection with the adoption of these provisions the Joint Committee Staff asserted that "Congress intended that this exception apply only if the transfer qualifies for capital gain treatment under section 1235. The exception under section 483 of prior law was held to apply to the transfer of any patent described in section 1235(a), without regard to the other requirements of section 1235." Staff of Joint Comm. on Taxation, 98th Cong., General Explanation of the Revenue Provisions of the Deficit Reduction Act of 1984, 123 n.44 (Comm. Print 1984). Does the statutory language adequately express this intention?

3. Of course the main thing to be learned from *Busse* transcends its narrow holding in any event. Patents originally raised very similar issues to those raised by copyrights. *Busse* mainly illustrates the legislative response to those issues in the patent context. Why is that response so very different than in the case of copyrights? Is there any adequate justification for the difference? If not, which response makes better sense?

COMMISSIONER v. FERRER
304 F.2d 125 (2d Cir. 1962)

Before Friendly, Smith and Marshall, Circuit Judges.

FRIENDLY, Circuit Judge. This controversy concerns the tax status of certain payments received by José Ferrer with respect to the motion picture "Moulin Rouge" portraying the career of Henri de Toulouse-Lautrec. The difficulties Mr. Ferrer must have had in fitting himself into the shape of the artist can hardly have been greater than ours in determining whether the transaction here at issue fits the rubric "gain from the sale or exchange of a capital asset held for more than 6 months," Internal Revenue Code of 1939, §117(a)(1) and (4), as the Tax Court held, 35 T.C. 617 (1961), or constitutes ordinary income, as the Commissioner contends. We have concluded that neither party is entirely right, that some aspects of the transaction fall on one side of the line and some on the other, and that the Tax Court must separate the two.

In 1950 Pierre LaMure published a novel, "Moulin Rouge," based on the life of Toulouse-Lautrec. He then wrote a play, "Monsieur Toulouse," based on the novel. On November 1, 1951, LaMure as "Author" and Ferrer, a famous actor but not a professional producer, as "Manager" entered into a contract, called a Dramatic Production Contract, for the stage production of the play by Ferrer.

The contract was largely on a printed form recommended by the Dramatists Guild of the Authors League of America, Inc. However great the business merits of the document, which are extolled in Burton, Business Practices in the Copyright Field, in C.C.H., 7 Copyright Problems Analyzed (1952) 87, 109, for a court, faced with the task of defining the nature of the rights created, it exemplifies what a contract ought not to be. Its first six pages include eleven articles, some introduced by explanatory material whose contractual status is, to say the least, uncertain. Here the last of these pages was preceded by three single-spaced typewritten pages of "Additional Clauses," one with a still further insert. Finally come 15 pages of closely printed "Supplemental Provisions," introduced by explanatory material of the sort noted. We shall thread our way through this maze as best we can.

By the contract the Author "leased" to the Manager "the sole and exclusive right" to produce and present "Monsieur Toulouse" on the speaking stage in the United States and Canada, and gave certain rights for its production elsewhere. Production had to occur on or before June 1, 1952, unless the Manager paid an additional advance of $1,500 not later than that date, in which event the deadline was extended to December 1, 1952. Five hundred dollars were paid as an initial advance against Author's royalties: the Manager was required to make further advances of like amount on December 1, 1951, and January 1, 1952. Royalties were to be paid the Author on all box-office receipts, on a sliding scale percentage basis.

Article Seventh said that "In the event that under the terms hereof the Manager shall be entitled to share in the proceeds of the Motion Picture and Additional Rights hereafter referred to, it is agreed that the Manager shall receive" 40% for the first ten years and diminishing percentages thereafter. Among the additional rights so described were "Radio and Television."

For the beginning of an answer whether the Manager would be so entitled, we turn to Article IV, §2, of the Supplemental Provisions. This tells us that "In the event the Manager has produced and presented the play for the 'Requisite Performances and Terms,' the Negotiator shall pay the Manager" the above percentages "of the proceeds, from the disposal of the motion picture rights." Article VI, §3, contains a similar provision as to payment by the Author of the proceeds of the "additional rights" including radio and television. The "Requisite Performances and Terms" are defined in Article XIII, §9(b); we shall say more about the "Negotiator" hereafter.

Further provisions put flesh on these bones. Article IV, §1(a), says that "The title" to the motion picture rights "vested in the Author, as provided in Article VIII hereof." Article VIII says, even more broadly, "The Author shall retain for his sole benefit, complete title, both legal and equitable, in and to all rights whatsoever (including, but not by way of limitation, the Motion Picture Rights . . . Radio and Television Rights . . .)," other than the right to produce the play. The Motion Picture Negotiator, a person appointed by the Council of the Dramatists Guild, Article V, §§1 and 6, has power to dispose of the motion picture rights. However, he may not do this without the written consent of both Author and Manager "prior to the time the play has been playing for any of the respective periods of time referred to in Article XIII, Section 9(b) hereof," Article IV, §1(b). This prohibition serves a double purpose — it protects the Manager from dilution of the value of the right to produce the play through too early exhibition of a picture, and it promotes realization of the enhancement in the value of the motion picture rights normally resulting from successful dramatic production. Doubtless for similar reasons, the Author could not, without the consent of the Manager, permit the release of radio and television rights until first-class production of the play had ceased. Article V, §1(b), decrees that the Manager shall "have no right, title or interest, legal or equitable, in the motion picture rights, other than the right to receive the manager's share of the proceeds. . . ." Article V, §1(c), lays down that if the Manager deems "himself aggrieved by any disposition of motion picture rights, he shall have no recourse, in law or in equity," against a purchaser, a lessee, or the Negotiator; "the Manager's sole recourse . . . shall be against the Author and only by arbitration as provided hereunder." Article V, §1(d), says it again: "No claim of the Manager, howsoever arising, shall constitute a cloud on the title to the motion picture rights; and a purchaser or lessee thereof shall have the right to deal freely and exclusively with the Author and Negotiator. . . ."

Having been somewhat upstaged by these provisions, the Manager then returns toward the center under other clauses. The Negotiator must confer with him, as well as with the Author, on every step in the disposition of the motion picture rights. "It is desirable that the price shall be mutually satisfactory to both Author and Manager," Article V, §2(a). If the Manager does not like an offer the Negotiator is planning to accept, he has an opportunity to turn up a better one, ibid. All moneys received for the motion picture rights are to be deposited in a special account, Article V, §3. An insert to one of the "Additional Clauses" provides that if the Manager desires, the Author, not later than three weeks after the New York opening of the play, will "discuss a proposed deal for the Manager to acquire" the motion picture rights. Finally, another "Additional Clause" prescribes that "All dramatic, motion picture, radio and television rights in the novel Moulin Rouge shall merge in and with the play during the existence of this contract," and if the Manager produces and presents the play for a sufficient period, "throughout the copyright period of the play."

Shortly after signature of the Dramatic Production Contract, John Huston called Ferrer to ask whether he would be interested in playing Toulouse-Lautrec in a picture based upon "Moulin Rouge." On getting an affirmative indication, Huston said he would go ahead and acquire the motion picture rights. Ferrer replied, in somewhat of an exaggeration, "When you get ready to acquire them talk to me because I own them."

Both Huston and Ferrer then had discussions with LaMure. Ferrer expressed a willingness "to abandon the theatrical production in favor of the film production, provided that, if the film production were successful, I would be recompensed for my abandoning the stage production." On the strength of this, LaMure signed a preliminary agreement with Huston's corporation. In further negotiations, Huston's attorney insisted on "either an annulment or conveyance" of the Dramatic Production Contract. LaMure's lawyer prepared a letter of agreement, dated February 7, 1952, whereby Ferrer would cancel and terminate the Contract. Ferrer signed the letter but instructed his attorney not to deliver it until the closing of a contract between himself and the company that was to produce the picture; the letter was not delivered until May 14, 1952.

Meanwhile, on May 7, 1952, Ferrer entered into a contract with Huston's company, Moulin Productions, Inc. ("Moulin"), hereafter the Motion Picture Contract. This was followed by an agreement and assignment dated May 12, 1952, whereby LaMure sold Huston all motion picture rights to his novel, including the right to exploit the picture by radio and television. Under this agreement LaMure was to receive a fixed sum of $25,000, plus 5% and 4% of the Western and Eastern Hemisphere motion picture profits, respectively, and 50% of the net profits from exploitation by live television.

The Motion Picture Contract said that Romulus Films Limited, of London, proposed to produce the picture "Moulin Rouge," that Moulin would be vested with the Western Hemisphere distribution rights, and that Moulin on behalf of Romulus was interested in engaging Ferrer's service to play the role of Toulouse-Lautrec. Under clause 4(a), Ferrer was to receive $50,000 to cover twelve weeks of acting, payments to be made weekly as Ferrer rendered his services. Ferrer's performance was to begin between June 1 and July 1, 1952. By clause 4(b), Ferrer was to receive $10,416.66 per week for each additional week, but this, together with an additional $50,000 of salary provided by clause 4(c), was "deferred and postponed" and was payable only out of net receipts. Finally, clauses 4(d) and (e) provided "percentage compensation" equal to stipulated percentages of the net profits from distribution of the picture in the Western and Eastern Hemispheres respectively — 117% of the Western Hemisphere net profits until Ferrer had received $25,000 and thereafter 12¾% (such payments to "be made out of sixty-five (65%) percent of the net profits," whatever that may mean), and 3¾% of the Eastern Hemisphere net profits. If Ferrer's services were interrupted by disability or if production of the picture had to be suspended for causes beyond Moulin's control, but the picture was thereafter completed and Ferrer's "acts, poses and appearances therein" were recognizable to the public, he was to receive a proportion of the compensation provided in clauses 4(c), (d) and (e) corresponding to the ratio of his period of acting to twelve weeks. The same was true if Ferrer failed to "conduct himself with due regard to public conventions and morals" etc. and Moulin cancelled on that account. The absence of any similar provision with respect to termination for Ferrer's wilful refusal or neglect to perform services indicates that all his rights, except that for compensation already due under clause 4(a), would be forfeited in that event. Over objections by the Commissioner, Ferrer offered testimony by Huston's attorney, who was also president of Moulin, that in the negotiation "it was said that the ultimate percentage payment to be made to Ferrer would be his compensation for giving up his interest in the dramatization guild," and a letter from the same attorney, dated March 3, 1953, confirming that in the negotiations with Ferrer's attorney "for the sale of the dramatic rights held by you to the property entitled 'Monsieur Toulouse' and the novel 'Moulin Rouge,' it was understood that the consideration for such sale price was the payments due, or to become due, to you under Clause 4(d) and Clause 4(e)," and also that LaMure "refused to sell the motion picture rights for the production of the motion picture known as 'Moulin Rouge' unless you sold the aforesaid dramatic rights." Ferrer's agent testified, again over objection, that the largest salary Ferrer had previously received for a moving picture appearance was $75,000.

Moulin's books showed $109,027.74 as a salary payment to Ferrer in August, 1953, and $178,751.46 at various later dates in 1953 as the payment of "Participating Interests" under clause 4(d).[1] Ferrer's 1953 return reported the former as ordinary income, and the latter, less expenses of $26,812.72,[2] as a long-term capital gain. The Commissioner determined a deficiency on the basis that the difference, $151,938.74, constituted ordinary income; from the Tax Court's annulment of that determination he has taken this appeal.

Section 117(a) of the 1939 Code, now §1221 of the 1954 Code, tells us, not very illuminatingly, that " 'capital asset' means property held by the taxpayer (whether or not connected with his trade or business), but does not include" four (now five) types of property therein defined. However, it has long been settled that a taxpayer does not bring himself within the capital gains provision merely by fulfilling the simple syllogism that a contract normally constitutes "property," that he held a contract, and that his contract does not fall within a specified exclusion, C.I.R. v. Gillette Motor Transport, Inc., 364 U.S. 130, 134-135 (1960); Surrey, Definitional Problems in Capital Gains Taxation, 69 Harv. L. Rev. 985, 988 (1956). This is easy enough; what is difficult, perhaps impossible, is to frame a positive definition of universal validity. Attempts to do this in terms of the degree of clothing adorning the contract cannot explain all the cases, however helpful they may

1. The record is silent on payments for Eastern Hemisphere profits under clause 4(e), or on whether there will be further payments for Western Hemisphere profits under clause 4(d): we suppose both these will come in later years.
2. The record does not disclose the nature of these expenses, but the Commissioner has not questioned them.

be in deciding some, perhaps even this one; it would be hard to think of a contract more "naked" than a debenture, yet no one doubts that is a "capital asset" if held by an investor. Efforts to frame a universal negative, e.g., that a transaction can never qualify if the taxpayer has merely collapsed anticipation of future income, are equally fruitless; a lessor's sale of his interest in a 999 year net lease and an investor's sale of a perpetual bond sufficiently illustrate why, as does Ayrton Metal Co. v. C.I.R., 299 F.2d 741 (2 Cir. 1962).

Perhaps we can get more help from analyzing the fact situations in cases in adjacent areas, including those decided since Judge Smith's careful review in C.I.R. v. Pittston Company, 252 F.2d 344 (2 Cir.), cert. denied, 357 U.S. 919 (1958), than from the language of the opinions. Putting aside Jones v. Corbyn, 186 F.2d 450 (10 Cir. 1950), which we have disapproved, C.I.R. v. Starr Bros., Inc., 204 F.2d 673, 674 (2 Cir. 1953) and whose status in its own circuit has now become rather doubtful, Wiseman v. Halliburton Oil Well Cementing Co., 301 F.2d 654, (10 Cir. 1962), a case to which we refer below, and C.I.R. v. Goff, 212 F.2d 875 (3 Cir.), cert. denied, 348 U.S. 829 (1954), which is only dubiously reconcilable with our *Pittston* decision, the principal relevant authorities on the two sides of the line in the Supreme Court and in the courts of appeals are as follows: There is no sale or exchange of a capital asset when a lessor receives payment for releasing a lessee from an obligation to pay future rent, Hort v. C.I.R., 313 U.S. 28 (1941). The same was true of the cancellation of an exclusive distributorship, C.I.R. v. Starr Bros., Inc., 204 F.2d 673 (2 Cir. 1953); Leh v. C.I.R., 260 F.2d 489 (9 Cir. 1958), although §1241 of the 1954 Code now rules otherwise if the distributor has a substantial capital investment therein. The transfer of exclusive agency rights to a third person likewise did not qualify, General Artists Corp. v. C.I.R., 205 F.2d 360 (2 Cir.), cert. denied, 346 U.S. 866 (1953); whether it now does if the capital investment requirement of §1241 is met is another question. The sale of oil payment rights, C.I.R. v. P.G. Lake, Inc., 356 U.S. 260 (1958), the temporary taking of a taxpayer's right to use his own transportation assets, C.I.R. v. Gillette Motor Transport, Inc., supra, and the surrender of an exclusive contract to purchase coal, C.I.R. v. Pittston Co., supra, do not meet the statutory test. Neither does the receipt of a lump sum in liquidation of a percentage of the gross receipts of motion pictures otherwise payable to a producer solely in return for personal services not yet performed, Holt v. C.I.R., 303 F.2d 687 (9 Cir. 1962). On the other hand, a lessee's surrender of his lease to the lessor, C.I.R. v. Golonsky, 200 F.2d 72 (3 Cir. 1952), cert. denied, 345 U.S. 939 (1953); C.I.R. v. McCue Bros. & Drummond, Inc., 210 F.2d 752 (2 Cir.), cert. denied, 348 U.S. 829 (1954), now in effect ratified by §1241 of the 1954 Code, his relinquishment of a right to restrict the lessor's renting to another tenant in the same business, C.I.R. v. Ray, 210 F.2d 390 (5 Cir.), cert. denied, 348 U.S. 829 (1954), and his release of his entire interest to a sublessee, Metropolitan Bldg. Co. v. C.I.R., 282 F.2d 592 (9 Cir. 1960), but see Voloudakis v. C.I.R., 274 F.2d 209 (9 Cir. 1960), constitute the sale or exchange of a capital asset. So does the abandonment of an option to acquire a partnership interest, Dorman v. United States, 296 F.2d 27 (9 Cir. 1961).

One common characteristic of the group held to come within the capital gain provision is that the taxpayer had either what might be called an "estate" in (*Golonsky, McCue, Metropolitan*), or an "encumbrance" on (*Ray*), or an option to acquire an interest in (*Dorman*), property which, if itself held, would be a capital asset. In all these cases the taxpayer had something more than an opportunity, afforded by contract, to obtain periodic receipts of income, by dealing with another (*Starr, Leh, General Artists, Pittston*), or by rendering services (*Holt*), or by virtue of ownership of a larger "estate" (*Hort, P.G. Lake*). We are painfully aware of the deficiencies of any such attempt to define the wavering line even in this limited area, but it is the best we can do. We add, with greater confidence, that more recent cases, such as *McCue Bros. & Drummond, Ray, Metropolitan*, and *Dorman*, have moved away from the distinction, relied upon to some extent in *Starr Brothers* and *General Artists*,[3] between a sale to a third person that keeps the "estate" or "encumbrance" alive, and a release that results in its extinguishment.[4] Indeed, although reasoning from another section of a statute so full of anomalies is rather treacherous business, we take §1241 of the 1954 Code as indicating Congressional disenchantment with this formalistic distinction. In the instant case we can see no sensible business basis for drawing a line between a release of Ferrer's rights to LaMure for a consideration paid by Moulin, and a sale of them, with LaMure's consent, to Moulin or to a stranger who would then release them. Moulin's attorney, as we have seen, did not care a fig whether there was "an annulment or conveyance" of the Dramatic Production Contract. Tax law is concerned with the substance, here the voluntary passing of "property" rights allegedly constituting "capital assets," not with whether they are passed to a stranger or to a person already having a larger "estate." So we turn to an analysis of what rights Ferrer conveyed.

Two issues can be eliminated before we do this. We need no longer concern ourselves, as at one time we might have been obliged to do, over the alleged indivisibility of a copyright; the Commissioner is now satisfied that sales and exchanges of less than the whole copyright may result in capital gain, Rev. Rul. 60-226, 1960-1 Cum. Bull. 26. See also Gitlin & Woodward, Tax Aspects of Patents, Copyrights and Trademarks (1960 rev.) 18-19; Sargoy, Formalities and Ownership, 9 Bull. Cr. Soc. 20,

---

3. These cases could well have been decided on the basis that the taxpayer held only a contract right giving him an opportunity to earn future income.

4. We say this despite certain language in Leh v. C.I.R., 260 F.2d 489 (9 Cir. 1958) and in Holt v. C.I.R., 303 F.2d 687 (9 Cir. 1962), both of which, like the cases referred to in footnote 3, validly rested on the absence of a "capital asset."

43 (1961); Surrey & Warren, Federal Income Taxation, Cases and Materials (1960) 753. Neither do we have in this case any issue of excludability under §117(a)(1)(A), now §1221[(a)](1); Ferrer was not in the "trade or business" of acquiring either dramatic production rights or motion picture rights.

When Huston displayed an interest in the motion picture rights in November, 1951, Ferrer was possessed of a bundle of rights, three of which are relevant here. First was his "lease" of the play. Second was his power, incident to that lease, to prevent any disposition of the motion picture rights until June 1, 1952, or, on making an additional $1,500 advance, to December 1, 1952, and for a period thereafter if he produced the play, and to prevent disposition of the radio and television rights even longer. Third was his 40% share of the proceeds of the motion picture and other rights if he produced the play. All these, in our view, Ferrer "sold or exchanged," although the parties set no separate price upon them. To be sure, Moulin had no interest in producing the play. But Ferrer did, unless a satisfactory substitute was provided. Hence Moulin had to buy him out of that right, as well as to eliminate his power temporarily to prevent a sale of the motion picture, radio and television rights and to liquidate his option to obtain a share of their proceeds.

(1) Surrender of the "lease" of the play sounds like the transactions held to qualify for capital gain treatment in *Golonsky* and *McCue Bros. & Drummond*, see §1241 of the 1954 Code. Such cases as Wooster v. Crane & Co., 147 F. 515 (8 Cir. 1906), Underhill v. Schenck, 238 N.Y. 7, 143 N.E. 773, 33 A.L.R. 303 (1924), and Kirke La Shelle Co. v. Paul Armstrong Co., 263 N.Y. 79, 188 N.E. 163 (1933) are a fortiori authority that courts would have enjoined LaMure, or anyone else, from interfering with this, unless the Dramatic Production Contract dictated otherwise. None of its many negations covered this basic grant. Ferrer thus had an "equitable interest" in the copyright of the play.

The Commissioner did not suggest in the Tax Court, and does not here, that this interest or, indeed, any with which we are concerned in this case, fell within §117(a)(1)(C) of the 1939 Code, now §1221[(a)](3), excluding from the term "capital asset" "a copyright; a literary, musical, or artistic composition; or similar property; held by — (i) a taxpayer, whose personal efforts created such property. . . ." He was right in not doing this. In one sense the lease of the play was "created" simply by the agreed advance of $1,500. If it be said that this is too narrow an approach and that we must consider what Ferrer would have had to do in order to make the lease productive, the result remains the same. Although the Dramatic Production Contract demanded Ferrer's personal efforts in the play's production, much else in the way of capital and risk-taking was also required. Yet the legislative history, see S. Rep. No. 2375, 81st Cong., 2d Sess., printed in 2 U.S. Code Cong. Serv. p. 3053 (1950), shows that §117(a)(1)(C), initially added by the Revenue Act of 1950, 64 Stat. 906, 933, was intended to deal with personal efforts and creation in a rather narrow sense.[5] See Stern v. United States, 164 F. Supp. 847, 851 (E.D. La. 1958), aff'd per curiam, 262 F.2d 957 (5 Cir.), cert. denied, 359 U.S. 966 (1959); McPeters, Taxation of Literary Property Income, 12 Mercer L. Rev. 370, 375-380 (1961); and Rev. Rul. 55-706, 1955-2 Cum. Bull. 300. Ferrer's role as producer, paying large sums to the theatre, the actors, other personnel, and the author, is not analogous to that of the writer or even the "creator" of a radio program mentioned by the Committee. Moreover, the dramatic producer does not normally "sell" the production to a single purchaser, as an author or radio program "creator" usually does — he offers it directly to public custom.

We see no basis for holding that amounts paid Ferrer for surrender of his lease of the play are excluded from capital gain treatment because receipts from the play would have been ordinary income. The latter is equally true if a lessee of real property sells or surrenders a lease from which he is receiving business income or subrentals; yet *Golonsky* and *McCue Bros. & Drummond* held such to be the sale or exchange of a capital asset, as §1241 now provides. Likewise we find nothing in the statute that forbids capital gain treatment because the payment to Ferrer might be spread over a number of years rather than coming in a lump sum; although prevention of the unfairness arising from applying ordinary income rates to a "bunching" of income may be one of the motivations of the "capital gain" provisions, the statute says nothing about this. Compare Burnet v. Logan, 283 U.S. 404 (1931). Finally, with respect to the lease of the play, there was no such equivalence between amounts paid for its surrender and income that would have been realized by its retention as seems to lie at the basis of the Tenth Circuit's recent refusal of capital gain treatment in Wiseman v. Halliburton Oil Well Cementing Co., 301 F.2d 654 (1962), a decision as to which we take no position.

(2) Ferrer's negative power, as an incident to the lease, to prevent any disposition of the motion picture, radio and television rights until after production of the play, was also one which, under the cases previously cited, as well as Harper Bros. v. Klaw, 232 F. 609, 613 (S.D.N.Y. 1916) and Manners v. Morosco, 252 U.S. 317 (1920), would be protected in equity unless he had contracted to the contrary, and would thus constitute an

5. The Committee introduced its discussion by referring to persons "in the profession of writing books, or creating other artistic works." It then discussed the previous law, whereby an "amateur" can sell "his book or other artistic work" after holding it for 6 months, and thereby receive "long-term capital gain treatment on the product of his personal effort," p. 3097. The bill therefore provided "that when any person sells a book or other artistic work which is the product of his personal effort his income from the sale is taxed as ordinary income." At p. 3140, the Committee characterized its handiwork as follows:

"Under the committee amendment, a person who writes a book or creates some other sort of artistic work will be taxed at ordinary income rates, rather than at capital-gain rates, upon gain from the sale of the work regardless of whether it is his first production in the field or not. The amendment made by section 211(a) will also exclude from the capital asset category any property similar to that specifically named; for example, a radio program which has been created by the personal efforts of the taxpayer. . . . The interest of a sole proprietor in such a business enterprise as a photographic studio is not 'similar property' even though the value of the business may be largely attributable to the personal efforts of the sole proprietor."

"equitable interest" in this portion of the copyright. Although we should not regard Articles IV, §1 (a) and VIII as outlawing equitable relief to protect the rights granted as to the play, a literal reading of Article V, §1(c), quoted above, would negate Ferrer's power to enjoin disposition of the motion picture rights prior to production of the play and would remit him to arbitration—a consequence serious from the standpoint of definition of a capital asset, especially in view of the emphasis we placed in *Pittston*, 252 F.2d at 348, on the unavailability of injunctive relief there. In the absence of authority, we should not read the clause so broadly; we would construe it as relating to disputes as to the manner of disposition of the rights after the Negotiator had become entitled to dispose of them, not as closing the door on the only effective method for protecting the Manager's important interest against premature disposition. As a practical matter, this feature of the Dramatic Production Contract "clouded" LaMure's title, despite the Contract's contrary assertion. Huston would not conclude with LaMure and LaMure would not conclude with Huston unless Ferrer released his rights; Huston's attorney testified that a contract like Ferrer's "imposes an encumbrance on the motion picture rights." Ferrer's dissipation of the cloud arising from the negative convenant seems analogous to the tenant's relinquishment of a right to prevent his landlord from leasing to another tenant in the same business, held to be the sale or exchange of a capital asset in *Ray*. What we have said in (1) with respect to possible grounds for disqualification as a capital asset is a fortiori applicable here.

(3) We take a different view with respect to the capital assets status of Ferrer's right to receive 40% of the proceeds of the motion picture and other rights if he produced "Monsieur Toulouse."

We assume, without deciding, that there is no reason in principle why if the holder of a copyright grants an interest in the portion of a copyright relating to motion picture and other rights contingent on the production of a play, or, to put the matter in another way, gives the producer an option to acquire such an interest by producing the play, the option would not constitute a "capital asset" unless the producer is disqualified by §117(a)(1)(A), now §1221[(a)](1). Although the copyright might not be such an asset in the owner's hands because of that section or §117(a)(1)(C)(i), now §1221[(a)](3)(A), the latter disqualification would not apply to the producer for reasons already discussed, and the former would not unless the producer was a professional. However, it is equally possible for the copyright owner to reserve the entire "property" both legal and equitable in himself and agree with the producer that a percentage of certain avails shall be paid as further income from the lease of the play—just as the lessor of real estate might agree to pay a lessee a percentage of what the lessor obtained from other tenants attracted to the building by the lessee's operations. In both instances such payments would be ordinary income. If the parties choose to cast their transaction in the latter mold, the Commissioner may take them at their word.

Here the parties were at some pains to do exactly that. LaMure was to "to retain for his sole benefit, complete title, both legal and equitable, in and to all rights whatsoever" other than the right to produce the play. Ferrer was to "have no right, title or interest, legal or equitable, in the motion picture rights, other than the right to receive the Manager's share of the proceeds"; even as to that, he was to have "no recourse, in law or in equity" against a purchaser, a lessee, or the Negotiator, but only a right to arbitration against the Author. We cannot regard all this as mere formalism. The Contract is full of provisions designed to emphasize the Negotiator's freedom to act — provisions apparently stemming from a fear that, without them, the value of the motion picture rights might disintegrate in controversy. McClintic v. Sheldon, 269 App. Div. 356, 55 N.Y.S.2d 879 (1st Dept. 1945), aff'd, 295 N.Y. 682, 65 N.E.2d 328 (1946), greatly relied upon by the taxpayer, does not show that, despite the contrary language of the Contract, Ferrer had, or ever would have, an affirmative equitable interest in the motion picture or other rights, as distinguished from his temporary negative "encumbrance" on them. Although the Appellate Division's opinion contains some remarks as to the equitable interest of a licensee in a copyright, these were not essential to the holding, namely, that "the clear language" of the agreement entitled the producer to the moneys there in question. Moreover, examination of the papers on appeal shows that the contract between the producer and the author in that case was an earlier form not containing the extensive negation of equitable property interests present here.[6]

It follows that if Ferrer had produced the play and LaMure had sold the motion picture, radio and television rights for a percentage of the profits, Ferrer's 40% of that percentage would have been ordinary income and not the sale or exchange of a capital asset. The decisions in *Hort* and *Holt* point to what would seem the inevitable corollary that if, on the same facts, Ferrer had then sold his rights to a percentage of the profits for a lump sum, that, too, would have been ordinary income, see Herman Shumlin, 16 T.C. 407 (1951). The situation cannot be better from Ferrer's standpoint because he had merely a contingent right to, or an option to obtain, the 40% interest; the case differs from Dorman v. United States, supra, in that there the option was to acquire what would admittedly have been a "capital asset."

The situation is thus one in which two of the rights that Ferrer sold or exchanged were "capital assets" and one was not. Although it would be easy to say that the contingent contract right to a percentage of the avails of the motion picture, radio and television rights was dominant and all else incidental, that would be viewing the situation with the inestimable advantage of hindsight. In 1952 no one could tell whether the play might be a huge success and the picture a dismal failure, whether the exact opposite would

6. The "Additional Clause" summarized at the end of our analysis of the Dramatic Production Contract does not call for a different conclusion, as Ferrer urges. This simply protected Ferrer against LaMure's dealing with the novel without regard to Ferrer so long as LaMure did not deal with the play; the clause did not alter the character of Ferrer's rights with respect to LaMure's copyright.

be true, whether both would succeed or both would fail. We cannot simply dismiss out of hand the notion that a dramatic production, presenting an actor famous on the speaking stage and appealing to a sophisticated audience, might have had substantial profit possibilities, perhaps quite as good as a film with respect to a figure, not altogether attractive and not nearly so broadly known then as the success of the picture has made him now, which presumably would require wide public acceptance before returning production costs. At the very least, when Ferrer gave up his lease of the play, he was abandoning his bet on two horses in favor of a bet on only one.

In such instances, where part of a transaction calls for one tax treatment and another for a different kind, allocation is demanded. Helvering v. Taylor, 293 U.S. 507 (1935); Ditmars v. C.I.R., 302 F.2d 481 (2 Cir. 1962). If it be said that to remand for this purpose is asking the Tax Court to separate the inseparable, we answer that no one expects scientific exactness; that however roughly hewn the decision may be, the result is certain to be fairer than either extreme; and that similar tasks must be performed by the Tax Court in other areas, see Webster Investors, Inc. v. C.I.R., 291 F.2d 192 (2 Cir. 1961); Meister v. C.I.R., 302 F.2d 54 (2 Cir. 1962) [determination of portion of purchase price attributable to goodwill].

Still we have not reached the end of the road. The Commissioner contends that, apart from all else, no part of the payments here can qualify for capital gain treatment, since Ferrer could receive "percentage compensation" only if he fulfilled his acting commitments, and all the payments were thus for personal services. Citing C.I.R. v. Dwight's Estate, 205 F.2d 298, 301 (2 Cir.), cert. denied, 346 U.S. 871 (1953), the Commissioner says it was error for the Tax Court to rely on extrinsic evidence to vary the written contract.

Although the parties have taken opposing positions on the applicability of the "parol evidence rule" to a dispute involving a stranger to the contract, a question discussed by Professor Corbin in his usual illuminating fashion in 3 Contracts (rev. ed. 1960) §596, cf. 9 Wigmore, Evidence (3d ed. 1940) §2446, at p. 150, and see, with respect to tax controversies, Stern v. C.I.R., 137 F.2d 43, 46 (2 Cir. 1943); Scofield v. Greer, 185 F.2d 551, 552 (5 Cir. 1950); Landa v. C.I.R., 92 U.S. App. D.C. 196, 206 F.2d 431, 432 (1953); Mustard v. United States, 155 F. Supp. 325, 332 (Ct. Cl. 1957); Thorsness v. United States, 260 F.2d 341,345 (7 Cir. 1958); Cooper Foundation v. O'Malley, 121 F. Supp. 438, 444 (D. Neb. 1954), no such issue is here presented. No one argued the contract provided anything other than what was plainly said. Huston's attorney did not assert that Ferrer would become entitled to the percentage compensation without fulfilling his acting commitment; what the attorney said in his testimony, as he had earlier in his letter, was that Ferrer was selling two things to Moulin—his services as an actor and his rights under the Dramatic Production Contract—and that the parties regarded the payments under clauses 4(a), (b) and (c) as the consideration for the former and those under clauses 4(d) and (e) as the consideration for the latter.

On the basis of this evidence the Tax Court found that the percentage compensation was not "to any extent the consequence of, or consideration for, petitioner's personal services." In one sense, this is hardly so. Under the Motion Picture Contract, Ferrer would receive no percentage compensation if he wrongfully refused to furnish acting services, and none or only a portion if, for reasons beyond his control, he furnished less than all. Since that must have been as plain to the Tax Court as to us, we read the finding to mean rather that Ferrer and Moulin adopted the percentage of profits formula embodied in clauses 4(d) and (e) as an equivalent and in lieu of a fixed sum payable in all events for the release of the Dramatic Production Contract. If they had first agreed on such a sum and had then substituted the arrangement here made, it would be hard to say that although payments under their initial arrangement would not be disqualified for capital gain treatment, payments under the substituted one would be. Ferrer was already bound to play the role of Toulouse-Lautrec, at a salary implicitly found to constitute fair compensation for his services; adoption of a formula whereby his receipt of percentage compensation for releasing his rights was made contingent on his fulfilling that undertaking does not mean that the percentage compensation could not be solely for his release of the Contract. The Tax Court was not bound to accept the testimony that this was the intent — it could lawfully have found that the percentage compensation was in part added salary for Ferrer's acting services and in part payment for the release. However, it found the contrary, and we cannot say that in doing so it went beyond the bounds to which our review of its fact findings is confined, Internal Revenue Code of 1954, §7482(a); F.R. Civ. Proc. 52(a). Since, on the taxpayer's own evidence, the percentage compensation was for the totality of the release of his rights under the Dramatic Production Contract, allocation is required as between rights which did and rights which did not constitute a "capital asset."

We therefore reverse and remand to the Tax Court to determine what portion of the percentage compensation under clauses 4(d) and (e) of the Motion Picture Contract constituted compensation for Ferrer's surrendering his lease of the play and his incidental power to prevent disposition of the motion picture and other rights pending its production, as to which the determination of deficiency should be annulled, and what part for the surrender of his opportunity to receive 40% of the proceeds of the motion picture and other rights as to which it should be sustained. The expenses allowed as basis must likewise be allocated. Doubtless further evidence will have to be taken unless the parties can reach some practical adjustment.

It is so ordered.

Questions

1. One way to read *Ferrer* is as an essay on contract rights as capital assets. It cites many of the most important cases. Does it succeed in rationalizing

them? Is the analysis in terms of estate, encumbrance, and option a happy one?

2. Was it necessary or wise for the court to deal separately with Ferrer's different rights under the dramatic production contract? Are the court's reasons sound for concluding that the right to share in motion picture profits was not a capital asset? Is it not that very right, after all, which is most apt to be purchased and sold by an investor other than an active participant in play or movie production, and in that sense at least, the most like a capital asset?

3. Should the government in *Ferrer* have cited *Corn Products* and the related cases dealing with losses in Chapter 20B? Is it not clear that Ferrer was in, or was at least entering into, the business of producing a play, and that his reasons for acquiring his rights under the first contract were solely to enable him to carry on that business? If he had suffered a loss, would his deduction have been limited by §1211?

4. Even if Ferrer's rights under the dramatic production contract did amount to a capital asset, is there something wrong with the decision? After all, what he is receiving in the end is simply his share of the profits from a venture in which he has been actively and personally engaged. Is the fact that he originally started out to make a play instead of a movie, and then delayed any formal change in his plans for six months and a few days, sufficient to transform part of his share of the movie profits into capital gain?

Assuming the contract rights are a capital asset, what would the government's strongest argument(s) be? Are any of the following persuasive?

(a) Ferrer exchanged his rights under the dramatic production contract for other rights under the motion picture contract. If any gain were realized and recognized on that exchange, it might be taxable at capital gain rates. But the fact of such an exchange does not operate to transform profit realized by exploitation of the new rights from ordinary income into capital gain.

Would it strengthen this argument to assert that the exchange of rights itself was a like-kind exchange under §1031?

(b) Ferrer's transaction with Huston and LaMure is predominantly one of entering into a new venture to produce a motion picture; liquidation or abandonment of the stage production is only incidental. Part of Ferrer's contribution to the new venture are his rights under the dramatic production contract. But the fact that a participant contributes a capital asset does not operate to transform part of his share of the profits from a common venture into long-term capital gain.

(c) Ferrer's exchange of rights under the dramatic production contract for rights in connection with the movie production is in effect a kind of modification of rights with respect to the underlying property rather than a real exchange or disposition. Such a modification of rights does not operate to transform part of all the profits accruing thereafter into capital gain.

(d) Ferrer's rights to share in the profits of the motion picture are conditioned upon his performance of services. Therefore, what he has amounts to an employment contract. His terms of employment may be more favorable because his rights under the dramatic production contract put him in a favorable bargaining position. But it is unrealistic to conclude that part of his compensation is, therefore, taxable at capital gain rates.

(e) The case simply presents none of the bunching or acceleration of tax liability for which the capital gain provisions are meant to provide relief.

5. Is the court's analysis in *Ferrer* too abstract? Could the court have concerned itself more directly and concretely with the case itself? Would it be fair to suggest that the court's legal concepts and categories are mainly a distraction, like learned discussion of the emperor's clothes, from judging the case at hand?

References

A. Receipt of a Lump-sum Payment for a Future Income Stream: A. Andrews, Disposition of a Life Estate in Realty: What Are the Implications of Revenue Ruling 72-601?, 40 J. Taxn. 26 (1974); DelCotto, "Property" in the Capital Asset Definition: Influence of "Fruit and Tree," 15 Buffalo L. Rev. 1 (1965); Joyce & DelCotto, The AB (ABC) and BA Transactions: An Economic and Tax Analysis of Reserved and Carved Out Income Interests, 31 Tax L. Rev. 121 (1976); Lyon & Eustice, Assignment of Income: Fruit and Tree as Irrigated by the *P.G. Lake* Case, 17 Tax L. Rev. 293 (1962); Note, Distinguishing Ordinary Income from Capital Gain Where Rights to Future Income Are Sold, 69 Harv. L. Rev. 787 (1956); Note, The *P.G. Lake* Guides to Ordinary Income: An Appraisal in Light of Capital Gains Policies, 14 Stan. L. Rev. 551 (1962); Wilkinson, ABC Transactions and Related Income Tax Plans, 40 Texas L. Rev. 18 (1961).

B. Receipt of Payments out of a Future Income Stream: Chirelstein, Capital Gain and the Sale of a Business Opportunity: The Income Tax Treatment of Contract Termination Payments, 49 Minn. L. Rev. 1 (1964); DelCotto, "Property" in the Capital Asset Definition: Influence of "Fruit and Tree," 15 Buffalo L. Rev. 1 (1965); Eustice, Contract Rights, Capital Gain, and Assignment of Income — The *Ferrer* Case, 20 Tax L. Rev. 1 (1964); Kinsey, Bootstraps and Capital Gain — A Participant's View of *Commissioner v. Clay Brown*, 64 Mich. L. Rev. 581 (1966); Lanning, Tax Erosion and the "Bootstrap Sale" of a Business, 108 U. Pa. L. Rev. 623, 943 (1960); Morreale, Patents, Know-How and Trademarks: A Tax Overview, 29 Tax Law. 553 (1976); Note, A Comparison of the Tax Treatment of Authors and Inventors, 70 Harv. L. Rev. 1419 (1957); Note, Tax Problems of Bootstrap Sales to Exempt Foundations: A Comprehensive Approach, 18 Stan. L. Rev. 1148 (1966).

Appendix — *Rates of Return and Effective Rates of Tax on Investments*

1. Rates of Return

(a) *The basic case.* Consider a residential building which is to cost $1 million and to produce net rental income (after deducting all expenses except federal income taxes, depreciation, mortgage interest, and amortization) of $124,000. The building is to have an $800,000 mortgage with fixed annual payments of $105,000, to be applied first to interest at 12 percent on the unpaid principal and then to reduction of principal. The building will be depreciated over 27.5 years using the straight-line method. §168(b)(3)(B) & (c). First year operations can then be projected as follows.

Cash Flow		Taxable Income	
Net rent	$124,000	Net rent	$124,000
Interest	(96,000)	Interest	(96,000)
Principal payment	(9,000)	Depreciation	(36,364)
Pretax yield	$ 19,000	Taxable income (loss)	$ (8,364)
Tax saving @ 35%	2,927		
After-tax yield	$ 21,927		

The pretax yield in the first year is $19,000, or 9.5 percent of the $200,000 equity investment. The after-tax return may be more, since it may include the tax saving resulting from the tax loss of $8,364.[1] For a taxpayer with a marginal rate of 35 percent that would be $2,927,[2] and the total cash return in the first year would be $21,927 or about 11.0 percent on the net $200,000 investment.

But of course the figures will change after the first year, and an adequate appraisal requires a projection throughout the whole anticipated period of investment. Assume that net rental income remains constant. Since mortgage payments are also constant, the pretax yield will remain at $19,000 a year. The tax loss, however, will decrease each year, since the amount of the mortgage payments allocable to interest will decline. Because after-tax return is a function of tax loss, it too will decline. In fact the declining tax loss will switch over to a gain in year seven and grow rather rapidly thereafter, and so the after-tax cash flow will drop below $19,000 at that time, and continue to decline. See Table A-1.

When taxable income exceeds cash flow, investors are apt to consider selling. It is not uncommon for a new building in a good location to sell even well after its construction for a price at or above cost — $1 million in this case. The cash flow from the sale will consist of the sale proceeds ($1 million) minus the remaining mortgage balance ($642,061) and any tax resulting from gain on the sale. If the building sells for original cost, then gain will just equal accumulated depreciation ($363,636); the tax will be at the 25 percent maximum rate for section 1250 property, and the tax will be $90,909, leaving net cash flow of $267,030 ($1,000,000 − $642,061 − $90,909), as shown on the next-to-last line of Table A-1.

The whole after-tax cash yield on this investment would therefore be $195,494 over ten years, plus $267,030 from the sale, from an initial cash investment of $200,000. This represents a cash profit of $262,524. Spread evenly over ten years this would be an average of $26,252 a year, or about 13.13 percent.

Dollars received early, however, are worth more than dollars received later, and a more careful evaluation must take that into account. What we want is the rate of return represented by the cash flow that is received in exchange for the original investment of $200,000. The question is, what compound interest rate, when applied to the outstanding balance of the $200,000 investment, would generate sufficient funds to allow annual withdrawals equal to the cash flow shown, just exhausting the account with the last withdrawal? Such a rate of return, being implied by or inherent in a

---

1. Today the tax loss might well be disallowed under the Passive Activity Loss limitation in §469 (see Chapter 16C above), but we are interested here to see what kinds of effects that provision guards against. Or, to make it current, assume the taxpayer has other passive income sufficient to absorb these losses without running into the limitation.

2. For taxable years beginning in 2009 the overall limitation on itemized deductions would operate to increase the taxpayer's income subject to the top rate by 1 percent, resulting in an effective marginal rate of 35.35 percent (35 percent nominal rate plus an add on of 1 percent of 35 percent). §68(a), (f). Section 68 is scheduled to terminate in 2010.

TABLE A-1
Taxable Income and After-Tax Cash Return Projected over Ten Years

(1)	(2)	(3)	(4)	(5)	(6)	(7)
Year	Beginning Mortgage Balance	Mortgage Interest Paid	Mortgage Principal Paid	Taxable Income (Loss)	Tax Saving (or tax) at 35%	After-Tax Cash Yield
1	$ 800,000	$ 96,000	$ 9,000	$ (8,364)	$ 2,927	$ 21,927
2	791,000	94,920	10,080	(7,284)	2,549	21,549
3	780,920	93,710	11,290	(6,074)	2,126	21,126
4	769,630	92,356	12,644	(4,719)	1,652	20,652
5	756,986	90,838	14,162	(3,202)	1,121	20,121
6	742,824	89,139	15,861	(1,503)	526	19,526
7	726,963	87,236	17,764	401	(140)	18,860
8	709,199	85,104	19,896	2,532	(886)	18,114
9	689,303	82,716	22,284	4,920	(1,722)	17,278
10	667,019	80,042	24,958	7,594	(2,658)	16,342
Totals		$892,061	$157,939	($15,698)	$5,494	$195,494
Sale for $1M			642,061	363,636	(90,909)	267,030
Grand totals		$892,061	$800,000	$347,939	($85,415)	$462,524

particular cash flow pattern (schedule of the timing and amount of receipts) rather than given as a parameter, is called the *internal rate of return.*

One way to estimate an internal rate of return is to take each year's cash flow separately and calculate its present value. The present value of a future payment depends upon the interest rate and the time to payment according to the formula $1/(1 + i)^t$, where i is the rate of interest per compounding period (here years) and t is the number of periods (years) until payment is due. (Figure A-1 at the end of this Appendix applies this formula to show the present value of $1 at different interest rates and different numbers of years hence.) Column (2) of Table A-2 simply lists the schedule of after-tax cash flow computed in column (7) of Table A-1. The initial investment occurs at the start of the first year and as an outlay of funds is represented by a negative number; the year 10 receipt ($283,372) is the sum of the final year after-tax return from operations ($16,342) plus the after-tax sale proceeds ($267,030). Column (3) of Table A-2 converts each cash flow entry to present value using a 10 percent compound annual interest (discount) rate. Observe that the total present value of the receipts is almost $26,000 more than the investment—this positive balance indicates that the 10 percent test rate is too low. Column (4) of Table A-2 again converts each cash flow entry to present value, this time using a 12 percent interest rate. Now the total present value is a small negative balance (–$456), which indicates that the 12 percent discount rate is too high, but only slightly. Column (5) uses a test rate of 11.95 percent, which is closer still but just a tad low. This iterative process of approximating the internal rate of return ever more precisely is

TABLE A-2
Internal Rate of Return Illustration

(1)	(2)	(3)	(4)	(5)	(6)
	After-Tax	PV	PV	PV	PV at
Year	Cash Flow	at 10%	at 12%	at 11.95%	11.9623%
0	$(200,000)	$(200,000)	$(200,000)	$(200,000)	$(200,000)
1	21,927	19,934	19,578	19,587	19,585
2	21,549	17,809	17,179	17,194	17,191
3	21,126	15,872	15,037	15,057	15,052
4	20,652	14,105	13,125	13,148	13,142
5	20,121	12,493	11,417	11,443	11,436
6	19,526	11,022	9,892	9,919	9,912
7	18,860	9,678	8,531	8,558	8,551
8	18,114	8,450	7,316	7,342	7,336
9	17,278	7,328	6,231	6,256	6,250
10	283,372	109,252	91,238	91,646	91,546
Totals	$ 262,524	$ 25,944	$ (456)	$ 150	$ 0

tedious and time consuming, but modern spreadsheet programs include financial functions that will perform it automatically given a schedule of cash flows. The actual internal rate of return of this investment is, to six significant figures, 11.9623 percent, as column (6) demonstrates.

Question

How much would the building have to sell for at the end of ten years to bring the rate of return up to an even 12 percent? Or down to an even 10 percent?

(b) *Adding a second mortgage.* Often an investor in real estate will seek to borrow more than 80 percent of the price, and a similar rate-of-return analysis will show why. Suppose the investor above could obtain a 16 percent $150,000 second mortgage with no amortization of principal. The $24,000 annual interest on the second mortgage would turn the $19,000 annual pretax cash return into an annual pretax deficit of $5,000. However, it would also increase the tax loss by $24,000 each year, so that the net effect on after-tax cash return, at a 35 percent tax rate, would be a decrease of only $15,600. In addition, the net sales proceeds, like the cash cost, would decrease by $150,000. The whole after-tax return would therefore be $39,494 ($195,494 − $156,000) over ten years and $117,030 ($267,030 − $150,000) on sale. This represents a cash profit of $106,524 ($39,494 + $117,030 − $50,000) on an initial cash investment of $50,000, or an average over ten years of about $10,652 or 21.3 percent a year. Because most of the cash is not received until the end, however, the internal rate of return in this case is 15.675 percent.

Questions

1. Can you explain why taking a second mortgage at 16 percent interest has the effect of raising the return on equity from 11.962 to 15.675 percent?

2. How high would the interest on the second mortgage have to run before that mortgage would fail to increase the after-tax rate of return on the equity?

2.   Effective Rates of Tax on Investment

The effective rate of tax on any particular investment can be defined as the amount by which the tax reduces the rate of return, expressed as a percentage of the pretax rate of return. For example, if the after-tax rate of return on an investment as computed above were 15 percent, while the rate of return on the same investment in the absence of income tax were 20 percent, the effective rate of tax would be 25 percent ([20 – 15]/20).

(a) The pretax cash return on the investment above, without the second mortgage, would be $19,000 a year for ten years, and then $357,939 ($1,000,000 – $642,061 unpaid mortgage principal) on sale. That yields an internal rate of return of approximately 13.653 percent. The income tax therefore decreases the rate of return from 13.653 percent to 11.962 percent, and the effective rate of tax is 12.39 percent ([13.653 – 11.962]/ 13.653), a little more than one-third of the nominal rate of 35 percent.

(b) In the absence of income tax, but with the second mortgage, the investment above would produce a loss of $5,000 per year, since interest on the second mortgage exceeds the cash flow by that amount. On sale, however, without income tax, the investor would get $207,939 ($1,000,000 sale price – $642,061 first mortgage – $150,000 second mortgage) for an original investment of $50,000 plus additional investments of $5,000 annually for ten years. That represents a gain of $107,939 on a total outlay of $100,000, but none of the return comes until the end. This translates into a pretax internal rate of return of 9.908 percent.

An after-tax rate of return of 15.675 percent on an investment that would yield only 9.908 percent for a tax-exempt charity represents an effective rate of tax of *negative* 58.21 percent ([9.908 – 15.675]/9.908). A negative income tax for the needy indeed!

Question

The second mortgage lowers the pretax rate of return from 13.653 percent to 9.908 percent (which seems normal enough), while it raises the after-tax rate of return from 11.962 percent to 15.675 percent. Why is this?

3. Before and After 1986

These relationships were much more dramatic prior to 1986, for several reasons: Tax rates were higher, depreciation was faster, and gain on sale was taxed at a capital gain rate substantially below the ordinary income rate. The combined effect of a 50 percent rate, a 60 percent capital gain deduction, and 18-year straight-line depreciation on the example under discussion would be to produce a rate of return of 16.285 percent without the second mortgage, and 40.009 percent with it. These represent effective rates of taxation of *negative* 19.3 percent and *negative* 303.8 percent, respectively. These figures are all shown on the first line of Table A-3.

On the other hand, immediately after enactment of the Tax Reform Act of 1986 these effects were considerably muted: Ordinary income and capital gain rates were set at 28 percent and the depreciable life of residential real estate was stretched out to 27.5 years. The Internal Rates of Return (IRRs) and Effective Rates of Tax (ERTs) for this regime are shown on the third line of Table A-3, labeled "1987-1990."

Present law represents something of an intermediate position. The top rate on ordinary income is 35 percent, which is in between 50 and 28. The marginal rate on capital gain from depreciable real estate is 25 percent, which is in between 20 and 28. The capital gain preference in this case in present law is a difference of 10 percentage points or 28.6 percent of the ordinary income tax. That is distinctly less than the pre-1986 differential of 30 percentage points or 60 percent, but obviously more than the zero differential immediately thereafter. Most of the IRRs and ERTs shown in Table A-3, with or without the second mortgage, are likewise intermediate.

But notice that with no mortgage the rankings of the three regimes are quite different. Significantly, the 1987-1990 regime exhibits the lowest ERT and highest IRR by a considerable margin, a distinction it loses in both cases with mortgages.

4. Analysis

Tax shelter tax savings are commonly attributed to three effects, which are illustrated in this discussion and Table A-3: (1) tax deferral, (2) conversion of ordinary income into capital gain, and (3) leverage. In fact these three effects are intensely interrelated, and the remaining lines in Table A-3 represent an effort to sort them out.

The line labeled "No Tax" is taken as an analytical starting point. It shows the effects of leverage in the absence of tax, and it is the reference line

TABLE A-3

Internal Rates of Return and Effective Rates of Tax for Various Tax Regimes

(1)	(2) No Mortgage	(3)	(4) 12% First Mortgage Only	(5)	(6)	(7) 16% Second Mortgage Too	(8)	(9)
	IRR	ERT	ATCB	IRR	ERT	ATCB	IRR	ERT
Pre-1986 (50% OI; 20% CG; 18 yrs)	8.219%	33.7%	6.0%	16.285%	−19.3%	8.0%	40.009%	−303.8%
Present Law (35% OI; 15% CG; 27.5 yrs)	8.727%	29.6%	7.8%	11.962%	12.4%	10.4%	15.675%	−58.2%
1987-1990 (28% OI; 28% CG; 27.5 yrs)	9.285%	25.1%	8.6%	11.566%	15.3%	11.5%	11.675%	−17.8%
No Tax	12.400%	0.0%	12.0%	13.653%	0.0%	16.0%	9.908%	0.0%
Tax at 35% on both OI & CG								
No depreciation	8.060%	35.0%	7.8%	8.854%	35.2%	10.4%	6.489%	34.5%
27.5-year SL	8.474%	31.7%	7.8%	10.947%	19.8%	10.4%	12.455%	−25.7%
18-year SL	8.707%	29.8%	7.8%	12.396%	9.2%	10.4%	20.270%	−104.6%
Tax at 35% on OI & 15% on CG								
27.5-year SL	8.973%	27.6%	7.8%	12.889%	5.6%	10.4%	18.181%	−83.5%
18-year SL	9.468%	23.6%	7.8%	15.285%	−11.9%	10.4%	27.455%	−177.1%

Where:

ATCB is the After-Tax Cost of Borrowing for each mortgage separately;

IRR is the after-tax Internal Rate of Return on equity ("No Tax" IRR gives pretax rate); and

ERT is the Effective Rate of Tax reflected in the difference between after-tax IRR and no-tax IRR.

Facts: Residential rental realty on leased land; cost $1,000,000. Net rental income before mortgage interest or income taxes: $124,000. Sold after ten years for original cost. First mortgage: $800,000, 12% interest, fixed annual payments of $105,000. Second mortgage: $150,000, 16% interest, no principal amortization.

for computing ERTs above and below it throughout the table. Deferral and conversion cannot occur in the absence of tax.

The next line is for a *correct* 35 percent income tax. "Correct" in our simple example means no depreciation, since it has been assumed that the property sells for original cost. This line shows that without deferral (unreal depreciation, even if recaptured at the same rate as deducted) or conversion, leverage has no significant effect — ERTs remain very close to the stated rate of 35 percent and IRRs go up and down in rough proportion to those for no tax. The remaining lines reintroduce depreciation over 27.5 and 18 years, first with no capital gain preference and then with a 15 percent rate on capital gains.

First consider deferral, even without conversion. This means depreciation of any sort in this simple example, and it is illustrated on the next two lines (as well as the 1987-1990 line above). Columns (2) and (3) show that deferral alone produces a modest reduction in ERT below the stated rate. Columns (5), (6), (8), and (9) show how that reduction can be greatly magnified by leverage, so that 95 percent debt financing on the figures given pushes the ERT below zero whether the depreciation period is 18 or 27.5 years.

Columns (4) and (7) may give the best insight as to how this happens. They are headed *ATCB* which stands for After-Tax Cost of Borrowing. In each case the figure is simply 12 percent or 16 percent reduced by the ordinary income tax rate. In the lower half of the table that is constant at 35 percent, so the figures remain at 7.8 and 10.4 percent for the first and second mortgages, respectively. In the top three lines ATCBs vary because the top marginal rates differ.

What these show in each case is that the cost of borrowing is reduced by the full ordinary income tax rate. But with deferral the ERT on the investment viewed separately from the debt (column (3)) is pushed lower, with the result that the IRR on the investment viewed separately (column (2)) is reduced less by the tax than is the ACTB.

Leverage is essentially about making money by borrowing at a lower cost than the return one makes by investing the borrowed funds. Look down columns (2) and (4) comparing the figures on each line. If the IRR in column (2) exceeds the ATCB in column (4), then the IRR in column (5) will be higher than in column (2). And in general, the greater the difference between columns (2) and (4), the greater is the increase in column (5). And the same relationships hold among columns (5), (7), and (8) with respect to adding the second mortgage. Notice on the third line (the 1987-1990 tax regime), for example, that the IRR with first mortgage only and the ATCB for the second mortgage both begin with the figures "11.5," and so the IRR with second mortgage is barely affected. (Why is it then that the ERT drops 33.1 percentage points, from +15.3 percent to −17.8?)

The last two lines reintroduce a capital gain preference of 20 points (57.1 percent). One question is whether to prefer a capital gain rate preference to an acceleration of depreciation. The answer depends, of course, on how much of each. Table A-3 indicates that it also may depend on how things are financed. Look at the fourth line up from the bottom — no capital gain preference and 27.5-year depreciation. Then look at the next two lines to compare the effects of going back to 18-year depreciation or reintroducing a 20-point capital gain preference. Looking in column (3) it appears that the reduction in ERT is 1.9 percentage points from shortening depreciation, and 4.1 points from introducing the capital gain preference. But now look at the bottom line — it shows that the effect of doing both is a reduction of 8.1 percentage points, which is considerably more than the sum of the parts.

And then explore to the right. Leverage, as expected, magnifies the distortions as computed without debt financing. But it also leads to a change, in this case, in the relative effects of single changes. With both mortgages, a shortening of depreciable life from 27.5 years to 18 produces a bigger benefit than a 20 percentage point reduction in the tax rate on capital gains.

Compare the top and bottom lines in the table. They both have 18-year depreciation, but the ordinary income and capital gains rates are higher in the pre-1986 regime (top line). With no mortgage that has the expected effect of making IRR higher and ERT lower when the tax rates are lower (bottom line). But look what happens with the first mortgage in place, and even more with the second. Why?

Questions

1. In view of the enormous reduction in tax shelter effects produced by the 1986 reduction in marginal rates, depreciation deductions, and capital gain relief, was it necessary and appropriate also to enact the Passive Activity Loss limitation in §469? See Chapter 16C. How would the PAL limitation affect the results reflected in Table A-3?

2. How should one read Table A-3 in reference to the question of distortion in allocation of resources? In simpler terms, do the high IRRs and negative ERTs on the right-hand side of that table provide a good measure of the degree to which income tax treatment is likely to produce an over-allocation of resources to residential rental realty? Or is it likely that the occurrence of investment will depend primarily on the relation between prospective gross returns (12.4 percent in the foregoing example) and interest costs (12 percent or a blend of 12 and 16), which is unaffected by tax treatment of the borrower-owner? How should one go about finding an answer to this question?

3. Do any of the figures in this appendix suggest any other changes in behavior that might be induced by income tax treatment? Would an investor be well-advised, for example, to consider selling after seven years instead of ten? Find the optimum period after which to sell, assuming the building could be sold for $1 million at any time. Will the answer differ depending on whether either or both mortgages are in effect?

Figure A-1

Present Value of a Future Payment

(annual compounding at various interest rates)

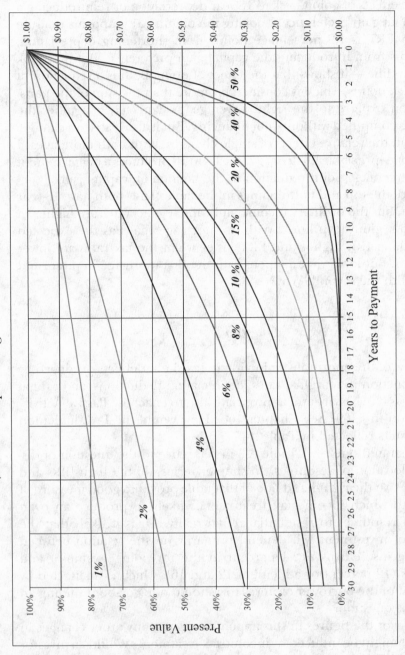

Each curve in Figure A-1 represents a prevailing market interest rate for the obligation in question, without regard to what the instrument says about interest. If prevailing interest rates remain unchanged, then the value of the future payment will increase as time goes by, along the corresponding curve in the chart, somewhat like a bank account accruing interest at the specified rate.

If the prevailing market interest rate changes, however, then the present value must be found on the curve that corresponds with the new market rate. Thus an increase in prevailing interest rates will require shifting to a lower curve on the chart, which may represent a substantial loss in value, particularly if the payment is still a long time off.

Table of Cases

Italics indicate principal cases.

Table of Statutes

Table of Treasury Regulations, Revenue Rulings and Procedures, and Miscellaneous IRS Pronouncements

Italics indicate principal rulings.

Index